# Eastern Christianity in Its Texts

# Eastern Christianity in Its Texts

Cyril Hovorun

t&tclark

LONDON • NEW YORK • OXFORD • NEW DELHI • SYDNEY

T&T CLARK
Bloomsbury Publishing Plc
50 Bedford Square, London, WC1B 3DP, UK
1385 Broadway, New York, NY 10018, USA
29 Earlsfort Terrace, Dublin 2, Ireland

BLOOMSBURY, T&T CLARK and the T&T Clark logo are trademarks of
Bloomsbury Publishing Plc

First published in Great Britain 2022



Cover Photographs: Egyptian Encaustic Icon at Benaki Museum, Athens photographed by
Cyril Hovorun, Stone Texture © vlntn/AdobeStock
Cover design by Nicky Borowiec



A catalogue record for this book is available from the British Library.

Library of Congress Cataloging-in-Publication Data.
Names: Hovorun, Cyril, editor.
Title: Eastern Christianity in its texts / [editor] Cyril Hovorun.
Description: London; New York: T&T Clark, 2022. | Includes bibliographical references
and index. | Identifiers: LCCN 2021048826 (print) | LCCN 2021048827 (ebook) |
ISBN 9780567682918 (hb) | ISBN 9780567682901 (paperback) |
ISBN 9780567682932 (epub) | ISBN 9780567682925 (epdf)
Subjects: LCSH: Orthodox Eastern Church–History. | Orthodox Eastern
Church–History.–Sources.
Classification: LCC BX290 .E275 2022 (print) | LCC BX290 (ebook) |
DDC 281.9–dc23/eng/20220128
LC record available at https://lccn.loc.gov/2021048826
LC ebook record available at https://lccn.loc.gov/2021048827

ISBN: HB: 978-0-5676-8291-8
PB: 978-0-5676-8290-1
ePDF: 978-0-5676-8292-5
ePUB: 978-0-5676-8293-2

Typeset by Deanta Global Publishing Services, Chennai, India
Printed and bound in Great Britain

# Contents

# Figures

# Note on Quotes

The book is tailored around texts that come from different eras and areas. They have survived in many languages. I cared to use the most updated critical editions of these texts, whenever they are available. These editions are acknowledged in the list of primary sources at the end of the book. I also tried to utilize the best scholarly translations, which I sometimes had to modify. These translations are listed among the primary sources and in the bibliography. In several cases, I translated texts myself.

# Introduction

This book imitates ancient florilegia—collections of extended quotes from the theological authorities of the past. This is an annotated florilegium: all quotes have been explained and supplied with pretexts and contexts. The genre of florilegia flourished from the fifth century on, during the Christological controversies (see Horster & Reitz 2018: 440–1). Its purpose was to corroborate particular theological points. While composing this book, I also had some theological points in mind.

One is a critique of the critique of what has been called "scholasticism." This notion has many meanings and connotations. In modern Orthodox theology, since Georges Florovsky (1893–1979) began forging his "neo-patristic synthesis," "scholasticism" has been mostly perceived as a Western *pseudomorphosis*—a distortion of the original Eastern style of doing theology (see Gavrilyuk 2014: 171). It has become a fashion to construct an ostensibly "genuine" Orthodox theology by deconstructing "scholasticism."

In this book, I reconstruct scholasticism. I try to rebuild it on the bedrock of the so-called categories: generalizations that help reduce to fewer ordered commonalities a dizzyingly chaotic multiplicity of things and phenomena surrounding us. Categories help me to rearticulate classical theological maxims and articulate new ones. My project, therefore, can be called "neo-scholastic."

It resembles and yet differs from the nineteenth-century Roman Catholic neo-scholasticism (see Heynickx et al. 2018). The latter aimed at restoring the original Thomism, adjusting it to modernity, and contesting alternative methods of the contemporary Roman Catholic theology, such as the ones based on German idealism. My "neo-scholasticism" redraws the dialectical perimeter of the classical philosophical and theological thinking, reintroduces the early Eastern patristic scholasticism, and argues that this scholasticism can be relevant to today. I believe this is the next step after the "neo-patristic synthesis." Like the latter, it reconnects modernity with the church's fathers and mothers. However, it does so by affirming and not rejecting scholasticism.

## Categories

Categories were "voices" (φωναί, *voces*), through which ancient thinkers vocalized their beliefs. Studying categories has become a distinct discipline—logics or dialectics.

Whenever in this book we mention either logics or dialectics, we imply their classical meaning of an intellectual framework that frames speculative thinking by the means of the canon of categories set up by Aristotle and his commentators.

Most classical categories were rendered in pairs. The most important of them is the one of commonality and particularity. This pair can be discerned in the pre-Socratic philosophy, in Plato's differentiation between common invisible ideas and their particular manifestations in visible things. Aristotle perfected this differentiation. He considered particularities and commonalities as innate in everything and identified them as beings' first and second essences correspondingly. He also elaborated on the gradation of commonalities: there are more common commonalities, which he called "genera," and more particular commonalities, which he called "species."

Following Aristotle, we call generalizations "categories." Generations of commentators on the Aristotelian corpus, who represented various philosophical schools, adjusted the Aristotelian "categories" to their lines of thought. The neo-Platonic philosopher Porphyry of Tyre, who flourished in the late third century AD, became particularly famous because of his adaptation of the Aristotelian categories. His rendition turned to a golden standard of the classical logics. Christian theologians appropriated this standard and developed on its basis the earliest form of Christian scholasticism. A prominent early sixth-century theologian and scholastic, Severus of Antioch, used to say that a good theologian has to be "trained in Aristotle's *Categories* and in similar texts of outside philosophers" (quoted by Theodore of Raïth, *Praeparatio* 10; Diekamp 1938: 200.14–16). Theologians could disagree with one another on various theological issues, but they agreed that categories can help them resolve those issues. Some issues were indeed successfully resolved when logical categories were applied to them.

Such was a church-dividing issue debated during the fourth century—about how one God can be simultaneously the Father, the Son, and the Holy Spirit. Theologians who disagreed on this issue did not necessarily understand the Trinity differently. The classical categories of commonality and particularity helped them to arrive at a common denominator. They identified in God one commonality, which they eventually agreed to call *ousia*, and three particularities, which they agreed to call hypostases. These categories, thus, helped to restore consensus in the church and its unity. Early scholastics, one could conclude, functioned as a means of ecumenical reconciliation. Early Christian ecumenism was unthinkable without scholastic categories.

Such a success of the early Christian scholasticism can be explained by the metaphysical neutrality of the categories. Aristotle had secured this neutrality by distilling logics, as a purely intellectual exercise, from the Platonic metaphysics. Neo-Platonists enhanced the metaphysical neutrality of the Aristotelian logics, even though they emphatically professed polytheistic metaphysics. The metaphysical neutrality of the logical categories made them applicable to any metaphysics, including monotheistic ones. Jewish and Muslim scholars used them to prove something opposite to what the neo-Platonists had held—that God is one. Christian theologians had used the same Aristotelian-Porphyrian categories to solve more nuanced dilemmas of oneness and plurality in God and his incarnation. On their basis, they developed the categories of *hypostasis/prosopon* and *ousia/physis*, which enabled them to distinguish between the three persons of the Trinity and God's one essence, as well as between two natures and one person of Jesus Christ.

## Scholasticism

The mobilization of the Aristotelian-Porphyrian categories for the purposes of Christian theology created momentum for the emergence of Christian scholasticism. It was born and flourished first in the East. The original language of the scholastic theology was Greek, from which it was translated to Syriac, Coptic, Arabic, Armenian, Georgian and other oriental languages, as well as to Latin. Greek categories, both directly and indirectly (through Syriac and Arabic translations), influenced Western scholasticism, which flourished several centuries after its Eastern original.

Modern polemists against scholasticism, especially among the Orthodox theologians, target primarily its Western derivative and tend to ignore its Eastern original. They accuse scholasticism of being speculative and secularizing. These accusations could be justifiable, but only partly. Indeed, scholastics can mortify spiritual life by diverting a human being from a direct relationship with God. However, this is an abuse of an instrument, which in the first place was designed to enhance the relationship with God by explaining it. As with any instrument, it can be misused, which does not cancel its original usefulness. This also applies to the presumably secularizing effect of scholasticism. Christian theologians initially employed this instrument precisely because it was secular—in the sense that it did not admix polytheistic metaphysics to the Christian monotheistic spirituality. From this perspective, logical categories originally featured positive secularity. They became instruments of negative secularity, when they were used to attack any metaphysics, for example in the case of logical positivism. Instead of trashing the misused instrument, I suggest recycling it.

Moreover, I argue that by throwing scholastics away, we cannot understand our theology in the same way as it had been articulated by the church fathers. When we remove classical Christian texts from the scholastic context, we lose some of their important points. Paradoxically, by rejecting scholasticism as a *pseudomorphosis*, theologians arrive at other *pseudomorphoses*, such as the personalistic interpretation of the Trinity. This interpretation, in contrast to the patristic one, ascribes more value to the divine persons than to God's one essence. As a result, Christian monotheism can be compromised.

I believe scholasticism still features a tremendous potentiality of creativity for modern theology. To demonstrate this, I offer a fresh outlook at the church. It is based on the classical scholastic categories. In the logical framework of scholasticism, we can properly understand the role of communities in the church. In my interpretation, they constitute the particularities or "hypostases" of the church's universal nature. From the same logical perspective, one can better understand why the Christian East always contested the Western claims of universal jurisdiction for the church of Rome. Such claims confuse the church's particular modalities with its universal nature. From the Eastern perspective, the Western church continues to be local and particular, and cannot be identified with the ecclesial commonality.

Scholastics, when properly applied, can give a solution to such theological dilemmas as the one between human agency and predestination for salvation. Speaking scholastically, salvation can be interpreted as either common or particular. The incarnation of God made common salvation possible for everyone. However, to appropriate this salvation and make it particular, each person has to make his or her own decision. The particularization of the common salvation, thus, is impossible without human agency. Such "scholastic" interpretation of salvation coheres with the Orthodox concept of synergy between God and human beings, with the Eastern ascetic practices, and the theology of deification-*theosis*.

Classical logical categories, in my opinion, may also help to address the modern issues of racism, nationalism, sexism, and other forms of discrimination. Discrimination is often based on the assumption that some groups of people are ontologically different from other groups. In the Antiquity, for example, men, women, children, and slaves were perceived as sharing in different humanities. In our time, similar ideas underpin racism or sexism. Discrimination is based on a mistaken particularization of common humanity. This mistake can be corrected, if the correct distinction between the categories of particularity and commonality is applied. According to such distinction, all human beings, regardless of their gender, race, nationality, sexual orientation, and so on, equally share in the same common human nature. Everyone particularizes this nature to the same extent, which eliminates a possibility of ontological differentiation between various social groups. Such differentiation can be social or cultural, but not based on any assumed natural differences within humanity.

## Tradition *versus* Traditionalism

Another agenda permeating this book differentiates between two attitudes to tradition. One confuses it with the Revelation and perceives it in absolutist terms. This attitude has been called "traditionalism." If traditionalism were applied to the tradition it venerates in the period when this tradition was formed, this would have impeded the formation of this tradition. Another attitude takes tradition with the same creativity that had produced this tradition in the first place. Such attitude is more faithful to tradition than traditionalism is. Traditionalism is eager to preserve old forms of tradition and often disregards its original meaning. Tradition, when perceived according to its original meaning, reinvents itself. The point that this book has been designed to prove is that the best of the Eastern Christian theology was creative and innovative: it found new linguistic forms to express the same Revelation. In contrast to the stereotype, orthodoxy is innovative and heresy is traditionalist.

The roots of traditionalism grow from the polytheistic Antiquity, particularly from its concept of "golden age." The earliest recording of this concept occurs in Hesiod's *Works and Days* (90–120) and was apparently known before him (see Baldry 1952). Hesiod identified five ages in the history of humankind: golden (*chryseon genos*, χρύσεον γένος), silver, bronze, heroic, and iron (127–201). The next one was worse than the previous one, except the heroic age, which was better than the preceding bronze one. Roman poets followed Hesiod's model and streamlined his timeline. According to Ovid (43 BC–17/18 AD), for example, *each* next age was worse than the previous one (*Metamorphoses* I 89–150).

Christianity was despised by many educated pagans as a product of the latest and, therefore, worst of the ages. One of the arguments that its adversaries railed against Christianity was its novelty. Such, for instance, was the point of the pagan middle-Platonic philosopher Celsus, who flourished in the late second century. He was a "conservative intellectual" who promoted "traditional values" (Wilken 2003: 95). He criticized Christianity on the grounds that it was a novelty, which threatened the values of the Greco-Roman civilization.

Christianity's lack of traditionalism, perceived as a threat to traditional values, incited some Roman emperors, such as Decius (r. 249–51) and Diocletian (r. 284–305), to launch anti-Christian persecutions. Some Christian apologists responded: it is not bad per se to introduce something new to the stagnating society. Novelty is not tantamount to evil—in contrast to what many pagans believed. Such was, for example, the response given by the author of the *Letter to Diognetus*. Other apologists, who complied with the classical concept of "golden age," struggled to demonstrate that Christianity has ancient roots that go back to "better" ages. There were two strategies to make such a point. One was biblical: Christianity is based on the ancient Jewish revelations, which are contemporary or even more ancient than the Greek ones. The second strategy was to go even further back in history and to trace the common roots of the Christian Revelation and the Greek wisdom. Both stem from the divine Logos, who partially revealed the truth to the Greeks, through the "seminal logos" (Justin, *Apologia* II 7, 13), and recently completely disclosed it to the Christians. This strategy also assumed that Christianity is not a novelty but the fulfillment of the antique past.

The latter apologetic strategies, combined with the appropriation of the Greek idea of the "golden age," made Christians adopt the traditionalist attitude to novelties as something suspicious. As Christianity grew older and its past became longer, Christians began preferring what is old to what is new. During doctrinal disputes, theologians who disagreed with one another developed a custom to accuse opponents of novelty. Novelty gradually evolved to be associated with heresy, while orthodoxy became identified with an imagined dogmatic "golden age." Such an age never existed though. Most doctrines, which later would become accepted as orthodox, were novelties in the periods of their formation: they were rendered through neologisms. However, in the posterior period of reception, they would be regarded as old and, therefore, trustworthy. Theology always added something new, but this new, to be accepted, had to be camouflaged as old. Nevertheless, the idea that any *nouvelle théologie* is bad by default, and the old theology is good, has little to do with Christianity per se, which is indeed a "new commandment" (Jn 13:34) and a radical breakup with many traditions of the past.

Notwithstanding the ever-renewing character of the Eastern Christian theological tradition, I intend to demonstrate the continuity of this tradition from its inception to our days. This continuity is not linear though. There were disruptions in it, as, for example, within the neo-Nicaean and neo-Chalcedonian traditions. Both were intended to clarify orthodox points and both had factions that went astray from orthodoxy. This book demonstrates that theological voices, even the most celebrated ones, did not sing a Byzantine chant: a monotonic curve against the *isokratema* of the tradition. These voices often went polyphonic and sometimes even atonic. They sound similar not only to Bach and Beethoven, but sometimes to Schoenberg and Stravinsky. A project that I had a chance to participate in from 2013 through 2019, organized by the *Internationales Wissenschaftsforum der Universität Heidelberg* and called *Die Polyphonie der Theologien der Kirchenväter* (published in the special volume of the *Evangelische Theologie* 79/5 (2019)), aimed at demonstrating exactly this—a diversity in patristic voices.

## Book's Structure

This book is structured in accordance with the traditional theological rubrics. Its first chapter, *Milestones*, describes the historical paths of Eastern Christianity: from the primitive apostolic communities to what Francis Fukuyama has described as "the end of history" (Fukuyama 2020)—the collapse of the classical ideologies. My historical survey stops short before the post-Soviet era begins and offers only a few glimpses in it. This is because I avoid analyzing modern theologians who live.

The chapter is focused on how the church's structures and theological traditions have been shaped by its interaction with political systems. I argue that Christianity emerged as a nonconformist movement in a hostile environment of the global Roman

Empire. The hostility between the church and the empire was mutual (see *Romanitas versus Christianitas* and *Christianitas versus Romanitas*). One of the reasons for such hostility was the incompatibility between the Roman and Christian political theologies. The former deified political power, while the latter was eschatological. Nevertheless, as it evolved, the church began absorbing Roman elements to its structures and self-perception. I have explored these evolutional processes in more detail in my earlier books on ecclesiology (Hovorun 2015a; Hovorun 2017).

Rapprochement between the church and the empire culminated in what was later called "symphony"—an idealistic vision of a complete coherence between them. I argue that this was a millennialist vision that envisaged a 1,000-year-long Christ's kingdom on earth. This vision transformed both the church and the empire. It forged the ecclesial and imperial self-awarenesses into a single theopolitical vision, which to a great extent substituted the church's eschatological vision.

The church adopted many elements of Roman statehood, including its administrative grid and hierarchical ethos. Within the empire, the church substituted traditional republican institutes. For example, under the church-state symphony, the senate turned more to a decoration, while the church snapped up some of its political roles. Symphonic mentality that the church had adopted outlived the Roman Empire and survived in the Eastern Christianity to our day. It explains, for example, the church's collaboration with modern autocracies. In this book, I refer to some cases of such collaboration but explore them in more detail in another book (Hovorun 2018).

Despite symphonic fusion of self-awarenesses, the innate apostolic nonconformism survived within imperial Christianity—in the form of monasticism. I argue that monasticism emerged as a nonconformist movement within the church being assimilated into the empire. In its nonconformist capacity, monasticism opposed some teachings promoted by the empire, such as dyophysitism or iconoclasm. Monastics often resisted abuses against the church by the state.

The church-state symphony, on the one hand, and its critique, on the other, played a crucial role in divisions within global Christianity during the first millennium. As a result, three separated fellowships emerged in the East: Byzantine, Eastern Syriac (or "Nestorian," now known as the Church of the East), and Oriental. I argue that fellowship or commonwealth is the basic ecclesial structure in the Christian East. In contrast to premodern Western Christianity and modern Roman Catholicism, which can be presented as a pyramid, Eastern Christianity's structures consist not of one, but of several pyramids. Within these pyramids, power has been strictly stratified and centralized. At the same time, the pyramids of the local churches are not subordinate to each other but relate to each other as a fellowship or commonwealth.

Relationship between local churches is based on consent and not coercion. While this system of interchurch relations is more consistent with the Christian ethos, it is more fragile than the hierarchical system, which can be observed in the Roman Catholic Church. The consent-based system works well only when the local churches are responsible enough to understand common good and able to sacrifice their local interests for its sake. The moderator of the common action—the patriarch of Constantinople in the case of the Byzantine fellowship—should be patient enough to communicate with local churches in noncoercive manner. The moderating church should be more selfless than other local churches.

Eastern Christianity had experienced separation from the state long before the modern processes of disestablishment began: first in the Persian Empire, then in the Arab caliphates, and later in the Mongolian, Central Asian, Safavid, Mughal, and Ottoman empires. Some Orthodox churches that had not experienced separation from the state under the Muslim rule eventually became disestablished under Communist rule. Despite these experiences of living separately from the state, Orthodox churches, especially in the Byzantine fellowship, still have phantom longing for the Byzantine style of symphony. Such longing infects these churches with ideologies (see the subchapter *-isms*), such as nationalism, Byzantinism, traditionalism, and so on.

In the end of the chapter, I argue that ideological polarization affected most Orthodox theological trends during the twentieth century. For example, the Russian religious philosophy and Eucharistic ecclesiology are more liberal, while neopatristic synthesis and its most recent neo-Palamist update are more conservative. These trends constitute projections of the modern culture wars. I believe that the idea of culture war is applicable even to premodern theological trends. For example, it gives a clue to better understand the early Christian attitudes to the Greco-Roman culture or to the figure of Origen. I try to revisit the history of Eastern Christian thinking from the perspective of modern political and public theologies.

In the book's second chapter, *Dialectics*, I approach theological texts through the category of meta-language. It is both dialectical and linguistic, consisting of logical categories linked syntactically. Meta-language resembles languages we speak; it features lexemes, grammar, and syntax. At the same time, it can be easily rendered to any spoken or written language—because it articulates universal categories. Meta-languages have meta-dialects. Each particular Christian tradition expresses itself through a distinct meta-dialect, which is usually different from the normative theological language. I explore this difference with the assistance of sociolinguistics. Sometimes, theological differences between traditions can be explained by what kinds of meta-dialect they use. Sometimes, using different meta-dialects incurs deeper differentiations and even alienations in theology.

Normative Christian meta-language was shaped by a synthesis between the Christian Revelation and the Greco-Roman culture. The most important source of it was the dialectics elaborated upon by Aristotle and his later commentators. As was mentioned earlier, Christians chose the neo-Platonic edition of the Aristotelian categories to articulate their teaching. Neo-Platonism became the fabric, from which Christian theologians tailored clothes for the Revelation. They thus demonstrated a remarkable open-mindedness and forgiveness. In the third century, neo-Platonism had been mobilized to campaign against Christianity. It ideologically underpinned the "Great persecution" under Diocletian. The neo-Platonist Porphyry became "the prophet of the Great Persecution" (Frend 2008: 485). He instrumentalized neo-Platonism to attack the Christian doctrine, on the assumption that they are completely incompatible. This assumption was wrong. Christians extracted from neo-Platonism its logical component and left aside its metaphysics. Paradoxically, Porphyry became the most popular pagan philosopher among Christian theologians.

Based on the Aristotelian-Porphyrian logics, Christians constructed their own categorial taxonomies. These taxonomies included the pairs of commonality and particularity, distinction and separation, potentiality and actuality, which Christian theologians modified from their pagan originals. They combined the older Aristotelian categories of differences and properties with the newer neo-Platonic categories of participation and unity. All these categories proved to be crucial in the theological controversies about the Trinity and the incarnation.

Crucial for Christian anthropology was differentiation between what is given and what is assigned to human beings. This differentiation rides on the specifically Christian idea of the world being created by God. Human beings have been created with innate potentialities, which they must actualize. Their most important potentiality is the images of God (*imago Dei*), which makes them equal to God (*isotheon*/ἰσόθεον) and having freedom of choice (*autexousion*/αὐτεξούσιον).

Modern Orthodox theology has to a significant extent abandoned the classical logical framework, following the rejection of scholasticism. This, on the one hand, helped modern Orthodox theologians to adjust themselves to the contemporary philosophical frameworks, such as personalism and existentialism. On the other hand, they lost an adequate understanding of the original scholastic categories, such as hypostasis and nature. These categories were redefined, not always helpfully. New categories were added to the nomenclature of basic theological categories, such as "sophia" and Eucharist. I argue that these categories have their advantages and disadvantages. At the end of the chapter, I demonstrate how the new categories have affected modern theology.

Differences between commonality and particularity, potentiality and actuality underpin the book's third chapter, *Salvation*. In this chapter, I differentiate between common/potential and particular/actual salvations. The former became possible because of the incarnation of the divine Logos. By becoming a human being, God saved the common human nature, that is, he offered everyone a possibility of salvation. This salvation, however, does not work automatically, but should be individually appropriated. In other words, to be actualized, it must become particularized.

Human agency is crucial in the process of the actualization of salvific potentiality. Without human input, this process is impossible. That is why it requires *synergy* between human beings and God—a fundamental category in Eastern Christian soteriology. Synergy for the sake of salvation begins with choosing one of two paths: of life or of death. This is an ancient idea that goes back to the Pythagoreans and the *Yahad* community in Qumran. It was explicated in one of the earliest Christian texts, *Didaché*.

Eastern Christian authors presented following the path of life as moving up and forward, or toward the center, where there is God. In the latter case, moving to God means getting closer to one another. Ascetic writers insisted that a person cannot stand still in his or her spiritual development. He or she goes either forward or backward. Christian spiritual writers upgraded the pre-Christian aretology and hamartology. They introduced a differentiation between sins and passions, and defined passionlessness as the *telos* of the virtuous life. They believed that both virtues and passions develop in sequences. The book explores these sequences.

Eastern Christianity has developed various ascetic techniques to achieve the *telos* of spiritual life, such as Jesus prayer. Byzantine hesychasm offered comprehensive and sophisticated theories and practices of spirituality. Yet, hesychasts considered these practices not an end in itself but a path to *theoptia* (vision of God) and *theosis* (deification), which are the ultimate particularizations of the common salvation.

Soteriology constitutes the most comprehensive framework for all other theological disciplines. It is more important than the dialectical framework of categories. Christian theology *can* be comprehended and articulated without classical categories. However, outside the soteriological framework it completely loses its raison d'être. The church fathers found solutions to theological issues on the soteriological basis. For example, they identified components of the humanity appropriated by God through the incarnation, by applying the criterion of what had to be saved in the human nature. Inside the soteriological framework, theological opinions are dogmas, which must be upheld in the orthodox way. Without the orthodox take on these dogmas, a particular salvation is in peril. Outside the soteriological framework, theological opinions are *theologoumena*—optional ideas unnecessary for salvation.

Chapters 4 and 5 of the book present theological dogmas that Eastern Christianity regards as a mandatory precondition for salvation. One must uphold in the orthodox way the teaching about the Trinity and the incarnation. Theological enchiridia usually present these two dogmas as separate theological disciplines. In fact, Trinitarian theology and Christology are inseparable from one another. Jesus Christ is a central figure in both.

At the same time, Eastern theology differentiates between *theologia* and *oeconomia*. The former reflects on God in his uncreated divine existence, while the latter—on his relationship to the world that he had created. I explore *theologia* and *oeconomia* by answering two sets of "big questions" relevant to each of them. The classical Eastern

Christian Triadology and Christology can be scaled down to these questions. Questions for *theologia* are:

*Who* is God?
*What* is God?
*How* God's whos? are linked to each other and how they together are related to God's what?

*Oeconomia* features similar "big questions":

*Who* is Jesus Christ?
*What* is Jesus Christ?
*How* his divinity and humanity are united?

In the church's history, it took a long time and a lot of pain to answer these questions. I argue that convincing answers were given by theologians and received by communities only when the scholastic Aristotelian-Porphyrian categories were applied to both *theologia* and *oeconomia*. Particularly helpful were differentiations between commonality and particularity, as well as distinction and separation. Theologians significantly upgraded some other categories, which had a rudimentary presence in the pre-Christian logical taxonomies, such as unity, activity, and volition.

The bottom line of the theological inquiries from the third through the seventh century was solving the dilemma of oneness and plurality in the triune God and his incarnation in the person of Jesus Christ. Sometimes, solving one theological riddle opened new issues and divisions in the church. For example, the councils of Nicaea (325) and Chalcedon (451), crucial in answering the aforementioned questions, caused further splits in the church. Most church hierarchs and theologians first did not accept the Nicaean language. They are misleadingly called "Arians." I consider them conservatives who could not accept an innovative theological meta-language promulgated by the Nicaea. Another conservative group, this time consisting of the followers of the Alexandrian Archbishop Cyril, did not accept the council of Chalcedon, which for them also was too innovative.

Neo-Nicaean and neo-Chalcedonian movements emerged as attempts to overcome the divides caused by the Nicaea and the Chalcedon. However, within these movements, new divisions emerged. Thus, the neo-Nicaean Cappadocians contested their neo-Nicaean confederates Apollinaris of Laodicea and Diodore of Tarsus. The neo-Chalcedonian movement almost three centuries later divided into the monoënergist/monothelite and dyoënergist/dyothelite factions. Eventually, the Cappadocian take on neo-Nicaeanism and the Maximian dyoënergist/dyothelite take on neo-Chalcedonianism prevailed in the official church. These takes were endorsed by two councils held in the imperial capital: in 381 and 680–1.

Both Trinitarian and Christological controversies were effectively theological "civil wars" that caused schisms, including the greatest one during the first millennium—between the followers and adversaries of the councils of Ephesus and Chalcedon. These schisms disrupted the imperial peace, *Pax Romana*. Emperors tried to preserve and restore the church's unity, with the goal to sustain the state's integrity. This goal incited them to what can be called "Byzantine ecumenism."

This ecumenism antedates the modern "ecumenical era" by sixteen centuries. Unlike the latter, it was often enforced by coercion. To sustain the church's unity, Christian emperors did not hesitate to apply the rough methods of their pagan predecessors. At the same time, they also tried to bring opponents to the same table for a dialogue. Emperor Justinian, for example, introduced the earliest form of ecumenical dialogue for the adversaries and supporters of the Chalcedon. Imperial authorities also promoted rapprochement between divided theological groups through councils. Countless councils happened during the period of Trinitarian/Christological controversies, for which reason I call it the period of *synodomachia*.

Some of these councils were ecumenical—in two senses. First, they were pan-imperial and thus represented the entire *oecumene*—the Greco-Roman world. Second, they aimed at the restoration of the Christian unity and thus were ecumenical in the modern sense of the word. Probably the earliest council of this sort was convened by Constantine only one year after he had signed the Edict of Milan (313). In 314, he initiated a bishops' meeting in Arles to give a solution to the Donatist schism, which ravaged the western part of northern Africa—what is now known as the Maghreb.

A decade later, Constantine initiated a similar council to give a solution to another issue, which this time emerged in the eastern part of northern Africa. This issue is usually called "Arianism." I call it "Alexandrian controversy." A pan-imperial council convened by Constantine in Nicaea in 325 was to put an end to that local controversy. Although the emperor left it to bishops to decide who was right and who was wrong, he seemed to favor the party of the Alexandrian archbishops. Nicaea extinguished the fire of the local Alexandrian controversy. However, from its ashes, a new global controversy was ignited, which I call "Nicaean controversy." This time, Constantine chose to support the anti-Alexandrian party.

The rationale of Constantine's policies regarding both Alexandrian and Nicaean controversies was more political and ecumenical than theological. This explains his ostensible inconsistency. Politically, the idea of a hierarchical relationship between the Father and the Son, which was promoted by the adversaries of Nicaea, served better a new monarchical model, which the emperor implemented to redefine imperial power in the framework of the Christian state. Ecumenically, he came to believe that not the nonconformist archbishop of Alexandria Athanasius, but a more diplomatic archbishop of Nicomedia Eusebius, who later would become the archbishop of Constantinople, and his followers—the "Eusebians," could better secure *Pax Romana*.

Constantine's son and successor Constantius II believed the same. Like his father, he tried to reconcile the supporters and opponents of the council of Nicaea. However, he believed that Nicaea per se cannot be a platform of reconciliation. He instead designed his own platforms. Constantius set up a pattern of rapprochement, which resembles the modern ecumenical movement. The pattern was as follows: first, to gather theologians for informal consultations to work out a certain common theological language. Then a working group assembled, in the form of a small council, which adopted a "consensus document." Then a larger "ecumenical" assembly would approve this document as official. Based on the results of such gathering, the emperor issued a decree, which gave the document the status of a law.

Constantius initially tested this pattern in the 340s. In 341, he assembled a relatively small council in Antioch, which adopted several editions of a new creed to replace the Nicaean creed. The new creed did not contain the term "consubstantial," which disturbed many conservative bishops and theologians, who regarded it as too philosophical and unbiblical. After that, the emperor tried to pass this creed at an "ecumenical" council in Serdica in 343. The council, however, did not bring the desired reconciliation. Then Constantius undertook a second ecumenical attempt in the 350s, following the same scheme. First, he consulted theologians, who suggested a new theological language. This language carefully avoided any reference to the term "essence" (*ousia*, οὐσία). A working group then met in 357 in Sirmium and drew up a new creed. It was tested at more formal councils—in the same Sirmium and then in the Thracian city of Nikē (the city was intentionally chosen to sound like Nicaea) and, finally, in Constantinople. This is how the first "Nikēan-Constantinopolitan" creed was adopted. It substituted the Nicaean term "consubstantial" (*homoousios*, ὁμοούσιος) with the term "alike" (*homoios*, ὅμοιος). The emperor made this creed a law by his decree. Finally, Constantius convened "ecumenical" councils in Seleucia and Rimini, which formally accepted the "Nikēan-Constantinopolitan" creed as mandatory in the imperial church.

A similar ecumenical process took place during the Christological debates. The council of Chalcedon tried to ecumenically reconcile two approaches to the Incarnation: "Logos-flesh" (*Logos-sarx*, Λόγος-σάρξ) and "Logos-human being" (*Logos-anthropos*, Λόγος-ἄνθρωπος), which epicentered correspondingly in Alexandria and Antioch. Instead of reconciliation, however, the council caused further divisions. These were divisions between conservative and more open-minded followers of Cyril of Alexandria. For the former, the Chalcedon deviated from Cyril's Christology. For the Chalcedonians, this council remained faithful to Cyril, but interpreted him in a creative way.

To bridge post-Chalcedonian divisions, Emperor Justinian, whom I consider as the greatest figure in the Byzantine ecumenism, designed a theological project, which we nowadays call neo-Chalcedonianism. It featured both theological and political aspects. Theologically, neo-Chalcedonianism comprised the meta-dialects of both Cyril of Alexandria and Chalcedon. Politically, it condemned Origen and the "three chapters." Neo-Chalcedonianism put its own theological accents—on the logical categories of property (*poiotes*, ποιότης; *idiotes*, ἰδιότης), activity (*energeia*, ἐνέργεια) and will (*thelema*, θέλημα).

To promote his ecumenical project, Justinian consulted prominent theologians of his time, such as Severus of Antioch and Leontius of Byzantium, and held an ecumenical council, in 553 in Constantinople. This one was probably the most "ecumenical" (in the modern sense of ecumenism) among ecumenical councils. It was designed from the beginning to the end with the sole goal to bridge gaps between the divided ecclesial groups. From this perspective, the council of Constantinople 553 was opposite to the least "ecumenical" (in the modern sense of ecumenism) councils of Ephesus in 431 and 449, which promoted the interests of only one, Alexandrian, party. The neo-Chalcedonian project, initiated by Justinian and continued by his successors, after internal controversies and crises mentioned earlier, was reconfirmed by the ecumenical council of Constantinople in 680–1.

Neo-Chalcedonianism failed to reconcile the divided church in the sixth-seventh centuries. However, it became a basis for reconciliation between the Byzantine and Oriental fellowships in the end of the twentieth century, when their representatives signed Agreed Statements in 1989 in Anba Bishoy Monastery (Egypt) and in 1990 at the Center of the Ecumenical Patriarchate in Chambésy (Switzerland). Only in our time, the ecumenical project of Justinian seems to begin working.

In contrast to the common stereotype, Christological issues were not exhausted by the end of the seventh century, when monoënergism/monothelitism was tackled by the sixth ecumenical council. Christological debates continued in the next century, in the form of iconoclasm. This was essentially a Christological controversy because it discussed the implications of the incarnation. Iconodules argued that icons are possible because God became a human being. I explain the details of these discussions in the end of the chapter on the incarnation.

Iconoclasm was the highest point of mingling religion and politics in the Byzantine era. Symphony, state-sponsored protectionism, lucrative privileges that hierarchs and clergy received from the empire—these and other factors had contributed to the fusion of the church and the state to a single theopolitical entity (see Hovorun 2015a: 37–68). Such fusion blurred the ecclesial self-awareness and made it indistinguishable from the Roman civil identity. As a result, Eastern Christian theologians rarely reflected on the church as a phenomenon distinct from the empire. While other theological discourses flourished in highly creative ways, the Byzantine ecclesiology remained rudimentary.

Symphony impoverished the early Christian ecclesiology, which had been expressed, often poetically, through rich imagery. In the ecclesiological chapter,

*Church*, I explore some early images of the church. I also argue that Modernity created a powerful momentum for the Orthodox ecclesiology to reemerge after the centuries-long staying in the shadow of the empires. The ecclesiological awakening began in nineteenth-century Russia and continued during the twentieth century (see Hovorun 2015a: 79–94). This process coincided with the Orthodox churches leaving the shadow of empires and facing the necessity to live on their own.

The chapter also explores how the Orthodox churches faced Christian divisions without relying on the state's support. I mentioned earlier that the Byzantine ecumenism was framed by the Byzantine state. Byzantine ecumenical activities targeted primarily the "Great Schism I" caused by the Christological controversies in the fifth century. When the Eastern Roman Empire weakened and eventually disappeared, the global ecumenical agenda became gradually dominated by Western Christianity, where the Roman see, supported by new ambitious political powers, such as the Frankish quasi-empire, launched its own ecumenical projects. These projects were based on the ecclesiology, which had been in making since at least the papacy of Gregory I (in office 590–604). The new Roman ecclesiology envisaged for the Roman see primacy established as *jus divinum* and jurisdiction identical with the universal church. Such Western ecclesiological shift followed the changes in the perception of ecclesial structures and how they are related to the church's nature.

The distinction between the church's nature and structures frames the ecclesiological Chapter 6 of the book. I have developed this distinction in more detail in my earlier ecclesiological study *Scaffolds of the Church* (Hovorun 2017). The church's nature constitutes a sanctifying core of the ecclesial phenomenon. It is like the star in an imagined ecclesiological planetary system. Structures are like planets and moons, which can reflect the star's light but cannot shine on their own. The church's structures can also be presented as scaffoldings surrounding a building. They help maintain it but are not a part of it. These scaffoldings include such ecclesial institutions as patriarchates, dioceses, autocephalies, canonical territories, and so on. They are handmade structures and did not emerge miraculously. They reflect a centuries-long process of ecclesial evolution. During this process, some ecclesial structures were obliterated, some invented, and others reinvented.

The structures' provenance from various sociopolitical environments, primarily the Roman Empire and its political derivatives, enables a critical approach to them. They should be criticized when they fall short of their original purpose to serve the church's nature. The church's history demonstrates many such shortcomings. In this book, I explore some of them and try to explain why the corruptness of the church's hierarchy does not contradict the ideal of the one, holy, catholic, and apostolic church. In my judgment, the ecclesiological ideal corresponds to the church's nature, while corruptness—to its structures. The nature and structures cannot be separated but only distinguished from one another. Their distinction constitutes a starting point for the project of critical ecclesiology, which I develop together with my colleagues at University College Stockholm (Enskilda Högskolan Stockholm).

The ecclesiological chapter is focused on the division between the Western and Eastern Christianities, which I call the "Great Schism II." It explores the precedents and roots of the second great schism in the "Great Schism I," which had divided Eastern Christianity since the fifth century. In that century, one of the earliest East-West divides bisected Syria. Later, it moved to the Balkans, which since then has become a territory of regular religious and political contestations. Both schisms were underpinned by political processes; theological differences were more a pretext for them.

A major theological issue that divided the East and the West during the Middle Ages was "Filioque"—a theological statement that the Holy Spirit proceeds from the Father "and from the Son"—in Latin *filioque*. I explore this issue in detail to showcase how the church's divisions emerge and can be healed. The issue of Filioque is rooted in the Nicaean controversy. The West traditionally followed the wording of the original Nicaean creed, which presented the Son as begotten "from the essence" of the Father. This implied that the Holy Spirit also proceeds from the common essence of the Father and the Son. The East, however, was not satisfied with the original Nicaean formulation and eventually updated it at the council of Constantinople in 381. The neo-Nicaean theology implied that both the Son and the Spirit come from the hypostasis of the Father. The difference between the old Nicaean and the neo-Nicaean wordings for the provenance of the Son and the Spirit propelled the issue of Filioque to church-dividing.

Christian Antiquity was remarkably tolerant to differences in local ecclesial practices and theological expressions. That is how the Western Filioque, which emerged in Spain during the pro-Nicaean campaigns, was tolerated for a long time in the East. During the Middle Ages, local churches became less tolerant of their differences. The West, as a result, began imposing the Filioque on the East, while the East resisted and began rejecting Filioque as a heresy. These polemics added to the growing divergence between the East and the West regarding the aforementioned ecclesiological issues, such as primacy and jurisdiction.

In the medieval ecumenical era, which succeeded the Byzantine one and was dominated by the church of Rome, the latter *forced* the East to accept the Filioque and Rome's universal jurisdiction and primacy. The so-called uniate councils, held from the thirteenth through the seventeenth centuries, became the main platform for exercising the coercive medieval ecumenism. All of them failed to achieve a sustainable reunification of the church.

The "uniate" approach to ecumenism marked an era, which Ernst Troeltsch called "das konfessionelle Zeitalter der europäischen Geschichte" (Troeltsch 1906: 29) or simply confessionalism. Confessionalism was instigated by the European Reformations. Eastern Christianity, which had yielded the ecumenical lead to Rome long ago, now could only choose between theological menu sets offered by the Western Christianities, without offering attractive dishes of its own. Orthodox theologians sided with the causes of either Reformation or counter-Reformation. I tell in detail a story about the "confession" composed by Cyril Lucaris and reactions to it—to explain how Eastern Christianity became confessionalized. It continues to be like that even after the Western "confessions" began deconstructing confessionalism during the modern ecumenical era. The role of the Orthodox churches in the ecumenical movement during the twentieth century was rather passive, with a few exceptions, such as the encyclical letter *Unto the Churches of Christ Everywhere* promulgated by the Ecumenical Patriarchate in 1920. At the end of the ecclesiological chapter, I showcase both ecumenical enthusiasm and skepticism through some Orthodox representatives of both attitudes.

The final chapter of the book, *World*, focuses on the ancient cosmological debates. They were both internal and external for the church. Externally, Christian theologians engaged with neo-Platonic philosophers on the world's createdness. This discussion took place mostly in Alexandria. It convinced the neo-Platonists to believe in the world's eternity more firmly than even their teacher Plato did, while Christians came to believe in the world's createdness more firmly than even the Bible had said.

Internally, the Christian community became divided by the issue of *apokatastasis*—the idea that every angelic or human being that ever lived in the world, will be eventually saved and reconciled with God. Several prominent theologians of the past shared this idea, including Origen and Gregory of Nyssa. In our day this idea continues to be popular, even though *apokatastasis* was condemned as a heresy. For example, Ilaria Ramelli advocates for this idea from the patristic perspective (Ramelli 2013), while David Bentley Hart—from the perspective of moral theology and metaphysics (Hart 2019). To prove their points, both provide revised translations of the scriptural and patristic texts. Hart even undertook a new translation of the New Testament (Hart 2017).

Another issue that divided the early church and continues tantalizing modern Christians is dualism. This is a worldview that polarizes the world. Instead of seeing the world as a colorful spectrum, dualism presents it in black and white. Dualistic worldview perceives evil as nested in some commonalities—not as an individual choice of particular intelligent beings. For example, it often perceives the female commonality as the vessel of inherent corruption. In other words, it identifies evil with parts of the world: evil is resident in things or places. Such a take on evil is materialistic and fatalistic. Human beings, to avoid evil, are requested not to observe what choices they make but to avoid touching certain things and staying in certain places.

The roots of the dualistic worldview go to the ancient polytheistic cosmogonies, which I explore in the chapter. Dualistic cosmogonies usually ascribe the origins of the world to two principles: a good and an evil one. These principles produced respectfully good and evil parts of the world, which have been antagonistic since the beginning. There is an ongoing battle between the good and evil parts of the world on a cosmic scale. Human beings can participate in this battle. However, this participation is more mechanic and magical than ethical. Magics—an attempt to manipulate the divine—is intrinsically dualistic.

From the pagan cosmogonies and cosmologies, dualism was smuggled into Christianity, even though dualistic and Christian worldviews are incompatible on the molecular level. For Christianity, evil is not an ontological but a moral category. It exists because intelligent beings choose it and not because some god created it. In other words, evil does not reside somewhere in the world, but is an outcome of free choices. The only polarization in the world that Christianity admits is the one between the created and uncreated. Even this polarization, however, has been bridged by Jesus Christ. The created world after the Fall remains ontologically good: there are no dark or unclean spots in it.

Although dualism is incompatible with Christianity, the former still parasitizes within the latter. In different times dualism took different forms: the so-called Gnosticism, Marcionism, Manichaeism, Montanism, Eutychean monophysitism, various mystical sects, such as Paulicians and Bogomils (see Runciman 1961), and so on. Dualism has survived the disenchantment of the world in the period of Modernity and continues tormenting the church in our days. Some forms of modern fundamentalism are dualistic. Modern dualists tend to see the world outside the church as the residence of evil or the evil incarnated. They sometimes associate such substantial evil with the West, heterodox groups, or modern civilization. Similarly to ancient Manichaeans, they imagine themselves taking part in the cosmic battle of the "Orthodox civilization" against the "godless West." Dualism also inspires modern anti-ecumenical movement, which is seen, from the dualistic perspective, as a compromise with the resident evil embodied in the "heretic" groups.

Since the first Christian centuries, dualism has been a challenge for every Christian generation. It remains appealing to many Christians despite the fact that the church had condemned its many forms. After each condemnation, it reincarnates in new forms. Dualistic worldview is childish and oversimplifying. It can be overcome only when a Christian grows up spiritually. This is probably why it continues existing in the church—to instigate its members to mature.

The dualistic worldview tends to ontologize differences between human beings and their groups: men *versus* women, one nation or race against other nations or races, one social class against another social class, clergy against laity, and so on. For example, misogynism, including its Christian forms, often rides on the dualistic assumption that female nature encapsulates evil. From the same perspective, black people are seen by racists as inherently inclined to do evil. As was mentioned earlier, the dialectical category of common nature, in which particular beings participate, can help overcome discrimination, including the one based on dualism. Indeed, if all human beings, regardless of their race, nation, gender, and so on, participate in the same humanity, which has been created good, then no one can be libeled as ontologically evil.

In the last part of the chapter, I address some anthropological issues, both ancient and modern. I discuss the composition of human nature from the perspective of Greek philosophy and patristic theology. I focus on the idea of *imago Dei* in humankind. I also concentrate on the issue of freedom and argue that the church fathers perceived it in the double way (see Hovorun 2019)—similarly to how they differentiated between commonality and particularity, potentiality and actuality, the given and the assigned for the creation. One sort of freedom, which the church fathers often denoted by the word *autexousion* (αὐτεξούσιον), corresponds to the image of God and constitutes the given potentiality pertinent to the common human nature. No human individual can be deprived of it. Another sort of freedom, usually designated as *eleutheria* (ἐλευθερία), is contingent on the human will and choices a person makes. It corresponds to the likeness to God and constitutes the assigned actuality realized by a particular individuum.

Finally, I discuss some aspects of human rights. I showcase what ancient Christian authors held regarding slavery, gender inequality, and racism. Some of their opinions were controversial. Nevertheless, the scholastic categories of commonality and potentiality, which the fathers relied upon, can enhance the modern idea of equal rights for all human beings. Everyone is eligible for equal rights because he or she shares in the common human nature. These rights stand for the sort of freedom that the ancient authors called *autexousion*—the unalienable human autonomy. At the same time, human rights cannot secure what the ancients called *eleutheria*. This sort of freedom can be achieved only through spiritual exercises and volitional efforts—in response to the salvific grace of God.

## Periodization

This book is underpinned by the assumption that, while the Christian Revelation remains the same, theological reflections on it constantly evolve. Each theological topic discussed in the book is presented through evolutionary phases marked by three periods: Antiquity, Middle Ages, and Modernity. It would be too speculative to draw clear demarcation lines between these imagined periods. Such a periodization is a modern contract. It reflects the way we imagine the past but not how the peoples in the past imagined the global timeline. The transition from one period to another was unnoticeable for the generations who lived then. However speculative it is, the tripartite periodization helps us understand better the evolution of Christian theology.

Let us briefly overview each period in more detail. Christianity was born in the era, which Peter Brown identified as Late Antiquity (Brown 1971). In contrast to the earlier Antiquity, this period was marked by globalization driven by the expanding Roman Empire and by the convergence of different lines of thinking. Neo-Platonism, which would profoundly influence the meta-language of Christian theology, was one of many fruits of such convergence. After the church converged with the Greco-Roman world, the Late Antiquity can be also called "Christian Antiquity." During this period, the church's theological reflections evolved from the apostolic and prophetic eschatology to scholastics. Such evolution happened first in the East and later expanded to the West.

Under the influence of classical Antiquity, Christianity came to appreciate texts and traditions. In a sense, texts are opposite to immediate experiences and the idea of tradition is opposite to the imminence of God's coming. Antiquity helped the church begin thinking of itself in the terms of centuries and not only centuries of centuries. By adopting the classical idea of tradition, the church learned to reproduce itself for many generations ahead and connect them with many generations before. Texts became the prime medium for keeping Christian generations and eras together. Antique *paideia* taught the church to use this medium, and Christianity was a good student.

Christian theologians developed a universal meta-language with the purpose to articulate the Revelation. To construct a distinctively Christian meta-language, they borrowed some elements from the Stoic and neo-Platonic meta-languages, primarily their basic lexemes, that is, logical categories. Because of these categories, Christianity became Hellenized and scholasticized. In contrast to popular stereotype, as was mentioned, scholasticism is a product of Antiquity and not of the Middle Ages, which only perfected it.

Late Antiquity taught the church to appreciate diversity. The Mediterranean civilization learned to enjoy diversity not long before the emergence of Christianity, soon after Rome had conquered and absorbed to its melting pot various cultures, languages, religions, and walks of life. Initially, Christianity could survive only as a part of the tolerated diversity. Together with Judaism, it constituted a monotheistic minority within the polytheistic majority. The Christian strategy of survival at this stage was to advocate for diversity and minorities' rights. This strategy did not survive the legalization of Christianity by the Roman Empire. Once a religious majority, the church often applied to the minorities the same methods it had experienced when it was itself a minority.

Christianity borrowed from the Greco-Roman world not only the appreciation of diversity but also elements hardly compatible with the original apostolic ethos. These elements included the idea of hierarchy and the coercive methods of persuasion. The church, which originally featured affinity with republicanism, developed a political theology that justified monarchical authoritarianism. This theology, instead of discarding the pagan Roman political religion altogether, adopted it and produced its Christian edition. In the former, emperors were gods. In the latter, a sole imperial ruler became the image of one God.

Some Late Antique tendencies receded, and others accelerated during the Middle Ages. The politicization of religion, coercion as a method of persuasion, and the church's stratification into hierarchies reached their highest points. As a result, both the medieval church and society became rebuilt to hierarchical pyramids. In contrast to Antiquity, which valued plurality, the Middle Ages preferred uniformity: in theological thinking, ritual practices, and administrative structures (see Galvão-Sobrinho 2021). The church was not anymore in dialogue with external cultures and philosophies but substituted them with its own culture and philosophy. The mechanisms of power-sharing, which constituted a part of the symphonic deal between the state and the church in the period of Late Antiquity, were weakened during the Middle Ages. In the East, the state dominated the church—in contrast to the West, where the papal authority fought for and eventually won superiority over the state.

Justus Henning Böhmer (1674–1749) described these two models as "Papo-Caesaria" and "Caesaro-Papia" (Böhmer 1756: 10–11). He oversimplified and exaggerated, because he extrapolated to the Antiquity and Middle Ages a distance between the church and the state, which had emerged in the period of Modernity. Before Modernity, such a distance did not exist. During the Late Antiquity and Middle Ages, both in the East and the West, there was no gap whatsoever between the state and the church, politics and religion. At the same time, Böhmer was right in sensing that the equilibrium between the church and state, as it had emerged in the Antiquity, became unbalanced during the Middle Ages, in both the East and the West.

The medieval era, as we perceive it from our perspective, landed first at the East and later at the West. The earliest form of Christian scholastic theology, as mentioned, was articulated in the Greek language. Tendencies toward hierarchization and stratification within the church and society also emerged first in the East. For instance, the practice of electing bishops by communities was replaced by the practice of appointing them first in the East and later in the West. Although the West began building its ecclesial and social pyramids after the East, the Western pyramids eventually became higher and stronger than their Eastern prototypes. This can be illustrated by the institute of papacy. It was first established in Egypt and later planted in Italy. Roman papacy monopolized authority piecemeal to the extent that was never known in the East. Although the patriarchs of Constantinople became the highest hierarchs in the Eastern church, their primacy was significantly limited by emperors. They also had to share authority in the church with other patriarchs and councils.

The medieval abuses of uniformity and hierarchism became fatal for the church's unity. The churches of Rome and Constantinople, which during the Middle Ages grew to be the two largest and highest ecclesial pyramids, could not stand another pyramid next to themselves. Once allies during the first great schism against the churches of Alexandria and Antioch, now they broke up their relations. They were unable to tolerate one another, because they had developed similar lust for power, coercive ethos, and monopolies on religious uniformity. These and other negative medieval tendencies culminated in the second great schism, which outlived the age that had born it.

The two largest medieval churches, Rome and Constantinople, could not stop on their own to pursue even more power. Some external circumstances had to interfere to reverse the tide from hierarchization to emancipation. The Eastern church had experienced hierarchization prior to the Western church. In a similar way, the wave of emancipation arrived at it approximately half a century before it reached the West. This wave came from the conquest of the Eastern Roman Empire by the Ottomans in the mid-fifteenth century. Islam is fundamentally egalitarian (see Lindholm 2002: 11). Its equalizing power imposed by new masters, weakened or obsoleted many earlier hierarchical structures, which the Orthodox church had amassed during the symphonic centuries. The church was forced to return to its roots. It learned anew to appreciate communities and laypeople, who now mattered for the survival of the church more than before. The waves of the Reformation in the sixteenth century brought similar effects upon the Western church.

If emancipation is a feature of Modernity, then the Modernity knocked on the church's doors first in the East and only later in the West. However, other fruits of Modernity, such as rationalism and secularism, appeared first in the West and then were imported from there to the East. While Western modernization was geared in the seventeenth century, similar processes in the East were delayed by approximately two centuries. After the fall of Byzantium and before the arrival of Modernism, the Eastern churches were intellectually lethargic. Most texts produced in this period were copies, paraphrases, or compilations of the texts from the creative era of Late Antiquity. Moralistic texts for mass consumption were preferred to complicated and speculative theological treatises. The invention of print did not encourage Eastern authors to write creatively, in the manner that the contemporary Western theologians did. Only the territories, where the East met the West, such as Ukraine or Transylvania, could be seen as an exception. These were the territories of religious rivalry, which instigated theological creativity.

The advance of the Enlightenment to the Eastern territories and the processes of Westernization and secularization triggered by it forced the Orthodox churches to be more creative theologically. Eastern theologians of that time perceived the Age of Reason as both a challenge and an opportunity. For most of them, it threatened the traditional ways of life and thinking. Some theologians, however, accepted the challenge of the Enlightenment and adapted its ideas to their milieu. Both its supporters and adversaries utilized intellectual instruments and methods that the Enlightenment offered. These methods changed forever the way in which Orthodox theologians thought of their traditions and wrote their texts.

In either endorsing or contesting the Modernity, the Orthodox theologians often plagiarized: they borrowed Western ideas and formulas without acknowledging them. Moreover, they often presented these ideas as genuinely Orthodox and sometimes utilized them to attack the West. Not quite ethical, this approach was nevertheless more creative than methods that had dominated the Eastern theological landscape since the Middle Ages.

One of such Western ideas appropriated without proper acknowledgment was that of nation. This category had become an intrinsic part of the project of Modernity and is secular in its origin. In the East, however, it substituted the traditional principles of religious fellowship. For example, in the Ottoman Empire, nations succeeded *millets*—groups of people sharing in the same religious tradition. Despite its provenance from the secular Western Enlightenment, the category of nation, in the Eastern Christian context, became almost identical with the concept of the church. Eastern Christian nationalism became an alter ego of modern ecclesial self-awareness.

Nationalism was not the only Western secular ideology, which has been appropriated by the church and turned to a quasi-theological doctrine. The Orthodox churches have borrowed a lot from culture wars waged in the secularized Western societies. For instance, many of them have identified themselves with the Western secular ideology of conservatism. They proclaim it a new Orthodoxy, while condemning liberalism as a modern heresy of sorts.

## Identities

The title of this book declares that it is about "Eastern Christianity." Indeed, it is focused on the texts produced in the "East." It is difficult, however, to identify where the "East" begins and where it ends. In this book, the meaning of the "East" depends on the period. During the Christian Antiquity, it meant primarily the eastern part of the Roman Empire, as well as the empires and kingdoms to its east. During the Middle Ages, the East included what remained of the Roman Empire, the Slavic states in the Balkans (an area contested at that time by the West and the East) that pretended to be the Roman Empire, the vast state of Rus', and the territories under the Muslim control. In modern times, the mass migration from the Christian East to the New World made "Eastern Christianity" a global phenomenon. It is not Eastern anymore geographically, but only in the terms of identity.

In the book, I generally avoid referring to and explaining the texts coming from the Latin or modern "West." As we increasingly understand nowadays, the division between the East and the West is more an intellectual construct than a historical reality. I follow this construct for only one reason—to not make this thick volume thicker. At the same time, I try to demonstrate that both the West and the East were always in more interaction than we have accustomed to believing.

I argue that "Eastern Christianity" is a modern concept shaped by relatively recent political developments, such as the emergence of the nationalistic ideology which urges the "Eastern" Christians to identify themselves with the "East." The same modern and ideologically charged is the concept of "Byzantium." It was coined in the European early modern scholarship to counterpose the "West" to the "East," "Byzantium" to the Roman Empire (see Kaldellis 2019: 11–17). However, Byzantium *was* the Roman Empire. After its Western part collapsed in the early fifth century, the empire continued to exist in the East for more than 1,000 years. The imperial framework, thus, shaped Eastern Christianity more than what it did to the West. I use the term "Byzantium" in the technical sense signifying the Eastern Roman Empire.

Although "Byzantium" constituted the core of the "Eastern Christianity," it could not exhaust the latter. Some "Eastern" parts had left the Roman dominion and developed strong anti-Byzantine attitudes and identities. They are often called "Oriental." The term "Oriental Christianity" is as confusing as the term "Eastern Christianity." It derives from the name of the Roman diocese of *Oriens* established by Emperor Diocletian in the late third century AD. Its capital was Antioch. This was one of the richest, both economically and culturally, provinces of the Roman Empire.

In the aftermath of the Christological controversies in the fifth and sixth centuries and the Persian-Arab invasions in the seventh century, the largest part of this province was lost for the Roman Empire. Most of its Christian population developed their own theological and cultural identity, often by counterpoising themselves to Constantinople. In parallel to Greek, which they were forgetting, they preferred to speak their own languages, until Arabic became their new *lingua franca*. They established independent ecclesial structures, which we now know as the Church of the East and the Oriental churches. This book explores the history and texts of various "Oriental" traditions in such languages as Coptic, Syriac, Armenian, Ethiopian, Parthian, Sogdian, Chinese, and Arabic.

Cultural identities intertwined with theological opinions. In combination, both contributed to the fragmentation of the single Christian community. Some of its fragments became connected with the names of charismatic leaders and theologians: Valentinians, Arians, Donatists, Nestorians, Cyrillites, Severans, Jacobites, Theodosians, Maximites, Maronites, and so on. Some of them vanished in the centuries and others evolved to continue keeping Christians away from each other, such as, for example, "Nestorian" and "Monophysite" identities. Early Christian identities evolved from theological to political. In our time, they have taken such forms as *Romiosynē*, *Panhellenism*, *Svetosavlje*, "Russian world," and so on. These ideological forms incur further fragmentation to the already fragmented Eastern Christian world.

There is an identity that underlines all Eastern Christian traditions—Orthodoxy. In this book, I use "Orthodox" or "Orthodoxy" with capital "O," when this term and its derivatives imply identity. In its minuscule form, "orthodox" was one of many predicatives that described the ideals of the Christian community. This term was never mentioned in the Bible but had been used in classical philosophy since Aristotle (see *Ethica Nicomachea* 1151a). In the fourth century, this Aristotelian term was employed by the Athanasian party for self-identification and counterposition vis-à-vis its adversaries. Epiphanius of Salamis, for example, contradistinguished the "orthodox" (ὀρθόδοξος) against the "Arians" (*Panarion* 340). Later, the council of Chalcedon and neo-Chalcedonian theologians applied it to identify their belief in the two natures of Christ.

Even prior to the term "orthodox," the term "catholic" became popular in both the East and the West. Like "orthodox," "catholic" was not a biblical term. It had been frequently used by the Ancient Greeks and Hellenistic Jews (see Philo, *De Abrahamo* 4). Such early Christian authors as Justin introduced it to the theological curriculum. In the dialogue with Trypho, he spoke about the "common" (*katholiken*, καθολικήν) resurrection of all (*Dialogus cum Tryphone* 81), as well as about the following "common and particular judgements" (καθολικὰς καὶ μερικὰς κρίσεις) (*Dialogus cum Tryphone* 102). Irenaeus applied this word to the church (*Adversus haereses* III 11) and made catholicity a predicative of the Christian community.

Both categories "catholic" and "orthodox," in minuscule forms, were among the terms borrowed from the classical philosophy to become the keywords of the Christian theology, together with such terms as *ecclesia* or *hypostasis*. However, from predicatives commonly used in both the East and the West, they turned to distinct and sometimes even antagonistic identities, by which the Eastern and Western churches have consolidated themselves against each other. The West, on the one hand, transformed the predicative "catholic" to an identity with the purpose to stress the assumed universal jurisdiction of the Roman see. The East contested this jurisdiction and, in the confessional era, tried to secure its own place among the Western confessions by identifying itself with the predicative of "orthodoxy."

In the times before "orthodoxy" and "catholicity" turned to identities, the majority of Eastern and Western Christians commonly identified themselves as Romans (see Kaplanis 2014: 97). The Quran has a special surah dedicated to the "Byzantines," which is titled "Sūrat ar-Rūm," that is, "Roman" (surah 30). The Chinese called all forms of ancient Christianity—even those ones that had developed an anti-Byzantine identity—"the illustrious religion of Romans" (*Daqin Jingjiao*/大秦景教). The Roman identity survived the Roman Empire. After it fell in 1453, the Christians under Ottoman rule became organized into a self-reliant group, which was called *millet-i Rûm*. Modern Turks even now call the Ecumenical Patriarchate "Roman": *Rum Ortodoks Patrikhanesi*. In modern Greece, in some remote villages, locals still call themselves not Greeks but "Romans" (*romioi*).

The "Orthodox" identity replaced the "Roman" one in the Christian East only during the era of confessionalism (see Hovorun 2015b). Both "Catholic" and "Orthodox" identities, as identities, in our days rather impede the restoration of Christian unity and reduce the self-understanding of the Western and Eastern churches as the universal church of Christ. The "Orthodox" identity locked the self-awareness of the Orthodox to the East. It became included in the self-designation of most local Eastern churches: Russian Orthodox Church, the Orthodox Church of Greece, Orthodox Church in America, Syriac Orthodox Church, Malankara Orthodox Syrian Church, and so on.

Identities can be stronger than the theologies that had formed them. When there are no theological reasons anymore for staying divided, Christians still cannot detach themselves from the identities that keep them separated. The dialogue between the Eastern and Oriental churches has demonstrated this convincingly. The two sides of the dialogue reached in 1990 an agreement that there are no theological issues anymore that would impede their reconciliation. Nevertheless, the two churches stay divided, because primates do not dare to declare to their people that the other side is not heretic. The reconciliation seems to be impossible, because it would insult people's identities, which have been shaped through the rejection of the other side since at least the fifth century.

Identities, on the one hand, can be helpful in consolidating and preserving the integrity of various Christian groups. On the other hand, they can substitute theology and disintegrate the church's unity. In the latter case, they turn against the church's nature. That is probably why Christ challenged the identities that had underpinned his contemporary environment, such as, for instance, those of Pharisees, Sadducees, or Samaritans. Moreover, he did not assign any identity to his disciples, except the identity of disciples (Lk. 14:26). Even this identity was not quite an identity, as it did not guarantee discipleship. Thus, when Peter (Mt. 16:23) and Judas (Mt. 26:25) betrayed Christ, they acted with their identity as disciples. To avoid divisions in the early Christian community, Paul urged the Corinthians to identify themselves not with "Paul" or "Apollos" or "Cephas," but with Christ (1 Cor. 1:10-13).

Identities can turn on the church because all Christian identities are not revealed but constructed. They emerged in the course of history. Some of them vanished. Some survived but changed their original meaning. Identities were initially constructed for good reasons and with the best intentions. However, as all human constructions, they can turn against their original rationale. This indeed happened in history and not infrequently. To avoid the abuses of identities, those who subscribe to them should from time to time revisit their original meaning and historical reasons for their appearance. This is what this book tries to do.

# I

# Milestones

# I.1

# From *Qahal* to *Ekklesia*

It all began as Jesus had predicted—as a mustard seed: a small grain that grows to a big plant (Mt. 13:31-32; Mk 4:30-32; Lk. 13:18-19). That is how a small group of Jesus' disciples transmorphed to liquid-like movements and then to the rigidly structured universal church (see Ward 2013; Korner 2017; Porter & Pitts 2018). Originally, it was a small Jewish sect. After painful debates and without complete consensus, the disciples decided to step out from the Jewish enclosure to the Greco-Roman world.

**Figure 1.1** The church of St. Peter at the place, where, according to legends, the earliest Christian community in Antioch met. This community consisted of both Jews and Gentiles.

Source: Photo by the author.

# Metaphors of the Church

*Ekklesia* was originally a metaphor, through which the early community of Jesus' disciples began imagining themselves in the Greco-Roman context. The symbolic meaning of *ekklesia* comprised two identities that this community had adopted: Jewish and Gentile. On the one hand, "the church of God" (*ekklesia Theou*, ἐκκλησία Θεοῦ) translated the biblical *qahal Yahweh*—the people of God (see Deut. 23:2, Judg. 20:2, 1 Chron. 28:8, Neh. 13:1; Mic. 2:5). On the other hand, it referred to the Greek political culture, where *ekklesia* was a key institution of representative democracy. Free and wealthy males of a *polis* met in its *ekklesia* to make political decisions (see Beck 2013: 391–2).

The word *ekklesia*, thus, reflected the mixed Judeo-Christian character of the early Jesus' movements. At the same time, the adoption of this word by Jesus' movements as an exclusive self-definition marked the so-called parting—the process of distancing between those who received and those who rejected Jesus as the promised messiah. This process accelerated in the second century. It ignited what has been misleadingly called Christian anti-Jewish polemics. It was rather an intra-Jewish debate. Numerous debates of this sort engulfed Jewish communities before and after Jesus. These communities were often divided by the controversial figures, such as Bar Kokhba (second century), Moses of Crete (fifth century), Abu Isa (eighth century), Alrui (twelfth century), Abulafia (thirteenth century), Sabbatai Zevi (seventeenth century), Jacob Frank (eighteenth century), and others who pretended to be messiahs. The controversy about Jesus did not initially differ from other intra-Jewish messianic debates, until Jesus' movements grew to a religion that distanced itself from Judaism.

**Figure 1.2** *Ekklesiasterion*—the place of *ekklesia* on Delos. In most Greek cities, *ekklesia* met in theaters. On Delos, it met in a roofed building, which is now destroyed (see Whitehead 1994: 61–2).

Source: Photo by the author.

## Early Christian Networks

The more the Christian *ekklesia* departed from Judaism, the more it expanded throughout the Roman Empire on its own, outside the existent Jewish networks. Apostles and their disciples established new communities, which formed new networks—the earliest supra-communal ecclesial structures. Since then, the church has been perceived in two ways: as a community and supra-communal structures that help managing groups of communities. Originally, most networks of communities were connected with either apostolic or other charismatic personalities.

The earliest known network was Pauline. Paul personally established its communities and took care of them. He stitched them together, often by sending them letters. Some of his epistles circulated even before the Gospels were written. After Paul died, his communities continued exchanging letters, sometimes in the name of Paul. The book of Acts also emerged as an internal document of the Pauline network and chronicled its evolution.

Another well-attested network of communities is associated with John. The book of Revelation, composed not necessarily personally by the son of Zebedee, was intrinsically

**Figure 1.3** A fragment of the apostolic Acts (17:9-17). This Greek papyrus was produced between 200 and 250 AD in Egypt. Chester Beatty Library in Dublin.
Source: Photo by the author.

connected with the "seven churches" in the western part of Asia Minor (Rev. 1:4–3:20)—the main locus of the Johannine network. This network was distinct from other early Christian networks in many ways. For example, its stories about Jesus, recorded in the Gospel according to John, had a different perspective from the synoptic stories. Generally speaking, what we know as "the New Testament" is effectively a collection of documents by and about early Jesus' various movements and networks.

In contrast to the apostles, a leader of the Christian community in Antioch Ignatius did not establish communities, but he took care of some of them on his way to Rome at the turn of the second Christian century. He had been arrested in the capital of Syria and brought for trial to the imperial capital, where he died as a martyr. While traversing Asia Minor, Thrace, and Macedonia, Ignatius wrote letters to some local communities: in Antioch, Ephesus, Magnesia, Tralles, Smyrna, Philadelphia, Philippi, and Rome. These communities probably did not constitute an "Ignatian network." Nevertheless, the way Ignatius treated them was similar to how the apostles had taken care of their networks. For example, he addressed the Christian community in Philadelphia in the Pauline style:

> Ignatius, who is also called God-bearer, to the church of God the Father and of the Lord Jesus Christ that is in Philadelphia of Asia, that has received mercy and been founded in the harmony that comes from God, that rejoices without wavering in the suffering of our Lord and that is fully convinced by all mercy in his resurrection; this is the church that I greet by the blood of Jesus Christ, which is an eternal and enduring joy, especially if they are at one with the bishop and with the presbyters with him, and with the deacons who have been appointed in accordance with the mind of Jesus Christ—those who have been securely set in place by his Holy Spirit according to his own will. (*Ad Philad.* 282–3)

**Figure 1.4** The supposed tomb of John in Ephesus, now Selçuk in Turkey (see Harrison & Welborn 2018).
Source: Photo by the author.

Networks of Christian communities, connected with charismatic personalities, continued emerging and growing. Three generations after Ignatius, the bishop of Corinth Dionysius (in office during the 160s–170s) established his own network (see Concannon 2017). Its center was in Corinth. The Corinthian community had originally belonged to the Pauline network. Dionysius built his network on its top and incorporated such cities as Athens in Attica, Sparta in Peloponnesus, Knossos and Gortyna in Crete, and Nicomedia and Amastris in Asia Minor; even Rome became affiliated with the Dionysian network. We know about this network from a series of letters that Dionysius sent to the communities in these cities. In contrast to the Ignatian correspondence, Dionysius' letters have not survived, and we know about them only from Eusebius, who quoted some of them (see on the role of letters in Late Antiquity Allen & Neil 2020). Here is an excerpt from a Dionysian letter to the Roman community quoted by Eusebius:

> This has been your custom from the beginning, to do good in manifold ways to all Christians, and to send contributions to the many churches in every city, in some places relieving the poverty of the needy, and ministering to the Christians in the mines, by the contribution which you have sent from the beginning, preserving the ancestral custom of the Romans, true Romans as you are. Your blessed bishop Soter has not only carried on this habit but has even increased it, by administering the bounty distributed to the saints and by exhorting with his blessed words the brethren who come to Rome, as a loving father would his children. (*Historia ecclesiastica* IV 23)

One of the issues that Dionysius addressed in his network was the teaching of Marcion. Marcion originated from Pontus in Asia Minor, being born at the end of the first century. His family owned a successful business. After his conversion to Christianity, he invested his entire fortune to the cause of promoting Christianity—as he understood it. Marcion moved from Asia Minor to Rome around AD 140. There, he began disseminating his peculiar dualistic ideas and was confronted by the local catholic community. In response, he established his own network of communities, which he endowed with his capital. His was the first recorded network of communities, which did not supplement but competed with the existent networks. This was one of the earliest cases of church schism.

## Roman Structures

Networks were a primitive supra-communal structure. As the Christian church evolved, its structures became more sophisticated. Their evolution followed the administrative patterns and grids of the Roman Empire. There was a quantum leap in this evolution, when the structures from community-based switched to territory-based. The earliest networks mentioned earlier were attached to communities. Paul, Ignatius, and Dionysius stitched together communities regardless of which corner of the Roman Empire they were located. In the third century, the church in its majority adopted a different principle of organization: territoriality. Only communities on the same territory could be grouped together, regardless of their origins and affiliations. New supra-communal structures were built on the top of the extant networks and imitated the Roman administrative structures.

The earliest Christian supra-communal structure that followed the Roman principle of territoriality became known as "metropolitan." The church's "metropolises" (μητροπόλεις) mimicked Roman provinces. Bishops in the Roman provincial capitals became "metropolitan bishops," or metropolitans. They were entrusted with the task of coordinating activities and resolving issues in the local communities that had happened to be located within the boundaries of the same imperial province. The metropolitan system was approved by the first ecumenical council in Nicaea (325).

It was later upgraded to the "diocesan" system. This system relied on the larger territorial units of the Roman Empire—dioceses, which had been introduced by Diocletian in the 280s. Each imperial diocese included several provinces. The local churches, as they grew in numbers, became regrouped to larger units as well, now managed from the capitals of the imperial dioceses. The modern term "diocese" is a rudiment of the "diocesan" model of the church administration. In the fifth century, the so-called patriarchal system was built on the basis of the "diocesan" system. The most important imperial hubs, which had also played special role in the early Christian history, became "patriarchal" sees. They were five and came to be known together as "pentarchy" (πενταρχία): five principal sees (see Φειδᾶς 1969). The patriarchal sees have been sorted out in particular order, called "diptychs" (δίπτυχα): first the see of Rome, then Constantinople, Alexandria, Antioch, and Jerusalem. The "patriarchal" system survives until our days, with some modifications.

# I.2

# *Romanitas versus Christianitas*

When looked at retrospectively, the administrative grid of the Christian church that imitates Roman patterns seems natural. However, from the perspective of early Christianity, it would have looked peculiar. The early church was incompatible with the Roman state by many parameters, including administrative models. Christianity emerged in the period, when the Roman state turned from republic to empire, with a permanent dictator on its top. Rome was busy substituting its horizontal republican structures with the vertical monarchal ones, while Christianity developed horizontal networks. Christian theologians emphasized freedom as the basis of spiritual life. Rome, in contrast, advanced in coercion as the foundation of Roman spirituality.

## Roman Political Religion

Notwithstanding their differences, the Roman Empire followed the Roman Republic in treating politics and religion as inseparable. From this perspective, Roman society was not different from any ancient society. At the same time, the republic and the empire differed in their approach to the state-religion relations. In the republican period, the Roman authorities usually sought public consent for many religious practices. It was not exactly freedom of consciousness in the modern sense, but some sort of freedom regulated by republican institutions, such as the senate. The imperial Rome, however, demanded from its subjects more conformism in religious matters. It became a rule that monarchs regulated religious beliefs, implementing the principle *cuius regio, eius religio*. Such a role was instituted in their official function as "highest priest," *pontifex maximus*. The senate usually approved without further questions the religious initiatives of a monarch. Religious conformism, thus, became one of the pillars of the *Pax Romana* (see Rüpke & Woolf 2020; Rüpke 2012). In contrast to Roman conformism, the original Christian attitude to the state was nonconformist. Christianity, at least in its initial intentions, supported the idea of the freedom of consciousness. This freedom was crucial for the survival of Christianity

**Figure 1.5** Emperor as *pontifex maximus*. A second century AD statue from Perge. Antalya Archeological Museum.
Source: Photo by the author.

in the Roman Empire. Without the freedom of consciousness, Christianity did not have many chances to compete with the state religion or numerous philosophical schools, which often were also religious sects.

The roots of the early Christian nonconformism are Jewish. Less than a century before Christ was born, Rome had finally conquered Judea. Roman authorities ruled it either through their local proxies, such as the Herodian dynasty, or directly through procurators. The Jews regularly rebeled against the Roman rule (see Schäfer 2003). Their anti-Roman nonconformism framed the mission of Christ. Many of those who perceived him as the messiah wanted him to be their king. At the same time, some of those who were against him, provoked him to demonstrate disloyalty to the Roman state, to accuse him of treachery. Christ had to disappoint the former and to deal with the latter. He made it clear that his kingdom is "not of this world" (Jn 18:36). At the same time, he urged to give back to Caesar what is Caesar's (Mk 12:13-17). Christ effectively made the religion he preached neither confronting nor conforming with politics but transcending it. He introduced a radical differentiation between religion and politics, probably unprecedented for his time. Such a differentiation became a basis for the later Christian nonconformism.

**Figure 1.6** Julius Caesar (first century AD). Archaeological Museum of Corinth.
Source: Photo by the author.

As mentioned, when Christianity emerged, the Roman political system was undergoing a radical transformation from republic to monarchy. This transformation caused the Roman civil religion to turn to a political religion (see Riedl 2010). Civil religion secures social cohesion based on values and rites that look religious, but in fact are political. It requires some degree of public consent. Political religion also secures social cohesion based on ostensibly religious values and rites but in a more coercive way. Roman republican institutes regulated the public cult and received feedback from various strata of the Roman society. From the time of Julius Caesar, civil religion evolved to a political religion. Monarchs, consequently, exercised an increased role in the religious life of their subjects, in the capacities of both the regulators (as *pontifex maximus*) and objects (as *divinus*) of public worship.

The veneration of different aspects of monarch's personality—his image, *genius*, *numen*, and *persona*—became the core of the Roman political religion. The idea that monarchical power is divine and should be venerated accordingly is coeternal with the idea of monarchical power as such (see Oakley 2008). It was not completely out of blue that, soon after Julius Caesar initiated the transformation of republic to monarchy, the senate voted for several remarkable initiatives that were supposed to enhance his political status through religious attributes and rituals. For example, after having granted Caesar the title *dictator perpetuo*, the senate established quadrennial festivals in his honor and ordered installing his statues in the state-controlled temples. The republican mint began producing coins with Caesar's image and references to his assumed descent from Venus, through Aeneas. Never an alive person appeared on the coins minted by the Roman Republic. After Caesar was assassinated in the senate in March 44 BC, his grieving supporters began offering sacrifices *to* him and not just *for* him. They raised an altar at the place, where his body was put on pyre.

His adopted son and successor Octavian endorsed the growing cult of Julius Caesar as a divine personality. After the senate deified Caesar in 42 BC, Octavian constructed a temple to him. He intended to project the cult of the "divine Caesar" upon himself. Indeed, Octavian soon became called "the son of god" and was officially exempted by the senate from other mortals. In 27 BC, the senate bestowed upon him the title "Augustus." This title corresponded to the Greek "Sebastos" (Σεβαστός), which previously applied exclusively to gods. As Dio Cassius remarked, this title implied that Octavian "was more than human" (*Historiae Romanae* VI 53.16). Octavian was careful enough to avoid being overtly venerated as a god, at least in Rome. However, in the remote corners of his empire, locals soon began worshipping him as a deity. After Octavian died, the senate declared him a god.

Augustus has been credited, if not for inventing, at least for upgrading the Roman imperial cult. After him, most Roman emperors were deified. Sometimes they also arranged deification-*apotheosis* (ἀποθέωσις) for the members of their families: parents, siblings, in-laws, and even lovers. For example, Caligula (r. AD 37–41), the great-grandson of August, made goddess Julia Drusilla (AD 16–38), who was his sister and an assumed lover. Hadrian (r. AD 117–38) created a whole religious cult of his boyfriend Antinous.

During the early decades of the Roman monarchy, worshipping the emperor was camouflaged, indirect, and optional, at least in Rome. After Caligula, it became increasingly overt and mandatory. In contrast to Julius Caesar and Octavian Augustus, Caligula demanded his *apotheosis* while he was still alive. He built his new palace to be extended to the podium of a temple. This was to convince the Roman people that in his palace a god lives—that is, Caligula himself.

The legitimate source of such deifications was always the senate. Even the "divine" emperors could not deify others but had to ask the senators to do this. Paradoxically, a republican institution that survived under the monarchy, the senate came to play a leading role in promoting the imperial cult, which became the core of the monarchial and anti-republican ideology. The magics of the imperial cult boosted the legitimacy of the imperial authority in general and of individual emperors in particular. This

**Figure 1.7** Hadrian's boyfriend Antinous. After he drowned in the Nile, the emperor deified him. In Egypt, Antinous was identified with Osiris and venerated as Osirantinous. A second century AD statue from Perge. Antalya Archeological Museum.
Source: Photo by the author.

**Figure 1.8** *Ara pacis Augustae*—an altar propagating the divine nature of the Roman imperial power. Museum of the *Ara Pacis* in Rome.
Source: Photo by the author.

cult would remain "the only element of the old civic ritualism that still had vitality" (Scheid 2014: 279) in the time, when other Roman religious practices would become relativized or obsolete.

All emperors after Julius Caesar made sure they themselves and the traditional Roman gods are properly worshipped together. Both the imperial and traditionalist cults were regarded as essential for sustaining the cohesion of the Roman society and the strength of the Roman state. The imperial cult boosted the legitimacy of the imperial power, while the cult of traditional deities secured *pax deorum*—peace with gods. These two cults became intertwined. Emperors came to be perceived as mediators between the Roman people and the Roman gods. They ensured that peace with gods, *pax deorum*, translates to peace in the empire, *Pax Romana*. Those who refused to participate in either imperial or traditionalist cults were believed to upset gods and endanger the Roman peace. They were accused of "misanthropy" (μισανθρωπία)—hating the human race (see Johnson 2010: 34). Romans believed that such "misanthropes" incur divine wrath on the humankind.

## Persecutions under Nero

This was one of the reasons why Romans did not like Jews. They extrapolated their Judeophobia (see Schäfer 1998: 180–96) to Christians. For as long as Christians were seen as a Jewish sect, they enjoyed the protection of the laws that exempted Jews from public sacrifices and other mandatory pagan practices. Around the mid-first century, however, Romans began realizing that Christians are not the same as Jews. Parting from Judaism made the Christian community vulnerable and led to the first specifically anti-Christian persecutions.

It happened under Emperor Nero (54–68). In July 64, three of Rome's fourteen districts were wiped away by what would be called the Great Fire (see Malitz 2008: 66–76; Barrett 2020). Other seven districts were severely damaged. Countless lives were lost. Many accused Nero of doing little about this catastrophe. Some even believed he was behind it. Indeed, he took an advantage of the destruction of the capital's center, where he soon began building his new gigantic palace, the "Golden House" (*Domus aurea*). Nero had to divert public dissatisfaction from himself to someone else.

He chose the relatively small Christian community of Rome to be scapegoats for the fire. Nero knew Christians were disliked by most Romans, similarly to Jews. At the same time, they were different, as the Romans began realizing. Therefore, the laws protecting Jews did not apply to them. Nero utilized these factors to his own advantage. He acted as a "brilliant populist" (Strauss 2019: 82). In his private estate at what is now Vatican, he staged a performance with Christians as main actors. Some of them were dressed in animal skins and torn apart by dogs—in the resemblance of the myth of Actaeon. Others were crucified or burned. These were well-calculated acts of populism aiming at calming down and distracting people's anger. However, these performances only partially satisfied the Roman plebs, and their distracting

**Figure 1.9** Inside Nero's *Domus aurea* in Rome.
Source: Photo by the author.

effect did not last long. Public dissatisfaction with Nero soon resumed growing, and he eventually had to commit suicide in 68.

## Martyrdom of Peter and Paul

According to the later apocryphal reports, apostles Peter and Paul died during the persecution that followed the Great Fire (see Eastman 2019). One of these reports is known as the *Acts of the Holy Apostles Peter and Paul*. The Acts were composed in the fifth or sixth centuries in Rome and exist in Latin and Greek editions. They have incorporated earlier traditions and accounts. At the same time, they stressed what was important for the Roman church in that period. On the one hand, the Acts synchronized the deaths of the two apostles, even though the earlier reports had presented them as two different events. On the other hand, they promoted the figure of Peter as superior to Paul, which marked the acceleration of the Peter-based ecclesiology in the West on the eve of the Middle Ages.

Nero played a central role in the martyrdom of both Peter and Paul, according to the Acts. They present him as acting in the interest of the Jews. Nero reportedly held long conversations with Peter and Paul on Christian teaching and eventually sentenced them to death. The Acts first tell the story of Paul's execution. The document has blended this story with another ancient story, about Perpetua:

> Peter and Paul were led away from the presence of Nero after they received their sentence. They led Paul three miles outside the city in order to decapitate him, and he was bound in irons. The three soldiers guarding him were of a large race. After they left the gate and had traveled about the distance of a bow shot, a pious woman came to meet them. When she saw Paul being dragged along and bound in chains, she felt great pity for him and wept bitterly. The name of the woman was Perpetua, and she had only one eye. Seeing her crying, Paul said to her, "Give me your scarf, and as I am returning I will give it back to you." She took the scarf and gave it to him willingly.
>
> The soldiers approached the woman and said to her, "Why do you want to lose your scarf, woman? Do you not know that he is going to be beheaded?" Perpetua said to them, "I adjure you, by the well-being of Caesar, to place this scarf on his eyes when you cut off his head." And it happened in that way. They decapitated him at the estate called Aquae Salvias, near the pine tree. But just as God wished, before the soldiers returned, the scarf, which was covered with blood, was given back to the woman. As soon as she put it on, immediately and at that moment her eye was opened.

The story proceeds with the circumstances of Peter's death:

> As for the soldiers who had led away holy Peter, as soon as they came to crucify him, the blessed one said to them, "Because my lord Jesus Christ came down from heaven

**Figure 1.10** Peter and Paul in the Catacombs of Domitilla in Rome.
Source: Photo by the author.

to the earth and was raised up on an upright cross, as for me—whom he deigned to call from the earth to heaven—my cross must place my head down to the ground and my feet directed toward heaven. Because I am not worthy to be on a cross in the way my lord was, turn my cross upside down." They immediately inverted the cross and nailed his feet upward. (In Eastman 2015: 307–9)

# Pliny the Younger

After Nero, there were no centrally imposed persecutions against Christians for a long time. Christians continued to be a minority group, which was hated by the majority. Dealing with this minority was left to the provincial authorities, as a policy of subsidiarity. The correspondence between a governor in Asia Minor Pliny the Younger and his patron Emperor Trajan testifies to that. Pliny was supposed to decide on his own how to treat Christians under his jurisdiction. At the same time, using his proximity to the emperor, he asked him to confirm that what he was doing was right. He informed Trajan that he would interrogate the Christians and spare them, "when they had repeated after me a formula of invocation to the gods and had made offerings of wine and incense to your statue (which I had ordered to be brought

**Figure 1.11** Emperor Trajan, a second century AD statue from Perge. Antalya Archeological Museum.

Source: Photo by the author.

into court for this purpose along with the images of the gods), and furthermore had reviled the name of Christ" (*Ep.* 96). If they refused to do so, Pliny would send the Roman citizens for trial in Rome and would punish others on the spot. This punishment was usually capital. Trajan approved this line. Later, Emperors Hadrian and Antoninus Pius confirmed that this was the official line of the Roman state.

# Martyrdom of Polycarp

One of such local persecutions, in conformity with Pliny-Trajan correspondence, happened in the 150s in Smyrna. The bishop of the city Polycarp was tried and executed by local authorities. The story of his martyrdom became a model for later Christian martyrologies. It contains not only an account of Polycarp's death but also a theology of martyrdom. At the core of this theology is the idea of sacrifice. This sacrifice is an imitation of Christ on the cross. The structure and messages of Polycarp's martyrdom imitate the Gospels. Based on these parallels, the authors of the *Martyrium Polycarpi* suggested a chain of imitations: martyrs imitate Christ and all Christians should imitate martyrs:

> We are writing you, brothers, about those who were martyred, along with the blessed Polycarp, who put an end to the persecution by, as it were, setting a seal on it through his death as a martyr. For nearly everything leading up to his death occurred so that the Lord might show us from above a martyrdom in conformity with the gospel.
>
> For Polycarp waited to be betrayed, as also did the Lord, that we in turn might imitate him.

Police found Polycarp in a house in the countryside, where he was hiding. They brought him to Smyrna and started interrogations. What follows is a testimony that the only requirement on which the authorities insisted was to offer sacrifices to the emperor:

> The chief of police Herod, along with his father Nicetas, met him and transferred him to their carriage. Sitting on either side, they were trying to persuade him, saying, "Why is it so wrong to save yourself by saying 'Caesar is Lord,' making a sacrifice, and so on?" He did not answer them at first; but when they persisted, he said, "I am not about to do what you advise." <. . .>
>
> The proconsul became more insistent and said, "Take the oath and I will release you. Revile Christ." But Polycarp responded, "For eighty-six years I have served him, and he has done me no wrong. How can I blaspheme my king who has saved me?"

The authorities persuaded Polycarp to make a minimal gesture of loyalty to the emperor by offering a formal sacrifice to his "genius." When Polycarp refused, they proceeded to tortures:

**Figure 1.12** A Roman priest from the Archeological Museum in Izmir (Smyrna). Priests could also perform other public offices, including judicial ones.
Source: Photo by the author.

> Immediately the instruments prepared for the pyre were placed around him. When they were about to nail him, he said, "Leave me as I am; for the one who enables me to endure the fire will also enable me to remain in the pyre without moving, even without the security of your nails." <. . .>
>
> When he sent up the "Amen" and finished the prayer, the men in charge of the fire touched it off. And as a great flame blazoned forth we beheld a marvel—we to whom it was granted to see, who have also been preserved to report the events to the others.
>
> For the fire, taking on the appearance of a vaulted room, like a boat's sail filled with the wind, formed a wall around the martyr's body. And he was in the center, not like burning flesh but like baking bread or like gold and silver being refined in a furnace. And we perceived a particularly sweet aroma, like wafting incense or some other precious perfume.
>
> Finally, when the lawless ones saw that his body could not be consumed by the fire, they ordered an executioner to go up and stab him with a dagger. When he did so, a dove came forth, along with such a quantity of blood that it extinguished the fire.

After Polycarp's death, a new phase of drama began, now related to his remnants. For Christians, the body of a martyr was a precious relic. The authorities knew this and made sure they destroy it. They burned the body of Polycarp. However, the Christians managed to save some of his bones, which they brought to their community for veneration:

> But the jealous and envious Evil One <. . .> made certain that his poor body was not taken away by us, even though many were desiring to do so and to have a share in his holy flesh.
>
> So he incited Nicetas, the father of Herod and brother of Alce, to petition the magistrate not to hand over his body, "Lest," he said, "they desert the one who was crucified and begin to worship this one." <. . .>
>
> When the centurion saw the contentiousness caused by the Jews, he placed Polycarp's body in the center and burned it, as is their custom.
>
> And so, afterwards, we removed his bones, which were more valuable than expensive gems and more precious than gold, and put them in a suitable place. (*Martyrium Polycarpi*)

The remnants of martyrs became the earliest sacred subjects for Christians. Christians originally did not have sacred places of worship and usually met at homes. They often brought the bones of martyrs to those homes, where they also baptized new members of communities, studied the Scripture, and participated in Eucharistic meals. Sometimes they also met at burial places, such as abandoned catacombs, where martyrs' remnants had been interred. Graves of martyrs, thus, became liturgical places utilized for Eucharist. Only after the legalization of Christianity in the early fourth century, communities began meeting in public places, such as basilicas. Christians brought the relics of martyrs to their new public spaces of worship. Nowadays, this tradition survives as a custom to place a martyr's relic to the *antimension*—a piece of cloth upon which the liturgy is performed.

**Figure 1.13** An early Christian burial place inside the catacombs on the Aegean Island of Milos.

Source: Photo by the author.

**Figure 1.14** Emperor Decius on a Roman coin. Archäologische Museum at the University of Münster in Germany.
Source: Photo by the author.

## Persecutions under Decius

For a long time, the Roman policies toward Christians followed the principle of subsidiarity and remained a responsibility of local authorities. The situation changed in the mid-third century, when Decius became the emperor in 249. He soon applied new religious policies, which led to the unprecedented persecutions of Christians. His motifs remain unclear. One can guess, however, that he strove to reinforce the traditional Roman values and thus to enhance the cohesion of the Roman society.

To enforce his new policies, Decius promulgated an edict that commanded all his subjects to participate in public rituals, which included offering sacrifices to the common gods and to the genius of the emperor (see Rives 1999). Edict was a law intended for all people and not just officials. Jews were exempted, but Christians were not. According to new policies, they were allowed to keep in private their religious practices. At the same time, publicly, they were mandated to demonstrate their loyalty to the state and their commitment to common good by participating in sacrifices. Those who refused were warned to be severely punished. Local administrations were instructed to make sure that everyone participates in rituals, which had to be certified by a *libellus*. Such *libelli* have been excavated in Egypt, including the following one:

> To the commission in charge of the sacred victims and sacrifices of the city. From Aurelius L<. . .>thion, son of Theodore and Pantonymis, his mother, of the same city. I have always and without interruption sacrificed and poured libations to the gods, and now in your presence in accordance with the decree I have poured a libation, and

> sacrificed, and partaken of the sacred victims, together with my son Aurelius Dioscorus and my daughter Aurelia Lais. I request you to certify this for me below. Year one of Imperator Caesar Gaius Messius Quintus Traianus Decius Pius Felix Augustus, Payani 20 (June 14, 250). (*P. Oxy* IV 658; Knipfing 1923: 366)

Many Christians received such *libellus*. Some of them did not see a problem in sacrificing. Many of those who saw a problem could not stand threats or tortures. Some scholars argue that the majority of Christians sacrificed for one or another reason (see Rebillard 2017a: 53). In the early church, they became known as *lapsi*—"the fallen." Even some church leaders apostatized, such as the bishop of Smyrna Euctemon. There were much more *lapsi* than martyrs—"hordes" of them (Frend 2008a: 415). Their readmission to the church became a serious issue provoking deep divisions in the Christian communities. Decian persecutions shocked the church. They also caused aftershocks in the form of schismatic movements such as Novatianism (see Papandrea 2011; Gülzow 1975), which applied rigorism to the *lapsi*.

The neo-Platonic philosopher Porphyry, in his work *Against the Christians*, testified of thousands (μύριοι) persecuted Christians (*Contra Christianos*, fr. 36). W. H. C. Frend believed that the real number of victims was about ten times less: hundreds and not thousands (Frend 2008a: 413). These numbers included some prominent figures, such as the bishops of Rome Fabian, of Antioch Babylas, and of Jerusalem Alexander. Bishops of Alexandria Dionysius and of Carthage Cyprian escaped trials. Origen was tortured but then released. His health was so damaged, however, that he died three years later.

## Martyrdom of Pionius of Smyrna

The persecutions under Decius were documented in the Martyrdom of Pionius of Smyrna. Pionius was a presbyter of the local church. Local authorities arrested him together with other members of his community. The account of his trial is based on immediate witnesses (see Rebillard 2017b: 47–50). It in particular demonstrates the prototypical role that the martyrdom of Polycarp played for the posterior martyrs and martyrologies:

> On the second day of the sixth month, at the beginning of a great Sabbath, on the anniversary of the blessed martyr Polycarp, during the persecution of Decius, Pionius a presbyter, Sabina a confessor, Asclepiades, Macedonia, and Limnus a presbyter of the universal church were arrested.

Pionius and his companions were prepared for arrest: they had celebrated Eucharist. It is remarkable that, according to the text, they used water instead of wine, which indeed sometimes happened in the early church (see McGowan 2007). The text also mentions the edict of Decius:

> After they had prayed and taken the holy bread and water on the Sabbath, Polemon the neokoros (a warden in a temple of the imperial cult) came to them, accompanied by those who were appointed with him to seek out Christians and drag them to sacrifice and eat the sacrificial meat. And the neokoros said: "You know very well the emperor's edict that commands you to sacrifice to the gods." And Pionius said: "We know God's commandments, in which he orders us to adore him alone." Polemon said: "Come, then, to the agora, and there you will obey." Both Sabina and Asclepiades said: "We obey the living God."

The official who interrogated the Christians threatened to send to a brothel the women who were with Pionius:

> Polemon said: "Obey us, Pionius." Pionius said: "I wish I could persuade you to become Christians." They laughed a lot and said: "You cannot have us be burnt alive." Pionius said: "It is much worse to burn after death." And as Sabina was smiling, the neokoros and the men with him said: "You laugh?" And she said: "If God wills it, yes. For we are Christians, and whosoever trusts in Christ unreservedly will laugh in joy for ever." They say to her: "You then are going to suffer what you do not want. For women who do not sacrifice are sent to the brothel." And she said: "The holy God will take care of this."

All interrogations followed a formal protocol. This protocol included offering sacrifices to the emperor as the minimal requirement:

> Then the neokoros Polemon started his interrogation, saying: "Sacrifice, Pionius." Pionius said: "I am a Christian." Polemon said: "What sort of god do you worship?" Pionius said: "The almighty God, who created heaven and earth and everything in these and all of us, who provides us with all things in abundance, whom we know through Christ, his Word." Polemon said: "Then at least sacrifice to the emperor." Pionius said: "I do not sacrifice to a man, for I am a Christian."
>
> Then he interrogated him on record, saying: "What is your name?" The secretary was writing everything down. He answered: "Pionius." Polemon said: "Are you a Christian?" Pionius said: "Yes." Polemon the neokoros said: "Of which church?" He answered: "Of the universal church (τῆς καθολικῆς), for there is no other church with Christ."

The last question was not accidental. The official was apparently aware about divisions between various Christian groups. When Pionius was thrown to the prison cell, he found there someone from "the Phrygian sect," that is, a Montanist. The officials in the meantime continued convincing Pionius to sacrifice. They urged him to follow the example of his bishop Euctemon, who had already done so. They also brought in an orator, who tried to persuade the Christians with philosophical arguments.

Pionius, in response, invoked the example of Socrates implying a parallel between his death and the death of the Christian martyrs:

> Rufinus, a man who had an excellent reputation as an orator, was present and said: "Stop, Pionius, being vainglorious." But Pionius said to him: "These are your speeches? These are your books? Socrates did not suffer in such a way from the Athenians. Now every man is an Anytus and a Meletus.[1] In your opinion, were they vainglorious Socrates, Aristides, Anaxarchus, and all the others, because they practiced philosophy, justice, and perseverance?" When Rufinus heard this he fell silent.

Pionius asked to be tried by the proconsul—the governor of the province. This request had to be duly met according to the law. After having been tried at the proconsul's office, Pionius was sentenced to death:

> And it was read from a tablet in Latin: "As Pionius confesses himself to be a Christian, we have commanded that he be burnt alive."
>
> Pionius went to the arena eagerly because of the zeal of his faith. When the commentariensis was present, he undressed willingly. Then as he observed that his own body was sound and in good shape, he was filled with a great joy, looked to heaven, and thanked God for keeping him thus. And he laid down on the cross and let the soldier drive in the nails. When he was nailed on, the public slave said to him again: "Change your mind, and the nails will be removed from you." And he answered: "Indeed, I felt that they are in place." And after thinking briefly, he said: "For this reason, I am eager to awake more quickly," revealing the resurrection of the dead. So they set him upright on the cross, and next also a presbyter called Metrodorus, one of the sect of the Marcionites. And it so happened that Pionius stood on the right and Metrodorus on the left, but they both faced east.
>
> And when they had brought the tinder and piled the wood around in a circle, Pionius closed his eyes so that the crowd presumed he had expired.
>
> But he was secretly praying and when he came to the end of his prayer he opened his eyes. Now, as the flames were rising, he uttered his last Amen with a joyful face and said: "Lord, receive my soul."

## The Great Persecution under Diocletian

After Decius was killed in the war with Goths in 251, the persecution paused and then resumed for a short while under Valerian (253–60). Two generations of Christians after Valerian lived in relative peace, until what has been called "the Great Persecution" became initiated by Emperor Diocletian (reigned 284–305, died after

---

[1] Anytus and Meletus were known to be among the accusers of Socrates.

**Figure 1.15** Emperor Diocletian on a Roman coin. Archäologische Museum at the University of Münster in Germany.
Source: Photo by the author.

abdication in 311; see Shin 2019). This persecution was what Thomas Fuller called the darkest hour of the night before the dawn. It was the most cruel and systemic of all persecutions in the early Christian era.

There was no obvious motivation moving this persecution. Diocletian had been the ruler of the empire for twenty years and managed to restore peace and order to it. He successfully redesigned its structure and shared power with three other rulers. As a soldier and a pragmatist to his bones, he did not prioritize religion in his policies. At the same time, probably his pragmatism urged him to deal with the "Christian question."

By the time of Diocletian's rule, this question grew sizable. The estimated 10 percent of the empire's population practiced Christianity, most of them in the cities and many in the noble and military classes. Diocletian, who strove to restore the empire's integrity, believed that Christians threatened it. Indeed, they rejected the so-called traditional values of the Roman society, which for Diocletian were safeguarded by the Greco-Roman religion (see Ando 2008). Diocletian's program of the empire's restoration included the invigoration of the traditional Roman piety and the oppression of new cults.

As a good Roman soldier, Diocletian was superstitious. Superstition grows when the chances to lose one's life are high and do not much depend on one's choices. For this reason, for example, Roman soldiers could refuse to fight, if sacred chicken did not peck greedily. Roman generals also practiced divination and consulted oracles before going to a battle. Following this military custom, Diocletian regularly inquired with the Apollonian oracle at Didyma on the southwestern shore of Asia Minor (see Johnston 2009: 82–90). It seems this was his favorite oracle whom he trusted (see Frend 2008a: 490).

**Figure 1.16** Apollo's temple that hosted oracle in Didyma. Modern Didim in Turkey.
Source: Photo by the author.

The neo-Platonic Iamblichus left a testimony about the ritual of inquiring with an oracle. Before the session, the *mantis* would stay for three days in the inner part of the temple. She would purify herself by fasting and bathing. After that,

> either she is filled with divine radiance when she holds the staff that [Apollo] has given to her, or she foretells the future when she sits on an axle, or she receives the god when she dips her feet or her skirt into water or when she is affected by vapors from the water. But in any case, having been prepared and made fit by all of these things for the reception [of the god] from outside, she partakes [of the god]. (In Johnston 2009: 85)

During one of such divinations, according to Lactantius, the Didyma oracle responded to the augur sent by Diocletian in hostile tones about Christianity (*De mortibus* XI 7). Apparently, the oracle's harsh words were not the reason but might be a trigger for Diocletian to launch a campaign against the Christians. Another trigger was the fire that twice started in his palace. Palatial Christians were blamed for it. W. H. C. Frend called it the "Reichstag fire" (Frend 2008a: 491), which gave Caesar Galerius, who hated Christians, a strong argument to push Diocletian to punishing them.

Diocletian was not a sole instigator of the "Great persecution." It was a shared responsibility of the tetrarchy (see Rees 2004). A surprising fact about the tetrarchs was their common origins from those parts of the Balkans, which would become

Yugoslavia and Bulgaria. Diocletian was born in what is now Croatia. His co-augustus Maximian (286–305) came from what is now Serbia. Diocletian's caesars, Constantius (293–305) and Galerius (293–305), were both born in what is now Bulgaria. Some Christians accused Galerius and not Diocletian of initiating the persecutions. Some blamed for that Galerius' mother, Romula—a Dacian woman from what is now Serbia. She was claimed to be fanatically devoted to her gods and hating Christians. Constantius Chlorus, first a caesar and later an augustus in the tetrarchy, also originated from Bulgaria. His son Constantine was born in Naissus—Niš in modern Serbia.

The tetrarchs, despite their differences and disagreements, shared the same vision of a great empire, whose integrity is safeguarded by the traditional Roman religion and values. Religious novelties were regarded a threat. In this vein, Diocletian first turned on the Manichaeans—an eclectic and dualistic religion that had arrived at the Roman Empire from Persia. He promulgated an edict that banned Manichaeanism and proscribed burning its leaders and books (see Dignas & Winter 2007: 28; Fournier & Mayer 2020: 115–16). In its motivating part, the edict stated: "It is the greatest crime to wish to undo what once has been fixed and established in antiquity, and holds to its course and is possessed of proper status" (in Frend 2008a: 478). This is a clear indication that Diocletian and other tetrarchs saw Manichaeanism as a dangerous novelty. They also suspected the Manichaeans as potential collaborators and the agents of influence of Persia—Rome's archenemy.

**Figure 1.17** A spot in Niš—the birth city of Constantine the Great.
Source: Photo by the author.

Christians also represented a new religion, which challenged the Roman traditional piety. After having dealt with the Manichaeans, Diocletian turned on them. In February 303, he signed an edict with measures against the followers of Jesus. The document was posted at the forum in Nicomedia—the city of Diocletian's court. A Christian reportedly pulled it down. He also publicly uttered accusations against Diocletian. This was enough to arrest him and roast alive.

Diocletian initially did not intend to shed Christian blood—he only wanted to protect traditional values. His algorithm of dealing with the Christians was like the one of Decius. Diocletian substituted subsidiarity with a centralized religious policy regarding religious minorities, including Christians. He also started purging army and decimate clergy. Eusebius described Diocletian's anti-Christian measures as follows:

> It was the nineteenth year of the reign of Diocletian, and the month Dystrus, or March, as the Romans would call it, in which, as the festival of the Saviour's Passion (i.e., Christian Easter) was coming on, an imperial letter was everywhere promulgated, ordering the razing of the churches to the ground and the destruction by fire of the Scriptures, and proclaiming that those who held high positions would lose all civil rights, while those in households, if they persisted in their profession of Christianity, would be deprived of their liberty. Such was the first document against us. But not long afterwards we were further visited with other letters, and in them the order was given that the presidents of the churches should all, in every place, be first committed to prison, and then afterwards compelled by every kind of device to sacrifice.

Contrary to his initial intentions, Diocletian eventually surpassed Decius in the numbers of killed and tortured. Eusebius gave an account of what those who had refused to comply with the imperial decrees had to endure:

> Each underwent a series of varied forms of torture: one would have his body maltreated by scourgings; another would be punished with the rack and torn to an unbearable degree, whereat some met a miserable end to their life. (*Historia ecclesiastica* II 8.2)

Similarly to the Decian persecution, the "Great persecution" produced more Christian apostates than martyrs and confessors. However, not all those who fell did so by their will. Some were tricked. Eusebius described some tricks to make Christians to sacrifice without consent:

> One man was brought to the abominable and unholy sacrifices by the violence of others who pressed round him, and dismissed as if he had sacrificed, even though he had not; another who did not so much as approach or touch any accursed thing, when others had said that he had sacrificed, went away bearing the false accusation in silence. A third was taken up half-dead and cast aside as if he were a corpse already; and, again, a certain person lying on the ground was dragged a long distance by the

> feet, having been reckoned among those who had voluntarily sacrificed. One cried out and with a loud voice attested his refusal to sacrifice, and another shouted aloud that he was a Christian, glorying in his confession of the saving Name. Another stoutly maintained that he had not sacrificed, and never would. Nevertheless these also were struck on the mouth and silenced by a large band of soldiers drawn up for that purpose, and with blows on their face and cheeks driven forcibly away. So great store did the enemies of godliness set on seeming by any means to have accomplished their purpose. (*Historia ecclesiastica* II 8.3)

The *lapsi* overwhelmed the church. Many orthodox rigorists refused to receive back their fallen brethren. A reactionary movement similar to the earlier Novatianism engulfed both the western and the eastern parts of the church. In the West, this movement became known as Donatism (see Miles 2018). It sprang from the Latin-speaking Africa. The Greek-speaking Africa produced its own version of rigorism—Melitianism (see Hauben 2017).

## Martyrology

Scholars keep arguing how big was the difference between the actual persecutions and how they came to be perceived in the Christian community. Eusebius of Caesarea, whose *Ecclesiastical History* is the main source on both the persecutions and their reception in the fourth-century church, presented them like a horror movie with killings and tortures happening every minute. Other Roman sources, however, indicate that between 64 and 250 persecutions were sporadic and local—they usually were not enforced by centralized imperial policies. They were not an average Christian experience (see Watts 2015: 39). Until the mid-third century, most Christians experienced not much violence but rather social marginalization (see Moss 2012: 51).

The early Christian perception of the persecutions is important, because it made a significant contribution to the evolution of the church's self-awareness (see Hovorun 2015: 37–68). Christians claimed that they are different from other religious groups in the Roman Empire, because they have martyrs. Indeed, the Christian church had more martyrs than other religious groups in the empire (see Middleton 2020). However, it was not only Christianity that perceived itself as the religion of martyrs. Both the Greco-Roman and Jewish religious groups had and cherished their own martyrs.

For example, both Greek and Roman public had been fascinated by Achilles, who went to the Trojan War knowing that he would die there. Intellectuals revered Socrates, who had died for the truth he preached. For them, he was "the world's first recorded martyr" (Smith 1999: 23). There were also female figures who were

**Figure 1.18** An early depiction of the Roman martyr Achilleus. Catacombs of Domitilla.
Source: Photo by the author.

**Figure 1.19** Dying Achilleus by Ernst Herter. Achilleion Palace on the Island of Corfu.
Source: Photo by the author.

venerated for their beliefs and the way they died, including Iphigeneia, Polyxena, and Antigone. The Greco-Roman pagan culture, thus, had its own martyrs. They influenced, to an extent, the Christian perception of martyrdom. For example, as was mentioned, Pionius of Smyrna referred to Socrates as an ancient martyr.

Joseph Flavius had promoted Jewish martyrs (*Contra Apionem* II 226–8). He meant primarily those Jews who had perished in the revolt against the Seleucids in the mid-second century BC, led by the Maccabee family. Christians came to appreciate whom they called the Maccabee martyrs. They included the Maccabee's feast day to their calendars and the books of Maccabees from the Septuagint to their own biblical canon. In contrast to the West, which has kept only two of the Maccabees books, the Christian East keeps three of them. In addition, the Ethiopian biblical canon has preserved three unique books different from the Septuagintic Maccabees, called *Meqabyan* (Selassie 2008).

# I.3
# *Christianitas versus Romanitas*

The Christian theology of martyrdom absorbed elements of both Greco-Roman and Jewish martyrologies. Even more elements of the Greco-Roman and Jewish cultures were appropriated by the Christian apologists. In the early Christian communities, martyrdom was perceived as a mission of witnessing about Jesus Christ. Such a mission has been encoded in the word *martyr* (μάρτυρ)—"a witness." Another way of witnessing, which did not necessarily lead to sacrificing life, was apologetics. Candida Moss has observed "the bleeding of apologetics into martyrdom literature and martyrdom literature into apologetics" (Moss 2012: 16). Indeed, martyrdom and apologetics were intertwined in the early Christian centuries. Some Christians witnessed about their faith by blood and some—by ink. Some did both.

Early Christian apologists pursued two goals: minimal and maximal. The minimal goal was to convince their pagan interlocutors, whether real or imagined, that Christians are not inferior to any other religious group in the Roman Empire. The maximal goal was to demonstrate that Christians are superior in their beliefs and behavior. Apologists usually responded to the outbreaks of persecutions, as well as to less violent pressure and injustice that the church experienced from the Roman authorities and public. In most cases, apologetic texts addressed popular stereotypes about Christians spread among less-educated strata. Less frequently, apologists engaged with elites and discussed sophisticated matters. Popular stereotypes included the Christians' alleged incest, ritual infanticide, and even cannibalism. More sophisticated metaphysical discussions evolved around the idea of one God, the relation of Jesus to this one God, and the theological status of idols.

## Addressing Roman Emperors

Some apologies were addressed to emperors—usually those more educated and interested in philosophy. Thus, two Christians petitioned Emperor Hadrian directly during his sojourn in Athens, in 124 or 125. One of the petitioners, Aristides would

**Figure 1.20** A bust of Antoninus Pius at the Ny Carlsberg Glyptotek in Copenhagen. Source: Photo by the author.

send an updated apology also to Antoninus Pius. Two generations later, in the mid-170s, another Christian intellectual based in Athens, Athenagoras, sent an apology to Marcus Aurelius and his son Commodus. The most famous apology addressed to an emperor was the one by Justin. It is noteworthy that Justin's apology mentions among its addressees not only Emperor Antoninus Pius, but also the Roman senate: "To the emperor Titus Aelius Adrianus Antoninus Pius Augustus Caesar; to his son Verissimus the philosopher (i.e., Marcus Aurelius); to Lucius the philosopher, by birth son of Caesar and by adoption son of Pius, an admirer of learning; to the sacred senate and to the whole Roman people; in behalf of those men of every race who are unjustly hated and mistreated."

# Justin

Justin was born in Samaria to a non-Jewish family. He received a classical Greek education, which helped him navigate through various philosophical schools of his time: Stoic, Peripatetic, neo-Pythagorean, before he ended up in the middle Platonism. His intellectual journey earned him nickname "philosopher." Justin did not stay for long with the Platonists and eventually converted to Christianity. He acknowledged that the example of Christian martyrs had urged him to consider such conversion. He eventually martyred himself, around 165. His two apologies (which some scholars see as two parts of the same text) constitute a remarkable sample of this genre in the Christian literature. Justin addressed both the popular stereotypes about Christians and the "big" metaphysical questions. He insisted that Christians should be tried fairly:

> Common sense dictates that they who are truly pious men and philosophers should honor and cherish only what is true, and refuse to follow the beliefs of their forefathers, if these beliefs be worthless. For, sound reason not only demands that we do not heed those who did or taught anything wrong, but it requires that the lover of truth must choose, in every way possible, to do and say what is right, even when threatened with death, rather than save his own life. You hear yourselves everywhere called pious men and philosophers, guardians of justice and lovers of learning: whether you really deserve this reputation will now become evident. Indeed, we have come not to flatter you with our writings or to curry your favor with this discourse, but to ask that, after an accurate and thorough examination, you hand down a decision that will not be influenced by prejudice or by the desire to please superstitious men; a decision that will not be the result of an irrational impulse or of an evil rumor long persistent, lest it become a judgment against yourselves. As far as we (Christians) are concerned, we believe that no evil can befall us unless we be convicted as criminals or be proved to be sinful persons. You, indeed, may be able to kill us, but you cannot harm us. (*Apologia* I 1-3; Justin 2008: 33–4)

## Celsus

Approximately a generation after Justin, a Platonic philosopher Celsus undertook a first systemic deconstruction of Christianity. He did so in the treatise *True Doctrine*. Many of its passages have survived as quotes in Origen's *Against Celsus*. Some scholars believe Celsus had been incited to write his work by the work of Justin. Celsus not only "read Christian writings," but also "understood what he read" (Wilken 2003: 101). Unlike other pagan critics of Christianity, he addressed not only Christian practices, but delved to theological matters, which only a few Christians were able to discuss.

## Origen

For about eighty years, there were no Christian theologians to respond to Celsus, until a catechist from Alexandria, named Origen, picked up each of Celsus' arguments against Christians. Origen instructed those who wanted to convert to

Christianity, mostly by explaining the Jewish and Christian Scriptures. He was also an apologist who defended Christianity from pagan accusations. At the same time, he undertook a gigantic project of synthesizing classical and Christian wisdom. Out of this synthesis, which had begun as an apologetical effort, the classical Christian theology was born. There was virtually no theological topic which would become crucial in the posterior Christian theology and was not addressed by Origen. Origen introduced the standard of theological thematology, coined language to articulate it, and gave solutions to many issues stemming from it. Not all solutions suggested by Origen were received by the later generations of Christian theologians. Nevertheless, his theological thinking continues framing various Christian traditions.

Origen was born in Alexandria, in the family of a Christian martyr. His father Leonides died during the persecutions under Septimius Severus in 202. A wealthy Christian women became Origen's patron. She sponsored his studies. He reportedly studied under the Platonic philosopher Ammonius Saccas. His co-student was the founder of neo-Platonism Plotinus. After he graduated, Origen first became a teacher and later a scholarch of the Christian catechetical school in Alexandria. His tenure did not last long, until Origen decided to pursue ascetic life. He thus set a pattern for the posterior generations of Christian youth: after completing studies, to isolate themselves for spiritual purification. In solitude, he reportedly castrated himself. After living as a hermit, he returned to the active service to his church. However, his relations with the bishop of Alexandria Demetrius became tense. Origen left Egypt and moved to Syria. He was ordained a priest in Caesarea of Palestine. This made Demetrius of Alexandria jealous, accusing him of heresies. Such accusations accompanied Origen until the end of his life and continued for centuries after his death. During the persecutions under Decius, in 250, Origen was arrested and tortured. He survived, but did not live long after that, and died in 253 or 254.

## Porphyry

Origen became so famous in Syria that even Julia Mammaea, the mother of Emperor Alexander Severus and the most powerful woman in the Roman Empire, wanted to see him and reportedly inquired about Christianity. A less known at that time philosopher Porphyry also came to listen to Origen. He later grew to a major figure in neo-Platonism. After attending Origen's lectures, he remained unimpressed. Eusebius of Caesarea has preserved Porphyry's impressions of Origen:

> This kind of absurdity (i.e., Christian teaching) must be traced to a man whom I met when I was still quite young, who had a great reputation, and still holds it, because of the writings he has left behind him, I mean Origen, whose fame has been widespread among the teachers of this kind of learning. For this man was a hearer of Ammonius,

> who had the greatest proficiency in philosophy in our day; and so far as a grasp of knowledge was concerned he owed much to his master, but as regards the right choice in life he took the opposite road to him. For Ammonius was a Christian, brought up in Christian doctrine by his parents, yet, when he began to think and study philosophy, he immediately changed his way of life conformably to the laws; but Origen, a Greek educated in Greek learning, drove headlong towards barbarian recklessness; and making straight for this he hawked himself and his literary skill about; and while his manner of life was Christian and contrary to the law, in his opinions about material things and the Deity he played the Greek, and introduced Greek ideas into foreign fables. (*Historia ecclesiastica* II 6.19; Oulton 1932: 56–9)

Porphyry, on the one hand, acknowledged the synthetic work of Origen, who tried to reconcile Christian doctrine with classical culture. On the other hand, he believed the result of this synthesis was not successful. Porphyry apparently had a chance to read Origen's apology *Against Celsus*. It is quite possible that this reading incited him to produce his own critique of Christianity. It seems that Porphyry knew the Christian Scriptures and doctrine in more detail than Celsus did. After all, by the second half of the third century, when Porphyry flourished, Christianity had developed a more sophisticated theology, which became more available to readers with various backgrounds. With more dexterity than Celsus, Porphyry criticized most points of this theology. He expounded them in a treatise, which later would become known as *Against Christians*, but has been lost to us. In another treatise that has been also lost, *Philosophy of Oracles*, Porphyry developed an apology of the traditional Greco-Roman religion in counterposition to Christianity. He wrote: "The greatest fruit of piety is to honor the divine in accordance with what has been handed down from the fathers (κατὰ τὰ πάτρια)" (*Ad Marcellam* 18).

Christianity, in contrast to *ta patria*, was a novelty. As was mentioned, novelties were the heresies of the ancient world. All new religious teachings and practices were heretical by default. Christianity, with its radical program of changes, appeared as an arch-heresy to any Roman patriot. Eusebius preserved a fragment from Porphyry blaming Christians for introducing novelties:

> What forgiveness shall they be thought to deserve, who have turned away from those who from the earliest time, among all Greeks and Barbarians, both in cities and in the country, are recognized as gods with all kinds of sacrifices, and initiations, and mysteries by all alike? <. . .> And to what kind of punishments would they not justly be subjected, who deserting the customs of their forefathers have become zealots for the foreign mythologies of the Jews? (In Eusebius, *Praeparatio Evangelica* I 2; Gifford 2002: 5b)

The key phrases in this passage are "earliest time" and "customs of forefathers." These keywords expressed what Porphyry, as a Roman patriot, valued and what he believed Christians violated. He wrote to his wife in his older years: "The greatest fruit of piety is to worship God according to the tradition of one's fathers" (in Wilken 2003: 128). From this perspective, Christians were unpatriotic nontraditionalists. They did not seem to be upset about such perception (see Arnobius, *Adversus nationes* II 67).

The critique of Porphyry was by far more challenging for the Christians than any other anti-Christian invectives that the earlier apologists had to deal with. Best theological minds of that time addressed various accusations articulated by Porphyry (see Magny 2016). The most comprehensive apologies were produced by Eusebius of Caesarea and Apollinaris of Laodicea. Eusebius wrote twenty-five and Apollinaris thirty books against Porphyry. None of them has survived. Only Eusebius' *Preparation of the Gospel* survives, which deals with some Porphyry's points and includes many fragments from his anti-Christian work.

# Roman Antichrists

Many Christians interpreted the persecutions as caused not by Rome's failure to implement its own laws and principles of justice, but by the inherent evilness of the Roman state. They often perceived this state in dualistic terms. According to this perception, the reality around us is dichotomized in black and white, evil and good. The evil is substantial; it can be touched and should be avoided physically. Rome

**Figure 1.21** Emperor Nero. Archaeological museum of Corinth.
Source: Photo by the author.

was such substantiated evil for those Christians who perceived it in dualistic terms. For them, the Roman Empire was also the kingdom of the antichrist. Hippolytus, who was a leader of the conservative faction in the Roman church, compared this city with the beasts from the books of Daniel (7:3-8) and Apocalypse (23:29) (see Schmidt & Nicholas 2017). According to the same dualistic worldview, there were Roman rulers, who were regarded antichrists par excellence, such as Emperor Nero (see Malik 2020; Maier 2013).

# I.4
# Christianity Accommodates Rome

In parallel to the dualistic worldview that rejected the Roman world altogether, many Christians developed a more appreciating attitude to it. They accepted Rome as an unavoidable reality, which they have to deal with anyways, until Jesus would come. The more the coming of Jesus was delayed, the larger was the number of such Christians. They found a *modus co-vivendi* with Rome, which was expressed in the anonymous letter to Diognetus. This letter was composed approximately in the time of the martyrdom of Polycarp. It became a golden standard of equilibrium between otherworldliness of Christianity and its openness to the contemporary society, even if the latter is not Christian:

> For Christians are no different from other people in terms of their country, language, or customs.
>
> Nowhere do they inhabit cities of their own, use a strange dialect, or live life out of the ordinary.
>
> They have not discovered this teaching of theirs through reflection or through the thought of meddlesome people, nor do they set forth any human doctrine, as do some.
>
> They inhabit both Greek and barbarian cities, according to the lot assigned to each. And they show forth the character of their own citizenship in a marvelous and admittedly paradoxical way by following local customs in what they wear and what they eat and in the rest of their lives.
>
> They live in their respective countries, but only as resident aliens; they participate in all things as citizens, and they endure all things as foreigners. Every foreign territory is a homeland for them, every homeland foreign territory.
>
> They marry like everyone else and have children, but they to not expose them once they are born.
>
> They share their meals but not their sexual partners.
>
> They are found in the flesh but do not live according to the flesh.
>
> They live on earth but participate in the life of heaven.
>
> They are obedient to the laws that have been made, and by their own lives they supersede the laws.
>
> They love everyone and are persecuted by all.

> They are not understood and they are condemned. They are put to death and made alive.
>
> They are impoverished and make many rich. They lack all things and abound in everything.
>
> They are dishonored and they are exalted in their dishonors. They are slandered and they are acquitted.
>
> They are reviled and they bless, mistreated and they bestow honor.
>
> They do good and are punished as evil; when they are punished they rejoice as those who have been made alive.
>
> They are attacked by Jews as foreigners and persecuted by Greeks. And those who hate them cannot explain the cause of their enmity. (*Ad Diognetum* 5; Ehrman 2003: 139–41)

Some Christian authors went further and suggested considering the Roman world not only as something to be tolerated but as a part of God's plan about the church. This standpoint copied a trend in the contemporary Jewish attitude to the Roman rule as providential for the Jews. Those Christians who followed this line argued that the Roman Empire gave Christianity an opportunity to rapidly grow and reach the most remote corners of earth. One of such apologists of Rome was Origen. He, on the one hand, was a staunch nonconformist, as this can be seen in his *Exhortation to Martyrdom*. On the other hand, he praised Augustus for unifying the empire:

> God was preparing the nations for his (Jesus') teaching, that they might be under one Roman emperor, so that the unfriendly attitude of the nations to one another, caused by the existence of a large number of kingdoms, might not make it more difficult for Jesus' apostles to do what he commanded them when he said, "Go and teach all nations" (Mt. 28:19). It is quite clear that Jesus was born during the reign of Augustus, the one who reduced to uniformity, so to speak, the many kingdoms on earth so that he had a single empire. It would have hindered Jesus' teaching from being spread through the whole world if there had been many kingdoms, not only for the reasons just stated, but also because men everywhere would have been compelled to do military service and to fight in defence of their own land. This used to happen before the times of Augustus and even earlier still when a war was necessary, such as that between the Peloponnesians and the Athenians, and similarly in the case of the other nations which fought one another. Accordingly, how could this teaching, which preaches peace and does not even allow men to take vengeance on their enemies, have had any success unless the international situation had everywhere been changed and a milder spirit prevailed at the advent of Jesus? (*Contra Celsum* II 30; Chadwick 2009: 92)

# Roman Roads

Indeed, apostles, later Christian missionaries, and bishops, who hit the road to preach the Gospel, take care of communities, and gather for church councils, had many good reasons to be thankful to the Roman state for providing them with the comprehensive network of roads. These roads were made accessible for everyone and could bring anyone everywhere (see Kolb 2019). Other civilizations of antiquity could not dream about such luxury. They had roads, but these roads were either for elites or did not go where people had to go. The Roman Empire offered an unprecedented mobility to all its inhabitants, including Christians.

Owing to its roads, the Roman Empire became universal. Such an ambition did not exist from the beginning, however. The initial Rome's aspirations were modest and did not go beyond Italy. Only after the Punic wars (264–146 BC), the Roman state began growing to occupy first the western Mediterranean. After the Macedonian, Seleucid, Achaean, and Mithridatic wars, the Roman rule extended to the eastern Mediterranean world. Rome, thus, materialized the Greek dream of cosmopolis—a universal *politeia* that embraced the entire universe—*oecumene* (see Harte & Lane 2013; Richter 2011). It became an "empire without end," in the words of Virgil (*Aeneid* I 278–9). The Roman Empire and the Christian church came to share the same limitless centrifugal dynamism of expansion. This shared dynamism also incited many Christians to appreciate the Roman world.

# Eusebius

The Christian appreciation of the Roman Empire culminated in the writings of a bishop of the Palestinian city Caesarea, Eusebius (in office *c.* 314–39/40). He followed the line of Origen, with whom he was intellectually connected through his mentor Pamphilus of Caesarea (second half of the third century–309). Eusebius produced the first Christian political theology and can be regarded the father of this discipline. His politico-theological vision to a significant extent shaped the self-perception of the church, as well as the models of its relations with the state.

First, Eusebius exploited the still fresh memories of many Christians about persecutions. Some scholars believe he exaggerated the persecutions in order to emphasize how beneficial for the church the conversion of the Roman Empire to Christianity became (see Moss 2014). He retold the story about the church's sufferings under the pagan emperors and made it an ideologeme (Cameron & Hall 1999: 35). This ideologeme was designed to stress the uniqueness of Constantine among other Roman emperors. Every Roman ruler tried to present himself as special. Eusebius presented Constantine as special, because he had put an end to the persecutions (see Damgaard 2013). Second, Eusebius exploited the expectations of the early Christians for the second coming of Christ. Eusebius interpreted the conversion of the empire to Christianity as a fulfillment of these expectations. Although Christ did not come in person, he came to act politically through his proxies—the emperors. His kingdom became incarnated in the Roman Empire, after the latter embraced Christianity. The Roman kingdom now reflected the Kingdom of God. Christian millennialism, popular in the first centuries, was transformed to a political theology, where the Christian emperor and his kingdom occupied the central place.

The idea that the political realm can reflect the sphere of the divine was neo-Platonic. Neo-Platonism facilitated the transformation of the early Christian expectations for the second coming to the idea of the Roman Empire as the reflection of Christ's kingdom. Neo-Platonism also helped the early Christians to confront dualism, which inspired many of them to see the empire as the kingdom of the antichrist and an incarnation of evil. Neo-Platonic philosophy opposed such an idea and promoted instead the idea that evil is nonexistential and therefore could not be ontologically incarnated in anything, including the state. Eusebius, who propagated the idealistic millennial kingdom, relied on such neo-Platonic thinking.

Although known as a church historian, Eusebius was primarily a spin doctor. In his writings, he not only reconstructed the past, but also constructed the present and future. Sometimes, his past was also constructed, like, for example, in the way he presented the persecutions. The most elaborate construction of Eusebius, however, was the figure of Emperor Constantine per se. It is unlikely that Eusebius had many chances to have a private conversation with Constantine (see Barnes 2006: 261–75). Unlike his namesake Eusebius of Nicomedia, he was not a courtier. The less Eusebius knew Constantine personally, the more imagination he used to depict his figure. He admixed a lot of messianic hue to his depiction of the first Christian emperor. For Eusebius, Constantine was a new Moses and a living image of God's rule (see *Historia ecclesiastica* II 9.9; Oulton 1932: 363; Van Nuffelen 2013: 145). He was chosen by God to demonstrate how God himself rules the universe:

> God himself, whom Constantine honoured, by standing at Constantine's side at the beginning, the middle and the end of his reign, confirmed by his manifest judgement, putting forward this man as a lesson in the pattern of godliness to the human race. As the only one of the widely renowned Emperors of all time whom God set up as a huge luminary and loud-voiced herald of unerring godliness, he is the only one to whom God gave convincing proofs of the religion he practised by the benefits of every kind which were accorded him. <. . .> Making him the model of his own monarchical reign, he appointed him victor over the whole race of tyrants and destroyer of the God-battling giants, who in mental frenzy raised weapons against the Sovereign of the universe himself. (*Vita Constantini* I 4; Cameron & Hall 1999: 69)

# I.5

# Rome Accommodates Christianity

The real Constantine, it appears, was quite different from how he had been described by Eusebius (see Siecienski 2017; Barnes 2011). In his political behavior, Flavius Valerius Constantinus—so was his full name—was closer to Augustus than to Moses. Raymond van Dam is right in asserting that "before Constantine was a Christian emperor, he was a typical emperor" (Van Dam 2009: 11). As a son of Constantius, who had been first a caesar and later an augustus in Diocletian's tetrarchy, Constantine after the death of his father imposed himself on the tetrarchy. After having been eventually received as a member of this elite club, he later on destroyed the tetrarchic system of power-sharing and monopolized all imperial power. He reduced tetrarchy to monarchy after having won the battles at Milvian Bridge against Maxentius in 312 and near Chrysopolis against Licinius in 324. He repressed not only his brother-in-law Licinius, but also his son Crispus, whom he had first proclaimed a caesar and later would order to poison. Constantine's second wife Fausta suspiciously died in an overheated bath. Posthumously, he sentences both of them to something worse than death—*damnatio memoriae*. Many emperors before Constantine did the same to their foes and relatives. Constantine's faith, it seems, did not doubt this Roman tradition.

## *Sol Invictus*

Constantine "was every inch a Roman" (Strauss 2019: 288). In the Roman culture, among the strongest interpersonal bonds was the one between mother and son. The relationship between Constantine and his mother Helen was not an exception. Helen was to Constantine what Livia Drusilla was to Tiberius, Agrippina the Younger to Nero, and Julia Domna to Caracalla. All these women exercised enormous political power in the empire and influenced beliefs, moral principles, and political preferences of their sons. Probably it was through Helen that Constantine was initiated to Christianity.

**Figure 1.22** Constantine's arch in Rome. He ordered a huge statue of *Sol invictus* to be installed between the arch and Colosseum.

Source: Photo by the author.

**Figure 1.23** Constantine's statue in York, near the spot where his army proclaimed him an emperor.

Source: Photo by the author.

After he became the sole ruler of the empire, Helen was his informal coruler. In the Eastern Christian hagiology, Constantine and Helen are inseparable as two equal-to-the-apostles. They became personifications of the state patronage of the church.

There were other wise advisers to Constantine who instructed him in faith. One of them was Lactantius (*c.* 240–320), a Christian philosopher and educator. Constantine met him in Nicomedia—at that time Diocletian's capital. Later, Constantine invited Lactantius to Trier, where he became a tutor of Constantine's son Crispus. In Nicomedia, Lactantius apparently had many opportunities to converse with Constantine on the matters of faith (see Shelton 2014; Digeser 2000). He also provided an account of Constantine's life (Lactantius 1998)—more balanced than the one by Eusebius. In the later years, Constantine had other spiritual and theological mentors, such as Hosius of Cordoba and Eusebius of Nicomedia. The latter baptized Constantine upon his deathbed in 337.

Constantine became a conscious Christian probably around 312 or later. His conversion was not instantaneous, but gradual. An important landmark of his spiritual journey was the cult of the "invincible sun" (*sol invictus*) (see Halsberghe 1972), which had been brought to Rome from Syria by Antoninus "Elagabalus" (218–22). In 274, Emperor Aurelian made this cult an official religion, in parallel to the traditional Roman cult. It is difficult to say when or even if Constantine left this cult. *Sol invictus* appears on Constantine's arch in Rome and his coins. He even suggested to name after the sun the day of the week dedicated to the resurrection of Christ, Sunday (*dies solis*).

Constantine's conversion apparently happened at the court of Diocletian in Nicomedia. Formally, the son of a tetrarch was there in the service of the tetrarchy's president. Informally, he was a hostage who secured the loyalty of his father Constantius. After his conversion, Constantine could not openly practice his faith in the environment that was increasingly anti-Christian. He kept silent in the period of the Great persecution, which had its epicenter in Nicomedia. Later, he would have to explain himself why he was doing nothing about the persecutions (see his letter to the provincials of the East, quoted by Eusebius in *Vita Constantini* II 50; Cameron & Hall 1999). Constantine began coming out as a Christian only after he was proclaimed *augustus* by his troops in York.

When he launched a military campaign to secure his position in the tetrarchy, Constantine put the Christian sign *chi-rho* on his personal banner. Before the battle at the Milvian Bridge, he ordered his troops to put the same sign on their shields. Against many odds and the strategic advantage of his rival Maxentius, Constantine won this battle. Eusebius vividly described Constantine's triumphal entrance to Rome after his victory:

> He entered Rome with hymns of triumph, and all the senators and other persons of great note, together with women and quite young children and all the Roman people,

> received him in a body with beaming countenances to their very heart as a ransomer, saviour and benefactor, with praises and insatiable joy. <. . .> Straightway he gave orders that a memorial of the Saviour's Passion should be set up in the hand of his own statue; and indeed when they set him in the most public place in Rome holding the Saviour's sign in his right hand, he bade them engrave this very inscription in these words in the Latin tongue: "By this salutary sign, the true proof of bravery, I saved and delivered your city from the yoke of the tyrant; and moreover I freed and restored to their ancient fame and splendour both the senate and the people of the Romans." (*Historia ecclesiastica* II 9.9; Oulton 1932: 362–5)

Constantine not only propagated Christian symbols but also made practical steps to make easier the life of the Christians in the empire. He, thus, ordered to stop enforcing the earlier anti-Christian edicts. However, he was not the only tetrarchy member who did so. In 311, Galerius, who had been a staunch persecutor, changed his attitude toward Christians. He promulgated an edict, which effectively allowed the Christians "to exist" (Frend 2008a: 513). At the same time, he did not restore their properties or rights. It is noteworthy that the edict of 311 made it clear that the earlier anti-Christian measures had been inspired by caring for the "institutions of the ancients" (Frend 2008a: 510). In other words, Christians had been persecuted because they were believed to stand for religious novelties and, as such, constituted a threat to the traditional Roman values.

**Figure 1.24** Tapestry with *chi-rho* symbol (fifth to sixth century). Benaki Museum in Athens.

Source: Photo by the author.

# The Edict of Milan

In 313, Constantine held a meeting in Milan with his Eastern co-emperor at that time, Licinius. In the vein of Galerius' edict of 311, they together promulgated a similar document, through which they apologized for the mistreatment of the Christians by the previous regime and outlined measures to restore properties and statuses of those Christians who had been mistreated. They even promised to pay them some compensation from the imperial budget. This document was important, but not as crucial for the conversion of the empire as many believe. It was only one of several legal steps over several years that led to the legalization of Christianity and the restoration of justice and freedom of consciousness for religious minorities. Both Lactantius and Eusebius quoted the text adopted in Milan:

> When I Constantine Augustus and I Licinius Augustus had come under happy auspices to Milan, and discussed all matters that concerned the public advantage and good, among the other things that seemed to be of benefit to the many,—or rather, first and foremost—we resolved to make such decrees as should secure respect and reverence for the Deity; namely, to grant both to the Christians and to all the free choice (ἐλευθέραν αἵρεσιν) of following whatever form of worship they pleased, to the intent that all the divine and heavenly powers that be might be favourable to us and all those living under our authority. Therefore with sound and most upright reasoning we resolved on this counsel: that authority be refused to no one whomsoever to follow and choose the observance or form of worship that Christians use, and that authority be granted to each one to give his mind to that form of worship which he deems suitable to himself. (*Historia ecclesiastica* II 10.5; Oulton 1932: 446–7)

# Civil War

Licinius would not continue respecting the edict that he and Constantine had signed in Milan. He occasionally persecuted Christians in the eastern part of the empire. An episode of such persecutions became classical in the Christian hagiography. It was described as a story about "forty martyrs of Sebaste"—a group of Christian soldiers from the *Legio XII* stationed near the city of Sebaste in Asia Minor. To make them denounce their Christianity, their superiors made them standing naked in the freeze of winter. They would allow to warm up in the bath nearby only those who would denounce their Christianity. This story was told by Basil of Caesarea in his sermon delivered at the martyrium of the forty martyrs in Basil's cathedral city Caesarea in Cappadocia:

> When that godless and impious edict was promulgated, to not confess Christ or to expect danger, every kind of punishment was threatened, and great and savage was the

> wrath aroused by the judges of iniquity against the pious. Plots and tricks were stitched together against them, and various kinds of torments were practised, and the torturers were implacable, the fire was prepared, the sword sharpened, the cross put together, the pit, the wheel, the whips. Some fled, others gave in, others vascillated. Some were terrified before their ordeal by the threat of it alone; others, having come close to the torture, became dizzy; others, having embarked on their struggles, then were unable to hold out until the end of their pains, shrinking from exhaustion in the middle of their suffering, like people tossed on the sea, and the wares of patience they already possessed were shipwrecked.

Basil proceeded to telling how the Christian soldiers were stripped and made standing in the cold of the winter. One of them could not bear and deserted:

> One of the number, sinking in the face of the terrible events, deserted and left, to the unspeakable grief of the saints. However, the Lord did not allow their prayers to be ineffectual. I mean that the man who had been entrusted with guarding the martyrs, while he was getting warm in a gymnasium nearby, observed what was going to happen and was prepared to welcome the fugitive soldiers. <. . .>
>
> While they were suffering, he observed what was about to happen. He saw a strange sight—powers coming down from the sky, and distributing huge gifts to the soldiers, as if from an emperor. They distributed the gifts to all the others, but they left just one man without a present, judging him unworthy of heavenly honours. He immediately gave up the fight in the face of trouble, and went over to the enemy. It was a pitiful sight for the just—the soldier turned fugitive, the valorous man taken prisoner, the sheep of Christ caught by wild beasts. And the most pitiful thing was that he missed out entirely on eternal life and could not even enjoy this life, because immediately his flesh was consumed by the wave of heat. And the one who loved life fell, having transgressed in vain, while the public executioner, as he saw him give way and run to the baths, put himself in the place of the deserter, threw off his clothes and joined in with the naked men, shouting the same cry as the saints: "I am a Christian."

At the dawn, after having stayed in cold all night, the soldiers were still alive:

> As the day began, while they were still breathing they were delivered over to the fire, and the remains of the fire were scattered on the river. (In Allen 2003: 66–74)

Such episodes of anti-Christian violence became a pretext (but not necessarily the reason) for Constantine to turn upon his co-emperor Licinius. They stopped collaborating and began competing. Their competition became a civil war around 324, when Constantine prevailed and had Licinius executed. After his victory, Constantine abolished tetrarchy and became the sole ruler of both eastern and western parts of the Roman Empire (see Vanderspoel 2020). This gave him an opportunity to push even further his pro-Christian policies. For example, he brought back from exile those who had been persecuted, and restored social statuses and properties of all Christians:

> All such as exchanged their native land for exile because they did not despise that faith in the Deity to which they had consecrated themselves with their whole souls, being subjected to harsh sentences of judges, at whatsoever time it happened to each, or such as were included in curial registers, not having been reckoned in their number previously, let them be restored to their ancestral place and customary contentment, and give thanks to God the liberator of all. Or such as were deprived of their goods and, afflicted by the loss of all their existing wealth, have hitherto been living in straitened circumstances, let them be given back their old dwellings and birthright and properties, and enjoy to the full the beneficence of the Supreme. <. . .>
>
> Those also who were condemned either to labour under harsh conditions in mines, or to perform menial tasks at public works, let them exchange incessant toils for sweet leisure, and now live an easier life of freedom, undoing the infinite hardships of their labours in gentle relaxation. But if any have been deprived of their civil liberty and suffered public dishonour, then let them, with the gladness appropriate considering they have been parted by a long exile, take up again their former rank and make haste back to their native lands. (Letter to the provincials of Palestine quoted by Eusebius in *Vita Constantini* II 30, 32; Cameron & Hall 1999: 106–7)

Constantine had to be cautious in pursuing new religious policies. Eighty to 85 percent of his subjects were still practicing pagans. Constantine could not afford to irritate them too much. The foundation of the survival of any Roman emperor was public popularity. Those emperors who were losing public support would soon lose their throne or life. It was vital for Roman emperors to be popular, and many successful emperors were talented populists and demagogues. The religious politics of Constantine were contrary to populism and could have easily cost him throne and possibly life. His religious reforms would be popular only with about ten percent of the population.

In his letter to the provincial governors in the East, Constantine acknowledged that his policies would go against the majority feelings (quoted by Eusebius in *Vita Constantini* II 48; Cameron & Hall 1999: 112). He also realized that he could not dismantle at once the over-three-millennia-old pagan infrastructure, which consisted of hundreds of thousand temples and shrines, an army of priests and their families whom they had to feed. His religious reform would radically affect the lifestyle and beliefs of millions of people who were surrounded by millions of gods' images and referred to these gods every time they performed any public or private interaction. Roman society was not at all secular or lukewarm to pagan religion. And it would not give up on this religion easily.

To navigate between the imperatives of his faith and the political necessity to survive pagan protests, Constantine chose the strategy of toleration. He started with accusing his

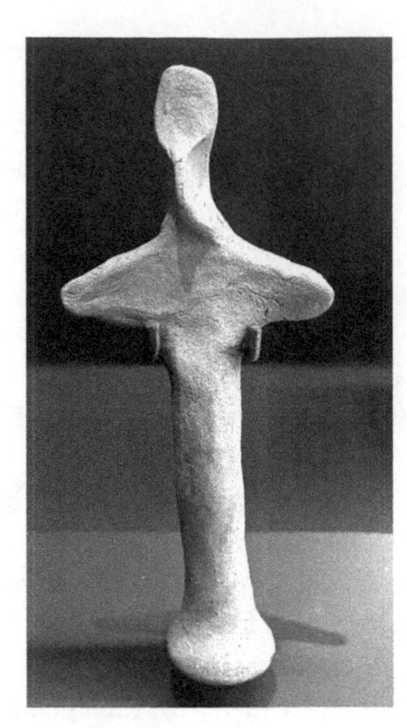

**Figure 1.25** A terracotta idol excavated at Troy.
Source: Photo by the author.

predecessors of intolerance: "I held the previous Emperors as exceedingly harsh." Constantine was particularly critical of Diocletian, whom he accused of launching a persecution against Christians out of blue, when the empire was at peace. He called the Great persecution a "civil war": "When all divine and human affairs were alike at peace, civil wars were rekindled by them" (letter to the provincials of the East quoted by Eusebius in *Vita Constantini* II 49; Cameron & Hall 1999: 112). Constantine made it clear that he was resolved to avoid a civil war between Christians and pagans. He also made it clear that, on the one hand, he disagreed with the pagan beliefs. On the other hand, he did not want to disturb them but wanted them to enjoy peace. He explicitly allowed the pagans to practice their religion. In contrast to his predecessors, Constantine proclaimed religious tolerance, and not traditional values, as a foundation of *Pax Romana*:

> For the general good of the world and of all mankind I desire that your people be at peace and stay free from strife. Let those in error, as well as the believers, gladly receive the benefit of peace and quiet. <. . .> May none molest another; may each retain what his soul desires, and practise it. (Letter to the provincials of the East quoted by Eusebius in *Vita Constantini* II 56; Cameron & Hall 1999: 113)

# *Pontifex Maximus*

Moreover, Constantine continued performing some of his duties as *pontifex maximus*—the chief priest of the Greco-Roman religion. In this capacity, for example, he approved new members of the priestly college in Rome and participated in some pagan rituals. Only as late as in 326, when he visited Rome to celebrate his twentieth anniversary as emperor, he refused to sacrifice to Jupiter publicly. In province, he continued to passively support the Greco-Roman cults. For example, about ten years after he refused to sacrifice to Jupiter in Rome, he nevertheless endorsed paganism in the community of Hispellum (now Spello) in Umbria. This community approached him with an initiative to adopt Constantine's name, Flavia Constans, and to construct a pagan temple dedicated to him and his family. Constantine approved both initiatives. He also allowed the local pagan priest to inaugurate festivals and gladiatorial fights:

> You most earnestly request that <. . .> we shall give a name from our cognomen to the community, which now has the name Hispellum and which you state is contiguous to and lying along the Flaminian Way and in which a temple of the Flavian Family is being built, of truly magnificent workmanship worthy of the greatness of its name; and that there that priest, whom Umbria selects annually, shall exhibit a festival of both stage plays and gladiatorial shows <. . .>: our assent is gladly granted to your prayer and desire. (*Hispellum rescript*; Johnson 2012: 241–2)

Constantine, in the meantime, made sure that the key imperial cities looked more Christian. He founded several churches on the outskirts of Rome. It is noteworthy that Constantine was careful to use the imperial and not public lands for those constructions. The most important of those church, in the Lateran, still stands there and continues serving as the cathedral for the bishops of Rome. Constantine also

**Figure 1.26** Inside the Lateran "Constantiana basilica."
Source: Photo by the author.

built shrines to the martyrs, again mostly on the outskirts of Rome. He cautiously promoted the new religion, and cautiously increased his personal distance from the old one.

## Constantinople

Constantine could only use a limited space to make Rome looking more Christian. The eternal city remained too pagan and grew too unfavorable to Constantine—his popularity with the local population had dramatically fallen. The emperor was also bothered by the senate, which never missed a chance to remind him of the old religion and old republican traditions. For these reasons, Constantine preferred to spend time in other imperial cities, such as Trier, Milan, Thessalonica, and Sofia in modern Bulgaria, which he reportedly called "my Rome" (*Serdica mea Roma est*). When he and his court stayed in one of those cities, they became the emperor's capitals. Constantinople was initially envisaged as one of such emperor's capitals, not a substitute for Rome. Its purpose, in addition to be the first entirely Christian city of the empire, was to provide a base for military campaigns against Persia and troublemaking tribes to the north. Only with the passage of decades, Constantinople evolved to the new Rome (see Pigott 2019).

The place and name for this city was chosen based on multiple precedents. The rumors held that Julius Caesar had planned to move his capital to northwest Asia

**Figure 1.27** Excavations of Troy near Çanakkale in Turkey.
Source: Photo by the author.

Minor, somewhere close to Troy. This plan fitted the imperial ideology, famously promoted by Virgil. His *Aeneid* became a founding myth of the Roman *Empire*. Diocletian, two and half centuries later, accomplished Julius' dream and moved his capital to Nicomedia, which was not far from the supposed place of Troy. Other emperors, instead of establishing a new capital, reestablished the old one. Commodus ritually reestablished Rome and changed its name after himself, to Colonia Lucia Annia Commodiana. Nero before him had entertained the idea of renaming Rome to Neropolis.

All these precedents were amalgamated in Constantinople, which was built on the top of the old Greek colony of Byzantion. It was located close to ancient Troy and thus marked a symbolic tribute to the assumed prototype of the old Rome (see Van Dam 2010). Another reason for choosing this place might be its proximity to Chrysopolis, where Constantine in 324 defeated Licinius and thus became the sole ruler of the empire. Licinius had made Byzantion his residence. Choosing this place for his residence certified Constantine's victory over his rival. To make his victory even more visible and the new city entirely Christian, as he intended, Constantine ordered demolishing most extant urban infrastructure of the old city, including pagan shrines. Constantinople was inaugurated as a completely new city through Christian rites on May 11, 330 (see Falcasantos 2020; Grig & Kelly 2012; Bassett 2004; Dagron 1984; Dagron 1974).

## Model of Tolerance

Even in this Christian city, there was enough room left for pagans. Many of them took key positions in the imperial administration and education. Unless they were fanatical about their religion, pagans did not experience discrimination from the Christianized imperial authorities. The famous pagan rhetor Libanius in the end of the fourth century recollected with nostalgia the times of Constantine in Constantinople, where he had begun his career as an educator:

> While I was still a boy, the ruler who held a reign of terror in Rome was brought down by the leader of an army of Gauls—Gauls who, originally worshippers of the gods, turned against them and attacked them. He, after overcoming the person who had infused new life into the cities, thought it to his own advantage to recognize some other as a god, and he employed the sacred treasures on the building of the city upon which his heart was set. For all that, he made absolutely no alteration in the traditional forms of worship, but, though poverty reigned in the temples, one could see that all the rest of the ritual was fulfilled. (Libanius, *Oratio* XXX 6; Norman 1977: 104–7)

# I.6

# Persecutions against the Greco-Roman Religion

## Constantius II

Libanius changed his tone when he came to describe the religious policies of Constantine's son Constantius II (337–61):

> To his (i.e., Constantine's) son passed the government, or rather the shadow of it, for the reins of power were held by others who, through their control of his earliest upbringing, had gained a supremacy absolutely equal to his own. He (i.e., Constantius II), then, ruling under orders from them, was induced to adopt several misguided policies, in particular, the banning of sacrifices. (Libanius, *Oratio* XXX 7; Norman 1977: 106–7)

Indeed, Constantius gradually departed from his father's ways of balancing between promoting his own religion and tolerating other religions. In the beginning of his tenure, he continued the policies of tolerance but abandoned them toward the end (see Stenger 2020). Constantius eventually ordered closing all pagan temples and prohibited all public sacrifices. Perpetrators were proscribed the confiscation of property and sometimes even capital punishment. Constantius knew that local authorities often ignored the imperial orders against pagan practices. He enforced his orders by threatening those governors who sabotaged them:

> It is Our pleasure that the temples shall be immediately closed in all places and in all cities, and access to them forbidden, so as to deny to all abandoned men the opportunity to commit sin. It is also Our will that all men shall abstain from sacrifices. But if perchance any man should perpetrate any such criminality, he shall be struck down with the avenging sword. We also decree that the property of a man thus executed shall be vindicated to the fisc. The governors of the provinces shall be similarly punished if they should neglect to avenge such crimes. (*Codex Theodosianus* XVI 10.4; Pharr 1952: 472)

**Figure 1.28** Instead of destroying pagan sanctuaries, Christian authorities prohibited access to them and left them to collapse naturally. This happened, for instance, to the temple of Poseidon in Sounion near Athens.
Source: Photo by the author.

In 356 in Milan, Constantius promulgated a similar edict with the same proscriptions. This edict was promoted with some apparent symbolism attached to it. It was signed in the same city where Constantine had issued in 313 his own edict in support of Christians. Like the earlier edict of Milan was cosigned by Constantine's coruler Licinius, Constantius made his caesar Julian cosign the edict of 356. Despite these superficial similarities, the Edict of Milan 356 was quite a departure from the edict of 313. The latter proclaimed the freedom of consciousness, while the former effectively rejected it.

Constantius did not proceed, however, to destroying pagan temples—in the pre-dynamite era, this demanded a lot of money and labor. There are also no reports about any executions of the perpetrators. Moreover, Constantius' policies targeted primarily urban paganism and allowed the rural temples to function as venues for festivals. It seems that what Constantine really tried to achieve was to lock up urban paganism in homes and other private places. This per se was a major blow to the Greco-Roman religion, which was public in its very nature. Constantius calculated that confining it to private spaces would eventually suffocate it. He was right in his calculations.

# Julian

Constantius tipped the balance that had been set by Constantine, to the Christian advantage. This backfired after Constantius' death. The pagan rebellion, which Constantine had been afraid of, eventually happened. It was led by someone unlikely—Constantine's nephew Julian, who had been brought up as a Christian (see Rebenich & Wiemer 2020). It seems that for several years, Julian practiced paganism in secret, while publicly he pretended to be a Christian. He even had to cosign with Constantius the edict of 356 that reinforced anti-pagan policies and proscribed capital punishment for their violators.

Julian's rise to power was against many odds, which made him believe that he was chosen for a mission. He perceived his mission as the restoration of the pagan *ancien régime*. Julian, on the one hand, became a nonconformist rebel against the established religion, which Christianity had become under Constantius. On the other hand, his rebellion was for the sake of traditional Roman values. Christianity for Julian, like earlier for Porphyry, was a novelty that disrupted the smooth flow of Roman history. He accused Christians of "abandoning the religion of your forefathers" (ἀπολιπόντες τὰ πάτρια) (*Contra Galilaeos*; Wright 1923: 388).

Julian's worldview was framed by neo-Platonic philosophy. After Porphyry, this philosophy was aggressively anti-Christian. In contrast to its parental Platonic and Aristotelian schools which tolerated but not promoted polytheism, neo-Platonism was intentionally polytheistic. In the time of Julian, neo-Platonism was not yet Christianized. Julian adopted its polytheistic thrust, which made him a fervent pagan. He publicized his intimate experiences with gods in a letter to the Athenians, where he revealed how he learned about being elected as emperor:

> It was already late, when about sunset the news was brought to me, and suddenly the palace was surrounded and they all began to shout aloud, while I was still considering what I ought to do and feeling by no means confident. My wife was still alive and it happened, that in order to rest alone, I had gone to the upper room near hers. Then from there through an opening in the wall I prayed to Zeus. And when the shouting grew still louder and all was in a tumult in the palace I entreated the god to give me a sign; and thereupon he showed me a sign and bade me yield and not oppose myself to the will of the army. (*Ἀθηναίων τῇ βουλῇ καὶ τῷ δήμῳ*; Wright 1913: 282–3)

After becoming the emperor, Julian focused on the restoration of paganism throughout his empire. He made all pagan shrines again accessible for worship. He also significantly upgraded functions and structures of the Greco-Roman religion. He reshaped it following the model of the Christian church. For example, Julian appointed priestly governors in provinces—in the imitation of Christian bishops. Higher priests were instructed to appoint local priests—in the way that bishops ordained priests. Following Julian's reforms, the Greco-Roman religion in its structure resembled more the Christian church than the pre-Constantinian priest colleges. Julian effectively established a "pagan church" that never existed before.

As for the Christian church, Julian did not oppress it directly. Instead, he decided that the best strategy would be to sow chaos among Christians. He utilized the ongoing theological debates about the council of Nicaea, which had become particularly divisive under Constantius II, as an instrument to dig inter-Christian divisions deeper. He brought back from exile bishops representing antagonistic groups. After they returned to their sees, they resumed fighting each other. Julian smartly calculated that the church was unable to manage its own matters on its own anymore. Without the interference of the state, he hoped, the church would inevitably collapse because of internal divides.

Julian prohibited Christians to teach in the state-endowed schools. Christian students could study there, but only with pagan professors. Julian's justification for this policy was that, when Christians use pagan philosophers, such as Plato or Aristotle, they act as hypocrites. Only pagans, according to Julian, could be sincere and consistent in teaching pagan philosophy. He unwillingly sided with the Christian conservatives, who rejected pagan wisdom whatsoever.

Julian hoped that he would restore the pre-Constantinian *Pax Romana* by restoring the disturbed—so he believed—*pax deorum*. His messianic policies, however, depleted the treasury and destabilized the Roman administrative system. The Constantinian system of political stability based on tolerance was shaken first by Constantius and even more by Julian. The traditional Roman values did not spell their stabilizing magic anymore. Julian's tenure ended sooner than he expected. He so much believed in his mission that he wanted to prove himself being elected by gods by going to a risky campaign against Persia. There he was killed in 363.

## Jovian

Constantius' and Julian's failure to produce sustainable religious policies demonstrated that such policies had to stay within the frame of tolerance: the state's favors to Christianity and paganism had to be balanced. The policy of balancing was restored by Jovian (in office 363–4) and continued by his successors. Jovian neither reinstated Constantius' ban on sacrifices nor closed the temples which had been reopened by Julian. Both the Greco-Roman religion and Christianity were endowed with state funds. These policies lasted for about one generation.

## Theodosius

The balance between Christianity and paganism was tipped in favor of Christianity by Emperor Theodosius (in office 379–95). This Spanish general was promoted to emperor with the goal to defeat Goths. He failed to reach this goal and looked for other sources of legitimacy for himself. He opted for religion as a source of his legitimacy. In the main religious conflicts of his time—between the followers and adversaries of the council of Nicaea, as well as between Christians and pagans—Theodosius abandoned the position of an impartial moderator held by his predecessors and threw himself to support one side against the other. He supported the Nicaeans and built for them a platform to defend their doctrine—an ecumenical council, which he convened in 381. The emperor also reproached pagans through a series of actions and inactions.

In particular, Theodosius promulgated laws that enhanced the earlier legislation prohibiting sacrifices and attending temples. He dropped the imperial title of *pontifex maximus*, which all his Christian predecessors had preferred to keep. In another rupture with the earlier Christian emperors, he dissolved the order of the Vestal virgins in Rome. Theodosius did not directly order destroying temples, but he informally encouraged Christian assaults against them. During his tenure, Christian activists destroyed two crucial sacred places of the Greco-Roman religion: the temple complexes of Apollo in Delphi and of Serapis in Alexandria. Theodosius did nothing to prevent these destructions.

Pagan reactions to any assault or restriction had been imminent since Constantine. Such reactions immediately followed both actions and inaction of Theodosius. A senior member of the senate in Constantinople, Themistius, tried to convince the emperor to allow the pagan religion to breathe. The same begging voice was heard from Antioch, where Libanius wrote a long apology encouraging the emperor to continue the policies of tolerance practiced by his predecessors (Libanius, *Oratio* XXX; Norman 1977). In Alexandria, pagan mob rioted, being led by the philosopher Olympus and grammarians Helladius and Ammonius (see Watts 2017). Rufinus of Aquileia described how pagans occupied the premises of the main African sanctuary, Serapeum. They captured some Christians and forced them to make sacrifices. Those who refused were tortured. Rufinus rendered this religious conflict in the terms of a civil war:

> The two peoples (i.e., Christians and pagans) were at open war. Our side (i.e., Christians) far outweighed the other in numbers and strength, but was rendered less violent by religious restraint. As a result, when many of ours had been wounded repeatedly, and some even killed, [the pagans] took refuge in a temple as a sort of stronghold, taking with them many Christians whom they had captured. These they forced to offer sacrifice on the altars which were kindled; those who refused they put to death with new and refined tortures, fastening some to gibbets and breaking the legs of others and pitching them into the caverns which a careworn antiquity had built to receive the blood of sacrifices and the other impurities of the temple. (*Eusebii Historiarum continuatio* XI 22; Amidon 2016: 463)

In this war, pagans did not have a chance to win. Christians eventually captured Serapeum and demolished it. Some scholars believe that this demolition was a landmark event, which indicated that paganism was not anymore the political and cultural backbone of the empire (see Watts 2015: 2–4). Theodosius realized that this was an opportunity for him to abandon the policy of tolerance without endangering the stability of his realm. He looked at the Christian-pagan battlefield as a general. When he saw that the virtual Christian army is stronger and more numerous than the pagans, he led it to an attack. His calculations were correct: paganism was not as resilient as it used to be under Julian. It could not anymore undermine the legitimacy

**Figure 1.29** The ruins of the temple complex dedicated to the Greco-Egyptian deity Serapis—Serapeum, in Alexandria.
Source: Photo by the author.

of the emperors who led attacks against it. Under Julian, paganism demonstrated that it could not anymore be the platform of *Pax Romana*. Under Theodosius, it demonstrated that it could not anymore threaten the *Pax Romana*, which had been reestablished on the Christian platform. Now Christianity enjoyed a monopoly in securing peace across the Roman world.

## Shenoute

The civil war between Christians and pagans, in the meantime, continued in the province. One of its violent episodes is described in the *Life of Shenoute*—a charismatic abbot of the "White Monastery Federation" in Upper Egypt, near the city of Panopolis, now Akhmim. When he was elected an abbot of the White Monastery in 385, he united it with two other communities nearby: the Red Monastery and a nunnery. This "Federation" became the most famous in the Coptic world. Shenoute, who was reportedly an abbot for around eighty years, claimed that he had direct revelations from God. His behavior was of a "monastic prophet" (Brakke & Crislip 2019: 5). Although he was fluent in Greek and had received decent classical education, he preferred to write in Coptic.

Shenoute was a militant campaigner for the religious monopoly of Christianity. While chasing both overt and crypto-pagans, he invoked the will of the emperor:

"The present righteous emperors who rule the earth, have decreed in their edicts to demolish and to dig out the foundations of what remains, until no stone among them is left on top of any other stone" (in Emmel 2008: 179). Shenoute targeted the former governor of the city of Thebes Flavius Aelius Gessius. The Coptic abbot publicly accused Gessius of practicing idolatry in secret. To prove this, he raided his private residence. The following fragment from his Coptic *Vita* describes what happened there:

> We (i.e., a group of Christians led by Shenoute) made an example of him (i.e., Gessius) by removing his idols from a private chamber during the night quietly even though the doors protected them securely. <. . .> It was Jesus who enabled us to open the doors as He wanted. It was also He who led us through the atrium and up the stairway of that house until we came upon those abominations hidden away. And it was He who made straight our entry and our exit. We received neither iron key nor wooden key nor key-ring from any of his people, and we had with us no tool of any sort for opening, but we opened those great doors that were very securely fastened. <. . .> The door by which we entered the private chamber on the [second storey, where] those [vain] things (i.e., the idols) were kept, popped out, [not] because we put our shoulders to it and pushed with force, <. . .> but when I grasped it, it fell by coming off its hinges, and we carried it away easily. We did not suffer any hurt, and we did not stumble [at all] in that house, which is full of darkness because also the lord of that house is dark. (In Emmel 2008: 168)

Constantius II had forced paganism to abandon the public square and confine itself to private spaces. Paganism from a public religion, thus, turned to private. In the reversal move, Christianity from private became public. These processes began under Constantine and were accelerated under his son Constantius. Julian undertook to bring paganism back to the public space and to drive Christianity back to private life, but this attempt was short-lived. Paganism was again confined to privacy under Theodosius. The aforementioned story told by Shenoute shows that some Christian zealots tried to purge paganism even from private spaces, like the one where Gessius kept his idols. This meant total extermination of the Greco-Roman religion.

When there is a war, enemies are often dehumanized. The civil war between Christians and pagans in Egypt was not an exception. Shenoute in his *Discourses* also dehumanized pagans. He developed a moral theology, which excluded pagans and heretics from God's love. For Shenoute, this was because they were not quite human:

> If you say that the Lord accepts sinners and eats with them, rather it is necessary to understand why—[is it] so that they might believe in him or so that they might blaspheme against call the sinners to repentance? Don't you see the indication of their love; for the one who has called them, that is, that all the tax collectors and sinners were approaching him so that they might hear him? If you invite an unbeliever, and he comes to the supper of your God, and he eats from the good things that he has sown,

**Figure 1.30** Although Shenoute was against everything pagan, elements of both Egyptian and Hellenic pagan culture were used in the decoration of Shenoute's Red Monastery.

Source: Photo by the author.

saying, "I have prepared them," then well and good. If an unbeliever invites you to dinner, and you too eat with him as your Lord Jesus did, your cup is divided. <. . .>

Good fathers said, "You shall not curse any human being" (see Num. 22:12). But in fact they are not human beings, and if they are human beings, they are human beings who deserve to be cursed by those who say, "We are Christians," because they have cursed him who created them. <. . .> If it's appropriate to curse the snake, it's even more appropriate to curse the children of that snake, which the Lord cursed at the beginning because it deceived Eve and caused Adam to stumble in paradise, just as now these accursed people cause many to stumble and scandalize those who cannot understand that they belong to Satan. (*Discources* V 6; Brakke and Crislip 2019: 267, 272–3)

# Survival of Greco-Roman Religion

Although pagans were oppressed and even dehumanized, they survived for a long time. The traditional Greco-Roman religion continued to be practiced until the end of the Christian Antiquity and the beginning of the Middle Ages. This religion survived in social bubbles, just as Christianity had survived in bubbles before Constantine.

**Figure 1.31** Pagan elements in the altar of an Orthodox chapel on the Aegean Island of Leros.
Source: Photo by the author.

Some of these bubbles were intellectual, grouped around philosophical schools. When the pagan schools were closed down, paganism continued to be practiced in private households. While pagan temples stood abandoned, people kept a lot of images and statues of gods in their private places. For example, there was enough of them in the 480s in Alexandria to keep bonfire burning for most of the day. Even more enduring were traditional festivals, such as Lupercalia that continued until the fifth century in Rome and until the tenth century in Constantinople. Some primitive forms of paganism have survived until our days, being blended with Christianity in the popular piety.

# I.7

# Symphonies

## The Church between Monarchy and Republic

The Roman state changed its political system from republican to monarchical several decades before Christ. Even as monarchy, however, the Roman Empire pretended to function as a republic. Such republican institutes as the Roman senate and regional magistrates continued playing an important role in the empire's political life. Emperors were obliged to show at least formal respect to and consult the senate. Since the murder of Julius Caesar, many figures in the Roman political system had not abandoned hopes to restore the full republic.

The conversion of the Roman Empire to Christianity created a momentum for its re-republicanization.[1] However, this momentum was not materialized in the traditional republican forms. One of the reasons was because most advocates for traditional republican institutes remained convinced pagans. Another reason could be that many Christians, even after Constantine, continued entertaining the idea that the empire is alien to them—their memories about the persecutions were still vivid. It took a generation or two before most Christians began perceiving the empire as their home and wanting to take care of it. Before that would happen, they hesitated to invest themselves in sustaining and improving imperial structures.

When Christians realized that the Roman Empire is not their prison or temporary abode but home, they reimagined its structures of power in more Christian ways. Many of them envisaged the Christianized Roman Empire to be more transparent, egalitarian, with more participation and representation of people. This would be a republican vision.

---

[1]Anthony Kaldellis convincingly argues that the bottom line of the Byzantine political system was republican and not monarchical; see Kaldellis 2015.

**Figure 1.32** Apostles in senatorial togas. Catacombs of Domitilla in Rome.
Source: Photo by the author.

Even if such republican vision existed indeed, it was subsumed by another vision articulated by Eusebius of Caesarea. He suggested an upgrade to monarchy instead of dismantling it. In his oration addressed to Constantine, Eusebius bluntly advocated for monarchy against returning to republic. He argued that Christians should prefer monarchy, because it is ostensibly closer to monotheism:

> Lastly, invested as he (i.e., Constantine) is with a semblance of heavenly sovereignty, he directs his gaze above, and frames his earthly government according to the pattern of that Divine original, feeling strength in its conformity to the monarchy of God. And this conformity is granted by the universal Sovereign to man alone of the creatures of this earth: for he only is the author of sovereign power, who decrees that all should be subject to the rule of one. And surely monarchy far transcends every other constitution and form of government: for that democratic equality of power, which is its opposite, may rather be described as anarchy and disorder. Hence there is one God, and not two, or three, or more: for to assert a plurality of gods is plainly to deny the being of God at all. There is "one King"; and his Word and royal Law is one: a Law not expressed in syllables and words, not written or engraved on tablets, and therefore subject to the ravages of time; but the living and self-subsisting Word, who himself is God, and who administers his Fathers kingdom on behalf of all who are under him and subject to his power. (Eusebius, *De laudibus Constantini* 3.5-6; Stevenson & Frend 2013: 417–18)

The rationale of monarchical power, which Eusebius promoted, certainly cohered with the expectations of Constantine, who had adopted Christianity not with the purpose to water down his authority, but to boost it. And Constantine was delivered what he had aspired for. The church, through the people like Eusebius, endorsed Constantine as the sole ruler of both the East and the West. After Constantine, Byzantine basileuses concentrated the legislative, executive, and judicial powers to the extent that their pagan predecessors could only dream of (see Φειδᾶς 1991: 155–6).

In contrast to his pagan predecessors, Constantine could not pretend to be god and had to abandon the imperial cult—the source of legitimacy for the previous emperors. A new theological mechanism of enhancing his legitimacy was designed instead to secure divine status for the imperial office. This office was reimagined as a reflection of the one God. The idea that the imperial office is an image of the divine authority was not a Christian invention. Some pagan emperors, who preferred to avoid being proclaimed deities while alive, promoted themselves as images of one of the Olympian gods. Trajan, for example, called himself *optimus maximus*—a title reserved exclusively for Zeus/Jupiter. Pliny the Younger presented Trajan as Jupiter on earth (*Panegyricus* 80; Radice 1969). In contrast to the Christian emperors, however, a pagan emperor was one of many gods or an image of one of them. A Christian monarch became the only image of the one God, as Eusebius of Caesarea elaborated upon in his oration dedicated to Constantine:

> The only begotten Word of God reigns, from ages which had no beginning, to infinite and endless ages, the partner of his Father's kingdom. And our emperor ever beloved by him, who derives the source of imperial authority from above, and is strong in the power of his sacred title, has controlled the Empire of the world for a long period of years. Again, that Preserver of the universe orders the whole heaven and earth, and the celestial kingdom, consistently with his Father's will. Even so our emperor whom he loves, by bringing those whom he rules on earth to the only begotten and saving Word renders them fit subjects for his kingdom. And as he who is the common Saviour of mankind, by his invisible and Divine power as a good shepherd, drives far away from his flock, like savage beasts, those apostate spirits which once flew through the airy tracts above this earth, and fastened on the souls of men; so this his friend, graced by his heavenly favour with victory over all his foes, subdues and chastens the open adversaries of the truth in accordance with the usages of war. He who is the pre-existent Word, the Saviour of all things, imparts to his followers the seeds of true wisdom and salvation, makes them at the same time truly wise, and understanding the kingdom of their Father. Our emperor, his friend, acting as interpreter to the Word of God, aims at recalling the whole human race to the knowledge of God; proclaiming clearly in the ears of all, and declaring with powerful voice the laws of truth and godliness to all who dwell on the earth. Once more, the universal Saviour opens the heavenly gates of his Father's kingdom to those whose course is thitherward from his world. Our emperor, emulous of his Divine example, having purged his earthly dominion from every stain of impious error, invites each holy and pious worshipper within his imperial mansions, earnestly desiring to save with all its crew that mighty vessel of which he is the appointed pilot. (*De laudibus Constantini* 2.1-5; Stevenson & Frend 2013: 416–17)

The pagan imperial cult framed the history of Christianity both before and after the empire's conversion, in different ways though. Before, this cult was the main driving force of the persecutions: Christians who refused to recognize the emperors' divine status were treated as criminals. After the fourth century, the old imperial cult merged with the new Christian political theology. This theology reimagined a Christian emperor as the image of God and a mediator between the Kingdom of God and his own kingdom (see García Ruiz & Quiroga Puertas 2021; Burgersdijk & Ross 2018; Dagron 2003). The concept of an emperor as *imago Dei* framed all posterior church-state relations, as well as the concept of the church per se.

## The Idea of Symphony

Although Eusebius envisaged the church as a part of the one-God-like monarchy, the real role of the church sometimes resembled the role that the Roman senate had played in the heydays of the Roman Republic. The church became a gravity center in the system of checks and balances on the imperial power. This system became known as "symphony" (see Hovorun 2016). It comes from the Greek word *symphonia* (συμφωνία), which has a synonym of *synallelia* (συναλληλία). These two words describe an intended partnership in sharing power between the church and state.

As a partner of the empire in power-sharing, the church received its share in privileges. Its clergymen were exempted from public services (*munera*) and some taxes. They also regularly received state subsidies. Their important legal privilege was to be judged by church courts. Bishops were endowed with the legal power to notarize slaves' manumission. They were also allowed to use imperial facilities, such as post services, for free. This helped them to attend church councils. Councils were costly, and because the state generously paid for them, the church was able to have many of them. Constantine and his successors sponsored copying and circulating the Jewish and Christian Scriptures. This was also very expensive. They subsidized building magnificent basilicas. Constantine, for example, built from scratch vast worship complexes in Jerusalem and Bethlehem. His mother Helen personally supervised this work. The most magnificent construction project of the first millennium was accomplished by Justinian, who sponsored and personally supervised building the cathedral of St. Sophia in Constantinople.

## Legitimacy

The emperors' motivation to make the church participating in power-sharing and provide it with privileges was not altruistic. They expected that the church in return would enhance their legitimacy. In the Roman Empire, during both pre-

Christian and Christian periods, there were no clear rules accepted by everyone and securing the succession of power. There were many ways to ascend the imperial throne and even more ways to fall from it. Most of these ways were not regulated by law. In their ascension to the throne and then keeping it, emperors could rely more on legitimacy than legality. Not so much the law, as the reception by different constituencies, secured power for individual rulers. They desperately needed support from army, aristocracy, and people to gain and stay in power. The mission of the church in creating and maintaining legitimacy for Christian emperors was, therefore, crucial.

Neither pagan nor Christian Roman Empire was ever secular. It always related to the divine, in many ways. Divine was the main source of legitimacy for all Roman rulers, be they pagan or Christian. Those emperors were regarded successful who were believed to be endorsed with what the Chinese call "heavenly mandate." A Chinese traveler to Byzantium in the seventh century made a characteristic observation about how the Byzantines perceived the legitimacy of their rulers:

> Their kings are not men who last. They choose the most capable and they put him on the throne; but if a misfortune or something out of the ordinary happens in the Empire, or if the wind or the rain arrive at the wrong season, then they at once depose the emperor and put another in his place. (新唐書 [New Book of Tang] 198; Hirth 1975: 52)

Such perception of legitimacy had deep roots in the pre-Christian Roman statehood. Pagan Roman rulers were expected to make sure that "peace with gods" (*pax deorum*) translated to the well-being of the Roman people (*salus populi romani*) and the peace across the Roman world (*Pax Romana*). The same idea, somehow modified, survived in Christianity, where the emperor became the image of one God and a mediator between the heavenly and earthly kingdoms. If his subjects felt that there was a harmony between heaven and earth, the emperor's legitimacy increased.

The Christian empire inherited many pagan devises of securing the heavenly mandate for the emperors. One of them was the idea that emperors are exempted from the rest of the humankind and endowed with a special divine status. In the pagan times, emperors were proclaimed gods. In the Christian times, they were perceived as images of God in a way, which was different from how all human beings are the images of God. Pagan emperors often consulted oracles and stars about matters of state governance. Many Christian emperors retained astrology as their favorite way of knowing God's will (see Wisniewski 2020). All these instruments of securing the heavenly mandate were secondary in comparison with what could be provided by the church. However, to use the legitimizing power of the church, the state had to share with the church some political power.

**Figure 1.33** Maria *Salus Populi Romani*. A Byzantine icon in the Roman Basilica of Santa Maria Maggiore.

Source: Photo by the author.

**Figure 1.34** Astrological disc from Perge. Antalya Archeological Museum.

Source: Photo by the author.

## Power-sharing

The "symphonic" system of power-sharing, of which the church became an essential part, was codified in two major collections of Byzantine law: *Codex Theodosianus*, named after Theodosius II (in office 402–50), who together with Valentinian III (in office 419–55) codified the imperial legislation from Constantine through the beginning of the fifth century, and *Corpus iuris canonici*, collected by Justinian (in office 527–65). Justinian went further than any other emperor before him in making coherent the systems of the ecclesial and imperial legislation. He systematically applied the norm, which before him was enacted sporadically and according to which all decisions of the church adopted at its major councils—the so-called canons—would become enforced as state laws. This norm was, on the one hand, beneficial for the church, because all its decisions were implemented by default through the state mechanisms. On the other hand, this meant that the church could not adopt canons, which would be incoherent with the imperial policies.

Several laws collected in the Theodosian and Justinianian codices, defined the systems of power-sharing and legitimization in both Western and Eastern parts of the Roman Empire. They in particular regulated privileges and benefits that the state offered to the church. The Theodosian codex, for example, postulated the depravation of the pagan priests of their statuses and privileges:

> If any privileges have been granted by ancient law to civil priests, ministers, prefects, or hierophants of the sacred mysteries, whether known by these names or called by any other, such privileges shall be completely abolished. Such persons shall not congratulate themselves that they are protected by any privilege, since their profession is known to be condemned by law. (*Codex Theodosianus* XVI 10.14; Pharr 1952: 474)

These statuses and privileges were transferred to the Christian clergy and hierarchy:

> We direct that priests, deacons, subdeacons, exorcists, lectors, doorkeepers, and likewise all persons who are of the first rank in the Church shall be exempt from the compulsory public services that are incumbent on persons. (*Codex Theodosianus* XVI 2.24; Pharr 1952: 444)

As another decree from the same codex explained, the Christian clergy was exempted from public services, including taxation, because the empire "is sustained more by religion than by official duties and physical toil and sweat" (*Codex Theodosianus* XVI 2.16; Pharr 1952: 443). The latter idea was explicated by Justinian. In the preamble to his novella 6, the legislator stated:

> The greatest gifts that God, in his celestial benevolence, has bestowed on mankind are priesthood and sovereignty, the one serving on matters divine, and the other ruling over

> human affairs, and caring for them. Each proceeds from one and the same authority, and regulates human life. Thus nothing could have as great a claim on the attention of sovereigns as the honour of priests, seeing that they are the very ones who constantly offer prayer to God on the sovereigns' behalf. Hence, should the one be above reproach in every respect, and enjoy access to God, while the other keeps in correct and proper order the realm that has been entrusted to it, there will be a satisfactory harmony, conferring every conceivable benefit on the human race. We therefore have very great concern for the honour of priests, as well as for the truth of theological doctrine; as long as they maintain that honour, our confident belief is that, through it, great gifts will be bestowed on us by God, and that as well as keeping firm possession of what we hold, we shall also gain what has not yet come to us, even now. All would go duly and well, provided that the first step in the matter is taken in a way correct and pleasing to God; and we believe that that will be so, if only observance of the sacred canons is maintained in the manner that the apostles, justly celebrated as the venerable eyewitnesses and ministers of the divine word, have handed down, and as the holy fathers have maintained and taught. (*Corpus iuris civilis*; Miller & Sarris 2018: 97–8)

This is believed to be the standard definition of the Byzantine symphony, which actually uses the word "symphony." This piece refers to God as the source of legitimacy for the imperial power ("sovereignty"), through the intercession of the church ("priesthood"). The two powers, "sovereignty" and "priesthood" are clearly distinguished: the former cares for the "human affairs," while the latter, for the "matters divine." Yet, they are supposed to be in harmony with one another and share the same responsibility for "human life." The emperors who take care of the "honour of priests," through such caretaking hope for "great gifts" from God. This was a way to say that the emperors shared with the church power, to receive for themselves more legitimacy.

# Constantian Symphony

Some Christian emperors were more and others less consistent with the symphonic model of power-sharing. For example, Constantius II developed a "paranoid inability to share power" (Watts 2015: 89). After Constantine died in 337, his three sons became *augusti*: Constantine II, Constans, and Constantius II. Even though they were originally supposed to share power, they couldn't. In the civil war that followed (see Lewis 2020), Constantius emerged as the sole ruler of the empire. For that he eliminated several relatives. His cousin Julian, who would later succeed him as emperor, accused him of tyranny (Baker-Brian & Tougher 2020: 3). Such accusation, which had been used since the Athenian democracy, in both Greek and Roman political cultures meant that a ruler did not want to share power with any other person or institution.

Constantius, on the one hand, overprotected and patronized the church. On the other hand, he tried to unshare the power, which his father Constantine had shared with it. This embarrassed many in the church. A leading hierarch of that time, the archbishop of Alexandria Athanasius came to an open clash with the emperor. One of the reasons of the clash was doctrinal: Constantius conducted policies that marginalized the council of Nicaea, which Athanasius held as the keystone of orthodoxy. This, however, was not the only reason for the conflict between the two men. Athanasius tried to protect the share in power, which was reserved for the church by Constantine and which Constantius wanted to take back.

## Theodosian Symphony

In contrast to Constantius, Theodosius did not want all power for himself. Instead, he divided his power into two pieces. In 395, the Roman Empire formally and for good split into two parts, each led by Theodosius' two sons, Arcadius in the East and Honorius in the West. Theodosius also enhanced and expanded the senate; its role in the empire became more substantial. Finally, he allocated more power for the church. In the episode of clash with Ambrose of Milan, who had imposed on him an interdict, he accepted the authority of Ambrose to do that. There was another episode that demonstrates how serious Theodosius was about political independence of the church. After he convoked in 381 a council, which would become known as second ecumenical, he did not show up there himself but let the bishops decide on their own. He did so in contrast even to Constantine, who was present during the sessions of the council in Nicaea. On a general note, it seems that all ecumenical councils were convened by the emperors who respected the model of power-sharing with the church. The ecumenical councils as such were a product of this model.

## Pentarchy

Another product of this model was the aforementioned system of *pentarchy*. This system functioned as a supplement and sometimes a substitute for councils. It was designed to secure the unity of the universal church through a "symphony" between its independent primates—the patriarchs, as well as through their "symphony" with both the Western and Eastern parts of the Christian Roman Empire. It should be noticed that the primates of the church outside the Roman Empire, like in Persia, Armenia, or Georgia, were excluded from *pentarchy*, which was a club for the Roman primates only. For this reason, the primates outside the Roman milieu were not called patriarchs—a title reserved for the club members only but held the title of "catholicos."

As was mentioned, the "patriarchal" system gradually replaced the earlier "metropolitan" and "diocesan" systems of the church administration. Patriarchates were built on the basis of the largest imperial structures of that time: prefectures. In contrast to the preceding "metropolitan" and "diocesan" systems, this system was not completely coherent with the political grid of the Roman Empire. It was a compromise between the current political system and the apostolic past of the church. For this reason, for example, the politically insignificant city of Jerusalem was endowed with the status of patriarchate along such political heavyweights as Alexandria and Antioch.

The council in *Trullo*, also known as *Quinisext* (Πενθέκτη), confirmed the transition of the church to the patriarchal system. It was convened in 691 by Emperor Justinian II in his palace. Its sessions took place in a domed chamber—*trullus*, hence is the council's name. Justinian II belonged to the group of ambitious emperors, who, for the sake of prestige and legitimacy, wanted to convene their own ecumenical councils. The problem for Justinian II, however, was that the previous ecumenical council was convened only ten years ago. Therefore, he positioned his council as sorting out the unfinished business from the two previous ecumenical councils. Hence is its second name: the Fifth-Sixth council. In its canon 36, it postulated the pentarchy in its accomplished form:

> Renewing the laws laid down by 150 holy fathers, who had gathered in this God-protected and imperial city, and by the 630, who had been convened in Chalcedon, we define that the see of Constantinople shall enjoy equal primacies (πρεσβείων) with the see of the older Rome, and in ecclesiastical matters shall be celebrated as the latter, being second after it. After [Constantinople] shall be numbered the see of the great city of Alexandrians, then that of Antioch, and afterwards the [see] of the city of Jerusalemites. (My translation from Φειδᾶς 1997: 161–2)

Theodore the Studite, a Byzantine monk who lived in Constantinople in the eighth to ninth centuries, provided one of the rare witnesses about how the pentarchy worked in solving issues:

> We are not discussing worldly affairs. The right to judge them rests with the Emperor and the secular tribunal. But here it is question of divine and heavenly decisions and those are reserved only to him to whom the Word of God has said: "Whatsoever you shall bind upon earth, will be bound in Heaven and whatsoever you shall loose on earth, shall be loosed in Heaven" (Mt. 16:19). And who are the men to whom this order was given?—the Apostles and their successors. And who are their successors?—he who occupies the throne of Rome and is the first; the one who sits upon the throne of Constantinople and is the second; after them, those of Alexandria, Antioch and Jerusalem. That is the Pentarchic authority in the Church. It is to them that all decision belongs in divine dogmas. The Emperor and the secular authority have the duty to aid them and to confirm what they have decided. (*Ep.* 478; translated by E.A. Quain in Dvornik 1979: 101)

Approximately at the same time, the Byzantine patrician Baanes explained the system of pentarchy as a divine institution, *jus divinum*. According to this interpretation, patriarchates are not a product of the evolution of ecclesial administrative structures, but have been established directly by God:

> God founded His Church on the five patriarchs and in the Gospels He defined that it could never completely fail because they are the chiefs of the Church. In effect Christ had said: "and the gates of Hell shall not prevail against her," which means: if two of them should happen to fail, they will turn to the three others; if three of them happen to fail, they shall address themselves to two others; and if by chance, four of them come to failure, the last, who dwells in Christ Our God, the Chief of all, will restore again the rest of the body of the Church. (In Mansi XVI 140–1; Dvornik 1979: 102)

The West accepted such an idea of pentarchy, with some reservations. It reserved for the bishop of Rome some exclusivity among the five patriarchs. According to Anastasius Bibliothecarius,

> Just as Christ has placed in His body, that is to say, in His Church, a number of patriarchs equal to the number of the senses in the human body, the well being of the Church will not suffer as long as these sees are of the same will, just as the body will function properly as long as the five senses remain intact and healthy. And because, among them, the See of Rome has precedence, it can well be compared to the sense of sight which is certainly the first of the senses of the body, since it is the most vigilant and since it remains, more than any of the other senses, in communion with the whole body. (In Mansi XVI 7; Dvornik 1979: 104)

Some rudiments of this Roman self-perception as a part of the pentarchic system continued to exist until our days. The title of the "Patriarch of the West" was dropped by Pope Benedict XVI only in 2006.

Sometimes, pentarchy malfunctioned. This happened, for example, in the case of monothelitism. This doctrine, promulgated by the imperial court in Constantinople in the seventh century, was endorsed by all five patriarchal sees, including that of Rome. Nevertheless, many in the church resisted it as heretic. Only a council could lead the church from the dead-end, where in this case it had been misled by the institute of pentarchy.

Either in the framework of pentarchy or in that of conciliarity, the patriarchs were in constant touch with each other. They tried to solve various church issues together, before there would emerge an urgent need to solve them through a council. Their joint efforts were facilitated by imperial authorities, which encouraged and sometimes moderated this institute of church governance. In this sense, pentarchy was an effective institute of symphony and power-sharing: patriarchs shared responsibility with one another and with their partners in the political system. None of them originally pretended to have a universal jurisdiction or exclusive rights. Even the church of Rome interpreted itself in this way in the period, when pentarchy was emerging.

# Theopolitical Unity

The imperial system of checks and balances, where the church played a crucial role, sometimes supplementing and sometimes substituting other republican institutes, such as the senate, continued to function for more than a thousand years. Around the mid-fourteenth century, Gregory Palamas described the church as "coming together" with the state and the *politeia* (ἐκκλησία καὶ βασιλεία καὶ πολιτεία πᾶσα σχεδὸν εἰς ταὐτὸ συνελθόντες) (*Orationes apologeticae* V 5). The word *politeia* usually applied to the traditional republican institutes of the Roman Empire. Gregory, thus, suggested that the church should cherish symphony with both the imperial and republican institutes. He confirmed that the church conflated "in almost everything" with the Roman political structures. Their conflation formed what can be called "a theopolitical unity."

In the end of the same fourteenth century, this conflation was concisely epitomized and promoted as the only possible model for church-state relations by the patriarch of Constantinople Anthony IV (in office 1389–90, 1391–7), in his letter to Grand duke of Moscow Basil I (1371–425). In this letter, Anthony referred to the roles that the emperors played in the Byzantine church, such as convoking ecumenical councils and making the canons of the church imperial laws. In return, the church boosted the emperors' legitimacy through various rituals:

> The Emperors convoked the ecumenical councils; by their own laws they sanctioned what the divine canons said about the correct dogmas and the ordering of the Christian life; they determined by their decrees the order of the episcopal sees and set up their boundaries. The church ordained the Emperor, anointed him, and consecrated him Emperor and Autocrat of all the Romans, that is, of all Christians. My most exalted and holy autocrat is by the grace of God the eternal and orthodox defender and avenger of the church. (In Wolff 1959: 299)

This is an ideal picture of the Byzantine symphony, where the state and the church act in complete harmony. However, the concluding sentence to this passage is peculiar: "It is not possible for Christians to have a church and not to have an Emperor." These words mean that a thousand years of symphonic relationship led the church and the state to a situation where they did not perceive themselves anymore on their own: their consciousnesses have conflated to a single theopolitical self-awareness (see Hovorun 2015: 37–68). This theopolitical self-awareness has become a common feature of the Byzantine fellowship of churches. Its rudiments survive to our days. That explains why, in the eyes of the Church of the East and the Oriental fellowship, the Byzantines are "Melkites"—the "royal" Christians. Even when separated from the state, the "Melkite" churches instinctively seek a partnership with political authorities, be they democratically elected governments or dictatorships.

**Figure 1.35** Double-headed eagle—the symbol of Byzantine symphony. Mystras archaeological site.
Source: Photo by the author.

# Isaurian Symphony

The idyllic picture of symphony between the church and the state presented by Patriarch Anthony to Grand duke Basil does not contain any black spot of abuse. In reality, however, there were many such spots in the Byzantine history. For example, the symphonic system of power-sharing was seriously tested under the Isaurian dynasty (717–802). This dynasty became notorious for promoting iconoclasm. It also tried to monopolize as much power as possible, at the expense of the traditional stakeholders, including the church. The Isaurian emperors unilaterally introduced a new practice and theology regarding the veneration of icons. By controlling popular piety and theological narratives of the church, they wanted to reinstate absolute authority in both political and ecclesial matters. To make this claim more convincing, Leo III, the founder of the dynasty, assumed for the imperial office the capacities, which had been traditionally reserved for the church hierarchs only. He reportedly stated: "I am emperor and priest." Emperors before Leo assumed some kind of ecclesiastical status for themselves. Constantine had famously called himself a bishop over those outside, as reported by Eusebius:

> On one occasion, when entertaining bishops to dinner, he (i.e., Constantine) let slip the remark that he was perhaps himself a bishop too, using some such words as these in our hearing: "You are bishops of those within the Church, but I am perhaps a bishop appointed by God over those outside." In accordance with this saying, he exercised a bishop's supervision over all his subjects, and pressed them all, as far as lay in his power, to lead the godly life. (Eusebius, *Vita Constantini* IV 24; Cameron & Hall 1999: 161)

Leo, however, meant something different. He understood "priesthood" in the sense of the Justinianian novella, that is, as the church itself. In his perception, he was a bishop "of those inside" the church, "not the secular arm of the Church, but high priest as David's heir" (Dagron 2003: 158). This was certainly an attempt to steal something that belonged exclusively to his partner in power-sharing—the church.

# I.8

# Critiques of Symphony

## Policies of Intervention

Some emperors not only deprived the church of its share in power but also imposed themselves on the church and interfered in its internal matters. The church hierarchs had invited them to such interference in the first place. As early as in 270, bishops asked Emperor Aurelian (r. 270–5) to help them solve an internal issue caused in Antioch by its bishop Paul Samosatean. Paul had preached an adoptionist Christology and was deposed by the council of Antioch in 268. However, he refused to vacate the see. The church reached out for imperial help to get rid of him. The pagan emperor, however, kept distance and left it to the Christians to resolve their own issues.

With the conversion of the Roman state to Christianity, emperors became more involved in the internal ecclesial issues—initially because of the church's inability to solve them on its own. Soon after Constantine became the ruler of the West, he faced the problem of the Donatist schism, which had divided the church in the Latin-speaking Africa and spread further throughout his dominion. He first gave the bishop of Rome Miltiades a carte-blanche to solve this problem but was not satisfied with the results. Then Constantine took the matters into his own hands and convened a council in Arles in 314. This was the first church council ever called by an emperor.

Constantine intervened only when bishops too were insisting for him to step in or unable to solve their problems on their own. Even then, his main concern was not so much to side with a faction he believed to be orthodox but to reconcile antagonist factions. In contrast to many bishops, who wanted to protect orthodoxy "by removing the diseased limb," Constantine, in the words of H.A. Drake, protected it "by binding wounds" (Drake 2021: 118). Such were his policies regarding the Arian crisis and the Nicaean controversy that followed.

Later emperors, in contrast to Constantine, perceived interventions to the church matters not as an exception, but as a rule. They often intervened on their own initiative, without being invited. Some of them tried to avoid siding with one of the arguing sides and promoted reconciliation. Others became partisan.

At the end of the fourth century, Emperor Theodosius seemed to enjoy his role as an arbiter in matters of faith. He contributed to the theological debates not only as an emperor but also as an expert in theology. The laws Theodosius promulgated are theologically richer than the church-related decrees of his predecessors. On the one hand, this demonstrates that theology as such became richer. On the other, the legalistic language of Theodosius' laws cannot conceal his fascination about theological debates:

> We direct that none of the Eunomians and the Arians or the adherents of the dogma of Ethius (Aëtius) shall have the right to build churches in the municipalities or in the country. But if this right should be rashly presumed by any person, the aforesaid house, wherever such forbidden constructions have been made, and also the estate or private landholding shall immediately be vindicated to the resources of Our fisc. All places also which have received either the abode or the ministers of this sacrilegious doctrine shall immediately become fiscal property. (*Codex Theodosianus* XVI 5.8; Pharr 1952: 452)

<. . .>

> We command that the Apollinarians and all other followers of diverse heresies shall be prohibited from all places, from the walls of the cities, from the congregation of honorable men, from the communion of the saints. They shall not have the right to ordain clerics, they shall forfeit the privilege of assembling congregations either in public or private churches. No authority shall be granted to them for creating bishops; moreover, persons so appointed shall be deprived of the name of bishop and shall forfeit the appellation of this dignity. They shall go to places which will seclude them most effectively, as though by a wall, from human association. Moreover, We subjoin to the foregoing provisions that to all the aforesaid persons the opportunity to approach and address Our Serenity shall be denied. (*Codex Theodosianus* XVI 5.14; Pharr 1952: 453)

Church councils and theologians defined orthodoxy. The emperor, however, came to decide who would represent this orthodoxy across his dominion. Theodosius appointed Damasus of Rome and Peter of Alexandria as representing the standards of the orthodoxy that had been defined by the council in 381:

> It is Our will that all the peoples who are ruled by the administration of Our Clemency shall practice that religion which the divine Peter the Apostle transmitted to the Romans, as the religion which he introduced makes clear even unto this day. It is evident that this is the religion that is followed by the Pontiff Damasus and by Peter, Bishop of Alexandria, a man of apostolic sanctity; that is, according to the apostolic discipline and the evangelic doctrine, we shall believe in the single Deity of the Father, the Son, and the Holy Spirit, under the concept of equal majesty and of the Holy Trinity.

> We command that those persons who follow this rule shall embrace the name of Catholic Christians. The rest, however, whom We adjudge demented and insane, shall sustain the infamy of heretical dogmas, their meeting places shall not receive the name of churches, and they shall be smitten first by divine vengeance and secondly by the retribution of Our own initiative, which We shall assume in accordance with the divine judgment. (*Codex Theodosianus* XVI 1.2; Pharr 1952: 440)

Theodosius would later add more names to the list of those who personified orthodoxy (see *Codex Theodosianus* XVI 1.3; Pharr 1952: 440). The two original names on the emperor's list, Damasus and Peter, were popes representing the Western and Eastern parts of the empire. The emperor intended to divide it to two empires, and he wanted each of them to have a person who represented and promoted the synodally approved orthodoxy. Imperial politics, thus, came to include both identifying and promoting the criteria of orthodoxy.

Theodosius' contemporaries believed that one can be saved only through the orthodox faith. In other words, upholding orthodoxy became a condition sine qua non for the individual appropriation of the universal salvation. Theodosius projected this belief to the empire: the integrity of the entire state depends on how successfully it promotes the orthodox doctrine. This idea would dominate the political theology and practice of the Roman Empire and its imitators up to the modern age, especially in the Christian East. The so-called *Synodikon* of Orthodoxy captured it in one phrase: "this is the faith which has sustained the Universe" (*Τριῴδιον Κατανυκτικόν* 1856: 135).

Sustaining the empire by upholding orthodoxy, however, came at a price. The legislation that defined the standards of orthodoxy, tended to impose them on the imperial subjects by coercion and not persuasion. Orthodoxy was not people's private business anymore, because the peace and prosperity of the empire depended on it. In the aftermath of the theological controversies during the fourth century, the presumably Christianized empire came back to the pagan idea that people can be coerced to a set of beliefs defined by the state—not for the sake of the people, but for the sake of the state.

Emperors after Theodosius continued issuing laws to promote doctrines, which they believed to be orthodox. While Theodosius complied with the decisions of the ecumenical council of 381, which he had convened, some of his successors went against theological decisions adopted at ecumenical councils. Thus, Basiliscus (r. 475–6) in his *Encyclical* (475) and *Anti-Encyclical* (476), as well as Zeno (r. 474–91) in his *Henotikon* (482), effectively tried to unilaterally revise the decisions of the council of Chalcedon.

Some emperors managed to get their theological opinions confirmed by an ecumenical council. Justinian was the most successful among them. He promoted a doctrine, which modern scholars call neo-Chalcedonianism. This doctrine elaborated on a theological language that bridged the Chalcedonian and anti-Chalcedonian formulas. Justinian made the church to support his neo-Chalcedonian project at a council, which became known as the fifth ecumenical.

# Athanasius

When the empire interfered in the church matters, there were always those in the church who felt happy and those who resisted the interference. Those objecting often perceived the intervention of the state as a violation of the established symphonic relationship between the church and the state (see Kahlos 2019). For example, the archbishop of Alexandria Athanasius, who was a protagonist of the Nicaean faith, criticized the policies of Constantius II as both anti-Nicaean and violating the rights of the church. Hilary of Poitiers and Lucifer of Cagliari, in their invective treatises (see Flower 2016: 37), blamed Constantius for the same. Athanasius and his Nicaean confederates accused Constantius of violating the freedom of speech and the internal freedom of the church from the state. Athanasius argued that the only way of solving theological issues should be through persuasion, not coercion. It should be noted that Athanasius himself had been accused of coercive practices against the Melitians, but preferred to not mention this.

Athanasius also did not mention the coercive promotion of the Nicaean faith by Constantius' father Constantine. The archbishop of Alexandria had personally experienced the Constantinian policies of coercion. Nevertheless, Athanasius rejected Constantius' intrusion to the matters of doctrine as a "novel practice." What follows is his implicit critique of Constantius' attempts at revising the system of power-sharing that had been established by Constantine:

> The emperor summoned them (i.e., bishops) and ordered them to subscribe against Athanasius and be in communion with the heretics. When they were amazed at this novel practice and said that it was not an ecclesiastical canon, he immediately replied: "Whatever I want, let that be deemed a canon. The so-called bishops of Syria allow me to speak in this way. Either obey or be exiled."
>
> On hearing these words, the bishops were utterly astonished. Stretching their hands up to God, they employed much freedom of speech towards him (i.e., Constantius) as well as arguments, teaching him that the kingdom was not his, but belonged to God, who had given it, and they told him to fear God, because he might suddenly take it away. They threatened him with the Day of Judgement and told him not to corrupt ecclesiastical affairs, nor to involve the Roman empire in the government of the church, nor to introduce the Arian heresy into the church of God. But he neither listened, nor allowed them to say anything else, but threatened them even more, bared his weapon against them and commanded that some of them be taken away. But, like Pharaoh, he changed his mind yet again. So the holy men shook off the dust, looked

> up to God and did not fear the emperor's threat or surrender when the sword had been unsheathed. Instead they received exile as the performance of a service in their religious ministry.

Athanasius describes the protestations by the Nicaean bishops as corresponding to the Constantinian model of power-sharing. These bishops had their own opinion, which they openly and fearlessly communicated to the emperor. In contrast to them, Athanasius presents the non-Nicaean bishops as encouraging the emperor to violate the healthy church-state partnership based on respect and consent:

> The truth is proclaimed not with swords and javelins and soldiers, but by persuasion and advice. What sort of persuasion is it when there is fear of the emperor? Or what sort of advice, where anyone who rejects it receives exile and death? When David was king and had his enemy in his power, and his soldiers wanted to kill this man, he prevented them not by his power, but, as Scripture says, by persuading them with arguments and not allowing them to rise up and kill Saul (see 1 Sam. 26). But this man (i.e., Constantius) has no arguments and so he compels everyone through his power, revealing to all that their (i.e., the non-Nicaean bishops') wisdom is not in accordance with God, but is merely human, and that those who follow the beliefs of Arius truly have no king but Caesar. (*Historia Arianorum* 33–4; Flower 2016: 67–8)

# Maximus

Three centuries after the clash between Athanasius and Constantius, another prominent theologian, Maximus the Confessor, criticized imperial authorities on the same matter. He accused these authorities of trespassing the red line, beyond which the interference of the state to the matters of the church was unacceptable. He objected to the doctrines, which later would become known as monoënergism and monothelitism. According to these doctrines, Christ has two natures, one activity (*energeia*/ἐνέργεια) and one will. These doctrines continued the neo-Chalcedonian project of Emperor Justinian and had the same political expedience: to bridge the rapidly widening gap between the Chalcedonian and anti-Chalcedonian Christians. Both monoënergism and monothelitism were conceived and promoted together by the church and state. They were initiated by Emperor Heraclius (r. 610–41) and endorsed by his symphonic partners, primarily the patriarch of Constantinople Sergius (in office 610–38). Heraclius promulgated the new doctrines by the imperial *Ekthesis* in 638. Ten years later, in 648, Constans II (r. 641–68) published another imperial decree, *Typos*. Both documents defined which theological issues can be discussed, and which must not. Maximus believed that by trying to censor theological discussions, imperial authorities trespassed the demarcation line between the church and the state:

> No emperor was able to persuade the Fathers who speak of God to be reconciled with the heretics of their times by means of equivocal expressions. Instead they employed clear and authoritative expressions, and ones that corresponded to the teaching that was being inquired into, saying plainly that it is the mark of priests to make an inquiry and to define on the subject of the saving teachings of the catholic church.

Maximus made this statement at his trial for political disloyalty. The state's prosecutors then asked him a crucial question: "Well then, isn't every Christian emperor also a priest?" Maximus answered:

> No, he isn't, because he neither stands beside the altar, and after the consecration of the bread elevates it with the words: "Holy things for the holy"; nor does he baptize, nor perform the rite of anointing, nor does he ordain and make bishops and presbyters and deacons; nor does he anoint churches, nor does he wear the symbols of the priesthood, the pallium and the Gospel book, as [he wears the symbols] of imperial office, the crown and purple. (In Allen & Neil 2002: 57)

Maximus, thus, responded to the tendency of his time, which culminated two generations later, in iconoclasm. This was a tendency to concentrate in the imperial

**Figure 1.36** Assumed relics of St. Maximus the Confessor at the assumed place of his exile, near the town of Tsageri in Georgia.

Source: Photo by the author.

office all power, including the one previously allocated to the church. As a former high-ranked imperial official, Maximus knew how important for both the state and the church is to uphold the system of checks and balances. He also advocated for the church to share in power. From this perspective, he was a republicanist. As a theologian, Maximus wanted to preserve the autonomy of the church from the state. For the imperial authorities of his time, however, both the system of checks and balances and the autonomy of the church, infringed the sovereignty of the emperor. Maximus, as a result, was accused of treason and died in exile.

# John of Damascus

As mentioned earlier, the system of checks and balances between the church and the state was violated particularly by the iconoclast emperors, who wanted to concentrate all power in their hands. The church objected. A Palestinian monk John from a Damascus-based Christian family of Mansur became a staunch critic of such violation. He lived outside the empire and was in a better position than Maximus to criticize its political authorities for intervention in the matters of the church (see Hovorun 2019). He enjoyed the protection of the caliphate, and the Byzantine authorities could not reach him for prosecution. This emboldened John to openly criticize the Byzantine religious politics under the iconoclast emperors:

> Kings have no right to make laws for the church. As the apostle says, "God has appointed in the church first apostles, second prophets, third pastors and teachers" (1 Cor. 12:28) "for the equipment" of the church (Eph. 4:12). No mention of kings! Again: "Obey your leaders and submit to them, for they are keeping watch over your souls and will give an account" (Heb. 13:17). Again: "Remember your leaders, those who spoke the word of God to you; consider the outcome of their way of life and imitate their faith" (Heb. 13:7). It was not kings that spoke the word of God to us, but apostles and prophets, pastors and teachers. When God instructed David to build his house, he added: "You shall not build a house for me, for you are a man of blood" (1 Chron. 22:8). And the Apostle Paul declares: "Pay to all what is due to them, honor to whom honor is due, respect to whom respect is due, tax to whom tax is due, revenue to whom revenue is due" (Rom. 13:7).
>
> Kings have responsibility for political welfare, pastors and teachers for the state of the church. And this, brothers, is a raid. Saul tore the cloak of Samuel, and what became of him? God tore the kingdom from him, and gave it to David, a man of self-restraint. Jezebel pursued Elijah, and the swine and dogs licked up her blood, and the prostitutes washed in it (1 Kings 22:38 [misremembered]). Herod destroyed John, and was eaten by worms and perished. Now the blessed Germanus (the patriarch of Constantinople), a shining example in life and word, is beaten up and exiled, together with many other bishops and fathers, whose names are unknown to us. Is not this an

act of brigands? (*Orationes de imaginibus tres* II 12; O. O'Donovan & J.L. O'Donovan 1999: 213–14)

# Photius

Resistance to the abuses of the church by the state in the period of iconoclasm contributed to a clearer definition of the patriarchal authority and a better understanding of how it is different from the imperial authority (see Stratoudaki-White 2000). The patriarch of Constantinople Photius should be credited for strengthening the patriarchal institute in the capacity of a counterbalance to the imperial institutes. His activities as a patriarch enhanced the position of the church in the system of power-sharing, which had been damaged by the iconoclasts. His intentions can be interpreted as contributing to the process of the restoration of republicanism in the empire that had become overwhelmingly autocratic.

These intentions can be discerned in the collection of laws called *Introduction to the Law* (*Eisagoge tou nomou*/Εἰσαγωγὴ τοῦ νόμου, sometimes inaccurately referred to as *Epanagogé*/Επαναγωγή; see Aerts et al. 2001; Schminck 1986). The collection was initiated by Emperor Basil I (r. 867–86) and intended to replace the iconoclast collection *Ecloga*. Photius is believed to be behind the norms of the *Eisagogé* related to the church-state relations. With more clarity and precision than similar imperial documents before, the *Eisagogé* defined the institutions of imperial and patriarchal power, as well as the ways they should relate to each other. Regarding the emperors, the document stated:

> The emperor is a legal authority, a blessing common to all his subjects, who neither punishes in antipathy nor rewards in partiality, but behaves like an umpire making awards in a game. (§1)
>
> The aim of the emperor is to guard and secure by his ability the powers that he already possesses; to recover by sleepless care those that are lost; and to acquire by wisdom and by just ways and habits those that are not [as yet] in his hands. (§2)
>
> The end set before the emperor is to confer benefits: this is why he is called a benefactor; and when he is weary of conferring benefits, he appears, in the words of the ancients, to falsify the royal stamp and character. (§3)
>
> The emperor is presumed to enforce and maintain, first and foremost, all that is set out in the divine scriptures; then the doctrines laid down by the seven holy councils; and further, and in addition, the received Romaic laws. (§4)
>
> The emperor ought to be most notable in orthodoxy and piety, and to be famous for holy zeal. <. . .> This [he will do] by observing the [doctrine of the] identity of being in the three substances of the Godhead, indivisible and illimitable, and the union of the two natures substantially in the one Christ. (§5) <. . .>

> In his interpretation of the laws he must pay attention to the custom of the state. What is proposed contrary to the canons [of the church] is not admitted as a pattern [to be followed] (§7). (*Eisagogé* II; Geffert & Stavrou 2016: 116–17)

These articles clearly restrict the role of emperors to *preserving* the orthodox doctrine. They cannot amend the doctrine and should comply with the canons of the church. In other words, emperors should not intervene in the patriarchal responsibilities. These responsibilities are defined as follows:

> The attributes of the patriarch are that he should be a teacher; that he should behave equally and indifferently to all men, both high and low; that he should be merciful in justice but a reprover of unbelievers; and that he should lift up his voice on behalf of the truth and the vindication of the doctrines [of the church] before kings, and not be ashamed. (§4)
>
> The patriarch alone must interpret the canons passed by the men of old and the decrees enacted by the holy councils (§5). (*Eisagogé* III; Geffert & Stavrou 2016: 117)

The latter statement makes clear the demarcation line between the imperial and patriarchal authorities: the former should comply with the way in which the latter interprets the "canons" and "decrees" of the church. The *Eisagogé* asserted the idea of symphony as harmony similar to the one between human body and soul:

> As the constitution consists, like man, of parts and members, the greatest and the most necessary parts are the emperor and the patriarch. Therefore the peace and felicity of subjects, in body and soul, is the agreement and concord of the kingship and the priesthood in all things (§8). (*Eisagogé* III; Geffert & Stavrou 2016: 118)

This formula of symphony is symmetric and rooted in the Chalcedonian Christology. It connects the church-state relations with the incarnation of God, who has become united with humanity in Christ in the same way as soul and body are united in a human being. At the same time, the *Eisagogé* presented a patriarch as "a living and animate image of Christ" (Πατριάρχης ἐστὶν εἰκὼν ζῶσα Χριστοῦ καὶ ἔμψυχος) (§1). The latter phrase marked a disruption of the tradition of symphony that went back to Eusebius, who considered emperor, not bishops, to be the image of Christ. Such interpretation of symphony rescaled the balance between the imperial and ecclesial authorities in the favor of the latter. Under Leo VI (r. 886–912), who succeeded Basil, *Eisagogé* ceased to be a law (in case it was ever adopted as law). It is noteworthy that the same Leo VI stripped the senate of those rudimentary responsibilities that it had had. His novella 47 explained how the senate had participated in sharing power, and now it does not anymore:

> In the past, when the domain of the state was different, the order of things was also different. Not everything was secured by the care of the emperor, but the senate had

> responsibility to discuss and decide on some matters. <. . .> Under the circumstances of that time, this law was necessary. Now, however, when everything depends on the emperor and, with help of God, everything is controlled and administered by the royal care, that law does not offer any usefulness. (In Τρωϊάνος 2007: 172–5)

It seems that Leo VI was not ready to share power either with the church or with the senate to the same extent that Theodosius or Justinian had envisaged this. When the church, as a republican institute in the empire, was deprived of its share in power, this also affected other, less powerful, republican institutes, such as the senate. Emperors, who interfered in the internal church matters, such as doctrine, effectively infringed on its republican role in the state. The church's autonomy, thus, secured its republican role in the state and preserved republicanism in the empire.

# I.9
# Monasticism

## Nonconformist Movement

While most of the Byzantine patriarchs, with only a few exceptions, did not mind or even endorsed the interference of the state in the matters of the church, many educated monks objected to such violations of symphony. Maximus the Confessor, John of Damascus, Theodore the Studite, and others were vigilant about the mechanisms of power-sharing and the church's autonomy.

As was mentioned earlier, in the symphonic relationship with the state, the church was supposed to counterbalance the monarchy of the Christian emperors. It supplemented and often substituted the traditional republican mechanisms, such as the senate. However, like the senate had done earlier, the church's hierarchy eventually conformed with the state and often failed to check the power of emperors. At the same time, a power remained within the church that resisted hierarchical conformism. This was monasticism. Monastic communities struggled to preserve the mechanisms of power-sharing when the official hierarchy gave up on them. Monks were the guardians of the symphony between the church and the state when the latter violated it. Nonconformism is encoded in the very nature of monasticism.

The monastic movement started as nonconformist in the period when the church began embracing the Roman Empire and conforming with it. Those Christians who had strong beliefs that the church is not of this world and who disagreed with the ostensible assimilation of Christianity in the Greco-Roman world pursued their own lifestyle. They fled to the desert, established independent communities, and tried to live a life, which they wanted to embed Christian ideals without any impediment, including the one coming from the state. Monks were Christian maximalists who tried to avoid any compromise with the empire. Early monasticism, thus, emerged as a nonconformist movement that aimed at establishing a particularly Christian *politeia*.

The vision that drove early monasticism in this sense was opposite to the one shared and articulated by Eusebius. That is why a founding monastic text, the *Life of*

*Antony* by Athanasius of Alexandria, as Raymond van Dam noticed, was a response of the Christian nonconformism to Eusebius' *Life of Constantine* (see Van Dam 2009: 318). In his political theology, of which monasticism was amalgamation, Athanasius substituted the figure of Constantine with the figure of Antony. *Vita Antonii* was effectively an ideological program, which promoted an alternative polity to Eusebius' "Leviathan" of the ostensibly "Christianized empire."

The collection of short stories and sayings of the Egyptian monks, the *Apophthegmata*, corroborated Athanasius' political theology, by praising monks who avoided engaging with political figures. This was a metaphorical way to say to the church: avoid embracements by the empire. A story of abba Moses clearly signaled such a message:

> The governor [of a province] once heard of Abba Moses and off he went to Scete to see him. When some folk reported the matter to the elder, he got up to run away into the marsh but they met him and said: "Tell us, old man, where is Abba Moses' cell?" "What do you want from him?" he said to them; "he is crazy." When the governor came into the church, he said to the clergy: "I am hearing things about Abba Moses and have come to see him and here an old man who was going into Egypt met us. We said to him: 'Where is Abba Moses' cell?' and he said to us: 'What do you want from him? He is crazy.'" The clergy were sad when they heard this; they said: "What sort of a person was this old man who said these things against the holy one?" "He was elderly, wearing old clothes, tail and black," they said, and the clergy said: "That is Abba Moses; he said

**Figure 1.37** An icon of Abba Arsenius from the monastery of Our Lady Baramus in Wadi El Natrun, Egypt.
Source: Photo by the author.

> those things so he would not meet you." The governor went his way having reaped great benefit. (Moses 8; Wortley 2014: 195)

Monks demonstratively ignored and even humiliated imperial officials, in contrast to the church hierarchs who flirted with them, like in another story from the *Apophthegmata*:

> The blessed archbishop Theophilus [of Alexandria] once visited Arsenius together with an official and he asked the elder if they might hear a saying from him. After remaining silent for a little, the elder answered him: "If I say something to you, will you observe it?" They agreed to observe it, then the elder said to them: "Wherever you hear Arsenius is, do not come near." (Arsenius 7; Wortley 2014: 41)

## Virginity the Countercultural

Christian monasticism was countercultural to the Greco-Roman society in many ways—not just in rejecting its political and social hierarchies. It was also scandalous because of promoting abstinence from sexual life (see Binns 2020: 18). The ancient society knew some forms of institutionalized female virginity, such as the order of virgins serving the goddess of hearth Vesta (see Beard 2004). This was, however, rather an exception from the ancient norms, which envisaged the main function of women as producing and taking care of children. As for men, their virility was a basic virtue in classical antiquity (see Foxhall & Salmon 2011) and as such was opposite to virginity. Christian monasticism challenged the traditional Greco-Roman values of procreativity and virility.

Various forms of abstinence from sexual life were widely practiced in the early Christian communities before the emergence of monasticism. Christian widows were discouraged to remarry; those who decided to remain virgins were protected by the communities. Even spouses often decided to live together without having sex. Virginity was institutionalized and became an ecclesial structure (see Elm 2004). Sometimes preserving one's virginity was included in the baptismal vows.

Early Christians preferred to abstain from sexual relationships for different reasons. For many, it was a shortcut to salvation. For some, it did not make sense to start a family, given that Jesus would be coming very soon. For others, it was a way of liberation from the restrictions and burdens imposed by the social norms of Antiquity (see Binns 2020: 19). According to these norms, women, especially of lower social standing, were supposed to serve men and deliver them children. Christianity showed women a way to be more than that: to serve a community as its equal members, as well as to utter voice and wisdom appreciated by others.

**Figure 1.38** Vestal virgins. Museum of *Ara Pacis* in Rome.
Source: Photo by the author.

# Emancipatory Movement

When the church began reconciling with the empire, the monastic movement took over the earlier forms and institutions of abstinence, charity, and equality. This movement opposed the new tendencies in the now official church to conform with the Greco-Roman sociopolitical patterns, including those of hierarchism and inequality. Richard Paul Vaggione is right to call the early monasticism "the most popular and vital lay movement of its day" (Vaggione 2000: 196). Some rudiments of the original monastic emancipatory momentum have been preserved to our days. When in the eighteenth or the nineteenth century, for example, the patriarchs of Constantinople retired to Mount Athos, they sometimes abstained from performing any sacred service and lived there as simple monks. Monasticism is still the only institution in the Eastern Christianity, where women may have a hierarchical rank—that of abbess (*hegoumene*). The installation of abbesses is similar to the enthronement of male hierarchs. They are allowed to wear a pictorial cross on their chest—as the priests do.

The *politeia* that early monastic communities pursued was not only *alternative* to the one that was emerging from the conflation of the state and the church but was also envisaged as *ideal*. Monastics tried to implement in their communities what they believed the church is supposed to be. In this regard, monasteries were established not as alternatives to the official church but as ideal models of the church. All members of an ideal monastic community were supposed to be equal, sharing in the common possession without having anything of their own, and obeying an elder whom they had elected. These ideals were hardly achievable in reality but monks never gave up on trying.

# Jewish Precedents

In contrast to many other institutions of the church, Christian monasticism had a little to owe to the Greco-Roman antiquity. Vaggione is right again when he calls it a "*non-Hellenic* ascetic revolution" (Vaggione 2000: 182). At the same time, monasticism effectively made available to us many pieces of the Greco-Roman Antiquity. Most classical pre-Christian texts survived because they were copied in the monasteries. However, monasteries in their life copied a little from Antiquity. Christian monasticism inherited more from the Jewish precedents, such as Nazirites, Therapeutae, and Essenes.

We have learned many details about the Essene community from the scrolls discovered in the mid-twentieth century in the Qumran caves on the northern shore of the Dead Sea. The community's rationale and lifestyle in many respects are similar to the later Christian monasticism. Both featured the idea of separation from the world, nonconformism, and puritanism. These ideas can be seen, for example, in the following text from Qumran:

> They shall separate from the congregation of the men of injustice and shall unite, with respect to the Law and possessions, under the authority of the sons of Zadok, the Priests who keep the Covenant, and of the multitude of the men of the Community who hold fast to the Covenant. Every decision concerning doctrine, property, and justice shall be determined by them. (1QS 5:1–3; Campbell 2008: 80–1)

Jewish-Christian influences were not a one way road. Christian monastic wisdom also left an impact on the later Rabbinic literature. Michal Bar-Asher Siegal has demonstrated convergence between Egyptian monasticism and Babylonian Talmudism (Bar-Asher Siegal 2013). Illustrative in this regard is the story about Rabbi Shimon bar Yohḥai. He lived in the early second century. In the fifth century, his story was retold within the confines of the Persian Empire in the way that resembled Christian stories about early monks in Egypt:

> For R. Yehudab, R. Yose, and R. Shimon were sitting, and Yehudah, a son of proselytes, was sitting near them. R. Yehudah commenced [the discussion] by observing, "How fine are the works of this people (i.e., the Romans)! They have made streets, they have built bridges, they have erected baths." R. Yose was silent. R. Shimon b. Yohai answered and said, "All that they made they made for themselves; they built market-places, to set harlots in them; baths, to rejuvenate themselves; bridges, to levy tolls for them." Now, Yehudah the son of proselytes went and related their talk, which reached the

> government. They decreed: "Yehudah, who exalted [us], shall be exalted, Yose, who was silent, shall be exiled to Sepphoris; Shimon, who censured, let him be executed."
>
> He and his son went and hid themselves in the Beth Hamidrash (i.e., the place of study), [and] his wife brought him bread and a mug of water and they dined. [But] when the decree became more severe, he said to his son, "Women are of unstable temperament: she may be put to the torture and expose us."
>
> So they went and hid in a cave. A miracle occurred and a carob-tree and a water well were created for them. They [would strip their garments and] sit up to their necks in sand. The whole day they studied; when it was time for prayers they robed, covered themselves, prayed, and then put off their garments again, so that they should not wear out. (*Babylonian Talmud, Shabbat* 336 [AB]; Bar-Asher Siegal 2013: 134–5)

As Bar-Asher Siegal has argued, this fifth-century story about second-century Jews was remodeled according to the patterns borrowed from the Christian ascetic literature. The latter had been imported to Persia from Egypt in Syriac translations. The Christian story behind the story of Rabbi Shimon bar Yoḥḥai was the one about the Christian hermit Paul:

> During the persecutions of Decius and Valerian, when Cornelius at Rome and Cyprian at Carthage shed their blood in blessed martyrdom, many churches in Egypt and the Thebaid were laid waste by the fury of the storm. <. . .> While such enormities were being perpetrated in the lower part of the Thebaid, Paul and his newly married sister were bereaved of both their parents, he being about sixteen years of age. <. . .> His brother-in-law conceived the thought of betraying the youth whom he was bound to conceal. <. . .> The young man had the tact to understand this, and, conforming his will to the necessity, fled to the mountain wilds to wait for the end of the persecution. He began with easy stages, and repeated halts, to advance into the desert. At length he found a rocky mountain, at the foot of which, closed by a stone, was a cave of no great size. He removed the stone (so eager are men to learn what is hidden), made eager search, and saw within a large hall, open to the sky, but shaded by the wide-spread branches of an ancient palm. The tree, however, did not conceal a fountain of transparent clearness, the waters whereof no sooner gushed forth than the stream was swallowed up in a small opening of the same ground which gave it birth. <. . .> Accordingly, regarding his abode as a gift from God, he fell in love with it, and there in prayer and solitude spent all the rest of his life. The palm afforded him food and clothing. (Schaff & Fremantle 2017: 315–16)

# Egypt

This story, which influenced the later rabbinic literature, was about a person, who is one of the earliest Christian hermits, Paul of Thebes. One generation after him, the most famous Coptic anchoret was born, whose name was Antony. Like Paul, Antony

**Figure 1.39** First Christian hermits Paul and Antony. A modern Coptic wall painting in the Anba Bishoy Monastery in Wadi El Natrun, Egypt.

Source: Photo by the author.

**Figure 1.40** Coptic inscriptions inside a pharaonic tomb in the Valley of the Kings near Luxor.

Source: Photo by the author.

**Figure 1.41** A fourth-century parchment with the Pachomian letters in Greek. Chester Beatty library in Dublin.
Source: Photo by the author.

**Figure 1.42** The remains of the fifth-century basilica in the Red Monastery, which flourished under Archimandrite Shenoute.
Source: Photo by the author.

lived in the Egyptian desert (see Görg 2011). His life was promoted by Athanasius as a model of the ideal Christian lifestyle. Its main feature was staying in solitude, far from people. The original monasticism, thus, was a hermitic movement (see Dunn 2003: 13). First hermits lived in abandoned buildings, such as Egyptian tombs, or in caves. This kind of monasticism flourished in the delta of the Nile.

Another monastic lifestyle became known as *coenobitic*—from the Greek *koinobia* (κοινόβια)—"living together." This type of monasticism was invented also in Egypt and became popular in its upper part. A retired soldier Pachomius is credited for introducing this type. His military background helped him to organize monks in disciplined communities. Pachomian communities flourished between the 320s and the 360s.

One or two generations later, in the same area of Upper Egypt, Archimandrite Shenoute expanded his own monastic network, which became formative for the Coptic Christianity (see López 2013).

# Syria

From Egypt, monasticism was imported to Syria. Countless monastic hermitages and over a hundred communities flourished in the vicinity of Edessa and Nisibis, especially in the area known as Tur Abdin, which is translated as "The Mountain of Servants" (see Rahmani 2008). It became a monastic heartland of Syriac Christianity. Syriac monasticism was close to Antonian anchoritism. At the same time, Syrian hermits usually did not detach themselves from local communities. Syrians also developed their own forms of asceticism, such as stylitism. Stylites spent years on the top of a pillar (στυλίς). From these platforms, they offered spiritual counseling to numerous pilgrims (see Schachner 2010). The first "fools for Christ" also appeared in Syria. They pretended to be fools to be mocked and humiliated by crowds (see Saward 2007).

# Palestine

Jerusalem and its vicinity became another epicenter of monasticism. Among those who brought monasticism to Jerusalem was Hilarion (291–371). Originally from Gaza, he studied in Alexandria and visited Antony in his desert. After having returned to Gaza, Hilarion implemented there the Egyptian monastic lifestyle. Barsanuphius and John were other famous ascetics who flourished in Gaza in the early sixth century. Mar Saba (439–532) founded monasteries in the vicinity of Jerusalem and in the Judean Desert. The best known of them is the Lavra at the Kidron Valley.

**Figure 1.43** An Ethiopian monk from Debre Libanos.
Source: Photo by the author.

Palestinian monasticism flourished from the late fifth through the late sixth century, when thirty-five monasteries were founded in the area (see Binns 2020: 84).

## Ethiopia

Both Coptic and Syriac monasticism influenced the Ethiopian tradition. Monasteries there were founded from at least the early sixth century. The country's first monks are remembered as "nine Syrian saints." One of them, Za-Mikael, was known as coming from a Pachomian community in Egypt. During this first wave of monastic movement in Ethiopia, several monasteries were established in hardly accessible mountains, such as Debre Damo. Another wave of the monastic movement is connected with the name of Täklä Haymanot (see Haile 2012). He was initiated to monasticism at the Debre Damo. In the 1280s, he established his own monastic community, which would become known as Debre Libanos. This monastery continues playing a central role in the life of the Ethiopian church.

## Asia Minor

Monasticism also flourished in Asia Minor. However, until quite late, monastic communities there were not even called monasteries. They performed spiritual exercises, studies, and social work in balanced proportions. They were not much separated from lay communities and ecclesial administration that managed them (see Binns 2020: 74). Bishops, such as Basil of Caesarea, managed them. Basil gave these communities a rule.

As the new imperial capital, Constantinople, grew, it attracted increasing numbers of monks. They came from all over the empire. Monastic individuals and communities of Constantinople played a significant role in both ecclesial and imperial politics. They often advocated for and practically enhanced the role of the church in the system of power-sharing. Their inspiration came from the original monastic nonconformism. For example, a Syrian monk Isaac, who came to the city in the late 370s, used every opportunity to annoy Emperor Valens because of his support to Arianism. Valens had to eventually imprison Isaac.

A more fundamental political role was played by the capital's monastic communities, such as the one of the so-called sleepless (*akoimetoi*/ἀκοίμητοι) monks. They were called so because they worshipped in shifts without pauses. The Studion monastery also became famous and important. It was established in 781 by a family. A Studite abbot from this family, Theodore, became particularly famous for his nonconformism. Theodore wanted to plant in Constantinople the coenobitic traditions of Egypt and Palestine. On their basis, he drafted his own rule. This rule became so popular that most monastic communities in the East eventually adopted it. In particular, the Studite rule framed the newly established monastery of caves in Kyiv. From there, it was disseminated throughout other Slavic monasteries.

The Studite monastery played a pivotal role in overcoming iconoclasm. Iconoclasm, as was mentioned, was a part of the imperial policy aimed at reducing the participation of the church in power and concentrating all power in the hands of the emperors. The Studites, while polemicizing against the iconoclast theology, also defended the share of the church in the Byzantine political system. Eventually they achieved their goal. They also dramatically increased the prestige of monasticism. Late Byzantine Christianity, as a result, became more monastic-centric. For example, the number of bishops from monks dramatically increased. Eventually it would become a norm that all Eastern bishops should be monks.

## Crisis of Medieval Monasticism

The Byzantine monasticism after iconoclasm demonstrated its high potentiality to affect the legitimacy of the emperors. Some of them considered monasteries as a more effective source of political legitimacy than even the official church hierarchy, which to a significant extent had been compromised by collaborating with the iconoclast emperors. Later Byzantine emperors began investing in the monasteries more than their predecessors did and expected from them to support and boost their legitimacy. They particularly hoped that such legitimizing role would be played by a relatively new monastic *politeia* located not far from Constantinople—on the Chalkedikė peninsula. It is commonly known as Mount Athos or Holy Mountain (see Speake 2018). Hermits and small monastic communities had lived there since at least the ninth century. However, the Athonite monasticism boomed when emperors endorsed local communities with vast resources and prestigious statuses. The first monastery to receive a special imperial status was the Great Lavra. It was funded by Emperor Nicephore II Phokas (r. 963–9). Other emperors after him continued providing for this and other monasteries, which had been established nearby. In return, the Athonite monasticism became royal and loyal to the Byzantine rulers. Even nowadays, these monasteries preserve the most significant treasures and legacies of the Byzantine Empire. Seen from this perspective, however, the Athonite monasticism has departed far from the original monastic nonconformism of the Egyptian desert.

Even further from the original monastic ideals departed the Russian monasticism. Its crisis culminated in the controversy between the so-called "possessors" and "non-possessors" (*stiazhateli/nestiazhateli*). The controversy lasted about a century from the 1480s through the 1580s and epicentered in two monasteries: Volotskiy and Belozerskiy. The "possessors" led by Joseph of Volotsk (1439–1515) argued that monasteries, to fulfil their mission better, can and should have possessions: lands, villages, and slaves. Their opponents led by Nil of Sora (1443–1508), strongly disagreed. This controversy was effectively about whether monasticism should be conformist or nonconformist. The conformist faction of Joseph won.

## *Via Tertia*

Throughout its entire history, Eastern monasticism featured three main lifestyles. In addition to anchoritism and communal monasticism mentioned earlier, there was always a third way of monastic life. This *via tertia* of monasticism often changed forms and names and was often under the fire of criticism and sanctions by the church. Nevertheless, it always survived and continues to be practiced in our days. In Egypt, such monks lived in tiny communities in separate households. They decided for themselves how they wanted to live. Clusters of such small communities were called "lavras."

In modern Eastern monasticism, this lifestyle became known as *idiorythmia* (ἰδιορυθμία). "Idiorythmic" monks live in communities yet enjoy a significant individual autonomy. They may have their own possessions, can be paid from the monastery for their services, buy their food, and eat on their own. Until recently, idiorythmic monasteries constituted a majority of the Athonite communities. After these monasteries converted to coenobia, the idiorythmic lifestyle was preserved in sketes. The Athonite sketes even now follow a middle path between coenobitic monasteries and anchorites-kelliotes. Monks in the sketes live in small communities under the guidance of an elder. These communities take care of themselves. They participate in the common liturgy on Sundays and feasts together with other communities of the skete.

In the Christian East, there were always monks who constantly moved from place to place. They sometimes were called *boskoi* (βοσκοί)—"herdsmen" or the "ones who eat herbs." Sozomen described this sort of monks in Syria:

> When they first entered upon the ascetic mode of life, they were denominated shepherds, because they had no houses, ate neither bread nor meat, and drank no wine, but dwelt constantly on the mountains, and passed their time in praising God by prayers and hymns, according to the canons of the church. At the usual hours of meals, they each took a sickle, and cut some grass on the mountains; and this served for their repast. Such was their course of life. (Sozomen & Philostorgius 1855: 299)

Wondering monks continue browsing through the cities and villages until our days. Some of them have become famous, such as Kosmas of Aetolia (1700/1714–79) or the anonymous Russian pilgrim, who lived in the mid-nineteenth century and composed an influential book *The Way of a Pilgrim: Candid Tales of a Wanderer to His Spiritual Father* (Zaranko & Louth 2017). Some monks on the Mount Athos, after having stayed for some time in one hut (καλύβα), would burn it and move to another one. They do so to avoid attaching to one place and became known as *kavsokalyvites* (καυσοκαλυβίτες)—"the ones who burn their huts." In the Soviet era, when most monasteries were closed, most monks lived at homes or wondered. Some of them educated people in religion, and some disseminated controversial ideas.

In Eastern Christianity, there were always monks who did not want to live in an organized way. They often loitered in big cities, looking for alms and scandalizing local people with their behavior and teaching. The church repeatedly adopted measures to discipline them, without much success. At the same time, unorganized monks had more freedom than established ones to follow the original call of the monastic movement: to be nonconformist and countercultural.

# I.10

# Eastern Christian Fellowships

## I.10.1 Oriental Fellowship

Monasticism played a crucial role in the formation of the "Oriental" tradition in Eastern Christianity. The "Orient" was diverse. Many civilizations left their imprints on its peoples and cultures. Its peoples spoke different languages, such as Coptic, Syriac, Armenian, Ethiopian, and others, and had various religious backgrounds. During the Late Antiquity, most of these peoples adopted Christianity and Greek as their *lingua franca*. At the same time, they developed and often demonstrated allergic symptoms to uniformity, which was often imposed upon them by the imperial center.

### Eastern and Western Syriac Christianity

An example of such diversity is the difference between the Western and Eastern Syriac traditions. This difference evolved and exists even in our days, as a clash between the Syriac and Assyrian identities. Both identities have the same root, which grew from the Christian community in Antioch. Since the Hellenic times, both Western and Eastern Syrians were bilingual: they spoke Greek and the dialects of the Aramaic. Yet, they became polarized by different ways of interpreting the incarnation of God.

The Eastern Syrians interpreted the unity of divinity and humanity in Christ as rather imaginary. They tended to consider a man Jesus as a self-sufficient being, who has been adopted by the Logos. For them, number two, which symbolized the reality of both his divinity and humanity, applied to Christ more appropriately than number one, which indicated his unity. The Western Syrians, in contrast, came to believe that the only number applicable to Christ is one. They stressed the ultimate integrity of Jesus, with his divinity and humanity being only distinguished in one's imagination. In reality, they constituted one being. In other words, for the Western Syrians, Christ's duality was more imagined than his unity, which for them was more real. For the Eastern Syrians, on the contrary, Christ's duality was more real than his imagined unity. There were also Syrians, who believed that the numbers one and two are applicable to Christ in equal proportions.

## The Chalcedon

This third Syriac faction, which was also the smallest one, subscribed equally to the two main Christological councils: the ones in Ephesus (431) and in Chalcedon (451). In contrast to them, Eastern Syrians accepted neither Ephesus nor Chalcedon, while the Western Syrians opposed only the Chalcedon. Both these groups can be called non-Chalcedonians. The Western Syrians can be also called anti-Chalcedonians. Sometimes, they call themselves "Miaphysites." The name "Monophysite," which is often applied to them by their opponents, is not correct. This name historically applied to the followers of Archimandrite Eutyches, who is condemned by both Eastern and Western Syrians.

The intra-Syriac conflict was an instance of the larger divide in global Christianity, which became known as the first great schism. This schism divided the church into three fellowships: Nestorian, Oriental, and Chalcedonian. Eastern Syrians constituted the core of the former one. The Oriental fellowship included the majority of Western Syrians and Egyptians (Copts), together with Ethiopians and Armenians. The churches clinging to Rome and Constantinople formed a backbone of the Chalcedonian fellowship.

The rejection of the council of Chalcedon became a basic feature of the Oriental identity. Severus, who was born not far from Western Syria and became the archbishop of Antioch, founded Oriental theology and created the earliest narratives formative for the Oriental identity. His letters played a key role in the formation of this identity. Severus originally composed his letters in Greek, but they have survived only in the Syriac translation. This translation was accomplished in the seventh century by a Syrian presbyter from Nisibis Athanasius, who thus responded to the request of Bishop Matthew of Berrhoea and Bishop Daniel of Edessa. In a letter addressed to Bishop Constantine, Severus among other things warned his followers against any compromise with the Chalcedon:

> All, so to speak, have the one object only, to bring to naught the *typos*[1] or formula of satisfaction which seemed good to the pious king, which he also sent to Flavian, the prelate of the city of Antiochus, and either altogether to remove and abolish it, or to cut away some of its exactitude, because they do not intend to drink the still water, as says Ezekiel, but strive to foul it with their own feet, in order that the sheep which have learned to hear the voice of the Good Shepherd, and to drink "the water of Shiloah that goeth softly," may not be able to avoid the pollution of the drink. Which John of Claudioupolis also tried to do when he came here. When he received me in the house of the glorious Patrick, the Master of the Soldiers, and conversed with me by order of

[1]An edict promulgated by Emperor Constans II in 648; it prohibited theological discussions on the issue of activities and wills in Christ.

our pious king, he said, "There ought to be introduced into the formula of satisfaction this statement, 'We receive the synod at Chalcedon, not as a definition of faith, but as a rejection of Nestorius and of Eutyches.' Thus both those that are pleased with the Synod will not be angry, and you will receive contentment in that the doctrines which offend you are rejected." But I said, "This argument is silly, and the offspring of a drunken mind. Who is there among right-minded persons who will accept and praise us on account of this disturbance and confusion? If the Synod of Chalcedon introduced the doctrine of Nestorius into the churches, though it called Nestorius 'of small intelligence' in order to entice and deceive those that are more simple, how can we say that it rejected the opinion of Nestorius? But, if the formula of satisfaction in so many words rejects the doctrines of the Synod and of the impious Tome of Leo, which are the life blood of the abomination of Nestorius, how can we honestly say that we accept this synod as against Nestorius? <. . .>

"What then? Were not those at Chalcedon rightly moved against Eutyches? Why, [if] you accept them on this point, do you think them fit <. . .> an anathema?" [But] I said, "What I am about to say is strange, but nevertheless true. It is especially for this reason that we say that they are men that deserve anathema, because they unnecessarily extended the heresy of Eutyches. Owing to the fact that they wished to heal the disorder in an unintelligent way by means of an opposite infection, I mean by the evil impiety of Nestorius, thenceforward those who were infected with the belief in a phantasy, seeing that they were inviting them to man-worship, recoiled from this vicious remedy, and thought themselves all the more pious, and carried their own corruption further. But, if they had been cured and healed by means of right doctrines, they would perhaps have abandoned their infection." (Brooks 1903: 4–6)

## Monasticism and the Chalcedonian Divisions

In contrast to the Byzantine church, whose hierarchical figures often had a political background, most bishops who formed the structures of the Oriental churches had a monastic background. The anti-Chalcedonian movement was endorsed by the majority of monks, especially in the cradles of monasticism, Egypt and Syria. In Egypt, the monastic network of Archimandrite Shenoute was among the factors that kept the majority of Copts on the side opposite to the Chalcedon. In Syria, a similar role was played by the monastic communities of Tur Abdin.

Palestinian monasticism was also initially anti-Chalcedonian. The way the Palestinian monks treated their bishop Juvenal illustrates a broader monastic attitude to Chalcedon that prevailed in the East. Juvenal went to Chalcedon with a strong resolution to oppose the dyophysite theology. At the council, he unexpectedly changed sides and returned to Palestine as a Chalcedonian. This infuriated many monks in the area. The abbot of the monastery at the Mount of Olives Gerontius famously claimed: "God forbid that I should see the face of Judas the traitor" (*Vita Petri Iberi* 32; Horn 2006: 147). This reaction has been recorded in the life of Peter the

Iberian, an influential monastic and prominent proponent of anti-Chalcedonianism. Peter was originally from Georgia or, as it was called at that time, Iberia. He was brought up at the court of Theodosius II (r. 408–50) in Constantinople. When he went for pilgrimage to Jerusalem, he decided to stay there as a monk. His life has preserved his own reactions to Juvenal's "apostasy":

> When it came to a meeting of the Fathers with the unholy Juvenal, the blessed Theodosius, that monk whom the believers eventually made archbishop in Jerusalem, also boldly put to shame the apostasy which happened in Chalcedon. [He held authority] as one who had been present the whole time and knew all the things that had been performed [there]. When he laid out Juvenal's obvious hypocrisy and apostasy, Juvenal was furious and commanded a certain *decurion*, one of those who were following him, to deal secretly with [Theodosius] as a revolutionary and [as] one who resisted the emperor's will. As that one (i.e., the *decurion*) was about to do so, the blessed Peter, still being a monk and not [yet] having the dignity of the office of bishop, was inflamed with zeal. He knew that one, however, from [his time at] the court. He threw his stole around his neck and said to him with the strength of a prophecy, "You [there], do you dare to act as mediator concerning the faith and speak about all of it? Did you not do these and other [things] in that night? I am the least of all the saints who are here. [But if] you seek [to do so], I will speak and immediately fire will come down from heaven and will destroy you and those who belong to you." When that one (i.e., the *decurion*) was in fear and was shaking, knowing who he (i.e., Peter the Iberian) was, he fell down at his feet, asking him in front of everyone, "Forgive me, Lord Nabarnugi! (The Georgian name of Peter) I did not know that your Holiness is here." And thus he let the blessed Theodosius go, no longer daring to speak again or do [anything] against the saints. He took Juvenal and returned to Caesarea. (*Plerophoriae* 56; Horn 2006: 85–6)

Peter became the bishop of Maiuma. After a short while he went to Egypt, where he stayed as a hermit for twenty years. He participated in the consecration of the anti-Chalcedonian archbishop of Alexandria Timothy Aelurus in 457. In 475, Peter returned to Palestine, where for a while he was the only anti-Chalcedonian bishop. He eventually managed to establish an anti-Chalcedonian ecclesial structure in this region.

## Anti-Chalcedonian Raison D'être

There were many reasons why the groups that could not accept the council of Chalcedon decided to have their own church. These groups mixed theology with politics and social concerns, which was a common phenomenon in the pre-secular era. Only a small group of theologians were upset by the language of two natures that the Chalcedonians applied to Christ. Some intellectuals also resisted the policies of uniformity, which the central imperial and ecclesial authorities imposed from Constantinople on the empire's periphery. As was mentioned earlier, peoples on the margins of the empire enjoyed their difference from the center and cherished their diversity.

However, most adversaries of Chalcedon did not know much about its theology and did not care about diversity. They had other reasons to oppose the controversial council. Monks and those who surrounded them, for instance, considered the Chalcedonian faith to be too politicized. They believed this faith had been imposed upon the church by the imperial authorities. In the vein of the monastic nonconformism, they rejected Chalcedonianism as polluted by various political agendas. This explains why the anti-Chalcedonian movement enjoyed such strong support in the monastic circles. There was significant monastic support to the Chalcedon too, but most monasteries in Egypt and Syria rejected the Chalcedon. The anti-Chalcedonian movement was monastic par excellence. Consequently, this movement became nonconformist. Chalcedonians, from the anti-Chalcedonian perspective, were "melkites"—the people of the king. Their goals, in the anti-Chalcedonian eyes, were more political than spiritual.

Most followers of the anti-Chalcedonian doctrine in Egypt and Syria were poor peasants. They usually spoke only Coptic or Syriac and did not have access to the sophisticated theological arguments articulated in Greek. Their immediate experience was not that of theological incorrectness or spiritual impurity that the Chalcedon represented to its adversaries among the literati and monks, but of injustice. Injustice often came from the authorities, who in their majority were Chalcedonians. Therefore, the anti-Chalcedonian movement on the grassroots level was effectively a peasant revolt ignited by social injustice.

This revolt can be also interpreted in postcolonial terms. The eastern and southeastern provinces of Byzantium were effectively colonies, which Rome had occupied several centuries before. The Greek language and culture, in which the imperial theology had been articulated, were alien for most locals in Egypt and Syria. They wanted to speak their own language and to have their own theology. Because the Chalcedonian theology for many of them was imperial and colonial, the anti-Chalcedonian reaction to it was effectively anti-imperial and anti-colonial. Of course, the anti-Chalcedonians did not perceive their resentment in the modern postcolonial terms, but they should have felt this way.

Armenians had some additional reasons to not accept the Chalcedon. These reasons were also not entirely theological. A part of the Armenian people lived in their own state. The degree of its political independence and its size varied in different periods, but it was usually squeezed between the Roman and Persian Empires and exposed to the rivalry between them. Their geopolitical situation urged the Armenian rulers to be careful not to associate themselves too closely with the Romans and their imperial theology. Armenia wanted to prove to Persia that it was not a Byzantine ally. At the same time, the Armenian state did not want to be completely associated with the sort of anti-Chalcedonianism hosted by the Persians—for the sake of preserving

**Figure 1.44** Exterior of the Holy Cross cathedral of the Armenian Catholicosate of Aghtamar. Van Lake, Turkey.
Source: Photo by the author.

its political autonomy. For which reason, for example, the Armenians rejected the mainstream Severan interpretation of miaphysitism. They tried to navigate between the Byzantine Chalcedonianism and anti-Byzantine anti-Chalcedonianism and wanted to coin their own Christological formulas. Such formulas were adopted at the councils in the ancient capital of Armenia, Dvin.

## Parallel Structures

For various theological, political, and social reasons, the anti-Chalcedonian population of Egypt and Syria rejected the ecclesial policies of Constantinople, which were epitomized in the decisions of the council of Chalcedon. They did not accept Chalcedonian bishops and wanted a hierarchy "unpolluted" by the compromises with the imperial theology. Soon, however, they faced the problem of reproducing their hierarchy. Some older bishops died, and others deserted to the Chalcedonian side. To provide their flocks with pastors, the adversaries of the Chalcedon had no other choice but to consecrate new bishops. They decided to proceed to consecrations without the consent of the imperial authorities. This was an act of nonconformism. It also meant a schism.

The anti-Chalcedonians did not originally intend to have their own church. They hoped the pro-Chalcedonian tide would soon change, and Constantinople would eventually reject the Chalcedon. In such case, the anti-Chalcedonian hierarchy would continue to be a part of the universal church in communion with the rest of the global Christianity. They saw the pro-Chalcedonian tide as resembling the pro-Arian tide one century earlier. Then, the heretic hierarchy also constituted a majority in the church and was backed by the state. There was, however, an orthodox hierarchy in parallel to the Arian one, which eventually prevailed. Something like this, the anti-Chalcedonian hierarchs hoped, would happen with the Chalcedon.

Their hopes were never materialized. Constantinople persisted in promoting the council of Chalcedon and took draconian measures against those opposing it. There were periods of more accommodating policies that the imperial center demonstrated to the anti-Chalcedonians, but they were short and insufficient. The anti-Chalcedonians eventually faced a difficult dilemma: either to accept the doctrine, which they regarded as heretical, or to build their own hierarchy and ecclesial structures, which meant a schism in the church. Both choices were bad for them. They decided that the former option was worse. In result, the anti-Chalcedonian fellowship of churches emerged in parallel to the Chalcedonian one (see Frend 2008b).

## Collaboration

The anti-Chalcedonian ecclesial structures developed primarily in Egypt and Syria, where they had the support of the majority of the population. Their development was significantly restrained by the authorities in Constantinople. These authorities were afraid that parallel ecclesial structures, disloyal to the ecclesial center in Constantinople, endangered the integrity of the empire. Indeed, the anti-Chalcedonian masses, led by their own hierarchy, without much hesitation embraced intruders to the Roman soil, even though they were of different religions.

After Islam emerged at the beginning of the seventh century as an energetic centrifugal movement, it surprisingly quickly conquered territories, which for centuries remained Persian and Roman, or were contested by those two superpowers. Such a swift spread of Islam, which for its followers was a miracle proving that God was with the Muslims, could be also explained by historical circumstances. One of them was the consequence of the devastating war between the Roman and Persian Empires in the period between 602 and 628 (see Wakeley 2018: 84–92). This war exhausted both states and their armies and created a political void, which was quickly filled by Arab tribes. These tribes crashed both Persians and Byzantines, with the decisive victories in the battles at al-Qadisiyyah and Yarmouk in 636. After these battles, the Arabs quickly conquered almost the entire Middle East. The Arab army consisted not only of Muslims but also of Persian and Christian *al-mujāhidīn*, who joined it for various reasons (see Wakeley 2018: 49–68). The mixed composition of the Arab armies became an additional argument for the Christians in the Middle East to accept them.

Many anti-Chalcedonian Christians initially perceived the Arab conquerors as liberators from what they called "the Chalcedonian darkness."[2] They preferred the Muslim ignorance of the nuances of their theological beliefs to the coercion that the Byzantine emperors had imposed in order to convert them to the Byzantine orthodoxy. The medieval *History of the Patriarchs of the Coptic Church of Alexandria* (Evetts 1907), composed in Arabic to edify the Coptic community, clearly demonstrated polarization between Coptic and Byzantine attitudes to the Arab army under the command of ʿAmr ibn al-ʿĀṣ al-Sahmī, who had conquered Alexandria in 641. The Byzantine troops were under the command of the Chalcedonian archbishop of the city, Cyrus (in office 630–42). They made every effort to defend Alexandria, but Cyrus eventually decided to surrender. The *History* presents Cyrus as having committed suicide after the sack of the city, which was not true. The anti-Chalcedonian archbishop of Alexandria Benjamin demonstrated a different attitude to the Arab conquerors. During the siege of the city, he was hiding in exile. When Alexandria fell, Benjamin returned and, according to the Coptic historian, was honored by the Muslim general:

> When Amr took full possession of the city of Alexandria, and settled its affairs, that infidel, the governor of Alexandria (i.e., Archbishop Cyrus), feared, he being both prefect and patriarch of the city under the Romans, that Amr would kill him; therefore he sucked a poisoned ring, and died on the spot. But Sanutius, the believing dux, made known to Amr the circumstances of that militant father, the patriarch Benjamin, and how he was a fugitive from the Romans, through fear of them. Then Amr, son of Al-Asi, wrote to the provinces of Egypt a letter, in which he said: "There is protection and security for the place where Benjamin, the patriarch of the Coptic Christians is, and peace from God; therefore let him come forth secure and tranquil, and administer the affairs of his Church, and the government of his nation." Therefore when the holy Benjamin heard this, he returned to Alexandria with great joy, clothed with the crown of patience and sore conflict which had befallen the orthodox people through their persecution by the heretics (i.e., the Chalcedonians), after having been absent during thirteen years, ten of which were years of [Emperor] Heraclius, the misbelieving Roman, with the three years before the Muslims conquered Alexandria. <. . .>
>
> Sanutius went to the commander and announced that the patriarch had arrived, and Amr gave orders that Benjamin should be brought before him with honour and

[2]A phrase attributed to the Coptic pope of Alexandria Anastasius (in office 605–16); see Evetts 1907: 481.

veneration and love. And Amr, when he saw the patriarch, received him with respect, and said to his companions and private friends: "Verily in all the lands of which we have taken possession hitherto I have never seen a man of God like this man." For the Father Benjamin was beautiful of countenance, excellent in speech, discoursing with calmness and dignity.

Then Amr turned to him, and said to him: "Resume the government of all your churches and of your people, and administer their affairs. And if you will pray for me, that I may go to the West and to Pentapolis, and take possession of them, as I have of Egypt, and return to you in safety and speedily, I will do for you all that you shall ask of me." Then the holy Benjamin prayed for Amr, and pronounced an eloquent discourse, which made Amr and those present with him marvel, and which contained words of exhortation and much profit for those that heard him. (Evetts 1907: 485–97; see Swanson 2010: 7)

## Under Crescent

The Arab conquest of the Middle East created a new environment for the Oriental churches. On the one hand, these churches were able to finalize constructing hierarchical structures independent from Constantinople. They also received a better opportunity to develop theology and culture in their own languages, without censorship from the Greco-Chalcedonian center. At the same time, they found themselves enclosed in ghettos within the caliphate. For the most part of their later history, most Oriental churches lived in such ghettos, which were slowly but steadily dwindling. The Middle Eastern Christian ghettos continue shrinking in our days. The only exception was the Ethiopian church, which for most of its history lived under the protectorate of the Christian emperors.

## Modern Oriental Churches

Only in the twentieth century, after the collapse of the Ottoman Empire and the new opportunities for emigration, Oriental Christians were able to leave their ghettos and began planting their communities in the free world (see Stetter & Nabo 2020). The Oriental churches, as a result of emigration, became truly global. The modern global fellowship of the Oriental Orthodox churches does not have a *prima inter pares* church—in contrast to the fellowship of the Byzantine churches, which has its ecumenical patriarchate. Connectedness between the Oriental churches is looser than the relations between the Byzantine ones. The Oriental fellowship features less imperial legacy and more self-reliance than the Byzantine one.

The Coptic church is perceived by many in the Oriental fellowship as its informal leader. Copts constitute a majority of the Christian minority in Egypt (see Agaiby et al. 2021; van Doorn-Harder 2017). The administrative center of the Coptic church is in Cairo. For centuries, this church supervised the church in Ethiopia. In the middle of the twentieth century, the Ethiopian Tewahedo Church became autocephalous—formally independent from the Coptic church. After Eritrea became independent from Ethiopia in 1993, the church there proclaimed its own autocephaly.

The Syriac church has its historical territories in Syria, Turkey, Iraq, and Lebanon, with its center in Damascus since 1959. Similarly to the Coptic church in Ethiopia, the Syriac church had its branch in India, mostly in the southern state of Kerala. One of the Syriac churches there, the Malankara Jacobite Syrian Church, is still in unity with the Syrian Patriarchate in Damascus. Another Indian church, the Malankara Orthodox Syrian Church, had proclaimed its autocephaly, which is predictably not recognized by the Syriac metropolis in Damascus.

The Armenian church has two centers: the Western Armenian in Beirut and the Eastern Armenian in Etchmiadzin, in the vicinity of the capital of the Republic of Armenia, Yerevan. The Armenian church, thus, has two leaders (*Catholicoi*), who are formally independent of each other. Yet, the Catholicos in Etchmiadzin is regarded superior to his counterpart in Lebanon. There is also an Armenian patriarch in Constantinople, who represented the Armenian millet during the Ottoman period. Such divisions of leadership within the Armenian church were caused by the genocide of the Armenian people at the beginning of the twentieth century.

**Figure 1.45** The "mother church" of the Armenian Apostolic Church in Etchmiadzin, Armenia.

Source: Photo by the author.

# I.10.2 Church of the East

## Antiochian Theology

The common denominator of all Oriental churches is their focusing on the rejection of "Nestorianism." The latter identity derives from the name of the patriarch of Constantinople Nestorius (in office 428–31). He represented the people who in their majority spoke Syriac and lived in the eastern part of what then constituted Syria. These people had been instructed in the Scriptures and theology by such teachers as Aphrahat (*c.* 270–345), Ephrem (*c.* 306–73), Diodore (*c.* 330–90), and Theodore of Mopsuestia (*c.* 350–428/29). They preferred to interpret the Scriptures literally, historically, and realistically. They tried to avoid allegories, which they considered a too speculative method of exegesis. In modern terms, they were closer to the analytical than phenomenological way of thinking. Such was the way they looked, for example, at the Gospels' stories about Jesus: as a "son of man" (see Mt. 4:2; Mk 23:19; Lk. 5:24; Jn 2:3) whose humanity was as complete and real as his divinity. Both divine and human realities of Jesus were more real, as it were, than their unity, which looked to them more speculative.

"Nestorian" identity is misleading. "Nestorianism" was elaborated theologically not by the patriarch of Constantinople Nestorius, but by some brighter Syrian theologians, such as Theodore of Mopsuestia. The name "Theodoreans" would suite them better than "Nestorians." However, because Nestorius, who enthusiastically promoted the "Theodorean" doctrine, was the highest hierarch, the subscribers to this doctrine were called after his name. Nestorius was a zealous fighter against heresies. As often happens to such fighters, he ended up condemned as a heretic. This happened at the council of Ephesus in 431. As the rejection of the council of Chalcedon (451) would define the identity of the Western Syrian Christians, so the rejection of the council of Ephesus defined the Eastern Syriac identity. This identity was and remains anti-Ephesian. Although the Western Syrians perceived Chalcedon as a "Nestorian" council, the real "Nestorians" did not accept it either. "Non-Chalcedonianism," therefore, could be an umbrella term for both "Nestorians" and miaphysite anti-Chalcedonians.

## Borderland

The Nestorian identity succeeded a series of earlier identities that had evolved in Antioch and its vicinity. Syrian Christians lived in the borderland, which often changed political affiliations: Roman, Parthian, Sassanian, Arab, and so on. It featured one of the early borderlines that came to divide the East and the West. This line dissected Syria in western and eastern parts. To its east, there were non-Roman

**Figure 1.46** Border between modern Turkey and Syria—an early borderline between the West and the East.
Source: Photo by the author.

states hostile to the Roman Empire and its Christianity. These states reshaped the Christian churches on their territories and alienated them from the Greco-Roman Christianity, which, from their perspective, was "western." Much later, the East-West divide moved westward and dissected Illyria. That later borderline would eventually mark the schism between the "Latin" and the "Greek" churches. However, in the time, when Christianity was being divided in Syria, the "Latin West" and the "Greek East" belonged to the same "West."

During 363–4, the Roman Empire lost vast territories toward the east from Antioch to the Persian Empire. Antioch remained in Western Syria. Nisibis (modern Nusaybin in Turkey), 500 kilometers to the east, emerged as the intellectual center of Eastern Syria. Even before having been taken by the Persian Sassanids, Nisibis hosted a prominent school of exegesis (see Becker 2006; Vööbus 1965). Ephrem the Syrian (*c.* 306–73) was among its most famous teachers. After Nisibis became Persian, however, he moved onto Roman soil and eventually settled in Edessa. Immigrants from Nisibis enhanced the theological school in Edessa, which became known as "the School of the Persians." This school made a major contribution to a Christology, which envisaged a self-sufficient humanity in the loose unity with divinity in Christ. In 489, this school was closed by the Byzantine authorities, who considered it not complying with the imperial orthodoxy. Most school's faculty moved back to the Persian soil and reestablished a school in Nisibis. They were gladly received by the local Bishop Narsai (d. *c.* 500), who provided them with facilities and became a master of the school. The school of Nisibis continued as an intellectual center of the Eastern Syriac Christianity during the sixth and early seventh century. It featured several prominent scholarchs, such as Abraham of Beth Rabban (sixth century) and Ḥenana (d. *c.* 610). A number of prominent hierarchs in the Church of the East were its graduates, including the Catholicoi Isho'yahb I (d. 595), Isho'yahb II of Gdala (d. *c.* 646), and Isho'yahb III of Adiabene (d. 659).

## Persian Symphony

These Catholicoi finalized the formation of the autocephalous Church of the East. Even before the council of Ephesus, the Christian community in Persia enjoyed a high degree of autonomy from the churches in the Roman Empire. It had its primates, Catholicoi, who resided in the Sassanian capital Seleucia-Ctesiphon. Persian Catholicoi were elected by local synods and were not accountable to other ecclesial authorities. A council of the Persian church in 424 formally declared its independence from the "Western" churches, that is, the churches in the Roman Empire. It also forbade its bishops and clergy to appeal to the churches in the West. The Persian autocephaly, thus, was the earliest one similar to the modern concept of ecclesial autocephaly.

While unaccountable to the "Western" churches, the Persian church had to give account to the Persian shahs, even though they were not Christians. The Sassanid dynasty (225–651), under which Christianity flourished on the Persian soil, held Zoroastrianism as its official religion in a way similar to the Byzantine symphony. The Roman and Persian Empires were two archrivals. Their animosity defined the Persian policies to the Christians, who were often seen as Roman agents and collaborators. To dissipate such suspicions, the local Christian community was eager to demonstrate its loyalty to the Persian authorities. No doubt, there were Christian sympathizers and collaborators with Byzantium, but they constituted a minority. The church's leadership tried to establish some sort of symphony with the Persian rulers, with very limited success though (see Payne 2015; Young 1974).

The Persian church more yielded to than gained from this "symphony." On the one hand, for example, in 410, Shah Yazdgard I (r. 399–420) convoked a council, which was attended by the bishops of his empire. He imitated Roman emperors who had done the same. This council formally accepted the decisions of the council of Nicaea in 325 and was beneficial for the church. On the other hand, Persian rulers often interfered to the internal ecclesiastical matters more violently than their Roman counterparts. Thus, Shah Khosrau II (r. 590–628) deliberated between the options of choosing the next Catholicos or not to choosing anyone at all. Like in the Roman

**Figure 1.47** Zoroastrian ossuary decorated with Nestorian crosses—an illustration of inter-religious exchanges in Persia. Afrasiyab Museum in Samarkand.
Source: Photo by the author.

Empire, some prominent church hierarchs ascended to their positions straight from the political service to the Persian Empire. Such was the case, for instance, of Catholicos Aba I (in office 540–52), who before baptism was a high-ranked Zoroastrian official.[3]

Toward the end of the fifth century, the councils of the Persian church confirmed its theological autonomy from the "Western" churches by promoting a strong dyophysite Christology. A motivation behind such strong dyophysitism was not only theological but also political: the Church of the East struggled to demonstrate its loyalty to Persia and its difference from the Greco-Roman imperial Christianity. Approximately at the same time, the monopoly of the Eastern Syriac church on Persian soil was contested by Western Syriac Christianity, which confessed strong miaphysitism. The rivalry between the two Syriac traditions was not only theological but also political. Both Christian groups appealed to the Persian authorities with the claim that only they represented the genuine Christian truth. There were some debates in the presence of governors and even shah. The most famous one occurred in 612, under the presidency of Shah Khosrau II.

The Western Syrians appealed to the Persians by emphasizing their strong monastic traditions. The Eastern Syrians, to match this appeal, had to enhance their own monasticism, which had been weak. Abraham of Kashkar (490–588) reformed the Eastern Syriac monasticism following the Egyptian pattern. Around 570, he founded on Mount Izla a monastery, which became known as the "Great Monastery" (see Jullien 2009). Eastern Syriac monasticism would be eventually able to produce some prominent spiritual writers, such as Isaac of Nineveh.

---

[3]Some Zoroastrian officials after conversion to Christianity ended up as martyrs. For example, the Church of the East venerates martyr Mar Qardagh, who was such a convert under Shapur II (309–79); see Walker 2006.

Isaac was born on the Arabian Peninsula, in what is now Qatar, in the seventh century. He was elected a bishop of Nineveh, now Mosul in Iraq, sometime between 661 and 681. The primate of the Church of the East then was Catholicos George, who consecrated Isaac. He remained in this office for five months only. After that he retreated to what is now southeast Iraq. He lived there for the rest of his life as a hermit in the vicinity of the monastery of Rabban Shabur.

Isaac's writings, which survive in three parts (see Brock 2006: viii–xiv), became popular across all Christian traditions: Byzantine, Syriac, Coptic, Ethiopian, Catholic, Anglican, and so on. Isaac originally wrote in Syriac. Soon a collection of his writings was translated in Greek in the Byzantine monastery of St. Sava in Palestine. Its excerpts were included in the popular medieval anthology *Evergetinos* (eleventh century). During the Middle Ages, the Greek translation was translated further into Georgian, Arabic,[4] and Slavonic languages. From Arabic, the texts of Isaac were also translated to the Ethiopian Geʿez. From the Christian East, the texts of Isaac migrated to the West. They were first translated to Latin (from Greek), and then, by the early sixteenth century, to Portuguese, Catalan, Spanish, French, and Italian. The Greek publication in 1770 became a basis for translations in Romanian (1781), Modern Greek (1871), and Russian (1854) languages. From Russian, Isaac was translated to Japanese (1910).

Isaac flourished in the Persian cultural milieu under Arab rule. By his time, the Sassanid dynasty ceased to exist. Khosrau II was the last independent ruler of Persia. After him, the empire collapsed first under the Byzantine attacks and then was conquered by the Arabs. Muslim rulers established their authority over both Eastern and Western Syrians. Under new political circumstances, the two Syriac groups often forgot or did not pay attention to their theological differences in the past.

The Eastern Syriac experience of survival under the Persian and later the Arab, Central Asian, and Mongolian rulers, eventually benefited the entire Eastern Christianity. This was an experience of disestablishmentness, when the church becomes separated from the state. The Persian church still enjoyed some partnership with the state, but not to the extent of merging with it, as it had happened in Byzantium. The experience of disestablishmentness that the Persian church had as early as in the fourth century is prototypical for the modern model of the "wall" between the church and the state. It is possible to conclude, therefore, that both symphony and disestablishmentness are originally Eastern models of the church-state relations. Only later they were replicated in the West.

[4]Some Arabic translations were also made directly from Syriac.

# Silk Road Christianity

The Eastern Syriac church in Persia developed remarkable missionary activities. The scale of these activities can be compared with the apostolic era when Christianity spread throughout the Roman Empire. In a similar manner, the Church of the East rapidly spread throughout the Persian Empire, its vassal states, and beyond (see Lieu & Thompson 2019; Saint-Laurent 2015). In the early fifth century, this church expanded its jurisdiction in the Arabian Peninsula (see Gilman & Klimkeit 2016: 77–90). Soon the entire Asian subcontinent, from Persia to China, became an area of Nestorian Christianity.

As the apostles and their disciples relied on Roman roads to evangelize the empire, so the Persian Christians utilized the Silk Road to disseminate their own tradition. All religions in the region used this road to expand (see Foltz 1999). Persian Christians planted their religion in Sogdiana, which hosted the crucial hubs of the Silk Road. By 650, they had established a diocesan center in Samarkand—the Sogdian capital. Local rulers demonstrated remarkable tolerance to minorities, including Christians.

Many Christian texts were translated to the Sogdian language—the *lingua franca* of the Silk Road. Some of them were found as far away as in the Chinese Turfan (see Sims-Williams et al. 2014). One such document, in Sogdian, tells a story about the missionary activities of Bishop Bar Shabba in Central Asia:

> He (i.e., Bishop Bar Shabba) bought land and water and built citadels, hostels and houses and laid out gardens, <. . .> and he settled serving brothers and sisters there, in the area of Fars up to Gurgan (i.e., bishopric Hyrcania), in the area of Tus (i.e., one of the three bishoprics of Parthia), in Abarshar, in Serachs (a place at the border of

**Figure 1.48** A "Nestorian" stone from Balasagun—the Sogdian city on the Silk Road, in modern Kyrgyzstan.

Source: Photo by the author.

> Margiana), in Mervrod (i.e., Merv), in Balkh (ancient capital of Bactria) and in Herat and Sistan. He built churches there and built everything necessary [for the Christian community]. And he also had presbyters and deacons settle there. And they began to teach and to baptise, by the grace of the Holy Spirit, and by the authority and power which they had received from the pious Lord Bar Shabba. <. . .> And the proclamation of Christ the Vivifier became great in all areas. They became priests, and Christianity was strengthened. And they praised his name in all the areas up to many distant realms. To the Lord Bar Shabba, the pious Bishop, power and might was given <. . .> over the unclean spirits. (In Gilman & Klimkeit 2016: 211)

Persian monks introduced literacy to some Silk Road peoples. For instance, they constructed alphabet and grammar for the local Turkic nomads, on the basis of the Syriac language. They also baptized some Turkic tribes. A local chronicle of the middle-seventh century described these activities as follows:

> And Elijah (Elias), Metropolitan of Merv, converted a large number of Turks. <. . .> About this Elijah <. . .> it is related that when travelling in the countries situated beyond the border line (of the river Oxus) he was met by a king who was going to fight another king. Elijah endeavoured with a long speech to dissuade him from the fight, but the king said to him, “If thou showest to me a sign similar to those shown by the priests of my gods, I shall believe in thy God.” And the king ordered the priests of the demons who were accompanying him, and they invoked the demons whom they were worshipping, and immediately the sky was covered with clouds, and a hurricane of wind, thunder, and lightning followed. Elijah was then moved by divine power, and he made the sign of the heavenly cross, and rebuked the unreal thing that the rebellious demons had set up, and it forthwith disappeared completely. When the king saw what Saint Elijah did, he fell down and worshipped him, and he was converted with all his army. The saint took them to a stream, baptised all of them, ordained for them priests and deacons, and returned to his country. (In Gilman & Klimkeit 2016: 216)

Bishops, priests, and monks used the Silk Road not only to preach the Gospel but also for trade and even industrial espionage. Procopius of Caesarea (d. *c.* 565) reported on some monks who had brought the secrets of producing silk to Constantinople from China, which he called *Serinda* (Σηρίνδα):

> Certain monks, coming from India and learning that the Emperor Justinian entertained the desire that the Romans should no longer purchase their silk from the Persians, came before the emperor and promised so to settle the silk question that the Romans would no longer purchase this article from their enemies, the Persians, nor indeed from any other nation; for they had, they said, spent a long time in the country situated north of the numerous nations of India—a country called Serinda—and there they had learned accurately by what means it was possible for silk to be produced in the land of the Romans. Whereupon the emperor made very diligent enquiries and asked them many questions to see whether their statements were true, and the monks explained to him that certain worms are the manufacturers of silk, nature being their

**Figure 1.49** The site of a Persian monastery near Urgut, Uzbekistan. Monks moved here from Persia seeking the protection of the Sogdian kings and bringing enlightenment to local Iranian and Turkic peoples.

Source: Photo by the author.

> teacher and compelling them to work continually. And while it was impossible to convey the worms thither alive, it was still practicable and altogether easy to convey their offspring. Now the offspring of these worms, they said, consisted of innumerable eggs from each one. And men bury these eggs, long after the time when they are produced, in dung, and, after thus heating them for a sufficient time, they bring forth the living creatures. After they had thus spoken, the emperor promised to reward them with large gifts and urged them to confirm their account in action. They then once more went to Serinda and brought back the eggs to Byzantium, and in the manner described caused them to be transformed into worms, which they fed on the leaves of the mulberry; and thus they made possible from that time forth the production of silk in the land of the Romans. (Procopius, *De bellis* VIII 17; Dewing 1928: 226–31)

From the seventh century on, the Church of the East added new dioceses in Hulwan, Herat, Samarkand, as well as India and China. Catholicos Timothy I of Baghdad (in office 780–823), whose jurisdiction covered probably the largest territory in the history of Eastern Christianity, was reported at the beginning of the ninth century to overseeing nineteen metropolitans and eighty-five bishops in most parts of Asia. In his words, he had to care about "the Indians, the Chinese, the Tibetans, and the Turks" (in Norris 2006: 134).

Culturally, these areas were diverse. Timothy's flocks expressed themselves in the languages such as Aramaic, Persian, Sogdian, Arabic, Chinese, and others. The

Persian church was flexible enough to not completely stick to its Syriac roots. It adapted itself to the cultures beyond the Syriac and Persian worlds. Such ability for inculturation owes, to a great extent, to the disestablished character of this church in the Persian Empire. Loose connections with the state did not tie up this church to only one culture, as it had happened in Byzantium. The Byzantine church was usually lukewarm when it came to missionary activities outside the Roman Empire. In contrast to the Byzantine church, the Church of the East tirelessly dispatched missionaries beyond its traditional area, to the Far East.

## *Jing Jiao*

Some of these missionaries reached China under the Tang dynasty (618–907), which was remarkably open to foreign cultures and religions (see Hovorun 2014). The Tang Emperor Taizong (r. 626–49) granted the Nestorians permission to preach Christianity in his dominion. The religion they preached became known to the locals as "the Luminous Religion" (景教). We know from the sources that a Persian monk Olopun (Abraham) established in the Chinese capital of that time, Xi'an, a monastery. He was officially recognized as a "national priest" under Emperor Gaozhong (r. 649–83).

**Figure 1.50** The "Valley of Tang Poetry" in Xi'an, celebrating the cultural richness and diversity of China under the Tang dynasty.

Source: Photo by the author.

Olopun's story is a part of the brief chronicle of the early Chinese Christian community. This chronicle has been inscribed on the famous "Nestorian stele" raised in Xi'an in 781. Most inscriptions of the stele are in Chinese, but there is also a Syriac text carved on its margins. This text refers mostly to the persons who were related to erecting the stele:

> Adam, Deacon, Vicar-episcopal and Pope of China. In the time of the Father of Fathers, the Lord John Joshua, the Universal Patriarch.
>
> In the year of the Greeks one thousand and ninety-two, the Lord Jazedbuzid, Priest and Vicar-episcopal of Cumdan the royal city, son of the enlightened Mailas, Priest of Balkh a city of Turkestan, set up this tablet, whereon is inscribed the Dispensation of our Redeemer, and the preaching of the apostolic missionaries to the King of China.
>
> Adam the Deacon, son of Jazedbuzid, Vicar-episcopal.
>
> The Lord Sergius, Priest and Vicar-episcopal.
>
> Sabar Jesus, Priest.
>
> Gabriel, Priest, Archdeacon, and Ecclesiarch of Cumdan and Sarag. (In Horne 1917, vol. 12: 392)

The Chinese part of the inscription presents a creed and a brief description of some Christian rituals. Some articles of the Xi'an creed are peculiar, like the one that God created the world from primordial substance:

> Behold the unchangeably true and invisible, who existed through all eternity without origin; the far-seeing perfect intelligence, whose mysterious existence is everlasting; operating on primordial substance he created the universe, being more excellent than all holy intelligences, inasmuch as he is the source of all that is honorable. This is our eternal true Lord God, triune and mysterious in substance. He appointed the cross as the means for determining the four cardinal points, he moved the original spirit, and produced the two principles of nature; the somber void was changed, and heaven and earth were opened out; the sun and moon revolved, and day and night commenced; having perfected all inferior objects, he then made the first man; upon him he bestowed an excellent disposition, giving him in charge the government of all created beings.

The creed continues with explaining evil—a difficult subject for contemporary Chinese philosophy. The text mentions sixty-five sects, that is, religious doctrines:

> Man, acting out the original principles of his nature, was pure and unostentatious; his unsullied and expansite mind was free from the least inordinate desire; until Satan introduced the seeds of falsehood, to deteriorate his purity of principle; the opening thus commenced in his virtue gradually enlarged, and by this crevice in his nature was obscured and rendered vicious; hence three hundred and sixty-five sects followed each other in continuous track, inventing every species of doctrinal complexity; while some pointed to material objects as the source of their faith, others reduced all to

> vacancy, even to the annihilation of the two primeval principles, some sought to call down blessings by prayers and supplications, while others by an assumption of excellence held themselves up as superior to their fellows; their intellects and thoughts continually wavering, their minds and affections incessantly on the move, they never obtained their vast desires, but being exhausted and distressed they revolved in their own heated atmosphere; till by an accumulation of obscurity they lost their path, and after long groping in darkness they were unable to return.

In what follows, the inscription refers to the Trinity and the incarnation. It strangely describes the Trinity as "divided in nature." While speaking of the Messiah, it stresses his Syriac origin, as well as the Persian background of the Magi who came to venerate him. The authors intended to emphasize the importance of the Syriac and Persian background of Jing Jiao, without diminishing the culture of their Chinese hosts. Moreover, the text implies the usefulness of Christianity for good governance—something highly valued by the Chinese:

> Thereupon, our Trinity being divided in nature, the illustrious and honorable Messiah, veiling his true dignity, appeared in the world as a man; angelic powers promulgated the glad tidings, a virgin gave birth to the Holy One in Syria; a bright star announced the felicitous event, and Persians observing the splendor came to present tribute; the ancient dispensation, as declared by the twenty-four holy men [the writers of the Old Testament], was then fulfilled, and he laid down great principles for the government of families and kingdoms; he established the new religion of the silent operation of the pure spirit of the Triune; he rendered virtue subservient to direct faith; he fixed the extent of the eight boundaries, thus completing the truth and freeing it from dross; he

**Figure 1.51** Bilingual inscriptions in Chinese and Syriac.
Source: Photo by the author.

opened the gate of the three constant principles, introducing life and destroying death; he suspended the bright sun to invade the chambers of darkness, and the falsehoods of the devil were thereupon defeated; he set in motion the vessel of mercy by which to ascend to the bright mansions, whereupon rational beings were then released, having thus completed the manifestation of his power, in clear day he ascended to his true station.

The next portion of the text is dedicated to the sources of the Revelation, the sacraments of baptism and Eucharist, as well as some liturgical and ascetic practices. It is noteworthy that the statement condemns slavery and inequality:

Twenty-seven sacred books [the number in the New Testament] have been left, which disseminate intelligence by unfolding the original transforming principles. By the rule for admission, it is the custom to apply the water of baptism, to wash away all superficial show and to cleanse and purify the neophytes. As a seal, they hold the cross, whose influence is reflected in every direction, uniting all without distinction. As they strike the wood, the fame of their benevolence is diffused abroad; worshiping toward the east, they hasten on the way to life and glory; they preserve the beard to symbolize their outward actions, they shave the crown to indicate the absence of inward affections; they do not keep slaves, but put noble and mean all on an equality; they do

**Figure 1.52** The top part of the "Nestorian stele."

Source: Photo by the author.

> not amass wealth, but cast all their property into the common stock; they fast, in order to perfect themselves by self-inspection; they submit to restraints, in order to strengthen themselves by silent watchfulness; seven times a day they have worship and praise for the benefit of the living and the dead; once in seven days they sacrifice, to cleanse the heart and return to purity.
>
> It is difficult to find a name to express the excellence of the true and unchangeable doctrine; but as its meritorious operations are manifestly displayed, by accommodation it is named the Illustrious Religion. Now without holy men, principles cannot become expanded; without principles, holy men cannot become magnified; but with holy men and right principles, united as the two parts of a signet, the world becomes civilized and enlightened.

The Xi'an inscription continues with the history of the Christian community in China, with emphasis on the imperial recognition of Jing Jiao:

> In the time of the accomplished Emperor Tai-tsung, the illustrious and magnificent founder of the dynasty, among the enlightened and holy men who arrived was the most-virtuous Olopun, from the country of Syria. Observing the azure clouds, he bore the true sacred books; beholding the direction of the winds, he braved difficulties and dangers. In the year of our Lord 635 he arrived at Chang-an; the Emperor sent his Prime Minister, Duke Fang Hiuen-ling; who, carrying the official staff to the west

**Figure 1.53** The "Nestorian stele" in its full height at the Beilin Museum in Xi'an.
Source: Photo by the author.

border, conducted his guest into the interior; the sacred books were translated in the imperial library, the sovereign investigated the subject in his private apartments; when becoming deeply impressed with the rectitude and truth of the religion, he gave special orders for its dissemination.

In the seventh month of the year AD 638, the following imperial proclamation was issued:

Right principles have no invariable name, holy men have no invariable station; instruction is established in accordance with the locality, with the object of benefiting the people at large. The greatly virtuous Olopun, of the kingdom of Syria, has brought his sacred books and images from that distant part, and has presented them at our chief capital. Having examined the principles of this religion, we find them to be purely excellent and natural; investigating its originating source, we find it has taken its rise from the establishment of important truths; its ritual is free from perplexing expressions, its principles will survive when the framework is forgot; it is beneficial to all creatures; it is advantageous to mankind. Let it be published throughout the Empire, and let the proper authority build a Syrian church in the capital in the I-ning May, which shall be governed by twenty-one priests. When the virtue of the Chau Dynasty declined, the rider on the azure ox ascended to the west; the principles of the great Tang becoming resplendent, the Illustrious breezes have come to fan the East.

The Chinese inscription concludes with an ode in verses:

The true Lord is without origin,
Profound, invisible, and unchangeable;
With power and capacity to perfect and transform,
He raised up the earth and established the heavens.

Divided in nature, he entered the world,
To save and to help without bounds;
The sun arose, and darkness was dispelled,
All bearing witness to his true original.

The glorious and resplendent, accomplished Emperor,
Whose principles embraced those of preceding monarchs,
Taking advantage of the occasion, suppressed turbulence;
Heaven was spread out and the earth was enlarged.

When the pure, bright Illustrious Religion
Was introduced to our Tang Dynasty,
The Scriptures were translated, and churches built,
And the vessel set in motion for the living and the dead;
Every kind of blessing was then obtained,
And all the kingdoms enjoyed a state of peace.

When Kau-tsung succeeded to his ancestral estate,
He rebuilt the edifices of purity;

Palaces of concord, large and light,
Covered the length and breadth of the land.

The true doctrine was clearly announced,
Overseers of the church were appointed in due form;
The people enjoyed happiness and peace,
While all creatures were exempt from calamity and distress.

When Hiuen-tsung commenced his sacred career,
He applied himself to the cultivation of truth and rectitude;
His imperial tablets shot forth their effulgence,
And the celestial writings mutually reflected their splendors.

The imperial domain was rich and luxuriant,
While the whole land rendered exalted homage;
Every business was flourishing throughout,
And the people all enjoyed prosperity.

Then came Suh-tsung, who commenced anew,
And celestial dignity marked the Imperial movements.
Sacred as the moon's unsullied expanse,
While felicity was wafted like nocturnal gales.

Happiness reverted to the Imperial household,
The autumnal influences were long removed;
Ebullitions were allayed, and risings suppressed,
And thus our dynasty was firmly built up.

Tai-tsung the filial and just
Combined in virtue with heaven and earth;
By his liberal bequests the living were satisfied,
And property formed the channel of imparting succor.

By fragrant mementoes he rewarded the meritorious,
With benevolence he dispensed his donations;
The solar concave appeared in dignity,
And the lunar retreat was decorated to extreme.

When Kien-chung succeeded to the throne,
He began the cultivation of intelligent virtue;
His military vigilance extended to the four seas,
And his accomplished purity influenced all lands.

His light penetrated the secrecies of men,
And to him the diversities of objects were seen as in a mirror;
He shed a vivifying influence through the whole realm of nature,
And all outer nations took him for example.

The true doctrine, how expansive!
Its responses are minute;

How difficult to name it!
To elucidate the three in one.

The sovereign has the power to act!
While the ministers record;
We raise this noble monument!
To the praise of great felicity.

This was erected in the 2d year of Kien-chung, of the Tang Dynasty (i.e., A.D. 781), on the 7th day of the 1st month, being Sunday.

Written by Lu Siu-yen, Secretary to Council, formerly Military Superintendent for Tai-chau; while the Bishop Ning-shu had the charge of the congregations of the Illustrious in the East. (In Horne 1917, vol 12: 381–91)

Nestorian Christianity demonstrated an extraordinary ability of inculturation. Christians assimilated in China and reached prominent positions in the Chinese society. After the open-minded and tolerant Tang dynasty declined, Christianity declined as well.

**Figure 1.54** Nestorian bronze crosses from the Inner Mongolia during the Yuan dynasty. They were collected by F. A. Nixon, a British postal commissioner in Beijing during the 1930s–40s. Now the collection is on display at the Hong Kong University.
Source: Photo by the author.

It resurged under the Mongolian dynasty of Yuan (1206–368), which was imposed by the Kublai Khan (r. 1260–94), the grandson of Genghis Khan (1162–227). Kublai's mother, Sorghaghtani, was an Eastern Syrian Christian. Through her, this version of Christianity became one of the court religions in Dadu—Yuan's new capital, which is now Beijing. Kublai Khan himself, according to the Syrian Catholicos Gregory Bar Hebraeus (1226–86), was a "lover of the Christians" (Barhebraeus 2003: 439). Around 30,000 Christians were reported to live in China at that time and held important political positions. Among them, for instance, we know about Mar Sergius, a "Nestorian" governor of the city of Chinkiang, which is located between Nanjing and Shanghai.

Under the Yuan dynasty, the Church of the East to some degree reached the goal it had unsuccessfully tried to achieve at the court of the Persian shahs—to become established. However, this achievement came at a price. When the Mongolians were forcefully replaced by the Han dynasty of Ming in 1368, Eastern Christianity was eradicated from the Chinese soil as well. Because of the unreserved affiliation with the political regime, several successful centuries of Christian inculturation in China ended with the almost complete oblivion of Eastern Christianity in this country.

## Indochina

Kublai Khan tried to expand his rule far beyond China. He unsuccessfully attacked Japan and Java and was successful in conquering territories in Vietnam

**Figure 1.55** Eastern Syriac crosses found in a Mongolian edifice called Kyanzittha-Umin in Old Bagan, now Myanmar. Charles Duroiselle, who discovered this panel, identified eight Nestorian crosses on it. The crosses were painted, most probably, in the thirteenth century. See Bautze-Picron 2018.

Source: Photo by the author.

and Myanmar. His army defeated the empire of Pagan at Ngasaunggyan in 1277. Wherever the Yuan rule reached, it left traces of the Nestorian Christianity. One can see them, for instance, in the ancient capital of the Pagan Empire. Just like in Han China, this Christianity disappeared from these territories when the invaders were gone.

## I.10.3 Byzantine Fellowship

In contrast to the Persian church, the Byzantine church was not much interested to evangelize peoples outside its empire. The Romans identified the Roman Empire with the entire world (*oecumene*). The Christian church had emerged in this empire, converted it to Christianity, and now was comfortable within its confines. Most Byzantine missions, therefore, happened within the empire, not outside it.

### Mission among the Slavs

The most successful Byzantine mission, among the Slavs (see Stephenson 2004; Fine 1983; Dvornik 1970), was initially internal. Slavs were nomadic and seminomadic tribes, which began infiltrating the Roman soil in the sixth century AD. Some tribes, which would become known as southern Slavs, settled in the mountainous terrain of the Byzantine Balkans. Most of them preferred countryside and did not make trouble to the cities. Some, however, became troublemakers, especially after they allied with the Avars (see Pohl 2018). In 626, for example, they besieged Constantinople (see Hurbanič 2019).

Slavs gradually organized themselves into political entities. One of them was a short-lived Samo Empire, which was effectively a union of the western Slavs organized and managed by a Frankish merchant Samo (r. 623–58). Southern Slavs formed their own political entities. One of them was the so-called Bulgarian Empire. It was founded in the end of the seventh century by the Turkic Bulgars and absorbed many southern Slavs. Together, they built their state on the territory, which the Romans considered their own (see Fine 1983). To make things more complicated, the Western and Eastern Romans argued with each other about this territory, which at that time was called Illyria. After the formal division of the Roman Empire into eastern and western parts by Theodosius in 395, Eastern Illyria became administratively subordinated to Rome, with its administrative center in Thessalonica. Ecclesially, however, Constantinople continued exercising its authority over this region, to the much dismay of the church of Rome.

The Bulgars, who had established themselves in the disputed territory, exploited the rivalry between Rome and Constantinople to their own advantage. The Bulgarian

**Figure 1.56** A Glagolitic inscription in the Roman-Catholic cathedral in Zagreb, Croatia. The Glagolitic alphabet was in the church use in Croatia until recently.
Source: Photo by the author.

Khan Boris (r. 852–89), who made Christianity the official religion of his state, played a game of alliances with both Rome and Constantinople, until he secured autocephaly for the newly established Bulgarian church (see Sophoulis 2012; Hopkins 2009). The Bulgar rulers also decided to develop a distinct Slavic style of Christianity. It had to be different from both Byzantine and Frankish Christian styles, through which Christianity had been brought to the Bulgarian people in the first place. Bulgars preferred the Scripture, liturgy, and theology to be articulated in their own language, which became known as church Slavonic. The language was first rendered in the Glagolitic alphabet designed by two well-educated missionaries from Thessalonica, Constantine (826–69) and Methodius (815–85). Constantine, before he died, became a monk and was given a new monastic name Cyril. The two brothers designed an alphabet to reflect the nuances of Slavic pronunciation. The Greek alphabet was unable to render such Slavic sounds as ʂ̪, t̠͡ɕ, ʐ, ɕː, ʑː, or ɨ (according to the International Phonetic Alphabet). The first Slavic alphabet, Glagolitsa, looked completely different from the Greek or Latin alphabets. This was an implicit political message about the desire of the Slavs to preserve cultural and political distance from both centers of Christianity of that time—Rome and Constantinople.

The Glagolitic alphabet, however, turned out to be too complicated for Slavs and was replaced by Cyrillic alphabet. Although it is called after the name of Cyril-Constantine, the Thessalonian brothers did not design it. It was constructed by their disciples who were commissioned for this task by the son of the Bulgarian ruler Boris, Simeon I (r. 893–927). The Cyrillic alphabet is based on Greek, with some elements from the Glagolitic for the sounds not found in Greek. Its syntax completely imitates the Greek syntax. From the Bulgarian kingdom, the Cyrillic alphabet and the standardized written Slavonic language spread to other southern and eastern Slavic peoples. It was used for translating Greek and Latin texts and for writing, but not so much for oral usage.

In the meantime, the eastern Slavs formed their own state, which became known as Rus'. As in the case with the Samo and Bulgarian states, the eastern Slavic state was ruled not by Slavs, but by foreigners. In this case, it was a Rurik dynasty from what is now Sweden. This dynasty gave the Slavic state its Scandinavian name, Rus'. The dynasty of Rurikids ruled over various eastern Slavic principalities and states until the beginning of the seventeenth century, when it was replaced by the Romanov dynasty in the Moscow tsardom.

**Figure 1.57** Ruins of a church in Sigtuna, the center of the Swedish state in the time, when the Rurikids came to rule Rus'.

Source: Photo by the author.

Scandinavian rulers assembled the eastern Slavic tribes and principalities to a state, which would become the largest and one of the most powerful in Europe during the eleventh and twelfth centuries. This state was established as pagan. In its religious policies, it copied the Scandinavian models. Its dynamics also resembled the Viking style of expansionism. While the western Scandinavians systematically raided the Christian kingdoms in Britain, the eastern Scandinavians did the same to their southeast. They reached as far as Constantinople. Rus', under the Scandinavian leadership, also bothered the Eastern Roman Empire with regular raids.

In addition to fighting Rus' back, the Byzantine diplomacy attempted to make it an ally. Although Constantinople did not claim that the Rus' lands were Roman—in contrast to the Bulgarian kingdom—it set an ultimate goal of including this Slavic state to the Byzantine Commonwealth (see Obolensky 1971). Both political devises and Christian mission were used for that end. These combined efforts of the Byzantine political and ecclesial diplomacy were successful. The ruler of the state at that time, Volodimer (r. 980–1015), received baptism from the Byzantines. First, the population of Rus' capital, Kyiv, and then the entire state were converted to the Eastern Roman version of Christianity. Often the conversion was done in a medieval way—without asking consent of those who received it. Christianity became an established religion of the Slavic states. New churches were established in the image and likeness of the Byzantine church. The Slavic states also adopted the Byzantine model of symphonic relations with these churches.

The *Prime Chronicle of Rus'*, composed by the Kyivan monk Nestor, tells the story of Volodimer's baptism. The story begins with Volodimer's assault against the Byzantine colony of Chersonesus in Crimea (now the city of Sevastopol):

> After a year had passed, in 6496 (988), Vladimir proceeded with an armed force against Kherson, a Greek city, and the people of Kherson barricaded themselves therein. Vladimir halted at the farther side of the city beside the harbor, a bowshot from the town, and the inhabitants resisted energetically while Vladimir besieged the town. Eventually, however, they became exhausted, and Vladimir warned them that if they did not surrender, he would remain on the spot for three years.

In addition to conquering a Byzantine city, Volodimer wanted the Byzantine princess Anna for wife. Otherwise, he threatened to besiege Constantinople. The Byzantine diplomacy, however, turned its military disadvantage to political advantage, with the help of the church. The Eastern Romans requested Volodimer to baptize, if he wanted to get what he desired:

> Vladimir and his retinue entered the city, and he sent messages to the Emperors Basil and Constantine, saying, "Behold, I have captured your glorious city. I have also heard

that you have an unwedded sister. Unless you give her to me to wife, I shall deal with your own city as I have with Kherson." When the Emperors heard this message they were troubled, and replied, "It is not meet for Christians to give in marriage to pagans. If you are baptized, you shall have her to wife, inherit the kingdom of God, and be our companion in the faith. Unless you do so, however, we cannot give you our sister in marriage." When Vladimir learned their response, he directed the envoys of the Emperors to report to the latter that he was willing to accept baptism, having already given some study to their religion, and that the Greek faith and ritual, as described by the emissaries sent to examine it, had pleased him well. When the Emperors heard this report, they rejoiced, and persuaded their sister Anna to consent to the match. They then requested Vladimir to submit to baptism before they should send their sister to him, but Vladimir desired that the Princess should herself bring priests to baptize him. The Emperors complied with his request, and sent forth their sister, accompanied by some dignitaries and priests.

Vladimir was baptized in the Church of St. Basil, which stands at Kherson upon a square in the center of the city, where the Khersonians trade. The palace of Vladimir stands beside this church to this day, and the palace of the Princess is behind the altar. After his baptism, Vladimir took the Princess in marriage. Those who do not know the truth say he was baptized in Kiev, while others assert this event took place in Vasil'ev, while still others mention other places.

**Figure 1.58** What remains of the Pochaina River, a suggested place of the baptism of the Kyivans under Volodimer.

Source: Photo by the author.

After having received baptism, Volodimer initiated a radical religious reform throughout his dominion, by replacing paganism with Christianity. He began with a mandatory baptism of Kyiv's population:

> When the Prince arrived at his capital, he directed that the idols should be overthrown, and that some should be cut to pieces and others burned with fire. He thus ordered that Perun should be bound to a horse's tail and dragged down Borichev to the stream. He appointed twelve men to beat the idol with sticks, not because he thought the wood was sensitive, but to affront the demon who had deceived man in this guise, that he might receive chastisement at the hands of men. Great art thou, oh Lord, and marvelous are thy works! Yesterday he was honored of men, but today held in derision.
>
> While the idol was being dragged along the stream to the Dnieper, the unbelievers wept over it, for they had not yet received holy baptism. After they had thus dragged the idol along, they cast it into the Dnieper. But Vladimir had given this injunction, "If it halts anywhere, then push it out from the bank, until it goes over the falls. Then let it loose." His command was duly obeyed. When the men let the idol go, and it passed through the rapids, the wind cast it out on the bank, which since that time has been called Perun's sandbank, a name that it bears to this very day.
>
> Thereafter Vladimir sent heralds throughout the whole city to proclaim that if any inhabitants, rich or poor, did not betake himself to the river, he would risk the Prince's displeasure. When the people heard these words, they wept for joy, and exclaimed in their enthusiasm, "If this were not good, the Prince and his boyars would not have accepted it." On the morrow, the Prince went forth to the Dnieper with the priests of the Princess and those from Kherson, and a countless multitude assembled. They all went into the water: some stood up to their necks, others to their breasts, and the younger near the bank, some of them holding children in their arms, while the adults waded farther out. The priests stood by and offered prayers. There was joy in heaven and upon earth to behold so many souls saved. (In Hazzard Cross & Sherbowitz-Wetzor 1953: 111–13; 115–17)

## Medieval Slavic "Roman Empires"

The Slavic kingdoms in the south and east of Europe, which had been incorporated to the Byzantine Commonwealth by adopting Christianity as their established religion, eventually faced the temptation of substituting Byzantium in this commonwealth. Slavic rulers contested the Byzantine basileuses and claimed their status for themselves. The unquestionable axiom of medieval political philosophy held that there could be only one Christian empire, the Christendom, in the entire world. Other states that pretended to hold the imperial status could not be parallel empires, but had to prove that they have more rights than Byzantium to call themselves the Roman Empire. In other words, they could not supplement Byzantium, but had to substitute it.

Among such pretenders were the Carolingian Francia in the Western Europe, as well as Bulgaria and Serbia in the Southern Europe. The Bulgarian ruler Simeon I in 913 claimed for himself the title of "the Emperor and Autocrat of all Bulgarians and Romans," which he perceived as equal to the title of the Roman emperors in Constantinople. Such assumed imperial status was amalgamated in the title "tsar," a Slavicized rendition of "caesar." Since the first Bulgarian state, the Slavic rulers, who pretended to be successors to the Roman emperors, have been called "tsars."

Later, a Serbian "tsardom" emerged as another Slavic version of the Roman Empire. Serbian ruler, *župan*, Stefan Dušan (r. 1331–55) proclaimed himself the emperor ("tsar") of the Serbs, Romans, and Bulgars (*car Srba i Grka i Bugara*). He also rebranded his courtiers in the Byzantine manner, such as *despotes*, *caesars*, *sebastocratores*, *domestikoi*, *protovestiarioi*, and so on. He and his successors copied other Byzantine institutions in an attempt to substitute Byzantium. One of them was patriarchate. In 1219, Constantinople had granted the Serbian church honorary autocephaly (ψιλῷ ὀνόματι) (see Γόνης 1996: 67). In 1346, Stefan Dušan convoked in his capital Skopje a council, which unilaterally proclaimed the Serbian church a patriarchate. Simultaneously, he was crowned an emperor. Both acts meant a declaration that Serbia has become a new Roman Empire.

Stefan encoded this new assumed imperial status in what would be known as the *Dušan's Code* or *Zakonik*—a collection of laws that copied and imitated the codices of the earlier Roman emperors. The Code was adopted in 1349 in Skopje. It was supplemented and amended by Dušan's successors (see Fine 1983: 314). The Code legally confirmed the autocephaly of the Serbian church: "And the Tsar's churches shall not be subject to the Great Church" (Article 27; Burr 1949: 203). The "Great Church" here is the Patriarchate of Constantinople. The Code called the Serbian

**Figure 1.59** A medieval fortress (Kale) in Skopje, where Stefan Dušan was crowned Roman emperor.
Source: Photo by the author.

church "the Tsar's churches." Like earlier with the Bulgarian church, the medieval Serbian autocephaly became an attribute, through which the state pursued imperial status. The political status of the Serbian autocephaly is clear from the model of governance, which was imposed on the church. The *Dušan's Code* stated regarding this: "And the Lord Tsar and the Patriarch and the Logofet (a chancellor of the Byzantine and then the Serbian court) shall govern the churches and none other" (Article 25; Burr 1949: 203). A medieval autocephalous church, thus, was usually governed by a hierarchical order consisting of political authorities at its top and bottom. Ecclesial authorities were sandwiched between them.

## The "Mongolian" Rus'

More than a century later, another medieval autocephaly was proclaimed to support claims for the succession to the Roman Empire, by the rulers of Moscow. These rulers also claimed their succession to the Kyivan state of Rus'. However, more directly their authority originated from the Mongolian Empire. The Muscovite state emerged from and succeeded one of the *uluses* of the Mongol Empire, the Golden Horde. This *ulus* had been established in the mid-thirteenth century and was responsible for the occupation of Rus'. In 1240, the Mongols led by Batu Khan (r. 1227–55) sacked the capital of Rus' during their European campaign. By that time, Rus' had effectively become a confederation of feudal principalities, with rather nominal authority of the grand *knyaz'* of Kyiv. During their European campaigns, the Mongols occupied most of these principalities.

The Mongolian invasion to Rus' was described in several ancient chronicles. The Mongols were called "Tatars," and the authors of these chronicles confessed that they had known nothing about them. They provided several accounts of the Mongolian invasion, including the following one from the *Chronicle of Lavrentiy*:

> In the same year (1223 AD), some nations came, about which no one exactly knows who they are, where they came from, what is their language, what kind of tribe they are, and of what faith. And they call them Tatars, and some say—Taurmen, and others—Pechenegs. Some say that these are the nations about which Methodius, the Bishop of Patara, has reported that they came out of the Etrievskaya desert, located between east and north. <. . .>
>
> And the Russian princes set out on a campaign, and fought with the Tatars, and were defeated by them, and a few only escaped death. Whoever had the lot to survive, they fled, and the rest were killed. The good old prince Mstislav was killed, and the other Mstislav, and seven more princes died, and many boyars and ordinary soldiers were killed. They say that only ten thousand people of Kyiv died in this battle. <. . .>
>
> In the same year (1237), in winter, godless Tatars came from the eastern countries to the Ryazan land through forest, and began to conquer the Ryazan land, and captured it up to Pronsk, and took the entire Ryazan principality, and burned the city, and killed their prince. And some of the captives were crucified, others were shot

**Figure 1.60** The pre-Mongolian (twelfth century) church of St. Peter and Paul in Smolensk, Russia.
Source: Photo by the author.

> with arrows, and others were tied behind their hands. They gave many holy churches to the fire, burned monasteries and villages, and took considerable spoils from everywhere. <. . .>
>
> The Tatars set their camps near the city of Vladimir, and in the meantime they went and took Suzdal, and plundered the church of the Holy Mother of God, and burned the prince's court with fire, and burned the monastery of St. Dmitry, while others they plundered. They killed the old monks, and nuns, and priests, and the blind, and the lame, and the hunchback, and the sick, and all the people, but the young monks and nuns and priests, and priests' wives, and deacons, and their wives, and daughters, and sons—they took them all away to their camps. <. . .>
>
> Bishop Mitrofan, the wife of [prince] Yuri with their daughter, as well as their daughters-in-law, grandchildren, and others, the wife of [prince] Vladimir with children, and many boyars with ordinary people locked themselves in the church of the Holy Mother of God. And they were burned there without mercy. (*The Lavrentiy's Chronicle*; Дмитриева 1981: 133–9)

The northeastern principalities of former Rus' became vassals of the Golden Horde—the western *ulus* of the Mongolian Empire. Through the Horde, they were a part of the superstate ruled by the Mongolian Yuan dynasty from Beijing. In other words, this part of former Rus' was formally incorporated to the Chinese Empire and continued to be so until the Yuan dynasty was succeeded by the Ming dynasty. After approximately fifty years of tight control by the Mongols, the northeastern principalities received a relative autonomy. For example, they were allowed to collect their own taxes. At the same time, the rulers of these principalities were appointed by and accounted to the khans in Sarai—the capital of the Golden Horde.

There was a significant political and cultural assimilation between the Mongol-controlled Russian vassals and their overlords. The political elites in the former Rus' principalities adopted many methods and norms of the Mongolian politics. At the same time, they preserved their Byzantine faith and Slavic language.

## The "Lithuanian" Rus'

The southwestern principalities of what used to be the state of Rus', even though they had been battered by the Mongols, remained relatively independent, until they were included into the Grand duchy of Lithuania. Some scholars believe that Lithuania was an unproclaimed empire of sorts (see Norkus 2019). It was not a monolithic state and gladly accommodated ethnic and religious diversity of its peoples. The Lithuanian political system created favorable conditions for the peoples of Rus'. Most of the western Rus' principalities joined the Duchy and transformed it to Orthodox and Slavic in its majority. Only some principalities, such as Novgorod and Pskov, preferred to remain independent republics. Nevertheless, they had active interactions and trade with Lithuania. After the Grand duchy of Lithuania united in 1385 with

**Figure 1.61** The gates to the historical center of Vilnius with the medieval symbols from the Grand Duchy of Lithuania.

Source: Photo by the author.

the Kingdom of Poland, it became a less friendly environment for the Orthodox Christians.

The ruined Kyiv found itself on the territory controlled by Vilnius. This was an important symbolical asset, which allowed the Grand duchy of Lithuania to claim succession to the formerly powerful Kyivan state of Rus'. In a sense, the Duchy was Rus'. This "Lithuanian" Rus' counterposed itself to the "Mongolian" Rus', which remained under the control of the Golden Horde. The two Rus'es, as it were, developed hostility to each other, which in a sense continues to our days. Although they had belonged to the same state before the Mongolian invasion, after the invasion they grew quite different in their mentality and political culture. The Mongol-controlled principalities, which would become the core of modern Russian Federation, constituted an Asian frontier facing the West. The Lithuania-controlled principalities, in their turn, found themselves at the European frontier facing the East. The latter continue to exist as modern Ukraine and Belarus'. The name of Ukraine, which means borderland, reflects this role (see Plokhy 2016).

## Two "Clones" of the Kyivan Church

The rivalry between the "Lithuanian" and "Mongolian" Rus'es affected the ecclesial structures on the territories of the former Kyivan state. After this state was converted to Christianity in the late tenth century, the Patriarchate of Constantinople established there its *Metropolia*: a large structure that included several dioceses. The heads of this structure, the metropolitans of Kyiv, were confirmed and sometimes elected in Constantinople. After the destruction of the Kyivan state, when two parts of it found themselves in the Mongol and Lithuanian states, each part wanted the metropolitan of Kyiv for itself. Sometimes the metropolitan commuted between the two states, but this did not always work, especially in the periods of tensions between them.

The ecclesial see of Kyiv had to be "cloned," as it were. As a result, sometimes there were two metropolitans of Kyiv. Neither of them stayed in Kyiv. A Kyivan metropolitan for the Mongolian part stayed first in Vladimir-upon-Klaz'ma, later in Moscow, and sometimes in Tver. He nevertheless continued holding the title of the metropolitan of Kyiv. The "Lithuanian" metropolitan of Kyiv stayed in different cities of the Grand duchy, such as Galych, Novgorodok, Vilnius, and sometimes Kyiv.

Both "cloned" metropolitans of Kyiv were under the jurisdiction of the patriarchs of Constantinople, until 1448. Then, the Grand duke of Moscow Basil II (r. 1425–62) unilaterally promoted to the "Mongolian" Kyivan see his own candidate, Jonas, without asking Constantinople for consent. This was a de facto proclamation of autocephaly of the Moscow part of the Kyivan church. However, the Eastern patriarchates did not recognize the autocephalous church of Moscow, which for about one and half centuries effectively remained in a schism with the rest of the Byzantine fellowship of churches. In 1589, during his visit to Muscovy, the patriarch of Constantinople Jeremiah II (1572–9, 1580–4, 1587–95) eventually recognized the independence of the church of Moscow and elevated it to the patriarchal rank.

In the meantime, the Ruthenians—so the contemporary Western sources called the Orthodox descendants of Rus' who had become subjects of the united commonwealth of Poland and Lithuania,—experienced increasing restrictions and oppression. The Polish policies that favored Roman Catholicism, prevailed over the Lithuanian policies of toleration. The Polish state, in cooperation with Rome, forced the Orthodox Ukrainians and Belarusians to a union, which was signed in Brest in 1596 (see Groen & Bercken 1998). The sociopolitical conditions for the Orthodox deteriorated, which caused a violent rebellion led by Bohdan Khmelnytsky (1595–1657). As a result, the first modern Ukrainian state was founded. The Orthodox church in this state continued to be under the jurisdiction of Constantinople. This jurisdiction did not last long.

In 1654, Khmelnytsky signed a treaty with the Muscovite tsardom and joined it on the condition of preserving Ukrainian autonomy. The church followed the cause. In 1686, the Patriarchate of Constantinople transferred to the Moscow patriarchs the right to consecrate the metropolitans of Kyiv, after they had been elected by their Ukrainian constituencies. The Ukrainian church, however, had to remain under its original jurisdiction and to commemorate the patriarchs in Constantinople:

**Figure 1.62** The historical residence of metropolitans in Kyiv, Ukraine.
Source: Photo by the author.

> We order that the holy diocese (ἐπαρχία) of Kyiv should subject itself (ὑποκειμένη) to the holy patriarchal throne of the great and God-saved city of Moscow. It means that the metropolitan of Kyiv is to be consecrated (χειροτονεῖσθαι) there, whenever there is a need, by the blessed patriarch of Moscow. <. . .>
>
> Whenever this metropolitan of Kyiv preforms in this diocese the divine, holy, and bloodless sacrifice, let him among the first to commemorate the honorable name of the ecumenical patriarch (τοῦ οἰκουμενικοῦ πατριάρχου), who is the source (πηγή), the beginning (ἀρχή), and [stands] above all (ὑπερκειμένου πάντων) parishes and dioceses; then [he can commemorate] the patriarch of Moscow, who is his (i.e., metropolitan's) elder (γέροντος αὐτοῦ). (Copy of the letter from the patriarch of Constantinople Dionysius and the Synod about the transfer to the patriarch of Moscow of the right to consecrate the metropolitan of Kyiv. Constantinople, June 1, 1686; in Чснцова 2020: 394)

The Moscow Patriarchate, however, did not respect the conditions of the transfer. Soon it began treating the church in Ukraine as its own jurisdiction and eventually absorbed it completely. As earlier, in the case of proclaiming itself autocephalous, the Moscow church did not have the consent of Constantinople for the effective annexation of the Metropolia of Kyiv. In October 2018, the Ecumenical Patriarchate annulled the transfer to Moscow of jurisdiction over Kyiv. The Kyivan Metropolia, as it existed from the baptism of Rus' through the seventeenth century, was restored under the jurisdiction of Constantinople. Based on this Metropolia, an autocephalous Orthodox Church of Ukraine was established in December 2018.

## Paul of Aleppo's Travelogue

In the mid-seventeenth century, a deacon from Aleppo named Paul took several snapshots of various Eastern Christian milieus across Southern and Eastern Europe. He accompanied his father, the patriarch of Antioch Macarius, who during the 1650s–60s made fundraising tours to the Orthodox lands. His final destination was Muscovy—so Paul called this country, as it was the custom in his time. On his way there, the patriarch traversed several other countries. Paul's account of the patriarch's itinerary was written in Arabic. Its original text has been published in *Patrologia orientalis.*

Paul began his travelogue with a description of the Greek quarter of Istanbul, Fener. He provided some valuable insights into the lifestyle of the ecumenical patriarchs:

> We alighted in the apartments of Cyrillus the Alexandrian,[5] afterwards Patriarch of Constantinople; which are of singular beauty, and were built by him for his own use,

[5]Cyril Lukaris, the patriarch of Alexandria from 1601; the patriarch of Constantinople in 1620–3, 1623–33, 1633–4, 1634–5, 1637–8.

and adorned with a variety of marble, and coloured tiles, and crystal. They are, at the highest part of the buildings, comprised in the Patriarchal palace. <. . .>

After the Patriarchs had distributed the *Antidora* (blessed bread distributed in the end of the liturgy) they left the church: and having given their benediction to the assistants, while the bearer of the silver-candlestick cried out the *Polychronion*, or Long Life, to each, they ascended to the Divan, the Janissaries going before them with their staves; and sat upon two thrones, in their robes, surrounded by the Metropolitans, Priests, and Archons. Upon the table were placed two crystal cups of wine and spirits, and twelve dishes of Indian ware, heaped with meats, according to the number of the Apostles. The first that drank was the Constantinopolitan, whilst the singer chanted for him the Πολυχρόνιον. Then he said a prayer for the Metropolitans and the rest of the assistants, and wished them a health to each in his place. Afterwards the Antiochian did in like manner; and the heads of the Clergy, &c. Then the two Patriarchs distributed biscuit among the assembly; and we ascended to the banquet, in a room above the Divan, which has many windows looking over the sea, and commanding a magnificent prospect. (Belfour 1836: 35–6)

Another interesting description provided by Paul, is that of Bulgaria, which at that time was a part of the Ottoman Empire:

We arrived at a small town of Bulgarian Christians, called *Iglitsa*, in the middle of the river Danube. There is a road to it by land, and it is under the Mahometan Government; but we saw crosses erected in it, by the sides of the roads and upon their tombs. There is a church in the town, and the hogs feed at large in the streets.

From this place we came to a town called *Majina* (*Matchin*) upon the bank of the Danube, containing four hundred and twenty houses of Bulgarian Christians. It is the last under the Mahometan Government, and is in the Pashalik of Silistria. It has Turkish Commissioners, and a Cadi (a Muslim judge). (Belfour 1836: 42)

Paul also left detailed descriptions of Moldavia and Wallachia, which are now parts of Romania. At that time, they were autonomous principalities under Ottoman supervision. They had their own rulers, whom Paul calls "Begs." He described in detail how the patriarch of Antioch was received by the "Beg" of Moldavia in the capital of his principality, Iaşi:

On the afternoon of Sunday <. . .> we went to see his Highness the Beg, as he entered the town, amid the ringing of all the bells. In the evening, he sent some bread to our Lord the Patriarch, to bless, that he might have it brought back to him the next morning. The following day came Yoáni Boyar, the Saljdar, and all the Begs, who had met us on our arrival, accompanied by about fifty soldiers, or Janissaries, all clothed in red. With them came a royal coach, drawn by six grey horses; in which they placed the Patriarch, after they had robed him in his Mandya (bishop's mantle). I was seated at the door, and held up the crosier. The soldiers then marched before us, two and two, till we entered the Corta, in their language, that is, the palace; and approached the steps of the Divan, between rows of troops. Here the Patriarch alighted, and went up the staircase, whilst they held his train; and I, as usual, went before him. All the Grandees came forth to receive him in the outer hall, and in the second intermediate. The Beg came to meet him from the inner hall, appropriated to himself, and kissed his hand. The Patriarch kissed the Beg's forehead, according to custom, and gave him his benediction: and they sat down. The Beg, from the greatness of his love and friendship for him, wept more than once. We all of us made our obeisances to the ground before the Beg, and kissed, first his right hand, then the left; as we did afterwards at going out. The Beg then remained conversing with the Patriarch, and expressing his sentiments of veneration and love towards him for about an hour, and much delighted his grateful heart. Hereupon the Patriarch blessed him; and, taking his leave, departed. They placed him again in the coach, as before, and we returned to the convent. (Belfour 1836: 52–3)

Paul was a deacon, and many of his observations were made from the perspective of a deacon. That is why he paid much attention to the liturgical details, especially when they differed from the Middle Eastern customs:

It is remarkable, that in Moldavia and Wallachia, and in all the country of the Cossacks (i.e., Ukraine), as far as Moscow, they stand in the church from the beginning of the service to the end, morning and evening, in all seasons, with their heads uncovered, particularly in presence of a Patriarch, or Chief Priest, or Abbot, or even an ordinary

**Figure 1.63** The Orthodox cathedral in modern Iaşi.

Source: Photo by the author.

> Priest: for in all these countries they wear calpacks of felt, with fur, even the Princes and Grandees. The ladies also, in Moldavia, wear calpacks of red velvet, with sables; but in Wallachia, and among the Cossacks, with a white handkerchief; and the richest, with ornaments of pearls. (Belfour 1836: 50)

The next stopover of Macarius and his entourage was in the land of the Cossacks—so Ukraine was often called at that time. Paul described the habits of the Ukrainians as distinct from their neighbors':

> We beheld in them acts of religion which excited our astonishment: and God help us, for the length of their prayers and chaunts and masses! But nothing surprised us so much as the sweet voices of the little boys, as they sang in company with the men, with all their heart and might. We observed in this people an excellent custom, which exists all over these regions of the Russians or Cossacks; and we were inclined to admire any good practice that we discovered among them. All, except a very few of them, know the prayers by heart, and the order of the service, and the chaunting, even to the greatest part of the women and girls. Beside this, the Priests give instruction even to the orphan children, and do not suffer them to go about without knowledge. (Belfour 1836: 164–5)

Paul remarked how relaxed and easygoing were the people in the "land of Cossacks":

> On Tuesday, the third of the month Tamoz, we took leave of the Metropolitan, and descended to the city of Kiov, after the Metropolitan had sent word to them first, and

**Figure 1.64** The church and residence of the Ukrainian het'mans in Baturyn, on the banks of the Seym River.
Source: Photo by the author.

> they had prepared for us a large apartment. To precede us, he despatched a body of Grandees and Archons, armed, and on horseback, as usual; and on our descent we were met by a great number of Priests and Deacons, in their robes, and with banners and torches, who conducted us into a magnificent stone church in the centre of the market-place, with five cupolas in the shape of a cross, and dedicated by the title of "The Assumption of Our Lady." Then they walked before us to a large hotel, where we alighted.
>
> In this district the Grandees are numerous, and their trains are great: and these Grandees of Kiov carry in their hands staves of the bamboo-cane, of considerable thickness, and others of different kinds; as do also the inferior Lords and rich men.
>
> And now they began to bring us mead and beer, in large barrels, drawn in carts; and an abundance of strong spirits. Bread they furnished us in loads: and fish in quintals, from the plentiful cheapness of it among them; and its immense variety of shape and colour astonished us: for, as we before mentioned, the great River Niepros (i.e., Dnieper) is near them, and many ships sail out of it. (Belfour 1836: 236–40)

In the end, Paul gave a detailed account of Muscovy, which was their final destination:

> On the morning of Thursday the twentieth of Tamoz, which was the Festival of St. Elias the Prophet, and the completion of the two years since our departure from Aleppo, we arose; and having travelled other five miles, over wild deserts and through extensive forests entirely destitute of water, in the course of which progress we had occasional glimpses of the city of Potiblia (i.e., Putivl') from a great distance, we passed the extreme boundary of the Cossack territory, and came to the bank of the river called Sayimi the Deep (now Seem); which is the first line of frontier of the Muscovite territory. (Belfour 1836: 258–9)

Paul described some Muscovite liturgical practices and cultural habits. One of them was the way of blessing waters, on the feast of Theophany. Paul complained about how the patriarch had to do this blessing in the dead of winter:

> When the Patriarch came to that part of the service where he was to dip the cross in the water three times, several layers of ice had already been formed upon it, and it became necessary to break through them. This was done with brazen pitchers; and after the third immersion, all the people took of the water in their vessels from the holes which they had dug, and gave to their horses to drink.
>
> Thousands and thousands of persons had assembled from the villages, having heard that it was the intention of the Patriarch of Antioch to bless the water. Then the Patriarch came out upon the platform; and began to asperge the Grandees first, and afterwards the Clergy. In consequence of the intense cold, it was wonderful to see the drops of water freeze on the bristles of the hogs, as he sprinkled them: and on the sleeves and collars of the people these drops became like glass spangles shining in the light. Even the beards and mustaches of the men were covered and whitened with hoar-frost, their breath instantly freezing as it issued from their

> nostrils; nor could the icicles be removed without such violence as almost to draw the hairs along with them. The sun was risen; but no hope arose to us that we should be able to go through the hardships of this day, and we abandoned ourselves to despair. God, however, was pleased to assist us and save us, though our hands and feet and noses were nearly bitten off by the frost, notwithstanding the tight fur gloves which were doubled on our hands, and the thick fur boots which inclosed our feet and legs, besides the many fur cloaks with which we were entirely enveloped. But the great wonder was, to behold all, whether Clergy or laity, standing bareheaded in this intense cold, from the earliest hour of the morning until we went forth from mass in the evening.
>
> At the conclusion of the ceremony on the river, we returned the way we came; our Lord the Patriarch sprinkling the men and women on the right and left, until we arrived at the great church. All this time the bells of all the churches were ringing, both as we went and returned; and under the steps of the Cathedral, one of the Priests stood to incense the Clergy one by one, as they entered. Last of all, the Patriarch ascended the steps; and having entered the church, we took our station in the porch &c. At the end of the service we were so much affected by the cold, that we were unable to perform mass in the Cathedral; and therefore went up into the higher church, which they had warmed with stoves from the preceding evening. Here we celebrated the holy mysteries, and there was an ordination of Priests and Deacons. We were detained until evening, cursing our very souls from weariness and starvation. (Belfour 1836: 254–355)

Paul described the Muscovite customs with admiration. However, from time to time he gave away the disappointment of the Antiochian delegation with some of them. For example, they insisted on seeing the tsar, with no avail for a long time. Another custom that Paul observed was keeping their national matters in secrecy from foreigners, even if this foreigner is a patriarch:

> We were therefore in great distress, perplexity, and doubt; particularly as we were shut up in close confinement, without a single person to inform us what the Emperor was doing, or where he was, or what was passing in the world; for the Muscovites are all, from the highest to the lowest, of a silent disposition; and this is the only disagreeable part of their character. They will tell nothing to a foreigner whatever, either good or bad, of their own affairs: even to our Lord the Patriarch, when he condescended to ask the chief Officers and Priests, or even the common people, concerning the circumstances of the Emperor, not one would give the smallest information: all their answer was, "We do not know." The very children were perfectly instructed in the like dissimulation. How surprising is the strictness of such discipline, and that in the mouths of all of them there should be but one tongue! We were afterwards given to understand, that every Muscovite is sworn upon the Cross and the Gospel, and bound, on pain of excommunication by the Patriarch, not to reveal their national affairs to foreigners; but should they gain any intelligence from or concerning strangers, they are obliged to communicate it to the Emperor. (Belfour 1836: 259)

## Tsardom

Paul called the Muscovite ruler "an Emperor." This flattering title reflected the way in which these rulers perceived their power: they pretended to be the successors of Roman emperors. Their political self-perception had undergone a significant evolution since Mongol times. As was mentioned earlier, in those times, the northeastern dukes were vassals of the Golden Horde. The Moscow dukes used their close relations with their Mongol sovereigns to overcome other vassals. Most successful in this regard was Ivan I Kalita (r. 1325–40). He made the small principality of Moscow the richest and most influential among other Russian vassal states of the Golden Horde. He used as leverage bribes and intrigues at the capital of the Horde, Sarai.

Ivan's grandson Dimitriy, nicknamed Donskoy, challenged the rule of the Mongols. He won a decisive battle against the ruler of the Golden Horde, Mamai (1335–80), at the Kulikovo field near the Don River (hense is his nickname) in 1380. Although this victory did not liberate the northeastern principalities from the Mongol dependence completely, it radically changed the character of their dependence. A century later, the principalities got rid of the Mongol rule altogether, under the leadership of Moscow.

Soon after the Muscovite state became completely independent, it began looking for a new political ideology to facilitate its expansion. The Moscow rulers found this ideology in imitating the Eastern Christian empire, which just had been conquered by the Ottomans. Following the earlier examples of the Bulgarian and Serbian rulers, the Muscovite rulers assumed for themselves the role of Roman emperors. Ivan III (r. 1462–1505), the first ruler independent from the Mongols, was also the first to pretend to be an emperor. He adopted the Byzantine title of "autocrator" (*samoderzhets*), began using the Byzantine double-headed eagle for his coat of arms, and married a niece of the last Byzantine emperor Constantine XI Palaeologus, Zoë Palaeologina (while in Moscow, she changed her name to Sophia).

More importantly, Ivan unilaterally proclaimed independence from Constantinople for that part of the Kyivan church, which had its center in Moscow. As was mentioned, the Muscovite autocephaly was recognized by other Orthodox churches almost one and half centuries later, under Tsar Boris Godunov (r. *c.* 1585–98). It is noteworthy that when the ecumenical patriarch Jeremiah arrived in Moscow, Boris offered him to stay in his tsardom permanently. Jeremiah declined the offer, which revealed Moscow's political plan to accomplish the *translatio imperii Romani* through *translatio ecclesiae Constantinopolitanis* to Muscovy. Having an independent church in the tsardom of Moscow was a political act, similar to the earlier proclamations of autocephaly by the Bulgarian and Serbian rulers. In this sense, the Muscovite autocephaly was typologically political—an attribute of a growing empire with the pretension to substitute the Roman Empire, which had recently collapsed.

To substantiate their claims for *translatio imperii*, the Moscow rulers actively borrowed from the depository of the Byzantine rites and ideologies. For example, when Ivan III decided to officially proclaim his grandson Dimitriy as his successor, he crowned him following the Byzantine rite. Dimitriy, however, did not succeed Ivan on the Moscow throne. This throne was taken by Ivan's son from Sophia, Basil III. Basil continued the policies of his father in promoting the Moscow principality as a successor to the Byzantine Empire. He insisted to be addressed as "tsar"—the title that the southern Slavic rulers had used when they pretended to be successors to the Byzantine emperors.

The Moscow church was busy articulating an ideological justification for the Muscovite tsardom as a new Christian empire. The republic of Pskov, which Basil annexed, played a particularly important role in the formation of the Russian imperial ideology. A monk from Pskov named Filofey wrote epistles to Basil's officials and the tsar himself. He argued that Moscow should be understood as "the third Rome" (see Poe 1997; Kortschmaryk 1971). In his epistle to a courtier Mikhail Misyur'-Munekhin, for example, Filofey described Basil III as a ruler who

> in the entire world is the only tsar for the Christians and the ruler of the holy God's thrones, of the holy catholic and apostolic church, which emerged instead of the Roman and Constantinopolitan [churches] and which exists in the God-saved city of Moscow. <. . .> [It] is the only in the world that shines brighter than the sun. <. . .> All Christian kingdoms reached their end and came together in one single kingdom of our sovereign. According to the prophetic books, this is the Roman kingdom, because two Romes fell and the third one stands still, while there will be no fourth one. (In Синицына 1998: 345)

The idea of Moscow as the "third Rome" was manipulative, because Constantinople, according to the official Byzantine ideology, was not regarded as a "second," but as the "new" Rome. Nevertheless, the new Muscovite ideology, elaborated by the church, was eventually accepted in the Christian East. When the Ecumenical Patriarch Jeremiah II visited Moscow to confirm its autocephaly, he also reportedly confirmed the ideology of the "third Rome." In his address to the tsar, according to the Muscovite sources, he stated:

> Since the old Rome fell because of the Apollinarian heresy, and the Second Rome, which is Constantinople, is possessed by the godless Turks, thy great Russian Tsardom, pious Tsar <. . .> is the Third Rome <. . .> and thou alone under heaven art called the Christian Tsar in the whole world for all Christians. (In Wolff 1959: 305)

Moscow's political style appeared increasingly Byzantine, in both rituals and symbols. However, the Moscow rulers, now called tsars, often acted as Mongolian khans: insidiously and cruelly. The most notorious in his cruelty was the son of Basil III, Ivan IV (r. 1547–84), who was nicknamed accordingly, as "Terrible." He preferred to appear and behave as a Byzantine basileus. He even wanted to be anointed as a basileus. However, this rite was for the first time applied to his successor Theodore I (r. 1584–98). As historians note, it is not only Ivan IV who should be called "terrible"; his predecessors and some successors on the throne of Moscow deserve the same label.

## Imperial Russia

Under John IV, Muscovy became officially Russia. Before him, it is historically incorrect to call Muscovy Russia. However, the state of John the Terrible was not yet formally an empire, but the "Russian Tsardom." It was proclaimed empire by Peter I Romanov (r. 1682–1725) on October 22 (November 2, according to the Gregorian calendar), 1721. Since its foundation, the Russian Empire functioned based on the medieval concept of *translatio imperii*: as an assumed successor of the Eastern Roman Empire. Russia was indeed the only Eastern Christian state in the world, except only Ethiopia being such a state for the anti-Chalcedonian tradition. All other Orthodox peoples lived in the empires, which were not Orthodox or even Christian. Most of them were under Ottoman rule.

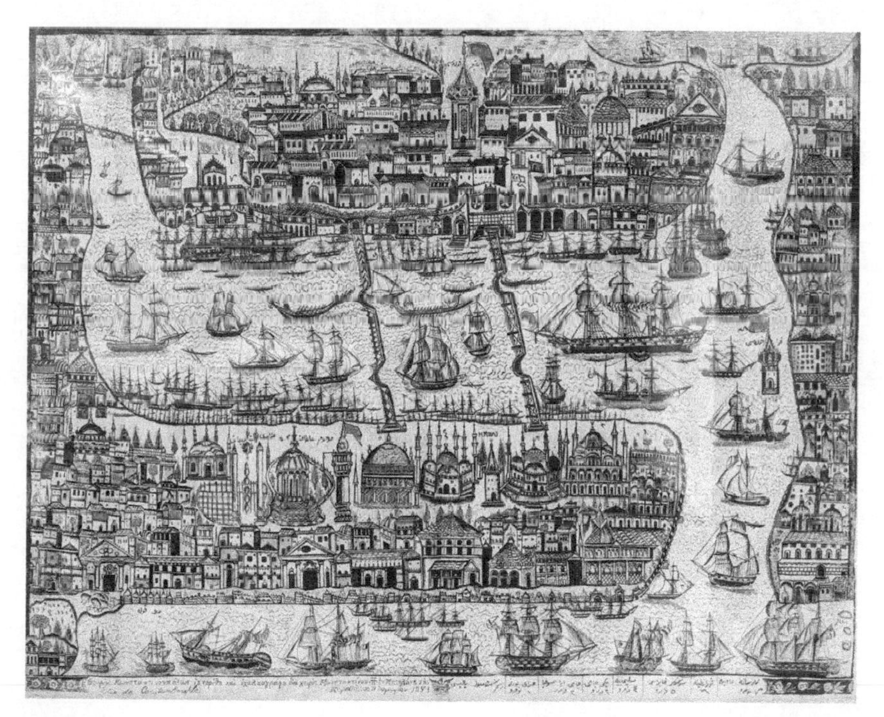

**Figure 1.65** Constantinople. Engraving by Konstantinos Kaldis (1851). Benaki Museum in Athens.

Source: Photo by the author.

Russian and Ottoman Empires became archrivals. Most of the dozen Russo-Ottoman wars were primarily about who would control Constantinople. There were also other reasons for the Moscow-Ottoman conflicts, such as control over the Straits of Bosphorus and Dardanelles. Both Russian and Ottoman political philosophies were built on the Byzantine axiom: whoever controls Constantinople is eligible to claim imperial status. The wars, therefore, were waged not only for territories and peoples but also for identities. Their competition for the Byzantine imperial legacy ceased only when the Russian and Ottoman Empires collapsed, which happened almost simultaneously.

Following the Young Turk Revolution in 1908 and the Bolshevik Revolution in 1917, Turkey and Russia became secular states. Among other things, this meant they did not pretend anymore to be successors to Byzantium. The Soviet Russia supported the Turkish Republic (since 1923), with explicit hope that it would join the global proletarian revolution and with implicit rejection of the theory of "third Rome." At the same time, the Turkish state, under the leadership of Mustafa Kemal Atatürk (*c.* 1881–1938), moved its capital away from Istanbul to Ankara. This was a symbolic act of the rejection of the Roman imperial legacy. Atatürk also abolished the caliphate, which meant that Turkey ceased to be not only the Roman Empire but also the global Muslim empire.

# I.11

# The Wall

Both Soviet Russia and Kemalist Turkey built a high wall between the state and religion as a part of their modernization programs. They followed the Western models of modernization and separation between the church and state. A need for such separation in Western Europe emerged as a result of the wars that followed the Reformation. The most notorious of them was the Thirty Years' War (1618–48). European states fought each other implementing the ancient principle *cuius regio, eius religio*. These wars, which claimed millions of lives, triggered the process of separation between the state and the church. Thomas Hobbes (1588–1679) explored the possibility of such separation in his treatise *Leviathan* (1651, revised Latin edition 1668). He personified the state as the biblical monster Leviathan (Job 41:1; Pss. 74:14, 104:26; Is. 27:1) and envisaged its role as an arbiter in religious quarrels. To function as such an arbiter, the state had to secularize. Secularity became an intrinsic feature of Modernity.

Across the Atlantic, the situation was similar. Some North American states originally supported particular Christian denominations and did not tolerate others. For example, the congregationalists of New England persecuted Quakers, Baptists, and Anglicans. In the southern states, Anglicans harassed Baptists and Puritans. Huguenots were not welcome in Florida and Jews, in New York. All other states, except Maryland, oppressed the Catholics. Religion-driven clashes between these states were probably not as violent as they were in Europe. Still, they made miserable the life of religious minorities in some states. One such minority group was a Baptist community in Danbury, Connecticut. This community was regularly harassed by the congregationalist majority of the state. The third president of the United States, Thomas Jefferson (in office 1801–09), penned in 1802 a consoling letter to this community. In this letter, he suggested to build a wall, which would separate the churches from the state and thus would protect Baptists and other oppressed minorities throughout the country. Jefferson's wall was envisaged as accommodating in a single state the absolutist claims coming from rather exclusivist religious groups, each pursuing its own theocratic utopia.

President James Madison (in office 1809–17), who succeeded Jefferson, developed what can be called a theology of the separation between the state and the church. This

**Figure 1.66** "The Pioneers' Village" in Salem, Massachusetts, established in 1630. One of the earliest congregationalist "micro-theocracies" in New England.
Source: Photo by the author.

theology underpinned the First amendment drafted by Madison and postulating the freedom of consciousness. Madison argued that it is more in the interest of the church than in the interest of the state to be parted from each other. The state can err in religious matters and thus can divert the church from the path of truth. The state also impedes the mission of the church more than facilitates it. Therefore, if the church wants to be faithful to God and successfully develop its mission, it should stay separate from the state.

# I.11.1 The Persian Wall

It is commonly believed that the Hobbsean and Jeffersonian models of separation between the church and the state constitute the archetypes of the modern church-state relations. In fact, such archetypes had emerged more than a thousand years prior to the Western Modernity, in the Antique Christian East. The archetypes of both unity and separation between the church and the state are Eastern. Only later were they reproduced in the West. As was mentioned earlier, established Christian communities experienced separation from the state for the first time in the Persian Empire. Many Christian communities that had been established in the Roman setting, under Persian rule, were effectively disestablished. They lost their privileges that they had enjoyed in the Roman Empire. However, now they felt freer in holding beliefs that they regarded orthodox. Disestablishmentness taught the Christian communities in Persia to live without the state support and to tolerate other religions.

# I.11.2 The Arab Wall

Even more, the Christian groups in the East had to learn such lessons with the rise of Islam. Many Christians who lived on both Roman and Persian soil welcomed new

Arab masters. They hoped that, unlike their previous Byzantine masters, the Muslim leaders would completely abstain from interfering in their theology. The Nestorian Catholicos Isho'yahb III, for example, expressed such hope in 650:

> These Arabs, whose God has now given sovereignty over the world, are disposed towards us as you know. They are not opposed to Christianity. Indeed, they respect our religion and honor the priests and the saints of our Lord and they give aid to the churches and monasteries. (In Tolan 2013: 13)

Caliphs indeed did not interfere in the internal matters of the Christian communities. Earlier Christian encounters with what has been called paleo-Islam (see Al-Azmeh 2014: 358–497), that is, pro-Islamic beliefs before Muḥammad, as well with Muḥammad himself,[1] set a pattern for the Muslim policies toward Christians and Jews—the "people of the Scripture" (*ahl al-Kitāb*). In this capacity, they were "protected people" (*ahl al-ḏimmah*).

In contrast to Christianity or Judaism, there is no natural gap between religion and politics in Islam. In political Islam, politics and religion cohere to a greater extent than they did in Byzantium. Christians could not hope for the slightest share in the power of a Muslim state. Muslim states did not need the church as a source of legitimacy. The only political usefulness that the church could have was to keep Christian communities organized and under control. For the sake of such control, Muslim states established a relationship with the church of sorts. They promised Christian communities some protection in exchange for their submission.

Such relationship was codified in what has been called the "Pact of Umar" (*shurūṭ ʿUmar*). The roots of this document go back to the period of the early Arab conquests, for which reason it bears the name of ʿUmar ibn al-Khaṭṭāb (r. 634–44)—an early caliph and conqueror. It reflects the practice of conquest, when a besieged city had two options: to resist the conquerors and be taken by force (*ʿanwatan*) or to surrender and be spared. In the latter case, the city's population was eligible for an agreement (*ṣulḥān*) that guaranteed some safety (*amān*) in exchange for submission. The original versions of the Pact settled the conditions of Christian surrender.

Several centuries later, when Muslims and the conquered Christians developed a stable modus vivendi in the political frame of the caliphate, the earlier agreements from the period of conquests were codified and modified. These codifications applied primarily to the areas, where Muslim and Christian communities lived together. There were areas, however, which were completely Christian, and the Pact did not affect them. Christians in these areas preserved for long time their lifestyle without

---

[1]According to the mid-eighth-century biography of Muḥammad written by Ibn Isḥāq, in his teens he met a Nestorian monk named Baḥīrā.

much change. In contrast to the earlier codifications of the Pact, which emphasized harmony between the two communities, its later editions stressed a distinct and inferior social status of the Christians. These editions were designed to minimize the Christian influence on Muslims. One of the later versions of the Pact, named after al-Ṭurṭūshī, made sure that Christians feel their inferiority and do not practice or demonstrate their religion publicly:

1. We (the document was written as if from the Christians) shall not build, in our cities or in their neighborhood, new monasteries, churches, convents, or monks' cells, nor shall we repair, by day or by night, such of them as fall in ruins or are situated in the quarters of the Muslims.
2. We shall keep our gates open wide for passers-by and travelers. We shall give board and lodging for three days to all Muslims who pass our way. We shall not give shelter in our churches or in our dwellings to any spy, nor hide him from the Muslims.
3. We shall not teach the Qurʾān to our children.
4. We shall not manifest our religion publicly nor convert anyone to it. We shall not prevent any of our kin from entering Islam if they wish it.
5. We shall show respect towards the Muslims, and we shall rise from our seats when they wish to sit.
6. We shall not seek to resemble the Muslims by imitating any of their garments, the *qalansuwa* (a hood), the turban, footwear, or the parting of the hair. We shall not speak as they do, nor shall we adopt their *kunyas* (a component in an Arabic name, such as *abū*).
7. We shall not mount on saddles, nor shall we gird swords nor bear any kind of arms nor carry them on our persons.
8. We shall not engrave Arabic inscriptions on our seals.
9. We shall not sell fermented drinks (nor shall we keep pigs in their vicinity).
10. We shall clip the fronts of our heads.
11. We shall always dress in the same way wherever we may be, and we shall bind the *zunnār* (sashes of a particular color) round our waists.
12. (a) We shall not display our crosses or our books in the roads or markets of the Muslims (nor shall we conduct processions on Palm Sunday and Easter).
    (b) We shall only use clappers in our churches very softly (and we shall not display the cross on them).
    (c) We shall not raise our voices in our church services or in the presence of Muslims, nor shall we raise our voices when following our dead.
    (d) We shall not show lights on any of the roads of the Muslims or in their markets.
    (e) We shall not bury our dead near the Muslims.

13. We shall not take slaves who have been allotted to the Muslims.
14. We shall not build houses overtopping the houses of the Muslims. (In Thomas 2018: 87–8)

The Pact aimed at making Christianity a private religion—something it used to be before Constantine. After Constantine, Christianity substituted Greco-Roman religion in the public square. After Umar, the Christian religion was substituted there by Islam.

The Pact strictly prohibited the conversion of Muslims to Christianity, while Christians were encouraged to convert to Islam (see Hurvitz 2020). One of the most effective instruments of conversion to Islam was the religious tax imposed on non-Muslims, *jizyah* (جِزْيَة). For poor Christian families, this was quite a burden. Only the Christian middle and upper classes could afford to remain Christians. To force such families to conversion, the Pact envisaged measures of public humiliation. They were to demonstrate their inferiority even to the lowest classes of Muslims. All Christians became second-class citizens in the Muslim society, even when they constituted a majority in it. Because of such restricting measures, the Christian majority in the lands controlled by Islam was gradually reduced to a minority. As Sidney Griffith has remarked, "The history of Christians under Muslim rule is a history of continuous, if gradual, diminishment" (Griffith 2010: 14).

# I.11.3 The Ottoman Wall

The principles of the Pact of Umar were implemented, with variations, in all Islamic states. They continue to be implemented in some societies with Muslim majority, often as unwritten rules and unofficially, even to our days. The Ottoman Empire adopted and advanced them in the most sophisticated way, through a complex system of laws and regulations. This empire was the most advanced Islamic state ever. Its ambition was to conquer the entire European continent. On the one hand, it embodied the principles of political Islam, which considers religion and politics as inseparable. On the other, it accommodated large non-Muslim groups, including Christians of various Eastern denominations. In comparison with other contemporary European states, which tended to be highly centralized and uniformed, the Ottoman Empire was more diverse. It relatively easily granted autonomy to groups and territories within its borders.

## The Osmans

The Ottoman State began as a humble Turkic principality (*beylik*) in Asia Minor. Among its early leaders was Osman (*c.* 1258–325), who gave his name to the dynasty that founded the empire. During the thirteenth and the first half of the fourteenth centuries, the Osman or Ottoman (from the Arabic spelling of Osman's name,

**Figure 1.67** The mausoleum of the founders of the Osman dynasty in Bursa, ancient Prousa—one of the early Ottoman capitals. The Byzantine monastery of St. Elias was reconstructed by the Osmans to host their mausoleum.

Source: Photo by the author.

*ʿUthmān* (عثمان)) dynasty prevailed over most other principalities in Asia Minor and the Balkans.

# Fall of Constantinople

In May 1453, after several weeks of besieging Constantinople, the troops of the young Ottoman sultan Mehmed II (1432–81) breached through its walls. There are some contemporary accounts of this historical event (see Philippides & Hanak 2020; Melville-Jones 1972). A later comprehensive summary of these accounts can be found in an anonymous Greek chronicle from the early 1600s:

> [Sultan Mehmed] rushed, like a wild beast, toward [Constantinople] with a countless multitude, from land and sea. The land was filled with men and horses while the sea was full of long ships, the greatest number possible. They manned the ships with individuals from the regions of the emperor by the Black Sea. They had been recruited by force. When the ships arrived, they were prevented from entering the harbor by the chain [stretched across the mouth by Byzantine defenders]. So they resorted to a marvelous and astonishing tactic: they unfurled the sails, put the oars in their places, and dragged the ships over land. A multitude of countless soldiers pulled the ships to

the very high hills to the accompaniment of drums and trumpets and then dragged them down to the sweet waters. Thus, they took command of the harbor. Then they constructed quays with empty containers and planks <. . .> and attacked the walls of the city, as there was nothing to prevent them.

Thus, he besieged the city by land and sea. [The Sultan] destroyed with the big cannon the section of the walls from the Gate called Charsia to the Gate of Saint Romanos. Many sections of the walls were brought down. Those sectors were fortified nevertheless with stockades made of brushwood and cotton. There happened to be present, in those days, a nobleman from Genoa called Giustiniani <. . .> [who said,] "I can guard the demolished sector with my soldiers; I will defend it for the name of Christ." <. . .> This nobleman took his position and fought for many days, preventing them from entering the fortifications. But observe our sin and God's departure: while he was at his post fighting, a shot from an arquebus hit him on the right leg; he collapsed like a corpse. His own men took him, went to the ships, made sail, and escaped as far as the island of Chios, where he died. It was rumored that he had been shot from within the fortifications but no one knows how it really came about.

While the nobleman was still alive, the Constantinopolitans decided to send a vessel in the night with forty young men on board to set fire to the armada in secret. <. . .> But the Franks <. . .> who were befriending the Turks, discovered this and lit a fire on top of the tall tower. So they brought their cannons from the galleys and sank the vessel. Thus those admirable young men drowned.

The Constantinopolitans were at a loss; there was nothing that they could do against such a countless multitude (almost one man against one thousand). When the demolished sector failed to be approached by the mob, the Constantinopolitans realized that a strong attack would be launched on the following day. So they came out to the outer fortifications, as they feared that they would come close to the great walls. The Turks charged, entered the demolished sector, took charge of the great walls, and raised their standard on the towers. But the army of the city was outside. When they heard the shouting and saw the standards on the towers, they rushed to enter through the Charsia Gate in order to expel the Turks. And they perished in the press; they could not enter because of the dead bodies blocking the entrance (the gates of Charsia and of Saint Romanos were congested, all the way up to the arches). Later, the captives, women and children, could not be brought out but had to be lowered by rope from the walls.

So the capture of the renowned city took place in the year 6961, on May 29, Tuesday morning. (*An Anonymous Greek Chronicle*; Philippides 1990: 43–51)

## Rise of the Ottoman Empire

The fall of Constantinople marked a radical change in the configuration of both Islamic and Christian worlds. For the former, it was a "conquest" (*fethi*) and a symbol of Islam's might, while for the latter it was "fall" (*halōsis*) that caused a lasting trauma. *İstanbul'un Fethi*—the "conquest of Constantinople," encouraged the Ottomans to

**Figure 1.68** A ferryboat on Bosporus whose name celebrates the "conquest" of Constantinople in 1453.
Source: Photo by the author.

claim global leadership in the Muslim *ummah*. They built their political theology on the Byzantine idea that whoever controls Constantinople is the ruler of the universal empire. After they established control also over Mecca and Medina in 1517, the Ottoman "sultans" (literally "rulers") claimed for themselves the status of caliphs. Gradually, almost all Muslim principalities in Europe, North Africa, and Middle East recognized Ottoman superiority.

There were two other Muslim empires to the east of the Ottomans: the Safavid Empire based in Persia (1501–1722) and the Mughal Empire based in India (1526–1739). The Ottoman and Safavid Empires often had tensions and sometimes even wars with each other. They diverged on the interpretation of Islam. The former protagonized Islam's Sunni version, while the latter, Shia. Their rivalry resembled the older antagonism between the Roman and Persian Empires. To insult the Safavid dynasty and emphasize their leadership in global Islam, the Ottomans claimed for themselves the title of the Persian shahs: the king of the kings. In the Turkish, this title was rendered as *Sulṭānü's-Selāṭīn*—"the sultan of sultans."

## Qayser-i Rûm

The Ottoman sultans adopted another imperial title, *Qayser-i Rûm*—"the Caesar of the Romans." They did so after they conquered Constantinople and, in this way, claimed that their Muslim empire was a rightful successor to the Roman Empire. For the Byzantine Christians, however, that empire ended with the fall of Constantinople. The polity that had been founded in Latium, presumably by

**Figure 1.69** Christ the Pantocrator from Mystras. This image, which expresses the Byzantine millennialist political theology, was produced in the period of the dramatic decline of Byzantium.
Source: Photo by the author.

the descendants of the Trojans, and then moved its center to Troy's vicinity, in Constantinople, ceased to exist after twenty-two centuries of glorious history. For Eastern Christians, the fall of Constantinople was the end of history and of the millennial Kingdom of God on earth. Curiously, the Christian Roman Empire indeed lasted about 1,000 years.

In contrast to the millennialist expectations, however, it did not end with the coming of Christ. A ruler that came claimed that Jesus is just a prophet, not God. For many Byzantines, Mehmed the Conqueror was an antichrist. Historian Michael Ducas (*c.* 1400–after 1462) summarized what these Byzantines thought about him:

> He (Mehmed), the Antichrist before Antichrist (ὁ πρὸ τοῦ ἀντιχρίστου ἀντίχριστος), the destroyer of Christ my shepherd, the enemy of the Cross and of those who trust in the One who was fixed upon it, his face wreathed in friendship, like a true disciple of that Satan who once took the form of a serpent, received their embassy, and wrote out new treaties. He swore by the god of their false prophet, and by the prophet whose

> name he bore, by his heathen books and by his angels and archangels, that he was their friend, and would remain for the whole of his life a friend and ally of the city and its ruler Constantine, together with all the country around it and its dependencies. (*Historia Turcobyzantina* 33.12; Melville-Jones 1972: 61)

People like Ducas could not accept a new reality. For them, despite its claims, the Ottoman state represented the opposite to everything they believed to be Roman. Some other Byzantines, however, believed that the history did not end with the sack of Constantinople. They developed positive thinking about it—like the one that had allowed many Christians in the third and fourth centuries to accept the pagan Roman Empire. One such Roman was Michael Kritovoulos (*c.* 1410–70), from the eastern Aegean Island of Imvros. He undertook an ambitious task to historicize Mehmed's rule and presented it in positive light. The style of his *History of Mehmed the Conqueror* resembles the encomiastic historiography applied to the Byzantine basileuses. Kritovoulos utilized the best of the Byzantine rhetoric to eulogize Mehmed, as this can be seen in the letter of dedication that he addressed to the sultan:

> To the Supreme Emperor, King of Kings, Mehmed, the fortunate, the victor, the winner of trophies, the triumphant, the invincible, Lord of land and sea, by the will of God, Kritovoulos the Islander, servant of thy servants.
>
> Seeing that you are the author of many great deeds, O most mighty Emperor, and in the belief that the many great achievements of generals and kings of old, nor merely of Persians and Greeks, are not worthy to be compared in glory and bravery and martial valor with yours, I do not think it just that they and their deeds and accomplishments, as set forth in the Greek historians and their writings from contemporary times and up to the present, should be celebrated and admired by all, and that these should enjoy everlasting remembrance, while you, so great and powerful a man, possessing almost all the lands under the sun, and glorious in your great and brilliant exploits, should have no witness, for the future, of your valor and the greatest and best of your deeds, like one of the unknown and inglorious ones who are till now unworthy of any memorial or record in Greek; or that the deeds of others, petty as they are in comparison to yours, should be better known and more famed before men because done by Greeks and in Greek history, while your accomplishments, vast as they are, and in no way inferior to those of Alexander the Macedonian, or of the generals and kings of his rank, should not be set forth in Greek to the Greeks, nor passed on to posterity for the undying praise and glory of your deeds. (*Ep. ad Mechmet II*; Kritovoulos 2019: 3)

Kritovoulos chose to walk in the shoes of Eusebius. He tried to sell to the Christians an empire, which they saw as hostile and incompatible with their faith. To make himself more convincing, he referred to the authority of the first ecumenical patriarch under the Muslim rule, Gennadius Scholarius (1400–73):

> During that period he (Mehmed) called back Gennadius, a very wise and remarkable man. He had already heard much through common report about the wisdom and prudence and virtue of this man. Therefore, immediately after the capture he sought for him, being anxious to see him and to hear some of his wisdom. And after a painstaking search he found him at Adrianople in a village, kept under guard in the home of one of the notables, but enjoying great honors. For his captor knew of his virtue, even though he himself was a military man. <. . .>
>
> In the end, he made him Patriarch and High Priest of the Christians, and gave him among many other rights and privileges the rule of the church and all its power and authority, no less than that enjoyed previously under the emperors. He also granted him the privilege of delivering before him fearlessly and freely many good disquisitions concerning the Christian faith and doctrine. And he himself went to his residence, taking with him the dignitaries and wise men of his court, and thus paid him great honor. And in many other ways he delighted the man. <. . .>
>
> Furthermore the Sultan gave back the church to the Christians, by the will of God, together with a large portion of its properties. (*Historiae* 5-8; Kritovoulos 2019: 94–5)

Kritovoulos presented Mehmed as a leader who cared about his new subjects. In this vein, the sultan picked up for the Christians of the city a new religious leader whom they would trust and made him their patriarch. Kritovoulos rendered his description in terms familiar to the Byzantines. For him, the new religious policies of Mehmed were similar to the traditional relationship between the church and the state in Byzantium. The new *Qayser-i Rûm* even chose a patriarch—just as the caesars before him had done in the frame of the Byzantine symphony. Kritovoulos believed himself and tried to convince his Roman fellows that Mehmed acted in the best interests of the Christian community of Constantinople.

Indeed, Gennadius Scholarius was respected in Constantinople. However, Mehmed's concern was not so much to give Christians the best leader, but to make sure that this leader serves his agenda. The sultan feared the intervention of the Western powers, that they could deprive him of his trophy—the Roman capital. This was the main reason why he promoted to the patriarchal office a public figure, who was outspoken in the criticism of the West. Gennadius was such a person. He had participated in the council of Ferrara-Florence, where he turned anti-Latin. Since then, he had repeatedly condemned the so-called Latinophrones—those Eastern Romans who sought the restoration of unity with Rome:

> Wretched Romans, how you have gone astray! You have rejected the hope of God and trusted in the strength of the Franks; you have lost your piety along with your city which is about to be destroyed. Lord have mercy on me. I testify before you that I am innocent of such transgression. Know, wretched citizens, what you are doing. Along with your impending captivity, you have forsaken the faith handed down from your

> fathers and assented to impiety. Woe unto you when you are judged! (*Historia Turcobyzantina* 36.3; Geanakoplos 1984: 388)

This kind of rhetoric was exactly what Mehmed needed to stabilize his rule in Constantinople, without being threatened by an alliance between the Byzantines of Constantinople with the Westerners. Gennadius played his role well. Many Christians eventually accepted that the sultan's turban for them is better than the papal tiara.[2] Centuries earlier, the anti-Chalcedonian Christians in Egypt and Syria were in the same way convinced by their religious leaders that Muslim Arabs were better for them than the Chalcedonian Romans. In the meantime, Mehmed gave back to the Christians only some churches that they had lost. The most important of them, Hagia Sophia, was transformed into a mosque. Since then, it has become a symbol of conquest.

## Muslim Symphonies

Kritovoulos presented the new mode of church-state relations under the Ottomans as an update of the Byzantine symphony. However exaggerating this might be, all three Muslim empires of the early modern period—Ottoman, Safavid, and Mughal—developed modes of relations with the Christian communities, which can be called, to use the wording of Sidney Griffith, "harmonious *convivencia*" (Griffith 2010: 22; see also Goddard 2020). This *convivencia* sometimes could be indeed quite harmonious, but more often was a mere symbiosis, or worse. The Mughals, especially under Akbar (r. 1556–1605), applied a remarkably tolerant policy to the non-Muslim religious groups in Hindustan (see Chatterjee 2014). They called this policy *sulh-i kull*, meaning "universal peace" or "absolute toleration." For a long time, the Mughals did not even impose *jizyah* on the Christians. The Safavids, in contrast, were usually intolerant to other religions in Iran, with rare exceptions (see Tiburcio 2020). The Ottomans balanced between these two policies (see Baer et al. 2009). They called their own policies *istimalet*, which can be translated as "trying to persuade" (see Barkey 2005). In other words, the Ottomans' main concern was to persuade non-Muslims to accept Islam, without much forcing them to conversion.

Unlike their Christian predecessors, the Muslim rulers did not need the church as a source of legitimacy. At the same time, the Ottoman sultans went further than other Muslim leaders in sharing some power with the church leaders: not on the imperial level, however, but locally. In its relations with the church, the Ottoman state more consistently than the earlier Arab states applied the principle of subsidiarity.

[2] This was a popular saying at that time, ascribed to the last Grand duke of the Byzantine Empire Loukas Notaras (1402–53).

It delegated to patriarchs and hierarchs a lot of responsibilities to manage both the ecclesial and the administrative matters of their communities, under only a general supervision of the Muslim authorities.

## Ethnarchs

Since the times of pentarchy, the key role in the church administration has been played by patriarchs, but they had to share their power with the synod. The role of the synod in the Ottoman period was the same or even greater than in the Byzantine past. Synod became a major stakeholder in the system of power-sharing within the Christian communities. It could do things that previously the emperors did, such as dethroning patriarchs. Patriarchs and their synods shared the following responsibilities, as Steven Runciman summarized them (Runciman 2003: 171–2):

1. Patriarch and his synod in the Ottoman period retained complete control over all ecclesial institutions and their possessions.
2. Together they elected and dismissed bishops. At the same time, all appointments to the hierarchy, including the patriarchal see, had to be confirmed by the Ottoman authorities. There was, therefore, a sort of synergy between the church and Muslim authorities.
3. In the spirit of this synergy, Ottomans could not prosecute any bishop without the permission of the patriarch.
4. In all cases relevant to clergy, including prosecuting crime, the church courts had exclusive jurisdiction.
5. As for the Christian laypersons, the ecclesial courts judged their cases only if they had some religion connotations, such as related to family, inheritance, and so on.
6. If both plaintiff and defendant were Christians, the ecclesial court could hear even cases related to money and property.
7. Ottoman courts could hear appeals to the decisions of the ecclesial courts, if one or both sides were not satisfied with these decisions. Ottoman judges (*kadı*) also heard cases involving treason, murder, and theft. However, if clergy were involved in such cases, they were still judged by ecclesial courts.

The most important bureaucratic task that the Ottomans expected patriarchs and bishops to perform, was to make sure that Christian individuals and institutions paid their taxes. Hierarchs became tax farmers (*mültezim*) (see Papademetriou 2015: 11), representing in this capacity the Muslim state. The church hierarchy effectively became a part of the Ottoman bureaucracy, although in a different way than it had been in the Byzantine Empire.

## May the Ottomans Be Praised

The church leaders had many reasons to be satisfied with the Ottoman "symphony." Some of them praised the Ottoman rule as superior even to that of Byzantium. Patriarch of Jerusalem Anthimus (1788–1808) could not contain his enthusiasm in the following panegyric:

> See how clearly our Lord, boundless in mercy and all-wise, had undertaken to guard once more the unsullied Holy and Orthodox faith. He raised out of nothing this powerful empire of the Ottomans, in place of our Roman Empire which had begun, in a certain way, to cause to deviate from the beliefs of the Orthodox faith, and he raised up the empire of the Ottomans higher than any other kingdom so as to show without doubt that it came about by divine will, and not by the power of man. <. . .> The almighty Lord, then, has placed over us this kingdom, "for there is no power but of God," so as to be to the people of the West a bridle, to us the people of the East a means of salvation. For this reason he puts into the heart of the sultan of these Ottomans an inclination to keep free the religious beliefs of our Orthodox faith and, as a work of supererogation, to protect them, even to the point of occasionally chastising Christians who deviate from their faith, that they have always before their eyes the fear of God. (*Διδασκαλία πατερική*; Ramet 1988: 46)

## Serving the Caliphate

According to the Muslim normative documents, such as the "Pact of Umar," Christians were not supposed to hold high administrative positions in an Islamic state. Indeed, some Muslim regimes, such as the Mamluk Sultanate in Egypt, consistently enforced such policies. Others were more flexible. As a result, there were many examples when not only church leaders but also lay Christians enjoyed considerable administrative authority. Christian laypersons could serve at various levels of the Muslim political establishment and society, as doctors, translators, businessmen, and so on.

Such was the family of John of Damascus, Mansur, whose members were responsible for collecting taxes in Damascus (see Awad 2018). An Eastern Syrian ʿAlī ibn Rabban al-Ṭabarī (d. *c.* 865) was a doctor and secretary to several ʿAbbasid caliphs. One of them, al-Mutawakkil (r. 847–61), made al-Ṭabarī a *nadīm*—a special companion. Al-Ṭabarī eventually converted to Islam. Fāṭimid caliphs in North Africa also relied in their administration on Christians. They especially valued Armenians and promoted some of them as high as to viziers.

Even more the Ottomans relied on the experienced Byzantine professionals. For example, two prominent members of the imperial Palaeologus family became viziers at the court of Mehmed II: Hass Murat Pasha and Mesih Pasha. However, they had to convert to Islam before taking such high positions. A class of the so-called phanariotes (*fenerliler*) flourished at the Ottoman court. They were called so after the name of the quarter in Istanbul, *Fener*, where many Christians lived. The patriarchal offices moved there and remain in the same place to our days.

## I.11.4 Disestablishmentness: Pro Et Contra

Not just groups and individuals in the church were benefited by the Ottoman regime. The church in general received numerous benefits from the separation from imperial power and from living on its own. These benefits are comparable with the ones that the Western church would receive from the Reformation half a century later. Because of the separation, theologians felt freer to defend the truth as they understood it. It is not a coincidence, for example, that the most substantiated theology of icons was articulated within the caliphate, by John of Damascus. He had more liberty than his Byzantine colleagues to criticize the iconoclastic policies of the Roman emperors.

The Muslim rule created a powerful momentum for emancipation within the church. It made the church's hierarchy and clergy closer to the people and communities. Laypeople again became important for the church. Hierarchs, clergy, and lay became more aware that they constitute the church together. Confusion between the church and the state, which the Byzantine symphony featured, dramatically decreased under the Ottomans. The pre-Constantinian ecclesial self-awareness reemerged within the Eastern churches.

At the same time, there were also numerous disadvantages for the church, stemming from being a suppressed minority in the Muslim state. Literacy among the Christian population dramatically dropped, while Christian literati lost interest and capacity for high-level theological reflections. This propelled superstitions and ignorance among the faithful and facilitated their conversion to Islam.

Heavy taxation (*jizyah*) forced poor Christian families to receive Islam. Sometimes they practiced two religions: Islam publicly and Christianity privately. Such families have been called crypto-Christian. They were similar to crypto-Jews who superficially converted first to Christianity and later to Islam but continued practicing Judaism. Crypto-Christians usually did not hold their double identity for a long time and eventually embraced Islam completely.

Conversion and reconversion from Islam to Christianity was punished with death. In rare cases, reconversion to Christianity was permitted, if the original conversion to Islam had been nonconsensual. Some reconverted Christians were prosecuted and punished with death. Christians considered them as "new martyrs" (Νεομάρτυρες). Several dozens of such Christians were executed for apostasy in the Arab caliphates and Turkic empires. Among them, for example, are Stamatios from Volos (1680), Theodore from Lesbos (1784), Theodore from Samothraki (1835), and others.

**Figure 1.70** A Janissary—a portrait by the Flemish painter Jean Baptiste Vanmour (1671–1737). Rijksmuseum in Amsterdam.
Source: Photo by the author.

The Ottomans practiced *devşirme*—collection of children from Christian families, mostly in the Balkans. It was a form of taxation imposed on Christians, the so-called blood tax. Such children were completely separated from their families and never reunited with them. They were trained for Ottoman bureaucratic and military elites. Those who proved to be good soldiers were enlisted to the imperial guard of Janissary. This military corps resembled the Roman praetorian guard. In this sense, to join the Janissary corps was a social lift, which even some Muslims dreamed to use. However, ascending this social lift came at a price, as these "new soldiers"—that is what the word *yeñiçeri* means—were brought up as Muslims and had loyalty only to their sultan. They cut off every connection with their parents, people, and faith. A Serb named Konstantin Mihailović from Ostrovica was contemporary to the siege of Constantinople. He was captured and had a chance to closely observe the upbringing of the Janissaries. He recorded his observations in Serbian language:

> Whenever the Turks invade foreign lands and capture their people an imperial scribe follows immediately behind them, and whatever boys there are, he takes them all into the Janissaries and gives five gold pieces for each one and sends them across the sea. There are about two thousand of these boys. If, however, the number of them from enemy peoples does not suffice, then he takes from the Christians in every village in

> his land who have boys, having established what is the most every village can give so that the quota will always be full. And the boys whom he takes in his own land are called *cilik*. <. . .> And at the court there are about four thousand Janissaries. (In Rodriguez 2015: 432)

The positive tendency of emancipation within the church under the Ottoman rule, when laypeople received more voice in the church, had its downside effect. A small lay group of the Phanariotes effectively monopolized control over the church. They managed appointments of new bishops and even patriarchal elections, often for money. They thus contributed to the spread of corruption in the church.

Corruption became a chronic problem of the Ottoman Empire and badly affected the churches in it. Responsibilities to collect and handle tax money, as well as donations from private sponsors, such as Phanariotes, tempted hierarchs to systemic abuses. For example, they developed a custom to bribe Ottoman officials to be promoted to higher ecclesial offices. Even the candidates to the patriarchal office competed with one another by offering higher bids (*bakšiš*) to the imperial authorities. The Ottomans encouraged this sort of corruption in the church. In result, during the Ottoman period, patriarchs usually stayed in their office between one and three years, before they were overbid by others (see Papademetriou 2015: 214). A huge pyramid of corruption was constructed, which pushed cash to flow from communities through various episcopal offices up to the office of the patriarch. The final beneficiaries of the cash flow were various Ottoman bureaucrats and the sultan himself. Such a pyramid of corruption was described in a complaint dating 1796:

> Those who in this century rise to office in the hierarchy are slaves and servants either of the patriarch or of the higher clergy. <. . .> [They] slave for their superiors with great patience, in the hope of becoming the successors of their own superior or to become bishops of another diocese. And when the chief priest of a diocese dies, immediately the lobbying begins in force, some going to the patriarch, some going to the senior clergy, some to the notables and their wives, and often to the magnates, and of the many one is lucky and receives the office. But as such as he succeeds, many expenses follow him, five, ten, fifteen thousand grosia. Some of these expenses are occasioned by gifts to the go-betweens, some to the Porte, some to the higher clergy, all with I.O.U.s. And if perhaps the diocese also has old debts from the previous incumbents, he promises [repayment of] all these, with 15 percent [interest] at least—and there is not a diocese that does not have debts of 10 or 20 thousand grosia. This new bishop, then, without having 50 grosia of his own, falls into an abyss of debt. He comes to the diocese and has no other way of repaying his debts and of holding the high office. <. . .> And no one dares to oppose him in the customary ecclesiastical revenues or gifts, those from ecclesiastics, priests and monasteries, as those from the laity. And with this power, immediately he arrives in the diocese, he begins to seek from the villages help for his new high priestly office of from 50 to 100 grosia, from the

monasteries of from 100 to 200 grosia, from the priests, some 10, some 15 grosia and so on, all excessive amounts. The poor cannot resist, fearful of excommunications, curses and exclusion from church, the notables are ashamed of the daily coffee and pipes and gifts. The ağas do not object, for he says to them: "It is the custom, as my predecessor took it, so do I want it." (In Clogg 1976: 65–6)

# I.12 Russian Modernity

While some Eastern churches had experienced separation from the state as early as during the Late Antiquity, most of them faced a new form of separation with the coming of Modernity. In the premodern times, the churches were usually separated from the state, because the latter had preferred another religion or Christian confession as its partner. In modern times, most states became secular.

In most countries of the free world, secularization was milder and looked more like a boycott of religion. Religion was not persecuted there. Democratic states in many cases have preserved some formal or informal partnership with the church. Sometimes, the churches have retained their established status, such as in the case of the Orthodox Church of Greece.

The situation was different in the countries of the Soviet bloc. Most of them, by a remarkable coincidence, had been Orthodox and featuring symphonic relationship with the church. Under the pressure of the communist ideology, which had declared religion "the opium of the people," these states reversed symphony with the churches to its opposite—persecutions.

Whether in the form of persecution or boycott, the process of secularization implies privatization of religion. Religion is more or less forcefully pushed from the public square and confined to private homes. It ceased to be a source of legitimization for political authority. Moreover, some political authorities, on both sides of the Iron Curtain, made secularization a new source of their legitimacy. They also hardly allowed the church to share in any power.

For the Eastern Christian churches, leaving the public square was not a completely new experience, as we have demonstrated earlier. Christianity emerged as a private religion, in the period when all spaces were completely occupied by the Greco-Roman religion. Owing to Constantine and his successors, Christianity turned public. Initially, it shared Roman fora with the traditional polytheistic religions. Gradually, Christianity forced its competitors to vacate the fora. As pieces of the Roman Empire went under Muslim control, Christianity had to yield public spaces to Islam. Eventually, only in the Russian Empire, the church enjoyed monopoly in the public space.

Nevertheless, even in the tsarist Russia, the church was restricted in its public activities. After the reforms of Peter I, the Russian church became a part of the imperial machinery, with limited freedom to decide on its own. The institute of patriarchs was substituted by the Holy Synod, which effectively acted as a proxy agent for the imperial administration. *Ober-prokuror*—a secular official accountable to the tsar—controlled the Synod completely. The church, as a result, played more a decorative role in the Russian public square. It provided the empire with legitimacy; the empire, however, did not share power with the church.

The situation changed after the Russian Republic substituted the empire, following the February Revolution of 1917. This republic lived short and, after the October Revolution of 1917, was replaced by the Bolshevik dictatorship. During these several republican months, the Russian church enjoyed unprecedented freedom.

The church seized new opportunities provided by the republican regime and convened a council in Moscow. In the imperial period, the Russian church was not allowed to hold its councils. The Moscow council, which continued its work through 1918, became a landmark in the modern history of Eastern Christianity. On the one hand, it continued a series of the mixed clerical-laic assemblies (Κληρικολαϊκές συνελεύσεις) in the Balkans during the nineteenth century. On the other hand, the "Local council of the Orthodox Russian Church"—so it called itself, adopted guidelines for a church living in the situation of separation from the state and escalating secularization. The council offered an emancipatory program of *aggiornamento*, which anticipated a similar program of the Vatican II (see Destivelle 2015; Cunningham 2002). Among other important decisions, the Moscow council of 1917–18 postulated the following:

> The Orthodox Church in Russia is independent from the state regarding the doctrines of faith and morality, regarding worship, internal church discipline and in its relations with other autocephalous Churches. On the basis of its dogmatic and canonical principles, it exercises the rights of self-definition and self-control in the matters of church legislation, management and judgement. (Article 2 from the definition of the council on December 2, 1917; Священный Собор Православной Российской Церкви 1918)

A secretary of the council, Sergiy Bulgakov (1871–1944), who would become one of the most prominent Orthodox theologians in the twentieth century, advocated for the separation of the church from the state as a precondition for a successful *aggiornamento*. Following the Madisonian train of thought, he argued that separation is beneficial for the church:

> Separation of Church and state, under different forms, has replaced the ancient alliance. This separation, at first imposed by force, has been accepted by the Orthodox Church also, for it corresponds with its dignity and its vocation. <. . .> The liberty <. . .> is now

> the regime most favorable to the Church, most normal for it; it frees the Church from the temptations of clericalism and assures it development without hindrance. Doubtless this system is valid only provisionally, depending upon its historic usefulness. <. . .> New dangers, new difficulties arise in this way, analogous to those which existed at the time of the alliance between Church and state. The Church may be led to interfere in party politics: the latter, in its turn, may divert the Church from its true path. But an essential advantage remains: the Church exercises its influence on souls by the way of liberty, which alone corresponds to Christian dignity, not by that of constraint. (Bulgakov 1988: 162–4)

Bulgakov warned that the separation of the church from the state also has its reverse side: the church becomes more vulnerable to partisan ideologies. The phenomenon of ideology is deeply embedded in Modernity. It was designed as secular and originally intended to substitute religion. In this sense, ideology and religion are supposed to be incompatible. Nevertheless, in their modern history, the churches often embarked on secular ideologies. For some churches, ideology to a significant extent substituted theology.

# I.13
# National Awakening and Nationalism

## Nationalism as Ideology

The most popular ideology in the Eastern Christian milieu is nationalism (see Kedourie 1996: xiii). Nationalism is an ideology in the sense that it can mobilize masses of people and drive them to political goals, such as the unity of a people or the formation of a national state. To achieve these goals, the nationalist ideology may employ religious symbols and traditions. It nevertheless remains profoundly secular, under the religious guise. Nationalism is rooted in Romanticism. Most modern nations have been constructed on idealized past: for the Greeks, for example, it was Ancient Athens and Byzantium, for the Bulgars and Serbians—their medieval empires, for the Armenians—the Cilician kingdom, and so on. Because Christianity was a part of this past, it also became a part of the national and nationalistic narratives. For many nationalists, Christianity has lost its own value and is appreciated only as a part of the imagined past.

A specific precondition of the Eastern Christian nationalism is a tradition of structuring the church locally. In contrast to the Christian West, where Roman papacy substituted locality with universal jurisdiction, the Eastern churches remained organized around particular *loci*. Locality continues defining Christianity in the East. Under the influence of nationalist ideology, locality, in the form of the church's autocephaly, contributes to the self-determination of the Orthodox peoples.

## Millets

Another precondition for Eastern Christian nationalism is the way, in which religious minorities were structured in the Ottoman Empire. As was mentioned earlier, the Ottomans applied to these minorities the principle of subsidiarity. Their religious leaders were endowed with responsibilities to manage their internal life and represented them to the central authorities. In the early Ottoman period, these minorities were called *tâ'ife*—a group, class, or a tribe, or *cema'at*—a religious congregation. In the later period, they became known as *millet* (see Kenanoğlu 2017). An Armenian translator (*dragoman*) for the Swedish embassy in Istanbul, Muradcan Tosunyan (1740–1807), reported on the way the religious minorities were organized in his time:

> The tributary subjects are divided into three peoples: The Greeks (Roum), the Armenians (Ermeni) and the Israelites (Yahudi). They are different in all things, culture, language, usage, and character. Each has its own spiritual leader. Those of the first two have the title patriarch, Patrik. The Jews call theirs Grand Rabi, Khakham Baschy. The primates are elected from among the notables of their people, lay and clergy. But, they need to be confirmed by the sultan. Their jurisdiction is at the same time spiritual and temporal. Whenever there is a need to punish an individual of their religion, they have the right to imprison him, without any other formality but to report it to the state. It is through this body that these primates shall publish all ordinances relating to their respective nations. (In Papademetriou 2015: 35)

## *Tanzimat*

The millet system was completed in the period of the *Tanzimat* reforms (1839–76) (see Özyasar 2019). Western powers pressed the Ottomans to carry out these reforms. Among other goals, the *Tanzimat* intended to equalize the rights of non-Muslims with the Muslims. As a first step in this direction, Sultan Abdülmecid (r. 1839–61) declared by his edict (*hatt-i sharif*) of Gülhane that all inhabitants of the empire are protected by the Ottoman law. The next step was the abolition of *jizyah* and of capital punishment for apostasy from Islam, in 1840. The *hatt-ı humayun* of 1856 established formal equality for all citizens regardless of their religion.

The *Tanzimat* reforms indeed improved conditions for the Eastern Christian minorities in the Ottoman Empire. At the same time, they facilitated the transformation of their originally religious identities to ethnic ones. The process of such transformation began even before the reforms started. Thus, it had led to the creation in 1832 of an independent Greek state, following the liberation revolution of 1821.

## Phyletism

The *Tanzimat* reforms created a stronger momentum for some other Orthodox nations in the Balkans for their own national struggles. One of such nations was Bulgar. Even before gaining their independence from the Ottoman Empire, the

Bulgars declared in 1870 independence of their church from the Ecumenical Patriarchate. They followed the pattern established by the Greeks. After having declared their independence in 1821, the Greeks proceeded to declaring autocephaly from the Patriarchate of Constantinople in 1833. Since then, autocephaly had become an attribute of an Orthodox state seeking liberation from an empire. This created a new model of autocephaly different from the older medieval model, when autocephaly was perceived as an attribute of an emerging empire.

The response of the Ecumenical Patriarchate to both Greek and Bulgarian declarations of autocephaly was negative. It was a response of the institute that safeguarded both its own interests and the interests of the empire. The church of Constantinople did not recognize the Greek autocephaly for almost twenty years, until 1850. During this time, the Ecumenical patriarchate did not maintain communion with the Church of Greece. Its reaction to the Bulgarian attempt at independence was more severe: the entire church was excommunicated. The Ecumenical patriarchate restored its communion with the Church of Bulgaria only in 1945.

In 1872, the patriarchate convened a "Great local council" in Constantinople, which condemned "phyletism." This neologism literally means "tribalism." Initially, it had a narrow meaning referring to attempts at establishing national ecclesial jurisdiction in parallel to the existent jurisdictions—something that the Bulgars in Constantinople and elsewhere in the Ottoman Empire tried to do. Later, "phyletism" came to denote more broadly the ideology of nationalism as influencing ecclesial policies. The council's own definition of phyletism is as follows:

> We denounce, penalize, and condemn phyletism (φυλετισμόν), i.e., tribal differentiations (φυλετικαὶ διακρίσεις), national rows (ἐθνικὰς ἔρεις), envies (ζήλους), and confrontations in the church of Christ, as opposite to the teaching of the Gospel and to the sacred canons of our blessed Fathers. (Article 1 of the *Definition*; in Καρμήρης 1968: 1015)

# Nations against Empires

The council of 1872 condemned nationalism from the imperial perspective. Its standpoint corresponded to the policies of the Ottoman Empire that oppressed the national awakening of its minorities. Same policies were implemented by all the empires of that time, where the Eastern Christians lived as religious minorities, including Habsburg and British ones. Even the Russian Empire, despite its phyletistic ideology of Panslavism (see Erickson 2013), mostly supported the Patriarchate of Constantinople in its struggle to preserve integrity.

National awakening of the Orthodox minorities in the nineteenth-century's empires was initially a liberation movement. It created a momentum for a better social cohesion and more equality within a nation. It utilized and reshaped the ancient institute of autocephaly to secure national cohesion and equality. Autocephaly in the nineteenth century, thus, became effectively an anti-imperial instrument of decolonization. In this spirit, some—not all—Orthodox nations managed to achieve their independence and secured autocephaly for their churches. Thus, the Church of Romania in 1865 and the Church of Serbia in 1920 were assembled from the parts that had belonged to the Ottoman and Habsburg Empires.

The liberation momentum that drove national awakening and autocephalist movements had its downsides. New autocephalous churches, which were established in the spirit of anti-colonialism, soon found themselves completely dependent on their national states. The Church of Greece, which had been an archetype for the anti-colonial autocephalies of the modern time, also set a pattern of complete submission to the state. The decree of its independence, promulgated in 1833, made sure that the king is the leader (ἀρχηγός) of the church in administrative matters (Article 1); the members of the Synod (which, by the way, is of the kingdom and not of the church (Ἱερᾶ Σύνοδος τοῦ Βασιλείου τῆς Ἑλλάδος)) are appointed by the government (Articles 2–3) and make oath to the king (πίστιν εἰς τὸν Βασιλέα) (see Κωνσταντινίδης 2000: 16).

The emancipatory national awakening often turned to nationalism, understood as ethnic exclusivism. While in the empires, the oppressed nations struggled for more inclusivity for themselves. After having liberated themselves from the imperial yoke, however, they often adopted policies that oppressed their minorities and neighbors. In the Ottoman and Habsburg Empires, the Orthodox nations of Greeks, Bulgars, Serbs, Romanians, and so on fought together for their liberation. Having achieved freedom, they turned on each other. This happened during the Balkan Wars (see Yavuz & Blumi 2013; Hall 2010; Gerolymatos 2003). In the First Balkan War, which lasted from October 1912 through May 1913, the coalition of the Orthodox ex-Ottoman nations of Bulgaria, Serbia, Greece, and Montenegro together attacked the Ottoman Empire. However, in the second war, which started immediately after the first one, in June 1913, the Orthodox nations began fighting each other: Bulgaria attacked Serbia and Greece, while the Romanians and Ottomans attacked Bulgaria.

# I.14
# Turkish Genocides

## Armenian National Awakening

There were nations who won in their fight against empires, and nations who lost. The nation that lost most was Armenia. About one and half million Armenians perished in the genocide. Armenia is one of the most ancient nations in the world. It was the first nation in world history to adopt Christianity as the state religion. During the Antiquity and Middle Ages, the Armenian people had its states, but also lived in the large empires: Roman, Persian, and Muslim ones. In the nineteenth century, most Armenians lived in the Ottoman and Russian Empires.

National ideology, which was born in the West and spread to the East, also affected the Armenians. The Greek liberation Revolution of 1821 triggered similar processes in the Armenian community. Intellectuals like Nahabed Rusinian (1819–76) helped planting the Western national ideology in the Armenian soil. This soil was under Ottoman and Russian jurisdictions—at the intersection of their vital geopolitical interests. Both rival empires were afraid of the Armenian national awakening. They considered it a threat for themselves, but also an opportunity to use it against each other.

The Armenians adopted two different approaches to these empires. The active minority wanted to have their own state. This was a program of the Social Democrat Hunchakian Party (or simply Hunchak Party). More popular was the Armenian Revolutionary Federation, also known as *Dashnaktsutyun*. It did not focus on the Armenian independence but envisaged a harmonious and autonomous coexistence of the Armenian people with the two empires. This was a vision shared by most Armenians.

## Ottoman Empire against Nations

The Armenians were benefited by the *Tanzimat* reforms and actively contributed to them. For example, an Armenian intellectual Krikor Odian (1834–87) was one of the drafters of the Ottoman constitution (1876), which constituted the culmination of the reforms. However, following the defeats in the war with Russia during 1877–8, the Ottomans reversed the reforms. Sultan Abdülhamid II (r. 1876–1909) reestablished absolute rule and abolished the constitution. He also developed paranoia about the assumed separatism of the Christian minorities, primarily the Armenians. He suspected that they wanted to create their own state in Anatolia, just as the Bulgars had created their state in the Balkans. Most Armenians, it seems, did not want this, but this did not help them. Abdülhamid decided to preventively punish them. He did not make direct orders, but used various proxy groups, such as Kurds, Chechens, and Circassians, to kill Armenians and force them to leave their lands. It is estimated that during the anti-Armenian pogroms in the period of 1894–6, between 100,000 and 300,000 Armenians died. Other Christian minorities suffered as well, including Greeks and Assyrians.

## Young Turks

The reactionary politics of Abdülhamid II targeted not only Christian minorities, but also progressivist Turks. In 1889, they established the Committee of Union and Progress (CUP) and became known as "Young Turks." They wanted the *Tanzimat* reforms to continue and Turkey to be included to the family of the European nations. In 1908, they carried out a successful revolution and forced the sultan to restore the constitution of 1876. The sultan had also to share power with the CUP. In 1913, as the result of a coup d'état, the CUP led by Mehmed Talât (1874–1921) and Ismail Enver (1881–1922) assumed the entire power in the state.

The Young Turks accused the sultanic ancien régime of inefficiency, losing the Balkan War, and oppressing minorities. Initially, their agenda was coherent with the agendas of such parties as *Dashnaktsutyun*. In 1909, the Dashnaks signed an agreement with the Young Turks, where they pledged to safeguard "the sacred Ottoman fatherland from separation and division." The CUP's ideology was national: it marked the national awakening of the Turkish peoples who got tired of their empire. They wanted a modernized national state.

However, after the Young Turks assumed all political power, they changed their attitude to the Christian minorities and national politics. From an inclusivist and emancipatory, they turned to an excluding and oppressive power. Something similar had happened in the Balkans to the Eastern Christian nations, which originally were driven by the ideas of emancipation, and, after establishing their national states, they turned increasingly nationalistic and oppressive. Following the same trajectory, the Turkish national awakening transformed to Panturkism.

It was similar to the contemporary ideologies of Pangermanism or Panslavism. Panturkism or Panturanism meant that the centripetal forces holding the Turkish state together were Turkish language and culture, and not the existent borders or even Islam. Other national identities, including Slavic, Armenian, and even Arabic, were perceived as dangerously centrifugal. The Turkish state in this period was constantly challenged by the Western powers and Russia. The Young Turks, consequently, developed the same paranoia about the ostensible collaboration of the Ottoman Christians with these powers that earlier Abdülhamid had demonstrated.

## Genocide under the Young Turks

Although earlier the Young Turks had criticized the Ottoman sultanate for violence against minorities, they eventually arrived at even worse policies. The CUP's government adopted the old practices of arresting, torturing, killing, and raping. They invented a new method of mass killings: death marches. Local administrations were instructed to group up minorities, which the central government wanted to extinguish, in columns and forced them to walk hundreds of miles to a desert. Most people in these columns died of dehydration, hunger, diseases, and exhaustion. Many were killed by gangs and looters. Those who survived the march were gathered in concentration camps in Syria and exterminated. Victoria Barutjibashian was one of many witnesses of such mass deportations. Her family was forced to leave Erzurum. Together with other Armenian families, they formed a column, which was soon robbed by a gang. The following day, the Turkish gendarmes

> separated the men, one by one, and shot them, <. . .> every male above fifteen years old. By my side were killed two priests, one of them over ninety years of age.

Gangsters, who were assisted by locals,

> took all the good-looking women and carried them off on their horses. <. . .> Among them my sister, whose one-year-old baby they threw away; a Turk picked it up and carried it off. <. . .> My mother walked till she could walk no farther, and dropped by the roadside on a mountain top. (In Morris & Zeevi 2019: 177–8)

Victoria survived because she decided to convert to Islam. For many Christians, this was the only escape. At some point, the Turkish authorities decided not to spare even the converts, believing their conversion to be insincere.

Although the Armenians were killed and persecuted before and after the Young Turks, the CUP's policies were the cruelest. The extermination of the Armenians

**Figure 1.71** Religious leaders commemorating the centennial of the Armenian genocide at the Memorial (*Tsitsernakaberd*) in Yerevan.
Source: Photo by the author.

under the Young Turks constitutes the core of the Armenian genocide (see Hovannisian 2017; Hovannisian 2014; Freedman 2009). Rafał Lemkin (1900–59) is known to having been moved by the Turkish crimes against the Armenians to coin the word "genocide."

## Genocide of (As)Syrians

Although Turkish nationalists hated the Armenians most, they also purged other Christian minorities, such as Greeks and Assyrians/Syrians. The latter, before the First World War, counted more than half a million people on the Ottoman territories. They spoke Turkish but also used Syriac language, especially in their worship. They included the representatives of the historical Western and Eastern Syriac communities, that is, both supporters and adversaries of the council of Ephesus (431). Many of them differentiated between the Syriac and Assyrian identities. The Turks, however, treated them in the same way. In the period between 1914 and 1924, most of them were killed or forced to leave their homelands.

Tur Abdin became the epicenter of what has been branded as the Assyrian genocide, *Sayfo* (see Gaunt et al. 2019; Travis 2017; Yacoub & Ferguson 2016). In June 1915, most Armenian and Assyrian males of the ancient city of Nusaybin (Nisibis) were arrested and then executed. A few days later, Christian women were also slaughtered, some of them in a stone quarry. In August of the same year, a local Syriac Jacobite community was decimated, together with its bishop. A member of the Assyrian community, Judad Abdarova, left one of many testimonies about the Turkish atrocities against this community:

> They were beaten from all sides and ordered to become Muslims, but they refused. Before my eyes Hurshid Bey (i.e., a Turkish or Kurdish commander) shot my sons with a pistol. <. . .> I tried to protect my husband, hut Hurshid Bey kicked me in the face, knocking out two teeth. Then he shot my husband with six bullets <. . .> Hurshid Bey ordered that the corpses be smeared with excrement. Over the following four days dogs ate the corpses. Then Hurshid ordered that the corpses be thrown in the latrine. <. . .> Hurshid had the whole village burned and twelve people killed. <. . .> All the women, virgins, and children were taken captive and brought to the village of Atis. There they had to choose: Islam or death. 150 women and girls were forced to become the wives of Hurshid Bey's relatives. Of all the prisoners, only I remained, because Hurshid Bey knew that I was the cousin of the patriarch. <. . .> I was on the road for two days. I was so tired that I had to leave two of my small children under a tree. <. . .> I know nothing of their fate. My small daughter died of hunger on the way. (In Morris & Zeevi 2019: 375–6)

**Figure 1.72** The streets of the ancient Nisibis, now Nusaybin in Turkey.
Source: Photo by the author.

Judad Abdarova was spared because she was a cousin of the patriarch. A few years later, even the patriarch's life would not be spared. In 1918, Kurds murdered the Assyrian Catholicos Mar Shimun XIX Benyamin (1887–1918), together with dozens of his supporters.

## Genocide of Greeks

The (As)Syrians were not affected by the nationalist ideas as much as the Greeks. The independent Greek state was a constant source of nationalistic aspirations for the Ottoman Greeks. In Greece of that time, the so called Great Idea became a governmental program. This idea envisaged the expansion of the Greek state to the territories, which in the past belonged to the Greeks, particularly in Asia Minor. Millions of Greeks lived on those territories, especially in Constantinople, Smyrna, and the coast around it, as well as on the southern coast of Black Sea—Pontus.

Many Pontic Greeks entertained the idea of their own state, which could eventually join Greece. During the First World War and especially after the Greek army landed in 1915 in Smyrna, the Turkish government became highly concerned, to the degree of paranoia, about the threat coming from Pontus. The governmental reactions to the Pontic separatism, be it real or imagined, were the same as to the potential Armenian separatism: they led to what has been called Pontic genocide. The Young Turks

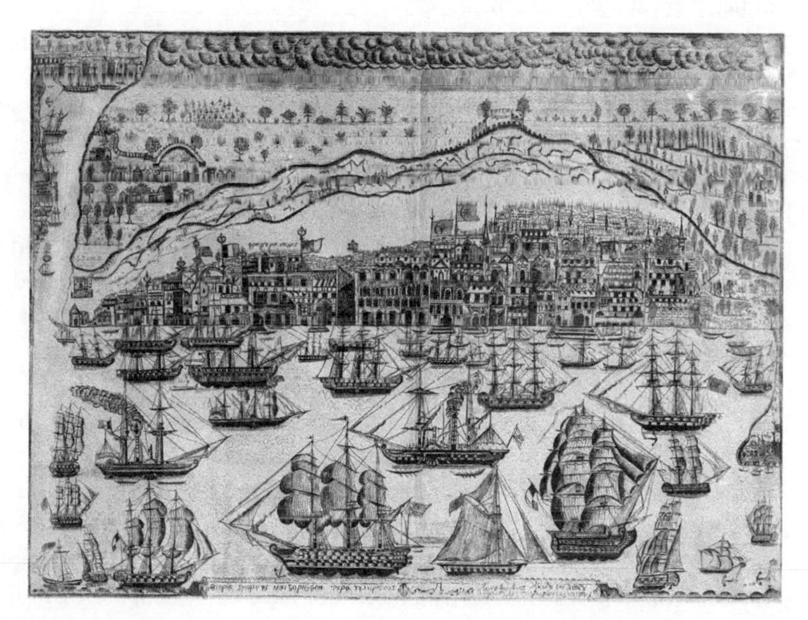

**Figure 1.73** Smyrna. Engraving by Konstantinos Kaldis (1845). Benaki Museum in Athens.

Source: Photo by the author.

applied to the Pontic Greeks the same methods of exterminations as they did to the Armenians, including death marches.

The Ottomans began massively uprooting Greeks even before the Armenian genocide. In the first half of 1914, between 100,000 and 200,000 Greeks were displaced, mostly from the northwestern coast of Asia Minor. The Turks harassed the Greeks, forcing them to leave their homes and emigrate to Greece. During the First World War, more than half a million Greeks left their homeland. After the war, between 1919 and 1923, more than a million Greeks were killed or relocated. During 1923–4, most of those who had stayed had to leave in the frame of populations' exchange. They went to Greece, while the Muslims from Greece moved to Turkey.

The ethnic cleansing began under the Ottomans in the 1890s, culminated under the Young Turks in 1915–16, and continued after the Turkish Republic was established in 1923. It diminished the Christian population of Asia Minor by four million. What happened to these millions has been summarized in a conversation of a Pontic girl Sano Halo with a local priest, as it was recorded by Sano's daughter Thea in her best-selling autobiographical novel:

> In Karabahçe, in the ruined house where we had first taken shelter, I found the priest from our village sitting with a small group of people. I recognized his apple cheeks above his long, thick beard. He still wore the robe, now patched here and there. His shoulders stooped as if the robe itself weighed him down.
>
> As I entered the dimly lit room, he looked up at me. His face was illuminated by a few candles that sat lighted on the floor.
>
> "You've been crying," he said. "Come sit here with us and tell me what has happened."
>
> Again I burst into tears and try as I might, I couldn't speak.
>
> "Bring her some tea," he said to one of the women. "Come sit beside me and rest and when you are ready, you will tell me."
>
> I sat beside him choking back my tears until finally my heaving chest became calm as I listened to his gentle voice in our own language.
>
> "General Mustafa Kemal has pushed the Greeks out of Smyrna," he said to the group gathered around him, continuing where he had left off when I entered. "They are saying the Greeks burned the city before retreating, but others say it was not the Greeks, but the Turks themselves who deliberately set the fire. Only the Turkish quarter was left standing in Smyrna."
>
> "Does it mean that we are lost forever in this place then, Father?" one man asked. "Will we never be able to go home?"
>
> "I don't know, son," the priest said. "It's not a good sign. If the Greeks lose . . ." He broke off and shook his head. "They have moved many of the Greeks to Greece. At least those living on the western coast. But many more have died or were slaughtered. They say that many thousands of Armenians too have been slaughtered in the east. The Greek forces have been very strong until now. It's a major defeat. We can only wait and see."
>
> "Are they getting rid of all the Christian population, Father?" another man asked.

**Figure 1.74** Interior of an abandoned Greek church in Cappadocia.
Source: Photo by the author.

"It looks like that is so. Perhaps it is only a matter of time before they chase the rest of these Assyrians out also, and any other Christians living here in the south. We will have to move on too."

I curled up beside him on the mat where he sat, wondering where I would go, and soon fell asleep, lulled by his voice. (Halo 2001: 291–2)

# I.15
## -isms

Not only the Turkish authorities should be blamed for the atrocities against the Christian minorities. These atrocities were often provoked by the Christian states, which sought to infringe on Turkish sovereignty. They were driven by the ideologies that made references to the Roman/Byzantine Empire. In their expansionism, these Christian states usually used the pretext of protecting Christian population, but in effect were inspired by various forms of Romanism/Byzantinism.

## Byzantinism

Such Byzantinist ideology of "Moscow—the third Rome," for example, incited Russia to go to war against Turkey in 1877–8. The Ottoman defeat in this war led to the curtailment of the *Tanzimat* reforms. Italy waged similar wars against Turkey in Libya (Tripolitana) and the Dodecanese Islands in the eastern Aegean Sea in 1911–12. The Italian government thus hoped to restore pieces of the ancient Roman Empire. Some Orthodox nations in the Balkans that had recently emerged from the Ottoman Empire rushed to restore their own imagined medieval empires and thus ignited the Balkan Wars. These wars shocked the Young Turks and forced them into making a U-turn in their national policies—toward the genocides. The so-called Great Idea (Μεγάλη Ἰδέα) (see Koslin 1958), which was a form of Byzantinism, drove the Greek government to the shady enterprise of occupying the Turkish heartland in Anatolia. This enterprise led to the "Micrasian catastrophe," when the Greek army had to abandon Asia Minor (see Milton 2009). Most local Greeks who remained there after the earlier ethnic cleansing had to leave their homelands. All these catastrophes and genocides were a price paid for various forms of Byzantinism.

Irresponsible dreams about the restoration of Byzantium urged the Orthodox churches to support various dictatorships during the twentieth century, especially in the interwar period. The ideology of Byzantinism, for instance, underpinned the semi-fascist regimes of General Ioannis Metaxas (r. 1936–41) and the so-called Black

Colonels (1967–74) in Greece, as well as of King Carol II (r. 1930–40) and General Ion Antonescu (r. 1940–4) in Romania (see Deletant 2006). Numerous Romanian bishops and priests in the interwar period identified themselves with the fascist "Legion of Archangel Michael" (*Legiunea Arhanghelului Mihail*). The very name of this movement, "Legion," was a reference to the conquest of Dacia by Roman legions. Romanian fascism (see Bejan 2020) was a form of Byzantinist ideology.

## Orthodoxism and Traditionalism

A prominent Romanian theologian Nichifor Crainic (1889–1972) articulated the basics of the fascist and semi-fascist ideologies, which some Orthodox churches embraced during the twentieth century (see Morariu 2020). There is a revival of such ideologies in the twenty-first century. They have become known under the umbrella name of "Orthodoxism" (see Clark 2018: 113–15). Orthodoxisms usually consist of two ingredients: Byzantinism and nationalism. Such a combination per se is peculiar. Byzantium was a multinational entity and, as such, incompatible with the ethnic exclusivism of modern nationalist ideologies. Nevertheless, Orthodox ideologues, such as Crainic, managed to pack Byzantinism and nationalism into a single ideology, close to fascism and Nazism:

> A great river of orientalism, then, flowed in the riverbed of our people's soul. Byzantium and Kiev took their tool as it passed by, flowed underneath Orthodoxy—that import, which in time developed into the reservoir of our primitive forces. [Orthodoxy] thus forms part of our people's wealth and constitutes yet a power by which our patriarchal mentality, our native genius, differentiates itself from and resists the currents of European civilization, so fresh in their historical origin. (Crainic 1924: 185; Biliuță 2007: 52)

The combination of Byzantinism and nationalism amplified anti-Semitism in some Orthodox countries, especially during the interwar period. Most conservative Orthodox public thinkers in the period before the Holocaust were openly anti-Semitic. Crainic, for instance, went as far as arguing that Jesus Christ could not be a Jew (see Romocea 2011: 135). He described the clash between the liberal and conservative factions in the contemporary society as a "war of the Talmud against the Gospel of Christ":

> Europe today is not stirred by a simple social war, nor by an ideological war. Today Europe is stirred by the war of the Talmud against the Gospel of Christ. The democratic regime of the last century, its unlimited liberties in paroxysm after world peace, has given the Jewish people an insane courage and the messianic frenzy of the White Horse. <. . .> Since the French revolution, Judaism has won success after success, and its progressive domination in the world is blinding it to its limitations. However, these

> excesses of an immoderate people will be the downfall of Judaism. (Crainic 1997; 143; Biliuţă 2007: 70)

Crainic called himself and his confederates "traditionalists" (Crainic 1996: 126–7). Traditionalism has become another face of the same ideology of Byzantinism-Orthodoxism. The Orthodox churches during the twentieth century endorsed fascist regimes in their own and other countries, because these regimes appealed to the traditional values. The problem of traditionalism, in addition to legitimizing dictatorships, is that it substitutes the Tradition in the sense of Revelation being transmitted to and through the church, with the idolatrous veneration of the past. It is usually selective about what exactly in the past it wants to worship. The criteria for such selection are often shaped by ideological conservatism, which many Eastern Christians confuse with Orthodoxy.

# I.16
# Eastern Christianity and Communism

Most Eastern European nations, which in the interwar period developed right-wing dictatorships, after the Second World War switched to the opposite left-wing ideologies. The leftist regimes were instated and supported by the Soviet Union. The churches in these countries had to accommodate themselves to the new political realities and sometimes made a U-turn in their ideological preferences. Most hierarchs chose to collaborate with the new regimes, even though the latter had declared themselves atheist. Official theologians, following the ideological mainstream, invented theological justification for the leftist ideologies. For example, they drew parallels between communism and Christianity, stressing communal life, equality, and sharing property. Similarly to Eusebius with the Roman Empire and Kritovoulos with the Ottoman Empire, some Russian hierarchs and theologians became advocates for the Soviet atheist quasi-empire.

## Soviet Persecutions

Both Russian revolutions of 1917, in February and October, polarized the Russian church and led to divisions and schisms within it. These schisms were along ideological lines. One part of the church remained faithful to the ideals of the Russian monarchy. This part organized itself in what would become known as the Russian Orthodox Church Outside Russia (ROCOR). Another part complied with the republican ideals of the February Revolution. That revolution, as was mentioned earlier, opened a door to the short-lived Russian democracy and republic. The Great council of Moscow 1917–18 encapsulated the republicanism of the February Revolution. The ideals of the republic and of the Great council survived in a part of the Russian church abroad, which became known as the Russian exarchate of the Ecumenical Patriarchate. The Moscow Patriarchate—the third part of the Russian Orthodoxy—eventually developed symbiosis with the Soviet regime and the communist ideology.

This church accommodated itself to the new Soviet realities with great pain and many sacrifices. A considerable number of its members did not accept these realities. They either were killed by the Soviet regime or ended up in the underground (see Fletcher 1971). Some of the former became known as "new martyrs" (*novomucheniki*), while many of the latter broke relations with the official church and formed several sects.

Repressions against the church began soon after the Bolsheviks took power in their hands on October 25 (November 7) of 1917. The leader of the Bolshevik Revolution, Vladimir Lenin (1870–1924), promulgated in January (February according to the Gregorian calendar) of 1918 a decree, which radically separated the church from the state. Following the decree, the Bolshevik authorities launched a campaign of confiscating ecclesiastical properties. Soon, the first victims of the persecutions fell, including senior hierarchs: Metropolitans Vladimir of Kyiv (1848–1918) and Veniamin of Sankt Petersburg (1873–1922).

The persecutions culminated during the so-called "Great terror" of 1937–8 instigated by Joseph Stalin. They became less intensive, when the Second World War began. By 1939, only around 100 churches remained open in the entire Soviet Union, out of about 60,000 in 1917 (see Shevzov 2004). Approximately 400 bishops were persecuted and 300 died. Thousands clergymen and over half a million laypersons perished in the Soviet prisons and the system of forced labor camps coordinated by the "Main Directorate of Camps" (GULAG). Of them, over 36,000 are regarded martyrs, according to the database of the St. Tikhon's Orthodox Humanitarian University (http://martyrs.pstbi.ru/).

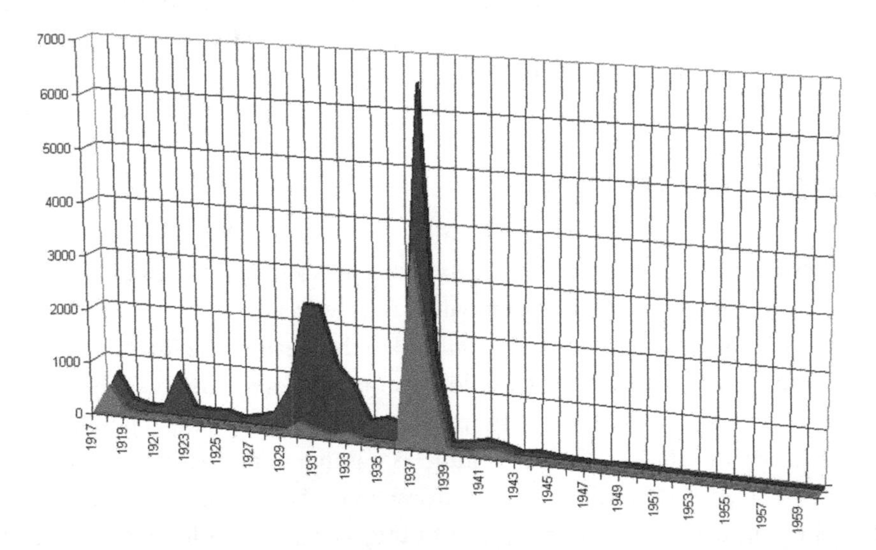


**Figure 1.75** Soviet persecutions against the Russian Orthodox Church. The darker field shows the numbers of arrested lay- and clergymen, while the lighter field shows the numbers of deaths.

Source: The Database of "new martyrs" by St. Tikhon's Orthodox University, http://martyrs.pstbi.ru/mgstat.html [accessed on June 6, 2021].

# Patriarch Tikhon

The first new martyr recognized by the Russian Orthodox Church was its Patriarch Tikhon Bellavin (1865–1925) (see Kenworthy 2015). He was elected by the Great council of Moscow in 1917 and led this church during the troublesome early years of the Communist regime. Tikhon refused to collaborate with this regime, just as he refused to collaborate with its opponents—various monarchist movements that fought for the restoration of tsardom. In January 1918, he promulgated a pastoral letter, which condemned the oppressive Communist policies towards the church:

> The Holy Orthodox church of Christ is at present passing through difficult times in the Russian Land; the open and secret foes of the truth of Christ began persecuting that truth, and are striving to destroy the work of Christ by sowing everywhere in place of Christian love the seeds of malice, hatred, and fratricidal warfare. The commands of Christ regarding the love of neighbor are forgotten or trampled upon; reports reach us daily concerning the astounding and beastly murders of wholly innocent people, and even of the sick upon their sick-beds, who are guilty perhaps only of having fulfilled their duty to the Fatherland, and of having spent all their strength in the service of the national welfare. This happens not only under cover of the nocturnal darkness, but openly in daylight, with hitherto unheard of audacity and merciless cruelty, without any sort of trial and despite all right and lawfulness, and it happens in our days almost in all the cities and villages of our country, as well as in our capital, and outlying regions (Petrograd, Moscow, Irkutsk, Sevastopol, and others). <. . .>
>
> Recall yourselves, ye senseless, and cease your bloody deeds. For what you are doing is not only a cruel deed; it is in truth a satanic act, for which you shall suffer the fire of Gehenna in the life to come, beyond the grave, and the terrible curses of posterity in this present, earthly life.
>
> By the authority given us by God, we forbid you to present yourselves for the sacraments of Christ, and anathematize you, if you still bear the name of Christians, even if merely on account of your baptism you still belong to the Orthodox church.
>
> I adjure all of you who are faithful children of the Orthodox church of Christ, not to commune with such outcasts of the human race in any matter whatsoever: "cast out the wicked from among you" (1 Cor. 5:13). (In Maclear 1995: 329–30)

# Sergianism

Less than ten years later, the *locum tenens* of the patriarchal throne, Metropolitan Sergiy Stragorodsky (1867–1944) promulgated a completely different kind of statement. This time, it was not condemning, but appeasing the Communist regime. The statement was published in the central Soviet newspaper *Izvestia* on August 18, 1927. It is regarded as one of the most striking examples of conformism in the history of Christianity, which has been branded "Sergianism" after the metropolitan's name:

> At present our Orthodox Church in the [Soviet] Union possesses not only canonical, but also fully legal, centralized administration consonant with civil laws. We furthermore hope that this legalization will be gradually extended to the lower ecclesiastical administrations: archdiocesan, regional, etc. Is it necessary to enlarge upon the significance of the consequences of the change that has occurred in the status of our Orthodox Church, of her clergy, and all her functionaries and institutions?
>
> Let us raise our grateful prayers to the Lord who has been so gracious to our holy Church. Let us also express, on behalf of the entire nation, our gratitude to the Soviet government for this attention to the spiritual needs of the Orthodox population, and at the same time let us assure the government that we will not abuse its confidence reposed in us.
>
> Addressing ourselves, with God's blessing, to our synodal labors, we clearly realize the magnitude of our task. <. . .> We need to show not in words, but in deeds, that not only people indifferent to Orthodoxy, or those who reject it, may be faithful citizens of the Soviet Union, loyal to the Soviet government, but likewise the most fervent adherents of Orthodoxy, to whom it is as precious with all its canonical and liturgical treasures as truth and life. We wish to remain Orthodox and at the same time to recognize the Soviet Union as our civil fatherland whose joys and successes are our joys and successes, and whose misfortunes are our misfortunes. Every blow directed against the Union, be it war, boycott, or any other common disaster, or even a hole-and-corner murder <. . .> we acknowledge as a blow against us. (In Maclear 1995: 358–9)

Metropolitan Sergiy hoped that through the compromises with the Soviet state, he would secure the survival of the church. By the Second World War, the Russian church was almost extinguished. It reemerged after the Second World War (see Kalkandzhieva 2017), when Joseph Stalin decided to revise his anti-religious policies and make them more tolerant. He wanted to boost the acceptance of the Soviet regime in the traditionally Orthodox areas, which he controlled or wanted to control, such as the Middle East and Eastern Europe. Official representatives of the Moscow Patriarchate were allowed to travel abroad, with the task to showcase the alleged Soviet freedom of consciousness. In the meantime, ordinary members of the church continued suffering and being persecuted. The Soviet policies to the church turned more tolerant around 1988, when the state-sponsored pompous celebrations of the millennium from the baptism of Kyiv. The church could enjoy its freedom only after the collapse of the Soviet Union in 1991 (see Митрофанов 2021; Pospielovsky 1984).

# Ethiopia

Some Oriental churches also found themselves under the Communist regime, such as the Armenian Apostolic Church in the Armenian Soviet Socialist Republic. The Oriental church that suffered from the Communist regime most was the Ethiopian Tewahedo Church. For most of its history, it enjoyed the protection of the state. In the middle of the twentieth century, the state secured its formal independence (autocephaly) from the Coptic church.

Things changed in 1974, when, with the help of the Soviet Union, the military regime of Derg (from "committee" or "council" in Amharic) toppled Emperor Haile Selassie I (1892–1975) (see Persoon & Jezek 2014). The emperor had sustained a traditional symphony with the Ethiopian Tewahedo Church in the way close to the Byzantine model of church-state relations. When the Derg seized all power, it dismantled this model. Derg's leader Colonel Mengistu Hailemariam (b. 1937) established a military dictatorship. Despite its leftist ideology, in many regards it was similar to the right-wing military dictatorships in Europe. In contrast to the latter, the Derg did not make the church a source of its legitimacy. At the same time, in contrast to the Soviet Union, it did not try to get rid of the church altogether.

Instead, the Derg preferred to keep the church under its control and to manipulate it. For this purpose, the regime removed disloyal hierarchs and provided the loyal ones with financial sponsorship—instead of nationalized assets that had supported the church in the past. The state also began paying salaries to the clergy. In return, the

**Figure 1.76** The offices of the Ethiopian patriarchate in Addis Ababa.

Source: Photo by the author.

Derg requested complete obedience, even though it had declared separation from the church. When the primate of the church, Abune Tewophilos (1910–79, patriarch since 1971) consecrated three bishops without the governmental consent, he and these bishops were imprisoned. The synod was forced to elect Tewophilos' replacement, Abuna Täklä Haymanot (1918–88). He was an ascetic with no interest in politics—the Derg needed exactly this kind of leadership for the church. Abune Tewophilos, in the meantime, spent three years under arrest. His coprisoner Aberra Jambre wrote about him in his memoirs:

> It was the afternoon of March 12, 1976, while we were milling around disconcertedly in the open enclosure of the prison, when the spiritual father of Ethiopia, Abune Theophilos, the Patriarch of the Ethiopian Orthodox Church, the highest church-man in the Land, was rudely shoved into this cage. He was manhandled, abused, hands chained together, barefoot. The prisoners froze where they were. One, distressed by what he saw, explained, "Goodbye Ethiopian humanism and spiritualism." (Gambaré 2005: 1)

In August 1979, Abune Tewophilos was strangled with electric wire, and his body was burned. The Ethiopian church remained under the Communist control until the fall of the Derg regime in 1991.

# I.17

# Orthodox Theology in the Twentieth Century

During the twentieth century, Orthodox countries lived through captivity by various totalitarian ideologies: communist, nationalist, fascist, and Nazist. These ideologies have left their footprint on the theological developments in these countries (see Ladouceur 2019). Churches under communism could not develop theology properly, being enclosed in their ghettos. Mainstream theology in the nationalist or fascist settings was effectively enslaved by ideologies and sometimes itself turned to an ideology.

## Theology in Diaspora

Orthodox theology could develop relatively unrestrained only in the so-called diaspora, that is, primarily in the Western Europe and the New World. Mass emigration there from the Middle East and Eastern Europe was propelled by Turkish genocides, the collapse of the Austro-Hungarian and Russian Empires, and economic crises in the traditional countries of the Eastern Christian traditions (see Teule & Verheyden 2020; Emerson et al. 2020). Particularly the Bolshevik Revolution of 1917 caused dramatic changes in the theological landscape of the Eastern Christianity. Most prominent theologians left Russia and emigrated to both East and West: China in the East and Yugoslavia, France, the United States, and other countries in the West. In Paris, they established in 1925 St. Sergius Orthodox Theological Institute, which became the center of advanced Orthodox theological studies. The Institute's faculty developed an approach to theology, which became known as "Paris school." This was a method of open engagement with the secular and heterodox environments. Paris school demonstrated that Orthodox theology can be successful outside the imperial frameworks.

In 1938, a new theological institution was founded in the State of New York. It became known as St. Vladimir's Orthodox Theological Seminary. Some prominent

**Figure 1.77** The church of St. Sergius Orthodox Theological Institute in Paris.
Source: Photo by the author.

theologians moved from France to the United States, bringing with them the methods and principles of the "Paris school." Fr. Georges Florovsky (1893–1979), who served as the seminary's dean in the 1950s, facilitated the transmission of the theological traditions from France to the United States. The seminary flourished under the leadership of Fr. Alexander Schmemann (1921–83) and Fr. John Meyendorff (1926–92), who also had started their theological careers in Paris. The Greek immigrants to the United States established their own educational institution, the Holy Cross Greek Orthodox School of Theology. It was founded in 1937 in Connecticut and later moved to Massachusetts. Since 1961, the Armenian St. Nerses seminary has been training priests and advancing Armenian theology in the State of New York. In addition to the confessional seminaries and institutes, departments and centers at universities have made a significant contribution to advancing Eastern Christian studies.

## Ideological Polarization

The ideological polarization, which shaped the twentieth century, affected also Orthodox theology. It was mentioned that theology in the traditional Orthodox countries often aligned with their dominant ideologies. In the diaspora, Orthodox theology was also affected by ideologies, but in more subtle ways. It had either "liberal" or "conservative" tilts.

The "liberal" trend in the Orthodox theology is more welcoming to new ideas from outside. It tries to synthesize the Orthodox past with the contemporary philosophical and theological ideas, even if they are not Orthodox or Christian. The "conservative" trend in Orthodox theology is also open to new ideas. However, it tries to rediscover these ideas inside its own tradition, in the past. It is usually suspicious of borrowing from other cultures and theological traditions.

These trends sometimes clash with one another in what has been called "culture wars." The Orthodox "culture wars" often echo and imitate similar "wars" in the Western, especially American, societies. They ideologically polarize communities and often cause splits in them. Members of these communities engaged in the culture wars, often perceive their ideological opponents as heretics, while their own ideological preferences they regard as orthodox.

## Russian Religious Philosophy

One of the earliest "liberal" theologies in the Orthodox setting was the so-called Russian religious philosophy (see Emerson et al. 2020). It addressed fundamental theological questions with the help of the contemporary philosophical languages and produced some remarkable intellectual syntheses. The "Russian religious philosophy" began developing outside the official system of the theological education in the Russian Empire—in parallel to the so-called academic theology. After the Bolshevik Revolution, it continued developing in diaspora, mostly in Paris.

The imperial academic theology had been cultivated in the specially designed academic spaces: "spiritual"[1] theological academies. In the Russian Empire during the nineteenth century, there were four such academies: in Sankt Petersburg, Moscow, Kyiv, and Kazan. Their common ancestor was the theological collegium established in 1615 in Kyiv by Metropolitan Petro Mohyla (1596–1647). The imperial academies followed the Humboldtian model of higher education popular in the nineteenth century.

Toward the end of that century, rationalism and positivism (see Feichtinger et al. 2019) became fashionable among the educated Russians and challenging for the Russian church. The academic theology in the Russian Empire had to a significant extent embraced the methods of rationalism and positivism. Based on these methods, it struggled to solve what was perceived as the dilemma between faith and reason. However, because the system of the Russian theological education was encaged in the narrow "spiritual estate" and had a limited outreach to the wider society, its contribution to the intellectual discussions of that time was limited.

[1] "Spiritual" means that such academies were founded for the education of the "spiritual" estate of the realm—a formal stratum in the Russian society during the imperial time, which included clergy and their families.

**Figure 1.78** The building of the theological academy in Kazan, Russia.
Source: Photo by the author.

More effective were theological responses coming from the secular estates of the upper and urban middle classes. Many intellectuals from these classes were interested in theological matters, without having ever studied in the theological academies. They studied at universities, where they learned Western intellectual culture, and applied it to the traditional Orthodox theology. Their efforts at synthesis between traditional Orthodox theology and contemporary philosophy, primarily German idealism, were branded as the "Russian religious philosophy." Although official academic theology and unofficial religious philosophy had different social and intellectual backgrounds, they converged in many points:

1. Both theologies aimed at achieving a synthesis between faith and rationality.
2. Both tried to reconnect the traditional Russian culture with modernity.
3. Both promoted a confessional approach to theology. At the same time, they demonstrated sympathy to ecumenism, even before ecumenism was officially inaugurated in the 1910s.
4. They were not anti-Western by default and widely utilized the foreign and heterodox sources.
5. The main source and inspiration for both was contemporary German scholarship. The theological academies widely used the methods of the German liberal theology, such as rational critique based on studying sources and historical evidence. The "religious philosophy," in turn, preferred the German idealistic philosophy.

German idealism particularly influenced the founder of the Russian religious philosophy, Vladimir Solovyov (1853–1900). He aimed at creating a comprehensive system of thought similar to the German universal theories developed in the early nineteenth century. In his system, Solovyov combined rationalism with the classical theology and esoteric mysticism.

Pavel Florensky (1882–1937), another key figure in the Russian religious philosophy, tried to bridge the Orthodox theology also with the contemporary culture and aesthetics. He was in touch with the poets and other creative figures of the Russian cultural "Silver Age." He tried to replicate their style in theology. This style featured rich metaphors. The stylistics of Florensky's theology was highly metaphoric as well.

Sergiy Bulgakov (1871–1944) was less metaphorical and more theological than any other representative of the Russian religious philosophy (see Arjakovsky 2006). While Solovyov produced a system of philosophical knowledge with multiple references to theology, Bulgakov developed a systematic theology with multiple references to philosophy. In addition to synthesizing theological and philosophical knowledge, Bulgakov attempted at synthesizing the Russian religious philosophy with the Russian academic theology.

## Neopatristic Syntheses

The subtle liberalism of the Russian religious philosophy was contested by the subtle conservatism of what has been branded as "neopatristic synthesis" (see Gavrilyuk 2014: 4–5). It became another major trend in twentieth-century Orthodox theology. This trend was reactive, similarly to the classical political conservatism, which also emerged as a reaction to political liberalism. While conservative in its demeanor, the "neopatristic synthesis" was in many regards theologically innovative.

It has been constructed by Georges Florovsky, a historian by training, who emigrated to the West after the Bolshevik Revolution. Florovsky officially inaugurated his theological method of synthesis at the theological congress in Athens in 1936. He suggested bridging tradition and modernity, faith and reason in the way which was an alternative to the one suggested by the Russian religious philosophy.

In the term "neopatristic" coined by Florovsky, the "patristic" refers to the Tradition, and the "neo" to modernity. The word "synthesis" promised a bridge between the past and the present. In this sense, Florovsky's agenda was not much different from the agenda of Bulgakov and other figures in the Russian religious renaissance. However, in contrast to Bulgakov and his liberal confederates, Florovsky criticized intellectual borrowing from the Western theological or philosophical repositories. He called the results of such borrowing "pseudomorphosis." For him, "pseudomorphoses" impede the Orthodox tradition to engage with modernity. Therefore, for the sake of successful synthesis, the church should distill the Eastern traditions from any Western influences on them.

Florovsky rendered his intellectual solutions to the theological dilemmas of his time in geographical terms. He identified truth with the East and falseness, with the

West. He thus continued the geopolitical line of thinking, which he had subscribed to and then abandoned—Eurasianism.[2] This was a political ideology, which considered Russia as a self-sufficient civilization alternative to both West and East. Florovsky eventually denounced this ideology in his article "The Eurasian Temptation."[3] However, some strains of Eurasianism remained in his posterior work, including his project of "neopatristic synthesis."

## Ideological Divisions in Greece

Antagonism between more liberal and more conservative trends can be spotted not only in diaspora, but also in the traditional Orthodox countries. For example, since the beginning of the twentieth century, the fellowship of theologians "Life" (*Zoï*/Ζωή) has been an important religious institution in Greece. It was ideologically conservative and endorsed restrictive and even dictatorial forces in the Greek society (see Γιανναρᾶς 2011: 106). In 1959, the fellowship "Savior" (*Sotir*/Σωτῆρ) separated from the "Life" as its more liberal counterpart. Such polarization within the Greek "brotherhoods" propelled the emergence of a more creative "theology of the 60s" (see Καλαϊτζίδης 2008; Μεταλληνός 1989). It was more liberal than *Sotir* and eventually turned to the theological mainstream of the afterwar period.

## Ideological Divisions in Romania

The Romanian theology after the Second World War also became more liberal than what it used to be in the interwar period. At that time, Romania switched from fascist to communist ideology. In contrast to the Soviet Union, the Romanian communist regime did not openly persecute the church. At the same time, it oppressed groups and individuals who attempted at revival of theology or spirituality. Such was the group that became known as "Burning bush" (*Rugul Aprins*) (see Giocas & Ladouceur 2007). It consisted of lay intellectuals, monks, and clergymen. The group studied the spiritual traditions of the past, particularly hesychasm. At the same time, it sought to build bridges to the modern society. From this perspective, it was relatively liberal. This is despite the fact that some of its members were ex-members of the fascist Iron Guard. In 1958, most members of the group were arrested. Some of them died in the prison, including its founder Alexandru Teodorescu (1896–1962; monastic name, Daniel).

---

[2]Florovsky was a coauthor of the Eurasian manifesto *Exodus to the East* published in 1921: *Исход к Востоку. Предчувствия и свершения. Утверждение евразийцев*, София: Типография Балкан.

[3]Published in the periodical *Современные записки* (Modern Notes), Paris, 34 (1928): 312–46.

## Eucharistic Ecclesiology

Some trends in the Orthodox theology during the twentieth century were interchangeably conservative and liberal. This was the case of the so-called Eucharistic ecclesiology (see Nichols 1989). During the Middle Ages, this ecclesiology contributed to the stratification in the church (see Hovorun 2015: 129–30). As a result, the wall between clergy and laypeople became higher. In the modern time, however, the Eucharistic ecclesiology helped in pulling down this wall. It became an emancipatory doctrine, which refocused the church's attention on communities. Modern Eucharistic ecclesiology gained its liberating momentum from Nikolay Afanasiev (1893–1966) and Alexander Schmemann (1921–83). However, in the recent decades, Eucharistic ecclesiology again began underpinning the growing stratification and conservatism in the church.

# II

# Dialectics

# II.1

## Three Words

The main source for studying Christianity in its various forms and traditions are texts. Texts are ostensibly immanent to Christianity, but this is a superficial impression. There was a time when there was Christianity without Christian texts. First-generation Christians, in their majority, did not need texts to share their experience of God's revelation in Jesus Christ. They expected Jesus to come back soon after his resurrection and ascension. Therefore, they did not see much sense in writing down texts—who would read them if Jesus was coming?

Only after an increasing number of Christians came to realize that Jesus was not returning soon, first Christian texts were written down. Christians still expected Jesus rather soon. However, now they accepted that his coming might be delayed. In the case of such delay, they decided to pass their knowledge and experience to new converts and the next generation. Still, they regarded their texts as a temporarily backup of the collective memories shared within the community. As time passed, this temporary backup ossified into the venerated Tradition. Dozens of Christian generations in the centuries that followed would perceive it as an incarnation of the divine Revelation.

The earliest Christian texts were most probably penned by Paul. He did not meet Jesus personally when the Messiah preached in Judea. This was probably one of the reasons why Paul relied on written testimonies and cared to leave them for others. Paul composed his first texts for Jews like himself, and for the Gentiles outside the Jewish community.

As the oral stories about Jesus, on the one hand, had multiplied, and on the other, had become more fictional, the community of Jesus' disciples authorized four stories, which were written down and became known as "good news"—the *euangelia* (εὐαγγέλια). These stories were intended for those who did not have access to genuine oral witnesses about Jesus' life and teaching. Stories about Jesus and the first generation of disciples, as well as their writings, were included in what would become known as the Christin Scriptures, or the New Testament. Together with the Jewish scriptures, the Christian scriptures came gradually to be perceived by the Christian community as the Revelation of God.

**Figure 2.1** Paul with his writings. An Egyptian icon (seventh to eighth century). Benaki Museum.
Source: Photo by the author.

They became one of three types of word written down in Christian texts. This was the type of the word directed from God to humanity. Another type was the word that Christians directed to God. This word could be individual and communal: delivered as prayer and liturgy. By applying the third type of the written word, Christians shared with one another their experiences of God. This type became known as theology. In contrast to the Revelation and prayer, which are vertical types of word, theology is a horizontal word.

Christ himself employed these three kinds of words. He himself was the divine Word, who revealed to his disciples everything he heard from his Father (Jn 15:15). He also uttered human words of prayer to the Father (Mk 14:32; Lk. 22:44; Jn 18:1). Finally, he communicated to his fellow human beings his immediate experience of the Father. He made sure to use the language understandable by his contemporaries. Jesus thus produced theology and was the first Christian theologian—in addition to being the source of the Revelation on which his theology reflected.

The church, as the continuation of Jesus' presence among his disciples, became and continues to be the depository of all three types of communication. Thus, the church has treasured the recorded pieces of Revelation from Jesus. The same church added to the New Testament accounts and documents about its own evolution in the early decades after Jesus. Furthermore, the church offered hermeneutics to these pieces of

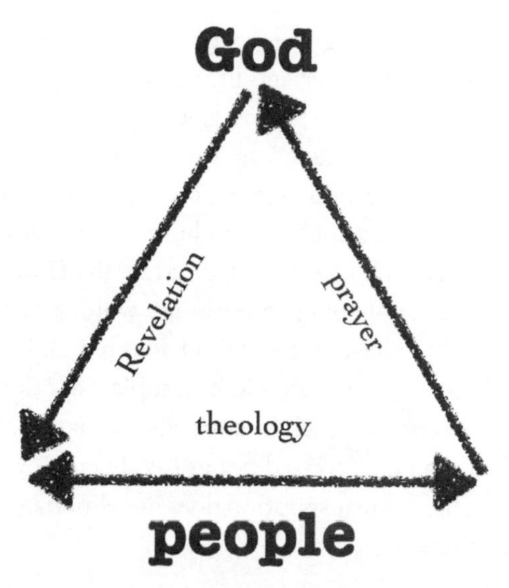


**Figure 2.2** Three words that circulate between God and human beings.

Revelation and historical accounts through God-inspired men and women, known as fathers and mothers of the church. Their most important task, and the commonest genre of patristic literature, was to interpret the words coming from God to humanity.

In the church, the human word *toward* God took a shape of communal worship, of which liturgy constitutes the most important part. Liturgical traditions and practices are human reactions to God's revelations and divine activities in the church known as sacraments. The church has also authorized a rich variety of prayers, for which reason in Eastern Christianity, even personal prayers usually follow preset patterns and utilize pre-drafted texts.

Finally, the church has accumulated a vast corpus of theological witnesses. They are texts that contain human words addressing fellow human beings. These words reflect human experiences of the divine and are tailored to fit particular contexts. For this reason, all church theologies are contextual: they were articulated under particular historical circumstances and responded to particular issues that had emerged in the church.

Theology, as a human word addressing other human beings about God, can be articulated in many ways and by different teaching authorities—*magisteria*. It may stem from the decisions of the church councils and circular letters of hierarchs, from polemical treatises and homilies by the fathers of the church, from spiritual advice uttered by ascetics, and so on. All these are the genres of theological literature. They are diverse and pluriform. Most theological genres have been exemplified in this book.

Although Revelation, liturgy, and theology are three distinct types of the words that circulates in the church, they are not completely different or separated from one another. The Scriptures and liturgy are expressed in theological languages, and theology borrows from the Scriptures and liturgy. Additionally, all three-word types utilize the same lexemes and formulas. The Scriptures, liturgy, and theology, therefore, can be distinguished but not separated from each other.

Theology is an inherent function of the church. Without theology, the church cannot fulfill its mission. It cannot be the church in the full sense of the word. Theology, especially patristic theology, is inspired by the Holy Spirit, who dwells in the church. At the same time, theology is a human word, and as such is limited and sometimes deficient. That it is a word about God does not make it divine or infallible. Theological word, therefore, can and should be a subject of critical analysis. The texts of the highest church authorities, such as councils, patriarchs, bishops, fathers, and mothers of the church, should be treated not as the divine Revelation, but as a God's inspired human word. The divine inspiration does not eliminate human shortcomings in reflecting on God's Revelation.

# II.2

# Knowledge of and about God

Following the same train of thought, one can assume that knowledge *about* God is different from the knowledge *of* God. The former can be speculative and does not necessarily presuppose a direct relationship with God, while the latter is impossible without such relationship. Since the time when the earliest Christian texts were penned, theologians have drawn a clear demarcation line between these two kinds of knowledge. They wrote theological texts with a disclaimer that these texts cannot substitute the immediate experience and knowledge of God.

Such was in particular the point made by Justin—an early Christian thinker and martyr, who flourished in the mid-second century. The Christian knowledge *of* God, he believed, constitutes the basis of true philosophy, that is, of the true knowledge *about* God. Justin discussed the distinction between these two types of knowledge in his imagined dialogue with an educated Jew called Trypho. He modeled this text after Platonic dialogues—a genre of fictional literature whose purpose was to test philosophical assumptions. An assumption that Justin wanted to test was that the direct knowledge of God is superior to any indirect philosophical reflection about God. Answering the question of Trypho, "Can the philosophers speculate correctly or speak truly of God, when they have no knowledge of Him, since they have never seen nor heard him?" Justin made his point: "But the Deity <. . .> cannot be seen by the same eyes as other living beings are. He is to be perceived by the mind alone, as Plato affirms, and I agree with him" (*Dialogus cum Tryphone Iudaeo* 2-3).

The idea of seeing God with spiritual sight became popular in Eastern Christian literature. Theophilus of Antioch, who lived in the same second century, made clearer the distinction between physical and spiritual sights. Only with the soul's eye one can see God and thus have a direct knowledge of him:

> But if you should say, "Show me your God," I may reply to you, "Show me your man and I will show you my God." You must show me that the eyes of your soul can see and that the ears of your heart can hear. For just as those who see with bodily eyes contemplate the affairs of life on earth and distinguish things that differ, such as light from darkness, white from black, ugly from beautiful, rhythmical and metrical from unrhythmical and unmetrical, beyond the metre from truncated; and similarly with

> things that fall under the sense of hearing, sounds that are shrill or deep or sweet; just so, the ears of the heart and the eyes of the soul are potentially capable of beholding God.

Theophilus stressed that seeing God depends not only on the availability of spiritual eyes but also on the condition of one's soul. Soul, to contemplate God, should be clean from sins, just as physical eyes should be healthy to be able to see:

> For God is seen by those who are capable of seeing him, once they have the eyes of the soul opened. All men have eyes, but some have eyes which are hooded by cataracts and do not see the light of the sun. Just because the blind do not see, however, the light of the sun does not fail to shine; the blind must blame themselves and their eyes. So you also, O man, have cataracts over the eyes of your soul because of your sins and wicked deeds. (*Ad Autolycum* 2; Grant 1970: 4–5)

A century later, Origen explained that a person, through spiritual senses, can perceive God and taste spiritual food coming from him:

> For just as in the body there are the different senses of tasting and seeing, so are there, as Solomon says, divine faculties of perception. One of them is the seeing and contemplating power of the soul, the other, a faculty of taste for receiving spiritual food.

However, spiritual senses can be dysfunctional. They then cannot perceive God or taste spiritual food. Their condition is similar to dead body:

> For just as in bodily death the senses decay so that no one receives anything further through the body, neither hearing nor smelling nor tasting, or through the touch, so too with the person who loses the spiritual senses in the soul so as not to see God nor hear the Word nor smell the sweet fragrance of Christ nor taste the goodness of the Word of God (cf. Heb. 6:5): such persons are rightly called dead. This was the way the coming of Christ found us, but he has given us life through his grace. (In Balthasar & Daley 2018: 221)

Three centuries later, an unidentifiable author, who wrote under the pen-name Dionysius the Areopagite, asserted that the knowledge of God is so much superior to any other kind of knowledge that it cannot even be called knowledge:

> It might be more accurate to say that we cannot know God in his nature, since this is unknowable and is beyond the reach of mind or of reason. But we know him from the arrangement of everything, because everything is, in a sense, projected out from him, and this order possesses certain images and semblances of his divine paradigms. We therefore approach that which is beyond all as far as our capacities allow us and we pass by way of the denial and the transcendence of all things and by way of the cause of all things. God is therefore known in all things and as distinct from all things. He is known through knowledge and through unknowing.

> Of him there is conception, reason, understanding, touch, perception, opinion, imagination, name, and many other things. On the other hand he cannot be understood, words cannot contain him, and no name can lay hold of him. He is not one of the things that are and he cannot be known in any of them. He is all things in all things and he is no thing among things. He is known to all from all things and he is known to no one from anything. (*De diuinis nominibus* 7.3; Luibheid 1987: 107–8)

This was a sort of religious agnosticism that stresses the superiority of knowing God over knowledge about God. The Dionysian agnosticism was probably not completely different from the modern agnostic ideas. Both acknowledge that what is said about God cannot adequately describe what God could really be. In contrast to modern agnostics, however, Pseudo-Dionysius asserted the existence of God in the strongest possible terms. For him, the word "existence" is too weak to apply to God. In comparison with the created existence, God does not exist.

Knowledge is not an end in itself, even when it is the immediate knowledge of God. For a Byzantine thinker from the seventh century, Maximus the Confessor, knowledge should resolve in love:

> If an intellective being is moved intellectively, that is, in a manner appropriate to itself, then it will necessarily become a knowing intellect. But if it knows, it surely loves that which it knows; and if it loves, it certainly suffers an ecstasy toward it as an object of love. If it suffers this ecstasy it obviously urges itself onward, and if it urges itself onward, it surely intensifies and greatly accelerates its motion. And if its motion is intensified in this way it will not cease until it is wholly present in the whole beloved, and wholly encompassed by it, willingly receiving the whole saving circumscription by its own choice, so that it might be wholly qualified by the whole circumscriber, and, being wholly circumscribed, will no longer be able to wish to be known from its own qualities, but rather from those of the circumscriber, in the same way that air is thoroughly permeated by light, or iron in a forge is completely penetrated by the fire, or anything else of this sort. (*Ambiguum ad Joh.* VII 10; Maximus 2014: 87–9)

# II.3 Theological Meta-languages

This book focuses on the texts that communicate knowledge *about* God, that is, theology. As with any communication, the theological one requires a medium. We will call it *meta-language.* Prefix *meta-* means that this medium is based on conventional languages and can be adopted by them. While conventional languages consist of lexemes and syntactic structures, theological categories and formulas constitute the Christian meta-language. This meta-language has originated from the Christian East. Its vocabulary is based on ancient Greek and includes such lexemes as *hypostasis*, *synergy*, *symphony*, *ekklesia*, and so on.

## Meta-lexemes

The Greek-based Christian meta-language has been transmitted to and mixed up with other ancient languages, such as Syriac, Coptic, Armenian, Georgian, Ethiopian, Slavonic, and so on. Metalinguistic categories and formulas were sometimes translated and sometimes transliterated to these languages. For example, the category of *hypostasis* (ὑπόστασις) has been transliterated in Coptic as ϩⲩⲡⲟⲥⲧⲁⲥⲓⲥ and in Slavonic as **ѵпостáсь**. In the classical Armenian (Grabar), the word *yent'akacut'yun* (**ենթակացութիւն**) was constructed to literally render the Greek *hypostasis*, with the prefix *yent'* corresponding to the Greek ὑπό, and the root *kacut'yun*, to the Greek στάσις. This literal translation circulated in parallel to the original Armenian words *andzn* (**անձն**) and *dem/k'* (**դէմ(ք)**).

Theological meta-lexemes were transmitted to other languages with as little changes as possible, to ensure the correct rendition of their original meaning. The purpose of theological meta-language, thus, was to secure the common understanding of basic categories. Yet, in each linguistic environment, these categories were perceived with different connotations. Sometimes, these connotations led to misunderstandings and caused controversies. For example, Patriarch Photius, who flourished in the second half of the ninth century, believed that the incorrect rendition

**Figure 2.3** A fifth-century Georgian inscription in the Bolnisi Sioni Cathedral.
Source: Photo by the author.

of the Greek terminology into Latin had caused theological disagreements between the East and the West:

> The Latin [language when it was used to] expressing the holy teaching of our Fathers did not furnish a pure and exact vocabulary precisely befitting the [Greek] concept, both on account of the deficiency of the language and because of its inability to cover the wide range of Greek; and for many it was causing the suspicion that false religion was incorporated in the faith, as the limitations of the [Latin] words do not suffice to interpret the [Greek] sense precisely. (Photius, *De spiritu sancti mystagogia* 87; Kinzig 2017, vol. 4: 326)

Theological disagreements were caused not so much by the vocabulary, as by the grammar of the meta-language. Meta-grammar is a set of rules about how to use theological terminology. For instance, according to the traditional grammar of the theological meta-language, the category of "hypostasis" can be applied to anyone and anything, while the synonymous category of "prosopon"—only to persons. If "hypostasis" is applied only to persons, as it is often the case in modern personalist thinking, this is an illiterate usage of the traditional meta-grammar. Another example: the term "consubstantial" (ὁμοούσιος) applies to both the Trinity and the incarnation. Applying this term to the Trinity only would be illiterate.

The formula of the double consubstantiality of the Son, namely that he is consubstantial with the Father according to his divinity, and with us according to his humanity, is a syntactic structure. Theological meta-language, thus, features its own syntax, which regulates formulas. The creed, for example, consists of several syntactic structures: "the only-begotten Son of God," "one holy catholic and apostolic Church," and so on. In contrast to these credal formulas, which were received by consensus, some syntactic structures caused disagreements. For example, the Chalcedonians held the Christological formula "composite hypostasis" in contrast to the anti-Chalcedonian formula "composite nature."

# Meta-dialects

Differences in the meta-syntax, meta-grammar, and various semantic connotations of the meta-vocabulary, contributed to the formation of theological meta-dialects. Meta-dialects are the spoken theological languages of particular Eastern Christian traditions. Their bottom line is the same: it is biblical and patristic. However, local cultures, political circumstances, preferred epistemologies, and philosophies created differentiations in the same Christian meta-language.

Theological meta-dialects may differ from each other in the usage of various categories and formulas. This does not, however, necessarily mean that they understand these categories and formulas differently. In other words, some theological differences can be explained by different languages, or more precisely meta-dialects, they use. At the same time, they may use the same formulas, but imply different semantics. The Chalcedonians and anti-Chalcedonians, for example, agree that the syntactic structure of "one incarnated nature of the Word of God" can be used in describing Christ. Nevertheless, for the Chalcedonians, this formula was synonymous with the lexeme "hypostasis," while for the anti-Chalcedonians, with "nature."

The concept of meta-language and its dialects can be helpful in answering the question: Do the antagonistic theological doctrines differ in semantics or in grammar? In other words: Is their faith different or they only have different expressions for the same faith? Another relevant question is: Do those who speak the same meta-dialect necessarily have the same faith? The answers to both questions can be both yes and no.

Some theologians always sensed that many theological differences have to do more with language than theology. This is, in particular, a popular belief in our days regarding the schism between the Chalcedonian and non-Chalcedonian churches. Some theologians in the past shared the same belief. For example, the Chalcedonian theologian Nazif Ibn Yumn (ninth century; see Nasrallah 1974) and anti-Chalcedonian Ali ibn Dawud al-Arfadi (eleventh century; see Troupeau 1969) agreed that they were separated by terminology and not theology. Their common experience of facing Islam helped them to arrive at such a conclusion.

According to this approach, theological differences are underlined by the usage of the meta-language, rather than different faiths. This approach follows the line in the Greek philosophy that was drawn by Heraclitus. This pre-Socratic philosopher reportedly claimed: "The lord whose is the oracle at Delphi neither speaks nor hides his meaning, but gives a sign" (Fr DK B93; Diehls & Kranz 1996: 172). Although Heraclitus was referring to the way the pythian priestesses uttered their prophecies, this reference is metaphorically applicable to the Christian meta-language: theological lexemes are not containers but pointers toward theological truth. Therefore, theologians may use different terms and formulas, and yet they speak of the same truth.

An alternative interpretation holds lexemes as containers of truth. Such an interpretation goes back to Plato's *Cratylus*. According to Socrates and Cratylus in this dialogue, names can adequately express the essence of things, because they "belong to things by nature" (390e). This implies that those who use same words to describe reality understand reality in the same way. Following *Cratylus*' line, the fourth-century Christian theologians Aëtius of Antioch and Eunomius of Cyzicus argued that some names of God can capture his essence. They believed that the name "unbegotten," for example, reveals this essence in the most adequate way. For them, therefore, the Son of God cannot be God, because he bears a different name, "begotten." Since the Father's and the Son's names are antonymous, Aëtius and Eunomius argued, their essences must be completely different; only the Father's essence can be regarded as properly divine.

Some other theologians, including the Cappadocian fathers, contested this train of thought. Although the Father and the Son have different names, they argued, the essence of the Trinity is the same. This is because, first, names apply to individuals and not to their essence. Second, names are like tags, which *mark* what they are attached to, but do not *explain* its content. One of the Cappadocians, Gregory of Nyssa, made this point clear by referring to the possibility of translating words to other languages. If words were identical with what they mean, any translation would have been impossible:

> It appears however that the nonsensical attack Eunomius has composed against conceptual thought has held us back like sticky, glutinous mud, and will not let us get to grips with more useful topics. How could one pass over that earnest and carefully reasoned philosophy, where he says that "not only in the things made is the majesty of the Designer expressed, but also in their names is the wisdom of God displayed, he having fitted the appellations individually appropriately to each thing made." He may have read this himself, or learnt it from someone who had read it, in Plato's dialogue *Cratylus*, and because of his dearth of ideas, I suppose, has stitched together his own nonsense with the rubbish he found there, doing the same as those who collect food by begging. Just as they get a little bit from each of their benefactors and gather their food of many different kinds, so Eunomius' book, for want of the true bread, laboriously gathers together scraps of verbs and nouns from all over the place, and for that reason, resonating with the literary beauty of the Platonic style, he thinks it right to adopt his philosophy as the Church's doctrine.
>
> How many words, please tell me, are used to name the created firmament among different nations? We call it *ouranos*, the Hebrew *shamaim*, the Latin *caelum*, and other names the Syrian, the Mede, the Cappadocian, the Moor, the Thracian and the Egyptian, nor would it be easy to count the different names which occur in use nation by nation for the sky and other things. Which of these, tell me, is the naturally fitting name, by which the magnificent wisdom of God is displayed? If you promote the Greek above the rest, the Egyptian may object and propose his own; if you give priority to the Hebrew, the Syrian will put forward his own word against it; the Roman will not yield priority to

> these, nor will the Mede accept that his own should not come first, and every one of the other nations will demand that his own should have priority over the rest. What follows? The theory will not convince, when it is divided between so many words by the disputants.
>
> "But from these things," he says, "as it were from laws publicly established, it is apparent that God appointed suitable and particular names for the natures." What a grand doctrine! What privileges the theologian bestows on the divine teachings! People would not begrudge them to the bath-men. In their case we let them make up words for the operations they are engaged in, and no one has dignified them with godlike honours, when they invent names for many things they produce, like foot-baths, hair-strippers, hand-towels, and many more of the same, names which by "fitting naturally" reveal the object by the meaning of the words. (*Contra Eunomium* II 403-9; Karfíková et al. 2008: 150–1)

The polemics against Aëtius and Eunomius may help us clearer identify the features of theological meta-languages:

1. That a meta-language expresses eternal divine truth does not make it eternal or divine or even truth per se.
2. Theology does not deliver truth. A theological meta-language only points to where truth can be found and helps establishing a relationship with it. This relationship cannot be possessive.
3. A theological meta-language can point in the wrong direction. A traveler can also misread the sign and take a wrong path.
4. There is no meta-language that can claim monopoly to express truth.
5. A meta-language, in which the Revelation, prayer, and theology are expressed, is not given by God. It is a human construct. In the best case, it is a result of synergy between human agency and divine grace.
6. Even if people speak the same theological meta-language, this does not ensure they mean the same theology.
7. Meta-language is not a theological golden standard. It is a changeable reality, which both is defined by and defines contexts.

# Socio-metalinguistics

The latter feature of the theological meta-language can be better understood from the perspective of sociolinguistics. This discipline is different from classical linguistics, which treats language as a golden standard normative for its bearers. According to Steven Pinker, "Linguists often theorize about a language as if it were the fixed protocol of a homogeneous community of idealized speakers, like the physicist's frictionless plane and ideal gas" (Pinker 2008: 74). Theological meta-dialects are often perceived in the same way: as ideal constructs, which are believed to adequately and fully express the divine realities. Such a perception of meta-dialects is one of the reasons for the clashes between traditions: each of them believes that its meta-dialect is the only golden standard of theology.

In contrast to linguistics, which holds languages as static and ideal, sociolinguistics treats them as social realities that constantly change. It is descriptive rather than prescriptive (see Wardhaugh & Fuller 2015: 3). From the standpoint of sociolinguistics, the way in which a language is spoken, speaks about its speakers and communities they belong to. Theological meta-dialects also reveal not only divine realities but also what are those who relate themselves to these realities. Theological meta-dialects are contextual and not self-explanatory, conditional and not unconditional, polyphonic and not monophonic. It would have been possible to avoid many church schisms, if theological expressions were looked at through sociolinguistic prism.

This does not mean that all Christian divisions have been caused by the absolutization of theological expressions. Indeed, some schisms happened, because theologians confused metalinguistic expressions with their semantics. At the same time, there were also real semantic incompatibilities between theological expressions. The historical divisions in Christianity were complex phenomena that included both confusion between truth and its language, and the real differences in understanding truth. To understand whether the difference was only linguistic or also theological is always a difficult task.

The things became even more complicated when some differences that had emerged as metalinguistic grew to semantic ones, that is, affecting the content of faith. This happened because of the phenomenon described by analytic philosophy: languages not only describe reality but also define and amend it. Under the pressure of language, initial terminological differences eventually led to the formation of different doctrines and traditions. For example, Severus of Antioch and Leontius of Byzantium might have argued about metalinguistic matters, such as whether we should apply to Christ only number one or also number two. However, the real theological distance between their followers became bigger than it was initially between these two figures, because the language they adopted to express their faith eventually affected faith.

# Modern Theological Meta-languages

The evolution of the theological meta-language and its dialects continues to our day. This evolution not only affects relations between traditions but also occurs within traditions. For instance, in the Roman Catholic theology during the last two centuries, there was a competition between the meta-dialects of neo-scholasticism (also known as neo-Thomism), German idealistic philosophy, and the "New theology" (*Nouvelle théologie*). During the nineteenth century, neo-scholastic theology suppressed the theological dialect emerging from the idealistic philosophy. Neo-scholasticism wrestled also with the "New theology," when it appeared in the 1930s, and was close to extinguishing the latter, with the administrative leverage from the Vatican. The Second Vatican council changed the tide, and the meta-dialect of the "New theology" prevailed over the neo-scholastic meta-dialect. It continues to dominate the Catholic theological scene to our days.

Similar conflicts, based on clashes between different meta-dialects within the same tradition, occur also in the Eastern Christian world. For example, in the nineteenth century in Russia, theological academies had elaborated the mainstream theological meta-dialect. Lay theologians, mostly from the Slavophile movement, such as Aleksei Khomyakov, designed a new meta-dialect based on the German idealistic philosophy. Unlike the academic meta-dialect, the idealistic theological language survived the Bolshevik revolution of 1917 and flourished in the diaspora. The twentieth century was marked by the antagonism between the meta-dialects of the Russian religious renaissance and the neopatristic synthesis. Fr. Georges Florovsky, who had invented the latter, was a linguistic purist. He hoped to distill a theological meta-language, which would be purified of all external borrowings, primarily the Western ones. Florovsky wanted to express in his ideal theological language an ideal state of mind, which he called patristic *phronema* (see Florovsky 1960: 188). As a result, he constructed his own meta-dialect. In the recent decades, Florovsky's neopatristic meta-dialect was modified to the neo-Palamite one. As Andrew Louth has noticed, neo-Palamism mirrors the role that neo-scholasticism has played in the West (Louth 2015: 179). In sum, each tradition features its own meta-dialect, these meta-dialects constantly evolve, and some lines of their evolution are similar.

Modern theological meta-dialects express not only theological ideas but also political ideologies. Catholic neo-scholasticism, for example, was utilized in the anti-modernist campaigns, while *Nouvelle théologie* is often associated with liberal thinking. The same ideological polarity, dressed in theological dialects, can be observed in the Orthodox milieu. Here, conservative theologians and church figures often use both neopatristic synthesis and neo-Palamism as ideological banners. Russian religious philosophy and its derivatives, in contrast, are usually perceived as liberal projects (see Suslov & Uzlaner 2020).

# II.4
# Metalinguistic Syntheses

The concept of meta-language may help us better understand the idea of the evoluton of theology. In the process of such evolution, the core of Christian beliefs remained the same. What evolved was primarily the meta-language, which expressed religious beliefs. At the same time, because languages not only express reality but also amend it, the theological meta-language influenced the faith of communities that had adopted it.

Meta-language is both a medium that allows Christianity to communicate with the world outside and a barrier between them. It functions like a membrane: it absorbs some elements and repulses others. There are three basic sources that have contributed to the formation of the Christian meta-language: Jewish scriptures and traditions, political culture and social ethos of the Greco-Roman world, and its philosophy.

## Sources of the Christian Meta-language

Bible became the main source of the Christian meta-language and its fabric. All Christian authors weaved biblical language into their own theology. They also interpreted the Bible in multiple commentaries. Biblical commentaries constitute the largest part of patristic literature. The use of the Bible in the patristic texts was so broad that it made it possible to reconstruct the entire Bible from the patristic sources, in the frame of the project *Biblia Patristica* (http://www.biblindex.mom.fr/). This project is one the best illustrations of how the meta-language of the Christian theology is intertwined with the biblical language.

Although the initial momentum of Christianity was nonconformist and apolitical, as the church grew it adopted a lot of structures and principles from its political environments, particularly the Roman one. It also expressed itself in the Greco-Roman political terms. The word for the church, ἐκκλησία/*ecclesia*, can illustrate this best. This word was borrowed from the political culture of classical Greece, where it meant a gathering of the citizens of a Greek *polis*. In Christianity, it came to mean the gathering of the citizens of the Kingdom of God.

Following the conversion of the Roman Empire to Christianity in the fourth century, *politeia* and *ekklesia* conflated into a singular theopolitical polity. In this polity, the church and the state shared the same purposes, methods, self-awareness, and language. Both expressed themselves through a common meta-language, which thus was not only theological but also theopolitical. It included theological, legal, and political categories.

The Roman state contributed to the common theopolitical vocabulary with such terms as "diocese," "jurisdiction," and so on. The church borrowed these terms from the Roman state to name its own administrative structures. Because language not only reflects but also defines reality, these linguistic borrowings influenced the church's structures. They propelled the church to assimilation with the political institutions of the Roman Empire.

The church, in return, contributed its own lexemes to the common theopolitical meta-language that it shared with the empire. The category of "hierarchy" became particularly successful and popular in the political philosophies of the Christian Roman state and all its successors and imitators. This category was adopted to the Christian meta-language from neo-Platonism. Through the Christian neo-Platonic metaphysics, it became a basic principle of both political philosophy and praxis of the Christian states.

Even when the earliest community of Jesus' followers was still confined within Judea, Biblical and Talmudic languages did not cover all its needs. From its earliest years, it needed Greek culture to communicate with the Hellenists—Jews who spoke and thought in Greek. Some Hellenists were among the earliest converts to Christianity, such as deacon Stephen (Acts 6:5–8:2). They needed their new faith to be articulated in the language, which they understood better than the traditional Jewish culture. When Christianity crossed the threshold of the Jewish world and stepped into the vast Greco-Roman world, rendering Christianity in the language of this world turned from optional mandatory. Paul and Luke were among the first Christians who realized this (see Rowe 2016: 4–5).

Christianity entered a huge marketplace where various doctrines competed with one another (see DesRosiers & Vuong 2016). Those doctrines were not a kind of philosophy we know now: a purely intellectual and secular exercise for a few who are intellectually concerned about big questions. Ancient philosophical schools offered all-in-one packages that included explanations of God(s), world, and human life, glued together by ethical principles and religious practices—everything that one needed for a fulfilled life. Christianity, for many, was just another philosophical sect that had little chance of standing up against the well-established philosophical franchises, such as Stoicism or Platonism. Justin the "philosopher" explained through

**Figure 2.4** An avenue in ancient Ephesus (see Black et al., 2020), modern Selçuk in Turkey, where Justin had his imagined dialogue with Trypho: "One morning as I was walking along a broad avenue, a man, accompanied by some friends, came up to me and said: 'Good morning, Philosopher.' Whereupon, he and his friends walked along beside me" (*Dialogus cum Tryphone Iudaeo* 1).

Source: Photo by the author.

his personal story what a seeker of ultimate truth faced in the second century, after he or she departed for spiritual odyssey:

> I placed myself under the tutelage of a certain Stoic. After spending some time with him and learning nothing new about God (for my instructor had no knowledge of God, nor did he consider such knowledge necessary), I left him and turned to a Peripatetic who considered himself an astute teacher. After a few days with him, he demanded that we settle the matter of my tuition fee in such a way that our association would not be unprofitable to him. Accordingly, I left him, because I did not consider him a real philosopher. Since my spirit still yearned to hear the specific and excellent meaning of philosophy, I approached a very famous Pythagorean, who took great pride in his own wisdom. In my interview with him, when I expressed a desire to become his pupil, he asked me, "What? Do you know music, astronomy, and geometry? How do you expect to comprehend any of those things that are conducive to happiness, if you are not first well acquainted with those studies which draw your mind away from objects of the senses and render it fit for the intellectual, in order that it may contemplate what is good and beautiful?" He continued to speak

> at great length in praise of those sciences, and of the necessity of knowing them, until I admitted that I knew nothing about them; then he dismissed me. As was to be expected, I was downcast to see my hopes shattered, especially since I respected him as a man of considerable knowledge. But, when I reflected on the length of time that I would have to spend on those sciences, I could not make up my mind to wait such a long time. In this troubled state of mind the thought occurred to me to consult the Platonists, whose reputation was great. Thus it happened that I spent as much time as possible in the company of a wise man who was highly esteemed by the Platonists and who had but recently arrived in our city. Under him I forged ahead in philosophy and day by day I improved. The perception of incorporeal things quite overwhelmed me and the Platonic theory of ideas added wings to my mind, so that in a short time I imagined myself a wise man. So great was my folly that I fully expected immediately to gaze upon God, for this is the goal of Plato's philosophy. (*Dialogus cum Tryphone Iudaeo* 2)

Christians like Justin were eager to prove that their Christian "philosophy" is superior to the existent philosophical schools. For this purpose, they had to render Jesus' teaching in the language understandable by educated pagans. That is how Christian meta-language began growing—by absorbing lexemes from the polytheistic cultures. The process of incorporation of classical philosophy to Christian theology was not linear. It required special skills of discernment. In the first place, philosophy had to be distilled from its religious beliefs: lexemes were detached from their original pagan semantics. The distilled metalinguistic forms were vetted and only the metaphysically neutral ones were admitted for inclusion to the Christian theological vocabulary. Late Byzantine Archbishop of Thessalonica Gregory Palamas (1296–357) described this process as like cooking a snake:

> In the case of the secular wisdom, you must first kill the serpent, in other words, overcome the pride that arises from this philosophy. How difficult that is! "The arrogance of philosophy has nothing in common with humility," as the saying goes. Having overcome it, then, you must separate and cast away the head and tail, for these things are evil in the highest degree. By the head, I mean manifestly wrong opinions concerning things intelligible and divine and primordial; and by the tail, the fabulous stories concerning created things. As to what lies in between the head and tail, that is, discourses on nature, you must separate out useless ideas by means of the faculties of examination and inspection possessed by the soul, just as pharmacists purify the flesh of serpents with fire and water. Even if you do all this, and make good use of what has been properly set aside, how much trouble and circumspection will be required for the task! Nonetheless, if you put to good use that part of the profane wisdom which has been well excised, no harm can result, for it will naturally have become an instrument for good. But even so, it cannot in the strict sense be called a gift of God and a spiritual thing, for it pertains to the order of nature and is not sent from on high. (*Pro hesychastis*, I 1.21; Palamas 1983: 29)

# Love and Hate to Pagan Culture

It took a long time, a lot of tries, and many failures before the Christians learned how to cook the snake of pagan philosophy. The adoption of pagan philosophy to Christian theology can be described in a dialectical way. There were figures and tendencies that rejected classical culture. Other figures and tendencies received it, often overenthusiastically. These thesis and antithesis paved a path to syntheses: classical wisdom would be accepted conditionally and in a distilled form. Even then, however, it remained thoroughly camouflaged: the syntheses often omitted references to the classical works, from which they borrowed.

Rejection was a very early Christian reaction to the Greco-Roman world and its culture. As early as in the end of the first Christian century, Clement of Rome, in his letter to the Christians in Corinth, spoke about Christ's (*Ad Corinthios* 21.8.2) and God's (*Ad Corinthios* 62.3.4) *paideia* that had replaced the pagan *paideia*. Such standpoint reached its peak in the writings of Tatian the Syrian, whom Werner Jaeger has characterized as the "champion of anti-Hellenism" (Jaeger 1962: 34). Tatian was born in "Assyria," that is, somewhere in Mesopotamia or Syria. He received there a

**Figure 2.5** Third-century papyrus with a fragment of Tatian's *Diatessaron* (P. Dura 10, the Beinecke Rare Book & Manuscript Library at Yale University).
Source: Photo by the author.

good Greek education. After trying different philosophical schools in different places, he ended up in Rome as a convert to Christianity. There, he was initiated to the Christian theology under the guidance of Justin. He did not, however, inherit Justin's open-mindedness, but developed hostility to the Greco-Roman culture. Tatian eventually joined a conservative sectarian group of the "Encratates" and became its leader.

Tatian is also known for forging the four Gospels to a single story, "the gospel according to the four" (τὸ διὰ τεσσάρων εὐαγγέλιον). It is better known by abbreviation, *Diatessaron* (Διατεσσάρον). Tatian's compilation became so popular that it was soon translated from original Greek to Arabic, Persian, Latin, and other ancient languages. It was used for personal studies and liturgy. The earliest Greek fragment of the *Diatessaron* was discovered in Dura Europos—a Roman city in Syria abandoned in the 250s. Together with other artifacts found during the excavations, a fragment of papyrus with the *Diatessaron* is held at Yale University.

Tatian developed a caustic criticism of the ancient Greek paideia in his *Address to the Pagans*. He mocked virtually every philosophical authority of the antiquity:

> What that is distinguished have you produced by your philosophizing? Who among the real enthusiasts is innocent of self-display? Diogenes by boasting of his tub prided himself on his self-sufficiency; he ate raw octopus, was seized with pain and died of an internal obstruction because of his intemperance. Aristippus, walking about in a purple robe, abandoned himself to luxury under a cloak of respectability. Plato while philosophizing was sold by Dionysius because of his gluttony.[1] Aristotle, too, after ignorantly setting a limit for providence and defining happiness in terms of his own pleasures, used to fawn in a very uncultured way on that wild young man Alexander, who in true Aristotelian fashion shut his own friend up in a cage, because he refused to prostrate himself, and carried him about like a bear or a leopard. At least he was completely obedient to his master's teaching, displaying his manliness and valour in drinking parties and transfixing his closest friend with a spear and then weeping and starving himself in a show of grief, in order not to be hated by his friends. His modern disciples, too, are good for a laugh; they exclude providence from any part in sublunary affairs, yet themselves, being nearer the earth than the moon and living underneath its course, provide the care that providence fails to give; and those who have neither beauty, nor wealth, nor physical strength, nor good birth, these, according to Aristotle, have no happiness. Let men like this go on with their philosophizing.
>
> I have no use for Heraclitus and his boast "educated myself," because he was self-taught and arrogant, nor do I think much of his trick in hiding his work in the temple of Artemis, in order to achieve publication later in a mysterious way. For the pundits

---

[1] It was believed at that time that Plato, after becoming an enemy of the Sicilian tyrant Dionysius, was handed over to a Spartan. That Spartan brought him to Aegina, where he was put up for sale as a prisoner of war.

> say that the tragedian Euripides went down and read it, and from memory revealed the obscurity of Heraclitus to the devotees piecemeal. His manner of death showed up his ignorance, for he was stricken with dropsy, and being a practitioner of medicine on the same lines as his philosophy he smeared himself all over with excrement; when it hardened it caused cramp all over his body, and after convulsions he died. Nor can I accept Zeno and his revelation that after the holocaust the same men rise again to behave exactly as before—I mean Anytus and Meletus to prosecute, Busiris' to kill his guests and Heracles to labour over again. In his treatise on the holocaust he introduces more rogues than righteous, of whom there are only a few, not many; only one Socrates and Heracles and others like them. You will find that his wicked are much more numerous than his good, and he portrays God as creator of evil, who turns up in sewers and worms and doers of things unmentionable. The volcanic eruptions in Sicily showed up Empedocles' boastfulness, in that he was no god and lied in claiming that he was.[2] And I have no more respect for Pherecydes' old wives' tales, or Pythagoras's takeover of his doctrines, or Plato's copying of them—whatever some people say. For who would appeal to Crates's "dog-marriage"? Who would not rather stop his ears to such arrogant and crazy talk, and turn to a serious quest for the truth? So do not be swept away by the august crowds of those who love noise rather than wisdom. They express views that contradict one another, and each says whatever comes into his head. And there are many causes of friction between them, for each one hates his fellow and they hold different views, each taking up an exaggerated position out of self-importance. Another point: they ought not to have kowtowed to the eminent in anticipation of their elevation to sovereignty, but have waited for the great to come to them. (*Oratio ad Graecos* 2-3; Whittaker 1982: 5–9)

Surprisingly, Tatian spared from this list of shame only one key thinker of antiquity, Socrates. He probably made this exception not because he liked Socrates, but as a tribute to his teacher Justin, who seemingly had exceptional respect for Socrates. Justin was the first Christian author who made an explicit reference to Socrates.[3] For him, Socrates was a "good (σπουδαῖος) man" (*Apologia* II 7). As a good man, he was hated by bad men and demons—just like Christians are. Justin had drawn a parallel between Socrates and Christian martyrs. For him, Socrates and Christians rejected false gods and exposed demons hiding behind these gods. In retaliation, demons inspired dishonest people to kill both Socrates and Christians:

> Led by unreasonable passion and at the instigation of wicked demons, you punish us inconsiderately without trial. But the truth shall be told, for the wicked demons from

---

[2]According to legends, Empedocles jumped into the Mount Etna to make others think of him as a god, but Etna erupted and cast up one of his sandals.

[3]There are also references in the works of Clement of Rome, who lived earlier. However, these references belong to spurious homilies. The author of these homilies appreciated the figure of Socrates and called him "the wisest among all men" (*Homiliae* V 18-19).

ancient times appeared and defiled women, corrupted boys, and presented such terrifying sights to men that those who were not guided by reason in judging these [diabolical] acts were panic-stricken. Seized with fear and unaware that these were evil demons, they called them gods and greeted each by the name which each demon had bestowed upon himself. But, when Socrates attempted to make these things known and to draw men away from the demons by true reason and judgment, then these very demons brought it about, through men delighting in evil, that he be put to death as an atheist and impious person, because, they claimed, he introduced new divinities. And now they endeavor to do the very same thing to us. And not only among the Greeks were these things through Socrates condemned by reason (logos), but also among the non-Hellenic peoples by the Logos Himself, who assumed a human form and became man, and was called Jesus Christ. (*Apologia* I 5)

The reason why Justin invoked the example of Socrates' trial is clear. In the period of the Greco-Roman Antiquity, Socrates enjoyed "the status of a cultural icon" (Charalabopoulos 2007: 105). Execution of Socrates by the council of Athens in 399 BC was among the most remembered and most formative events for the posterior Antiquity. There was a consensus that he was accused on wrong grounds, and his death was presented as a classical example of injustice. In the time when Justin composed

**Figure 2.6** Socrates from the Odysseus Palace on Ithaka.
Source: Photo by the author.

his apologies, the trial and death of Socrates were still widely discussed among the learned Greeks and Romans, such as, for instance, Albinus of Smyrna or Favorinus of Arelate. Justin employed such a perception of Socrates' death to demonstrate that Christians are also accused on wrong grounds and experience the same injustice. He argued that Socrates was accused of "atheism" because he promoted one deity instead of many gods from the Athenian pantheon. Christians were persecuted for exactly the same reason.

Justin addressed his apology not only to pagans but also to Christians. He wanted to convince his fellow co-believers that there is a big value in the pagan wisdom. Just as he was the best example to demonstrate to the pagans that they were wrong in judging Christians, Justin believed the same figure could convince the Christians that they were sometimes wrong in rejecting pagan culture wholesale. The Socrates argument reveals the implicit agenda of Justin's apologetical project. Its explicit side clearly addressed prejudices that pagans had toward Christians. The implicit side tackled the prejudices that Christians had toward pagan wisdom. Justin's apologies imply that the Christians in his time often rejected this wisdom in wholesale—just because it was pagan.

Justin introduced a differentiation between the layers of the Greco-Roman culture. Some of them are indeed toxic and should be rejected altogether. Others, however, contain seeds of genuine wisdom, sparks of truth coming from the One God. Justin

**Figure 2.7** A façade of the library of Celsus in Ephesus. Built in the early second century AD as the third largest book storage of the ancient world. The library is believed to have contained around 12,000 manuscripts.

Source: Photo by the author.

called them "a part of the seminal word" (σπερματικοῦ λόγου μέρος; *Apologia* II 7, 13). Christians, who believe in the Word of God, should appreciate those who bear in themselves the seeds of the divine Word, including Socrates. Even though such figures as Socrates did not believe in Christ, because they lived before him, they could be called Christians:

> Those who lived by reason (μετὰ λόγου) are Christians, even though they have been considered atheists: such as, among the Greeks, Socrates, Heraclitus, and others like them; and among the foreigners, Abraham, Elias, Ananias, Azarias, Misael, and many others whose deeds or names we now forbear to enumerate, for we think it would be too long. So, also, they who lived before Christ and did not live by reason were useless men, enemies of Christ, and murderers of those who did live by reason. But those who have lived reasonably, and still do, are Christians, and are fearless and untroubled. (*Apologia* I 46)

At the same time, the knowledge that the so-called Christians before Christ have is incomplete and often simply false. Only the truth revealed by Christ to his faithful is complete and incorrupt:

> I am proud to say that I strove with all my might to be known as a Christian, not because the teachings of Plato are different from those of Christ, but because they are not in every way similar; neither are those of other writers, the Stoics, the poets, and the historians. For each one of them, seeing, through his participation of the seminal Divine Word, what was related to it, spoke very well. But, they who contradict themselves in important matters evidently did not acquire the unseen [that is, heavenly] wisdom and the indisputable knowledge. The truths which men in all lands have rightly spoken belong to us Christians. For we worship and love, after God the Father, the Word who is from the Unbegotten and Ineffable God, since He even became Man for us, so that by sharing in our sufferings He also might heal us. Indeed, all writers, by means of the engrafted seed of the Word which was implanted in them, had a dim glimpse of the truth. For the seed of something and its imitation, given in proportion to one's capacity, is one thing, but the thing itself, which is shared and imitated according to His grace, is quite another. (*Apologia* II 13)

# Syntheses

Justin indicated a direction where to look for the divine seminal word in the pagan wisdom. Theologians from Alexandria hit the road and walked down it. Two headmasters of the Christian school in Alexandria, Clement and Origen, became the most consistent apologists of the classical culture and promoters of its integration in Christian theology. They saw the pagan culture, which they separated from pagan religion, as a colossal project of the divine providence aimed at teaching the

**Figure 2.8** A church of St. Eleutherius in Athens, also known as "Little Metropolis," is famous for the combination of pagan and Christian elements in its decoration. This is a fragment of such decoration.
Source: Photo by the author.

fallen humankind right ways of thinking and behaving. Christianity upgraded this project to a completely new level. At this level, knowledge about God comes directly from God and reveals God without deficiency. For the Alexandrian theologians, Christianity was not a rejection but a fulfillment of the Greek wisdom, just as it was the fulfillment of the Jewish law. The original source for both wisdoms, Greek and Jewish, was the divine Logos, who became incarnated as Jesus Christ. This idea is implied in an early Alexandrian hymn "To the Educator." It praises two "breasts of the Word," who nourishes the entire humankind:

The footsteps of Christ
Are pathway to heaven,
Of ages unbounded,
Everlasting Word,
Light of eternity,
Well-spring of Mercy,
Who virtue instills
In hearts offering God
The gift of their reverence,
O Jesus, our Christ!
Milk of the bride,
Given of heaven,
Pressed from sweet breasts—
Gifts of Thy wisdom—
These Thy little ones
Draw for their nourishment;

With infancy's lips
Filling their souls
With spiritual savor
From breasts of the Word.[4]

The Alexandrian effort of synthesis was appreciated by the church in its most part. However, some Alexandrian ideas, primarily about the beginning and the end of the world (the head and the tail of the snake, according to Gregory Palamas), were rejected. They include what has been called *apokatastasis* or "restoration" of the entire world to its original condition. The idea of the cyclical restoration of the world constituted a leitmotif in the teachings of the pre-Socratics, Plato, Aristotle, Pythagoras, Stoics, and middle- and neo-Platonists. Hellenistic Jews, such as Philo of Alexandria, were also familiar with it (see Ramelli 2013: 1–10). Origen tried to recast it from the perspective of the Christian Revelation. In his interpretation, it came to mean that, eventually, the cycles of restoration should end up in a final *apokatastasis*, when all enemies of God will be reconciled with him: "The end (τὸ τέλος) will be at the so-called *apokatastasis*, in that no one, then, will be left an enemy (ἐχθρόν)" (*Com. in Ioh.* I 16.91; Ramelli 2013: 3). The idea of apokatastasis, as a synthesis between the pagan and Christian outlooks, was not appreciated by the majority in the church.

More successful was the synthesis between the Stoic idea of *logos* and the Christian revelation about the Triune God. Origen forged this synthesis as an answer to the question: How is the existence of the Son of God compatible with Christian monotheism? Origen's take on logos implied that the divine Word is distinct from the Father and at the same time inferior to him. This interpretation triggered controversies in the fourth century about whether the divine being is hierarchical.

Origen's controversial ideas about *apokatastasis* of all beings and hierarchy in God, compromised his unprecedented synthetic work. He, on the one hand, "had given the Christian religion its own theology in the style of the Greek philosophical tradition" (Jaeger 1962: 74). In other words, he is the most important creator of the comprehensive theological meta-language, a *lingua franca* for all posterior generations of theologians. On the other hand, in his synthesis, he made some mistakes, which to a significant extent compromised his entire synthetic project in the eyes of the later generations.

Some theological mistakes cast a shadow on another colossal synthesizing project. Two Apollinarises, father and son, both of the Alexandrian provenance, undertook in the fourth century an ambitious task of rendering the entire Christian scriptures and stories in classical poetic meters and genres, such as dialogue and tragedy. They

---

[4]*Hymn to the Educator*, one of the earliest pieces of Christian poetry. It was added to the end of Clement's *Paedagogus*: Clement of Alexandria 2008: 276.

did so in reaction to Emperor Julian's (r. 361–2) ban on Christians to study ancient philosophy and culture: if Christians are denied access to this culture, they have to create their own culture in the image and likeness of the classical one. Church historian Sozomen reported with admiration about this ambitious undertaking by Apollinarises:

> Apollinarius <. . .> employed his great learning and ingenuity, in which he even surpassed Homer, in the production of a work in heroic verse, on the antiquities of the Hebrews from the creation to the reign of Saul. He divided this work into twenty-four parts, to each of which he appended the name of one of the letters of the Greek alphabet. He also wrote comedies in imitation of Menander, tragedies resembling those of Euripides, and odes on the model of Pindar. In short, he produced within a very brief space of time a numerous set of works, which, in point of excellence of composition and beauty of diction, may vie with the most celebrated writings of Greece. Were it not for the extreme partiality with which the productions of antiquity are regarded, I doubt not but that the writings of Apollinarius would be held in as much estimation as those of the ancients. The comprehensiveness of his intellect is more especially to be admired; for he excelled in every branch of literature, whereas ancient writers were proficient only in one. (*Historia ecclesiastica* V 18; Sozomen & Philostorgius 1855: 233)

Both the Origenian and Apollinarian projects of synthesis were colossal. Both were rooted in the Alexandrian tradition of learning. Both were not uncritical about the classical knowledge. Origen, for instance, contested many points of this knowledge in his treatise *Contra Celsum*, while Apollinaris reportedly composed a thirty-volume oeuvre against Porphyry. Both, however, failed to receive unquestionable recognition by the church.

**Figure 2.9** Volumes in the patriarchal library in Alexandria.
Source: Photo by the author.

A fully acceptable synthesis between Christian revelation and pagan culture, which completed the Origen's undertaking to create a universal theological meta-language, was achieved by the so-called Cappadocian fathers: Basil of Caesarea, Gregory of Nazianzus, Gregory of Nyssa, and Amphilochius of Iconium. They are called "Cappadocians" because their provenance was from this rough heartland of Asia Minor.

Similarly to the Alexandrians a couple of generations earlier, the Cappadocians tried to distill what is useful from what is useless in the ancient wisdom. Their attempt was more successful than the Alexandrian one. The success of the Cappadocian synthesis was secured not by a different method, but by a more cautious and consistent application of the same method that Origen had applied and which Jaeger has called "Christian neoclassicism" (Jaeger 1962: 75). As a token of the appreciation of Origen's method, Basil of Caesarea and Gregory of Nazianzus compiled a collection of excerpts from Origen, which they named *Philokalia*. Basil explained how this method works, in his *Address to Young Men on the Right Use of Greek Literature*—"the charter of all Christian higher education for centuries to come" (Jaeger 1962: 81):

> But that this pagan learning is not without usefulness for the soul has been sufficiently affirmed; yet just how you should participate in it would be the next topic to be discussed.

Basil goes more specific about what can be useful and edifying for the Christian youth in the classical poetry. He also warns what lessons from this poetry to avoid:

> First, then, as to the learning to be derived from the poets, that I may begin with them, inasmuch as the subjects they deal with are of every kind, you ought not to give your attention to all they write without exception; but whenever they recount for you the deeds or words of good men, you ought to cherish and emulate these and try to be as far as possible like them; but when they treat of wicked men, you ought to avoid such imitation, stopping your ears no less than Odysseus did, according to what those same poets say, when he avoided the songs of the Sirens. For familiarity with evil words is, as it were, a road leading to evil deeds. On this account, then, the soul must be watched over with all vigilance, lest through the pleasure the poets' words give we may unwittingly accept something of the more evil sort, like those who take poisons along with honey. We shall not, therefore, praise the poets when they revile or mock, or when they depict men engaged in amours or drunken, or when they define happiness in terms of an over-abundant table or dissolute songs. But least of all shall we give attention to them when they narrate anything about the gods, and especially when they speak of them as being many, and these too not even in accord with one another. For in their poems brother is at feud with brother, and father with children, and the latter in turn are engaged in truceless war with their parents. But the adulteries of gods and their amours and their sexual acts in public, and especially those of Zeus, the chief and highest of all, as they themselves describe him, actions which one would blush to mention of even brute beasts—all these we shall leave to the stage-folk.

**Figure 2.10** Rough terrain of Cappadocia.
Source: Photo by the author.

Then Basil makes similar distinctions regarding pagan prose. One has to approach it in the same selective way that bees choose flowers:

> These same observations I must make concerning the writers of prose also, and especially when they fabricate tales for the entertainment of their hearers. And we shall certainly not imitate the orators in their art of lying. For neither in courts of law nor in other affairs is lying befitting to us, who have chosen the right and true way of life, and to whom refraining from litigation has been ordained in commandment. But we shall take rather those passages of theirs in which they have praised virtue or condemned vice. For just as in the case of other beings enjoyment of flowers is limited to their fragrance and colour, but the bees, as we see, possess the power to get honey from them as well, so it is possible here also for those who are pursuing not merely what is sweet and pleasant in such writings to store away from them some benefit also for their souls. It is, therefore, in accordance with the whole similitude of the bees, that we should participate in the pagan literature.

Basil ends his admonition with the words of Hesiod about the hardships and rewards of achieving virtuous life:

> And since it is through virtue that we must enter upon this life of ours, and since much has been uttered in praise of virtue by poets, much by historians, and much more still by philosophers, we ought especially to apply ourselves to such literature. For it is no small advantage that a certain intimacy and familiarity with virtue should be

engendered in the souls of the young, seeing that the lessons learned by such are likely, in the nature of the case, to be indelible, having been deeply impressed in them by reason of the tenderness of their souls. Or what else are we to suppose Hesiod had in mind when he composed these verses which are on everybody's lips, if he were not exhorting young men to virtue?—that "rough at first and hard to travel, and full of abundant sweat and toil, is the road which leads to virtue, and steep withal." (*De legendis gentilium libris*; Deferrari & McGuire 1934: 387–93)

## Stoic Language

The lexeme "virtue," which Basil invokes in his admonition, he borrowed from the vocabulary of the classical philosophy. It was especially dear to the Stoics, who supplied Christian theology with plenty other lexemes. Christian ascetic authors particularly appreciated the Stoic moralistic terminology. Such Stoic notions as passion (πάθος) and passionlessness (ἀπάθεια), together with others, became keywords in the Christian ascetic literature. Justin presented Christianity as the true philosophy in the same way as the Stoics propagated their lifestyle (see Rowe 2016: 5).

Stoic influence on the Christian literature was particularly strong during the first hundred years of Christianity. Paul in his deliberations on law and sin in the Romans (Rom. 7:7–8:13) employed the Stoic juxtaposition of law and sin (see Engberg-Pedersen 2016; Thorsteinsson 2010). In the 1 Corinthians (11:14), he referred to another Stoic notion, that of natural order. He quoted the Stoic philosopher Aratus in his sermon at Areopagus: "Yet he (God) is actually not far

**Figure 2.11** A marble bust of Paul (fourth to fifth centuries). Musei Vaticani.
Source: Photo by the author.

from each one of us, for 'In him we live and move and have our being'; as even some of your own poets have said, 'For we are indeed his offspring'" (Act 17:27–28). Indeed, the idea of human kinship to God and God's immanent presence in human life was important in Stoicism. In the same 1 Corinthians, Paul employed the Stoic concept of "spirit" (*pneuma*/πνεῦμα) while explaining the resurrection in "a spiritual body" (1 Cor. 15:44) (Engberg-Pedersen 2010: 9). Because of these and other striking parallels between Paul and Stoics (see Dodson & Briones 2017), it was easy to sell to the Christian readership as genuine the pseudepigraphic correspondence between Paul and Seneca, a leading figure in the Latin Stoicism (see Dodson & Briones 2017).

John was also under considerable Stoic influence (see Engberg-Pedersen 2018; Engberg-Pedersen 2016). He made the concept of "logos" central to his Gospel. The same concept had been central in the Stoic philosophy. Stoics described by "logos" the active principle of reality, which activates all beings and makes them coherent with one another and the universe. It was one of the ways to describe the single deity, as the Stoics understood it. "Logos" was synonymous for them with the "designing fire" and *pneuma*—other names of their deity (see Long 2011: 240). The Stoic "logos," however, unlike the Logos in John, was impersonal.

## Platonic Language

Stoicism had a potentiality to become the main supplier of philosophical ideas and lexemes for the Christian theological meta-language. During the first century of the church, it actually *was* the main supplier of theological terminology for the New Testament and subapostolic authors. This corresponded to the overall dominance of Stoicism on the Greco-Roman philosophical scene at that time. However, the things started changing after the first century AD, when Thrasyllus of Alexandria recirculated the works of Plato, and Platonism made its coming back to the market of ideas in what scholars identify as its "middle" form (see Dillon 2017). Upgraded Platonism accumulated enough intellectual resources to replace Stoicism as the main supplier of philosophical ideas for the entire Greco-Roman milieu, including the church. Alexandria was the epicenter of this takeover.

Christian theology soon readjusted itself to the new philosophical mainstream (see Hampton & Kenney 2020). The first known headmaster of the Alexandrian school, Pantaenus, had been a Stoic philosopher before his conversion to Christianity. His successor, Clement, aligned with Platonism and became a broker of the special partnership between Christian theology and middle-Platonic philosophy (see Heath 2020). Clement declared that Plato was a better guide for Christians than any other pagan philosopher, including Stoics:

**Figure 2.12** A sixth century AD mosaic of Alexandria and Memphis from Gerasa, Jordan. Yale University Art Gallery.
Source: Photo by the author.

> I long for the Lord of the winds, the Lord of fire, the Creator of the world, He who gives light to the sun. I seek for God Himself, not for the works of God. Whom am I to take from you as fellow worker in the search? For we do not altogether despair of you. "Plato," if you like. How, then, Plato, must we trace out God? "It is a hard task to find the Father and Maker of this universe, and when you have found Him, it is impossible to declare Him to all." Why, pray, in God's name, why? "Because He can in no way be described." Well done, Plato, you have hit the truth. (*Protrepticus* 6; Butterworth 1919: 152–5)

Origen, who succeeded Clement as the scholarch in Alexandria, also favored middle Platonism, even though he continued using Stoic philosophy (see L. Roberts 1970). Simultaneously, he criticized those elements in Platonism, which he believed to be incompatible with Christianity (see Edwards 2018).

Christian theologians abandoned Stoicism and aligned with Platonism not only because the latter had become more fashionable than the former. The main problem of Stoic philosophy for the Christians was its materialistic take on God. Platonism, in contrast, offered a picture of the transcendent and nonmaterial divinity. This picture better corresponded to the Judeo-Christian metaphysics. Christians appreciated the differentiation between the visible and invisible worlds that Platonism offered. The invisible world of ideas, according to Plato, was totally different from the world that we perceive with our bodily feelings. The two worlds are separated from one another as much as one can imagine: they belong to the opposite poles of existence. Although both worlds are real, the invisible world of ideas is more real than what we feel as real—the visible world around us. Plato helpfully placed human beings to the framework of this differentiation: human soul has kinship with the world of ideas, while body is a part of the visible world. Christians also appreciated Plato's intuition that human knowledge about the ideal world is not so much gained as it is disclosed. This intuition corresponded to the Christian idea of Revelation.

Although many Platonic ideas were close to Christianity, Christians felt them belonging to a different religious worldview. A polytheist in his social life, Plato was not monotheistic enough in his philosophy. Only well-intended monotheists could see in Plato's "idea of good" (ἡ τοῦ ἀγαθοῦ ἰδέα; *Respublica* 505a3) a reference to one God. Both ideal and material worlds were eternal for Plato, which clashed with the Judeo-Christian concept of the world being created *ex nihilo*. The idea of circulation and transmigration of human souls could not be reconciled with the Christian anthropology either.

Christians encountered the "middle" edition of Platonism, which flourished from the first century BC through the second century AD, when it was in the process of being upgraded to neo-Platonism. After a couple of centuries of skepticism and relative detachment from religion—something close to what we could render by the modern term of "secularization"—middle Platonism reconnected with the religious traditions of the Greek polytheism and tried to revitalize its spirituality. Neo-Pythagoreanism and oriental religious cults contributed to this metaphysical turn in the middle Platonism, which can be called ancient post-secularism.

This turn and specifically Platonic takes on the beginning and the end of the world and soul constituted a difficult dilemma for the Christian theologians. Many of them loved many aspects of Platonism, for which reason they have been branded as "Christian Platonists." However, none of them could fully identify themselves with proper Platonism. For this reason, some scholars have criticized the concept of "Christian Platonism" and argue that some of the so-called Christian Platonists were in effect "Christian anti-Platonists" (see Dörrie 1976: 522). This argument makes sense—those early theologians, who have been called "Platonists," would never call themselves like that.

The proximity of Platonism to Christianity and yet their incompatibility in some crucial points, made them difficult partners. Many Christians saw Platonism as deceitful, easy to be confused with the Christian orthodoxy. In result, while some theologians loved Platonism, many hated it. Others were confused. This love-hate relationship between Christianity and Platonism was rarely honest. Even the great "Christian Platonist," Gregory of Nyssa, called Plato's ideas "rubbish" (see Rist 2020). Those who had sympathies with Plato, usually preferred to hide them and to pretend they do not care or dislike him. Those theologians who demonstrated too much enthusiasm about Plato were sometimes disciplined by the church. For example, a council that took place in Constantinople in 1082 dealt with the case of the court philosopher John Italus, who openly demonstrated admiration for Platonism and used Platonic ideas without expected caution. The result was a conciliar condemnation of John and all those

> who pretend to be pious, while without shame and piety they bring to the Orthodox Catholic Church the impious teachings of the Greeks about human souls, heavens, earth, and other creatures. <. . .>
>
> Those who prefer the foolish and so-called wisdom of pagan philosophers and follow them in accepting the reincarnation of human souls or think that [souls], similarly to the irrational animals, get destroyed and turn into nothing; they thus reject the resurrection of the dead, the judgement, and the final retribution for the deeds in the present life. <. . .>
>
> Those who teach that matter is without beginning—together with ideas—or coeternal with God the creator of everything, that heavens and earth, as well as the rest of the creatures, are eternal and without beginning, and will remain unchangeable. <. . .>
>
> Those who receive Greek teachings and study them not only for the sake of education, but who follow their wrong opinions. <. . .>
>
> Those who, <. . .> by taking the Platonic ideas as true, claim that matter, as something self-sufficient, was formed by itself, and thus challenge the sovereign freedom of the Creator. (My translation from the *Τριῴδιον Κατανυκτικόν* 1856: 138)

# Aristotelian Language

In the Hellenistic period, many regarded renewed Aristotelianism as a via media between the ultra-metaphysical middle Platonism and ultra-physical Stoicism. Aristotle's works were rediscovered in the first century BC, when Andronicus of Rhodes published a new edition of the Aristotelian corpus. From the second century AD, there was a boom in commentaries on the Aristotelian treatises. These commentaries were produced not only by neo-Peripatetics but also by the followers of other philosophical schools, including middle-Platonic and Stoic (see Sorabji 1990: 1). This was also a time when Christian theologians became interested in Aristotle. Bishop of Laodicea Anatolius in the third century was among the earliest Christian admirers of the Stagirite thinker.

Some Christian authors hesitated to embrace Aristotle, because of his assumed pragmatism (see Edwards 2019: 100). He was accused of denying God's providence and focusing on the things pertinent to this world. Soon, however, theologians realized that this is not a disadvantage, but rather an advantage. Those theologians who felt intoxicated with the Platonic metaphysics could choose Aristotle as less metaphysical and therefore safer for the Christian orthodoxy. In contrast to Platonism, Aristotelianism did not interfere with the Christian metaphysics.

Aristotelianism was safer, but not safe. John Philoponus (*c.* 490–570), for example, was condemned for relying on Aristotle's categories too much. He studied in the neo-Platonic school of Alexandria as one of the Christian disciples of the pagan schoolmaster Ammonius. While following the neo-Platonic line of the school, he particularly valued the Aristotelian component in it. In this sense, he can be called neo-Aristotelian. Philoponus applied the Aristotelian categories more consistently than other Christian theologians did. He identified the Aristotle's first essence, which signified particularity, with the essence as it became perceived in the theological debates during the fourth and fifth centuries. He concluded that God has three essences, while Christ—only one (see Lang 2001). As a result, the ecumenical council held in Constantinople in 680–1 condemned Philoponus posthumously.

Those theologians who enjoyed Aristotle's sober and systematic approach, including such enthusiasts of his teaching as John Philoponus, did not buy him in wholesale. They treated in different ways his writings on logics and physics on the one hand and his metaphysical treatises on the other. They particularly valued the corpus of logical texts known as *Organon*. In this corpus, they paid special attention to the treatise *Categories*. Theodore Metochites (1270–332) explicitly stressed the value of Aristotle's logical and physical treatises and warned against his metaphysical works (*Γνωμικαὶ σημειώσεις* 11 & 12). Nicholas the bishop of Methone explained why the Byzantine theologians made such differentiation. He drew parallels between Plato's ideas and Aristotle's category of commonality. Both are generalizations of particular beings. The difference, however, is that for Plato those generalizations were real, while for Aristotle imagined and theoretical. For Aristotle, the commonalities of beings and things exist in our mind only and not as an objective reality. In the terms of the later Christian logics, Plato's ideas are hypostases, while Aristotle's categories are not—they generalize and conceptualize real hypostases:

> Plato, the most prominent among the sages of the Hellenes, fabricates certain "Ideas"; this is how he calls the genera and the species. For this reason, he claims that some of these Ideas are more universal henads, whereas others are more particular [henads]; but he does not introduce them as having no real existence. <. . .> Quite on the contrary, insofar as he claims that these are primary and self-subsistent substances or natures, [and are such] to the highest degree the more universal [henads], which give existence to the more particular, he proclaims them to be first and second gods and says that the rest of beings acquire their existence from them. But the extraordinarily wise Aristotle, who came immediately after him in time, rejected Plato's doctrine abundantly; he successfully named Plato's arguments in favour [of the existence] of the Ideas "twitterings," because they do not contribute anything to our comprehension of being and differ in nothing from empty noises, which are useless for the production of harmony. This is why the philosophers who succeeded Aristotle in the Peripatos (i.e.,

> the ancient commentators) declared that these very ideas are simply concepts [in our thought]. (*Or.* 6: Golitsis 2019: 37)

Christian theologians gradually came to prefer Aristotle to Plato, because his logics and physics were easier to distill from metaphysics. It was also easier than in the case of Plato to render the Aristotelian philosophy to a Christian theological meta-language. This metaphysics-free meta-language could be safe enough to be applied to the Christian metaphysics. Michael Psellus (*c.* 1018–82) explained this in his letter to John Xiphilinos:

> As for syllogisms (τοῦ δὲ τῶν συλλογισμῶν εἴδους), I have not yet despised this kind (εἶδος), even though I wish I could despise them, so that I could see the Lord in [His own] kind (ἐν εἴδει), and not in riddles. To exercise syllogisms, my brother, is neither a dogma alien to the church nor a paradoxical point made by those who think philosophically but is only an instrument of truth and a discovery of a thing that is inquired. And if someone does not want to approach the right reason in a more logical way (λογικώτερον) or does not wish to eat solid food, but instead wants to drink only milk, as a Corinthian did, should we, who in writings cope to explain the [divine] discourses in a more exact way, be proscribed to do so? (My translation from ep. 202)

Syllogisms that Michael was talking about are logical categories. He stressed their instrumental character and metaphysical neutrality. In contrast to Platonism, they do not distort Christian metaphysics.

## Neo-Platonic Dialect

The mainstream Christian theology came to express itself neither through pure Platonism nor through pure Aristotelianism, but through what scholars call neo-Platonism. Neo-Platonists did not regard themselves as "neo-Platonists," but plain "Platonists." They believed they faithfully continued the line of Plato. Therefore, in this book we call them "neo-Platonists" and not "Neoplatonists," as there is a custom. Their Platonic identity was most important for the neo-Platonists, for which reason we prefer the "Platonist" and not the "neo" part of the word to begin with capital letter. It was not a different Platonism, but an update to its previous versions.

Following the trend of that time, to look for points of convergence rather than cherishing divergencies between various philosophical teachings, neo-Platonists tried to build bridges from Platonism to other doctrines, primarily Aristotelianism and Stoicism (see Hadot 2015). The Aristotelian categories helped in this undertaking as a language that proved to be acceptable in various philosophical

**Figure 2.13** The famous painting by Raphael "The School of Athens" presents Platonism and Aristotelianism as seen from the neo-Platonic perspective, that is, compatible and engaged with one another in the same way as Plato and Aristotle could walk and talk together. Musei Vaticani.
Source: Photo by the author.

schools. The neo-Platonist Porphyry of Tyre (234–309), for example, chose categories as an instrument of reconciliation between Platonism and Aristotelianism. He even had to contest on this point his teacher Plotinus (*c.* 205–60), who, while accepting the Aristotle's categories to some extent, believed that they are irrelevant to Plato's world of ideas. When applied to the physical world, according to Plotinus, the Aristotelian categories had to be modified to fit Plato's physics (see Evangeliou 2016: 8–9). Porphyry, in contrast to Plotinus, was ready to accept the Aristotelian categories without any special adjustment to Platonism. He developed his point about compatibility of Aristotelianism and Platonism also in the treatises *On the School of Plato and Aristotle Being One* and *On the Difference Between Plato and Aristotle.*[5]

Porphyry's disciple Iamblichus (*c.* 240–325) made a step further and applied Aristotle's categories to the invisible world of ideas. Moreover, he insisted that these

[5]In case they are two different texts. Neither of them has survived. Only fragments have been preserved in the Arabic treatise by Ḥasan Muḥammad ibn Yūsuf ʿĀmirī: السعادة والاسعاد في السيرة الانسانية [*On Seeking and Causing Happiness*], edited by Mujtabá Mīnuvī (Wiesbaden: F. Steiner, 1957).

categories are applicable to the realm of ideas first and foremost (see in Simplicius 2000: 363.29–364.6). Iamblichus' neo-Platonism was highly metaphysical and infused with polytheistic spirituality. Porphyry himself was a convinced and practicing pagan. Similarly to the middle Platonism, neo-Platonism was explicitly religious and, as such, clearly contrasted itself to the Christian spirituality (see Addey 2014).

Nevertheless, while a practicing pagan and convinced anti-Christian, Porphyry tried to keep his personal religious convictions unmixed with the categories, which thus preserved metaphysical neutrality. This allowed Christians, and later Muslims and Jews, to borrow that part of his neo-Platonic teaching, which was least religious and mostly logical. This was the Aristotelian component in neo-Platonism. What scholars now call Christian Neoplatonism, therefore, should be better called Christian neo-Aristotelianism.[6]

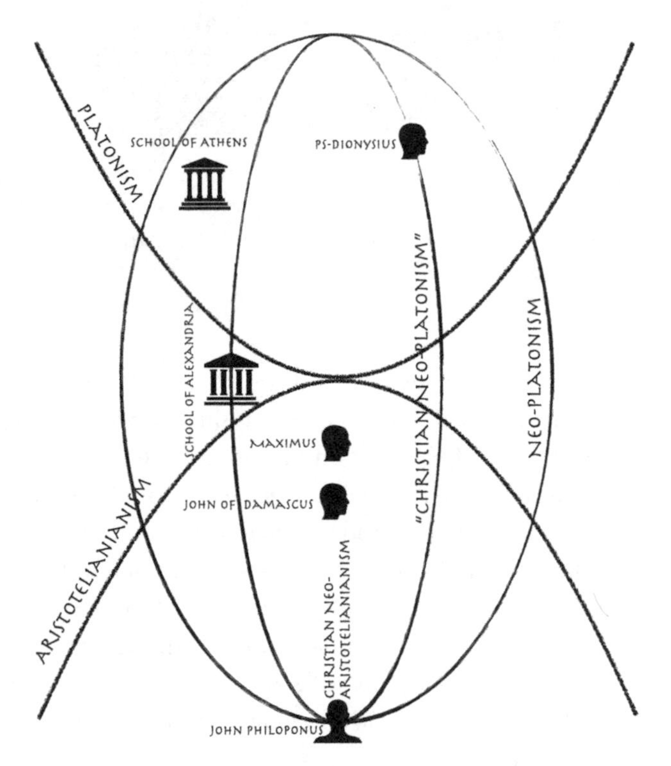


**Figure 2.14** Christian neo-Platonism and neo-Aristotelianism.

[6]This dialectical neo-Aristotelianism is not to be confused with rhetorical, ethical, metaphysical, and political Neoaristotelianisms. Rhetorical Neoaristotelianism was developed within the Chicago school of rhetorical criticism. It is based on Aristotle's *Poetics* and promotes narratives as communicative acts and not simply rhetorical structures. Ethical Neoaristotelianism is based on Aristotle's concept of virtue and updates it for

There were also some proper Christian neo-Platonists. Ps.-Dionysius the Areopagite was one of them. He introduced to the Christian theology the neo-Platonic concept of "hierarchy" (ἱεραρχία). In the original pagan neo-Platonism, this concept helped to sort out many gods to hierarchical ranks. Proclus (*c.* 410–85), a devoted polytheist, was particularly good in constructing those "divine hierarchies" (see Hovorun 2017: 132–44). Ps.-Dionysius applied the principle of hierarchy to the angels: he sorted out angels in hierarchical ranks similar to the ranks of gods in the pagan neo-Platonism.

modern times, as an alternative deontology and consequentialism. Metaphysical Neoaristotelianism addresses the modern concepts of substance. Political Neoaristotelianism is a political theory that explains society and political systems as based on a given ethos.

# II.5
# Eastern Logics

Categories constitute the basic structure of the theological meta-language.[1] Aristotle presented them as linguistic phenomena. He begins his *Categories* with describing "things that are *said*." They include such *grammatical* forms as homonyms, synonyms, and paronyms (*Categoriae* 1-2; Barnes 1984: 3). Posterior commentators on Aristotle continued developing categories as philological by their nature. Antique lexicographers and grammarians described categories as elements of speech. They appear in this capacity, for example, in the *Onomasticon* by Julius Pollux and in the grammatical treatises by Aelius Herodianus (both flourished in the second century AD in Egypt). As was mentioned, late antique and medieval interpreters of the Aristotelian categories called them "voices" (φωναί, *voces*), that is, elements of language. Christian theologians also perceived theological categories as grammatical forms. Theodore Studite, for instance, presented them as forms of noun:

> The general term "man" (ἄνθρωπος) is a common noun (προσηγορικὸν ὄνομα), but "Peter" and "Paul," to give an example, are instances of proper (κύριον) noun. So the particular individual can be called by the common name as well as by his own proper name. For instance, Paul is also called "man." In consideration of what he shares with other individuals of the same species (ὁμοειδέσιν), he is called man; but with regard to his own hypostasis, he is called Paul. If, therefore, the incarnate Christ were called merely God or man by scripture, then he would merely have assumed our nature in general; and, as we demonstrated previously, our nature cannot subsist unless it is contemplated in an individual manner. However, Gabriel said to the Virgin, "Behold, you will conceive in your womb, and bear a son, and you will call his name Jesus." Thus, Christ is called not only by a common name, but also by a proper name, and this distinguishes him from all other men in virtue of his hypostatic properties, and because of this he is circumscribable. (*Adversus iconoclastas* III 18; Cattol 2015: 94)

[1]See Luhtala 2005: 15–16. According to Ebbesen, the logical late antique standard corresponded to the grammatical late antique standard (Ebbesen 2007; see also Usacheva 2017: 73–114).

# Handbooks of Logics

During Late Antiquity and Middle Ages, categories constituted the main subject of studies in logics and, in this capacity, an introduction to philosophy. The most famous *Introduction* (Εἰσαγωγή) to philosophy based on Aristotle's *Categories* was composed by Porphyry of Tyre.[2] Unlike some other neo-Platonists, Porphyry did not believe that the Aristotelian categories had to be adjusted to Platonism. He accepted them at face value. At the same time, he wanted to make them more comprehensive, so that any philosophical school could use them. To make them simpler, he boiled down the ten original Aristotelian categories to five: genera, species,[3] differences, properties, and accidents. For this reason, medieval commentators called Porphyry's *Introduction* "Five voices" or "Five terms" (*Quinque voces*).

Porphyry's *Introduction* became an instant classics. It was translated to most languages of Antiquity. Its original Greek text has come down to us in over 150 manuscripts. Numerous commentaries mushroomed on this commentary on Aristotle soon after it was published. Being composed as a teachable handbook, the *Introduction* became a basis for many other handbooks. Dozens of generations of students began their studies in philosophy with Porphyry's book in hands. As Jonathan Barnes, who translated it in English, has remarked, "Other philosophical introductions may have sold more copies: none has had—or is likely to have—a longer career" (Porphyry 2003: ix).

# Reception of Pagan Logics

Being designed on the basis of Aristotelian philosophy in the framework of neo-Platonism with elements of Stoicism, categories, as formulated by Porphyry, became a universal logical instrument appropriated by various philosophical sects and in Christianity. Moreover, it became the most popular pagan text for the generations of Christian students. Despite Porphyry's aggressive anti-Christian propaganda in his polemical treatise *Against the Christians* (Berchman 2005; Hoffmann 1994), Christian theologians and educators believed that he was "the sanest of all the Neoplatonists" (Blumenthal 1993: 82). Christians preferred to keep a blind eye on what Porphyry

---

[2] *Introduction* is not the only logical treatise of Porphyry. He wrote a longer commentary on Aristotle's *Categories*, but it has not survived. Iamblichus' disciple Dexippus (flourished in the mid-fourth century; Dexippus 2014) summarized and quoted some of its points. Simplicius of Cilicia (flourished *c.* 530) also made references to Porphyry's commentaries (see Simplicius 2000).

[3] This was Cicero's favorite rendering of Plato's *eidos* (εἶδος) and *idea* (ἰδέα) into Latin, which is also used in modern European languages (see Cassin 2014: 1031–7).

had written about Christianity, as far as his logical apparatus did not compromise Christian metaphysics.

Christian theologians continued elaborating on categories creatively, following primarily the Porphyrian *Introduction*. They ignored some of his categories, refurbished others, and added new ones. Controversies from the fourth through the ninth centuries urged theologians to constantly rethink and, if needed, modify the canon of the categories. Particularly the neo-Chalcedonian Christology was productive in amending and enriching this canon.

Among those who contributed to the creative rethinking of the categories were Leontius of Byzantium, Ephraim of Antioch, Theodore of Raith, Athanasius Gammolo of Antioch, Maximus the Confessor, Anastasius of Sinai, John of Damascus, and Theodore Abū Qurrah. Some Christian theologians, such as Maximus the Confessor, touched on the categories occasionally—in his own words, in the "letter-writing" (*Op*. 21; Törönen 2007: 18), but these were the touches of a genius.

# Alexandrian Neo-Platonism

Alexandria was a place where Christianity met neo-Platonism and where the earliest Christian commentaries on Aristotle's *Categories* and Porphyry's *Introduction* were published. These commentaries came from the Alexandrian school of neo-Platonism, whose leadership chose to collaborate with the church and, if not to completely comply with, at least to pretend to be Christian. In this regard, it was different from the Athenian school of neo-Platonism, which demonstratively remained pagan, until it was dissolved by Justinian. Some Alexandrian neo-Platonic professors even received baptism and had Christian names, such as Elias and David.

These two neo-Platonists lived in the sixth century and were disciples of the pagan scholarch Olympiodorus. They composed commentaries on Aristotle and Porphyry (Gertz 2018). We do not know if these professors were Christians by conviction or pretension (see Wildberg 1990: 39–41). Their surviving texts are not different from the texts by overtly pagan neo-Platonists, save scarce hints to the creation of the world (see Muradyan 2015: 117). We know that one of the latest neo-Platonic philosophers in Alexandria, who flourished in the beginning of the seventh century, before this school was closed down following the Arab conquest of Egypt, was also Christian. His name was Stephen. We know about Stephen that he penned a commentary on Aristotle's logical treatise *De interpretatione*.[4]

[4]Mossman Roueché argues that Stephen should not be identified with an author who lived in the same time in Constantinople and is known as Ps.-Elias (Roueché 2012).

**Figure 2.15** A female figure with a warship on her head—the symbol of Alexandria. A second century BC mosaic from the Alexandria National Museum.
Source: Photo by the author.

# Theodore of Raith

In contrast to the Alexandrian approach to the dialectics, which had only lightly refurbished categories from the Christian perspective, a more radical rethinking of the logical apparatus was accomplished in the environment of the Palestinian monasticism. Geographically, this environment had two epicenters: within the triangle Raith-Pharan-St. Catherine's monastery on the Sinai peninsula and in the vicinities of Jerusalem. Theologically, it was neo-Chalcedonian. This was a trend in the Chalcedonian theology, which sought rapprochement with the anti-Chalcedonian Christians through the theological language of Cyril of Alexandria. There were two factions in the neo-Chalcedonian movement: monoënergist/monothelite and dyoënergist/dyothelite. The former accepted two natures and single activity and will in Christ, while the latter two natures, activities, and wills.

A Sinaite monk Theodore of Raith[5] belonged to the monoënergist faction in the neo-Chalcedonian movement. From the perspective of his Christological

[5]He is usually referred to as "Theodore of Raithu" or "Theodore of Raithou," but this reference is clumsy, as "Raithu" is genitive of the original Greek name of his town, Ραϊθός, which is best transliterated as Raith. Therefore, the correct way to address him is "Theodore of Raith." Most scholars nowadays believe that Theodore of Raith is the same person as Theodore of Pharan. Franz Diekamp, who critically published the *Preparation* in 1938 (Diekamp 1938), was the first who suggested that the two Theodores are the same person. Werner

preferences, he redefined the traditional neo-Platonic categories. Theodore has authored the earliest known handbook of logics, which was Christian not only in appearance but also in content. It was composed sometime between 580 and 620, and is titled *Preparation* (*Proparaskevé*/Προπαρασκευή).[6] In its structure and size, it was similar to Porphyry's *Introduction*. However, Theodore did not blindly copy the Aristotelian-Porphyrian categories, as was the custom in his days, but reworked them in a creative way.

# Anastasius of Sinai

A neo-Chalcedonian theologian from the opposite—dyoënergist—faction, who also lived on the Sinai peninsula, Anastasius, composed his own manual of Christian logics. He flourished two or three generations after Theodore, in the second half of the seventh century. Anastasius of Sinai lived most of his life outside the Byzantine Empire. This gave him freedom to polemicize against the imperial orthodoxy of that time—monothelitism. Anastasius demonstrated outstanding rhetorical skills. He also showed himself as a remarkable logician. In the late 680s, bits and pieces of Anastasius' writings were compiled under one cover titled *The Guide* (Ὁδηγός, *Viae dux*). Its substantial part explains logical categories, which are needed to understand the Eastern take on the natures, activities, and wills in Christ. This work was critically edited and published in 1981 by Karl-Heinz Uthemann.

# John of Damascus

Another neo-Chalcedonian dyothelite theologian who lived in Palestine, John of Damascus, produced a less colorful and original, but more inclusive and systematic logical introduction to the Orthodox theology. This introduction is called *Dialectica*.[7] It is a part of the summa titled *The Fountain Head of Knowledge* (Πηγὴ γνώσεως). This book is based on the earlier compilations, including *Doctrina patrum de*

Elert (Elert 1951: 71–3) found convincing arguments to support this hypothesis, which was also endorsed by Hans-Georg Beck (Beck 1959: 382–3). Some scholars, however, believed that the two Theodores are different persons. Such was the opinion of Marcel Richard in his article on Theodore in the *Dictionnaire de théologie catholique* (vol. 15.1, 1946. Paris: Librairie Letouzey et Ané: 284). Athanasios Nikas, who wrote on Theodore doctoral thesis at the University of Athens and produced the most detailed study of the *Preparation* (Νίκας 1981), aligned with Richard's hypothesis. However, Nikas' arguments are not convincing and ignore clear indications of Theodore's monoënergism in his *Preparation*.

[6] Sometimes it is also referred to as Περὶ τῆς ἐνσαρκώσεως (*On the Incarnation*).

[7] There are shorter (earlier) and longer (later) editions of the *Dialectica* published by Bonifatius Kotter (Kotter 1969: 51–146).

**Figure 2.16** The icon of John Damascene by Ioannis Tzenos (1682). Byzantine Museum of Antivouniotissa on Corfu, Greece.
Source: Photo by the author.

*incarnatione verbi* (Diekamp 1981), which was falsely ascribed to Anastasius of Sinai. The *Dialectica* consists of three parts: the exposition of the logical categories in the light of the previous commentaries on Aristotle's *Categories*; commonalities and differences between categories; and original categories as they had been put together by Aristotle (see Louth 2002: 40). In contrast to his predecessors who tried to reduce and simplify categories, John's method was to include in his taxonomy as many categories as possible, in all their complexity and diversity. Like his predecessors, he applied categories to solve various theological problems.

# Theodore Abū Qurrah

John's line in theology and logics was continued by Theodore Abū Qurrah, who transmitted the Palestinian dialectical tradition to the Arabic milieu. Theodore was born in Edessa in the 750s. At that time, the city was under the rule of the Abbasid caliphs. His family belonged to a Chalcedonian community. Theodore learned

**Figure 2.17** Medieval ruins in Harran, province Şanlıurfa in modern Turkey.
Source: Photo by the author.

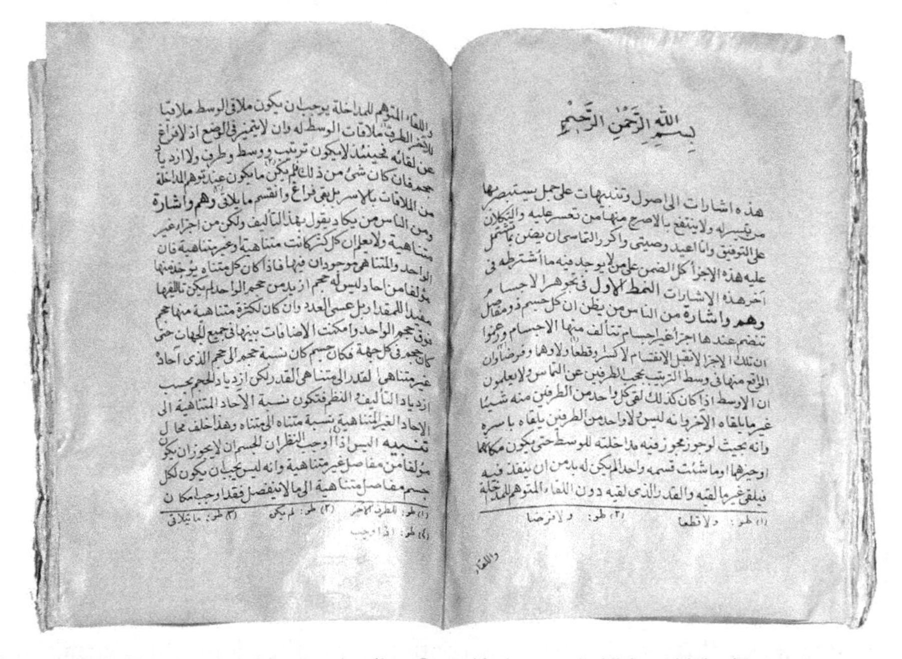

بسم الله الرحمن الرحيم

**Figure 2.18** The book of logics by Ibn Sīnā (Avicenna). Khiva, Uzbekistan.
Source: Photo by the author.

Arabic, which he used to compose his theological treatises. He thus became one of the earliest Christian authors who wrote in Arabic and is regarded as one of the founders of the Arabic Christian terminology and literature (see Roggema & Treiger 2020). Theodore was connected with St. Sabas monastery in the proximity of Jerusalem, served as a bishop of Harrān, until he was deposed for unspecified reasons. He flourished theologically in the period between 785 and 829 (see Griffith 1993: 148).

Theodore continued John of Damascus' line in many ways. He followed in the steps of John in advocating for Chalcedonian and dyothelite Christology, as well as in supporting icons. Theodore continued and eventually surpassed John in engagement with Muslim theology. He proved himself to be "extremely innovative in <. . .> attempt to articulate a new vision of Christian identity using the language and conceptual tools of Muslim theologians" (Lamoreaux 2002: 25). Less innovative but still solid were Theodore's exercises in logics. He transmitted to Arabic the key categories elaborated upon by the Byzantine and Palestinian theologians. Theodore's work was continued later in the Middle Ages by Muslim theologians.

## Syriac Logics

In parallel to the Byzantine and Palestinian lines of logics, distinct dialectical lines were developed in the Syriac world, both its Western and Eastern parts (see Watt 2019; King 2010). Eastern Syrians composed their handbooks in the Aristotelian-Porphyrian logics from as early as the mid-sixth century. Among them, Paul the Persian (fl. around 550), a convert from Zoroastrianism who worked at the Persian court in Seleucia-Ctesiphon, penned an *Introduction to the Study of Logics*. Two generations later, Abā of Kashkar (fl. around 600) left commentaries on the entire Aristotelian corpus of logics, according to ʿAbdišo. Silvanus of Qardu, who flourished in the early seventh century, compiled *Extracts from Profane Books and from the Philosophers*. Theodore bar Kōnī and Īšōʿbōkt of Rēv Ardašīr, who lived in the late eighth century, left numerous scholia on Aristotle's *Categories*, with their application to the Christological discussions. The Persian school of Nisibis and some Mesopotamian monasteries, such as Qenneshre, became centers of studies in the Aristotelian-Porphyrian logics (see Metselaar 2019: 13–14).

In the Western Syriac milieu, the adversaries of the council of Chalcedon developed their own logical apparatus. Sergius of Reš'aina (d. 536) left seven books *To Theodore, on the Aim of the Logic of Aristotle*, and a one-book summary *To Philotheos, on the Categories of Aristotle*. Athanasius of Balad (d. 687–8) composed an *Introduction to Logic*, where he focused on Aristotle's *Prior Analytics* and touched on the *Categories* and *De interpretatione*. Jacob of Edessa (d. 708) defined key logical

**Figure 2.19** A mosaic with Syriac inscriptions, Zeugma Museum in Gaziantep, Turkey. It demonstrates how the Greco-Roman and Syriac cultures became intertwined in the period of Late Antiquity.
Source: Photo by the author.

categories in his *Encheiridion*. George of the Arabs (d. 724) and David bar Paul (fl. around 785) left notes on the *Categories*, which remain unpublished in manuscripts. Gregory Bar Hebraeus (d. 1286) undertook a colossal task of summarizing the entire Aristotelian philosophy in his *Cream of Wisdom*. He compiled a shorter summary of Aristotle's *Organon* in the *Book of the Pupils of the Eye*.

# II.6

# Dialectical Taxonomies

As was mentioned, the original Aristotelian taxonomy of categories consisted of ten items. Porphyry reduced them to five. He also made clear explanations about how each category relates to others:

> Of predicates, some are said of only one item—namely, individuals (for example, Socrates and "this" and "that"), and some of several items—namely, genera and species and differences and properties and 20 accidents (those which hold commonly not properly of something). Animal, for example, is a genus; man a species; rational a difference; laughing a property; and white, black, sitting are accidents.
>
> Genera differ from what is predicated of only one item in that they are predicated of several items. Again, they differ from what is predicated of several items—from species because species, even if they are predicated of several items, are predicated of items which differ not in species but in number. Thus man, being a species, is predicated of Socrates and of Plato, who differ from one another not in species but in number, whereas animal, being a genus, is predicated of man and of cow and of horse, which differ from one another not only in number but also in species. (*Isagoge* 1; Barnes 2003: 4)

The Porphyrian *voces* were tuned up to better express the Christian doctrine. For example, Christian dialectical taxonomies often ignored the difference between "genus" (*genos*/γένος) and "species" (*eidos*/εἶδος). While these degrees of commonality were important for Aristotle, Porphyry, and other neo-Platonists, Christians preferred to speak about commonality in general, as "the common" (*to koinon*/τὸ κοινόν). They rendered the category of commonality in new terms, such as "essence" (*ousia*/οὐσία)[1] and "nature" (*physis*/φύσις).

---

[1]I prefer to translate *ousia* as "essence" and not "substance," because the latter can be easily confused with "hypostasis," which is literally rendered as "substance." As some ancient experts in logics explained, *ousia* derives from the verb "to be" (*einai*/εἶναι), for which reason it is more appropriate to translate it with the word "essence," which also derives from the Latin "to be" (esse). See Theodore of Raith, *Preparatio* (Diekamp 1938: 201 = Νίκας 1981: 204).

While speaking about the category of "differences" (*diaphorae*/διαφοραί), which in the neo-Platonic logics helped, among other things, differentiating between *genus* and species, Christians reapplied this category to stress the ontological chasm between the uncreated and created worlds, and how these two worlds have been united in Christ. This sort of utilization of "differences" was unthinkable in the neo-Platonic tradition, for which the world was uncreated.

Christians reimagined also the category of properties (*idiotes*/ἰδιότης, *poiotes*/ποιότης). They applied it primarily to the incarnation and connected it with the category of nature. The fourth Porphyrian category of property was expanded by Christians to include activity (*energeia*/ἐνέργεια) and volition (*thelesis*/θέλησις). The original Aristotelian categories of *energeia* (ἐνέργεια) and *dynamis* (δύναμις) have been modified and listed in the Christian dialectical taxonomies in a new fashion. Christian theologians occasionally used the distinction between properties (*idioma*/ἰδίωμα) and accidents (*symbebekos*/συμβεβηκός), but not as systematically as the neo-Platonists did.

Christians emphasized three logical functions, which in the neo-Platonic taxonomies had been rudimentary. First, they paid much attention to the differentiation between distinction and separation. This differentiation played an important role in the debates about the Trinity and the incarnation. For example, three divine persons are not separated but distinguished. Two natures in Christ are also distinguished but not separated.

Second, during the debates about the veneration of icons, the idea of image (*eikōn*/εἰκών) was upgraded to a distinct logical category. This idea preexisted in the classical thought, but only in Christianity it became thoroughly studied from both theological and philosophical perspectives. The difference between the uncreated and created world underlined the Christian take on image, which was understood as a bridge between the two worlds.

Finally, Christians utilized in a creative way the neo-Platonic concept of participation (*metoché*/μετοχή). They used both categories of image and participation to make clear the connection between the created and uncreated worlds. Participation is a more ontological sort of connection, in contrast to more epistemological connection provided by image. The difference between participation and image is similar to the two kinds of knowledge: knowing God and knowing about God. By knowing God, we participate in him. We render our knowledge about God through images.

## Common and Particular

The most important of all categories, in both pagan and Christian philosophies, were commonality and particularity. These two categories framed the entire classical Christian theology. Outside their framework, patristic thought cannot be comprehended adequately.

Peripatetic philosophy should be credited for elaborating on these categories in the first place. Aristotle suggested two ways of defining commonality and particularity in beings: one is philological and another ontological. According to the philological approach, commonality is what can be said of similar beings. From this perspective, both particularity and commonality can be applied to subjects and their properties:

> Of things there are:
>
> (a) some are said of a subject but are not in any subject. For example, man is said of a subject, the individual man, but is not in any subject.
>
> (b) Some are in a subject but are not said of any subject. (By "in a subject" I mean what is in something, not as a part, and cannot exist separately from what it is in.) For example, the individual knowledge-of-grammar is in a subject, the soul, but is not said of any subject; and the individual white is in a subject, the body (for all colour is in a body), but is not said of any subject.
>
> (c) Some are both said of a subject and in a subject. For example, knowledge is in a subject, the soul, and is also said of a subject, knowledge-of-grammar.
>
> (d) Some are neither in a subject nor said of a subject, for example, the individual man or the individual horse—for nothing of this sort is either in a subject or said of a subject. Things that are individual and numerically one are, without exception, not said of any subject, but there is nothing to prevent some of them from being in a subject—the individual knowledge-of-grammar is one of the things in a subject. (*Categoriae* 2; Barnes 198: 3)

Ontological approach is more specific, as it applies to the category of "essence" (οὐσία). Aristotle differentiated between two kinds of essence: primarily and secondary ones. The former corresponds to particularity, while the latter to commonality. Commonality per se can be more common or more particular. In the former case, it is called "genus" (γένος), while in the latter "species" (εἶδος):

> A substance (οὐσία)—that which is called a substance most strictly, primarily, and most of all—is that which is neither said of a subject nor in a subject, e.g. the individual man or the individual horse. The species in which the things primarily called substances are, are called secondary substances, as also are the genera of these species. For example, the individual man belongs in a species, man, and animal is a genus of the species; so these—both man and animal—are called secondary substances. (*Categoriae* 5; Barnes 1984: 4; see Mignucci 2019: 128–56)

Distinction between commonality and particularity continued to be entertained in the philosophical schools after Aristotle's works had been archived and remained in oblivion for a couple of centuries. Stoic philosophers in particular took over this distinction (see Brumberg-Chaumont 2014: 69–71; Sorabji 2006: 83–93; Gourinat

2000). They developed on its basis an idea of "individual quality" (τὸ ἰδίως ποιόν) (see *Stoicorum Veterum Fragmenta* 395). The Stoics stressed particularity over commonality and applied the former primarily in their physics.

Apollonius Dyscolus (second century AD) summarized the Stoic distinction between commonality and particularity by defining two kinds of nouns, common and proper ones: "The institution of nouns was devised for [the signification] of qualities, whether common, for instance 'man,' or peculiar, for instance 'Plato'" (*Syntax* II 22; my translation based on F. W. Housegolder's in Brumberg-Chaumont 2014). Apollonius noticed that proper and common nouns can be distinguished by the article. The former do not need it as much as the latter do: "Proper nouns, because they have in themselves their particularity (ἰδιότητα) do not need the article in the same manner as those [nouns] to which a common conception (κοινὴ ἔννοια) belongs" (*Syntax* I 112; my translation based on F. W. Housegolder's in Brumberg-Chaumont 2014). Apollonius also noticed that particular beings answer the question "who?" (τίς) (*Syntax* I 31).

Differentiation between commonality and particularity resurged in the frame of neo-Platonism (see Chiaradonna 2014), particularly in the works of Porphyry. Porphyry, as was mentioned, in developing his categories relied on Aristotle, utilized some Stoic concepts, and added to them his own ideas. He presented the categories of commonality and particularity as a hierarchical pyramid with three steps: genus on the top, species in the middle, and individual beings at the bottom:

> In each type of predication there are some most general items and again other most special items; and there are other items between the most general and the most special. Most general is that above which there will be no other superordinate genus; most special, that after which there will be no other subordinate species; and between the most general and the most special are other items which are at the same time both genera and species (but taken in relation now to one thing and now to another). (*Isagoge* 2; Barnes 2003: 5–6)

Porphyry sorted out all his categories as a pile, with "the upper items being always predicated of the lower" (*Isagoge* 2, 8; Barnes 2003: 8, 14). Such hierarchization of categories fitted the neo-Platonic way of thinking, which was inherently hierarchical. Porphyry appreciated commonality more than particularity (see Zachhuber 2014b: 93). For him, particular is ontologically inferior to common. He made another important observation about the nature of particularity: it is a bundle of particular qualities:

> Such items are called individuals because each is constituted of proper features the assemblage of which will never be found the same in anything else—the proper features of Socrates will never be found in any other of the particulars. (*Isagoge* 2; Barnes 2003: 8)

This idea became popular among the Christian theologians in the classical era. Following Porphyry, they often defined hypostasis as a result of the conflation of properties. However, this idea is counterintuitive to the modern perception of individuality, which we tend to regard as a source and not a result of various individual qualities.

Christian theology adopted the distinction between commonality and particularity as a part of its strategies to defend monotheism. This distinction, which had been elaborated by convinced polytheists, became useful in proving that God is one, even though he is Trinity. The oneness and plurality of the Christian God have been harmonized with the assistance of the categories of commonality and particularity. The so-called neo-Nicaean theologians were particularly successful in such harmonization. Apollinaris of Laodicea was among the first who explained the oneness of God as commonality, and God's plurality as the unity of three particularities (see Zachhuber 2014c: 428):

> We call one *ousia* not only that which is numerically one, as you say, and that which is in one circumscription, but also, specifically, two or more men who are united as a family (γένος): thus two or more can be the same in *ousia*, as all men are Adam and [thus] one, and the son of David is David being the same as him; in this respect you rightly say that the Son is in *ousia* what the Father is. For in no other way could there be a Son of God, given that the Father is confessed to be the one and only God, but in some way like the one Adam is the primogenitor of men and the one David the originator of the royal dynasty. In this way, then, both [the idea of] one antecedent genus and [that of] one underlying matter in Father and Son can be removed from our conceptions, when we apply the prodigenital property to the supreme principle and the clans derived from a primogenitor to the only-begotten offspring of the one principle. For to a certain extent they resemble each other: there is neither one common genus term of Adam, who was formed by God, and us, who were born of humans, but he himself is the principle (ἀρχή) of humanity, nor matter common to him and us, but he himself is the starting point (ὑπόθεσις) of all men. (In Basil of Caesarea, *ep*. 362; Zachhuber 2020: 26)

Apollinaris was among the first theologians who realized the universal applicability of the distinction between communality and particularity to both the Trinity and the incarnation. He also coined suitable terminology. In the classical Aristotelian-Porphyrian tradition, particularity was usually called "individuality" (ἄτομον) or "something existing in a particular way" (τὸ κατὰ μέρος). Apollinaris used the word "person" (πρόσωπον) to denote the particularities of the Father and the Son. He applied this term also to the incarnated Word, Jesus Christ (see Spoerl 1991: 353).

Apollinaris could not yet clearly differentiate between communality and particularity. For example, he interpreted the Father as the exclusive bearer of the divine essence, while the Son, for him, participates in the divine essence only by the virtue of his begottenness from the Father. In Christ, Apollinaris identified the nature as a category, in which commonality and particularity mix up. Therefore, Christ's nature for him was one.

In contrast to Apollinaris, his younger neo-Nicaean confederate Basil of Caesarea stressed that the Father and the Son equally share in the divine essence. To make clear that "essence" should not be mixed up with any particularity, Basil specified that commonality features the "logos of essence" (τῆς οὐσίας λόγος). To avoid confusing particularity with commonality, he applied to them different terms: *ousia* (οὐσία) for commonality and hypostasis (ὑπόστασις) for particularity:

> If we have to state briefly our own opinion, we shall say this that the relation the common item has to the particular, *ousia* has to hypostasis. For each of us partakes of being (εἶναι) through the common formula of being (τῆς οὐσίας λόγῳ), but he is one or the other through the properties (ἰδιώμασιν) attached to him. So also there (sc. in the Godhead) the formula of being is the same, like goodness, divinity and what else one may conceive of: but the hypostasis is seen in the properties of fatherhood or sonship or the sanctifying power. (*Ep.* 214; Zachhuber 2020: 38)

Basil probably did not coin the dialectical pair *ousia-hypostasis*. Before Basil, it had appeared around 358 in the West, in the treatise *Against Arius* by Gaius Marius Victorinus (see Zachhuber 2014a: 56). Victorinus was interested in the neo-Platonic categories and produced Latin translations of Aristotle's *Categories* and *On Interpretation*, as well as of Porphyry's *Introduction*. Therefore, it should not be a surprise that he applied in a creative way the neo-Platonic distinction between commonality and particularity to the Trinitarian theology (see Henry 1950). Yet, Victorinus mentioned that the "Greeks" had done this before him. Whether he meant Basil, or Apollinaris, or someone else is unclear. Clear is that Basil convinced many in the East that the logical pair *ousia-hypostasis*, standing for commonality and particularity correspondingly, can help resolve the seemingly unresolvable dilemma between the oneness and plurality of God.

In Basil's letter 38, which many scholars ascribe to Gregory of Nyssa (see Zachhuber 2020: 15), its author gives a more detailed explanation about his choice of terms. The reason why he has chosen the word "hypostasis" has to do with its root "stasis" (στάσις), which among other things means position and foundation. Hypostasis is something that makes something or someone real and substantial:

> The indefinite notion of "ousia" (substance), which by reason of the generality (τῆς κοινότητος) of the term employed discloses no "sistence" (στάσιν); it is the conception which, by means of the specific notes that it indicates, restricts and circumscribes in a particular thing (πρᾶγμα) what is general (τὸ κοινόν) and uncircumscribed (ἀπερίγραπτον). (*Ep.* 38)

It was mentioned that, following Porphyry, some Christian theologians understood the uniqueness of each hypostasis as a result of the conflation of particular qualities (see Zachhuber 2020: 54). Basil or Gregory stated in this regard in the same epistle 38:

> By all these means—the name, the place, the peculiar qualities of his character, and his external attributes as disclosed by observation—the description of the subject of the story becomes explicit. But if he had been giving an account of the substance, there would have been no mention of the aforesaid things in his explanation of its nature; for the same terms would have been used as in describing Baldad the Sauhite, Sophar the Minnaean, and each of the men mentioned in the narrative (see Job 2:11). (*Ep.* 38)

The Cappadocian theologians demonstrated that both terms *ousia* and *hypostasis* can be truly universal. They are applicable not only to God or Christ but to any alive being and any being whatsoever. Because of their clarity and universality, these terms became accepted as the theological *koine* and constitute basic theological categories to our days.

In neo-Platonism, as it was mentioned, there was a hierarchy between the categories of commonality and particularity. The former was regarded superior to the latter. This superiority of the common can be explained by the Platonic legacy in neo-Platonism. Commonality was considered as belonging to the world of ideas, which in Platonism is more valuable than the visible world that consists of particular beings. Arius and his followers in the fourth century, although they did not employ the categories of commonality and particularity explicitly, implicitly reversed the neo-Platonic hierarchy of categories. For them, the particularity of the Father and the Son made more sense than their commonality. For this reason, they rejected the term "consubstantial" (ὁμοούσιος) and believed the Son to be inferior to the Father.

In contrast to them, neo-Nicaeans established an equilibrium between commonality and particularity—as ontologically equal categories. Neo-Nicaeans regarded these categories as applying to God simultaneously and to the same extent. The three persons of God share in commonality to the same degree as they feature particularity. The author of the epistle 38 made such equilibrium clear:

> It is impossible in any manner to conceive of a severance or separation whereby either the Son is thought of apart from the Father or the Spirit is parted from the Son; but there is apprehended among these three a certain ineffable and inconceivable communion and at the same time distinction, with neither the difference between their persons disintegrating the continuity of their nature, nor this community of substance confounding the individual character of their distinguishing notes. <. . .>
>
> The same thing is both joined and separated (τὸ αὐτὸ καὶ συνημμένον καὶ διακεκριμένον εἶναι), and if, as though speaking in riddles, we devise a strange and paradoxical sort of united separation (διάκρισίν τε συνημμένην) and disunited connection (διακεκριμένην συνάφειαν). (*Ep.* 38)

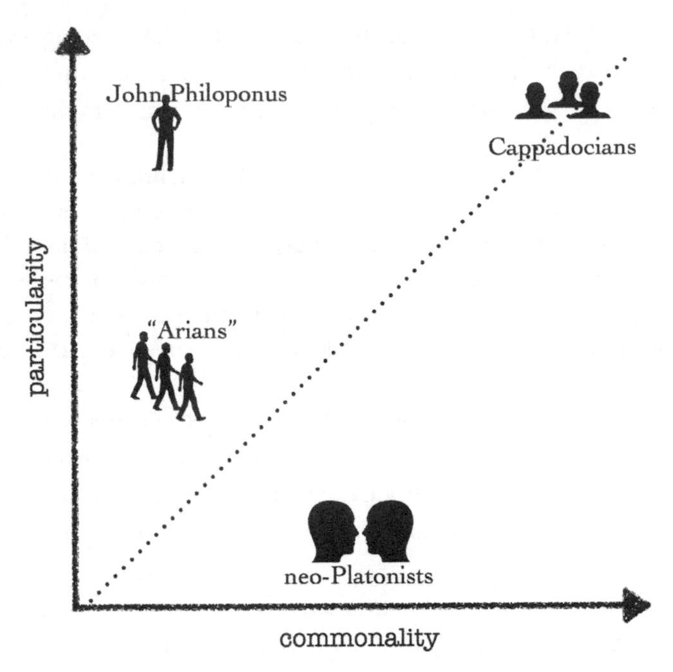


**Figure 2.20** This chart schematically demonstrates how different doctrines balanced the categories of commonality and particularity.

The equilibrium between commonality and particularities in the Trinity, which had been established by the Cappadocian fathers, was disturbed by a Christian neo-Aristotelian, John Philoponus. He valued particularities more than commonalities: "Species and genera are posterior to particular individuals" (*Fr.* 1; Erismann 2014: 148). In this point, Philoponus broke away from the Platonic legacy in neo-Platonism, which valued the world of ideas more than the world of real things. He also unwillingly concurred with Arius and his confederates, who had ostensibly stressed the particularities of the Father and the Son at the expense of their commonality. Philoponus went even further than that: he claimed that in God only particularities are real, while commonality is merely an intellectual construct.

John Philoponus was an original thinker with a systematic and critical approach even to what he valued. Thus, he respected his neo-Platonic teacher Ammonius and admired Aristotle. Yet, he criticized both neo-Platonic and Peripatetic schools—from the Christian perspective on creation. At the same time, Philoponus criticized some Christian points—from the perspective of the Aristotelian logics. He built his critique on the presupposition that commonalities cannot exist without particularities. In a fragment that has survived in Syriac, Philoponus asserted: "Nothing which is called 'common' has existence of its own apart from the particular: there exists only this horse, only this man, only this angel" (*Contra Themistium*, fr. 22; Erismann 2014: 148). As a matter of fact, only particularities exist, while commonalities are imagined:

> Each common thing is constructed by our intellect from particulars. For this reason, the Ancients called such things posterior and intellectual beings. For, correctly speaking, Peter, John and every individual man are animal and substance, and the same goes for this horse and that ox. However, these names passed from these (particulars) to what is called genera and species, that is, from things which subsist in substance to those which are inferred by our intellect.
>
> This is why the important physicist, Aristotle, says: the universal either is nothing or is posterior. Nothing, because no universal has a proper existence, and our idea about them is not, correctly speaking, a substance. Particulars are called principal and first substances, whereas that which is said of many, i.e., genera and species, is called substance only in a secondary way. And this is why, when we speak not metaphorically, but properly, we call hypostases "substances." (*Contra Themistium*, fr. 1; Erismann 2014: 148)

The assumption that commonality can exist only as long as particularities exist, is correct. This assumption was held by many other theologians. Maximus the Confessor, for instance, stated characteristically that "if all the particular are destroyed <. . .> also the universals will be destroyed with them" (*Ambiguum ad Joh.* X; Törönen 2007: 142). However, this presupposition led Philoponus to a controversial conclusion that an individual being does not share anything real with other individual beings of the same nature:

> This common nature of man, in which no one man differs from any other, when it is realised in any one of the individuals, then is particular to that one and is not common to any other individual. <. . .> Thus that rational mortal animal which is in me is common to no other animal. <. . .> Thus that rational mortal animal which is in me is not common to any other man. Neither would the animal nature which is in this particular horse be in any other. (*Arbiter* 7, quoted by John of Damascus in *De haeresibus* 5; Erismann 2014: 147)

This train of thought brought Philoponus to the conclusions, which have been rejected by the church. He assumed that (1) God is not one, but three realities, and his oneness is imagined and that (2) the reality of Jesus Christ is single and therefore he could have only one essence. The latter statement had important soteriological ramifications. For Philoponus, the humanity of Christ did not share commonality with the rest of the humankind—not in any real sense. His humanity constituted an exclusive and singular particularity with his divinity. This meant that the salvific effect of the incarnation was confined to this particularity of Jesus and could not be extended to other human beings.

This was too much even for the miaphysites, who also had claimed that Christ had one nature. The mastermind of this theological group, Severus of Antioch, in contrast to Philoponus, insisted that Christ, in his humanity, is consubstantial with the rest of humankind. Severus paid particular attention to the distinction between the categories of common and particular. Following Porphyry and Gregory of Nyssa, Severus explained particularity as a bundle of properties:

> The set of properties of Peter is one; the fact that he is from the little village of Beth-Saida, the son of John, the brother of Andrew, and a fisherman of skill, and after these things, an apostle, and because of the orthodoxy and firmness of his faith had been newly named "Rock" by Christ. But another is the set of properties of Paul, the fact that he is from Cilicia, that he used to be a Pharisee, that he was taught and learned the law of the fathers at the feet of Gamaliel, and that after having persecuted, he preached the Gospel <. . .> *and all these other things that are written concerning him in a history.* In the same way hypostasis does not deny genus or ousia or abolish it, but it sets apart and limits in particular icons the one who subsists. For in ousia and in genus Peter is a man as is Paul; but in propriety he is distinguished from Paul. (*Hom.* 125; Chesnut 1976: 11–12)

In contrast to Philoponus, who was a consistent neo-Aristotelian, other miaphysites followed the logical line of Porphyry and other neo-Platonists. Regarding logics, they were on the same page with their theological opponents from the dyophysite camp. At the same time, they had their preferred neo-Platonic logicians. They particularly favored a professor at the Alexandrian neo-Platonic school David.

David received an unprecedented reception in Armenia, where he has become an intellectual hero. The Armenian tradition presents David, anachronistically, as a disciple of Mesrop Maštocʿ (mid-fourth century–439 or 440) and Catholicos Sahak (Isaac) the Great (*c.* 345–439). He was believed to having won theological contests in

**Figure 2.21** A manuscript with the Armenian translation of Aristotle's *Categories*. From the collection of the Mesrop Mashtots Institute of Ancient Manuscripts (*Matenadaran*) in Yerevan, Armenia.

Source: Photo by the author.

Athens and Constantinople, together with Movsēs Xorenacʿi. For these reasons, Armenians called him "invincible." Four of David's philosophical treatises have survived in Armenian translation: *Prolegomena philosophiae*, commentary on Porphyry's *Introduction*, commentary on Aristotle's *Categories*, and commentary on Aristotle's *Analytics*. The Greek original of the latter has been lost.

David, in his commentary on Porphyry, argued that commonalities "are not in bare thought but subsist." At the same time, "they are not bodies but incorporeal" (*On Porphyry's Introduction* 9; Muradyan 2015: 123). He criticized those who rejected the reality of commonalities:

> There was doubt among some old masters, e.g. Antisthenes. For Antisthenes said: "I see a man, not humanity, I see a horse, not horsehood, I see a bull, not bullhood." He said so trying to show that particulars and sensibles exist whereas universals and intelligibles do not exist. Rejecting this we claim that not all beings are objects of the senses. For if only those that are objects of the senses are beings then, since the divine, reason and the soul are not objects of the senses, they are not beings. Besides, we must not believe the senses for they do not report the truth. Note that the sun, although it is many times larger than the earth, appears inch-sized and that the senses see an oar in the water as broken. (*On Porphyry's Introduction* 6; Muradyan 2015: 109–11)

It should be noted that David contemplated relationship between commonalities and particularities not in the Cappadocian way, but rather in the spirit of classical neo-Platonism. Thus, he believed that the category of commonality is more "honorable" than particularities: "Universals are, as they are always and in the same manner, more honourable" (*On Porphyry's Introduction* 5; Muradyan 2015: 97). In this point, David departed from the equilibrium between the two categories established by the Cappadocians and their followers.

David is credited with the logical framework, in which Armenian theologians preferred to articulate their theology. One of them, Khosrovik Targmanich, lived between 630 and 730. He was a key figure in articulating Armenian Christology. His theology underpinned the decisions of the council of Manzikert in 726, which defined the theological profile of the Armenian Christianity. Categories played an important role in Khosrovik's theology. For example, he explained the difference between commonalities and particularities as follows:

> Into four are divided the names that are said about existing things: the general, the whole, the individual and the each one. Let us leave others aside for a moment and say a few words about the each one that will help for the understanding the [notions] that I am going to propose. The each one is denoted by the following: from the location, parents, actions and passions. Now all these [properties] are combined separately in each one, and the collection of them together are not seen in another. Don't we see all these properly suitable for our Lord and Savior: the name—being Jesus Christ, location—Nazareth, parent—the Holy Virgin, kind—the appearance by which He

> knew others and was known, action—the wonders that He made among people, passions—baptism, crucifixion, burial, resurrection in three days, ascension to heavens and further things? (Khosrovik 2019: 53–5)

Chalcedonians had their own preferred logicians. One of them was Theodore of Raith. Similarly to Khosrovik, Theodore paid a particular attention to the differentiation between commonalities and particularities, and how they relate to other categories. For example, Theodore defined "essence" (οὐσία) as everything that exists in self-sufficient way (αὐθυπόστατον), that is, in itself (καθ᾽ ἑαυτό) and not for (δι᾽ ἄλλο) or in (ἐν ἑτέρῳ) anything else. To exist (εἰς τὸ ὑπάρχειν), *ousia* does not need anything from outside (ἔξωθεν αὐτοῦ). The synonym of the word "essence" is "nature" (φύσις). It is not, however, a complete synonym, as there is a subtle difference between them. "Nature" features dynamism; it embeds the principle of movement or stillness (κινήσεώς τε καὶ ἠρεμίας) (see *Preparatio*; Diekamp 1938: 202 = Νίκας 1981: 206). Theodore cohered with Apollinaris of Laodicea, who also considered "nature" as imbued with dynamism.

**Figure 2.22** Frescos in the Holy Cross cathedral of the Armenian Catholicosate of Aghtamar. Van Lake, Turkey.

Source: Photo by the author.

"Essence" and "nature" are a pair of synonyms that denote common existence. There is a corresponding pair of synonyms that denote particular existence: "hypostasis" (ὑπόστασις) and "person" (πρόσωπον). As Theodore put it, "on the one hand, the essence (οὐσία) means [that] something is common (κοινόν); on the other hand, hypostasis (ὑπόστασις) [means] particular (ἴδιον)" (see *Preparatio*; Diekamp 1938: 204 = Νίκας 1981: 210). The notion of particularity, according to Theodore, includes the notion of commonality, but not the other way around. He put it in this way:

> The name of essence (τὸ τῆς οὐσίας ὄνομα) does not always contain [the notion of] hypostasis. At the same time, [the notion] of hypostasis always contains also [the notion] of essence (οὐσία). (My translation from *Preparatio*; Diekamp 1938: 205 = Νίκας 1981: 212)

Theodore of Raith followed the line of Porphyry in defining the category of hypostasis. Similarly to the latter, he considered it to be "a bundle of accidents" (τὸ τῶν συμβεβηκότων ἄθροισμα) (see *Preparatio*; Diekamp 1938: 205 = Νίκας 1981: 212). The difference between the categories of hypostasis and *prosopon* is similar to the difference between *ousia* and *physis*. The key differentiator between them is the category of *energeia* (ἐνέργεια), which can be translated as activity or operation. A person makes himself or herself known to others through activities. Activities basically differentiate one person from another:

> Person is someone who through [his or her] own deeds (ἐνεργημάτων) and properties (ἰδιωμάτων) shows [him or herself] clearly as different from other [persons] of the same nature (ὁμοφυῶν). (My translation from *Preparatio*; Diekamp 1938: 206 = Νίκας 1981: 214)

Similarly to the category of "hypostasis," which is a bundle of accidents, "person" can be described as consisting of the bundle of activities. Theodore, thus, tightly links activities (ἐνέργειαι) with "person" (πρόσωπον). In this point, he follows the monoënergist thread in the neo-Chalcedonian theology. In contrast to this thread, the dyoënergist neo-Chalcedonians linked activities to the category of nature, and not person. Maximus the Confessor, who was a protagonist of the dyoënergist neo-Chalcedonianism, bluntly criticized Theodore for defining the category of person through activities:

> I read the book of Theodore of Pharan on essence and nature, hypostasis and person, and the rest of the chapters; and as an introduction it is perhaps not altogether useless. But in the chapter on person and hypostasis, rather than following the rules concerning them, he seems to be following himself, as he calls the activity hypostatic. And it is in this that he has let his reason grow dark, namely, in giving to the person *qua* person the activity which characterizes nature. (*Op*. 10; Törönen 2007: 28)

Theodore, thus, tailored categories to make them fitting his doctrinal preferences. Connecting "activity" with "person" was one of such preferences. Another logical statement was tuned up to corroborate the Chalcedonian formula of one hypostasis in two natures. For Theodore, an essence can be combined with another essence into a single hypostasis. Something like this happened following the incarnation. At the same time, in contrast to the Nestorian teaching, a hypostasis cannot be combined with another hypostasis into a single being. Such a combination of hypostases can produce only a group of beings. In the modern terms, such combination can be only sociological, not ontological:

> An essence put together (συντεθειμένη) with [another] essence produces one hypostasis. However, an hypostasis put beside (παρατιθεμένη) another hypostasis [produces] neither essence nor hypostasis, but a composite group (περιληπτικόν τι σύστημα), such as for instance demos, choir, crowd, multitude of people, army and so on. (My translation from *Preparatio*; Diekamp 1938: 215 = Νίκας 1981: 232)

Before Theodore, Leontius of Byzantium had found other ways to explain the same idea. Like Theodore, Leontius redefined the classical categories to make them fit his theological preferences. Unlike Theodore, however, he did not present them in a systematic way, as a handbook. Leontius was a strict Chalcedonian, not a neo-Chalcedonian. He insisted that we must speak of two natures only and not about one and two natures. To prove his point, he utilized the category of *enhypostaton* (ἐνυπόστατον).

This term had probably been coined by Irenaeus and certainly used by Origen (see Gleede 2012: 13–15). It became popular in the fourth century, especially in the works of Epiphanius of Salamis. Cyril of Alexandria also included it to his theological vocabulary (*Thesaurus*; PG 75, 101), together with the terms *enousios* (ἐνούσιος) (*Thesaurus*; PG 75, 105, 257, 260, 261, 360) and *ousiodes* (οὐσιώδης) (*Thesaurus*; PG 75, 549), which later would be utilized by Leontius.

By elaborating on the category of *enhypostaton*, Leontius addressed an objection, which had been brought up by his miaphysite opponents: if the natures are two, then hypostases in Christ should be two too, because a nature cannot exist without its own hypostasis. Leontius agreed that there are no unhypostatic (ἀνυπόστατον) natures. He also agreed that the common and particular in Christ should be clearly differentiated—fortunately, such a differentiation had been an axiom for all disputing theological factions since at least the fourth century.

In addition to this common wisdom, Leontius suggested to differentiate between particularity and commonality in Christ as between hypostasis and *enhypostaton* (ἐνυπόστατον). "Hypostatic" would be the best translation for this term (see Anastasius of Sinai, *Viae dux* II 3; Uthemann 1981: 38). Leontius characterized commonality as in need to be substantiated and particularized through hypostasis, and for this reason, "hypostatic" (ἐνυπόστατον). This was an ingenious logical twist, which implied that any essence can be substantiated either through its own or another hypostasis.

This twist had immediate Christological ramifications: Christ's humanity is hypostatic not on its own, but through the hypostasis of the Word. It should be noted here that "nature" (φύσις) was not for Leontius the same category as "essence" (οὐσία): the categories of "hypostasis" and "essence" conflate in the category of "nature," which signifies the completeness (τὸ τέλειον) of a being (see Zhyrkova 2017: 200). The classical excerpt that explains the category of *enhypostaton* and its relation to other categories can be found in the beginning of Leontius' polemical treatise *Against the Nestorians and the Eutycheans*:

> Hypostasis, gentlemen, and the hypostatic (ἐνυπόστατον) are not the same thing, just as essence and the essential (ἐνούσιον) are different. For the hypostasis signifies the individual (τὸν τινά), but the hypostatic the essence (οὐσίαν); and the hypostasis defines the person (πρόσωπον) by means of peculiar characteristics (τοῖς χαρακτηριστικοῖς ἰδιώμασι), while the hypostatic signifies that something is not an accident (συμβεβηκός), which has its being (τὸ εἶναι) in another (ἐν ἑτέρῳ) and is not perceived by itself. Such are all qualities (ποιότητες), those called essential (οὐσιώδεις) and those called non-essential (ἐπουσιώδεις); neither of them is the essence, which is a subsistent thing (πρᾶγμα ὑφεστώς)—but is perceived always in association with an essence, as with color in a body or knowledge in a soul. He then who says, "There is no such thing as an anhypostatic (ἀνυπόστατος) nature," speaks truly; but he does not draw a correct conclusion when he argues from its being not-anhypostatic (μὴ ἀνυπόστατον) to its being an hypostasis—just as if one should say, correctly, that there is no such thing as a body without form (ἀσχημάτιστον), but then conclude incorrectly that form is body, not that it is seen in the body. There could never, then, be an anhypostatic nature—that is, essence. But the nature is not a hypostasis, because it is not a reversible attribution; for a hypostasis is also a nature, but a nature is not also a hypostasis: for nature admits of the predication of being, but hypostasis also of being-by-oneself (καθ' ἑαυτὸν εἶναι), and the former presents the character of genus (εἴδους), the latter expresses individual identity. And the one brings out what is peculiar to something universal (καθολικοῦ πράγματος), the other distinguishes the particular (τὸ ἴδιον) from the general (τοῦ κοινοῦ). To put it concisely, things sharing the same essence (τὰ ὁμοούσια) are properly said to be of one nature, and things whose structure of being is common; but we can define as "hypostasis" either things which share a nature but differ in number, or things which are put together from different natures, but which share reciprocally in a common being. I say that they share being (κοινωνοῦντα τοῦ εἶναι), not as if they completed one another's essence, as happens with essences and with things that are essentially predicated of them—which are called qualities—but insofar as the nature and essence of each is not considered by itself but with the other, to which it is joined and assimilated. One finds this in various things, not least in the case of soul and body, whose hypostasis is common but each of whose natures is individual, with a different way of being. (*Contra Nestorianos et Eutychianos* 1; Daley 2017: 132–5)

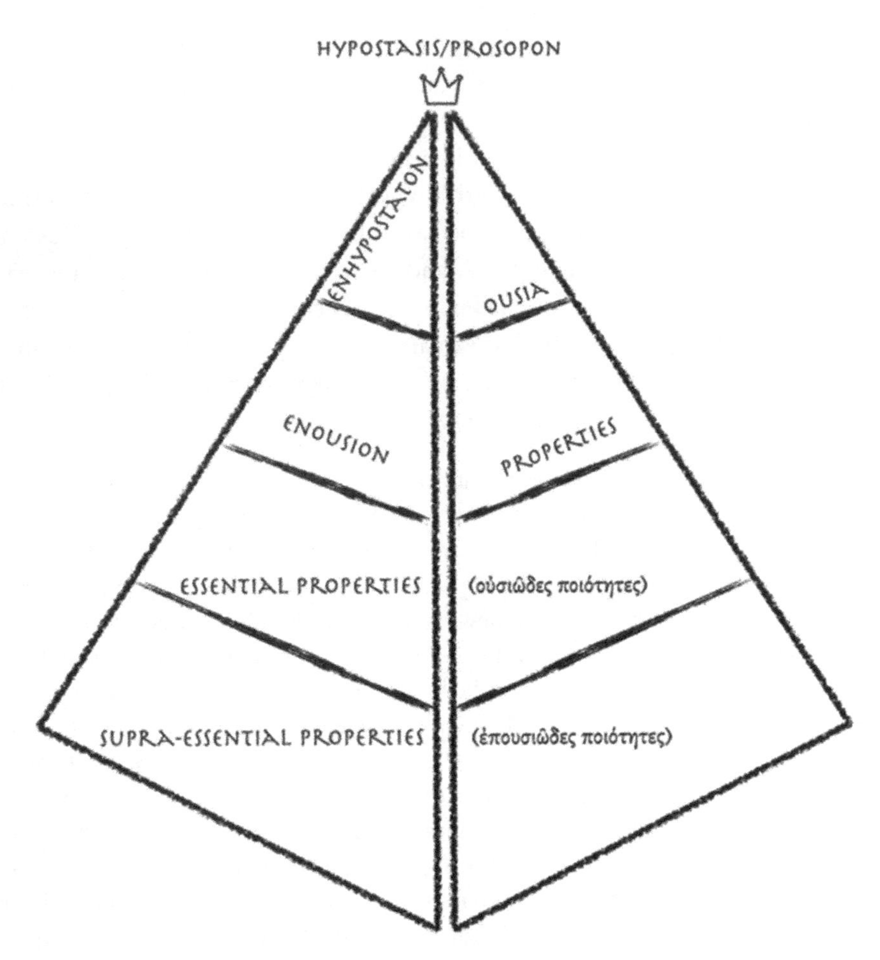


**Figure 2.23** The ontological hierarchy of categories according to Leontius of Byzantium.

Nevertheless, this ingenious and elegant construction seems to have a serious logical flaw. The miaphysite opponents of Leontius based their statement that two natures would necessarily lead to two hypostases, on the assumption that the categories of nature and hypostasis feature the same ontological status and weight: they are equal in the hierarchy of categories. In their assumption, they followed the line drawn by the Cappadocians, who had equalized the ontological statues of commonality and particularity. Leontius, in contrast to them, followed the neo-Platonic hierarchization of categories. On the top of the ontological pyramid, he placed the category of hypostasis as signifying the particular and real existence of a being (τί or τίς). Below it is the category of essence (οὐσία), which signifies common existence. Leontius implied that essence is ontologically inferior to hypostasis, by characterizing it through an adjective "hypostatic" (ἐνυπόστατον). In the hierarchy of grammar, adjectives are below nouns. The derivative and adjective status of the *enhypostatos*-

*ousia* is a clear indication that it is less valuable than the category of hypostasis. Below the essence/*enhypostaton* in the hierarchy of categories, there is the category of properties (ποιότητες), which Leontius characterized by the adjective "essential" (ἐνούσιον). The category of properties has its own hierarchy: properties can be more or less substantial (οὐσιῶδες or ἐπουσιῶδες).

Why ordering the categories of hypostasis and essence in the way Leontius did is problematic? It underestimates the equality of these categories, which was central to the neo-Nicaean theology: God is one to the same extent as he is three, and his threeness is not superior to his oneness, or vice versa. If the essence of one God is the *enhypostaton* of the three persons of the Trinity, then God is more three than he is one. In other words, the concept of *enhypostaton*, applied to God, can potentially undermine monotheism.

Maximus the Confessor, on the one hand, continued Leontius' line in advocating for two natures in Christ. He excelled in logical innovation, which he put to the service of his Christology. On the other hand, Maximus adhered to neo-Chalcedonianism (see Hovorun 2015c) and therefore was more flexible than Leontius regarding one nature in Christ. In this point, Maximus stood closer to Theodore of Raith, who was also neo-Chalcedonian. At the same time, Maximus and Theodore belonged to two opposite factions within neo-Chalcedonianism: Theodore was monoënergist, while Maximus criticized monoënergism from the perspective of dyoënergism.

In approaching logical categories, Maximus generally followed classical taxonomies. Yet, he applied a fresh outlook at what was regarded traditional. In particular, he suggested an original way of describing the category of common nature. For Maximus, this category is not just an idea in one's mind, but a reality that relates to God. He called this reality *logos* (or *logoi* in plural). Neo-Platonic philosophers had been speaking about the "logos of nature" (λόγος φύσεως) prior to Maximus.[2] The Cappadocians and Cyril of Alexandria had used the same phrase to denote commonality. Maximus unpacked further the theological meaning of this phrase. For him, God had had these *logoi* even before the world was created and used them as a blueprint for creation. Each *logos* corresponds to a common nature and becomes particularized in individual things. This idea helped Maximus to solve the problem, which had been posed by John Philoponus: how commonalities can exist apart of human imagination. Maximus made the category of common nature a logical part of the story about the world's creation:

> The many logoi are one Logos, seeing that all things are related to Him without being confused with Him, who is the essential and personally distinct Logos of God the Father, the origin and cause of all things. <. . .>

[2]Porphyry, *Εἰς τὰ ἁρμονικὰ Πτολεμαίου ὑπόμνημα*; I. Düring, 1932: 152. As Melchisedec Törönen has observed, in his teaching about *logoi*, Maximus comes closest to neo-Platonism (Törönen 2007: 8).

> From all eternity, He contained within Himself the pre-existing logoi of created beings. When, in His goodwill, He formed out of nothing the substance of the visible and invisible worlds, He did so on the basis of these logoi. By his *word (logos) and His wisdom He created* and continues to create *all things* (see Wis. 9:1-2)—universals as well as particulars—at the appropriate time. We believe, for example, that a logos of angels preceded and guided their creation; and the same holds true for each of the *beings and powers* (see 1 Pet. 3:22) that fill the world above us. A logos of human beings likewise preceded their creation, and—in order not to speak of particulars—a logos preceded the creation of everything that has received its being from God. (*Ambiguum ad Joh.* VII 15–16; Maximus 2014: 95–7)

To explain how God created things from *logoi*, Maximus employed the Aristotelian distinction between potentiality and actuality:

> In the wisdom of the Creator, individual things were created at the appropriate moment in time, in a manner consistent with their logoi, and thus they received in themselves actual existence as beings. For God is eternally an active creator, but creatures exist first in potential, and only later in actuality. (*Ambiguum ad Joh.* VII 19; Maximus 2014: 101)

Beings are the particularizations and actualizations of the preexistent and potential *logoi*—commonalities. They are the "ways" (*tropoi*/τρόποι), in which *logoi* become particularized. The defining feature of the *tropoi* is that they are numerical and measurable:

> If the substance of all beings—and by "all" I mean the vast multitude of beings—cannot be infinite (for it has as a limit the numerical quantity of the many beings that circumscribes both its principle and mode of being, since the substance of all beings is not limitless), then neither can the subsistence of particular things be without circumscription, for each is limited by all the others, owing to the laws of number and substance. (*Ambiguum ad Joh.* X 93; Maximus 2014: 295)

In contrast to *logoi*, particularities exist in place and time:

> Who does not know that every kind of being whatsoever, with the sole exception of the Divine (which strictly speaking is beyond being), presupposes the concept of a "where," which in absolutely every instance necessarily requires the related concept of a "when"? For it is not possible for a "where" to be thought of separately from a "when" (for they belong to those things that are simultaneous, and do not exist apart from their mutual conditioning). If however, a "when" cannot in any way be separated from a "where" (together with which it is of a nature to be contemplated), then all things are subject to the category of "where," since all things exist in a particular place. (*Ambiguum ad Joh.* X 91; Maximus 2014: 293)

As we can see, Maximus did not add any new category to the classical taxonomies. At the same time, he rethought connections between the existent categories in innovative ways. For him, they are not speculations of human mind, but a part of the divine creation and *oeconomia*.

Anastasius of Sinai continued the line of Maximus regarding most theological issues, and of Theodore, in building his dialectical taxonomy. At the same time, he used his sources creatively. He enriched the classical canon of categories with new ones. For example, he added "form" (μορφή) (*Viae dux* II 3) to "nature" (φύσις) and "essence" (οὐσία), to describe commonality; and "character" (χαρακτήρ) (*Viae dux* II 3) to "hypostasis" (ὑπόστασις) and "person" (πρόσωπον), to describe particularity. He also applied to hypostasis the term "proper" (ἴδιον) (*Viae dux* II 3), which Theodore of Raith had used for the category of property.

Most Christian innovations and additions to the traditional Aristotelian-Porphyrian taxonomies were caused by the disputes about the unity of divinity and humanity in Jesus Christ. John of Damascus, who summarized the Christological doctrine, also procured the completest catalogue of categories. He tried to include there most dialectical definitions known by his time. John began his *summa categoriarum* by defining a basic category, which was usually skipped by other logicians, a being: "Being is the common name for all things which are" (*Dialectica* 4; Chase 1958: 13). The most important logical distinction for John was the one between commonality and particularity. In this point, he was not different from other logicians:

> There is that which is more particular and is numerically different, as, for example, Peter, an individual, a person, and a hypostasis. This signifies a definite person. For, when we are asked who this man is, we say that he is Peter. The term "other" signifies the same thing, for Peter is one and Paul is another. Likewise the terms "he," "this," and "that"—these and such others as stand of themselves are applied to the individual.
>
> But that which includes the individuals is called *species* and is more general than the individual, because it does include several individuals. An example would be man, because this term includes both Peter and Paul and all individual men besides. This is what is called nature and substance and form by the holy Fathers. Now, that which includes several *species* is called *genus*, an example of which is animal, for this includes man, ox, and horse, and is more universal than the species. Moreover, both species and genus were called *nature* and *form* and *substance* by the holy Fathers. Furthermore, the species—that is, the nature and the substance and the form—does not produce something which is "other" or something which is "of another sort," but rather "another" of the same sort. (*Dialectica* 5; Chase 1958: 17–18)

Distinction between commonality and particularity, which had been initially articulated in Greek, was transmitted to the oriental languages. In Syriac, for example, it is rendered through the terms *qnoma* and *parsopa* for particularities, and *itya/ituta* and *kiana/*

*kyana* for commonalities (see Awad 2015: 143). The term *ituta* is also synonymous with the "being" (τὸ ὄν) (see Possekel 1999: 56). Some Syrian authors distinguished between *itya* and *ituta*. For the Eastern Syrian theologian Babai the Great (*c.* 551–628), for instance, the divine *itya* is accessible for human comprehension, while *ituta* is not (see Metselaar 2019: 148). *Kiana* can be interpreted as particularity or commonality depending on the doctrinal view on the incarnation. As for the *parsopa*, Syriac authors hesitated to apply this term to the three persons of God, because it sounded for them modalistic and connotating appearance more than reality.

Syriac categories, alongside their Greek originals (see Gutas 1998), became a source of Arabic theological terminology (see Griffith 2002). Both Chalcedonian and non-Chalcedonian Syrian theologians contributed to the formation of the Arabic categories, which became appropriated also by Muslim and Jewish theologians. In the ninth century, three theologians representing different Christological doctrines, made particular contributions to the Arabic logics: Theodore Abū Qurrah—from the Chalcedonian, Habib Abū Ra'ita (see Graf 1951) from the anti-Chalcedonian, and ʿAmmār al-Baṣrī—from the Eastern Syriac perspectives.

They rendered *qnoma*, which refers to particular being, as *uqnūm*, while person/*parsopa*, as *shakhs*. A particular being, which in the patristic language was denoted by the term "hypostasis," in Arabic was also put as *dat khassa*. *Kiana*, which usually translates Greek *physis*, has been rendered as *kayan*. Commonality expressed by the Greek *ousia* and Syriac *etuta*, was rendered to the Arabic as *jawhar*. Syrian theologians also transmitted various *differentiae*: *ittisal* for "unity" (*henosis*), *tabayon* for "distinction" (*diakrisis*), and *iftiraq* for "separation" (*diairesis*).

# Difference

The triad of logical functions "unity–distinction–separation" became fundamental in the classical Christian theology. Unity is a result or process of bringing two or more items together. It should not be confused with oneness. In contrast to unity, oneness is not necessarily composed. Distinction means a speculative or imagined differentiation within the unity. In contrast to it, separation means an empirical or often physical differentiation. In other words, distinguishable items cannot be moved away from each other, while separable items can. These were the Christian elaborations on the traditional Aristotelian-Porphyrian category of "differences" (διαφοραί/*differentiae*).

In both pagan and Christian dialectical taxonomies, "differences" played an auxiliary role: they explained relation between commonality and particularity. The Alexandrian Christian neo-Platonist David underlined this secondary role of *differentiae* in the following comment on Porphyry:

> [Porphyry] reasonably never mentioned difference, property and accident. For it was sufficient for him to mention genus and species because genus and species pervade the other three. Now by discussing genus and species he includes also the others. For the difference has a genus and a species. (In Muradyan 2015: 127)

Christian theologians, on the one hand, followed the definitions of "differences," which had been elaborated upon in the Aristotelian-Porphyrian taxonomies. Such, for example, was the summary of this category by John of Damascus:

> *Difference* is that which is predicated of several things specifically different in respect to their particular sort, and it is included in the definition as essential. This is that which cannot *be* and *not be* in the same species and cannot *not be* in the species to which it belongs. When present, it assures the existence of the species; when absent, the species is destroyed. Also, it is impossible for it and its opposite to be in the same species. Thus, for example, the rational cannot *not be* in man, because that which is irrational is not man. When it is present, it constitutes the nature of man; when it is absent, it destroys it, because that which is irrational is not man. Now, one must know that this is called essential, natural, constituent, and distinguishing, and specific difference, essential quality, and natural property of a nature. (*Dialectica* 5; Chase 1958: 19)

On the other hand, the category of "difference" was heavily employed in the Christological debates. It helped to demonstrate how divinity and humanity preserve their differences in Christ without compromising his unity. As a result of the debates, the classical Aristotelian-Porphyrian *differentiae* were redressed in many creative ways. One of them was a difference between the existence as "someone and someone else" (ἄλλος καὶ ἄλλος) and "something and something else" (ἄλλο καὶ ἄλλο). Such differentiation had been introduced by Porphyry (Porphyry, *Isagoge* 4.1) and then significantly elaborated upon by the Christians. Theodore of Raith summarized the result of the Christian elaboration as a difference between the "essential" and "hypostatic" differences (*Preparatio*; Diekamp 1938: 216–17 = Νίκας 1981: 234–6):

1. "Essential" (οὐσιώδης or ἰδιαίτατα) is a kind of difference that differentiates between different natures. It makes them distinguished as "something and something else" (ἄλλο καὶ ἄλλο).
2. "Hypostatic" differences apply to particular beings. They can be of two sorts:
   - 2.1. One sort is a hypostatic difference of the "common" sort (κοινῶς). It differentiates one hypostasis from another, as "someone and someone else" (ἄλλος καὶ ἄλλος).
   - 2.2. The other sort of hypostatic difference is "proper" (ἰδίως). It applies to the same individual being that may change and adopt various accidents (συμβεβηκότα) under various circumstances.

Maximus the Confessor continued this line and explained the difference between the "essential" and "hypostatic" differences in the following statement:

> The Fathers, then, say that an "essential quality," in the case of the human being, for instance, is rationality, and in the case of horse, neighing. A "hypostatic quality," on the other hand, of a particular human being is, [for instance], being snub-nosed or hook-nosed, and that of a particular horse, being dapple-grey or chestnut. Similarly, "quality" is considered in all the other created essences and hypostases, commonly and individually, that is, in general and in particular, and by it the difference, that exists between species and between individuals, is made known, as it clarifies the truth of things. (*Op.* 21; Törönen 2007: 23–4)

The category of "essential" difference was pivotal in emphasizing the paradox of the incarnation. Opposite *differentiae*, which characterize two completely different natures, became united in the single being of Jesus Christ. Theologians described Christ in the terms that excluded each other, such as created and uncreated, mortal and immortal, circumscribed and uncircumscribed. These terms were nothing else but *differentiae*. They went back to Porphyry, who in these terms had differentiated human beings from gods: "The differences of rational and of mortal are found to be constitutive of man, those of rational and of immortal of god" (*Isagoge* 3; Barnes 2003: 10). In contrast to Porphyry, for whom contrary differences cannot mix (*Isagoge* 13; Barnes 2003: 18), Christian theologians pointed out that these differences, when combined, could only save the humankind through the incarnation.

"Hypostatic" differences can be measured in numbers. Numbers constitute a sort of *differentiae* that became particularly important in the Christian theology. While all theologians had consensus that the "substantial" differences, such as "mortal and immortal," are united in Christ, they disagreed on the numerical hypostatic differences. They argued with one another whether Christ had *one* or *two* hypostases and natures. Disagreements on numerical differences caused major schisms in the church. That is why it is not a surprise that theologians were focused on them. John of Damascus paid a particular attention to the category of numbers. For example, he identified three ways, in which number "one" can be defined:

> The term "one" is used in three ways. Either it will be one in genus, as, for example, we say that man and the horse are generically one and the same, because they belong to one genus, namely, the animal. Or it will be one in species, as we say that, since Socrates and Plato belong to one species, man, they are specifically one and the same. Or it will be one in number, as we say that Socrates is in himself one, being distinct from all other men. (*Dialectica* 37; Chase 1958: 63)

The Cappadocians had applied this numeric difference to God. Basil of Caesarea, for example, explored how the oneness of God correlates with three divine persons. He argued that the number "three" does not introduce any division in one God:

> Against those who accuse us of tritheism, let us answer that we confess that there is only one God—not in number but in nature. For everything that is called one in nature is not one absolutely, nor is it simple in nature, God, however, is universally confessed to be simple and not composite. Therefore he is not one in number. What I mean is this. We say that the world is one in number, but it is not one by nature, nor is it simple, for we divide it into its constituent elements—fire, water, air and earth. Again, a human is said to be one in number. We often speak of one person, but this person is a compound of body and soul, and not simple. Similarly we talk of one angel in number, but not one by nature and not simple, because we think of an angel as a being who also possesses sanctification. Therefore, if everything that is one in number is not one in nature, and that which is one and simple in nature is not one in number, and if we call God one in nature, how can the issue of number be raised against us, when we exclude it from that blessed and spiritual nature? Number relates to quantity and quantity only makes sense in terms of bodily nature. We believe that our Lord is the creator of bodies and therefore that every number refers to things that have received a material and finite nature. (*Ep*. 8.2; Bray 2009: 39–40)

Leontius of Byzantium added to this argument that numbers do not divide what they enumerate. As number "three" does not divide the Trinity, so number "two" does not divide Jesus Christ:

> If everywhere and in every way, number introduces division, then surely number will be the cause of division, not division the cause of number; and one of two conclusions follows: either not to count anything which is united, or not to unite anything which is counted. And why is it not ridiculous to ascribe this kind of power to number, when every number naturally reveals the quantity of things, not their nature or any kind of relationship among them? (*Epaporemata* 8; Daley 2017: 316–17)

## Property

Another Aristotelian-Porphyrian category that the Christian theologians actively utilized was property. There was a consensus among both pagan and Christian logicians that this category is intrinsically and primarily connected with commonality, however the latter is called. Porphyry, for example, remarked that "common to properties and inseparable accidents is the fact that without them the items on which they are observed do not subsist" (*Isagoge* 16; Barnes 2003: 19). Basil of Caesarea also observed that properties (ἰδιότητες/ἰδιώματα), "being added onto the substance (οὐσία) like marks or forms, distinguish what is common by means of individual characteristics (τοῖς ἰδιάζουσι χαρακτῆρσι)" (*Contra Eunomium* II 28; Ayres 2004: 198). Because of the connection of property with communality and yet its predictive character, David called this category "post-substantial": "species is substantial, whilst a property and an accident are post-substantial" (in Muradyan 2015: 97).

Some properties are actualized in particular ways and as such characterize particular beings. Maximus the Confessor distinguished between properties "natural" and "hypostatic." In application to God, he identified them as following:

> Natural qualities are God's being: all-holy, omnipotent, all-perfect, more than complete, self-sufficient, self-ruling, all-ruling, and the like natural and divine things that are said, things proper to God alone as being beyond being.
>
> "Hypostatic qualities" are: that of the Father, unbegottenness; that of the Son, begottenness; and that of the Holy Spirit, procession. [Both kinds of qualities] are also called "properties," on the grounds that they naturally or hypostatically belong to this one [nature or hypostasis] and not to another. Out of these [qualities] are put together essential and hypostatic differences, and as I said, they are applied properly speaking to all created beings by nature, but only in a manner of speaking to God. (*Op.* 21; Törönen 2007: 24)

Theodore of Raith identified four kinds of property:

1. Properties that belong to the nature, but not to every individual who participates in this nature. For example, the property to heal or to build is inherent in the human nature, but not every human being is a doctor or a builder.
2. Properties that everyone who shares in the same nature obtains sooner or later, but does not have them all the time. This is, for example, the property of having gray hair.
3. Properties that characterize every individual of a given nature, but not only of this nature. For example, all human beings have two legs, but birds also have them.
4. Finally, there are properties that characterize all human beings and only them. Such is the ability to laugh. As Theodore put it, "if something is a human being, [he or she is] capable of laughing; and if something is capable of laughing, [that being is] human" (*Preparatio*; Diekamp 1938: 218 = Νίκας 1981: 238).

It should be noted that all sorts of properties (ἴδιον), according to Theodore, are "natural" (φύσει ἐστίν). This feature of properties had been observed prior to the Christological controversies, but became an undisputed axiom as a result of them. This axiom states: all properties are related to common natures, even though they can be observed in individual hypostases. If the nature changes, so its property does, and vice versa.

Unlike property (ἴδιον), which correlates with the nature, accident (συμβεβηκός) is a nonessential (μὴ οὐσιῶδες) characteristic of a being. It correlates with the individual mode of existence, which subsists in hypostasis (ὑποκειμένη τῇ οὐσίᾳ ὑφίσταται). Accidents (συμβεβηκότα) could be concrete deeds or lack of them, such as walking, sleeping, speaking, being ill or having a snub nose (*Preparatio*; Diekamp 1938: 218 = Νίκας 1981: 238).

Within the category of natural properties, Christian theologians identified the subcategory of motion (κίνησις). In Aristotle, who first studied motion systematically, this subcategory was a part of physics (see Gill & Lennox 2017). In Christian theology, it became a part of dialectics. The category of "motion" helped the fathers of the church to explain not only Christological issues but also spiritual life and the world. Maximus the Confessor, for example, distinguished between the physical and spiritual or intelligible kinds of motion:

> The motion of intelligible beings is an intelligible motion, whereas that of sensible beings is a sense-perceptible motion. According to those who have examined these matters carefully, no being in principle is devoid of motion (including beings that are inanimate and merely objects of sense perception), for these experts affirm that all things move in either a linear, circular, or spiral manner. All motion, in other words, unfolds in simple and composite patterns. If then, coming into being must necessarily be posited before beings can begin to move, it follows that motion is subsequent to the manifestation of being, for it is something that the intellect perceives only after the apprehension of being.

In exploring motion, Maximus applied the Aristotelian idea of the prime unmoved mover (see Aristotle, *Physics* VIII 5; also Louth 1996: 207, n. 96; Mitralexis 2017: 141) as the first and final cause of all kinds of motion:

> Motion which is impelled toward its proper end they call either a "natural power," or else a "passion," that is, a motion that "passes from one thing to another," having impassibility as its end, or an "effective activity," having self-perfection as its end. Yet nothing that has come into being is its own proper end, insofar as it is not self-caused, for if it were, it would be uncreated, without beginning, and without motion, having no way of being moved toward something else. For that which is self-caused transcends the nature of beings, since it exists for the sake of nothing else. Hence the definition of it is true, even though it was expressed by a man who was an outsider to the faith: "The end is that for the sake of which all things exist; it, however, is for the sake of nothing." And nothing that has come into being is perfect in itself for if it were, it would be devoid of activity, having no want or need of anything, since it owes its origin to nothing outside itself. Hence that which is perfect in itself is, in some manner, uncaused. In the same way, nothing that has come into being is impassible, for this belongs only to what is unique, infinite, and uncircumscribed. That which is impassible is in no way subject to the movement of the passions, for there is nothing that it desires, neither can it be moved by desire toward something else. Therefore no created being which is in motion has yet come to rest, either because it has not yet attained its first and sole cause, to which it owes its existence, or because it does not yet find itself within its ultimate desired end. (*Ambiguum ad Joh.* VII 6-7; Maximus 2014: 81–3)

Maximus called motion a "natural power." He thus recapitulated the tradition that went back to the Cappadocians, who had also regarded motion a "movement of nature" (φύσεως κίνησις). They identified this motion with natural activity (ἐνέργεια)—another notion that derived from Aristotle. Christian theology, however, modified the notion of *energeia*. In Aristotle, *energeia* was a part of the binary "potentiality-actuality" (δύναμις-ἐνέργεια) (see Bechler 1995). In Christianity, it turned to a self-sufficient category that predicates nature, as one can see in the following passage from Gregory of Nyssa:

> We say that one works metal or wood, or carries out another of such activities. Therefore, language presents at once both the art and he who exercises the art, so that if one separates one thing, the other cannot subsist. If then, the two realities are thought one together with the other, that is activity itself and he who acts through it, how is it that in this case one says that on the first substance (τῇ οὐσίᾳ τῇ πρώτῃ) follows activity that produces the second substance, as if mediating in itself between the one and the other, without being confused with the first according to nature, nor being tied to the second? For [the activity] is separated from the first by the fact of not being a nature, but a movement of nature (φύσεως κίνησις), and is not united to that which results because it does not have as proper result a simple activity, but an active substance. (*Contra Eunomium* I; Jaeger 1960: I, 88.4–17; Maspero 2007: 40)

In the course of the controversy about the activities (ἐνέργειαι) of Jesus Christ during the 630s–40s, activity as the motion of nature became the most discussed logical category. In the dialectical taxonomies of that time, it was reshelved as a subcategory of the category of property (see Hovorun 2008: 160–1). Sophronius of Jerusalem, for instance, underlined the intrinsic connection of activities with natural properties in his encyclical epistle:

> For, as each nature in Christ preserves without omission its property, in the same way each form (μορφή) acts in communion with the other whatever is proper to it (τοῦθ' ὅπερ ἴδιον ἔσχηκε). (In $ACO_2$ $II^1$ $442^{14\text{-}16}$)

Maximus the Confessor was even more explicit in attributing *energeiai* to the category of natural properties:

> It is surely necessary for natural things to correspond with their appropriate natures, for how it is possible for the energy of a created nature to be uncreated, without beginning, infinite, creative, and sustaining? And the reverse: how is it possible for the uncreated and eternal nature to be created, a thing made, tried and compelled by other things? (*Disputatio* 341a; Maximus the Confessor 2014: 61)

For Anastasius of Sinai, *energeia* is "a natural power (δύναμις) and movement of each essence" (*Viae dux* II 4; Uthemann 1981: 44). It is so closely connected with nature that the very names of various natures derive from their activities:

> [The name] "God" does not show us the very essence of the Creator, which is incomprehensible and unnamed, but he is said God because of his contemplative activity. The same is with the [name] "angel," which does not reveal the essence as such and the existence of their nature, but [angels] have their name from their messaging activity and service. Also a human being is not called *anthropos* because of his essential property, but from "look up" (ἄνω θρεῖν τὴν ὦπα) he is called "ἀνωθρώοπος." (*Viae dux* II 4; Uthemann 1981: 46)[3]

The category of activity served the theologians during the seventh century in their argument that Christ has two natures. If one could clearly distinguish two sorts of activities in Christ—divine and human—then one would prove that the natures in Christ are two. With this purpose in mind, Anastasius of Sinai produced a detailed catalogue of Christ's activities. On the one hand, they are distinctively human, such as the forming of Christ's body in Mary's womb, the strengthening of his nerves, bones, hands, and legs, his circumcision, seeking his mother's breast, switching from milk to solid food, crying, cooing, and creeping, then walking and uttering his first words. In the more mature age, Jesus demonstrated such purely human activities as growing hair, nails, and teeth, hunger, sleep, fatigue, bodily discharges, including spitting, sweating, and bleeding (*Opera* 2 VIII 3). On the other hand, Christ demonstrated activities impossible for human beings, such as moving a star to guide the Magi, shedding light on shepherds, being worshipped by angels (*Opera* 2 VIII 5), and enabling the Virgin to lactate (*Viae dux* XIII 5).

*Energeia* was regarded as any active manifestation of nature. All passive manifestations of nature were called *pathos* (πάθος), usually translated as passion. Like *energeia*, *pathos* is a natural property, but features lack of motion. Anastasius drafted a list of such motionless passions of Christ, including the insensibility of Christ's body in the tomb (*Opera* 2 VIII 3), his speechlessness (ἀφθεγξία) either when he was a baby (*Viae dux* XIII 7) or when his body was dead (see *Opera* 2 VIII 3), as well as being wrapped in linen cloth (*Opera* 2 VIII 3).

Anastasius of Sinai defined will as a distinct category similar to the category of activity. According to this definition, "Will (θέλημα) is the longing of intellectual essence to what is desired" (*Viae dux* II 3). Anastasius distinguished three kinds of will: divine, angelic, and psychic. In the case of human beings, he differentiated between "natural" and "gnomic" (γνωμικόν) wills. The former sort of will is innate and permanent, such as will for life (φιλόζωον), while the latter is ceaselessly changing and depending on opinions that a human being may have at the moment (*Viae dux* II 4). The issue of gnomic will was debated in the course of the monothelite controversy during the seventh century and continues attracting attention of modern theologians.

---

[3] See the definition of human beings in the *Etymologicon* of Orion: "A human being is called [so] because of looking up (ἄνω θρεῖν, ἤγουν ὁρᾶν), or to walk straight (ἀνορθροῖ περιπατεῖν)" (in Sturz 1973: 174).

Another important logical function in high demand by Christian theologians during the classical era was distinction between distinction and separation. This function became particularly popular during the theological debates from the fourth through the seventh centuries. However, it was introduced to Christian epistemology prior to those debates.

In the third century, Origen had differentiated between reality and intellectual elaboration on this reality. He called the latter *epinoia* (ἐπίνοια), which can be translated as "thinking upon." Its meaning was opposite to *hypostasis*, which for Origen meant real and not speculative existence (see Kritikos 2007: 411–12). *Epinoia*, therefore, is an intellectual exercise, which helps discerning theoretical aspects of reality. This exercise does not separate these aspects, which in reality constitute one being. Gregory of Nyssa applied the Origenian concept of *epinoia* to distinguish God's activities (ἐνέργειαι) (see Mateo-Seco & Maspero 2009: 71). For Gregory, *epinoia* constitutes a creative power of conceptualizing thought (see Mateo-Seco & Maspero 2009: 303).

Gregory, who was probably the author of the aforementioned letter 38 from Basil's collection, similarly to Origen counterposed *epinoia* to cutting in pieces (τομή) and separation (διαίρεσις) (*ep*. 38). He used the word *diakrisis* (διάκρισις) as a synonym of *epinoia*. *Diakrisis* literally means "judging through" and implies a purely intellectual, not a physical process. This process is the only acceptable one in deliberations about God:

> Since we must use the words which individualize the three (persons in the Trinity) in order that we may keep free from confusion the distinction (διάκρισιν) we shall make when dealing with the Trinity, with this aim in view we shall not include in our discussion of the individualizing element any general speculation, such as the quality of being uncreated, beyond comprehension, and so forth, but we shall investigate only those qualities by which the conception (ἔννοια) of each person in the Trinity will be conspicuously and sharply marked off from that which results from the study of all three together. (*Ep*. 38)

For the author of the epistle 38, thus, the Trinitarian persons can be only distinguished and not separated from each other and from their common essence:

> Faith teaches us to understand that which is separated in person (ἐν ὑποστάσει) but at the same time united in substance (ἐν τῇ οὐσίᾳ). Since, therefore, reason has distinguished (ὁ λόγος ἐνεθεώρησεν) an element common to the Persons of the Trinity as well as an element peculiar to each, what reason shows is common is referred to the substance, and the Person (ὑπόστασις) is the individualizing note of each member of the Trinity. (*Ep*. 38)

Cyril of Alexandria made the logical operation of distinction a keystone of his Christological construct. Unity of Christ was ultimately important for him. At the

**Figure 2.24** The icon of Cyril of Alexandria by Emmanuel Tzanes (1654). Byzantine Museum of Antivouniotissa on Corfu, Greece.
Source: Photo by the author.

same time, he acknowledged the completeness of Christ's divinity and humanity. Cyril harmonized Jesus' unity and duality by stressing that the latter can be only contemplated in thought (τῇ θεωρίᾳ μόνῃ) (*Quod unus sit Christus* 736.27). Cyril, thus, arrived at the key point of his Christology that divinity and humanity in Christ are only theoretically distinguished, and cannot be separated from each other. They are also distinguishable from Christ's hypostasis.

That they are distinguishable does not make them ephemeral. Both divinity and humanity remain real in Christ, but their reality is shared and subsists as the singular reality of the incarnated Logos. David, in his Armenian commentary on Porphyry, explained what contemplation in one's thought means:

> Let us state what "in thought" means. Thought is that whose origin is our thought and whose destruction is our forgetting. For example, when someone thinks in his thought about a goat-stag, which nature has not created but which our thought, violating nature, thought of as of an animal [composed] of a stag and a goat which nature did

> not know, and, when remembering it, he creates it in thought and, when forgetting it, brings about its destruction. (In Muradyan 2015: 73)

This definition of what is distinction was helpful only to some extent. Christian theologians would not agree that forgetting something would destroy the distinction. In such case, ignorance about the incarnation of the Logos would have endangered this incarnation with obliteration.

More helpful was a definition of what is distinction provided by Theodore of Raith. In line with the Cappadocians, he counterposed *epinoia* (ἐπίνοια) and *diairesis* (διαίρεσις). He elaborated on two cases of differentiation: when essences are united in a single hypostasis, and when hypostases are united with one another. In the former case, essences are distinguished and their difference exists only in one's mind (ἐποινίᾳ). In the latter case, however, hypostases can be united only in one's mind, while in reality (ἔργῳ δὲ καὶ πράγματι) they stay separated from each other (*Preparatio*; Diekamp 1938: 215 = Νίκας 1981: 232). Of course, Theodore meant created hypostases, and not the divine ones.

# Unity

The idea of distinction helped Christian theologians to explain how oneness and plurality can be together in God and Christ. Distinction is a key to understand the category of unity, which, as was mentioned, is not identical with oneness. Oneness is not necessarily composed, while unity always is. Unity presupposes at least two components that come together. In contrast to "oneness," "unity" features dynamism. Unity *brings* separate parts together. The Greek word *henosis* (ἕνωσις), which the English words "unity" or "union" translate, derives from the verb *henoō* (ἑνόω)—"to make one." The suffix -ωσ- in the word "unity" (ἕνωσις) indicates its verbal origins. The verbal origins of either "unity" or "union" in English are not so obvious.

Even before the Christian theological debates, neo-Platonists struggled with the same issue as the Christians would do: how to harmonize oneness with plurality, including in the sphere of the divine. On the one hand, neo-Platonists acknowledged and venerated multiple gods. On the other, they believed that plurality, both cosmic and divine, is driven to the One. Porphyry, to address this issue, suggested a notion of "unity without confusion" (ἀσύγχυτος ἕνωσις). He illustrated this notion by the example of body and soul united in human beings.[4] Porphyry thus contested the

[4]Scholars believe that a fragment from Nemesius' *De natura hominis* (Morani 1987: 44) on this matter belongs to Porphyry (Törönen 2007: 116, n. 3).

Stoic concept of "confusion" (σύγχυσις), which implied blending together various elements of plurality.

In a completely different context, Cyril of Alexandria contested a similar idea of divinity and humanity of Christ being "confused." He employed the Porphyry's expression "unity without confusion" (see *In Lucam* (in catenis); PG 72, 484). Cyril developed a rich vocabulary of theological lexemes signifying unity, such as unity "according to hypostasis" (καθ' ὑπόστασιν) (see *fr. ad Hebraeos*; Pusey 1872: 395) and "according to person" (κατὰ πρόσωπον) (see *fr. ad Hebraeos*; Pusey 1872: 377), as well as "natural" (φυσική) (see *De sancta Trinitate dialogi*; de Durand 1976–1978: 462), "essential" (οὐσιώδη) (*In Joannem*; Pusey 1872, vol. 2: 102), and "ultimate" (ἄκρον ἕνωσιν) (*In Joannem*; Pusey, 1872, vol. 2: 638) unity.

To express the same kind of "ultimate unity," Maximus the Confessor utilized the term "interpenetration" (περιχώρησις). This term was first used by Gregory of Nazianzus. Maximus made it a keyword in his theological language. He applied it primarily in Christology, to describe how completely different natures have become united in the person of Jesus Christ:

> And this is truly marvellous and astounding to all: the same one is wholly among men remaining entirely within its own nature, and the same one being wholly among the divine remains completely unmoving from its natural properties. For according to the teaching of our Fathers inspired by God this was an interpenetration (περιχώρησις) of the natures, and of their natural properties, one into the other, but not a change or declension (μεταχώρησις ἢ μετάπτωσις) on account of the union—which is proper to those who malevolently turn the union into confusion. (*Disputatio Bizyae cum Theodosio*; Törönen 2007: 122–3)

Maximus summarized his understanding of unity in an insightful commentary on the image of flying sharp sickle from the book of Zechariah (5:1–4):

> "Sickle" is, therefore, our Lord Jesus Christ, the only-begotten Son and Logos of God, who in himself is and ever remains simple by nature but who for my sake became composite by hypostasis, as he knows how, through assuming flesh animated by an intelligent soul. He neither accepted a fusion (σύγχυσις) into one nature on account of his utter hypostatic union with the flesh, nor was he severed into a duality of Sons due to his utter natural difference from the flesh. By "utter" (lit. "edge" of the sickle) of the hypostatic union I mean the absolute undividedness, and by the "utter" of natural difference the complete unconfusion and unchangeability. <. . .> For the union was of two natures into one hypostasis, not into one nature, so that the hypostatic oneness is shown to result by union from the natures which have come together, and the difference in natural particularity of the natures united in an unbreakable union is believed to remain free from every change and confusion. (*Quaestiones ad Thalassium* 62; Törönen 2007: 120–1)

Anastasius of Sinai tried to generalize the concept of unity in a similar way. He identified five sorts of it:

> Unity is a sharing concourse (κοινωνικὴ συνδρομή) of separate things. It is called unity (ἕνωσις) because of pushing to one (εἰς ἓν ὦσαι), i.e., to force things together. There are five sorts of unity: (1) confusing (συγχυτική), as in the case of wine and water; (2) divided (διαιρετή), as in the case of one human being to another; (3) related (σχετική), as in the case of peoples [who share the same] faith; (4) affirmative (θετική), as in the case of [one piece of] gold to another; (5) the unity of Christ, which is above all the mentioned [sorts of unity] and called "according to hypostasis" (καθ'ὑπόστασιν). (*Viae dux* II 5)

John of Damascus explained in more detail the category of "unity according to hypostasis," which had been pivotal in the theological language of Cyril of Alexandria and was adopted to the neo-Chalcedonian Christological language:

> Hypostatic union produces one compound hypostasis of the thing united and that this preserves unconfused and unaltered in itself both the uniting natures and their difference as well as their natural properties. Moreover, this has no hypostatic difference with itself, because those characteristic differences of the things uniting, by which each of them is distinguished from others of the same species, become its own.

While elaborating on "hypostatic unity," John employed the classical model of a human being as a unity of body and soul:

> Thus it is with the hypostasis in the case of the soul and the body, for here one hypostasis is made of both—the compound hypostasis of Peter, let us say, or of Paul. This keeps in itself the two perfect natures—that of the soul and that of the body—and it preserves their difference distinct and their properties unconfused. And in itself it has the characteristic differences of each, those of the soul, which distinguish it from all other souls, and those of the body, which distinguish it from all other bodies. These, however, in no wise separate the soul from the body, but they unite and bind them together, at the same time marking off the one hypostasis composed of them from all other hypostases of the same species. Moreover, once the natures become hypostatically united, they remain absolutely indivisible. And this is so because, even though the soul is separated from the body in death, the hypostasis of both remains one and the same. For the constitution in itself of each thing at its beginning of being is a hypostasis. Therefore, the body remains, as does the soul; both always having the one principle of their being and subsistence, even though they are separated.

The reason why the category of "hypostatic unity" was introduced was to explain the incarnation:

> It is further necessary to know that it is possible for natures to be united to each other hypostatically, as in the case of man, and that it is also possible for the hypostasis to assume an additional nature. Both of these are to be observed in Christ, because in

> Him the divine and human natures were united, while His animate body subsisted in the pre-existent hypostasis of God the Word and had this for a hypostasis. It is, however, quite impossible for one compound nature to be made from two natures or for one hypostasis to be made from two, because it is impossible for contrary essential differences to exist together in one nature. This is because it is of the very nature of these to distinguish from each other the natures in which they exist. (*Dialectica* 66; Chase 1958; 104–5)

# Potentiality and Actuality

Eastern Christian cosmology and anthropology relied on the binary of the given and the assigned. The given is innate in the human nature and cannot be taken away. It corresponds to various commonalities pertinent to human nature. At the same time, the category of assigned is more particular. It constitutes the goal or *telos* that each human individual is expected to eventually achieve. What is assigned is not what is given but is based on the given. The given should grow to the assigned *telos*.

The patristic binary of the given and the assigned is similar to the classical binary of potentiality and actuality. The latter goes back to Aristotle. He explained the difference between potentiality and actuality as follows:

> We have distinguished in respect of each class between what is in fulfilment and what is potentially; thus the fulfilment of what is potentially, as such, is motion—e.g. the fulfilment of what is alterable, as alterable, is alteration; of what is increasable and its opposite, decreasable (there is no common name for both), increase and decrease; of what can come to be and pass away, coming to be and passing away; of what can be carried along, locomotion. (*Physica* III 201a10-14; Barnes 1984: 343)

Aristotle applied to various forms of potentiality such terms as *dynamis* (δύναμις) and *hexis* (ἕξις). He called various forms of actuality *energeia* (ἐνέργεια) and *entelecheia* (ἐντελέχεια). Zev Bechler helpfully rendered the relation of potentiality to actuality in Aristotle as *X*able to *X* (Bechler 1995: 7). For example, the potentiality of life (an *X*) is in fact the ability to live (*X*able). Differentiation between potentiality and actuality helped Aristotle to explain motion (κίνησις). The process of moving converts potentiality to actuality and helps beings to reach their *telos*. The latter, for Aristotle, is the "eventual actuality" of the potentialities embedded in a being (see Bechler 1995: 2).

Christian theology defines the *telos* of human life as related to Christ. This *telos* has been rendered in many ways: salvation, deification, spiritual perfection, passionlessness, freedom, likeness to God, and others. All these notions relate to the actuality of human life. This actuality is based on the potentiality, with which God had endorsed the human nature through the act of creation.

Eastern Christian theology has developed a sophisticated language to describe the binary of potentiality and actuality applicable to the human existence. One of them is the binary of the divine image and likeness. It derives from Genesis 1:26: "And God said, Let us make man in our image, after our likeness." *Imago Dei* here is the potentiality, which is embedded in the common human nature. It is the given, which has been designed to lead a human being to the *telos* of the likeness. Likeness in this case is individual, not common—as far as it is a particular actualization of the common potentiality of the *imago*.

The same logic can be applied to the category of freedom. Eastern Christian authors distinguished freedom as a common potentiality and particular actuality. They usually called the former *autexousion* (αὐτεξούσιον) and the latter *eleutheria* (ἐλευθερία). *Eleutheria* as freedom in Christ is the ultimate *telos* of the Christian life. It is, however, impossible without the potentiality of the *autexousion*.

The same ultimate *telos* of human life has been perceived in the Eastern Christian spiritual traditions as divinization or *theosis* (θέωσις). An individual human being can reach this *telos* after applying much effort to actualize the potentialities embedded in the human nature. Eastern theologians called the potentiality of *theosis* as *isotheon* (ἰσόθεον) or "equality to God." *Isotheon* is a faculty pertinent to the entire humankind and cannot be taken away.

In sum, *imago*, *autexousion*, *isotheon* are among the potentialities (*X*ables) embedded in the common human nature. They become appropriated and actualized (*X*s) by individual human beings. In such case, they convert to various forms of the Christian *telos*, including God-likeness, *eleutheria*, and *theosis*. We will explore these binaries of potentialities and actualities in more detail in the chapters that follow.

# Participation

An important grammatical structure of the theological meta-language spoken in the Christian East, is participation or *metoché* (μετοχή). Similarly to such logical functions as *diaphorae*, *metoché* connects other categories with one another. This logical operator was elaborated upon by Plato and became an important part of the major philosophical discourses after him. Plato utilized it to link the ideal world of ideas to this world. Things, for him, *participate* in ideas (see especially *Parmenides*). Aristotle was skeptical about the immanence of ideas in things through participation. Yet, he did not reject the idea of participation altogether (see Tollefsen 2012: 13–22).

This idea became a keystone in the neo-Platonic philosophy, where it had a wide range of applications: from the emanation of one to many, to connecting particularities with commonalities. Porphyry, for example, explained the relationship between common and particular with the assistance of the category of participation:

"Particular men participate equally in man and also in the difference of rational" (*Isagoge* 11; Barnes 2003: 16).

Christians also used the idea of participation to explain how various categories relate to one another. Gregory of Nyssa, for instance, described common nature as "undivided and permanent and perfect that is not divided in the individuals that participate (μετέχουσιν) in it" (*Ad Ablabium*, Mueller 1958: 41; Maspero 2007: 3). The Christian usage of the idea of participation was not confined to logics only but was applied to a wide array of topics: from the *theosis* of human beings to the symphony between the church and the state. In the former case, *theosis* is a result of the human participation in the divine being. In the latter case, the Byzantines believed that symphony between the church and the state is achievable because both participate, each in its own way, in the Kingdom of God.

# Eastern Scholasticism

Categories, as they had been defined by Aristotle and interpreted by his numerous commentators, both pagan and Christian, served as a basic matrix of thinking during the Antiquity and Middle Ages, until Modernity. These categories were crucial in shaping Christian theology. Theology, rendered in categories, became known as scholasticism. We have demonstrated that scholasticism was born and flourished first in the Christian East, from at least the fourth century. Through the works of such theologians as Leontius of Byzantium, Severus of Antioch, Theodore of Raith, Maximus the Confessor, Anastasius of Sinai, and John of Damascus, Eastern scholasticism evolved to its most refined form. These theologians were proponents of high scholasticism, which marked Byzantine theology during the sixth to eighth centuries. Only later, the Eastern scholasticism became appropriated in the West and developed there as a copy of the Eastern scholasticism. Western high scholasticism flourished during the thirteenth to fourteenth centuries—seven centuries after its Eastern prototype.

# II.7

# Modern Categories

Since the beginning of Modernity, traditional logical categories have been often discarded as "scholastic," outdated, and irrelevant. They fell victims to such opposite processes as secularization and religious renewal.

Secularists disdain them as the expressions of premodern metaphysics. The irony, however, is that these "scholastic" categories were originally secular—as much as they could be in the pre-secular era. As was mentioned, Christian theologians appropriated them from neo-Platonism, because they were metaphysically neutral. However, as Christian theology evolved, the categories turned inseparable from the metaphysics they expressed. When the Enlightenment contested Christian metaphysics, the "scholastic" categories were attacked as well. German idealistic philosophy substituted them with a new frame of thinking (see Altman 2014; Ameriks 2005). In result, the Aristotelian-Porphyrian dialectics was replaced with the Hegelian one (see Rescher 2013; McKenna 2011).

Christian "scholasticism" became rejected not only by secularists but also by modern theologians, both conservative and liberal ones. Eastern Christianity entered the period of Modernity with dismantled and rudimentary system of theological education, which was not anymore able to reproduce high late antique and medieval theology, of which scholastics was an inseparable part. In result, the dialectical/scholastic framework of theology became often misunderstood and caricatured. For gnoseomachic pietists, it turned opposite to spirituality and even a threat to salvation. Conservative ideologists interpreted it as a Western construct incompatible with the Eastern ways of thinking. More open-minded theologians associated scholasticism with archaism. *Aggiornamento*, for them, was possible only when scholasticism is completely shrugged off.

An Orthodox anti-scholastic campaign was launched in the mid-nineteenth century, when the Slavophiles tried to identify features of the assumed "genuine" Eastern thinking and to purge it from the assumed Western influences. Scholasticism was then identified as Western and alien to the Orthodox mindset. The Slavophile movement put in motion liberal Russian religious philosophy and conservative neopatristic synthesis. They could not stand each other on many issues, but surprisingly converged in their critique of "scholasticism."

**Figure 2.25** Personification of dialectics. A tombstone at St. Peter's basilica in the Vatican.
Source: Photo by the author.

Georges Florovsky was particularly outspoken in his criticism. He identified three stages of the assumed scholastic impact on the Orthodox theology: in the seventeenth, eighteenth, and nineteenth centuries (Gavrilyuk 2014: 179). During the seventeenth century, the Catholic version of scholasticism was propelled to Russia through Ukraine. Florovsky criticized particularly the role of the Kyiv-Mohyla Academy:

> In practically every respect the Kiev collegium (i.e., Kyiv-Mohyla Academy) represents a radical break with the traditions of earlier schools in West Russia (i.e., Ukraine). <. . .> Its students were hardly initiated into the heritage of the Orthodox East. Scholasticism was the focus of teaching. And it was not simply the ideas of individual scholastics that were expounded and assimilated, but the very spirit of scholasticism. (Florovsky 1979: 78)

In the eighteenth century, scholasticism was reintroduced to Russia, following the reforms of Peter I the Great. This form of scholasticism was Protestant. Its proponent was the Archbishop of Novgorod Feofan Prokopovych (in office 1725–36), who had Ukrainian background. For Florovsky, "Feofan did not simply borrow from seventeenth-century Protestant scholasticism, he belonged to it" (Florovsky 1979: 124). The final form of the Russian scholasticism in the nineteenth century, according to Florovsky, was inspired by German idealism.

Florovsky considered overcoming scholasticism as one of the most urgent tasks for the contemporary Orthodox theology. Most theologians from different ideological camps agreed with him. They looked for alternatives to the seemingly outdated

Aristotelian-Porphyrian logics. As a result, some new categories have been appropriated in the modern Orthodox theology as its new dialectical frame.

# Sophia

One of them was the category of *sophia*-wisdom. As such, this category was not new. It is a modification of the Stoic notion of spirit-*pneuma* (see Osler 2005). This notion was adopted to the Jewish Stoicism, particularly the apocryphal *Wisdom of Solomon* (see Winston 2011). One can also draw parallels between the *sophia* in the Russian religious renaissance and Maximus the Confessor's theology of *logoi*. Although seemingly ancient, the category of *sophia* in the Russian theology during the twentieth century was brand new. This applied to all new categories in the modern Orthodox theology: they pretend to represent the ancient patristic legacy, but in fact are new and turn out to be closer to the modern Western philosophical concepts.

Liberal Russian religious philosophers agreed with their more conservative counterparts that scholasticism is outdated and irrelevant. They started looking for a new framework to interpret God, creation, human beings, church, and so on. The concept of *sophia* became for them a substitute of scholastic categories. They perceived this concept not so much as logical but mystical. Thus, Vladimir Solovyov (1853–900) reported that he had contemplated *sophia* through three revelations: first, as a nine-year-old boy at a liturgy in Moscow, then a young man in the British Museum, and finally in the Egyptian desert. He described the latter revelation in the following verses:

> "Go then to Egypt!" sounded a voice inside me.
> To Paris! And then steampower bore me southward. <. . .>
>
> I waited, meanwhile, for the promised meeting,
> And suddenly, one night when all was still,
> I heard, just like the wind's cool breath, these words:
> "I am there in the desert. Go to meet me."
> I had to walk. <. . .>
>
> Surely, you must have been laughing at me when I,
> Attired in tall top-hat and warm overcoat in the desert,
> Was taken, by sturdy bedouins, for a demon,
> Provoking a shiver of fear in them and thus
> Was nearly killed.
> When, in the Arab manner, noisily,
> Sheiks of two tribes held a council to decide
> My fate, then later tied my hands together
> Like a slave's and without mincing words

Led me some distance off, and generously
Untied my hands—and then departed. Now
I'm laughing with you, my beloved: gods and men alike
Can laugh at troubles once they've passed.
By that time the mute night had descended
Directly to the earth. Around me I heard
Only the silence, and saw the darkness
Between the little starry flames.
Lying upon the ground, I looked and listened. <. . .>

Long I lay there in a frightened slumber, till
At last, I heard a gentle whisper: "Sleep, my poor friend."
Then I fell into a deep sleep; and when I waked
The fragrance of roses wafted from earth and heaven.
And in the purple of the heavenly glow
You gazed with eyes full of an azure fire.
And your gaze was like the first shining
Of universal and creative day.
What is, what was, and what will be were here
Embraced within that one fixed gaze. . . The seas
And rivers all turned blue beneath me, as did
The distant forest and the snow-capped mountain heights.
I saw it all, and all of it was one,
One image there of beauty feminine. . .
The immeasurable was confined within that image.
Before me, in me, you alone were there.
O radiant one! I'm not deceived by you.
I saw all of you there in the desert. . .
And in my soul those roses shall not fade
Wherever it is the billows of life may rush me.
A single instant! Then the vision was hidden
And into heaven's dome the solar sphere began its rise.
The desert was silent, but my soul was praying
And church bells kept on ringing in my soul. ("Three meetings"; Solovyov 2014: 106–9)

Fr. Pavel Florensky (1882–1937) described *sophia* as experienced in the similar context of solitude, when he was staying in a small lonely house:

This is the "Great Being," not that to which Auguste Comte prayed, but one that is truly great: It is the actualized Wisdom of God, *hokhmah*, *Sophia*.

Sophia is the Great Root of the whole creation (cf. *pasa hē ktisis*, Rom. 8:22). That is, Sophia is all-integral creation and not merely all creation. Sophia is the Great Root by which creation goes into the intra-Trinitarian life and through which it receives Life Eternal from the One Source of Life. Sophia is the original nature of creation, God's creative love, which is "shed abroad in our hearts by the Holy Spirit which is

> given unto us" (Rom. 5:5). For this reason, the true I of a deified person, his "heart," is precisely God's Love, just as the Essence of Divinity is intra-Trinitarian Love. For everything exists truly only insofar as it communes with the God of Love, the Source of being and truth. If creation is torn away from its root, an inevitable death awaits it. Wisdom itself says: "For whoso findeth me findeth life, and shall obtain favour of the Lord. But he that sinneth against me wrongeth his own soul: all they that hate me love death" (Prov. 8:35-36).
>
> With regard to creation, Sophia is the Guardian Angel of creation, the Ideal person of the world. The shaping reason with regard to creation, Sophia is the shaped content of God-Reason, His "psychic content," eternally created by the Father through the Son and completed in the Holy Spirit: God thinks by *things*. (Florensky 1997: 237)

Philosophers and theologians who employed the category of *sophia* were criticized by their more traditionalist peers. They were accused even of introducing the fourth hypostasis of *Sophia* to the Trinity, which was not what they meant, of course. In 1935, the Moscow Patriarchate and the Russian Orthodox Church Outside Russia (ROCOR), which disagreed with one another on many other issues, converged in officially condemning "sophiology" and those who promoted it, primarily Fr. Sergiy Bulgakov (1871–1944).[1]

# Persona

The same thinkers who introduced to the Orthodox theology the *sophia*-language, adopted a theological language based on the category of *persona*. In contrast to the former, the latter language became widely accepted in the Orthodox milieu as its *lingua franca*. Most Orthodox thinkers during the twentieth century articulated their theology in the personalist language.[2]

Personalism in some points resembles Platonism and neo-Platonism. For example, personalists counterpose personality and nature in the same way as Platonists counterposed the invisible and visible worlds. In the neo-Platonic way, personalism promotes a hierarchy of ontological statuses: personal mode of existence, being marked by freedom, is superior to the "natural" mode framed by necessity. Similarly to the Porphyrian interpretation of particularity as a bundle of properties, personalists

---

[1]In the same year, a Russian conservative theologian Archbishop Seraphim Sobolev (1881–950) published a book against "sophiology": Архиепископ Серафим (Соболев), *Новое учение о Софии Премудрости Божией* [A New Teaching about Sophia the Wisdom of God] (София, 1935).

[2]The most outspoken Orthodox theologian who follows the personalist line is Christos Yannaras (b. 1935). See especially: Γιανναρᾶς 2016; Γιανναρᾶς 2006; English translation: Yannaras 2007.

perceive personhood as a bundle of relations. In the words of the Greek theologian Nikos Nissiotis (1924–86),

> The identity (which is correspondent to personhood), as dependent on self-consciousness—as far as self-knowledge is based on inter-subjectivity (διυποκειμενικότητα)—is not allowed to be understood as an absolute self-likeness (αὐτομοιότητα) and self-unity (αὐτοενότητα) in the isolation of the Self in itself; they should not be considered as a rationalized Ego.
>
> The identity can be achieved as an open possibility of the subject through a conscious relationship with another one, as well as through the dialectical relation with him and with the objective reality of the world. The identity can function only through such relationship. The difference and distinction from the other one and other things in the outer world, as well as different projections of Ego towards outside (such as emotion, volition, feeling), which become united in the self-awareness through consciousness, underline even more the dialectical process in the course of the search for identity. (Νησιώτης 1996: 24; see also Asproulis 2018)

The success of personalism among the Orthodox has been secured by its vague character: unlike classical categories, personhood and its derivatives have been never clearly defined. Moreover, from the personalist perspective, definitions are not applicable to personhood whatsoever. Personalism, being a Western philosophy, became popular among the Orthodox, including anti-Westernists, also because of the deliberate confusion of the idea of personhood with the patristic category of hypostasis. Orthodox personalists have claimed that the category of personhood is genuinely Eastern because it is centered around the Eastern concept of hypostasis. This concept makes the Orthodox theology superior to the assumed Western scholasticism.

None of these claims is correct. First, the way, in which the category of personhood is understood in the modern theology, is different from the way how hypostasis was understood in the classical theology. As we have demonstrated, the latter was framed by the Aristotelian-Porphyrian "scholastic" logics, while the former emerged to a significant extent as a rejection of this logics. The personalistic take on personhood was influenced more by modern psychoanalysis than by patristic theology.

Second, although some modern Orthodox theologians believe personalism to be genuinely Eastern and ancient, its intellectual roots are modern Western. Methodists and liberal Catholics have made a particular contribution to it. Orthodox personalism echoes such Western personalists as Borden Parker Bowne (1847–1910), who founded the Boston school of personalism, William Stern (1871–1938) (see Stern 1906), Emmanuel Mounier (1905–50), who was the author of *A Personalist Manifesto* (Mounier 1938), Ralph Tyler Flewelling (1871–1960) (see Flewelling 1915; Flewelling 1952), who founded the Californian school of personalism, and many others. Flewelling also launched a journal of the personalist movement, *The Personalist*, which since its beginning in 1920 has been hosted at the University of Southern California in Los Angeles.

**Figure 2.26** University of Southern California (USC) in Los Angeles, originally affiliated with the Methodist church, is an informal center of the global Personalist movement.
Source: Photo by the author.

In the West, personalism emerged as a reaction to positivism (see Feichtinger et al. 2019). Its popularity climaxed after the two world wars, as an alternative to the totalitarian ideologies. These ideologies valued masses over individualities. In contrast to them, personalism emphasizes individuality. In the Orthodox milieu, personalism spearheaded the emancipation of the church life, for which reason it became popular among more liberal thinkers. From this perspective, the idea of personhood can be seen as a banner of liberal theology that can be easily carried across confessional borders.

As was mentioned earlier, modern Orthodox theologians tend to present the category of person as equivalent to the classical category of hypostasis. In fact, however, the modern personalist concept of personhood is closer to the classical category of *logos*. Personalism usually counterposes personhood to "nature," which in this context is closer not to the classical category of commonality, but to the idea of "flesh" (*sarx*/σάρξ). In the classical Christian interpretation that goes back to John (1:14), "flesh" is inferior to the "logos"—in the same way as "nature" is inferior to "persona," according to modern personalism. The modern personalistic pair of categories "person-nature," thus, is closer to the classical binary of "*logos-sarx*" than to "hypostasis-essence."

Yet, there is some correspondence between the modern personalistic and classical patristic takes on the category of hypostasis. They converge in interpreting *enhypostaton*. As was explained earlier, this category was utilized by the Byzantine logicians, such as Leontius of Byzantium, in the sense that implied inferiority of *enhypostaton*, understood as essence, vis-à-vis hypostasis. In contrast to this take, the neo-Platonists interpreted particularity as inferior to commonality. Most Christian theologians in Antiquity did not admit such stratification of categories. For the Cappadocians, as was mentioned, the categories of commonality and particularity

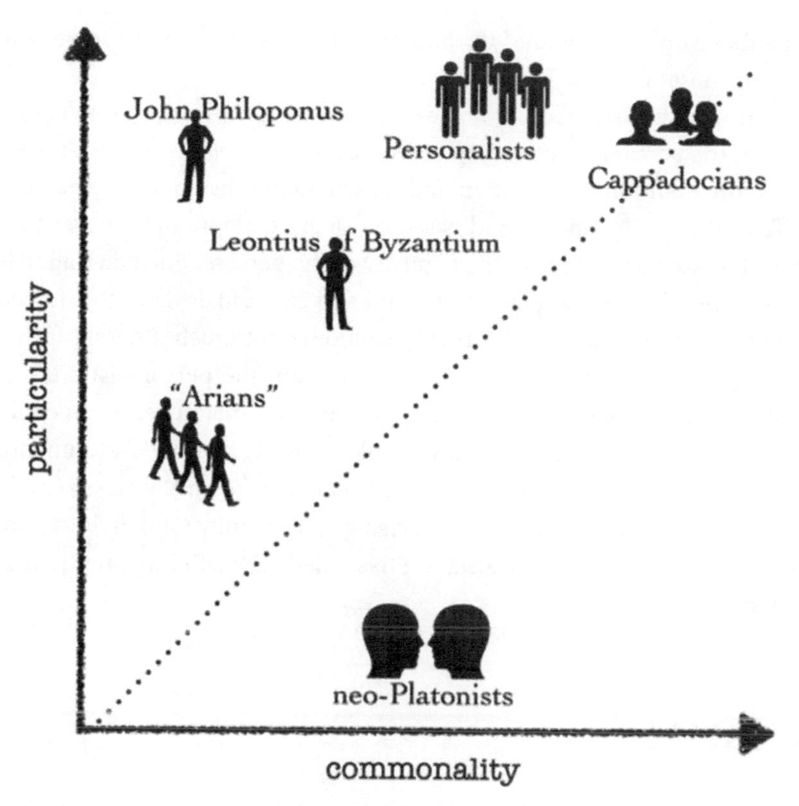


**Figure 2.27** Personalists value the category of particularity more than commonality. In this regard, they stand closer to Leontius, Philoponus, and the "Arians" than to the Cappadocians.

were on the same ontological level. Modern personalism, in contrast to the Cappadocians, favors the category of person and undermines the category of nature. In this regard, it is closer to the standpoint of Leontius.

Nevertheless, in some points, personalism misunderstands the Leontius' category of *enhypostaton*. Modern Orthodox personalists tend to interpret the prefix *en-* as signifying the inclusion of nature to hypostasis. Such interpretation underlines the assumed inferiority of nature to hypostasis: a container is larger than its content. From the same perspective, when something or someone is evolving hypostatically, they are improving their existence. Such existentialist interpretation of hypostasis is far from the original patristic one. According to the original patristic reading of the category of *enhypostaton*, its prefix *en-* does not mean inclusion, but substantiation: a common essence becomes substantiated and particularized—not included in something else or elevated to a higher level of existence. In other words, *enhypostaton* does not mean "in-hypostatic," but plainly "hypostatic." Such a confusion in interpreting *enhypostaton* became possible, when theology was extracted from the traditional scholastic framework—on the assumption that such framework is incompatible with the "genuine" Orthodoxy. This extraction led to some dangerous pseudomorphoses in theology.

For example, the assumed ontological superiority of "person" over "nature," as it stems from the personalistic reading of the category of *enhypostaton*, appears to be distorting the traditional Trinitarian and incarnational theologies. If the hypostases of the Trinity are to be understood based on such assumption, then the oneness of God could be seen as inferior to the triplicity of the persons. Such an understanding unbalances the oneness and plurality in God and can lead as far as to tritheism. The personalistic interpretation of the Trinity would be not much different from that of John Philoponus. In application to the incarnation, the personalistic take on the differentiation between person and nature would not be helpful either. It could mean that the personality of Jesus is more valuable than his divinity and humanity. The latter are natures and, according to the personalistic take on the category of nature, bear in them an assumed ontological deficiency. If humanity (and divinity!) in Christ has such deficiency, then the incarnation has failed. The latter assumptions amount to a Christological heresy.

# Eucharist

Eucharist is another category that became popular in the modern Orthodox theology. This category has been applied to most theological fields, but primarily to ecclesiology. Eucharistic ecclesiology resembles personalism in shaping the Orthodox theology during the twentieth century (see Ware 2011). Usually, personalists also appreciate Eucharistic ecclesiology. Like personalism, this ecclesiology is rooted in the Western theology.[3] While personalism stresses the central role of personhood in the world, Eucharistic ecclesiology emphasizes Eucharist in the life of the church. The Russian theologian in diaspora, Nikolay Afanasiev (1893–1966), who was a proponent of this ecclesiology,[4] explored "the eucharistic understanding of the Church" and its many ramifications:

> The royal priesthood of the members of the Church found expression in the eucharistic assembly. Upon entering the Church, each member of the Church is ordained into the ministry of priest, in order to serve in the Church "our God and Father." This priestly ministry of all members of the Church was the basis of all the variety of ministries that we find in the original Church. <. . .>

---

[3]Roman Catholic theologian Henri de Lubac claimed in 1953: "The Eucharist makes the church" (Lubac 1953: 115–16; see also McPartlan 1996).

[4]See Wooden 2019. The modern protagonist of the Eucharistic ecclesiology is Metropolitan John Zizioulas (born 1931). There are also critics of this ecclesiology, such as John Erickson (see Erickson 2011).

> In the light of eucharistic ecclesiology, the problem of the appearance of the episcopate, which until now seems to have been unsolvable, is not essentially a problem, especially if one omits the problem of the term [itself]. The ministry of bishops is original and, as the ministry of presidency, is included in the eucharistic concept of the Church. The traditional view of the bishop [episcopacy] is confirmed by what we know about Church life in early Christianity. <. . .>
>
> [E]arly Christianity did not know the external-universal concept of the Church. This was not due to the primitiveness of its dogmatic thought, but because of its eucharistic ecclesiology. The fullness of the Church was fully revealed in every local church with its Eucharistic assembly. The church is one, but its unity in empirical life is manifested in the form of many local churches.
>
> The eucharistic assembly is the assembly of the people of God in Christ. Founded at the Last Supper, the Eucharist is actualized after the sending down of the Spirit. The Spirit is the beginning and the foundation of the life of the Church. Charisms are gifts of the Spirit, without which neither ministry nor life in the Church is possible. *The fullness of grace—omnis gratia—* belongs to the Church and the Church is the fulness of grace. "The Church of God in Christ" is the Church of the Holy Spirit.[5]

Eucharistic ecclesiology was originally designed as a liberal instrument of emancipation—similarly to personalism. Nikolay Afanasiev envisaged it as an affirmation of priesthood for all believers. Nevertheless, conservative circles accepted it as well when they saw it as an opportunity to affirm their Orthodox identity and to confirm the hierarchical authority in the church. Indeed, the Eastern Christianity focuses on liturgy more than its Western counterpart. That is how Eucharistic ecclesiology, despite its Western provenance, became associated with the East. Interpreted from the same conservative perspective, Eucharist ecclesiology promotes the bishops' office as ontologically superior to other church offices. According to this interpretation, hierarchy is rooted in the life of the Trinity. Besides, because Eucharist is performed either by a bishop or in his name, the exclusivity of Eucharist is projected to the exclusivity of the episcopal office.

Eucharist as a category, therefore, can be ambivalent. Its interpretations may have self-excluding ramifications in the life of the church. As we have demonstrated, the same happens to other modern categories, which have substituted the classical ones—following the anti-scholastic campaigns. The new categories can be applied to modern theology in a less controversial way when they become harmonized with the old ones. A synthesis between the new and the classical dialectical frameworks is one of the actual tasks for modern theologians. This task can be achieved only if Orthodox theology rehabilitates scholasticism.

[5]Abstract to the thesis of Archpriest N. N. Afanasiev, "Church of the Holy Spirit"; found in the archives of St. Sergius' Institute in Paris and published by Wooden 2019: appendix 3, pp. 482–3.

# Salvation

# III.1

# The Fall

Christian theology is teleological. The *telos* it aims at is the salvation of both humankind and individual human beings. All domains of Christian theology, including Triadology, Christology, ecclesiology, anthropology, cosmology, and so on, have been developed in the framework of soteriology (see Twomey & Krausmüller 2010). "Soteriology" derives from the Greek word *soteria* (σωτηρία)—"salvation." Classical Christian theology was driven not by curiosity and knowledge for the sake of knowing, but by concerns for the salvation of the world and human beings in it. We can hardly find classical theological topics irrelevant to such concerns. Soteriological perspective makes theology different from modern scientific inquiry. The latter wants to understand and give explanations to everything, while the former—primarily to the matters relevant to salvation.

Salvation presupposes peril, from which someone must be saved. In Christianity, this peril is the "Fall"—a catastrophe of cosmic scale, which has affected the entire created world. The original purpose of this world, and of human beings in it, was to achieve the increasingly perfect unity with God. This everlasting journey toward perfection was disrupted by the transgression of God's commandment. Human beings, in result, became unable to achieve unity with God. In the Scriptures, this is described as expulsion from Paradise, sufferings, and eventually death. In the Western theological tradition, the outcome of the Fall has been portrayed as "original sin," understood as an ontological alienation of the human nature from what it had been originally created by God. In the East, theologians did not use this notion (see Romanides 2018).

## Melito of Sardes

One of them, the bishop of Sardes in Asia Minor Melito, gave a detailed account of the Fall in a poetic form. This is the earliest comprehensive summary of the Fall in the Christian literature. Melito flourished in the 160s–80s. He was a talented poet and a good theologian. His most famous work is a long homily in verses titled *On Pascha*

(Περὶ Πάσχα), which was discovered and published in the mid-twentieth century. Melito described the Fall by paraphrasing relevant passages from the Scripture:

When God in the beginning had made the heaven and the earth
and all the things in them by his word,
he fashioned from the earth man,
and gave him a share of his own *breath*.
This man he set in the paradise eastward
*in Eden, there* to live in bliss,
laying down this law for him by his command:
"Of every tree in the paradise by all means eat,
but of the tree of knowing good and evil
you shall not eat;
and on the day you eat
you shall certainly die."
But the man, being naturally receptive of good and evil,
as a clod of earth is of seed from either side,
accepted the hostile and greedy adviser,
and by touching the tree he broke the command
and disobeyed God.
So he was cast out into this world
as into a convicts' prison.

Then, Melito proceeds to describing the consequences of the Fall in almost baroque style:

This man having become very prolific and very long-lived,
when through the tasting of the tree he was dissolved
and sank into the earth,
an inheritance was left by him to his children;
for he left his children as inheritance
not chastity but promiscuity,
not imperishability but decay,
not honour but dishonour,
not freedom but slavery,
not royalty but tyranny,
not life but death,
not salvation but destruction.

Melito explored every detail of sinful behavior resulted by the Fall. However, he did not render this behavior in the terms that would resemble "original sin":

The destruction of men upon earth became strange and terrible.
For these things befell them:
they were seized by tyrannical sin,
and were led to the lands of the lusts,
where they were swamped by insatiable pleasures,
by adultery,

by promiscuity,
by wantonness,
by avarice,
by murders,
by bloodshed,
by wicked tyranny,
by lawless tyranny.
For father took up sword against son,
and son laid hands on father,
and impiously smote the breasts that nursed him;
brother killed brother,
guest and host wronged each other,
friend murdered friend,
and man slew man with tyrannous right hand.
So all men became upon the earth either manslayers
or parricides
or infanticides
or fratricides.
But the strangest and most terrible thing occurred on the earth:
a mother touched the flesh she had brought forth,
and tasted what she had suckled at the breasts;
and she buried in her belly the fruit of her belly,
and she wretched mother became a terrible grave,
gulping, not kissing, the child she had produced.
Many other things, strange and quite terrible and quite outrageous,
took place among mankind:
father for child's bed,
and son for mother's,
and brother for sister's,
and male for male's,
and one man for the next man's wife, they neighed
like stallions.

Sin has not altered human nature, but left a "mark" (ἴχνος) in every human soul:

At these things sin rejoiced,
who in the capacity of death's fellow worker
journeys ahead into the souls of men,
and prepares as food for him the bodies of the dead.
In every soul sin made a mark,
and those in whom he made it were bound to die.
So all flesh began to fall under sin,
and every body under death,
and every soul was driven out of its fleshly dwelling.

And what was taken from earth was to earth dissolved,
and what was given from God was confined in Hades.
And there was separation of what fitted beautifully,
and the beautiful body was split apart.
For man was being divided by death;
for a strange disaster and captivity were enclosing him,
and he was dragged off a prisoner under the shadows of death,
and desolate lay the Father's image. (*De pascha* 47–55; in Hall 1979: 25–31)

# Sophrony Sakharov

After Melito, most Eastern theologians explained sin as a catastrophe of cosmic scale. It affects the entire created world—not in the sense of modifying its nature, which remains ontologically good, but by causing sufferings and catastrophes in it. Modern spiritual writer, Sophrony Sakharov (1896–1993), explained the Eastern reading of sin in modern terms:

> What does the Christian understand by sin?
>
> Sin is primarily a metaphysical phenomenon whose roots lie in the mystic depths of man's spiritual nature. The essence of sin consists not in the infringement of ethical standards but in a falling away from the eternal Divine life for which man was created and to which, by his very nature, he is called.
>
> Sin is committed first of all in the secret depths of the human spirit but its consequences involve the individual as a whole. A sin will reflect on a man's psychological and physical condition, on his outward appearance, on his personal destiny. Sin will, inevitably, pass beyond the boundaries of the sinner's individual life, to burden all humanity and thus affect the fate of the whole world. The sin of our forefather Adam was not the only sin of cosmic significance. Every sin, manifest or secret, committed by each one of us affects the rest of the universe. (Sakharov 1999: 31)

# Common and Particular Salvations

Human beings were powerless to change their sinful condition. A radical intervention from God was needed to make such change. Thus, God became man, to save humankind from enslavement to sin and the inevitability of death. This universal salvation, from the Eastern perspective, does not automatically translate to individual salvation. The former has become given, while the latter must be earned—through the individual synergy of human beings with God.

This paradox of salvation, which is given and yet should be achieved, can be explained by applying to it the logical framework of commonality and particularity, as well as of the given and the assigned. In this framework, salvation can be distinguished as common and particular. Common salvation has been secured by the incarnation of God in the person of Jesus Christ. Its saving effect applies to the entire humanity. Its universal character is conditioned by the fact that God has adopted not an individual, but the common human nature. The incarnation does not automatically secure the particular salvation of each individual Christian. Such salvation requires collaboration between divine and human agencies.

Several ancient theologians made explicit references to the common and particular sorts of salvation. Clement of Alexandria, for example, spoke about "general" and "single cases" of salvation, which are "ordered by the Lord of the universe for the purpose of universal salvation." In the frame of this universal salvation, God leads "each being to what is better" (*Stromata* VII 2.12; Ramelli 2013: 124). Gregory of Nyssa also referred to the "common salvation of the nature" (κοινὴ σωτηρία τῆς φύσεως):

> The same Only-Begotten God causes the man who is united (ἀνακραθέντα) to him to rise, at once separating the soul from the body and reuniting anew the two: in this way is realized the common salvation of nature (ἡ κοινὴ γίνεται σωτηρία τῆς φύσεως). For this he is called Author of life (ἀρχηγὸς ζωῆς). In fact, the Only-Begotten God, dying for us and rising, has reconciled to himself the cosmos, ransoming with flesh and blood, as of prisoners of war, all of us, who through ties of blood (διὰ τοῦ συγγενοῦς ἡμῶν αἵματος) have part in him. (*Antirrheticus adversus Apollinarium* 154.11-18; Maspero 2007: 21)

John Climacus, a monk from the Mount Sinai who flourished in the first half of the seventh century, also referred to the universal salvation in his classical work *The Ladder of Divine Ascent*:

> God is the life of all free beings. He is the salvation of all, of believers or unbelievers, of the just or the unjust, of the pious or the impious, of those freed from the passions or caught up in them, of monks or those living in the world, of the educated or the illiterate, of the healthy or the sick, of the young or the very old. He is like the outpouring of light, the glimpse of the sun, or the changes of the weather, which are the same for everyone without exception. (John Climacus 1982: 74)

We partake in this common salvation in a particular manner. Jesus himself explained particular salvation: "From the days of John the Baptist until now, the kingdom of heaven has been subjected to violence (βιάζεται), and violent people (βιασταί) have been raiding it" (Mt. 11:12). "Violence" here means personal efforts to gain individual salvation as an appropriation of the common salvation. Common salvation is one for all, but particular salvation presupposes a unique path that everyone takes on his or her way to God. It is impossible for all to follow the same path. Such paths are as many as individuals who want to appropriate the common salvation.

At the same time, an individual way of participation in common salvation should not be interpreted that salvation is individualistic. On the contrary, it is communal. A person partakes of it by developing relationships with other human beings. The "neighbor" is a means sine qua non for one's salvation. The founder of the Eastern monasticism, Antony of Egypt, used to say in this regard: "Life and death depend on our neighbor: for if we win over our brother, we win over God, but if we offend our brother, we sin against Christ" (Antony 9; Wortley 2014: 32). For the same reason, belonging to the church is also a necessary condition for salvation. Church secures the communal character of the individual participation in the common salvation.

Common and individual aspects of salvation cannot be separated from each other—they are only distinguished. Therefore, common salvation is not effective for an individual when it is not particularized. Without being embodied through an individual appropriation and effort, it remains a mere potentiality. In a similar way, particular salvation is impossible without common salvation: in such case, there is nothing to participate in. It means that no one can be saved if there is no common salvation offered by Jesus Christ. In other words, individual salvation is possible only in Christ.

# III.2

# Two Paths

An individual, who through baptism receives access to common salvation, should cover a distance to arrive at particular salvation. That is how the metaphor of a *path* toward salvation became popular in Christianity. This was a metaphor about not one, but two paths: one toward salvation, and the other toward perdition. The metaphor of two paths is one of the earliest in the Christian literature. From as early as the second century, it appeared in such works as the *epistle of Barnabas* and *Epitome of the Apostolic Commands*. In these texts, the metaphor of two paths was employed for catechetical purposes. Those preparing for baptism were explained that there are two paths ahead of them. Baptism opens to them the path toward salvation, but there is still a danger to continue walking the path of perdition.

In the fourth century, the massive influx to the church of people with different motivations made individual pre-baptismal instructions scarcer. Consequently, references to two paths gradually disappeared from the catechetical literature. At the same time, they reappeared in the monastic literature. People who sought perfection in solitude, understood themselves as following the path of life. They also realized that the danger of a path of death was always immanent for them. The fifth-century Coptic *Life of Shenoute* and the sixth-century Latin *Rule of Benedict* exemplify the transition of the idea of two paths from baptismal to monastic literature.

It should be also mentioned that Christians were not original in entertaining the idea of two paths. Pythagoreans had preached their lifestyle as an alternative to the path of evil. They used symbol Y for a point, at which a person should choose, which of two paths he or she should follow. In the Jewish literature, the same idea was articulated first in the book of *Psalms* (1:1); then it appears in the *Testaments of the Twelve Patriarchs*, *Testament of Levi* (19), and *Testament of Asher* (1:6-8). In Judaism, the idea of two paths had the same trajectory as in Christianity: from common practice to special use in the elitist ascetic communities. A Jewish community that called itself *Yahad*, instructed its novices about two paths, according to the *Community rule* that survived in the Qumran collection.

# Qumran

Most probably, this was one of the Essene communities (Ἐσσαῖοι or Ἐσσηνοί).[1] Adults who joined it were probed during three years of novitiate and then took oath of allegiance to the community. They had to share their property, observe Jewish rites (among which ablutions were of particular importance), study Torah, and practice asceticism. *Yahad* was a charismatic and pietistic group, with some dualistic tilt. Teaching about two ways of life was fundamental for it and reflected this tilt:

> He created man to rule the world and placed within him two spirits so that he would walk with them until the moment of his visitation: they are the spirits of truth and of deceit. From the spring of light stem the generations of truth, and from the source of darkness the generations of deceit. And in the hand of the Prince of Lights is dominion over all the sons of justice; they walk on paths of light. And in the hand of the Angel of Darkness is total dominion over the sons of deceit; they walk on paths of darkness. <. . .>
>
> These are their paths in the world: to enlighten the heart of man, straighten out in front of him all the paths of true justice, establish in his heart respect for the precepts of God; it is a spirit of meekness, of patience, generous compassion, eternal goodness, intelligence, understanding, potent wisdom which trusts in all the deeds of God and depends on his abundant mercy. <. . .> And the reward of all those who walk in it will be healing, plentiful peace in a long life, fruitful offspring with all everlasting blessings, eternal enjoyment with endless life, and a crown of glory with majestic raiment in eternal light.
>
> However, to the spirit of deceit belong greed, sluggishness in the service of justice, wickedness, falsehood, pride, haughtiness of heart, dishonesty, trickery, cruelty, much insincerity, impatience, much foolishness, impudent enthusiasm for appalling acts performed in a lustful passion, filthy paths in the service of impurity, blasphemous tongue, blindness of eyes, hardness of hearing, stiffness of neck, hardness of heart in order to walk in all the paths of darkness and evil cunning. And the visitation of all those who walk in it will be for an abundance of afflictions at the hands of all the angels of destruction, for eternal damnation by the scorching wrath of the God of revenges, for permanent terror and shame without end with the humiliation of destruction by the fire of the dark regions. And all the ages of their generations [they shall spend] in bitter weeping and harsh evils in the abysses of darkness until their destruction, without there being a remnant or a survivor for them. (*Community Rule/Manual of Discipline*, 1 QS III.17-IV.14; Tigchelaar & García Martínez 1999)

---

[1]The name of the group derives from a Semitic word, possibly the Aramaic חסיא (*hasya*) or its Hebrew equivalent חסידים (*Hasidim*), which mean "pious," or from the Aramaic אסיא (*asya*), which means "healer," or from עושין (*osin*) ("doers"), an abbreviation of the phrase עושי התורה (*ose ha-torah*)—"doers of the Torah."

# *Didaché*

Some scholars believe that the Qumranic rhetoric of two paths influenced *The Lord's Teaching through the Twelve Apostles to the Nations* (Διδαχὴ Κυρίου διὰ τῶν δώδεκα ἀποστόλων τοῖς ἔθνεσιν), or simply *Didaché* (see Myllykoski 2015: 437–42). It was composed in Greek in Western Syria. It is one of the earliest Christian texts. Some believe it is *the* earliest Christian text (see Павлов 2017: 17). It survives almost completely in the eleventh-century manuscript (*Codex Hierosolymitanus* 54), which was published in 1883 by the metropolitan of the Ecumenical Patriarchate Philotheos Vriennios (1833–1917).[2]

This is a didactic document, hence its title *Didaché*. It teaches on sacraments, with focus on baptism and Eucharist, church organization, and the *eschaton*—Christ's second coming. *Didaché* reflects the Judeo-Christian character of the community, in which it was composed, with the Gentile component in it unstoppably growing. The largest part of the text is moralistic. It epitomizes Christian morality through the imagery of two paths:

> There are two ways, the one of life and the one of death; the difference between the ways is great.
>
> Now the way of life is this. First you shall love the God who made you, secondly your neighbour as yourself, and whatever you would not wish done to you, do not do to anyone else.
>
> The instruction of these maxims is this: Bless those who curse you, and pray for your enemies, fast on behalf of those who persecute you. For what is the merit of loving those who love you? Do not even the gentiles do the same? But love those who hate you, and you shall have no enemy.
>
> Abstain from fleshly and worldly lusts. If any one gives you a blow to your right cheek, turn the other to him also, and you will be perfect. If anyone obliges you to go a mile, go with him two; if anyone takes away your cloak, give him your coat also. If anyone takes what is yours from you, do not ask for it back, for you are unable.
>
> Give to everyone who asks from you, and do not ask it back; for the Father wishes to give to all from his own graces. Whoever gives in accordance with the commandment is blessed, for he is free of guilt; but woe to anyone who receives. For anyone in need who receives is free of guilt; but anyone who receives when not in need shall stand trial as to why he received and for what purpose; and when in prison shall be examined

[2]The official version of the discovery of the monument holds that the metropolitan of Serres (later of Nicomedia) Philotheos Vriennios (1833–1917) found it in the library of the representation (*metokhion*) of the Patriarchate of Jerusalem in Istanbul, in 1873. Ten years later, in 1883, Philotheos published the text. However, there is a more nuanced version of the events preceding the publication. According to this version, the text was discovered not by Philotheos, but by a professor at the theological school of the Ecumenical Patriarchate on the Isle of Halki (Heybeliada). Philotheos later used this manuscript to produce a publication under his name.

concerning the things that he has done, and shall not depart thence until he has paid back the last cent.

But on this it was also said: "Let your alms sweat in your hands until you know to whom you are giving." <. . .>

My child, you shall remember both night and day the one who speaks to you the word of God. You shall honour him as a master. For inasmuch as the dominion is discussed, the Lord is there. You shall seek out daily the presence of the saints, that you may find refreshment in their words. You shall not bring about schism, you shall reconcile those who are disputing, you shall judge justly, you shall not show partiality in rebuking any transgression. You shall not be divided in your mind, whether it will be or not. <. . .>

You shall not forsake the commandments of the Lord. You shall preserve what you have received, neither adding nor subtracting. You shall confess your transgressions in the assembly, and you shall not come to prayer with an evil conscience. This is the way of life.

Yet the way of death is this.

First of all it is evil and beset by cursing. Murders, adulteries, lusts, fornications, thefts, idolatries, charms, sorceries, magic, robberies, falsities of witness, hypocrisies, double-heartedness, trickery, arrogance, malice, selfishness, greed, base speech, jealousy, insolence, haughtiness and pretence, persecutors of the good, haters of the truth, lovers of falsity, unaware of the reward for righteousness, not associating with the good or with just judgement. Those who lie awake, not for good but for evil, far from generosity or patience, loving foolishness, pursuing a reward, showing no pity to the poor, doing no labour for the downtrodden, unaware of the one who made them, murderers of children, corrupters of what God has formed, turning away the needy, treading down the afflicted, advocates of the rich, lawless judges of the poor, utterly sinful. Children, may you be rescued from all of these. (In Stewart-Sykes 2011: 35–9)

# Life of Shenoute

The moralistic style of the *Didaché* made it popular in the monastic circles in both East and West. In the West, for instance, it influenced the Benedictine rule. In the East, it found its way to the monastic teachings of Archimandrite Shenoute. His *Vita* makes frequent references to two paths in application to monastic life:

> He (i.e., Shenoute) always used to teach us that the way was easy. The way is a double one, one leading to life and the other to death with a huge difference between the two. The way to life is this: before all else, love the Lord your God with all your heart, with all your soul and with every thought. Love your neighbour as yourself in all your thinking.
>
> Whatever you would not wish done to you, do not do to anyone else. So act thus. These are the deeds (to be observed) one by one with the first of them being, do not

kill, do not fornicate, do not make yourself impure by loving impurity, do not act sinfully, do not steal, do not practise sorcery, do not bring about an abortion for a pregnant woman through a potion and do not kill her newborn, do not covet the goods of your friend and your relative, do not break an oath, do not speak falsely, do not speak evil of anyone lest the Lord grow angry with you. Do not be changeable, do not speak false or empty words, do not hold back anything from a labourer's wage lest he seek help from the Lord and is heard by Him as the Lord Jesus the Messiah is not far from us. My child, do not take by force, do not loot or be a usurer or wickedly disavow [a debt]. My child, do not be proud, for the proud man is detested by God. Do not speak ill of your friend, your relative or your rival, for if you act thus God will love him more than you. My child, do not hate any person for they are the image and likeness of God. If somebody slips and takes a false step falling into sin, reprimand him among yourselves alone as other kinsfolk have done and love him as yourself. Flee from every evil, do not associate with him who does bad things lest your life be reduced and you die before your allotted time. My child, do not be envious or jealous, do not mislead, for these teach man to kill. My child, do not let your zeal be for lust as lust leads to adultery. My child, do not utter obscene words, do not have covetous eyes for they make false witness. My child, do not ask, "what is it?" or "why is it?," for (questioning) leads to the worship of idols. Do not count the hours for unhappiness, sighing, anxiety and fear fall on those who act thus. My child, do not receive incanters and magicians hospitably and do not approach them or have conversation with them, for any man who frequents them does not draw near to God. My child, do not be a liar, for falsehood leads to theft. My child, do not be a lover of silver, do not boast, for from these is born the desire to kill. My child, do not grumble, for grumbling leads to blasphemy. My child, do not be small-minded, do not think with evil intent but be gentle, for the gentle inherit the earth. My child, be patient, long-suffering, merciful, simple-hearted and faithful in all actions: be good, always fearful and trembling before the words and commands of God. Do not be proud-hearted but always modest. Do not grow close to the rich but associate with people who are devout and humble, for the prophet David owed his salvation to humility many times. Whenever good or evil happen to you, receive it with gratitude for you know that nothing happens to you without the will of God, your God. My child, remember the word of God within your heart, night and day, for the Lord is present wherever anyone mentions his name and He is eternally worthy of respect and praise. My child, follow the path of purity at all times to become strong and powerful in its excellent system and enjoy its sweet words and delightful tales. My child, do not seek discord or argument among your fellow men but seek to make peace among those in disagreement. Then judge with justice and do not be embarrassed to reprimand the criminal for his faults or the sinner for his sin. My child, do not open your hand to receive nor close it to avoid giving. Be careful to act as long as you are able, giving to the poor in exchange for your many sins. Indeed, do not be changeable when you give and if you give do not be saddened nor be regretful if you act mercifully. You might well know that it is Jesus the Messiah who pardons sins and recompenses the honest and the faithful man. My child, do not turn your face from the poor but give according to your power. Share with all who are troubled and in need, for if we share our perishable goods with the disenfranchised we shall share with them in goods which are lasting and eternal. If we follow these recommendations we may travel along the road of life and the blessed path to eternity which belongs to the one king, the Lord Jesus the Messiah who is generous to those who desire him.

As to the way of death, whoever follows its track and walks in its paths shall die the death of a bad man because of all its evil deeds which are: cursing, murder, pillage, violence, hypocrisy and every bad deed. Have we not explained it [all] lest someone be led astray and fall in the road of death and travel its paths to bad deeds for the man untried in such things grows proud.

This is the teaching which our holy father, Anba Shenoute, always used to teach us on every occasion and it is this, our children, we have explained to you at this time. (Translated by Posy Clayton in Stewart-Sykes 2011: 122–4)

# III.3

# Dynamics of Virtue

The more the Christian theology advanced, the more sophisticated and nuanced the imagery of the two paths became. The Aristotelian concept of motion contributed to the evolution of this image. Maximus the Confessor employed the category of motion to explain spiritual progress. According to Maximus, spiritual life cannot be static, but permanently evolves. The momentum for spiritual movement springs from God, to whom everyone longs as the ultimate destination:

> It belongs to beings <. . .> to be moved toward that end which has no beginning, and to cease from their activity in that perfect end which is devoid of all quantity and passively to experience the Unqualified, without being or becoming it in essence, for everything which has come to be and is created is clearly not absolute. <. . .>
>
> If then, rational creatures are created beings, then surely they are subject to motion, since they are moved from their natural beginning in being, toward a voluntary end in well-being. For the end of the motion of things that are moved is to rest within eternal well-being itself, just as their beginning was being itself which is God, who is the giver of being and the bestower of the grace of well-being, for He is the *beginning and the end*. For from God come both our general power of motion (for He is our beginning), and the particular way that we move toward Him (for He is our end). (*Ambiguum ad Joh.* VII 9-10; Maximus 2014: 85–7)

## Movement Up and Forward

For Gregory of Nyssa, the moment a person pauses in moving forward, he or she immediately begins moving backward. In spiritual life, one cannot stand still, but always moves: either forward or backward. The only alternative to spiritual regress is spiritual progress. If there is no progress, there is always regress.

The destination is spiritual perfection. It is like horizon: a person can get closer to it, but never reaches it. This should not stop one from moving forward and up. Such direction was allegorically indicated by Moses in his ascending to the Mount Sinai.

**Figure 3.1** Moses. A wall-painting from an Egyptian church (seventh to eighth centuries). Benaki Museum in Athens.

Source: Photo by the author.

For Gregory, Moses' ascension was an icon of a human soul advancing in spiritual perfection:

> Bodies, once they have received the initial thrust downward, are driven downward by themselves with greater speed without any additional help as long as the surface on which they move is steadily sloping and no resistance to their downward thrust is encountered. Similarly, the soul moves in the opposite direction. Once it is released from its earthly attachment, it becomes light and swift for its movement upward, soaring from below up to the heights.
>
> If nothing comes from above to hinder its upward thrust (for the nature of the Good attracts to itself those who look to it), the soul rises ever higher and will always make its flight yet higher—by its desire of the heavenly things straining ahead for what is still to come, as the Apostle says (Phil. 3:13).
>
> Made to desire and not to abandon the transcendent height by the things already attained, it makes its way upward without ceasing, ever through its prior accomplishments renewing its intensity for the flight. Activity directed toward virtue causes its capacity to grow through exertion; this kind of activity alone does not slacken its intensity by the effort, but increases it.
>
> For this reason we also say that the great Moses, as he was becoming ever greater, at no time stopped in his ascent, nor did he set a limit for himself in his upward course. Once having set foot on the ladder which God set up, as Jacob says (Gen. 28:12), he continually climbed to the step above and never ceased to rise higher, because he always found a step higher than the one he had attained. <. . .>

This truly is the vision of God: never to be satisfied in the desire to see him. But one must always, by looking at what he can see, rekindle his desire to see more. Thus, no limit would interrupt growth in the ascent to God, since no limit to the Good can be found nor is the increasing of desire for the Good brought to an end because it is satisfied. (*De vita Mosis* 219–39; Katz 2013: 217–9)

Almost three centuries after Gregory, one monk John lived at the foot of the Sinai and often ascended it. To present spiritual progress, he used the image of ladder. John thus wanted to stress that spiritual progress is like a systematic work: one particular step follows another one. If one tries to jump over several stairs of such spiritual ladder, one can easily fall down. This was a point that John wanted to emphasize in his letter to another John, the abbot of the monastery of Raïth. John "of the Ladder" (Climacus/τῆς Κλίμακος)—so he became known to the posteriority, alluded to the story about Patriarch Jacob's dream at Bethel, when he "saw a stairway resting on the earth, with its top reaching to heaven, and the angels of God were ascending and descending on it. There above it stood the Lord" (Gen. 28:12-13).

John Climacus presented spiritual development similarly to ascending a ladder:

Ascend, my brothers, ascend eagerly. Let your hearts' resolve be to climb. Listen to the voice of the one who says: "Come, let us go up to the mountain of the Lord, to the house of our God" (Isa 2:3), Who makes our feet to be like the feet of the deer, "Who sets us on the high places, that we may be triumphant on His road (Hab 3:19). Run, I beg you, run with him who said, "Let us hurry until we all arrive at the unity of faith and of the knowledge of God, at mature manhood, at the measure of the stature of Christ's fullness" (Eph 4:13). (John Climacus 1982: 291)

John envisaged spiritual ladder as having three sections: (1) breaking up with the world, (2) fighting passions and pursuing virtues, and (3) uniting with God.[1] Thirty steps of this ladder lead a person to the love of God, which John held as the ultimate *telos* of Christian life. These steps are following:

stage 1: break with the world
step 1: renunciation
step 2: detachment
step 3: exile

stage 2: virtues and passions
*fundamental virtues*
step 4: obedience
step 5: repentance
step 6: remembrance of death
step 7: joyful sorrow

[1]I follow the systematization of the "ladder" by Chryssavgis 2004: 28–9.

*struggle against passions*

*(a) passions that are predominantly non-physical*
step 8: anger
step 9: malice
step 10: slander
step 11: talkativeness
step 12: falsehood
step 13: despondency

*(b) passions that are predominantly physical and material*
step 14: gluttony
step 15: lust
steps 16-17: avarice

*(c) passions that are predominantly non-physical and spiritual*
steps 18-20: insensitivity
step 21: fear
step 22: vainglory
step 23: pride (including blasphemy)

*higher virtues of the "active life"*
step 24: simplicity
step 25: prayer
step 26: discernment

stage 3: union with God
step 27: stillness
step 28: prayer
step 29: dispassion
step 30: love

The hardest part of ascending is its beginning:

> Violence (see Mt. 11:12) and unending pain are the lot of those who aim to ascend to heaven with the body, and this especially at the early stages of the enterprise, when our pleasure-loving disposition and our unfeeling hearts must travel through overwhelming grief toward the love of God and holiness. It is hard, truly hard. There has to be an abundance of invisible bitterness, especially for the careless, until our mind, that cur sniffing around the meat market and revelling in the uproar, is brought through simplicity, deep freedom from anger and diligence to a love of holiness and guidance. Yet full of passions and weakness as we are, let us take heart and let us in total confidence carry to Christ in our right hand and confess to Him our helplessness and our fragility. We will carry away more help than we deserve, if

> only we constantly push ourselves down into the depths of humility. (John Climacus 1982: 75–6)

After these initial stages of hardship, going up becomes easier. An ascetic should pass through all stages, more or less in the order described by John. In the end, he or she will be rewarded with the gift of divine love. John found nice and convincing words to describe this gift at the final, thirtieth, step of his ladder:

> The man who wants to talk about love is undertaking to speak about God. But it is risky to talk about God and could even be dangerous for the unwary. Angels know how to speak about love, but even they do so only in proportion to the light within them.
>
> "God is love" (1 Jn 4:16). But someone eager to define this is blindly striving to measure the sand in the ocean.
>
> Love, by its nature, is a resemblance to God, insofar as this is humanly possible. In its activity it is inebriation of the soul. Its distinctive character is to be a fountain of faith, an abyss of patience, a sea of humility.
>
> Love is the banishment of every sort of contrariness, for love thinks no evil. <. . .>
>
> Someone truly in love keeps before his mind's eye the face of the beloved and embraces it there tenderly. Even during sleep the longing continues unappeased, and he murmurs to his beloved. That is how it is for the body. And that is how it is for the spirit. A man wounded by love had this to say about himself—and it really amazes me—"I sleep (because nature commands this) but my heart is awake (because of the abundance of my love)" (Song of Songs 5:2). You should take note, my brother, that the stag, which is the soul, destroys reptiles and then, inflamed by love, as if struck by an arrow, it longs and grows faint for the love of God (see Ps. 41:1). <. . .>
>
> He who loves the Lord has first loved his brother, for the latter is proof of the former. Someone who loves his neighbor will never tolerate slanderers and will run from them as though from a fire. And the man who claims to love the Lord but is angry with his neighbor is like someone who dreams he is running. <. . .>
>
> Love grants prophecy, miracles. It is an abyss of illumination, a fountain of fire, bubbling up to inflame the thirsty soul. It is the condition of angels, and the progress of eternity. (John Climacus 1982: 286–9)

Spiritual writer a generation younger than John, Isaac of Nineveh, also used the image of ladder to describe the spiritual development of a person. Such ladder is hidden in human soul. This idea helped Isaac to present spiritual development as a paradox: to ascend the ladder, one needs to descend down to his or her soul: "The ladder to the Kingdom is hidden within you, and within your soul. Dive down into your self, away from sin, and there you will find the steps by which you can ascend up" (*Hom.* 2 B12; Brock 2006: 2). After reaching the top, one will meet God's love. Isaac is completely coherent with John in setting the *telos* of the Christian asceticism as love. The love of God is stronger than any sin:

> Just as a grain of sand will not balance in the scales against a great weight of gold, such too is the case with God's justice when it is weighed against His compassion. When compared with God's mind, the sins of all flesh are like a handful of sand thrown in the sea. (*Hom.* 50 B345; Brock 2006: 16)

## Movement toward the Center

Some fathers described the movement of human beings toward God not only in linear, but also in circular fashion. A Palestinian abbot Dorotheus, who lived in the sixth century, presented this movement as inscribed in the "circle of love." The closer the points on the circumference get to the center, the shorter is the distance between them. It can also be put the other way around: the shorter is the distance between points on the same circumference, the closer they approach the circle's center. The same equation applies to the spiritual life: the closer we approach to God, the shorter is the distance to our neighbor, and vice versa:

> Suppose we were to take a compass and insert the point and draw the outline of a circle. The center point is the same distance from any point on the circumference. Now concentrate your minds on what is to be said! Let us suppose that this circle is the world and God himself is the center; the straight lines drawn from the circumference to the center are the lives of men. To the degree that the saints enter into the things of the spirit, they desire to come near to God; and in proportion to their progress in the things of the spirit, they do in fact come close to God and to their neighbor. The closer they are to God, the closer they are to one another; and the closer they are to one another, the closer they become to God. Now consider in the same context the question of separation; for when they stand away from God and turn to external things, it is clear that the more they recede and become distant from God, the more they become distant from one another. See! This is the very nature of love. The more we are turned away from and do not love God, the greater the distance that separates us from our neighbor. If we were to love God more, we should be closer to God, and through love of him we should be more united in love to our neighbor; and the more we are united to our neighbor the more we are united to God. May God make us worthy to listen to what is fitting for us and do it. For in the measure that we pay fitting attention and take care to carry out what we hear, God will always enlighten us and make us understand his will. (Dorotheos of Gaza 1977: 139)

For Maximus the Confessor, a person does not initiate movement toward God, but responds to God's movement toward the person. All trajectories, by which a person approaches God, originate from God:

> According to the creative and sustaining procession of the One to individual beings, which is befitting of divine goodness, the One is many. According to the revertive,

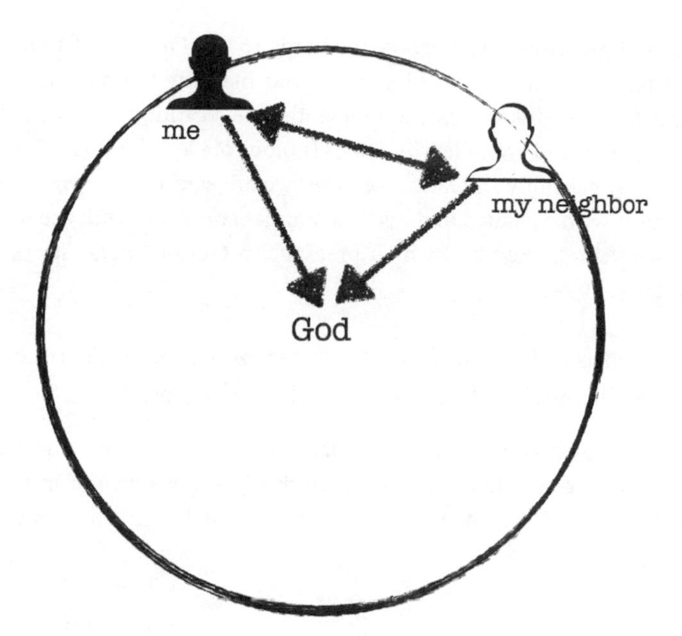


**Figure 3.2** Simultaneous movement of a person to God and neighbor, according to Dorotheus of Gaza.

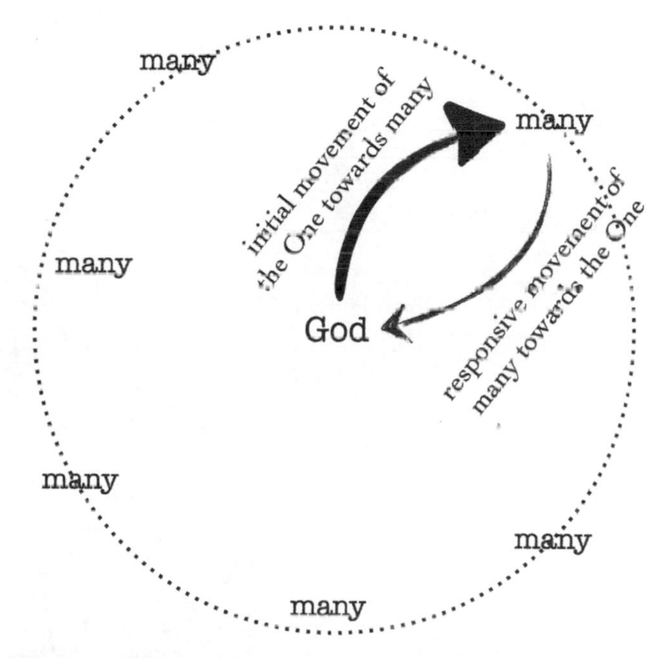


**Figure 3.3** God by his movement to many incites the movement of many to God, according to Maximus the Confessor.

> inductive, and providential return of the many to the One—as if to an all-powerful point of origin, or to the center of a circle precontaining the beginnings of the radii originating from it—insofar as the One gathers everything together, the many are One. We are, then, and are called "portions (μοῖρα) of God" because of the logoi of our being that exist eternally in God. Moreover, we are said to have "flowed down from above" because we have failed to move in a manner consistent with the logos according to which we were created and which preexists in God. (*Ambiguum ad Joh.* VII 20; Maximus 2014: 101–3)

The following words of Isaac of Nineveh summarize various trajectories that human beings follow while moving closer to God and one another:

> With the love of God a person will draw close to a perfect love of fellow human beings. No one has ever been able to draw close to this luminous love of humanity without having first been held worthy of the wonderful and inebriating love of God. (X 33-34; Brock 2006: 34)

# III.4
# Synergy

The metaphors of walking a path or moving to a destination presuppose free choice and strong will. Such movement would be impossible without human agency, which contributes to synergy between human person and God, when they cowork in making one's eternal salvation possible. These metaphors also emphasize that salvation is a process, not an instantaneous event. They imply that there can be degrees of salvation, as there are different distances that a person can cover while walking or moving. All these connotations, implied by the metaphor of two paths, became explicated by various ascetic authors.

The individual participation in salvation means that human freedom is its unavoidable prerequisite. Human beings participate in the common salvation individually through their personal decisions. Maximus the Confessor stated that, in as much as freedom is the only explanation of evil and sufferings, the same freedom is the only door to salvation and joy in Christ (see *Disputatio cum Pyrrho* PG 91, 325). Salvation is impossible without free engagement of an individual. Any salvation imposed by force is not saving. It can be a simulacrum of salvation, but not salvation proper. Therefore, coercion and salvation are incompatible. As Origen put it, "If you take away the element of free will from virtue, you also destroy its essence" (*Contra Celsum* IV 3; Origen 2009: 186). Gregory of Nyssa explained this in more detail:

> If you divide in two a stick—since nothing hinders explaining with a material example the mystery of the economy of the Incarnation—and the ends of the [two] pieces of the stick are joined on one side, necessarily the whole cut part of the stick, through the junction and binding into one of the extremities, will be reunited to the whole, as it is reunited to the other extremity. In this way, in him (Christ) the union of soul and body accomplished in the resurrection guides by conjunction (κατὰ τὸ συνεχές) the whole human nature, divided by death into soul and body, to the natural union (πρὸς συμφυΐαν) by the hope of the resurrection, uniting the combination of that which was divided. And this is what Paul says: "Christ is risen from the dead, first fruit of those who are dead" (1 Cor. 15:20), and "as all of us died in Adam, so all will receive life in Christ" (1 Cor. 15:22). In fact, following the example of the stick, our nature was split

> by sin from the limit enacted by Adam, since by death the soul was separated from the body, but the humanity of Christ (τοῦ κατὰ τὸν Χριστὸν ἀνθρώπου) was united into one nature alone (συμφυομένης). Therefore we die together with him who died for us, and with this I do not refer to the necessary and common death belonging to our nature. For this happens even if we wish it not. But, since one must die with him who died by his own will, it is good for us (αὐτοῖς) to think of that death that comes through free choice (ἐκ προαιρέσεως). In fact it is impossible to imitate that which is voluntary by that which is necessarily imposed. Since then, the death that is imposed on each of us by our nature comes to pass, and that necessarily, whether we wish or do not, one cannot hold as voluntary that which is necessary; therefore in another mode we die together with him who died voluntarily, that is being buried in the mystical waters through baptism. It is said in fact, that "through baptism we were buried together with him in death" (Rom. 6:4), so that from the imitation of death can also follow the imitation of the resurrection. (*Antirrheticus adversus Apollinarium* 226.6–227.9; Maspero 2007: 24–5)

The category of freedom explains the distinction between common and particular salvations mentioned earlier. Common salvation depends completely on God and has been accomplished by his incarnation. Particular salvation requires both divine and human agencies. Human beings corroborate their particular salvation by their consent and effort. The idea of human agency as a condition sine qua non for salvation is early. Justin explained it in the second century:

> God knows in advance that some will be saved by repentance, even though they may not yet be born. In the beginning he made the human race with the power of thought, of choosing the truth and of doing right, so that no one has any excuse before God, for they have been born with reason and the power to reflect. If anyone refuses to believe that God cares for these things, he is either insinuating that God does not exist or else asserting that he delights in vice or is like a stone, indifferent to virtue or vice, which mean nothing to him but only to human beings. To say that would be the greatest profanity and wickedness. (*Apologia* I 28; Bray 2009: 55)

Isaac of Nineveh captured the same idea in one sentence: "God is compassionate, and He loves to give, but He wants us to be the reason for His giving" (*Hom.* 24 B181; Brock 2006: 10). Maximus the Confessor unpacked this idea with the help of the categories of commonality and particularity. For him, the ways (*tropoi*) of particularization of the common human essence can be three: being (εἶναι), well-being (εὖ εἶναι), and eternal well-being (ἀεὶ εὖ εἶναι) (*Ambiguum ad Joh.* VII 10). The first mode of existence is pertinent to the human nature and does not depend on human agency. The second and the third modes, however, feature such dependence. It is up to us (but not only) to transform our being to either well-being or ill-being. In the afterlife, these two modes will become either eternal well-being or eternal ill-being. To achieve the eternal well-being, one has to apply persistent effort and collaborate with the divine grace. A medieval Byzantine mystical writer Symeon the New Theologian described his own persistence in seeking God:

> I never turned back. . .
> I did not slow down my running
> But with all my strength,
> With all my power
> I searched for Him Whom I did not see.
> I looked around the roads
> And behind the fences, to discover where He might appear.
> I was filled with tears
> And I asked everyone
> Who had ever seen Him
> The prophets, Apostles and Fathers
> I asked them to tell me
> Where they had ever seen Him.
> And when He spoke with me,
> I started running with all my strength
> And I saw Him totally,
> And He united Himself entirely with me. (*Hymn* 29.81-129; Alfeyev 2000: 54)

Divine and human contributions to the particular salvation are not equal. Divine one is more substantial than human. Still, it does not work without even minimal human effort. At the same time, human effort, however intense it is, means nothing without leverage from God. A modern Greek Orthodox saint, Païsius the Hagiorite (Eznepidis, 1924–94), suggested a metaphor of divine-human synergy. According to this metaphor, human efforts are like a sequence of zeros. They can be many, yet regardless of how many they are their sum equals to zero for the salvation. Only when God comes and puts one in front of zeros, they receive value for the particular salvation:

> Our works are zero, and our virtues are a series of zeros. We should try to continuously add zeros and to ask Christ to put one in front of them, to become rich. If Christ does not put one in the beginning, our work is in vain. (Παΐσιος Ἁγιορείτης 1999: 160)

Païsius the Hagiorite mentioned "virtues"—a fundamental category in both Greek pre-Christian and Christian thought. In the latter, it means a persisting intention and acquired habit to do good deeds, as commanded in the Scriptures. Eastern theologians developed a sophisticated system of "aretology." According to this system, virtues can be directed to God, other human beings, and self. The virtues related to God include preaching the God's word and worshipping. In the Eastern Christianity, worship is an important prerequisite of salvation, which is endangered

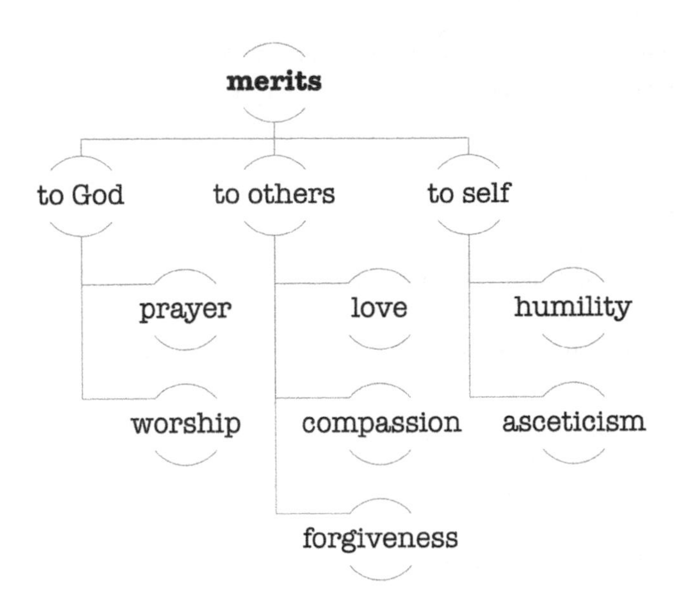


**Figure 3.4** Taxonomy of merits.

if a person does not attend divine services. Virtues related to others include love, works of charity, compassion, and forgiveness. When a person judges others and does not forgive, this creates a chasm between the common and individual salvations for that person. Finally, an important virtue in relationship to self is asceticism—various forms of self-restriction.

# III.5
# Sins and Passions

Opposite to virtues are sins and passions. In the Christian East, spiritual writers often differentiated between these two categories. Sins, for them, are accomplished actions—something one has done. Passions are intentions and habits that cause sins. In the Aristotelian categories, passions are potentialities, while sins are actualities. Passions do not necessarily produce sins. However, when infected by a passion, a person can commit a sin anytime. Therefore, the Eastern ascetic practices try in the first place to tackle passions and then sins. When passions are eradicated from soul, a person becomes "passionless" (ἀπαθής). Isaac of Nineveh described this state in the following passage:

> Just as the sun's rays are sometimes hidden from the earth by thick cloud, so for a while a person may be deprived of spiritual comfort and of grace's brightness: this is caused by the cloud of the passions. Then, all of a sudden, without that person being aware, it is all given back. Just as the surface of the earth rejoices at the rays of the sun when they break through the clouds, so the words of prayer are able to break through to drive the thick cloud of the passions away from the soul. (*Hom.* 13 B124; Brock 2006: 8)

## Evolution of Passions

Eastern ascetic tradition has thoroughly examined in every detail the process of genesis and evolution of passions. This process begins with a thought (*logismos*/λογισμός). The person does not bear moral responsibility for the *logismoi* approaching him or her. *Logismos* is not a sin yet. Abba Poemen from the Egyptian desert explained this to a novice:

> A brother came to Abba Poemen and said to him: "Abba, I have many *logismoi* and am in danger from them." The elder took him out into the open air and said to him:

> "Inflate your chest and hold the winds" (Prov. 30:4), but he said: "I cannot do that." The elder said to him: "If you cannot do that, neither can you prevent the *logismoi* from coming: your [task] is to withstand them." (Poemen 28; Wortley 2014: 232)

Among the sources of the *logismoi* are demons, other human beings, or a person himself or herself. The initial stage, when a sinful thought approaches one's mind, is called "insult" (*prosbolé*/προσβολή). Ascetic writers accentuated the importance of this stage for the further development of a passion. It is the easiest stage to get rid of it because the sinful intention is not yet rooted in the human mind. They advised Christians to carefully examine thoughts approaching them and cast them away as soon as possible. When *logismoi* are not expelled in time, "conjunction" (*syndyasmos*/συνδυασμός) between mind and thought can occur. At this stage, a passion begins planting itself in one's soul. It first plunges to mind. At the next stage of consent (*synkatathesis*/συγκατάθεσις), the human will complies with the sinful thought.

Consent is probably the most crucial point in the evolution of a passion. It is a rubicon, after crossing which a person bears full moral responsibility. Before this point, a human being is not yet guilty for his or her actions. After this point, whatever a human being does turns either to merit or to sin. Before giving his or her consent, a person cannot be praised or blamed for what he or she does or intends.

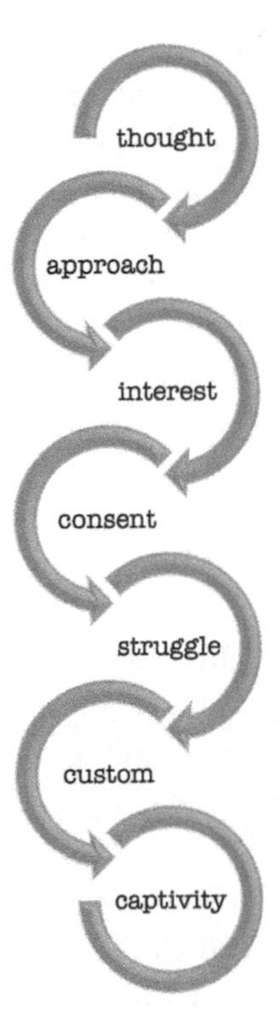


**Figure 3.5** Genesis of a passion.

Following the consent to sin, the next stage of struggle (*palē*/πάλη) begins. At this stage, the soul tries to get rid of the sinful thought. However, now it is harder to eradicate, as it has planted roots in soul. The sinful thought grows and becomes an acquired property (*hexis*/ἕξις) of the soul, which develops to captivity (*aechmalosia*/αἰχμαλωσία). In the modern language, this stage could be called addiction. In the language of ancient asceticism, it was called "passion" (*pathos*/πάθος).

# Taxonomy of Passions

Christian theologians shelved particular passions to taxonomies, which resemble the logical taxonomies. The taxonomies of passions helped to trace connections and dependences between them. A taxonomy produced by Evagrius of Pontus (345–99) is the most famous one. It includes gluttony, impurity, avarice, sadness, anger, acedia, vainglory, and pride:

> There are eight general and basic categories of thoughts in which are included every thought. First is that of gluttony, then impurity, avarice, sadness, anger, acedia, vainglory, and last of all, pride. It is not in our power to determine whether we are disturbed by these thoughts, but it is up to us to decide if they are to linger within us or not and whether or not they are to stir up our passions.
>
> The thought of gluttony suggests to the monk that he give up his ascetic efforts in short order. It brings to his mind concern for his stomach, for his liver and spleen, the thought of a long illness, scarcity of the commodities of life and finally of his edematous body and the lack of care by the physicians. These things are depicted vividly before his eyes. It frequently brings him to recall certain ones among the brethren who have fallen upon such sufferings. There even comes a time when it persuades those who suffer from such maladies to visit those who are practicing a life of abstinence and to expose their misfortune and relate how these came about as a result of the ascetic life.
>
> The demon of impurity impels one to lust after bodies. It attacks more strenuously those who practice continence, in the hope that they will give up their practice of this virtue, feeling that they gain nothing by it. This demon has a way of bowing the soul down to practices of an impure kind, defiling it, and causing it to speak and hear certain words almost as if the reality were actually present to be seen.
>
> Avarice suggests to the mind a lengthy old age, inability to perform manual labor (at some future date), famines that are sure to come, sickness that will visit us, the pinch of poverty, the great shame that comes from accepting the necessities of life from others.
>
> Sadness tends to come up at times because of the deprivations of one's desires. On other occasions it accompanies anger. When it arises from the deprivation of desires it takes place in the following manner. Certain thoughts first drive the soul to the memory of home and parents, or else to that of one's former life.
>
> Now when these thoughts find that the soul offers no resistance but rather follows after them and pours itself out in pleasures that are still only mental in nature, they

then seize her and drench her in sadness, with the result that these ideas she was just indulging no longer remain. In fact they cannot be had in reality, either, because of her present way of life. So the miserable soul is now shriveled up in her humiliation to the degree that she poured herself out upon these thoughts of hers.

The most fierce passion is anger. In fact it is defined as a boiling and stirring up of wrath against one who has given injury—or is thought to have done so. It constantly irritates the soul and above all at the time of prayer it seizes the mind and flashes the picture of the offensive person before one's eyes. Then there comes a time when it persists longer, is transformed into indignation, stirs up alarming experiences by night. This is succeeded by a general debility of the body, malnutrition with its attendant pallor, and the illusion of being attacked by poisonous wild beasts. These four last mentioned consequences following upon indignation may be found to accompany many thoughts.

The demon of acedia—also called the noonday demon—is the one that causes the most serious trouble of all. He presses his attack upon the monk about the fourth hour and besieges the soul until the eighth hour. First of all he makes it seem that the sun barely moves, if at all, and that the day is fifty hours long. Then he constrains the monk to look constantly out the windows, to walk outside the cell, to gaze carefully at the sun to determine how far it stands from the ninth hour, to look now this way and now that to see if perhaps [one of the brethren appears from his cell]. Then too he instills in the heart of the monk a hatred for the place, a hatred for his very life itself, a hatred for manual labor. He leads him to reflect that charity has departed from among the brethren, that there is no one to give encouragement. Should there be someone at this period who happens to offend him in some way or other, this too the demon uses to contribute further to his hatred. This demon drives him along to desire other sites where he can more easily procure life's necessities, more readily find work and make a real success of himself. He goes on to suggest that, after all, it is not the place that is the basis of pleasing the Lord. God is to be adored everywhere. He joins to these reflections the memory of his dear ones and of his former way of life. He depicts life stretching out for a long period of time, and brings before the mind's eye the toil of the ascetic struggle and, as the saying has it, leaves no leaf unturned to induce the monk to forsake his cell and drop out of the fight. No other demon follows close upon the heels of this one (when he is defeated) but only a state of deep peace and inexpressible joy arise out of this struggle.

The spirit of vainglory is most subtle and it readily grows up in the souls of those who practice virtue. It leads them to desire to make their struggles known publicly, to hunt after the praise of men. This in turn leads to their illusory healing of women, or to their hearing fancied sounds as the cries of the demons—crowds of people who touch their clothes. This demon predicts besides that they will attain to the priesthood. It has men knocking at the door, seeking audience with them. If the monk does not willingly yield to their request, he is bound and led away. When in this way he is carried aloft by vain hope, the demon vanishes and the monk is left to be tempted by the demon of pride or of sadness who brings upon him thoughts opposed to his hopes. It also happens at times that a man who a short while before was a holy priest, is led off bound and is handed over to the demon of impurity to be sifted by him.

> The demon of pride is the cause of the most damaging fall for the soul. For it induces the monk to deny that God is his helper and to consider that he himself is the cause of virtuous actions. Further, he gets a big head in regard to the brethren, considering them stupid because they do not all have this same opinion of him.
>
> Anger and sadness follow on the heels of this demon, and last of all there comes in its train the greatest of maladies—derangement of mind, associated with wild ravings and hallucinations of whole multitudes of demons in the sky. (*Practicus* 6-14; Evagrius Ponticus 1970: 16–20)

Evagrius' taxonomy of passions became popular and was swiftly disseminated across the monastic networks. John Cassian brought it to the West. He also modified some pieces of the Evagrian original. For instance, he swapped anger and sorrow. The Evagrian taxonomy became known in the West as "seven deadly sins." In the original, however, they were not seven (but eight), not deadly (but curable), and not sins (but passions).

# Antidote Virtues

Experts in spiritual life concluded that each passion can be cured by a correspondent virtue. Virtues, therefore, were also organized to taxonomies. Theologians agreed that the most dangerous passion on the top of any taxonomy is pride (*hyperiphania*/ὑπεριφάνια). Only genuine humbleness could eradicate this deadly passion. A classical maxim on this is ascribed to Antony of Egypt:

> Abba Antony said: "I have seen all the snares of the evil spread out on earth and I said with a sigh: 'Who can pass these by?' and I heard a voice saying to me: 'Humble-mindedness.'" (Antony 7; Wortley 2014: 32)

Antony referred to humility as a condition sine qua non for salvation in one of his own letters[1]: "If you do not have great humility throughout your heart and in all your mind, in all your soul and in all your body, you cannot inherit the kingdom of God" (*ep.* VI 110; Rubenson 1997: 224).

Humbleness can cure not only pride, but all passions, as Isaac of Nineveh explained. Moreover, virtues can be beneficial for soul only when they are accompanied by humility. Without humility, virtues can be poisonous:

[1] These letters were originally written in Coptic and then translated into most languages used by Christians in Antiquity. Samuel Rubenson compiled on the basis of the extant translations a *textus receptus* of the letters (Rubenson 1997).

> Humility, even without ascetic labours, expiates many sins. Ascetic labours that are not accompanied by humility, however, are not only of no benefit, but they actually bring upon us much harm. (*Hom.* 72 B499; Brock 2006: 24)

For Isaac, the source of humility is God himself. The coming of Christ was a manifestation of the ultimate divine humbleness:

> Humility is the robe of divinity: for when God the Word became Incarnate He put on humility and thereby communicated with us by means of our human body. Accordingly, everyone who is truly clothed in humility will resemble Him who descended from the height, hiding the radiance of His greatness and covering up His glory by means of His low estate. (*Hom.* 82 B574; Brock 2006: 26)

Together with pride, a grave transgression was regarded judging others. Some ascetics believed that it was equal to condemning self to eternal sufferings. They warned against this sin in many edifying stories, like the following one from the *Apophthegmata*:

> There was at that time a meeting at Scetis about a brother who had sinned. The Fathers spoke, but Abba Pior kept silence. Later, he got up and went out; he took a sack, filled it with sand and carried it on his shoulder. He put a little sand also into a small bag which he carried in front of him. When the Fathers asked him what this meant he said, "In this sack which contains much sand, are my sins which are many; I have put them behind me so as not to be troubled about them and so as not to weep; and see here are the little sins of my brother which are in front of me and I spend my time judging them. This is not right, I ought rather to carry my sins in front of me and concern myself with them, begging God to forgive me for them." The Fathers stood up and said, "Truly, this is the way of salvation." (Ward 1984: 199–200)

In tune with this story, Isaac of Nineveh instructed his followers:

> Do not hate the sinner, for we are all guilty. If it is for the sake of God that you feel moved, then weep for that person; why should you hate him? Or perhaps, if it is his sins you are hating, then pray for that person, so that you may imitate Christ who never got angry with sinners, but prayed for them. (*Hom.* 50 B356; Brock 2006: 20)

Maximus the Confessor applied the categories of commonality and particularity to sort out virtues. Some of them are more generic, and others are more particular. More generic virtues, which correspond to the category of genus, are love and humility (see *ep.* 12; Törönen 2007: 168). Love for Maximus is "a virtue which is universal and more generic than other virtues, and which is divided into six species" (*Quaestiones ad Thalassium* 40; Törönen 2007: 170).

# *Apatheia*

Virtues lead a person to *apatheia* (ἀπάθεια) or passionlessness. It is a human condition when a particular person lives according to the universal human nature—in the way God had designed this nature. Passionlessness is not the same as emotionlessness. Unlike the latter, the former does not exclude feelings, but harmonizes them with God's will. In other words, passionlessness is the lack of abuses of emotions. The concept of *apatheia* was not originally Christian: it had been first developed in Platonism and Stoicism. Christians borrowed it from these philosophical systems.

Evagrius of Pontus offered the most advanced Christian take on *apatheia*. He made it the core of his ascetic philosophy. For him, what true knowledge is to the human mind, passionlessness is to soul: "The glory and the light of the intellect is knowledge, whereas the glory and the light of the soul is *apatheia*" (*Kephalaia gnostica* I 80; Evagrius Ponticus 2015: 75). Passionlessness is also a mandatory precondition for obtaining true knowledge: "The ascetic soul that, thanks to God's grace, has won and is detached from the body will find itself in those regions of knowledge where the wings of its *apatheia* will bring it" (*Kephalaia gnostica* II 6; Evagrius Ponticus 2015: 90).

True knowledge, for Evagrius, always comes with love. Together, they constitute wisdom: "The one who is going to see written things needs light, and the one who is going to learn the wisdom of beings needs spiritual love" (*Kephalaia gnostica* III 58; Evagrius Ponticus 2015: 174). Love is a state of soul, which is congenial with passionlessness: "Charity-love is the excellent state of the rational soul, a state in which the soul cannot love anything that is among corruptible beings more than the knowledge of God" (*Kephalaia gnostica* I 86; Evagrius Ponticus 2015: 77).

# III.6
# Spiritual Battles

To transform passions to virtues and to pass from the way of perdition to the way of life requires much effort. Some ascetics compared it with a battle. As a battle against demons, passions, and the self, the spiritual life was presented by the Orthodox spiritual writers who lived in the nineteenth century, Nicodemus the Hagiorite (1749–1809) and Theophanes the Recluse (1815–94). Nicodemus translated from Italian to Greek the book *The Spiritual Combat* (Il combattimento spirituale) by the Italian Theatine Lorenzo Scupoli (*c.* 1530–1610). He paraphrased the Italian original and omitted what he considered to be unsuitable for his Orthodox readers. Theophanes did the same with the Russian translation of the book, which was produced based on the Greek publication. He thus censored the book even more than Nicodemus had done. Nicodemus and Theophanes, nevertheless, deemed the book of Scupoli to capture the essence of the Orthodox spiritual battles:

> If you want to gain speedy and easy victory over your enemies, brother, you must wage ceaseless and courageous war against all passions, especially and pre-eminently against self-love, or a foolish attachment to yourself, manifested in self-indulgence and self-pity. For it is the basis and source of all passions and cannot be tamed except by constant voluntary self-inflicted sufferings and by welcoming afflictions, privations, calumnies, persecutions by the world and by men of the world. <. . .>
>
> So this spiritual warfare of ours must be constant and never ceasing, and should be conducted with alertness and courage in the soul; they can easily be attained, if you seek these gifts from God. So advance into battle without hesitation. Should you be visited by the troubling thought of the hatred and undying malice, which the enemies harbour against you, and of the innumerable hosts of the demons, think on the other hand of the infinitely greater power of God and of His love for you. (Scupoli 1978: 110)

At the core of this battle is repentance—*metanoia* (μετάνοια) in Greek, which literally means "change of mind." Just as the genesis of a passion is regarded as a process evolving in stages, so repentance also is a process with stages. Gregory Palamas defined these stages as follows:

**Figure 3.6** The Aegean Island of Naxos, where Nicodemus was born and where he came in touch with the Western spiritual literature.
Source: Photo by the author.

> The awareness of common transgressions leads to self-accusation; this in turn results in sorrow for sinfulness, which Paul called godly sorrow. This godly sorrow naturally is followed by a broken-hearted confession and supplication before God and the promise of avoidance of evil from then on; and this is repentance. (In Athanasopoulos 2015: 3)

Spiritual battle is hard and painful. According to Gregory of Nyssa, this "pain is measured by the amount of evil in each person" (*Dialogus de anima et resurrectione*; Gregory of Nyssa 1967: 242). In the beginning, the spiritual fighter may have such a despair that he or she may think it is impossible to win. However, with some persistence, the battle becomes more bearable, as a modern Coptic ascetic Mattá al-Miskin (Matthew the Poor, 1919–2006) assured in his masterpiece of the Eastern Christian spirituality, *Orthodox Prayer Life*:

> In the outset of practicing retreat, the flesh will be ill at ease and the mind will revolt, for the flesh and the mind will feel the darkness of the grave, where the soul will be still suffering in travail and discomfort while trying to break loose from the prison of the flesh and the darkness of its senses. One may thus encounter unease at the beginning of one's solitude, but this is the crucial point, which calls for faith and patience. It is not so difficult for the soul to endure such an experience, for it will soon feel that the light is at hand and that behind the darkness of the grave there lies the glory of the resurrection. (Mattá al-Miskin 2003: 199)

Spiritual battle involves not only soul but also body. Ascetics made their spiritual recommendations on the assumption, widely believed in the ancient world, that soul and body are intrinsically connected with one another (see Inwood & Warren 2020). According to this belief, the purity of soul makes the body pure. That is what Jesus meant when he was saying: "Your eye is the lamp of your body. When your eye is healthy, your whole body is full of light, but when it is diseased, your body is full of darkness" (Lk. 11:34). The opposite is also true, according to the Eastern tradition: sinful or virtuous motions of body affect the purity of the "eye"—soul. This is the basic assumption of asceticism, which is a set of restricting practices applied to body, with the goal to affect soul.

## Antony

In the Eastern Christian literature, there are some detailed descriptions of the spiritual battle. The earliest is the *Life of Antony* composed by Athanasius of Alexandria. It is a constructed narrative—just as most narratives that Athanasius had produced. Athanasius constructed this narrative with two political purposes in mind: to contest Arius, who had been popular in the monastic circles, and pro-Arian Eusebius, who propagated the Arian teaching at the imperial court. As with his other narratives, Athanasius' story about Antony was enthusiastically received in the church and became an archetype for similar descriptions of monastic life. Here is Antony's story in the interpretation of Athanasius:

> When Antony entered the church again and heard the Lord saying in the Gospel "Do not be concerned about tomorrow" (Mt. 6:34), he could no longer bear to remain there, so he left and distributed his remaining things among those less well off. His sister he entrusted to well-known and faithful virgins, giving her to them to be raised in virginity, while from that time on he devoted himself to ascetic discipline in front of his home, watching over himself and practicing patient endurance. There were not yet monasteries in Egypt neighboring on one another, and no monk at all knew the remote desert; each one who wished to watch over himself spiritually would practice ascetic discipline by himself not far from his own village.
>
> Now there was at that time an old man in the neighboring village. From his youth he had practiced the solitary life of an ascetic. When Antony saw him, he emulated him in goodness. So, like him, Antony began his ascetic practice by staying in places outside that village. While there, if he heard about someone who was seriously practicing ascetic discipline somewhere, he would go like the wise honeybee and search out that person, and he would not return again to his own village unless he had seen him. Thus he was like someone who received provisions from that person for travelling the road to virtue. (*Vita Antonii* III 1-4; Athanasius of Alexandria 2003: 61–3)

Antony began living an ascetic life. He immediately experienced a strong setback. Athanasius described in colors the first diabolic attack against Antony:

> The Devil, who hates and envies what is good, could not bear to see such purpose in the young man so he now initiated his customary practices against Antony also. First, he attempted to lead him away from his ascetic discipline, filling him with memories of his possessions, his guardianship of his sister, the intimacy of his family, love of money, love of honor, the pleasure that comes from eating various kinds of foods, and the other indulgences of life, and finally the difficulty of living virtuously and the great suffering that that entails. He demonstrated for Antony the body's weakness and the long life ahead of him. In short, he raised up in Antony's mind a great dustcloud of thoughts, wanting to separate him from his ability to make correct choices.
>
> But when the Enemy saw how weak he himself was in the face of Antony's resolve, and even more how he was being thrown to the ground by the determination of that man and tripped up by his faith and cast down by Antony's unceasing prayers, he then took courage from the weapons strapped around his belly. Boasting about these (for these are the first snares that he lays against the young), the Enemy advanced against the young man, disturbing him at night and bothering him so much during the day that even those who were watching could see that there was a struggle being waged between the two of them.
>
> The Devil whispered foul thoughts, but Antony rebuffed them with his prayers; the Devil titillated him, but Antony, as though he were blushing, fortified his body through

**Figure 3.7** Antony and Athanasius: a modern Coptic wall painting in the Anba Bishoy Monastery in Wadi El Natrun, Egypt.

Source: Photo by the author.

> faith and fasting. But the Devil stood his ground, the wretch, and now dared to take on the form of a woman at night and imitated all of a woman's ways, solely for the purpose of deceiving Antony. But Antony, reflecting on Christ in his heart and the goodness he had through him, and reflecting on the spiritual insight given to him by his soul, extinguished the Devil's deceitful coals. Once again, however, the Enemy whispered soft pleasures in Antony's ear, but Antony, as though angry and grieving, pondered in his heart the threat of fire and the worm's punishment. Placing these thoughts in opposition to the Devil, Antony bypassed his insinuations unharmed. All these things happened to the shame of the Enemy. He who had thought he would become like God was now mocked by a mere youth; he who had vaunted himself against flesh and blood was being rebuffed by a flesh and blood human being. For working with Antony was the Lord, who for us bore flesh and gave the body victory over the Devil so that each of those who struggle like Antony can say "It is not I but the grace of God that is in me" (1 Cor. 15:10). (*Vita Antonii* V 1-7; Athanasius of Alexandria 2003: 65–9)

# Silouan

A similar experience has been described by another influential spiritual narrator, this time from the twentieth century. Sophrony Sakharov wrote a spiritual biography of his mentor, monk Silouan Antonov from Mount Athos (1866–1938). Sophrony described in a dramatic style the spiritual battle that Silouan endured at the beginning of his spiritual journey. This description is not dissimilar from the one that Athanasius had made about Antony:

> Long and fervent prayer sometimes brought a measure of peace to Simeon's (so was Silouan's name at that time) soul. But then insidious thoughts would whisper, "You pray, and maybe you will be saved. But supposing you do not find your father or your mother in heaven, or those you love—even there you will have no joy."
>
> Ideas like these shook the novice and agitated his heart—he lacked the experience to understand what exactly was happening to him.
>
> One night a strange light filled his cell, even piercing his body so that he saw his entrails. "Accept what you see," came the insidious suggestion. "It proceeds from grace." But his soul was troubled. The prayer within him continued unceasing but the spirit of contrition had gone—so completely that he laughed during the prayer. He hit himself a sharp blow on the forehead with his fist. The laughter stopped but still the spirit of contrition did not return and his prayer went on without it. Now he understood that something was wrong.
>
> After this vision of strange light devils began to appear to him and naively he talked to them "as if they were people." Gradually their assaults increased. Sometimes they said to him, "You are holy now," but at other times, "You will not be saved." Brother Simeon once asked one of these devils, "Why do you contradict yourselves so? Sometimes your cry is that I am holy, and then you say that I shall not be saved." The devil's mocking answer was, "We never tell the truth."

The alternation of these diabolic insinuations, first exalting him with pride to heaven, then hurling him into the depths of eternal perdition, brought the young novice near despair, and he prayed with the utmost intensity. He slept briefly, in snatches. Physically strong—a real Hercules—he did not lie down to sleep but spent all his nights in prayer, either standing or sitting on a backless stool. Only when he was worn out with fatigue did he fall asleep where he sat, for a quarter of an hour or so, and then stand up again and resume his prayer. So it would continue. Usually he only slept an hour-and-a-half to two hours in the twenty-four. <. . .>

Month after month went by and the torturing assaults of the devils never slackened. His spirits began to fail, he was losing heart, while despair and the fear of perdition gained ground. More and more often was he possessed by the horror of hopelessness. Anyone who has gone through something of the kind knows that no mere human courage or power can hold out in this spiritual battle. Brother Simeon foundered and reached the final stages of desperation. Sitting in his cell before vespers, he thought, "God will not hear me!" He felt utterly forsaken, his soul plunged in the darkness of despondency. Sick at heart, he remained in this black hell for about an hour.

That same day, during vespers in the Church of the Holy Prophet Elijah (adjoining the mill), to the right of the Royal Doors, by the ikon of the Saviour, he beheld the living Christ.

In a manner passing all understanding the Lord appeared to the young novice whose whole being was filled with the fire of the grace of the Holy Spirit—that fire which the Lord brought down to earth with His coming.

The vision drained Simeon of all his strength, and the Lord vanished. (Sakharov 1999: 24–6)

# III.7
## Jesus Prayer

The despair caused by spiritual battle, if handled properly, can become a springboard for prayer. Metropolitan of Sourozh Anthony Bloom (1914–2003) insightfully remarked:

> The day when God is absent, when He is silent—that is the beginning of prayer. Not when we have a lot to say, but when we say to God, "I can't live without You, why are You so cruel, so silent?" This knowledge that we must find or die—that makes us break through to the place where we are in the Presence. If we listen to what our hearts know of love or longing and are never afraid of despair, we find that victory is always there the other side of it. (Bloom 1971: 17)

**Figure 3.8** The funeral of Metropolitan Anthony Bloom in London on August 13, 2003.

Source: Photo by the author.

Prayer transforms despair to repentance. A classical Eastern prayer of repentance is the one ascribed to Ephrem the Syrian. It is read in churches during the Great Lent. In the words of Alexander Schmemann, it "is the simplest and purest expression of repentance in all its dimensions: desire for purification, desire for improvement, desire for a real change in relations with other people" (Schmemann 1977: 16). Here is the text of this prayer:

> O Lord and Master of my life, take from me the spirit of sloth, despair, lust of power, and idle talk.
>
> But give rather the spirit of chastity, humility, patience and love to Thy servant.
>
> Yea, O Lord and King, grant me to see my own sins and not to judge my brother; for Thou art blessed unto ages of ages. Amen. (In Schmemann 1977: 15)

In the triangle of relationships between God and the faithful mentioned earlier, prayer differs from both Revelation and theology.

According to this triangle, prayer is a human response to God, based on the human experience of the divine. As a Russian saint from the eighteenth century, Tikhon of Zadonsk (1724–83), used to say, "When you are reading the Gospel, Christ God speaks to you. When, while reading, you pray, you are speaking to him. What a sweet conversation!" (*Симфония* [Concordia]: 321). Although different from theology, prayer is not detached from it. They support and depend on each other. Evagrius of Pontus famously stated: "If you are a theologian, you will pray truly. And if you pray truly, you are a theologian" (*De oratione* 61; Bingaman & Nassif 2012: 119).

The Christian East developed many forms of prayer, both private and public. Their variety is dazzling. It is a custom among Orthodox Christians to use not their own

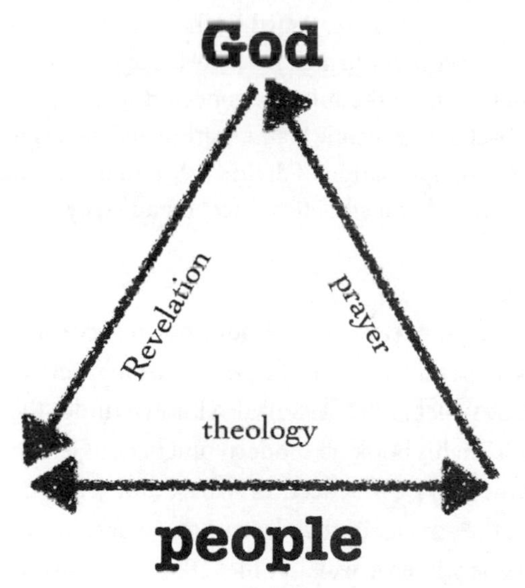


**Figure 3.9** Three words that circulate between God and human beings.

words for prayer, but pre-drafted prayers, usually ascribed to authoritative spiritual figures. Many of those prayers are pseudepigraphic. Despite the rich variety of pre-drafted prayers, some spiritual authors recommended using simple words. Elder (*starets*) Makariy Ivanov (1788–1860) from the Russian monastery of Optina, instructed his correspondents: "God does not demand complexities; a simple and humble prayer pleases him" (*Душеполезные поучения* [Edifying admonitions]: 306).

The simplest way of addressing God that the Christian East has invented is called "Jesus prayer." It is called so because the invocation of the name of Jesus Christ constitutes its core. There are longer and shorter versions of it. According to the Synodical Tome from the fourteenth century, this prayer should read as follows: "Lord Jesus Christ, Son of God, have mercy on me" (*Tomus synodicus* I 47; PG 151, 689). It can also be one word longer: "Lord Jesus Christ, Son of God, have mercy on me a sinner." Its short version reads: "Lord, have mercy." It may contain just the invocation of Jesus' name: "Lord Jesus Christ." Sophrony Sakharov explained comprehensively each part of the prayer:

> The complete formula of the Jesus Prayer runs like this: *Lord, Jesus Christ, Son of God, have mercy upon me, a sinner*, and it is this set form that is recommended. In the first half of the prayer we profess Christ-God made flesh for our salvation. In the second we affirm our fallen state, our sinfulness, our redemption. The conjunction of dogmatic confession with repentance makes the content of the prayer more comprehensive.
>
> It is possible to establish a certain sequence in the development of this prayer. First, it is a verbal matter: we say the prayer with our lips while trying to concentrate our attention on the Name and the words. Next, we no longer move our lips but pronounce the Name of Jesus Christ, and what follows after, in our minds, mentally. In the third stage mind and heart combine to act together: the attention of the mind is centred in the heart and the prayer said there. Fourthly, the prayer becomes self-propelling. This happens when the prayer is confirmed in the heart and, with no especial effort on our part, continues there, where the mind is concentrated. Finally, the prayer, so full of blessing, starts to act like a gentle flame within us, as inspiration from on High, rejoicing the heart with a sensation of divine love and delighting the mind in spiritual contemplation. This last state is sometimes accompanied by a vision of Light. (Sakharov 1977: 113)

Jesus prayer is convenient, because one should not reserve special time and place to practice it. It can be said in full voice, in whisper, or just in mind. It can be repeated under any circumstances. Lev Gillet (1893–1980), also known under the pseudonym "A Monk of the Eastern Church," in his book on modern practices of Jesus prayer remarked: "The invocation of the Name may be practiced anywhere and at any time. We can pronounce the Name of Jesus in the streets, in the place of our work, in our room, in church, etc. We can repeat the Name while we walk" (Gillet 1953: ii). Païsiy Velichkovsky (1722–94) even suggested to keep praying in lavatory (*Крины* [Kriny]: 28).

Jesus prayer is designed to become automatic and never ceasing in the mind of the praying person. Even while doing other things, the person keeps it running in the corner of his or her mind. To internalize it in this way, the person has to repeat it ceaselessly. The process of the internalization of Jesus prayer has been described in the fictional popular anonymous collection of stories published under the title *The Way of a Pilgrim: Candid Tales of a Wanderer to His Spiritual Father*. These are the stories about a wondering ascetic who visited different places and met different people in the mid-nineteenth-century Russia, in order to learn the "ceaseless prayer." Here is how the pilgrim learned it:

> For a whole week, in the solitude of my hut, I practised saying the Jesus Prayer 6,000 times every day, pushing all cares to one side and ignoring all thoughts, however they might rage; my only concern was to fulfil the starets' instructions precisely. And do you know what happened? I became so accustomed to the prayer that if I stopped repeating it for even a short while I felt that something was missing, as though I had lost something; I began the prayer again and instantly everything would become easy and filled with joy. If I met someone, I found I had no desire for conversation and wished only to find myself once more in solitude to say the prayer, so accustomed had I become to it in a week.
>
> As I had not visited him for ten days, the starets came to call on me himself; I explained my state to him. He listened carefully and said: "Now that you have become accustomed to the prayer, take care to maintain and deepen this habit. Do not waste your time, and with God's help resolve unfailingly to complete twelve thousand prayers a day; guard your solitude, rise early, retire late, and come to me every two weeks for advice."
>
> I set out to do as the starets had enjoined me. On the first day, I barely managed to complete my 12,000-prayer rule by late evening. On the second day, I completed it easily and with delight. At first, the unceasing repetition of the prayer tired me; my tongue felt numb, my jaw was stiff—but not unpleasantly so. Then came a slight, sharp pain in the roof of my mouth, an ache in my left thumb with which I counted the prayer rope, and an inflammation of the whole hand right up to my elbow, which felt quite pleasant. What is more, all of this seemed both to rouse me and to urge me on to yet greater efforts in prayer. For five days or so, I faithfully repeated 12,000 prayers daily and deepening the habit brought me both enthusiasm and delight.
>
> One day, early in the morning, the prayer itself seemed to wake me. I got up intending to recite the morning prayers, but my tongue could hardly pronounce the words while my desire strained of its own accord to say the Jesus Prayer. And when I began to say it, all became easy and joyful; my lips and tongue seemed to formulate the words by themselves, without being urged on by me! I was glad the whole day long, as though I were detached from everything, as though I were in another world, and I easily completed the 12,000 prayers by early evening. I longed to carry on repeating the prayer, but dared not do more than the starets had ordered. For the next few days I continued to call upon the name of Jesus Christ, drawn towards it with the same ease. (Zaranko & Louth 2017: 11–12)

**Figure 3.10** A rope for Jesus prayer.
Source: Photo by the author.

Jesus prayer can be done in any place, any way, and under any circumstances. At the same time, there are also special techniques for it, which go centuries back. According to these techniques, preferred for prayer is sitting on a low stool, with knees slightly higher than hips. The body should be leaned forward, and the head kept down. Eyes may be fixed on the area of navel. Normally, the strongest hand holds a prayer rope. With his or her fingers, a person draws one knot per each prayer. While uttering the first half of the prayer, a person usually inhales, and at the second half exhales. Sophrony Sakharov described this technique as follows:

> The monk, having suitably settled his body, pronounces the prayer with his head inclined on his chest, breathing in at the words "Lord Jesus Christ, (Son of God)" and breathing out to the words "have mercy upon me (a sinner)." During inhalation the attention at first follows the movement of the air breathed in as far as the upper part of the heart. In this manner concentration can soon be preserved without wandering, and the mind stands side by side with the heart, or even enters within it. This method eventually enables the mind to see, not the physical heart but that which is happening within it—the feelings that creep in and the mental images that approach from without. With this experience, the monk acquires the ability to feel his heart, and to continue with his attention centred in the heart without further recourse to any psychosomatic technique. (Sakharov 1977: 112–13)

During the Middle Ages, the technique of Jesus prayer became a subject of controversies. The way the monks on the Mount Athos sat and concentrated under their chest during prayer, embarrassed some other monks, including a Greek monk from *Magna Graecia* in Italy, Barlaam (*c.* 1290–1348). He was a scholar in classical philosophy, who also pursued a political program. This program was humanistic and envisaged the restoration of Hellenism in Byzantium. Barlaam's political ideas found much sympathy among the literati and politicians in Constantinople, where he arrived in 1338. John Cantacuzenus, at that time the "grand domestic" of Emperor Andronicus III (1297–1341), appointed him a professor to the imperial university (see 1974b: 81–2).

Barlaam saw the practice of Jesus prayer as a magic ritual that intends to force God to appear to the makers of Jesus prayer. He called them "navel-worshippers," because, as he caricatured them, they stare at their navel, breathe in and breathe out, and eventually see the light coming from their belly. Barlaam might have met monks who explained him Jesus prayer in such simplistic terms. However, other monks rebuked this mockery. Gregory Palamas, for instance, stressed that the technique of prayer does not secure seeing God. It is up to God to reveal himself to the person who prays. Techniques only help prepare soul for receiving the revelation of the divine light (see Mantzarides 1996: 211).

Another controversy related to Jesus prayer erupted in the imperial Russia in the beginning of the twentieth century. It started in the Russian community of St. Panteleimon at the Mount Athos and from there spread to the empire, which eventually had to interfere with military force to quench the disputes. A group of monks came to argue that, by invoking the name of Jesus, they partake in Christ's divinity. For them, Jesus' name was divine not metaphorically, but ontologically. Among the leaders of this group, there were monks Hilarion Domrachyov (*c.* 1845–1916) and Antoniy Bulatovich (1870–1919). Their arguments were contested by the official Russian theologians and condemned by the Synod of the Russian church. Two prominent hierarchs of that time, Metropolitan Antoniy Khrapovitsky (1863–1936) and Archbishop Nikon Rozhdestvensky (1851–1919) became the frontliners of polemics against those who were called *imyaslavtsy*, the "name-worshippers." The opponents of the *imyaslavtsy* were called *imyabortsy*—"fighters against the name." The movement in support of the "worshippers of the name" continued after the Bolshevik revolution of 1917, now mostly in the underground. Among the intellectual leaders of this controversial group at that time were Mikhail Novosyolov (1864–1938) and Aleksey Losev (1893–1988). Following is an excerpt from the theological deliberations about the name of Jesus by the leader of the "name-worshippers," monk Hilarion Domrachyov:

> If this name (i.e., Jesus) is not God then why does it possess omnipotent power that produces great and glorious works, even independently of the holiness of life of those who pronounce it? This, by the way, can be seen from the words of the Lord, "many will say to me in that day: 'Did we not prophecy in your name and by your name cast out demons and by your name worked miracles?' And then I will tell them: 'I never knew you; depart from me all workers of iniquity'" (Mt. 7:22-23). In these words is

found a new proof, having all power of indisputable persuasiveness, that in the name of Jesus Christ, God's omnipotent power is present and therefore this very name is God himself. <. . .>

For the believer who loves the Lord and always prays to him, the name of the Lord Jesus Christ is as it were he himself, our divine savior. And this great truth is really sensed best of all when one practices the Jesus Prayer of mind and heart. In the practice of the Jesus Prayer of mind and heart, done in a repentant attitude of soul and in deep contrition, with your heart's feeling you really hear and perceive that Jesus Christ's name is he himself our divine savior Jesus Christ, and it is impossible to separate the name from the person named. Rather, they merge into identity and interpenetrate one another and are one. <. . .>

With time and from long practice [my recitation of the Jesus Prayer] began to contract and finally stopped on the three words "Lord Jesus Christ." It became impossible to pronounce more than this; all was superfluous and somehow wouldn't fit into the system of internal feeling. But what an inexpressible, purely heavenly, sweet feeling in the heart, unattainable by any of the people of this world! These three divine words as it were became incarnate, became clothed in divinity; in them vitally, essentially, and actively was heard the presence of the Lord himself, Jesus Christ. For the sake of this [prayer] I decisively left every other spiritual exercise, whatever it might have been: reading and standing and prostrations and psalm singing. It constitutes my service both day and night. In whatever situation I find myself—walking, sitting, and lying—I only diligently try to carry in my heart the sweetest name of the Savior; even often just two words: "Jesus Christ." (In Dykstra 2013: 24–7)

# III.8
# Hesychasm

## *Hesychia*

Although controversies about Jesus' name were noisy, invoking this name is supposed to bring calmness to one's soul and mind. In the Eastern Christian literature, this calmness has a special term: *hesychia* (ἡσυχία) (see Meyendorff 1974a). Spiritual writers began referring to *hesychia* as early as in the period of the initial Egyptian monasticism:

> A brother asked Abba Rufus: "What is *hesychia* and what benefit is there in it?" The elder said to him: "*Hesychia* is remaining in a cell in fear and conscious awareness of God, refraining from rancor and arrogance. That kind of *hesychia* is the mother of all virtues; it protects the monk from the fiery darts of the enemy, preventing him from being wounded by them. Yes, brother, do acquire [*hesychia*], keeping in mind the exit at your death, for you know not at what hour the thief will come (Lk. 12:39). In a word: keep a watch on your own soul." (Rufus 1; Wortley 2014: 279)

*Hesychia* is an outcome of the reunification of "mind" with "heart." This reunification, according to Gregory Palamas, brings "stability of mind and of the surrounding world, abandonment of things below, initiation to things above, concentration of thoughts on that which is good. Hesychia is indeed an action, leading to true contemplation, or the vision of God" (*Hom.* 53.33; Mantzarides 1996: 210).

## *Theoptia*

*Hesychia*, thus, causes *theoptia* (θεοπτία)—the contemplation of God (see Boersma 2018). Maximus' scheme, when God moves the movement of creature to himself, applies also to *hesychia*—the lack of movement. The divine silence instills silence in hesychasts' mind. In result, they have their mind reunited with God through *theoptia*. Ps.-Dionysius had described this causality even before Maximus, in a prayer to the Trinity:

> Trinity!! Higher than any being,
> any divinity, any goodness!
> Guide of Christians
> in the wisdom of heaven!
> Lead us up beyond unknowing and light, up to the farthest, highest peak
> of mystic scripture,
> where the mysteries of God's Word
> lie simple, absolute and unchangeable
> in the brilliant darkness of a hidden silence.
> Amid the deepest shadow
> they pour overwhelming light
> on what is most manifest.
> Amid the wholly unsensed and unseen
> they completely fill our sightless minds
> with treasures beyond all beauty. (*De mystica theologia* I 1; Luibheid 1987: 134)

Vision of God, *theoptia*, was regarded in the East as a real experience opposite to imagination. Ascetics instructed to avoid any kind of imagination as spoiling the possibility of *theoptia*. Such classical Eastern attitude to imagination is opposite to the Western medieval attitude, which often encouraged applying imagination in spiritual practices. The East avoided imagination in order to keep spiritual sight clear for theophanies. Here is a description of one of such theophanies to Symeon the New Theologian. Symeon shared with his spiritual mentor the first appearance of God to him:

> If there exists someone who has explained this to him before, since he has already come to know God, he comes to that person and tells him: "I have seen!" [The elder] asks: "What did you see, my child?"—"A light, my father, a sweet sweet light; and my mind does not know how to describe it to you. <. . .> At once the space of my cell vanished and the world disappeared. I was left alone with this light. <. . .> There was ineffable joy, which is still in me, and great love and desire, so that streams of tears flowed out of me, as you see now." And he answers and tells him: "It is He, my child" (*Orationes ethicae* V 294-310; Alfeyev 2000: 22)

## Palamas *versus* Barlaam

The experience of the divine light became a subject of the theological controversy in the fourteenth century. It included discussions on the techniques of ceaseless prayer. This controversy became known as "Palamite"—after the name of the archbishop of Thessalonica Gregory Palamas, who was the theological mind and administrative muscle behind the hesychast cause (see Russell 2020; Papademetriou 2004). The Palamites claimed that the light they contemplate is God himself. It is uncreated and thus totally different from any other light experienced in the created world. They identified this light as "deifying grace," "power and universal operation of the Trinity," or just "energy" (see Lossky 1983: 157). Theological points underpinning the hesychast practices have been articulated in the *Hagioritic Tome*. It was drafted by Gregory Palamas and promulgated in the name of Athonite monks:

> The light of the intelligence is different from that which is perceived by the senses. In fact perceptible light reveals to us objects which are subject to the senses, while intellectual light serves to manifest the truth that lies in thought. Therefore sight and intelligence do not perceive one and the same light, but it is fitting that each of the faculties should act according to its nature and within its limits. However, when those who are worthy receive grace and spiritual and supernatural power, they perceive by the senses as well as by the intellect that which is above all intellect . . . how? That is known only by God and those who have had the experience of his grace. (In Lossky 1983: 162; see also Blackstone 2018)

Anti-Palamites rejected both the hesychastic techniques of prayer and the idea that God can be seen through the uncreated light. They argued that this light is not God: it is created, in contrast to the uncreated God. The protagonist of the anti-Palamite party, Barlaam of Calabria, disagreed with Palamas and his followers. For him, the light stems from human mind—in the best case. In the worst case, it is a dangerous delusion. Quite a few Byzantine intellectuals aligned with Barlaam, including a theologian from Bulgaria, Gregory Akindynos (*c.* 1300–48). Originally a disciple of Palamas, Akindynos switched to Barlaam's side. A series of councils were held in Constantinople from 1341 through 1351, which sided with Palamas.

## Barlaam *versus* Aquinas

Barlaam's initial target, however, was not Palamas, but Western theologians. He contested the idea, which had become popular in the West, that God can be perceived in his essence. This idea was articulated by Thomas Aquinas (1225–74). Chapter 12 in his *Summa theologica* is dedicated specifically to the question: "How God is known by us?" Thomas argued that it is wrong to believe that "no created intellect can see the essence of God" (*Summa theologica* I 12.1; Aquinas 2013: 49). In 1336, Pope Benedict XII (in office 1334–42) promulgated a constitution *Benedictus Deus*, which confirmed this theological point. Barlaam energetically engaged in polemics against this point. He insisted that it is impossible to contemplate God, who always remains transcendent to human knowledge and will continue to be so in the afterlife:

> Thomas and everyone who reasons as he does thinks that there is nothing inaccessible to the human mind; that we believe that this opinion comes from a soul of demoniacal and evil pride; for most divine things transcend human knowledge. (In Meyendorff 1974b: 84)

# Divine Darkness

Barlaam's and Aquinas' positions on God's accessibility were irreconcilable. Gregory Palamas suggested a *via media* between them, even though he probably had been unaware about Thomas's theology (see Pacella 2015: 200; Searby 2018; Williams 1999). The Palamite theology addressed the dilemma: how God can be simultaneously accessible and inaccessible. This dilemma is rooted in the Scriptures, which contain seemingly inconsistent statements. On the one hand, God reveals himself to Moses: "You cannot see my face, for man shall not see me and live" (Ex. 33:20). Paul wrote to Timothy about the same: "He who is the blessed and only Sovereign, the King of kings and Lord of lords <. . .> dwells in unapproachable light, whom no one has ever seen or can see" (1 Tim. 6:15-16). 1 John repeats this point: "No one has ever seen God" (4:12). On the other hand, the same author of 1 John promised to his readers: "Beloved, we are God's children now, and what we will be has not yet appeared; but we know that when he appears we shall be like him, because we shall see him as he is" (1 Jn 3:2).

The Palamite solution to this dilemma was offered through the differentiation between two classical categories from the Aristotelian-Porphyrian logical taxonomies, in their edition circulated after the monoënergist-monothelite controversy during the seventh century: God's essence (οὐσία) and activity (ἐνέργεια) (see Athanasopoulos & Schneider 2013). Divine essence is completely inaccessible for contemplation or knowledge by any created being, while the divine activities (ἐνέργειαι) communicate to human beings both knowledge and experience of God. With the reference to the story about Jesus' transfiguration on the Mount Tabor, Gregory Palamas argued that Christ appeared to his disciples

> not revealing his essence—for it is invisible and appears nowhere, even though it is present everywhere. He is not experienced in his essence, he does not reveal it, nor does he bestow it—it would be blasphemy to think it—but in a most mysterious manner, he shines upon them the radiance of his proper nature and grants them to participate in it. (*Orationes antirrheticae contra Acindynum* IV 14.36; Mantzarides 1996: 213)

Following the Palamite controversies in the fourteenth century, the idea that God is accessible through his divine activities and inaccessible in his essence became a significant theological differentiation between the East and the West. This idea is rooted in the earlier Eastern Christian literature. Gregory of Nazianzus, for instance, distinguished between two modes of existence of God: God himself and what surrounds him: "Only the intellect (νοῦς) might roughly depict Him, however, in some obscure and mediocre manner, and not in His nature, but in what is around Him" (in Alfeyev 2000: 157).

In the fourth century, the philosophical term *ousia*, debated in the course of the Nicaean controversy, came to denote the unaccessible aspect of the divine being. Gregory of Nyssa, for example, stated: "The divine nature in itself, that is what it is by essence (κατ᾽οὐσίαν), is above every capacity of intellectual comprehension, being inaccessible and unapproachable by conjectural reasonings" (*Orationes viii de beatitudinibus* 140.15–7; Maspero 2007: 31). In line with this statement, Maximus the Confessor, on the one hand, postulated that the essence of God cannot be perceived, because such a perception would imply limiting what is uncreated by what is created:

> The blessed and holy Godhead, according to its essence, is beyond ineffability and unknowability, for it infinitely transcends all infinity. To the beings which exist after it, the Godhead does not leave behind even the slightest trace of itself that can be apprehended by them, giving up to none of them anything of itself that could be used to form a concept about how, or to what extent, it is at once a Monad and a Trinity, since by its nature the uncreated cannot be contained by any created thing, nor can the unlimited be circumscribed as an object of thought by things that are limited. (*Ambiguum ad Joh.* X 78; Maximus 2014: 271)

On the other hand, God can be accessed through his activities: "We do not know God from His being but from the magnificence of His handiwork and His providence for creation. Through these as through mirrors we perceive His infinite goodness and wisdom and power" (*Capita de caritate* I 96; Maximus the Confessor 1978: 151).

A metaphor that was often employed in the Christian East to describe the inaccessible divine essence is that of the "divine darkness" (*gnophos*/γνόφος, *skotos*/σκότος) (Meyendorff 1974b: 84). This is not darkness in the sense of the lack of light but in the sense of "super-light" that remains beyond every perception. It can be illustrated by the so-called "black holes"—spaces in the universe with so intense energy that it cannot leave their confinements. The forces of gravity keep the light from slipping and being observed, for which reason such spaces appear to be "black." Origen explained the paradox of the "divine darkness" in his commentaries to John:

> We must point out that darkness is not always intended in a bad sense in Scripture. Sometimes we should understand it as being something good. The heretics have failed to understand this, and as a result they have said the most shameful things about the Creator of the world. <. . .> We must therefore show how and when darkness is meant in a good sense. In Exodus it is said that darkness, tempest and clouds

> surround God, and in Psalm 18, "He made darkness his secret place." If we consider the amount of speculation and knowledge about God, which is beyond the power of human nature to take in, <. . .> we discover how he is surrounded by darkness. For he is beyond the power of human nature to comprehend. (*Commentarii in Iohannem* II 23; Bray 2009: 47)

Gregory of Nyssa addressed the paradox of the "divine darkness," together with the dilemma of inaccessibility and accessibility of God, by referring to two biblical stories about Moses. Moses, on the one hand, was able to contemplate God in the burning bush. On the other hand, God appeared to him as darkness on the Mount Sinai. Maximus explicated this imagery further:

> Thus, again, Moses followed God who called him, and passing beyond everything here below he *entered into the dark cloud, where God was* (Ex. 20:21), that is, into the formless, invisible and incorporeal state, his intellect free from any relationship to anything other than God. Having entered this state (to the extent that this is granted to human nature), he received, as a prize worthy of that blessed ascent, knowledge encompassing the genesis of time and nature. Taking God Himself as the type and exemplar of the virtues, he modeled himself on Him, like a picture expertly capturing the likeness of the archetype, and as such he came down from the mountain. Shining with glory, he showed his face to those below as a sign of the grace he received, freely giving and presenting himself to them as one who had become an image of the divine archetype. And he made this clear by explaining to the people what he had seen and heard, and by handing down the mysteries of God in written form for those who were to come after him, as a kind of God-given inheritance. (*Ambiguum ad Joh.* X 15; Maximus 2014: 173)

# Kollyvades

Through the Palamite controversies, Byzantine theology reached its intellectual pinnacle. After the fall of Constantinople in 1453, both spirituality and theological reflections on it declined. There was a revival of both at the end of the eighteenth century, in the form of what has become known as Kollyvadic movement. This movement started at Mount Athos, having been caused by some minor liturgical practices, such as the commemoration of the dead on Sundays. It outgrew its initial ritualism and turned to a large-scale revival of the ancient monastic practices, including Jesus prayer and hesychasm.

The two protagonists of the movement, Macarius Notaras of Corinth (1731–1805) and Nicodemus the Hagiorite (1749–1809), produced a collection of texts written from the third through the fifteenth centuries and dedicated to the advanced forms of Eastern Christian spirituality. They collected these texts, commented on them, and

**Figure 3.11** The cave on the Island of Chios where Macarius Notaras spent the last years of his life.
Source: Photo by the author.

published (see Hovorun 2020). As Lev Gillet has put it, *Philokalia* became a "Summa of the Jesus Prayer" (Gillet 1987: 67). Through its multiple editions and translations to modern languages, it made the elitist spiritual practices of the past available to everyone. As a result, Jesus prayer and other meditative practices, which had been elaborated in the monastic circles, became widely known in our days, in all Christian traditions.

# III.9
## *Theosis*

Hesychasm was the next iteration in the evolution of the ancient doctrine of *theosis* (θέωσις), that is, divinization. This doctrine is rooted in the New Testament. It was advanced by Athanasius of Alexandria, who, to prove the true divinity of the Son, employed a theological maxim that Christ's humanity became divinized.

The Christian doctrine of *theosis* in many points, even if superficially, resembled some traditions of classical philosophy and religion. Greek mythology brought up many examples of *apotheosis* when humans beings were believed to have crossed the divide between mortals and immortals. Immortality was synonymous with divinity. Heroes were celebrated as mortals who had achieved the divine status of immortals.

Some ancient authors believed that parts of human nature are inherently divine. Pindar, for instance, claimed that "we do have some likeness to immortals in mighty mind of nature" (Pindar, *Nemea* VI 4-5). According to Plato, if a philosopher cultivates the godlike part of his nature, he can achieve deification. In such a case, his "soul brings calm to the sea of desires by following Reason <. . .> and by contemplating the true and divine" (*Phaedo* 85a-b). Socrates was an example of such a philosopher. For both of his biographers, Plato and Xenophon, his deification was marked, for instance, by him possessing his own *daimonion* (see *Apologia Socratis* 31c40, 41; *Euthyphro* 3b; *Alcibiades* I 103; *Euthydemus* 272). Stoics agreed that Socrates was a model of deification (Epictetus, *Encheiridion* XXII 51). Because there was a consensus that all philosophers should follow Socrates' model, many perceived deification as the ultimate destination of every true philosopher.

Neo-Platonists described this destination in detail. Plotinus, for example, gave an account of his personal experience of "identifying with the divine":

> Often I have woken up out of the body to my self and have entered into myself, going out from all other things; I have seen a beauty wonderfully great and felt assurance that then most of all I belonged to the better part; I have actually lived the best life and come to identity with the divine; and set firm in it I have come to that supreme

**Figure 3.12** Heracles, who had been transformed from mortal to immortal through *apotheosis*. A statue from Perge, now in the Antalya Archeological Museum.
Source: Photo by the author.

**Figure 3.13** Socrates. Library of the Trinity College in Dublin.
Source: Photo by the author.

> actuality, setting myself above all else in the realm of Intellect. Then after that rest in the divine, when I have come down from Intellect to discursive reasoning, I am puzzled how I ever came down, and how my soul has come to be in the body when it is what it has shown itself to be by itself, even when it is in the body. (*Enneades* IV 8.1; Plotinus 2014, v. 4: 397)

The more there were points of convergence between the Christian and pagan takes on divinization, the more the Christian authors stressed the difference between them. For this reason, they avoided to use the term *apotheosis* (ἀποθέωσις) and instead coined the term *theosis* (θέωσις) (see Lenz 2007: 61). For them, Christian *theosis* is possible only because of the incarnation. As in the incarnation God appropriated humankind, so all human beings can appropriate divine qualities through their participation in the incarnation. They can become like God, without however turning to God.

*Theosis* can be interpreted from the perspective of the logical categories of commonality and particularity. Common *theosis* has been the one described in Psalms: "You are 'gods'" (Ps. 82:6)—a phrase repeated by Jesus in Jn 10:34. 2 Pet. 1:3 could be also interpreted as a reference to the common divinization envisaged for the entire humankind. This common divinization can be appropriated individually only through the synergetic effort. As a result, only some achieve particular divinization. In Eastern Christianity, they are regarded as saints.

# *Isotheon*

*Theosis* can be also perceived from the dialectical perspective of differentiation between what is given and what is assigned to human nature. *Theosis* is the ultimate assignment for every human being. At the same time, every human being has a Godlike part in his or her nature, which in the patristic literature has been denoted as *isotheon* (ἰσόθεον) or "being-equal-to-God." *Isotheon* is a given precondition for *theosis*. The difference between *isotheon* and *theosis* can be rendered through the categories of potentiality and actuality. *Isotheon* as a feature of the common human nature and its potentiality constitutes a ground for the actualization of particular *theosis* for an individual human being.

The word *isotheon* was widely used in classical antiquity. It was essential in Greek mythology and referred to demigods and heroes. Dramatic and hermeneutical texts often used it to praise their protagonists, such as Odysseus (see *Scholia in Odysseam* V 35d). In the period of Late Antiquity, neo-Platonic philosophers made occasional references to *isotheon*. Iamblichus, for example, stated that "god-equal deeds" (ἰσόθεα ἔργα) cannot be done without the help of gods (*De mysteriis* III 18).

In the patristic literature, Cyril of Alexandria connected *isotheon* with the image of God (see *Epistulae paschales* X 1). For Gregory of Nyssa, it was the fundamental

**Figure 3.14** Odysseus from Odysseus Palace on Ithaka.
Source: Photo by the author.

human capacity of making choices—*autexousion* (*De mortuis non esse dolendum* 54). Hesychius summarized this patristic tradition in his *Lexicon*, where he defined *isotheon* as "immortal soul" (*Lexicon* I 956). The "equal-to-God" soul becomes Godlike in the process of deification—*theosis*.

## Incarnational framework

The original patristic framework for *theosis* was incarnational and cosmic. Irenaeus of Lyon spoke about the *theosis* of the entire world. It became possible because of the incarnation of the Word in the person of Jesus Christ. Through the incarnation, God embraced the entire universe with the purpose to bring it to unity with himself. For Irenaeus, God "became what we are, to make us what he is" (*Adversus haereses* V 1.2-5). In other words, there is a reciprocity and causality between the incarnation and divinization. The former causes the latter, and the latter mirrors the former.

Irenaeus called God's embracement of the entire created world, *recapitulatio* or *anakephalaeosis* (ἀνακεφαλαίωσις). This was a reference to Paul, who had spoken about God's plan "to unite (ἀνακεφαλαιώσασθαι) all things in him (Christ), things in heaven and things on earth" (Eph. 1:10). Irenaeus' concept of *recapitulatio* implied that God had incarnated for the sake of the salvation of human beings and of the entire universe: "The entire flesh of the entire humankind" and the whole world entered under the head of Christ (*Adversus haereses* I 2.1).

By the fourth century, the idea of divinization became widely accepted in Christian theology. Athanasius of Alexandria employed it in his polemics against Arius. He used the point of Irenaeus with the reversal logical causality: given that we get divinized, the Logos was true God. Otherwise, our divinization would have been impossible. In fact, the entire rationale of Christian life depends on the possibility of *theosis*:

> He became man that we might become divine; and he revealed himself through a body that we might receive an idea of the invisible Father; and he endured insults from men that we might inherit incorruption. He himself was harmed in no respect, as he is impassible and incorruptible and the very Word and God, but he cared for and saved suffering men, for whom he endured these things, by his impassibility. And, in short, the achievements of the Saviour effected through his incarnation are of such a kind and so great, that if anyone wished to expound them he would be like those who gaze at the vast expanse of the sea and wish to count the number of its waves. (*De incarnatione* 54; Athanasius of Alexandria 1981: 269)

Gregory of Nazianzus boiled down this idea to one poetical phrase:

> And since, then, God is made man,
> So man is perfect as God,
> and that is my glory. (*Carmina dogmatica* X 5-9; McGuckin 2007: 101)

The idea of divinization was important for Gregory, who frequently used the word *theosis*. He acknowledged that this word is not biblical. It is the same theological neologism as *homoousios* or *hypostasis*. Still, Gregory could not resist using it, because it was so well fitting what he wanted to describe as an outcome of the incarnation. He spoke of *theosis*, for example, in an oration dedicated to Athanasius of Alexandria:

> Whoever has been permitted to escape from matter, and from the fleshly cloud (or should we call it a veil?) by means of reason and contemplation, so as to hold communion with God, and be associated with the purest light (in so far as human nature can attain to it): such a man is truly blessed: both in terms of his assent from here, and in terms of his deification there, a deification which is conferred by true philosophy, and by virtue of his rising above all the duality of matter through that unity which is perceived in the Trinity. (*Oratio* XXI 2; McGuckin 2007: 103)

The Syrian poet and theologian Ephrem (see Wickes 2019) expressed the same idea in more verses:

> It is He who was begotten of Divinity,
> according to His nature,
> and of humanity,

which was not according to His nature,
and of baptism,
which was not his habit.
So that we might be begotten of humanity,
according to our nature,
and of divinity,
which is not according to our nature,
and of the Spirit,
which is not our habit. (In Christensen & Wittung 2007: 147)

## The Spirituality of *Theosis*

The writings of Ps.-Dionysius the Areopagite constitute a landmark in the Christian theology of *theosis*. This pseudonymous author made this theology his central topic and a departure point for exploring other theological topics. Being a neo-Platonist, Ps.-Dionysius in the Platonic way spoke about "godlike minds" that ascend to the archetype (ἀρχίθεος) and become similar to him. As a Christian, however, he specified that this archetype has names: the Father and the Son. Ps.-Dionysius went further than any Christian theologian before him in asserting that a human being can become not only Godlike but also Fatherlike and Sonlike. At the same time, he stressed that there is always an unsurmountable chasm between God and creatures, however godlike the latter can become:

> The procession of our intellectual activity can at least go this far, that all fatherhood and all sonship are gifts and on the celestial powers. This is why Godlike (deiform, θεοειδεῖς) minds come to be and to be named "Gods" or "Sons of Gods" or "Father of Gods." Fatherhood and Sonship of this kind are bestowed by that supreme source of Fatherhood and Sonship on us brought to perfection in a spiritual fashion, that is incorporeally, immaterially, and in the domain of mind, and this is the work of the divine Spirit, which is located beyond all conceptual immateriality and all divinization, and it is the work too of the Father and of the Son who supremely transcend all divine Fatherhood and Sonship. In reality there is no exact likeness between caused and cause, for the caused carry within themselves only such images of their originating sources as are possible for them, whereas the causes themselves are located in a realm transcending the caused, according to the argument regarding their source. (*De diuinis nominibus* II 8; Ivanovic 2016: 127–8)

Maximus the Confessor identified the moving force of deification—love. Love is reciprocal: God's love to mankind moves God to become a human being and then inspires human love to God. Out of love to God, human beings move to him and become deified:

> He himself by grace is and is called God, just as God by His condescension is and is called man for the sake of man, and also so that the power of this reciprocal disposition might be shown forth herein, a power that divinizes (θεοῦσαν) man through his love for God, and humanizes (ἀνθρωπίζουσαν) God through His love for man. And by this beautiful exchange, it renders God man by reason of the divinization (θέωσιν) of man, and man God by reason of the Incarnation of God. For the Logos of God (who is God) wills always and in all things to accomplish the mystery of His embodiment. (*Ambiguum ad Joh.* VII 22; Maximus 2014: 105–7)

Maximus thus added an important nuance to the basic thesis that God became a human being to make a human being divine. He presented the loving reciprocity between God and human beings as two distinct ages: the age of the incarnation and the age of the divinization of human beings:

> He would become man—in a manner known to Him—and at the same time make man God through union with Himself, and thus He wisely divided the ages, determining that some would be for the activity of His becoming man, and others for the activity of making man God. (*Quaestiones ad Thalassium* XXII 2; Maximus the Confessor 2018: 150)

Maximus described the age of *theosis* as mirroring the process of incarnation:

> We must henceforth await those other ages that are to come for the actualization of the mystical and ineffable divinization of human beings, in which "God will show the overflowing riches of His goodness to us" (Eph. 2:7), completely and actively effecting divinization in those who are worthy. For if He Himself reached the limit of his mystical activity of becoming man,—becoming like us in every way but without sin (Heb. 4:15), and having descended into the lowermost parts of the earth (Eph. 4:9) to where the tyranny of sin had driven man—then there will certainly also be a limit of God's mystical activity for the divinization of man in every way (with the obvious sole exception of any identification of man with God's essence), making man like Himself and raising him beyond all the heavens (Eph. 4:10; Phil. 2:9) to where the natural grandeur of grace dwells and calls fallen man through the infinity of goodness. (*Quaestiones ad Thalassium* XXII 4; Maximus the Confessor 2018: 151)

For Maximus, the age of *theosis* has not arrived yet. The age we live now is the one "of the flesh." It is different from the "age of the Spirit, which will come about after this present life" (*Quaestiones ad Thalassium* XXII 7; Maximus the Confessor 2018: 152–3). The present age is framed by the laws of nature. In the future age of *theosis*, the natural limits will be overcome:

> We will become the very thing that is not in any way the outcome of our natural capacity, since nature does not possess the capacity to grasp what is beyond nature.

For nothing created is by its nature capable of actualizing divinization, since it cannot grasp God. For this is the property of divine grace alone, that is, to grant the gift of divinization proportionately to created beings, brightly illumining nature by a light that transcends nature, actively elevating nature beyond its own proper limits through the excess of divine glory. (*Quaestiones ad Thalassium* XXII 7; Maximus the Confessor 2018: 153)

Symeon the New Theologian described how *theosis* affects human beings and experiences. Similar to Plotinus, he revealed his personal experience of divinization. Eucharist was the source of this experience:

My hand is Christ, and my foot is Christ. <. . .>
And I, miserable, am a hand of Christ and a foot of Christ.
I move my hand, and it is the whole Christ who is my hand
(Since we should think that the divine divinity is undivided),
I move my foot, and behold, it shines like He Himself.
Do not say that I am blaspheming, but rather accept this
And venerate Christ, Who makes you such! <. . .>
Thus, you have recognized my finger to be Christ
And even my pudendum—did you not tremble, did you not feel shame? <. . .>
When you said that Christ is like my uncomely member I suspected that you pronounced blasphemy! (*Hymni* XV 141–77; Alfeyev 2000: 266–7)

A century after Symeon, a Coptic monk and later Bishop Paul of Bush (Būlus al-Būshī, *c.* 1170–250), in a similar way connected the incarnation, Eucharist, and *theosis*. He did this in Arabic—soon after it had replaced Coptic in the life and worship of the Christian community in Egypt. Paul's writings marked the renaissance of Christian literature in Arabic under the Ayyubid rule in Egypt. Here are Paul's deliberations on Eucharist, which are similar to those by Symeon:

Then, after that, [God] added to us favor in relation to the state Adam was in before his error, and he gave us his life-giving body, just as he said, "I am the life-giving bread, which came down from heaven. Whoever eats of this bread will live forever!" (Jn 6:51). Then, he told us what the bread is when he said, "The bread that I give is my body, which I offer up for the life of the world" (Jn 6:51). Indeed, he even added to that an announcement, saying, "If you have not eaten the body of the Son of Man, nor drunk his blood, there is no eternal life in you" (Jn 6:53). His statement, "in you," means that it (i.e., eternal life) comes to existence in your essential nature (i.e., essence). It is not external to you, nor is it alien to you. He settled that matter when he said, "Because my body is true food, and my blood is true drink whoever has eaten my body and has drunk my blood remains in me, and I in him" (Jn 6:55-56). As for his statement "true food," [he said] that because his divinity is united with his body. He has been united with the holy bread and has transformed it into his body, in truth and not [merely] in likeness. Then he said the greatest thing when he made the statement, "Just as the living

> Father sent me, and I have life on account of the Father, so too whoever eats me lives on account of me" (Jn 6:57). He did not need to say here, "whoever eats my body," because he already had established that in the preceding statement. He said first, "the living bread" (Jn 6:51), and informed us that that bread was truly his body. Then, he said third, "whoever eats me" (Jn 6:57). He means [here] that he is God incarnate, and his divinity is not differentiated from his humanity. Whoever partakes [of the Eucharist] in a worthy manner and with faith, [God] resides in him and gives him the life that he gave to the body united to him. (*De incarnatione* 8; Davis 2007: 171–2)

The idea of divinization is particularly strong in the Coptic spirituality and theology. A modern Coptic spiritual writer, Matthew the Poor (Mattá al-Miskin, 1919–2006), continued the centuries-long Coptic reflections on *theosis*. Similarly to Paul of Bush, Matthew wrote in Arabic:

> There has occurred a change, which the Fathers term as deification, through the mediation of Christ. Human nature has undergone a heavenly re-creation from water and from the Spirit. It has achieved a state of union with God through grace. <. . .>
>
> The deification (θεοποίησις) that the Fathers had in mind does not mean the change of the human nature into a divine one. Rather, it means qualifying human nature for life with God in a communion of love. This is accomplished by lifting the serious barrier that severs the life of man from that of God—namely, sin. This takes place through our ablution and sanctification by the blood of Christ and our partaking of his Body. For this reason, deification—or union in its perfect sense as a life with God—cannot be fulfilled except at the resurrection from the dead. But we have been granted means of grace, commandments, and a divine power by which to conquer sin, the world, and the life of this age. We have thus a new door opened before us. Through this door we can have—here and now—a foretaste of the union with God in communion of love and in obedience.
>
> Therefore, the union of man with God, or deification, is a legitimate aim to seek. This is due to the preexisting union between divinity and humanity in the incarnation. It is Christ, then, who has set it before us as an aim. (Mattá al-Miskin 2003: 104–7)

This is a comprehensive summary of the Eastern Christian teaching about *theosis*. Divinization of human beings is possible because of the incarnation and constitutes the *telos* of the Christian life. It overarches (see Louth 2007: 35) the purpose of salvation. Not unlike the sin, which does not change human nature ontologically, *theosis* does not alienate it from its original logos either. It changes, however, the modality—*tropos*—of the human existence, and makes it fit what God intends about humankind.

# IV

# Trinity

# IV.1

# *Theologia* and *Oeconomia*

The mystery of how humankind has become united with God, of which Mattá al-Miskin was talking, constitutes the core of the mystery of salvation. Eastern Christianity consistently stresses on the inseparable connection between the two mysteries, like in the following passage from Maximus the Confessor:

> From before the ages He determined that we should exist in Him. In order for us to attain this most blessed end, He gave us a mode by which we could make proper use of our natural powers. However, man voluntarily chose to reject this mode by misusing his natural powers, and in order to prevent man from becoming completely estranged from God, He introduced another mode in its place, more marvelous and befitting of God than the first, and as different from the former as what is above nature is different from what is according to nature. According to the faith held by all, this was the mystery of the supremely mystical sojourn of God among human beings. *For if*, as the holy apostle says, *the first covenant had remained blameless, there would have been no occasion for a second* (see Heb. 8:7), and it is perfectly clear to all that the mystery accomplished in Christ *at the end of the age* (see Heb. 9:26) is nothing other than the proof and fulfillment of the mystery which our forefather failed to attain at the beginning of the age. (*Ambiguum ad Joh.* VII 38; Maximus 2014: 133)

Teaching about how God became a human being is connected with the teaching about the salvation of humankind—not only ontologically but also epistemologically. Theologians believed that a correct (orthodox) opinion about God and his incarnation is a mandatory condition for particular salvation. When a person develops a wrong idea about God, his or her chances to be saved become thin. In other words, knowing God not only defines our knowledge about God, but also depends on the latter.

As was mentioned, teaching about salvation—soteriology—framed all theological debates during the Late Antiquity and Middle Ages. From this perspective, classical theological disciplines can be presented as a Russian doll. Soteriology is the largest doll. It contains Christology, that is, teaching about God's incarnation, which, in turn, contains the Trinitarian doctrine, that is, teaching about God in his eternity. Such structure of theology is different from the conventional way it is presented in the classical theological *summae*, where the Trinitarian theology goes first and Christology follows.

Seen in the light of soteriology, Trinitarian theology and Christology are intertwined. They can be distinguished, but not separated. Their distinction reflects the existence of God in his self and God's existence toward "outside" (*ad extra*), that is, the created world. The Hegelian-Kierkegaardian philosophical language renders this distinction as between what is transcendent and what is immanent. Such rendition reflects the anthropocentric point of view: *we* see how God is transcendent for *us*, and he becomes immanent to *us* through his various theophanies. Eastern Christian tradition places the same distinction to the theocentric perspective: God exists in the uncreated universe and reaches out to the created world. To demonstrate this dynamic, theologians used the language that featured such keywords as *theologia* (θεολογία) and *oeconomia* (οἰκονομία).

*Theologia* is everything that can and cannot be said about the uncreated. *Oeconomia* consists of God's activities directed at the created world. Most disciplines from the modern nomenclature of theologies: Christology, ecclesiology, cosmology, ecotheology, political and public theologies, and so on—describe *oeconomia*.

*Theologia* and *oeconomia* are related to each other. This relationship stems from the creation of the world by God and has been enhanced through the incarnation of God. Maximus the Confessor commented on this relationship stressing that *oeconomia* opens doors to *theologia*:

> In becoming incarnate the Word of God teaches us the mystical knowledge of God (θεολογίαν) because he shows us in himself the Father and the Holy Spirit. For the full Father and full Holy Spirit are essentially and completely in the full Son, even the incarnate Son, without being themselves incarnate. Rather, the Father gives approval and the Spirit cooperates in the incarnation of the Son who effected it. (*Orationis dominicae expositio*; Berthold 1985: 103)

The distinction between *theologia* and *oeconomia* helps better understand the dilemma of inaccessibility and accessibility of God, as well as two meanings of the Holy Spirit. *Theologia* applies to the divine existence. In this existence, God's essence is beyond reach by any creature and the Holy Spirit is the third hypostasis of the Holy Trinity. Although proceeding from the Father, the Holy Spirit is distinct from and equal to the Father and the Son. *Oeconomia*, in contrast, postulates God as accessible for human mind and experience, through the divine activities (ἐνέργειαι). The Holy Spirit, from this perspective, appears as the common activity and manifestation of the Holy Trinity.

# IV.2

## Oneness and Plurality

The first axiom of the Christian *theologia* is that God is one. The second axiom is that the one God is personal. Christian monotheism, therefore, is personalistic. Christianity inherited its monotheism from the Jewish religion and treasured it as its core belief. The church's monotheistic self-consciousness sharpened during the persecutions in the first centuries of Christianity. Monotheistic religions constituted an oppressed minority in the midst of the polytheistic majority of the Roman Empire.

This minority struggled to survive, sometimes literally. Christian martyrs died for confessing one God. Christian intellectuals invented sophisticated arguments polemicizing against the idea of many gods. In most cases, they addressed vulgar and anthropomorphic forms of popular paganism. Aristides, for instance, wrote:

> God possesses neither anger nor indignation, because there is nothing that can stand against him. <. . .> God is not born or made. His nature always stays the same and has no beginning or end. God is immortal, perfect and incomprehensible. When I say that God is perfect, I mean that there is no defect in him and that he has no need of anything. On the contrary, everything else needs him! <. . .> He has no name, because everything that has a name is a creature. He has no form or body parts and is neither male nor female. (*Apologia* 1; Bray 2009: 54)

The unidentifiable author of the letter to Diognetus followed the same train of thought:

> Come and take a good look at those whom you claim are gods. Is not one of them a stone, just like the ones we walk on? Is not another brass, no different from those vessels that we use every day? Is not a third wood, and that already rotten? Is not a fourth silver, which has to be guarded in case it is stolen? Is not a fifth iron, eaten away by rust? Is not a sixth earthenware, no more valuable than the cheapest cooking pot? Are these not all made of corruptible matter? Are they not fabricated by means of iron and fire? Did not the sculptor fashion one of them, the brazier a second, the silversmith a third and the potter a fourth? Was not each one of them, in its primitive state before the artisans got hold of them, subject to change? Would they not have become pots or whatever, if they had met with different artisans? Are they not all deaf, blind, lifeless,

**Figure 4.1** An altar with household deities in Pompei.
Source: Photo by the author.

> without feeling, motionless and corruptible? These are the things you call gods—you worship them, you serve them, and in the end you become altogether like them! (*Epistula ad Diognetum* 2; Bray 2009: 44–5)

In parallel to the vulgar paganism practiced by uneducated people, there was a sophisticated paganism. Educated polytheists, on the one hand, were skeptical about the vulgar beliefs of masses. On the other hand, they readjusted polytheistic views in accordance with contemporary philosophies, particularly middle and neo-Platonism. Their gods migrated from Mount Olympus to the invisible world of ideas: from physical they turned metaphysical. Divine powers and personalities from Homer's and Hesiod's stories became philosophical concepts and artistic allegories. Christian polemics against such upgraded paganism had to readjust accordingly. For example, Origen dealt with the metaphysical polytheism of the middle Platonist Celsus by developing an emphatically monotheistic metaphysics:

> In giving an account of the attitude to idolatry as characteristic of Christians he (Celsus) even supports that view, saying: "Because of this they would not regard as gods those that are made with hands, since it is irrational that things should be gods which are made by craftsmen of the lowest kind who are morally wicked. For often they have been made by bad men." Later, when he wants to make out that the idea is commonplace and that it was not discovered first by Christianity, he quotes the saying of Heraclitus which says: "Those who approach lifeless things as gods act like a man who holds conversation with houses" (*Fr.* B5). I would reply in this instance also, as in

> that of the other ethical principles, that moral ideas have been implanted in men, and that it was from these that Heraclitus and any other Greek or barbarian conceived the notion of maintaining this doctrine. He also quotes the Persians as holding this view, adducing Herodotus as authority for this (*Historiae* I 131). We will also add that Zeno of Citium says in his *Republic*: "There will be no need to build temples; for nothing ought to be thought sacred, or of great value, and holy, which is the work of builders and artisans" (*Testimonia et fragmenta* 265). Obviously therefore, in respect of this doctrine also, the knowledge of what is right conduct was written by God in the hearts of men. (*Contra Celsum* 4-5; Origen 2009: 8–9)

Origen argued that the idea of one God is more natural than polytheism. He pointed out that many philosophers in the past had arrived at some form of monotheism. Michael Frede, who has studied the Greco-Roman monotheism, agrees with Origen: "Almost all philosophers in late antiquity were monotheists" (Frede 2011: 143; see also Athanassiadi & Frede 2008). This does not mean that they rejected the many gods of popular religiosity. Neo-Platonists, for example, emphasized the idea of the One and simultaneously sacrificed to the gods from the traditional Greco-Roman pantheon. The One hovered above the traditional gods and transcended them in many regards. A middle-Platonic philosopher Alcinous, who flourished in the second century AD, described this supreme deity in his *Handbook of Platonism* as

> ineffable and graspable only by the intellect. <. . .> Since he is neither genus, nor species, nor differentia, nor does he possess any attributes, neither bad (for it is improper to utter such a thought), nor good (for he would be thus by participation in something, to wit, goodness), nor indifferent (for neither is this in accordance with the concept we have of him), nor yet qualified (for he is not endowed with quality, nor is his peculiar perfection due to qualification) nor unqualified (for he is not deprived of any quality which might accrue to him. (*Didaskalikos* 10)

Alcinous described the supreme deity as exempted not only from the chronicles of Olympus but also from the framework of logics. In contrast to the One, the Olympians were perceived as subjects to the dialectical categories. From this point of view, the logics can be seen as a divine construct—not simply an invention of the human mind. Dialectical categories were divine. They played a role of a sacred perimeter, which the gods never left. In a sense, logics was a "superior deity" itself. However, and this was Alcinous' point, there is a deity, which is higher than even the "superior deity" of the divine categories.

Early Christian apologists, including Origen, utilized references to the supreme deity to promote the oneness of God. In contrast to pagan monotheists, they insisted that God's oneness is incompatible with the plurality of the divine.

However, soon they had to resolve the dilemma of the divine oneness and plurality in their own communities. To intellectually sustain Christian monotheism against

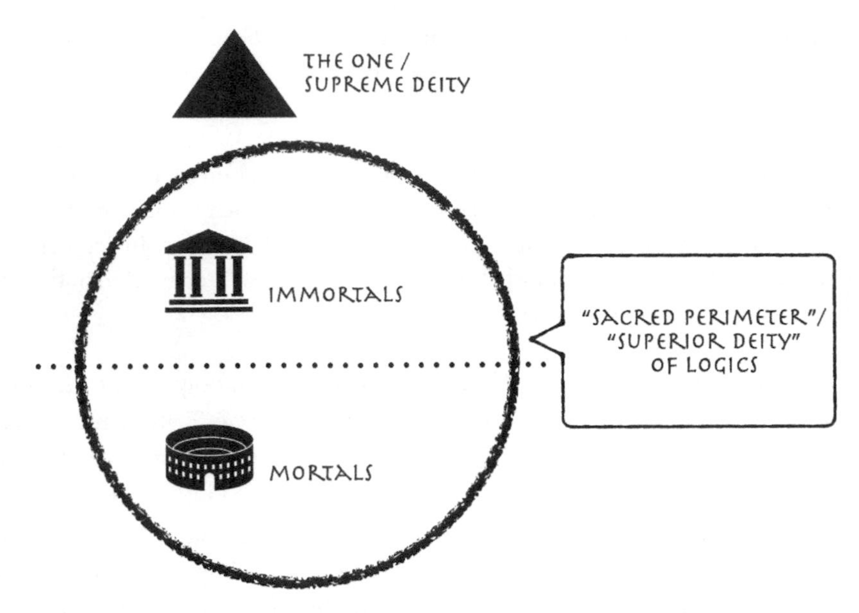


**Figure 4.2** The "superior deity" of logics.

internal challenges appeared to be harder than to criticize pagan polytheism or to advocate for the Jewish style of monotheism. In contrast to the latter, the Christian God became incarnated, which made Christian apologists facing the issue of the divine plurality.

Indeed, has the whole God become man or a part of him remained outside the incarnation? If the latter is true, then the one God must feature some plurality. Even if the whole God became a human being, Jesus seems to be different from the God whom he addressed as his Father. This again implies some plurality in the Christian God. The enigmatic Holy Spirit added to God's plurality. The divine oneness and plurality seemed to many Christian intellectuals like the opposite categories, or a thesis and antithesis in the terms of modern dialectics. A synthesis of these two categories was not a trivial task. It would require to prove the equation, which seemed absurd:

$$1+1+1=1$$

The task was even more complicated. To what extent Jesus was different and similar in comparison with us? If Christ is like us and simultaneously God, how could he be one? There had to be some plurality in him, in addition to oneness. In other words, theologians had to prove the following equation as well:

$$1+1=1$$

The Messiah, thus, featured at least two dialectical pairs of oneness and plurality. Each pair corresponded to *theologia* (1+1+1=1) and *oeconomia* (1+1=1). Both equations were eventually solved. Logical categories played a crucial role. Before arriving at the solution, however, theologians were often divided into antagonizing groups focused on only one side of each equation. Some insisted on oneness and diminished the role of plurality, and vice versa. Before they could reach equilibrium, the church went through a lot of quarrels, exiles, sufferings, deaths, schisms, and even wars.

# IV.3
# Big Questions

## Three Big Questions of *Theologia*

Debates on the two aforementioned dialectical pairs significantly diminished the spectrum of theological inquiries in the period of the Christian Antiquity. Their logical framework became a Procrustean bed for theology, which was reduced to three questions in each pair. The dialectical pair, which corresponds to *theologia*, can be triangulated to three big theological questions:

1. Who is God?
2. What is God?
3. How God's *whos?* are connected to each other and how they together are related to God's *what?*

Eastern theologians played a leading role in answering these questions. Their answers were based on the logical categories, primarily those of commonality and particularity:

1. *Who is God?*—God is three persons called "hypostases" (ὑποστάσεις): the Father, the Son, and the Holy Spirit. The logical category of particularity, thus, helps answering this question.
2. *What is God?*—God is one *ousia* (οὐσία), a word that can be translated as "essence." The category of commonality is a clue to answering this question.
3. The difference between distinction and separation is a key to the third big question. The persons and the essence are only distinguished but not separated from one another. The persons are distinguished both from each other and from the essence.

As was mentioned earlier, Christian theologians cared to sustain an equilibrium between the categories of commonality and particularity—in contrast to the pagan logicians who valued commonality more than particularity. Such an equilibrium was important to secure the equation between the oneness and plurality in God, and to preserve the Christian monotheism. Gregory of Nazianzus, for example, emphasized that in the triune God, we have to perceive trinity and unity simultaneously, without putting them in any chronical or logical order:

> When I speak of God, you must be illumined at once by one flash of light and by three. Three in individuality, hypostasis or person—choose whatever name you like—but one in respect of the substance, which is the Godhead. They are divided without division, so to speak, and they are united in diversity. The Godhead is one in three, and the three are one. (*Or.* 39.11; Bray 2009: 51)

Maximus the Confessor followed the same line:

> This is not, however, a causal explanation of the cause of beings, which is itself beyond all being, which is itself beyond all being, but the demonstration of a pious opinion about it, since the Godhead is a Monad (but not a dyad), and a Trinity (but not a multitude), for it is without beginning, bodily form, or internal strife. For the Monad is truly a Monad: it is not the origin of the things that come after it, as if it had expanded after a state of contraction, like something naturally poured out and proliferating into a multitude, but is rather the inherently personal reality of the consubstantial Trinity. And the Trinity is truly a Trinity not the sum of a divisible number (for it is not an aggregation of monads, that it might suffer division), but the inherently essential subsistence of the three-personed Monad. The Trinity is truly a Monad, for such it is; and the Monad is truly a Trinity for as such it subsists, since there is one Godhead that in essence is a Monad and in subsistence a Trinity. (*Ambiguum ad Thomam* I 2-3; Maximus 2014: 9–11)

## Three Big Questions of *Oeconomia*

Just as the discussions about one God were reduced to three basic questions, the same reduction happened to the discussions about Jesus Christ. The three basic questions pertinent to *oeconomia* were the following:

1. *Who* is Jesus Christ?
2. *What* is Jesus Christ?
3. *How* have his divinity and humanity been united?

Most answers to these questions were again given in the East, with the assistance of the logical categories. They can be summarized as follows:

1. Jesus is the Son of God, the second hypostasis of the Holy Trinity. His oneness corresponds to the category of particularity—in contrast to the triune God whose oneness corresponds to commonality.

2. Jesus is true and complete God, as well as true and complete human being. Both his divinity and humanity are the same as the divinity of the Father and our humanity (except sin). Jesus' plurality, thus, corresponds to the category of commonality—in contrast to the triune God whose plurality corresponds to particularity.
3. His divinity and humanity come together through the hypostatic unity. In this unity, the two Jesus' commonalities are only distinguished, but not separated. They are also only distinguished, but not separated, from Jesus' hypostasis. Differentiation between the categories of distinction and separation, thus, is the key to the equation between oneness and plurality in Jesus: 1+1=1. The same differentiation sustains the Trinitarian equation 1+1+1=1.

Gregory of Nazianzus articulated these answers in a comprehensive way in his most famous Christological text, the first letter to the presbyter Cledonius. He relied on the formulas coined by Irenaeus of Lyon (see *Adversus heareses* III 14) and perfected them. Gregory's answer to the question: who is Jesus?—is one Son. Gregory rendered the oneness of the Son as a pronoun "other" in masculine—*allos* (ἄλλος). For the sake of convenience, we will translate this word as "someone." This "someone" is different from "something" (more precisely, pronoun "other" in neutral—*allo* (ἄλλο)), which applies to both divinity and humanity. *Allo* answers the question: What is Jesus Christ? Gregory established an intrinsic connection between the *who* and the *what* in Jesus by applying the same pronoun "other" in masculine and neutral correspondingly:

> Whoever introduces two Sons, the first one from God the Father and the second from the mother, but not one and the same [Son], loses the adoption promised to those who believe in right way. Because God and human being are two natures (as there are soul and body), but not two sons or two Gods. There are neither two human beings, even though Paul spoke about the inner and outer man. To put it briefly: the Savior is from "something" and "something else" (ἄλλο), because invisible and visible, timeless and temporal are not the same. [He] is not the "someone" and "someone else" (ἄλλος)—let it not be so. Both constitute one by mixture (τῇ συγκράσει): God being inhumanated (ἐνανθρωπήσαντος) and the human being being deified (θεωθέντος)—or however one can put it. I say "something" and "something else" (ἄλλο) in the way reverse of what applies to the Trinity. There we have "someones" (ἄλλος) to avoid confusion of hypostases, but not "something" and "something else" (ἄλλο), because the three are one and the same as divinity. (*Epistula theologica* 101.18-23; translation is mine)

Not all Christological terms coined by Gregory would become accepted by the following generations of theologians. Some terms were eventually rejected, such as "mixture" (*synkrasis*/σύγκρασις). By this term, Gregory wanted to answer the third Christological question: *how* divinity and humanity became united in the person of Jesus Christ. Gregory's term was misread by the theologians such as Eutyches, who concluded on its base that humanity mixed up with divinity and thus changed to something else. Gregory did not imply this. He, nevertheless, cared to stress the intrinsic unity of Jesus, which he explicated in the same epistle to the presbyter Cledonius:

> We do not separate the human being from the Godhead. Instead, we postulate one and the same [Son], originally not a human being, but God and Son: only and pre-eternal, unmixed with body and all that belongs to the body. In the end [he became] a human being, having been assumed for our salvation, passible in flesh, impassible in Godhead, circumscribed in body, uncircumscribed in spirit, the same earthly and heavenly, visible and contemplated, contained and uncontained, so that by [uniting] the whole humanity to himself as God he could recreate the whole humanity, which had fallen under sin. (*Epistula theologica* 101.13-15; translation is mine)

In the seventh century, when the Christological controversies came to a conclusion, Maximus the Confessor epitomized the debates about the incarnation in the same comprehensive way that Gregory had done three centuries earlier. Each word in Maximus' phrases is well-calibrated and can be unpacked to volumes:

> Out of His infinite longing for human beings, He has become truly and according to nature the very thing for which He longed, neither suffering any change in His own being on account of His unutterable self-emptying, nor altering or diminishing anything whatsoever from human nature on account of His ineffable assumption of the flesh. The combination of these established the constitution of His human nature both "above mankind"—for He was divinely conceived without the participation of a man—and "after the manner of men," in a human way, for He was born "according to the law of conception," and thus "the One who is beyond being came into being by taking upon Himself the being of humans." For He did not simply project to our mind's eye an imaginary appearance of Himself in the form of flesh, <. . .> but He became "that which in the entirety of its essence is truly man," clearly by the assumption of human flesh endowed with an intellectual soul, united to Him according to hypostasis. (*Ambiguum ad Thomam* V 4; Maximus 2014: 35)

# IV.4

# Christological Blueprints

Eastern theology has developed a sophisticated speculative apparatus to demonstrate how divinity and humanity became united in Christ. At the same time, Orthodox Christology always kept in mind that Jesus Christ is one: he was seen and interacted with by people around him as a single reality. Within this reality, Eastern theologians only intellectually contemplated the distinction between divinity and humanity. Most theological discourses on the incarnation can be summarized as the pattern in the figure 4.3. The same pattern can be identified in the majority of the Eastern Christologies. It can also be rendered as the following formula (see figure 4.4):

$$1=1+1=1$$

## Earliest Christologies

This theological pattern goes back to the Gospels. Synoptic evangelists described Jesus as a historical figure who conversed with people around him and was treated as any other human being. The picture of Jesus penned by Matthew, Mark, and Luke, corresponds to the initial "1" in the aforementioned formula. John begins his Gospel differently—by introducing duality of Logos and flesh (Jn 1:1,14). He, thus, stresses the "1+1" part of the pattern. This part implies two poles: spiritual and material, uncreated and created, divine and human. Despite their polarity, these two components constitute unity. John concluded his Gospel by reconfirming Jesus' unity by telling a story of how he appeared to the seven after the resurrection (Jn 21). This story corresponds to the final "1" in the formula 1=1+1=1.

Early Christian theologians followed the same pattern. Ignatius of Antioch, for instance, described Jesus in the Johannian bipolar terms:

> There is one physician, both fleshly and spiritual, born and unborn, God come in the flesh, true life in death, from both Mary and God, first subject to suffering and then beyond suffering, Jesus Christ our Lord. (*Ep. ad Eph.* 7)

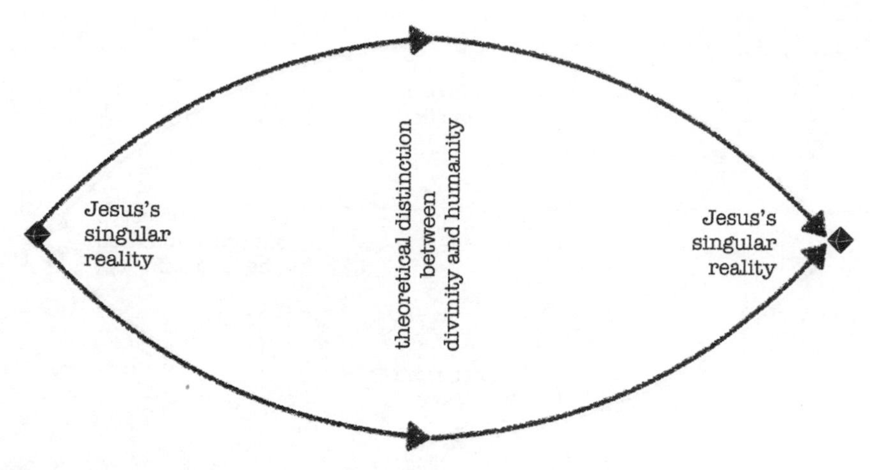


**Figure 4.3** Basic Christological pattern.

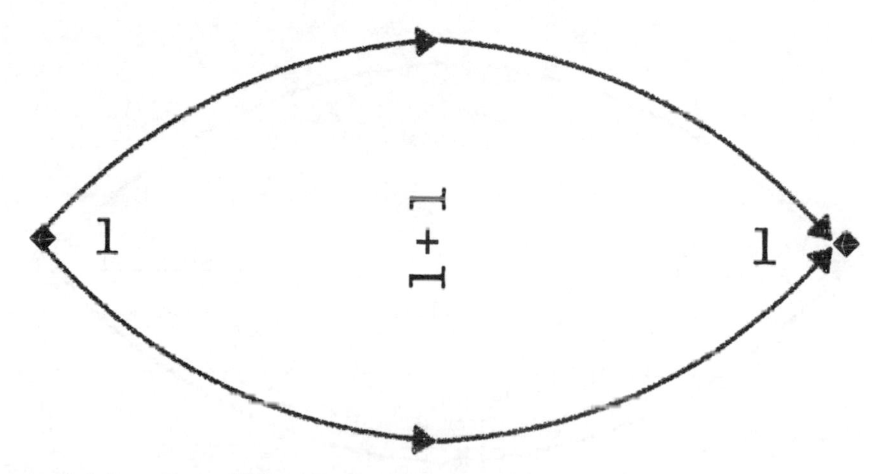


**Figure 4.4** Equation of Christ's singularity.

Ignatius stressed that Jesus Christ is the same being (the same "one physician"). Because he is a single being, Ignatius spoke about God in flesh and true life in death. Later, this trope would be called *communicatio idiomatum*—exchange of natural properties. Ignatius' train of thought followed the Christological pattern from the Gospels.

Melito of Sardes also stressed Jesus' singularity by referring to the single "mystery of Pascha." This single mystery at the same time featured some duality:

> It is new and old,
> eternal and temporary,
> perishable and imperishable,
> mortal and immortal,
> this mystery of the Pascha. (*De pascha* 7-12; Hall 1979: 3)

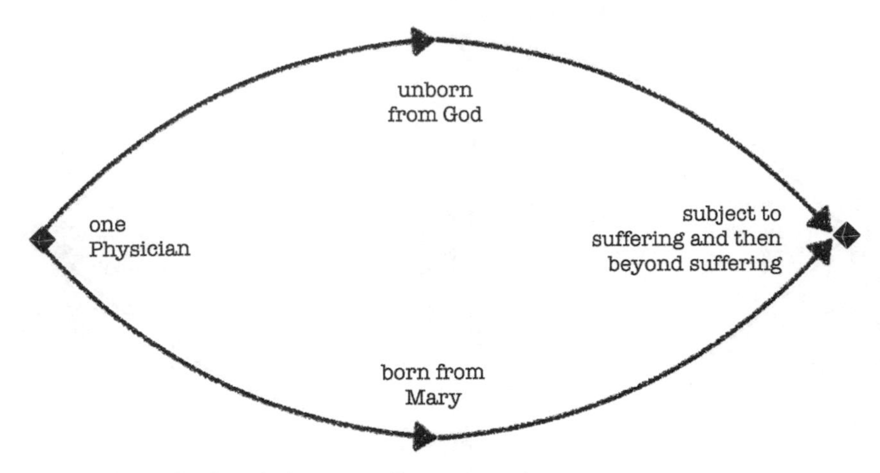


**Figure 4.5** Christ's singularity according to Ignatius.

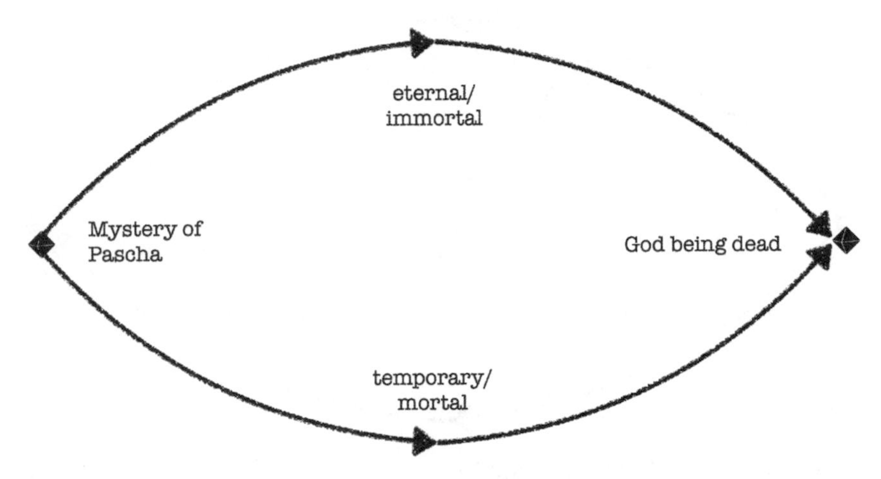


**Figure 4.6** Christ's singularity according to Melito.

Melito's strategy of emphasizing Christ's unity was designed to demonstrate how remote from each other are the poles that Jesus united in himself. Melito went as far as to proclaim "the death of God" on the cross (*De pascha* 597; 735). Melito, thus, stressed both the ultimate divergence and the ultimate convergence, both duality and singularity of Christ. Like Ignatius, Melito implied the same subject in Christ, who suffers and remains beyond suffering.

# Dualistic Christologies

Speaking about "the death of God," Melito stressed the reality of both divinity and humanity in Jesus Christ. This reality was doubted by some early Christian groups, which later would be called Gnostics and Docetists. Their main point was that the humanity of Jesus could not be identical with ours. It was more spiritual and less material. Some of them went as far as to suggest that it was imagined: Jesus appeared to his disciples as a human being, but in reality, he was not. Hence is the name of this group: Docetists—from *dokeo* (δοκέω), which in this context can be translated as "to seem" or "to imagine." These groups could not accept the full materiality of Jesus, because their views were dualistic. They believed that the material world, or at least some parts of it, are inferior or even opposite to the spiritual world. A spokesman of these groups, Valentinus, stated:

> He (i.e., Christ) was continent, enduring all things. Jesus practiced divinity; he ate and drank in a special way, without excreting his solids. He had such a great capacity for continence that the nourishment within him was not corrupted, for he did not experience corruption. (*Fr.* 3; Dunderberg 2008: 74)

Valentinus came from Egypt to Rome at the end of the 130s. Many local Christians became his followers and joined his school. He even ran for the bishop of Rome but was defeated by a more popular candidate. The ideas promoted by the Valentinian school were to a significant extent dualistic. We know about them from their critics, such as Irenaeus of Lyon and Tertullian, and from the original texts that survived in the Nag Hammadi library. Valentinus' Christology was registered as one of the earliest heresies.

The earliest Christian community had used the word "heresy" in a positive sense, as a welcomed diversity of opinions and practices. Paul urged the community in Corinth to acknowledge and appreciate diversity, which he called "heresies" (αἱρέσεις) (1 Cor. 11:19). Some degrees and forms of diversity, however, were regarded as not so good. In his epistle to the community in Galatia, Paul listed "heresies" in line with "sexual immorality, impurity and debauchery; idolatry and witchcraft; hatred, discord, jealousy, fits of rage, selfish ambition, dissensions, and envy; drunkenness, orgies, and the like" (Gal. 5:19-21). It seems that the author of 2 Peter was aware of both meanings of heresy and referred to the negative one by adding the word "destructive" (ἀπωλείας) to it (2 Pet. 2:1). This phrase implies that there are also "heresies" that are not destructive.

With the growth of various dualistic opinions—"heresies"—about the incarnation, this word became associated with only negative connotations. Heresy came to mean a wrong interpretation of the incarnation. Most heresies, including the dualistic ones, challenged the basic orthodox idea of the incarnation: true God became truly human, to save us from sin and death through the intrinsic unity between divinity and humanity. Every heresy tried to create an unsurmountable obstacle between God and humankind. Heresies are dangerous because they make the universal salvation either incomplete or inaccessible for individuals. Early Christological heresies triggered the emergence of Orthodoxy (see Casiday & Louth 2006). Both concepts of heresy and Orthodoxy were born in the same framework of the early Christological controversies and continue to relate primarily to the incarnation. The other way around is also true: the incarnation defined and continues to define what is Orthodoxy and what is heresy.

## Irenaeus

Irenaeus of Lyon was one of the earliest theologians who defined both orthodoxy (*regula fidei*) and heresy, in his multivolume treatise *Adversus haereses*. He approached them from the perspective of the incarnation. Irenaeus in particular argued that Jesus Christ is a mediator between God and humankind (see Briggman 2019). His mediation secures salvation for the latter by restoring its communion with divinity:

> Therefore, as I have already said, he caused man to become one with God. For unless a man had overcome the enemy of man, the enemy would not have been legitimately vanquished. And again; unless God had freely given salvation, we would not now possess it securely. And unless man had been joined to God, he could never have became a partaker of incorruptibility. For it was incumbent upon the Mediator between God and men, by his relationship to both, to bring both to friendship and concord, and present man to God, while he revealed God to man. For, in what way could we be partakers of the adoption of sons, unless we had received from him through the Son that fellowship which refers to himself, unless his Word, made flesh, had entered into communion with us? Wherefore also he passed through every stage of life, restoring to all communion with God. (*Adversus heareses* III 19; Stevenson & Frend 2013: 132)

To make the world's salvation possible, Jesus had to be not an imagined creature, as many dualists believed, but a real human being. The reality of Jesus' humanity is one of the preconditions sine qua non for salvation. Another precondition is that Christ is real God. The same mandatory condition for salvation is the unity of the divinity and humanity. To stress this unity, Irenaeus coined a formula, which would become classical: "one and the same Christ" (εἷς καὶ ὁ αὐτός). He also distinguished between unity and duality in Jesus by different forms of the pronoun "other," as was mentioned earlier. Irenaeus marked the unity of Christ with this pronoun in masculine (ἄλλος):

> The apostles did not preach God as someone (ἄλλος); and Christ who suffered and rose, as someone else; and the one who raised and stayed away from sufferings, as again someone else. [They preached instead] one and the same (ἕνα καὶ τὸν αὐτόν) God Savior and Jesus Christ, who has risen from the dead. (*Adversus heareses* III 14; translation is mine)

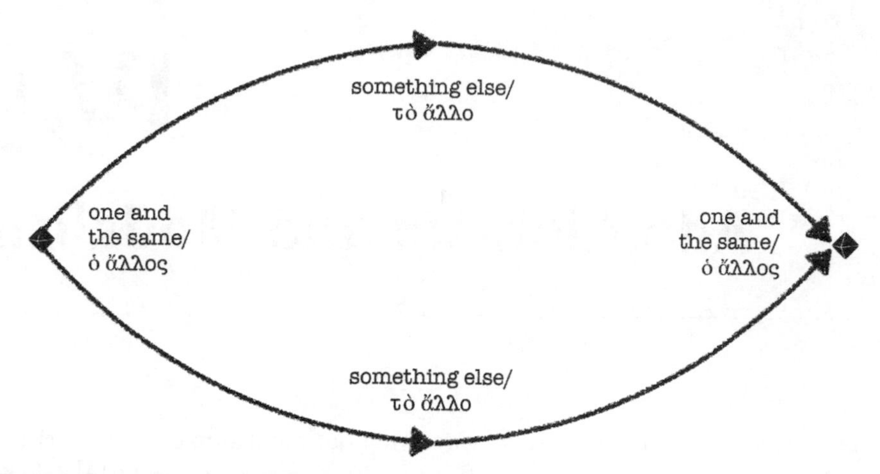


**Figure 4.7** Christ's singularity according to Irenaeus.

In parallel to Christ's singularity marked by the pronoun "someone" (ἄλλος), Irenaeus marked duality in Christ by the pronoun "something" (ἄλλο). He argued that God adopted the same creation (ἄλλο) as we are, to save it from sin and death: "Why God did not adopt soil, but made the creation to come from Mary?—[He did so] to avoid making another creation or something else (ἄλλο) to be saved" (*Adversus heareses* III, 33; translation is mine). The pattern of the incarnation that Irenaeus promoted is similar to the pattern of Ignatius and Melito.

# IV.5

# Adoptionism and Modalism

Two generations after Irenaeus, a controversy about the nature of Jesus Christ was ignited in Syria. It can be regarded as the first in the series of classical Christological debates, which continued through the seventh century. The controversy was initiated by the bishop of Antioch Paul, known as Samosatean. Paul reportedly promoted the idea that Jesus Christ was a mere man, who after his baptism was adopted by God to sonship. This doctrine became known as adoptionism. Adoptionism was a strategy of safeguarding monotheism. It was a way of harmonizing the idea of one God with the divine plurality manifested in Jesus Christ. The basic monotheistic stratagem of adoptionism was that one God adopted a man, without compromising the divine singularity.

Adoptionism was known in the early church before Paul the Samosatean. For instance, Theodotus of Byzantium, also known as Tanner or Cobbler (flourished in the late second century), had reportedly preached similar ideas at the end of the second century. Because of the prominent position of Paul as the leader of the church of Antioch, this church had to deal with him in councils. Several local councils discussed adoptionism during the 260s. Finally, one of them condemned Paul in 268. The council of Antioch 268 became one of the earliest fora, where multiple parts of the empire-wide Christian community were represented to discuss incarnational theology. It also articulated some earliest Christological formulas, like that Jesus was "by nature true and perfect God, and was not afterwards made God out of man" (in Socrates, *Historia ecclesiastica* II 19; Sample 1979: 24).

A monotheistic strategy opposite to adoptionism became known as "modalism." According to this strategy, the oneness of God is sustained by the assumption that the Father, the Son, and the Holy Spirit are modalities of the same God. Plurality in God, therefore, is apparent, not real. One of the earliest theologians who expressed such opinion was Noëtus of Smyrna—possibly the bishop of this city. Noëtus suggested that the one God can manifest himself in the modalities, and not entities. He believed that seeing God as two beings, the Father and the Son, was dualistic—like seeing him as the good God and the Demiurge. Modalities might seem opposite to each other, such as invisibility and visibility, incomprehensibility and comprehensibility, immortality and mortality. In effect, however, they belong to the same God, who shows himself in different ways on different occasions.

The critics of the modalist monotheism objected that in such a case the Father would suffer in the same way as the Son suffered. This paradox was called *Patripassianism*, meaning "the suffering Father." Modalists were also accused of promoting God's "monarchy" (μοναρχία), that is, the teaching that there is one God-monarch, who appears in different manifestations. Such teaching came to be associated with Sabellius, who perfected it in the 220s, in the capacity of the head of Noëtus' school in Rome. It is noteworthy that Sabellius was probably the one who introduced to the Christin theology the term *prosopon* (πρόσωπον), which, through Apollinaris of Laodicea, would become a keyword in the posterior Christological debates.

# IV.6
# Subordinalism

Alternative to both adoptionism and modalism/monarchianism was a theology based on the distinction between the God and his Logos, or, more specifically, between the Father and the Son. This strategy of bridging monotheism and the incarnation, oneness and plurality in God, goes back to the Gospel according to John and its Logos-theology. The Johannian strategy can be sketched as follows. There is the Father—the eternal God who has no cause for his existence, but himself is the cause of everyone and everything. He is primarily the cause of the Son, or Logos, who manifests the Father. This Logos became incarnated, without separating from the Father. Such scheme, on the one hand, safeguards monotheism. On the other hand, it combines monotheism with plurality in God and gives explanation to the incarnation.

Origen protagonized this strategy, which emerged as the only orthodox alternative to both adoptionism and modalism. He thus solved the equation 1+1+1=1. Eusebius of Caesarea mentions in his *Church History* an episode, when Origen encountered a bishop from Bostra, Beryllus, who had reportedly believed that the Son did not exist before the incarnation (*Historia ecclesiastica* VI 33.1–3). Origen converted Beryllus to his own interpretation of the incarnation. His basic idea was that the Logos exists eternally and is always with the Father. Origen explicitly rejected both modalist and adoptionist options of safeguarding monotheism, as he explained in his commentary on John:

> Many people who wish to be pious are troubled because they are afraid that they may proclaim two Gods and, for this reason, they fall into false and impious beliefs. They either deny that the individuality of the Son is other than that of the Father by confessing him to be God whom they refer to as "Son" in name at least (i.e., modalism), or they deny the divinity of the Son and make his individuality and essence as an individual to be different from the Father (i.e., adoptionism). (*Commentarii in Iohannem* II 16; Origen 1989: 98)

The alternative offered by Origen was based on the idea that the Logos is a reality distinct from the reality of the Father. He rendered the reality of the Logos through the words that strongly emphasized both reality and particularity: *hypothesis* (ὑπόθεσις), *hypokeimenon* (ὑποκείμενον), and *hypostasis*. The Logos is a "thing" (πρᾶγμα) and not an intellectual construct. He and the Father exist together not in the mind of philosophers—*kat'epinoian* (κατ' ἐπίνοιαν), but in reality—*kath'hypostasin* (καθ' ὑπόστασιν).

Origen suggested an ingenious solution to the Trinitarian dilemma. This solution shaped the entire theological tradition after him. For him, the birth of the Son from the Father was not a one-time event, but it happens eternally without disruption. This means that the Logos is always the Son of the Father:

> So, if I call your attention to the case of the Saviour, that the Father did not beget the Son and release him from his generation but ever is begetting him, I shall present a similar statement in the case of the just man also. But let us see who the Saviour is. He is "effulgence of his (i.e., the Father's) glory" (Heb. 1:3). The "effulgence of glory" has not once been begotten and is no longer begotten. But as far as the light is productive of the effulgence, to so great an extent the effulgence of the glory of God is being begotten. Our Saviour is the "Wisdom of God" (1 Cor. 1:24). And Wisdom is the "effulgence of eternal light" (Wis. 7:26). If therefore the Saviour is ever being begotten, and for this reason says, "Before all hills he begets me" (Prov. 8:25)—not "before all hills he has begotten me," but "before all hills he begets me"—and the Saviour is ever being begotten of the Father. (*In Jeremiam* IX 4; Stevenson & Frend 2013: 229)

The strategy of harmonization between the oneness and plurality of God, suggested by Origen, was received enthusiastically. However, soon this strategy became a source of controversies. Indeed, the idea that the Logos is coexistent with the Father as a distinct reality can be interpreted in different ways. One interpretation would imply that the Father and the Logos are coeternal and equal to each other. Others would consider such an interpretation as compromising monotheism. They instead suggested seeing the Father as superior to the Son and the only God in the proper sense. This interpretation has been branded as subordinalism—the idea that the Son is not equal, but subordinate to the Father.

Origen himself aligned with the latter interpretation of the relationship between the Father and the Son. He envisaged a hierarchical order in their relationship. Only the Father is the God in the proper sense: "the God over all" (ὁ ἐπὶ πᾶσι θεός) and "self-God" (αὐτόθεος). He is also the God with the definite article: *ho Theos* (ὁ Θεός). The Logos is a different sort of God—without the definite article *ho* (ὁ):

> But since the proposition, "In the beginning was the Word," has been placed first, perhaps it indicates some order (τάξις); in the same manner, next, "And the Word was with God," and third, "And the Word was God." Perhaps he says, "And the Word was with God," then, "And the Word was God," that we might understand that the Word has become God because he is "with God." John has used the articles in one place and omitted them in another very precisely, and not as though he did not understand the precision of the Greek language. In the case of the Word, he adds the article "the," but

> in the case of the noun "God," he inserts it in one place and omits it in another. For he adds the article when the noun "God" stands for the uncreated cause of the universe, but he omits it when the Word is referred to as "divine." For as the God who is over all (ὁ ἐπὶ πᾶσι θεός) is "the God" and not simply "God," so the source (πηγή) of reason in each rational being is "the Word." That reason which is in each rational being would not properly have the same designation as the first Reason, and be said to be "the Word." (*Commentarii in Iohannem* II 12-15; Origen 1989: 98)

There can be an overstretched interpretation of these words, which would fit the posterior Nicaean doctrine, with the persons of God being signified by the definite article (ὁ Θεός) and the God's essence (οὐσία) being denoted by the word θεός without article. Such an interpretation, although orthodox, would be anachronistic for what Origen meant. What he meant was a clear idea of an order (τάξις) between all three hypostases of the one God:

> We are persuaded that there are three hypostases, the Father, the Son, and the Holy Spirit, and we believe that only the Father is unbegotten. We admit, as more pious and as true, that the Holy Spirit is the most honored of all things made through the Word, and that he is [first] in rank of all the things which have been made by the Father through Christ. Perhaps this is the reason the Spirit too is not called son of God, since the only begotten alone is by nature a son from the beginning. The Holy Spirit seems to have need of the Son ministering to his hypostasis, not only for it to exist, but also for it to be wise, and rational, and just, and whatever other thing we ought to understand it to be by participation in the aspects of Christ which we mentioned previously. (*Commentarii in Iohannem* II 75-6; Origen 1989: 114)

Origen was not the first who introduced the idea of subordination in God. His predecessor in the school of Alexandria, Clement, implied a similar order in the relationship between the Father, the Son, and the Holy Spirit. It is noteworthy that Clement drew a parallel between the Christian Trinitarian perception of God and the monotheistic perception of the divine, which he discerned in Plato's *Timaeus*:

> And the address in the Timaeus calls the creator, Father, speaking thus, "You Gods of gods, of whom I am Father and the Creator of your works." So that when he says, "Around the king of all, all things are, and because of Him are all things; and he [or that] is the cause of all good things; and around the second are the things second in order; and around the third, the third," I understand nothing else than the Holy Trinity to be meant; for the third is the Holy Spirit, and the Son is the second, by whom all things were made according to the will of the Father. (*Stromata* V 14.102-3)

Justin also had believed that Plato implied the highest deity (first God). He drew a parallel between the Platonic and Christian theology, in a way similar to how different grades of deity are ordered against each other:

> Plato said that the Power next to the first God was placed crosswise in the universe. And as to his speaking of a third, he did this because he read <. . .> "that the Spirit of

> God moved over the waters" (Gen. 1:2). For he gives the second place to the Logos which is with God <. . .>; and the third place to the Spirit who was said to be borne upon the water, saying, "And the third around the third." (*Apologia* I 60.7)

Origen, thus, built on a solid and respected tradition of subordinalism, which had been articulated by the previous generations of theological authorities. After Origen, this tradition became mainstream. It is not coincidence, therefore, that the earliest council that dealt with the Christological issues, Antioch 268, also adopted a subordinalist interpretation of the Trinitarian relationships. According to Athanasius, this council, on the one hand, chose a correct track to interpret the dynamics of the incarnation: it is "God who became a man," and not "a man who became God." On the other hand, the council implied a degree of inferiority of the Son vis-à-vis the Father (Sample 1979: 24).

# IV.7

# The Alexandrian Controversy

The two interpretations of the Father-Logos relationship, which emerged from Origenism, namely the hierarchical and egalitarian ones, were destined to clash with one another, sooner or later. A chain reaction within the nucleus of the Origenist Trinitarian theology was triggered at the turn of the fourth century. It led to a series of explosions.

The earliest of them has been identified as the Arian controversy. Probably it is more appropriate to call it Alexandrian controversy. It began as a quarrel between the archbishop of Alexandria Alexander and a group of presbyters under his jurisdiction. A presbyter called Arius was the leader of the group.

There were dozens, if not hundreds, of such quarrels in the church of that time. They were usually caused by the rapid transformations of the administrative structures in the church and by the redistribution of authority. However, no one had such far-reaching consequences as this one. It outgrew Egypt, and soon the entire empire was engulfed in it.

At this stage, the "Alexandrian" controversy became "Nicaean." It was discussed at a council in Nicaea, which later would become recognized as ecumenical. This council tried to figure out which interpretation of Origen's take on the Logos was orthodox. Although the council adopted a common theological formula, disputes continued in its aftermath.

Motivations of those involved in the post-conciliar controversy varied. Quite a few contested the council of Nicaea and simultaneously distanced themselves from Arius. That is why, although featuring common topics, arguments, and language, the Arian and Nicaean controversies should be distinguished.

The Nicaean controversy triggered the first Origenist controversy in the end of the fourth century (see Clark 1992). This was understandable given that both Nicaean and non-Nicaean parties appealed to Origen. More importantly, the Nicaean controversy paved a path to the controversies, which we call "Christological." The chain reaction of these controversies would be extinguished as late as in the ninth century. By then, the church was half-decayed, that is, divided into multiple schisms. Some of them healed, and others have lasted to our days.

Fortunately, the Alexandrian controversy, followed by the Nicaean controversy, did not lead to a lasting schism, even though the church balanced on its verge during the fourth century. There were multiple breaks in communion and mutual anathemas between local churches, but their communion was eventually restored. The unity of the church was preserved by the efforts of the imperial authorities and responsible bishops, who valued unity more than their partisan agendas.

## Many Rationales of the Controversy

The Alexandrian/Arian controversy began around 318 or maybe a couple of years later. There were some cultural and spiritual preconditions for the quarrel between Alexander and Arius. The latter was from Libya—to the west from Egypt. These two regions had a political and cultural rivalry. Such rivalries often happen between neighbors. As a result, Arius enjoyed support from the Libyan bishops, who emboldened him to wrestle with the Egyptian bishop.

There were also misunderstandings about the role that the archbishop of Alexandria was expected to play. In the early centuries, the Alexandrian church was among the most democratic ones, with the bishop of the city being *primus inter pares*—the first among equal presbyters. Only later, the Alexandrian church would become a pioneer of the papacy. Such a highly centralized papacy can be observed even in our days in the churches of Alexandrian descent: Coptic and Ethiopian. In the third century, bishops of Alexandria began to be called popes (πάπας)—one century prior to the bishops of Rome (see Louth 2007: 75). The transition from the democratic to the hierarchical model of the church leadership coincided with the time of the Arian controversy. It seems that Alexander consistently promoted monoëpiscopacy, while his opponents stood against it as a novelty. Arius advocated for the venerated democratic traditions of the Alexandrian church. That is probably why he was supported by approximately a third of his fellow Alexandrian presbyters (see Lyman 2021: 51).

Adversaries usually presented Arius as a promoter of theological innovations (καινοτομία; see Athanasius, *De synodis Arimini in Italia et Seleuciae in Isauria* IX 2 and elsewhere)—by that time this had become a heavy charge. Arius, however, perceived himself as something the opposite—"a defender of traditional orthodoxies" and "a committed theological conservative" (Williams 2001: 115, 175). He wrote about himself in *Thaleia*: "These are the things I have learned from the men who partake of wisdom, the keen-minded men, instructed by God, and in all respects wise" (in Williams 2001: 85). He meant primarily the spiritual authorities of his time, such as Gregory of Neocaesarea (*c.* 213–70) and Lucian of Antioch (*c.* 240–312).

Arius was a charismatic figure with the aura of self-righteous traditionalism. There were speculations about his affinity with the pietistic Melitians. He also enjoyed

**Figure 4.8** A wooden icon of an Egyptian bishop. Alexandria National Museum.
Source: Photo by the author.

popularity among ascetics (see Mönnich 1950) and was admired by lay devotees who surrounded him in dozens. These devotees lived in a community close to the church "Baucalis" in Alexandria, where he was a pastor. This church had the relics of Apostle Mark. This fact added to the prophetic self-confidence of Arius. Even his appearance inspired reverence, according to Epiphanius, who did not sympathize with his style:

> He was unusually tall, wore a downcast expression and was got up like a guileful serpent, able to steal every innocent heart by his villainous outer show. For he always wore a short cloak and a dalmatic, was pleasant in his speech, and was constantly winning souls round by flattery. (*Panarion* III 154; Epiphanius 2013: 335)

Many Arius' confederates perceived the inferiority of the Son to the Father—his key theological point—as a part of the venerated past, both socially and theologically. Socially, the Egyptian society was (and remains) patriarchal, with the dominant role of *paterfamilias*. It was natural, therefore, for the Egyptians to see the figure of the Father as superior to the Son. Theologically, many Alexandrians, since at least Clement, had regarded the Son as subordinate to the Father. Subordinalism, thus, had become an Egyptian local theological tradition. Therefore, many conservative Alexandrian clergymen and laypeople considered Alexander and his young deacon Athanasius as innovators and a threat to the traditional values of the Alexandrian Christian community.

Indeed, Alexander and Athanasius went against many established traditions (Lyman 2021: 49). For example, the term "consubstantial" (*homoousios*/ὁμοούσιος), for which they advocated in application to the Trinity, was a bold innovation. It was not biblical but borrowed from pagan philosophy. It would be not, therefore, an exaggeration to say that in the quarrel between Arius and Alexander, charismatic and hierarchical, traditionalist and innovative mentalities clashed with each other. In the church of that time, hierarchism was still an innovation.

Despite its cultural and spiritual underpinnings, the Alexandrian controversy was primarily theological. The two prelates argued about the relationship between the Father and the Son. Alexander preached that they are coeternal. For Arius, Alexander undermined Christian monotheism. Despite their differences in interpreting the relationship of the Son to the Father, Alexander and Arius shared surprisingly many theological prerequisites, such as loathe to adoptionism and modalism, as well as the Origenist outlook at the Logos as a reality distinct from the Father's.

# A Bishop against His Priest

One of the impediments in studying Arius' theology is that we can hardly discern his own ideas from what has been ascribed to him by his opponents. We cannot be sure even about his quotes, as most of them have been passed by his enemies. In the vast corpus of the documents related to the fourth-century controversies,[1] we can trust only a few texts as genuinely representing the views of Arius. One of them is *Thaleia*—a theological treatise in verses, through which Arius expounded his views on the incarnation. Some fragments from this treatise have survived, including the following one:

> The Unbegun appointed the Son to be Beginning of things begotten, and bore him as his own Son, in this case giving birth.
> He has nothing proper to God in his essential property, for neither is he equal nor yet consubstantial with him.
> Wise is God, since he himself is Wisdom's teacher.
> There is proof enough that God is invisible to all, and to those through the Son and to the Son himself the same [God] is invisible.
> I will say exactly how the Invisible is seen by the Son:
> By the power by which God can see, and in proper measures,
> the Son sustains the vision of the Father as is right.

[1]See the series of publications by De Gruyter. The series was started by Hans-Georg Opitz in 1934 (*Urkunden zur Geschichte des Arianischen Streites 318-328*): https://www.degruyter.com/view/mvw/ATHANWB3T1-B [accessed on June 7, 2021].

> Or rather there is a Trinity with glories not alike;
> Their existences are unmixable with each other;
> One is more glorious than another by an infinity of glories.
> The Father is essentially foreign to the Son because he exists unbegun.
> Understand then that the Unity was, but the Duality was not, before he existed.
> So straight away when there is no Son, the Father is God.
> Thus the Son who was not, but existed at the paternal will,
> is only-begotten God, and he is distinct from everything else.
> Wisdom existed as wisdom by the will of a wise God. (In Athanasius, *De synodis Arimini in Italia et Seleuciae in Isauria* 15; Stevenson & Frend 2013: 374)

Even from this short passage, which represents Arius' later views, it is possible to conclude that he envisaged a structural, ontological, and epistemological disparity between the Father and the Son. The former is unbegun, while the latter is begotten. Their existence is unmixable, for which reason the Son cannot be said to be *homoousios* with the Father. The distance between the Father and the Son is kept by the Father' will—the same will that preserves the distance between God and creature. The Son is the beginning, and a part, of the "things begotten," even though he is different from the rest of the created world. Before this world came into existence, there was a time without the Son. The Son is so different from the Father that he cannot comprehend his nature. Inability to see the nature of the Father puts the Son on the same scale with the rest of the world.

Alexander and Athanasius contested Arius' points. Just as it is unrealistic to distinguish between what Arius wrote himself and what he was ascribed by his opponents, so it is hardly possible to distinguish the ideas of Alexander from those of Athanasius. Some texts signed by Alexander were in fact penned by Athanasius. This would become a common practice in the church and continues to our days. With only a few exceptions, church hierarchs do not compose their own texts, but commission them to ghostwriters. Athanasius was such a ghostwriter for Alexander. He, for example, authored the following encyclical letter signed by Alexander:

> Who, hearing in the Gospel of "the only-begotten Son" (Jn 3:16, 18), and that "through him all things were made" (Jn 1:3, see Rom. 11:36), will not hate those who proclaim that the Son is one of the things that were made (ποιήματα)? How can he be one of the things which were made through himself? Or how can he be the only-begotten, if he is reckoned among such created things? And how could he come into existence from nothing when the Father has said, "My heart has spewed out a good word (λόγος)" (Ps. 45:2); and "I begot you from the womb before the morning star" (Ps. 110:3)? Or how can he be unlike the Father in essence (οὐσία) when he is the perfect image and radiant glory of the Father (Heb. 1:3) and says, "He that has seen me, has seen the Father" (Jn 14:9)? Again how if the Son is the Word and Wisdom of God, could there

be a time when he did not exist? That is equivalent to their saying that God was once without the Word and without Wisdom.

How can one be mutable and susceptible of change who says of himself, "I am in the Father, and the Father is in me" (Jn 10:38; 14:10, 11); and "I and the Father are one" (Jn 10:30); and again through the prophet, "Look at me because I am, and I have not changed" (see Mal. 3:6)? If someone can use this expression of the Father himself, it would be even more fittingly spoken concerning the Word, because he was not changed when he became man, but as the apostle says, "Jesus Christ, the same yesterday, today, and forever" (Heb. 13:8). So who could persuade them to say that he was made on our account, when Paul wrote that "for him and through him all things exist" (Rom. 11:38)?

One need not wonder at their blasphemous assertion that the Son does not perfectly know the Father. For once they decided to fight against Christ, they reject also his own voice when he says, "As the Father knows me, even so I know the Father" (Jn 10:15). But if the Father only partially knows the Son, it is clear that the Son can only partially know the Father. But if it would be improper to say this, and if the Father does perfectly know the Son, it is also clear that just as the Father knows his own Word, so also the Word knows his own Father, whose Word he is. (*Epistula encyclica*; https://www.fourthcentury.com/urkunde-4b/ [accessed on January 22, 2021])

Athanasius invested in the anti-Arian polemics his theological mind, while Alexander engaged administrative mechanisms. He inaugurated a long period of countless councils, which focused on discussing the relationship between the Father and the Son. The period of the Nicaean controversy was a ceaseless *synodomachia*.

## Synodomachia

The earliest anti-Arian councils, held in Alexandria in 320 and 322 under the presidency of Alexander, condemned Arius. The dissident presbyter did not yield. He solicited support from outside Egypt: in his native Libya and in Syria. Two prominent hierarchs of that time endorsed his cause: Eusebius of Nicomedia and Eusebius of Caesarea. They made sure that local councils in their dioceses vindicate Arius (in 321). At this stage, Emperor Constantine stepped in. He first urged the Alexandrian prelates to stop quarreling. When his admonitions did not work, he appointed his trusted person, the bishop of Cordoba in Spain Hosius (*c.* 256–357/58) to sort the crisis out.

Hosius sided with Alexander. He supported his cause in 324 at another local council in Alexandria and at a local council in Antioch. Hosius presided at both councils. The latter council was summoned in early 325 by the bishop of Antioch Eustathius, who became a protagonist of anti-Arian polemics. The council of Antioch promulgated the earliest anti-Arian creed:

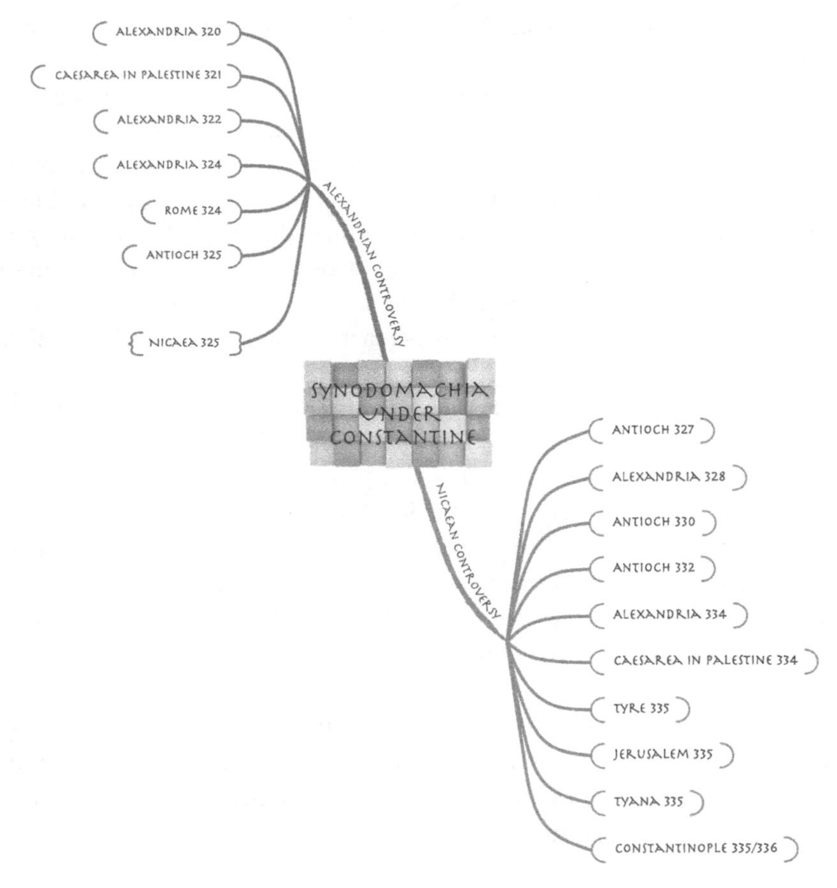


**Figure 4.9a** "Synodomachia" under Constantine.

The faith is <. . .> to believe in one God, the Father Almighty, incomprehensible, immutable and unchangeable, governor and administrator of all, just, good, Maker of heaven, earth, and of all the things in them, Lord of the Law, of the Prophets, and of the New Testament;

and in one Lord Jesus Christ, only-begotten Son, begotten not from that which does not exist, but from the Father, not as something made, but as properly an offspring, and begotten in an ineffable and indescribable manner, because only the Father who begot and the Son who was begotten know [it]. For "no one knew the Father except the Son, and [no one knew] the Son except the Father" (Mt. 11:27; Lk. 10:22), [the Son] who exists eternally and did not previously not exist.

For we have learnt from the holy Scriptures that he alone is the express image (see Heb. 1:3), not unbegotten (as "from the Father" signifies), nor by adoption (for it is impious and blasphemous to say this). Rather, the Scriptures say him to be properly and truly begotten such that we believe also that he is immutable and unchangeable; but not that he was begotten or came into being by volition or by adoption (whereby it would be clear that he existed from that which does not exist), but as it befitted him that he was born; nor according to a similarity of nature or commixture with anything

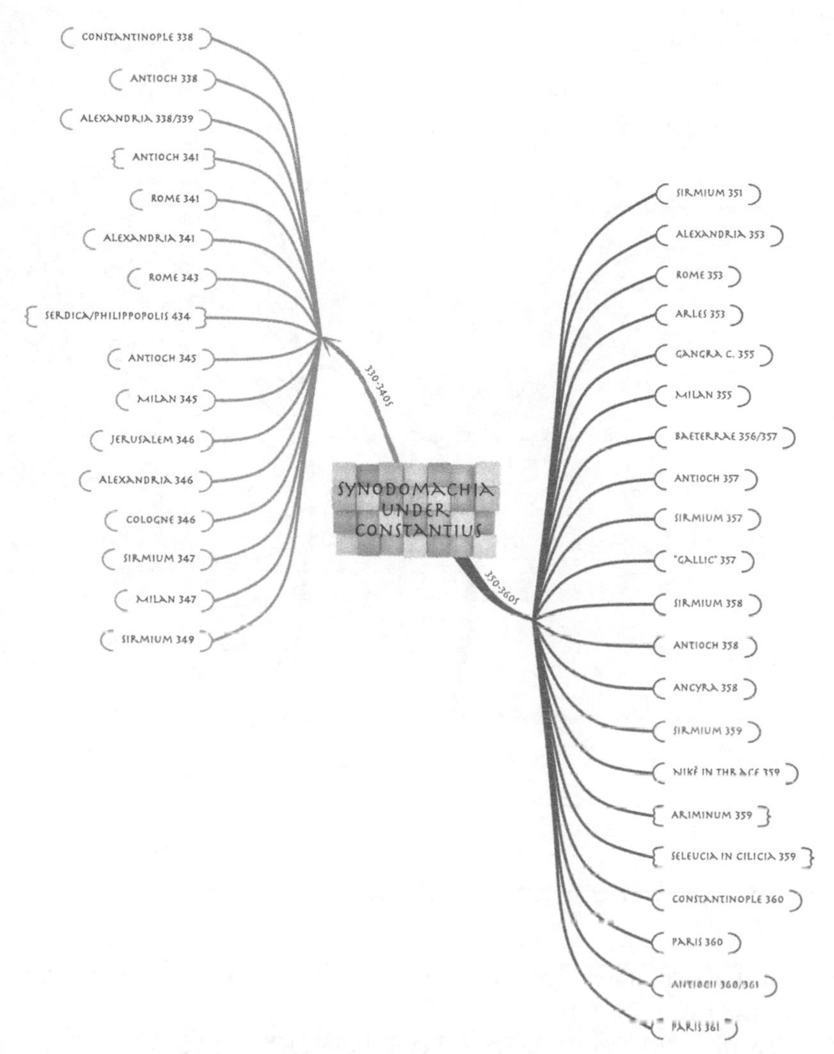


**Figure 4.9b** "Synodomachia" under Constantius.

which came into existence through him (which it is not lawful to think), but, since it transcends all reflection or understanding or reasoning, we confess him to have been begotten from the unbegotten Father, the God Word, true light, righteousness, Jesus Christ, Lord and Saviour of all. He is the express image, not of the will or of anything else, but of the paternal hypostasis itself (see 2 Cor. 4:4; Col. 1:15; Heb. 1:3).

But this Son, God the Word, was also born in flesh from Mary the Theotokos, assumed a body, suffered, died, rose again from the dead, was taken up into heaven, sits "at the right hand o f the Majesty most high" (Heb. 1:3), [and] will come "to judge the living and the dead" (2 Tim. 4:1; 1 Pet 4:5).

Furthermore, as also [in the case of] our Saviour, the holy Scriptures teach us to believe also one Spirit, one catholic Church, the resurrection of the dead, and a

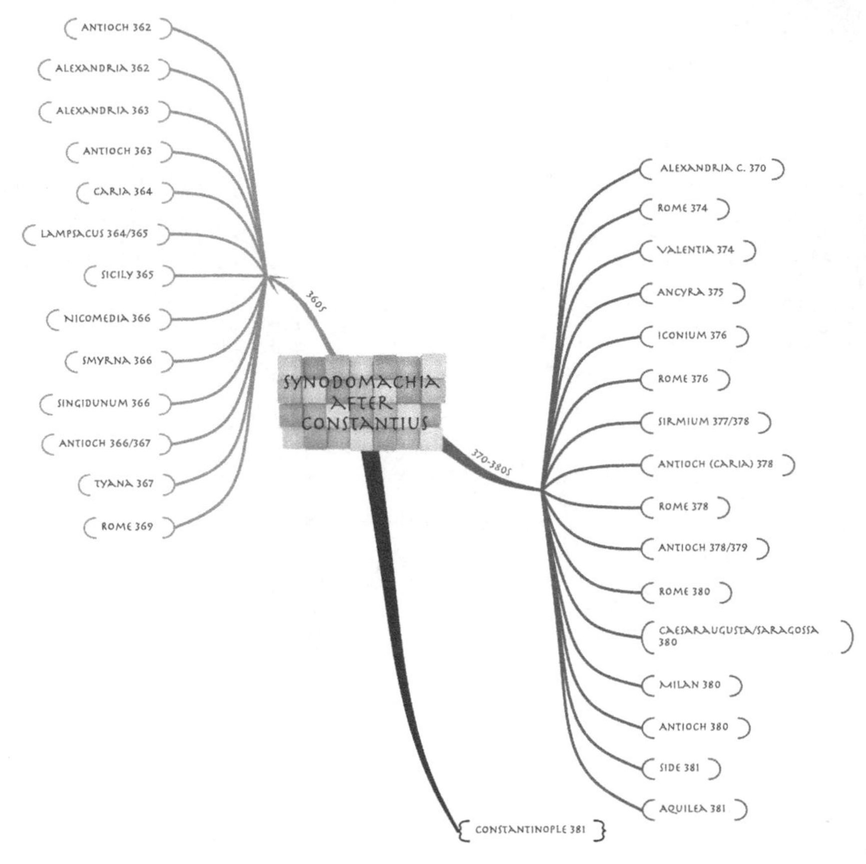


**Figure 4.9c** "Synodomachia" after Constantius.

judgement of retribution according to what someone has done in the body, whether good or bad (see 2 Cor. 5:10).

We anathematize those who say, believe, and preach God's Son to be a creature or originated or made, and not as truly begotten, or that there was when he was not; we believe, indeed, that he was and is and that he is light; but along with them [we anathematize] those who suppose he is immutable through his own act of will, just as [we anathematize] those who also derive his birth from that which does not exist and [say] that he is not immutable in nature as is the Father. For as the express image of the Father (see Heb. 1:3), just in all things, so in this respect particularly, is our Saviour proclaimed. (In Kinzig 2017, vol. 1: 277–8)

# Nicaea

Councils were a common practice in the early church. All of them had been local. It means that bishops from the vicinity gathered to discuss issues pertinent to their own communities. In rare cases did they discuss the issues that troubled the wider church. One of the reasons why the scope of the early councils was narrow and local was because most bishops could hardly make a long way to the capital or even provincial centers. Such trips were expensive and logistically complicated.

Roads were crucial for practicing the church's conciliarity. The very word "council"—*synodos* (σύνοδος)—was coined with roads in mind. Its root is "road"—*hodos* (ὁδός). *Syn-odos* (σύν-οδος), therefore, is a common undertaking by those who together hit a road. Roads that traversed the empire in every direction were a unique Roman innovation. Unlike other empires, the Roman Empire made its roads accessible to everyone and not just to chosen elites. The Roman roads went everywhere, making the imperial administrative structures sustainable and manageable from one capital city.

In the situation of being an illegal religion, Christianity could hardly afford to have councils of large scale, because mass locomotion of Christian bishops and their acolytes, especially from the remote corners of the Roman Empire, was risky, fatiguing, and expensive. The situation changed after Christianity became legal. Constantine offered bishops funds to travel, allowance for meals, and the imperial posting facilities. In the words of H. A. Drake, this was "akin to providing first-class passage on a supersonic transport today" (Drake 2021: 115). All these measures and facilities made possible what would become known as ecumenical councils.

"Ecumenical" means that local churches from the entire *oecumene*—the Greco-Roman world—sent their representatives to such councils. These councils could be

**Figure 4.10** A Roman road at Ostia Antiqua near Rome.
Source: Photo by the author.

also called "pan-imperial." They were imperial also in the sense that they were convoked by emperors. Emperors sometimes participated in such councils personally. After the councils had taken decisions, emperors issued decrees that made these decisions a mandatory law.

Constantine convoked such a council in the Bithynian city of Nicaea in the late May or June of 325. His original plan was to hold the council in Ancyra, but then he decided to move it closer to Nicomedia and Byzantion (which was not yet inaugurated as Constantinople), where he preferred to stay. He did not choose Nicomedia to avoid the conflict of interests—the bishop of the city Eusebius was an outspoken supporter of Arius. Besides, Nicaea was a splendid town with a beautiful lake and gardens. Constantine wanted the bishops to enjoy themselves.

Bishops from the entire *oecumene* and beyond, like the Persian Empire, came to Nicaea to discuss the Alexandrian controversy. Most of them were from the East. There were also some Western representatives, including Constantine's special envoy on theological issues, Hosius from Cordoba, who presided over and moderated the council. Athanasius, who attended the council as Alexander's acolyte, mentioned 318 participants, with a symbolic reference to 318 men in the personal army of Abraham (Gen. 14:14). The real number of participants was between 250 and 300.

**Figure 4.11** Nicaea was located on the eastern shore of the beautiful Lake Askania. Now it is Iznik in Turkey.

Source: Photo by the author.

The council held its sessions not on church premises, but, most probably, inside the imperial residence. Constantine attended the sessions personally. However, he did not moderate them or vote. He acted more like a hospitable host who cared about the best possible conditions for his guests' productive work and entertainment. At the same time, he participated in the discussions. Some bishops, therefore, thought twice before they would speak in front of the emperor.

The council acted in the capacity and followed the procedures of a Roman court. It deliberated on the pleadings of two parties, represented by Alexander and Arius. Both parties were present and their arguments heard. Each party had its advocates. Arius, for instance, had twenty-two bishops who aligned with him, according to Philostorgius. This number included such heavyweights as Eusebius of Nicomedia and Eusebius of Caesarea. Alexander had more followers, including Eustathius of Antioch and Marcellus of Ancyra. Many, if not most, bishops, however, hardly understood the nuances of the debates and were not sure which side to align with. Nevertheless, after deliberations, of which we do not have recordings, the council judged to support Alexander's pleading.

A drafting committee composed a creed, which corresponded to the earlier confessions promoted by Alexander (and penned by Athanasius). Structurally, this creed addressed both *theologia* and *oeconomia*. It begins with a strong monotheistic

**Figure 4.12** The hall in the imperial palace in Nicaea, where the council took place, might have looked like the interior of Constantine's basilica in Trier, which initially was not a church, but an imperial office.

Source: Photo by the author.

statement of God's oneness. It continues with explaining God's plurality, including the incarnation and a minimalistic reference to the Holy Spirit. It is noteworthy that the original Nicaean definition consisted of both affirmative and condemning parts. The latter was dropped in the version of the creed that would be revised at the council of Constantinople in 381. The original Nicaean version of the creed contained the following articles:

> We believe in one God, the Father Almighty, Maker of all things both visible and invisible;
>
> and in one Lord Jesus Christ, the Son of God, begotten (γεννηθέντα) from the Father, only-begotten (μονογενῆ), that is, from the essence (ἐκ τῆς οὐσίας) of the Father; God from God, Light from Light, true God from true God, begotten, not made, consubstantial (ὁμοούσιον) with the Father; "through whom all things came into being" (Jn 1:3; 1 Cor. 8:6), both things in heaven and things on earth; who for us humans and for our salvation descended, became incarnate (σαρκωθέντα), was made human (ἐνανθρωπήσαντα), suffered, on the third day rose again, ascended into the heavens, will come "to judge the living and the dead" (2 Tim. 4:1; 1 Pet. 4:5);
>
> and in the Holy Spirit.
>
> The catholic and apostolic Church anathematizes those who say, "There was when he was not," and, "He was not before he was begotten," and that he came to be from nothing, or those who claim that the Son of God is from another hypostasis or substance, (or created,) or alterable, or mutable. (Modified translation from Kinzig 2017, vol. 1: 290–1)

Bishops were asked to sign the creed and comply with the council's decisions—similarly to how the litigating parties are supposed to accept the court's judgment. Those who did not comply were excommunicated, including Arius and two bishops: Theonas of Marmarica and Secundus of Ptolemais. Several bishops, who had supported Arius, accepted the decisions of the majority, including Eusebius of Nicomedia and Eusebius of Caesarea.

This does not mean they gave up on the Arian cause. Eusebius of Nicomedia, for example, admitted the condemned presbyter to communion. This angered Constantine, who sent Eusebius in exile. Soon, however, Eusebius restored Constantine's confidence in him. He returned to his see and added to his political weight—to the extent that he would be entrusted with baptizing the emperor at his deathbed in 337. After having regained Constantine's ear, Eusebius convinced him that readmitting Arius to communion would serve peace in the church and the empire better than rejecting him. He was wrong. Arius was rehabilitated, but this did not bring the promised piece.

# IV.8

# The Nicaean Controversy

The controversy did not stop after Arius died in 336. Now, however, the church's attention shifted from the figure of the Alexandrian presbyter to the legacy of the Nicaean council. Athanasius rendered the ongoing controversy as Arian, but this was more a polemical trope. He aimed at tarnishing Nicaea's adversaries by associating them with the toxic name of the condemned dissident.

## The Nicaeans

Athanasius emerged as the chief guardian of the Nicaean legacy. He should be credited for inspiring the posterior perception of the council of 325 as one of the most important events in the church's history. Such later perception of the council was different from the way it was perceived by its contemporaries. For them, it was one of many councils that were called to address a local issue. Even the emperor's participation did not make it unique. The council of Arles in 314 had been the first church's gathering summoned by Constantine.

For Athanasius, however, the Nicaea was unique. He should be probably credited for constructing its identity as an "ecumenical council." This identity was later accepted by the church. Athanasius dedicated his entire life to protect and promote the Nicaean legacy. For its sake, he endured multiple condemnations and exiles. Thus, in 335, he was condemned at the council of Tyre and exiled to Trier. After Constantine's death in 337, he returned to Egypt and after two years again had to flee, this time to Rome. He was repeatedly justified by the councils in Rome (340) and in Serdica (343, at the council's Western session), and condemned by the councils in Antioch (341) and the Eastern session of the council in Serdica (343). After spending short periods of time in Alexandria, he was exiled again by Emperors Constantius II in 356, Julian in 362–3, and Valens in 365–6.

Athanasius was creative in protecting and promoting the Nicaean legacy. He explicated it in his numerous theological writings, including *On Incarnation*. At the beginning of this treatise, Athanasius explains how God created human nature, which is mortal, while he intended it to be incorruptible. If the first human couple kept the commandments of God, they would have advanced to *theosis*—a key notion in Athanasius' theological system. However, because they transgressed God's commandment, human beings who sprang from Adam and Eve, could not advance spiritually. Instead, they became subjects to death:

> We must, when speaking of the manifestation of the Saviour to us, speak also of the beginning of mankind, in order that you may know that our own cause was the reason of his coming, and that our own transgression called forth the mercy of the Word, so that the Lord came even to us and appeared among men. For we were the cause of his incarnation, and for our salvation he had compassion to the extent of being born and revealed in a body. God, then, had so created man and willed that he should remain in incorruptibility. But when men had disregarded and turned away from the understanding of God, and had thought of and invented for themselves wickedness, as was said in the first part (see *Contra gentes* 3), then they received the condemnation of death which had been previously threatened, and no longer remained as they had been created, but as they had devised, were ruined. And death overcame them and reigned over them. For the transgression of the commandment turned them to what was natural, so that, as they had come into being from non-existence, so also they might accordingly suffer in time the corruption consequent to their non-being. For if, having such a nature as not ever to exist, they were summoned to existence by the advent and mercy of the Word, it followed that because men were deprived of the understanding of God and had turned to things which do not exist—for what does not exist is evil, but what does exist is good since it has been created by the existent God—then they were also deprived of eternal existence. But this means that when they perished they would remain in death and corruption. For man is by nature mortal in that he was created from nothing. But because of his likeness to him who exists, if he had kept this through contemplating God, he would have blunted his natural corruption and would have remained incorruptible. (*De incarnatione* 4; Athanasius of Alexandria 1981: 144–5)

In what follows, Athanasius explains why God had to incarnate. Only by receiving what is ours—Athanasius uses the word "body" for it—God could save it from corruption and death. Body, thus, was an instrument of salvation. It must be capable of death—to allow the immortal God to die in it:

> For this reason the incorporeal and incorruptible and immaterial Word of God came to our realm; not that he was previously distant, for no part of creation is left deprived of him, but he fills the universe, being in union with his Father. But in his benevolence towards us he condescended to come and be made manifest. For he saw that the rational race was perishing and that death was reigning over them through corruption, and he saw also that the threat of the transgression was firmly supporting corruption over us, and that it would have been absurd for the law to be dissolved before it was fulfilled. He saw also the impropriety of what had occurred, that the creatures he

> himself had made should perish, and he saw the excessive wickedness of men, and that they were gradually increasing it against themselves and making it intolerable, and he saw too the liability of all men in regard to death. Therefore he had pity on our race, and was merciful to our infirmity, and submitted to our corruption, and did not endure the dominion of death. And lest what had been created should perish and the work of the Father among men should be in vain, he took to himself a body, and that not foreign to our own. For he did not wish simply to be in a body, nor did he wish merely to appear, for if he had wished only to appear he could have made his theophany through some better means. But he took our body, and not simply that, but from a pure and unspotted virgin ignorant of a man, a body pure and truly unalloyed by intercourse with men. For he, although powerful and the creator of the universe, fashioned for himself in the virgin a body as a temple, and appropriated it for his own as an instrument in which to be known and dwell. And thus taking a body like ours, since all were liable to the corruption of death, and surrendering it to death on behalf of all, he offered it to the Father. And this he did in his loving kindness in order that, as all die in him, the law concerning corruption in men might be abolished—since its power was concluded in the Lord's body and it would never again have influence over men who are like him—and in order that, as men had turned to corruption, he might turn them back again to incorruption and might give them life for death, in that he had made the body his own, and by the grace of the resurrection had rid them of death as straw is destroyed by fire. (*De incarnatione* 8; Athanasius of Alexandria 1981: 151–3)

In what follows, Athanasius is coming to his main point: demonstrating that Christ was true God. He asked himself a legitimate question: Why the Logos, after having been incarnated, did not die immediately, but lived and preached for several years? The answer Athanasius gives is simple: to demonstrate through miracles and his teaching that he indeed is the Son of God:

> For since men's reason had descended to sensible things, the Word submitted to being revealed through a body, in order that he might bring men to himself as a man and turn their senses to himself, and that thenceforth, although they saw him as a man, he might persuade them through the works he did that he was not merely a man but God, and the Word and Wisdom of the true God. This Paul wished to indicate when he said: "Be firm and grounded in love, that you may be able to understand with all the saints what is the breadth and length and height and depth, and that you may know the love of Christ which transcends knowledge, in order that you may be filled with all the fullness of God" (Eph. 3:17-19). For the Word spread himself everywhere, above and below and in the depth and in the breadth: above, in creation; below, in the incarnation; in the depth, in hell; in breadth, in the world. Everything is filled with the knowledge of God. For this reason, not as soon as he came did he complete the sacrifice on behalf of all and deliver his body to death, and resurrecting it make himself thereby invisible. But by means of it he rendered himself visible, remaining in it and completing such works and giving signs as made him known to be no longer a man but God the Word. For in two ways our Saviour had compassion through the incarnation: he both rid us

> of death and renewed us; and also, although he is invisible and indiscernible, yet by his works he revealed and made himself known to be the Son of God and the Word of the Father, leader and king of the universe. (*De incarnatione* 16; Athanasius of Alexandria 1981: 173)

Athanasius speaks about Christ dying on everyone's behalf, to resurrect all. This is a clear reference to the common human nature, which partakes in the common salvation provided by Christ's death and resurrection:

> So the body, as it had the common substance of all bodies, was a human body. Even if it had been constituted by a new miracle from a virgin only, nevertheless it was mortal and died in the fashion of those similar to it. But through the coming of the Word into it, it was no longer corruptible according to its nature, but because of the Word who was dwelling in it, became immune from corruption. And the two things occurred simultaneously in a miraculous manner: the death of all was fulfilled in the Lord's body, and also death and corruption were destroyed because of the Word who was in it. For there was need of death, and death on behalf of all had to take place in order that what was owed by all men might be paid. Therefore, as I said above, the Word himself, since he could not die, for he was immortal, took to himself a body which could die in order to offer it as his own on behalf of all and in order to take upon himself the suffering for all men, through his coming into it "to destroy him who held the power of death, that is the devil, and to deliver all those who through fear of death had been all their lifetime subject to bondage" (Heb. 2:14-15).
>
> So, since the common Saviour of all has died for us, no longer do we the faithful in Christ now die as before according to the threat of the law, for such condemnation has ceased. But as corruption has ceased and been destroyed by the grace of the resurrection, now in the mortality of the body we are dissolved only for the time which God has set for each man, in order that we may be able to "obtain a better resurrection" (Heb. 11:35). For like seeds which are sown in the ground we do not perish when we are dissolved, but we rise again as plants, since death has been destroyed by the grace of the Saviour. (*De incarnatione* 21; Athanasius of Alexandria 1981: 185)
>
> That death has been dissolved and that the cross was a victory over it and that it is no longer powerful but truly dead, is demonstrated in no uncertain manner and is clearly credible by the fact that it is despised by all Christ's disciples and everyone treads it underfoot and no longer fears it, but with the sign of the cross and in the Christian faith they trample on it as on a dead thing. For formerly, before the divine coming of the Saviour occurred, all used to weep for the dead as if they were lost. But now that the Saviour has raised up his body death is no longer to be feared, but all believers in Christ tread on it as something non-existent and would rather die than deny their faith in Christ. For they really know that when they die they do not perish but live and become incorruptible through the resurrection. (*De incarnatione* 27; Athanasius of Alexandria 1981: 199–201)

**Figure 4.13** The icon of Athanasius of Alexandria (*c.* 1718). Byzantine Museum of Antivouniotissa on Corfu, Greece.
Source: Photo by the author.

In his polemical effort, Athanasius had some heavy-weighing allies. One of them was the bishop of Ancyra Marcellus. Although a staunch anti-Arian, he had his reservations regarding the council of Nicaea (see Parvis 2006: 5; Barnard 1980: 63). As was mentioned, this council was a battlefield between the Origenist parties. In contrast to them, Marcellus was an old-school pre-Origen monotheist, suspicious of any Origenist differentiation applied to one God. This did not, however, make him a Sabellian, as some had accused him. Marcellus acknowledged the Logos in the undivided unity with the Father:

> By saying, "in the beginning was the Word," he shows that the Word was in the Father as a power. <. . .> By saying, "and the Word was with God," he teaches that the Word was with God as an [or "in"] energy. <. . .> And by saying that the Word was God he teaches that one should not divide the Godhead, since the Word is in him and he is in the Word. For he says, "The Father is in me and I am in the Father." (*Fr.* 70 (52); Ayres 2004: 64)

At the same time, Marcellus implied an evolution of the undivided divine monad to a triad:

> If the Word were to appear to have come from the Father Himself and has come to us and "The Holy Spirit <. . .> proceeds from the Father," and again the Savior says

> concerning the Spirit that "He will not speak on His own authority (ἀφ' ἑαυτοῦ), but whatever He hears He will speak, and He will declare to you the things that are to come. He will glorify me, for He will take what is mine and declare it to you," doesn't the monad in this ineffable statement appear clearly and obviously to broaden into a Trinity without in any way suffering division? (In Eusebius, *De ecclesiastica theologia* III 4.2; Eusebius of Caesarea 2017: 305)

This idea scared some of his fellow anti-Arians, including Athanasius. Even more they were scared by his idea that the Kingdom of Christ would eventually end. The credal statement "Whose Kingdom shall have no end" is directed against Marcellus. It addresses Marcellus' belief that in the end the Son will disunite from the man in Jesus Christ and will return to the Father (see Cartwright 2012: 177). This idea means that Christ had two subjects: the Logos and a man Jesus, who had some autonomy from God. In this point, Marcellus also diverged from Athanasius, who advocated for the intrinsic unity of the Logos and flesh in the undivided person of Jesus Christ.

Christ's human completeness, which Marcellus implied, was endorsed by another anti-Arian, the bishop of Antioch Eustathius. He called Jesus a "God-bearing human being" (ἄνθρωπος θεοφόρος, *homo deum ferens*). In contrast to the Athanasian picture of Christ with a rather passive flesh, Christ's humanity, according to Eustathius, was active and full of glory:

**Figure 4.14** The historical center of Ancyra, now Turkey's capital Ankara, where Marcellus was a bishop.
Source: Photo by the author.

> The God-bearing man, who thought to sustain the passion of death of himself for the benefit of human beings, received indeed the prize of the struggle, so to speak, and honour and power and, when it is received, glory, which he never had previously. (*Fr.* 93a; Parvis 2006: 59)

Eustathius, like Marcellus, detested Origen. He even wrote a treatise *On the Witch of Endor*, where he criticized the hermeneutical method of the Alexandrian teacher (see Trigg 1995). Both Eustathius and Marcellus believed that Origen had compromised God's singularity. Both were staunch proponents of such singularity, which they called "one hypostasis." In equation between the divine oneness and plurality, they emphasized the former.

At the same time, they disagreed with one another on some theological points, such as the end of Christ's kingdom. In contrast to Marcellus, Eustathius contemplated a pre-incarnational and pre-cosmic Logos, who is the image of the Father. Jesus' humanity, in turn, is the image of the Logos and, thus, the image of the Father's image:

> For Paul did not say "conformed to the Son of God," but "conformed to the image of his Son," showing that the Son is one thing and his image is something else. For the Son, bearing the divine tokens of the Father's virtue, is image of the Father. Since also those who are born—like begotten from like—appear [to be] true images of their begetters. But the human being whom he wore is image of the Son. (*Fr.* 68; Parvis 2006: 58)

## Anti-Nicaeans and Non-Nicaeans

The anti-Arian party, thus, was diverse. Its members agreed that Arius was wrong, but disagreed on many other issues, including their attitude to the council of Nicaea. It would probably be too much of a stretch even to call them a single party. The same applies to the assumed "Arian" party. Athanasius tried to persuade his contemporaries that there was one. He argued that a clique of confederates conspired against the council of Nicaea and wanted to substitute its theology with the teaching of their mentor and hero, Arius. Athanasius counterattacked the adversaries of the council by smearing them with "Arianism." His take on the events surrounding the Nicaean controversy is not much different from a conspiracy theory.

Modern scholars, however, doubt that there was a single "Arian" party. Those theologians who shared some ideas of Arius disagreed on many other ideas—with him and one another. Most of the assumed "Arian" theologians did not even want to associate themselves with his name. At the council of Antioch in 341, for example, the presumably "Arian" bishops complained about this libel in their letter to Pope Julius:

> We have neither become followers of Arius—for how should we who are bishops follow a presbyter?—nor have we embraced any other faith than that which was set

> forth from the beginning. But being both examiners and judges of his faith, we admitted him to communion rather than following him; and you will recognize this from what we are about to state. (In Athanasius, *De synodis Arimini in Italia et Seleuciae in Isauria* 22; Stevenson & Frend 2012: 10)

Rowan Williams is right that Arius "was never unequivocally a hero for the parties associated with his name" (Williams 2001: 82). For the assumed "Arians," Arius "was to be seen as a witness to, not a source of, tradition," according to Richard P. Vaggione (Vaggione 2000: 42). They believed that this tradition was apostolic and had been testified by many venerable authorities of the past. They did not need Arius to authorize this tradition.

Some of those whom Athanasius branded as "Arians" were staunch anti-Nicaeans. They believed that the council was wrong—not so much because it had condemned Arius, but because it put the Father and the Son on the same scale. Other "Arians" believed that this council was neither a mistake nor a success in articulating the orthodox doctrine. They doubted the Nicaean neologism "consubstantial" and continued seeking better formulas to explain the relationship between the Father and the Son. Sometimes, they appreciated the Nicaea more and sometimes, less. This party should be called not "Arian," but "non-Nicaean."

To be more precise, this was not even a party, but rather a trajectory or a loose alliance that linked hierarchs and theologians of otherwise different opinions. Their bottomline was doubts about the Nicaea and lack of doubts about the validity of the imperial policies. The majority of those who followed the non-Nicaean trajectory objected more to the Nicaean meta-language than to its semantics, while staunch anti-Nicaeans could accept neither the council's meta-language nor its semantics. This is probably the main difference between the two alliances.

The Nicaean skeptics constituted a majority in the Christian East during most of the fourth century. They perceived themselves as respectful moderates who avoided what they believed to be either Arian or Athanasian extremities. In contrast to the skeptical non-Nicaeans, both Nicaeans and anti-Nicaeans were in minority. Only for these two theological minorities, the council of Nicaea constituted a landmark, whether positive or negative. All three groups had also different attitudes to Athanasius. For the anti-Nicaeans, he was a heretic; for the non-Nicaeans, an annoying troublemaker; and for the Nicaeans, a champion of their faith.

In contrast to the East, in the West, both Athanasius and the Nicaea were significantly more popular. There were many devoted Nicaeans there, including bishops of Rome, who also offered Athanasius a helping hand. The Westerners, however, often failed to grasp the nuances of theological discussions in the East. Following Athanasius' conspiracy theories, they believed that all Eastern non-Nicaeans were Arians. In the same simplified way, many Eastern non-Nicaeans believed that the Western supporters of Athanasius were Sabellians. Incautious

Western support to Marcellus of Ancyra contributed to the otherwise unjustified Eastern suspicions about the West.

## The "Eusebians"

"Arian" was not the only theological identity constructed by Athanasius. He also coined the term "Eusebians" (οἱ περὶ Εὐσέβιον) (see *De decretis Nicaenae synodi* III 2.5 and elsewhere). For the bishop of Alexandria, they were the same "Arians" who, after Arius died, continued their anti-Nicaean conspiracies, now under the patronage of the bishop of Nicomedia Eusebius (see Gwynn 2007). Athanasius epitomized the assumed Eusebian theology in his *First Oration Against the Arians*:

> Not always was God a father; but there was once when God was alone, and not yet a father; later He became a father. Not always was the Son; for since all things came to be out of nothing (ἐξ οὐκ ὄντων), and since all things are created (κτισμάτων) and made (ποιημάτων) and came to be, thus also the Word of God Himself came to be out of nothing, and there was once when He was not. And He was not until He was generated, but He too had a beginning of creation. For he (Arius) says that God was alone, and not yet was the Word, nor the Wisdom. Then, wishing to fashion us, thereupon He made a certain one and named Him Word and Son and Wisdom, so that He might fashion us through Him. Thus he says that there are two Wisdoms, one proper and coexisting (συνυπάρχουσαν) in God, [and] that the Son was originated in this Wisdom, and only as partaking (μετέχοντα) of this is named Wisdom and Word. For Wisdom, he says, came into existence in Wisdom by the will of the wise God. Thus also he said there was another Word than the Son in God, and the Son again as partaking of this is Himself named Word and Son according to grace. And this too is a thought proper to their heresy, as is shown in other writings of theirs, that there are many powers. And the one in God is proper by nature (φύσει) and eternal; [but] Christ again is not the true power of God, but He also is one of those who are called powers, one of which indeed, "the locust" and "the caterpillar," is called [in Scripture] not only the power, but the great power. [And] many others also are like the Son, concerning whom David also sang, saying "Lord of the powers" (Ps. 24:10). And just as everything else, thus the Word too is changeable by nature, and He remains good by His proper free will, while He wishes. Therefore when He wishes, He too is able to change, just as we are also, being of changeable nature. For because of this, he (Arius) says, God who foreknew that He would be good, gave in advance to Him this glory, which He would have afterwards from virtue. Thus from His works, which God foreknew, He made Him such as He would come to be.
>
> He (Arius) has dared to say again that the Word is not true God. Although indeed He is called God, He is not true [God], but by participation of grace, [and] thus He, just as also all others, is called God only by name. And since everything is foreign (ξένων) and unlike (ἀνομοίων) to God according to essence (κατ' οὐσίαν), thus also

> the Word is alien and unlike (ἀνόμοιος) in everything to the essence and distinctive quality of the Father, [but] He is proper to generated and created things and is one of them. Afterwards, just as a successor to the recklessness of the devil, he (Arius) has laid down in the *Thalia* that therefore even to the Son the Father is unintelligible (ἄῤῥητος), and the Word is able to neither see perfectly nor know precisely His own Father. But indeed what He knows and He sees, He knows and He sees according to His own measure, just as also we know according to our own power. For the Son, too, he (Arius) says, not only does not precisely know the Father, for He is wanting in comprehension, but also the Son Himself does not know His own essence. And [Arius says] that the essences (οὐσίαι) of the Father and of the Son and of the Holy Spirit are separate by nature and estranged and divided and alien and do not participate in each other; and so he asserts that they are unlike (ἀνόμοιοι) altogether from each other by [their] essences and by glory into infinity. Thus as to likeness (ὁμοιότητα) of glory and essence, he says that the Word is entirely foreign from both the Father and the Holy Spirit. For in such words has the impious one spoken; and he has said that the Son is distinct according to Himself and without participation according to anything of the Father. (*Oratio contra Arianos* I 5-6; Gwynn 2007: 180–1)

Athanasius constructed the "Arian"/"Eusebian" theology as a speculation, which he then targeted in his polemical works. He ignored some substantial theological differences within the assumed "Arian"/"Eusebian" group, including divergency between Arius and Eusebius of Nicomedia (see Gwynn 2007: 169). The only surviving full text by the latter, his letter to Paulinus of Tyre, demonstrates this divergency. In this letter, Eusebius appears to be more agnostic about the origins of the Son and less categorical about his difference from the Father than what Athanasius ascribed to the "Arians":

> We have never heard that there are two unbegotten beings, nor that one has been divided into two, nor have we learned or believed that the unbegotten has ever undergone any change of a corporeal nature. On the contrary, we affirm that the unbegotten is one. One also is that which exists in truth by him, yet was not made out of his substance, and does not at all participate in the nature or substance of the unbegotten, entirely distinct in nature and in power, and made after perfect likeness both of character and power to the maker. We believe that the mode of His beginning not only cannot be expressed by words but even in thought, and is incomprehensible not only to man, but also to all beings superior to man.
>
> These opinions we advance not as having derived them from our own imagination, but as having deduced them from Scripture, whence we learn that the Son was created, established, and begotten with respect to his essence and his unchanging, inexpressible nature, in the likeness of the one for whom he has been made. <. . .>
>
> If the Son had been from him or of him, as a portion of him, or by an emanation of his substance, it could not be said that the Son was created or established. <. . .> For that which is from the unbegotten could not be said to have been created or founded, either by him or by another, since it is unbegotten from the beginning.

> But if the fact of his being called "the begotten" gives any ground for the belief that, having come into being of the Father's substance, he also has from the Father likeness of nature, we reply that it is not of the Son alone that the Scriptures have spoken as begotten, but that they also thus speak of those who are entirely dissimilar to God by nature. <. . .>
>
> There is, indeed, nothing which shares his substance, yet every thing which exists has been called into being by his will. For there is God on the one hand, and then there are the things towards (πρός) his likeness which will be similar to the Word, and these things which have come into being by [his] free will. (Quoted in Theodoret, *Historia ecclesiastica* I 6; modified translation by GLT from NPNF2)

If there was a "Eusebian" group, then the bishop of Caesarea in Palestine Eusebius would have more rights to be regarded as its member than many other assumed "Eusebians." He shared with his Nicomedian namesake not only the subordinalist outlook at the Son and reservations about the Nicaea but also unreserved conformism with the imperial policies. Out of such conformism, Eusebius of Caesarea signed the Nicaean decisions, even though he disagreed with their theological language. He explained to his flock in Palestine that he had accepted the Nicaea to comply with the emperor's will (Sozomen, *Historia ecclesiastica* I 21). After the council, Eusebius did not go against this will, but tried to influence it. In coordination with Eusebius of Nicomedia, he convinced the emperor that, for the sake of the Roman piece (*Pax Romana*), it is better to follow the middle way between theological extremities. From his perspective, both Athanasius and the Nicaea represented one of such extremities.

The other extremity was modalism. Eusebius believed that both the modalist and Athanasian theologies, each in its own way, failed to express the Christian monotheism. Only subordinalism, for him, could sustain the one God's transcendence to everything and everyone. Eusebius argued that the Christian God is separated from all other "inferior systems" by an unsurmountable chasm:

> But inspired instruction says that the highest of good things, who is himself the course of all things, is beyond all understanding. Wherefore he surely is inexpressible, unspeakable, and nameless, greater not only than all language, but even then all conception, not to be confined in a place nor existing a body, not in the heavens or the sky, or in any part of the universe, but everywhere and beyond everything, set apart in an ineffable depth of knowledge. The divine account teachers to recognize this one alone as truly God, separated from all bodily existence, different from all inferior systems. (*De laudibus Constantini* XII 1; Robertson 2007: 39)

If God is one, then the Son, according to Eusebius, cannot be identical with God. The Son comes from the will of the Father and is his image. He is also a "bond" (*desmos*/δεσμός) between the Father and the world (*Demonstratio evangelica* IV 2; *De laudibus Constantini* XII 7), standing between the Father and the created world. In this capacity of a mediator between them (Robertson 2007: 37), the Son is identical neither with the Father nor with the world. Eusebius located the Son's position in the hierarchy of existence by such formulas as "the perfect creature of the perfect one" (τὸ τέλειον τελείου δημιούργημα) and "the wise edifice of the wise one" (σοφοῦ σοφὸν ἀρχιτεκτόνημα) (*Demonstratio evangelica* IV 2).

The Son is not *the* God in the unconditional sense. He is God conditionally, owing to his bondage with the Father. The Word "is declared to be God of God by his communion with the Unbegotten that begot him, both the first and the greater" (*Demonstratio evangelica* IV 15; Robertson 2007: 52). Eusebius borrowed such differentiation between the Father and the Son from Origen, who had spoken about the Father as *the* God, and the Son as God without definite article "ho" (ὁ). Eusebius also borrowed from Origen the idea of hierarchy in the Trinity. In the hierarchical order of God, the Son is below the Father:

> Father precedes the Son, and has preceded him in existence, and as much as he alone is unoriginate. The One, perfect in himself and first in order as Father, and the cause of the Son's existence, receives nothing towards the completeness of his Godhead from the Son: the Other, as a Son begotten of him that caused his being, came second to him, whose Son he is, receiving from the Father both his being, and the character of his being. (*Demonstratio evangelica* IV 3; Robertson 2007: 49)

In a similar way, the Holy Spirit is inferior to both the Father and the Son:

> The Savior himself said all these things about himself would be tremendous and irremediable stupidity. For through these [statements] the Savior himself clearly taught that the Holy Spirit exists as another besides himself, outstanding in honor and glory and privileges, greater and higher than any [other] intellectual and rational being (for which reason he has also been received into the holy and thrice-blessed Trinity). Yet he is surely subordinate to [the Son]. (*De ecclesiastica theologia* III 5.16-18; Eusebius of Caesarea 2017: 311)

In the imagined "Eusebian" party, the greatest theological mind was Asterius the Cappadocian, also know as Sophist. He was not a hierarch and could not be one. He had apostatized during the persecutions. Although he was admitted back to the church, according to the rules of that time he could not become a clergyman. Nevertheless, he flourished as a lay theologian and preacher. His theological treatise *Syntagmation* (Συνταγμάτιον) has not survived. We have only its fragments, quoted mostly by Athanasius. According to these fragments, Asterius professed only the Father to be unbegotten and without beginning. Although the Son is not coeternal with the Father, the Father always had the Son as preexisted knowledge (in Athanasius, *De synodis Arimini in Italia et Seleuciae in Isauria* 19). Asterius admitted only the Father as the true God, while the Son is his creature (ποίημα):

> For the blessed Paul did not say that he proclaimed Christ (1 Cor. 1:23) his proper power or his wisdom, that is, the God's, but rather, without the qualification [of the article], "power of God and God's wisdom" (1 Cor. 1:24), proclaiming that there is another power which is proper to the God himself, which is innate to him and co-exists with him in an unbegotten way, able to beget, clearly, Christ and able to create the whole world. On this subject he taught in the epistle to the Romans, saying: "From the creation of the world his invisible things, namely, his eternal power and divinity, have been clearly perceived, understood by the things that have been made" (Rom. 1:20). For just as no one would say that the divinity mentioned here is Christ, but rather it is the Father, so too I think "his eternal power" (Rom. 1:20) is not the "only-begotten God" (Jn 1:18), but rather it is the Father who begot him. And he teaches that there is another power and wisdom of God which is manifest through Christ clearly and recognized through the very works of his service (Heb. 1:14). <. . .>
>
> And yet, "his eternal power" (Rom. 1:20) and wisdom, which the thoughts of the truth declare to be beginningless and unbegotten, must surely be one and the same. But there are many which are individually created by him, of which Christ is the "firstborn" (Col. 1:15) and "only-begotten" (Jn 1:18). All alike, however, depend on their possessor, and all the powers are rightly said to be of the one who created and uses them. For example, the prophet says that "the locust," which became a punishment sent for human sins, is designated by the God himself not only a "power" of God, but also "great" (Joel 2:25). And moreover the blessed David in most of the psalms urges not only "angels," but also "powers," to praise the God (Ps. 102:20–1). And indeed encouraging "all" [of them] to the hymn [of praise], he describes their great number and does not refuse to call them "ministers of God" and teaches them "to do his will" (Ps. 102:21). (*De synodis Arimini in Italia et Seleuciae in Isauria* 18; DelCogliano 2015: 633–4)

This excerpt can be seen as a bottom line of otherwise diverse theologies, which Athanasius branded as "Arian" and "Eusebian." We can hardly comprehend this diversity, because only fragments of the "Arian"/"Eusebian" texts have survived. There were some other figures who shared the same subordinalist outlook on the relationship between the Father and the Son. They also had the same reservations about the council of Nicaea. Theognis of Nicaea, Narcissus of Neronias, Patrophilus of Scythopolis, Maris of Chalcedon, George and Theodotus of Laodicea, Paulinus of Tyre, Athanasius of Anazarbus, Flacillus of Antioch, Ursacius of Singidunum, Valens of Mursa, et al. were among them.

## Christological Implications

As was mentioned earlier, the dilemma of oneness and plurality in God relates to the dilemma of oneness and plurality in Jesus Christ. Both dilemmas were addressed by the supporters and adversaries of the Nicaean council. One can observe tendencies in their approaches to these dilemmas. For example, those theologians who tended to see an ontological disparity between the Father and the Son also tended to diminish Jesus' humanity (see Haugaard 1960: 251). According to Epiphanius, "Arians, <. . .> who say that the Son of God is a creature and that the Holy Spirit is the creature of a creature," simultaneously maintain "that the Savior took only flesh from Mary and not a soul" (*Panarion* 69; Epiphanius 2013: 215).

There are also some firsthand witnesses about the Christological minimalism of the "Arians." Eusebius of Caesarea, for instance, condemned Paul the Samosatean on the grounds that "he asserted a human soul" in Christ (*De ecclesiastica theologia* I 20). This accusation implies that Eusebius did not assert a human soul in Christ. A prominent hierarch of the later generation, who followed the line of Eusebius, the archbishop of Constantinople Eudoxius, affirmed that Jesus lacked human *psyché*. We have an explicit written testimony from him about Jesus,

> who was made flesh, but not man (σαρκωθέντα, οὐκ ἐνανθρωπήσαντα). For He did not take a human soul, but became flesh so that God have dealings with us men through flesh as through a veil <. . .> not a complete man, but God in place of a soul in flesh. (In Haugaard 1960: 253)

Eusebius' soteriological framework, in which he studied the incarnation, was different from the Nicaean one as well. Thus, in contrast to Athanasius, who explained the incarnation by the necessity to redeem sin, Eusebius, in his *Demontratio Evangelica*, did not mention the Fall or sin at all. He did not render Christ's mission in the terms of universal salvation, that is, as aiming at saving the common human nature. For him, this mission was rather pietistic and didactic. Unlike Athanasius, who spoke about Christ as second Adam, Eusebius preferred to compare him with Moses, who taught Jews to worship one God.

Christological opinions within the Nicaean camp were not completely coherent—they varied from minimalist to maximalist. Some Nicaeans, including Athanasius, preferred to call Christ's humanity "flesh" (σάρξ). They utilized the Christological language of the council of Antioch (325), which had condemned both Arius and Eusebius of Caesarea and depicted Christ in minimalist strokes, with his activities being reduced to sufferings and death:

> This Son, God the Word, having been born in flesh from Mary the Mother of God and made incarnate, having suffered and died, rose again from the dead and was taken up into heaven, and sits on the right hand of the Majesty most high, and is coming to judge the living and the dead. (In Stevenson & Frend 2013: 380)

On the other side of the Nicaean spectrum, there were theologians like Marcellus of Ancyra, who presented Christ in maximalist terms—as an autonomous human being united with the Logos.

Eventually, the Nicaean Christological minimalism and maximalism converged in the *Tome to the Antiochians*, which was composed by Athanasius and authorized by the council of Alexandria in 361. It equated the terms of "incarnation" (*sarkosis*/σάρκωσις) and "inhumanation" (*enanthropesis*/ἐνανθρώπησις) (*Tomus ad Antiochenos*; PG 26, 805).

## Political Implications

Since at least the beginning of the twentieth century, it has been noted that the theological interpretations of God in the fourth century could be translated to political doctrines (see Peterson 1935). Indeed, some theological takes on the Trinity might have served as legitimizing or delegitimizing mechanisms for the authorities of the converted empire. They substituted the traditional pagan mechanisms of legitimization, such as apotheosis of emperors. After the imperial office, following the conversion of the pagan state to monotheism, was reinterpreted as reflecting the power of one God, the doctrine of God became the cornerstone of the early Christian political theologies.

The council of Nicaea promoted the equality of the three persons in the Trinity. At that moment, this idea was endorsed by Emperor Constantine. That period coincided with the transition from shared to absolute monarchy. The model of shared authority had been established by Emperor Diocletian in the form of tetrarchy. After the death of his father Constantius, Constantine was admitted to the tetrarchy as its minor stakeholder. Although all tetrarchs shared "the same essence of imperial rule" (Van Dam 2021: 27), in reality they were not equal. Constantine had to struggle to ascend to the same level with other emperors. This might be the optics, through which he looked at the discussions in Nicaea in 325. The Trinitarian model promoted by this council, corresponded to the tetrarchic model of power that Constantine had known before he became the sole ruler of the empire in 324.

After the council of Nicaea, Constantine got gradually used to his role of the sole ruler. He appointed his sons as his corulers but kept them under strict control. Probably his increasingly absolutist take on imperial power was one of the reasons why Eusebius of Nicomedia and his confederates succeeded to make him inclined to the hierarchical model of the Trinity, with the Father being on the top of the divine pyramid of power. This model better corresponds to how Constantine envisaged his own power. Of course, we do not have testimonies that Constantine thought this way. This is a speculation, but a plausible one.

Most Constantine's successors during the fourth century, especially his son Constantius II, upheld a strictly monarchical model of political power. Simultaneously and probably not coincidentally, they supported non- and anti-Nicaean groups in the church. The fourth-century Christian emperors seemed to be interested in the hierarchical disparity between the Father and the Son to the same extent as they procured a distance between themselves and their corulers. The monarchy of the Father underpinned their own political models.

Both political and theological models, as well as imperial policies regarding the Nicaea, changed under Theodosius I (in office 379–95). He demonstrated more eagerness to share power than his predecessors. In the spirit of egalitarianism, he decided to divide the empire into two parts: western and eastern. He also gathered a council that confirmed the Nicaea (in 381) and its egalitarian triadology. At the same time, having lost the source of legitimacy for the imperial power in the monarchical triadology, Theodosius had to find another source. He found such a source in upholding the orthodoxy of faith, even if this faith projected anti-hierarchical models of power. The imperial political theology, thus, could embrace the Nicaean egalitarianism as orthodox, without weakening the legitimizing power of theology.

## Problematic *Ousia*

The majority of those, whom Athanasius described as "Arians," constituted a theological mainstream during the decades that followed the Nicaea. We do not know whether all of them were subordinalists. It seems, however, that they all were concerned about the theological language, which the council of Nicaea had chosen to express its theology. They believed this language was neither biblical nor traditional. They particularly hesitated about the term "essence" (οὐσία) and objected that the Son is "from the substance" (ἐκ τῆς οὐσίας) of the Father and consubstantial (ὁμοούσιος) with him.

The non-Nicaeans had several reasons to question the term *ousia* and its derivatives. It sounded to them as one of those logical categories that by the time of the council had become fashionable among pagan philosophers. Middle and neo-Platonists widely applied the word *ousia* in their own polytheistic theology. Therefore, for most traditionalist bishops, the Nicaean formulas "from the substance" or "consubstantial" had a too-modernist, too-intellectualist, and too-pagan demeanor. Some of them knew that Plotinus, Porphyry, and Iamblichus had utilized *homoousios* to describe the mode, in which human soul is related to the One. For some, derivatives from the word *ousia* featured materialistic and carnal connotations—they encouraged popular paganism. Some might have perceived references to *ousia* as compromising the personal character of God.

To understand the latter point, we need to go forward to the twentieth century. Many modern Orthodox theologians claim that a characteristic feature of Eastern Christianity, in contrast to Western Christianity, has been the superiority of hypostasis over nature, or, in other words, of the personal over the essential. Such assumptions are anachronistic, with modern personalism projecting its own ideas to the patristic era. Nevertheless, such a projection makes sense in one point: proto-personalistic attitudes have some affinity with the views of Arius and some non-Nicaeans. The latter objected to the Nicaea because they believed it had overstressed "essentialism" in God. To avoid such essentialism, they insisted that the Father begets the Son through his will. Will, for them, has to do with personality and not with essence, which is always subject to necessity.

We may only assume that such personalistic concerns underpinned the non-Nicaean standpoint. We can be sure, however, that the term *homoousios* is completely incompatible with the subordinalistic idea shared by many non-Nicaeans. Athanasius was right when he pinpointed subordinalism as a common denominator between moderate and radical non-Nicaeans. They agreed that God consists of three realities with a significant ontological distance between them. These realities, if they are real, cannot constitute one *ousia*. They cannot be equal but are structured hierarchically. Only one of them, the Father, could be regarded *the* God. Other realities, of the Son and the Spirit, are not the God, but images of the Father. Having agreed on this bottom line, different anti- and non-Nicaean groups could disagree on naming those three realities, measuring the ontological distance between them, and defining in which way and sense the Son and the Spirit are God.

## Post-Nicaean "Ecclesiastical Civil War"

The council of Nicaea was designed to bring peace to the church—as any ecumenical council would intend to do. Instead, similarly to some posterior ecumenical councils, the first ecumenical council triggered new divisions. The aftermath of the Nicaea was described as an "ecclesiastical civil war" (Williams 2001: 75). An important aspect of this war was the "battle of councils"—*synodomachia*.

As we have mentioned, *synodomachia* began before 325. The council of Nicaea was supposed to lull it, but instead made it more intense. The councils that followed the Nicaea, in most cases, tried to revise it. As early as in 328, a council gathered in Nicomedia attempted at substituting the Nicaean creed with a new one that promoted subordinalism in God (according to Philostorgius, *Historia ecclesiastica* II 7). The pendulum of support from both political and ecclesial establishments swung away from the Nicaea.

### Seeking for New Nicaea and Creed

For half of the fourth century, both establishments remained convinced that neither the Nicaea nor the doctrine it contested could secure peace. Even Constantine, who considered the Nicaea a highlight of his ecclesial policies, eventually became lukewarm to it. During his lifetime, this council continued to be respected pro forma, but its theology was not.

After Constantine died, even the pro forma support was withdrawn. Political and ecclesial establishments began vigorously searching for a *via media* between what they believed to be the extremities of "Nicaeanism" and "Arianism." The pattern of searching was nevertheless Nicaean: by convening an ecumenical council, which would adopt a binding creed. This creed, however, had to be different from the Nicaean. Following this pattern, Constantine's successor Constantius II summoned in 341 a council—with the idea that it would be substitutive for the Nicaea. The occasion for this gathering was the dedication of the Golden basilica in Antioch.

The council of Antioch in 341 promulgated four definitions of faith. The second one, called the "Dedication creed," became particularly important and had a lasting effect on the post-Nicaean controversies. This creed was designed as a middle way between the Arian and Nicaean faith. On the one hand, it affirmed that the Son

> was begotten before the ages from the Father, God from God, whole from whole, sole from sole, perfect from perfect, King from King, Lord from Lord, living Word (cf. Jn 1:4; 1 Jn 1:1), living Wisdom, true Light (cf. Jn 1:9; 1 Jn 2:8), Way, Truth, Resurrection, Shepherd, Door, both unalterable and unchangeable. (In Kinzig 2017, vol. 1: 343–4)

This series of epithets, applicable to the Son and derivative from the Father, is Nicaean. Not Nicaean in the Antiochian creed is the absence of the term *homoousios*. Instead of it, the creed refers to the "precise image" (ἀπαράλλακτον εἰκόνα) of the Father's "divine *ousia*."

Soon after the council of Antioch adjourned its sessions, a fourth version of its creed was adopted. This time, it did not mention the term *ousia* or any of its derivatives whatsoever, even in application to the Father. It contained a rather minimalistic and emphatically monotheistic statement, which was supposed to be upheld across the empire:

> We have learnt from the beginning to believe in one God, the God of the universe, both the Demiurge and Governor of all things, both those intelligible and those perceptible;
>
> and in one only-begotten Son of God, subsisting before all ages and coexisting with the Father who begot him, "through whom" also "all things" both visible and invisible "came into being" (Jn 1:3; 1 Cor. 8:6; Col. 1:16); who "in the last days" (Heb. 1:2) according to the Father's good pleasure descended and assumed flesh from the Virgin; and having fully accomplished all his Father's will, he suffered, was raised, ascended into the heavens, sits at the right hand of the Father, will come again "to judge the living and the dead" (2 Tim. 4:1; 1 Pet. 4:5), and remains King and God forever.
>
> And we also believe in the Holy Spirit.

If it is necessary to add this, we also believe about the resurrection of the flesh, and eternal life. (In Athanasius, *De synodis Arimini in Italia et Seleuciae in Isauria* XXII 3-7; Kinzig 2017, vol. 1: 345)

The Westerners, however, did not buy into this Eastern minimalism. They wanted their counterparts in the East to be clearer about the relationship between the Son and the Father and more appreciating the Nicaea. They were also upset about how the East treated Athanasius, whom they regarded the champion of the Nicaean legacy.

A growing alienation between the two parts of the church urged Constans and Constantius—the Western and Eastern rulers correspondingly—to resolve it by a joint council. They decided to have it in the city of Serdica. Now the capital of Bulgaria Sofia, at that time it was a meeting point between the two parts of the empire. The council was supposed to calibrate the universal creed to make it acceptable across the empire.

The Western bishops wanted to add to the council's agenda discussions about Athanasius and other deposed Eastern Nicaeans. The Eastern bishops considered this to be an interference in their business and left Serdica. They gathered in the city nearby, Philippopolis, where they confirmed their charges against Athanasius and his confederates. The Western bishops did the opposite and declared the disgraced Nicaeans to be orthodox. The council of Serdica, which was planned to be reconciliatory and ecumenical, only deepened divisions in the church.

Constantius II planned to use Serdica to promote in the West the abbreviated (fourth) version of the Antiochian creed from 341. He did not give up on this agenda after the Serdica failed. Two years later, he convened another council in Antioch, with the purpose to unpack the laconic fourth edition of the Antiochian creed. The "unpacked" creed was called *Macrostichon*, literally meaning "long lines." This text epitomized the non-Nicaean mainstream of the 340s. It characteristically lacked references to the category of *ousia* and its derivatives:

Those who say that the Son is from nothing, or is from another hypostasis and is not from God, and that "there was a time or age when he was not," the catholic and holy Church regards as alien.

Likewise those who say that there are three Gods, or that Christ is not God, or that before the ages neither the Christ nor the Son of God existed, or that Father, Son, and Holy Spirit are the same, or that the Son is unbegotten, or that the Father did not beget the Son by choice or will, the holy and catholic Church anathematizes.

For neither is it safe to say that the Son is from nothing (since this is nowhere spoken of him in the divinely inspired Scriptures), nor indeed from any other hypostasis pre-existing alongside the Father, but we declare him to be genuinely begotten from God alone. For the divine Word teaches that what is unbegotten and unbegun is one, the Father of Christ.

But neither may one consider there to have been any interval of time prior to him, dubiously claiming from non-scriptural texts, "There was once when he was not," but rather [one should say that] God alone has timelessly begotten him; for both times and ages came to be through him.

Nor must we deem the Son to be co-unbegun and co-unbegotten with the Father, for no one can be properly called Father or Son of a co-unbegun and co-unbegotten being. But we acknowledge both that the Father, who alone is unbegun and unbegotten, begot [the Son] in a manner inconceivable and incomprehensible to all, and that the Son has been begotten before ages, and thus he is not himself unbegotten like the Father, but has a beginning in the Father who begot him, for "God is the head of Christ" (1 Cor. 11:3).

Nor again, in confessing three realities and three persons of the Father, the Son, and the Holy Spirit according to the Scriptures, do we therefore make three gods, since we acknowledge the self-sufficient and unbegotten, unbegun and invisible God to be only one, the God and Father of the only-begotten, who alone both has being from himself, and alone bestows [being] bountifully upon all others.

Nor again, in saying that the Father of our Lord Jesus Christ is the one and only God, the only ungenerate [one], do we therefore deny that Christ also is God before ages, as do the followers of Paul of Samosata, who say that only later, after the incarnation, he progressed to be made God, because in nature he had come into being as a mere man. For we acknowledge that even though he was subjected to God the Father, nonetheless, having been begotten from God before the ages, he is perfect and true God according to nature, and not [begotten] from man and after these things [becoming] God, but becoming man from God for our sake and never having been deprived of being God.

The *Macrostichon* creed continues with a remarkable theology of the Logos. It states that the Word of God is different from any other word available to human experience, be it verbal or nonverbal. It is a "hypostatic word," meaning that it is real and yet distinct from the Father. This statement is especially intriguing, provided that the creed rejects the idea of the Logos coming from the hypostasis of the Father:

We <. . .> regard him not as simply God's spoken or mental Word, but as the living God Word, existing in himself, and Son of God, and Christ, both existing and abiding with his Father before ages (not in foreknowledge [only]), and serving him in all things for the framing of things both visible or invisible; rather, he is the enhypostatic Word (ἐνυπόστατον λόγον) of the Father, and God from God.

In the end, the *Macrostichon* creed states that the Logos is begotten through the will of the Father and subordinate to him. It, thus, accentuates the hierarchical relationship between the Father and the Son:

Likewise those who irreverently say that the Son has been begotten not by choice nor will (thus encompassing God with a necessity which excludes choice and purpose such that he begot the Son unwillingly) we consider most-irreligious and alien to the Church, in that they have dared to define such things concerning God, beyond the common notions concerning him, what is more, also beyond the intention of the divinely inspired Scripture. For we, knowing that God is absolute and his own Lord, have piously accepted that he begot the Son voluntarily and freely. <. . .>

Believing then in the all-perfect, most-Holy Triad, that is, in the Father, the Son, and the Holy Spirit, and saying both that the Father is God and that the Son is also God, yet we confess in them, not two Gods, but one dignity of godhead and one exact harmony of dominion. [We confess] both that the Father alone completely rules over all things and over his Son, and that the Son is subordinated to the Father. But, aside from [the Father], [the Son] rules after him (i.e., the Father) over all things which came into being through himself and bestows the grace of the Holy Spirit unsparingly upon the saints at will of the Father. For the sacred oracles have transmitted to us this account of the monarchy towards Christ. (In Athanasius, *De synodis Arimini in Italia et Seleuciae in Isauria* XXVI 1-9; Kinzig 2017, vol. 1: 362)

The *Macrostichon* creed, on the one hand, professed that the Father and the Son are inseparable from each other (οὐδὲ χωρίζομεν). In contrast to the earlier "Arianism," it rejects either chronological or ontological disparity between the Father and the Son. On the other hand, the Son exists in the alike way (*homíōs*, ὁμοίως) to the Father: "Yet, in saying that the Son exists in himself, [and] both lives and exists in a manner like the Father [does], we do not for that reason separate him from the Father."

## Constantius' Ecumenical Pattern

The adverb "in the alike way," *homíōs* (ὁμοίως), became a theological keyword during the 350s. This adverb contains a rudiment from the Nicaean term *homoousios*. By using this adverb, the non-Nicaeans minimally acknowledged the vocabulary of the Nicaea, on the one hand. On the other hand, by excluding the second part of the *homoousios*, they continued purging the undesired connotations that the word *ousia* had accumulated since 325. A new theological language based on the keyword *homoios* was embraced and promoted further by Emperor Constantius II.

After he defeated in 353 the Western "usurper" Magnentius, Constantius became the sole ruler of the East and the West. Now it was his direct responsibility to bridge these theologically divided parts of his empire. A new start was needed for peace-building process, which he had implemented since 341. As Sara Parvis put it, the emperor intended "to wipe the theological slate clean and begin again" (Parvis 2021: 252). For this purpose, he employed the new *homoian* language, which was different from the language of the previous decade. In contrast to the latter, it completely excluded the category of *ousia*. Constantius nevertheless continued applying the same reconciliatory pattern that he had implemented during the 340s. This pattern still works in the modern ecumenical movement and can be seen as Constantius' know-how.

As the pattern's first step, preliminary theological consultations harvest opinions from competing trends. On their basis, a relatively small and therefore manageable local gathering drafts an agreed statement. During the 340s, such local gathering was the council of Antioch in 341, which produced the Dedication creed. On its basis, a small drafting group composed its "fourth" version, which would be promoted as a typical ecumenical "consensus document." Finally, this "consensus document" is sent out for consideration and acceptance by large constituencies, which are not in full unity with one another. For this purpose, Constantius convened an "ecumenical" council in Serdica in 343. That council, as we have seen, did not work. For this reason a fresh ecumenical start was needed in the 350s.

## The Homoian Movement

As a new start, as was mentioned, Constantius decided to promote the *homoios*-based language as a potential platform for reconciliation. He first consulted theologians, such as Basil of Ancyra. Then a relatively small gathering, convened in 357 in Sirmium (now Sremska Mitrovica in Serbia), drafted on the basis of the *homoios* language a "consensus document"—similarly to what the council of Antioch had done in 341. This document explicitly banned any reference to the *ousia*-based terminology:

> Since some, or, rather, many persons are disturbed by questions concerning substance, what is called in Greek *ousia*, that is, to make it understood more exactly, *homoousion* (ὁμοούσιον) or what is called *homoiousion* (ὁμοιούσιον), there ought to be no mention [of this] at all; nor ought it be proclaimed for this reason and for this consideration, that it is not contained in the divine Scriptures, and because it is beyond men's knowledge and because no one can describe the Son's generation, as it is written, "Who can describe his generation" (Is. 53:8; cf. Acts 8:33)? For it is plain that only the Father knows how he begot his Son, and the Son how he has been begotten by the Father.

The document confirmed the hierarchical relationship of the Father and the Son, which had been a bottomline of both anti- and non-Nicaean trajectories since 325:

> There can be no question [for anyone] that the Father is greater [than the Son], for no one can doubt that the Father is greater in honour, dignity, glory, majesty, and in the very name of Father, as the Son himself testifies, "The Father that sent me is greater than I" (cf. Jn 5:37; 6:44; 7:28; 8:16,26; 12:49; 14:24,28).
>
> No one is ignorant that it is catholic doctrine that there are two persons of Father and Son, and that the Father is greater, and the Son has been subordinated to the Father together with all things which the Father has subordinated to him (cf. 1 Cor. 15:28). (In Hilary of Poitiers, *De synodis* 11; Kinzig 2017, vol. 1: 404–8)

The Sirmium "consensus document" became a basis for formal creeds, which were designed to substitute both the Nicaean and Dedication ones. Two years later, another council in Sirmium promulgated a definition, which became known as "Dated" (also known as the fourth creed of Sirmium). After having been confirmed by the imperial decree, it became the official confession of the *homoian* mainstream. In its Christological part, the "Dated" creed expressed belief

> in one only-begotten Son of God, before all ages, before all beginning, before all conceivable time, and before all comprehensible thought begotten from God without passion; by whom the ages were framed and all things came into being; who was begotten as the only-begotten, the only one from the only Father, God from God, similar to the Father who begot him according to the Scriptures; whose birth no one knows except only the Father who begot him.

In the end, the text offers an explanation why the word *ousia* was deliberately omitted. This word is not wrong per se but was often misunderstood. Besides, it is not biblical and traditional. In its stead, the similarity of the Son to the Father "in all things" (κατὰ πάντα) was suggested:

> As for the term "substance" (τὸ δὲ ὄνομα τῆς οὐσίας), which was used by our fathers for the sake of greater simplicity, but not being understood by the people has caused offence since the Scriptures do not contain it, it seemed desirable that it should be removed, and that henceforth no mention at all should be made of substance in reference to God, since the divine Scriptures have nowhere made mention of the substance of the Father and the Son. But we say that the Son is similar (ὅμοιον) to the Father in all things, as the holy Scriptures also affirm and teach. (In Kinzig 2017, vol. 1: 413–15)

To make the text even more comprehensive, its explanatory part was shortened and the phrase "in all things" (κατὰ πάντα) was removed. This edition of the *homoian* creed was voted for in the same year 359 at the council in Nikē, in Thrace (the city was chosen to sound like Nicaea). In this redaction, the "creed of Nikē" was adopted a year later by the council held in the imperial capital and thus became the "creed of Nikē-Constantinople."

The next step for Constantius and the bishops he relied upon was to make the *homoian* creed accepted by wider constituencies. For this purpose, the emperor convened two councils with the intended status of ecumenical. He undertook something similar to the botched "ecumenical" council of Serdica in 343. Now Constantius learned from his mistakes and made sure that the new "ecumenical" councils succeed.

In the East, such council met in September 359 in the Cilician Seleucia (modern Silifke in Turkey) and adopted the "Nikē-Constantinopolitan creed." It was harder to convince Western bishops to sign this *homoian* creed. They were summoned to the Italian coastal city of Ariminium (now Rimini) a few months prior to the council in

Seleucia. Their majority initially predictably rejected a new creed and demanded to restore the Nicaean creed. However, after negotiations, pressure, and deceptions, most of them yielded and accepted the new *homoian* creed. Some did this out of convictions and others as a compromise for the sake of peace. This was a triumph of Constantius' policies directed at the reconciliation of the church.

## Homoiousians

In contrast to modern ecumenical practices, Constantius' ecumenical methods were coercive. He forced all bishops in the West and the East to subscribe to the creed adopted at Ariminium and Seleucia. However, his coercive policies caused a strong pushback. Negative reactions to homoianism increased after Constantius' death in 361. A growing number of theologians, now not only in the West but also in the East, began considering coming back to the *ousia*-based terminology. They formed groups which became known as *homoiousians*—from the term *homoiousios* (ὁμοιούσιος), that is, "of similar essence." The bishop of Ancyra Basil became a protagonist of this group.

Basil based his theology on the idea that the Son is the image of the Father. He envisaged their relationship as less hierarchical than the *homoians* would like. Still, for Basil, the Father and the Son are two separate, and not simply distinguished, entities. From this perspective, he followed the general non-Nicaean line by giving more weight to the divine plurality than to God's oneness. As most of his contemporaries, he could not yet equalize them.

**Figure 4.15** Ariminium, modern Rimini in Italy.

Source: Photo by the author.

Basil managed his theology to be approved by a local council held in Ancyra in 358. The council proclaimed the "Son's likeness to the Father according to substance" (in Radde-Gallwitz: 145). In its definition, it stressed that "the concept of likeness does not lead the Son to sameness with the Father" (in Radde-Gallwitz 2017: 145–6). At the same time, the likeness in essence implies that the Son cannot be perceived as the creation by the Father:

> We believe, therefore, in the Father and the Son and the Holy Spirit, not in the Creator and Creature. For "creator and creature" is one thing, and "father and son" is another. <. . .> Being Father of his only-begotten Son he is not understood as creator but as a Father who has begotten. (In Radde-Gallwitz 2017: 138–9)

Most non-Nicaeans, similarly to Basil of Ancyra, saw the Son as a creator and not a creation. At the same time, Basil, like most other non-Nicaeans, admitted a distance between the Father and the Son. This distance mirrors the distance between the humanity of the Son and the rest of the humankind:

> Since it is obvious that what is like can never be the same as that which it is like, this is proof that by "coming to be in the likeness of human beings" the Son of God did indeed become a human, but he did not become the same as a human in all respects, and by coming to be "in the likeness of the flesh of sin" he came to be in the passions which are the causes of sin in the flesh, we mean, hunger, thirst, and the rest, but he did not come to be in the sameness of the flesh of sin. <. . .>
>
> By "coming to be in the likeness of human beings," he was both a human and not a human in every respect: human insofar as he did indeed assume human flesh (for "the Word became flesh"), but not human since he was not begotten like human beings (for he is not from insemination and copulation).
>
> Similarly, the Son who was before all ages is indeed God inasmuch as he is Son of God, just as he is human inasmuch as he is Son of Man, but he is not the same as the God and Father who begot him, just as he is not the same as a human being, inasmuch as he is without emission or passion, inasmuch as he is without insemination and [sexual] pleasure. (In Radde-Gallwitz 2017: 144–5)

That the mode of relations between the Trinitarian persons is mirrored in the mode of relations between the humanity of Christ and the rest of humankind was Basil's profound insight. However, this insight corroborated the interpretation of the incarnation that envisaged an estrangement between Jesus' humanity and ours. Such estrangement became the main theological concern during the next century.

## Heteroousians

The ecumenical undertakings of Constantius II, who tried to reunite the post-Nicaean church, was based on coercion and ambiguous euphemisms. The term *homoios* was the basic euphemism and the keyword of mainstream theology during the 360s. It worked for the majority of the non-Nicaeans, who did not have a clear understanding of how the Father and the Son are related to each other. It did not work, however, for those who did have such understanding, namely the strict Nicaeans and the strict anti-Nicaeans. Although the theological terminology promoted during the 340s–60s was designed to cover both groups, it concealed for these groups more than it intended to reveal about God.

A strictly anti-Nicaean theologian, named Aëtius, eventually became ultimately annoyed by the official theological euphemisms. He decided to cut it straight to the truth—as he perceived it. He saw his mission to do a no-nonsense theology—in the prophetic spirit of a revelation that he believed he had received from God. Aëtius was sure that he had cognized the essence of God and could adequately render this essence in theological terms. He was convinced that, because the essence of God is accessible to human mind and can be adequately expressed in language, theological terms should not be blurred by political correctness and euphemisms. Theology must express the divine in a straightforward way. Aëtius insisted that such terms as *homoousios*, *homoiousios*, and *homoios* do not adequately express what God is. The only term that reveals the relationship between the Father and the Son with pristine clarity was for him *anomoios* (ἀνόμοιος)—"unlike." This term had been around in the theological discourses since at least the 320s (see Vaggione 2000: 175). Aëtius made it a key word of his theological language.

For this reason, his opponents soon libeled him and his followers as "anomoians." Aëtius believed this libel did not express what he stood for, because, he stressed, he accepted the Son to be unlike the Father only according to the essence (κατ᾽οὐσίαν), but not in all regards. That is why scholars have suggested calling Aëtius' group "heteroousians" (see Ayres 2004: 13), that is, the ones who believe in different essences of the Father and the Son.

"Heteroousians" were radical anti-Nicaeans (see Williams 2001: 82). They insisted that the Father and the Son, while sharing many features, including being called God, differed from each other in a radical way, by having two heterogeneous essences. From this perspective, only the Father can be called God in the proper sense of the word: he is "the unbegotten God" (ὁ ἀγέννητος θεός) (Aëtius, *Syntagmation* 2; Wickham 1968: 540). The Son, in contrast to him, is the "begotten hypostasis" (γεννητὴ ὑπόστασις) (Aëtius, *Syntagmation* 36; Wickham 1968: 544). The Father and the Son thus, are two completely separate entities, in a strictly hierarchical relationship with one another:

> If the ingenerate (unbegotten, ἀγέννητος) Deity is superior (κρείττον) to all cause, he must for that reason be superior to origination (γένεσις); if he is superior to all cause clearly that includes origination, for he neither received existence from another nature nor conferred it on himself; if he did not confer existence on himself (not because of

> ineffectiveness of nature but by virtue of his complete transcendence of cause) how could anyone grant that the nature which is posited is indistinguishable in essence from the nature which posited it, when such a substance does not admit of origination?
>
> If the Deity remains everlastingly in ingenerate nature, and the offspring is everlastingly offspring, then the perverse doctrine of the "homoousion" and the "homoiousion" will be demolished; incomparability in essence is established when each nature abides unceasingly in the proper rank of its nature. (*Syntagmation* 2-4; Wickham 1968: 545)

By considering the Father and the Son as two separate entities and placing them in hierarchical order, Aëtius concurred with the earlier positions of Arius and the "Eusebians." At the same time, he did not consider himself an Arian, and rightly so. For both Arius and the "Eusebians," God is inaccessible for human knowledge. Aëtius held the opposite: God's essence is knowable thoroughly.

This idea was elaborated upon by Aëtius' secretary and disciple Eunomius, who was one generation younger. Less charismatic and more systematic than his mentor, Eunomius achieved a prominence that made the Aëtius' opponents to call his movement not "Aëtian," as it should be, but "Eunomian." This is probably because he established an independent ecclesial structure.

Eunomius furthered Aëtius' idea of God's cognoscibility and tied it tightly to one of God's names, which Aëtius had favored as well, namely "ingenerate" or "unbegotten" (ἀγέννητος). Eunomius and Aëtius believed that this one is unique among other divine names. It is not an invention of human mind (ἐπίνοια), but the quintessence of the objective truth (ἀλήθεια) about the divine existence:

> When we say "Unbegotten," then, we do not imagine that we ought to honour God only in name, in conformity with human invention; rather, in conformity with reality, we ought to repay him the debt which above all others is most due God: the acknowledgement that he is what he is. Expressions based on invention have their existence in name and utterance only, and by their nature are dissolved along with the sounds [which make them up]; but God, whether these sounds are silent, sounding, or have even come into existence, and before anything was created, both was and is unbegotten. (*Apologia* 8)

The divine name "unbegotten" applies to the Father's essence only, according to Eunomius. It is unlike other words which have been produced by human creativity and consequently dissolve in thin air immediately after they are uttered. Through this unique word, we access the divine essence and can intimately communicate with God. If this word were like other words, our very faith would have been a phantasy. Moreover, through the word "unbegotten," we can cognize God to the same extent that he knows himself. Socrates Scholasticus ascribed to Eunomius the following shocking statement:

> God does not know anything more about his own essence than we do, nor is that essence better known to him and less to us; rather, whatever we ourselves know about it is exactly what he knows, and, conversely, that which he knows is what you will find without change in us. (*Fr*. 2)

This statement went against the mainstream philosophical and theological tenets, both pagan and Christian. It was more radical than even Plato's theory of language in *Cratylus* (see DelCogliano 2010: 62). In this dialogue, Plato seemingly aligned with the position of Cratylus, who had claimed that names reflect the nature of things, though *imperfectly* (see *Cratylus* 383a4–b2). In contrast to Cratylus, Eunomius insisted that the name "unbegotten" *perfectly* reflects God's nature.

At the same time, Eunomius' statement cohered with a more general Platonic idea that there is a homogeneity between the world of ideas and our perception of them. Through the *logoi*, we can access the unseen and partake in it. Christian Revelation gave all human beings indiscriminately the fullness of knowledge of God. Having been squared with the Christian idea about the absolute Revelation of God, the Platonic idea that language partially expresses the nature of things led Eunomius to the conclusion: what the pagans could conceive about God only partially, Christians can access in fullness. The fullness of the Christian participation in the divine implies, therefore, the fullness of knowledge of God—because, as the Platonists had held it, knowledge is participation.

There are some unavoidable deficiencies in Eunomius' epistemology. To identify them, one may follow the distinction between the categories of commonality and particularity. According to this distinction, knowledge of God can be either common or particular. The former one is given in all possible fullness to the entire humankind through Jesus Christ. The latter one is appropriated individually by each Christian, to limited measures. The word "Unbegotten," in its Eunomian interpretation, effectively translates the common knowledge of God to a particular knowledge obtained by everyone according to each one's individual capacity. Although Eunomius stressed that this is the knowledge *of* God, and not *about* him, he confused the common knowledge of God with the particular knowledge and made the translation of the former to the latter automatic. This automatism is secured by the magic word "unbegotten."

Eunomius treated the divine names as portals, and not windows, to the divine. His opponents insisted that the names are only signposts showing a way toward God. Gregory of Nyssa, for example, called names "guides" (ὁδηγίαι; *Ad Ablabium quod non sint tres dei* 43) and "semantic indications of what is happening" (αἱ σημαντικαὶ τῶν γινομένων προσηγορίαι) (*Contra Eunomium* II 269). They do not bring an individual in immediate touch with the divine reality, but rather show a way to this reality. Also, instead of *what* is God, they reveal *how* (ὅπως ἐστιν) he is (*Contra Eunomium* I 15). Eunomius confused the essence and activities of God regarding the process of cognizing God. This is a paradox, given how much innovation he applied to distinguish between the essence and activity (ἐνέργεια) in other regards. Indeed, Eunomius envisaged (and rightly so) a complete correspondence between them, in the way which would have been appreciated by the later generations of the Orthodox theologians. Yet, he did not make use of this helpful distinction in his epistemology and insisted that human beings cognize the essence, but not the activity of God. This mistake was indicated by Basil of Caesarea, who stressed that we could cognize God through his activities, but not in his essence:

> We know the greatness of God, and his power, and his wisdom <. . .>, not his very substance. <. . .> The concept of God (ἔννοια) is gathered by us from the many attributes which we have enumerated. <. . .> We say that from his activities (ἐνέργειαι) we know our God, but his substance itself we do not profess to approach. For his activities descend to us, but his substance remains inaccessible. <. . .> Knowledge of his divine substance is, then, knowledge of his incomprehensibility (ἀκατάληψις). (*Ep.* 234; Ayres 2004: 195–6)

As Basil has indicated, such divine names as "unbegotten" apply not to the essence of God, but to his personality. In other words, they express God's particular properties. Basil drew a parallel between this divine name and human names:

> [Eunomius] thinks that "the difference in substance is made clear by the distinctions in names." But what sane person would agree with the logic that there must be a difference of substances for those things whose names are distinct? For the designations of Peter and Paul and of all people in general are different, but there is a single substance for all of them. For this reason, in most respects we are the same as one another, but it is only due to the distinguishing marks considered in connection with each one of us that we are different, each from the other. Hence the designations do not signify the substances, but rather the distinctive features that characterize the individual. (*Contra Eunomium* II 3.29-4.9; DelCogliano 2010: 191)

In contrast to the "unbegotten" Father, the Son, for Eunomius, is "begotten." This word is the Son's unique and essential signifier. As in the case with the name "unbegotten," the name "begotten" is not an invention of human mind (ἐπίνοια), but an objective truth revealing the essence of the Son:

> We do not understand his essence to be one thing and the meaning of the word which designates it to be something else. Rather, we take it that his substance is the very same as that which is signified by his name, granted that the designation applies properly to the essence. We assert, therefore, that this essence was begotten—not having been in existence prior to its own coming to be—and that it exists, having been begotten before all things by the will of its God and Father. (*Apologia* 12)

Because the two divine names, "unbegotten" and "begotten," are antonyms, they imply two completely different essences. This was the crucial point, in which Eunomius' epistemology and ontology converged:

> If <. . .> "the Unbegotten" is based neither on invention nor on privation, and is not applied to a part of him only (for he is without parts), and does not exist within him as something separate (for he is simple and uncompounded), and is not something different alongside him (for he is one and only he is unbegotten), then "the Unbegotten" must be unbegotten essence.
>
> But if God is unbegotten in the sense shown by the foregoing demonstration, he could never undergo a generation which involved the sharing of his own distinctive nature with the offspring of that generation, and could never admit of any comparison or association with the thing begotten. (*Apologia* 8-9)

That the essences of the "unbegotten" and the "begotten" are different does not mean that they are different in every regard. Eunomius stressed that, in contrast to what his enemies ascribed to him, he did not believe that the Father and the Son are completely unlike (*anomoioi*). There are many things that they share, including other names, such as "light," "life," "power," and so on. Yet, even though these names are nouns and their grammatical status therefore is higher than adjectives', they do not indicate the difference between the Father and the Son, whose difference is indicated by the adjective "unbegotten":

> But perhaps someone who has been goaded by all this into responding will say, "Even granting the necessity of paying attention to the names and of being brought by them to the meanings of the underlying realities, still, by the same token that we say that the unbegotten is different from the begotten, we also say that 'light' and 'light,' 'life' and 'life,' 'power' and 'power' are alike with respect to both." Our reply is not to substitute the rod for an answer in the manner of the admirer of Diogenes (for the philosophy of the Cynics is far removed from Christianity), but rather to emulate the blessed Paul who said that we must correct our opponents with great patience. Our response, then, to such a person is to say that the one "light" is unbegotten and the other begotten. (*Apologia* 19)

The same difference that exists between the "unbegotten" and "begotten" essences applies to the difference between the "Begotten" and the "Comforter" (Παράκλητος), which looks like a specific name of the Holy Spirit. The essence of the Spirit is inferior to the essences of both the Father and the Son:

> He is third in both dignity and order, we believe that he is third in nature as well, for the dignities of the natures have not been bestowed on each in turn the way political office is among human beings, nor is the order of their creation the reverse of that of their essences. Rather, the order of each conforms harmoniously to its nature, so that

the first in order is not second in nature and the first in nature is certainly not allotted second or third place in the order.

Now if this order is in fact the best as regards the creation of the intelligible beings, and the Holy Spirit is third in the order, he cannot be first in nature since that "first" is "the God and Father" (for sure it would be both ridiculous and silly for the very same thing to occupy first place at one time and third at another, and for both the one worshipped and the one "in whom" he is worshipped to be identical, that is, in accordance with the Lord's own statement, "God is spirit, and those who worship him must worship in spirit and truth"), nor is he identical with the Only-begotten (otherwise he would not have been numbered after him as possessing his own substance, since the Saviour's own voice is sufficient proof of these things, when he expressly says that the one who would be sent to bring to the Apostles' remembrance all that he had said and to teach them would be "another"), nor is he something numerically other than God but nevertheless unbegotten (for the Unbegotten "from whom all things" came to be is "one and only"), nor yet is he some other distinct from the Son but nonetheless an "offspring" (for our Lord, "through whom are all things," as says the Apostle, is "one" and "only-begotten"), rather, he is third both in nature and in order since he was brought into existence at the command of the Father by the action of the Son. He is honoured in third place as the first and greatest work of all, the only such "thing made" of the Only-begotten, lacking indeed godhead and the power of creation, but filled with the power of sanctification and instruction. (*Apologia* 25)

# IV.9
# Cappadocian Synthesis

## Thesis, Antithesis, and Synthesis

For most of the fourth century, theologians struggled to strike a right balance between the thesis of God's oneness and the antithesis of the divine plurality. Based on these thesis and antithesis, they tried to produce a synthesis of God's unity. The dialectical process of reaching such synthesis started as early as in the 260s, with the discussions propelled by modalism and adoptionism. This process continued for about a century, with a milestone of the council of Nicaea in 325. In the 360s, the so-called neo-Nicaean theologians succeeded in producing a synthesis that would become a common platform for the accepted *theologia*.

During this century-long process, most theologians, with only a few exceptions, emphasized either oneness or plurality in God, without reaching an equilibrium between them. Eustathius of Antioch and Marcellus of Ancyra, for instance, were focused on safeguarding the oneness of God. Their formula of divine unity presupposed more oneness and less plurality in God. For this reason, they preferred to speak about one "hypostasis" of God, in the sense of singular reality. On the other side of the theological spectrum, the proponents of the extreme heteroousian theology Aëtius and Eunomius stressed plurality in God, at the expense of unity.

There were several attempts to reach a synthesis between the two extremes. *Homoian* language, for example, was designed to articulate such syntheses. However, this language did not last long as an accepted theological *lingua franca*. It failed to find the right balance between oneness and plurality in God (see Lenski 2002). It stressed plurality more than oneness and thus made the divine unity too loose. A problem of this synthetic language was the hesitation to embrace the category of *ousia* and its derivatives, such as *homoousios*. Athanasius of Alexandria insisted that this category was crucial, but almost no one listened to him. Theologians were afraid to rely on a nonbiblical category borrowed from pagan wisdom. For this reason, they hesitated to accept the council of Nicaea, which made the term *homoousios* a keystone of its theology. This was a conservative fear to embrace new ideas and to think out of the box.

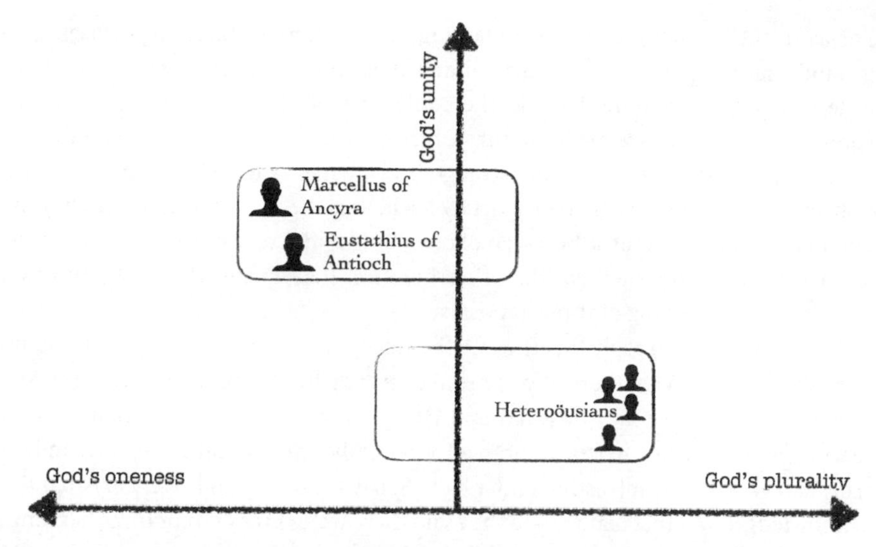


**Figure 4.16** Finding equilibrium between God's oneness and plurality.

Only when Christian theologians admitted the applicability of the logical categories to the divine, they felt a solid ground under their feet in approaching the dilemma between oneness and plurality in God. As a result, during the 360s, attitudes to the category of *ousia* and to the council of Nicaea began shifting to more appreciating. Even some convinced non-Nicaeans started wondering if coming back to the Nicaea could be a way out of the painful theological experiments that had failed. That is how a new theological consensus commenced growing based on the Nicaea. Modern scholarship has branded this consensus as neo-Nicaean. This was a synthesis, and not a repetition of the original Nicaean thesis. It acknowledged some anti-Nicaean sensitivities and reinterpreted the Nicaean terminology in a new logical framework.

# Council of Alexandria 362

Athanasius, who remained an adamant guardian of both the letter and the spirit of the Nicaea, initiated a process of its rethinking. In 362, he convened a council in Alexandria, which came up with new theological ideas and formulas. The council promulgated a document, which was sent to the church of Antioch as a gesture of reconciliation. It has been called the *Antiochian Tome*. In modern terms, this text can be regarded as ecumenical and convergent, as it tried to bridge the gap between two different theological languages. Indeed, through this text, Athanasius tried to reach out to the Antiochians, who were traditionally cautious regarding the Nicaea. He thus responded to the high demand for ecumenical rapprochement, which marked the era of Constantius II. Among other things, the *Antiochian Tome* stated:

> For as to those whom some were blaming for speaking of three hypostases, on the ground that the phrase is unscriptural and therefore suspicious, we thought it right indeed to require nothing beyond the confession of Nicaea, but on account of the (present) contention we made inquiry of them, whether they meant, like the Arian madmen, subsistences foreign and strange, and alien in essence from one another, and that each hypostasis was divided apart by itself, as is the case with creatures in general and in particular with those begotten of men, or like different substances, such as gold, silver, or brass;—or whether, like other heretics, they meant three beginnings and three gods, by speaking of three hypostases.
>
> They assured us in reply that they neither meant this nor had ever held it. But upon our asking them "What then do you mean by it, or why do you use such expressions?," they replied, Because they believed in a Holy Trinity, not a trinity in name only, but existing and subsisting in truth, "both a Father truly existing and subsisting, and a Son truly substantial and subsisting and a Holy Spirit subsisting and really existing do we acknowledge," and that neither had they said there were three gods or three beginnings, nor would they at all tolerate such as said or held so, but that they acknowledge a Holy Trinity but One Godhead, and one beginning, and that the Son is coessential with the Father, as the Fathers said; while the Holy Spirit is not a creature, nor external, but proper to and inseparable from the essence (οὐσία) of the Father and the Son.
>
> Having accepted then these men's interpretation and defence of their language, we made inquiry of those blamed by these for speaking of one hypostasis, whether they use the expression in the sense of Sabellius, to the negation of the Son and the Holy Spirit, or as though the Son were non-substantial or the Holy Spirit impersonal. But they in their turn assured us that they neither meant this nor had ever held it, but, "We use the word hypostasis thinking it the same thing to say hypostasis or Essence (οὐσία)"; "But we hold that there is One, because the Son is of the Essence of the Father, and because of the identity of nature. For we believe that there is one Godhead, and that it has one nature, and not that there is one nature of the Father, from which that of the Son and of the Holy Spirit are distinct." Well, thereupon they who had been blamed for saying there were three Subsistences (ὑποστάσεις) agreed with the others, while those who had spoken of one Essence, also confessed the doctrine of the former as interpreted by them. And by both sides Arius was anathematized as an adversary of Christ, and Sabellius and Paul of Samosata, as impious men, and Valentinus and Basileides as aliens from the truth, and Manichaeus as an inventor of mischief. And all, by God's grace, and after the above explanations, agree together that the faith confessed by the Fathers at Nicaea is better than such phrases, and that for the future they would prefer to be content to use its language. (In Stevenson & Frend 2012: 95–6)

In contrast to the *homoian* councils from the 350s, the Alexandrian council was not afraid of employing both terms *hypostasis* and *ousia*. It suggested they should be used simultaneously regarding different levels of the divine existence: *ousia*—in relation to oneness and commonality, and hypostasis—to plurality and particularity.

## Commonality and Particularity

This idea was a key to the neo-Nicaean synthesis. In this synthesis, the category of God's oneness related to the category of commonality, and the idea of divine plurality—to the category of particularity. By employing the categories of commonality and particularity, theologians did not have anymore to choose between oneness and plurality in God but could equate them—as far as these categories apply to different levels of the divine existence. These levels do not exclude but supplement each other, in the same way as commonality and particularity in principle cannot exist without each other.

Before the Nicaean controversy, theologians did not pay much attention to the differentiation between commonality and particularity, which, as we saw earlier, had been crucial in the Peripatetic, Stoic, and neo-Platonic logics. The Nicaean controversy urged Christian thinkers to employ these and other philosophical categories. They constituted a framework of the neo-Nicaean synthesis. This synthesis cannot be properly understood without them.

## Separation and Distinction

The Aristotelian-Porphyrian logical framework provided a framework to solve another fourth-century's issue, about the unity of God. As was mentioned, the category of unity harmonizes oneness and plurality. There can be more and less unity. Applying the difference between distinction and separation helped Christian theologians to figure out the right proportions of God's unity.

All beings feature commonality and particularity as distinguished, and not separated, from each other. In a similar way, the oneness/commonality and plurality/particularity in God are only distinguished from one another. The divine particularities (hypostases), which constitute God's plurality, are also only distinguishable, but not separable from each other. Therefore, an ontological disparity between the Unbegotten and the Begotten does not exist. Athanasius struggled to prove this idea by advocating for the Nicaean term *homoousios*. He did not, however, succeed much in convincing the majority of the bishops to accept the theological language of the Nicaea.

## Cappadocian Innovations

The council of Alexandria 362 and Athanasius who stood behind it only hinted at a solution based on the distinction between commonality and particularities in God.

A full and well-elaborated synthesis based on this distinction was offered by the Cappadocian theologians. They interpreted the Nicaea in a creative way, by placing its theology in the neo-Platonic logical framework. Conservative theologians often criticized them for that. Basil, for instance, complained that he and his confederates were called by their traditionalist opponents "innovators, revolutionaries, and wordsmiths" (*De spiritu sancto* VI 3; Basil of Caesarea 2011: 39). As a matter of fact, they were innovators and revolutionaries in theology.

Theirs was a logical revolution. As was mentioned, they distinguished between the common and particular aspects of the divine being, and denoted the former as *ousia*, while the latter, as hypostases. In the traditional Greek dialectics, these two terms were synonymous. The Cappadocians, by employing two synonyms, stressed that the commonality and particularities in God are distinguished and not separated from each other. One of the earliest clear distinctions between *ousia* and hypostasis in application to God can be found in Basil's letter to Amphilochius of Iconium:

> Now *ousia* and hypostasis have the same difference that the common has with the particular, as, for example, the animal has with such-and-such human being. Therefore, in the case of the divinity we confess, on the one hand, one hypostasis, so that the formula of its being is not defined in diverse ways, but, on the other hand, a distinct hypostasis, so that we may have an unconfused and clear notion about the Father, Son, and Holy Spirit. For when we fail to grasp the characteristics that have been defined for each, for example, fatherhood, sonship, and holiness, and instead confess God on the basis of the common notion of being, it is impossible to give the account of the faith in a sound way. So then, that which is distinct must be added to the common; one must confess the faith in this way. What is common is the divinity; what is distinctive is fatherhood. Joining these together, one must say: "I believe in God the Father." And again in the confession of the Son one must do the same thing: join what is distinctive together with the common and say: "[I believe] in God the Son." And likewise in the case of the Holy Spirit, one must form the utterance according to the logic of the expression and say: "I believe also in the divine Holy Spirit." In this way, then, the unity is completely preserved by the confession of the one divinity and what is distinct to the persons is confessed by the definition of the distinguishing marks that are considered in connection with each of them. Those who claim that *ousia* and hypostasis are the same are compelled merely to confess different persons (πρόσωπα), and by avoiding any mention of three hypostases they are found not to have escaped the evil of Sabellius, who on the basis of an utterly confused notion attempted to differentiate the persons by saying that the same hypostasis changed its form to meet the need arising on each occasion. (*Ep.* 236 6; modified transl. by Mark DelCogliano in Radde-Gallwitz 2017: 232)

Solutions offered by Basil and other Cappadocians raised some new questions. One of them was: If God is three equal persons, does this not imply that there is still an ontological distance between them? Such a distance is preserved, for example, when three human beings stand next to each other. These humans, being three hypostases, share the same nature. Why then the Trinity, who is three hypostases sharing one essence, is not three gods, just as three human persons are separate beings? The Cappadocian solution, thus, implied a challenge to Christian monotheism. One of the Cappadocians, Gregory of Nyssa, addressed this challenge in a treatise sent to Bishop Ablabius.

The argument of Gregory goes as following. Indeed, all human beings constitute not multiple but one common nature—similarly to the divine persons who share in the same essence of one God. There is, however, a difference between human nature and the common essence of God. A key to understanding the difference between them is, for Gregory, the category of activity (ἐνέργεια), which he also borrowed from the nomenclature of the Aristotelian logics. Each human individual has his or her own activity, while the activity of God is one. This activity stems from the essence and not from the persons. Nevertheless, because the persons and essence are only distinguishable and not separable, the hypostases of the Trinity participate in the single activity of God—each in his own way. As Giulio Maspero nicely put it, the single activity of the triune God follows the pattern "from-through-in" (ἐκ-διά-ἐν (Maspero 2007: xvi)): from the Father, through the Son, and in the Holy Spirit. That is how Gregory described this pattern:

> Regarding the divine nature, we have not learned that the Father accomplishes something by himself, in which the Son does not participate, or that the Son in his turn operates something without the Spirit. But every activity (ἐνέργεια), which from God is propagated to creation and is called according to the various conceptions, has origin from (ἐκ) the Father, continues (πρόεισι) by means of (διά) the Son and is accomplished in (ἐν) the Holy Spirit. For this reason the name of activity is not divided in the multiplicity of those who act, since the care of something is not exclusive to each one in particular. But all that is realized, regarding either our providence or the economy and order of the universe, is realized in a certain manner by the Three, but they are not in fact three the things that are realized. (*Ad Ablabium quod non sint tres dei* 48.13-14; Maspero 2007: 53)

Gregory of Nazianzus, in addition to the single activity, which he called "the identical movement" (ταὐτότης κινήσεως), listed among the factors of the unity of God's essence the coherence of will, the same honor of the nature, and the convergence of the divine persons with their source—the Father:

> Monotheism, with its single governing principle, is what we value—not monotheism defined as the sovereignty of a single person (after all, self-discordant unity can become a plurality) but the single rule produced by equality of nature (φύσεως ὁμοτιμία), harmony of will, identity of action (ταὐτότης κινήσεως), and the convergence towards their source of what springs from unity <. . .> though there is

> numerical distinction, there is no division in the being. For this reason, a one eternally changes to two and stops at three—meaning the Father, the Son and the Holy Spirit. In a serene and non-temporal, incorporeal way, the Father is parent of the "off-spring" and originator of the "emanation" <. . .> [but] we ought never to introduce the notion of involuntary generation. (*Or*. 29.2; Ayres 2004: 245)

In the framework of polemics with the heteroousians, the Cappadocians insisted that the divine names, such as "unbegotten" and "begotten," apply to the hypostases, and not the essence of God. This, however, did not answer the question, to what extent do the names reveal the nature of what they signify? In the case of the Cappadocian theology, this question could be articulated as follows: to what extent do the divine names reveal the persons of the Trinity? Gregory of Nazianzus suggested that the names reveal not the persons as such, but their relations to each other:

> "Father" is a name neither of substance nor of activity, but of relationship, of the manner of being (σχέσεώς δὲ καὶ τοῦ πῶς ἔχει), which holds good between Father and Son. Just as with us these names indicate kindred and affinity, so here too they designate the sameness of stock, of parent and offspring. (*Or*. 29.16; Ayres 2004: 247)
>
> In what particular, then, it may be asked, does the Spirit fall short of being Son? If there were not something missing, he would be Son. We say there is no deficiency—God lacks nothing. It is their difference in, so to say, "manifestation" or mutual relationship, which has caused the difference in names. (*Or*. 31.9; Ayres 2004: 247)

Each personal name, thus, implies a process expressed by a verb: to beget, to be begotten, to proceed. The Father is Father because he gives birth to the Son. The Son is Son, because he is born from the Father. And the Holy Spirit proceeds from the Father. The processes of "birth" and "procession" are metaphors that underline the uniqueness of each person through their relationship to each other.

One and half century later, Leontius of Byzantium described the persons of the Trinity as three pairs of relations. Each person has a relationship with two others. These relationships are six in sum:

> We perceive six relationships (σχέσεων), the two of the Father to the Logos and the Logos to the Father, the two of the Logos to the flesh and the flesh to the Logos, and the two of Christ to us and us to him, there are three universal pairs.
>
> And the first relationship of pairs is the same as that which is third from the first, next after the middle pair; for as the end pairs are linked within themselves, so they are opposed to the middle pair. And the opposite is true of the middle one: for as it differs within itself, so it is linked with the end pairs, and as it is linked within itself, so it differs from the end pairs. (*Contra Nestorianos et Eutychianos* 4; Daley 2017: 146–9)

# Father's Monarchy

There was another difficulty in the neo-Nicaean theology, which had not been a difficulty for the non-Nicaean theologians. For the latter, the Father is the cause of the Son and therefore is naturally superior to him. The neo-Nicaeans, who insisted on the total equality of the divine persons, had to accommodate this equality with causality. In other words, if the Father is the cause of the Son and the Holy Spirit, how they can be equal? The neo-Nicaean answer to this question was that in God, unlike in human experience, causality does not imply hierarchy. Although the Father is the cause of the Son and the Holy Spirit, he is equal with them. This is the only acceptable idea of monarchy, which could be applied to the Trinity from the neo-Nicaean perspective.

Gregory of Nazianzus addressed this paradox by explaining that there are three basic ideas about God: anarchy, polyarchy, and monarchy. The former two are pagan and cannot be accepted by the Christians. For the Christians, only monarchy is acceptable. However, this monarchy is not singular and personal, but natural and shared. It is a result of the full coherence of the divine persons who share one will and activity:

> We most respect monarchy. However, this is not a monarchy, which is defined by one person, <. . .> but the [monarchy], which is set together (συνίστησι) by the single honor of the nature, coherence of knowledge, identical movement, and the convergence towards one of those who are from [this one]. (*Or*. 29.2; translation is mine)

Gregory applied to the divine monarchy the verb *synistesi* (συνίστησι). Because of the prefix *syn*-, it implies a composed and not a singular character of the divine monarchy. As composed, this monarchy should be based on unity. Unity, as we have discussed earlier, is not identical with the oneness of God. Unity brings together God's oneness and plurality. The Father, for Gregory, is not only the source of diversity in the Trinity, by being the cause of the Son and of the Holy Spirit, but also the guarantor of the unity of God, that is, of the perfect convergence between the oneness and plurality:

> The three have one nature—God. The principle of unity (ἕνωσις) is the Father, from whom the other two are brought forward and to whom they are brought back, not so as to coalesce (συναλείφεσθαι), but so as to cleave together (ἔηεαθαι). (*Or*. 42.15; Ayres 2004: 246)

The divine monarchy, which Gregory advocated for, is, thus, nonhierarchical. Gregory rejected any gradation in relations between divine persons. For him, it is impossible to say that there is a great Spirit, a greater Son, and the greatest Father (μεγάλου καὶ μείζονος καὶ μεγίστου). Any hierarchical perception of the Trinity, which he called a "ladder," would not be "leading up to heaven, but bringing one down from heaven" (*Ep*. 101.67; translation is mine).

# The Holy Spirit

In the hierarchical models of God promoted by Origen, Arius, Eusebii, and even more Aëtius and Eunomius, the Holy Spirit had the lowest status. Such belief became associated with the name of the archbishop of Constantinople Macedonius (in office 342–6, 351–360), even though it had been articulated long before him. Even the council of Nicaea had not contested the perception of the Spirit's status as inferior to the Father and the Son. The Nicaean *horos* was lapidarian in this regard, stating only the belief "in the Holy Spirit," without specifying his relationship to the Father and the Son.

Only during the 360s, neo-Nicaean theologians became more explicit in supporting the idea of the equality of the Holy Spirit to the Father and the Son. Such egalitarian pneumatology became a characteristic feature of neo-Nicaean theology. Among the earliest voices articulating it, was Didymus the Blind's. He originated from Alexandria and tried to reconcile Origen's Trinitarian theology with the Nicaea. In particular, he advocated for the full divine honor that the Holy Spirit shares with the Father and the Son:

> Next, so that no one separates the Holy Spirit from the will and fellowship of the Father and the Son, it is written: "For he will not speak on his own accord, but he will speak as he hears" (Jn 16:13). The Savior said something similar to this about himself: "As I hear, so I judge" (Jn 5:30). And elsewhere: "The Son is not able to do anything on his own accord, but only what he sees the Father doing" (Jn 5:19). For if the Son of the Father is one, not according to the error of Sabellius who confuses the Father and the Son, but according to their inseparability of essence or substance, then he is unable to do anything without the Father. The works of separate individuals are distinct, but when the Son sees the Father working, he is himself also working, yet working not in a second rank and after him. After all, the works of the Son would begin to diverge from those of the Father if they were not performed by equals. (*De spiritu sancto* 160–1; Plaxco 2016: 214)

Didymus' pneumatology became inspirational for Basil of Caesarea, who dedicated to the Holy Spirit a significant part of his books against Eunomius and a special treatise *On the Holy Spirit*. Basil argued that the Holy Spirit is the same God as the Father and the Son. They are equal even from the perspective of the divine monarchy. Basil insisted that there is no order in the Trinity. Otherwise, the persons would have been counted as first, second, and third. Such "sub-numeration," as Basil called it, would lead to admitting three separate gods:

> For those who insist on saying that there is a sub-numeration into first, second, and third, let them know that they have introduced the polytheism of the errant Greeks into the undefiled theology of the Christians. For the evil of sub-numeration leads to nothing other than a confession of a first, second, and third God. (*De spiritu sancto* 18.47; Basil of Caesarea 2011: 83)

Instead of being numbered as third, the Holy Spirit, in Basil's interpretation, is "one"—in the same way as the Father and the Son are "one":

> One is the Holy Spirit, and he is proclaimed singly. He is joined through the one Son to the one Father, and through himself, he completes the famed and blessed Trinity. That he is not ranked in the multitude of creation but rather, uniquely named makes clear enough his kinship with the Father and the Son. For he is not one among many; rather he is one. As the Father is one, and the Son is one, so also the Holy Spirit is one. Therefore, the Holy Spirit is as far from created nature, as—it is reasonable to say—a monad is from the composites that have plurality. He is made one with the Father and the Son in the way that a monad has kinship with a monad. (*De spiritu sancto* 18.45; Basil of Caesarea 2011: 81)

In the spirit of logical *differentiae*, Gregory of Nyssa specified hypostatic characteristics pertinent to the Holy Spirit:

> The Holy Spirit, who in the uncreated nature is in communion (κοινωνίαν) with the Father and the Son, is nevertheless distinguished in his turn by his proper characteristics. To not be that which is contemplated properly in the Father and the Son is his most proper characteristic and sign: his distinctive property in relation to the preceding does not consist in being in an unengendered mode (ἀγεννήτως), nor in an only engendered mode (μονογενῶς), but to be in the mode of constituting a whole (εἶναι δὲ ὅλως). He is conjoined to the Father by the fact of being uncreated, but is distinguished in his turn by the fact of not being Father as he is. United to the Son by the uncreated nature and by the fact of receiving the cause of existence from the God of the universe, he is distinct from him in his turn by the peculiarity of not subsisting hypostatically (ὑποστῆναι) as the Only Begotten of the Father and by the fact of being manifested by the Son himself (δι᾽αὐτοῦ τοῦ υἱοῦ πεφηνέναι). But further, since creation subsists by means of the Only Begotten (διὰ τοῦ μονογενοῦς), so that one does not think that the Spirit has something in common with it due to the fact that he is manifested by the Son, he is distinguished from creation since he is invariable, immutable and without need of any external good. (*Contra Eunomium* 108.7-109.5; Maspero 2007: 177)

Gregory was inspired by a fourth-century spiritual writer from Mesopotamia whose name was Macarius or Symeon and who is referred to as Pseudo-Macarius (see Plested 2004). In the time when this idea was not widely held yet, he stated that the Holy Spirit is uncreated (Ps.-Macarius I 50.1.7-8; Berthold 1973). Because the Holy

Spirit is God, he can sanctify human beings. For Ps.-Macarius, seeking sanctification through the Spirit constitutes the main driving force of spiritual life.

# Council of Constantinople 381

Emperor Theodosius I seized the momentum of the neo-Nicaean movement as potentially consolidating for the church and the state. To enhance this momentum, he convened in 381 in Constantinople a council. This council did not have the ambition to be equal to other "ecumenical" councils, such as Nicaea or even Serdica and Ariminium/Seleucia. In contrast to the earlier post-Nicaean councils, which undertook to compose a new creed, Constantinople 381 concentrated on interpreting the existent creed of Nicaea.

This interpretation accommodated many (but not all) sensitivities of the groups that had disagreed with the Nicaea. For example, it dropped the original Nicaean "from the essence (ἐκ τῆς οὐσίας) of the Father" and anathemas. At the same time, it kept the keyword "consubstantial," which was quintessential for the belief in the equality and inseparability of the divine persons—the key notions in the neo-Nicaean theology.

More importantly, Constantinople 381 reframed the Nicaean creed based on the Aristotelian-Porphyrian logics. The oneness and plurality of God were rearticulated in the categories of commonality and particularity. In this frame, the Nicaean condemnation of those believing that "the Son of God is from another hypostasis" had to be eliminated. Otherwise, it contradicted the neo-Nicaean definition of hypostasis.

The council also added the anti-Marcellan formula, "and his kingdom will have no end." It unpacked the Nicaean lapidarian "and in the Holy Spirit." The Constantinopolitan article on the Spirit reflected the "high pneumatology" as it had been developed by the theologians like Didymus the Blind and Basil of Caesarea. Although it did not say explicitly that the Holy Spirit is consubstantial with the Father and the Son—something that the high neo-Nicaean pneumatology had stated—it apparently meant it.

Rather surprisingly, the definition of faith adopted at the council in Constantinople did not circulate widely. The only contemporary official reference to this creed was the letter promulgated by the council in Constantinople in 382. It explained the rationale of the council, which would become known as the second ecumenical:

> [Nicaea] is the faith of our baptism; it is the faith that teaches us to believe in the name of the Father, of the Son and of the Holy Spirit. According to this faith there is one

> Godhead (θεότης), Power (δύναμις), and Substance (οὐσία) of the Father and of the Son and of the Holy Spirit; the dignity being equal, and the majesty being equal in three perfect hypostases, i.e. three perfect persons (πρόσωπα). Thus there is no room for the heresy of Sabellius by the confusion of the hypostases, i.e. the destruction of the personal properties (ἰδιότητες); thus the blasphemy of the Eunomians, of the Arians, and of the Pneumatomachi is nullified, which divides the substance (οὐσία), the nature (φύσις), and the godhead (θεότης), and superimposes onto the uncreated consubstantial and coeternal Trinity a separate nature, created, and of a different substance. (In Theodoret, *Historia ecclesiastica* V 9; Ayres 2004: 258)

The creed adopted in Constantinople in 381 resurfaced only seventy years later, at the council of Chalcedon in 451. From this perspective, it can be called a Chalcedonian creed. In the Eastern tradition, however, it is a custom to call it "Nicaean," even though it is not identical with the original Nicaean creed. This is because the council in Constantinople made a point that it was not adopting a new creed but confirmed the old Nicaean one. This creed is also called Nicaean-Constantinopolitan.

The Chalcedonian version of the creed from 381 reads:

> We believe in one God, the Father Almighty, Maker of heaven and earth, of all things visible and invisible;
>
> and in one Lord Jesus Christ, the only-begotten Son of God, begotten from the Father before all ages. Light from Light, true God from true God, begotten, not made, consubstantial with the Father; through whom all things came into being; who because of us humans and because of our salvation descended from the heavens; became flesh from the Holy Spirit and the virgin Mary; became man; was crucified for us under Pontius Pilate, suffered, and was buried; on the third day rose again according to the Scriptures; ascended into the heavens; sits at the right hand of the Father; and will come again with glory to judge the living and the dead; of whose kingdom there will be no end;
>
> and in the Holy Spirit, the Lord and life-giver, who proceeds from the Father, who is jointly worshipped and glorified with the Father and the Son, who spoke through the prophets;
>
> in one, holy, catholic, and apostolic Church.
>
> We confess one baptism for the remission of sins.
>
> We look forward to the resurrection of the dead and the life of the world to come. Amen. (Council of Chalcedon, *actio* III 14; Kinzig 2017, vol. 1: 511–12)

The Nicaean controversy after the council of 381 became less intense but did not cease. Not all anti- and non-Nicaeans accepted its decisions, especially in the West. This was a tragic irony. During the earlier decades, when almost no one in the East was talking about the Nicaea, most Western bishops insisted on its validity. The situation

**Figure 4.17** The Mausoleum of Theodoric the Great, an "Arian" (rather *homoian*) ruler of the Ostrogothic Kingdom. Ravenna, Italy.
Source: Photo by the author.

changed after the council of Ariminium in 359. A significant number of the Western bishops accepted its *homoian* language and continued speaking this language even when the East abandoned it. *Homoian* theology remained popular among the Goths. After the "sack of Rome," it transformed to their proto-national identity, which helped them to differentiate themselves from the Romans (see Buchberger 2017).

# V

# Incarnation

# V.1

# Neo-Nicaean Christology

The focus of the pro-Nicaean theologians, of both older and younger generations, was on the divinity of the Logos. Some of them viewed Christ's humanity with their peripheral vision. Gradually, this humanity moved from the periphery to the center of the theological discussions among the neo-Nicaeans. This happened because some of them applied quite controversial strategies to corroborate their pro-Nicaea arguments. Christological controversies were triggered mostly by the arguments within the neo-Nicaean camp. Brothers-in-arms, who previously chased hand in hand all forms of hierarchism and subordinalism in the Trinity, now found themselves in the opposite trenches.

## Apollinaris of Laodicea

One of those who alienated himself from other neo-Nicaeans was Apollinaris of Laodicea. His family originated from Alexandria. This fact marked his theological style and language. He was born sometime between 310 and 315 and received a very good education. He emerged as a talented, original, and prolific author. It seems he had a touch of scribomania, which sometimes annoyed even his friends (see Basil, *ep.* 263.4). He demonstrated ambition not only in theology, but also in church politics. Quite a few disciples were attracted by him. He tried to transform their fellowship into a church movement. This movement ended up as a sect.

A council in Rome condemned Apollinaris in late 377 or early 378. This condemnation was confirmed by subsequent councils of Alexandria (377/378) and Antioch (379). In the winter of 383/384, and then in 388, the imperial office forbade the Apollinarian movement altogether. Its founder died soon, sometime before 392 (see Spoerl 1991: 53). The condemnation of Apollinaris meant that the huge corpus of his writings was not reproduced in copies and eventually vanished. Only one work has survived in full, "Particular Faith" (*Fides secundum partem*/Κατὰ μέρος πίστις), because it had been falsely ascribed to Gregory of Neocaesarea.

Apollinaris flourished theologically during the 360–70s. This was a period, when, on the one hand, the non-Nicaean movement became polarized by the heteroousian twist. On the other hand, some responses to this movement from the neo-Nicaean party proved to be ambiguous, like in the case of Apollinaris. He fought on two fronts: against Aëtius and Eunomius on the anti-Nicaean front, and against Marcellus of Ancyra and Eustathius of Antioch on the pro-Nicaean front. Apollinaris' style was polemical. He began his *Fides secundum partem* with a tirade of condemnations:

> Most hateful and alien to the apostolic confession are those who say that the Son is an addition to the Father, which arises from what does not exist and from a principle that is sent out, and who think the same about the Holy Spirit; those who say that the Son is deified and that the Holy Spirit is sanctified by a gift of grace; those who compare the name of the Son to that of slaves and "the first-born of the creation" (Col. 1:5), saying in this way that He likewise both exists out of what is not and was created first, and not confessing that the Father possesses a unique only-begotten Son, who has given Himself to be reckoned among mortals and in this sense is counted "first-born"; those who limit the begetting of the Son from the Father in a human way to a measured interval of time, and do not confess that the age of the Begetter and of the Begotten is without beginning; those who introduce three disparate and alien objects of worship, although there is only one legitimate object of our religion, which we possess, having received it from on high through the Law and the prophets, and which was confirmed by the Lord and proclaimed by the apostles. No less alien are those who do not confess the Trinity of three *prosopa* (πρόσωπα) in accordance with the truth, but who impiously imagine the three-fold reality in a monad resulting from synthesis and think that the Son exists as Wisdom in God just as human wisdom, through which humanity is wise, exists in a man, and represent Him as Word in a manner similar to a spoken or mental word and not a single, unique hypostasis. (Ch. 1; Spoerl 1991: 378–9)

Since the 340s, Apollinaris had been a *fidèle lieutenant* (Cavallera 1905: 5) of Athanasius of Alexandria and for some time enjoyed a reputation of a "staunch Nicene theologian" (Beeley 2011: 378). He belonged to the first generation of neo-Nicaeans, between the generations of Athanasius and Basil. Apollinaris defended the Nicaean language to its last syllabus, including, of course, the term *homoousios*. He defined this term as referring to "one Son, true God from true God, who possesses the Father's divinity by nature, that is to say, who is consubstantial with the Father" (*Fides secundum partem* 27; Spoerl 1991: 388). At the same time, Apollinaris sometimes projected subtle subordinalism (see Spoerl 1991: 355; Zachhuber 2014: 433) in such statements as the following: "Divinity is a characteristic of the Father" (*Fides secundum partem* 14–15; Spoerl 1991: 383) and "Let the ὑπόστασις of the Father be acknowledged by the title of 'God'" (*Fides secundum partem* 17; Spoerl 1991: 384). Although he criticized Origen, in these and other statements he sounded like an Origenist.

Following the Origenian train of thought, which had also Athanasius and most other pro-Nicaeans boarded on it, Apollinaris embraced what can be called "anthropological minimalism." It rendered Christ's humanity as "flesh" (σάρξ). This did not necessarily reduce the fullness of this humanity to "flesh," but certainly opened doors to such reductionism. Following this common Alexandrian trend, Apollinaris stressed that what united with divinity, was "flesh":

> He gave Himself to human flesh, which He took from Mary. <. . .> He was united to the flesh according to human likeness, so that the flesh was made one with the divinity, while the divinity took on the passibility of the flesh in fulfillment of the mystery. After the dissolution of death, a perpetual impassibility and unchanging immortality surrounded the holy flesh, for the original human beauty was assumed into the power of the divinity, and is provided to all in the fellowship of the faith. (*Fides secundum partem* 2; Spoerl 1991: 379)

Most theologians who participated in the Logos-related controversies during the fourth century had some opinions about Jesus' humanity. However, as was mentioned, these opinions remained on the margins of their main argument: that Logos is God. Apollinaris linked Christological opinions with this Trinitarian postulate. This was an innovative and ingenious move, which propelled Christology to the center of theological deliberations.

Apollinaris built on an assumption, commonly upheld by most pro-, non-, and anti-Nicaeans, that Christ's humanity is better to be called "flesh." He concluded from this assumption that Christ did not have the intellectual part of humanity, which the Greeks called *nous* and Christians *logos*. If there is an agreement on this point, Apollinaris suggested, then it can serve as an undeniable argument that the Logos is true God. Because only in such case Christ did not need human logos. In other words, if the divine Logos were a creature, then he would have coexisted in Christ with the human logos. But he is not a creature. Therefore, he had to substitute the human logos.

Apollinaris concluded that the human logos was absent in Christ and used this suggestion to prove that Christ's Logos was divine and consubstantial with the Father. The minimalistic language of "human flesh" in Christ perfectly corroborated this conclusion. Apollinaris had to make some additional clarifications. He suggested a formula of any human being as, roughly speaking, flesh (σάρξ) plus mind (νοῦς). Human *nous* was for him equivalent to logos. However, his understanding of *nous* was inconsistent—sometimes it included human *psyché* and sometimes not (see Spoerl 2021: 284). He called the full human nature "the incarnated mind" (ἄνθρωπος νοῦς ἔνσαρκος ὤν) (*Fr*. 69; Lietzmann 1970: 220). In the case of Christ, this means that he was not a complete human being, but "the divine spirit united to flesh" (*Anakephalaiosis* XVI 244.2-5; Spoerl 1991: 273).

Apollinaris built on the classical tradition of distinguishing three parts in human nature: body, mind, and soul. It went back to Plato's differentiation between the rational, irascible, and appetitive (λογιστικόν, θυμικόν, ἐπιθυμητικόν) faculties pertinent to all human beings, as well as the Aristotelian categories of what is vegetative, sense-perceptive, and rational. Such tripartite differentiation within human nature became accepted by Christian authors. Gregory of Nyssa, for instance, stated approximately in the time of Apollinaris: "Our vital faculty" features "three different varieties—one which receives nourishment without perception," that is, bodily capacities, "another which at once receives nourishment and is capable of perception, but is without the reasoning activity," which corresponds to psychic capacities, "and a third rational, perfect, and co-extensive with the whole faculty"—the reference to mind (*De opificio hominis* 14; Gregory of Nyssa 2016: 23). For Gregory of Nazianzus, "Our mind <. . .> is a complete thing, governing the soul and body" (*Ep.* 101; Gregory of Nazianzus 2002: 159–60). Therefore, "Godhead with only flesh, or even with only soul, or with both of them, is not man if lacking mind which is the even better part of man" (*Ep.* 101; Gregory of Nazianzus 2002: 159).

Apollinaris' argument might have been convincing for some non-Nicaeans to accept the idea of Christ's being homoousios with the Father according to divinity—we do not know about their reactions. But we know that by this argument he disappointed his neo-Nicaean confederates—their feedback was negative. His former confederates began thinking on counterarguments against Apollinaris. They entered the door that he had opened. A long period of controversies about Christ's humanity commenced.

Apollinaris' input to the Christological controversies was not only negative but also quite helpful, and sometimes even ingenious. He effectively designed a new Christological meta-dialect, which outlived him and was appreciated even by his opponents. In effect, some key Apollinarian terms and formulas have been appropriated to the Christological meta-*lingua franca*, which we still use in our days.

One of the keywords in this *lingua* is *prosopon* (πρόσωπον). The closest modern rendering for it is "person." However, because the modern meaning of person has many psychoanalytic and personalistic connotations, it should be used with caution. Apollinaris used the word *prosopon* to designate particular existence in the one God and in Jesus Christ (see Spoerl 1991: 353). Owing to Apollinaris, the term *prosopon* became popular in the traditional Trinitarian and Christological languages. With redefined semantics, it is still one of the most popular terms in modern Orthodox theology.

Another helpful category, on which Apollinaris elaborated, is *physis* (φύσις). It is related to *ousia* (οὐσία). Both terms correspond to the category of commonality. Johannes Zachhuber has argued that Apollinaris was the one who introduced the logical differentiation between commonality and particularity in the Eastern theology (see Zachhuber 2014: 428). Whether he was first or not, Apollinaris certainly applied this differentiation in a helpful way.

He implied a subtle difference between *physis* and *ousia*. *Ousia* is more abstract and static. It applies to any common essence, just as hypostasis applies to any particular being. *Physis*, in contrast to *ousia*, applies to a *dynamic* common essence, which is capable of moving on its own (αὐτοκίνητον). *Physis* is an active *ousia* (see Spoerl 1991: 290). In other words, it is *ousia* plus activity (ἐνέργεια). Activity-*energeia* is another notion that Apollinaris introduced to the Christological debates. It occupied a central place in these debates during the sixth and seventh centuries.

Apollinaris also coined a helpful formula of Jesus' double consubstantiality. According to this formula, Christ is consubstantial with the Father through his divinity and with us through his humanity. This was a rhetorical trope to support the Nicaean term "consubstantial" (ὁμοούσιος). As we demonstrated earlier, the neo-Nicaean party, of which Apollinaris was a prominent member, put this term on its banners against the anti- and non-Nicaean alliances. Following his hypothesis that Christology underpins Trinitarian theology, Apollinaris enhanced the idea of the Son being consubstantial with the Father by the idea of the Son being consubstantial with humankind. He in particular wrote:

> Thus [Christ] is both *homoousios* with God according to the invisible spirit (even the flesh being included in the title because it has been united to him who is *homoousios* with God), and again *homoousios* with human beings (even the godhead being included with the body because it has been united to what is *homoousion* with us). The nature of the body is not altered by its union with him who is *homoousios* with God and by its fellowship with the title of "*homoousios*," just as the nature of the godhead has not been changed by its fellowship with the human body and by bearing the designation of the flesh that is *homoousios* with us. (*De unione* VIII 188; Spoerl 2021. 293)

The Apollinarian idea that both divinity and humanity in Christ remained unchangeable after the incarnation became another basic axiom of the posterior orthodox Christology. Cyril of Alexandria adopted this idea from Apollinaris, together with the language of the double consubstantiality of Christ. Cyril concurred with Apollinaris in promoting the intrinsic unity of Jesus Christ.

Apollinaris was passionate about this unity and cared to articulate it in the most comprehensive and convincing ways. To stress Christ's unity, Apollinaris utilized the Irenaean catchphrase: "one and the same" (εἷς καὶ ὁ αὐτός) (see *Fragmenta in Joannem* (in catenis) 38). For him, both "what is corporeal" and "what is divine" apply to the "whole" Christ. Jesus' "distinctive characteristics" (τὰ ἴδια) do not compromise his "unity" (ἕνωσις) (*De unione* 17; Beeley 2011: 382). This train of thought is similar to the one of Ignatius, Melito, and Irenaeus. However, in contrast to the latter, it misses an active and intellectual human element, which resides in the human *nous*. Apollinaris' rendition of Irenaeus' Christological scheme would be as in the figure 5.1.

Apollinaris regarded Christ as an alive unity (ἑνότης ζωτική) (*Fr.* 144; Lietzmann 1970: 242). It is dynamic, not static, and full of life and movement. This life and

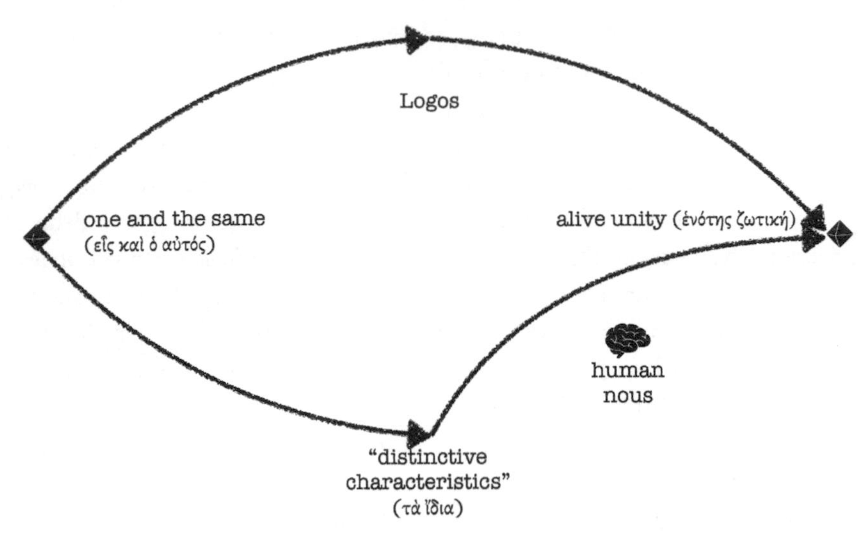


**Figure 5.1** Christ's singularity according to Apollinaris.

movement, however, had divine provenance. Christ's humanity itself, for Apollinaris, remained passive. Therefore, it cannot be called "nature," because the term "nature" is reserved only for active essences. Only in intrinsic unity and combination, Jesus' divinity and humanity can be regarded as one "nature." Apollinaris explicitly stated that Christ is "one nature, one hypostasis, one activity (ἐνέργεια), one *prosopon*, the whole God, and the same is whole human being (ὅλος ἄνθρωπος ὁ αὐτός)" (*De fide et incarnatione* 6; Lietzmann 1970: 199). The bishop of Laodicea, thus, can be credited for inventing the "miaphysite" one-nature Christological meta-language.

Apollinaris stressed Christ's unity in polemics with another neo-Nicaean, Diodore of Tarsus. He objected Diodore's language of duality in Christ. Apollinaris counterposed his concept of one *prosopon* and one nature to the concept of two *prosopa* and natures, which he ascribed to Diodore. Christ, for him, "is neither two *prosopa* nor two natures" (*Fides secundum partem* 31; Spoerl 1991: 389). Christ is also not "two sons"—something that Diodore indeed claimed. Apollinaris stated in this regard:

> We confess that the same is perfect Son of God and the same Son of Man, that His *prosopon* is one and that the worship of the Word and of the flesh that He assumed is one. (*Fides secundum partem* 28; Spoerl 1991: 388)

The single worship of Christ became a big issue in the polemical exchange between Apollinaris and Diodore. Apollinaris assumed about Diodore that with his theology of double Christ he would imply two kinds of worship: one addressing God and another addressing man in Christ. This assumption was wrong, because Diodore in fact asserted only one worship of Christ. Moreover, this worship, in his theology, became a crucial link that connected divinity and humanity in Jesus. Apollinaris nevertheless claimed, with Diodore in mind:

> We worship the purple because of the one who wears it, the temple because of the one who indwells it, the form of a servant because of the form of God, the lamb because of the High Priest, the one who was assumed because of the one who assumed, the one who was fashioned in the Virgin's womb because of the Creator of all. Confess the true facts of the matter, and, then, attribute a single honour. A single worship is not blasphemous if the facts of the matter are confessed. You say that there is one worship, but by means of this one worship you introduce blasphemy—if the singleness of worship is understood as a singleness of essence (*substantia*). (Quoted by Severus of Antioch, *Contra impium Grammaticum* III 25; Spoerl 1991: 274)

Apollinaris implied Diodore in another accusation—against those who believe that in the incarnation a mere man was adopted by the Logos. Apollinaris insisted that a different formula of unity should be used instead: of God who became incarnate: "Certain persons, attempting to overturn our faith in our Lord Jesus Christ, greatly troubled us by not confessing that He was God incarnate but a man joined to God" (*Fides secundum partem* 29; Spoerl 1991: 389). Formulas "God incarnate" and "one nature" became ingredients of a catchphrase that would become the most debatable in the centuries that followed: "one nature of the incarnated God Word" (μία φύσις Θεοῦ Λόγου σεσαρκωμένου).

## Diodore of Tarsus

Diodore, in responding to accusations from Apollinaris (see Spoerl 1991: 274), on the one hand, agreed that the worship of Christ is single. On the other hand, he argued, the ground for such worship is different from Apollinaris'. For the latter, it was an ontological unity between the Logos and flesh. For Diodore, it was the unity through grace and honor. Diodore implied a wide autonomy of Jesus' humanity. For him, Christ was God and a man: "someone and someone else" (ἄλλος καὶ ἄλλος) (see Greer 1966: 335).

Diodore was born around 330 in Antioch and received the best possible education of his time in Athens. As it was the case with the Cappadocians, who also studied in Athens, upon his return home Diodore dedicated himself to the life of asceticism and contemplation. He continued his ascetic practices even after he returned to active life as a teacher and church hierarch. He took care of an ascetic community (ἀσκητήριον) in Antioch. Among the younger members of this community under his spiritual and theological guidance, there were John Chrysostom and Theodore of Mopsuestia—two major theological personae in the following generation.

**Figure 5.2** Mountains surrounding Antioch, a possible place of Diodore's *asketerion*.
Source: Photo by the author.

Diodore became a prolific author focused on biblical hermeneutics. He also composed dogmatic, polemical, astronomical, and chronological works. His writings were praised by Basil (see *ep*. 135.1). None of them has survived, however, because of his posterior condemnation. His only fully extant text is the *Commentary on the Psalms*. Diodore represented the Christian community of Antioch in confronting the anti-Christian policies of Emperor Julian. Julian was irritated by Diodore and spilled out few caustic words about him:

> Diodorus, a charlatan priest of the Nazarene (*Nazarei magus*), when he tries to give point to that nonsensical theory about the womb by artifices and juggler's tricks, is clearly a sharp-witted sophist of that creed of the country-folk. A little further on he says: But if only the gods and goddesses and all the Muses and Fortune will lend me their aid, I hope to show that he is feeble and a corrupter of laws and customs, of pagan Mysteries and Mysteries of the gods of the underworld, and that that new-fangled Galilaean god of his, whom he by a false myth styles eternal, has been stripped by his humiliating death and burial of the divinity falsely ascribed to him by Diodorus.

Julian mentioned his days together with Diodore during their studies in Athens. He remembered how Diodore's ascetic lifestyle affected his health—something that Julian interpreted as a punishment from gods:

> The fellow sailed to Athens to the injury of the general welfare, then rashly took to philosophy and engaged in the study of literature, and by the devices of rhetoric armed

> his hateful tongue against the heavenly gods, and being utterly ignorant of the Mysteries of the pagans he so to speak imbibed most deplorably the whole mistaken folly of the base and ignorant creed-making fishermen. For this conduct he has long ago been punished by the gods themselves. For, for many years past, he has been in danger, having contracted a wasting disease of the chest, and he now suffers extreme torture. His whole body has wasted away. For his cheeks have fallen in and his body is deeply lined with wrinkles. (*Ep*. 55)

The church of Antioch was divided by the controversies around the council of Nicaea. Diodore took active part in the controversies as a pro-Nicaean theologian. For this reason, he experienced persecutions and exile. In 378, he was ordained a bishop of Tarsus. He attended the councils of Antioch in 379 and of Constantinople in 381. There, he played a central role in the condemnation of Apollinaris. Owing to his pro-Nicaean stand, Diodore was proclaimed the standard of orthodoxy by Emperor Theodosius I (*Codex Theodosianus* XVI 1.3). He passed away in the early 390s.

According to various polemicists against Diodore, he invented different ways to explain the distance between the divinity and humanity in Jesus. *Collectio Palatina*, a compilation produced in the early sixth century from the polemical works and translations by Marius Mercator (flourished in the first half of the sixth century), informs us that Diodore believed that the man in Christ was anointed, while the Word who in-dwelt in him, did not have to be anointed. The man in Christ was perfect, but still needed anointment, like one of us:

> The man Jesus is anointed, our Lord, the Word, is not anointed. For the Word is greater than Christ, because Christ became great through wisdom. The Word is from above; Jesus Christ is a man from hence. Mary did not bear the Word (for Mary was not before the ages), but she wore a man like us, yet better in all things, because from the Holy Spirit. (*Collectio Palatina* PD 4; Behr 2017: 268–9)

At the same time, the presence of God in Jesus was different from his presence in the God-inspired men and women:

> The God Word did not dwell in him who is from the seed of David as he did in the prophets. For by grace they enjoyed a certain and a moderate measure of the Holy Spirit, but this one continually remained in the things in which they were sometimes, and he was filled with the glory of the Lord and [his] wisdom. (*Collectio Palatina* PD 6; Behr 2017: 268–9)

Diodore applied the language of indwelling, assuming, and vesting-in to explain how God united with a man in the person of Jesus Christ. This language became normative for many of his followers in the Antiochian tradition:

> We adore the purple [garment] because of the one clothed [in it], and the temple because of the one who dwells [in it]; the form of the servant because of the form of

> God; the lamb because of the high priest; the one assumed because of the one who assumes; the one formed in the virginal womb because of the creator of all. Once these things have been confessed, offer one veneration; a single adoration will not be harmful, if you have first [these] things. Even [if you have not confessed these things] you say one veneration; but by the one veneration you will introduce blasphemy, as, if there is one adoration, so also there is one substance. (*Collectio Palatina* PD 6; Behr 2017: 270–1)

Leontius of Byzantium, who in his earlier years admired Diodore's work but later turned against him, saved for us some quotes from his treatise *Against the Synousiasts*. Here, Diodore explored the idea of sonship in Christ. For him, according to Leontius, the son of Mary participates in the divine sonship of the Logos. As a man, Jesus is the Son by grace, but not by nature:

> The human being born of Mary was Son by grace, God the Word is [Son] by nature; that which is by grace is not also [so] by nature, and that which is by nature is not also [so] by grace. The characteristics of sonship and glory and immortality by grace will suffice for the body taken from among us, since he has become the temple of God the Word; let it not be raised up beyond its nature, and let not God the Word be treated with arrogance, rather than with the gratitude we owe him. And what is this arrogance? Compounding him with his body, and thinking that he needs the body for perfect sonship. God the Word himself did not want to be David's son himself, but his Lord; but that his body should be called David's son, he not only did not refuse, but for this reason came among us. (Quoted by Leontius of Byzantium, *Deprehensio et Triumphus super Nestorianos* 38; Daley 2017: 494)

The idea of sonship led to heated debates about the identity of Mary: Did she give birth to God (*theotokos*) or to a mere man (*anthropotokos*)? These terms became the keywords of the Christological exchanges during the fifth century. Leontius of Byzantium informs us that for Diodore, it was inappropriate to consider Mary as the mother of God:

> And when there is discussion of natural begettings, let not God the Word be thought son of Mary. For mortal naturally begets mortal, and the body that which is of the same substance; and God the Word did not experience two births, one before the ages and one in the latter days. (Quoted by Leontius of Byzantium, *Deprehensio et Triumphus super Nestorianos* 39; Daley 2017: 496)

Most extant references to Diodore's writing have survived in the works of his enemies, which makes one to suspect them of bias and exaggeration. There is, however, an extant quote, which comes from a friendly source, the metropolitan of Tyana Eutherius, who wrote in the early fifth century. Eutherius presented Diodore not as a theological rigorist, who insists on only one way of expressing his beliefs, but a flexible thinker, who can accept several readings of a dogma. Thus, Mary, according to Eutherius, could be for Diodore both *theotokos* and *anthropotokos*—depending on how we interpret her role in the incarnation:

> Certainly Mary is to be called "Mother of God" because of the union, for the seed of Abraham is "mighty God" (Isa. 9:6) because of the union with the God Word, confessing in truth also "mother of man." For if, by nature, Mary is mother of man, [she is Mother of God] not as if it were the birth of [the divine] nature, but because that which is from David is man conjoined to the God Word. (*Ep. ad Alexandrum Hierapol.*; Behr 2017: 160)

*Theotokos* and *anthropotokos* for Diodore are theological synonyms, which express the same understanding of Mary: she gave birth to a human being who received God.

Diodore was a remarkable theologian with solid reputation because of his significant input in defending the Nicaean faith. He was a key figure in the neo-Nicaean circles. However, the trajectory of his reception in the church, especially in the wake of the later Christological controversies, was not linear. It mirrored the theological trajectory of his enemy Apollinaris. Both, because of their peculiar views on the way how the Logos united with humanity in Jesus Christ, were rejected by the church, notwithstanding their substantial contributions to the Nicaean cause. There is a difference between them, however. The legacy of Apollinaris was ostracized in all posterior traditions, while the legacy of Diodore became appreciated in the tradition of the Church of the East. There, he is venerated as one of the three "Greek Doctors," together with Theodore of Mopsuestia and Nestorius of Constantinople.

## Gregories

From within the same neo-Nicaean milieu, to which both Apollinaris and Diodore belonged, they were criticized by the Cappadocians, who were frustrated by their takes on the incarnation. Gregory of Nazianzus, for example, dedicated to such criticism his two letters to the presbyter Cledonius (*epp.* 101 and 102). He targeted Christologies that, on the one hand, divide Christ into two subjects and, on the other, unite him at the expense of his humanity. For Gregory, both these thesis and antithesis are unacceptable.

Gregory uttered ten anathematisms against Diodore's teaching. He rejected the idea of partition of one Christ, who, for Gregory, is the same subject for divinity and humanity. He also condemned contemporary forms of adoptionism, which means that there preexisted a human being who was later assumed by God to sonship. Gregory insisted on Mary's identity as the mother of God and thus underlined the unity of divinity and humanity in Christ:

> We do not part the human being from the Godhead; no, we affirm and teach one and the same God and Son, at first not man but alone and pre-eternal, unmixed with body and all that belongs to the body, but finally human being too, assumed for our salvation, the same passible in flesh, impassible in Godhead, bounded in body, boundless in spirit, earthly and heavenly, visible and known spiritually, finite and infinite: so that by the same, whole man and God, the whole human being fallen under sin might be fashioned anew.
>
> Whoever does not accept Holy Mary as the Mother of God has no relation with the Godhead.
>
> Whoever says that he was channeled, as it were, through the Virgin but not formed within her divinely and humanly ("divinely" because without a husband, "humanly" because by law of conception) is likewise godless.
>
> Whoever says the human being was formed and then God put him on to wear him is condemned: this is not God's birth but the avoidance of birth.
>
> Whoever imports two "sons," one from God the Father, a second from the mother and not one and the same Son, loses the adoption promised to those who believe aright. Two natures there are, God and man (since there are both soul and body), but not two "sons" or two "Gods"; though Paul spoke of the "inner" and "outer" man, we are not dealing with two human beings. In sum: the constituents of our Savior are different things (since invisible and visible, timeless and temporal, are not the same), but not different people—God forbid! The pair is one by coalescence, God being "in-manned" and man "deified"—or however we are to put it. (*Ep.* 101.4-5; Gregory of Nazianzus 2002: 156–7)

Gregory targeted also some linguistic choices of Diodore, such as the unity of God and man in Christ "by honor." Gregory rhetorically presented this unity by honor as dishonored:

> God is dishonored by the view that he was not born for us at all, nor nailed to the cross, and, obviously, was neither buried nor arose, as some perverse "lovers of Christ" have thought, but receives honor only here on earth, where honor is in reality dishonor. The result is that he is cut, or combined, into two sons. (*Or.* 22.13; Beeley 2011: 397).

In contrast to Diodore's views, as Gregory of Nyssa explained, both honor of God and the dishonors through which Christ's humanity went through are applicable to the entire Christ. Because of the conjunction (*synapheia*/συνάφεια) and connaturality (*symphyia*/συμφυΐα) of the divinity and humanity in Jesus, what is said of God can be also said of human being, and vice versa:

> It is clear that the blows are of the servant in whom the Lord is, while the honours are on the other hand of the Lord, that the servant is enveloped in (περὶ ὃν ὁ δοῦλος). In such a manner, by conjunction (συνάφεια) and connaturality (συμφυΐα) the effects of the one and the other become common, since the Lord takes upon himself the bruises of the servant, and the servant is glorified with the honour of the Lord. In fact for this

> reason, one says that the cross is of the Lord of glory and that every tongue proclaims that "Jesus Christ is Lord, to the Glory of God the Father" (Phil. 2:11). (*Contra Eunomium* III, 131.8-16; Maspero 2007: 23)

The Cappadocians also turned on another former neo-Nicaean fellow, Apollinaris. Their anti-Apollinarian polemics helped them elaborate on formulas which became theological classics. For example, Gregory of Nazianzus coined his famous formula "Whatever has not been assumed remains unhealed" (τὸ γὰρ ἀπρόσληπτον ἀθεράπευτον). It means that if there is a part of the human nature that has not been included in the incarnation, then that part cannot be saved from sin and death. Here is the full phrase from Gregory's epistle to Cledonius:

> Whatever has not been assumed remains unhealed; and whatever has been united with God, receives salvation. If Adam has fallen in his half, that half gets assumed and saved. If, however, he has fallen in his wholeness, he whole gets united with the [Logos who was] born and gets saved in his wholeness. (*Ep.* 101.32-33; translation is mine)

Gregory of Nyssa took the same idea and looked at it from an unusual angle. Not just all parts of human nature should be included in the incarnation—for the salvation to take effect—but also the beginning and the end of human life, that is, birth and death, should become a part of God's inhumation:

> And since human life has two limits, that from which we have a beginning and that in which we have an end, he who heals our entire life (ζωῆς) necessarily embraces us through the two extremes, grasping both our beginning and our end, to lift, from both, he who is fallen. (*Ep.* 3.25; Maspero 2007: 20)

In contrast to Apollinaris, the Cappadocians employed the language of two natures in Christ (see Beeley 2011: 402). In his epistle to Cledonius, for example, Gregory of Nazianzus spoke of "two natures: God and human being" (φύσεις μὲν γὰρ δύο Θεὸς καὶ ἄνθρωπος) (*ep.* 101.21). At the same time, as Gregory clarified, these two natures do not mean two subjects (ὁ ἄλλος) in Christ. Rather, the two natures are "meeting in one thing":

> What [Christ] was he set aside; what he was not he assumed. Not that he became two things, but he deigned to be made one thing out of two. For both are God, that which assumed and that which was assumed, the two natures meeting in one thing. Yet there are not two sons: let us not give a false account of the blending. (*Or.* 37.2; Beeley 2011: 401).

Christ, thus, is a single subject of everything that he did and suffered as both God and a human being. Gregory clearly articulated the idea of two natural activities in Christ that have a single subject. This idea would occupy the center of theological discussions three centuries later:

> He was begotten (ἐγεννήθη), but he was also born (ἐγεγέννητο) of a woman. <. . .> He is baptized as a human being, but he remitted sins as God. <. . .> He thirsted, but he cried out, "If anyone is thirsty, let him come to me and drink" (Jn 7:37-38). <. . .> He prays, but he hears prayer. He weeps, but he makes weeping to cease. <. . .> As a sheep he is led to the slaughter, but he is the shepherd of Israel. <. . .> He dies, but he gives life, and by death destroys death. He is buried, but he rises again. (*Or.* 29.19-20; Beeley 2011: 403)

Gregory of Nazianzus hesitated to consistently apply to the incarnation the same theological terminology that he had applied to the Trinity, namely the terms "hypostasis" and *ousia*. At the same time, he acknowledged that the way we should see Christ is reverse of the Trinity (see *ep.* 101; Gregory of Nazianzus 2002: 157). He felt safe to link the two cases by the pair of pronouns "someone–something" (ἄλλος–ἄλλο). In the Trinity, there are someone and someone else (ἄλλος καὶ ἄλλος)—not something and something else (ἄλλο καὶ ἄλλο). The case of the incarnation is the opposite: there, there are something and something else (ἄλλο καὶ ἄλλο), but not someone and someone else (ἄλλος καὶ ἄλλος) (*ep.* 101.20-21). Apollinaris, whom Gregory contested, was more consistent in applying the neo-Nicaean terminology to Christ, including hypostasis and *prosopon*.

The neo-Nicaeans, thus, while agreeing on what kind of wording should render the commonality and particularity in the triune God, disagreed or were inconsistent in ascribing the same commonality and particularity to the incarnated Logos. This inconsistency caused confusion, which lasted until the end of the Christological controversies. Leontius of Byzantium complained about this confusion almost two centuries after the neo-Nicaeans. He quoted his opponents, who still insisted on the separate terminology for the Trinity and the incarnation, notably with reference to Gregory of Nazianzus:

> Admittedly hypostasis and essence or nature are not the same thing in reference to the Trinity; but in reference to the Incarnation they are the same as each other. For if the new aspect of the mystery has made the natures into something new, as the holy Gregory says, I think it will make new nomenclature for them as well, so that according to him the name and definition of each will fit both. (*Epilyseis* 3; Daley 2017: 276–7)

# V.2

# "Logos-anthropos"

Gregory of Nazianzus realized that Apollinaris had developed his faulty points, because the word "flesh" (σάρξ) was polysemantic. To avoid further misunderstandings, he redefined this word and narrowed its meaning. He explained it in a "synecdochic way" (συνεκδοχικῶς). This means that "the whole being is indicated by a part" (*ep.* 101.59). According to such synecdochic interpretation, "the entire flesh" (πᾶσα σάρξ) should be understood as "the entire human being" (πᾶς ἄνθρωπος) (*ep.* 101.57). In other words, the word "flesh" should not be understood literally. Otherwise, such theology would be called "flesh-worshipping"—as in the Apollinarian case. In contrast to "flesh-worshippers" (σαρκολάτρης), Gregory called himself a "human-worshipper" (ἀνθρωπολάτρης) (*ep.* 101.48).

Gregory differentiated between two theological paradigms, which Aloys Grillmeier identified as the "Word-flesh" (*Logos-sarx*) and the "Word-human being" (*Logos-anthropos*) Christologies (see Grillmeier 1975, vol. 1: 218 ff). These two paradigms are not much different. They differ in accents and do not reject most tenets of each other. Thus, the *Logos-sarx* Christology stresses the *unity* of divinity and humanity in Jesus Christ. The *fullness* of his humanity, however, remains on the periphery of its vision. In contrast to it, the *Logos-anthropos* paradigm pays attention to the completeness of Christ's humanity. Sometimes it envisages the unity of Christ as quite loose. At the same time, it emphasizes Jesus' human activities: his human side was not passive, as in the case of the *Logos-sarx* paradigm.

Different focal points of these two paradigms can be rendered in the terms of oneness and plurality. Jesus' oneness absorbed all attention of those who followed the *Logos-sarx* paradigm, while the *Logos-anthropos* theologians cared more to preserve the ontological plurality in Jesus. The difference between the two approaches can be also described in the terms of what is real and what is imagined in Christ. From the perspective of the *Logos-sarx* paradigm, the gravity of Christ's reality lays in his singular presence. What is imagined about him is the distinction between his divinity and humanity. For the followers of the *Logos-anthropos* theology, both divinity and humanity constitute two realities par excellence. What is more imagined is the bond between them. Despite these different accents, for both paradigms both

**Figure 5.3** A modern cityscape of ancient Antioch on the Orontes—the birthplace of the *Logos-anthropos* Christology. Now it is the city of Antakya in the Turkish province of Hatay.

Source: Photo by the author.

divinity and humanity are undeniable realities. They are only contemplated from different angles.

Only in their extreme forms do these two paradigms substantially differ from each other. The extreme *Logos-sarx* theology reduces Christ's humanity to body with only partial, if any, human emotionality and intelligence. The extreme *Logos-anthropos* Christological paradigm, on the contrary, insists on the complete humanity of Christ to the extent of presenting it as a self-sufficient being, which is capable of existing separately from divinity. Christ, from this perspective, is *a* human being (ἄνθρωπος), in the sense of an individual being.

# Theodore of Mopsuestia

The extreme *Logos-anthropos* Christology sprang from the writings of Diodore of Tarsus and was systematized by Theodore of Mopsuestia, who was one generation younger and his disciple. Theodore was born around 350 in Antioch, where he also received his education in the rhetorical school of Libanius. After finishing his studies, at the age of about twenty, he went under the spiritual and theological guidance of Diodore in his *asketerion*. There, he composed his first theological texts,

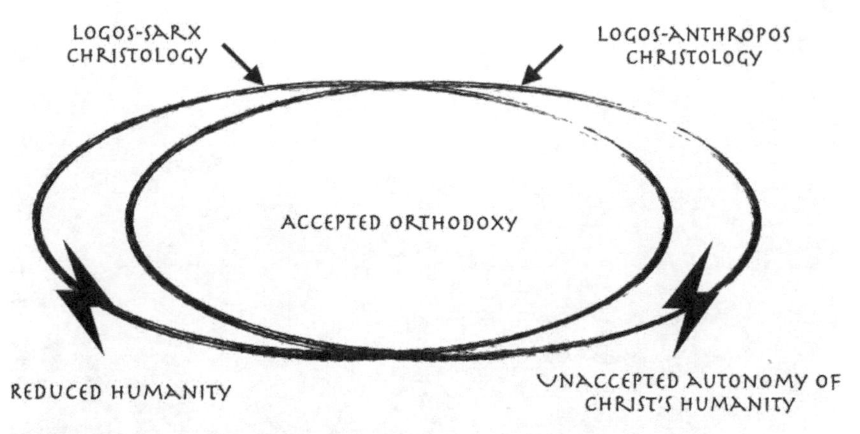


**Figure 5.4** *Logos-sarx* and *Logos-anthropos* Christologies.

which imitated Diodore's writings. When Diodore was consecrated a bishop in 378, Theodore became a more self-standing figure. In 383, he was ordained a priest for the church of Antioch. There, he flourished as a preacher and theologian, who made himself known for advocating for the Nicaean cause. During his time as a priest, he composed his most famous treatise, *On the Incarnation of the Lord*, which has survived in the Syriac translation. Theodore maintained a spiritual relationship with Diodore, who facilitated his election as a bishop of the Cilician city of Mopsuestia in 392. In Cilicia, Theodore spent thirty-six years, until he died in 428. He lived a quiet life and abstained from active involvement in church politics.

His exegetical work and advocating for the Nicaea earned Theodore a solid reputation among other neo-Nicaeans. His Christological writings, however, were more controversial and caused concern among many of his allies. Nevertheless, those concerned about his Christological tenets did not openly oppose him during his lifetime. Only after his death, some of his former admirers, such as Rabbula of Edessa, turned on his legacy. There were also apologists of his work, such as Rabbula's successor in Edessa, Ibas. Theodore was also appreciated in the theological school of Nisibis. Surprisingly, his theological reputation survived the council of Ephesus, which condemned Nestorius, and the council of Chalcedon, which confronted the opposite side to that of Theodore.

Only in the frame of neo-Chalcedonianism, which tried to build a bridge between the Chalcedonians and anti-Chalcedonians, the theological legacy of Theodore was sacrificed on the altar of the church's unity. The anti-Chalcedonians were upset by his writings and demanded his condemnation. A council, which was convened in 507 in Constantinople under Emperor Anastasius, condemned both Diodore and Theodore, together with Theodoret of Cyrus and Ibas of Edessa. The council of Antioch two years later repeated the condemnation. Emperor Justinian, who promoted rapprochement with the anti-Chalcedonians based on the neo-Chalcedonian formulas, in 544–5 issued an edict, which condemned the so-called three chapters.

**Figure 5.5** Cilician landscapes, which were familiar to Theodore.
Source: Photo by the author.

These "chapters" included the writings by Theodoret, the letter of Ibas to Mari, and the writings of Theodore of Mopsuestia. Theodore was the only one in this group who was condemned personally. The council of Constantinople in 553, which confirmed the neo-Chalcedonian initiatives of Justinian, repeated the condemnation of the "three chapters." The council's fathers found particularly harsh words for Theodore:

> After the blasphemies of Theodore of Mopsuestia and his impious creed had been read, the holy council said and exclaimed: "This creed was composed by Satan. Anathema to the writer of this creed! This creed together with its author was anathematized by the First Council of Ephesus.[1] <. . .> Anathema to Theodore of Mopsuestia! He attacked the gospels. He swore against the dispensation. Anathema to those who do not anathematize him! His defenders are Jews. His followers are pagans. Many years to the emperor! To the orthodox emperor many years! To the Christian emperor many years! This benefit was reserved for you [to bestow]. You have cast out the tares. You have purified the church. Theodore of Mopsuestia we all anathematize. Theodore and his writings we all anathematize." (Session IV 82; Price 2009: 270)

Theodore's legacy, while having been discarded in his native Greek milieu, became central in Eastern Syriac Christianity. There, he became a "Greek Doctor," also known as "the Interpreter" (*mpaššqānā*).

Theodore stressed plurality in Christ. He drew parallels between this plurality, which includes God and man, and the plurality observable in the created world. For him, the way, in which elements of the visible world remain separated from each

[1] This is not true—the council of Ephesus did not anathematize Theodore personally.

other, even though they can interact with one another, is an indication of the way, in which divinity and humanity are united in Jesus:

> The natures cannot enter into mutual opposition and that is why the Lord separated the natures from one another, put the fire on high and the earth below, and fenced off the waters by a wall of sand, as it were. And he separated them one from another; and he commanded that the waters should form a single group lest the waters, by intermingling with the nature of the earth, should swamp it and destroy those natures by their merger in it; and moreover lest [the waters] being vanquished by [earth] through their proximity to it should be annihilated because of its bulk, or the former, by prevailing over the fire, should consume its nature, and, again, lest the earth should vanquish the fire so as to lift it off in it. (In Behr 2017: 441)

Even if elements mix up, their natures remain intact. This happens in the case of human body, for example. Its functionality consists of the activities of elements that constitute it. At the same time, elements as such do not disappear or change their nature:

> We often use the word "mixture" of the human being who results from a mixture constituting a body, of the four elements although no visible feature of earth is present nor is exhaled air perceived in it nor fluid water. But their mixed operation results in the subsistence of our body when the force of their operation is mixed—that is, of heat and of cold and of dryness and of dampness—in accord with the wisdom of their Blender, and constituted for the maintenance of bodies. This does not happen by their natures—of fire and earth and air and water—being mixed. For if this were to occur, the elements would disappear for ever because existing entities would be receiving only partial natural subsistence. For the natures cannot stick together because they possess mutual contrariety of operations. No, in their intermingling indeed they would be destroyed. (In Behr 2017: 443)

Theodore explained how these analogies work in Christ. His two natures remain clear-cut different. At the same time, they act in such a way that they appear as one. Their unity is loose but still meaningful. Theodore exemplified it by a wife and her husband, who constitute one flesh (Mt. 19:6). This example was unacceptable for Theodore's opponents, who preferred to present Christ's unity through the analogy of body and soul in a human being. Nevertheless, even in the unity understood as marriage, Theodore insisted, Jesus' sonship and lordship are preserved as singular—contrary to what others accused him of:

> It is not the case that we say two natures in Christ, we would by necessity assert two Sons or two Lords, since it is proved to be extreme folly to think this? For all things whatsoever which are two in one respect, and one in another, do not destroy the division between them by the unity. For "I and my Father are one" (Jn 10:30); but not, because one, negating the properties of each. And, in another place, speaking of husband and wife: "They are not two, but one flesh" (Mt. 19:6); but it is not the case

> that because husband and wife are one flesh, they are no longer two. For they remain two, because they are two, and are one, because they are one. In the same way here: they are two by nature, but one by conjunction: two by nature, because of the great difference between the natures; but one by conjunction, because of the invisible veneration that is received by the one assumed together with the one assuming, just as he remains in his own temple. For all things whatsoever which are said to be two, thereupon involve the essence of two, [even] when one is believed to be not differentiated from the other, because it receives the term "two" and the connumeration. <. . .>
>
> Thus also here, if each of them were by nature Son and Lord, they could be called, in a certain manner, two sons and lords, according to the number of persons; but since this one is indeed by substance Son and Lord, that one is acknowledged to be neither Son nor Lord by substance; but by the conjunction which he had with him, he is known to have participated in the same, and therefore we say one Son and Lord, principally understanding him to be Son and Lord who by substance is believed and said to be both truly, but embracing in thought the one also who is inseparably conjoined to him and by an ineffable union with him is reckoned to participate in the Son and Lord. And so, wheresoever the divine Scripture calls him who was assumed "Son," it is to be said that we call him "Son" because of the relationship of union to the one who assumed. <. . .>
>
> We understand him to be Son, not because he is called Son in himself, but because of that union which he has with the one who is truly Son such a thing is said. The Creator had pity on the lost creature and forms the infant without a commixture [of himself], leads him to the adult state, introducing, in a believable way, the appearance of growth belonging to the process of nature, but invisibly being united with him. He was not absent, when he was formed; he was not separated, when he was born, speaking of the conjunction, being both present in his acts and also preserving [with him] wherever he guards, without sin, his connection. (*Collectio Palatina* PT 8; Behr 2017: 262–5)

Theodore described the unity of divinity and humanity in Christ as conjunction. This was a sort of unity which was like touching one another or cohabitating under the same roof. Theodore described this mode of unity as "relative" (ἕνωσις σχετική), which can be also rendered as "relativist." Such unity became possible because God willed it. For this reason, Theodore also called such unity to be "by benevolence" (ἕνωσις κατ'εὐδοκίαν). It is opposite to another type of unity, which he called "essential" (κατ' οὐσίαν) (in Diekamp 1981; 305) and which he could not accept in Christ.

It was indicated earlier that Theodore's teacher, Diodore, used theological synonyms, such as *theotokos* and *anthropotokos*. Theodore suggested that some terms could be also used as theological homonyms: they can signify different realities depending on their context. One of such homonyms was *prosopon*. It had been widely circulated by Diodore's opponent, Apollinaris. Theodore had to redefine it to make it fit his theology. For him, in application to any particular being except Christ, *prosopon* is identical with hypostasis and means someone's particular existence. In application to Christ, however, *prosopon* additionally means the unity of two beings. We can find such definition in a fragment from Theodore's polemical treatise *Against Eunomius*, which has survived in a Syriac manuscript in the Cambridge University Library (*or.* 1319):

> *Prosopon* is used in a twofold way; for either it signifies the hypostasis, and that which each one of us is, or it is conferred upon honour, greatness, and worship; for example: "Paul" and "Peter" signify the hypostasis and the *prosopon* of each one of them, but the *prosopon* of our Lord Christ means honour, greatness, and worship. For because the God Word was revealed in humanity, he was causing the glory of his hypostasis to cleave to the visible one; and for this reason, the *prosopon* of Christ declares it (i.e., the *prosopon*) to be [a *prosopon*] of honour, not of the *ousia* of the two natures. {For the honour is neither nature nor hypostasis, but an elevation to great dignity which is awarded as a due for the cause of the revelation.}[2] What purple garments or royal apparel are for the king is for the God Word the beginning which was taken from us without separation, alienation, or distance in worship. Therefore, as it is not by nature that a king has purple robes, so also neither is it by nature that the God Word has flesh. For anyone who affirms the God Word to have flesh by nature [predicates that] he has something foreign to the divine substance by undergoing alteration by the addition of a nature. But if he has not flesh by nature, how does Apollinarius say that the same one is in part consubstantial with the Father in his divinity; and the same [in part] consubstantial with us in the flesh, so that he may make him composite? For he who is thus divided into natures becomes and is found [to be] something composite, by nature. (In Behr 2017: 228–9)

Theodore's theological system was elegant and attracted many followers. At the same time, it alarmed many, who saw it as compromising the soteriological framework of classical theology. To understand their concern, we should look at this system from the logical perspective of commonality and particularity. Theodore's opponents interpreted his theology as implying that the Logos had assumed not the common but a particular human nature: a person named Jesus. In such a case, the salvific effect of the incarnation would benefit only that particular person and not the entire humankind. In other words, Theodore's Christological model presupposed particular salvation only for Jesus, but not universal salvation for all of us. Moreover, even Jesus' salvation was under question, because his unity with God was too loose and superficial. The divinity and humanity in Jesus remained too distant from each other to engage the latter to salvation. Theodore's Christology, thus, became

[2]Scholars believe this is a gloss interpolated by someone else.

perceived as soteriologically weak. It was eventually condemned under the brand of "Nestorianism."

## Nestorius of Constantinople

The legend says that Nestorius, on his way from Antioch to Constantinople, where he would be enthroned as the capital's archbishop, made a stop in Mopsuestia. There he met Theodore and spent with him a few days, receiving his counsel in theological and ecclesial matters (see Evagrius Scholasticus, *Historia ecclesiastica* I 2; Evagrius Scholasticus 2000: 10). Soon after that, Theodore died. Nestorius, however, continued his line—to the extent that the teaching, which had been elaborated upon by Theodore and should be associated primarily with his name, became known after Nestorius, as "Nestorianism."

Nestorius' intellectual input to "Nestorianism" was insignificant. This doctrine had been founded by Diodore of Tarsus and perfected by Theodore of Mopsuestia. At that time, however, doctrines were often named not after the original thinkers who articulated them, but by their high-ranked promoters among the hierarchs. "Nestorianism" was not an exception. It was called so because Nestorius became the archbishop of the imperial capital and did a lot to disseminate it.

Syriac sources identify Nestorius' birthplace in Germanicaea (Kahramanmaraş in the southeast of modern Turkey). Although his milieu was Syriac, he apparently did not master the language, which would eventually preserve many of his writings. He received a classical Greek education in Antioch. His theological formation happened in the same milieu and absorbed its trends. When he became the archbishop of Constantinople, he saw his role to be an ambassador of the Antiochian school.

Nestorius was born in the early 380s and belonged to the generation next after Theodore of Mopsuestia. Theologically, he was a son of Theodore and grandson of Diodore. Although the Nicaean faith had become a theological mainstream in the time he was born, in the mature age he continued fighting the remaining pockets of non-Nicaeans. After he moved in 428 to Constantinople as its bishop, he launched a series of militant campaigns against all those whom he regarded "heretics." He went as far as burning down the surviving *homoian* ("Arian") churches. Very soon, however, he had to taste himself the fruits of hatred he had sown.

Almost immediately after his election to the throne of Constantinople, Nestorius set against himself many in both the capital city and the provinces of the Eastern Roman Empire, especially in Egypt. Anti-Nestorian unrest was triggered by public statements that he personally and his clergy had made about Mary, namely that she cannot be called *theotokos*. Unlike more sophisticated issues about Christ's unity, this was a more comprehensive matter that touched on popular devotion. Church historian Socrates described both Nestorius' intolerant zeal and vehement public reactions to it:

> Nestorius was brought from Antioch, being greatly lauded by most people for his temperance: but of what sort of disposition he was in other respects, those who possessed any discernment were able to perceive from his first sermon.
>
> Being ordained on 10 April, under the consulate of Felix and Taurus, he immediately uttered those famous words, before all the people, in addressing the Emperor, "Give me, O Emperor, the earth purged of heretics, and I will give you heaven as a recompense. Assist me in destroying heretics, and I will assist you in vanquishing the Persians."
>
> Now although these utterances were extremely gratifying to some of the multitude, who cherished a senseless antipathy to the very name of heretic; yet those, as I have said, who were skillful in predicting a man's character from his expressions, did not fail to detect his levity of mind, and violent and vainglorious temperament, inasmuch as he had burst forth into such vehemence without being able to contain himself for even the shortest space of time; and to use the proverbial phrase, "before he had tasted the water of the city," showed himself a furious persecutor. Accordingly on the fifth day after his ordination, having determined to demolish a chapel in which the Arians were accustomed to perform their devotions privately, he drove these people, i.e. the Arians, to desperation; for when they saw the work of destruction going forward in their chapel, they threw fire into it, and set it alight and the fire spreading on all sides destroyed many of the adjacent buildings. A tumult accordingly arose on account of this throughout the city, and the Arians made preparations to take revenge: but God the Guardian of the city suffered not the mischief to gather to a climax. From that time, however, they called Nestorius "incendiary," and it was not only the heretics who did this, but those also of the household of faith. For he could not rest, but seeking every means of harassing those who did not embrace his own sentiments, he continually disturbed the public tranquility. (*Historia ecclesiastica* VII 29: Stevenson & Frend 2012: 330–1)

The archbishop of Alexandria Cyril grasped the momentum of public dissatisfaction with Nestorius and led a massive attack against him. Many factors contributed to the clash between the two primates, which turned out to be fatal for the church's unity. The traditional theological difference between the *Logos-sarx* and *Logos-anthropos* Christological paradigms was not the only one and probably not the most important reason for their fight. Political rivalry between Alexandria and Constantinople ignited it to a great, if not a greater, extent. The expansionist policies of Nestorius did not help to calm down this rivalry.

At that time, the zone of political influence of the archbishops of Constantinople was limited to the capital's vicinities. The Alexandrian zone was much larger and included the entire northeastern Africa. Nestorius tried to expand the territory of his own influence and used his native Antiochian theology as a vehicle of expansion. He began promoting the doctrine, which he believed to be orthodox, far beyond the

**Figure 5.6** Petra in modern Jordan—the place of exile of Nestorius.
Source: Photo by the author.

territories that had been under his jurisdiction. This irritated some neighboring churches. On their behalf, Alexandria spearheaded an attack against the archbishop of Constantinople.

The attack culminated in 431, when Cyril of Alexandria presided over a council in Ephesus that investigated Nestorius' teachings and policies. In parallel, in the same city, John of Antioch held his own gathering, which intended to support Nestorius' cause. The archbishop of Constantinople, however, attended neither of the two gatherings. Instead of picking up the fight, Nestorius decided to step down. The emperor approved his resignation in the same year 431. Nestorius went back to Antioch and lived there in a monastery. In 435, by an imperial order, he was exiled to Petra in modern Jordan and later was sent to Egypt. He died there at around 450.

In the last years of his life in Egypt, Nestorius composed the *Book of Heraclides of Damascus*, also known as *The Bazaar of Heraclides*, which has survived in the Syriac translation. This is an apologetical treatise in the form of dialogue. Nestorius gave his account of the events that surrounded the council in Ephesus and explained his Christological views. Among other things, he accused Cyril of introducing new terminology, including the word *theotokos*.

This term was not completely new, as it had been occasionally used in Egypt since at least the third century.[3] It seems that Origen, for example, made references to

[3]John Rylands Papyrus 470 from the University of Manchester is often mentioned as a third-century reference to the "Theotokos." It contains the prayer "Under your mercy we take refuge, Theotokos," which continues to be popular among Eastern Christians in our days. However, now the papyrus is attributed after the sixth century.

"theotokos" in his biblical commentaries (see *Fragmenta in Lucam* (in catenis) 41b). However, Nestorius either did not know or did not acknowledge earlier references to this term. He complained to his imagined interlocutor Sophronius:

> I have convicted him (i.e., Cyril of Alexandria) of lying concerning the Fathers, of having said that the Fathers called the holy Virgin the mother of God (i.e., *Theotokos*), without even making mention of the birth itself? For the sake of these things have you treated me as an adversary? Let none show favour unto any man. But if this phrase (i.e., *Theotokos*) has been employed in the discussion about the Faith by the Fathers at Nicaea, with [the aid of] whom he combats against me, read it; or if it has been spoken by any other Council of the orthodox. For it is of the heretics, all of whom fight against the divinity of Christ, but it has not been spoken by those who have adhered to the faith of the orthodox. But if it were shown to have been said by a Council of the orthodox, then even I should confess that I have been condemned as one who was on the opposite side. But if no one has used this phrase, thou hast risen up against them all to introduce into the Faith with boldness a new phrase which has not been accepted. (*Liber Heracleidis* II 10; Nestorius 1925: 174–5)

## Disputes about Theotokos

In this passage, Nestorius presents himself as a traditionalist, who safeguards the legacy of the council of Nicaea and the patristic tradition. Cyril, from his perspective, had introduced an unacceptable novelty to the Orthodox faith. Apparently, Nestorius did not realize that the Nicaean term *homoousios* had also been a novelty. In a sense, the word *theotokos* in the fifth century became what the word *homoousios* used to be in the fourth century: an innovative term promoted by creative theological minds. Nestorius was not such a creative mind. He was a Nicaean traditionalist who did not understand the creative and innovative impulses of the council he tried to protect. He did not understand the creative potentiality of the term *theotokos* either.

Nestorius promoted the terms *Christotokos* and *anthropotokos* as better expressions of the incarnation. He only reluctantly accepted the term *theotokos* as optional, under the pressure from his Antiochian confederates and by the fact that it had been used by Theodore of Mopsuestia and Theodoret of Cyrus.

Quite remarkably, the council of Ephesus did not use this term in its official documents. It would appear in the conciliar texts quite later (see Price 2019: 68–9). This could mean that the fathers of the council hesitated to use this theological neologism, to avoid possible unrest among traditionalists.

Cyril of Alexandria, it seems, was not afraid of traditionalists. He demonstrated a remarkable creativity in experimenting with the lexeme *theotokos*, by which he wanted to stress the intrinsic unity of the Logos and humankind in Christ. Soon after the council in Ephesus condemned Nestorius, Cyril preached a sermon, which was built around the term *theotokos*. It became known as "the most famous Marian sermon of antiquity" (O'Carroll 1982: 113):

> Resplendent is the assembly I see, with all the holy men eagerly assembled, summoned by holy Mary, Theotokos and ever-Virgin. Even though I was in great distress, the presence of the holy fathers has changed that into joy. Now is fulfilled in us that sweet saying of the psalmodist David, "Behold! What is good or what is delightful, compared to brethren dwelling in unity?" (Ps. 132:1). Rejoice, therefore, with us, holy and mystic Trinity that has summoned all of us here to this church of Mary Theotokos. Rejoice with us, Mary Theotokos, the venerable treasure of the whole world, the inextinguishable lamp, the crown of virginity, the sceptre of orthodoxy, the indestructible temple, the container of the Uncontainable, the Mother and Virgin, through whom in the holy gospels is pronounced blessed "he who comes in the name of the Lord" (Mt. 21:9). Rejoice, you who contained the Uncontainable in your holy and virginal womb, through whom the holy Trinity is glorified and worshipped throughout the world, through whom heaven is glad, through whom angels and archangels exult, through whom demons are put to flight, through whom the devil the tempter fell from heaven, through whom the fallen creature is received back into heaven, through whom the whole creation, caught in the madness of idolatry, has come to the knowledge of the truth, through whom holy baptism comes to those who believe, through whom is the oil of gladness, through whom churches have been founded throughout the world, through whom nations are led to repentance. Why should I say more? Through whom the only-begotten Son of God has shone as a light "to those seated in darkness and in the shadow of death" (Lk. 1:79), through whom the prophets spoke, through whom the apostles proclaim salvation to the nations, through whom the dead are raised, through whom kings exercise their rule. <. . .> Who among men is able to describe the much-hymned Mary? (*Hom.* IV; Price 2019: 74)

It would be an anachronism to assume that Cyril in his preaching was moved by pure Marian devotion.[4] His main motivation was Christological and soteriological. Indeed, if Mary is *Theotokos*, then the unity between God and humankind has become real and close enough to make salvation for every human being possible. If she is not *Theotokos*, however, then the unity is loose and cannot secure salvation for the humankind. As Richard Price correctly remarked, "the whole scheme of salvation unravels if the Virgin is denied the title of *Theotokos*" (Price 2019: 74). The devotion to Virgin Mary, as we know it now in both East and West, reached its present degrees and forms later, as the aftermath of the debates in the fifth century about her identity. Christology and soteriology prepared the soil, from which the later Marian cult sprang.

[4]Such a devotion was admittedly already popular in his time (see Constas 2002).

**Figure 5.7** An ancient icon of the Theotokos in the Red Monastery in Egypt, which flourished in the time of the controversies about Mary's identity. This icon was painted as a theological statement in support of the pro-Theotokos party.
Source: Photo by the author.

# Persian Christology

The followers of Archbishop Nestorius, after he was condemned in Ephesus, were expelled from the Roman soil. Ironically, they were welcomed by the Persians, whom Nestorius had wanted to destroy. In the Persian Empire, the "Nestorian" Christology flourished without the same impediments it experienced in Byzantium. First, the school in Nisibis and later in Seleucia-Ctesiphon became the centers of its studies. The formulations elaborated in these schools and adopted by the councils of the Eastern Syriac church, varied from a less to a more radical dyophysitism—a theological teaching and language speaking about two natures in Christ. For example, the council of 605, held by Catholicos Gregory I (in office 605–9), who prior to his primacy had been a teacher at the school of Seleucia-Ctesiphon, adopted the following Christological formula:

> One and the same [with the creeds of Nicaea and Constantinople] is our opinion and faith in the holy Trinity and the mysteries of the *mdabbranuta* (i.e., divine providence,

*oekonomia*) of our Lord in the body. [It is the faith] which our Fathers have taught us and shown to us; it consists for us in the confession of the one divine nature (*kyana*), the eternal Being (*itya*), Creator of all created things, cause of all, having no beginning and possessing no end, <. . .> and revealed <. . .> by means of his beloved Son, whom he had made heir of everything and in whom he had made known concerning the Trinity of his *qnome*, which are without beginning and without change, a single Divinity, unattainable, a single eternal nature who is known in three *qnome*, of the Father and the Son and the Holy Spirit. Who, through the first fruits from us (1 Cor. 15:23), effected the liberation and renovation of our race, for "the form of God assumed the form (*demuta*) of a servant" (Phil. 2:7), according to the apostolic utterance, and in him he perfected and completed his exalted *mdabbranuta* for the sake of our salvation: the form of God in the form of a servant, one Son, our Lord Jesus Christ, through whom everything was made, perfect God and perfect man, perfect God in the nature of his divinity, perfect man in the nature of his humanity. Two natures, of divinity and of humanity, the divinity being preserved in what belongs to it, and the humanity in what belongs to it; and they are united in a true union (*hdayuta*) of the one *parsopa* of the Son, Christ. And the divinity perfected the humanity through the suffering, as it is written, while suffering, change and alteration of any sort did not enter into his divinity. (Chabot 1902: 209–10; Brock 2008: 140)

This definition could be accepted in Byzantium. It reflected the tendency in the Eastern Syriac church to find ways of rapprochement with the Byzantine church. This tendency, however, did not last long and was soon substituted with a more radical edition of dyophysitism. Such an edition was articulated, for instance, by Babai the Great (*c.* 551–628)—the unofficial leader of the Eastern Syriac church in the late decades of the Sassanid dynasty. He made it clear that Christ had two *qnome*, which should be understood as hypostases: Babai ascribed three *qnome* to the Trinity. Christ's two *qnome* came together in a *prosopon* (*parsopa*) of filiation:

Thus God the Word, who is an infinite *qnoma* like the Father and like the Holy Spirit is also uniting in this venerable union with the finite *qnoma* of his human being whom he assumed over his *parsopa*—like fire in the thorn bush—in one *parsopa* of filiation, without confusion, without mixture, without admixture; while the properties of those two natures are preserved in their *qnoma*: in one conjunction of the one Lord Jesus Christ, the Son of God. (*Liber de unione* II 7; Metselaar 2019: 151)

Babai explained in more detail what kind of unity did Christ's two *qnome* have:

This venerable, marvellous, ineffable union has therefore all these ways and is above all these in a different way: unsearchable and exceeding the parts that limit each other: it is not by a conjunction from outside alone, and not by an inclusion and limitation from inside, and not at a distance according to the *parsopa*, and not by the will while [the parts] keep distance, but the infinite [is] in the finite and they remain without

> confusion, without mixture, without admixture, without composition and without parts.
>
> This union is not with a distance, neither is it a limited union, a compulsory one or a passive one, but rather a voluntary one and one according to the *parsopa*, to [the benefit of] the one venerable *mdabbranuta* in one conjunction and indwelling and union of the assuming with the assumed. And the conjunction [is] without confusion and the indwelling [is] without limitation. For unitedly God dwells unlimited in his humanity which is limited, like the sun in a shining pearl, in one union. (*Liber de unione* VI 21; Metselaar 2019: 152)

In contrast to the definition by the council of 605, this statement by Babai was rather unacceptable for the Chalcedonian dyophysites, because it clearly introduced two particularities (*qnome*) in Christ. At the same time, it contained a strong affirmation of unity, which might have been accepted in Byzantium. In contrast to what the Byzantines thought about the Nestorians, the latter did not accept double sonship in Christ. Babai made it explicit (see Metselaar 2019: 156).

At the same time, Babai was ambivalent about Mary's titles. As was mentioned, they became a big issue that divided the Eastern Syrians from the Western Syrians, Copts, and Byzantines. Both the anti-Chalcedonians and Chalcedonians accused the Nestorians of their unwillingness to call Mary *Theotokos*, the "one who gave birth to God." Babai, however, explained that the term "Mother of God" is applicable to Mary to the same extent as the term "Mother of a human being." His point was that neither of these terms is exclusive:

> God the Word is consubstantial with the Father, and because of the union (*hdayuta*) the blessed Mary is called Mother of God (*yaldat alaha*) and Mother of Man: Mother of Man according to her own nature, but Mother of God because of the union which he had with his humanity, which was his temple at the beginning of its fashioning and was begotten in union. Because the name "Christ" is indicative of the two natures in the *qnomatic* state of his divinity and his humanity, the Scriptures say that the blessed Mary bore Christ: not simply God in a disunited way, and not simply man, who was not put on by God the Word. (*Liber de unione* VII; Metselaar 2019: 155)

# V.3
# "Logos-sarx"

## Cyril

Nestorius' archenemy, Cyril, who caused so much trouble to the "Nestorians," was born at the same time as Nestorius, or was maybe a few years after him. Cyril's family was prominent in Alexandria, as his maternal uncle Theophilus was the archbishop of the city. Theophilus became famous for chasing after John Chrysostom and eventually having him condemned at the council "of the oak" in 403 and exiled (see Banev 2015). He trained his nephew Cyril for a prominent church career and had him engaged in the matters of church politics from his tender years. For example, Cyril was involved in the trial of John Chrysostom.

When Theophilus died in 412, Cyril easily succeeded him as the archbishop of Alexandria. At that time, such nepotism was already a norm in the church. It continues to be a widely spread practice in Eastern Christianity, when senior hierarchs promote their relatives, illegal sons, or even lovers to lucrative positions in the church hierarchy. Usually, these protégées do not merit pastoral or theological capacities. Cyril, however, like earlier Alexander's protégée Athanasius, was an exception. He by far exceeded his uncle as a theologian and pastor. The church recognized him as one of its greatest theologians.

In his ecclesial policies, Cyril inherited some violent approaches of his uncle, such as voluntarism, abuses of power, corruption, and intolerance to "the other." Although he was not directly involved in the killing of the Alexandrian neo-Platonic female philosopher Hypatia by the Christian zealots, he apparently enhanced the atmosphere of hatred in the city (see Norman & Petkas 2020; Dzielska 2002). Like his uncle, Cyril was suspicious about the political ambitions of the archbishops in Constantinople, especially when they had Syriac origins. Although he had to reconcile with the memory of John Chrysostom, probably under pressure from Rome, he found as his own prey Nestorius—another Syrian in Constantinople.

**Figure 5.8** Modern icon of St. Cyril of Alexandria painted by Olexandr Klymenko.
Source: From the author's personal collection.

# Attacks against Nestorius

Cyril began his assaults against Nestorius soon after the latter was elected as the archbishop of Constantinople. The Alexandrian archbishop brought up accusations against Nestorius' interpretation of the incarnation and Mary's identity, in the letter to Egyptian monks, which was intended for broader audiences. The attack was repeated in Cyril's paschal encyclical in the spring of 429. Later in the same year and during the following year, he sent direct letters to Nestorius, with increasingly harsh wording. Initially, Cyril concluded his letter to Nestorius with some nice words: "Christian love prompts me to write this even at this stage and I call on you as my brother" (*Ep. ad Nestorium* II 7; Cyril of Alexandria 1983: 11). His next letter, however, Cyril started with a completely different note: "You have scandalized the whole Church, have injected the ferment of bizarre and outlandish heresy into congregations not only at Constantinople but all over the world" (*Ep. ad Nestorium* III 1; Cyril of Alexandria 1983: 13). Cyril supplemented this letter with twelve anathemas, which were designed as sharp counterpositions to the corresponding points that Nestorius had allegedly stated:

1. Whoever does not acknowledge Emmanuel to be truly God and hence the holy Virgin "Mother of God" (Θεοτόκον) (for she gave fleshly birth to the Word of God made flesh) shall be anathema.
2. Whoever does not acknowledge the Word of God the Father to have been substantially united (καθ' ὑπόστασιν ἡνῶσθαι) with flesh and to be one Christ along with his own flesh, that is the same at once God and man, shall be anathema.
3. Whoever divides the subjects (ὑποστάσεις) in respect to the one Christ after the union, joining them together just in a conjunction (συναφείᾳ) involving rank i.e., sovereignty or authority instead of a combination involving actual union shall be anathema.
4. Whoever allocates the terms contained in the gospels and apostolic writings and applied to Christ by the saints or used of himself by himself to two persons or subjects (προσώποις δυσὶν ἢ γοῦν ὑποστάσεσι) and attaches some to the man considered separately from the Word of God, some as divine to the Word of God the Father alone, shall be anathema.
5. Whoever has the temerity to state that Christ is a divinely inspired man (θεοφόρον ἄνθρωπον) instead of saying that he is truly God as being one Son by nature, because the Word was made flesh and shared in flesh and blood like us, shall be anathema.
6. Whoever says the Word of God the Father is Christ's God or Master instead of acknowledging the same Christ at once God and man on the scriptural ground of the Word's having been made flesh, shall be anathema.
7. Whoever says that the man Jesus is under the control (ἐνηργῆσθαι) of God the Word and that the glory of the Only-begotten attaches to a different entity (ἑτέρῳ ὑπάρχοντι) from the Only-begotten, shall be anathema.
8. Whoever has the temerity to assert that the assumed man (ἀναληφθέντα ἄνθρωπον) should be worshipped along with God the Word, that one should be praised and be styled "God" along with another (the addition of "along with" will always entail this interpretation) instead of venerating Emmanuel with a single worship and ascribing to him a single act of praise because the Word has been made flesh, shall be anathema.
9. Whoever says that the one Lord Jesus Christ has been glorified by the Spirit, Christ using the force mediated by the Spirit as an alien force and having acquired from him the ability to act against foul spirits and to perform miracles on human beings instead of saying that the Spirit whereby he effected the miracles is Christ's own, shall be anathema.
10. Divine Scripture says Christ has been made "High Priest and Apostle of our confession" (Heb. 3:1) and "gave himself up for us as a fragrant offering to God the Father" (Eph. 5:2). So whoever says that it was not the Word of God personally who was made our High Priest and Apostle when he became flesh

and man as we are, but another woman-born man separate from him (ἕτερον παρ᾽αὐτόν ἰδικῶς), or whoever asserts he made the offering for himself too instead of for us alone (for he who knew no sin did not need an offering), shall be anathema.

11. Whoever does not acknowledge the Lord's flesh to be vitalizing (ζωοποιόν) and to belong to the very Word of God the Father but says it belongs to somebody different joined to him by way of rank or merely possessing divine indwelling (ἐνοίκησιν) instead of being vitalizing, as we said, because it has come to belong to the Word who has power to vivify everything, shall be anathema.
12. Whoever does not acknowledge God's Word as having suffered in flesh, been crucified in flesh, tasted death in flesh and been made first-born from the dead because as God he is Life and life-giving, shall be anathema. (*Ep. ad Nestorium* III 12; Cyril of Alexandria 1983: 28)

The purpose of the letter was provocative: it made Nestorius facing a difficult dilemma either to comply with the anathemas, which was unlikely, or to reject them and thus to expose himself to sanctions. Whatever he would choose would have severe consequences for him. Eventually the anathemas worked in the way Cyril wanted them to: Nestorius did not comply and was condemned at the council of Ephesus. The letter, however, had an unintended side effect: it embarrassed not only Nestorius but also many bishops in the East, especially in Syria. Many of them consolidated around Nestorius, even though earlier they hesitated to do so. The church, as a result, became polarized even further.

## Reconciliation with Antioch

After Cyril achieved his immediate goal, which was to bring Nestorius down, he tried to mend his relations with the Eastern bishops, primarily with the Archbishop John of Antioch. The Easterners wanted the same. The emperor facilitated their coming along. As a result of joint efforts, a formula of reunion was penned and adopted. It accommodated the sensitivities of both sides. On its basis, the sees of Alexandria and Antioch were reconciled in 433. The formula stated:

> Accordingly we acknowledge our Lord Jesus Christ, the only-begotten Son of God, to be perfect God and perfect man made up of soul endowed with reason and of body, begotten of the Father before the ages in respect of his Godhead and the same born in the last days for us and for our salvation of Mary the Virgin in respect of his manhood, consubstantial with the Father in Godhead and consubstantial with us in manhood. A union of two natures has been effected and therefore we confess one Christ, one

> Son, one Lord. By virtue of this understanding of the union which involves no merging, we acknowledge the holy Virgin to be "Mother of God" because God the Word was "made flesh" and "became man" and united to himself the temple he took from her as a result of her conception. As for the terms used about the Lord in the Gospels and apostolic writings, we recognize that theologians treat some as shared because they refer to one person, some they refer separately to two natures, traditionally teaching the application of the divine terms to Christ's Godhead, the lowly to his manhood. (*Ep.* 39.5; Cyril of Alexandria 1983: 222)

This formula stresses the fullness of Christ's humanity and its consubstantiality with the rest of humankind. It also speaks of "two natures" of one Christ, something Cyril usually hesitated to utter loudly. Many of his followers were seemingly puzzled or even scandalized that Cyril complied with this formula; they demanded explanations. Such explanations followed in a series of letters dispatched to several bishops. In his two letters to Bishop Succensus, for example, Cyril tried to explain, what "two natures" meant to him:

> If we consider <. . .> the mode of his becoming man we see that two natures have met (δύο φύσεις συνῆλθον ἀλλήλαις) without merger and without alteration in unbreakable mutual union—the point being that flesh is flesh and not Godhead even though it has become God's flesh and equally the Word is God and not flesh even though in fulfilment of God's plan he made the flesh his own. Whenever we take this point into consideration, therefore, we do not damage the concurrence into unity by declaring it was effected out of two natures (τὴν εἰς ἑνότητα συνδρομὴν ἐκ δύο φύσεων); however, after the union we do not divide (διαιροῦμεν) the natures from each other and do not sever the one and indivisible into two sons but say "one Son" and, as the fathers have put it, "one incarnate nature of the Word." So far, then, as the question of the manner of the Only-begotten's becoming man appears for purely mental consideration by the mind's eye (εἰς ἔννοιαν καὶ εἰς μόνον τὸ ὁρᾶν τοῖς τῆς ψυχῆς ὄμμασι), our view is that there are two united natures but one Christ, Son and Lord, the Word of God become man and incarnate. (*Ep. ad Succensum* I 6; Cyril of Alexandria 1983: 74–7)

# One Incarnate Nature of the Word of God

This passage is the only one, where Cyril speaks the language of two natures. He usually spoke of one nature. He preferred speaking of the "one incarnate nature of the Word of God" (μία φύσις Θεοῦ Λόγου σεσαρκωμένη).[1] He believed this formula

---

[1]Sometimes this formula was rendered in a different way: "one nature of the incarnate Word of God" (μία φύσις Θεοῦ Λόγου σεσαρκωμένου).

was coined by Athanasius of Alexandria. It might have been so, but it was not. It was circulated by Apollinaris of Laodicea and has amalgamated the crucial points of the *Logos-sarx* Christology.

Cyril became the protagonist of this Christology and made it a standard in Eastern Christianity. To make it acceptable, he had to make some important clarifications. First of all, he had to distance himself from the previous spokesperson of the *Logos-sarx* paradigm, Apollinaris. It was not an easy task, and Cyril was often suspected and accused of Apollinarism, especially in Syria. He did his best to assure everyone that he accepts the complete humanity in Christ, which is not "being diminished," "neither got smaller" (*Ep. ad Succensum* II 3; Cyril of Alexandria 1983: 89), but consists of "flesh endowed with life and mind" (*Ep. ad Succensum* II 5; Cyril of Alexandria 1983: 93). In contrast to Apollinaris, thus, Cyril envisaged Christ's humanity as not reduced or passive, but as having its own mind and full of its own life and activity. He stressed: "When we say 'flesh' we mean 'man'" (*Ep. ad Succensum* II 2; Cyril of Alexandria 1983: 87).

Still, Cyril's favorite word for Christ's humanity was "flesh." This is because this word served better his main point: stressing Christ's oneness. This oneness constituted the alpha and omega of Cyril's Christology. He believed that the unity of divinity and humanity is crucial for the salvation of humankind and cannot be compromised. Cyril implied three kinds of unity in Christ: his unity with the Father according to his divinity, his unity with all human beings according to his humanity, and the unity of his humanity and divinity in his person, which he called "hypostatic" (καθ' ὑπόστασιν) unity. To underline the latter sort of unity, Cyril called Jesus a "single alive being" (ἓν ζῷον) (*Ep. ad Succensum* II 5; Cyril of Alexandria 1983: 92).

## *Quod Unus Sit Christus*

The idea of Christ's unity is central to all Cyril's *oeuvres*. It is their *leitmotif*, to put in Wagnerian categories. This *leitmotif* comes back again and again, whatever he is writing on. One of his works is even titled *On the Unity of Christ*. It is one of his later and mature theological texts. He composed it in the form of a dialogue. Two unnamed interlocutors test the idea of unity from different perspectives. One of them presents the unity of divinity and humanity in Christ as a single reality. He argues that the word "unity" (*henosis*/ἕνωσις) is more appropriate in describing this reality than the word "conjunction" (*synapheia*/συνάφεια), which is preferred by the "Nestorians." Besides, unity does not impair or alienate the elements it unites:

> The term union in no way causes the confusion of the things it refers to, but rather signifies the concurrence in one reality of those things which are understood to be united. Surely it is not only those things which are simple and homogeneous which

> hold a monopoly over the term "unity," for it can also apply to things compounded out of two, or several, or different kinds of things. This is the considered opinion of the experts in such matters. How wicked they (i.e., the Nestorians) are, then, when they divide in two the one true and natural Son incarnated and made man, and when they reject the union and call it a conjunction, something that any other man could have with God, being bonded to him as it were in terms of virtue and holiness. (*Quod unus sit Christus*; Cyril of Alexandria 2000: 73–4)

Just as the noun "unity" describes the incarnation much better than the noun "conjunction," so the verb "has become" (ἐγένετο) is preferable to the verbs used by Cyril's opponents, such as "has dwelt in." The verb "has become" stresses the unity of divinity and humanity, to the point that the Logos has identified himself with humankind. This verb, however, may also imply that either the Logos or humanity have changed their nature. Cyril ruled out such connotation:

> The Only Begotten Word, even though he was God and born from God by nature, the "radiance of the glory, and the exact image of the being" of the one who begot him (Heb. 1:3), he it was who became man. He did not change himself into flesh; he did not endure any mixture or blending, or anything else of this kind. But he submitted himself to being emptied and "for the sake of the honor that was set before him he counted the shame as nothing" (Heb. 12:2) and did not disdain the poverty of human nature. As God he wished to make that flesh which was held in the grip of sin and death evidently superior to sin and death. He made it his very own, and not soulless as some have said, but rather animated with a rational soul, and thus he restored flesh to what it was in the beginning. He did not consider it beneath him to follow a path congruous to this plan, and so he is said to have undergone a birth like ours, while all the while remaining what he was. He was born of a woman according to the flesh in a wondrous manner, for he is God by nature, as such invisible and incorporeal, and only in this way, in a form like our own, could he be made manifest to earthly creatures. He thought it good to be made man and in his own person to reveal our nature honored in the dignities of the divinity. The same one was at once God and man, and he was "in the likeness of men" (Phil. 2:7) since even though he was God he was "in the fashion of a man" (Phil. 2:8). He was God in an appearance like ours, and the Lord in the form of a slave. This is what we mean when we say that he became flesh, and for the same reasons we affirm that the holy virgin is the Mother of God (Θεοτόκος). (*Quod unus sit Christus*; Cyril of Alexandria 2000: 54–5)

Cyril stresses that the purpose of such unity is the restoration of human nature and its eventual deification, which he calls "assimilation" with God. Without this unity, neither of them would be possible:

> The Son came, or rather was made man, in order to reconstitute our condition within himself; first of all in his own holy, wonderful, and truly amazing birth and life. This was why he himself became the first one to be born of the Holy Spirit (I mean of course

> after the flesh) so that he could trace a path for grace to come to us. He wanted us to have this intellectual regeneration and spiritual assimilation to himself, who is the true and natural Son, so that we too might be able to call God our Father, and so remain free of corruption as no longer owning our first father, that is Adam, in whom we were corrupted. (*Quod unus sit Christus*; Cyril of Alexandria 2000: 62)

# Cyril's Dialectics

The post-Ephesian Eastern Orthodoxy became gradually dominated by Cyril of Alexandria. His emphasis on Christ's unity and the language he had chosen to articulate this unity turned to a Christological golden standard across the East. Even Syria, in its western part, joined the growing consensus about Cyril's interpretation of the incarnation. Those Syrians who identified themselves with Diodore of Tarsus, Theodore of Mopsuestia, and Nestorius of Constantinople were gradually marginalized or condemned. More moderate Antiochians, such as Theodoret of Cyrus and Ibas of Edessa, tried to consolidate resistance to Cyril's theological domination, but eventually failed. Many "Nestorians" were pushed away from the Roman Empire. They had to emigrate to the Persian Empire and further to Central and East Asia.

The diversity of Christological opinions acceptable in the East was reduced to the relatively narrow spectrum of interpretations of Cyril's theology and language. As a result, all posterior Christological debates would continue not between the supporters and adversaries of Cyril (although exchanges between the Ephesians and the "Nestorians" would go on, they were increasingly hopeless), but between factions interpreting Cyril. Cyril provided them with plenty of room for deliberations and disagreements, as his theological language was often inconsistent and vague. As was mentioned earlier, he usually preferred the language of singularity regarding Christ, but occasionally also used the language of duality. This was confusing for many of his followers and became a reason for the splits between them.

Cyril used theological language not to set formulas, but for narratives. His followers, however, would treat his narratives more like formulas. Such a formalistic attitude to Cyril's language would lead to most Christological misunderstandings in the decades that followed. Cyril's own goal was to demonstrate in a convincing way that Jesus Christ as a living and life-giving reality is one. He cannot be divided or cut into parts. Only in one's thought and imagination can Christ's divinity and humanity be distinguished. The difference between distinction as a purely intellectual exercise and separation as a physical or ontological process was crucial for Cyril. He believed that Nestorius and his confederates separated God from a human being in Jesus.

Cyril, thus, applied the epistemological approach, which the neo-Nicaean theologians less than a century earlier had applied to the triune God. For them, God's hypostases are not separated, but only distinguished from each other. Together, they can be only distinguished from God's *ousia*. Their opponents—the "Arians"—envisaged a real, not imagined, ontological chasm between the Father and the Son. For Cyril, his own opponents professed a similar chasm between the divinity and humanity in Christ. This parallel probably made Cyril confident that he continued the Nicaean line.

Cyril implied another distinction in Christ, which had been important in the neo-Nicaean theology—that between the categories of commonality and particularity. The neo-Nicaean theologians had tagged the common aspect of God's existence with the word *ousia* and applied the word "hypostasis" to the Trinitarian particularities. It would be not too speculative to suggest that Cyril envisaged a similar differentiation between what is common and what is particular in Christ. He admitted complete and unalienable divinity and humanity as two commonalities in Christ. Simultaneously, he stressed Christ's singular particularity.

Cyril refused, however, to tag the commonalities and the particularity in Christ with the same terms that had been applied to the commonality and the particularities in the Trinity. His term for Christ's particularity was "nature" (φύσις) and not *ousia* or "hypostasis." This particularity denoted a singular reality of the "incarnated Logos," full of life, dynamism, and salvation. This reading of Christ's particularity was not too dissimilar from the one of Apollinaris. Like the latter, Cyril named it *physis*, because it grew (*phyō*/φύω) from the concurring (*syntrechouses*/συντρέχουσες) commonalities of divinity and humanity.

**Figure 5.9** A modern icon of Cyril Alexandria painted by Davor Džalto.

Such a choice of words caused confusion. Theologians after Cyril would be divided into interpretative groups that wrestled with one another in explaining what Cyril really meant. Those two groups can be identified as "miaphysites" and "dyophysites." These names should not be confused with later identities, which should be written with a capital letter: "Miaphysites," "Monophysites" or "Dyophysites." The "miaphysites" avoided binarities to describe the incarnation. They insisted that, because Cyril preferred the term "one nature," this term is the only permissible to describe Christ. They treated Cyril's theological narratives as terminology. These followers of Cyril can be called "Cyrillite conservatives"—they valued both the spirit and the letter of Cyril's writings. The "dyophysites" were more flexible and open-minded about Cyril's language. Because Cyril did use "two natures" (*dyo physeis*), they also allowed this phrase. Moreover, they interpreted Cyril's "one nature" language as implying two natures in one hypostasis.

# V.4
# Proclus of Constantinople

Such a "dyophysite" interpreter of the one-nature language was the archbishop of Constantinople Proclus. He was born in the capital city at around 390. Archbishop Atticus employed him as his secretary and ghostwriter. Soon he became a titular bishop with residence in Constantinople, where he preached with remarkable success. He could not be elected to the see of Constantinople, because he was already a bishop. However, the insistence of the emperor's sister Pulcheria helped to overcome this canonical obstacle, and Proclus became the archbishop in 434.

Although he had proven himself to be an opponent of Nestorius and his followers, Proclus' policies were mostly reconciliatory. He transferred to the city the relics of John Chrysostom and thus brought back to communion a group of his devotees who had refused to recognize any John's successor. When Proclus passed away in 438, he was loved by the majority of Constantinopolitans—a rather unusual phenomenon in the city, which was accustomed to being judgmental and capricious about its leadership.

Proclus' reconciliatory ethos can be discerned in the so-called *Tome to Armenians*. In 435, some Armenian churchmen approached him with questions about Theodore of Mopsuestia, whom they suspected of being the source of the Nestorian teaching. Although Proclus was anti-Nestorian, he avoided naming Theodore as the source of the problem—for the sake of peace. At the same time, he highlighted some of Theodore's opinions which he regarded as misleading. In the same text, Proclus suggested a reconciliatory interpretation of the phrase, which had been dear to Cyril and yet highly debatable among his contemporaries: "one nature of the incarnate God Word." He suggested to iron out the wording of "one nature" as effectively meaning "one hypostasis":

> Knowing and having been reverently taught only one Son, I confess only one hypostasis of God the Word made flesh (μίαν ὁμολογῶ τὴν τοῦ σαρκωθέντος Θεοῦ Λόγου ὑπόστασιν), the same one who in truth endured the passion and worked miracles. (*Tomus ad Armenios*; Constas 2002: 363)

Proclus repeated the same interpretation of Cyril's "one nature" formula in his homily on the incarnation:

> The same one (ὁ αὐτός) is God and man, truly with the Father with whom he is consubstantial, and alike in all ways (ὅμοιος κατὰ πάντα) unto his mother, sin excepted. The divine nature is uncreated, and the nature that he assumed from us is unadulterated (ἀνόθευτος). And he is the Son, because his two natures are not divided into two hypostases (οὐ τῶν δύο φύσεων εἰς δύο ὑποστάσεις διαιρουμένων), but [his] awesome dispensation has united the two natures in a single hypostasis (τὰς δύο φύσεις εἰς μίαν ὑπόστασιν ἑνωσάσης ἑαυτόν). (*Hom*. 23.11; Constas 2002: 363)

Proclus was the first theologian who finally applied to the incarnation the Cappadocian language that had described particularities and commonalities in the Trinity. He called Christ's particularity "hypostasis" and his commonalities—"natures" (φύσεις). This allowed Proclus, on the one hand, to remain faithful to Cyril. On the other hand, he extended his hand to those who could not ignore some binarity in Christ. Through the Proclean formula "one hypostasis–two natures," oneness and plurality/binarity were reconciled in Christ, just as oneness and plurality had been reconciled in the Trinity through the Cappadocian formula "one essence–three hypostases." The Proclean formula would eventually become the golden standard of the interpretation of Cyril in the Byzantine church.

# V.5

# Eutyches and Monophysitism

In parallel to the binarian interpretations of Cyril, there flourished singularian interpretations. They excluded references to number "two" in application to Christ and insisted on the Christological language based on the "one nature" formula. Some cases of such "miaphysite" interpretation were quite radical. One of them was the case of Archimandrite Eutyches.

He was a spiritual mentor and overseer of the monastic communities in the vicinity of Constantinople. His title "archimandrite" meant something like "a bishop for monks." He had not only spiritual authority of an "elder" (*gerontas*), but also an administrative authority similar to the bishop's, even though he was not consecrated to the episcopal rank. Eutyches was highly regarded at the court, where he offered spiritual counseling to the emperor. He was also a godfather of the influential eunuch Chrysaphius. In other words, he was that kind of seemingly ascetical personalities whom people in the establishment like to have by their side to continue doing what they were doing but with quieter conscience.

Eutyches enjoyed close relationship with Cyril. They exchanged letters, and Cyril shared with him some of his texts. Eutyches, however, read Cyril's texts in his own way, through the lenses of his ascetic experience. This experience taught him to distrust human nature and to rely on the correcting divine grace. It was not dissimilar from the Calvinist spirituality. He concluded from this experience that Christ's humanity cannot be similar to ours. As a result of the incarnation, it ought to be transformed to something less treacherous and vulnerable. Eutyches' ideas about the incarnation came not from highbrow intellectual deliberations, which he disregarded, playing a man of simple faith, but from his ascetic life. They were more appealing to crowds than the deliberations of learned theologians. In a sense, his were populist theology. He believed that when Cyril described Christ as "one-nature," he corroborated Eutyches' own monastic distrust of human nature. The "one-nature" language enhanced Eutyches' belief that Christ's humanity was different from ours—the Son of God could not be consubstantial with us. His humanity was deified not in the sense of appropriating divine properties, but in the sense of an ontological transformation to something which it had been not.

Of course, this was not what Cyril meant, because the Alexandrian archbishop had clearly stated that Christ's humanity did not change. Such a misreading of Cyril raised concerns about Eutyches' teaching in all camps, even antagonistic to each other. On the one hand, moderate Antiochians, such as Theodoret, rebuked Eutyches' tenets, without however pointing their finger at him.[1] On the other hand, even bishops from the strictly anti-Nestorian camp decided that it was too much and Eutyches had to be tried. So he was tried at an *endemousa* council, that is, an ad hoc gathering of bishops staying in or visiting Constantinople for any business (see Φειδᾶς 1971). Such councils were presided by the current archbishop of the city. The earliest recorded council of this sort, under the presidency of Archbishop Flavian, heard in 448 the case of Eutyches and found his Christological views unorthodox.

The ground for rejecting Eutyches' views was soteriological. If Christ's humanity is not the same as ours, then we lose access to the salvation he had offered—just like in the case of Nestorianism. It is only the personal alienated humanity of Christ, which is saved, but not our humanity, which remains outside salvation. Critique against Eutyches was based on differentiation between the ontological status of the human nature and sin. Sin cannot alienate the nature as such. Therefore, when Christ assumed human nature, he, on the one hand, purified it from sin. On the other, he did not change its ontological status.

In the case of Eutyches' Christology, two different soteriological aspects clashed, and two pictures of salvation became confused. The archimandrite was focused on ascetic practices and experiences—they constituted his big picture of salvation. However, from the perspective of orthodoxy, ascetic practices are only instruments that help individuals to appropriate the universal salvation offered by God through the incarnation. Eutyches, in contrast to this orthodoxy, substituted the universal salvation with the mechanisms of its transmission to the individual salvation. Unintentinally, he questioned the very purpose of God's incarnation.

[1]Theodoret addressed the teaching of Eutyches in his treatise *Eranistes*.

# V.6
# Ephesus II

Touching Eutyches was a risky business, as it could easily ignite monastic riots and cause dissatisfaction at the court. Indeed, when Eutyches, who had not accepted accusations, appealed to some major episcopal sees and demanded to be tried by nothing less than an ecumenical council, his request was satisfied by the emperor. A council with pretension to be ecumenical was convened in 449 in Ephesus. Its moderation was assigned to the successor of Cyril in Alexandria and his former archdeacon, Dioscorus.

Dioscorus imagined himself a new Cyril who has a historic mission to give the final battle royale against Nestorianism. In moderating the Ephesus II, he did what Cyril had done eighteen years earlier, but with less subtlety and more voluntarism. Dioscorus had attended the Ephesus I as Cyril's archdeacon and could observe his mentor's activities at the council as close as possible. At the Ephesus II, now himself the moderator of the council, he without hesitation manipulated witnesses and documents. It is not that such manipulations were unheard of at the councils, even ecumenical, but Dioscorus certainly overstepped what was acceptable. He, for instance, decided to skip reading the epistle sent by Pope Leo to Archbishop Flavian with judgments against Eutyches. He tried and accused without inviting the accused to the hearings, which was a violation of basic judicial principles. Even in the Coptic tradition, which holds Dioscorus as a hero and saint, his cunning and coercion are acknowledged as excessive. In the Byzantine tradition, the Ephesus II is regarded as a "robber" pseudo-council.[1]

Byzantines dismissed the Ephesus II not only because it had violated procedures (such things happened frequently), but also because of its theological content. The original goal of the council was to try Eutyches in the wake of his condemnation by the *endemousa* council a year earlier. Dioscorus, however, turned the trial of Eutyches, who was Dioscorus' friend, to the trial of those who had tried this archimandrite.

[1]The characterization *latrocinium* ("robber") was applied to this council by Pope Leo, who was upset that his letter had been ignored by Dioscorus.

**Figure 5.10** Ruins of Justinian's great basilica in Ephesus, built over the place where church councils met.

Source: Photo by the author.

Under Dioscorus' presidency, the council acquitted Eutyches and deposed Flavian. Dioscorus believed he was purging the church of the remnants of Nestorianism and thus finishing the work of Cyril. However, it looked more like a civil war between different factions of the Cyrillites. Those who had accepted Cyril as their unquestionable authority wanted to exterminate each other. The Ephesus II was a beginning of a long-lasting civil war between the Cyrillites, but not its end. The end was devastating for the unity of the church.

The two belligerent factions within the Cyrillite camp were the aforementioned "miaphysites" and "dyophysites." Both shared Cyril's accentuation of Christ's unity. At the same time, they differed about whether it is permissible to *speak* about his binarity. More conservative followers of Cyril insisted that the language to describe the incarnation should refer to only number "one." More flexible "dyophysites" suggested that this language can also use the word "two." At the Ephesus II, the Cyrillite faction of "miaphysites" enjoyed an unconditioned victory. The pendulum of their fortune, however, would swing away in a couple of years.

# V.7
# The Chalcedon

## Leo

The change of tide came from Rome. In parallel to the Eastern standard of Christology, the West developed its own standard. Both standards became personified: in the East by Cyril of Alexandria, while in the West by the pope of Rome Leo (390–461). Leo's most important Christological text, the aforementioned *Tome to Flavian*, marked the center of gravity for the Western Christology and influenced Christological developments in the East. This was a letter sent in response to the archbishop of Constantinople Flavian, who had asked Leo's consent with the condemnation of Eutyches at the *endemousa* council in Constantinople in 448. Leo gave his consent.

Provided with an opportunity, he amalgamated a Western take on the Christological issues discussed at that time. On the one hand, Leo concurred with Cyril in firmly postulating the unity of Christ, who is "true God, and the same is true human being; there is no deception in this unity" (*Epistula ad Flavianum*; ACO$_1$ II$^2_1$ 28.9-10). On the other hand, the Roman pope more emphatically than the Alexandrian pope differentiated between divinity and humanity in Christ. He called them *formae*. This was a stronger choice of words to stress their difference than even *naturae*/φύσεις:

> Each nature (*forma*) acts in communion with the other, as is fitting [for each of them], with the Word truly doing what belongs to the Word and the flesh carrying out what belongs to the flesh. The one shimmers with miracles, while the other succumbs to the injuries. (*Epistula ad Flavianum*; ACO$_1$ II$^2_1$ 28.12-14)

The language that Leo chose was even more vague than Cyril's language. First, *forma* is a notion that implies separation more than distinction: one *observes* two *formae* rather than *imagines* a difference between them. Second, it is unclear whether it is the *formae* or the one Christ who is the subject of his activities. The Latin phrase in Leo's *Tome*, "Agit enim utraque forma cum alterius communione quod proprium est," can be understood in both ways. *Forma* in this phrase could be both *nominativus* and *ablativus instrumenti*. If Leo used *forma* as *nominativus*, then it is the natures of Christ that constitute two subjects of his activities. In the case Leo meant *ablativus instrumenti*, it is a single Christ who acts (*agit*) through his natures. Leo does not make it clear what he meant. Maybe this ambivalence was his choice.

Certain is that Christ's binarity was as important for him as singularity. He viewed oneness and plurality in Christ as symmetrical. Such symmetry remains a distinct feature of the Western Christological orthodoxy even to our days. In contrast to it, the Eastern orthodoxy, since Cyril, has been asymmetrical, with Christ's oneness constituting the center of its gravity. One can observe these two angles of looking at the incarnation even now. For example, the Western Christological mainstream tends to see Cyril as a sometimes-peculiar theologian speaking confusing language. At the same time, most Eastern churches perceive the Alexandrian archbishop as an unquestionable criterion and a departure point for any further Christological discussions.

## The Chalcedon and Cyril

As was mentioned, Leo's *Tome to Flavian* was not brought to discussions at the council of Ephesus II in 449—to the pontiff's much dismay. It was read out, and much appreciated, at a council that met two years later, in 451 in Constantinople's suburb Chalcedon. This was another Cyrillite council, which followed the theological line of the late archbishop of Alexandria. The council of Chalcedon was hermeneutical—it interpreted Cyril's teaching. In this regard, it was similar to the council of Constantinople in 381, which was hermeneutical of the Nicaea. Even more the Chalcedon resembled the Ephesus II, which also interpreted Cyril's language. The difference between them, however, was that at the council of Chalcedon, a different faction from the Cyrillite camp took the upper hand—the "dyophysite" one. After having been defeated by the fellow Cyrillites from the "miaphysite" faction at the Ephesus II, the "dyophysites" regrouped and eventually managed to impose their own interpretation of Cyril's language at the Chalcedon. The card of Leo's letter played in their game.

## Proceedings

The council of Chalcedon became possible after Emperor Theodosius II (in office 402–50), who had completely supported Archbishop Dioscorus and the council of Ephesus II (see Millar 2007), fell from his horse while hunting and soon died. His sister Pulcheria (398/9–453), who disliked Dioscorus, married a general named Marcian (396–457), who was proclaimed emperor. Together, they endorsed the

Cyrillian "dyophysites." Pulcheria and Marcian imagined themselves as new Helen and Constantine. Not without influence of this imagery, they decided to summon an ecumenical council. They wanted to have it in Nicaea. Political circumstances, however, intervened, and the council was convened in Chalcedon—a capital's suburb. It was a convenient place with a short boat ride from the imperial palace. Now it takes only about half an hour to go by ferry from Kadıköy to Topkapı.

Council's presidium consisted of high-ranked officials with the patrician Flavius Anatolius as its head. Marcian and Pulcheria attended one of the council's sessions. Their attendance was staged to resemble a similar presence of Constantine at the council of Nicaea. Unlike in Nicaea, this time all motions and discussions during the sessions were meticulously recorded, so that the council of Chalcedon is regarded as one of the best-documented events in ancient history.

The number of bishops who attended the council was around 370. About one-third of them had participated in the Ephesus II. In Chalcedon, however, most Ephesus II delegates promptly realigned themselves to the new political situation. They rejected the suggestion to read out the proceeding of the Ephesus II, because their names would pop up in a negative light. This indicates how easy it was at that time to defect from the "miaphysite" to the "dyophysite" faction. It was easy not only because bishops were conformists but also because both factions spoke the same *lingua franca* based on Cyril's theology. The two factions soon developed distinct "miaphysite" and "dyophysite" meta-dialects of the same language. Later, they stopped understanding each other. Not because they became incapable, but because they refused to do so.

**Figure 5.11** Kadıköy, now at the heart of modern Istanbul. In the fifth century, Chalcedon was a suburb of Constantinople.

Source: Photo by the author.

# Horos

Imperial ambitions about the council included composing its own creed. The delegates first protested, but then yielded to the will of the emperor (and the empress). As a result, the following definition of faith was composed by a small drafting committee and then adopted by the plenary. It began with the usual rhetoric assuring that this definition does not introduce any novelty (even if it does):

> The sacred and great and universal synod by God's grace and by decree of your most religious and Christ-loving emperors Valentinian Augustus and Marcian Augustus assembled in Chalcedon, metropolis of the province of Bithynia, in the shrine of the saintly and triumphant martyr Euphemia, issues the following decrees.
>
> In establishing his disciples in the knowledge of the faith, our lord and saviour Christ said: "My peace I give you, my peace I leave to you" (Jn 14:27), so that no one should disagree with his neighbour regarding religious doctrines but that the proclamation of the truth would be uniformly presented. But the evil one never stops trying to smother the seeds of religion with his own tares and is for ever inventing some novelty or other against the truth. <. . .>
>
> We have renewed the unerring creed of the fathers. We have proclaimed to all the creed of the 318; and we have made our own those fathers who accepted this agreed statement of religion—the 150 who later met in great Constantinople and themselves set their seal to the same creed.
>
> Therefore, whilst we also stand by the decisions and all the formulas relating to the creed from the sacred synod which took place formerly at Ephesus, whose leaders of most holy memory were Celestine of Rome and Cyril of Alexandria, we decree that pre-eminence belongs to the exposition of the right and spotless creed of the 318 saintly and blessed fathers who were assembled at Nicaea when Constantine of pious memory was emperor: and that those decrees also remain in force which were issued in Constantinople by the 150 holy fathers in order to destroy the heresies then rife and to confirm this same catholic and apostolic creed.

At this point, the Nicaean-Constantinopolitan creed followed, which was the first full official record of it. After that, the Chalcedonian text tried to justify why something could be added to it. This is because new and false interpretations of the incarnation appeared after the council of 381 and they must be tackled. The delegates at the Chalcedon implied that they act in the spirit of Constantinople 381, which had not produced a new creed, but had interpreted the old (Nicaean) one:

> There are those who are trying to ruin the proclamation of the truth, and through their private heresies they have spawned novel formulas: some by daring to corrupt the mystery of the Lord's economy on our behalf, and refusing to apply the word "God-bearer" (*Theotokos*) to the Virgin; and others by introducing a confusion and mixture, and mindlessly imagining that there is a single nature of the flesh and the

> divinity, and fantastically supposing that in the confusion the divine nature of the Only-begotten is passible.
>
> Therefore this sacred and great and universal synod, now in session, in its desire to exclude all their tricks against the truth, and teaching what has been unshakeable in the proclamation from the beginning, decrees that the creed of the 318 fathers is, above all else, to remain inviolate. And because of those who oppose the holy Spirit, it ratifies the teaching about the being of the holy Spirit handed down by the 150 saintly fathers who met some time later in the imperial city—the teaching they made known to all, not introducing anything left out by their predecessors, but clarifying their ideas about the holy Spirit by the use of scriptural testimonies against those who were trying to do away with his sovereignty.

The Chalcedon proceeded with giving an account of the most recent Christological controversies. It emphasized the central role of Cyril of Alexandria in them:

> And because of those who are attempting to corrupt the mystery of the economy and are shamelessly and foolishly asserting that he who was born of the holy virgin Mary was a mere man, it has accepted the synodical letters of the blessed Cyril, pastor of the church in Alexandria, to Nestorius and to the Orientals, as being well-suited to refuting Nestorius's mad folly and to providing an interpretation for those who in their religious zeal might desire understanding of the saving creed.

After a rather long preamble, the council proceeded to the definition, which became famous for some and notorious for others:

> So, following the saintly fathers, we all with one voice teach to confess one and the same (ἕνα καὶ τὸν αὐτόν) Son, our Lord Jesus Christ: the same perfect (τέλειον) in divinity and perfect in humanity, the same truly God and truly human being (ἄνθρωπον), of a rational soul (ἐκ ψυχῆς λογικῆς) and a body; consubstantial (ὁμοούσιον) with the Father according to divinity, and the same consubstantial with us (ὁμοούσιον ἡμῖν) according humanity; like us in all respects (κατὰ πάντα ὅμοιον ἡμῖν) except for sin; begotten before the ages from the Father according to divinity, and in the last days the same for us and for our salvation from Mary, the virgin Theotokos (τῆς Θεοτόκου), according to humanity; one and the same Christ, Son, Lord, only-begotten, perceived (γνωριζόμενον) in two natures (ἐν δύο φύσεσιν) with no confusion (ἀσυγχύτως), no change (ἀτρέπτως), no division (ἀδιαιρέτως), no separation (ἀχωρίστως); at no point was the difference between the natures (τῆς τῶν φύσεων διαφορᾶς) taken away because of the union, but rather the property (ἰδιότητος) of each nature is preserved and concurs (συντρεχούσης) into a single *prosopon* (εἰς ἓν πρόσωπον) and a single hypostasis (μίαν ὑπόστασιν); he is not parted (μεριζόμενον) or divided (διαιρούμενον) into two persons (εἰς δύο πρόσωπα), but is one and the same only-begotten Son, God, Word, Lord Jesus Christ, just as the prophets taught from the beginning about him, and as the Lord Jesus Christ himself instructed us, and as the creed of the fathers handed it down to us.

Having added new distinctions to the creed of Nicaea-Constantinople, the council of Chalcedon forbade any further council to do the same:

> Since we have formulated these things with all possible accuracy and attention, the sacred and universal synod decreed that no one is permitted to produce, or even to write down or compose, any other creed or to think or teach otherwise. As for those who dare either to compose another creed or even to promulgate or teach or hand down another creed for those who wish to convert to a recognition of the truth from Hellenism or from Judaism, or from any kind of heresy at all: if they be bishops or clerics, the bishops are to be deposed from the episcopacy and the clerics from the clergy; if they be monks or layfolk, they are to be anathematized. (Modified translation based on Tanner 1990, vol. 1: 83–7)

## Language

The basis of the Chalcedonian meta-language is Cyrillian. The council's definition begins and concludes by emphasizing Christ's singularity, through Cyril's preferred catchphrase "one and the same" (εἰς καὶ αὐτός). At the same time, the definition avoids another catchphrase that Cyril preferred: "one incarnate nature of the Word of God" (μία φύσις Θεοῦ Λόγου σεσαρκωμένη). The council followed the hermeneutical line of Archbishop Proclus, by substituting Cyril's one *physis* with one hypostasis. The word *physis* was also added to the definition, but from a different context, namely from Cyril's outreach to the Easterners as an attempt at reconciliation after the Ephesus I. In the formula of reunion and the correspondence that followed, Cyril used the word *physis* in application to Christ's divinity and humanity. However, he preferred to put this word with the preposition "from" (ἐκ), and not "in" (ἐν). This was the only detour from the Cyrillian line.

The original first draft of the Chalcedonian definition was even more Cyrillian: "from two natures" (ἐκ δύο φύσεων). Although this draft has not survived, we know about it from the council's proceedings. On the insistence of the Roman delegation, the first draft was rewritten to its present form. This was a concession to the language of Pope Leo. Another concession to him was the symmetric use of four adverbs: "without division and separation" underlining Christ's unity, and "without confusion and change" underlining the distinctiveness of his divinity and humanity. All four adverbs were taken from the vocabulary of Cyril, but they were put symmetrically, which was unusual for Cyril. Nevertheless, both sets of adverbs were placed in the context of a purely intellectual contemplation (γνωριζόμενον) of any difference in Christ. All potentially explosive differentiations were sealed inside a safe logical container of the category of distinction as opposite to separation.

In sum, the overall frame of the Chalcedonian definition was Cyrillian. It stressed the unity of Christ. It was asymmetric, even though it featured some elements of

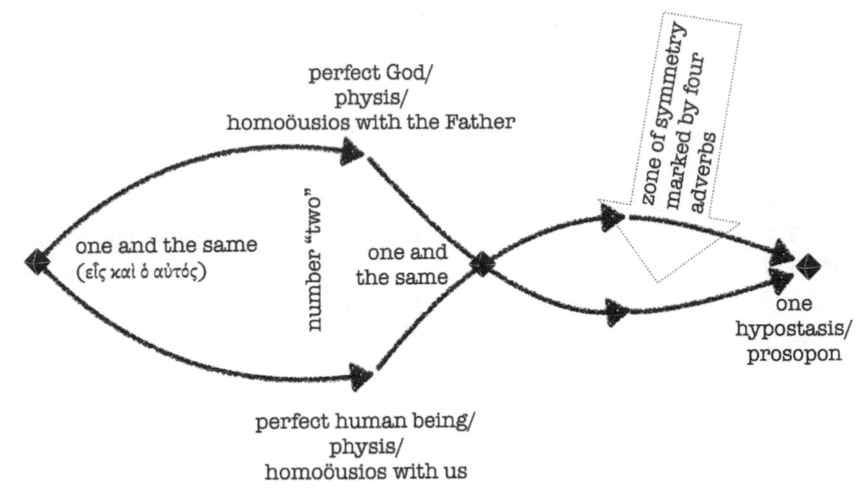


**Figure 5.12** Christ's singularity according to Chalcedon.

Christological symmetry, particularly through the usage of adverbs "with no confusion, no change, no division, no separation." This symmetry, however, was included in the larger asymmetric scheme, which started and ended with the statement of unity. The scheme of the Chalcedonian definition can be drawn as in the figure 5.12.

# Unfinished Businesses

Notwithstanding their common Cyrillite background, the council of Chalcedon was convened as an antithesis to the Ephesus II. It was called to correct and finalize the business that the latter could not accomplish. The "robber council" had been called to condemn Eutyches, which it failed to do. The Chalcedon picked up this pending issue and condemned the archimandrite. It also scrutinized the behavior of Dioscorus. His way of handling the Ephesus II was found unacceptable. Both this council and its president were condemned. Dioscorus was deposed and sent to exile. Probably anticipating what reactions from the "miaphysites" would follow its decisions, the Chalcedon did not condemn Dioscorus and the Ephesus II for wrong faith, but only for the violation of conciliarity. Over 100 bishops who had participated in the Ephesus II, now turned on Dioscorus. They made him a scapegoat for their own sins committed in Ephesus. This does not mean that Dioscorus was innocent, but he was certainly not the only one to be blamed for what had happened two years earlier.

# Canon 28

The council of Chalcedon worked with the active participation of the Roman legates, who represented Pope Leo. It accommodated many Western requests, even if they were risky for the integrity of the Christian East, such as the expression "in two natures." In result, Eastern bishops thought Rome owes them. In addition to that, Alexandria, the jealous rival of Constantinople and situational ally of Rome, was humiliated. Constantinople saw these factors as an opportunity to reward itself with extra privileges. That is how the canon 28 was drafted and adopted by a part of the council. It made more specific the rights that the archbishops of Constantinople exercised in the global Christianity:

> The fathers rightly accorded prerogatives to the see of older Rome, since that is an imperial city; and moved by the same purpose the 150 most devout bishops apportioned equal prerogatives to the most holy see of new Rome, reasonably judging that the city which is honoured by the imperial power and senate and enjoying privileges equalling older imperial Rome, should also be elevated to her level in ecclesiastical affairs and take second place after her. (Tanner 1990: 99–100)

The canon 28 was not a canonical novella. Before the Chalcedon, the council in Constantinople (381) had placed the see of the new capital on almost the same level with the see of the old capital (canon 3). The Chalcedon practically removed the "almost" and equalized Rome and Constantinople. Moreover, it explained why Rome and Constantinople should have their prerogatives in the first place: because of the political significance of the two capitals. No other explanations, such as apostolicity or role of Peter were given. This outraged Rome, whose delegates protested and refused to accept canon 28. This canon was ignored by the Western church until the fourth crusade (1202–4), when Rome used it as a justification for the installation of its marionette Latin patriarch in Constantinople.

The canon 28 made clearer the jurisdictional limits of Constantinople, which now included three dioceses: Pontus, Asia, and Thrace—all in the neighborhood of the capital. It also gave the archbishop of Constantinople a right to override metropolitans under him in taking care of the nomadic communities traversing the territories under their jurisdiction. In the twentieth century, mass migration to the West of Orthodox populations from the Southern and Eastern Europe, as well as from the Middle East, made the canon 28 important and controversial again. The church of Constantinople started interpreting it in the sense of endorsing the Ecumenical Patriarchate with an exclusive jurisdiction over the so-called diaspora. Such interpretation of the canon is contested by other local churches, especially those that have dioceses in diaspora.

## A Second Act of the "Civil War"

The council of Chalcedon turned out to be a second act of the "civil war" that ravaged camps of Cyril's followers, and it was not its final act. The Ephesus II in 449 was the first act of the same war, a sort of thesis in the dialectics of the post-Cyrillite theology. The Chalcedon was its antithesis. Although its intention was to reconcile different groups of Cyril's followers with one another and with the West, the result was rather the opposite. Yes, the West was satisfied with most outcomes of the council (except its canon 28). But conservative Cyrillites who cherished the exclusivity of the "one-nature" language, felt alienated further. Many of them were also "Nicene fundamentalists," as Michael Gaddis has put it (Price & Gaddis 2005, vol. 1: 47). It means that for them any addition to the Nicaean creed was anathema. They saw the Chalcedonian *horos* as such an addition.

From the Western perspective, the Chalcedon paved a *via media* between the extremities of Nestorianism and Monophysitism (now understood more like identities than doctrines). From the Eastern perspective, however, the Chalcedon stopped short before reaching the limits of the Cyrillite orthodoxy. For many Easterners, this council crossed the red line and ceased to be an authentic expression of Cyril's theology. For them, the Chalcedon polluted Cyril's faith with Nestorianism. From an intended reconciliatory event, the council turned to another apple of discord. As an eventual result, global Christianity split to "Chalcedonianism" and "anti-Chalcedonianism."

Originally, as we have seen, these were two factions of the followers of Cyril: "miaphysites" and "dyophysites." They represented two approaches to Cyril: a more conservative and a more liberal one. The "civil war" between these two factions was, from this perspective, a culture war. They alienated from each other so much that they denied the other side to be called Cyril's followers. Both parties eventually came to identify each other with those who had been enemies for both. Thus, the "miaphysites" called "Nestorians" their fellow Cyrillites who admitted binarity in Christ. The "dyophysites," in turn, identified the "miaphysites" with Eutyches—under the same libel of "Monophysitism." This resembles how a century earlier the Nicaeans identified all non-Nicaeans with Arians, while non-Nicaeans saw the Nicaeans as modalists.

# V.8

# Anti-Chalcedonian Résistance

## The Monastic Pillar of Anti-Chalcedonianism

Monastic movement, which emerged at the end of the third century as nonconformist résistance against rapprochement between the church and the Roman Empire, played a crucial role in the theological controversies that followed this rapprochement. Usually, monks sided with the parties oppressed by the state. For example, Antony endorsed Athanasius in his wrestling with the imperial machinery that promoted "Arianism" (see Antony's *ep*. IV 17; Rubenson 1997: 211).

Monastic involvement in the theological controversies increased when controversies focused on the incarnation. These controversies urged monastics to square theological concepts with ascetic experiences. It was mentioned earlier, for example, that Eutyches found Cyril's theological language helpful to describe the weakness of human nature as he realized it through his spiritual battles. Many other monks and nuns struggled to perfect their humanity and realized they could never reach the perfection of Christ's humanity. Consequently, many of them agreed with Eutyches that these two humanities are different.

After Eutyches was condemned by other Cyrillite parties, most monks and nuns sided with the "miaphysite" party, which, as they believed, better expressed their ascetic experiences. Besides, this party, following the death of Theodosius II, became oppressed by the imperial authorities, which redirected their support to the "dyophysite" party—to the extent that the latter became known as "melkite," that is, "king's" party. When the "miaphysite" leaders lost political and military back of the state, they turned to monasteries as their main human resource.

Many monks and nuns, who had identified their ascetic experiences with "miaphysite" theology, sublimated their spiritual militancy against sin to fighting "dyophysites." Sometimes they acted like hunweibins: raiding, crushing, beating, and lynching those whom they deemed to disagree with their understanding of salvation and theology. For example, in the wake of the council in 431, Cyril of Alexandria had deployed from Egypt to Ephesus groups of monks ready for direct action. They physically occupied the streets of Ephesus and helped Cyril secure control over the council. Dioscorus would do the same during the Ephesus II. The miaphysite monks became even more violent in Egypt after the council of Chalcedon. After the archbishop of Alexandria Dioscorus was condemned by the Chalcedon and succeeded by the pro-Chalcedonian Proterius (in office 451–7), Egyptian monks participated in his lynching.

The monastic communities of Upper Egypt, guided by Archimandrite Shenoute the Great, constituted the core of the anti-Chalcedonian movement. Together with Cyril, Shenoute had participated in the council of Ephesus in 431. Later, he allied with Archbishop Dioscorus. His monasteries became a hotbed of the anti-Chalcedonian résistance in Egypt. His reputation of a holy man and a prophet contributed to making anti-Chalcedonianism a part of the Coptic *psyché* and identity.

In Palestine, monks revolved against the bishop of Jerusalem Juvenal, after he had signed the Chalcedonian *horos*. He had to flee from his see to save his life. He was reinstated to his office only with the military support from the government, which added to the nonconformist determination of the anti-Chalcedonians. In contrast to Egyptian monasticism, the Palestinian monks and nuns did not resist the Chalcedon for long. Soon most monastic communities around Jerusalem switched to the "dyophysite" side. They remain to our day a pro-Chalcedonian enclave among the Syrian anti-Chalcedonian majority.

**Figure 5.13** A wall and ancient ruins of the White Monastery in Upper Egypt, a stronghold of the anti-Chalcedonian résistance under Archimandrite Shenoute.
Source: Photo by the author.

The Chalcedonian party had its own monastic supporters, even if they constituted a minority. In addition to the Palestinian monks, it enlisted Pachomian communities in Egypt and monasteries on the Sinai peninsula. The monastery of Sleepless monks in Constantinople became a pillar of this party. This community was established in the 420s. Its founder Alexander brought to Constantinople the traditions of the Syriac asceticism. He introduced a practice of nonstop worship by rotating groups of monks.

From the perspective of the anti-Chalcedonian party, monasticism saved faith from the Chalcedonian compromises with Nestorianism. Since then, monasticism has occupied central place in the Coptic and Syriac traditions. From the Byzantine perspective, however, monasticism contributed to the chaos and eventual schism within the Eastern Christianity. Probably because of such perception, the council of Chalcedon tried to discipline monastic communities by placing them under stricter episcopal authority.

## Pentarchy's Contribution to the Schism

The consolidation of episcopal power, however, did not prevent the schism either. In the fifth century, the institute of pentarchy began growing rapidly, with five senior sees accumulating unprecedented authority. The church was regrouped in five blocs with the centers in Rome, Constantinople, Alexandria, Antioch, and Jerusalem. These blocs became monolithic *inside*, while differences *between* them dramatically increased. Christological controversies amplified these differences and eventually disintegrated the system of pentarchy to two pieces. Alexandria and Antioch opposed Rome, Constantinople, and Jerusalem.

## Severus

A hierarch who occupied the see of Antioch, Severus, became the most prominent theologian of the anti-Chalcedonian group. He laid down the theological foundations of what is nowadays known as Oriental Christianity. The theological language he employed he had adopted from Cyril of Alexandria. In this sense, he was Cyril's interpreter. His hermeneutical approach to Cyril was rather conservative. For example, he insisted that speaking of "one nature" is the only way to describe Christ's unity. Severus' standpoint was strictly anti-Chalcedonian. At the same time, his rejection of the Chalcedon and his insistence on the "one nature" language were not blind. He was creative in substantiating why this language is the only applicable one to the incarnation. In particular, Severus relied on the Aristotelian-Porphyrian logics. His mentality was that of a lawyer and scholastic. His training in law helped him to think analytically. Severus became a master of formulas, which he constructed on the basis of clearly defined categories. One may see him as one of those early Byzantine scholastics who by several centuries predated the Western scholasticism.

Severus was born around 456 in the Pisidian city of Sozopolis, which is now Uluborlu in southwestern Turkey. He originated from a wealthy pagan family, which provided him with the means to receive the best education he could get. He first studied in Alexandria and then in Beirut, where he majored in law. While studying in Beirut, he became involved in the anti-Chalcedonian monastic circles and received there his baptism. Severus soon abandoned his professional career and retreated to the monastery of Peter the Iberian in Gaza. From coenobium, he advanced to solitude and spent some time in the desert. However, his deteriorating health conditions forced him to abandon the hermitic lifestyle. With the money of his family, he built his own monastery, in Maiuma near Gaza. Later, he was consecrated as a bishop of Antioch and immersed himself in ecclesiastical politics. Soon he became recognized as a leader of the anti-Chalcedonian party. Severus enjoyed the favors of Emperor Anastasius, who distanced himself from the Chalcedon. After Anastasius died in 518 and was succeeded by the pro-Chalcedonian Justin I (r. 518–27), Severus fell a victim to the new imperial policies. He was forced to abandon his see and fled to Egypt, where he spent the rest of his life, until he died in 528.

In his theological thinking, Severus was fixated on Christ's singularity. Like Cyril, who had rendered this singularity as "hypostatic unity," Severus also preferred this formula. The Chalcedonian theologians endorsed it as well. However, Severus stressed that his understanding of this Cyrillian formula is different from the Chalcedonian interpretation:

> We ourselves <. . .> believe and confess that the only-begotten Son of God, who is equal in essence to the Father through whose power all things existed, came down at the end of days and became incarnate and was made man—that is, he was united to flesh which had a soul possessed of reason and intelligence by means of a free and hypostatic union from the holy Spirit and from the ever-virgin Mary, Mother of God; and that his nature was one, even when the Word had become incarnate, just as the God-inspired men and mystagogues of the church have instructed us; and we know him as simple, and not compound, in that which he is understood to be God, and composite in that which he is understood to be man. For since we believe him to be Emmanuel, even the same God the Word incarnate out of two natures which possess integrity (I mean out of divinity and out of humanity), we know one Son, one Christ, one Lord. We do not affirm that he is known in two natures, as the Synod of Chalcedon declared as dogma, putting the expression "indivisibly" onto its declaration as a kind of apology. <. . .>
>
> But you can say that the Synod of Chalcedon understood the union as hypostatic, for it says in its definition that there is to be acknowledged "one and the same Christ and Son and Lord and only-begotten in two natures without confusion, without

> change, without separation, and without division; the difference of the natures being in no way taken away on account of the union, but rather the distinctive characteristic of each being preserved from two natures concurring together into one person *(prosopon)* and one hypostasis." But it is plain to all those who are even moderately educated and learned in the dogmas of orthodoxy that it is in the nature of a contradiction to say concerning the one Christ that on the one hand there are two natures, but on the other one hypostasis. For the person who speaks of "one hypostasis" necessarily affirms one nature as well. <. . .>
>
> Thus it is clear that those who were at Chalcedon, when they promoted the dogma that Christ is in two natures, threw in for us the term "one hypostasis" to lead to deception. For if there is one hypostasis, there is, in short, also one nature, as has been demonstrated before. (*Ad Nephalium* II; Allen & Hayward 2004: 59–64)

For Severus, the Chalcedonian "hypostatic unity" was in effect "prosopic unity" (ἕνωσις κατὰ πρόσωπον). This unity happens between individuals who preserve their own hypostases:

> When hypostases subsist by individual subsistence, as for instance, those of Peter and Paul, whom the authority of apostleship united, then there will be a union of prosopa and a brotherly association, not a natural union of one hypostasis made up out of two which is free from confusion.(*Ep.* II; Chesnut 1976: 13)

Severus ascribed such interpretation of Christ's unity to the Chalcedonians and condemned it as "Nestorian." This was a wrong attribution, of course. The Chalcedonians never accepted the sort of unity that Severus described as "prosopic."

The Chalcedonians were also sometimes unfair to Severus and confused his views with those of Eutyches. The latter was a heretic for Severus. The principal difference between the two of them was that, in contrast to Eutyches, Severus believed that Jesus' humanity remained the same as it had been adopted, without any ontological transformation to something else:

> We are not allowed to anathematize those who speak of natural properties: the divinity and the humanity that make the single Christ. The flesh does not cease to exist as flesh, even if it becomes God's flesh, and the Word does not abandon his own nature, even if he unites himself hypostatically to the flesh which possesses a rational and intelligent soul. But the difference is also preserved as well as the identity under the form of the natural characteristics of the natures which make up the Emmanuel, since the flesh is not transformed into the Word's nature and the Word is not changed into flesh. (*Ad Oecumenium* II; Meyendorff 2011: 40–1)

Both Christ's humanity and divinity are real, but they are not two realities. The reality of Christ is one. In other words, there is only distinction and not separation between divinity and humanity, and their differentiation can be perceived only speculatively. Severus thus followed the theological trope of Cyril, who had also distinguished divinity and humanity in Christ only intellectually. Difference between the logical operations of separation and distinction was crucial for Severus:

> Now when we affirm that he exists out of two natures or hypostases, separating as it were by thought alone those things from which he exists or is assembled by nature, we mean this: for it is not as if first of all there existed a duality of hypostases which was thus gathered together into one hypostasis, for this is both ignorant and impossible. For how can those things which subsist individually and separately, and exist in duality, be combined into one hypostasis? Now that which subsists as one entity as a result of being compounded without change from things differing from each other in kind and in substance—such as a reality of the sort that a human being represents, of soul and body—exists indeed in one hypostasis, but by means of reason alone allows those who make distinctions to perceive that he is assembled out of two natures, while he does not subsist in two natures or hypostases. For it is not possible to see each entity as it subsists in its own particular subsistence, but only what arises out of the composition of the individual entities, which is perfectly formed as one hypostasis. (*Contra impium Grammaticum* XI 22; Allen & Hayward 2004: 86)

For Severus, Christ's singular reality can be rendered by both words "hypostasis" and "nature"—in contrast to the Chalcedonians, who applied to it only the word "hypostasis." Severus preferred to call this reality "one composite nature" (see Lebon 1909: 319), while the Chalcedonians spoke about "composite hypostasis" instead of "composite nature." They avoided the latter expression by all means. Moreover, they introduced the formula "composite hypostasis" to replace the Severan formula of "composite nature," as this has been testified by Justinian: "If some say that since they speak of Christ as a single composite hypostasis, they should also speak of a single composite nature <. . .>—this is contrary to piety" (*Edictum rectae fidei* 144).

Severus and his Chalcedonian adversaries might have disagreed on whether the nature or hypostasis of Christ are composite, but they agreed that the word "composite" (σύνθετος) should be preferred to the word "mixture" (μίξις). "Mixture" sounded to both parties too Eutychean.

Both parties also agreed on adopting the term "theandric" in application to Christ, but they disagreed how to apply it. They borrowed this term from the letter of Ps.-Dionysius the Areopagite to Gaius. This letter stated that Jesus exercised his divine and human activities not separately from each other, but as "a certain new theandric activity" (καινήν τινα τὴν θεανδρικὴν ἐνέργειαν ἡμῖν πεπολιτευμένος) (*ep.* 4). Severus, who, in connection with this passage, made one of the earliest references to Ps.-Dionysius' work, suggested to apply the term "theandric" not just to Christ's activities, but also to his single nature and hypostasis: "We confess one theandric nature and hypostasis" (in Diekamp 1981: 309). In contrast to him, the Chalcedonians understood the term "theandric" as applicable to Christ's activities only and only in the sense of communication of two natural activities (*communicatio operationum*).

To demonstrate how the composite nature of Christ can be one, Severus employed Cyril's favorite model (see McKinion 2000: 188–98)—that of a human being. Just like body and soul are not distinct natures, but constitute one human nature, so Christ is one nature that unites divinity and humanity (see Chesnut 1976: 10). Moreover, whatever body or soul do or experience, we ultimately ascribe these activities and experiences to that individual and not to his or her components. In the same way, Severus argued, the one Christ takes credit for everything that either his divinity or humanity do or experience. In this point, he converged with the Chalcedonians, who also considered the single Christ as the ultimate subject of all his natural activities and wills.

The main commonality between Severus and the Chalcedonians was that both insisted on the unconditional singularity of Christ. The main difference between them was about how to use the number "two" in Christology. The Chalcedonians tried to cautiously combine it with Jesus' singularity, while Severus was completely allergic to this number. He believed there is no such an interpretation of the incarnation, which would make possible referring to number "two." Severus rejected all theological expressions that had a slightest hint of duality, such as, for instance, "single double nature" (μία φύσις διπλῆ) (*Ad Nephalium* I).

In the time of Severus, discussions about the number of natures in Christ came to a stalemate: neither side could convince the other side that its own number is correct. They therefore tried some different approaches to the same issue. The category of natural property was employed as a way of thinking out of the box. The Chalcedonian party tried this approach by introducing the so-called theopaschite formula. The neo-Chalcedonian movement that emerged from this attempt, made discussions about Christ's natural properties its signature topic. This shift of focus from one category to another made some people from the anti-Chalcedonian camp to doubt their tenets. For instance, Sergius the Grammarian, who initially was Severus' faithful follower, later on questioned his teacher's point about property, exactly on the dialectical grounds:

> If we speak of two properties, we are obliged also to speak of two natures. But if we suppose that the properties are undivided, neither do those (i.e., the dyophysites) divide the natures, but everywhere proclaim to us [natures] which are undivided. <. . .> Shall we speak of two properties, so that we may remove the foolishness of metousiasts (i.e., Eutycheans), flesh being understood as flesh, and divinity not descending to confusion? (*Ad Sergium* I; Torrance 2011: 2–3)

The anti-Chalcedonian party accepted the challenge to refocus on a new category. Severus became a leading theologian to discuss the natural properties of Jesus. While being uncompromisingly strict about the singularity of Christ's nature, Severus demonstrated more flexibility regarding the category of properties. He admitted some plurality applicable to them, which he called "particularities." He used the word "property" both in the singular and the plural. When he was speaking about the property in the singular, he confirmed that Christ is one being—no surprises here. His explanations became more nuanced, when he began speaking of properties in the plural. By these, he meant "properties of the flesh," "properties of the humanity," and "properties of the divinity of the Word" (*Ad Sergium* I; Torrance 2011: 150). By admitting particularities in Christ's single property, Severus wanted, first, to stress the reality of Christ's humanity, because—here he agreed with Sergius—there was a complete correspondence between nature and its property (*Ad Sergium* I; Torrance 2011: 151). Second, the concept of properties in the plural gave him a solution to the dilemma: How is it possible to speak simultaneously about the unity and plurality of Christ's nature? Severus, as it were, relieved the category of nature from such plurality and consolidated it in the category of properties. At the same time, he rejected to apply number two to Christ's properties, because, for him, this would inevitably lead to acknowledging the duality of his nature:

> If someone should wrongfully divide Emmanuel with a duality of natures after the union, there also occurs a division at the same time, along with the difference of the natures, and the properties are divided in every respect to suit the [two] natures. (*Ad Sergium* I; Torrance 2011: 150)

Admitting particularities in Christ's singular property allowed Severus to stabilize his model of incarnation. Nevertheless, this preserved some issues of this model unresolved, such as inconsistency between the nature and its property. Severus could not get rid of this inconsistency, because, if there is correspondence between property and nature—something that Severus admitted—the latter should feature the same particularities as the former. Severus, while acknowledging particularities of the natural properties, was not prepared to acknowledge them in the nature. This issue was spotted by Julian of Halicarnassus, who, like Sergius, had been Severus' disciple. He identified an inconsistency in his teacher's thought and concluded that it is possible to speak of the single property of the incarnate Logos only if Christ's body is incorrupt. Otherwise, the body's corruptibility cannot coexist in one property with the incorruptibility of the divinity. Severus rejected the idea of incorruptibility of Christ's body, but failed to convince Julian that corruptibility can be a part of the single property of Christ's nature. For Julian, this would simply imply two natures:

> If anyone divides up the one nature of the human being into what is unbodily and what is in the flesh and says: this [the flesh] is corruptible according to nature, even if it has not sinned, the soul in contrast escapes the condemnation to death; [whoever calls upon this analogy] in order to represent the Lord as "naturally corrupted" according to the flesh and as "incorrupt" according to the spirit (i.e., the Godhead), introduces by this means a duality of the Christs, the natures, the properties, and the sons: the one is [son] by nature, the other only in the applied sense. (*Anathema septimum* VII 62)

Julian recruited many followers to subscribe to his ideas. They were called *Aphthartodocetae* (Ἀφθαρτοδοκῆται), which literally means "those who believe in incorruptibility." At some point, their numbers exceeded even the numbers of Severus' followers. This unnerved Severus. He started a defamation campaign against Julian and called him a follower of Eutyches and Manes (see Severus, *Censura tomi Iuliani* 125–6), which of course was not true. Julian was simply more consistent than Severus in applying the logical categories. This helped him to become a more successful leader.

As was mentioned, Severus applied to Christology another logical category—activity (*energeia*/ἐνέργεια). Like his Chalcedonian counterparts, he regarded activities as natural properties and therefore completely correspondent with nature. Since Christ's nature was for him one, so was the *energeia*. His starting point in this regard was Ps.-Dionysius' phrase "a certain new theandric activity." Severus took this phrase as an argument in support of monoënergism:

> The statement of the utterly wise Dionysius the Areopagite, who says: "Since God has become a human being, he performed among us a new theandric activity," [means] the one composite [activity]; it cannot be interpreted other than as a rejection of every duality; and we confess the incarnate God, who operated in this new manner, as the one theandric nature and hypostasis and also as the one incarnate nature of the God-Logos. Because the reason of salvation, which has established new natures, together with them has established new appellations. So that if Christ is one, then we ascend, so to say, to a high mountain and profess one—because he is one—nature, hypostasis, and *energeia*, [which are also] composite; also we anathematize all those who, concerning this [question], teach about a dyad of natures and activities after the unity. (In Diekamp 1981: 309–10)

Such a take on Dionysius' monoënergist phrase was more adequate than the posterior dyoënergist interpretations that would claim that Dionysius in effect implied two activities in Christ. At the same time, just as with the logical category of natural properties, Severus distinguished between the "activity-in-the-singular" and the "activities-in-the-plural." He used different terms to mark this distinction: the former is an activity as such, *energeia*/ἐνέργεια, while the latter is its results, *energethenta*/ἐνεργηθέντα:

> There is one who acts (ἐνεργήσας), that is the Word of God incarnate; and there is one active movement which is activity (ἐνέργεια), but the things which are done (ἐνεργηθέντα) are diverse, that is, (the things) accomplished by activity. <. . .> And it is not that, because these things which were done were of different kinds, we say that conceptually there were two natures which were effecting those things, for as we have said, a single God the Word incarnate performed both of them. (*Ad Sergium* I; Grillmeier 1995, vol. 1: 165)

Severus, thus, again, like with properties, admitted some plurality of Christ's deeds, but rejected applying to them any duality. He also stressed that the only subject of all deeds is the same Jesus Christ. Jesus' singularity is the source of the singularity of his *energeia*. The idea of singularity of Christ's activity became crucial for the generations of Severus' followers. Sometimes, this idea overshadowed even the idea of one nature. For this reason exactly a century later, Emperor Heraclius (reigned 610–42) would construct on the basis of the Severan monoënergism his own monoënergist project. Heraclius' monoënergism was eclectic: it featured the Severan idea of one activity and the Chalcedonian idea of two natures. Later, Heraclius transformed this sort of monoënergism to monothelitism, which stressed a singular volitional capacity of Christ.

In the period when Severus flourished as a theologian, it was too early to discuss the category of will. Nevertheless, Severus touched on it as well, even if slightly. He did so in the context of his explorations of the category of property. Both will and activity are property's subcategories. Therefore, the will of Christ was for Severus single, just as his nature and its property, and activity. Like in the case of activity, Severus ascribed single will to Christ as the sole agent (*Ad Sergium* I; Torrance 2011: 152). This was a ground of his critiquing Leo, who, as mentioned earlier, probably implied two acting and willing subjects in Christ:

> If he (i.e., Leo) in spirit were to hold and confess the hypostatic union, he could not say that each of the two natures keeps its property without detraction, but he would say, like Cyril, that the Logos now and then permitted the flesh to suffer what is proper to it and to operate according to the laws of its nature. Thus the Logos would bear that as its own which is of the flesh, and still not relinquish what he has according to his essence (οὐσία), also not the superiority to suffering and his highest nobility. (*Contra impium Grammaticum* III 29; Grillmeier 1995, vol. 1: 162)

Those Christians in the East who did not accept the Chalcedon, were libeled by their adversaries as "Severans." "Severans" did not seem to object to this libel. Severus was their hero, and they were happy to be associated with him. He became one of the most venerated figures in both Egypt and Syria. A homily delivered by an unknown bishop of Assiut in Middle Egypt in the fifteenth century gives an idea about the extent of his veneration:

> The body of our father the great Abba Severus, remained in the city of Sahā for ten whole months and one day. Dorotheus the notable, who loved Christ—let His name be glorified—would wake up every day early in the morning and go to the city, prostate in front of the body of the saint and be blessed by him, and he had no desire to see the body leave the city, or to send it with a gladdened heart to the monastery of al-Zugāg as commanded by our father the holy Abba Severus. One night while he was sleeping in his bed, our father the holy Abba Severus appeared to him in a dream. He blessed

him and said to him: "O Dorotheus, my special beloved son, why have you forgotten what I commanded you?" He replied, "Never, never, my master and my father! For I have multiplied works of charity as you commended me." Father Abba Severus said to him, "Blessed are you. But I did not mean that; I meant that you have not transferred my body to Alexandria."

He said: "My father and my master, it is not out of negligence from me or forgetfulness but because I did not wish to be parted from your pure body." He said to him: "It is the will of God that my body should be kept in the monastery of the Enaton and that at the appointed time it should be translated to the monastery by the mountain of the city of Assiut just as I previously informed you. <. . .> Tomorrow morning when you awake, take care to send my body to Alexandria and the Lord will reward you for your trouble." Then he blessed him, granted him peace and disappeared from him.

And when Dorotheus woke up early in the morning, he took special care to do what he had been told and sent for a boat and put the body in it accompanied by some trusted people to take it to Alexandria, just as the saint had told him in the vision. He charged them not to enter in the canal but in the lake and from there they would sail to the shore. He gave them silver coins to cover their expenses and to build for it (i.e., the body) a suitable [resting] place.

When they arrived with the pure body a little to the north of Mūysā, they turned a little westward, but the water was not deep [enough] to keep them afloat and they became tired from pulling the boat. They tried hard to keep it afloat without success and were unable to cross. They became confused and worried and all their wisdom abandoned them (cf. Ps. 107:27). But God the lover of mankind, who had hidden the sons of Israel from the sight of their enemies and opened for them a way to cross in the midst of the Red Sea, protected the body of the saint, our father Abba Severus, from the dissidents. For they hated him in death as they had during his life because his sayings cut their hearts like a sword. Then He revealed a miracle by enabling the boat to sail in shallow water for six miles till they came to the place where they could go. Then they carried him to the monastery of al-Zugāg and they built for him a pleasant place where they kept him. There was great joy in the world, and especially in the city of Alexandria.

God made known miracles and wonders by the agency of his (i.e., Severus's) holy body. One of the saint's teeth had fallen when they wanted to shroud him in the monastery and some of monks at the monastery of al-Zugāg took it and wrapped it in a silk veil. It became a source of healing for those who were sick, for they would take it to the city and lay it over sick people and they would be healed. God gave this saint even greater fame after his death than he had enjoyed during his lifetime. (Youssef 2006: 69–73)

To the same extent as Severus was a hero for the adversaries of the Chalcedon, the followers of the council considered him their archenemy. For them, his name became a synonym of Eutyches, Nestorius, and even Jews. None of these comparisons was true, of course. Before condemning him, the Chalcedonians saw Severus as one

**Figure 5.14** Icon of Severus carved on the wooden doors at the monastery of St. Mary El-Sourian (Syrian) in Egypt.
Source: Photo by the author.

of the most capable theologians of his time. In the early 530s, he was invited to Constantinople for peace talks between the pro- and anti-Chalcedonian groups. After these talks failed, however, the *endemousa* synod held in Constantinople in May and June of 536, condemned Severus (see Brimioulle 2020). This synodal decision was ratified by an imperial edict later in August of the same year:

> Nor are we leaving unconfirmed by sovereign ratification the sentence justly issued on Severus,[1] which imposed on him an anathematisation proceeding from practically all the hierarchic and patriarchal authorities, with monastic approval. He had previously, against the sacred ordinances, seized the see of the most holy church of Theoupolis (i.e., Antioch), and created such complete turmoil, such all-pervading disorder, as to precipitate the most holy churches into a sort of truceless general warfare with each other, despite having been written to by our predecessors on the throne. His doctrines were involved, deceitful, blasphemous and foreign to orthodoxy; he created complete turmoil, and clung solely to the loathsome, unholy doctrines pertaining to the error of the two heresiarchs, Nestorius and Eutyches, and the mentors of each—doctrines that, while apparently quite opposed

[1]This passage implies Severus' dethronement by Justin in 518.

to each other, are actually heading towards a single impious end; and he stamped himself with their characteristic arguments. Each of the two doctrines we have just mentioned, those of Nestorius and Eutyches, which were derived from the pollutions of the Arians and Apollinarius, leads alike to the perdition of the soul, but they are mutually conflicting; he has nevertheless fallen, by some paradoxical malady, into both alike. Giving pride of place now to one, now to the other, he has seemed to make himself and his teachings into a collective sump for such aberrations.

Accordingly, he too is to be under the said anathematisation, justly imposed on him by virtually the whole patriarchal, priestly and monastic body of our realm, and to be expelled from Theoupolis. The holder of that see has ousted him for having taken control of it improperly in the first place: the previous holder of the high priestly office was still alive, and had had the acclamation of the most holy churches in his support, but had been deposed from office by his successor. Nor did he stop at that; but he has eventually been placed under general anathematisation from the orthodox catholic church, after filling our state with a quantity of blasphemous and forbidden books. We thus also forbid everyone to own any of his books. Just as it is not allowed to copy, or to own, books by Nestorius (because of predecessors as emperor, in constitutions of their own, decided that they were to be in the same category as Porphyry's discourses against Christianity), so no Christian is to keep the utterances or writings of Severus, either; they are to be profane, and foreign to the catholic church, and are to be burnt by their possessors—unless those who keep them are prepared to be in peril. They are not to be copied in future by any copyist whether of fine copies or of rapidly produced ones, nor by anyone else at all; they are to know that the penalty for those who copy his works will be amputation of the hand. We do not wish to let the blasphemy of his works leave its filthy mark on the time to come, as well.

Similarly, we comprehensively forbid him, too, to set foot in this sovereign city or its environs, or in any other of the more notable cities. He is to sit in solitary inactivity, not corrupting others or leading them into blasphemy, and not constantly scheming some new attack on true doctrines, by which he might aim to throw our most holy churches into turmoil again. (Miller & Sarris 2018: 381–3)

Severus was a prolific author. He wrote exclusively in Greek. However, almost (see Allen 1981) none of his texts survived in Greek because of the censorship imposed by the aforementioned edict. This prescription explains in detail how censorship worked in the aftermath of a conciliar condemnation. Severus' writings were translated into Syriac, Coptic, Ethiopian, and Arabic languages and thus survived.

## The "Monophysite" Identity

A manipulative trope to equalize Severus with Eutyches became popular in the Byzantine tradition. It contributed to a confusing identity, which the Chalcedonians even now often ascribe to the anti-Chalcedonians—the "Monophysites." It would be acceptable to call "monophysites" Eutyches and his immediate disciples, but it is unacceptable to identify modern Oriental Christians as "Monophysites." They prefer to be identified as "Miaphysites." This identity, on the one hand, indicates their adherence to the formula "one nature" (μία φύσις). On the other, it differentiates them from Eutyches.

Oriental Christians stand closer to the Chalcedonians than to the Eutycheans. Thus, both the Chalcedonians and Miaphysites accept that Jesus Christ features the completeness of divinity and humanity. Because of this, they call him consubstantial with the Father (according to his divinity) and with us (according to his humanity). Both groups share Cyril's standpoint that Christ's humanity did not alienate after the incarnation. The same applies to the divine and human properties of Christ—they did not mix up or change. Main difference between them is that the Chalcedonians describe the incarnation in the language of two natures, while the Miaphysites insist that the only applicable to Christ is Cyril's language of one nature. On these premises, they rejected the Chalcedon.

The way the Miaphysites for centuries saw the Chalcedonian Christians was similarly distorted. They confused them with the followers of Nestorius. Only in the twentieth century, both the followers and adversaries of the Chalcedon came together and openly discussed their theological differences. As a result of the dialogues, since 1964 (see Chaillot & Belopopsky 1998: 46–69), the two traditions have realized that they have in common more than they had thought. In their agreed statements, they acknowledge that their differences have been more linguistic than theological (see Chaillot & Belopopsky 1998: 60–6).

# V.9

# Leontius of Byzantium

Severus of Antioch developed a complicated system of arguments based on the logical categories with the purpose to prove that the only way to interpret Cyril's "one nature" language is to accept that Christ had only one nature. Severus' alter ego who opposed him with the precision of one's image in a mirror was his younger contemporary Leontius of Byzantium. Leontius believed that the only way to interpret Cyril's language of "one nature" is to understand it as "one hypostasis" and "two natures." From this perspective, he was an ardent proponent of the council of Chalcedon and a strict "dyophysite." Like Severus, Leontius was inventive in applying the traditional logical categories to prove his points.

Little is known about Leontius' life and personality (see Daley 2017: 1–24). He was born in Constantinople (hence his nickname "of Byzantium") in the last quarter of the fifth century. Judging from his writings, he received an excellent education. According to his own confession, in his younger years he was charmed by the teaching of Diodore of Tarsus and Theodore of Mopsuestia. At some point, he embraced the Chalcedonian faith. Since then, Leontius had been a strict follower of both the letter and spirit of the Chalcedon.

At some point, Leontius entered the monastic community of New Lavra near Jerusalem. There, he became involved in the controversy about Origen—as an assumed "Origenist." It is unclear what "Origenism" meant at that time. Most probably, arguments about Origen camouflaged a culture war between conservative/less-educated and open-minded/better-educated monks. Leontius fell a casualty in this culture war and was eventually expelled from the community by its abbot Sabas. Cyril of Scythopolis has described this episode in his *Life of Sabas*:

> [Sabas] included the destructive heresy of Origen in the rejection of the said heresies, since one of the monks with him, Byzantine by birth and named Leontius, who was one of those admitted with Nonnus into the New Laura after the death of the superior Agapetus, had been found embracing the doctrines of Origen; though claiming to support the Council of Chalcedon, he was detected holding the views of Origen. On hearing this and remembering the words of the blessed Agapetus, our father Sabas, acting with severity, expelled both Leontius and those with the views of Theodore and

> excluded them from his company, and asked the emperor to expel both heresies. (Cyril of Scythopolis 1991: 185)

Leontius' ostracization happened during his stay at his home city Constantinople on the business of his monastery. He decided to continue staying in the capital city, where he established his own *asketerion*. Probably for this reason, he would become known in the local circles as "Leontius the ascetic" or "the blessed hermit Leontius." He was granted access to the court and soon became a leading imperial expert on the Christological issues. Emperor Justinian included him to the commissions on dialogue with Severus and his party during the early 530s. In these commissions and through his writings, Leontius became known as a passionate adversary of the "one nature" language. He returned to Palestine for a short while, to come back to Constantinople following the ongoing "Origenist" controversy. Leontius died in Constantinople in 544, soon after Justinian promulgated the "anti-Origenist" edict (543).

# One Incarnated Nature

While advocating for the language of "two natures," Leontius had to explain what Cyril's language of "one nature" meant to him. Leontius could not simply discard Cyril's language, because in his time, that would automatically qualify as "Nestorianism." He approached this issue creatively and systematically:

> The "one nature of the Word, made flesh," has three [possible] meanings: either it is said by way of paradox, meaning that even though it is "made flesh" it is still only the one reality—in other words still without a body—just as a bronze statue has one nature of bronze, made into a shape; or [it is meant] as a change of essence, equivalent to "one nature of the Word turned into flesh," as one might speak of one nature of water turned to stone; or [it is meant to say] that the nature of the Word, being one, is not considered alone, by itself, but along with flesh. Now if they use this phrase according to the first [two] senses, the refutation of their impiety comes from their own words; for along with Apollinarius and Eutyches, they have done away with the Incarnation. But if they [use it] according to the last sense, why is the nature of the Word, which is associated with flesh, one in nature with the nature of the flesh which is associated with the Word, and why are they called one nature when they are not one in nature? (*Epaporemata* 17; Daley 2017: 320–3)

# Two Natures

Leontius demonstrated even more sophistry in proving his main point: there could be only two natures in Christ, and not one. He exploited a loophole between the logical categories of commonality and particularity. This loophole was identified by early neo-Platonists, such as Plotinus and Porphyry. They discovered it while exploring the cases, when a subject is one of a kind and does not share common nature with any other subject (see Adamson 2014). Leontius followed this neo-Platonic finding and applied it to contemporary Christology: if there is only one being of its kind, then that being does not have its own common nature. In application to Christ, this means that, because he is unique and there are no two or more Christs, he cannot have his own nature. Therefore, he can have only two natures:

> It is impossible to find an individual man who has a different essence from man in general (καθόλου ἄνθρωπον). But in the case of Christ, we cannot find this same set of relationships; for there is no species of "Christs," as there is of man, so that one of these, himself called "Christ" because he is in some way related as an individual to the general common "Christ" (καθόλου καὶ κοινὸν Χριστόν), is said to be one nature in reference to the rest and among the rest, so that we can call him both one and two natures, having the one appellation because of what is common and the other because of his parts—as we have seen in the case of ourselves. For since the reason which holds in our case is not found in his, it is impossible to transfer to him what is only a proper way of speaking for us. It is clear here in what respect man is called one and two natures: he has the one title because of his sharing in a species, and has the other because his parts remain unchanged. But in Christ's case, because he does not belong to a species, how can the two be called one? (*Contra Nestorianos et Eutychianos* V; Daley 2017: 152–3)

Another sophistry, this time from mathematical logics, helped Leontius to make the same point: there are two natures in Christ and not one. He reduced ad absurdum the argument that Christ has one nature by triangulating the relationships between the Father, the Son, and the humankind in the following way. These relationships can be presented as an equilateral triangle. Its sides represent the Father, the Logos, and human beings (Leontius referred to the latter as "flesh"). The triangle's angles represent relationships between these three realities and can be interpreted as natures. This is an innovative way to describe relations between the hypostases and natures. If the sides of the triangle are equal, so are the angles, that is, natures. This implies that, if Christ's nature is one, then it makes the Father's and human natures one and the same, which is absurd:

> Things which are equal to the same thing, they say, are equal to each other. Let us suppose, then, a diagram of an equilateral, acute-angled triangle. As the first side is related to the second, and the second to the third, so the first is related to the third. Draw the three sides, then, and put down three persons, one on each side, and you will find that as the first is related to the second, and the second to the last, so the first will be related to the last. Why do I say this? Because if you concede the right to speak of one nature of the Logos and the flesh, and it is acknowledged that the nature of the

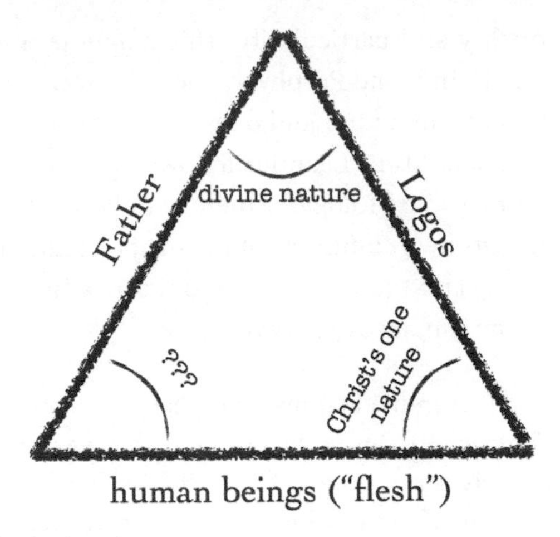


**Figure 5.15** Leontius' triangle.

> Logos and the Father is one, then you are granting that the nature of the flesh and the Father is one. (*Contra Nestorianos et Eutychianos* V; Daley 2017: 154–5)

Moreover, as Leontius argued, the very notion of unity, which is a bottom line of both Chalcedonian and anti-Chalcedonian theologies, could be valid only if different natures are involved in it. Unity cannot unite individuals of the same nature because, in the latter case, the idea of unity loses its sense:

> All beings of the same essence are joined together by the category of nature, and therefore are called "one nature," but beings of different essences tend to be joined by union, not by nature, but union and nature are not the same, then surely the product of both is not the same. (*Epaporemata* 26; Daley 2017: 328–9)

# V.10

## *Henotikon*

The logics-based sophistries that Severus and Leontius exchanged were smart and exciting for their followers, but they could only further alienate them from each other. Such an alienation constituted a major political problem for the Roman state. All the emperors had to deal with the issue of the church being divided by Christological debates. They tried to slow down the swaying pendulum, which was forcefully pushed by the Ephesus II and accelerated further by the Chalcedon. Their efforts to put the brakes on the discussions often had the opposite effect. This was the case of Emperor Zeno, whose strategy was to ban altogether the usage of controversial terms, such as *physis*. This strategy was similar to the imperial policies of Constantius II a century earlier, who prohibited the term *ousia* in theological formulas. Such policy became a feature of the *homoian* movement during the 350s, as we have seen. Zeno applied a similar strategy of censoring controversial theological terms in a document, which became known as *Henotikon* or "The Edict of Union."

The *Henotikon* was published in 482 as an imperial letter addressed to the church in Egypt. It became a product of collaboration between the emperor, the archbishop of Constantinople Acacius (in office 472–89), and the archbishop of Alexandria Peter Mongus (in office 477–90), who represented the large anti-Chalcedonian faction of Egypt. The *Henotikon* remarkably lacks any reference to the dialectical categories of commonality/particularity and distinction/separation, as well as to the terms "nature" and "hypostasis." It stresses the unity of Christ and his double consubstantiality. It also condemns both Nestorius and Eutyches, and confirms the centrality of Cyril's twelve anathemas.

The *Henotikon*'s choice of words regarding the Chalcedon was careful. It did not bluntly reject the council but made its acceptance conditional—if its definitions correspond to the aforementioned criteria of faith. The document relativized the Chalcedonian *horos* even further by absolutizing the Nicaean-Constantinopolitan creed. This creed is the only mandatory one, while the one adopted at Chalcedon cannot have the same authority:

For this reason, we were anxious that you should be informed that we and the most-holy churches of the orthodox in every quarter neither have held, nor do hold, nor shall hold, nor are aware of persons who hold to any other creed, doctrine, definition of faith, or faith than the aforementioned holy symbol of the 318 holy fathers, which the aforesaid 150 holy fathers confirmed. If any person does hold as much, we deem him an alien.

For we are confident, as we have said, that this [creed] alone is the preserver of our sovereignty. Upon their reception of one and the same [creed] all peoples who are deemed worthy of salvific illumination are baptized. All the holy fathers assembled at Ephesus, who further deposed the impious Nestorius and those who subsequently held his sentiments, also followed this [creed]. We also anathematize that Nestorius, together with Eutyches and all who entertain opinions contrary to the previously mentioned [fathers]; we also accept the so-called Twelve Chapters of Cyril, of God-beloved memory, archbishop of the catholic church of the Alexandrians.

We moreover confess the only-begotten Son of God, himself God, who truly became human, [namely,] our Lord Jesus Christ, who is consubstantial with the Father according to godhead and consubstantial with us according to humanity; having descended and become incarnate from the Holy Spirit and the ever-virgin Mary, the Theotokos, he is one Son and not two; for we affirm that both the miracles and the sufferings which he voluntarily endured in the flesh are those of the single, only-begotten Son of God, for we do not in any degree admit those who either make a division or a confusion, or introduce [the notion of] phantom, inasmuch as his sinless and true incarnation from the Theotokos did not produce an addition of a Son. For the Trinity persisted as a Trinity even after one [person] of the Trinity, God the word, became incarnate.

Therefore, knowing that neither the most-holy orthodox churches everywhere, nor the most-devout priests, who lead them, nor Our Own Sovereignty, have allowed or do allow any other creed or definition of faith than the aforementioned [holy] doctrine, you should unite yourselves thereto without hesitation.

Thus we write these things, not to set forth a new form of faith, but to assure you.

But we anathematize everyone who has thought or thinks anything different, either presently or formerly, whether at Chalcedon or in any other synod whatsoever, especially [the aforementioned] Nestorius and Eutyches, and those who maintain their doctrines. (In Kinzig 2017, vol. 3: 349–50)

The purpose of the *Henotikon* was to reach a compromise between the pro- and anti-Chalcedonian groups. It was a project with zero sum: the church's unity would be achieved at the expense of its doctrinal integrity. This approach did not work, however. The Chalcedonians were dissatisfied with the relativization of the council of Chalcedon. The church of Rome went as far as to break communion with the church of Constantinople. This became known as the Acacian schism—after the name of the archbishop of Constantinople who had drafted and promoted the *Henotikon*. At the same time, for some anti-Chalcedonian groups, which were pejoratively branded as "the Headless" (*Akephaloi*/Ἀκέφαλοι), the *Henotikon* was not anti-Chalcedonian enough. Even those who agreed to accept the *Henotikon* disagreed on how to interpret this document. For some, it was quite compatible, and for others completely incompatible with the Chalcedon. The church historian Evagrius described this chaotic situation as follows:

> And so, during this period, whereas the Synod at Chalcedon was neither openly proclaimed in the most holy churches, nor indeed universally repudiated, each of the prelates conducted himself according to his belief. And some adhered very resolutely to what had been issued at it, and made no concession with regard to any syllable of what had been defined by it, and did not even indeed admit a change of letter, rather, with great frankness they also recoiled from, and absolutely declined to tolerate communion with those, who did not accept what had been issued by it. Others, on the other hand, not only refused to accept the Synod at Chalcedon and what had been defined by it, but even encompassed it and the Tome of Leo with anathema. Others relied on the Henoticon of Zeno, and that even though they were at odds with one another over the one and the two natures, since some were deceived by the composition of the missive, while others inclined rather to greater peace. As a result all the churches were divided into distinct parties, and their prelates had no communion with one another. Consequently it came about that there were very many divisions both in the East and in the western regions and in Libya, since the Eastern bishops were not on terms with those in the West or in Libya, nor in turn were the latter with those in the East. The situation became more absurd. For the prelates of the East were not even in communion with each other, nor indeed were those directing the sees of Europe or Libya, and much less so with outsiders. (*Historia ecclesiastica* III 30; Evagrius Scholasticus 2000: 166–7)

In sum, Zeno's strategy to mute Christological discussions and to exclude from them such keywords as nature and hypostasis failed. This failure was similar to the similar *homoian* policies of Constantius II, who had also tried to reduce theological discussions by excluding the term *ousia* from them. A neo-Nicaean synthesis had been designed to rescue the church from the dead-end of homoianism in the fourth century. A neo-Chalcedonian synthesis one and a half centuries later helped the church to overcome, at least partially, the crisis caused by the censorship-based policies of Zeno.

# V.11

# Neo-Chalcedonianism

Just as the "neo-Nicaeans" did not call themselves so, so "neo-Chalcedonianism" is a modern technical term. It means a synthetic upgrade of the original Chalcedonian language. It functioned as a dictionary translating the language of the Chalcedon back to the language of Cyril. Neo-Chalcedonian approach was ecumenical—aiming at the reconciliation of antagonistic Cyrillite parties.

## Justinianian Ecumenism

Justinian, initially de facto and from 527 the de jure ruler of the Roman Empire, instead of imposing upon the arguing sides silencing and coercion, initiated theological dialogues between them. In the early 530s, he invited to Constantinople some anti-Chalcedonian churchmen, including Severus, to engage them in discussions with the Chalcedonian theologians, such as Leontius of Byzantium. Justinian made dialogue the main method of his ecumenical project. This does not mean that he abstained from using coercion altogether—something unthinkable in his time (see Gaddis 2005), but he certainly wanted also to convince and not just to force the opponents to arrive at an agreement.

While publicly positioning himself as a Chalcedonian, Justinian wanted to give the anti-Chalcedonians an impression that he is not against them. His wife Theodora helped him. Publicly, she appeared to align more with the adversaries of the council. She hosted them at her premises and was generous in supplying them with what they needed, including hers and the emperor's ear. It was a smart ecumenical strategy, when the royal family demonstrated to their subjects how supporters and adversaries of the Chalcedon could live together and love one another.

Justinian's political ambition was enormous. He dreamed of restoring the empire to its former glory. He realized that without restoring the church's unity, his political ambition would remain a utopia. Neo-Chalcedonianism was designed to make Justinian's political ambition a reality. It was, therefore, also a political project. At the same time, Justinian sincerely believed that his historical mission was to restore the church's unity—he was an enthusiast of ecumenism. If he succeeded in bringing the divided sides together, he hoped to be eligible for the heavenly mandate for his political and military undertakings. Justinian was instigated to believe in his special mission by the pandemic of bubonic plague, which broke out in 542–3 and was named after him, "Justinianic plague" (see Little 2009). Justinian contracted the disease but survived. His miraculous healing motivated him to work harder toward achieving the unity of the church.

Justinian did not want this unity with zero sum—at the expense of doctrinal integrity. He believed he could make it a win-win project, when the empire could be strengthened and the church could restore its integrity without sacrificing doctrine. Eventually, the empire under Justinian reached the highest point in its history. The restoration of the church's unity, however, was less successful—the Chalcedonian and non-Chalcedonian parties remained divided. Moreover, during Justinian's reign, the anti-Chalcedonians began consecrating their own hierarchy and set up church structures independent from the imperial ones. Notwithstanding this, the Justinianian neo-Chalcedonian ecumenical project produced a theological synthesis, which outlived its time and remains actual even in our days.

## Neo-Chalcedonian Meta-dialect

The main assumption of the neo-Chalcedonian project was that the difference between the followers and adversaries of the Chalcedon is superficial. At the bottom line, they understand the incarnation approximately in the same way, with the theology of Cyril of Alexandria constituting their common denominator. They disagree only in how they interpret him. The Chalcedonian interpretation of Cyril, which unpacked his formula "one incarnate nature of the Word" as "one hypostasis and two natures," was not acceptable for those Cyrillites who insisted on the language of "one nature." Neo-Chalcedonians, instead of solving the seemingly insolvable dilemma of either one or two natures, suggested that both languages can be valid—depending on how one interprets them. As was mentioned earlier, the council of Chalcedon per se was an interpretation of Cyril's theology. Neo-Chalcedonianism now interpreted the Chalcedon—in the light of Cyril. That is why it is sometimes also called "Cyrillian Chalcedonianism" (see Meyendorff 1987: 34f). It can be also called an interpretation of the interpretation.

Roman and Antiochian dyophysites contemplated the neo-Chalcedonian project as political and a rollback halfway toward the miaphysite theology. The mainstream Eastern theology, however, came to perceive the neo-Chalcedonian theology as a restoration of equilibrium within the Cyrillite Christological paradigm. It was mentioned earlier that for many Cyrillite theologians the Chalcedon came

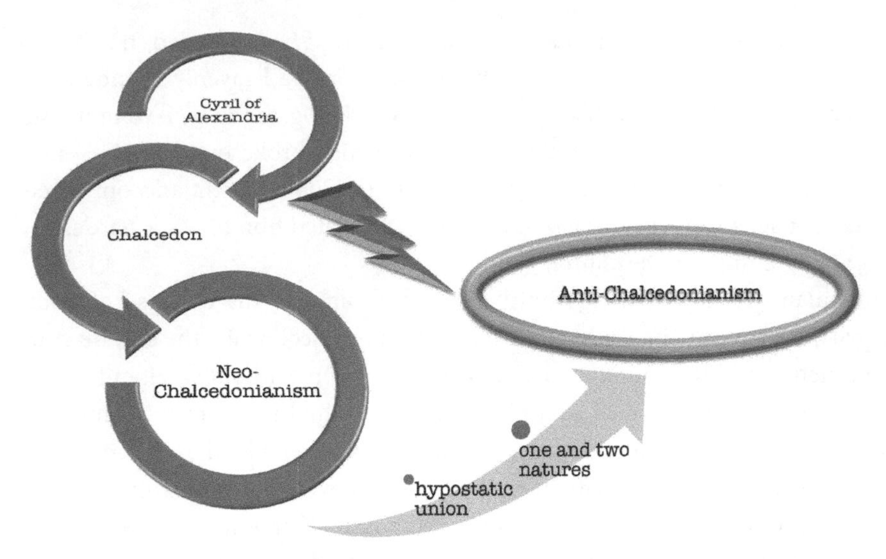


**Figure 5.16** Cyrillite factions from the neo-Chalcedonian perspective.

dangerously close to the edge of this paradigm. For some, it has crossed the red line with Nestorianism. Even many convinced Chalcedonians admitted that the Chalcedon could not be placed at the center of the Cyrillite paradigm. Neo-Chalcedonianism was designed to mark this center and indeed could be regarded as recalibrating both "one nature" and "two natures" interpretations of Cyril's theology.

The neo-Chalcedonian theological language was synthetic and perhaps even eclectic. It was a Christological Esperanto, which includes elements from different languages in order to remove linguistic barriers. Neo-Chalcedonian language was designed with the purpose to make the pro- and anti-Chalcedonian parties speaking the same theological language again. Regarding the traditional keywords of the theological debates, such as hypostasis and *physis*, neo-Chalcedonianism legitimized using both "one nature" and "two natures" lexemes. It also coined the phrase "composite hypostasis"—to stress both oneness and diversity in Christ. At the same time, it rejected the phrase "composite nature." In addition to these terms, the neo-Chalcedonian Christological Esperanto included such categories as property, activity, and will. These terms had already been a part of Christological discussions—since at least Apollinaris of Laodicea. However, in the neo-Chalcedonian theology, they moved from the periphery to the center of discussions.

## Scythian Monks

Neo-Chalcedonianism emerged from Scythia, somewhere around the Danube delta, on the territory of Dobrudja shared by modern Romania and Bulgaria. A group of monks from that region approached their compatriot Justinian with an idea of how to bridge the Chalcedonian and anti-Chalcedonian standpoints. They suggested speaking of Christ as "one of the Trinity who has incarnated and suffered" (*Christus unus ex Trinitate incarnatus et passus*). They believed this formula could reconcile dyophysites and miaphysites. Indeed, variations of the formula "Holy God, Holy Strong, Holy Immortal, *who was crucified for us*, have mercy on us!" had been dear to the miaphysites since at least the Chalcedon. For them, it stressed that the Word *became* a human being to the ultimate extent, so that sufferings could be ascribed to his divinity through *communicatio idiomatum*. The Scythian monks believed that the same formula could be interpreted in the Chalcedonian sense and rendered it in the way mentioned earlier.

The rationale of the Scythians was to leave behind the endless discussions about the natures of Christ and instead to focus on Christ's activities and sufferings. Justinian, whom they approached, first rejected this rationale, but soon realized its ecumenical potential and enthusiastically embraced it. Focus on activities in Christ became the signature of neo-Chalcedonianism. Another characteristic feature of the neo-Chalcedonian theology became the nonexclusive and interchangeable use of the formulas "one" and "two natures." Such a use was also suggested by the Scythian monks:

> In accordance with the tradition of the Holy Fathers, we confess our Lord Jesus Christ in two united and unconfused natures (that is, the natures of divinity and humanity), in one person or subsistence. We do not accept those who preach one incarnate nature of God the Word and who turn away from the faith of the venerable Chalcedonian council. Nor do we admit those who deceitfully profess two natures yet have difficulty in confessing the one incarnate nature of God the Word because they think that this is contrary to the profession of the two natures. Contrary to their opinion, the phrase "one incarnate nature of God the Word" signifies nothing other than two natures ineffably united, as the blessed Cyril (bishop of the city of Alexandria) wrote in his second letter to Succensus (bishop of Diocaesarea). (*Epistula Scytharum monachorum ad episcopos*; Fulgentius 2013: 26)

# The Only-Begotten Son

Justinian began energetically promoting the *unus ex Trinitate* formula and all its ramifications. His court theologians composed a liturgical hymn, which embedded the *unus ex Trinitate* wording and was supposed to be sung in both Chalcedonian and anti-Chalcedonian liturgies. Justinian's court succeeded in making the hymn well received by both communities. It remains at the center of the Byzantine liturgy as its third antiphon:

**Figure 5.17** St. Sophia in Constantinople built by Justinian. The neo-Chalcedonian hymn "Only-begotten Son" was probably sung first here.
Source: Photo by the author.

> Only-begotten Son and Word of God, who, being immortal, undertook to become incarnate from the Theotokos and always Virgin Mary for our salvation, who became a man immutably and was crucified, o Christ God, in death trampling upon death, being one of the Holy Trinity, praised together with the Father and the Holy Spirit, save us! (In Menze 2009: 174)

A similar hymn also continues to be used in the Oriental Syriac liturgy, where its authorship is ascribed to Severus of Antioch:

> I will magnify thee, o God my king, whose only-begotten Son who was immortal in his nature and came in grace for the life and salvation of the race of men and became incarnate of the holy and glorious pure virgin the mother of God Mary: he took a body without change and was crucified for us, even Christ our God, and by his death trampled under foot our death and destroyed it, who is one of the holy Trinity and is worshipped and glorified equally with his Father and his Holy Spirit. (In Brightman 1896, vol. 1: 77)

# Three Chapters

Neo-Chalcedonianism, in interpreting Cyril, made slightly different accents on his work, in comparison with the Chalcedon. Thus, Cyril's third letter to Nestorius, which was written in a rude language and included twelve anathemas, had been silently skipped at the council in Chalcedon. It resurfaced in the neo-Chalcedonian discourses. Simultaneously, the neo-Chalcedonians condemned some texts that criticized Cyril and had been spared by the Chalcedon. These texts came to be known as "three chapters": the writings of Theodore of Mopsuestia, the critical texts against Cyril by Theodoret of Cyrrus, and the letter by Ibas of Edessa to Mari "the Persian." The question, what to do with these texts, suddenly became central to the theological debates during the first half of the sixth century.

The Ephesus II had deposed Theodoret and Ibas, but the Chalcedon reinstated them, after they publicly condemned Nestorius. The neo-Chalcedonians, however, applied a hybrid approach to these figures. On the one hand, they spared them of personal condemnation. On the other, their writings, in which they had criticized Cyril and his twelve anathemas, were condemned. Emperor Justinian got himself personally involved in promoting the condemnation of the "three chapters." He issued a relevant edict in 543–4. Ten years later, he urged a council, which he convened in Constantinople and which would become known as fifth ecumenical, to confirm this condemnation (see canons 12–14; Price 2009, vol. 2: 124–6). He simultaneously suppressed any opposition to the condemnation and, more generally, to his neo-Chalcedonian undertakings, including the one coming from the bishop of Rome. Justinian forced Pope Vigilius (in office 537–55) to eventually accept the condemnation of "the three chapters"—despite his active unwillingness. A treatise from the mid-sixth century, falsely attributed to Leontius of Byzantium, *On the Sects*, describes the motivation of Justinian in condemning the "three chapters":

> Justinian, seeing that the Hesitants (i.e., Severans) inveighed against Theodoret and Ibas and rejected the council [of Chalcedon] because of them, anathematized them. The Hesitants ask us, "Why do you anathematize them? They are either good or evil. If they are good, why do you anathematize them? If they are evil, why did the council accept them? If you anathematize them as evil, what does that imply about the Council of Chalcedon, which accepted them and which you accept?" To this we reply that Justinian did this out of accommodation. For when, as we have said, he saw the Hesitants rejecting the council because of these men, he thought that, if he anathematized them, he would get the council accepted; and therefore he thought it appropriate to anathematize two individuals (even if they ought not to have been anathematized) so that he might bring about the reunion of all. This is why he anathematized them. Nevertheless, not even so did the Hesitants accept the council. (*De sectis*; Price 2009, vol. 1: 34–5)

# "Origenism"

Justinian's pattern in condemning "Origenism" was similar to his campaign against the "three chapters." He initiated this condemnation twice, in 543 and 553, and insisted on condemning both Origen's ideas and personality. In his letter to the council held in Constantinople in 553, the emperor described the "Origenist" views as follows:

> They (i.e., the contemporary "Origenists") assert that there were minds without any number or name, with the result that there was a henad of all the rational beings through identity of substance and operation and through power and their union with and knowledge of God the Word, and that when they reached satiety with divine love and contemplation, corresponding to the turning of each to what is worse, they clothed themselves with more subtle or denser bodies and were allotted names, and that this is the origin of the existence of the heavenly and ministering powers. Moreover, [they assert] that the sun, the moon and the stars, belonging themselves to the same henad of rational beings, became what they are through turning to what is worse, while the rational beings who for the greater part grew cold in divine love were named souls and were decked in our more dense bodies, and those who had reached the acme of evil were bound to cold and dark bodies and became and are named demons; and that from the state of the angels originates that of the soul, and from that of the soul that of demons and human beings, and from the whole henad of rational beings one mind alone remained undeviating and constant in divine love and contemplation, and it became Christ and King and a human being; and that there will be a total destruction of bodies with the Lord himself first shedding his own body and [then] of all the others; and that all will be raised again to the same henad and become minds (as they were in their pre-existence), when indeed the devil himself and the other demons are restored to the same henad, and when impious and godless human beings will be with godly and inspired men and the heavenly powers and will enjoy the same union with God that Christ too enjoys, just as in their pre-existence, with the result that there will be no difference at all between Christ and the remaining rational beings, neither in substance nor in knowledge nor in power nor in operation. (In the Byzantine chronicle by George the Monk and Cedrenus; Price 2009, vol. 2: 282–3)

The council of 553 followed the emperor's request and condemned both the person and the teaching of Origen (see Price 2009, vol. 2: 284–6). This was an anachronistic denunciation, which happened three centuries after Origen's death. Even during the fourth-century controversies surrounding the council of Nicaea and Origen's legacy, when there were much more reasons to blame Origen than in the time of Justinian, the church did not proceed to condemn him or his writings. In the sixth century, no additional theological reason emerged for such condemnation. Moreover, condemning Origen was seemingly irrelevant to the epic pan-imperial battles that concentrated on Christological issues.

Anti-Origenist campaign tackled local quarrels among marginal monastic groups, mostly in Palestine. These monks apparently entertained some Origenist ideas, such as *apokatastasis*. However, we cannot be sure that these monks were actually Origenists. Accusations against them, coming from their anti-Origenist adversaries, seem to be unreliable. For instance, the prominent anti-Origenist witch-hunter, Cyril of Scythopolis (see Stallman-Pacitti 1991), accused Leontius of Byzantium of being a champion of "Origenism." However, not a single passage in the surviving large bulk of Leontius' writings betrays a hint of Origenism. Moreover, in the only reference Leontius made to Origen, he described him as a theologian whom "we do not admire" (see Price 2009: vol. 2: 273).

It seems that "Origenism" became a label for a phenomenon, which in our days could be called "liberal thinking." In the monastic communities of that time, "liberalism" could primarily mean an interest in speculative theology and logical categories. Only a small fraction of monks could be characterized as "Origenists" according to these criteria. The majority was conservative, poorly educated, and hostile to intellectual inquiry. Origenist controversies in the sixth century, consequently, can be seen as an instance of ancient culture wars (see Clark 1992). During the Late Antiquity and Middle Ages, such wars were waged under various theological pretexts.

For Justinian, it seems, the "Origenist" controversies in Palestine provided a helpful pretext to appease the conservative anti-Chalcedonian monastic majority. This majority looked at the Chalcedon as a "liberal" assault against the traditional theology associated with the name of Cyril of Alexandria. The same group was also suspicious about Justinian's ecumenism, which he carried out as the neo-Chalcedonian project. As in our time most monks are anti-ecumenical, so they were in the time of Justinian. By condemning "Origenism," the emperor wanted to communicate to the conservative monastic masses a message that the Chalcedon was not a gathering of highbrow "liberal" intellectuals, and his own ecumenism is consistent with theological conservatism.

To satisfy the conservatives, thus, Justinian sacrificed the "three chapters" and Origen's writings. He also applied *damnatio memoriae* to Origen and Theodore of Mopsuestia. It seems that Justinian condemned Origen personally to justify the postmortem personal condemnation of Theodore: If Origen, who lived three centuries ago, could be condemned, why not Theodore? These condemnations, thus, became a tactical move in his strategy of winning a culture war. By winning this war, he hoped to enhance the integrity of his empire.

## Edict on Orthodox Faith

Notwithstanding this political rationale, Justinian was sincerely interested in theology. He dedicated his spare time to studying patristic texts and surrounded himself with good theologians who advised him on controversial issues. As a result, he eventually became able to produce his own theological statements, which, one should admit, are of good quality. Particularly impressive is his edict *On the Orthodox Faith*, which was published in 551. It contains key points of the neo-Chalcedonian language and theology, as they were envisaged by Justinian, such as the "theopaschite formula" *unus ex Trinitate*:

> Even after becoming man he is one of the holy Trinity, the only-begotten Son of God, our Lord Jesus Christ, composite from both natures; that Christ is composite we profess, following the teaching of the holy fathers. For as regards the mystery of Christ the union by composition excludes both merger and division, and protects the specific character of each nature, and presents one hypostasis or person of God the Word even with the flesh; he is one and the same, complete in Godhead and complete in manhood, not as in two hypostases or persons but acknowledged in both divine and human nature (so that both maybe one), complete God and complete man, the same Jesus Christ our Lord, glorified is one of the holy Trinity together with the Father and the Holy Spirit. (*Edictum rectae fidei*; Price 2009, vol. 1: 133–4)

Justinian propagated the term "composite hypostasis" and rejected "composite nature"—on the solid ground of the Aristotelian-Porphyrian logics:

> Nature and hypostasis are not the same. For all the holy fathers in harmony teach us that nature or essence and form is one thing and hypostasis or person another, and that nature or essence and form indicate the universal, while hypostasis or person indicate the individual. If some people say that, just as one composite hypostasis is attributed to Christ, so one must attribute one composite nature, we shall show that this is the alien to piety. (*Edictum rectae fidei*; Price 2009, vol. 1: 140)

## Council of Constantinople 553

This edict became a blueprint for the decisions of a big council that Justinian convened in Constantinople in 553. The council's purpose was to confirm the emperor's ecumenical initiatives and theological ideas. Although he demonstratively abstained from its sessions, Justinian designed them from the beginning to the end and made sure they followed his scenario. There was little improvisation at this gathering, which duly ticked the checklist drafted by the emperor, including the condemnation of the "three chapters" and "Origenism." The council's main task was to give its *imprimatur* to the neo-Chalcedonian Christology, which since then has become the Byzantine Christological mainstream. Neo-Chalcedonianism, thus, has been designed as a synthetic and ecumenical doctrine, underlined by a political agenda.

## Reception of Neo-Chalcedonianism

There was some tangible sabotage of the council both in the East and in the West, in both the Chalcedonian and anti-Chalcedonian camps. Some did not like the condemnation of the "three chapters," while others were embarrassed by the vandalization of Origen's legacy. For many, the council marked a partial restoration of miaphysitism and a dangerous revisionism of the Chalcedon. For their opponents, the council was not miaphysite enough. To suppress the opposition to the council, Justinian undertook active and often coercive measures.

These measures worked well for the Chalcedonians, who piecemeal arrived at the consensus that the neo-Chalcedonian council continued the line of the Chalcedon and did not disrupt it. Although Pope Vigilius resisted the council, his successors would eventually yield to accepting it, even if with reservations. The most prominent theologians in the generations that followed, such as Maximus the Confessor, Anastasius of Sinai, and John of Damascus, were already natural neo-Chalcedonians. The Byzantine church eventually received the council of 553 as ecumenical.

Less successful and more painful was the reception of the Constantinople 553 in the anti-Chalcedonian circles. Justinian's strategy behind the condemnation of the "three chapters" and "Origenism" did not work—these sacrifices were not sufficient for the conservative anti-Chalcedonians. The anti-Chalcedonians also did not buy into neo-Chalcedonianism, which for them was a Trojan horse of Nestorianism. They continued regarding Cyril and the Chalcedon worlds apart from each other.

Quite unexpectedly, however, the neo-Chalcedonian project attracted some interest of the Eastern Syrian Christians in the Persian Empire. On the one hand, in spite of the anti-Chalcedonian conviction that Justinian was Nestorian, for the proper Nestorians he was a monophysite. Babai the Great, for instance, presented him as a heretic and tyrant (see Metselaar 2019: 91). On the other hand, the same Babai picked up the Justinianian fight against "Origenism." He redirected it against his own opponents, such as the scholarch of the school in Nisibis Ḥenana of Adiabene (d. c. 610), whom he accused of "Origenism." Ḥenana, in his turn, applied the concept of composite *qnoma* of Christ, which was similar to the Justinian's concept of composite hypostasis. He seemed to appreciate quite a few lexemes from the neo-Chalcedonian meta-dialect. This appreciation, however, stirred an internal controversy in the Church of the East, which eventually rejected Ḥenana's ideas. Ironically, he was accused of Origenism because of the teaching that in Byzantium had been promoted by anti-Origenists. This episode is another illustration of how the accusations of "Origenism" were often brought against those of opposite opinions, which had little to do with the original ideas of Origen.

# V.12
# Monoënergism

Neo-Chalcedonianism demonstrated some tangible impact on anti-Chalcedonians only eighty years after the council of 553, which was the main forum of this movement. In 633, the Chalcedonian archbishop of Alexandria Cyrus managed to make some anti-Chalcedonian groups in Egypt to subscribe to the neo-Chalcedonian formulas and, on its basis, to share communion with the Chalcedonians. In dealing with the anti-Chalcedonians, Cyrus was authorized to use not only the power of theological persuasion, but also military force, which he readily applied. The theological component in Cyrus' strategy of persuasion utilized the theological language of Justinian, as it had been approved by the Constantinople 553. By applying both persuasion and coercion, Cyrus fostered what would become known as the "Alexandrian union" between pro- and anti-Chalcedonians. It was based on the following statement:

> If anyone, while using the expression "The one Lord is contemplated in two natures," does not confess that he is "one of the Holy Trinity" (ἕνα τῆς Ἁγίας Τριάδος), i.e., the Logos eternally begotten by the Father, who was made man in the last times; <. . .> but that he was "someone and someone else" (ἕτερος καὶ ἕτερος), and not "one and the same" (ἕνα καὶ τὸν αὐτὸν), as the most wise Cyril taught, "perfect in Godhead and the same perfect in humankind," and therefore contemplated "in two natures," "the same suffering according to one [nature] and not suffering according to the other [nature]" (τὸν αὐτὸν πάσχοντα καὶ μὴ πάσχοντα κατ'ἄλλο καὶ ἄλλο), as the same saint Cyril said, i.e., suffering as a human being in flesh, as far as he was a human being, but as God remaining incapable of suffering in the sufferings of his own flesh; and that this one and the same Christ and Son did both the divine and the human [things] (τὸν αὐτὸν ἕνα Χριστὸν καὶ Υἱὸν ἐνεργοῦντα τὰ θεοπρεπῆ καὶ ἀνθρώπινα) by one theandric activity (μιᾷ θεανδρικῇ ἐνεργείᾳ), <. . .> let him be anathema. (In ACO$_2$ II$^2$ 598.12-22)

The language of the Alexandrian union was neo-Chalcedonian and correspondent to the edicts of Justinian and the council of Constantinople in 553. There was, however, a theological neologism added in the end: "one theandric activity" (μία θεανδρικὴ ἐνέργεια). It was attached to the statement as an explanation of the key neo-Chalcedonian idea that the same Christ acted/suffered in accordance with his divinity and humanity. This explanation was added with a clear reference to the phrase from a letter ascribed to Dionysius the Areopagite: "a certain new theandric activity" (καινήν τινα τὴν θεανδρικὴν ἐνέργειαν ἡμῖν πεπολιτευμένος) (*ep*. 4). As was mentioned, the earliest reference to this phrase came from the anti-Chalcedonian circles of Severus of Antioch, who used it as a patristic proof that both Christ's nature and activity are single.

It was mentioned that the singularity of Christ's activity was for the Severans more singular than the singularity of Christ's single nature. In other words, they allowed more duality in the single nature of Christ than in his single activity. Cyrus of Alexandria used this tenet to approach Theodosians. The deal he offered them was the following: we, the Chalcedonians, accept your idea that Christ's activity is one, while you accept our idea that Christ's natures are two. At least some Theodosians accepted the deal. Cyrus could report to Constantinople good news:

> All the clergy of the Theodosian party of this city, together with all the civil and military persons of distinction, and many thousands of the people, on the third of June (of 633), took part with us, in the Holy Catholic Church, in the pure holy mysteries. (In $ACO_2$ $II^2$ 592.7-594.15)

This deal was not spontaneous, but well calculated and prepared in advance. Emperor Heraclius (r. 610–41) was behind it. He imagined himself a new Justinian (see Kaegi 2007). Heraclius inherited the empire divided by civil war, with lost territories and ceaseless military advances of its enemies from every direction. He had a moment of personal crisis, which was similar to what the plague had been for Justinian—by almost losing Constantinople to the joint forces of the Avars, Slavs, Bulgars from the northwest, and Persians from the east in 626. This siege was a civilizational shock for the Byzantines, who believed in the invincibility of their city almost as firmly as they believed in Christ. This shock marked their identity for centuries (see Hurbanič 2019: 3). Even now it echoes in the special worship of *Akathistos* hymn celebrated in the Greek churches during the Lent. A piece of the hymn addresses Mary on behalf of the impersonified capital city—the *Polis*:

> *Prooemium* I
> Having secretly received the command,
> the bodiless one went with haste to Joseph's dwelling,
> and said to her that knew not wedlock:
> "He who bowed the heavens and came down
> is contained unchanged but whole in you.
> I see him take the form of a servant in your womb;
> I stand in amazement and cry to you:
> Hail, bride unwedded."

*Prooemium* II
To you, our leader in battle and defender,
O Theotokos, I, your city, delivered from sufferings,
ascribe hymns of victory and thanksgiving.
Since you are invincible in power,
free me from all kinds of dangers, that I may cry to you:
"Hail, bride unwedded."

*Prooemium* III
We cease not, as is due, to hymn you,
Theotokos, and to say:
"Hail, favoured one." (Trypanis 1968: 29–30; Peltomaa 2001: 3)

The Byzantine *Akathistos* hymn influenced the Christian hymnography in the Oriental languages. An example of such influence is *Enzira Sebhet*—"The Harp of Glory" in Geʿez. It is a poem composed in the fifteenth century in Ethiopia. It reflects the surge in the veneration of the Theotokos in the wake of the reforms promulgated by king Zar'a Yaʿqob (r. 1434–1468), also known as Kwestantinos (Constantine) I. As a result of his reforms, the Theotokos's feasts in the Ethiopian church calendar outnumbered even the Byzantine calendar. The poem *Enzira Sebhet* clearly follows the pattern of the Byzantine *Akathistos* hymn:

I salute you, as once the angel Gabriel did,
saying:
"Hail, you who are blessed above all women;
Blessed is the fruit of your womb."
All shall bless you, all shall bend the knee
before you.
Seven times a day I praise you, telling of
your goodness,
From late at night to the break of day, from
morning to evening.
Save me from the drawn bow of hostile lips,
And from the arrow of the hostile tongue.
Preserve me from distress and save me from
calamity.
(McGuckin 2010: 72).
<. . .>
You are the Fortified City where the just live
in safety
And rest from all their afflictions.
You are the Seed of Justice, for the remnant
of the House of Israel.
You are the Beginning of Life and Salvation,

The cause of boasting among your people.
(McGuckin 2010: 27).
<. . .>
O Bride of Bethlehem, from the region of
Bethsaida,
Grant to me days of peace, as many as my
soul desires,
Until your Son shall come again to dispense
justice and retribution. (McGuckin 2010: 86)

While the celebrations based on the *Akathistos* hymn go back to the siege of 626, the hymn itself was probably composed in the period of the controversies about Mary's identity as *theotokos*, during the 430s. In a sense, this hymn is similar to the hymn "The only-begotten Son," which was promoted by Justinian. Both pieces of Byzantine poetry marked the largest ecumenical efforts undertaken in the end of the Late Antiquity. These efforts were directed at the restoration of unity between pro- and anti-Chalcedonian groups. Both Justinian and Heraclius needed this unity as a mandatory precondition for the territorial integrity of the empire. Both believed that they are chosen by God for accomplishing this holy mission.

In 626, Constantinople was besieged not only by the Avars, Slavs, and Bulgars but also by the Persians, who had swiftly advanced through Roman Mesopotamia,

**Figure 5.18** A medieval illuminated manuscript in the hands of a priest in the region of the Lake Tana, Ethiopia.
Source: Photo by the author.

**Figure 5.19** Ruins of Seleucia at the Zeugma—a midsize town in the Roman Mesopotamia, which often faced Persian military threat.

Source: Photo by the author.

**Figure 5.20** Underground towns were made and used by the local population in Cappadocia to hide from the Persian invaders. A hall in one such town.

Source: Photo by the author.

Persarmenia, and the Anatolian heartland. Before that, they had captured Jerusalem, damaged the church of Holy Sepulcher, and took with them as trophies the parts of Christ's cross, the holy lance, and other relics. This was a major blow to the legitimacy of the imperial power.

In their military campaign, the Persians had easily secured the collaboration of the anti-Chalcedonians by offering them privileges, which only the Chalcedonians could enjoy under Roman rule. The non-Chalcedonian Romans felt happy about the Persian rule—at least in the beginning. In the words of the anti-Chalcedonian archbishop of Antioch Athanasius I Gammolo (the Camel-Driver, in office 595–631), "The world rejoiced in peace and love," because the "Chalcedonian night" had passed away (Severus ibn al Muqaffa 1912: 481). Several years later, the Arabs would apply the same tactics with the same effect: they granted relative freedom to all oppressed non-Chalcedonian minorities. The massive defection of the non-Chalcedonian Romans to the Persians and Arabs urged the Byzantine officials, including Chalcedonian patriarchs, to focus even more on the restoration of the church's unity.

In elaborating on the policies of reconciliation, Heraclius followed his model emperor—Justinian. He employed the Justinianian neo-Chalcedonianism, after having tweaked it. Unlike Justinian, however, Heraclius was untrained in theology. He had to completely rely on experts, such as the archbishop of Constantinople Sergius (in office 610–38). With the full Heraclius' support, Sergius designed an upgrade of neo-Chalcedonianism. For this purpose, he consulted several prominent figures in both Chalcedonian and non-Chalcedonian camps.

The upgraded neo-Chalcedonianism was an elaboration on the "theopaschite" formula "one of the Trinity," who acts divinely and suffers humanly. The axiom, shared by pro- and anti-Chalcedonians, that both divine and human activities have the same subject, was interpreted as implying the single activity (ἐνέργεια) of Christ. The Heraclean neo-Chalcedonianism promoted the formula "one hypostasis/person of Christ—one activity—two natures" as a bottom line for all factions that had separated from each other since 431. Heraclius calculated that each faction would gain more than it would give up by subscribing to this bottom line. For the anti-Chalcedonians, for example, the idea of single activity had been more important than the idea of single nature. For the Chalcedonians, the idea of two natures was very important, but they were not sure what to believe about the activities, since there were no authoritative decisions of the church on this matter. Even the anti-Ephesian "Nestorians" could subscribe to this formula, because for them too Christ had two natures united under the umbrella of one *prosopon* and single activity. Exactly this rationale was employed by Cyrus in Alexandria, when he applied a monoënergist formula to approach the dissident groups of Egypt.

# Neo-Chalcedonian "Civil War"

The authors of the monoënergist formula, nevertheless, overestimated the flexibility of some Chalcedonians regarding Christ's activities. Soon after the "Alexandrian union" was signed, an alarm rang in Jerusalem. A Syrian monk Sophronius, who in 634 was elected a Palestinian patriarch, circulated his enthronement letter, which he used as an opportunity to criticize the Alexandrian statement. He, on the one hand, agreed that the subject of all activities in Christ is single:

> Visible and invisible, in the same way created and uncreated, bodily and unbodily, touchable and untouchable, circumscribed and uncircumscribed, earthy and heavenly, the same is the flesh endowed with an intellectual soul and divinity. (In $ACO_2$ $II^1$ 438.19-440.3)

On the other hand, the same Emmanuel acted according to his two natures. His activities are two different aspects correspondent to these natures:

> Emmanuel <. . .> acted according to something and something else (κατ'ἄλλο καὶ ἄλλο); as God, he is the same (ὁ αὐτός) [who did] the divine [things], while as a human being, he is the same [who did] the human things. In such a way, he wished to demonstrate himself to everybody as both God and a human being. (In $ACO_2$ $II^1$ 442.4-10)

In the light of these statements, Sophronius offered his own interpretation of the Ps.-Dionysian phrase "a certain new theandric activity," which seemingly contradicted his statements. The patriarch of Jerusalem suggested distinguishing three kinds of activities in Christ: divine, human, and theandric. He placed the latter between the two former ones (μέσιν τινὰ τάξιν ἐπέχουσιν) (in $ACO_2$ $II^1$ 456.12-13). In his interpretation, this was not a single activity, but a composition of two different and unconfused activities:

> We speak also about a common and so-called theandric activity (κοινὴν καὶ θεανδρικὴν λεγομένην ἐνέργειαν) of this power, which is not one, but has different origins and various [components] (οὐ μίαν ὑπάρχουσαν ἀλλ' ἑτερογενῆ καὶ διάφορον). (In $ACO_2$ $II^1$ 456.13-15)

Sophronius became a spokesperson of a neo-Chalcedonian group that disagreed with the monoënergist formula promoted by another neo-Chalcedonian group. This means that the neo-Chalcedonian party, whose rationale had been to heal divisions, instead found itself divided. Its division grew large and soon could be characterized as an intra-neo-Chalcedonian "civil war." In the standard *Dogmengeschicte*, it became known as the Monothelite controversy. The history of this controversy resembles the history of the neo-Nicaean disputes. At some point, the brothers-in-arms, who had fought the same enemies for the same Nicaean cause, turned on one another: the Cappadocians against Apollinaris of Laodicea, and together they turned on Diodore of Tarsus and Theodore of Mopsuestia. Now the neo-Chalcedonian theology, which emerged as a platform to tackle various misunderstandings regarding the Chalcedon, itself became a battlefield of internal misunderstandings.

## *Psephos*

At its initial stage, the "monothelite controversy" did not touch on the issue of wills and therefore cannot be called "monothelite." It concentrated solely on the issue of Christ's activities (*energeiai*/ἐνέργειαι) and therefore should be called "monoënergist." Contrary to the hopes of the imperial court, the opposition to the "one activity" formula did not fade away but only increased. Both political and ecclesial authorities in Constantinople did not wait long until the backfire would grow strong. The same year, 633, or maybe in the next year, they promulgated an "authoritative statement," *Psephos*, which prohibited speaking of either one or two activities. Instead, it suggested focusing on the single subject of these activities ($ACO_2$ $II^2$ 542.2-7). This was a policy of censoring theological discussions, which had been applied earlier, for example, by Constantius II and Zeno. It had not worked then and did not work now, however. Also, it quenched the ecumenical momentum of monoënergism.

## *Ekthesis*

An attempt to reignite the ecumenical momentum was undertaken in 638, when the imperial confession of faith, the *Ekthesis*, was promulgated as obligatory for the imperial church. This document was drafted by Sergius, who also backed it at an *endemousa* synod. The *Ekthesis* has been written in the clear neo-Chalcedonian language. It interchangeably used formulas "from two natures" and "in two natures," as well as the formula "one nature":

> Following the teaching of the holy fathers we praise Christ as being composite. For in regard to the mystery of [the person of] Christ the union by composition rejects both confusion and separation [between the persons], and it preserves the property of each nature, but shows one hypostasis and the one person of God the Word, animating the flesh with a rational soul. We do not introduce a quaternity in the place of a holy Trinity—by no means, for the holy Trinity did not accept the addition of a fourth person—but the one God the Word has become flesh from her (i.e., Mary). For it is not as if the person working miracles as God is one [person], while the one enduring

> sufferings is another person alongside [God]. Rather, we confess one and the same Son, both God and man, one hypostasis, one person, passible in the flesh, impassible in the godhead, the same [person] being both perfect [in godhead and perfect] in humanity; and that both the miracles and the sufferings which he voluntarily endured in the flesh are those of the same person.
>
> We, therefore, also confess one Christ from two natures, one Son, one Lord, one person, one composite hypostasis, and one nature of God the Word, which became incarnate, the flesh animated with a rational soul, as the inspired Cyril both thought and taught.

In the most neuralgic point of the document, where it addresses the issue of Christ's activities, it acknowledges disagreements. As a result, the *Ekthesis* prohibits using either "one activity" or "two activities" formulas, and, in this regard, reinstates the censorship of the *Psephos*. The only safe wording on this matter, according to the *Ekthesis*, is the one that affirms the same subject of all Christ's activities:

> We proclaim that both the miracles and the sufferings are those of one and the same person; we attribute all the operations [of Christ], divine and human, to one and the same incarnate God the Word; we render one worship to him who, for our sake, was voluntarily and truly crucified in the flesh, rose again from the dead, ascended into the heavens, and is both sitting at the right hand of the Father and will come again to judge the living and the dead. We do not at all allow that anyone should maintain or teach one or two operations in the Lord's divine incarnation, but rather, just as the doctrines of the holy and ecumenical councils handed down, we confess that one and the same only-begotten Son, our Lord Jesus Christ, the true God, does both divine and human things, and that every operation (ἐνέργεια), whether befitting God or man, proceeds from one and the same incarnate God the Word without division or confusion and refers back to one and the same [Word]. [We emphasize this] because the expression "one operation," although some of the fathers use it, still sounds strange to the ears of some and disquiets them. They suspect that it is suggested in order to sweep aside the two natures which are hypostatically united in Christ our God; and likewise the expression "two operations" causes many to stumble since it is not used by any of the holy and accepted teachers of the Church.

Unlike the *Henotikon* one and half centuries earlier, which had prohibited touching on the issue of natures, without offering an alternative, the *Ekthesis* suggested an alternative to the issue of activities, which was the category of will. The constructive proposal of the *Ekthesis* was to substitute the discussions on activities with the discussions on wills in Christ:

> It follows from that expression also to maintain two wills which are opposed to one another, as if God the Word desired to complete the salvific suffering, but his humanity resisted and opposed his will. And thus [they suspect that] two opposed wills would be introduced, which is impious and foreign to Christian dogma.

> For if the wicked Nestorius, although he tore apart the Lord's divine assumption of humanity and introduced two sons, did not dare to say that they had two wills (on the contrary, he declared that in the two persons which he invented there was only one will), how then can those who confess the right faith and recognize our Lord Jesus Christ, the true God, as one Son, admit [there to be] two wills in him, and that these [wills] are opposed to each other? Therefore, following the holy fathers in all things and so also in this, we confess a single will of our Lord Jesus Christ, the true God, such that his flesh, which was animated by a rational soul, never made any movement deriving from its own nature separately and of its own impulse in opposition to the will of God the Word, which was hypostatically united to it; rather [the flesh acted only] in the time, in the manner, and to the degree to which God the Word himself willed. (In Kinzig 2017, vol. 3: 386–8)

The rationale of substituting activities with wills in the Christological discussion was clear: while, indeed, patristic testimonies about Christ's activities can be ambiguous, Christ's will is certainly one, and it is identical with the will of God. Otherwise, human will, unlike human activity, would introduce disorder to Christ, as it is corruptible by its nature. It should be also noted that the category of will, in contrast to the category of activity, was borrowed not from the Aristotelian-Porphyrian nomenclature, but from the fourth-century disputes about the Logos: theologians then argued whether the Logos exists with or without the will of the Father. This means that the category of will looked more Christian and pious than the ostensibly pagan category of *energeia*.

When the logical category of activity was replaced by the category of volition, monothelitism substituted monoënergism on the imperial ecumenical agenda. The shift was approved by Pope Honorius (in office 625–38), who in response to Sergius wrote: "We recognize a single will of Lord Jesus Christ, because our nature is truly assumed by the Divinity" (in $ACO_2$ $II^2$ 551.14-16). The Christological formula of the *Ekthesis* can be summarized as follows.

> one hypostasis—two natures—one will—unknown number of activities in Christ.

# V.13
# Monothelitism

The monothelite formula of the *Ekthesis* was supposed to refresh the ecumenical project of Heraclius. Instead, it brought even less reconciliation than earlier the monoënergist formula could achieve. It raised a new wave of dissent within the neo-Chalcedonian camp. This time, the protagonist of résistance against the imperial dogma became a monk from Constantinople, Maximus. His basic point was that Christ has two wills. This is because one's will, similarly to activities, should be attributed not to hypostasis, but to nature. In Jesus, therefore, because the natures are two, activities and wills are two too. At the same time, Maximus agreed with his opponents that Jesus' hypostasis is the single ultimate subject of all his activities and wills. In other words, in contrast to the *Ekthesis*, Maximus' Christological formula could be summarized as follows:

one hypostasis—two natures—two wills—two activities in Christ.

## Many Maximus' Lives

Maximus was born in Constantinople around 580 and died in 662 in exile, in the western Georgia. He served at the imperial court, which he left to become a monk in the vicinity of Constantinople. Because of the siege of the imperial capital in 626, he left the banks of Bosphorus and moved to the shores of the Gulf of Tunis. He began commuting between Carthage and Palestine, where he met Sophronius. Sophronius, who was a generation senior to Maximus, apparently initiated him to polemics against monoënergism, which Maximus observed transforming to monothelitism. During his lifelong struggle against this new doctrine, Maximus found many allies in the West, including the Roman Pontiff Martin (in office 649–55). In 649, they together organized a council, which condemned monoënergism-monothelitism as heresy. Imperial authorities took this council as a political treason. Both Martin and Maximus were arrested, tried, and exiled. Maximus' first place of exile was in Thrace, and the second in Georgia, where he died in 662. Martin was exiled to the Tauric Chersonesus, where he died in 655.

There are two completely different accounts of Maximus' life. One was promoted in the Greco-Roman world, where his ideas eventually prevailed (after the ecumenical council in Constantinople in 680–1). This is a complimentary account that emphasizes Maximus' nobility and good standing in Byzantine society. The other one was made in the Syriac world. It presents Maximus as a wretch and outcast, who fully deserved his miserable fate. One can hardly recognize the same personality in these two accounts. The difference between them reflects the aforementioned "civil wars" waged by the interpretative groups who had different takes on the council of Chalcedon.

We will illustrate the post-monothelite Byzantine take on Maximus by the Georgian rendering of his *Vita*. A large part of Maximus' corpus has been translated to Georgian in the Middle Ages. The earliest recorded translations were made at the end of the tenth century by a Georgian monk Euthymius the Athonite. His work was followed up during the eleventh and twelfth centuries, primarily inside the walls of the Gelati school in western Georgia. There are three Georgian translations of Maximus' *Vita* that appeared in that period: the mentioned earliest and most extensive one by Euthymius; a *synaxarion* penned by George the Athonite in 1042–4; and the third account produced in the twelfth century anonymously by someone from Gelati.

All Georgian versions of Maximus' *Vita* are based on the Byzantine Greek sources, with emphasis on the last period of his life, which he spent in exile in Georgia

**Figure 5.21** The building of the medieval Gelati academy near Kutaisi in Georgia.
Source: Photo by the author.

(Khoperia 2015: 446–8). The Georgian texts have been published by Kornely Kekelidze (Kekelidze 1918: 60–103). Prior to the Georgian publication, the same scholar had published its Russian translation. The translation here is based on the Russian publication:

> This beautiful and much desired fertile soil of piety, a fruitful branch of asceticism and a chosen vessel of wisdom was born and brought up in the great city of Constantinople. His parents were noble and loving God. His father's name was John, and his mother's, Anna. They brought up their good son through the divine teaching and made him participant in the wisdom of philosophers. <. . .>
>
> At that time, there was a king Heraclius, who conquered Persia and killed the king of the Persians Khosroe; he liberated from captivity the patriarch of Jerusalem Zaccharias and by the grace of God brought back the precious wood of the cross, which had been taken from Jerusalem to Persia by Khosroe (i.e., Khosrau II Parviz, who reigned from 590 through 628); he also delivered to the royal palace a great treasure, to the glory of our Lord Jesus Christ and for the consolation of all faithful.
>
> The king heard from everyone about the wisdom, knowledge, and particular love to God of Saint Maximus. He called him and, having seen him, loved his piety and wisdom. He urged him to stay in the royal palace and distinguished him with the honor of being in charge of the king's literati; this honor being great and noticeable. This blessed man was pleasing to and loved by the King of heavens and particularly by the Greek king; he was respected by the senate and all patricians and generals; he was pleasing to and glorified by everyone.
>
> Long before that, a heresy of Severus and Dioscorus, the evil heretics-acephali, emerged. They rejected the two natures in Christ: the divine and the human ones—and preached one mixed nature and the ephemeral incarnation of the Lord. <. . .>
>
> King Heraclius, on his return from Persia after the great victories granted to him, entered Hierapolis in Syria. There was a Jacobite archbishop there, whose name was Athanasius (i.e., Athanasius I Gammolo). He was evil and cunning, full of all sorts of impiety and devoted to the Syriac magic. The king entered with him to discussions on faith and told: "If you recognize the council of Chalcedon, I will make you the patriarch of Antioch." The evil Athanasius cunningly recognized the mentioned council and cunningly confessed in Christ two natures united into one hypostasis. Then he asked the king: "So I confess two natures, but what would you say about will and activity: are there two or one will in Christ?" The king who was brought up in campaigns and battles, never heard such a word in the church. He took this question as strange, and for this reason he told Athanasius: "The word you are saying has not reached me yet. I will write to the patriarch, and you give me some time before I receive the answer." At that time, the patriarch in Constantinople was Sergius, who originated from Syria, from the Jacobite parents. He was brought up in Constantinople and, after having received Greek education, he reached the patriarchal office. Inside himself, however, he upheld the heresy and recognized one will and one activity in Christ. The cunning Athanasius knew this and asked the king this question, because he realized that if he

manages to persuade the king to accept one will and one activity, then there will be no confession of two natures. <. . .>

When all this happened, Maximus, the true philosopher, by deed, word, and understanding showed his love to wisdom. <. . .> He saw that the nets of the heresy were cast everywhere and the temptation by those who proclaim one nature, which had been suspended by great effort of the holy fathers, now resumes because of the carelessness and cunningness of those in power, who put the teaching on one will and one activity on paper and nailed it at the narthex of Saint Sophia. [As result,] he left the palace and distanced himself from every worldly deed. <. . .>

Having seen that the royal city and its neighborhoods are confused by the evil heresy, the God-bearing father many times addressed the king and the patriarch. He begged them to leave the evil heresy and to confess Christ in two natures, two wills, and two activities, complete according to both divinity and humanity. <. . .>

In the Orthodox Metropolia, in Rome, where the true faith was confessed, pope Theodore (i.e., Theodore I, in office 642–649) died, and the God-bearing and holy Martin (i.e., Martin I, in office 649–655) ascended to the throne of Peter. Then the blessed Maximus returned from Africa. Having come to Saint Martin, he aroused in him divine zeal. They convened a council of 150 bishops, condemned the heretics Sergius, Pyrrhus, Cyrus, Paul and their teaching, and loudly confessed in Christ two natures, two wills, and two activities. <. . .>

In the ninth year of his rule, Cosmas (i.e., Constans II Pogonatus, r. 641–668), the grandson of Heraclius, learned about everything what happened in Rome. Being angry, he sent there soldiers with order to bring to Constantinople Saint Martin and blessed Maximus. When the holy fathers arrived at the royal capital, Saint Martin underwent big tortures, abuses, and insults from the atheists. <. . .>

The king and the judges composed a sentence regarding these blessed fathers and sent it to the eparch. The eparch sat in the chair of the judges and ordered to bring the blessed [men]. When they came, he ordered to read out the sentence, where it was written: "We the God-protected king. . ." The sentence ended as follows: "then they will send you for eternal imprisonment to the Mingrelian lands." <. . .>

Then they inhumanly beat the slaves of God and cut their tongues and hands. According to the order they dragged them through the entire city and then they sent these holy confessors and martyrs to Mingrelia. When they brought them to the country of Mingrelians, they separated them from one another, because such was the order, and took away everything they had; they did not leave anything from what was given to them by God-loving people. Blessed Maximus fell severely ill, so he could not sit on a donkey or a chart. For this reason, the soldiers made a basket, put the saint man to it, and forced the outrunners to carry it. They enclosed him to the castle named h'Imar—close to the Ossetian country. Brother Anastasius was brought on a donkey and locked up in the Abkhazian castle called Kotori. Another Anastasius <. . .> was locked in the castle called Bokele on the board with Ossetia. Soon afterwards, the two brothers who had the same name were led out of these castles and sent [to other places. They sent] Anastasius the presbyter to a Svanetian castle. However, because of much distress and affliction, which he underwent in Byzantium and on the way, he had not reached that castle and died. With joy he ascended to the heavenly Kingdom on July 24. Anastasius the deacon was taken to the Tkverian castle in Abkhazia, where he stayed until the death of the king the torturer. After his death, he received a permission, came back to Greece, and told us everything that happened to them. He finished his life here in big ascetic labors and was honored together with his friends in the heavenly abode.

Holy and blessed Maximus, the true slave and confessor of Christ, who was imprisoned in the above-mentioned castle, stayed in it as an angel of God. <. . .> Four months after his imprisonment, an angel of God appeared to him and revealed about his departure from this world to God. The blessed [man] called the commander of the castle and others who were there and, having announced that he would depart from this world in seven days, wrote a letter to Anastasius the deacon. Anastasius the presbyter at that time was not alive. He handled [the letter] to the commander of the castle and asked him to send it to the mentioned brother after his death, something that the commander did indeed. We saw this epistle, which was full of spiritual grace. After that he (i.e., Maximus) stopped taking food; on the sixth day he felt some fever; and on the seventh day he gave his soul with joy to the hands of God, on August 13, Saturday. He thus reposed forever from distresses and afflictions, and received the crown of asceticism and martyrdom. Nearby that castle there was a monastery of St. Arsenius, where they buried his holy body to the glory of our Lord Jesus Christ. The Lord showed a great miracle: three bright lamps descended from heaven to the grave, where his holy body was buried, and remained there for the entire year, until the anniversary of his death.

**Figure 5.22** Ruins of a medieval castle at the border with Racha and Svanetia, where Maximus might have stayed in the last months of his life. Near Tsageri in western Georgia.

Source: Photo by the author.

> Those who stayed in the castle, the monastery, and neighborhood, saw those lamps and glorified God. They spread the word about this miracle from country to country. There were healings and many miracles happening at the grave of this blessed man every day. (Кекелидзе 1912: 451–79; translation is mine)

Maximus left a lasting footprint on Georgian popular culture and identity. It is observable even now. He remains a spiritual authority and a patron for local people. According to the local legends, which mix up Christian and pagan popular beliefs and which have been recorded by the Georgian anthropologist Lela Khoperia,

> The main place of his residence was the village of Dekhviri; according to one version of the legend, he lived in the hollow of a 1,000 year-old cult linden tree. Maximus was the ruler of the weather. "However clear the day might be, if he pointed his hand downwards, it would start raining; if [he pointed] upwards, the weather would be fine again." He also did his best to protect cornfields and hayfields from being ruined, and punished disobedient peasants who grazed their livestock in other people's cornfields and thus ruined their crops. There was only one person in the village who opposed him. Maximus warned this peasant to give up his evil practices and punished him several times, but he still would not obey. The conflict between the wicked peasant and Maximus ended with the murder of the saint. The frightened peasant tried to conceal traces of his crime and buried Maximus, but the corpse would not stay in the grave, and on coming back the murderer found him either sitting or lying on the ground. In

**Figure 5.23** Vicinity of Tsageri where Maximus most probably spent the final period of his life.

Source: Photo by the author.

> accordance with the conventions of legends, this was repeated three times, until a local woman (or the murderer) had a vision: Maximus requested that his corpse be tied to a sledge with a pair of unbroken, not castrated bulls (i.e., sacrificial bulls) harnessed to it, and wherever they stopped, there he had to be buried. The bulls stopped on reaching Muri, where the divine corpse settled down and found his final rest. In one version, the bulls died on reaching their destination; in another, they were killed as a sacrifice and boiled over the fire caused by the burning of the sledge, their meat being distributed among the villagers. After his interment, a church was built at this place dedicated to Maximus. (Khoperia 2015: 452–3)

Georgian legends about Maximus in some points are different from the Byzantine version his life. Even more different is the account of Maximus' life in his Syriac *vita*. It had been composed prior to the Greek *vita* and is contained in a manuscript dating back to the late seventh century. The manuscript indicates Gregory or George of Reš'aina as the author of this account. The title of the text warns that this is not a panegyric, but an invective: "The narrative concerning the wicked Maximos of Palestine, who blasphemed against his creator and his tongue was cut out." The manuscript not only interprets Maximus' life in a way different from the Byzantine interpretation—it presents a completely different factual account. According to this account, Maximus was born not in Constantinople and not from noble parents, but in Palestine from an extramarital affair between a Samaritan maker of linen and a Persian slave-girl. His entire life is presented as a sequence of mishaps, like in an ancient Greek tragedy:

> This Maximos was from the village of Ḥeṣfin, for it was there that this bitter tare was born, his father being a Samaritan from Sychar, while his mother was a Persian, the slave-girl of a certain Jew named Zadok from the town of Tiberias. Now the father of this Maximos used to go and sell his work in Tiberias—he was a maker of linen, and he sold luxurious goods—and when he was in Tiberias, next door to the house of Zadok, he committed adultery with the Persian slave-girl, for she was very pretty. And when she became pregnant she told him on the next occasion that he came to sell his work: "Either ransom me from my master before he notices my state and disgraces me, or I will inform on you at once, and they will seize you and you will become an object of ridicule and scorn; for I am certainly pregnant." He, being placed in an awkward position, took two hundred darics and ransomed her from Zadok her master.
>
> When his relations and fellow Samaritans saw what he had done they were in great consternation, and they all met together and told him: "Either allow us to burn this pregnant woman in order to remove the disgrace from us and our people, or we will expel you from our community." But he was unwilling to consent to them in this, saying "Although I agree to do what you want, I shall not carry it out today." They, however, were plotting to kill him, and the girl with him, secretly; but when he learnt of their plot against him, he made his escape by night, taking her with him. He arrived at the above-mentioned village of Ḥeṣfin and entered it, going to the house of a priest

> called Martyrios. He stayed with him for two years, and he and his wife were secretly baptized by him, Maximos' father receiving the name Theonas instead of Abna, and his mother the name Mary instead of ŠNDH—for that was her name in Persian. Now this Martyrios who baptized them was the son of the maternal uncle of Gennadios, the governor who was at that time in charge of Tiberias and all the surrounding area, and it was through his authority that he (i.e., Martyrios) escaped any punishment from the Samaritan people.
>
> When this fruit of wickedness (i.e., Maximus) was born, this priest Martyrios gave him the name of Moschion at baptism. The priest Martyrios also gave his parents a place in Ḥeṣfin, settling them near himself, on church property. Nine years later his father died of dropsy, leaving his children to the priest Martyrios to act as guardian (curator) to them. His mother also died a year after her husband, as a result of a fall from a pomgranate bush, leaving behind three children in all, two boys and one girl. His sister fell into the grate of a hearth and was badly burnt, as the result of which she died.
>
> The priest Martyrios took Moschion to the monastery of Palaia Lavra, where the abbot Pantoleon received him. His younger brother died in this monastery, three years after Moschion's noviciate, as the result of a bite he received from a vicious camel belonging to some orientals who were staying there; this occurred on the day of the adoration of the holy Cross. Moschion's teacher Pantoleon changed his name to Maximos, after the son of his (Pantoleon's) nephew, of whom he was very fond, but who had died while still a child: it was in memory of him that he gave the name to this rascal. (Brock 2018: 314–15)

This account is an allegorical presentation of how Syrian anti-Chalcedonians perceived Maximus and other Chalcedonians. For them, Chalcedonians—and Maximus as their prominent representative—were unrepentant Nestorians. By the seventh century, many Nestorians found refuge in the Persian Empire, where they were often treated as second-class people. A Persian slave-girl is an allegory for the Chalcedonians and other "Nestorians." Maximus' alleged father, Abna, allegorically represented what each theological party suspected about its opponents—crypto-Judaism. Accusations of being Jewish was a common polemical trope at that time. It continues to be so in our days among the Eastern Christians.

## Maximus' Theology

Maximus' figure is unique in Eastern Christianity. In the later Byzantine period, he was read and admired, but remained in the shadow of his imperial condemnation. In the medieval West, he was in the shadow of Dionysius the Areopagite, as an interpreter of the latter. In the post-Byzantine East, the dramatically declined theological and philosophical education made Maximus' work obscure and hardly accessible for understanding. Only in the modern scholarship, Maximus resurfaced as arguably the greatest Byzantine mind. Scholars in our time came to acknowledge and enjoy Maximus' creativity, thinking out of the box, and mastery in philosophy. He came to dominate the field of Eastern patristics.[1]

In his own context, Maximus was primarily a polemicist against monothelitism. One of his most famous engagements in polemics was a dispute with the former archbishop of Constantinople Pyrrhus, who had succeeded Sergius and then was forced from this office. While in the office, Pyrrhus continued the monothelite line of Sergius. Later, he came closer to the dyothelite tenets. The public dispute between two of them took place in Carthage in July 645. It was recorded either by Maximus himself or by someone from his entourage.

According to this recording, Pyrrhus started by postulating the intrinsic connectedness between nature and will, the latter being a property of the former. From the beginning to the end of the debate, the disputants stayed strictly within the frame of the Aristotelian-Porphyrian logics. From the perspective of this logics, Maximus argued, if the category of will is connected with the category of particularity—hypostasis, and not nature, then God should have three different wills. Maximus, thus, linked the Christological aspect of the category of will with its Trinitarian aspect. Indeed, prior to the monoënergist/monothelite controversy, there was a long tradition of considering the essence of one God as the source of both divine activities and volitions, which therefore are common for the three persons of God:

> Christ exists as God and as man by nature. Then did He will as God and as man, or only as Christ? If it were Christ who willed and initiated actions, being both God and man, then it is clear that, being one and the same, He willed dually and not singly. For if Christ be nothing else apart from the natures from which and in which He exists, then obviously He wills and operates in a manner corresponding to each of His natures, in other words, as each nature is capable of operating. And if he has two natures, then he surely must have two natural wills, the wills and essential operations being equal in number to the natures. For just as the number of natures of the one and the same Christ, correctly understood and explained, does not divide Christ but rather preserves the distinction of natures in the union, so likewise the number of essential attributes, wills, and operations attached to those two natures does not divide Christ either. For throughout both of his natures there flowed the same activity and purpose, to wit, our salvation. This introduces no division—God forbid!—but rather shows that they are preserved unimpaired, in their entirety, even in the union. <. . .>
>
> If one suggests that a "wilier" is implied in the notion of the will, then by the exact inversion of this principle of reasoning, a will is implied in the notion of a "wilier."

[1]See an overview of modern Maximian studies in Nichols 2019.

> Thus, will you say that because of the one will of the superessential Godhead there is only one hypostasis, as did Sabellius, or that because there are three hypostases there are also three wills, and because of this, three natures as well, since the canons and definitions of the Fathers say that the distinction of wills implies a distinction of natures? So said Arius! (*Disputatio cum Pyrrho* 13–15)

Attributing will to nature, however, incurred a serious difficulty, which was immediately grasped by the monothelites, who used it in their counterstrikes against the dyothelites. Namely, the volitional capacity of the human nature in such case appears to be not free, because everything associated with nature is bound by necessity. Maximus' response to this counterargument was that freedom as such, because every human being has it, belongs to the common human nature and not to individual hypostases. Maximus distinguished between the volitional capacity of the human nature and the way in which it is exercised. The latter is completely free of any necessity:

> The will and the mode of willing are not the same, just as the power of sight and the mode of perception are not the same. Will, like sight, is of nature. All things which have an identical nature have identical abilities. But the mode of willing, like the mode of perception—in other words, to will to walk or to will not to walk, and the perception of the right hand or of the left, or of up or down, or the contemplation of concupiscence or of the rational principles in beings—is only a mode of the use of a power, of the employment of will and of perception. And the same distinction may be applied to other things as well. These things demonstrate that they have, by nature, the will to eat or not to eat, to walk or not to walk. But these negatives are not applicable to the will as such, but only to the particular mode of willing. In other words, things come to pass by choices. If we assume that the things created by God and willed by Him pass out of existence, it does not follow that His essential and creative will, which is presupposed in those things, also passes out of existence. (*Disputatio cum Pyrrho* 23)

In the course of polemics, some monothelites, including Pyrrhus, suggested considering the single will of Christ as "gnomic" (γνωμικόν). This would be a will connected with Christ's capacity of reasoning (γνώμη). Trying to reach a compromise with the dyothelites, well-intended monothelites, such as Pyrrhus, would admit two natural wills in Christ, but under the single control of a more advanced and reasonable, as they believed, "gnomic will." Indeed, the concept of free gnomic will is more attractive than the concept of natural will, which was promoted by the dyothelites as restricted by necessity. Maximus, in his early writings, endorsed the idea of "gnomic will." Later, in the dispute with Pyrrhus, he remarked that this idea can be understood in many ways. The monothelite way of interpreting it, however, was not acceptable for him. Such an interpretation would mean that Christ developed opinions in the way human beings do—with limited knowledge, vulnerability, and mistakes. In contrast, Christ never had an opinion (γνώμη), but always had a perfect knowledge and an unmistakable judgment. Here is an exchange between Maximus and Pyrrhus on this issue:

> *Pyrrhus*: The gnomie is nothing else than the very thing which the blessed Cyril defined as "the mode of life."
> *Maximus*: Do you maintain that a good or evil mode of life is by choice or not?
> *Pyrrhus*: By choice, obviously.
> *Maximus*: Do we choose for ourselves, voluntarily and deliberately? Or involuntarily and without deliberation?
> *Pyrrhus*: Obviously, voluntarily and deliberately.
> *Maximus*: So then, the gnomie is nothing else than an act of willing in a particular way, in relation to some real or assumed good.
> *Pyrrhus*: I would regard this as a correct interpretation of the Patristic definition.
> *Maximus*: If this interpretation of the Patristic definition be correct, then in the first place it is not possible to say that this [appropriated will] is a gnomic will, for how is it possible for a will to proceed from a will? Thus, those who say that there is a gnomie in Christ, as this inquiry is demonstrating, are maintaining that he is a mere man, deliberating in a manner like unto us, having ignorance, doubt and opposition, since one only deliberates about something which is doubtful, not concerning what is free of doubt. By nature we have an appetite simply for what by nature is good, but we gain experience of the goal in a particular way, through inquiry and counsel. Because of this, then, the gnomic will is fitly ascribed to us, being a mode of the employment [of the will], and not a principle of nature, otherwise nature [itself] would change innumerable times. But the humanity of Christ does not simply subsist [in a manner] similar to us, but divinely, for He Who appeared in the flesh for our sakes was God. It is thus not possible to say that Christ had a gnomic will. (*Disputatio cum Pyrrho* 80–7)

Maximus concluded his argument with Pyrrhus on the category of will by referring to the polemics between Gregory of Nazianzus and Apollinaris of Laodicea. Gregory had pointed out that human mind sinned first and therefore should be assumed by God in the first place:

> Mind not only fell in Adam, but it was the "protopath," to use the term the physicians use in the case of first ailments. The very thing that had accepted the commandment did not keep the commandment. The very thing that did not keep it ventured its transgression. The very thing that transgressed stood in special need of salvation. The very thing that needed salvation was assumed. Therefore mind was assumed. (*Ep.* 101; Gregory of Nazianzus 2002: 161)

Maximus applied Gregory's point to the human will: if it is not included in the incarnation, it is left outside salvation. For Maximus, because sin had entered the human nature through Adam's will, this part of the human nature should be saved in the first place:

> If Adam when willing had obeyed, or while willing, considered, and after willing ate, then the faculty of will is the first thing in us that became subject to passion. So, if according to them the Word when He became incarnate did not have this [faculty of will] along with the nature, then I shall never be set free from sin. And if I cannot be freed from sin, then I have not been saved, since what is not assumed is not healed. (*Disputatio cum Pyrrho* 139)

Maximus, thus, followed the long tradition of approbating all theological ideas by applying to them the criterion of salvation. If an idea does not fit this criterion, it is either wrong or irrelevant. Maximus' method of theology was deeply rooted in soteriology.

## *Typos*

Monothelitism did not seem to have worked to the extent it was expected—just as monoënergism had not worked earlier. There were some instances of reunion between the non-Chalcedonians (including Nestorians!) with the Chalcedonians, but they were sporadic and not sustainable. Both imperial and ecclesial offices in Constantinople realized that, by supporting monothelitism, they were losing more than they were gaining. Particularly severe was the loss of the Western church, which, after the death of Honorius, reversed its policy of approving the Eastern monothelitism. The official Constantinople, consequently, decided to revoke the *Ekthesis*, which in 648 was removed from the narthex of Hagia Sophia and replaced with a new imperial document, *Typos*. This document banned using both number one and number two in application to both activities and wills of Christ:

> We declare to our orthodox subjects that, from the present moment, they no longer have permission in any way to contend and to quarrel with one another over one will and one energy, or two energies and two wills. ($ACO_2$ I 208.19-23)

The *Typos* was in line with the *Psephos* in 633–4 and earlier with the *Henotikon* in 482—the laws that had censored selected Christological topics under the threat of criminal prosecution. Censorship, however, could not solve the problems—only open discussions could tackle them.

## Lateran Council 649

Maximus and his Western confederates ignored the *Typos* and organized a council that openly addressed both issues of activity and will in Christ. This council was convened in 649 by Pope Martin in the papal basilica of St. John in the Lateran. Most delegates at the Lateran council—so it became known—were Italian bishops, who were joined by a small groups of Eastern monks, including Maximus. Maximus was the mastermind behind the council. The rationale of having such a council was to create a leverage against the seemingly consolidated position of the Eastern monothelites. Martin and Maximus wanted to make the emperor concerned about the anti-monothelite dissent in the West and to reconsider his support to the monothelite party in Constantinople. They used the council as a loudspeaker to broadcast to the East anti-monothelite arguments. The Western bishops, additionally, intended to secure more political and ecclesial freedom for themselves. Indeed, this council became a landmark in the evolution of Roman primacy, which Maximus endorsed.

Most Italian bishops, however, were theologically unfit to challenge the East. To their credit, they realized their limitations and agreed to outsource to Maximus taking care of the council's theology. Based on this mandate, Maximus staged a theological performance. Probably he did not go as far as Rudolf Riedinger has suggested, namely that he and his confederates had composed the acts prior to the council. Then the precomposed texts were simply read in the sessions of the council and duly signed by its participants (see Riedinger 1976). This would have made the council a pure manipulation. If it were so, Maximus' monothelite opponents would have quickly discovered this falsification and made it a part of their anti-dyothelite polemics. However, such accusations against dyothelites have never been recorded. It is also unlikely what Pietro Conte suggested, namely that bishops simply read the lines assigned to them by Maximus (Conte 1989). Such a farce would have been also discovered by the anti-Maximian propaganda. More likely is Richard Price's

**Figure 5.24** Papal Archbasilica of St. John in Lateran, Rome.
Source: Photo by the author.

suggestion that a selection of documents and some florilegia were prepared in both Greek and Latin prior to the council (Price 2016: 67–8). Speeches and motions were pre-drafted prior to each session and in the end amended to reflect the actual discussions.

The theologically richest points of the acts are pieces of Greek theology: written in Greek and intended for the Greek audience. Greek was the original language of most acts, with the Latin translation following it. Although the Lateran 649 happened in the West, it is a masterpiece of Eastern theology. The theological language, in which this council expressed itself, was mostly neo-Chalcedonian.[2] In fact, the Lateran 649 can be regarded as the only neo-Chalcedonian council of the Western church. At the same time, it was corrective of those deviations of neo-Chalcedonianism that had been caused by monoënergism and monothelitism. Following the vision of Maximus, who himself was a convinced neo-Chalcedonian struggling to correct this doctrine, the Lateran 649 tried to restore and to rehabilitate neo-Chalcedonianism. In this sense, it was an update to the first neo-Chalcedonian council, held in Constantinople in 553. The Lateran 649 confirmed the ecumenical status of the Constantinople 553, by referring to "ecumenical five councils." This was a precious confession, given that in the West the Constantinople 553 was often regarded as not-quite-ecumenical.

The Lateran 649 also marked the highest theological point in polemics against monothelitism, though this doctrine would be finally condemned more than thirty years later, by the sixth ecumenical council in Constantinople. The dyothelite theology of the Constantinople 680–1 was more lapidarian than the theology of the Lateran 649. Following the Maximian train of thought, the Lateran professed an intrinsic connection between Christ's two natures and his natural wills, operations, and properties. At the same time, it proclaimed Jesus' person as the only subject of his double wills and activities:

> Just as [we profess] his natures united without fusion or division to be two, so [we profess] the wills according to nature, divine and human, to be two, and his natural operations, divine and human, to be two, for a total and flawless confirmation that the one and the same our Lord and God Jesus Christ is truly by nature perfect God and perfect man apart from sin alone, and that he wills and operates our salvation both divinely and humanly, "as from of old the prophets and Jesus Christ himself taught us about him and the creed of our holy fathers has handed down," and simply all the holy and ecumenical five councils and all the approved teachers of the catholic church. (Preamble to the canons of the council adopted at its fifth session; Price 2016: 376)

[2]Almost half of the Christological definitions of the Lateran 649 were neo-Chalcedonian (see Price 2016: 379, footnote 484).

# Maximus' Trials

The Lateran council explicitly condemned monothelitism and those who promoted it, including the patriarchs of Constantinople Sergius, Pyrrhus, and Paul.[3] Maximus believed that it did this with the authority of an ecumenical council, the sixth in number. For the official Constantinople, however, it was not even a council, but an illegal gathering, because it violated the imperial law, the *Typos*, which had prohibited any discussions on the issues of activity and will in Christ. Martin and Maximus were arrested and tried as violators of law and conspirators against the imperial authority.

The protocols of Maximus' interrogations have survived and testify to his measured nonconformism. According to these protocols, Maximus recognized a unique role of the emperor in the church. Still, for him, this role was limited and could not go as far as the church's doctrine. Maximus denied the emperors the right to interfere in the matters of faith:

> No emperor was able to persuade the Fathers who speak of God to be reconciled with the heretics of their times by means of equivocal expressions. Instead they employed clear and authoritative expressions, and ones that corresponded to the teaching that was being inquired into, saying plainly that it is the mark of priests to make an inquiry and to define on the subject of the saving teachings of the catholic church. (In Allen & Neil 2002: 57)

Then Maximus was asked: "Well then, isn't every Christian emperor also a priest?" He replied to this provocative question bluntly:

> No, he isn't, because he neither stands beside the altar, and after the consecration of the bread elevates it with the words: "Holy things for the holy"; nor does he baptize, nor perform the rite of anointing, nor does he ordain and make bishops and presbyters and deacons; nor does he anoint churches, nor does he wear the symbols of the priesthood, the pallium and the Gospel book, as [he wears the symbols] of imperial office, the crown and purple. (In Allen & Neil 2002: 57)

Maximus, thus, protected the autonomy of the church in the matters of faith. In the words of Andrew Louth, "For Maximos, the Church, as defined by the true confession of faith celebrated in the Divine Liturgy of the Eucharist, is a sovereign body, with its own institutions. However deeply bound up with the Christian Empire it might be, it may not be confused with it" (Louth 2004: 118).

---

[3]See chapter 18 of the council's final definition (Price 2016: 381).

# Council of Constantinople 680–1

Even after monoënergism and monothelitism were condemned by the imperial council convened by Emperor Constantine Pogonatus (r. 668–85), Maximus was not rehabilitated. He was still considered a criminal that had trespassed the laws and questioned the imperial authority. The council, nevertheless, employed the full set of Maximus' arguments. On the basis of the Maximian theological criteria, it investigated the beliefs of the monothelite party, which participated in its sessions under the leadership of the patriarch of Antioch Macarius. The shadow mastermind of this party was one Stephan. It seems that Stephan composed a confession of faith, which Macarius presented to the council. Among other things, the confession stated:

> We say that the suffering belongs to the flesh (which clearly was not separated from the godhead, even though suffering did not belong to the godhead), and the operation belongs to God, even though he performed this [operation] through his humanity (that is, [through] the entirety of our lump) by the one and only divine will, as there was also no other will in him which either resisted or opposed his divine and powerful will. For it is impossible for two wills that are mutually contending or even similar to exist together and identically in one and the same Christ, our God. (In Kinzig 2017, vol. 2: 158)

The council deposed Macarius and interdicted the rest of the present monothelites. In the end, the council anathematized figures from the past who had contributed to the monothelite cause, including Pope Honorius, the patriarchs of Constantinople Sergius, Pyrrhus, Paul, Peter, and the patriarch of Alexandria Cyrus.

A curious episode occurred during the sessions of the council. A monk named Polychronius presented a book, which he claimed was revealed to him by God. It contained a monothelite confession. Polychronius promised to resurrect with it a dead body. He was provided with a dead body, but the book did not work. After he refused to rebuke monothelitism, he was condemned.

The council officially proclaimed two activities and volitions in Christ. This proclamation was wrapped in the wording from the Chalcedonian definition: Jesus' activities (ἐνέργειαι) and volitions (θελήματα) are united indivisibly, immutably, inseparably, and unconfusedly—just as the natures with which they are intrinsically connected:

> In him (i.e., Christ) two natural desires or wills and two natural operations [exist] indivisibly, immutably, inseparably, unconfusedly, according to the teaching of the holy fathers.
>
> We likewise proclaim that these two natural wills are not contrary the one to the other (God forbid!) as the impious heretics assert, but his human will follows without

> being resistant or reluctant, but rather being subject to his divine and omnipotent will. (In Kinzig 2017, vol. 2: 167)

The language of the Constantinople 680–1 was neo-Chalcedonian, like in the following statement:

> I proclaim his one hypostasis as composite; neither was one nature transformed or confused with another on account of the union, nor conversely does this ineffable union admit of any cleavage. For the synthetic or hypostatic union rejects both confusion and division; it both preserves the property of each nature and shows forth the one person of God the Word, even with the flesh. <. . .>
>
> I indeed confess the same Lord, our Jesus Christ, the true God; one [person] of the holy, consubstantial, and life-giving Trinity; crucified voluntarily on our behalf under Pontius Pilate, suffered; was buried, and on the third day rose again according to the Scriptures; ascended into the heavens, and sits at the right hand of Father. (In Kinzig 2017, vol. 2: 163)

The council of 680–1 was received across the Roman Empire as sixth ecumenical. It is sometimes called Constantinople III, as the third recognized ecumenical council held in the capital city (after the councils of 381 and 553). This council corrected the neo-Chalcedonian language and promoted it as a Christological *lingua franca*. Constantinople III put the end to the intra-neo-Chalcedonian "civil war," which was waged over the issues of activities and wills in Christ. The divided neo-Chalcedonian community became almost completely reconciled. The edition of neo-Chalcedonianism elaborated upon and promoted by Maximus was accepted as the only normative one. Other versions of neo-Chalcedonianism were discarded.

# The Maronites

Only a small monothelite community remained unreconciled. It would become known as Maronite. It was concentrated in Syria and apparently adopted its identity from the local monastery of St. Maron (Bêth Maron). Originally, this community was Chalcedonian. Under Heraclius, it embraced monoënergism-monothelitism as an imperial Orthodoxy. This group existed independently from other major Christian groups in the Orient, until it united with the Roman church in the twelfth century. It was the first successful union of an Eastern church with the papal see of Rome. Presently, the Maronite church is one of the Eastern Catholic churches *sui iuris*, with its own patriarch. The Maronites constitute a Christian majority in Lebanon and are present in other Middle Eastern countries. In recent decades, their diaspora dramatically increased its presence in the West (see Moosa 2005).

# Modern Neo-Chalcedonianism

While most Chalcedonian communities accepted the decisions of Constantinople III, most anti-Chalcedonian communities rejected it as crypto-Nestorian. Their main problem with this council was that it had condemned the idea of one activity in Christ. Even today, the Oriental churches feel less confident about Constantinople III than even about the Chalcedon. Nevertheless, the version of neo-Chalcedonianism promoted by Constantinople III became a basis for reconciliation between the Byzantine and Oriental fellowships of churches in our days.

These churches have been engaged in mutual ecumenical dialogues since the 1960s. They eventually agreed on theological formulas, which were articulated in the neo-Chalcedonian language and published as "Agreed Statements" in 1989 and 1990. Particularly important is the "Second Agreed Statement and Recommendations to Churches" discussed and signed at the Orthodox Center of the Ecumenical Patriarchate in Chambésy, Switzerland, in September 1990. An earlier version of this statement had been adopted in 1989 at Anba Bishoy Monastery in Egypt.

The key words of the Chambésy statement are neo-Chalcedonian, such as "hypostatic unity." The version of neo-Chalcedonianism that the statement utilizes is dyoënergist and dyothelite. On the one hand, it acknowledges two distinct volitions and activities in Christ. On the other, it postulates the single subject of these volitions and activities. The statement also allows double language for describing the unity of divinity and humanity in Christ. Each tradition is allowed to speak of either one or two natures in Christ, as far as they do not exclude each other's Christological formulas:

> Both families agree that the *hypostasis* of the Logos became composite (*synthetos*) by uniting to His divine uncreated nature with its natural will and energy, which He has in common with the Father and the Holy Spirit, created human nature, which He assumed at the Incarnation and made His own, with its natural will and energy.
>
> Both families agree that the natures with their proper energies and wills are united hypostatically and naturally without confusion, without change, without division and without separation, and that they are distinguished in thought alone (*te theoria mone*). <. . .>
>
> The Orthodox agree that the Oriental Orthodox will continue to maintain their traditional Cyrillian terminology of "one nature of the incarnate Logos" ("*mia physis tou Theou Logou sesarkomene*"), since they acknowledge the double consubstantiality of the Logos which Eutyches denied. The Orthodox also use this terminology. The Oriental Orthodox agree that the Orthodox are justified in their use of the two-natures formula, since they acknowledge that the distinction is "in thought alone" (*te theoria mone*). (In Chaillot & Belopopsky 1998: 63)

# V.14
# Iconoclasm

The monothelite controversy was not the last one in the series of Christological debates that had begun in the third century. These debates culminated in the issue of the veneration of icons. The so-called iconoclast controversy was provoked in the 720s by emperors from the Isaurian dynasty. Scholars continue arguing about their rationale to launch an anti-icon campaign. This campaign resembles the European Reformation 800 years later, but their rationales seem to be different. Unlike the Reformation, the iconoclasm was initiated as a movement from above and not from below.

## A Conservative Movement

Byzantine rulers perceived the prosperity and integrity of their state as contingent on the piety of their people. They considered their duty to make sure that their people please God. Otherwise, they knew, the divine wrath would punish them. They were sure that such punishment happened in the form of a large submarine eruption near the Isle of Thera (Santorini) in 726, which caused a lot of damage and loss of human life.

Emperor Leo III the Isaurian (r. 717–41) decided that this and some other misfortunes were caused by wrong popular practices of religion. He believed that, just as God had punished the people of Israel for venerating idols, so the Roman people are being punished for the ways they venerated icons. Apparently, there were indeed some practices of veneration which did not much differ from paganism. Such practices can be observed even in our days. Leo tackled them rather radically—by prohibiting icons altogether.

Iconoclasm was in many regards a conservative movement. Its intention was to dust off the genuine apostolic tradition. Iconoclasts regarded the veneration of icons as pagan dust that piled up during centuries. For them, icons are a novelty, which the early church did not know. This novelty is a sour fruit of compromises with the pagan

**Figure 5.25** The famous bay of Santorini was formed by one of the submarine eruptions.

Source: Photo by the author.

world. Icons compromise the Christian monotheism. Those who protect icons are effectively advocating for new practices—a very suspicious activity for any pious Christian.

## Dura Europos

Indeed, icons became popular in the church when Christianity engaged with the Greco-Roman world. Illustrative in this regard is the case of the house-church excavated in the Syriac town of Dura Europos. Discovered by a British military unit in 1920, the site was explored by various archeological teams during the 1930s. They established that in the 250s it was conquered and buried under a thick layer of earth by the Sassanids, who thus unwillingly preserved it for us. Sometimes, Dura Europos is compared with Pompei. When a Christian community was established in Dura Europos, it was a Roman military outpost with a diverse population. This community, whose majority consisted of pagan converts, interacted with various religious groups, both mono- and polytheistic. Near the Christian house, there were a synagogue and a mithraeum. Interactions between these groups can be observed in the decorations they used for their meeting places. The Jewish synagogue, for example, was lavishly decorated with images, despite the prohibition of images in Judaism.

The same iconic is the Christian house-church. It was originally built as a private residence. Around 240, it was renovated to be used by the local Christian congregation. This congregation met there for about fifteen years, until the town was destroyed by the Persians. Scholars believe that this building "remains the only extant nonfunerary ritual

**Figure 5.26** An image from the synagogue in Dura Europos, now at the Yale University Art Gallery.

Source: Photo by the author.

**Figure 5.27** The earliest icon depicting the "Good Shepherd" from Dura Europos, now at the Yale University Art Gallery.

Source: Photo by the author.

space from pre-Constantinian Christianity" (Peppard 2016: 15). Christians decorated the house's halls with inscriptions and paintings that illustrate various stories from the Gospels. These paintings are believed to be the earliest surviving Christian icons.

If the iconoclast emperors judged icons by what we know about Dura Europos, their complaints that icons were a relatively late novelty introduced to the church under the influence of paganism would have not been absurd. Modern scholarship corroborates the iconoclastic point that the veneration of icons is a relatively late tradition, which became noticeable in the fifth and sixth centuries (see Louth 2007: 44). The iconoclasts, thus, wanted to reset the norms of piety to the earliest and purest forms, uncompromised by paganism.

## Re-sacralization of Politics

By taking initiative to purge the church from assumed idolatry and reinstate the strict monotheistic piety, the iconoclast emperors intended to strengthen their authority, which had been desacralized in the aftermath of the earlier civil war and the administrative inefficiency of their predecessors. To resacralize their authority, they evoked the older tradition, which had bestowed some symbolic priestly identity upon the imperial office. Leo, for instance, reportedly called himself a king and a priest: "I am both a king and a priest" (βασιλεὺς καὶ ἱερεύς εἰμι) (see Dagron 2003: 161).

Another factor that possibly contributed to the Byzantine iconoclast policies was the rise of Islam. This radically iconoclastic religion had been a major challenge for Byzantium for a century now. The Byzantine rulers tried to face it not only through wars, but also through diplomatic and cultural engagement—a usual Byzantine approach to solving problems. Forbidding icons was an invitation to caliphs for political interactions.

**Figure 5.28** Iconoclastic internal decor has been preserved in some churches in Cappadocia, Turkey.

Source: Photo by the author.

A combination of these and other factors created a powerful iconoclastic momentum for a movement that lasted four generations, more than a century. It started in 726, when Leo III ordered that all sacred images across the empire should be destroyed. To enforce this order, he promulgated in 730 an edict. The patriarch of Constantinople Germanus I (*c.* 634–732) opposed the new imperial policies and had to resign. After Leo III died in 741, his son Constantine V (r. 741–75) continued the iconoclastic line of his father. He was reassured that he was on the right track after significant victories against the Arabs and Slavs. These victories enhanced the campaign against icons.

# Council of Hieria 754

In 754, Constantine V convened a church council to confirm the policies of his dynasty regarding sacred images. Bishops met in the palace of Hieria, after which the council became known as the council of Hieria. The gathering perceived itself as ecumenical and was one of the best attended in the church history. The council forbade icons and anathematized the "iconodules"—literally, "the slaves of icons."

There was a relatively brief remission of the imperial policies in support of icons from 786 through 815. It was initiated by Irene (*c.* 752–803), the daughter-in-law of Constantine V. She eventually became an empress. Under her patronage, an iconodulic council met in Nicaea in 787. It condemned the iconoclasts. It also made sure that people would perceive it as ecumenical—to contest the ostensibly ecumenical character of the council in Hieria. So, the council of Nicaea continues to be received even now—as seventh ecumenical.

Toward the end of the Isaurian dynasty, the Byzantine army experienced some significant defeats, which were interpreted as God's punishment for the compromises with iconolatry following Irene's rule. After the new Amorian dynasty came to power in 813, it restored iconoclasm. Leo V (r. 813–20), the founder of the dynasty, regarded the restoration of iconoclasm a key to military and political success. Iconoclasm was officially reinstated by a synodal decision in 815. This edition of the doctrine can be called neo-iconoclasm.

Both sides of the iconoclast controversy perceived themselves as successors of the fathers who had discussed the incarnation. This perception was clearly stated, for instance, by the iconoclastic council of Hieria:

> These holy and ecumenical six councils, therefore, expounding with piety and in a manner pleasing to God the doctrines of the unimpeachable faith of us Christians, instructed by the God-given gospels, have handed down that there is one hypostasis in two natures and wills and operations in the one Christ our Lord and God, and taught that of one and the same are both the miracles and the sufferings.

> We too, having investigated and come to understand these matters through much application and investigation and with the inspiration of the all-holy Spirit, have found that the unlawful art of painters blasphemes against this crucial doctrine of our salvation, that is, against the dispensation of Christ, and overturns the same holy and ecumenical six councils convoked and inspired by God, and that it reinstates Nestorius who divided into a duality of sons the one Son and Word of God who became man for our sake, and also Arius, Dioscorus, Eutyches and Severos, taught mingling and fusion in the two natures of the one Christ. (In Price 2018: 672)

The Christological argument that the iconoclasts invoked was as follows. Those who paint the image of Christ fall either to Nestorianism or to Eutycheanism—depending on how they interpret this image. If they interpret it as depicting only the human side of Christ, they thus dissect Christ into two autonomous parts—in the Nestorian way. If they say that they depict the whole Christ, then his humanity and divinity get mixed up on the icon in the Eutychean way. The only way to preserve the orthodox interpretation of the incarnation was to not attempt depicting it altogether. Iconoclasts argued that the orthodox doctrine of the incarnation, which was debated for centuries and eventually established with so much effort, is now endangered again by the iconodules.

The iconodules argued that the veneration of icons does not endanger the orthodox Christology. On the contrary, it naturally stems from this Christology. Icons visualize and confirm the reality of the incarnation: they are possible only if God has been truly incarnated. Moreover, icons corroborate the orthodox Christological formulas, particularly the distinction between the particularity (hypostasis) and commonalities (natures) in Christ. This distinction is a key to understand icons. Icons reflect primarily the singular particularity of Christ, and not his commonalities, that is, natures. From this perspective, the iconodules argued, the iconoclasts confuse the logical categories of particularity and commonality, and thus err against the orthodox Christology.

## John of Damascus

John of Damascus was particularly successful in connecting icons with Christology. He was a key figure during the first phase of the iconoclastic controversy. As was mentioned, John lived outside the imperial boundaries and probably never in his life set his foot on Roman soil. This gave him an advantage of freedom to contest imperial policies. John approached all theological topics systematically, based on the categories. Icons were not an exception. John elaborated on them as a distinct logical category. He explained the category of image vis-à-vis the idea of archetype, which image represents:

> An image is therefore a likeness and pattern and impression of something, showing in itself what is depicted; however, the image is certainly not like the archetype, that is, what is depicted, in every respect—for the image is one thing and what it depicts is another—and certainly a difference is seen between them, since they are not identical. For example, the image of a human being may give expression to the shape of the body, but it does not have the powers of the soul; for it does not live, nor does it think, or give utterance, or feel, or move its members. And a son, although the natural image of a father, has something different from him, for he is son and not father. (*Orationes de imaginibus tres* III 16)

John expounded his counterarguments against iconoclasm in three treatises against "those who attack the holy images." These treatises are both Christological and iconological. John summarized the Christological wisdom of his time and applied it to the concept of image. He first addressed the question, why images are needed at all? His answer is that images reveal the hidden reality, which is otherwise inaccessible for human experience:

> Every image makes manifest and demonstrates something hidden. For example, because human beings do not have direct knowledge of what is invisible, since their souls are veiled by bodies, or [knowledge] of future events, or of things distant and removed in space, since they are circumscribed by space and time, the image was devised to guide us to knowledge and to make manifest and open what is hidden, certainly for our profit and well-doing and salvation, so that, as we learn what is hidden from things recorded and noised abroad, we are filled with desire and zeal for what is good, and avoid and hate the opposite, that is, what is evil. (*Orationes de imaginibus tres* III 17)

However, not everything inaccessible for human experience can be reflected through images:

> Bodies can reasonably be depicted, as having shape and bodily outline and color. Angels and souls and demons, if without body or density, may yet be given shape and outline in accordance with their nature—for being intellectual, they are believed to be and act intellectually in intellectual places—they are therefore depicted in bodily form, as Moses depicted the cherubim, and as they were beheld by those worthy, the bodily image disclosing a certain incorporeal and intellectual vision. The divine nature is alone able and completely incomprehensible, without form or shape. (*Orationes de imaginibus tres* III 24)

John made a clear distinction between different kinds of veneration. The differentiation between "worship" (λατρεία) and "veneration" (προσκύνησις) is crucial for the entire iconoclastic debate. The former is appropriate only for God, while the latter can apply to holy subjects, including icons. John produced a taxonomy of subjects for veneration:

The first kind of veneration is that of worship, which we offer to God, who is alone venerable by nature (*Orationes de imaginibus tres* III 28). <. . .>

The second kind [of veneration] is that whereby we venerate creatures, through whom and in whom God worked our salvation, either before the coming of the Lord, or in his incarnate dispensation, such as Mount Sinai and Nazareth, the manger in Bethlehem and the cave, the holy place of Golgotha, the wood of the cross, the nails, the sponge, the reed, the holy and saving lance, the apparel, the tunic, the linen cloths, the winding sheet, the holy tomb, the fountain head of our resurrection, the gravestone, Sion the holy Mount, and again the Mount of Olives, the sheep gate and the blessed precinct of Gethsemane. These and suchlike I reverence and venerate and every holy temple of God and every place in which God is named, not because of their nature, but because they are receptacles of divine energy and in them God was pleased to work our salvation. And I reverence angels and human beings and all matter participating in divine energy and serving my salvation, and I venerate them because of the divine energy (*Orationes de imaginibus tres* III 34). <. . .>

The third kind [of veneration] is that whereby we venerate things dedicated to God, by which I mean the sacred Gospels and the other books [of Scripture]; "they were written down for our instruction, on whom the ends of the ages have come" (1 Cor. 10:11). It is clear, then, that patens and chalices, thuribles, lamps and tables: all these are to be reverenced. For see, when Baltasar made the people serve from the sacred vessels, how God destroyed his kingdom (see Dan. 5:3-4, 30) (*Orationes de imaginibus tres* III 35). <. . .>

The fourth kind [of veneration] is that whereby the images seen by the prophets were worshipped and also the images of things to come (for it was through a vision of images that they saw God), as Aaron's rod (see Num. 17:23) was an image of the mystery of the Virgin, and also the jar (see Ex. 16:33) and the table (see Ex. 25:23); and when Jacob bowed in veneration over the head of the staff (see Gen. 47:31), it was the figure of the Savior. (*Orationes de imaginibus tres* III 36)

## Council of Nicaea 787

John's iconology became a blueprint for the decisions of the second Nicaean council in 787. This council summarized many folia of the anti-iconoclastic treatises in a dense *horos*, which is both Christological and iconological:

We preserve without innovation all the traditions of the church that have been laid down for us whether written or unwritten. One of these is reproduction in painted images, as something that is in harmony with the narration of the gospel message for the confirming of the real and in no way phantasmal incarnation of God the Word, and which serves us by conferring the same benefit. For these two things provide indisputable proof of each other and give expression, to each other. <. . .>

We therefore decree with all care and precision that venerable and holy images, made in colours or mosaic or other fitting materials, in the same way as the figure of

**Figure 5.29** Restored church of St. Sophia in Nicaea (modern Iznik in Turkey), where the council of 787 supposedly took place.
Source: Photo by the author.

the honourable and life-giving cross, are to be dedicated in the holy churches of God, on sacred vessels and vestments, on walls and panels, in houses and in the streets—[namely] the image of our Lord and God and Saviour Jesus Christ, of our immaculate Lady the holy Theotokos, and of the honourable angels and all the holy and sacred men. For it is to the extent that they are constantly seen through depiction in images that those who behold them [the images] are spurred to remember and yearn for their prototypes. They are to be accorded greeting and the veneration of honour, not indeed the true worship corresponding to our faith, which pertains to the divine nature alone, but in the same way as this is accorded to the figure of the honourable and life-giving cross, to the holy gospels, and to other sacred offerings. In their honour an offering of incensation and lights is to be made, in accordance with the pious custom of the men of old. For the honour paid to the image passes over to the prototype, and whoever venerates the image venerates in it the hypostasis of the one who is represented. (In Price 2018: 564–5)

# Theodore the Studite

During the neo-iconoclastic period, under the Amorian dynasty, a key theological figure in the iconodulic camp was the abbot of the Studite monastery in Constantinople, Theodore (759–826). He was born and brought up in the capital city and belonged to its upper-class family. Its members were in the service of Emperor Constantine V. Theodore's maternal uncle, Plato, after imperial service became a monk. Theodore followed in his steps. He came to prominence in the wake of the scandal caused by the attempts of Emperor Constantine VI (r. 780–97) to remarry. This scandal became known as moechian (adultery) controversy and had iconoclastic ramifications. Constantine supported iconoclasm. Those who criticized his remarriages were also against iconoclasm. Theodore became the voice and mind of this party. His opposition activities, however, cost him trials and exiles.

Theodore's standpoint was nonconformist. He thus followed the line of the original monasticism. In the fifth century, this line had led to the great schism and thus was compromised in the eyes of many Byzantines. Theodore effectively rehabilitated nonconformist monasticism in Byzantium, after the empire acknowledged that Theodore was right in his advocacy for icons. He also restored the tradition of coenobianism, which had fallen to oblivion after its heydays in the Egyptian and Palestinian monasteries.

Two pillars of Theodore's iconodulic theology were Christology and logics. He demonstrated a remarkable command in the traditional Aristotelian-Porphyrian categories. He was a true scholastic who, together with other Byzantine scholastics, predated by long the Western scholasticism. In the way that resembles John of Damascus, Theodore employed the scholastic categories to elaborate on the category of image. For him, Christ features a singularity (hypostasis), which particularizes his humanity. This particularized humanity is circumscribable as an image:

> Given that according to the consensus of the church, we confess that the hypostasis of the Word has become the shared hypostasis of the two natures, and that it endows with a hypostasis the human nature that rests in it, together with the properties that differentiate it from the others belonging to the same species, we may then reasonably claim that the very same hypostasis is uncircumscribed according to the nature of the divinity, and that instead it is circumscribed according to the nature that it shares with us; this human nature does not have its own subsistence (ὕπαρξιν) in a person (πρόσωπον) that is self-subsistent and self-circumscribed outside the hypostasis of the Word, but in this very hypostasis—since there cannot be a nature that lacks a hypostasis (ἀνυπόστατος)—and it is contemplated and circumscribed in an individual manner. (*Adversus iconoclastas* III 22; Theodore the Studite 2015: 95–6)

The antonymic pair of terms "circumscribable-uncircumscribable" was added to the traditional set of Christological terminology and became crucial during the iconoclastic period. These terms are Christological. As Torstein Tollefsen has explained, "We have circumscription when something is discovered within the limits of bodily characteristics which may be identified as having appearance and a definite magnitude. It is further discovered in a definite place, has figure, and is coloured"

(Tollefsen 2018: 63). Theodore the Studite addressed this notion in the following passage, in response to an aporia of his imagined opponent:

> You appear to indulge in a word game when you bring forth your beloved term *uncircumscribable* (ἀπερίγραπτον). <. . .> Christ has not been generated as a mere man; no one who belongs to the number of the pious would ever say that he assumed one out of the members of the human race; rather, he assumed human nature as a whole, or the whole nature; and yet this nature was seen in an individual manner (ἐν ἀτόμῳ)—for otherwise how could he be seen?—and according to this nature he is then seen and described, touched and circumscribed, he eats and drinks, he grows and matures, works and takes a rest, sleeps and walks, experiences hunger and thirst, weeps and perspires, and does whatever else one who is a human being may experience at all. Therefore Christ is circumscribed, even if he is not a mere human being (he is not one of the many, but God become a human being); else those whom you follow, and who say that Christ only came in appearance and as it were in a phantasy, would be attacked by the swift dragons of heresy. And yet, if he is truly God made man, he is also uncircumscribed, so the impious dog who laughably suggests that Christ had his origin from Mary may be chased off. This is indeed the new mystery of the economy: an encounter (σύνοδος) has taken place between the divine and the human nature in the one hypostasis of the eternal Word, which preserves in an intact manner the properties of each in the undivided union. (*Adversus iconoclastas* I 4; Theodore the Studite 2015: 48)

## Triumph of Orthodoxy

The iconoclast project was closed for good after a strong-willed woman, Theodora, came to power. She empowered the iconodulic party led by Theodore. This party restored the veneration of icons at a council in 842. This council confirmed that the second council of Nicaea, and not of Hieria, should be regarded as the seventh ecumenical. The restoration of icons is still celebrated in the Byzantine churches every first Sunday of the Great Lent—as the Sunday or the Triumph of Orthodoxy. In fact, this is also a feast that celebrates the conclusion of the centuries-long disputes on the incarnation of God.

# VI

# Church

# VI.1

# *Extra Ecclesiam Nulla Salus*

The place where common salvation becomes appropriated individually as particular salvation is called church. The church makes the salvation of the entire humankind accessible for individual human beings. In other words, it actualizes the potentiality of universal salvation: in the church, salvation as an assigned task can become the given.

This does not mean that the universal salvation offered by the incarnated Word is confined to the church exclusively. It means that individuals can fully appropriate it within the church only. That is what the famous phrase of the Latin-speaking theologian from North Africa Cyprian (200–58) means: "There is no salvation outside the church" (*extra ecclesiam nulla salus*) (*ep.* 73.21). This phrase also became popular in the Christian East and was repeated many times on many occasions.

A human being participates in the church by his or her consent, which opens for him or her access to common salvation in Jesus Christ. Consent is a crucial element of membership in the church. It must always be clearly stated during initiation to the church—baptism. The rite of this sacrament presupposes that a person freely rejects the evil forces and accepts Christ. Even if someone is baptized without giving consent—as a baby, godparents should utter consent on the baby's behalf. As individuals enter the church by consent, so they should continue their Christian life based on consent and free acceptance of the church's teachings and sacraments. Consent and freedom, thus, constitute a platform for what the modern Russian theologian Sergiy Bulgakov (1871–1944) called "synergism" between the divine and human aspects of the church:

> The Church as Divine-humanity, as the body of Christ and the temple of the Holy Spirit, is a *union* of divine and creaturely principles, their interpenetration without separation and without confusion. In this sense, the Church is a *synergism*, where the divine principle descends to penetrate and attach itself to humanity, whereas the human principle ascends to the divine. Therefore, in practical terms, this synergism is a giving and a receiving of divine gifts. Combined, these gifts are *fullness*, whereas in their appropriation by personal reception, in their separateness, they represent different ministries. The growth of the body of the Church (Eph. 4:16), each member receiving his growth, is thereby accomplished. (Bulgakov 2002: 262)

Participation in the church is based on the freedom expressed by the Greek word *autexousion* (αὐτεξούσιον)—the unalienable and innate capacity to choose between good and evil. To be a member of the church, one must deliberately choose the former and reject the latter. This leads a person to obtain another kind of freedom, which is expressed by the word *eleutheria* (ἐλευθερία). This is a liberation from sin and death that only the church can provide. Freedom is a keystone in the edifice of the church. Without freedom, the church turns into a sect.

That the church processes the potentiality of common salvation to the actuality of individual salvation based on individual consent does not make the church an individualistic institution. The church makes individuals transcending their own individualism and incorporates them into communities. In the church, individual salvation is possible only in communities. Another modern Russian theologian, Aleksey Khomyakov (1804–60), branded this feature of the church as "conciliarity" (*sobornost'*/соборность). For him, "*Sobornost'* is an organic, living unity, the origin of which lies in the divine grace of mutual love" (Хомяков 1867: 101).

The church actualizes salvation not only for humankind but for the entire world. John Chrysostom called it "the pillar of the world":

> Here He speaks of the Dispensation on our behalf. Do not tell me of the bells, or of the holy of holies, or of the high priest. The Church is the pillar of the world. Consider this mystery and you will be awe-stricken: for it is indeed "a great mystery" and a "mystery of piety" and it is "undoubtedly great" because it is beyond question. Since in his direction to the priests he had stipulated nothing like the regulations in Leviticus he refers the whole matter to a Higher Being, saying, "God was manifest in the flesh." The Creator appeared incarnate. He was "justified in the Spirit." As it was written, "Wisdom is justified by her children," or because He practised no guile as the prophet says, "Because he has done no violence, neither was guile found in his mouth" (Is. 53:9). He was "seen of angels." Angels together with us saw the Son of God, not having seen Him before. Great, truly great, was this mystery.
>
> The dispensation on our behalf he calls a mystery, and well may it be called so, since it is not manifest to all. Indeed it was not manifest to the angels, for how could it, since "it was made known by the Church" (Eph. 3:10)? Therefore he says, "Undoubtedly, great is the mystery of piety." Great indeed it was. For God became man, and man became God. (*Commentarii in epistulam i ad Timotheum* 62.554; Halton 1985: 37–8)

John stressed the connection of the church with God's incarnation in the person of Jesus Christ. Indeed, the church continues the presence of Jesus Christ among the disciples after his ascension to the Father (Lk. 24:50) and keeps his promise: "I am with you always, to the end of the age" (Mt. 28:20). Through the church, its members participate in Christ's body, as Gregory of Nyssa explained, with reference to Col. 1:24:

> All of us, integrated into one and the same body, that of Christ, by means of participation become one body: his. When the Good has proceeded through all, then the whole of his body will submit to the life-giving Power, and thus the submission of this body is said to be the submission of the Son, who is mixed with his own body, which is the Church. (*Tunc et ipse filius*; Drecoll & Berghaus 2011: 460)

There is a reciprocal causality between the church and the incarnation. On the one hand, the church is possible and indeed happens because of the incarnation. On the other hand, the incarnation has happened to be continued in the church. The church distributes the saving effect of the incarnation to every corner of the Earth and every historical epoch, and reaches everyone. A modern Serbian theologian, Justin Popović (1894–1979), defined the church as

> the most complex organism in all the worlds; it comprises everything from all the worlds: that is why it is impossible to give an integral definition of the Church. Thus her most perfect definition is the God-man and He is her ineffable essence. The God-man embraces everything: from God to atoms. Everything is in God although everything is not God: it is precisely by Him and in Him that everything stays personal, original, on its own: in being and in essence and above all, in personality. For personality is the most mysterious mystery after God himself. (Popović 2013: 6)

# VI.2
# Images of the Church

In the first centuries of Christianity, there were not many theological reflections on the church. Much more the church reflected on the Trinity and the incarnation than on itself. Theoretical speculations on the church began booming as late as in Modernity. Still, even in our days, in the words of Georges Florovsky (1893–1979):

> It is impossible to start with a formal definition of the Church. For, strictly speaking, there is none which could claim any doctrinal authority. None can be found in the Fathers. No definition has been given by the Ecumenical Councils. In the doctrinal summaries, drafted on various occasions in the Eastern Orthodox Church in the seventeenth century and taken often (but wrongly for the "symbolic books"), again no definition of the Church was given, except a reference to the relevant clause of the Creed, followed by some comments. (Florovsky 1987: 57)

Instead of defining the church, Christians preferred to refer to it through symbols and metaphors. Paul Minear has identified about a hundred images of the church in the New Testament only (Minear 1960). Metaphors were applied to the church because they are not as reductionist as theories. They can be interpreted broadly enough to describe such multifaceted and dynamic phenomenon as the church. John Chrysostom captured this multifacetedness of the church in the following passage:

> Nothing is more abiding than the Church: she is your Salvation; she is your refuge. She is more lofty than the heavens; she is more far-reaching than the earth. She never grows old; she always stays in bloom. And so Scripture indicates her permanence and stability by calling her a virgin; her magnificence by calling her a queen; her closeness to God by calling her a daughter; her barrenness turned to fecundity by calling her "the mother of seven." A thousand names try to spell out her nobility. Just as the Lord is called by many names—Father, Way, Life, Light, Arm, Propitiation, Foundation, Gate, Sinless One, Treasure, Lord, God, Son, Only-Begotten, Form of God, Image of God—since one name could not hope to describe the Omnipotent, and many names give us some small insight into His nature, so the Church goes by many names. (*De capto Eutropio* 52.402; Halton 1985: 13)

The most popular metaphor for the church became "church"—ἐκκλησία. *Ekklesia* is not a technical term for the church, but a metaphor. This metaphor was borrowed from the Greek political culture. There, the word meant a gathering of representatives who discussed the matters of a *polis*. This word also translated the Hebrew *qahal Yahweh*—the "people of God" in the Greek Septuagint.[1] "People of God" became another image, through which the church imagined itself. The image favored by Jesus himself was the Kingdom of God.[2] The image that the church favored in the posterior centuries was the body of Christ. Various feminine images also became popular in the church's self-imagination, such as bride, mother, Mary, and so on. For Clement of Alexandria, for example, the church is both "virgin and mother—pure as a virgin, loving as a mother" (in Jay 1980: 59).

## The Female Church

An early Christian apocalyptic text penned by a Roman named Hermas presents the church through a series of appearances of a female figure. First, the church appears to Hermas as an old woman:

> I saw in front of me a large white chair made of snow-white wool. An older woman in a shining robe approached me with a book in her hands. She sat down by herself and greeted me.

The church encouraged Hermas, who was in distress, and warned him against some personal transgressions:

> When she <   > rose from the chair, four young men came to take up the chair and went off toward the East. She called me, touched my chest. <. . .> While she was still speaking with me, there appeared two men who took her by the arms and they went away to the East, just like the chair. But she left in a joyful mood and said to me as she left: "Be of good courage, Hermas!"

A year later, the church appeared to Hermas in a second vision:

> As I was going into the countryside at about the same time as the previous year, while walking along I remembered last year's vision, and again the spirit seized me and took me away to the same place as the previous year. <. . .>

---

[1] Exod. 19:5; Is. 43:20-21; Hos. 2:23. See Baily 1958; Minear 1960: 67–71.

[2] Mt. 12:28; 19:24; 21:31; 21:43; Mk 1:15; 4:11; 4:26; 4:30; 9:1; 9:47; 10:14; 10:15; 10:23-25; 12:34; 14:25; Lk. 4:43; 6:20; 7:28; 8:10; 9:27; 9:60; 9:62; 10:9; 10:11; 11:20; 13:18; 13:20; 13:28-29; 16:16; 17:20-21; 18:16; 18:17; 18:24-25; 21:31; 22:16; 22:18; Jn 3:3; 3:5.

> I saw before me the same elder lady that I had seen the previous year, walking and reading from a little book. She said to me: "Can you proclaim these things to God's elect?" I answered her: "Lady, I cannot remember so much, but give me the little book so I can copy it." "Take it," she said, "and return it to me."
>
> I took it to a certain place in the field and copied it all letter by letter because I was having trouble separating the syllables. When I had completed the letters of the little book it was suddenly snatched out of my hand—by whom, I did not see.

In a revelation, Hermas received an explanation of this vision:

> While I slept, a revelation came to me, brothers and sisters, from a handsome young man who said to me: "The elder lady from whom you received the little book—who do you think she is?" I answered: "The sybil." "Wrong," he said, "that is not who she is." "Then who is she?" I asked. "The church," he said. I said to him: "Then why is she elderly?" "Because," he said, "she was created before everything. That is why she is elderly, and for her the world was established." (Koester & Osiek 1999: 46–58)

Origen continued the line of thinking about the church as a heavenly entity that had existed since the inception of the world. He also called the church a "bride" but specified that this name applies to it only after the incarnation:

> You must please not think that she is called the Bride or the Church only from the time when the Saviour came in flesh: she is so called from the beginning of the human race and from the very foundation of the world—indeed, if I may look for the origin of the high mystery under Paul's guidance, even before the foundation of the world. For this

**Figure 6.1** An early Christian illustration of Hermas's vision in the catacombs of Naples, Italy.

Source: Photo by the author.

> is what he says: <. . .> “as He chose us in Christ before the foundation of the world, that we should be holy and unspotted in His sight” (Eph. 1:4). (*In Cant.* II 8; Jay 1980: 62)

The image of the church as a female figure became popular among early Christians. A late-second-century tombstone of a bishop from Asia Minor testifies to that. The inscription on the tombstone was quoted by Eusebius. A fragment of the original monument was found in 1883. It belongs to Avircius Marcellus, reportedly a bishop of Hieropolis in Phrygia, who died in the early 180s. According to the inscription, he visited various Christian communities of his time, including the one in Rome. Through various euphemisms, he described early Christian beliefs, including the one about the church. In the way that resembled Hermas, the inscription refers to the church as “a golden-robed and golden sandalled queen”:

> I, a citizen of the elect city, erected this tomb in my lifetime, that I might have clearly there a place for my body; my name is Avircius, a disciple of the pure Shepherd who feeds the flocks of sheep on mountains and plains, who has great all-seeing eyes; he taught me <. . .> faithful scriptures. To Rome he sent me to behold sovereignty and to see a queen, golden-robed and golden sandalled; a people I saw there which has a splendid seal, and I saw the plain of Syria and all the cities, and Nisibis, crossing the Euphrates; but everywhere I met with brethren; with Paul before me, I followed, and Faith everywhere led the way and served food everywhere, the Fish from the spring—immense, pure, which the pure Virgin caught and gave to her friends to eat for ever, with good wine, giving the cup with the loaf. These things I Avircius ordered to be written thus in my presence. I am truly seventy-two years old. Let him who understands these things, and everyone who is in agreement, pray for Avircius. No one is to put anyone else into my tomb; otherwise he is to pay the Roman treasury, 2,000 gold pieces and my good native city of Hieropolis 1,000 gold pieces. (Ramsay 2010: 722–3; Stevenson & Frend 2013: 122–3)

# In Syriac Poetry

In the early period, even more than in visions, the church appeared in poetry. Particularly the poets from the margins of the Greco-Roman world were fond of the church. The most prominent Western Syrian poet, Ephrem (*c.* 306–73), dedicated to the church a whole hymn, *On Paradise*. Dom Beck has titled this hymn *de ecclesia* (Beck 1960), because it is focused on the church as the paradise on earth:

> Rest firm on the Truth and fear not, my brothers,
> for our Lord is no weakling to fail us in trial;
> he is the power on which hangs the world and its dwellers.
> On him hangs the hope of his Church.

Who could ever cut off its heavenly roots?
Blessed be he whose power came down
and was made one with his churches!

Get yourselves, my brothers, the treasure of consolation
from the word of our Lord which he spoke of the Church:
"The bars of Sheol cannot conquer her."
If then she is stronger than Sheol,
who among mortals is able to frighten her?
Blessed be he who has magnified her, and turning
has tested her, to make her yet greater!

Then stretch out your hands towards the Branch of Truth!
Warriors' arms it has wearied, they could not bend it;
it bent down its summit, came down to the contest.
It tested the true who hung on it;
who hung but for profit dropped off and tell.
Blessed be he who made it come down,
to ascend in triumph! (In Murray 2004: 106–7)

In Eastern Syria, Aphrahat, who flourished in the first half of the fourth century, presented the church, also in Syriac language, as a colored bird. For him, such a bird is a symbol of many nations gathered into one community. The church, thus, is a "nation of nations" (*'ammâ d-men 'ammê*; see Murray 2004: 41):

> What is that coloured bird, I ask you? The coloured bird is the Church of the Nations. See why he called her coloured—because she is gathered from many tongues, and brought near from distant nations. And if you are still not persuaded that the Nations have become God's heritage, listen again to what Jeremiah says, calling the nations and rejecting Israel (Jer. 6:16-18 ff). <. . .> Therefore when the children of Israel would not listen to him, he turned to the Church of the Nations. (*Demonstrations* 12; Murray 2004: 57)

# In Coptic Poetry

Two generations later, the greatest Coptic author, Archimandrite Shenoute, in one of his discourses offered the following poetic description of the church:

Thus there is no measure of words for her and all her other secrets.
For she is one and she is a great multitude.
She is a virgin and a bride.
She is garden and a fountain.
She is a fertile land and she is a worker of land.

She is a people and she is a prophet.
She is an apostle and a saint.
She is a teacher and she is also a student.
She is a sister and she is a brother.
She is a child and she is an elder.
She is a daughter and a mother.
She is a house and she is also a city.
She is a sheepfold, going in through a door and going out from a door.
She is a shepherd to whose voice a sheepfold listens. Again she is a sheepfold listening to the voice of a shepherd.
She is a road on which people walk, and she is also a person walking on a road, that road leading to life.
And she is a slave who has a Lord, as it is written, "Serve the Lord in fear" (Ps. 2:11), and also, "Bless the Lord, all you slaves of the Lord" (Ps. 133:1), "Slaves, bless the Lord" (Ps. 112:1), "Praise his holy name" (1 Chr. 16:10).
She is a queen who has a multitude of slaves.
She is a child and she is also adult with breasts different from the breasts of all women who are on the earth.
She is a companion;
she is a perfect dove, a seed for sowing planted in a seed for a living fruit.
She is light coming from light.
She is a glory upon which the glory of the Lord comes.
She is a great multitude and a solitary. (*Discources* 1, 2, 3; Brakke & Crislip 2019: 50)

# In Armenian Poetry

In Armenia, Grigor Narekatsi (*c.* 950–1003/11) composed a litany for the church, which he compares with the Ark of the Covenant:

Gathered we all in the holy, universal, apostolic church,
we earthlings in circles, sing there in many groups,
praising with the myriads of spiritual beings, angelic;
we join the circles of the luminous kind.
We bless the One coming to you,
the Most Holy Trinity, [with whom] we plead. <. . .>

You (God) made her (church) glorious, radiant from the foundations [up],
brilliant, beyond the brilliance of the Ark.
And you adorned her beautifully, befittingly lavish,
the daughter of Sion that is above.
The many groups of singers there
join their voices with the heavenly ones.

We bless the One coming to you,
the Most Holy Trinity, [with whom] we plead.

A sanctuary built without hands, universal, holy,
you were established today in the midst of the universe, holy church,
a replica of the Garden where the work of creation—beautiful to behold—
[was accomplished], in the comfort of Eden,
[around] which—by the command of the Uncreated One—seraphim and cherubim
kept close watch over the passages to the tree of knowledge. <. . .>

Indescribable sanctuary, with incredible brightness
you were established today in the midst of the universe, holy church,
a replica of the high-domed ark
which the patriarch Noa—by the Creator's command—
built from the base up with fresh timber. <. . .>

A brilliant sanctuary, lit miraculously by the rays of the sun
in the midst of the universe today, holy church,
a replica of the [heavenly] sanctuary which the patriarch Abraham saw
when he was sitting at the threshold of heaven's gates
and gazing at heaven and earth—
[even] the Lord of Lords coming from there with his two angels
and drawing near to the shade of the tree
to reward his loved ones for their good deeds. <. . .>

Foursquare temple, magnificent in appearance,
radiating [your] light transparently
in the midst of the universe today, holy church,
a replica of the ark built by Moses
in the midst of the congregation of Israel. <. . .>

And now, may the Lord our God have mercy on us
according to his great mercy.[3]

[3]MH 12:691–94 [14:950–51]/TG 184–88, in Gregory of Narek, 2011. *The Festal Works*, annotated translation of the Odes, Litanies, and Encomia by Abraham Terian, Collegeville, MN: Liturgical Press: 120–6.

# VI.3

# Common and Particular in the Church

Not only poetic metaphors are applicable to the church but also scholastic categories. The dialectical distinction between commonality and particularity, which had become basic in the Trinitarian theology and Christology, was also applied in ecclesiology. It helps to differentiate between the universal and local churches. It is also a key to understand the difference between the common unchangeable "nature" of the church and its changeable accidents.

## Church Universal

The church's universal nature features shared faith in Jesus Christ, the presence of the Word of God in the Gospels and Eucharist, the deifying activity of the Holy Spirit, freedom-based human synergy with God in pastoral ministry, works of charity, and other instruments of salvation. Common salvation defines the universality of the church's nature. Like the former, the latter cannot be fragmented, cannot exist in one part of the church and be absent in another part of it. Ephrem the Syrian called the church's common nature "that universal branch" of vine, which has overshadowed the entire world (in Murray 2004: 112–3).

## Church Particular

In contrast to the Roman Catholic Church, which identifies the universal church with the see of Rome, the Orthodox churches believe that the universal church does not exist on its own, but only in particular churches. After the Roman Empire merged with Christianity, ecclesial particularity became synonymous with locality. In our days, locality is usually associated with the enormous structures of autocephalous churches. Metropolitan of Kyiv Petro Mohyla (1596–1647) in his *Catechism* interpreted the particularity of the church as the locality of the patriarchates:

> The Church is one, holy, catholic and apostolic, the Confession asserts; according to the Doctrine of the Apostle (2 Cor. 11:2), *I have espoused you to one Husband, that I may present you as a chaste Virgin unto Christ.* For like as Christ is only one, so His Spouse also can be but one; as is manifest from the Epistle to the Ephesians (4:5), One Lord, one Faith, one Baptism, one God and Father of all. <. . .> The Church does not apply this description of the Catholic Church to any one Place or See predominant over all others; for those are particular Churches which are in particular Places; As the Church of Ephesus, of Philadelphia, of Laodicea, Antioch, Jerusalem, Rome, Alexandria and others.

Peter contested the idea that Rome can be identified with the universal church and thus is different from the rest of the local churches. The only local church, for him, which comes close to such an exceptional role, is the church of Jerusalem—the Mother of the churches:

> However, among these particular Churches she may well be called the Mother who was honoured first with the Presence of Christ, and received eternal Life and Remission of Sins, and from which the Gospel was first preached and spread through the whole world. <. . .> The Church of Jerusalem, therefore, is without doubt the Mother and Princess of all other Churches: forasmuch as the Gospel was spread from her over the whole world. (In Bolshakoff 1946: 150)

Particular churches, in their original form, were not patriarchates or even dioceses, but communities. Communities, one could say, are hypostases of the universal church. The category of hypostasis means a particularity of the common nature. Communities are such particularities of the common nature of the church. Every community fully participates in this common nature and fully expresses it. There is nothing in the church's common nature, which would be missing in its particular nature—a community. Each community, at the same time, actualizes the common ecclesial nature in a particular way. If we apply the categorial language of Maximus the Confessor, we can distinguish between the communities' common "logos" and particular ways of their existence (*tropos hyparxeos*/τρόπος ὑπάρξεως). The way of particular existence is unique for each particularity. Particular communities constitute a plurality, which preserves its unity by participating in the oneness of the universal church.

Some early Christian writers went even further in atomizing the church. For them, every human soul that appropriates salvation can be regarded a church. The Syriac

*Book of Steps (ܟܬܒܐ ܕܡܣܩܬܐ)* speaks about the "church of heart" (see Murray 2004: 263). Anyone who has purified himself or herself and opened up for the indwelling grace of the Spirit becomes such a church. Ps.-Macarius explains this in one of his homilies:

> The word "church" is used of the individual soul, as well as of many; for the soul gathers together all her faculties and is thus a church to God. For the soul was fitted for communion with the heavenly Bridegroom, and mingles with the heavenly One. This is observed both of the many and of the one. (In Murray 2004: 270)

"Eucharistic ecclesiology," which became popular in the Christian East from the mid-twentieth century, synthesized the individual participation in the church with the idea of community as the church's particularity. A protagonist of this ecclesiology, Nikolay Afanasiev (1893–1966) (see Wooden 2019), pointed out that a community participates in the common nature of the church through the Eucharist:

> The unity of the local church itself is manifest in its one eucharistic assembly. The Church is one since it has one eucharistic assembly in which God's priestly people are gathered. Since Christ yesterday, today, and forever is one and the same, the multiplicity of the Eucharist in time does not divide the one body of Christ. In the same way, the multiplicity of eucharistic assemblies does not destroy the unity of God's Church, for in both space and time the eucharistic assembly remains one and the same. For primitive Christian consciousness the unity of the Church was not merely a dogmatic statement but a lived experience. Despite the increase of the number of local churches, the unity of the Church remained undisturbed, for they did not have different eucharistic assemblies but one and the same. Unity and fullness were not contained in the sum total of local churches nor in their confederation (which never existed), but rather in each local church.
>
> Being one in its fullness the Church always retained its internal universality, for each local church contained in itself all remaining local churches. What was done in one church was done in all remaining ones, for everything was done within God's Church and in Christ. Due to this catholic universality, the local churches were absolutely devoid of any isolation and provincialism. No single church could separate itself from the others for it could not separate itself from Christ. All were united to one another through love. Each of the churches was loved by all and all were loved by each one of them. (Afanasiev 2012: 4–5)

Eucharist is indeed an important medium that enables a particular church to participate in the universal nature of the church. Other manifestations of the universal nature of the church, such as faith, truth, holiness, the Scripture, and other sacraments, also connect a community with other communities and make them participate in the one church of Christ.

# Distinction between Common and Particular in the Church

The church's universal and particular aspects are not separated—they are only distinguished. To use the language of Cyril of Alexandria, we can imagine the difference between them only theoretically. We can apply to the church the difference between separation and distinction, which we studied earlier. Particular churches can be separated from each other but cannot be separated from the universal church: particular and universal churches can be only *distinguished* from each other. That is because particular churches *partake* in the universal church—to use the neo-Platonic terminology. When a particular church ceases partaking in the ecclesial common nature, it means that it falls out to schism or heresy. Schism and heresy, thus, separate a community or a group of communities from the universal church and make them nonchurch. This happens, when communities lose the common features of the church's nature, such as, for example, togetherness, same sacraments, faith, and so on.

# VI.4 Nature and Structures of the Church

We mentioned earlier the categories-based distinction between the church's nature and accidents (συμβεβηκότα). This distinction should not be confused with the distinction between the church's universal and particular aspects. The latter is the distinction between the universal church and its "hypostases," such as communities. Accidents are primarily the church's administrative structures. Their purpose is to preserve the unity of communities and to facilitate their participation in the common nature of the universal church.

## The Church's Binarity

The difference between the church's nature and accidents is similar to invariable and variable values in an equation. The nature remains the same, but its accidents can change depending on internal and external processes inside and outside the church. For example, communities have been a part of the church's nature since the apostolic times. In contrast to them, supra-communal structures, such as dioceses, patriarchates, and so on, emerged and evolved during the church's long historical journey. They are ecclesial accidents.

Our understanding of the Christological debates may help us also better understand the difference between the church's nature and structures. What comes from these debates is that, similarly to Christ's natures, the ecclesial nature does not change. Therefore, those elements of the church's life and functionality that were always there can be ascribed to the ecclesial nature. This idea is not new in Orthodox ecclesiology. Aleksey Khomyakov, for instance, spoke about the "outward immutability" (in Bolshakoff 1946: 145) as a feature of the church:

> The Church neither was at any time, nor could be changed, obscured, nor could she fall away; since in that case, she would have lost the spirit of truth. There could never be a time, when she received falsehood into herself. (In Bolshakoff 1946: 146)

The church Khomyakov was speaking about was the church's nature. In contrast to it, those elements that emerged in the church during its historical journey do not belong to the church's nature, but evolve around it. Sergiy Bulgakov identified the difference between these two aspects of the church as a polarity between the "ontological and institutional" (Bulgakov 2002: 262). Nikolay Afanasiev, in the same vein, differentiated between the dynamic life of the church and its static structures:

> As any organism, the Church has two principles: its static structure (constitution, organization) and dynamic life functions. Both of these principles are inseparable from each other and they cannot be studied separately, because there is no life without the organization, and there is no organization without life. (In Wooden 2019: 365)

This is an important testimony about the ecclesial nature and structures being inseparable from one another—in the same way as *ousia* and its accidents are only distinguishable. The difference between distinction and separation helps better understand how the administrative structures relate to the church's members and their communities.

## The Church's Nature

One of the most important unchangeable elements of the church's nature is faith in Jesus. This faith leads the members of the church to union with God and with one another. The church cannot be itself without faith in Jesus. Faith forms the church and is an inalienable feature of its nature. However, expressions of this faith evolved throughout the centuries. Therefore, various creeds and definitions, including the ones adopted at the ecumenical councils, cannot be seen as unchangeable—they are accidents of faith and the Revelation.

Through the ecumenical councils, the church confirmed the truth it had received through the Revelation from God. Truth is another important feature of the church's nature, which makes the church infallible. The infallibility of the church in whole, and not of any of its particular institutions, was emphasized by Aleksey Khomyakov:

> The Church knows nothing of partial truth and partial error, but only the whole truth without admixture of error. And the man who is living within the Church does not submit to false teaching or receive the Sacrament from a false teacher: he will not, knowing him to be false, follow his false rites. And the Church herself does not err, for

she is the truth; she is incapable of cunning or cowardice, for she is holy. (In Bolshakoff 1946: 146)

The Nicaean creed identified the church as one, holy, catholic, and apostolic. This is a list of marks of the church's nature. Although this list is not exhausting, it represents some important unchangeable aspects of the ecclesial phenomenon. Aleksey Khomyakov explained them:

> The Church is called *One, Holy, Collective, i.e., Catholic* and Oecumenical (in Slavonic *Sobornaya) and Apostolic*; because she is one and holy; because she belongs to the whole world, not to any, particular locality; because by her the whole human race and the whole earth are sanctified, and not only one particular nation or country; because her essence consists in concord and unity of spirit and life in all those her members, by whom she is acknowledged throughout the whole world; because, in fine, in the writings and the teachings of the Apostles, all the fullness of her faith, her hope and her love is contained. Hence it follows that, when a Christian community is called a local Church, as the Greek, Russian, or Syrian, such language denotes only the aggregate of those members of the Church, who live in such or such a country (as Greece, Russia, Syria, etc.), and by no means implies that any one particular community of Christians has power to formulate Ecclesiastical doctrines or to give to Ecclesiastical doctrine a dogmatic explanation without the concurrence of other communities; still less is it implied that any one particular community, or its pastor, can prescribe his own explanation to others. The grace of faith is not separate from holiness of life; and no one community, nor any one pastor can be acknowledged as the guardian of the whole faith, any more than any one pastor, or any one community can be looked upon as representing the holiness of all the Church. Nevertheless, every particular Christian community, without arrogating to itself the right of dogmatic explanation or teaching, has full right to change old rites and observances, and to introduce new, so long as it causes thereby no offence to other communities, but rather, on the contrary, waives its own opinion and yields to theirs in order that, what is innocent in one, and even laudable, may not seem blameable to another, and that brethren may not lead one another into the sin of doubt and discord. (In Bolshakoff 1946: 148–9)

The church's holiness stems from the holiness of God. In the church, God co-dwells with human beings. He imbues them and the entire world with his sanctifying and deifying grace. Gregory of Nyssa explained that the nature of the church, which he identified with "Christianity," is holy by imitating the nature of God:

> It is not possible for Christ not to be justice, purity, truth, and estrangement from all evil, nor is it possible to be a Christian, that is, truly a Christian, without displaying in oneself a participation in these virtues. If one might give a definition of Christianity we shall define it as follows: Christianity is an imitation of the divine nature. (*De professione Christiana ad Harmonium* 136; Halton 1985: 152)

The Holy Spirit, according to Maximus the Confessor, plays a special role in sanctifying the church:

> The Church of God, worthy of all praise, is a lampstand wholly of gold, pure and without stain, undefiled and without blemish, receptacle of the true light that never dims. <. . .> The lamp above her is the true light of the Father which lights up every man coming into this world, our Lord Jesus Christ, become light and called such. <. . .> And if Christ is the head of the Church according to human understanding, then he is the one who by his nature has the Spirit and has bestowed the charisms of the Spirit on the Church. <. . .> For the Holy Spirit, just as he belongs to the nature of God the Father according to his essence so he also belongs to the nature of the Son according to his essence, since he proceeds inexpressibly from the Father through his begotten Son. (*Quaestiones ad Thalassium* 63; Siecienski 2010: 77)

Cyril of Jerusalem explained the term "catholicity" as the church's ubiquity and universality. The church is "catholic," because it worships God in a true way. In this sense, the word "catholic" is synonymous with the word "orthodox," which means "correct worship" or "correct opinion" about God:

> This Church is called Catholic because it is spread throughout the world from end to end of the earth; also because it teaches universally and completely all the doctrines which men should know concerning things visible and invisible, heavenly and earthly; and because it subjects to right worship all mankind, rulers and ruled, lettered and unlettered; further because it treats and heals universally all sorts of sin committed by soul and body; and it possesses in itself every conceivable virtue, whether in deeds, words, or in spiritual gifts of every kind. (*Catechesis* XVIII 23; Halton 1985: 84)

The Western church has adopted the predicative "catholic" as its identity, while the Eastern churches adopted as their identity the predicative "orthodox." Some Eastern churches use for identity another church's "mark" from the Nicaean creed, "apostolic." Such is the Armenian Apostolic Church.

The idea of apostolicity was employed to counterpose the orthodoxy of the "catholic" church to numerous sectarian movements that mushroomed already in the first centuries of Christianity. Irenaeus of Lyon argued that various Gnostic groups cannot be regarded the church, because their teaching cannot be traced to the apostles. Only the true church in each corner of the world has the same apostolic faith:

> For the Church, though dispersed throughout the whole world, even to the ends of the earth, has received from the apostles and their disciples this faith: in one God, the Father Almighty, who made the heaven and the earth and the seas and all things that are in them; and in one Christ Jesus, the Son of God, who became incarnate for our

> salvation; and in the Holy Spirit, who proclaimed through the prophets the dispensations and the advents. <. . .>
>
> As I have already observed, the Church, having received this preaching, and this faith, although scattered throughout the whole world, yet, as if occupying but one house, carefully preserves it. She also believes these points of doctrine just as if she had but one soul, and one and the same heart, and she proclaims them, and teaches them, and hands them down, with perfect harmony, as if she possessed only one mouth. For, although the languages of the world are dissimilar, yet the import of the tradition is one and the same. For the churches which have been planted in Germany have not believed or handed down anything different, nor do those in Spain, nor those in Gaul, nor those in the East, nor those in Egypt, nor those in Libya, nor those which have been established in the central regions of the world. (*Adversus haereses* I 2-3; Stevenson & Frend 2013: 124–5)

For Irenaeus, Christian faith has authority not because it is old, but because it is preserved by the church. In the church, this faith is constantly regenerated:

> The preaching of the Church is everywhere consistent, and continues in an even course, and receives testimony from the prophets, the apostles, and all the disciples—as I have proved—through those in the beginning, the middle, and the end, and through the entire dispensation of God, and that well-founded system which tends to man's salvation, namely, our faith; which, having been received from the Church, we do preserve, and which always, by the Spirit of God, renewing its youth, as if it were some precious deposit in an excellent vessel, causes the vessel itself containing it to renew its youth also. For this gift of God has been entrusted to the Church, as breath was to the first created man, for this purpose, that all the members receiving it may be vivified; and the means of communion with Christ, that is, the Holy Spirit, has been distributed throughout it, the earnest of incorruption, the means of confirming our faith, and the ladder of ascent to God. (*Adversus haereses* III 38, Stevenson & Frend 2013. 125–6)

Irenaeus, importantly, did not identify the apostolic tradition with traditionalism. The former looks up to God, while the latter—back to the past. Traditionalism ossifies the past and does not allow the tradition to "renew its youth," to use Irenaeus' wording. Jaroslav Pelikan captured Irenaeus' idea of tradition in his famous catchphrase: "Tradition is the living faith of the dead, traditionalism is the dead faith of the living" (Pelikan 1984: 65).

# Ecclesial Structures

To ensure the apostolic character of the faith professed in communities and to keep these communities in communion with one another, the church developed supra-communal structures. In contrast to communities, supra-communal structures emerged at a later stage of the church's history. Because of this, they do not belong to the nature of the church. These structures are administrative and not charismatic in their nature. Their initial rationale was to facilitate communities to solve both internal and external issues. The original purpose of supra-communal structures, thus, is to serve communities. These structures were primitive in the beginning: they started as a network of neighbor communities. With the passage of time, however, supra-communal administrative structures became increasingly complicated. In their evolution, they imitated the administrative structures of the Roman Empire.

In the process of their evolution, some supra-communal structures deviated from their original rationale of serving communities. Instead, they often made communities serve them. Structures, which had been designed as an auxiliary for the church's nature, identified themselves with the church and made themselves more important than what they were supposed to serve. Such malfunctions in the supporting structures damaged some fundamental aspects of the church's nature, such as unity.

Particularly damaging were the malfunctions of the pentarchic system of patriarchates. The biggest schisms in the history of Christianity have been caused by quarrels between the patriarchates. In the fifth century, it was a schism between the sees of Rome, Constantinople, and Jerusalem on the one hand and Alexandria and Antioch on the other. In the eleventh century, it was a schism between the patriarchates of Rome and Constantinople.

Most schisms, particularly the latter one, were underpinned by arguments about the nature and practices of primacy.[1] In the fourth century, local churches reached a consensus that bishops of the old and new Romes should be regarded as "first among equals" (*primi inter pares*). In their tandem with bishops of the new Rome, bishops of the old Rome had a lead. Their senior status was accepted in the Christian East as well. Even after Rome and Constantinople broke their relations up, the archbishop of Thessalonica Symeon (*c.* 1381–1429) acknowledged that Rome could still hold primacy, as long as it also held the orthodoxy of faith:

> When the Latins say that the Bishop of Rome is first, there is no need to contradict them, since this can do no harm to the Church. If they will only show us that he has continued in the faith of Peter and his successors and that he possesses all that came from Peter, then he will be the first, the chief and head of all, the Supreme Pontiff. All these qualities have been attributed to the patriarchs of Rome in the past. His throne is apostolic and the Pontiff who sits there is called the successor of Peter as long as he professes the true faith. There is no right-thinking person who would dare to deny this. (*Dialogus contra omnes haereses* XXIII; PG 155, 120–1)

[1]See a fundamental study on primacy accomplished by the Saint Irenaeus Joint Orthodox-Catholic Working Group: 2019. *Serving Communion: Re-thinking the Relationship between Primacy and Synodality*, Los Angeles: Tsehai.

Symeon, together with other Byzantine theologians, concurred with the Roman narratives about the supposedly exclusive role of Peter among other apostles (see Dijkstra 2020). Toward the end of the Late Antiquity, these narratives were extrapolated to the primacy of the Roman bishops as alleged successors of Peter (see Demacopoulos 2013). These narratives contributed to the medieval concept that the Roman primacy stems from the very nature of the church. That is what Cardinal Thomas Cajetan (1469–1534) apparently meant when he stated: "The authority of the pope is immediately from God and revealed in Sacred Scripture" (*De divina institutione pontifucatus Romani Pontificis*; Burns & Izbicki 1997: 2).

The Christian East disapproved of such an interpretation of primacy. The Roman church, from the Eastern perspective, embodies the universal church to the same extent as other Eastern patriarchates do. Mark of Ephesus (1392–1444) remarked in this regard: "We consider the pope as one of the patriarchs" (in Gregory Mammas, *Responsio ad epistulam encyclicam*; PG 160, 200). While agreeing that the church of Rome is *prima inter pares*, the Easterners disagreed that any primacy, including the Roman one, is embedded in the church's nature.

The East preferred to see the criteria for choosing a particular church to be the first among equals, as political. Francis Dvornik called this the "principle of accommodation" (see Dvornik 1979: 27–39). It means that the church builds its administrative structures on the basis of political structures. As canon 28 of the council of Chalcedon put it, the Roman and Constantinopolitan sees took a lead among other churches, because they had been located in the centers of imperial "power and senate" (in Tanner 1990: 99–100). Canons 4 and 6 of the council of Nicaea (325), canon 9 of the council of Antioch (341), and canon 6 of the council of Constantinople (381) corroborated the same idea. Patriarch Photius summarized the "principle of accommodation" in his famous dictum: "The ecclesial rights and particularly those related to the borders of dioceses should change together with the civil domains and administration" (*ep.* 290.406-8; Photius 1985). In the same line, a late Byzantine theologian Nilus Cabasilas (*c.* 1298–1363) explained that a particular church enjoys primacy not because it has received it from God, but because other churches, in collaboration with imperial authorities, have endorsed it with such a privilege:

> The pope has indeed two privileges: he is the bishop of Rome <. . .> and he is the first among the bishops. From Peter he has received the Roman episcopacy; as to the primacy, he received it much later from the blessed Fathers and the pious emperors, for it was just that ecclesiastical affairs be accomplished in order. (*De primatu papae*; PG 149, 701)

The consensual interpretation of primacy, in contrast to the ontological interpretation, means that a church can claim and exercise primacy only when other churches have delegated this right to it. Consequently, in exercising its primacy, the *prima ecclesia* should consult other churches and cannot act unilaterally. Eastern theologians interpreted the unilateral activities of the Roman church, especially after the Gregorian reforms in the eleventh century, as a serious transgression that violated the consent-driven interchurch relations. As Andrew Louth has remarked, only after the Gregorian reforms we can properly speak about papacy (Louth 2007: 298). The archbishop of Nicomedia Nicetas, in his conversations held in 1136 with Bishop Anselm from northern Germany, opposed papacy as a regime of unilateral decisions. He argued that the church of Rome should return to consent-based relations with other churches:

> I neither deny nor do I reject the Primacy of the Roman Church whose dignity you have extolled. As a matter of fact, we read in our ancient histories that there were three patriarchal sees closely linked in brotherhood, Rome, Alexandria, and Antioch, among which Rome, the highest see in the empire, received the primacy. For this reason Rome has been called the first see and it is to her that appeal must be made in doubtful ecclesiastical cases, and it is to her judgment that all matters that cannot be settled according to the normal rules must be submitted.
>
> But the Bishop of Rome himself ought not to be called the Prince of the Priesthood, nor the Supreme Priest, nor anything of that kind, but only the Bishop of the first see. Thus it was that Boniface III, who was Roman by nationality, and the son of John, the Bishop of Rome, obtained from the Emperor Phocas confirmation of the fact that the apostolic see of Blessed Peter was the head of all the other Churches, since at that time, the Church of Constantinople was saying that it was the first see because of the transfer of the Empire.
>
> In order to make sure that all the sees profess the same faith, Rome sent delegates to each of them, telling them that they should be diligent in the preservation of the true Faith. When Constantinople was granted the second place in the hierarchy because of the transfer of the capital, this custom of the delegations was likewise extended to that see.
>
> We find that, my dear brother, written in the ancient historical documents. But the Roman Church to which we do not deny the Primacy among her sisters, and whom we recognize as holding the highest place in any general council, the first place of honor, that Church has separated herself from the rest by her pretensions. She has appropriated to herself the monarchy which is not contained in her office and which has divided the bishops and the churches of the East and the West since the partition of the Empire. When, as a result of these circumstances, she gathers a council of the Catholic faith, how can we be expected to accept these decisions which were taken without our advice and of which we know nothing, since we were not at that same time gathered in council?
>
> If the Roman Pontiff, seated upon his sublime throne of glory, wishes to fulminate against us and to launch his orders from the height of his sublime dignity, if he wishes to sit in judgment on our Churches with a total disregard of our advice and solely according to his own will, as he seems to wish, what brotherhood and what fatherhood can we see in such a course of action? Who could ever accept such a situation? In such

> circumstances we could not be called nor would we really be any longer sons of the Church but truly its slaves.
>
> If the authority of the Pope was such as described by Anselm what good could be served by Scripture, by studies and by Greek wisdom? If that is the way things are, the Pope is the only bishop and the only master.
>
> But if he wishes to have collaborators in the vineyard of the Lord, let him dwell in humility in his own primatial see and let him not despise his brothers! The truth of Christ has caused us to be born in the bosom of the Church, not for slavery but for freedom. (In Dvornik 1979: 145–6)

Seven centuries later, Aleksey Khomyakov expressed the same idea that both primacy and unity should be based on love and consent, and not on unilateral actions of one church:

> The bond of love was torn, the communion of faith (which cannot exist with different symbols) was rejected in fact I will not say: Was that lawful? The idea of law and lawfulness may do for casuists and disciples of the *jus Romanum*, but cannot do for Christians. But I will ask: Was that moral? Was it brotherly? Was it Christian? The rights of the Catholic Church were usurped by a part of it. An unmerited offence was given to unsuspecting brothers, who till that time had fought with the greatest perseverance and certainly the greatest ability for Orthodoxy. This action was certainly a most heinous sin, and a most shocking display of pride and disdain. (In Bolshakoff 1946: 102–3)

Because primacy is bestowed upon a chosen church through the consent of other churches, it can be revoked—by the same churches. That is how the East has interpreted what happened in the eleventh century. According to this interpretation, the Roman church was demoted from its primacy, which passed to the next church in rank—Constantinople.

# Hierarchy and Ministry

The issue of primacy in the church is the tip of the iceberg. The whole iceberg is the issue of hierarchy. The concept of hierarchy was imported to Christianity from the neo-Platonic theology. In this theology, which was emphatically polytheistic, deities were ranked hierarchically. Christian neo-Platonists, such as Ps.-Dionysius the Areopagite, on the one hand, rejected neo-Platonic polytheism, while, on the other, adopted its idea of "divine hierarchy."

The idea of hierarchy was a later addition to the teaching about the church—the early church did not know it. Earlier, we have stated that only those elements that *always* belonged to the church can be ascribed to its nature. Following this criterion, we can assume that hierarchy does not belong to the ecclesial nature but is its accident. It is a supportive structure—a scaffolding that helps maintaining a building but is not a part of it.

The auxiliary function of hierarchy does not mean that it is useless or necessarily harmful to the church. The church adopted this structure with the purpose to serve communities. Indeed, hierarchies keep complex structures in order. However, when hierarchs, instead of serving communities, force communities to serve themselves, the hierarchical principle turns against the church's nature and against the idea of ministry. Ministry can be easily confused with hierarchy, but it should not be. Hierarchy is a ministry's modality—its "how" and not its "what."

The amplitude of the interpretations of how ministry is exercised varied in the early church from egalitarian to segregationist. In the apostolic times, all faithful were believed to be priests, through the participation in the priesthood of Jesus Christ (1 Pet. 2:5). There was no laity, in fact, which is a later notion. Each member of the church could serve his or her community through various charismata, such as prophetic, teaching, working miracles, healing, supporting, interpreting tongues (1 Cor. 12), admonishing, benefactoring, and showing mercy (Rom. 12:6–8). In line with the Pauline testimonies, early Christian writers took the general priesthood of all church members as granted. For instance, Origen believed that all baptized members of the church "have been made priests" (*In Leviticum* IX 9; Jay 1980: 62). He asked his lay audience: "Do you not know that the priesthood is given to you also, that is to the whole Church of God, the people who believe?" Everyone, consequently, "must offer to God sacrifices of praise, prayers, pity, purity, righteousness, and holiness" (*In Leviticum* IX 1; Jay 1980: 61–2).

With the passage of time, ministry was separated from the rest of a community. Ministerial charismata were reduced to the threefold service of bishops, presbyters, and deacons. This service was focused on ministering sacraments. Particularly important became the ministry of bishop, whose office evolved from charismatic to administrative. Under bishops' overseeing, the originally horizontal networks of communities transformed to vertical hierarchical structures.

The system that contributed to this transformation has been called monoëpiscopacy. We can trace it back to the second century. Ignatius of Antioch is famous for advocating for it. However, what he envisaged was not yet a hierarchical structure. One can conclude this from the parallel that Ignatius draws between the relations between a bishop and his community on the one hand and the Father and the Son on the other. According to Ignatius, monoëpiscopacy should be not a vertically structured order, but a horizontally harmonized relationship:

> And so, just as the Lord did nothing apart from the Father—being united with him—neither on his own nor through the apostles, so too you should do nothing apart from the bishop and the presbyters. Do not try to maintain that it is reasonable for you to

> do something among yourselves in private; instead, for the common purpose, let there be one prayer, one petition, one mind, one hope in love and in blameless joy, which is Jesus Christ. Nothing is superior to him. (*Ad Magnes.* VII 1)

Monoëpiscopacy, on the one hand, helped the church to tackle multiple problems, both doctrinal and disciplinary. It proved to be effective in safeguarding the church's unity. At the same time, monoëpiscopacy led to stratification within the church, that is, to creating internal divisions between sacred orders and laity. The idea of laity emerged because of the growth of monoëpiscopacy. Ministry turned from a serving facility to the served end of the church.

These changes were immediately reflected in the language that described ministry. The lexemes denoting ministry, such as *episkopos*, *presbyteros*, and *diakonos*, had been initially used as adjectives. These offices were regarded as literally adjective to the church, that is, having to do with the church's accidents. With the growth of hierarchical stratification, adjectives turned to nouns: a bishop and a priest. This meant that these offices started to be perceived as pertinent to the church's nature. Only deacons remained servicing adjectives, both morphologically and ecclesiologically. However, deacons, from the servicemen of communities, turned to servicemen of bishops. Other clerical ranks became self-sufficient.

A sacramental and social chasm emerged between them and the rest of community. Stratification within the ecclesial body began developing as early as in the third century. Some testimonies from that period present the episcopal office as superior to the rest of the community. *Didascalia apostolorum*, a text composed in the third century, rendered this office in the pagan terms of high priests and kings:

> The bishops are your high priests. <. . .> He is minister of the word and mediator, but to you a teacher, and your father after God; he begot you through the water. He is your chief and your leader, your powerful king. He rules in the place of the Almighty. (*Didascalia apostolorum* IX 3-4; Johnson 2009: 229)

The episcopal office, thus, was remodeled according to the political and religious patterns of the Greco-Roman world. These patterns were polytheistic. Ps.-Dionysius the Areopagite should be credited for synthesizing pagan hierarchism with Christian monotheism. In contrast to pagan neo-Platonists, who considered gods as sorted out in a hierarchical order and who became an inspiration for Ps.-Dionysius, he applied this order to angels:

> These latter beings are nearer to God, since their participation in him takes so many forms. Compared with the things which merely are, with irrational forms of life and indeed with our own rational natures, the holy ranks of heavenly beings are obviously superior in what they have received of God's largess. Their thinking processes imitate the divine. They look on the divine likeness with a transcendent eye. They model their

> intellects on him. Hence it is natural for them to enter into a more generous communion with the Deity, because they are forever marching towards the heights, because, as permitted, they are drawn to a concentration of an unfailing love for God, because they immaterially receive undiluted the original enlightenment, and because, ordered by such enlightenment, theirs is a life of total intelligence. They have the first and the most diverse participation in the divine and they, in turn, provide the first and the most diverse revelations of the divine hiddenness. That is why they have a preeminent right to the title of angel or messenger, since it is they who first are granted the divine enlightenment and it is they who pass on to us these revelations which are so far beyond us. (*De caelesti hierarchia* IV 1-2; Luibheid 1987: 155–6)

The divine enlightenment flows through a cascade of angelic ranks. They pass what they receive from their superiors to those below them. Ps.-Dionysius applied the same idea to the ecclesial structures. What for the angels is divine enlightenment, for the "ecclesial hierarchs" are sacraments. Church members do not have direct access to this resource, but only through the chain of clergy. Within this chain, clerical orders have access to the sacraments through their superiors:

> The order of hierarchs <. . .> is that which fully possesses the power of consecration. In particular, it completes every hierarchic rite of consecration. It revealingly teaches others to understand, explaining their sacred things, proportionate characteristics, and their holy powers. The light-bearing order of priests guides the initiates to the divine visions of the sacraments. It does so by the authority of the inspired hierarchs in fellowship with whom it exercises the functions of its own ministry. It makes known the works of God by way of the sacred symbols and it prepares the postulants to

**Figure 6.2** A fresco from the Gelati monastery in Georgia, where the Ps.-Dionysian ideas about angelic and ecclesial hierarchies were meticulously studied during the Middle Ages.

Source: Photo by the author.

> contemplate and participate in the holy sacraments. But it sends on to the hierarch those longing for a full understanding of the divine rites which are being contemplated. The order of deacons purifies and discerns those who do not carry God's likeness within themselves and it does so before they come to the sacred rites performed by the priests. It purifies all who approach by drawing them away from all dalliance with what is evil. It makes them receptive to the ritual vision and communion. (*De ecclesiastica hierarchia* V 6; Luibheid 1987: 236)

Half a millennium after Ps.-Dionysius, the medieval Byzantine monk Nicetas Stethatos (*c.* 1005–90) from the Studite monastery adjusted the original Areopagitic hierarchy to the pentarchic system of his time. In his interpretation, the angelic "thrones," "cherubim," and "seraphim" correspond to the offices of patriarchs, metropolitans, and archbishops; the "lordships," "powers," and "authorities" are related to bishops, priests, and deacons; sub-deacons, readers, and monks stood for the ranks of "principalities," "archangels," and "angels" (see Louth 2007: 333–4). The church's structures evolved—so did the idea of hierarchy. This evolution confirms that hierarchy is an accident, not the essence of the church.

Ps.-Dionysius refrained from extrapolating the principle of divine hierarchy to political structures. Later political theologians, however, would gladly make such an extrapolation. The Ps.-Dionysian insight that everyone has access to divine resources not directly, but through mediators—when applied to political systems, meant that a monarch was the only source of political and social resources. People could have access to them through the hierarchy of nobility. Following this train of thought, both the church and society reached the peak of hierarchization during the Middle Ages.

Despite such hierarchization, the early egalitarian idea of the general priesthood of all survived in the church and resurfaced at the dawn of Modernity. For example, the metropolitan of Kyiv Petro Mohyla in the early seventeenth century regarded ministry as

> Twofold—the one *spiritual*, the other *sacramental*. Of the former, namely the *spiritual Priesthood*, all Christians in general are equally endowed, and do exercise it in common, according to that saying of St. Peter the Apostle (1 Pet. 2:9), *But ye are a chosen Generation, a royal Priesthoods, an holy Nation, a peculiar People.* <. . .> The *Priesthood*, which is a *Mystery*, is that which Christ committed to his Apostles; which is continued down unto this Day, by their laying on of hands, and by the laying on of Hands of the Bishops, who are the Successors of the Apostles, to dispense with divine Mysteries and to perform the Ministry for the Salvation of Mankind. (In Bolshakoff 1946: 162–3)

The idea that laity constitutes the ultimate magisterium, that is, the teaching authority of the church, also remained echeloned deeply in the ecclesial subconsciousness. It resurfaced from time to time, like in the case of the *Encyclical of the Eastern*

*Patriarchs* promulgated in 1848. This was a response to the letter that Pope Pius IX (in office 1846–78) had addressed "to the Easterners." Four Eastern patriarchs (of Constantinople, Alexandria, Antioch, and Jerusalem), together with the members of their synods, stated in their letter that "the protector of religion is the very body of the Church, even the people themselves."[2] In line with this letter, Aleksey Khomyakov, who praised it, highlighted the nonhierarchical character of the Orthodox magisterium:

> The unvarying constancy and the unerring truth of Christian dogma does not depend upon any Hierarchical Order: it is guarded by the totality, by the whole people of the Church, which is the Body of Christ. <. . .>
>
> No Hierarchical Order nor Supremacy is to be considered as a guarantee of truth. The knowledge of truth is given to mutual love. (In Bolshakoff 1946: 117–18)

Modern Orthodox theologians piecemeal returned to the idea of the general priesthood of all. This idea became central in the ecclesiology promulgated by Nikolai Afanasiev:

> Upon entering the Church, each member of the Church is ordained as a priest, in order to serve in the Church "to God and Father." This priestly ministry of all members of the Church was the basis of all the variety of ministries that we find in the original Church. (In Wooden 2019: 381)

> Two degrees of priestly ministry, extant in the church from apostolic times—where the first degree is the ministry of Christ as the high priest, and the second is the priestly ministry of all people—transformed into the two degrees of ecclesiastical hierarchy, where the first degree was assigned to the bishop, as the image (typos) of Christ at the Eucharistic assembly, and the second to all the people. (Afanasiev 2012: 233)

> We are not aware of how extraordinary and audacious the idea of the priestly ministry of all members of the Church is. This idea could not just have arisen in the human mind. Here we are on the lofty summits of the Spirit that feeble human thought cannot attain. For this reason both those who accept this teaching and those who would gladly reject it if it were not contained in the Scriptures, do not realize that it is only in and through this idea that the "fullness of grace" (*omnis gratia*) received by the Church can be expressed. The very life of primitive Christianity was based upon the ministry of all the members of the Church. The entire ecclesial organization grew out of this concept of ministry just as the ensuing fate of this organization has been bound up with the fate of this teaching. (Afanasiev 2012: 4)

[2]§17; Fordham Modern History Sourcebook: https://tinyurl.com/b24xk3zb [accessed on March 19, 2021]

# VI.5
# Great Schisms

## The Imperative of Unity

Oneness of the church is its birthmark and a part of its nature. It belongs to the ecclesial nature as its actuality. Church's unity is more like potentiality—it means that all those who believe in Jesus Christ will eventually belong to the same church. Oneness and unity of the church, therefore, are not the same. The church's unity as potentiality is implied in Jesus' prayer to the Father: "My prayer is not for them alone. I pray also for those who will believe in me through their message, that all of them may be one, Father, just as you are in me and I am in you. May they also be in us so that the world may believe that you have sent me" (Jn 17:21). Jesus did not *postulate* that his disciples are one, but *wished* them to be one. The difference between the church's oneness and unity is similar to the difference between oneness and unity in the Trinity and Jesus Christ: unity is supposed to equalize plurality with oneness. In the equations mentioned earlier, oneness stays for their right side, while unity—for the left:

1+1+1=1 (in the Trinity)
1+1=1 (in Jesus Christ)
1+1+1+1. . . +1=1 (in the church)

Cyril of Alexandria, while commenting on John, connected the unity of the Trinity and of Jesus with the unity of the church:

> Christ is taking the substantial unity which He has with the Father and the Father with Him as an image or model of that indestructible love, harmony and unity which obtains where there is real and deep concord. He thus indicates His wish that in the strength of the holy and substantial Trinity, we too should be commingled with one another, so that the whole body of the Church may be perceived as one, as moving in Christ, through the union of two peoples, towards the constitution of a perfect, single whole. (*Commentarii in Joannem* 11; Halton 1985: 40–1)

The Holy Spirit, for Cyril, also plays an important role in sustaining the church's unity. Being undivided, the Spirit keeps all the church members together and safeguards the global Christian community from divisions:

> With regard to union in the Spirit <. . .> we shall say again that we have all received one and the same spirit, namely the Holy Spirit, and are, so to speak, mingled with one another and with God. For though Christ makes the Spirit of the Father who is also his own Spirit to dwell in each of us individually, many as we are, yet the Spirit is one and undivided; and in that individuality which is his by nature he holds together in unity those spirits which are separated from unity one with another, showing them all to be as one in himself. For as the power of the holy flesh makes those in whom it may come to dwell to be of one body, in the same way, I hold, the one indivisible Spirit dwells in them all and binds them all into spiritual unity. (*Commentarii in Joannem* 11; Jay 1980: 79)

In the same vein, Aleksey Khomyakov derived the unity of the church from the unity of God:

> The Unity of the Church follows necessarily from the Unity of God, for the Church is not a multitude of persons as separate individuals, but an unity of Divine grace dwelling in a multitude of rational creatures, who submit themselves to grace. Grace is given also to them that are disobedient and that make no use of it, "who bury their talent in the earth"; but these are not in the Church. The unity of the Church is not an imaginary, nor allegorical, but a real and substantial unity, like that of many members in a living body. The Church is one, notwithstanding what to the apprehension of men still living upon earth seems like division. It is only in relation to man, from a human point of view, that the division of the Church into visible and invisible can be recognized; but her unity is real and absolute. (In Bolshakoff 1946: 142)

Modern Greek theologian Nikos Nissiotis described the church's unity as an imperative, which rests on all theological axioms: Trinity, creation of the world, incarnation, and universal redemption:

> Unity is not an attribute of the Church, but it is its very life. It is the divine-human inter-penetration realized once and for all in the Communion between Word and Flesh in Christ. It includes the act of Creation of man by the Logos; the reality of the Incarnation of this same Logos in man; man's redemption and regeneration through him, and the participation and consummation of all history in the event of Pentecost—when the Holy Spirit accomplished the communion of mankind in Christ.
>
> Therefore, the Church does not move towards unity through the comparison of conceptions of unity, but lives out of the union between God and man realized in the communion of the Church as union of men in the Son of Man. We are not here to

> create Unity, but to recapture it in its vast universal dimensions. Unity as union is the source of our life. It is the origin and the final goal of the whole Creation in Christ represented in his Church. We are not only moving towards unity, but our very existence derives from the inseparable union between the three persons of the Holy Trinity given to us as a historical event on the day of Pentecost. Therefore, unity, which is the essence of God's act in Creation, Incarnation and Redemption, and which is reflected in the historical life of the Church, constitutes the first chapter of an authentic ecclesiology. (Address to the III General Assembly of the WCC in New Delhi (1961); Patelos 1978: 11)

# The Tragedy of Schisms

The Christian church was always one, but Christians were never completely united. Since the apostolic era, there have been divisions in the global Christian community, which are called "schisms"—from the Greek word *schisma* (σχίσμα). From the Eastern Christian perspective, it is not correct to speak about divisions *of the church*, because the church is always one and cannot be divided. It is theologically more correct to speak about divisions *among Christians*. Such divisions have existed since the apostolic era.

Eastern attitudes to Christian divisions were not always the same. During the first millennium, Eastern churches cared about the preservation of the global Christian unity more than they cared about it in the second millennium, including modern times. Nevertheless, they still perceive the Christian divisions as a tragedy, even though, under the influence of confessionalism, they do not often render them in tragic terms. This feeling of tragedy was poetically expressed by the great Syrian theologian Ephrem in one of his songs:

> And for me in my misery
> intercede, O Church;
> I have grieved for thy divisions,
> may I rejoice in thy reunion!
> And with thee and under thy protection
> may I enter the Kingdom! (*Carmina Nisibena* 26; Murray 2004: 91)

It is easy, for Ephrem, to provoke a division, but very difficult to heal one. Nevertheless, God has power to bring the church back to unity:

> Lord, for a surgeon it is simple
> to cut off a limb,
> but it is not easy for him
> to fasten it back in its place;
> but for thee, Lord, both are easy,
> for thou art God. (*Carmina Nisibena* 27; Murray 2004: 91)

# Great Schism I

Ephrem was right: it may take months to provoke a schism and requires centuries to heal one. The longest schism in the Christian history happened in the East in the fifth century. This schism, which we may call great schism I, at that time had the largest scale that the Christian world had ever known. As a result of this schism, three Eastern commonwealths emerged: the Byzantine, the Oriental, and the Church of the East. We have explored these commonwealths in the first chapter, and their theological underpinnings—in the chapter on the incarnation.

# Great Schism II

This schism triggered a series of events, which eventually led to the second great schism—the division between the Eastern and Western churches. It is commonly believed that this schism happened in 1054. However, the processes of division had begun much earlier, several centuries prior to that date, and were not completed in the eleventh century. Some scholars believe that only the trauma of the fourth crusade and the sack of Constantinople by the Latins in 1204 made the Easterners mentally break up with the West (see Demacopoulos 2019: 129). One can even suggest that this schism reached its completion as late as in the eighteenth century.

**Figure 6.3** Palace of the Propagation of the Faith in Rome. It currently hosts the Congregation for the Evangelization of Peoples.

Source: Photo by the author.

In 1729, the congregation *Propaganda fide* formally prohibited participation in sacraments over confessional borders. In 1755, the Ecumenical Patriarchate issued a similar prohibition (see Hovorun 2019).

# Acacian Schism

The earliest cessation of communion between Rome and Constantinople that lasted several years, happened in the fifth century and has been called "Acacian schism." It lasted from 484 to 519 and was caused by the policies of Emperor Zeno to undermine the council of Chalcedon. The emperor was supported by the patriarch of Constantinople Acacius (in office 472–89). However, Pope Felix III (in office 483–92) considered this move a betrayal of orthodoxy and excommunicated the patriarch of Constantinople. The cessation of communion between the churches of Rome and Constantinople that followed can be formally defined as a "schism." It became an aftershock of the great schism I between the Byzantine and Oriental churches. It also created a dangerous precedent for the events that would happen a few centuries later.

# Eastern Illyria

Fortunately, the Acacian schism did not mutate into a larger division. It was eventually settled through the intervention of the imperial authority. The same authority, however, created political preconditions for a further alienation between the Eastern and Western churches. An apple of discord for the two parts of Christendom became the region sandwiched between Asia Minor and Italy—Eastern Illyria. As mentioned earlier, after Theodosius divided the Roman Empire into Eastern and Western parts, Eastern Illyria became administratively subordinated to Rome. Ecclesially, however, the church of Constantinople continued claiming its rights over it. These claims were contested by the church of Rome. Both political and ecclesial statuses of this territory were rearranged by later imperial decrees, so that the church of Rome was right to accuse Constantinople of political interventions. When Christianity was adopted by the Bulgars, who had settled in Illyria in the sixth–seventh centuries, the churches of Rome and Constantinople contested control over the Bulgarian church.

# Filioque

All Christian divisions were caused by the combination of theological, social, and political factors, in different proportions. It is difficult to say in what proportions did politics and theology contribute to the great schism II. The issue of Eastern Illyria was one of the political factors, while the controversy about *Filioque* was one of the theological factors of the schism (see Bucossi & Calia 2020; Coetzee 2014; Siecienski 2010; Oberdorfer 2001). *Filioque* is a Latin word, which means "and from the Son." This word was added in the West to the Nicaean creed: "We believe in the Holy Spirit, the Lord, the giver of life, who proceeds from the Father *and the Son*" (see *Catechism of the Catholic Church*, https://tinyurl.com/nhnxkzds [accessed on March 19, 2021]). One of the original purposes of this addition was to fight what at that time was perceived as Arianism and adoptionism. Both teachings were popular among the Goths, especially in Gaul, Spain, and Northern Africa. The anti-Arian polemics there continued even after Constantinople I (381). The rationale of this polemic can be summarized as following: if the Son is the source of the Holy Spirit—in a similar way as the Father is the cause of the Spirit—then the Son is equal to the Father.

The third council of Toledo (589) followed this rationale and anathematized everyone who "denies that he (the Spirit) is coeternal and coequal with the Father and the Son" and who "does not believe that he (the Spirit) proceeds from the Father and the Son (*a Patre et Filio procedere*)" (in Siecienski 2010: 69). Nine other councils of Toledo confirmed *Filioque* during the seventh century, together with some other Spanish councils, such as in Merida (666) and in Braga (675). The council of the English church in Hatfield (680) followed the cause. A milestone in the series of the synodal confirmations of the *Filioque* became the council in Gentilly in 767. At this point, Frankish kings picked up the issue of *Filioque* and soon turned it to a powerful political instrument. This instrument was forged through the synergy of the Frankish court and some Western theologians. One of them, Alcuin of York (*c.* 732–804), introduced the *Filioque* to the court liturgy at Aachen.

**Figure 6.4** Cityscape of Toledo in Spain.
Source: Photo by the author.

Frankish theologians relied on the tradition of the Filioque, which had existed since at least the third century. Augustine became the main authority in this tradition, even though he never used the word "Filioque" or similar. He interpreted the Spirit as the bond of love between the Father and the Son. His famous Trinitarian formula expresses the Trinity as "the lover" (*amans*)—"the beloved" (*amatus*)—"the love" (*amor*).[1] Among other theological authorities in the West who thought along this line, were Hilary of Poitiers, Ambrose of Milan, Leo of Rome, Fulgentius of Ruspe, Isidore of Seville, and others.

This Western line of thinking about the Spirit slightly diverged from the Eastern one, but this did not seem to bother the Easterners. Partially, because most of the Easterners were unaware about what the Westerners were writing. There was a lack of full theological exchange between the two parts of the Christian world. When the Easterners learned what the Westerners were thinking, they still preferred to tolerate the diversity of opinion and expressions.

At the same time, the Easterners kept insisting on their opinions and expressions. They framed the issue of the Holy Spirit through the differentiation between *theologia* and *oeconomia*. In the uncreated sphere of the divine existence, the Spirit proceeded from the Father only, while the Son contributes to the Spirit's procession to the created sphere. The Latins, in the Eastern opinion, were blurring the demarcation line between *theologia* and *oeconomia*. The Easterners preferred to describe the Father's hypostasis as the only cause of other hypostases in the Trinity, including the Holy Spirit. Gregory of Nyssa pointed this out:

> And saying "cause" and "from the cause" (αἴτιον καὶ ἐξ αἰτίου), we do not designate with these names a nature—in fact, one could not adopt the same explanation for a cause and for a nature—but we explain the difference according to the mode of being (κατὰ τὸ πῶς εἶναι). For, saying that the one is in a caused mode (αἰτιατῶς), while the other is without cause, we do not divide the nature according to the understanding of the cause, but we only demonstrate that neither is the Son without generation nor is the Father by generation. <. . .> Therefore, affirming in the Holy Trinity such a distinction, so as to believe that one thing is that which is cause and another that which is from the cause, we will not any longer be able to be accused of confusing in the communion of nature the relationship of the hypostases. (*Ad Ablabium* 56.11–57.7; Maspero 2007: 156)

The Latins tended to derive the existence of the Spirit from the divine essence (οὐσία). This tendency followed the original Nicaean creed, which had stated that

[1]In his *De Trinitate*, Augustine utilized other formulas as well, such as *mens—notitia—amor* (9.3.3); *res—visio—intentio* (10.2.2); *memoria—visio—volitio* (11.3.6-9); *memoria—scientia—voluntas* (12.15.25); *scientia—cogitatio—amor* (13.20.26); *memoria Dei—intelligentia Dei—amor Dei* (14.12.15). See Siecienski 2010: note 55, p. 237.

the Son comes "from the essence" (ἐκ τῆς οὐσίας) of the Father. The Easterners, in contrast, relied on the updated neo-Nicaean interpretation of the creed. According to this interpretation, the Son and the Spirit come from the Father's hypostasis, and not essence. Difference between the initial Nicaean and later neo-Nicaean terminology became one of the factors that contributed to the divergent Western and Eastern takes on the Filioque.

Although Eastern theologians preferred to derive the hypostases of the Son and the Holy Spirit from the hypostasis of the Father, they sometimes acknowledged a causal connection between the hypostases of the Son and the Spirit. This was not a mainstream Eastern line, but it was regarded as fitting the Eastern orthodoxy. Gregory of Nyssa made a relevant statement:

> If then one will falsely accuse the reasoning to present a certain mixture (μίξις) of the hypostases and a twisting by the fact of not accepting the difference according to nature, we will respond to this accusation that, affirming the absence of the diversity of nature, we do not negate the difference according to that which causes and that which is caused. And we can conceive that the one is distinguished from the other uniquely since we believe that the one is that which causes and the other that which is derived from the cause. And in that which is originated from a cause we conceive yet another difference: one thing it is, in fact, to be immediately from the first (ἐκ τοῦ πρώτου), another to be through (διά) that which is immediately (προσεχῶς) from the first. In this way the being Only Begotten remains incontestably in the Son and there is no doubt that the Spirit is from the Father, since the mediation of the Son (τῆς τοῦ Υἱοῦ μεσιτείας) maintains in Him the being of Only Begotten and does not exclude the Spirit from the natural relation with the Father. (*Ad Ablabium* 55.21–56.10; Maspero 2007: 153)

Maximus the Confessor continued this line. He was an Easterner who spent a lot of time in the Latin-speaking West. In his letter to Marinus, which was composed around 645, Maximus addressed the issue of the procession of the Holy Spirit. He, on the one hand, followed the mainstream Eastern train of thought and stressed that the Father is the only cause (μία αἰτία) of both the Son and the Holy Spirit:

> There is one God, because the Father is the begetter of the unique Son and the fount of the Holy Spirit: one without confusion and three without division. The Father is the unoriginate intellect, the unique essential Begetter of the unique Logos, also unoriginate, and the fount of the unique everlasting life, the Holy Spirit. (*Capita theologica et oeconomica* 4; Palmer et al. 1990, vol. 2: 165)

On the other hand, the Son, for Maximus, also contributes to the progress of the Spirit. The Son's causality vis-à-vis the Spirit, however, is different from the causality of the Father. Maximus differentiated between two causalities by applying to them two different verbs: *ekporeuesthai* (ἐκπορεύεσθαι) and *proienai* (προϊέναι) (see

Larchet 1998: 53). The former is in the passive voice (because of the suffix -σθαι) and presupposes a cause prior to it (because of the prefix ἐκ-), while the latter is in the active voice and presupposes an object ahead of it (because of the prefix προ-). The Holy Spirit proceeds (ἐκπορεύεσθαι) from the Father, who is the only cause of the Spirit and the active subject of the Spirit's procession. Spirit in this procession is a passive subject (hence is the passive voice of the verb ἐκπορεύεσθαι).

At the same time, the same Spirit progresses from the Father *through* (διά) the Son. In this process, the role of the Spirit is less passive: he is an active subject of the process (hence is the active voice of the verb προϊέναι). This process goes forward. The only possible direction for it is toward the created word. Maximus, thus, by reserving the verb with the prefix *ek-* to the Father exclusively, implies *theologia*. In the other verb, which also involves the Son, its prefix *pro-* implies God's stepping out to the created world—*oikonomia*. The very root of *-ienai* (-ιέναι—from *eimi* (εἰμι)), "to be," implies a field of activities for God, that is, the world. It is different from another word for being—*hyparhein* (ὑπάρχειν)—which would apply to God's own existence and which Maximus did not use. To summarize, by applying two verbs, Maximus differentiated between the two modalities of the origination of the Holy Spirit. One is intra-divine and caused by the Father only. The other one is forwarded extra-wise and presupposes the involvement of the Son.

Maximus designed this sophisticated hermeneutics with the purpose to reconcile the Eastern and Western approaches to the procession of the Holy Spirit. When he started commuting between East and West in seeking support for his dyothelite cause, he realized that these two approaches had diverged. He believed that the two approaches are bridgeable, and his intentions were "genuinely ecumenical" (Siecienski 2010: 11). Some other minds on both sides of the divide followed Maximus' line and were motivated by ecumenical intentions. In the East, there were moderate theologians like the archbishop of Nicomedia Nicetas (*c.* 1118–35) or Nicephorus Blemmydes (1197–1269). Nicetas, for instance, acknowledged that speaking about the procession of the Spirit also from or through the Son had been a line in the Eastern thinking, even though not a mainstream one:

> The wisest of the Greeks ascribe the first cause of procession properly to the Father, from whom the Son is properly by generation, and from whom the Holy Spirit is by procession. They moreover ascribe the procession of the same Holy Spirit to the Son, but not properly, because the Son is neither from his own self, nor is he the cause of his own self <. . .> nor is he the primary cause of the Holy Spirit <. . .> and therefore I concede that the Holy Spirit proceeds properly from the Father, who is from no one; from the Son, however, because the Son is also from the Father, he does not proceed properly. (See Anselm of Havelburg, *Dialogi* II 24; Siecienski 2010: 122)

In the West, Anastasius Bibliothecarius (*c.* 800/17–79) and John Scotus Erigena (*c.* 800–77) demonstrated similar open-mindedness to the Eastern standpoint.

Anastasius' case is interesting and, in some respects, mirroring the case of Maximus. Being born in the West, he learned Greek and became a connoisseur of Greek theology. He felt at home in both worlds. Although he became an opponent of Photius and many Byzantine traditions in his time, he appreciated the ecumenical intentions of Maximus. He also acknowledged that misunderstandings between the East and the West can be explained by different languages they use:

> We have translated also a passage from the letter of St. Maximus to the priest Marinus concerning the procession of the Holy Spirit. In it he said that the Greeks have in this matter become needlessly opposed to us since we do not at all say, as they pretend we do, that the Son is the cause and the principle of the Holy Spirit. On the contrary, in our preoccupation to assert the unity of substance of the Father and the Son, we say that the Holy Spirit, while he proceeds from the Father, also proceeds from the Son, understanding this procession as a mission. Maximus pleads with those who know the two languages to maintain peace. He says that both we and the Greeks understand that the Holy Spirit proceeds, in one sense from the Son, but that in another sense he does not proceed from the Son. He draws attention to the fact that it is very difficult to express this precise distinction in both Latin and in Greek. (In Dvornik 1979: 12–13)

Anastasius' opponent in the East, Photius, complained about the Latin language as incapable to capture some Greek concepts. He was particularly upset about how the Latins rendered the Greek ideas about the procession of the Holy Spirit from the Father:

> The Latin [language when it was used to] expressing the holy teaching of our Fathers did not furnish a pure and exact vocabulary precisely befitting the [Greek] concept, both on account of the deficiency of the language and because of its inability to cover the wide range of Greek; and for many it was causing the suspicion that false religion was incorporated in the faith, as the limitations of the [Latin] words do not suffice to interpret the [Greek] sense precisely. (*Mystagogia* 87; Kinzig 2017, vol. 4: 326)

Photius was not disposed toward the West ecumenically. Instead of finding points of reconciliation with it, he looked for excuses to disagree. In his time, the issue of Filioque grew political and, consequently, hardly bridgeable. The East was increasingly unprepared to tolerate Filioque, while the West made it from optional mandatory. Pope Leo III, for example, initially resisted the pressure of the Frankish court to introduce the Filioque to the Roman creed. He even ordered silver tablets with the creed without Filioque.[2] However, in his correspondence with the East, he

---

[2] *Liber pontificalis* describes this as follows: "Here (in St. Peter's cathedral), out of love and in defence of the orthodox faith, he (Leo) made two silver shields, on each of which the creed was inscribed, one in Greek letters and the other in Latin; they stand over the entrance to the tomb, on the right and on the left. They weigh 94

wrote, "We believe the Holy Spirit proceeds equally from the Father and the Son," and then added: "All must hold the correct and inviolate faith according to the Holy Roman Catholic and Apostolic Church" (*ep.* 35; Haugh 1975: 68).

The court theologians, in the meantime, employed the pretext of Filioque to accuse the Easterners of apostasy. The council convened in the Frankish capital Aachen in 809, proclaimed the Filioque "a central teaching of the Catholic faith," which "must be firmly believed and professed without doubt with a pure and sincere heart <. . .> by all the orthodox and faithful" (in Willjung 1998: 237). Ratramnus of Corbie (d. *c.* 868) brought the accusations for not upholding Filioque *ad personam*. In his *Contra Graecorum opposita Romanam Ecclesiam Infamantium*, he accused the contemporary Byzantine emperors Michael III (r. 842–67) and Basil I (r. 867–86) of heresy, blasphemy, and stupidity, because they did not comply with Rome's teachings.

Mirroring the Westerners, the Easterners also ceased to regard the Filioque as an acceptable theological option and began treating it as an unacceptable novelty. The *Vita* of Michael the Synkellos illustrates this shift in attitudes. Michael was a monk who lived in Palestine from around 809 to 846. He served as a secretary to the patriarch of Jerusalem Thomas. The *Vita* mentions some contemporary Eastern reactions to the "Frankish" ways of handling the Filioque issue:

**Figure 6.5** The Frankish cathedral in Aachen.
Source: Photo by the author.

pounds and 6 ounces" (98.84; Kinzig 2017, vol. 4: 324). Some scholars believe that Leo resisted the court, because he wanted to protect his political autonomy (see Siecienski 2010: 100).

> But in those days some priests and hermits of the nation of the Franks arose, speaking that which was set out in the divine creed by the 150 holy fathers who assembled together in Constantinople for the second council during the reign of Theodosius the Great against the most-ungodly Macedonius (who dared to blaspheme against the Holy Spirit): "And in the Holy Spirit, the Lord and life-giver, who proceeds from the Father and the Son." Thus they created no small confusion in the metropolis of Rome, since the pope of the Roman metropolis who was at that time in office took a stand and refused to add anything that had not been jointly expressed by the divine fathers in the divine creed.
>
> This pope sent letters to the great Patriarch Thomas in the holy city of Christ our God such that the latter might help [the pope's] endangered church by dispatching to him from his apostolic and priestly throne some men well endowed in speech and wisdom in order to resist those who stubbornly insisted on the addition made to the divine creed by the Franks. <. . .>
>
> Therefore, the aforementioned most-holy Patriarch Thomas took counsel with his orthodox and holy synod and with a meeting of the divine fathers who live in the desert of the holy city of Christ our God, and all made a unanimous decision such that they sent the great and holy Michael [the Synkellos] to the aforementioned pope in the greatest of all cities, Rome, that he might bring help to the Church of God, to shut up the gaping mouths of the godless Franks, to teach them to keep to the truth and not to speculate beyond what was permitted, and to follow the precise doctrine of the holy fathers which had been inspired by the Holy Spirit, [that is:] "Who proceeds from the Father" and, "Who is jointly worshipped and glorified with the Father and the Son." (Kinzig 2017, vol. 4: 313–14)

The reason why the Franks became so sensitive to the issue of Filioque was political. It had to do with the imperial ideology of that time. As was mentioned earlier, Romans believed that there can be only one empire, and that empire is Roman. The Byzantines believed that their emperor is the true and only Roman emperor, the ruler of the world. The Franks—a new power consolidating Western Europe—initially accepted this role of the Byzantine basileuses. However, at some moment they demonstrated an ambition to appropriate the imperial status for themselves. Charlemagne made a decisive step in this direction, when he was crowned by Pope Leo III on Christmas 800, as *Imperator Romanorum*.

Coronation by the pope, however, was only a part of the legitimization of the Frankish ruler as "emperor." According to the aforementioned political philosophy of that time, there could be only one Roman emperor in the world. Therefore, to complete his own legitimization as an emperor, Charlemagne had to delegitimize the Byzantine emperors. In other words, to become a legit emperor, Charlemagne had to prove that the emperors in Constantinople have lost their legitimacy.

His court ideologists and theologians (who usually were the same people, with Alcuin of York having a lead among them) elaborated arguments to prove

**Figure 6.6** The imperial crown of Charlemagne (replica) in Aachen.
Source: Photo by the author.

Charlemagne's claim. First, they used the fact that the Byzantine throne at that time was held by a woman, Empress Irene. They argued that only a man could be a proper emperor. In addition to this sexist argument, second, they utilized Filioque. Their train of thought was the following. Since at least Theodosius I, orthodoxy of faith had been one of the main factors of legitimacy for an emperor that distinguished him from usurpers. If the Frankish theologians could prove that Filioque was the only orthodox interpretation of the Trinity, they would claim that the Easterners, who did not hold it, were apostates and usurpers. Only the Frankish kings, who upheld the orthodox doctrine of Filioque, could claim to be true Roman emperors.

Under the pressure of this political ideology, Filioque from an optional *theologoumenon*, to use the phrase of the Russian scholar Vasily Bolotov (Болотов 1914: 31), turned to a mandatory doctrine with far-reaching political ramifications.[3]

[3]The collection of theopolitical treatises known as *Libri Carolini* or *Opus Caroli Regis* became a "Declaration of Independence" of Franks from the Byzantines (see Siecienski 2010: 92). The book in particular repudiated the confession of the Patriarch Tarasius of Constantinople (in office 784–806) that "the Holy Spirit is not from the

In the words of another scholar, Edward Siecienski, from "the obscure theological backwaters" that bothered only scholars, the issue of Filioque "quickly catapulted <. . .> to become a casus belli" (Siecienski 2010: 87). The trophy in this quasi-theological *bellum* that the Frankish kings had waged was the crown of the Roman Empire.

## "Photian Schism"

Easterners picked up the fight. They utilized the issue of Filioque for their own political purposes. Just as Charlemagne tried, through Filioque, to undermine the imperial legitimacy of the Byzantines, the latter did the same in the opposite direction. By insisting that Filioque is a heretical doctrine, the Byzantines presented Charlemagne as a typical usurper of the imperial status. These ideological underpinnings propelled an optional and neglected doctrine that had helped fighting pockets of Arians in some remote and obscure lands, to a prime theological issue that occupied the best Greco-Roman minds. Eventually, Filioque became perceived as a symbol of differences, either imagined or real, between the East and the West.

A protagonist of the Byzantine deconstruction of the Frankish theopolitical constructions, based on Filioque, was the patriarch of Constantinople Photius. He was both a statesman and a churchman. He clearly saw how politics and theology had been mixed in the Frankish take on Filioque. He also knew how to deconstruct the Franks and how to turn against them their own arguments. Although Photius, as we have mentioned earlier, defended some autonomy of the church from the state, when it came to the external threats, like from the Franks, he was an adamant patriot of his state.

Frankish attacks and Byzantine counterattacks led to a schism, which was called "Photian" (see Dvornik 1948). It was a cessation in communion between Rome and Constantinople, which had multiple pretexts, including disagreements on ritual practices. The Photian schism was shorter than the preceding Acacian schism: it lasted from 863 to 867. However, during the Photian schism, most arguments were elaborated upon, which later would be utilized for a much longer schism. Both Acacian and Photian schisms set unfortunate precedents for the great schism between the Eastern and Western churches that lasts until now.

Before the Photian schism, a rich diversity of beliefs and practices was tolerated in both the East and the West. The schisms reduced the space for pluralism. Each

Father and the Son according to the most true and holy rule of faith but proceeds from the Father through the Son" (Freeman & Meyvaert 2010: 345).

side now insisted that only its practices and beliefs are right, and the other side is wrong—even though earlier they did not bother themselves with differences. In this polemical spirit, Photius drafted a catalogue of the assumed Western mistakes. He disseminated it among his peers. In his encyclical letter to the Eastern patriarchs sent in 866, Photius informed them about the activities of the Western missionaries in Bulgaria. Among the unacceptable Latin practices and beliefs, Photius listed fasting on Saturdays, celibacy of priests, Chrismation by bishops, and, finally, the Filioque:

> The Bulgarians had not been baptized even two years when dishonorable men emerged out of the darkness (i.e., the West), and poured down like hail or, better, charged like wild boars upon the newly-planted vineyard of the Lord, destroying it with hoof and tusk, which is to say, by their shameful lives and corrupted dogmas. For the papal missionaries and clergy wanted these Orthodox Christians to depart from the correct and pure dogmas of our irreproachable Faith.
>
> The first error of the Westerners was to compel the faithful to fast on Saturdays. (I mention this seemingly small point because the least departure from Tradition can lead to a scorning of every dogma of our Faith.) Next, they convinced the faithful to despise the marriage of priests, thereby sowing in their souls the seeds of the Manichean heresy. Likewise, they persuaded them that all who had been chrismated by priests had to be anointed again by bishops. <. . .>
>
> They attempted by their false opinions and distorted words to ruin the holy and sacred Nicene Symbol of Faith—which by both synodal and universal decisions possesses invincible power—by adding to it that the Holy Spirit proceeds not only from the Father, as the Symbol declares, but from the Son as well. Until now, no one has ever heard even a heretic pronounce such a teaching. What Christian can accept the introduction of two sources into the Holy Trinity; that is, that the Father is one source of the Son and the Holy Spirit, and that the Son is another source of the Holy Spirit, thereby transforming the monarchy of the Holy Trinity into a dual divinity? <. . .>
>
> These so-called bishops thus introduced this foul teaching, together with other impermissible innovations, among the simple and newly-baptized Bulgarian people. This news cut us to the heart. How can we not grieve when we see before our eyes the fruit of our womb, the child to whom we gave birth through the Gospel of Christ, being rent asunder by beasts? He who by his sweat and suffering raised them and perfected them in the Faith, suffers the greatest pain and sorrow upon the destruction of his children. Therefore, we mourn for our spiritual children, and we will not cease from mourning. For we will not give sleep to our eyes until, to the extent that lies in our power, we return them to the House of the Lord.
>
> Now, concerning these forerunners of apostasy, common pests and servants of the enemy, we, by divine and synodal decree, condemn them as impostors and enemies of God. It is not as though we were just now pronouncing judgement upon them, but rather, we now declare openly the condemnation ordained by the ancient councils and

> Apostolic canons. If they stubbornly persist in their error, we will exclude them from the communion of all Christians. <. . .>
>
> But even if we did not cite all these and other innovations of the Romans, the mere citing of their addition of the *filioque* phrase to the Nicene Symbol of Faith would be sufficient to subject them to a thousand anathemas. (Photius 1983: 50–4)

## Primacy as *Jus Divinum*

Surprisingly, the list of Photius' complains misses an issue, which was really divisive and underpinning most other divisive issues between the East and West. This was the issue of primacy. As was explained earlier, the Western theologians interpreted the primacy of Roman bishops as a divine institution, established by the divine right (*jus divinum*). The East disagreed with such interpretation. It ascribed such divine right either to all patriarchates or to none of them. In the latter case, the Eastern theologians interpreted primacy as conventional—it stems not from God, but from the consent of other churches and imperial authorities.

## Universal Jurisdiction

The East also disagreed with the Western interpretation of primacy as based on the identification of the Roman see with the universal church. Such an identification was apparently facilitated by the Western discovery of Aristotle and his categories. As was said many times, the basic distinction, with which the Aristotelian logics enriched Christian theology, was the one between commonality and particularity. Medieval Western ecclesiologists effectively identified the Roman see with the common nature of the church, while they regarded other local churches as particularities of this nature. They also adopted the neo-Platonic outlook at the category of commonality, as more important than the category of particularities. Such outlook corroborated the growing Western consensus that the Roman church is more important than other local churches, including the patriarchate of Constantinople.

Such ideas can be traced in several documents and practices. One of them is *Donation of Constantine*—a forgery produced in the eighth century. It tells a legend that Pope Sylvester (in office 314–35) cured Emperor Constantine of leprosy and baptized him. In return, Constantine granted the pope primacy over the universal church (see Fried 2012).

The idea of the Roman universal jurisdiction was implemented in the Western church policies during the fourth crusade. After the Latins occupied Constantinople, the pope appointed a new patriarch for the capital city, under his jurisdiction. This move corresponded to the Western perception of the Roman church as an embodiment of the universal church. After the Byzantines restored their control over Constantinople, the Roman popes continued treating their patriarchs as their subjects. A small but telling episode during the council of Ferrara-Florence illustrates this attitude. The protocol of Pope Eugene IV (in office 1431–47) requested that the patriarch of Constantinople, while meeting the pope in person, should first kiss his shoe. This had been a requirement for all Western bishops. The patriarch understandably objected:

> Whence has the pope this right? Which synod gave it to him? Show me from what source he derives this privilege and where it is written? <. . .> This is an innovation and I will not follow it. <. . .> If the pope wants a brotherly embrace in accordance with ancient ecclesiastical custom, I will be happy to embrace him, but if he refuses, I will abandon everything and return to Constantinople. (Sylvester Syropulus, *Historiae* IV 33; Geanakoplos 1989: 235)

In the medieval Roman ecclesiology, the idea of Rome as the quintessence of the universal church became linked with the idea of particular salvation. The bull *Unam sanctam*, promulgated in 1302 by Pope Boniface VIII (in office 1294–1303) stated: "We declare, we proclaim, we define that it is absolutely necessary for salvation that every human creature be subject to the Roman Pontiff" (in Fordham Medieval Sourcebook: https://tinyurl.com/ut4fkc2k [accessed on March 19, 2021]). This bull also implied that any local church, to be the true church, has to subject itself to the see of Rome—just as every Christian, to be saved, has to recognize the pope.

Both ideas did not make sense to the Easterners. On the one hand, they also believed that the particular salvation is possible only in the universal church. On the other hand, since the church of Rome was for them a particular church, to confine salvation to only one particular church would be dangerous for salvation. Roman claims reduced the availability of salvation—just as ancient heresies did. It was if someone would say that one can be saved only in the church of Alexandria, and not in the church of Antioch. The Easterners, thus, objected the Western claims for universal jurisdiction on the soteriological grounds.

## Anathemas of 1054

At the turn of the second Christian millennium, neither the East nor the West could tolerate anymore their growing differences in interpreting primacy and jurisdictions. In 1009, the Patriarch Sergius II of Constantinople (in office 1001–19) and Pope Sergius IV (in office 1009–12) stopped commemorating each other. This was called the schism of two *Sergii*. It was a prelude to more dramatic events some fifty years later.

A chain of the events was triggered, when Pope Leo IX (in office 1049–54) sent to Constantinople Cardinal Humbert of Silva Candida (d. 1061), with a mission to secure Byzantine help against the Normans ravaging papal dominions in Italy. Although not a remarkable theologian himself, Humbert was a zealot of the new Roman ecclesiology. On the margins of political negotiations at the Byzantine court, the papal legates discussed some theological issues, including the Western practice of using unleavened bread in Eucharist. At that time, this issue seemed to be the most discussed one in the theological exchanges between the East and the West. Such exchanges were a sort of routinely performed rituals during political missions like this one.

Theological discussions did not go well. They were exacerbated by bad personal chemistry between Humbert and Patriarch Michael I Cerularius (in office 1043–59). The patriarch demonstratively mistreated the papal delegation. The unnerved cardinal did not grant it to Cerularius. On July 16, 1054, he rushed to the cathedral of St. Sophia, before the patriarchal liturgy started, and placed on the holy table the bull of excommunication of Michael and some other hierarchs close to the patriarch. After that, the Roman delegation immediately left the city.

Humbert could not anathematize a patriarch in the name of the pope, because Pope Leo IX, who had sent him, was already dead. Humbert acted in a fit of hysterics. He also wanted to demonstrate that, when he earlier in the discussions insisted on the Roman prerogatives, he meant it. Now he was applying these prerogatives in practice.

Same hysterical was the Constantinopolitan reaction. Michael immediately convened an *endemousa* synod, which condemned those who had dared to anathematize the patriarch. The emperor enhanced this decision with an edict. This document gives a sense of rage that engulfed Patriarch Michael. It also discloses both theological and political sensitivities in the relations between Rome and Constantinople at that time:

> Edict concerning the writ of excommunication placed on the altar by the Roman legates against the most holy patriarch, Lord Michael, in the month of July. <. . .>
>
> There now come some men who are wicked, abominable, and (for right believers) downright unspeakable, men who have come up out of the darkness. Having their origin in the West, they arrived in this devout and God-protected city, out of which the wellsprings of orthodoxy flow as from some deep and elevated place and the pure streams of right belief gush forth into the entire civilized world and the rivers water all the souls under the sun with correct dogmas. Bursting into it like lightning or an earthquake or a hailstorm or, to put it more appropriately, like a boar out of the forest, they tried to overthrow the orthodox message with a diversity of dogmas, so that they laid a writ on the sacramental altar of the great church of God, by which they pronounced an anathema on us, or rather on the orthodox church of God and all those orthodox who, simply because they have a desire to believe

correctly and to preserve the orthodox faith, have not been carried away by their false doctrines.

They also attack us on other grounds: that we refuse to shave our beards as they do and to alter the natural human appearance; also, that we do not decline to receive holy Communion from presbyters who are married; in addition to all this, that we are not willing to adulterate, with false reasoning and alien terminology as well as with overweening presumption, the sacred and holy creed, which has been endowed with unassailable authority by all the conciliar and ecumenical decrees; that we do not say, as they do, that the Holy Spirit proceeds from the Father and the Son (O, the machinations of the evil one!), but from the Father. <. . .>

[No one should demand] at the time of ordination that [a deacon] abstain from intercourse with his own lawful wife, lest we be compelled to insult marriage, which God has instituted and blessed with his own presence: as the voice of the Gospel cries out, "What God has joined together, let not man put asunder"; and as the apostle teaches, "Marriage is honorable in all things, and the marriage bed undefiled"; and "Are you bound to wife? Do not seek to be free." <. . .>

In addition to all of this and totally without understanding, they say that the Spirit proceeds not only from the Father but "also from the Son." For they do not get this statement from the evangelists, nor does this blasphemous dogma derive from an ecumenical council. For the Lord our God says, "the spirit of truth, who proceeds from the Father"; but the fathers of this novel piece of impiety say: "the Spirit, who proceeds from the Father and the Son." But once again they do not see that because the distinctive attribute of the Spirit is discerned in his proceeding from the Father, just as the distinctive attribute of the Spirit is discerned in his proceeding from the Father, just as the distinctive attribute of the Son is discerned in his being begotten, then if the Spirit proceeds also from the Son, as their wicked teaching maintains, the Spirit will be distinguished from the Father by more distinctive attributes than the Son is. For to come from the Father is common to the Spirit and the Son, but the procession from the Father is peculiar to the Spirit, though not also to the Son. <. . .>

In accordance with the dispensation of the orthodoxy-loving autocrat, the wicked writing itself, as well as those who perpetrated it and those who contributed to its composition and those who gave assistance to the perpetrators, were subjected to an anathema in the grand privy council and in the presence of the representatives of the emperor. The judgment took place on the fourth day, which is the first day of the present month. But on the twenty-fourth day of the present month of July <. . .> with a large crowd in attendance, an anathema was pronounced again upon the same wicked writing itself, as well as upon those who perpetrated it and wrote it and who gave any assistance or counsel to the deed. (In Pelikan & Hotchkiss 2003, vol. 1: 311–17)

Michael was as politically ambitious as his Western counterparts. He notoriously wore purple shoes—the imperial color. That is why he presented the assault against him as an attack on the imperial authority. He also identified the patriarchal office with the church itself—a common perception even in our days. In his eyes, as well as in the eyes of later generations, anathema against a patriarch meant anathema against the church. A minor episode caused by emotional incontinence of two ambitious hierarchs, thus, came down to history as a great schism. It was not so much this episode as such, as the medieval tendency to equate hierarchy with the church that made the great schism possible.

In the meantime, Michael Cerularius informed other Eastern patriarchs about what happened in the capital. Not all of them shared Michael's uncontrolled anxiety. Patriarch Peter III of Antioch, for instance, tried to calm down Michael and reminded him that the Latins are still "our brothers, even if from rusticity or ignorance they attain the same level of accuracy that we ask of our own people" (in Siecienski 2010: 116). Another prominent hierarch of that time, Archbishop Theophylact of Ohrid (*c.* 1050–1107; see Mullett 2016) also believed that the difference between the East and the West should not become a reason for break ups. He blamed the Eastern zealots who "through unmeasured zeal <. . .> and lack of humility" were quick to bring all sorts of accusations against the West, without thinking through them thoroughly (*Liber de iis in quorum Latini incusantur*; PG 126, 224).

## Lifting Anathemas in 1965

The anathemas of 1054 passed almost unnoticed by the contemporaries. However, they grew enormous in the perception of the further generations. Now we see them as a breaking point in the relations between the East and the West. Because of the tremendous symbolic significance of these anathemas in modern perception, there was an attempt to undo them. In December 1965, soon after the historic meeting of Patriarch Athenagoras of Constantinople (in office 1948–72) with Pope Paul VI (in office 1963–78) in Jerusalem (in January 1964), the two sees promulgated a joint declaration. It was read synchronically in the St. Peter's cathedral in Rome and the Patriarchal cathedral of St. George in Istanbul. The declaration stated:

1. Grateful to God, who mercifully favored them with a fraternal meeting at those holy places where the mystery of salvation was accomplished through the death and resurrection of the Lord Jesus, and where the Church was born through the outpouring of the Holy Spirit, Pope Paul VI and Patriarch Athenagoras I have not lost sight of the determination each then felt to omit nothing thereafter which charity might inspire and which could facilitate the development of the fraternal relations thus taken up between the Roman Catholic Church and the Orthodox Church of Constantinople. They are persuaded that in acting this way, they are responding to the call of that divine grace which today is leading the Roman Catholic Church and the Orthodox Church, as well as all Christians, to overcome their differences in order to be again "one" as the Lord Jesus asked of His Father for them.

2. Among the obstacles along the road of the development of these fraternal relations of confidence and esteem, there is the memory of the decisions, actions and painful incidents which in 1054 resulted in the sentence of excommunication leveled against the Patriarch Michael Cerularius and two other persons by the legate of the Roman See under the leadership of Cardinal Humbertus, legates who then became the object of a similar sentence pronounced by the patriarch and the Synod of Constantinople.
3. One cannot pretend that these events were not what they were during this very troubled period of history. Today, however, they have been judged more fairly and serenely. Thus it is important to recognize the excesses which accompanied them and later led to consequences which, insofar as we can judge, went much further than their authors had intended and foreseen. They had directed their censures against the persons concerned and not the Churches. These censures were not intended to break ecclesiastical communion between the Sees of Rome and Constantinople.
4. Since they are certain that they express the common desire for justice and the unanimous sentiment of charity which moves the faithful, and since they recall the command of the Lord: "If you are offering your gift at the altar, and there remember that your brethren has something against you, leave your gift before the altar and go first be reconciled to your brother" (Mt. 5:23-24), Pope Paul VI and Patriarch Athenagoras I with his synod, in common agreement, declare that:
   A. They regret the offensive words, the reproaches without foundation, and the reprehensible gestures which, on both sides, have marked or accompanied the sad events of this period.
   B. They likewise regret and remove both from memory and from the midst of the Church the sentences of excommunication which followed these events, the memory of which has influenced actions up to our day and has hindered closer relations in charity; and they commit these excommunications to oblivion.
   C. Finally, they deplore the preceding and later vexing events which, under the influence of various factors—among which, lack of understanding and mutual trust—eventually led to the effective rupture of ecclesiastical communion.
5. Pope Paul VI and Patriarch Athenagoras I with his synod realize that this gesture of justice and mutual pardon is not sufficient to end both old and more recent differences between the Roman Catholic Church and the Orthodox Church.[4]

---

[4]*Joint Catholic-Orthodox declaration of His Holiness Pope Paul VI and the Ecumenical Patriarch Athenagoras I, December 7, 1965*: https://tinyurl.com/w86z2d9a [accessed on March 19, 2021].

**Figure 6.7** Pope Paul VI and Patriarch Athenagoras by Angelo Biancini. Musei Vaticani.
Source: Photo by the author.

This declaration was a symbolic gesture. It did not mean, and was not intended to mean, restoration of communion between the two churches. It acknowledged that what happened in 1054 was a mutual excommunication not of the churches, but only of some individuals. The lifting of anathemas was appreciated by many in both churches, as a token of the restoration of trust between them. Some conservatives, however, perceived this event as an act of apostasy. They ascribed to it more significance than what was intended with this act.

# Filioque and the Personalist Hypothesis

In the twentieth century, more liberal Orthodox theologians came to believe that the divide between the East and the West was conditioned not by ecclesiological issues, but by different attitudes to the category of personality. They have asserted that the Eastern way of theological thinking is more personalistic, while the Western theology is more essentialist. It means that the Orthodox ostensibly value the particular dimension of beings, while the Catholics and Protestants—the dimension of commonality. This assumption is not correct.

As we have mentioned, both Eastern and Western theologians in the classical era agreed that the categories of particularities and commonalities should be equally applied to God and his incarnation. They disagreed, however, about how to interpret the procession of the Holy Spirit. The East considered the source of the Spirit to be the Father, while the West—the Father's *ousia*. This difference reflected the two versions of the Nicaean language. The Westerners relied more on its initial version, which professed the Son being begotten "from the essence" (ἐξ οὐσίας) of the Father. The Easterners, in contrast, used the updated neo-Nicaean language, which derived both the Son and the Spirit from the Father's hypostasis.

The modern personalist take on the classical theological languages, when it ignores scholastic logics, often alienates the original semantics of traditional terms. This has happened, for example, to the term "hypostasis." In classical theology, it was understood as a particular instance of a common nature. In modern personalistic theology, however, hypostasis turned to a modality of being *opposite* to nature. The modern personalistic dichotomization of hypostasis and nature is closer to the classical dichotomization between spirit and flesh.

Such substitution of semantics in the modern understanding of hypostasis has affected the modern Orthodox interpretations of the Filioque. According to such interpretations, all Western doctrines, including papal primacy, derive from the Filioque. Some Orthodox theologians go as far as to believe that the essentialist framework, amalgamated in the Filioque, has shaped the entire Western civilization, including its secular forms (see Γιανναρᾶς 2018). A Russian theologian in emigration, Vladimir Lossky (1903–58), asserted that Filioque should be considered a root of all other theological differences between the East and the West:

> Whether we like or not, the question of the procession of the Holy Spirit has been the sole dogmatic ground for the separation of East and West. All the other divergences which, historically, accompanied or followed the first dogmatic controversy about the *filioque*, in the measure in which they had too some dogmatic importance, are more or less dependent upon the original issue. (Lossky 1974: 71)

The most prominent modern Romanian theologian, Dumitru Stăniloae (1903–93), in his earlier writings followed the same personalistic hypothesis, which placed Filioque at the foundation of the East-West divide:

> In the West ecclesiology has become an impersonal, juridical system, while theology, and in the same way the whole of Western culture with it, has become strictly rational. The decline of the importance of the Spirit compared to that of the Son, a decline that can be traced back to the *filioque* and the near-reduction of the Spirit to the Son together constitute one reason why in the Roman Catholic Church there has been

> such infrequent mention of the presence and the activity of the Spirit. <. . .> The character of a juridical society has been imprinted upon the Church, a society conducted rationally and in absolutist fashion by the Pope while neglecting both the active permanent presence of the Spirit within her and within all the faithful, and also the presence of Christ bound indissolubly to the presence of the Spirit. (In Coman 2019: 49)

In the later years of his life, however, Stăniloae would doubt the personalistic hypothesis. He came to believe that, because of the ecumenical dialogue, the issue of Filioque ceased to have importance in the Orthodox-Catholic relations:

> Some advancements have been made in the dialogue between the Orthodox Church and the Roman Catholic Church. The primacy of the pope remains the major obstacle. <. . .> The Orthodox Church and the Roman Catholic Church are not divided by essential differences. In 1982, at the Munich meeting of the Orthodox and Roman Catholic delegates, which I attended together with metropolitan Antonie Plămădeală, I had the pleasure to see that everything we proposed was immediately accepted by cardinals and Catholic theologians. <. . .> They received the old formula of the Eastern Fathers, i.e., the Holy Spirit proceeds from the Father and abides in/shines forth from the Son. <. . .> I am of the opinion that in the *filioque* problem we got close to each other. <. . .> I believe that the dialogue between us on the *filioque* will continue to advance. The problem of the primacy of the pope remains though [to be solved]. The problem of the primacy is the most dangerous. (In Coman 2019: 86)

The Russian theologian Sergiy Bulgakov confessed that he also initially was under the spell of the personalistic hypothesis. However, as he studied the history behind it, he could not find historical evidence that Filioque shaped the civilizational differences between the East and the West. He eventually abandoned this hypothesis:

> It would have been natural to expect that the existence of such grave heresy, of such fundamental divergence, would permeate the entire life of the two churches and their entire doctrine. Over the course of many years, I have sought traces of this influence, and I have attempted to comprehend the *life*-significance of this divergence and to find out *where* and in *what* it is manifested *in practice*. And I must admit that I have not been able to find this practical *life*-significance and, more than that, I deny that there is any such significance. (Bulgakov 2004: 132)

Even Georges Florovsky, who liked to disagree with Bulgakov on many issues, in this point would embrace his position:

> With respect to the Western (Roman) theology, I, too, for myself, anyway, prefer cautious judgements. <. . .> I doubt very much the centrality of the *filioque* for the dogmatic development of the West, and I do not think that "papism" could derive

> from the *filioque*—that is, maybe you can "derive" it, but me as a historian, I'm not interested in logical deduction but in actual filiation of ideas. "Papism" already existed when the *filioque* was not yet even in prospect. (A letter to Archimandrite Sophrony Sakharov on May 15, 1958. In Krawchuk & Bremer 2014: 247)

The bottom line of these opinions is that Filioque cannot be considered an apple of discord between the East and the West. The discord is still there, but it is hidden in two different interpretations of how primacy is exercised in the church.

# Fourth Crusade

More than the anathemas of 1054, other events contributed to the great schism between the East and the West—particularly, the fourth crusade. It was envisaged by Pope Innocent III (in office 1198–1216), who initiated it as an ecumenical enterprise, through which the Latin West and Byzantium would join their efforts to reestablish Christian hegemony in the Holy Land. However, a coup d'état in 1195 and the following civil conflict in Byzantium changed the original plans. Alexius III Angelus (r. 1195–1203) replaced his brother Isaac II (r. 1185–95; 1203–4) as emperor. Isaac's son, who would become known as Alexius IV (r. 1203–4), went to the West, where he convinced the crusade's military leadership to help him to depose his uncle and to make him the emperor. In exchange, Alexius promised payment from the imperial coffers and army to attack Egypt.

Crusaders accepted Alexius' offers and diverted their way to the outskirts of Constantinople. They besieged the city in June 1203. Alexius' plan worked—his uncle had to flee, and he with his father took the throne as co-emperors. However, he could not deliver on his promises to the crusaders. Soon Alexius IV was murdered in another coup. Crusaders realized they would not receive what they had been promised. So they decided to take their promised payments on their own. On April 13, 1204, they seized the city and looted it. They looted with particular cruelty, probably having in mind an 1182 massacre of the Latins who lived in Constantinople. Nicetas Choniates (*c.* 1155–1215), a Byzantine statesman and historian, was a witness of the looting and provided a detailed account of it:

> The enemy, who had expected otherwise, found no one openly venturing into battle or taking up arms to resist; they saw that the way was open before them and everything there for the taking. The narrow streets were clear and the crossroads unobstructed, safe from attack, and advantageous to the enemy. The populace, moved by the hope of propitiating them, had turned out to greet them with crosses and venerable icons of Christ as was customary during festivals of solemn processions. But their disposition was not at all affected by what they saw, nor did their lips break into the slightest smile,

nor did the unexpected spectacle transform their grim and frenzied glance and fury into a semblance of cheerfulness. Instead, they plundered with impunity and stripped their victims shamelessly, beginning with their carts. Not only did they rob them of their substance but also the articles consecrated to God; the rest fortified themselves all around with defensive weapons as their horses were roused at the sound of the war trumpet.

What then should I recount first and what last of those things dared at that time by these murderous men? O, the shameful dashing to earth of the venerable icons and the flinging of the relics of the saints. <. . .> How horrible it was to see the divine body and blood of Christ poured out and thrown to the ground! These forerunners of Antichrist, chief agents and harbingers of his anticipated ungodly deeds, seized as plunder the precious chalices and patens; some they smashed, taking possession of the ornaments embellishing them, and they set the remaining vessels on their tables to serve as bread dishes and wine goblets. Just as happened long ago, Christ was now disrobed and mocked, his garments were parted, and lots were cast for them by this race; and although his side was not pierced by the lance, yet once more streams of divine blood poured to the earth.

The report of the impious acts perpetrated in the great church are unwelcome to the ears. The table of sacrifice, fashioned from every kind of precious material and fused by fire into one whole—blended together into a perfection of one multicolored thing of beauty, truly extraordinary and admired by all nations—was broken into pieces and divided among the despoilers, as was the lot of all the sacred church treasures, countless in number and unsurpassed in beauty. They found it fitting to bring out as so much booty the all-hallowed vessels and furnishings that had been wrought with incomparable elegance and craftsmanship from rare materials. In addition, in order to remove the pure silver which overlay the railing of the bema, the wondrous pulpit and the gates, as well as that which covered a great many other adornments, all of which were plated with gold, they led to the very sanctuary of the temple itself mules and asses with packsaddles; some of these, unable to keep their feet on the smoothly polished marble floors, slipped and were pierced by knives so that the excrement from the bowels and the spilled blood denied the sacred floor. Moreover, a certain silly woman laden with sins, an attendant of the Erinyes, the handmaid of demons, the workshop of unspeakable spells and reprehensible charms, waxing wanton against Christ, sat upon the synthronon and intoned a song, and then whirled about and kicked up her heels in dance. <. . .>

There were lamentations and cries of woe and weeping in the narrow ways, wailing at the crossroads, moaning in the temples, outcries of men, screams of women, the taking of captives, and the dragging about, tearing in pieces, and raping of bodies heretofore sound and whole. They who were bashful of their sex were led about naked, they who were venerable in their old age uttered plaintive cries, and the wealthy were despoiled of their riches. <. . .>

The sons of Ishmael did not behave in this way, for when the Latins overpowered Zion the Latins showed no compassion or kindness to their race. Neither did the Ishmaelites neigh after Latin women. <. . .> Thus the enemies of Christ dealt

> magnanimously with the Latin infidels, inflicting upon them neither sword, nor fire, nor hunger, nor persecution, nor nakedness, nor bruises, nor constraints. How differently, as we have briefly recounted, the Latins treated us who love Christ and are their fellow believers, guiltless of any wrong against them. (Niketas 1984: 312–20)

The sack of Constantinople by the crusaders caused an unprecedented shock to the Byzantines. It was not only a physical shock of massacre, pillaging, and looting but also a metaphysical one, caused by the fact that the city, which was never captured by enemy, fell. As was mentioned earlier, the Byzantines had an almost dogmatic belief that their *Polis* is invincible. The trauma from the fourth crusade and the sack of Constantinople remains deeply embedded in the consciousness and often subconsciousness of the Orthodox, especially in the Greek-speaking world. This memory still defines conservative Orthodox attitudes to the Catholic Church.

Pope Innocent III initially opposed the idea of detouring the crusade to Constantinople and besieging it. He believed that the crusaders must not touch any Christian city. He also believed that it would be anti-ecumenical. However, after the crusaders established control over the capital city, the pope saw this as God's providence that was helping him ironing out some pending ecclesial issues. He believed that God gave him an opportunity to finally impose on the Easterners the Roman vision of the papal authority as a divine institution with universal jurisdiction.

The pope also wanted to restore the church's unity—in accordance with this vision. The Latin Patriarchate of Constantinople fully embodied it. Ecumenical undertakings of that time relied on military force and political opportunities. Forcing into unity was considered a norm. Those who were forced were treated not as equals, but as subjects (see Demacopoulos 2019: 125).

# VI.6 Uniatism

Medieval ecumenism to a great extent continued the ecumenism of the Late Antiquity. However, it featured more mistrust and more coercion. In the era, when the Byzantine Empire was strong, the state usually initiated ecumenical projects. When Byzantium became weak and the Western church grew stronger, the latter began playing the leading ecumenical role. In its ecumenical activities, the Roman see followed its new ecclesiology, which presupposed identification of this see with the common nature of the church.

The so-called uniate councils embodied this ecclesiology. They usually aimed at bringing Eastern churches to union with Rome. These churches had to acknowledge and submit themselves to the universal authority and jurisdiction of the Roman bishops. Similar "uniate" councils happened in the Late Antiquity as well. One of them was the aforementioned monoënergist council in Alexandria in 633. Then, political and ecclesial authorities of Byzantium also forced schismatic groups to union. However, they forged unions on different ecclesiological grounds. "Schismatic" groups were invited to join the fellowships of the churches, but not to submit themselves to the church of Constantinople.

Soon after Emperor Michael VIII Palaeologus (r. 1261–82) took back Constantinople from the Latins (1261), he approached Rome with the request to restore communion between the churches. Michael desperately needed the Western military help, and unity with Rome was a key to get it. Rome, in response, asked the Byzantines to accept the Filioque.

Restoration of unity based on Filioque happened at the council convened in Lyon in 1272. It is regarded fourteenth ecumenical in the Roman Catholic Church and was presided by Pope Gregory X (in office 1271–6). The unity did not last long, however, as most Byzantines opposed it. They were supported by Michael's son, who became Emperor Andronicus II (r. 1282).

A second significant attempt at the restoration of unity happened at the council of Ferrara-Florence (1438–45), which is regarded a continuation of the council in Basel (began in 1431) (see Alberigo 1991). The Eastern delegation to the council was numerous, around 700 members, including the patriarch of Constantinople Joseph II (in office 1416–39) and Emperor John VIII Palaeologus (r. 1425–48). The Western part insisted that the Easterners should accept the Filioque and the Western interpretation of primacy. Most Easterners eventually accepted these conditions. A minority, led by the archbishop of Ephesus Mark Eugenicus (*c.* 1392–1444), also wanted unity, but at a higher price. Like earlier in the case of the council of Lyon, the Ferrara-Florence was eventually rejected by the Easterners.

The "uniate" councils failed, because their ecclesiological presumptions were the same as with the schism of 1054: the church is its hierarchs who decide on its behalf. The voice of laity was not taken into consideration. The medieval churches, like contemporary societies, were rigidly stratified, with minimum input from laypeople. Laypeople, however, did not always accept such passive role. They sometimes actively resisted the decisions taken on their behalf by hierarchs at the "uniate" councils. Attempts at the church's reconciliation, thus, fell victims to stratification within the churches.

This was particularly the case with the council of Brest in 1596. This council was convened on the territory of the Polish-Lithuanian Commonwealth (*Rzeczpospolita*), which consisted of the Catholic majority. This majority wanted to force the Orthodox minority to union with Rome. Such union was attempted at the Brest council.

This council thought of itself as a successor to the Ferrara-Florence council. It applied the same hierarchical model of taking decisions, without taking lay voices into consideration. The hierarchs of the Kyivan metropolia, under the jurisdiction of Constantinople, supported the union. They usually spoke on behalf of the Orthodox nobility, who sought more privileges for themselves, and not for the simple people.

**Figure 6.8** Ostroh Academy in Ukraine—one of the centers of Orthodox polemical theology in the early modern era.

Source: Photo by the author.

These people refused to accept theological concessions that their hierarchs had made at the "uniate" council.

"The union of Brest" awakened the grassroots theological creativity in the Orthodox lands of the *Rzeczpospolita*. The territory of modern Ukraine became a major center of Orthodox learning and writing in the period of early Modernity. Among the prominent Ukrainian authors of that time were Basil Malyushytsky, Christopher Philalet, Leontiy Karpovych, Job Boretsky, Zachary Kopystensky, and others.

An interesting case was Meletiy Smotrytsky (1577–1633). First, he was an ardent polemicist against the uniatism and later turned to its proponent. At the first stage of his polemical activities, he composed a treatise *Threnos, or the Lament of the Eastern Church*, where, in resemblance with Hermas' *Pastor*, he compared the Orthodox church in Ukraine with a suffering woman. This woman is abused by her children. Meletiy implied that Orthodox priests and bishops had betrayed her with another woman, the Catholic church:

Woe to me poor, oh my dear, as I am in misery, being deprived of every good,
oh my dear, and stripped of my garments, so that the shame of my body is in front of the world!
Trouble on me, as I am burdened by unbearable burdens!
My arms in shackles,
my yoke on the neck,
my legs tied,
the chains are on my hips,
the two-edged sword is above my head,
deep water is under my feet,
unquenchable fire surrounds me from the sides,
from each side there is screaming,
from each side there is fear,
from each side there are persecutions.
There is disaster in cities and villages,
there is trouble in fields and debris,
trouble in mountains and deeps of the earth.
There is no quiet place or shelter.
I spend my day in sores and wounds,
and night, in moaning and sighing.
In the summer, it is so hot that I faint,
and in the winter, it is cold that I die:
because I am completely naked and persecuted to death.
Once beautiful and rich, now I am ugly and poor.
Once a queen dear to the entire world, now I am despised and embarrassed by everyone. <. . .>
Now I became a laughing stock for the world,

**Figure 6.9** A bust of Meletiy Smotrytsky at the Ostroh Academy, Ukraine, where he was a graduate.

Source: Photo by the author.

while once I was wonderful to both humans and angels.
I was decorated before all, beautiful and sweet,
splendid as the dawn,
beautiful as the moon,
amazing as the sun,
the only child of my mother,
chosen as a spotless dove,
with no wrinkle or anything of that kind.
Fragrant myrrh is my name,
and my surname is the well of living water.
Having seen me, the daughters of Zion proclaimed me the most blessed queen.
In short, I was among the daughters of Zion what Jerusalem was among other cities —
like lily between the thorns, so I was between the girls.
The king, the best of the sons of men, desired my beauty and, having fallen in love with me, he united me with him in eternal marriage.
I gave birth to babies and raised them,
but they renounced me;
they became my shame.
For they stripped me of my garments and cast me out of my house naked:
they have taken away the beauty of my flesh and the embellishment of my head.
What is more!
Day and night they encroach upon my poor soul and constantly think how to destroy me.

O you, who stand before me,
you who look upon me!
Listen and weigh, where is a pain like mine?
Where is the anguish and pity similar to mine? <. . .>
My sons and my daughters, who I have raised, left me and followed another woman, who did not have pain for them,
so that they could be satisfied with her goods.
My priests became blinded,
my shepherds <. . .> turned numb,
my elders went mad,
my youth became feral,
my daughters went for fornication. (*Θρῆνος to iest lament iedyney świętej Powszechney Apostolskiey Wschodniej Cerkwie z obiasnieniem dogmat wiary*, published in 1610 by the Brotherhood of the Holy Spirit in Vilnius; translation is mine)

The council of Brest happened under the pressure of the administrative and military machine of the Polish state, which also violently implemented its decisions. Orthodox population, whose majority were peasants, perceived the union as a continuation of the violent policies of the state, which now wanted to grab not only their possessions and freedoms, but their very soul. These political oppressions provoked insurgencies of the Cossacks—military and paramilitary troops (insurgencies were acute in 1648–57; see Plokhy 2001). They were underpinned by religious resentment: their goal was to protect Orthodoxy from unionism. They resembled the religious wars in Europe in about the same time. Both conflicts were provoked by a mixture of religious, political, and social unrest.

Cossack wars in Ukraine were as violent as the oppressions that had provoked them. With similar violence that the Polish government had promoted uniatism, the repressive Soviet state tried to undo the Brest union after the Second World War. In 1946, the Soviet authorities organized a council in L'viv. This gathering dissolved the uniate Ukrainian Greek Catholic Church. Its members had either to join the Orthodox church or to hide in underground. Those who resisted were exiled. With the collapse of the Soviet Union, violence came back to the western regions of Ukraine, where many Orthodox churches were converted to Greek Catholic, sometimes without the consent of their members.

These issues became a subject for discussions at the Orthodox-Catholic dialogues. A session of this dialogue held in Lebanon in 1993, promulgated a statement, which condemned uniatism as a method of the Orthodox-Catholic rapprochement. It also condemned the use of violence in resolving disputes between the Orthodox and Eastern Catholics:

In the course of the centuries various attempts were made to re-establish unity. They sought to achieve this end through different ways, at times conciliar, according to the

**Figure 6.10** A monument to the leaders of the Ukrainian Cossack wars. Uman', Ukraine.

Source: Photo by the author.

political, historical, theological and spiritual situation of each period. Unfortunately, none of these efforts succeeded in re-establishing full communion between the Church of the West and the Church of the East, and at times even made oppositions more acute.

In the course of the last four centuries, in various parts of the East, initiatives were taken within certain Churches and impelled by outside elements, to restore communion between the Church of the East and the Church of the West. These initiatives led to the union of certain communities with the See of Rome and brought with them, as a consequence, the breaking of communion with their Mother Churches of the East. This took place not without the interference of extraecclesial interests. In this way Oriental Catholic Churches came into being. And so a situation was created which has become a source of conflicts and of suffering in the first instance for the Orthodox but also for Catholics.

Progressively, in the decades which followed these unions, missionary activity tended to include among its priorities the effort to convert other Christians, individually or in groups, so as "to bring them back" to one's own Church. In order to legitimize this tendency, a source of proselytism, the Catholic Church developed the

> theological vision according to which she presented herself as the only one to whom salvation was entrusted. As a reaction, the Orthodox Church, in turn, came to accept the same vision according to which only in her could salvation be found. To assure the salvation of "the separated brethren" it even happened that Christians were rebaptized and that certain requirements of the religious freedom of persons and of their act of faith were forgotten. This perspective was one to which that period showed little sensitivity.
>
> On the other hand certain civil authorities made attempts to bring back Oriental Catholics to the Church of their Fathers. To achieve this end they did not hesitate, when the occasion was given, to use unacceptable means.
>
> Because of the way in which Catholics and Orthodox once again consider each other in their relationship to the mystery of the Church and discover each other once again as Sister Churches, this form of "missionary apostolate" described above, and which has been called "uniatism," can no longer be accepted either as a method to be followed nor as a model of the unity our Churches are seeking.

At the same time, the Balamand declaration clearly recognized the right of the Eastern Catholic churches to exist and continue their pastoral work among their faithful:

> Concerning the Oriental Catholic Churches, it is clear that they, as part of the Catholic Communion, have the right to exist and to act in answer to the spiritual needs of their faithful. (*Uniatism, Method of Union of the Past, and the Present Search for Full Communion*: https://tinyurl.com/23h6hf85 [accessed on March 19, 2021])

# VI.7

# Era of Confessionalism

The council of Brest marked an active involvement of the Eastern churches in the process that became known as confessionalization (see Lieburg 2006). This was a religious, social, and political process that took place mostly in the Western Europe and had been triggered by the Reformation. The Reformation caused what could be called the third great schism in the global Christianity. In contrast to the first great schism, which had affected mostly the Eastern Christianity, and the second great schism, which had divided the Eastern and Western Christianities, the third great schism fragmented the Western Christianity. Fragments of the Western church identified themselves as different *confessions* of faith: Catholic, Lutheran, Calvinist, Presbyterian, Anabaptist, Anglican, and so on. They preferred to reflect on their differences with other "confessions" rather than on what they shared.

The confessionalized faith was articulated and circulated in articles of "confessions"—symbolic texts that tried to comprehensively summarize each group's credo, especially in contrast to the credos of other groups. The first symbolic text of this sort was the Augsburg Confession (1530), produced by what would later become known as Lutheranism. Among other important confessions from the churches of the Reformation are the Lutheran Schmalkald Articles (1537), the Formula of Concord (1577), the Book of Concord (1580); then the Reformed Helvetic Confessions (1536, 1566), the Gallican Confession (1559), the Belgic Confession (1561), Heidelberg Catechism (1563), and Canons of Dort (1619); the Presbyterian Westminster Confession (1648); and the Anglican Thirty-nine Articles (1571). The Roman Catholic Church felt urge to produce its own confession, which was adopted at the council of Trent (1545–63)—a high point of the so-called counter-Reformation. This council's canons and decrees, together with the *Professio fidei Tridentina* promulgated in 1564, constituted a confessional codification of the Roman Catholic faith. A series of Western councils that produced confessions during the sixteenth-seventeenth centuries resembles the synodomachia of the fourth-fifth centuries in the East. The Western synodomachia, however, was less ecumenical and incurred a more severe fragmentation of global Christianity.

The confessional fragmentation of the Christian West in the aftermath of the Reformation affected also the Christian East. Uniatism was one of its effects, but not the only one. In their anti-uniate polemics, Eastern theologians became preoccupied with the differences of the Orthodox "confession" from the Western confessions. In result, some confessional differences were exaggerated and some, invented. Orthodox theologians often borrowed from either Catholic or Protestant nomenclature of polemical tropes. In result, sometimes they redefined their Orthodoxy in either Protestant or Catholic terms.

# Cyril Lucaris

The earliest Orthodox "confession," which emulated Western "confessions," was produced by Patriarch Cyril Lucaris. He was born in 1572. From the early years of his life, he witnessed wrestling among Western confessions. His most immediate experience was that of counter-Reformation: first in his native Crete, which was under Venetian rule, then in Venice, and later in Padua, where he completed his graduate studies. In his mid-twenties, Cyril came to *Rzeczpospolita*, to help the local Orthodox to wrestle with uniatism. He found the local Orthodox population there in the condition of almost complete ignorance about their Orthodox doctrine. He taught in and directed a number of Orthodox educational institutions, which were established in Vilnius, L'viv, and Ostroh—with the goal to impede the spread of and conversion to Roman Catholicism.

His sour experiences of counter-Reformation pushed Cyril to align with the cause of the Reformation. He came to appreciate particularly its later Reformed edition. Following the model of Western "confessions," he produced his own one, which had a clear Calvinist demeanor:

> We believe that the best and greatest God hath predestinated his Elect unto glorie before the beginning of the World, without any respect unto their workes, and that there was other impulsive cause to this election, but onely the good will and mercy of God. In like manner before the world was made, he hath rejected whom he would; of which act of reprobation, if you consider the absolute dealing of God his will is the cause; but if you looke upon God's orderly proceeding, his justice is the cause, for God is merciful and just. (*Confessio fidei* 2)

After having been elected to the patriarchal throne of Alexandria and later Constantinople, Cyril became a proponent of what can be called "Orthodox Reformation." Some points of this Reformation program were rejected by the Orthodox church, and some became a norm, such as, for instance, having the Holy Scripture in vernacular translations. Cyril commissioned and edited the first Modern

Greek translation of the New Testament, which was published in Geneva. In his preface to this edition, Cyril stated that the Gospel, when accessible in vernacular language, is "a sweet message, given to us from heaven." All Christians should "know and be acquainted with all its contents." They also have to delve deep into the meaning of the Gospel's words, which is hardly possible, if these words are not written in an understandable language: "If we speak or read without understanding, it is like throwing our words to the window" (in Hadjiantoniou 1961: 94).

Cyril's Reformation also featured critiquing practices and beliefs that were regarded contrary to the Gospels and Orthodoxy. In his letter to the Dutch Calvinist theologian Johannes Uytenbogaert (1557–1644), Cyril referred to such practices as "liable to error." For him, "all such practices must be submitted to the scrutiny of the Scriptures and of the Holy Spirit" (letter to Johannes Uytenbogaert on October 10, 1613; Hadjiantoniou 1961: 41). Cyril might have referred here to the practice of indulgence. Although less known and spread not as widely as in the West, indulgences existed in the East. There, they were known as *synchorochartia* (συγχωροχάρτια), which literally means "forgiving papers." These certificates, which were believed to absolve sins, could be obtained in exchange for a fee. Only patriarchs could issue them—not bishops or priests. A confession of faith adopted at the council of Constantinople in 1727 confirmed the right of the patriarchs to promulgate indulgences:

> The power of the forgiveness of sins, which is termed by the Eastern church of Christ absolution certificates (συγχωροχάρτια) when given in writing, but by the Latins "indulgences" (ἰντουλγκέντζας), is given to the holy church by Christ. These absolution certificates are issued in the whole catholic church by the four most holy patriarchs: Constantinople, Alexandria, Antioch, and Jerusalem. (In Καρμήρης 1968, vol. 2: 867–8)

The Orthodox, in that period of time, were not as much against indulgences per se as against their monopolization by bishops of Rome. They insisted that the right to issue indulgences belongs to all members of the pentarchy. Even anti-Latin Orthodox theologians of that time endorsed indulgences. For example, Nicodemus the Hagiorite (1749–1809), in his letter to the bishop of Stagonas Païsius, who at that time stayed in Constantinople, asked him to procure from the patriarchate a *synchorochartion* for a "living" monastic, also named Nicodemus. He promised Païsius that he would send money to purchase the certificate as soon as he knows how much it would cost (letter dated April 1806; Ἡλιοῦ 1985: 22–3).

Indulgences as a means of earning money for patriarchates were condemned at the council of Constantinople in 1838. Like the council in 1727, this council was preoccupied with purging the church from the Latin influences. An encyclical letter promulgated by this council and signed by the patriarch of Constantinople Gregory VI (in office 1835–40; 1867–71) and the patriarch of Jerusalem Athanasius V (in office 1827–44), condemned the "horrid and unheard-of evil usage, originating in arrogance, by which the bishops of Rome employ the most holy, most sacred, and most awesome articles of belief of the sacred Christian Faith as a means to raise money" (in Καρμήρης 1968: 898). Despite such condemnations, the practice of selling "absolution certificates" lasted until the mid-twentieth century.

Cyril Lucaris did not endorse indulgences. He rebuked them in the spirit of his sympathies to the cause of the Reformation—as he explained in a private letter to Mark Antonio de Dominis (1560–1624), formerly a Catholic archbishop who converted to Protestantism:

> Having obtained, through the kindness of friends, some writings of Evangelical theologians, books which have not only been unseen in the East, but, due to the influence of the censures of Rome, have not even been heard of, I then invoked earnestly the assistance of the Holy Ghost, and for three years compared the doctrines of the Greek and Latin Churches with that of the Reformed. <. . .> Leaving the Fathers I took for my only guide the Scriptures and the Analogy of Faith. At length, having been convinced, through the grace of God, that the cause of the Reformers was more correct and more in accord with the doctrine of Christ, I embraced it.

Cyril was certainly in favor of the Reformed doctrine, without, however, buying it in wholesale. Thus, in the same letter he stated regarding the issues that divided Catholicism and Protestantism of his time:

> In the Sacrament of the Lord's Supper we fully believe that Christ is present, not illusorily and symbolically, but truly and in person, substantially and really, as is testified by the Word of our Lord, "which is given for you." With respect to the manner of the Presence, our Greek Church is at variance both with those who adopt the chimera of transubstantiation, and with the erroneous opinion of the Ubiquitaries. <. . .>
>
> As for Image Worship, it is impossible for me to say how disastrous it is under the present circumstances. <. . .> Not that I can say that, absolutely speaking, images are to be condemned, since, when not worshipped, they cannot do any harm; but I abhor the idolatry of which they are the cause to these blind worshippers. And although in my private prayers I have sometimes observed that the Crucifix was an assistance to my mind, as bringing more readily before it the Passion of our Lord, yet in view of the fact that the naive, to say nothing of some who are enlightened, are carried away from the true and spiritual worship and adoration which is due to God alone, I would rather that all would entirely abstain from this so dangerous handle of sin. <. . .>
>
> As for the invocation of Saints, there was a time when I too did not perceive how it overshadowed the glory of our Lord Christ. (Letter to Marco Antonio de Dominis on September 6, 1618; Hadjiantoniou 1961: 43)

Cyril was not only pro-Reformation but also overtly anti-counter-Reformation. Influential proponents of the Catholic cause in Constantinople considered him an enemy and tried to discredit him in the eyes of the Ottoman authorities. Eventually, the High Porte became convinced that the patriarch was in alliance with the Ukrainian Cossacks, who at that time were at war with the Ottomans. Sultan ordered executing Cyril, who was strangled on a boat in the Bosphorus in 1638.

Cyril Lucaris was caught in the crossfire between the Catholics and Protestants in the period of their bloodiest conflict—the Thirty Years War. He, on the one hand, fell a symbolic casualty of this conflict and confessionalism it propelled. On the other hand, he became a protagonist of confessionalism in the Orthodox milieu.

Confessionalism is hardly compatible with ecumenism. Yet, Cyril tried to be ecumenical, as much as his confessionalism allowed this. Thus, he insisted that Christian groups should not be misguided by confessional libels. A meticulous study of theological beliefs should precede any judgment. The following statement can be seen as Cyril's ecumenical credo:

> We abominated the doctrine of the Reformed Churches, as opposed to the Faith, not knowing in good truth what we abominated. But when it pleased the merciful God to enlighten us, and make us perceive our former error, we began to consider what our future stand should be. And as the role of a good citizen, in the case of any dissension, is to defend the juster cause, I think it all the more to be the duty of a good Christian not to dissimulate his sentiments in matters pertaining to salvation, but to embrace unreservedly that side which is most accordant to the Word of God. (Hadjiantoniou 1961: 42 3)

Cyril was not an ecumenist in the modern sense. In the spirit of his contemporary confessionalism, he distrusted other confessions. Surprisingly, he regarded non-Chalcedonian Christians, such as Copts and Assyrians, as the enemies of the Byzantine Orthodoxy. In his letter to Johannes Uytenbogaert, Cyril called them "the pests of the Orient" (Hadjiantoniou 1961: 37). The rhetoric of this Byzantine hierarch toward his Oriental fellow Christians was similar to the war of words between Catholics and Protestant in his time in the West. For Cyril, who used to be a Chalcedonian Patriarch in Egypt, his non-Chalcedonian fellow Christians, who together with his own community faced the same Muslim majority, were nothing more but what Trojans had used to be for Greeks (Hadjiantoniou 1961: 37). This metaphor illustrates what kind of ecumenism was possible in the early modern era: paranoic and proselytizing. Other Christians were regarded as enemies. Each confession tried to send its own Trojan horse to the camp of the enemy, to conquer it.

Cyril can be seen as one of the founding fathers of the Orthodox confessionalism. Following the pattern of Western confessionalism, he composed his own *confessio fide*. This "confession" was first printed in Geneva in March 1629, in Latin. Soon its Greek edition and its translations into French, English, and other European languages

**Figure 6.11** Artistic representation of Cyril Lucaris at the Ostroh Academy in Ukraine, where he was a rector.
Source: Photo by the author.

followed. Like most confessions of the era of confessionalism, the one composed by Cyril provoked a lot of debate in the Orthodox world and beyond it.

# Petro Mohyla

Lucaris' successor at the throne of Constantinople, Cyril II Kontares (d. 1640), convoked in September 1638 a synod, which condemned both Cyril Lucaris and his *confession*. Two years later, a council in the Moldavian city of Iaşi condemned Lucaris' *confession* as well. This council adopted its own version of the Orthodox confession. Its text was originally composed by a group of educated Ukrainian monks under the leadership of the rector of the theological academy in Kyiv, abbot Isaiah Kozlovsky-Trofymovych (d. 1651), who was also a friend and collaborator of the metropolitan of Kyiv Petro Mohyla. The latter edited the text and made it approved by the local council held in St. Sophia Cathedral in Kyiv. After that the text was sent to the Ecumenical Patriarchate for further approval.

The ruler of Moldavia Basil Lupu (1595–1661), who was also one of the most influential and richest political figures in the Christian East at that time, convened in his capital Iaşi in 1641–2 a council, which was attended by representatives from

**Figure 6.12** Entrance to St. Sophia Cathedral in Kyiv.
Source: Photo by the author.

almost the entire Christian East. Among other issues, they discussed the confession presented by Petro Mohyla. Mohyla could bring this text to the table in Iași because he originated from the ruling Moldavian family. The initial version of the confession, which had been composed by the Ukrainian monks, was elaborated upon by Greek theologians, who made some Latin formulas of the original text sound more traditionally Orthodox. In the form approved by the council in Iași, the confession was also approved by the four Eastern patriarchs.[1] It, thus, became an Eastern theological standard for the next two centuries.

Unlike the confession of Cyril Lucaris, whose structure is close to the Protestant confessions of that time, the confession of Petro Mohyla structurally replicated the catechism of the council of Trent. It also contained quite a few Latin ideas and formulas. There were more of them in the original Kyivan edition of the text, and they did not completely disappear after the editorial work done by the Greek theologians. Among other Trent-inspired issues, the Mohyla confession discussed the idea of authority in the church. It articulated this idea in the language that sounds Trentine, with the papal authority substituted by councils:

[1]Parthenius of Constantinople, Ioannikius of Alexandria, Macarius of Antioch, and Païsius of Jerusalem.

> Every Christian ought to submit himself and be obedient to the Church. This Christ himself teacheth: "If he neglects to hear the Church, let him be unto thee as an Heathen Man and a Publican" (Mt. 18:17). And the Church is so fully empowered, that she hath Authority, in her general Councils, to examine and warrant the Scripture, to inquire into the Behaviour and judge the Patriarchs, Popes, Bishops, and all others, and to inflict severe Canonical Punishment upon them according to their Offenses. (*Questio* 86; Mogila 1898: 68)

The Mohyla's confession, thus, put the church above the Scripture and any personal primacy, be it papal or patriarchal. At the same time, it clearly differentiated between the church's hierarchy and laypeople. For the latter, the confession stated, it is unlawful "to meddle with and thrust themselves into Spiritual Matters" (*Questio* 89; Mogila 1898: 70).

# Dositheus of Jerusalem

A generation later, the patriarch of Jerusalem Dositheus Notaras (in office 1669–1707) continued fighting against the Calvinist ideas of Cyril Lucaris and tried to find equilibrium between Catholic and Protestant positions regarding the controversial issues. In 1672, he convened a council in Bethlehem, which anathematized Cyril's *confessio*. Simultaneously, the council adopted its own confession authored by Dositheus. In some points, this confession was clearer on the controversial issues than Mohyla's confession. For example, regarding the issue of how the Tradition relates to the Scripture, this confession stated:

> We believe that the divine and sacred scripture is taught by God. And therefore we ought to believe it without doubting, yet not otherwise than as the catholic (καθοληκή) church has interpreted and delivered it. For every foul heresy does indeed receive the divine scripture, but interprets it perversely, using metaphors and homonymies and sophistries of human wisdom, confusing what ought to be distinguished and trifling with what ought not to be trifled with. For if we were to receive it otherwise, with each man holding every day a different sense concerning it, the catholic church would not, as she does by the grace of Christ, continue to be the church until this day, holding the same doctrine of faith and always believing it identically and steadfastly, but would be rent into innumerable parties and subject to heresies. <. . .> Therefore the witness of the catholic church is, we believe, not inferior in authority to that of the divine scripture. For one and the same Holy Spirit being the author of both, it is quite the same to be taught by the scripture and by the catholic church. Moreover, when anyone speaks from himself, he is liable to err, to deceive and be deceived. But for the catholic church, as never having spoken or speaking from herself but from the Spirit of God—who being her teacher, she is unfailingly rich forever—it is impossible to err in any

> way, or to deceive at all or be deceived; but like the divine scripture, she is infallible and has perpetual authority. (Translation by J.N.W.B. Robertson in Pelikan & Hotchkiss 2003, vol. 1: 615–16)

Some other apologetical efforts of Dositheus, however, look clumsy. Rather unfortunate is his attempt to justify indulgences (συγχωροχάρτια): "We have the custom and ancient tradition, which is known to all, that the most holy Patriarchs would give the people of the Church a certificate for the absolution of their sins" (in Παπαδόπουλος-Κεραμεῦς 1908: 133).

# VI.8

# Russian Ecclesiology

In the nineteenth century, confessionalism was still strong, but not as strong as earlier. Under the influence of secular philosophy, primarily German idealism, Orthodox theologians effectively rediscovered for themselves the phenomenon of the church. A Russian amateur theologian Aleksey Khomyakov is usually credited for such rediscovery. Khomyakov continued thinking in the terms of confessionalism. At the same time, he applied new ways of looking to the phenomenon of the church. He promoted a more "organic" ecclesiology, which he still employed to stress the differences between confessions:

> Romanism is an unnatural tyranny; Protestantism is an unprincipled revolt. Neither of them can be accepted. But where is unity without tyranny? Where is freedom without revolt to be found? They are both to be found in the ancient, continuous, unadulterated tradition of the Church. There a unity to be found more authoritative than the despotism of Vatican, *for it is based on the strength of mutual love*. There a liberty is to be found more free than the licence of Protestantism, for it is *regulated by the humility of mutual love*, There is the Rock and the Refuge. (In Bolshakoff 1946: 118; all italics by Khomyakov)

In parallel to such confessional thinking, a new ecumenical thinking was emerging. A rather conservative Metropolitan of Moscow Filaret Drozdov (1782–1867), who, by the way, did not appreciate the work of Khomyakov, was not as categorical in judging the Western confessions: "I will dare not to call as false any Church, which believes that Jesus is Christ. <. . .> My justified respect to the teaching of the eastern Church, he continues, does not mean that I judge or accuse western Christians and the western Church" (Дроздов 1886: 29, 35). Filaret admitted some saving grace outside the Orthodox church—an idea that undermined confessionalism: "An Orthodox Christian is supposed, in the spirit of love, to joyfully find outside of the Orthodox Church a preserved grace" (Дроздов 1886: 29, 35).

Another prominent hierarch of that time, Metropolitan Platon Gorodetsky of Kyiv (1803–91), coined a catchy phrase that would become a slogan of the modern ecumenical movement: "Our earthly walls do not reach the sky." He uttered this when he visited a Catholic congregation in the town of Korostyshev in Ukraine in 1884. He also called the Orthodox and the Catholic churches "cousins," anticipating the modern ecumenical language that calls churches of different traditions "sisters" (see Cohen 2017).

Later in the nineteenth century, the Russian Orthodox Church initiated the earliest ecumenical dialogues, which adopted new patterns of inter-Christian relations. These were the patterns of deliberations, based on the studies of the church history and critical approach to patristic sources. Text criticism, which developed in the biblical and patristic scholarship at that time, was laid at the foundation of the new ecumenical method. Critical method helped the Orthodox theology of that time to weaken the confessionalist grip on it.

A new ecumenical thinking beyond confessionalism was applied for the first time in the dialogue of the Russian church with the Anglican and Old Catholic churches. Among the features that attracted the Orthodox in these confessions was their rejection of the papal authority in the form that had been postulated by the Vatican I (1870). A leading Russian scholar at that time, professor of the Sankt Petersburg Theological Academy Vasily Bolotov, articulated some early principles of the modern Orthodox ecumenism. He did this as a member of the commission on the dialogue with the Old Catholics that had been established in 1892 by the Synod of the Russian church. Bolotov published in 1893 his twenty-seven theses on the principles of dialogue. He in particular differentiated between dogma, *theologoumenon*

**Figure 6.13** The grave of Metropolitan Platon Gorodetsky in St. Sophia Cathedral in Kyiv.

Source: Photo by the author.

(θεολογούμενον), and theological opinion. Theological opinion, for him, is any opinion expressed by any theologian in the past, without being endorsed by the authority of the church. *Theologoumenon*,

> in its essence, is the same theological opinion, but it is an opinion by those who are for any catholic more than mere theologians; these are the opinions of the Fathers of the one undivided church; these are the opinions of those men, among whom are rightly named the "teachers of the universe, *hoi didaskaloi tes oikoumenes* (οἱ διδάσκαλοι τῆς οἰκουμένης)."
>
> I consider *theologoumena* (θεολογούμενα) highly, but in no way do I exaggerate their significance; I think I differentiate them "quite sharply" from the dogma.
>
> The content of the dogma is true, while the content of *theologoumenon* (θεολογούμενον) is probable. The sphere of dogma is *necessaria*, while the sphere of θεολογούμενον is *dubia*. *In necessariis unitas, in dubiis libertas*! (Болотов 1914: 31)

Bolotov believed that Filioque is a *theologoumenon*. Moreover, both the moderate Eastern interpretation of the Filioque (in the sense of procession of the Holy Spirit "through the Son" (διὰ Υἱοῦ)) and a more radical Western interpretation of it (the Father and the Son are two causes of the Holy Spirit) are also *theologoumena*. Therefore, they cannot be considered as an obstacle for unity. What Bolotov considered an obstacle was the interpretation of the Roman primacy as it had been promulgated by the Vatican I. He believed that the restoration of unity with the Old Catholics, who had rejected Vatican I, was for the Orthodox possible, but it was impossible with the mainstream Catholics, because of their interpretation of papacy in the spirit of the doctrine of infallibility.

In parallel to the academic theology, which developed in the theological academies and had Bolotov as its prominent representative, Russian religious renaissance adopted its own take on ecumenism. This renaissance was more philosophical than theological, secular rather than ecclesial. The ecumenical approach of the Russian religious renaissance was more radical than the academic approach in relativizing the existent church divisions. Sometimes it rejected these divisions altogether.

A prominent figure in the Russian religious renaissance, Vladimir Solovyov (1853–1900), believed in the innate universality of the true Christianity. He criticized any particularization of the church. He believed that the mark of the true church is its care for a better society—without poverty and social injustice. He illustrated his views on differences between the Eastern and Western churches by retelling a legend about St. Nicholas and St. Cassian:

> A popular Russian legend tells how St. Nicolas and St. Cassian were upon a visit to the earth. On their journey they met a poor peasant who had got his wagon, with a load of hay upon it, stuck in the mud and was making fruitless efforts to get his horses on.
>
> "Let's go and give the good fellow a hand," said St. Nicolas.
>
> "Not I; I'm keeping out of it," replied St. Cassian, "I don't want to get my coat dirty."

**Figure 6.14** Decoration of the doors dedicated to Vatican I. Apostolic Palace in Vatican.

Source: Photo by the author.

> "Well, wait for me," said St. Nicolas, "or go on without me if you like," and plunging without hesitation into the mud he vigorously assisted the peasant in dragging his wagon out of the rut.
>
> When he had finished the job and caught his companion up, he was all covered in filth; his coat was torn and soiled and looked like a beggar's rags. St. Peter was amazed to see him arrive at the gate of Paradise in this condition.
>
> "I say! Who ever got you into that state?" he asked. St. Nicolas told his story.
>
> "And what about you?" asked St. Peter, turning to St. Cassian. "Weren't you with him in this encounter?"
>
> "Yes, but I don't meddle in things that are no concern of mine, and I was especially anxious not to get my beautiful clean coat dirty."
>
> "Very well," said St. Peter, "you, St. Nicolas, because you were not afraid of getting dirty in helping your neighbor out of a difficulty, shall for the future have two feasts a year, and you shall be reckoned the greatest of saints after me by all the peasants of holy Russia. And you, St. Cassian, must be content with having a nice clean coat; you shall have your feastday in leap-year only, once every four years."[1]

Archpriest Pavel Svetlov (1861–1945), who was a professor at Kyiv University, did not find any meaningful reason why all Christian churches should stay separated from each other. Divisions between all Christians, he believed, were caused by historical misunderstandings, and are preserved by confessional arrogance. In reality, however, all churches in both East and West constitute one universal Church of Christ (Светлов 1914: vol. 1: 209).

---

[1]Solovyov 1948: 39. St. Nicolas in the Orthodox tradition is celebrated twice a year: on May 9 and December 6. The feast day of St. John Cassian is on February 29.

**Figure 6.15** Grave of Nikolay Berdyayev in Clamart near Paris.
Source: Photo by the author.

Nikolay Berdyayev (1874–1948) adopted a different approach to the Christian divisions. For him, not a single extant church can pretend to identify itself with the universal church of Christ. All churches have their limitations, and all confuse their confessional identity with the universal revelation of Truth. Berdyayev's main target was confessionalism:

> A Confession, any Confession, is an historic individualisation of the one Christian Revelation, of the one Christian Truth. Since no Confession is able to be the full universal Truth, it is not able to be the Truth itself. A Confession is an historical category and it relates to an historical issue of the Divine-human religious process. A Confession is the confessing of faith in God by man, and not the full Truth revealed by God. And man himself adds on limitations to his confession of faith in God. A believer has an irresistible tendency to see a theophany in that which he himself has contributed to the historical religious process. His very own deeds appear to him like an objective truth revealed from without. National-historical faith-confessions in particular appear to be revelations objectively given. Church nationalism, although it were as vast as Latinism, is still an irresistible paganism within Christianity. A Christian is not able not to believe, that the Universal Church of Christ exists, and that in it are oneness, fullness and riches. But it is only partially, incompletely actualised in history, and much in it remains in a potential condition. Confessions with their own conjoining with nationalism and political forms, with their own limitations by certain types of thought and certain styles of culture are not able to pretend to be the contemporary actualised Universal Church, a contemporary expression of oneness and fullness. No confession in its human aspect is able to pretend to be the bearer of the fullness and

purity of Orthodoxy, Catholicity, and Evangelicity. Confessions always have limitations and often become ossified, obstructing the Spirit. No local Orthodox Church can pretend to be the bearer and expression of the fullness of Orthodoxy. The Orthodox Church exists as the true Universal Church, but this is not the Russian or the Greek Church, in which the Orthodoxy is subsumed. The Roman Catholic Church cannot pretend to be the bearer and expression of the fullness of Catholicity. And the many-denominationed Protestant Church cannot pretend to be the bearer and expression of the fullness and pureness of Evangelicity. People very often accept their own pride and self-conceit for faithfulness to Truth. But they become faithful not so much to Truth, as to themselves and their own limitations. (Бердяев 1933: 69–70; transl. by Fr. Stephen Janos, "Universality and Confessionalism": https://tinyurl.com/44u6ah6c [accessed on March 19, 2021])

# VI.9

# Era of Ecumenism

Despite these bold statements from individual thinkers, the Orthodox hierarchs in their majority continued to cherish confessionalism. The early twentieth-century turmoil, caused by the First World War, Russian revolutions, and Turkish genocides, pushed them to embrace more inclusive attitudes to other traditions. The new ecumenical spirit was captured by Berdyayev:

> We live in an universalist/ecumenical era, an era of world associations, religions, cultures, intellectualism, economics and politics. Worldly organisations, congresses, gatherings, diverse international meetings show the symptoms of a will detected everywhere for accord and association. This began after the bloody discord of the world war. Fierce nationalist passions still lacerate all the entire world. The sin and sickness of nationalism all still disfigure the Christian confessions. Already there is the possibility of yet a new war to torment the European nations. But never has there been such a yearning for unity, such a thirst for overcoming particularism and isolation. These worldly tendencies show themselves also in the life of Christian churches. The Ecumenical Question has become for Christian consciousness the question of the day. The Christian East issues forth from a condition of reticence and the Christian West as it were ceases to account itself the sole bearer of truth. Many write and speak about the coming-together of the divided parts of the Christian world, about the unification of the Church. They are beginning to be acutely aware, that the divisions and discords within Christianity is a great scandal before the face of an un-Christian even anti-Christian world. (Бердяев 1933: 69–70; transl. by Fr. Stephen Janos, "Universality and Confessionalism": https://tinyurl.com/44u6ah6c [accessed on March 19, 2021])

## Early Ecumenical Initiatives

It is usually believed that the modern ecumenical movement was launched at the conference on mission in Edinburgh in 1910. At that conference, new strategies of protestant mission were discussed, which envisioned cooperation instead of competition between churches. The Nobel Peace Prize winner John Mott (1865–1955) captured optimism that dominated the Edinburgh conference in the following words: "We go out <. . .> with a larger acquaintanceship, with deeper realization of this fellowship. <. . .> Our best days are ahead of us because we have a larger Christ" (Mott 1947: 19–20). The decades of ecumenical work that followed, demonstrated that ecumenical journey was not easy.

Orthodox churches joined the ecumenical movement with some reluctance. They looked at it as a Western and Protestant enterprise. To make ecumenism more acceptable by the Orthodox, the movement adopted some keywords from the traditional Eastern meta-language, such as *ecumene*, *kairos*, *koinonia*, and so on. The very word "ecumenism" has come from the Orthodox setting: *oecumene* meant the Greco-Roman universe dominated by the Eastern churches. The word *kairos* (καιρός) came to mean in the ecumenical language an ecumenical opportunity for the churches to get closer to each other. Finally, the goal of the ecumenical movement was defined as achieving full *koinonia* (κοινωνία)—communion between the churches.

Soon after the inception of the global ecumenical movement, the Orthodox churches, even if reluctantly, realized its potentiality and came up with their own initiatives. In 1920, the Ecumenical Patriarchate promulgated an encyclical letter *Unto the Churches of Christ Everywhere*. The letter referred to the newly established League of Nations (1919) and suggested to establish a similar inter-Christian organization to promote church unity. The encyclical listed a number of concrete proposals for achieving unity:

> Our own church holds that rapprochement between the various Christian Churches and fellowship between them is not excluded by the doctrinal differences which exist between them. In our opinion such a rapprochement is highly desirable and necessary. It would be useful in many ways for the real interest of each particular church and of the whole Christian body, and also for the preparation and advancement of that blessed union which will be completed in the future in accordance with the will of God. We therefore consider that the present time is most favourable for bringing forward this important question and studying it together. <. . .>
>
> Wherefore, considering such an endeavour to be both possible and timely, especially in view of the hopeful establishment of the League of Nations, we venture to express below in brief our thoughts and our opinion regarding the way in which we understand this rapprochement and contact and how we consider it to be realizable; we earnestly ask and invite the judgement and the opinion of the other sister churches in the East and of the venerable Christian churches in the West and everywhere in the world.
>
> We believe that the two following measures would greatly contribute to the rapprochement which is so much to be desired and which would be so useful, and we believe that they would be both successful and fruitful:
>
> First, we consider as necessary and indispensable the removal and abolition of all the mutual distrust and bitterness between the different churches which arise from the

tendency of some of them to entice and proselytize adherents of other confessions. For nobody ignores what is unfortunately happening today in many plates, disturbing the internal peace of the churches, especially in the East. So many troubles and sufferings are caused by other Christians and great hatred and enmity are aroused, with such insignificant results, by this tendency of some to proselytize and entice the followers or other Christian confessions.

After this essential re-establishment of sincerity and confidence between the churches, we consider,

Secondly, that above all, love should be rekindled and strengthened among the churches, so that they should no more consider one another as strangers and foreigners, but as relatives, and as being a part of the household of Christ and "fellow heirs, members of the same body and partakers of the promise of God in Christ" (Eph. 3:6). <. . .>

In our opinion, such a friendship and kindly disposition towards each other can be shown and demonstrated particularly in the following ways:

A. By the acceptance of a uniform calendar for the celebration of the great Christian feasts at the same time by all churches.
B. By the exchange of brotherly letters on the occasion of the great feasts of the churches' year as is customary, and on other exceptional occasions.
C. By close relationships between the representatives of all churches wherever they may be.
D. By relationships between the theological schools and the professors of theology; by the exchange of theological and ecclesiastical reviews, and of other works published in each church.
E. By exchanging students for further training between the seminaries of the different churches.
F. By convoking pan-Christian conferences in order to examine questions of common interest to all the churches.
G. By impartial and deeper historical study of doctrinal differences both by the seminaries and in books.
H. By mutual respect for the customs and practices in different churches.
I. By allowing each other the use of chapels and cemeteries for the funerals and burials of believers of other confessions dying in foreign lands.
J. By the settlement of the question of mixed marriages between the confessions.
K. Lastly, by whole-hearted mutual assistance for the churches in their endeavors for religious advancement, charity and so on. <. . .>

Being ourselves convinced of the necessity for establishing a contact and league (fellowship) between the churches and believing that the other churches share our conviction as stated above, at least as a beginning we request each one of them to send us in reply a statement of its own judgement and opinion on this matter so that common agreement or resolution having been reached, we may proceed together to

> its realization, and thus "speaking the truth in love, may grow up into Him in all things, which is the head, even Christ; from whom the whole body fitly joined together and compacted by that which every joint supplieth, according to the effectual working in the measure of every part, maketh increase of the body unto the edifying of itself in love" (Eph. 4:15,16). (*A New Translation of the 1920 Message of the Ecumenical Patriarchate* 1959)

Some of these proposals have become materialized, and some not. Some even provoked a schism inside the Eastern Christianity, like the one that suggested to have a uniformed calendar. Most Orthodox churches abandoned their traditional Julian calendar and adopted Gregorian. This step made some conservatives leave these churches. They formed schismatic "Old-calendarist" groups. These groups evolved to hierarchical structures parallel to the official ones, which they call "World Orthodoxy." They believe that the "World Orthodoxy" has compromised faith through ecumenism and became too worldly. Anti-ecumenism became a unifying platform for the networks of communities calling themselves "Genuine Orthodox Churches" (Γνήσιοι Ορθόδοξοι Χριστιανοί, Истинно Православные Церкви). Some of the "genuine" churches are in communion with each other, and others are not. They commonly reject the churches that participate in the ecumenical dialogues. They sometimes even do not recognize the baptisms and other sacraments in those churches. These networks resemble ancient schisms, which arose from moral rigorism, such as Donatism or Melitianism.

In 1910 in Edinburgh, Bishop Charles H. Brent (1862–1929) from the Episcopal Church in the United States suggested to convene a conference on what he called "faith and order." This idea was materialized only in 1927, when the First World Conference on Faith and Order was held in Lausanne, Switzerland. A Continuation Committee followed up and met almost every year afterward. The main purpose of the Faith and Order movement was to discuss the issues of Christian unity from the theological perspective. It ran in parallel to the Life and Work movement, which focused on the practical issues of Christian common action in charity.

The Orthodox churches contributed to the work of both movements from their beginning. However, they gave preference to the Faith and Order because of its focus on theology. A metropolitan from the Ecumenical Patriarchate, Germanos Strenopoulos of Thyateira (1872–1951), addressed the assembly in Lausanne with the following words:

> Brethren, on receiving the invitation of the Organizing Committee of the world Conference on Faith and Order seven years ago, the Orthodox Church answered readily by sending representatives from her particular Orthodox Churches to the preliminary Conference in 1920 at Geneva. That delegation of the Orthodox Church put before the Conference a united declaration in general terms of the teaching of their Church in the matter of faith and order, and at its conclusion recommended that

before any discussion of the reunion of the Churches in faith and order, a League of Churches should be established for their mutual co-operation in regard to the social and moral principles of Christendom. Further, when the Orthodox Church was invited a short time ago to take part through her representatives in the present Conference, although any of her particular Churches are in distress so grave as to threaten their very existence, she has hastened to send her delegation to it.

Accordingly, we, the undersigned, delegates of the Orthodox Church, being inspired by a sincere feeling of love and by a desire to achieve an understanding, have taken part in every meeting held here for the purpose of promulgating closer brotherhood and fellowship between the representatives of the different Churches and for the general good and welfare of the whole body of Christians. But while sharing the general labours of the Conference both in delivering addresses as arranged in the programme and in taking part in the open debates, as also in the work of the Sections, we have concluded with regret that the bases assumed for the foundation of the Reports, which are to be submitted to the vote of the Conference, are inconsistent with the principles of the Orthodox Church we represent. <. . .>

The Orthodox Church adheres fixedly to the principle that the limits of individual liberty of belief are determined by the definitions made by the whole Church, which definitions we maintain to be obligatory on each individual. This principle holds good for us not only as to the present members of the Orthodox Church, but also as to those who, in the future, may become united with it in faith and order. Moreover, the symbols which would be accepted by the united Church acquire their importance (in our conception as Orthodox) not only from the fact of their being historical witnesses of the faith of the primative Church, but above all because the Church has affirmed their validity in her Oecumenical Councils. It should be unnecessary for us to add that the Orthodox Church recognizes and accepts as an Oecumenical Symbol only the Creed of Nicea-Constantinople.

That which holds good for us in regard to the Oecumenical Symbol holds good also in regard to the dogmatic definitions of the Seven Oecumenical Councils, the authority of which no Orthodox would be justified in shaking.

Therefore the mind of the Orthodox Church is that reunion can take place only on the basis of the common faith and confession of the ancient, undivided Church of the seven Oecumenical Councils and of the first eight centuries. (In Patelos 1978: 79–81)

# Ecumenism during the Cold War

The proposal of the Patriarchal encyclical from 1920 to set up an international institution to promote ecumenism similar to the League of Nations could be materialized only after the Second World War, in the wake of the establishment of the United Nations. The World Council of Churches (WCC) was established in 1948 in Amsterdam. Geneva was chosen as the place for the WCC headquarters.

The majority of the WCC members are different churches representing the Reformation. Roman Catholic Church decided not to join the WCC. Orthodox churches, including Oriental ones, constitute its minority. It was decided from the beginning that Eastern autocephalous churches can be individual members of the WCC. Each would have its own vote.

In the spirit of this arrangement, some Orthodox churches took part in the Amsterdam meeting and others abstained. Those abstained gathered the same year in Moscow, to celebrate 500 years since the self-proclaimed independence of the Russian Orthodox Church. The Moscow council criticized recent ecumenical initiatives in Amsterdam and adopted a conservative agenda. Some churches that came to the Moscow meeting subscribed to its anti-ecumenical rhetoric sincerely, while some not quite so. They complied with the new Soviet policies to use ecumenical movement as an instrument of foreign politics. In the last years of Joseph Stalin, the interest of the Soviet state was to promote anti-ecumenism, because it was anti-Western, and, therefore, fitted the Cold War agenda.

The Soviet state capitalized on the fears shared by many Orthodox that the WCC would become a superchurch that would substitute the existent churches. It cannot be ruled out that some Protestant stakeholders of the WCC did not have such superchurch on their mind. For most Orthodox, however, such ecumenical scenario would mean apostasy. The fears and protests of the Orthodox, it seems, corrected the initial scenario, if it existed. Two years after its founding, the WCC, at its General

**Figure 6.16** The headquarters of the World Council of Churches in Geneva.
Source: Photo by the author.

Assembly in Toronto (1950), made necessary clarifications regarding what is its own nature. The key document adopted by the Assembly, *The Church, the Churches and the World Council of Churches: The ecclesiological Significance of the World Council of Churches*, stated that the WCC is not a quasi-church, but a fellowship of the churches that represent different traditions.

Under Nikita Khrushchev (leader of the Soviet state in 1953–64), Soviet policies regarding ecumenism changed. The Kremlin and its satellites in the Warsaw Pact encouraged the churches in their orbit to join the ecumenical movement. As a result, at the General assembly of the WCC in New Delhi (1961), some churches from the Communist bloc joined this ecumenical organization. The churches from this block, on the one hand, promoted through the WCC the political agenda of their political regimes. On the other hand, they sought protection from the oppression of the Communist state. Whatever was the motivation of the Orthodox churches to participate in the WCC, their voices in this organization became stronger after the General Assembly in New Delhi. They then issued a special statement with a common vision about the Orthodox participation in the ecumenical movement:

> The ecumenical problem, as it is understood in the current ecumenical movement, is primarily a problem of the Protestant world. The main question, in this setting, is that of "Denominationalism." Accordingly, the problem of Christian unity, or of Christian Reunion, is usually regarded in terms of an interdenominational agreement or Reconciliation. In the Protestant universe of discourse such approach is quite natural. But for the Orthodox it is uncongenial. For the Orthodox the basic ecumenical problem is that or schism. The Orthodox cannot accept the idea of a "parity of denomination" and cannot visualize Christian Reunion just as an interdenominational adjustment. The unity has been broken and must be recovered. The Orthodox Church is not a confession, one of many, one among the many. For the Orthodox, the Orthodox Church is just the Church. The Orthodox Church is aware and conscious of the identity of her inner structure and of her teaching with the Apostolic message (*kerygma*) and the tradition of the ancient undivided Church. She finds herself in an unbroken and continuous succession of sacramental ministry, sacramental life and faith. Indeed, for the Orthodox the apostolic succession of episcopacy and sacramental priesthood is an essential and constitutive, and therefore obligatory element of the Church's very existence. The Orthodox Church, by her inner conviction and consciousness, has a special and exceptional position in the divided Christendom, as the bearer of, and the witness to, the tradition of the ancient undivided Church, from which all existing denominations stem, by the way of reduction and separation. (In Patelos 1978: 97–8)

A key ecumenical figure in the Communist bloc was the metropolitan of Leningrad and Novgorod Nikodim Rotov (1929–78). He advocated for the participation of the Russian church in the WCC and promoted other ecumenical engagements for his church. During his tenure as a chairman of the Department of External

Church Relations (DECR) of the Moscow Patriarchate, he was regarded as the most influential official in the church. His vision of ecumenism, church-state relations, and the church's activities in the public space, shaped the policies of the Russian Orthodox Church regarding these issues for decades. His attitude to the ecumenical movement was sincere and, at the same time, instrumentalizing. He believed in the ideal of Christian unity and simultaneously used ecumenical fora to promote the interests of the Soviet state. Here is an example of Nikodim's ecumenical speech, which was delivered at the General Assembly of the WCC in Uppsala (1968). In this speech, he explained the rationale of the Russian participation in this organization:

> What was it then which incited the Russian Orthodox Church to join the World Council of Churches? My answer is this: firstly, the love of brethren who feel how baneful are the divisions between Christians, and who declare their desire to eliminate the obstacles to fulfilling the will of our Lord Jesus Christ "that they may all be one" (Jn 17:21). Secondly, awareness of the importance of coordinating the efforts of all Christians, in their witness and service to men in the complex conditions of the secularized world of today, subject to rapid changes, divided, but aspiring to unity. <. . .>
>
> The way in which the Russian Orthodox Church took the decision to join the WCC clearly indicates that this act was never considered as having an ecclesiologically obligatory meaning for the Orthodox conscience. It would be more exact not to speak of the Russian Orthodox Church "joining" the WCC, still less "being admitted" to the WCC, but rather of an agreement between the leaders of the Russian Orthodox Church and those of the World Council of Churches for representatives of the Russian Orthodox Church to enter into permanent collaboration with representatives of other Churches belonging to an association called the World Council of Churches. The Assembly held at New Delhi in 1961 gave its consent to a collaboration of this kind. (In Patelos 1978: 267–9)

Metropolitan of Sourozh Anthony Bloom (1914–2003) urged the ecumenical movement, while avoiding political partisanship, to demonstrate solidarity with the suffering churches. In his sermon at the meeting of the Central Committee of the WCC in Western Berlin, he addressed the Christian disunity in the following words:

> We are divided through sin but also through our conflicting loyalties. These we cannot abandon without denying our integrity. We stand separated before the table of the Lord. He calls us to come, but we dare not come together to His table, because to do this would be a lie. It would assert a unity which is lost, a oneness which is to be reconquered, but is not yet possessed. This oneness can come to us only as a gift from God when we have become true Christians, not only in our faith, but also in every manifestation of life.
>
> But is there nothing that we can do to accomplish together this commandment of Christ? Are we so hopeless, so ultimately divided at the Lord's table? <. . .>

Don't we hear Him speak to all of us and say: "Go into the world of men of your own free will, uncoerced, as I have done. Take upon yourselves all the limitations of the fallen world. Make your own all its pain, all its hunger, all its loneliness, all its misery, but make also your own all its love, all its beauty, all its incipient glory and abiding love. Live in the midst of men; but remain free from fear, from greed, from pride, from hatred. Live with and for them, live long, long lives." <. . .>

These things and many more are significant in the broken bread, in the cup shed. Until we follow in His steps and do these very things in remembrance of Him, it will not be given to us to share the holy meal which is the proclamation of His resurrection, which is the foretaste of the Kingdom of God. Let us do together all that we can already do together in faithfulness and obedience. Live and if necessary die, as Christ has taught us, both singly and in the great fellowship of the disciples of Christ. Then will we discover that the barriers which separate us will have fallen. (In Patelos 1978: 339–42)

# Ecumenical Skepticism

As was mentioned, many Orthodox look at ecumenism with suspicion or even condemn it. For some, ecumenism is a part of the global liberal agenda. Those who pursue a conservative agenda often position themselves as anti-ecumenists. For others, ecumenism is arch-heresy. Different attitudes to ecumenism, based on ideological preferences, have become a part of the culture wars waged in the Eastern Christian world.

All Orthodox churches have groups, which are more conservative and more liberal. Although conservatives usually criticize the official ecumenism, they sometimes develop their own ecumenical rapprochement—with conservative groups in other churches. They look not for the restoration of unity but for ideological alliances to enhance their positions to win their culture wars. The sort of ecumenism they pursue is "cultural" or "ideological." It features a strong political agenda, but undermines the traditional theological agendas of their churches. It also contributes to widening the chasm between ideological factions in their own churches.

"Ideological" ecumenism contributes to the growth of fundamentalism. Fundamentalism is a reaction of conservative groups within a religious community to modernization outside and inside the church. Fundamentalists usually have two fronts of fighting: one with the modernity in general, and the other one with those who seek *aggiornamento* of their religious traditions with the modern world. Fundamentalists consider such *aggiornamento* an unacceptable concession to the fallen world, a manifestation of apostasy. Ecumenism for them is a token of such apostasy.

Despite their antagonism, both open-minded and conservative Christian groups are well intended—each in its own way. They do care about the church's unity.

However, they interpret this unity differently. For the ecumenically minded groups, unity is the reintegration of the fragmented Christianity into one church. The anti-ecumenical groups primarily care about preserving the integrity of extant communities. They fear that any outreach or encounter with a different tradition can damage this integrity. Because of their conservative attitudes, they do not entertain any changes in the status quo of their communities.

The dialectics of ecumenical and anti-ecumenical approaches to the church's unity is a part of the dialectics of openness and closeness, which all Christian churches feature to different extents. This dialectics goes back to the apostolic times. The early Judeo-Christian community also had hot debates about whether to step out and reach to the pagan world, putting at risk its own integrity. Eventually, the party of the open-minded "ecumenists," with Paul as their spearhead, won, and Christianity became a universal religion. In a similar way, pro- and counter-ecumenical groups in all churches never ceased to argue: Can they talk to other churches or should they stay closed inside their own traditions? It seems that only through the efforts of ecumenical groups, the unity of the fragmented Christianity can be eventually restored. However, the conservative voices should be heard as well. Without this voice, the integrity of the existent communities can be in peril.

One of such conservative voices was Justin Popović's (1894–1979). He knew the ecumenical movement from within, and criticized it as a challenge to the integrity of the Eastern Christianity. He even called ecumenism a pan-heresy. Justin did not acknowledge the validity of the sacraments outside the Orthodox church. The only way of restoring church unity, for him, was when others convert to Orthodoxy and completely reject their previous tenets. This resembles a medieval pattern of doing ecumenism, which Justin applied to the modern inter-Christian relations:

> Ecumenism is the common name for the pseudo-Christianity of the pseudo-churches of Western Europe. It contains the heart of European humanism, with papism as its head. All of pseudo-Christianity, all of those pseudo-churches, are nothing more than one heresy after another. Their common evangelical name is pan-heresy. Why? Because through the course of history various heresies denied or deformed certain aspects of the God-man and Lord Jesus Christ; these European heresies remove him altogether and put European man in [Jesus'] place. In this there is no essential difference between papism, Protestantism, ecumenism, and other heresies, whose name is "Legion." <. . .>
>
> Protestantism? It is the loyal child of papism. It went from one heresy to another over the centuries because of its rationalistic scholasticism, and it is continually drowning in the various poisons of its heretical errors. In addition, papal haughtiness and "infallible" foolishness reign absolutely within it, ruining the souls of its faithful. First of all each Protestant is an independent pope when it comes to matters of faith. This always leads from one spiritual death to another; and there is no end to this "dying" since a person can suffer countless spiritual deaths in a lifetime.

Since this is the way things are, there is no way out of this impasse, for the Papist-Protestant ecumenism with its pseudo-church and its pseudo-Christianity, without wholehearted repentance before the God-man Christ and his Orthodox catholic church. Repentance is the remedy for every sin, the medicine given to man by the only friend of man—Christ.

Without repentance and admittance into the true church of Christ, it is unthinkable and unnatural to speak about unification of "the churches," about the dialogue of love, about intercommunion (which is to say, the common cup). <. . .>

The naked moralistic, minimalistic, and humanistic pacifism of contemporary ecumenists does only one thing: it brings to light their diseased humanistic roots, which is to say, their sick philosophy and feeble morality "according to the human tradition" (Col. 2:8). They reveal the crisis of their humanistic faith, as well as their presumptuous insensibility for the history of the church, i.e., for its apostolic and catholic continuation in truth and in grace. <. . .>

In Orthodox teaching about the church and the sacraments, the single most unique mystery is the church itself, the body of the God-man Christ, so that [the church] is the only source and content of all divine sacraments. Outside of this theanthropic and inclusive mystery of the church—the pan-mystery itself—there are no and cannot be any "mysteries"; therefore, there can be no intercommunion of mysteries. Consequently we can only speak about mysteries within the context of this unique pan-mystery, which is the church. This is because the Orthodox Church—as the body of Christ—is the source and the foundation of the sacraments and not the other way around. The mysteries, or sacraments, cannot be elevated above the church, or examined outside the body of the church. <. . .>

The Orthodox Church does not recognize the existence of other mysteries or sacraments outside of itself, nor does it recognize them as being mysteries, and one cannot receive the sacraments until one comes away from the heretical "churches" (i.e., the pseudo-churches) through repentance before the Orthodox Church of Christ. Until then one remains outside the church, un-united with it through repentance, remaining—as far as the church is concerned—a heretic and consequently outside the saving Communion. "What fellowship has righteousness with unrighteousness and what communion has light with darkness?" (2 Cor. 6:14) <. . .>

But you might ask: Will it be possible for this generation, this most erring, deluded generation in the history of man, to return to honesty and the truth? Can it? Would that the Christ they despise let this happen as soon as possible. But when will it happen?

It is only going to happen when our Western brothers start writing books glorifying Christ our God, and when their thousands of newspapers print praises of Christian virtues and Christian good works, instead of writing about crimes and blasphemies against the divine majesty and about the commerce of vile instincts. When this transformation takes place, then Western heretical humanity will be cleansed, and it will smell sweetly of heavenly incense.

Then we Orthodox Christians will rejoice because we will receive our returning brothers. (Popović 2013: 169–96)

Another important conservative voice that criticized ecumenism belongs to the Romanian theologian Dumitru Stăniloae. In his early writings, he repudiated the ecumenical movement altogether. However, as he began participating in the ecumenical meetings, he gradually changed his attitude to other confessions and the ecumenical movement in general. Toward the end of his life, he recognized some value in the Western Christian traditions and even articulated the principles of involvement in the ecumenical movement for the Romanian Orthodox church:

> God reveals himself and operates through different acts, words, and images, for He does not exhaust his own being in any of them. <. . .> Since God has considered these ways worthy to reveal himself, one should not disregard any of them. Yet one should not regard any of these ways <. . .> as fully expressing God, thereby excluding for the future other possible ways of revealing God. <. . .> One should not attach oneself to any or to all of them as to the final reality, as Bonhoeffer and Congar say, because all of them are penultimate. <. . .> This means that one must recognize all Christian ways of expressing God as having a certain value, but equally a certain insufficiency, or degree of relativity. Both these attitudes of Christian conscience can help us to advance on the path of unity between Christians. (In Coman 2019: 64)

# VI.10

# Church and World

The church was established with the ultimate goal to eventually engulf the entire world. The world's size indicates the potentiality of the church's mission: how big the church can grow. In the terms of quantity, the church potentially—τῇ δυνάμει, to put it in the logical categories—can be what the world actually is. The church also demonstrates what the world *can be* in the terms of quality. In other words, the world *potentially* (τῇ δυνάμει) is what the church is *actually* (τῇ ἐνεργείᾳ). In the *eschaton*, the world's and the church's potentiality and actuality should be equated.

Now, the world, on the one hand, is opposite to the church; it is an anti-church, as it were. The author of 1 John urged his readers: "Do not love the world or the things in the world. If anyone loves the world, the love of the Father is not in him. For all that is in the world—the desires of the flesh and the desires of the eyes and pride of life—is not from the Father but is from the world" (15–16). On the other hand, the mission of the church is to transform this anti-church into the Kingdom of God.

This mission becomes possible only if the church's dynamism is centrifugal, not centripetal. The centripetal church surrounds itself with high walls; its borderlines turn to well-guarded ditches. They become ever-expanding frontiers (see Hovorun 2017: 163–80), however, when the members of the church care to convert the potentialities of both the world and the church to actuality, by fulfilling the "great commission": "Go therefore and make disciples of all nations, baptizing them in the name of the Father and of the Son and of the Holy Spirit, teaching them to observe all that I have commanded you." (Mt. 28:19-20). The *Encyclical of the Holy and Great Council of the Orthodox Church* captured this idea:

> The apostolic work and the proclamation of the Gospel, also known as mission, belong at the core of the Church's identity, as the keeping and observation of Christ's commandment: "Go and make disciples of all nations" (Mt. 28:19). This is the "breath of life" that the Church breathes into human society and makes the world into Church through the newly-established local Churches everywhere. In this spirit, the Orthodox faithful are and ought to be Christ's apostles in the world. This mission must be fulfilled, not aggressively, but freely, with love and respect towards the cultural identity

> of individuals and peoples. (II 6; https://tinyurl.com/1tv2mre8 [accessed on February 13, 2021])

This council, convened in Crete in the period of Pentecost of 2016, is also known as Panorthodox. It epitomized several decades of the engagements of the Orthodox churches in the ecumenical movement and in the dialogue with the modern world. Its decisions reflect the complexity and often inconsistencies of such engagements. Nevertheless, as the *Message* of this council states,

> The Holy and Great Council has opened our horizon towards the contemporary diverse and multifarious world. It has emphasised our responsibility in place and in time, ever with the perspective of eternity. The Orthodox Church, preserving intact her Sacramental and Soteriological character, is sensitive to the pain, the distress and the cry for justice and peace of the peoples of the world. She "proclaims day after day the good tidings of His salvation, announcing His glory among the nations and His wonders among all peoples" (Ps. 95). (Article 12; https://tinyurl.com/1tv2mre8 [accessed on February 13, 2021])

# VII

## World

# VII.1

# Classical Cosmogonies

The idea of salvation and sanctification frames the Christian theories about the world—in the same way as it frames all other theological discourses. This idea differentiates the Christian teaching about the world from the Greek cosmology and cosmogony. Ancient Greek philosophers and Christian theologians spoke about the world in a similar language and used similar categories, such as *kosmos*, *arché*, matter, time, and so on. They often perceived them in different ways.

## Cosmogony as Theogony

Since at least Hesiod (flourished *c.* 700 BC), the Greeks connected the origins of the world (cosmogony) with the origins of gods (theogony). In this regard, the Greek cosmogony was not much different from the Egyptian or Hittite or Babylonian ones (see Sassi 2018: 33), which also explained the world through theogonic myths. The Greeks, however, made a leap forward and conceptualized theogonic myths to philosophical ideas. They began seeing the world as "parsimonious, invariant, consistent and natural" (Gregory 2007: 53). Such disenchanted Greek world was not quite Cartesian, because it continued to be imbued with the divine presence, which could take different forms.

## Soul of World

The Greeks continued seeing the world as an alive being. Although it did not have its persona, it certainly featured a soul. For example, Thales of Miletus (*c.* 625–546 BC), who among the first suggested a nonmythical explanation of the world, still envisaged this world to be ensouled. The world's "soul," which he also called "mind," was for him divine: "God is the mind (νοῦν) of the world (τοῦ κόσμου)" (in Aëtius doxogr., *De placitis reliquiae* 301). More than a century later, Anaxagoras of Clazomenae (*c.* 500–428/27 BC) introduced a distance between the world and the divine mind. The latter, for him, is "unlimited (ἄπειρον) and self-ruling (αὐτοκρατές) and has been mixed with no thing, but is alone itself by itself" (*fr.* B12; Anaxagoras 2007: 22–3).

# Motion

Soul explained why the world and its elements change. What we nowadays identify as fundamental interactions (gravitational, electromagnetic, strong, and weak), the ancient Greeks described as the world's soul. Plato was particularly insightful about this: "Soul drives all things in Heaven and earth and sea by its own motions" (*Leges* 897a). Motion, thus, became a precondition sine qua non for the world to become *kosmos*—beautiful and logical. Aristotle's physics was focused on motion. The world's motion or, in other words, change, does not have beginning—because, as Aristotle put it in his *Physics*, "every mover too is moved" (*Physica* III 2.202a). For Aristotle, this made the idea of the beginning of the world absurd.

# *Archai*

The idea that the *kosmos* emerged from preexistent "principles" or "beginnings" (*archai*, ἀρχαί), was shared by more or less all ancient Greek writers. For Homer (flourished in the ninth or eighth century BC), this preexistent something was the Ocean, "from whom the gods are sprung."[1] Homeric Ocean was a person-like deity. Thales degraded him to impersonal water (see Aristotle, *De caelo* II 13.294a).

The Orpheans saw the initial something as the darkness of the night: "I will praise night as the mother of gods and men" (*Orphica* III 1). Hesiod suggested that prior to this night, there was *chaos* (χάος), which is better to be translated as "chasm" and not "chaos": "First of all Chasm (Χάος) came to be. <. . .> From Chasm, Erebos and black Night came to be" (*Theogonia* 117).

The preexistence of *chaos* became the Newton's laws of the post-Hesiodic Greek physics. Anaximander (610–547 BC), who was one generation younger than Thales and who lived in the same Ionian city of Miletus, interpreted *chaos* as "the unlimited" (*apeiron*, ἄπειρον) (in Aëtius doxogr., *De placitis reliquiae* 277). "The unlimited" is the principle of everything, including gods, but has no its own beginning. As Aristotle explained, "There is no beginning of [the unlimited], but it is this which is held to be

[1] *Ilias* 14.200, 301. According to Plato's commentary, Homer "declared all things to be generated from flux and motion" (*Theaetetus* 152e; see *Cratylus* 402b).

**Figure 7.1** Okeanos and his wife Tethys, a second to third century AD mosaic from a house in Seleucia on the Euphrates. Now in Zeugma Museum, Turkey.

Source: Photo by the author.

**Figure 7.2** Double-sided herm of Aristotle. National Archaeological Museum in Athens.

Source: Photo by the author.

the beginning of other things." Moreover, "the unlimited," for Aristotle, is "both uncreatable and indestructible" (*Physica* III 2.203b).

## Kosmos *versus* Matter

The Greeks counterposed *kosmos* to *chaos* (see Gregory 2007: 1). From this perspective, the latter came to be interpreted in the sense of unordered matter. This matter, having been ordered, appropriates beauty and turns to *kosmos* (see Horky 2019). Counterposition between the ordered *kosmos* and unordered matter is called hylomorphism (see Manning 2013). It was a common belief shared by most non-Christian and some Christian thinkers in Antiquity (see Rasmussen 2019: 86). Aristotle rendered hylomorphism in logical categories:

> The word "*ousia*" (οὐσία) is applied, if not in more senses, still at least to four main objects; for the existence (τὶ εἶναι) and the common (καθόλου) and the genus (γένος) are thought to be the *ousia* (οὐσία) of each thing, and fourthly the subject (τὸ ὑποκείμενον). Now the subject is that of which other things are predicated, while it is itself not predicated of anything else. And so we must first determine the nature of this; for that which underlies a thing primarily is thought to be in the truest sense its *ousia*. And in one sense matter (ὕλη) is said to be of the nature of subject, in another, shape, and in a third sense, the compound of these. By the matter I mean, for instance, the bronze, by the shape the plan of its form, and by the compound of these (the concrete thing) the statue. Therefore if the form is prior to the matter and more real, it will be prior to the compound also for the same reason. (*Metaphysica* VII 3.1028b-1029a)

Long before Aristotle, Anaxagoras had suggested that the principle that caused the kosmic order was divine mind (νοῦς). Diogenes Laërtius (flourished in the third century AD) summarized his idea as follows: "All things were together; then came Mind and set them in order" (*Vitae philosophorum* II 6). "Set in order" here translates the verb *diekosmese* (διεκόσμησε), which can be also translated as "embellished" or "made kosmos." Plato defined this kosmic mind as demiurge (δημιουργός)—a designer of the world (see Broadie 2014):

> He was good, and in him that is good no envy ariseth ever concerning anything; and being devoid of envy He desired that all should be, so far as possible, like unto Himself. This principle, then, we shall be wholly right in accepting from men of wisdom as being above all the supreme originating principle of Becoming and the Cosmos. For God desired that, so far as possible, all things should be good and nothing evil; wherefore, when He took over all that was visible, seeing that it was not in a state of rest but in a state of discordant and disorderly motion, He brought it into order out of disorder, deeming that the former state is in all ways better than the latter. (*Timaeus* 30a)

**Figure 7.3** Plato. Library of the Trinity College in Dublin.
Source: Photo by the author.

Plato's physics was quite unique for his time, because it implied a significant degree of the world's createdness. The Platonic world was not as radically created as the Christian world, yet it was not as much uncreated as most ancient Greek philosophers before and after him assumed (see Sedley 2007).

## World's Eternity

Pre-Socratic Heraclitus (*c.* 544–484 BC) was among the first who stated clearly that the *kosmos* is eternal: it is "the same for all, no god or man made, but it always was, is, and will be" (*Fr.* 30; Heraclitus 1991: 25). Another pre-Socratic, Parmenides (*c.* 515–450 BC), substantiated the world's eternity by the logical conclusion that anything cannot come from nothing. Moreover, to say or even think anything about nothing would be an oxymoron: "Neither from what-is-not shall I allow you to say or think." In full contrast to it, "what-is" holds existential completeness, which cannot be taken from it: "What-is is ungenerated and imperishable; whole, single-limbed, steadfast, and complete (*fr.* 8; Parmenides 2011: 70–1). In the period of Christian Antiquity, this idea would be appropriated and elaborated upon by Ps.-Dionysius the Areopagite.

The most famous promoter of the idea of the world's eternity was Aristotle. He criticized those who either implicitly or explicitly affirmed the beginning of the world, including Plato. His argument was that even if matter was generated, it still should come from something else. Therefore, there always should be something else preceding any assumed creation:

> If it (i.e., matter) came to be, something must have existed as a primary substratum from which it should come and which should persist in it; but this is its own very nature, so that it will be before coming to be. For my definition of matter is just this—the primary substratum of each thing, from which it comes to be, and which persists in the result, not accidentally. (*Physica*, I 9.192a)

## *Ex Nihilo*

At the same time, if not the entire world, at least some of its aspects were perceived by the Greeks as having emerged *ex nihilo*—from nothing. Plato, for example, assumed that time has beginning. Aristotle famously blamed him for this assumption: "Plato alone asserts the creation of time, saying that it is simultaneous with the world, and that the world came into being" (*Physica* VIII 1.251b). For Aristotle, there cannot be time or space or anything else before, after, or beyond this world: "There is no

**Figure 7.4** Aristotle. Library of the Trinity College in Dublin.
Source: Photo by the author.

place or void or time outside the heaven" (*De caelo* I 9.279a). Since the world has no beginning or end, so the time is eternal: "There must always be time" (*Physica* VIII 1.251b). At the same time, even Aristotle was prepared to admit something, or rather someone, as the initial cause in the world. This is the Prime Mover (see Kosman 2017), who moves all other things, but is not moved by anyone or anything else:

> Whatever is divine, whatever is primary and supreme, is necessarily unchangeable. <. . .> There is nothing else stronger than it to move it—since that would be more divine—and it has no defect and lacks none of its proper excellences. Its unceasing movement, then, is also reasonable, since everything ceases to move when it comes to its proper place. (*De caelo* I 9.279a)

Both ideas, of the beginning of time and of the original Mover, would become important in the Christian theology. Another Greek idea would be appropriated by the Christians—that of the rationale and the ultimate goal of the world—its *telos* (τέλος).

## Teleology

A number of pre-Socratics, including Empedocles and Anaxagoras, expressed belief that the world has a rational driving force and a goal. They define the way in which the world is developing. Plato brought teleology to its logical end—the concept of Demiurge, who transforms the chaotic disorder to the beauty and rationality of the *kosmos* (see Plato, *Timaeus* 30a). Later Platonic and Stoic traditions followed this train of thought (see Reydams-Schils 1999). Christians would render teleology as providentiality, and *telos* as *eschaton* (see Burns 2020).

## End of the World

Most ancient Greeks believed that the world would not cease to exist—it can only be modified. Even Plato, while asserting that the *kosmos* has been formed by the Demiurge and thus has a beginning, believed that it has no end. To be more precise, the world can have end, if the Demiurge would have wanted it. However, because the world is perfect, there are no reasons for the Demiurge to destroy what he has created. The Demiurge himself assures in the *Timaeus*:

> Those works whereof I am framer (δημιουργός) and father are indissoluble save by my will. For though all that is bound may be dissolved, yet to will to dissolve that which is fairly joined together and in good case were the deed of a wicked one. (*Timaeus* 41b)

Plato's idea that the world has the beginning, but not the end, was criticized by Aristotle, who saw this idea as inconsistent. The Stagirite accused Plato of contradicting the axiom that if there is a beginning of something, there must be an end to it, and vice versa. Aristotle himself tried to be consistent with this axiom. He asserted that the world has neither beginning nor end:

> The heaven as a whole neither came into being nor admits of destruction, as some assert, but is one and eternal, with no end or beginning of its total duration, containing and embracing in itself the infinity of time. (*De caelo* II 1.283b)

# Multiverse

At the same time, Plato and Aristotle agreed that the world is one. They together opposed the idea of multiple worlds (see Rubenstein 2014; Warren 2004). Those who believed in multiverse usually held that the worlds are driven not by any rationale or *telos*, but by chance (see Aristotle, *Physica* II 4). Some of such philosophers suggested that several worlds can exist in parallel to each other. This was the opinion of Leucippus (flourished around 440 BC) and Democritus (flourished around 420 BC). Others believed in a consequent series of worlds.

# Cyclical Cosmogony

Empedocles (*c.* 495–435 BC) was particularly famous for introducing such a cyclical cosmogony (see O'Brien 2008): "Insofar as they (the worlds) never cease their continual exchange, so far they are forever unaltered in the circle" (*fr.* 8 (17); Empedocles 1981: 96–7). The circle itself, however, does not feature beginning or end. Empedocles stressed the importance of chance in moving forward the circle of the worlds' transformations (see Gregory 2007: 78): "And earth, anchored in the perfect harbors of Aphrodite, chanced to come together with them" (*fr.* 83 (98); Empedocles 1981: 125, 237). John Philoponus, who among the Christian theologians was most interested in the issues of cosmogony, left an important testimony about Empedocles' idea of mechanical chance:

> Empedocles says that it is by chance that air seized the upper position, all things having at one time been previously mixed together in the sphere, having been separated out by strife, each was carried to the place where it is now, not by providence, but by chance. Indeed, concerning the upward motion of the air he says: "Thus at one time it ran by chance, but many times it was otherwise." Water is now on top of the earth, but at another time, if it chanced to happen in another kosmos making, when

> again the kosmos is generated from the sphere, a different order and place would be obtained. He also says that most of the parts of animals were generated through chance as though through forethought. (*In Aristotelis physicorum libros commentaria* 261; Gregory 2007: 90)

The two moving forces behind the cyclical transformations that Empedocles advocated for are love (φιλότης) and strife (νεῖκος). The former contributes to unity and homogeneity of the world, while the latter to its diversity. When love increases, strife decreases, and vice versa. Any change in the proportions between love and strife makes the world to change. In the posterior patristic literature, Maximus the Confessor would have similar deliberations on how God's love brings the world to unity (see Törönen 2007). There is, however, a significant difference between the patristic and Ancient Greek takes on these moving forces. For Empedocles, strife and not love constitutes the reason why human beings exist: "Alas, poor unhappy race of mortal creatures, from what strifes and lamentations were you born" (*fr.* 114 (124); Empedocles 1981: 141–2, 279).

Cyclical cosmogony constituted the cornerstone of the Stoic cosmogony. For Stoics, the worlds succeed one another through *ekpyrosis* (ἐκπύρωσις): a preceding world being consumed by fire and the succeeding world being born from the same fire. Only one God and the matter, from which the world is formed, could survive this fire: "Matter and God are the only things preserved in the fire" (Alexander of Aphrodisias, *De mixtione* 226; Todd 1976: 142–3).

# VII.2

# Christian Cosmogonies

## Stoic Fire and the Book of Revelation

The Stoic idea of the world ending in or changing through fire correlates with the image of the end of this world in the book of Revelation: "A new heaven and a new earth" (Rev. 21:1) emerge after "Death and Hades were thrown into the lake of fire" (Rev. 20:14). The book of Revelation also speaks of Christ, whose eyes, in his second coming, will be "like a flame of fire" (1:14; 2:18; 19:12). This image resembles the Stoic idea that God is fire.[1] Such parallels are not surprising, given the influence of the Stoic language and imagery on Christian literature during the first and second centuries. Stoic motifs were particularly rich in the Johannine texts (see Engberg-Pedersen 2018; Buch-Hansen 2010).

## Christian Hylomorphism

Notwithstanding these similarities, the Christian interpretations of the beginning and the end of the world were different from what had been postulated in the pagan Antiquity. In contrast to the latter, most early Christian authors emphasized the creation of the world by one God from the complete zero—*ex nihilo*. They were clear on this point even more than the primary source of their cosmogony—the book of Genesis. Indeed, the first verses of this book are open-ended. The verse "The earth was without form and void, and darkness was over the face of the deep" (Gen. 1:2) can be interpreted in the Hesiodian or Orphic sense of the darkness of the night and *chaos* that preceded fashioning the *kosmos*. The first verse, "In the beginning, God created the heavens and the earth," also does not say explicitly that they were created

[1]See the testimony of the doxographer Aëtius: "The Stoics considered god to be an intelligent, designing fire, treading the path to the generation of the cosmos" (*De placitis reliquiae* 306; Gregory 2007: 189).

**Figure 7.5** Greek papyrus from Egypt (between AD 250 and 300) with Rev. 9:17–10:1. Chester Beatty Library in Dublin.
Source: Photo by the author.

*from nothing* (see Gregory 2007: 204-9; Anderson 2018), but may imply a Platonic Demiurge.

Because of such ambiguity of the Genesis' cosmogony, some Hellenized Jews and early Christians admitted the hylomorphic interpretation of creation, with God fashioning the world from the prime matter (see Winston 1971: 191–2). The Jewish book of the Wisdom of Solomon, which the Eastern Christian tradition includes to those allowed to be read in the church, *anagignoskomena*, speaks about God making the world from "formless matter" (ἀμόρφου ὕλης; 11:17). Philo of Alexandria (15–10 BC–AD 45–50), in interpreting Genesis 1:1-2, assumed God and matter to be two causes of creation, active and passive ones (see Sterling 2018).

In the same hylomorphic vein, Justin suggested that God created the world from preexistent matter: "God, in the beginning, created in His goodness everything out of shapeless matter for the sake of men" (*Apologia* I 10). Justin was so sure that hylomorphism could be a true orthodox teaching that he accused Plato of plagiarizing this idea from the Jewish prophets: "Plato plagiarized from our teachers when he affirmed that God changed shapeless matter and created the world" (*Apologia* I 59).

In contrast to hylomorphism, some Christian authors in the same second century asserted that the world has come from complete nothing. They adopted this idea under the influence of polemics against polytheism and quasi-Christian dualistic movements, such as Gnosticism and Manichaeism. Justin's disciple Tatian, who was an anti-Greek zealot, appears to be among the earliest Christian authors who clearly articulated the doctrine of the world's creation from complete scratch:

> The whole structure of the world, and the whole creation, has been produced from matter, and the matter itself brought into existence by God; so that on the one hand it may be regarded as rude and unformed before it was separated into parts, and on the other as arranged in beauty and order after the separation was made. (*Oratio ad Graecos* 52)

Theophilus of Antioch deconstructed both Platonic and Stoic cosmogonies and suggested in their stead an idea of the world coming to existence from nonexistence by the will of God:

> Some of the Stoics absolutely deny the existence of God or assert that if God exists he takes thought for no one but himself. Such views certainly exhibit the folly of Epicurus and Chrysippus alike. Others say that everything happens spontaneously, that the universe is uncreated and that nature is eternal; in general they venture to declare that there is no divine providence but that God is only the individual's conscience. Others, on the contrary, hold that the spirit extended through everything is God.
>
> Plato and his followers acknowledge that God is uncreated, the Father and Maker of the universe; next they assume that uncreated matter is also God, and say that matter was coeval with God. But if God is uncreated and matter is uncreated, then according to the Platonists God is not the Maker of the universe, and as far as they are concerned the unique sovereignty of God is not demonstrated. Furthermore, as God is immutable because he is uncreated, if matter is uncreated it must also be immutable, and equal to God; for what is created is changeable and mutable, while the uncreated is unchangeable and immutable.
>
> What would be remarkable if God made the world out of preexistent matter? Even a human artisan, when he obtains material from someone, makes whatever he wishes out of it. But the power of God is revealed by his making whatever he wishes out of the non existent, just as the ability to give life and motion belongs to no one but God alone. For a man makes an image but cannot give reason or breath or sensation to what he makes, while God has this power greater than his: the ability to make a being that is rational, breathing, and capable of sensation. As in all these instances God is more powerful than man, so he is in his making and having made the existent out of the non-existent; he made whatever he wished in whatever way he wished. (*Ad Autolycum* II 4)

Irenaeus of Lyon, in his polemics against quasi-Christian dualism, addressed the difference between the matter and the *kosmos* (see Steenberg 2008). For him, God is the creator of both. God first created matter, from which he formed the world:

> These [heretics], while seeking to explain the Scriptures and parables, introduce another, greater God above the God who is Creator of the world. <. . .> They make a collection of foolish discourses that they <. . .> might be thought to be able to tell us from where the substance of matter came, without believing that God made those

things that were made in order that all things might exist out of things that did not exist, just as he willed, making use of matter by his own will and power. (*Adversus haereses* II 10; Irenaeus 2012: 36)

# Origen

Among all Christian theologians, Origen offered the most comprehensive and nuanced cosmogony. As with many other Origen's ideas, his cosmology ignited heated discussions. It influenced the posterior generations of theologians, who nevertheless

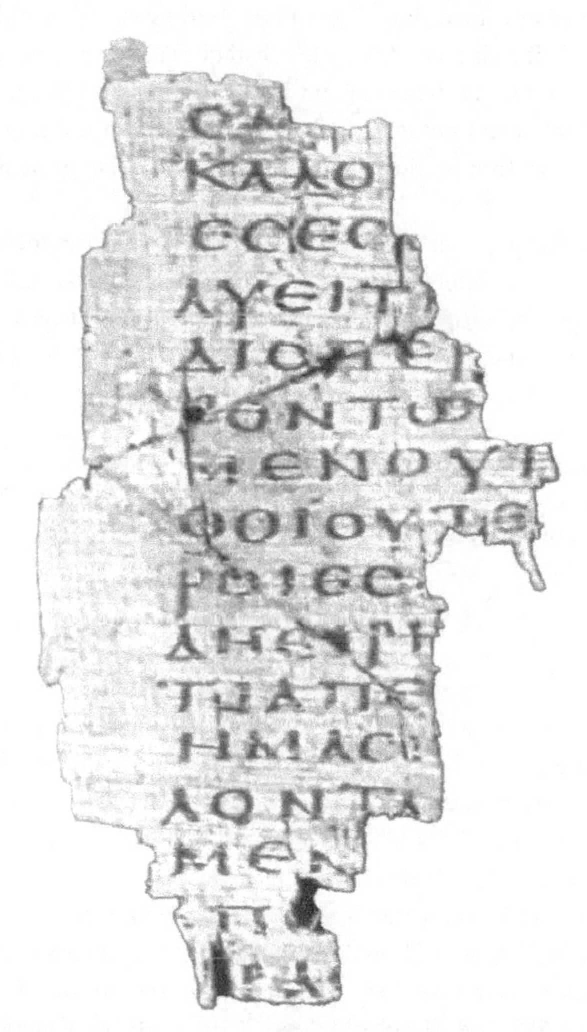

**Figure 7.6** Origen's commentary on Genesis 1:14. A fragment of fourth-century papyrus from Schøyen Collection, MS2634/2. Archäologische Museum of Münster University.

Source: Photo by the author.

acknowledged this influence through gritted teeth, if at all. Origen addressed almost the entire gamut of antique cosmologies, as well as various dualistic teachings of his time, such as the ones promoted by Hermogenes and Marcion. He composed a commentary on Genesis, which has not survived. Fortunately, we have his other cosmological work, *On First Principles*.

The title of this work refers to the issue that ancient cosmologists discussed most: what are the "principles" or "beginnings" (ἀρχαί) that caused this world. For Origen, this is God, who has created both the matter and the *kosmos*. Origen only partially followed hylomorphism. On the one hand, he differentiated between matter and *kosmos*. Matter was for him "that which underlies bodies, that is, that from which, with the inclusion and insertion of qualities, bodies exist." In other words, the prime matter for Origen is an undefinable substance lacking any perceptible quality. On the other hand, Origen was adamant in confessing God as the sole creator of both of them: "Matter did not exist and <. . .> God, when nothing existed before, caused to exist those things which he wished to exist" (*De principiis* II 1.4; Behr 2017: 150–1).

Just as God always gives birth to the Son, so he always creates the world: although these two processes are different for Origen, they are related to each other. Because God continues creating, Origen concluded, our world is not the only one. There were worlds before it, and there will be worlds after it (see Rubenstein 2014: 62–3). Each time, God creates a new world *ex nihilo*:

> God did not begin to work for the first time when he made this visible world, but that just as after its dissolution there will be another world, so also we believe others to have existed before this one was. (*De principiis* III 5.3; Behr 2017: 426–9)

# Basil

After Origen, the next quantum leap in studying cosmogony was made by Basil of Caesarea. Basil tried a new format of presenting this subject: a series of homilies under the title of *Hexaemeron*: on the six days of the creation of the world. Gregory of Nyssa supplemented the work of his older brother by treatises *Apologia in Hexaemeron* and *De opificio hominis* (see Marmodoro 2015). Basil's *Hexaemeron* became popular and was translated to Latin, Syriac (see Thomson 1995), Georgian, Armenian (see Thomson 2012), Arabic, and Slavonic languages. It also inspired other authors in different contexts to compose their own *Hexaemerons*. Among them, there were Jacob of Edessa (*c*. 640–708) (Jacob of Edessa 2010), Bede the Venerable (672/3–735; see Freibergs 1981), the Byzantine court poet George of Pisidia (flourished in the seventh century; see Olster 1991), Anastasius of Sinai (Anastasius of Sinai 2007), the exarch of Bulgaria John (ninth–tenth centuries; see Aitzetmüller 1975), and others.

**Figure 7.7** St. Basil. A monument at a Ukrainian Greek Catholic church in Kyiv.
Source: Photo by the author.

Basil, on the one hand, implicitly utilized quite a few ideas from the ancient cosmologies, while, on the other hand, explicitly refuted them (*Homiliae in hexaemeron* I 2; Basil of Caesarea 1963: 5). For example, he appropriated the famous Aristotelian axiom: "It is absolutely necessary that things begun in time be also brought to an end in time" (*Homiliae in hexaemeron* I 3; Basil of Caesarea 1963: 5). At the same time, based on this axiom, he deconstructed the Aristotelian idea of the world's eternity. Basil tirelessly repeated that the entire world has been created by God. This included matter, which for Basil cannot be coeternal with God:

> If matter itself is uncreated, it is, in the first place, of equal rank with God, worthy of the same honors. What could be more impious than this, that the most extreme

> unsightliness, without qualities, without form, unshapen ugliness (I have used, indeed, their own expressions) be considered worthy of the same superior ranking as the wise and powerful and all-good Craftsman and Creator of all things? (*Homiliae in hexaemeron* II 2; Basil of Caesarea 1963: 23)

This does not mean, for Basil, that matter as a category is just a pagan phantasy. On the contrary, he followed the hylomorphic line in differentiating between matter and its forms. In contrast to the antique authors, however, he claimed that both matter and material forms have been created simultaneously (*Homiliae in hexaemeron* II 3; Basil of Caesarea 1963: 24–5), and all things are a combination of both:

> Among us each art is definitely occupied with a certain material, as the art of metalworking with iron, and of carpentry with wood; and in them the substance is one thing; the form, another; and that made from the form, another. (*Homiliae in hexaemeron* II 2; Basil of Caesarea 1963: 23)

Basil applied to the Christian cosmology the classical distinction between commonality and particularity. He followed Aristotle, who also implied that matter is correspondent to the commonality, while things are its particularities. Basil followed the Greek train of thought also in describing time. Time, for him, concurs with and measures movements or changes in the visible world. This was another explicitly Aristotelian insight. However, in contrast to Aristotle, who believed in the world's eternity, Basil considered time as congruent with the creation and bracketed by its beginning and end:

> Adapted by nature to the world and to the animals and plants in it, the passage of time began, always pressing on and following past, and nowhere checking its course. In truth, is this not the nature of time, whose past has vanished, whose future is not yet at hand, and whose present escapes perception before it is known? Such also is the nature of all that has been made, either clearly growing or decaying, but possessing no evident settled state nor stability. Therefore, it was proper for the bodies of animals and plants, bound, as it were, by force to a sort of current, and maintained in a motion which leads to birth and corruption, to be possessed of the nature of time, which has the peculiar character natural to things which change. (*Homiliae in hexaemeron* I 5; Basil of Caesarea 1963: 9)

Time, thus, emerges together with the world—there was no time before the world. Even the beginning of the world was timeless: "The beginning of time is not yet time, on the contrary, not even the least part of it" (*Homiliae in hexaemeron* I 6; Basil of Caesarea 1963: 11). At the same time, even "before" the world was created and even "before" time, there was a spiritual world consisting of angels. This world is created too. However, its createdness is somehow different from the createdness of the visible world, because unlike the latter, which is framed by time, the former is framed by eternity. The angelic eternity transcends human time. Yet, it is different from the uncreated eternity of God:

> In fact, there did exist something, as it seems, even before this world, which our mind can attain by contemplation, but which has been left uninvestigated. <. . .> This was a certain condition older than the birth of the world and proper to the supramundane powers, one beyond time, everlasting, without beginning or end. In it the Creator and Producer of all things perfected the works of His art, a spiritual light befitting the blessedness of those who love the Lord, rational and invisible natures, and the whole orderly arrangement of spiritual creatures which surpass our understanding and of which it is impossible even to discover the names. (*Homiliae in hexaemeron* I 5; Basil of Caesarea 1963: 8–9)

Basil's cosmology is teleological. In contrast to the ancient Greek understanding of *telos*, Basil's teleology is also soteriological. For him, the purpose of the world is to teach human beings about God and to lead souls to salvation:

> The world was not devised at random or to no purpose, but to contribute to some useful end and to the great advantage of all beings, if it is truly a training place for rational souls and a school for attaining the knowledge of God, because through visible and perceptible objects it provides guidance to the mind for the contemplation of the invisible. (*Homiliae in hexaemeron* I 6; Basil of Caesarea 1963: 11)

## Athanasius

Basil stressed that God created the world by his will: "His will alone brought the mighty creations of the visible world into existence" (*Homiliae in hexaemeron* I 2; Basil of Caesarea 1963: 6). The idea that the existence of the world depends on the will of God goes back to as early as Plato (see *Timaeus* 41b), who believed that the existence of the world is contingent on the will (βουλήσεως) of the Demiurge: "Those works whereof I am framer and father are indissoluble save by my will (ἐμοῦ γε μὴ ἐθέλοντος)" (*Timaeus* 41b). This idea would become crucial in the theological controversies during the fourth century.

Athanasius of Alexandria, one generation prior to Basil, focused theological attention on the category of will and made it a cornerstone of polemics against those who admitted an ontological disparity and hierarchy between the Father and the Son. Athanasius' train of thought was the following. The Father gives birth to the Son without engaging his will—in the same way as for those who give birth, it is a natural process that does not require volition. In contrast to giving birth, creating things requires one's will. Through his will, the Father has created the world and human beings in it—in the same way as we apply volition to create anything. The category of will, as a result, became central in differentiating between birth and creation. The former applies to the Son, while the latter to the world.

Another category that helped Athanasius differentiating between the created and the uncreated was time. Arius and his confederates believed that there was a time gap between the existences of the Father and the Son. Because of this gap, it was impossible for them to speak about the Son as sharing the same essence (ὁμοούσιος) with the Father. Athanasius objected this idea and used the same time argument: there was no time when there was no Son; therefore, the Son is coeternal and consubstantial with the Father. The relationship between the Father and the Son is exempted from the time frame. This point was logically consistent with the idea that time applies to the created world only. From this perspective, Arius was wrong by describing the relationship between the Father and the Son through a timeline.

For the sake of his anti-Arian polemics, Athanasius had to stress the radical difference between the created and the uncreated realms. Never before him, the transcendence of God vis-à-vis the world was articulated with such clarity and emphasis. Athanasius studied the world's createdness in the soteriological and incarnational frameworks (see Conradie 2012). The following passage is explicit about how his cosmology related to soteriology:

> The nature of created things, having come into being from nothing, is unstable, and is weak and mortal when considered by itself; but the God of all is good and excellent by nature. Therefore he is also kind. For a good being would be envious of no one, so he envies nobody's existence but rather wishes everyone to exist, in order to exercise his kindness. So seeing that all created nature according to its own definition is in a state of flux and dissolution, therefore to prevent this happening and the universe dissolving back into nothing, after making everything by his own eternal Word and bringing creation into existence, he did not abandon it to be carried away and suffer through its own nature, lest it run the risk of returning to nothing. But being good, he governs and establishes the whole world through his Word who is himself God, in order that creation, illuminated by the leadership, providence, and ordering of the Word, may be able to remain firm, since it shares in the Word who is truly from the Father and is aided by him to exist, and lest it suffer what would happen, I mean a relapse into non-existence, if it were not protected by the Word. (*Contra gentes* 41; Athanasius of Alexandria 1981: 113–15)

In this statement, Athanasius first affirmed the creation of the world from nothing. Then he proceeded to the idea of the world as ontologically good, because it has been created by good God with best possible intentions. Despite being good, the world is perishable—it can return to nonexistence—something that Khaled Anatolios has called "creatio ad nihilum" (Anatolios 2018: 138). The mission of the Son is to save the world from such scenario and to maintain its existence. The idea of the world's maintenance and salvation by the Son, thus, helps Athanasius to demonstrate its createdness, and vice versa: the createdness of the world stresses its difference from the Son and his special role in maintaining and saving it. This role fits only God—not another creature. Athanasius, thus, arrived at his main theological point: the Son is true God consubstantial with the Father.

# Neo-Platonists

Athanasius and Plato agreed on some ideas about the world, namely, that (1) it is essentially good, (2) but needs maintenance; therefore, (3) God maintains the world through his will. The followers of Plato and Athanasius, however, radically diverged on whether the world is created. Following Athanasius, theologians made the world's creation *ex nihilo* a basic axiom of the Christian credo. They insisted on this axiom so much that their pagan opponents, primarily neo-Platonists, launched a vigorous campaign to promote the opposite idea—of the world's eternity.

While Alexandrian neo-Platonists tried to be more cautious in their pro-uncreatedness campaign, their Athenian colleagues became highly polemical against the Christian doctrine of creation *ex nihilo*. This was, by the way, one of the main reasons why the Alexandrian neo-Platonic school survived for longer than the Athenian school (see Watts 2008). Neo-Platonic philosophers were absorbed by their anti-Christian polemics so much that they had to depart from Plato. The vectors of the original Platonic and neo-Platonic cosmologies went in opposite directions: the former went toward the createdness, while the latter toward the uncreatedness of the world. When neo-Platonists realized this, they suggested interpreting the Plato's story about the Demiurge metaphorically (see Philoponus, *De aeternitate mundi contra Proclum*, 121, 223). On this point, they sided with Aristotle, who had suggested interpreting Plato in a similar way (*De caelo* I 10.279b).

The neo-Platonic take on the world's eternity had two options: either the *kosmos* always existed in parallel to God or it has emanated from God (see Gregory 2007: 219). Plotinus, for example, advocated for the latter option: "If there is anything after the First, it must necessarily come from the First" (*Enneades* V 4.1). God, thus, is the source of a series of emanations (see Greig 2020), which led to the emergence of matter and of the visible world from it.

The neo-Platonists made sure to be clear that the process of emanation excluded divine volition.[2] To point this out, neo-Platonist Sallustius (flourished in the mid-fourth century) stressed that as we cast shadows without applying our will, so God casts his shadow, which is the world (*De deis et mundo* VII 2). This image excluded any divine volition from the existence of the world whatsoever and was underpinned by the neo-Platonic anti-Christian agenda. This agenda, however, pushed neo-

[2]Later neo-Platonists would allow some volition on the lower levels of emanation.

**Figure 7.8** Plato. A Roman copy of the original from Plato's Academy. National Archaeological Museum in Athens.
Source: Photo by the author.

Platonism away from Plato, who had envisaged volition in the relationship between the Demiurge and the world.

## Philoponus

In response, Christians escalated further their criticism of the world's eternity and more insistently promoted the idea of its createdness *ex nihilo*. John Philoponus became a protagonist of this apologetical effort. Having studied in the Alexandrian neo-Platonic school, he became well versed in the classical cosmogonical debates. Philoponus reflected on them systematically from the Christian perspective in several works, including special treatises: *Against Proclus on the Eternity of the World*, which has survived, and *Against Aristotle on the Eternity of the World*, which has not. In his cosmological works, on the one hand, he tried to deconstruct the pro-eternity arguments (see Sorabji 1987b), and on the other, to construct a Christian procreation philosophical system.

Philoponus was inventive in both endeavors and relied more on the philosophical syllogisms than on biblical or patristic witnesses. He apparently addressed the audience that consisted not of pious Christians, but of pagan intellectuals. Philoponus heavily relied on Aristotle as regards categories. From this perspective, he was more a neo-Aristotelian than a neo-Platonist. As regards cosmogony, however, he unhesitatingly turned against Aristotle's standpoint on the eternity of both the *kosmos* and its matter. Philoponus criticized the following Aristotelian idea of infinity:

> If there was a becoming of every movable thing, it follows that before the motion in question another change or motion must have taken place in which that which was capable of being moved or of causing motion had its becoming. (*Physica* VIII 1.251b)

This idea of "extendible finitude" means that "however large a finite number you have taken, you can take more" (Sorabji 1987a: 168). Consequently, one can always add at least one moment before the assumed beginning of the world, and then another moment before that moment, and so on. For Aristotle, an infinite number of years has passed since the assumed beginning of the world to the present moment. The infinitude of this number proves that the world has no beginning.

Philoponus took the Aristotelian idea of "extendible finitude" as a leverage to prove the opposite. His argument had to do with the mathematical logics of his time: if the number of years that have passed since the beginning of the world is infinite, then the world has experienced the actual infinitude. This was impossible, because even for Aristotle, one cannot count infinite numbers. Moreover, each next year would increase this infinitude, which for Philoponus was also absurd:

> How, then, could it not be beyond every absurdity, if it is not even possible for the infinite to be traversed once, to postulate something ten thousand times greater that the infinite, or rather to postulate something infinite times greater than the infinite. (In Simplicius 2012: 78)

In contrast to Aristotle's standpoint, which was advocated by neo-Platonists, Philoponus argued that the "before" the beginning of the world does not need always to be understood in the temporal sense (see Gregory 2007; 219). One can also speak of the "before" in the sense of the cause that brought the world to existence (see Sorabji 2015).

The aforementioned quote from Philoponus has been preserved by Simplicius of Cilicia (*c.* 480–560). Philoponus and Simplicius had the same alma mater, the Alexandrian school of neo-Platonism, and the same teacher, Ammonius. Simplicius was probably a generation older than Philoponus. He could not hide his snobbery regarding his younger Christian colleague. In his treatises, he commented on Philoponus in the way haters leave their comments on social media in our days. Philoponus was for Simplicius a barking dog who defecates in the minds of his readers. Simplicius attacked Philoponus' arguments about the origins of the world, but not convincingly (Sorabji 1987a: 171).

Soon the debates between Christians and neo-Platonists on the origins of the world were disrupted. In 529, Emperor Justinian closed the neo-Platonic school in Athens. A century later, the Arab conquest of Egypt put the end to the Alexandrian school. These debates, nevertheless, continued in the Arab-speaking milieu.

Muslim scholars built their own procreation arguments based on the Byzantine polemics between Christians and neo-Platonists. One of them was a prominent Central Asian polymath Abū Naṣr Al-Fârâbî (*c.* 870–*c.* 950) who in the West became known as Alfarabius. In the Arab-speaking context, he was held as "the second teacher" after Aristotle (see Starr 2013: 12). Like Christian theologians, he tried to accommodate Aristotelian logics and neo-Platonism in his religious tradition. He was aware of similar attempts by Christians and engaged with them critically. For example, he questioned Philoponus' motivation for his anti-neo-Platonic polemics:

> One may suspect that his intention from what he does in refuting Aristotle is either to defend the opinions laid down in his own religion about the world, or to remove from himself the suspicion that he disagrees with the position held by the people of his religion and approved by their rulers, so as not to suffer the same fate as Socrates. (Mahdi 1967: 257)

# Ps.-Dionysius

Al-Fârâbî exaggerated Philoponus' neo-Platonic agenda hidden behind his anti-pro-eternity polemics. This agenda, however, is more apparent in the writings of another author who lived at the same time and who hid himself behind the name of Dionysius the Areopagite. There are scholars who believe that Philoponus was the real author of the *Corpus Dionysiacum* (see Чорноморець 2010: 75–202). Despite some unquestionable neo-Platonic points of convergence between them, however, there is also an irreconcilable divergency between the two Christian philosophers, which makes this hypothesis untenable. In applying logical categories, Philoponus was Aristotelian to a more extent than any other Christian neo-Platonist, including Ps.-Dionysius. Regarding the world's createdness, however, he was far more anti-Aristotelian and anti-neo-Platonist than Ps.-Dionysius could be.

In contrast to the majority of the known Christian theologians who have been branded as neo-Platonists, Ps.-Dionysius was a genuine neo-Platonist. Another proper neo-Platonist was Boethius (*c.* 477–524; see Marenbon 2015: 42–54). One of the most neo-Platonic features in Ps.-Dionysius' thinking was the idea of hierarchy, which he had borrowed from Proclus (see Hovorun 2017: 132–44). Another neo-Platonic element in Ps.-Dionysius is his apparent inclination to consider the world as emanating and being maintained not through the divine volition, but automatically (see Tollefsen 2012: 110–1). The world, for Ps.-Dionysius, is a shadow of God. This resembles the neo-Platonic image by Sallustius mentioned earlier:

> This essential Good, by the very fact of its existence, extends goodness into all things. Think of how it is with our sun. It exercises no rational process, no act of choice (οὐ λογιζόμενος ἢ προαιρούμενος), and yet by the very fact of its existence it gives light to whatever is able to partake of its light, in its own way. So it is with the Good. Existing far above the sun, an archetype far superior to its dull image, it sends the rays of its undivided goodness to everything with the capacity, such as this may be, to receive it. These rays are responsible for all intelligible and intelligent beings. (*De diuinis nominibus* IV 1; Luibheid 1987: 71)

There are no clear testimonies in Ps.-Dionysius' extant texts that he believed in the creation of the world *ex nihilo*. This does not necessarily mean that he did not believe in such creation. However, it certainly implies that Ps.-Dionysius' concerns about the world's createdness were remote from those of Philoponus. It seems these concerns were different also from the concerns of Maximus the Confessor, even though the latter was a Ps.-Dionysian apologist and promoter, who did not yield doubts about the authenticity of his name and thinking.

# Maximus

In contrast to Ps.-Dionysius, Maximus did care to demonstrate that the world has been created by God *ex nihilo* (see Tollefsen 2015; Louth 2013):

> For who, in contemplating the beauty and the magnificence of creation, does not immediately understand that God is the one who has brought all creatures into existence, since He is the Origin and Cause and Creator of all beings?" (*Ambiguum ad Joh.* X; Maximus 2014: 284–5)

Maximus explored various aspects of creation, holding as his departure point various cosmogonic issues discussed in Antiquity. One of them was the origin of motion. Maximus arrived at a conclusion that resembles that of Aristotle, namely that there is the First Mover behind any motion in the world. In contrast to Aristotle, however, he used the argument of the First Mover to support the createdness of the world:

> No motion is without beginning, since it is not without a cause. For its beginning is that which set it in motion, and its cause is the end that calls it and attracts it, and toward which it is also moved. But if the mover is the beginning of every motion of every thing that is moved, and if the cause toward which whatever is moved is carried along is the end (for nothing moves without a cause), then no being is unmoved, except the Prime Mover (for the Prime Mover is absolutely unmoved, since it is without beginning), from which it follows that no beings are without the beginning,

> since none of them is unmoved. Everything that in any way exists is in motion, except the sole, unmoved Cause that transcends all things. (*Ambiguum to Joh.* X; Maximus 2014: 286–7)

Not only particular things, for Maximus, are created from scratch, but also their commonalities, including the "most generic genus," which is the universe (see Törönen 2007: 140):

> But even what is called "substance" in a simple sense—not just the substance of things subject to generation and corruption, which moves according to generation and corruption, but the substance of all beings—has been set in motion and continues to move according to the principle and mode of expansion and contraction. For it is moved from the most generic genus through the more generic genera to particular species, through which and in which it is naturally divided, proceeding down to the most specific species, where its expansion comes to a limit, which circumscribes its being on the lower end of the scale. (*Ambiguum ad Joh.* X; Maximus 2014: 288–9)

Maximus, thus, connected physics with logics, by placing the categories of commonality and particularity to the creationist framework. He was not the first to observe this connectedness—it had been noticed by Aristotle. Maximus, however, offered a fresh outlook at this connectedness by identifying the commonalities of particular things with blueprints-*logoi.* They are similar to Plato's ideas and the Aristotelian/neo-Platonic category of species. Maximus suggested that God had the *logoi* of things before the creation. After having used them as blueprints for particular beings, God continues preserving *logoi* in existence:

> God, as He alone knew how, brought to completion the primary principles and the universal essences of the things that were brought into being. He nonetheless continues to work, not only to preserve the existence of these beings and essences, but also for the actual creation, growth, and sustenance of the individual parts that exist potentially within them. At the same time, He works providentially to bring about the assimilation of particulars to universals, until such time as He—having united the voluntary impulse of the particulars with the naturally more general principle of rational being through the movement of the particulars toward well-being—will unite them reciprocally to each other and to the whole universe in an identity of movement. And He will do this in such a way that the particulars will not differ in inclination from the universal, but that one and the same principle will be seen in all things, admitting of no division because of the modes predicated of each. (*Quaestiones ad Thalassium* II; Maximus the Confessor 2018: 97–8)

Maximus addressed the issue of time, which had been an intrinsic part of cosmology since Aristotle. We have seen earlier how it was dealt with by Philoponus. Maximus was clearer on it: whatever exists in a particular place is also framed by time. God, therefore, cannot be framed by time because he is omnipresent:

> The very being of beings itself does not exist simply or without qualities, but in a particular way, which constitutes its first form of delimitation—as well as a powerful demonstration that there is a beginning of beings and of their coming to be. Yet who does not know that every kind of being whatsoever, with the sole exception of the Divine (which strictly speaking is beyond being), presupposes the concept of a "where," which in absolutely every instance necessarily requires the related concept of "when"? (*Ambiguum ad Joh.* X; Maximus 2014: 290–3)

Maximus, thus, employed the entire arsenal of the philosophical instruments that the Antiquity before him had produced, to demonstrate that God created the world from nothing. At the same time, Maximus wanted to demonstrate that the world was created not to be alone, but to come back to God. Unity with God, which will never abolish the ontological chasm between the uncreated and created, constitutes the ultimate *telos* of the world's existence.

## Kosmas Indikopleustes

The sixth-century merchant Kosmas Indikopleustes brought up less theoretical and more empirical arguments that the world has been created. His point was: the world is limited, which makes it different from unlimited God. Somehow naïvely, he wanted to reach the end of the world and thus to demonstrate that those who believe

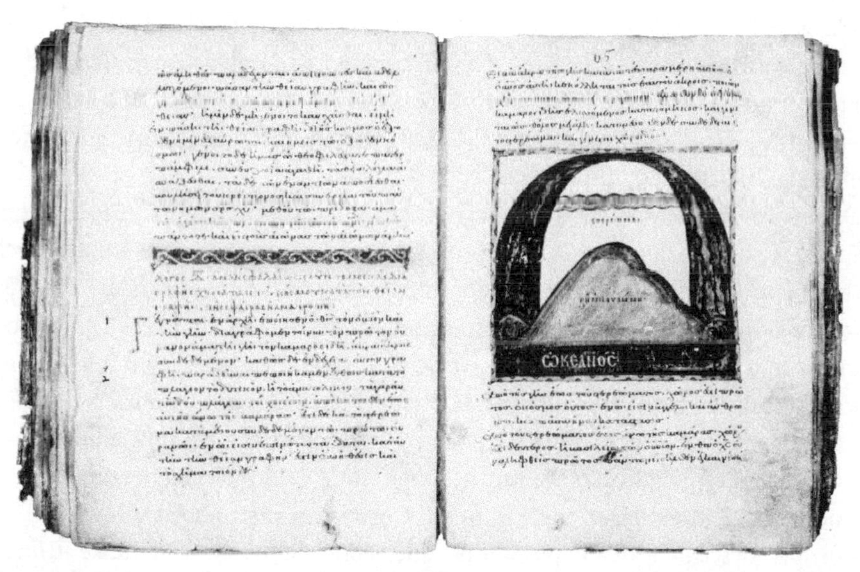

**Figure 7.9** A page (#68) from Sin. gr. 1186, which demonstrates that the Earth is rectangular, has a cupolum of heaven above it, which is divided by the firmament into two compartments.

Source: the website of the Library of Congress: https://www.loc.gov/item/00271076642-ms/ [accessed on February 10, 2021].

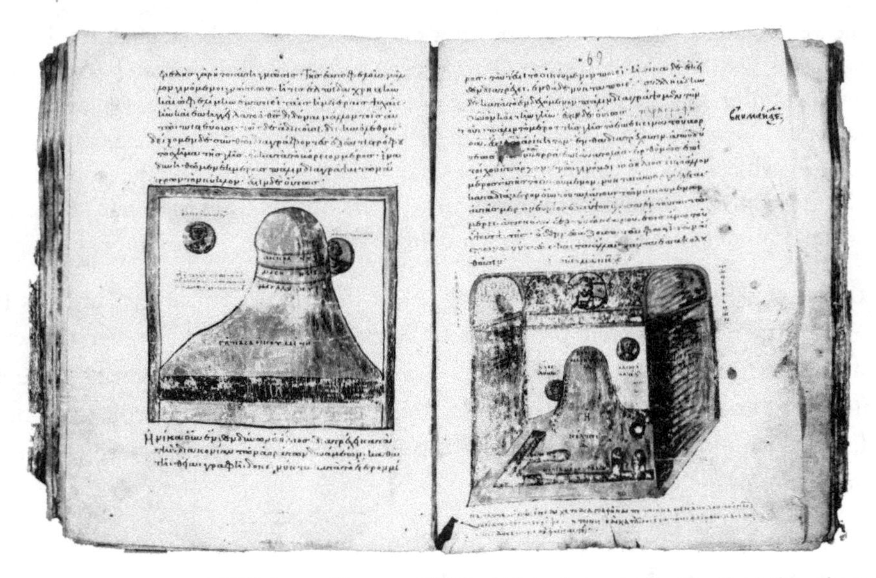

**Figure 7.10** A page (#73) from Sin. gr. 1186, which demonstrates that the shape of the kosmos is similar to the Ark of the Covenant.

Source: the website of the Library of Congress: https://www.loc.gov/item/00271076642-ms/ [accessed on February 10, 2021].

in the world's eternity are wrong. He had in mind particularly the neo-Platonists from Alexandria—his native city.

Alexandria was a departure port for Kosmas' explorations. He became one of the most traveled explorers of his time. His nickname, Indikopleustes, indicates that he had reached as far as India. At that time, the toponym India applied to a wide variety of territories, including Ethiopia and the Gulf. Therefore, it is unclear whether he had been to the Indian subcontinent.

During his journeys, Kosmas came in touch with Eastern Syrians—the theological antipodes of his Alexandrian compatriots. He knew some of them personally, such as the bishop of Chaldea Patricius and later the Persian Catholicos Mar Aba I the Great (in office 540–52). Kosmas utilized the knowledge that he had received from his journeys in the East to prove that the world is limited. He argued that it lies on a flat rectangular platform. This platform has a vault of heaven above it and is divided by firmament into two spaces. One is allocated for those who live now, and the other one—for whoever will live in the future Kingdom of God. The shape of the universe, Kosmas argued, is similar to the Ark of the Covenant constructed by Moses.

Kosmas described his explorations and conclusions in a treatise *Christian Topography* published sometime in the 540s. He designed rich illustrations to make his point (see Kominko 2013: 1). The original illustrations have not survived, but we have their medieval copies. One of them was produced in the twelfth century and is preserved in the St. Catherine's Monastery at Sinai (Sin. gr. 1186).

# VII.3

# Creation in the Image

A category that bridges ontologically different or even polarized entities and levels is image (see Squire 2009). Indeed, image connects such entities and levels without blurring demarcation lines between them. It is a window, not a door, from one world to another. Another window between worlds is symbol. The difference between image and symbol is that the former visualizes its prototype, while the latter conceptualizes it. Gregory of Nyssa explained the idea of image:

> Since he was created to take part (μέτοχος) in divine blessings, man must have a natural affinity with that object in which he has participation (μετουσία). It is just like an eye which, thanks to the luminous rays which nature provides it, is enabled to have communion (κοινωνία) in the light. <. . .> It is just so where is man, who since he was created to enjoy the divine blessings must have some affinity with that in which he has been called to participate. And so he has been endowed with life, reason, wisdom, and all those truly divine advantages so that each one of them should cause that innate desire of his to be demonstrated within him. Since immortality is one of those benefits that are appropriate to deity, it follows that our nature cannot be deprived even of this in its constitution, but must possess within itself the disposition to immortality in order that (thanks to this innate capacity) it might be able to recognize that which is transcendent far beyond it and might thus experience the desire for divine eternity. (*Oratio catechetica* 5; McGuckin 2007: 104–5)

Christian theologians were pioneers in using the category of image as a bridge stretching over the chasm between the uncreated and created worlds. Such usage was unknown in the pre-Christian antiquity, which did not differentiate between the uncreated and created worlds. The category of image became central in the Eastern Christianity, especially after the iconoclastic crisis. In the aftermath of this crisis, icons became identical with Orthodoxy itself. Long before that, the idea of the Roman Empire as an image of the Kingdom of God had been laid down at the foundations of the Eastern political theology. However, the field, where the category of image applied originally, was theological anthropology—the teaching about the human nature.

There was a patristic consensus that human beings have been created by God not out of blue, but in the image of the divine. The patristic opinions varied, however, as regards which aspect of the divine was the prototype for the human nature: God (*imago Dei*), the Trinity (*imago Trinitatis*), or Christ (*imago Christi*). Church fathers also had different opinions about what to regard as the image of God *in* the human nature: mind, soul, or also body. Finally, they sometimes identified the *image* and *likeness* of God (Gen. 1:26) and sometimes differentiated between them.

# Origen

One of the earliest Christian theologians who employed the category of image was Origen. He used this category to explain the relationship of the Logos to God, as well as the principles of cosmogony. Origen built a hierarchy of images: the Logos is the only exact and direct image of the Father, while human beings are images of God through the Logos. The Logos, therefore, is an immediate prototype or a "paradigm" (παράδειγμα) for men and women:

> Since the firstborn of all creation is the image of the invisible God (Col. 1:15), the Father is his beginning. And likewise also Christ is the beginning of those made according to the image of God.
>
> For if men are according to the image, and the image according to the Father, the "according to which" of Christ, on the one hand, is the Father, his beginning but, on the other hand, Christ is the "according to which" of men, who are made, not according to that of which Christ is the image, but according to the image. The statement, In the beginning was the Word, will fit the same paradigm. (*Commentarii in Iohannem* I 17.104-5; Origen 1989: 55)

Maximus the Confessor, in his usual way of thinking out of the box, concluded that the Logos, having been incarnated, became an image of himself:

> In His measureless love for mankind, there was need for Him to be created in human form (without undergoing any change), and to become a type and symbol of Himself presenting Himself symbolically by means of His own self, and, through the manifestation of Himself, to lead all creation to Himself (though He is hidden and totally beyond all manifestation), and to provide human beings, in a human-loving fashion, with the visible divine actions of His flesh as signs of His invisible infinity, which is totally transcendent, and secretly hidden, which no being, in absolutely any way whatsoever, can capture in thought or language. (*Ambiguum ad Joh.* X 77; Maximus 2014: 269)

Origen set up another line of thinking about the image, which would become widely accepted by later theologians: he differentiated between the image and likeness of God. In this differentiation, he employed the categories of given and assigned.

Image, according to Origen, has been given through creation, while likeness should be obtained by human beings through cooperation with God:

> For Moses, before all others, points to it when he describes the first creation of the human being, saying, "And God said, 'Let us make the human being in our image and likeness.'" Then he adds afterwards: "And God made the human being, in the image of God he made him; male and female he made them and he blessed them" (Gen. 1:26-28). The fact that he said, in the image of God he made him and was silent about the likeness, indicates nothing else except that the human being obtained the dignity of the image in his first creation, but the perfection of the likeness was reserved for him at the consummation; that is, that he might acquire it for himself by the exercise of his own diligence in the imitation of God, so that while the possibility of attaining perfection was given to him in the beginning through the dignity of the image, he should in the end, through the accomplishment of the works, complete in himself the perfect likeness. (*De principiis* III 6.1; Behr 2017: 440–1)

This differentiation between constant and changeable elements in human nature became important in posterior anthropology. It applied to human freedom, perfection, and other aspects of human being. The constant element in it is given by God and cannot be affected by any human decision. In contrast to it, the changeable element depends on human agency and synergy with God. In the categories of commonality and particularity, image and likeness can be seen as corresponding to these categories. Image, as pertinent to every human being, is a part of common human nature. Likeness, as gained individually, can be thus interpreted as a particularization of the image. Likeness is a particular instance of the image—its "hypostasis," as it were.

# Athanasius

Athanasius presented the Son as the image of the Father, and human beings as created in the image of the Son. In contrast to Origen, however, he did not consider the Son as inferior to the Father. He thus perceived the category of image as not necessarily introducing hierarchy between itself and its prototype. Unlike Origen, Athanasius did not differentiate between image and likeness in the human nature:

> Since he (i.e., the Father) is good he bestowed on them of his own image, our Lord Jesus Christ, and he made them according to his own image and likeness, in order that, understanding through such grace the image, I mean the Word of the Father, they might be able through him to gain some notion about the Father, and recognizing the Maker, might live a happy and truly blessed life. (*De incarnatione* 11; Athanasius of Alexandria 1981: 161)

The idea of the humanity being created in the image of the Son helped Athanasius to differentiate the created world from the uncreated Son—a central point in his anti-Arian polemics. The Son should not be confused with the rest of the creation, because the nature of image is usually different from the nature of its original:

> And, as some son of a king, when the father wished to build a city, might cause his own name to be printed (ἐγγραφῆ) upon each of the works that were rising, both to give security to them of the works remaining, by reason of the show of his name on everything, and also to make them remember him and his father from the name, and having finished the city might be asked concerning it, how it was made, and then would answer, "It is made securely, for according to the will of my father, I am imaged (ἐξεικονίσθην) in each work, for my name was made in the works"; but saying this, he does not signify that his own essence is created, but the impress (τύπον) of himself by means of his name. (*Oratio contra Arianos* II 4.79)

The uncreated image is different from the created one. Therefore, the image of the Son in relationship to the Father is different from his image in relationship to human beings. They are two different kinds of image:

> For in the Son is contemplated the Father's Godhead. And we may perceive this at once from the illustration of the Emperor's image (τῆς εἰκόνος τοῦ βασιλέως). For in the image (τῇ εἰκόνι) is the shape (τὸ εἶδος) and form (ἡ μορφή) of the Emperor, and in the Emperor is that shape (εἶδος) which is in the image (ἐν τῇ εἰκόνι). For the likeness (ὁμοιότης) of the Emperor in the image (ἐν τῇ εἰκόνι) is exact; so that a person who looks at the image (τῇ εἰκόνι), sees in it the Emperor; and he again who sees the Emperor, recognizes that it is he who is in the image (ἐν τῇ εἰκόνι). And from the likeness not differing, to one who after the image wished to view the Emperor, the image might say, "I and the Emperor are one; for I am in him, and he in me; and what you see in me, that you behold in him, and what you have seen in him, that you hold in me." Accordingly, he who worships the image (τὴν εἰκόνα), in it worships the Emperor also; for the image (ἡ εἰκών) is his form (μορφή) and appearance (τὸ εἶδος). Since then the Son too is the Father's Image (εἰκών), it must necessarily be understood that the Godhead and propriety of the Father is the being of the Son. (*Oratio contra Arianos* II 4.5)

The key to understanding the difference between the two kinds of images is the category of will. Human beings have originated as the image of God with the involvement of God's will, while the Son is the image of the Father without any involvement of God's will:

> Things originate have come to be "by favor and will," but the Son is not a work of will, nor has come after, as the creation, but is by nature the own Offspring of God's essence. (*Oratio contra Arianos* II 4.63)

As with other theological categories, Athanasius put image in the soteriological and incarnational framework. After the Fall, the image of God in the human beings became corrupted. The Logos came down to restore it. The incarnation, thus, became a part of the Son's assignment to take care of his image:

> It would not be right for those who had once partaken of the image of God to perish. What then was God to do, or what should have happened, except that he should renew again that which was in his image, in order that through it men might be able once more to know him? But how could this have been done, unless the very image of God were to come, our Saviour Jesus Christ? For neither by men was it possible, since they had been created in the image, nor by the angels, for neither were they images. So the Word of God came in his own person, in order that, as he is the image of his Father, he might be able to restore man who is in the image. (*De incarnatione* 13; Athanasius of Alexandria 1981: 165–7)

## Theodoret

Alexandrians placed *imago Dei* at the center of their theology and used this category to make their main theological points. Antiochian theologians followed in their steps but adopted a slightly different approach. One of the most prominent of them, Theodoret the bishop of Cyrus, paid particular attention to this category. We already mentioned him several times in the context of controversies about "three chapters." He was an extraordinary figure in the fifth-century theology who hardly fitted any trend of his time. From the posterior Chalcedonian perspective, Theodoret was quite orthodox. From the anti-Chalcedonian perspective, he was a Nestorian. Neo-Chalcedonianism sacrificed his theology for the sake of the church's unity. That is how some of his writings were condemned by the council of Constantinople in 553. At the same time, this council refused to condemn Theodoret in person.

Theodoret was born around 393 in Antioch and studied in the local theological school, which was under the influence of Diodore of Tarsus and Theodore of Mopsuestia. He adopted some of their views, but not to the extent to be rejected by the Chalcedonian theologians. In 423, Theodoret became a bishop in the city of Cyrus northeast from Antioch. As a bishop, he belonged to the faction of Syrian bishops who opposed those Egyptian bishops who had promoted the theology of Cyril of Alexandria. Theodoret was deposed by the second, "robber," council of Ephesus in 449 and then restored to his office through the intervention of Pope Leo. He played a visible role at the council of Chalcedon and died around 460.

Theodoret was primarily an exegete. He left comments, in his own words, on "all the prophets, the psalter, and the apostle" (*ep.* 82; Theodoret of Cyrus 2007: xx). His detailed reflections on *imago Dei* can be found in the *Questions on the Octateuch*.

They constitute two series of answers to the aporias from the eight books of the Old Testament: Genesis through Ruth, and then 1 Samuel through 2 Chronicles. Theodoret systematically expounded different interpretations of what does *imago Dei* mean. With some of them he concurred, and with others, did not. Thus, he disagreed with the Alexandrian point that the invisibility of human soul constitutes the image of God:

> Some commentators have referred the phrase "the image of God" to the invisibility of the soul; but they are mistaken. If the invisibility of the soul constituted God's image, angels and archangels, along with all the incorporeal and holy natures, would with greater reason be called God's images. After all, they are completely free of bodies and possess an invisibility that is quite uncompromised. (*Quaestiones in Octateuchum* (Genesis) XX 1; Theodoret of Cyrus 2007: 49)

At the same time, Theodoret rejected the idea that the human body is *imago Dei* (see *Quaestiones in Octateuchum* (Genesis) XX 1; Theodoret of Cyrus 2007: 49–50). For him, the image of God should be identified neither with the invisible nor with the visible parts of the human nature. Rather, it is a link and mediation between both:

> After completing the material and spiritual creation, the God of the universe formed man last and set him like an image of himself in the midst of the inanimate and the animate, the material and the spiritual, so that the inanimate and the animate might offer him their service as a kind of tribute, and the spiritual beings, by caring for him, might manifest their love for the Creator. (*Quaestiones in Octateuchum* (Genesis) XX 2; Theodoret of Cyrus 2007: 51)

*Imago Dei* is similar to the human word, which connects both visible and invisible parts of the human nature. It begins in and expresses the invisible side of a person and becomes accomplished through the mediation of the human body. As such, speaking constitutes the image of God:

> One might discover a further, more precise, resemblance in the human soul. This is both rational and vital. The mind begets the word, and with the word proceeds a breath, not begotten like the word, but always accompanying the word and proceeding with it when the word is begotten. (*Quaestiones in Octateuchum* (Genesis) XX 3; Theodoret of Cyrus 2007: 55)

Another important resemblance of human beings with God is human creativity. Just like God creates the world, men and women can craft amazing things. Creativity and innovation, thus, are an intrinsic part of *imago Dei*:

> In imitation of the Creator, man also creates houses, walls, cities, harbors, ships, dockyards, chariots, and countless other things, including likenesses of heaven, representations of the sun, moon, and stars, and images of people and brute beasts.

Nonetheless, the difference in creating is infinite. The God of the universe creates from both the existent and the non-existent, and, without effort or lapse of time, puts his intention into effect as soon he wills it. But a human being who sets out to make an object requires material, as well as tools, planning, consideration, time, effort, and the assistance of other trades. The builder requires a bronze smith, and the bronze smith a metallurgist and a charcoal maker, and all of these require woodcutters, while woodcutters require planters and farmers; every trade borrows what it needs from the others. Yet creating even in this fashion, the human being to some extent imitates the Creator as an image its archetype. (*Quaestiones in Octateuchum* (Genesis) XX 2; Theodoret of Cyrus 2007: 53)

# Anastasius

The neo-Chalcedonian theologian Anastasius of Sinai was among the most creative minds who elaborated on the idea of *imago Dei*. He reflected on this idea in several pieces known as sermons on the construction of human beings by God according to image and likeness. They were composed some twenty years after the council in Constantinople in 680/1 and critically published by Karl-Heinz Uthemann in 1985. In the first sermon from the series on the creation of human beings, Anastasius observed that being an image of God is the source of beauty for human personality; it is also the reason for its depth:

Those who want to unmistakably understand the God-created beauty of the person (προσώπου), can see the reflection of their own image and the features of person only in a clear mirror. Through which they approach the image of their own appearance and clearly see in it and through it the resemblance of their image and likeness. In the same way, as if looking in a mirror at the ray of the mind-contemplated sun, we clearly learn from within it the reflection, shape, and image of our nature, [which exists] according to the image and likeness [of God].

It seems to me that the composition of a human being inspires awe and is difficult to interpret. Many hidden secrets of God are reflected in it. As the eye easily observes what is beyond it, but cannot see itself, in the same way it is difficult for the eye of the human intellect to contemplate and to discover the reason of our creation (ὁ τῆς ἡμετέρας δημιουργίας λόγος). After the Creator accomplished the simple and most intellectual world of the invisible forces and then this material and visible [world], which is composed from four elements, he said: "Let us make the man in our image and after our likeness" (Gen. 1:26). Then he creates the alive being (ζῷον) as a mixed world, which is related to two worlds: composed from the bodiless, immortal, and incorruptible soul and from the material and visible body, which consists of four elements. After this has happened, the Scripture again says: "And God created man, in the image of God he created him" (Gen. 1:27). When it says God, it means the Father, the Son, and the Holy Spirit.

Anastasius summarized different opinions about what *imago Dei* may mean. It should be noted that he himself did not differentiate between the image and likeness of God:

> The exegetes have expressed many different opinions about this. Some said that the image and likeness of God is the human capacity for ruling and exercising power (τὸ ἀρχικὸν καὶ ἐξουσιαστικόν); others—that it is the intellectual and invisible quality of soul; others—when Adam became incorruptible and free of sin, others said that it was a prophecy about baptism. "Last of all, as though to one born at the wrong time" (1 Cor. 15:8), it came to me to express my opinion about this. First of all, one should ask why God did not name in his image and likeness the angels who are intellectual, immaterial, heavenly, and close to God. Because they are more than man in charge of the entire earth and of men. In their intellectual and heavenly choirs, they are also superior to the incorruptible, immaterial, invisible, the pure, and whatever else praiseful you can say about Adam.

Anastasius did not reject the idea that parts of a human being can be images of God. At the same time, he specified that human soul should be regarded as an image of the divine essence. Together with body, it symbolizes the incarnation of God:

> Is there anything more profound than what has been earlier said regarding the "according to the image" of man? Because the human being has obtained not only one image and likeness of God, but two, three, four, and five, which like in a mirror or through shadow, depict the mystery of the three-hypostatic God—not naturally, but symbolically. Additionally, the human being clearly pre-describes (προδιαγράφων) the incarnation of the one of this Holy Trinity—the Word of God. So that the naked soul is in the image of the naked divinity, while the composition of soul and body is after the likeness of the incarnation of the Word.

Anastasius elaborated on the idea that human being is an image of God not individually, but collectively. For him, Adam was the image of the Father, Eve—of the Holy Spirit, and their child (Anastasius did not specify whether this was Cain or Abel) stood for the Word of God. Adam was not born and had no cause except God, which makes him similar to the Father. Eve proceeded from Adam in the same way as the Holy Spirit proceeds from the Father. Finally, their son was born in a way similar to the Son of God. This interpretation of the first human family as the image of the Trinity goes back to Apollinaris of Laodicea (see Zachhuber 2014: 39) and the Cappadocians. Several other theologians elaborated on this image, including Syrians Theodore Abū Qurrah, Habib Abu Ra'ita, Dionysius Bar Salibi, and others. Anastasius' take on this image was the following:

> Let us go back to the beginning [of the Bible], from which as from the deepest source, we can learn what God has created not after the likeness of other intellectual beings, i.e., angels, but on the level (κατ' ἰσότητα) of animals that have soul (τῶν ἐμψύχων ζῴων), i.e., similar-in-their-ways (ὁμοιοτρόπους), ancient, and chief hypostases. I mean Adam, Eve, and the son who came from them. He made Adam without any

> [created] cause (ἀναιτίως) and birth, his second man—as the begotten son, and Eve—as the one who is neither begotten nor without cause. In a subtle, that is to say proceeding way (ἐκπορευτῶς), she came from the essence of Adam, who is without cause. She was thus substantiated (οὐσίωσε) in an inexpressible way. Did not these three heads, ancestral for the entire humankind, who are consubstantial hypostases, <. . .> symbolically become the images of the holy and consubstantial Trinity? Adam, who is without cause and birth, became the symbol (τύπος) and image (εἰκών) of God and Father, who is without cause and the cause of everything. His son pre-describes (προδιαγράφοντος) the begotten Son and the Word of God. Eva, who proceeds (ἐκπορευτή), means the hypostasis of the Holy Spirit who also proceeds (ἐκπορευτὴ ὑπόστασις). God did not breathe into her the breath of life (Gen. 2:7), because she is the symbol of the breath and life of the Holy Spirit, and also because she would receive, through the Holy Spirit, God, who is the true breath and life for everyone.
>
> One should therefore see and be excited that the unbegotten Adam did not have someone similar to him among the human beings, who would be without birth and cause. The same is with Eva, who proceeds. They are true symbols of the unbegotten Father and of the Holy Spirit. The begotten son [of Adam] had all human beings as brothers, who are begotten sons—in the symbolic image and likeness of Christ—the begotten Son, who became a man "firstborn" without seed "among many brothers" (Rom. 8:29). (*Sermo in constitutionem hominis secundum imaginem Dei* I 1.1-91; translation is mine)

In his second sermon from the series on the creation of human beings, Anastasius developed an idea that Adam was created in the image and likeness of Christ (*imago Christi*). God thus prefigured his own incarnation as early as during the creation of human beings and before their fall. Anastasius envisaged the following parallel between the creation of Adam and the incarnation of the Word: as God breathed into the dust his spirit and thus created Adam, so Christ was born as a result of the in-breathing of the Logos to the human flesh of Mary:

> Christ said, I shall make a man according to my image and likeness, and God made a man—he made him according to his image (Gen. 1:26). When I see how a human being was then created by God and how the divine, unspeakable, and life-giving breath, which comes from him, enters to that earthly and material body, I think about this symbol (τύπον) as the image, likeness, and prefiguration (προδιατύπωσιν) of Christ. Because the breath (ἐμφύσημα) that had come from the mouth [of God] implied the existence of the God Word, while what entered the dust—his true indwelling in flesh. <. . .>
>
> As the wisest and knowing about things before they happen, God pre-describes in Adam's construction and creation the image and symbol of his own incarnation, birth, and inhumation. He thus pre-shows his own composition as visible and invisible, mortal and immortal. So that a man, by seeing himself, would become undoubting and believing in Christ as visible and invisible, simultaneously God and human being, the same mortal and immortal, who is born from the Virgin. (*Sermo in constitutionem hominis secundum imaginem Dei* II 1. 35-45, 55-63; translation is mine)

# Microcosm

Men and women are not only the images of God—they also reflect the world around them. As Gregory of Nyssa's sister Macrina in the dialogue *On the Soul and the Resurrection* remarked, "Man is a microcosm, encompassing in himself the elements by which he is made complete" (Gregory of Nyssa 1967: 204). In this sense, a human being is also *imago mundi*—an image of the world.

Eastern theologians emphasized the connectedness between the *kosmos* and its image—microcosm. They believed that in the same way as human soul and body affect one another, whatever happens to human soul projects itself to the world. Holy souls sanctify the world around them, in the way Gerasimus of Jordan (fifth century), Cuthbert of Northumbria (634–87), or Seraphim of Sarov (1759–1833) did. Human sin, on the contrary, corrupts the surrounding world. Theophilus of Antioch in the second century explained this using the etymology of the Greek word "beast":

> Wild animals (θηρία) are so called from their being hunted (θηρεύεσθαι). They were not originally created evil or poisonous, for nothing was originally created evil by God; everything was good and "very good" (Gen. 1:31). The sin of man made them evil, for when man transgressed they transgressed with him. If the master of a house does well, his servants necessarily live properly; if the master sins, his slaves sin with him. Just so, it turned out that man, the master, sinned and the slaves sinned with him. Whenever man again returns to his natural state and so no longer does evil, they too will be restored to their original tameness. (*Ad Autolycum* II 17)

Christian theologians adopted the anthropocentric worldview, which went back to Homer and Hesiod (see Steiner 2010). They held that the world was created not for its own sake, but as a home for human beings. Adam and Eve entered their home after it had been prepared for them. The idea of the nature as home for human beings is embedded in the modern term *ecology*. This word comes from the Greek *oikos* (οἶκος), which means "house," "abode." Such an anthropocentric outlook at the world and human beings in it has been criticized by many modern environmentalists (see Boddice 2011). This critique is partially justifiable because human beings often abuse their central position in the nature. They selfishly exploit natural resources and undermine their harm to the environment. However, these numerous and grave abuses could be avoided, if anthropocentrism would be interpreted not as an opportunity to exploit nature, but as the responsibility to take care of it. Seen as duty and not privilege, anthropocentrism can be compatible with modern ecological thinking.

# VII.4
# Structure of Human Nature

Although patristic cosmology was anthropocentric, patristic theology was not. The fathers and mothers of the church rarely focused their attention on the composition of human nature in detachment from the larger soteriological and incarnational frameworks. In this regard, Christian theologians differed from the Greek philosophers, whose attention was absorbed by identifying elements of human nature. Notwithstanding their differences, Christian theology and Greek philosophy agreed upon differentiation between human body and soul, even though they often interpreted this differentiation in diverging ways.

The basis for the patristic understanding of the body-soul differentiation was biblical. Both the Old and the New Testaments provided the early Christian theologians with a wide array of meanings attached to such words as *nephesh* (נֶפֶשׁ) and *psyché* (ψυχή), standing for "soul"; as well as *gewiyyā* (גְּוִיָּה) or *gešēm* (גֶּשֶׁם) and *sōma* (σῶμα) standing for "body." Biblical theology differentiates between these two aspects of a human being (see Green 2008). In this, it cohered with the ancient Greek wisdom.

## Homer

Homer was among the earliest Greek authors who clearly distinguished soul from body. In most cases, soul, for him, was associated with life. At the same time, he spoke of soul as a continuation of human existence after death (see Davis 2011: 9). Homer described the death of Patroclus and then Hector as follows: "The end of death enfolded him; and his soul (ψυχή) fleeting from his limbs was gone to Hades" (*Ilias* 16.22). That for Homer soul was more than just biological life, is clear from the fact he never mentioned soul of animals.

**Figure 7.11** Homer from Troy Museum in Turkey.
Source: Photo by the author.

# Plato

When Plato made a clear-cut and radical differentiation between the ideal and empirical worlds, this differentiation was immediately applied to the two aspects of human beings, which had been introduced by Homer. Soul became perceived as consistent with the world of ideas, while the body as belonging to the material world. This was a radical departure from the standpoint of pre-Socratics, who had ascribed materiality to human souls. Because of that, they had believed that soul cannot survive the death of body. Plato criticized this idea.[1] He went further and suggested that soul not only does not end with the end of body but also does not begin with the beginning of body: it preexists.

For Plato, body is "a vehicle and means of transport" (*Timaeus* 44) for soul, which precedes body's birth and continues its journey after body's death. Without body, soul is naked (*Gorgias* 523e). Soul and body can be considered as two opposite poles of human existence. They are in permanent tension with one another. This tension can be seen in Plato's parable of the cave (*Respublica* 514a-520a). The

[1]See, for example, the exchange between Socrates and Glaukon in Plato's *Respublica* (608d–611c); see de los Ríos 2018.

**Figure 7.12** Artistic presentation of Plato's cave by Huan Yong Ping, *Caverne 2009*. From the exhibition *Plato in L.A. Contemporary Artists' Visions*. Villa Getty, Los Angeles.

Source: Photo by the author.

parable can be interpreted in the sense that philosophers see shadows in the cave because their souls are impeded by bodies. Only a soul, which has loosened its ties with its body through philosophical training, can come closer to seeing the things as they are.

# Aristotle

While Plato referred to soul on the margins of his philosophy, Aristotle made it a focus of his philosophical inquiry (see Boeri 2018; Granger 1996). He basically agreed with Plato about how soul and body are different (*De anima* III 429a). At the same time, Aristotle, unlike Plato, did not bother himself much with exploring the gap between them, but rather tried to demonstrate how they are connected and influence one another. For him, soul and body are parts of the whole (see Blumenthal 1993: 76). They are related to one another as sight to the eye, "for sight is the substance of the eye which corresponds to the account, the eye being merely the matter of seeing" (*De anima* II 412b).

Aristotle considered soul in the framework of logical and physical categories: as a motion and a form of particularity. Soul is the principle of motion. As motion, soul is pertinent to everything moveable—not just to human beings. Plants and animals also have souls, but of inferior kinds: nutritive and perceptive correspondingly. Human soul helps a human being to be aware of his or her motion. Self-awareness indicates the highest sort of soul, which only human beings feature. Aristotle explored various kinds of awareness, which human beings owe to soul, such as, for example, imagination and knowledge.

Soul, according to Aristotle, is related to body in a similar sense as the category of particularity is related to commonality: “Soul is the actuality of a body” (*De anima* II 412a). It is a bundle of capacities, such as nutritional, perceiving, and thinking ones (*De anima* II 413b). Aristotle differentiated between different bodies by the capacities of their souls. He, thus, applied his favorite method of analyzing things by sorting them out.

# Plotinus

The same method was applied to the analysis of soul by neo-Platonic philosophers (see Inwood & Warren 2020). Some of them did this in their commentaries on Aristotle’s *De anima*, including such authors as Iamblichus (*De anima*) and Simplicius (*In Aristotelis libros de anima commentaria)*. Plotinus developed an original teaching on soul in his *Enneads*. He considered soul in the framework of his basic idea that the world emanates from the One and comes back to the One. Human souls are a part of this process (see *Enneades* IV 9). They derive from the universal soul (ἡ τοῦ παντὸς ψυχή), which in turn emanates from the One through the universal intellect (νοῦς). Plotinus, thus, distinguished between soul and mind (see *Enneades* IV 8). Such a distinction became a common place in the Late Antiquity. It also played a crucial role in the Christian theological controversies, such as neo-Nicaean discussions about Apollinaris’ Christology.

Plotinus also suggested a *via media* between the Platonic radical differentiation between body and soul, and the Aristotelian way of considering them as parts of the whole (see Blumenthal 1993: 340). For Plotinus, human soul has an upper part, which is completely spiritual, and the lower one (Plotinus called it “nature”—*physis* (φύσις)), which is mixed up with body. Soul, thus, is a bridge between the ideal and empirical worlds. At the same time, soul, even in its lower part, cannot be located in a particular part of body. Plotinus compared the way that soul relates to body, with the way in which light or heat come from fire and fill in air (see *Enneades* IV 3).

Plotinus inaugurated not only the neo-Platonic line in the classical philosophy but also a specific neo-Platonic psychology. His line was followed by other neo-Platonists. The bottom line of their beliefs about soul was, on the one hand, a clear differentiation between body and soul. This differentiation was hierarchical: soul in this hierarchy stood higher than body. On the other hand, body and soul, for them, could not be regarded as irrelevant to each other—they are intrinsically connected.

# Alexander of Aphrodisias and Themistius

Some late antique thinkers interpreted soul and its relationship to body differently. For example, Alexander of Aphrodisias, who flourished in the early third century and extensively commented on the Aristotelian work, also left a remarkable commentary on *De anima*. His method of commenting was to be faithful to Aristotle's thought as much as possible. The same method was followed by a Byzantine statesman and philosopher Themistius. He lived in the fourth century and was admired as a politician by the Roman emperors, even though he did not convert to Christianity (see Heather & Moncur 2001; Vanderspoel 1995). Themistius left commentary on Aristotle's *De anima*, where he tried to establish what Aristotle meant, instead of ascribing to him his own ideas—in contrast to what many other neo-Platonic commentators on Aristotle did.

## Philoponus and Stephanus

There were also Christian commentators on *De anima*, whose method of interpretation did not much differ from that of Themistius. The aforementioned John Philoponus was in many regards more Aristotelian than Platonic. In his commentaries on the creation of the world, however, as we have seen, he turned radically against both Aristotelian and neo-Platonic standpoints that promoted the eternity of the world. In contrast to this, in his commentaries on Aristotle's *De anima (In Aristotelis libros de anima commentaria)*, which have survived, Philoponus seemingly aligned with most Aristotelian points, including those contradicting the Christian doctrine (see Blumenthal 1993: 59–60). The same and almost-complete lack of Christian reevaluation of Aristotle's take on soul can be observed in Stephanus—a baptized neo-Platonist, who taught first in Alexandria and later in Constantinople. Stephanus' *On De anima* has survived as a third book of Philoponus' commentaries (see Blumenthal 1993: 94).

## Origen

Origen was also under the influence of both Platonic and Aristotelian teachings on soul, but his intention was to produce a characteristically Christian psychology. He managed this, even though with some significant shortfalls. Origen's psychology is a part of his cosmogony, which he had produced in polemics with the pagan idea of the world's eternity. For him, all human beings have been created by God—not emanated from him. They had preexisted in the divine Logos, but only as blueprints:

> As a house and a ship are built or devised according to the plans of the architect, the house and the ship having as their beginning the plans and thoughts in the craftsman, so all things have come to be according to the thoughts of what will be, which were prefigured by God in wisdom, "For he made all things in wisdom" (Ps. 103:24). (*Commentarii in Iohannem* I 114; Origen 1989: 57)

Origen suggested that humanity preexisted in the Logos not just as a common nature, but as individual beings as well: "Without doubt all genera and spices always were [in the Logos], and perhaps even individual things" (*De principiis* I 4.5; Behr 2017: 88–9). In contrast to what many objected in "Origenism," Origen criticized those who believed that human soul could exist before body. From their beginning, all human beings consisted of soul and body, which can be only distinguished but not separated from one another: "Material substance is to be separated from them (souls) only in thought" (*De principiis* II 2.2; Behr 2017: 154–5). The prelapsarian body, always in unity with soul, was different from what we have now. It will be restored back to its prelapsarian state after the resurrection. The prelapsarian body is spiritual; its corporality is similar to the angelic corporality:

> We consider the quality of a spiritual body to be such as befits being inhabited not only by all holly and perfect souls, but also by that "whole creation" which "will be set free from the slavery of corruption" (Rom. 8:21). <. . .>
>
> From this statement, then, we can form a conjecture of what great purity, of what great refinement, and of what great glory is the quality of that body, if we make a comparison of it with those which now, although they are bodies celestial and most splendid, are yet made by hand and visible. But of the body it is said that it is "a house not made with hands but eternal in the heavens." Since, then, "things seen a temporal, but those not seen are eternal" (2 Cor. 4:18), all able to be seen, and have been made by hand and are not eternal, are very greatly surpassed in glory by that which is neither visible nor made by hand but is eternal. From this comparison, it may be conjectured how great is the beauty, how great the splendor, and how great the brilliance of a spiritual body. (*De principiis* III 6.4; Behr 2017: 444–7)

The Fall changed human body. This change, for Origen, was allegorized in the Scripture by the image of "skin tunics" (Gen. 3:21). The metaphor of tunics implies a change in the ontological status of human nature: it became mortal, thick, and dark. Skin tunics became "a symbol of the mortality which he (Adam) received because of his skin and of his frailty which came from the corruption of the flesh" (*In Leviticum* VI 2; Origen 1990: 120).

## Gregory of Nyssa

Another theologian who was as innovative as Origen in identifying the origins and structure of human nature was Gregory of Nyssa. He followed in the steps of Origen but avoided most of his mistakes. Gregory was helped by a clear differentiation between commonalities and particularities, which became available to the Christian theologians in the fourth century through the neo-Platonic dialectics.

Like Origen, Gregory placed anthropology in the frame of cosmogony. God had a blueprint for the entire humankind before the creation of the world. In contrast to Origen, however, Gregory believed that God created from this blueprint not all human beings at once in their ethereal bodies but the common nature of humankind. This common nature was first particularized in Adam. In her or his own time, each individual human being would particularize the common nature of humankind according to the preexistent plan:

> When the word says that God made man, the whole of humanity is indicated by the indefiniteness of the expression. For it is not named now Adam alongside the creature, as the history says in the following: but the name for the created man is not the particular (ὁ τίς), but the universal (ὁ καθόλου). Now we are led by the universal name of the nature to understand it so that by the divine foreknowledge and power all humankind was encompassed in the first creation. For it is necessary that God does not conceive of anything made by him as indefinite (ἀόριστον): but that all being has a certain limit and measure taken by the creative wisdom. As now the particular man (ὁ τὶς ἄνθρωπος) is limited by the quantity of his body, and the measure of his existence (ὑπόστασις) is his size which contains the surface of his body: so I think is the totality of mankind (ὅλον τὸ τῆς ἀνθρωπότητος πλήρωμα) in a way encompassed by a single body through the foreseeing power of the God of the whole. (*De opificio hominis* 16; Zachhuber 2014: 155)

Gregory stressed unity between body and soul. On the one hand, they are completely different: soul is spiritual, while body is material. On the other hand, they are not alien to each other and constitute a perfect unity (see Usacheva et al. 2020). For Gregory, the unity of body and soul is a key to the salvation of humankind through the incarnation of God:

> As the principle of death was in one and went through the entire human nature, in the same way also the principle of resurrection extends from one into the whole of humanity. For he who again united the soul, which had been assumed by himself, with its proper body by means of his power which had been mixed with both of those at their first constitution, mixed, in a more general way, the intelligible substance with the sensible so that the beginning (ἀρχή) is with consequence led to its perfection (πέρας). For when in that man, who was assumed by himself, the soul re-entered the body after the dissolution, the same kind of junction of the separated passed over from it as from a starting point (ἀρχή), as it were, potentially (τῇ δυνάμει) to the entire human nature. And this is the mystery of God's plan (οἰκονομία) with regard to his death and his resurrection from the dead: that, rather than preventing the separation of his soul and body by death according to nature's necessary development (ἀκολουθία), both would be reunited with each other in the resurrection; so that he might become in himself the meeting-ground both of life and death, having re-established in himself that nature which death had divided, and being himself the originating principle of the uniting of those separated portions. (*Oratio catechetica* XVI 48.2-49.16; Zachhuber 2014: 230)

Gregory dedicated to the unity of soul and body a dialogue *On the Soul and the Resurrection* (see Cadenhead 2018). He made his interlocutor his sister Macrina. Their conversation resembles the one between Socrates and his disciples in Plato's *Phaedo*. Gregory reserved the role of Socrates not for himself, but for his sister. In his time, it was an extraordinary step to put a female voice on the same scale with the voice of the father of philosophy. Like in *Phaedo*, the focus of the conversation between Gregory and Macrina is about the immortality of human soul.

Gregory and Macrina agreed that soul is attached to only one body: "The same body provides a frame for the same soul" (Gregory of Nyssa 1967: 246). Soul and body "have a single beginning" (Gregory of Nyssa 1967: 255). They separate for a short while in death and then will reunite in the resurrection. During lifetime and after death, soul is connected with the elements of body—regardless of whether these elements stay together or dissolve. Macrina, in responding to Gregory's question, argued that this happens in the same way as God takes care of all elements of the created world. As God is unmixed with creature, so soul remains always unmixed with body. Yet, soul accompanies body during and after life:

> Just as through the unspeakable wisdom of God appearing in all things we do not doubt that there is a divine nature and power in all being, so all things remain essentially themselves, and yet, if anyone should demand an account of the divine nature, the essence of God would be very far away from what is demonstrated and known in each thing in created nature, and yet it is agreed that the divine nature is present in these despite the difference. So it is not at all incredible, and the essence of the soul, although it is something else in itself (whatever it is conjectured to be), is not prevented from existing, despite the fact that those things contemplated in the universe under the heading of elements do not come together in it according to the logic of its nature. For, as has been said before, in the case of living bodies in which there is substance resulting from the mingling of the elements, there is, according to the logic of being, nothing in common between the simple and invisible essence of the soul and the coarseness of the body. Nevertheless, it is not doubted that the vital energy of the soul is present in the elements, diffused with a logic that is beyond human comprehension. Therefore, when the elements in the body are resolved into themselves, that which links it together through its vital energy does not perish. <. . .>
>
> The intelligible nature of the soul exists in the union of the elements and is not separated when they are dissolved. It remains in them and is not cut apart or extended by their separation. Nor is it broken up into bits and pieces in relation to the number of the elements. This is characteristic of a bodily and dimensional nature, whereas the intelligible and undimensional nature is not subject to dimensional effects. Therefore, the soul is present in those elements in which it once dwelt, there being no necessity for withdrawing it from its union with them. (Gregory of Nyssa 1967: 212–13, 215)

The relationship between one's body and soul, thus, is unique. It is maintained even when they are separated by death. A soul cannot be connected with another body. Macrina and Gregory strongly criticized *metempsychosis*—the idea that a soul can migrate from one body to another, including animals and plants. Such an idea had been supported philosophically since the pre-Socratics (see Inwood 2009) and continued to be a popular belief in the time of Gregory. Macrina addressed this issue in the following passage:

> Some <. . .> insult the human race by the idea of the community of animate beings, declaring that man and animal have the same soul in turn, that the soul changes bodies, always going on to what is pleasing to it, a bird, a fish, or a land animal after man, and that it returns from these to human form again. Others extend such nonsense even to trees, so that they think a life of wood is suitable for the soul. To others, it seems that the soul is always going from one human form to another and that human life goes on all the time with the same soul, that is, that the same souls now reside in these human forms and again in others continuously. (Gregory of Nyssa 1967: 246)

It is noteworthy that one of the arguments against *metempsychosis* was based on distinction between the categories of commonality and particularity. Macrina pointed out that if human souls migrate to other beings that share in different common natures, like animals or plants, then there is no much sense to speak about a human nature as such: "One nature in all things mingled with itself in a confused and disorderly unity" (Gregory of Nyssa 1967: 247).

The second century's apologist Athenagoras, who is believed to be the author of the treatise *De resurrectione*, had employed a similar argument. For him, human nature consists of soul and body. Therefore, to be preserved, it requires a unique and unchangeable relationship between a particular soul and a particular body. They should share the same departure point and the same final destination. Athenagoras used this as an argument in support of resurrection. For him, the possibility of resurrection is the only condition for human nature to remain whole:

> For if human nature universally considered is constituted by an immortal soul and a body which has been united with it at its creation; and if God has not separately assigned a creation and existence and course of life of this kind to the soul as such or to the body but to men who are made up of both, so that they might spend their life and come to one common end with the parts from which they are created and exist; then it is necessary, since all there is is one living being composed of two parts, undergoing all the experiences of soul and body, and actively carrying out whatever requires the judgement of the senses and of reason, that the entire concatenation of such phenomena leads to one end so that all these things—the creation of man, the nature of man, the existence of man, the deeds and experiences and way of life of man,

> and the end which suits his nature—might be fully integrated into one harmonious and concordant whole. (*De resurrectione* XV 2; Schoedel 1972: 123–5)

The partnership of a soul with its body never changes. So does the entire human nature—it remains the same regardless of the Fall, death, or resurrection (see Moss 2019). For Gregory of Nyssa, the fall of the first human couple has not incurred any ontological change in the human nature. In this point, he differed from Origen. Gregory's interpretation of the biblical story about the skin tunics (Gen. 3:21) demonstrates the difference. For Origen, this story meant the ontological change in the human nature. For Gregory, on the contrary, it meant that the nature has remained the same. What did change was what surrounds the nature. Gregory used the preposition "around" (περί) for this:

> For since Adam is living in us, we all, the individual human beings (οἱ καθ' ἕκαστον ἄνθρωποι), see each and all these tunics of skin round (περί) our nature, and also the transitory fig leaves of this material life which we have badly sewn together for ourselves after being stripped of our resplendent garments. (*De oratione dominica orationes* V 64.14–65.5; 66.8–15; Zachhuber 2014: 182)

# *Apokatastasis*

Origen and Gregory of Nyssa were on the same page in their interpretation of the universal salvation of the human nature. Since the early Christian centuries, there have been theologians who advocated for the "restoration of all" (ἀποκατάστασις τῶν πάντων). They believed that some Christians, who have lived pious life, would reach their salvation immediately. Others, including non-Christians, would reach salvation eventually, after having been purified in the afterlife. In the end, every human being who ever lived, as well as all demonic forces who had revolted against God, will reconcile with their Creator.

Among the earliest theologians who seemingly advocated for *apokatastasis* was Clement of Alexandria. Clement pointed out that God is good and cannot punish sinners. He rather corrects people through sufferings and pain, which do not last eternally:

> May these heretics, too, after learning from these notes, return to wisdom and turn to the omnipotent God. But if, like deaf snakes, they should refuse to listen to the song that is sung now, all recently, but is extremely ancient, may they be educated at least by God, by bearing his paternal admonitions; may they be ashamed and repent, and may it not happen that, behaving with obstinate disobedience, they must undergo the final and general judgment. For partial educative processes take place as well, which are called "corrections," which we, who belong to the people of the Lord, mostly encounter

> when we happen to be in a state of sin: we are corrected by divine Providence just as kids are by their teacher or father. God does not punish (τιμωρεῖται)—since punishment is the retribution of evil with further evil—but corrects (κολάζει) for the sake of those who are corrected, both in general and singularly. (*Stromata* VII 16.102; Ramelli 2013: 127)

In the same period of time in a different part of the Roman Empire, Syria, Bardaisan (*c.* 154–222) made similar claims. He, on the one hand, acknowledged that human beings have freedom to choose either good or evil. On the other hand, God is more powerful than their freedom and can override it in order to save them. For Bardaisan, this is a precondition of the universal reconciliation of everyone with God:

> Whenever God likes, everything can be, with no obstacle at all. In fact, there is nothing that can impede that great and holy will. For, even those who are convinced to resist God, do not resist by their force, but they are in evil and error, and this can be only for a short time, because God is kind and gentle, and allows all natures to remain in the state in which they are, and to govern themselves by their own will, but at the same time they are conditioned by the things that are done and the plans that have been conceived [by God] in order to help them. For this order and this government that have been given [by God], and the association of one with another, damps the natures' force, so that they cannot be either completely harmful or completely harmed, as they were harmful and harmed before the creation of the world. And there will come a time when even this capacity for harm that remains in them will be brought to an end by the instruction that will obtain in a different arrangement of things: and, once that new world will be constituted, all evil movements will cease, all rebellions will come to an end, and the fools will be persuaded, and the lacks will be filled, and there will be safety and peace, as a gift of the Lord of all natures. (In Ramelli 2013: 112–13)

Origen's take on the issue of *apokatastasis* was less moralistic and more ontological. For him, life is good and death is evil. Therefore, they cannot be put on the same scale: life always prevails. Unlike life, death cannot be eternal. Therefore, everyone will eventually get rid of death and reach eternal life:

> However, even if one may remain in sin, even if one may endure under the kingly power of death, I do not think that this reign of death is eternal as that of Life and Justice is, especially in that I hear from the Apostle that the last enemy, death, must be destroyed (1 Cor. 15:26). For should one suppose that the eternity of death is the same as that of Life, death will no longer be the contradictory opposite of Life, but equal to it. For "eternal" is not the contradictory of "eternal," but the same thing. Now, it is certain that death is the contradictory of Life; therefore, it is certain that, if Life is eternal, death cannot possibly be eternal. <. . .> For, when the death of the soul, which is the very last enemy, has been destroyed, also this common death (which, as I said, is a sort of shadow of the death of the soul) will necessarily be abolished, and the

> kingdom of death, along with death itself, will be destroyed. (*In epistulam Pauli ad Romanos* V 7; Ramelli 2013: 162)

Gregory of Nyssa, in his dialogue with Macrina on the soul and the resurrection, ascribed to his sister similar ideas. He agreed with her that some souls can be purified in this life, and some in the afterlife. In the latter case, they have to suffer in order to be purged by pain. Their idea of *apokatastasis* is quite close to the idea of purgatory as it was developed in the Middle Ages in the West:

> The virtuous life will be distinguished from the evil life by the fact that those of us who cultivated virtue will grow immediately into a perfect plant, while those whose virtues became faded and deformed through evil, having "fallen on the horns" as the saying goes (see Plato's *Leges* 853d), even if we are born again through the resurrection, will be harshly treated by the judge and will not be strong enough to return to the form of the original plant and become what we were before our fall into the earth. <. . .>
>
> After a long period of time, they will assume again the form which they received from God in the beginning. Blessed are those who come immediately to a complete perfection of growth. (Gregory of Nyssa 1967: 271)

The council that met in Constantinople in 553 rather unexpectedly occupied itself with some old ideas about the origins and the final destination of human beings. The council ascribed these ideas in wholesale to Origen, whom it also anathematized in person. Gregory of Nyssa was spared. Some ideas that the council condemned as "Origenism" can hardly, if at all, be found in Origen. Most of these ideas were polemical approximations to Origen's original ideas. It seems that the council dealt with some popular beliefs which circulated in the sixth century and had some remote resemblance with Origen's teaching. These popular ideas were articulated in the final definitions of the council:

> If anyone advocates the mythical pre-existence of souls and the monstrous restoration that follows from this, let him be anathema (§1).
>
> If anyone says that the origin of all rational beings was incorporeal and material minds without any number or name, with the result that there was a henad of them all through identity of substance, power and operation and through their union with and knowledge of God the Word, but that they reached satiety with divine contemplation and turned to what is worse, according to what the drive to this in each one corresponded to, and that they took more subtle or denser bodies and were allotted names such that the powers above have different names just as they have different bodies, as a result of which they became and were named some cherubim, some seraphim, and others principalities, powers, dominations, thrones, angels, and whatever heavenly orders there are, let him be anathema (§2).
>
> <. . .>
>
> If anyone says that the rational beings who grew cold in divine love were bound to our more dense bodies and were named human beings, while those who had reached

the acme of evil were bound to cold and dark bodies and are and are called demons and spirits of wickedness, let him be anathema (§4).

If anyone says that from the state of the angels and archangels originates that of the soul, and from that of the soul that of demons and human beings, and from that of human beings angels and demons originate again, and that each order of the heavenly powers is constituted either entirely from those below or those above or from both those above and those below, let him be anathema (§5).

If anyone says that the genus of demons had a double origin, being compounded both from human souls and from more powerful spirits that descend to this, but that from the whole henad of rational beings one mind alone remained constant in divine love and contemplation, and that it became Christ and king of all rational beings and created the whole of corporeal nature, <. . .> let him be anathema (§6).

<. . .>

If anyone says that the Lord's body after the resurrection was ethereal and spherical in form, and that the same will be true of the other bodies after the resurrection, and that, with first the Lord himself shedding his own body and [then] all likewise, the nature of bodies will pass into non-existence, let him be anathema (§10).

<. . .>

If anyone says that the heavenly powers, all human beings, the devil, and the spirits of wickedness will be united to God the Word in just the same way as the mind they call Christ, which is in the form of God and emptied itself, as they assert, and that the kingdom of Christ will have an end, let him be anathema (§12). (Price 2009: vol. 2: 284–6)

The council also anathematized those who believed that "there will be one henad of all rational beings, when the hypostases and numbers are annihilated together with bodies" (§14). This anathematism is intriguing. It pinpoints a real problem that underpinned some controversial ideas about the origins and the final destination of human beings. This problem is caused by insufficient distinction between the categories of commonality and particularity. No doubt, Origen did not believe that the particularities of the human nature—hypostases—would be annihilated after the resurrection. At the same time, he apparently confused the common and particular modalities of the humankind, when he assumed that all individual human beings have been created at once by God in a certain form. Gregory of Nyssa corrected him by saying that it was the common nature, which was created first, simultaneously with Adam. After that, every human being would come to this world and would participate in this common nature in her or his own time and place.

It seems that the teaching about *apokatastasis* is a result of confusion between the categories of commonality and particularity. It dwells on the axiom of the common salvation of humankind. This common salvation of the entire humankind should not be interpreted as a particular salvation of every human being. The idea of *apokatastasis*, however, does confuse the two aspects of salvation (i.e., of humankind and individual human beings), which should be kept distinguished. In other words, God assumed the entire humanity, and not individual human beings. The incarnated Logos was a unique individual being and cannot be confused with anyone else. He, thus, saved the common nature, which will continue to be close to him in the *eschaton*. This, however, will not incur automatic reconciliation of everyone with God only by the virtue of belonging to the common human nature. To be saved, a human being is expected to appropriate or particularize the common salvation. If she or he does so, then the common salvation becomes particular one and an individual enters the Kingdom of God.

# Nemesius

In the late fourth century, a comprehensive treatise on the human nature was composed as an attempt at the Christian evaluation of the available opinions on this matter expressed by the pagan and early Christian theologians. It was titled *On the Nature of a Human Being* (Περὶ φύσεως ἀνθρώπου)—similarly to a Hippocratic treatise, which had been commented upon by Galen (see Galenus 1969: 603). Many thought this treatise was composed by Gregory of Nyssa. It was translated under his name to the Armenian (see Morani 1990) and Arabic (see Khalil 1999) languages. However, its author was the bishop of Emesa (modern Homs) in Syria Nemesius. Almost nothing is known about him except his authorship of the treatise.

It summarized various opinions on the human nature. Yet, it merits a constructive and positive willingness to take the best from different schools of thinking, without prejudices and aggressive polemics. Nemesius included to his summary pre-Socratics, Plato, Aristotle, middle- and neo-Platonists Posidonius, Plotinus, Porphyry, Iamblichus, and quite a few Christian theologians before him, such as Origen, Apollinaris, Eunomius, Theodore of Mopsuestia, and others. With special fondness he referred to the work of the highest medical authority of his time, Galen, whom he called "the marvellous physician." Although Nemesius criticized particular points, both pagan and Christian, his purpose was not polemical. He wanted not to triumph over the opinions of others, but to draw a bottom line of various takes on human nature. Here is an example:

> If we have proved that the soul is neither a body nor an attunement nor a mixture nor any other quality, it is clear from this that the soul is some incorporeal substance. For that it exists is agreed by all. If it is neither body nor accident, it is clear that it is an incorporeal substance and none of those things that have their being in something else. For these come and go without the destruction of their substrate. But when the soul is separated from it the body is altogether destroyed. It is possible to prove that the soul is immortal using the same facts. For if it is neither a body, which was shown to be naturally able to be dispersed and perishable, nor a quality nor quantity nor anything else perishable, it is clear that it is immortal. There are many proofs of its

> immortality in Plato and the rest, but those are very difficult, hard to comprehend and scarcely well-understood by those brought up in these sciences. For us let the teaching of the sacred books suffice as a proof of the soul's immortality, for it is reliable in itself, since it is divinely inspired. But for those who do not accept the Christian writings it suffices to prove that the soul is none of those things that perish. For if it is none of the things that perish, and is imperishable, it is also immortal. (*De natura hominis* II 37; Nemesius 2008: 76–7)

In contrast to many other Christian theologians of his time, who borrowed ideas of ancient philosophers without acknowledging them and, at the same time, openly despised them, Nemesius acknowledged his sources and appreciated them, whenever he deemed them to be compatible with the Christian worldview. He explored with open mind "the borderline between pagan and Christian cultures" (Introduction to Nemesius 2008: 1).

His theological line, however, was not completely orthodox, if judged by the criteria of the posterior anthropology. On the one hand, Nemesius rejected the idea of *apokatastasis*. On the other, he accepted the existence of souls prior to bodies. His take on the relationship between soul and body is close to neo-Platonic. He pointed out the superiority of soul over body. At the same time, he followed Plotinus in stressing that soul does not sit in a particular place of the body, but engulfs and penetrates it as light penetrates air:

> As the sun by its presence transforms the air into light, making it have the form of light, and light is unified with the air, mixed with it without being compounded, in the same way the soul is unified with the body while remaining altogether uncompounded, differing only in that the sun, being a body and circumscribed in place, is not everywhere that its light is. <. . .>
>
> The soul, being incorporeal and not circumscribed in place, occupies as a whole the whole of its own light and of its body, and there is no part to which it gives light in which it is not present as a whole. For it is not controlled by the body, but itself controls the body; it is not in the body as in a vessel or a wine-skin, but rather the body is in it. (*De natura hominis* II 41; Nemesius 2008: 81–2)

Nemesius was a proponent of human agency. He stressed that human beings are free, and freedom constitutes an important part of the human nature. Freedom, for Nemesius, is a key to explain evil in the world:

> One surely cannot blame God for our being bad through having powers that admit of change. For vices do not reside in powers but in dispositions, and our dispositions follow our choice. So we become bad through our choice, and we are not bad by nature. (*De natura hominis* XLI 119; Nemesius 2008: 203)

# VII.5
# Dualism

## Pandora's Box

In the period of classical Antiquity, human agency was rarely invoked to explain evil. Other explanations were more popular (see Angier 2019), such as a story told by Hesiod about Pandora (see Sassi 2018: 32). According to this story, after the Titan Prometheus stole fire from Olympus, Zeus decided to retaliate. He ordered Hephaestus to create a woman, Pandora. She was made from earth in the image of goddesses (*Opera et dies* 62). Zeus sent her to Prometheus' brother Epimetheus, who had in his care an amphora (πίθος) containing all sorts of evil. While in Epimetheus' household,

> The woman removed the great lid from the storage jar with her hands and scattered all its contents abroad—she wrought baneful evils for human beings.

After that, Hesiod continues,

> countless other miseries roam among mankind; for the earth is full of evils, and the sea is full; and some sicknesses come upon men by day, and others by night, of their own accord, bearing evils to mortals in silence. (*Opera et dies* 57)

According to Hesiod, the human input to the emergence of evil in the world was minimal and passive. Gods and titans bore most responsibility for it. The posterior Greek culture followed this line and explained evil in deterministic terms. Active human synergy was almost impossible in containing evil and its consequences.

## Astral Determinism

Astral determinism, or astrology, was another popular explanation of evil: it held that celestial bodies control earthly matters and can cause human misfortunes (see

**Figure 7.13** Mediterranean amphorae from Sardinia—a crossroad of Punic, Phoenician, and Greek cultures. Hesiod might have had in mind such vessels when he told the myth about Pandora's "box."
Source: Photo by the author.

Denzey 2013; Beck 2008). Astrology was popular not only among polytheists but also among monotheistic Jews, Christians, and Muslims (see Stuckrad 2000). It survived the conversion of the Roman Empire to Christianity and became a part of everyday life and politics in Byzantium (see Magdalino 2017). Astral determinism, as an explanation of evil in the world, was upheld by the early quasi-Christian groups, which we now identify as Gnostic.

## Features of Gnosticism

"Gnosticism" is an umbrella term, criticized by some (see Williams 1999), which denotes a variety of deterministic and dualistic views. Gnostic groups, notwithstanding their diversity, featured some common intuitions about the origins of evil and the ways to overcome it. They tended to see the world in black and white, with evil being embedded in it ontologically. One had to be initiated to special knowledge, which often had a form of conspiracy theories, to be saved from the global evil. Gnosticism was elitist—only those predetermined had access to the saving knowledge.

## Gospel of Judas

The apocryphal *Gospel of Judas* is an example of Gnostic literature. This text was translated from Greek to Coptic some time between 220 and 340. It was discovered in the 1970s somewhere to the south from Cairo.[1] The gospel presents Apostle Judas telling "a secret story" about Jesus, whom all other apostles had misunderstood. It is a typical Gnostic text featuring dualism and conspiracy theories. It also refers to astrology. The word "star" has been used in this text more than in any other early Christian text.

According to the gospel's narrative, each of the twelve apostles had his own star. Judas' star was special; it secured for this apostle a special mission. Jesus told him about this mission: "Lift up your eyes and look at the cloud and the light within it and the stars surrounding it. And the star that leads the way is your star" (§§56-57; Ehrman et al. 2008: 44-5). Following his star, Judas handed Jesus to the Jewish high priests and in this way fulfilled Jesus' commandment to "sacrifice the man who bears" God. Judas' betrayal of Jesus, thus, was not a betrayal, but a mission. The apostle was led through this mission by his star, which predetermined it.

The *Gospel of Judas*, as all other Gnostic gospels, is dualistic. As mentioned, dualism was a popular way to explain the existence of evil in the world. The dualistic worldview renders evil in ontological terms—as embedded in the world and an intrinsic part of it. According to this worldview, evil has its own chemistry and physics, which are different from the chemistry and physics of good things. Evil can be touched and felt. It has its own matter, and matter itself is often perceived as evil. It is concentrated in special places and transmitted through special procedures. Evil is mechanical and features particular mechanisms of reproduction and dissemination. These mechanisms are magical and magics is usually dualistic.

## Gospel of Thomas

Another pseudepigraphic gospel, of Thomas, also features dualism. Like the *Gospel of Judas*, the *Gospel of Thomas* was originally composed in Greek and later translated in Coptic. Only a few fragments of the original Greek texts were found among the Greek papyri in the Egyptian village El-Bahnasa (the ancient town of Pr-Medjed (in Egyptian), Oxyrhynchus (in Greek), or Pemdje (in Coptic)). Its almost-complete Coptic translation was found among the Gnostic texts in Nag Hammadi. This is a modern town in the Upper Egypt. In the period of Late Antiquity, it was a center of Gnostic Christianity and monasticism. After the political and ecclesial authorities in Alexandria cracked down on Gnosticism, many of its texts were hidden on the banks of the Nile. These texts were discovered only in 1945.[2]

---

[1]See a thrilling story about this gospel's discovery and publication in Gathercole 2007: 8–23.
[2]See Robinson 1977. Brill publishes a series of Nag Hammadi and Manichaean Studies and maintains Nag Hammadi Bibliography Online: https://bibliographies.brillonline.com/browse/nag-hammadi-bibliography [accessed on June 7, 2021].

**Figure 7.14** The banks of the Nile at Nag Hammadi in Upper Egypt, close to the place where the Gnostic library was found in 1945.
Source: Photo by the author.

Although found in Egypt, the *Gospel of Thomas* might have been written in Syria or indeed in any part of the Roman Empire (Gathercole 2014: 124). The form of this gospel is different from the canonical Gospels. The latter are narratives with some direct quotes (*logia*) of Jesus, while the Thomas' gospel almost completely consists of Jesus' *logia*. We do not know who wrote them under the name of Thomas.

The gospel features a dualistic thinking. For example, the *logion* 56 presents the world as a corpse: "Jesus said, 'Whoever has come to know the world has found a corpse'" (in Gathercole 2014: 428). This comparison diminishes the ontological value of the world and counterposes it to the spiritual realm. The *Gospel of Thomas* also contains references to the secret and elitist knowledge—another typical Gnostic feature. Like in the *Gospel of Judas*, this secret knowledge has been communicated exclusively to the author of the gospel and remains hidden from other apostles:

> Jesus said to his disciples, "Compare me and tell me whom I resemble." Simon Peter said to him, "You are like a righteous angel." Matthew said to him, "You are like a wise philosopher." Thomas said to him, "Master, my mouth is completely unable to say whom you are like." Jesus said, "I am not your master. When you drank, you became drunk with the bubbling spring which I have dug." And he took him and withdrew, and spoke three words to him. When Thomas returned to his companions, they asked him, "What did Jesus say to you?" Thomas said to them, "If I told you one of the words which he spoke to me, you would pick up stones and throw them at me. But fire would come forth from the stones, and burn you." (In Gathercole 2014: 259)

The author of the gospel presented Peter and Matthew as wrong about Jesus' identity. Apparently, this was an allegorical way (see Gathercole 2014: 260–1) to say that the Christian communities who read the texts of Peter and Matthew, that is, catholic communities, were wrong in interpreting Jesus. Only the community that read this gospel of Thomas, that is, the Gnostic community, was right in interpreting him.

The gospel made it clear that it is alright to stay away from those who lack the hidden knowledge about Jesus. The following *logion* 77 implied that the true knowledge comes from separation, like a sliver that splits from a log: "Split a piece of wood—I am there" (in Gathercole 2014: 492). For the author of the gospel, Jesus himself endorsed such sectarian approach regarding other Christians: "A man said to him, 'Tell my brothers to divide my father's property with me.' He (Jesus) said to him, 'O man, who has made me a divider?' He turned to his disciples and said to them, 'Surely I am no divider?'" (in Gathercole 2014: 481). While the Christians who have limited or distorted knowledge of the divine may be many, those with advanced and true knowledge are a few: "One out of a thousand or two out of ten thousand" (in Gathercole 2014: 313). Those a few have been predestined to have access to this exclusive knowledge.

## Basilides

One of the earliest recorded representatives of the dualistic mentality was Basilides. He flourished in the 130s. His ideas came from the Alexandrian context, but he possibly developed them while staying in Antioch. Eusebius called Basilides a "Gnostic" (see Pearson 2008: 28). *Acta Archelai,* a fictional narrative about the bishop of a Mesopotamian city Carchar, Archelaus, ascribed to Basilides the following statement:

> Let us investigate what inquiries the barbarians have made about good and evil things, and what opinions they have formed on all these matters. For some of them have said that all things have two beginnings, to which they have associated good and evil, stating that these beginnings themselves are without beginning and unbegotten. In other words there was in the beginning Light and Darkness, which existed of themselves, which were not said to be begotten. (*Acta Archelai* 67.6–7; Pearson 2008: 7)

This can be seen as a classical definition of the dualistic worldview. It explains good and evil as "things." According to such explanation, each kind of these things has its own source and creator: good and evil ones.

## Marcion

Another representative of the dualistic worldview, Marcion, polarized the Scriptures. He suggested that not only parts of the world (he, for instance, believed that insects belong to the evil part of the world) but also the Scriptures have different ontological statuses. There are good Scriptures and bad Scriptures—depending on what deity they come from. The Jewish Scriptures revealed the evil god. This god is revengeful and cruel: he likes punishing those who do not obey him.

In contrast to him, the good god revealed himself as the Son in a number of texts that can be regarded specifically Christian Scriptures, including the Gospel of Luke (see Roth 2015) and some of Paul's epistles. Marcion excluded from his canon the epistle to Hebrews, as well as pastoral letters. He edited the rest of Paul's writings. In his only surviving direct quotation, Marcion praised the Christian Scriptures as coming from the good god: "Oh fullness of wealth, folly, might, and ecstasy, that no one can say or think anything beyond it, or compare anything to it!" (in Räisänen 2008: 105).

Marcion's good god is merciful and redeeming. He was punished, however, for his kindness by the evil god through crucifixion and death. Even in the hades, however, the good god continued his redemptive mission and saved all those who had been cast there by the god of the Jewish Scriptures. Marcion's approach to the word of the Bible was both fundamentalistic and dualistic.

By confronting Marcion's scriptural canon, the church was forced to develop its own New Testament canon. Without Marcion, this canon would probably continue to be vague for long time. Some scholars even believe that the church owes to Marcion the idea of a new testament as distinct from the old one (see Knox 1980). Marcion, who established his own church, also pushed the catholic communities to consolidate and develop their own ecclesial structures.

## Montanism

Similar quasi-church was established by the Montanists. They identified particular places as clean, and other places declared unclean. Montanism was a charismatic movement branded by its contemporaries as "prophecy" (see Eusebius, *Historia ecclesiastica* V 16.4; Clement of Alexandria, *Stromata* IV 13). It was nostalgic about the first decades of Christianity, when everyone was equal, often filled with the prophetic spirit, and waiting for the imminent second coming of the Lord. Montanism tried to encapsulate the evaporating charismata of the early Christian communities, and confined them to a particular place.

The Montanist movement emerged in the 150–60s in Phrygia, in the western part of Asia Minor. From there, it spread as far as to Italy and North Africa, and survived until the sixth century. Three persons have been reported as the founders of the movement: Montanus, who gave the movement his name, Prisca (or Priscilla) and Maximilla. Women were important in the Montanist movement. They were highest-ranked prophetesses and could minister sacraments, including Eucharist. Even God

**Figure 7.15** Ruins of the Montanist "New Jerusalem" in Phrygia.
Source: Photo by the author.

appeared to the Montanists as a female figure. A Montanist prophetess described one of such appearances in the following passage preserved by Epiphanius:

> Christ came to me dressed in a white robe, in the form of a woman, imbued me with wisdom, and revealed to me that this place is holy, and that Jerusalem will descend from heaven here. (*Panarion* 49.3; Marjanen 2008: 204)

This special place referred to in the dream was located on a deserted and rough terrain between the villages of Ardabau, Pepuza, and Tymion in Phrygia. This place was recently discovered by the research teams led by William Tabbernee and Peter Lampe near the Turkish city of Uşak (see Tabbernee & Lampe 2008). Montanists believed that this would be the place for the millennial kingdom promised by Jesus. It was exempted from the general condemnation of matter and provided spiritual healing and salvation for all those staying at it. After Montanus and his co-prophetesses died, their bodies were possibly buried in a shrine in Pepuza and venerated as relics (see Tabbernee 1997: 32). In the eyes of the Montanists, the relics of the founders added to the sacrality of this place.

# Manichaeism

An extremely dualistic worldview was embodied in Manichaeism. This was a syncretic religious movement that incorporated elements of Buddhism, Zoroastrianism, and

Christianity. It was born in Sassanid Persia and spread far to the east in China and to the west across the Roman Empire. It mimicked local religious traditions. In the East, it appeared as polytheism, while in the West it tried to look monotheistic. In India, for instance, the founder of Manichaeism Mani (around AD 216–76) was perceived as Buddha. On the Roman soil, however, he presented himself as the "apostle of Jesus Christ" and the "Paraclete." The Manichaean movement often affiliated itself with Marcionism and was perceived by many in this way. Although Manichaeism pretended to be a sort of Christianity, it never was. It featured a very different cosmology, theology, and Christology. As Iain Gardner and Samuel N. C. Lieu have remarked, it was "the first real 'religion' in the modern sense" (Gardner & Lieu 2004: 1), and thus should be perceived as very different from Judeo-Christianity.

The following account of how Mani after his death entered the Manichaean paradise, for example, looks Buddhist. This fragment shows the syncretic and polytheistic character of this religion. It was originally composed in Syriac and has survived in the Parthian translation:

> Just like a sovereign who takes off armour and garment and puts on another royal garment, thus the apostle of light (i.e., Mani) took off the warlike dress of the body and sat down in a ship of light and received the divine garment, the diadem of light, and the beautiful garland. And in great joy he flew together with the light gods that are going to the right and to the left [of him], with harp[-sound] and song of joy, in divine miraculous power, like a swift lightning and a shooting star (lit. splendid swift form), to the Pillar of Glory, the path of the light, and the moon-chariot, the meeting-place of the gods. And he stayed [there] with god Ohrmezd the father (i.e., the First Man). And he left the whole herd of righteousness (i.e., the Manichaean community) orphaned and sad, because the master of the house had entered *parinirvana*. (In Gardner & Lieu 2004: 88)

Mani perceived himself as the seal of all prophets before him, including Buddha, Zarathustra, and Christ (see Gardner 2020). He believed that his was the final revelation to the humankind, and he wanted to spread this revelation to the entire world. To some extent, he succeeded, as Manichaeism became quite popular from Rome and Carthage to Syria, India, and China.

In all these settings, Manichaeism was also persecuted. Mani was imprisoned by the Persian king Vahram I (r. 271–74) and died in bounds. Most Manichaean writings were destroyed, for which reason for a long scholars had to rely only on the accounts from the opponents of this religion. In the recent decades, they learned much more about Manichaeism from its original texts discovered in Medinet Madi and at the Dakhleh oasis in Egypt. These texts have survived in Coptic, as well as in Middle Persian, Parthian, Sogdian, Tocharian B, Uighur, and Bactrian.

Manichaeans believed that there is essentially good and essentially bad matter. The "Father of Greatness" was the master of the former, which in a sense was his extension, in the form of light. The "King of Darkness" was the master of the evil matter, which was imbued with carnality and conflict. According to the Manichaean cosmogonic myth, these two opposite kinds of matter occupied different parts of earth: the good one was in the North, East, and West, while the evil one in the South. They were separated by a border. Here is a brief account of this myth in a Manichaean psalm discovered in the Medinet Madi codex, in Coptic:

> When the Holy Spirit came he revealed to us the way of truth and taught us that there are two natures, that of light and that of darkness, separate one from the other from the beginning.
>
> The kingdom of light, on the one hand consisted in five greatnesses, and they are the Father and his twelve aeons and the aeons of the aeons, the living air, the land of light; the Great Spirit breathing in them, nourishing them with its light.
>
> However, the kingdom of darkness consists of five storehouses, which are smoke and fire and wind and water and darkness; their counsel creeping in them, moving them and raising them to make war with one another. (In Gardner & Lieu 2004: 176–7)

At some point, the dark part of the universe decided to conquer the bright part of it. To protect its kingdom, the "Father" decided to immobilize the forces of darkness by the means of the universal soul—in the polytheistic version of Manichaeism, it was a variety of deities. This procedure was a bit complicated. First, the "Father" evoked the "Great Spirit," who is also the "Mother of Life." The "Spirit" then called the "First Man," who is also the "Son." The "Father," the "Mother," and the "Son" constituted the Manichaean trinity, which was hierarchical and compartmentalized ontologically. Here is a fragment from the Manichaean gospel preserved in the Sogdian language, praising the Manichaean trinity:

> He has been praised and will be praised, the dearest-of-the-dear son, the life-giving [saviour] Jesus, head of all giving, support of the pure and perception of the wise. She has been praised and will be praised, the wonder-working Kanīgrōšān, who is the head of all wisdom. It has been praised and will be praised, the holy church, righteousness, by the power of the Father, god Zurwān, by the praise of the Mother [of Life], god Rāmrātux, and by the wisdom of the Son Jesus. Welfare and blessing upon the children of well-being and on the speakers and hearers of the trustworthy holy word. (In Gardner & Lieu 2004: 157–8)

The son engaged in the battle with the evil and was defeated in it, in order to overcome evil. He cast the soul (or his five divine sons, according to the polytheistic version) attached to him, and the latter, being essentially good, mixed up with the bad matter, to poison the latter. An eighth-century Eastern Syrian theologian Theodore bar Khoni provided an account of this point of the Manichaean doctrine, in Syriac:

> Then the Primal Man (i.e., the Son) gave himself and his five sons to be consumed by the five sons of darkness, like a man who has an enemy and mixes a deadly poison into

> a cake and gives it. He says that when they had partaken of the five nourishing gods, the latter's intellect was removed, and that due to the poison of the sons of darkness, they became like people who are bitten by an enraged dog or a snake. (In Gardner & Lieu 2004: 13–14)

This mixture of good and evil elements is the reality that human beings face everywhere, and they are themselves a part of this reality. Their task is to liberate the elements of light from the bounds of bad matter and send them up to special reservoirs: the Sun and the Moon. These are quintessentially good and completely different from planets and stars, which are concentrations of evil. To liberate the elements of light, Manichaeans had to literally eat them. They believed that the largest concentration of these elements was in fruits and vegetables. For this reason, they ate them as much as possible, sending the liberated light up and defecating evil matter down. At the same time, they avoided meat and wine, which, according to their beliefs, had critical concentrations of bad matter. They also avoided procreation, because they believed it contributed to the further particularization of the light and its incarceration within the dark matter.

Eventually, the Manichaeans hoped, the light will win over darkness, and all their particles will gather to where they belong, without ever mixing up again. Here is what the Coptic psalm from Medinet Madi says about this:

> All life, the relic of light wheresoever it be, he will gather to himself and of it depict a Statue. And the counsel of death too, all the darkness, he will gather together and paint its very self for a (bond?) for the ruler. In an instant the Living Spirit will come. <. . .> He will succour the light. However, the counsel of death and the darkness he will shut up in the tomb that was established for it, that it might be bound in it for ever. (In Gardner & Lieu 2004: 178)

# VII.6
# Anti-dualism

However eclectic, the Manichaean explanation of the world appeared captivating to the imagination of many. Its points of attraction were a colorful cosmology and dualism. Dualism is attractive, because it gives an easy explanation of evil and relieves human beings from the burden of responsibility for it. Gods and nature are to be blamed for the existence of evil. It is a spiritual populism of sorts, which renders the picture of the world as simplified bipolarity and blames others for people's own faults and misfortunes.

Young Augustine, together with many other pagans and Christians of his time, was enchanted by the Manichaean fantasy world. Later, it took a lot of effort for him to get away from the Manichaean dualistic worldview. It seems he did not get rid of it completely, and *dualistic* traces can be spotted in the way he polarized the presumably damaged nature and the divine grace. Notwithstanding this, Augustine contributed a lot to the polemics against dualism (see Augustine 2008; Oort 2013; Lauber & Johnson 2018: 181–98).

Long before Augustine, Irenaeus of Lyon focused on dualism in his polemical treatises *Against heresies*. For him, dualistic worldview was heretical in the original sense of heresy—an arch-heresy of sorts. In a fragment preserved by Andrew of Caesarea, Irenaeus (if it was indeed him) summarized such worldview through the concept of recapitulation. Irenaeus, as we have seen, spoke of recapitulation of the entire created world, in Christ. Global evil, for him, was in a similar way recapitulated by Christ's antipode and imitator, the antichrist:

> In the beast that must come the recapitulation of every injustice and deception is realised, that, once every power that has apostatised has joined in it, as in a big ocean, this can be thrown into the furnace of fire. It recapitulates in itself every manifestation of evil which took place even before the deluge due to the apostasy of the angels, and also recapitulates every idolatry even from before the deluge. <. . .> The name under which every apostasy, injustice, and evilness of the six thousand years is subsumed. (*Fr.* 23; Rousseau 1969: 81–2; Ramelli 2013: 100)

The recapitulation of the world in Christ, however, is stronger than the recapitulation of evil in the antichrist. The former is real, while the latter is ephemeral, for which

**Figure 7.16** Augustine. A Flemish fifteenth-century statue. Rijksmuseum in Amsterdam.

Source: Photo by the author.

reason the former is destined to prevail. Therefore, there is not an equilibrium between good and evil, as the dualists suggested, because their ontological statuses are opposite:

> In recapitulating all things, he has recapitulated also the war against our enemy, crushing him who at the beginning led us away as captives in Adam, trampling upon his head. This can be perceived in Genesis, where God said to the serpent, "And I will put enmity between you and the woman, between your seed and her seed; he shall be on the watch for your head, and you on the watch for his heel" (cf. Gen. 3:15). For

> from that time, he who should be born of a Virgin after the likeness of Adam was preached as keeping watch for the head of the serpent. (*Adversus heareses* V 21.1; Steenberg 2008: 187)

The oppositeness of the ontological statuses of good and evil was stressed by Origen. He identified goodness with existence itself. Whatever exists is good. Evil is both nongood and nonexistent:

> This is the same God the Savior honors when he says, "No one is good except the one God, the Father" (see Mk 10:18; Lk. 18:19). "The one who is good," therefore, is the same as "the one who is." But evil or wickedness is opposite to the good, and "not being" is opposite to "being." It follows that wickedness and evil are "not being." (*Commentarii in Iohannem* II 96; Origen 1989: 119)

Origen applied the categories of commonality and particularity to the discussion about the nature of evil. He rebuked the suggestion that some had made, according to which commonalities, such as species or genus, are equal with evil—because both are not substantial. For Origen, such suggestion sounded alarmingly dualistic, because it equated evil with aspects of the created world. Evil is "nothing" in a completely different sense than the logical categories:

> Some, therefore, because evil is unsubstantial (for it neither was from the beginning nor will it be forever), have understood these things to be the "nothing." And as certain Greeks say that the genus and species, such as living being and man, belong to the category of "no things," so they have supposed "nothing" to be everything which has received its apparent constitution neither from God nor through the Word. (*Commentarii in Iohannem* II 93; Origen 1989: 118–19)

By applying Origen's own language (as was mentioned, "hypostatic" meant for him real and substantial), we could say that, in contrast to commonalities, evil excludes any possibility of hypostatization. In other words, commonalities, such as species or genus, can be and in fact are hypostatic, while evil is not. Evil cannot have its own hypostases. In this, the orthodox doctrine expressed by Origen differed from the dualistic approach to ontology. For the latter, evil is hypostatic.

Athanasius of Alexandria continued the line of his great compatriot. For the primate of the Egyptian church, evil cannot be thought of as a part of the creation. In fact, it can be only a reversal of the creation. Evil happens, when a creature comes back to nonexistence (see Lauber & Johnson 2018: 165-80). Evil, therefore, does not exist in the world as a thing, but as a negation of such existence: "Evil neither came from God nor was in God. <. . .> It did not exist in the beginning, nor does it have any being" (*Contra gentes* 7; Athanasius of Alexandria 1981: 18-9). In coherence with his customary theological method, Athanasius placed the problem of evil in the incarnational framework. The purpose of the incarnation was to maintain human beings in existence and to prevent their slipping to the nonexistence of evil: "It would have been improper that what had once been created rational and had partaken of his Word, should perish and return again to non-existence through corruption" (*De incarnatione* 6; Athanasius of Alexandria 1981: 149).

Basil of Caesarea criticized the dualistic worldview in his *Hexaemeron*. Speaking about the darkness that was created by God (Gen. 1:2), he pointed out that this darkness is not something evil, because nothing of what has been created by God and what exists is evil by its nature—in contrast to what the dualists believed:

> They (i.e., the dualists) explain the darkness, not as some unlighted air, as is natural, or a place overshadowed by the interposition of a body, or, in short, a place deprived of light through any cause whatsoever, but, they explain the darkness as an evil power, or rather, as evil itself, having its beginning from itself, resisting and opposing the goodness of God. <. . .>
>
> Evil is not a living and animated substance, but a condition of the soul which is opposed to virtue and which springs up in the slothful because of their falling away from good. (*Homiliae in hexaemeron* II 4; Basil of Caesarea 1963: 26, 28)

The author hiding behind the pseudonym of Dionysius the Areopagite was more outspoken than any other theologian in the antiquity about the nonexistent nature of evil. He compared the nonexistence of evil with the nonexistence of God and explored similarities and differences between these two nonexistences:

> Evil is not a being; for if it were, it would not be totally evil. Nor is it a nonbeing; for nothing is completely a nonbeing, unless it is said to be in the Good in the sense of beyond-being. For the Good is established far beyond and before simple being and nonbeing. Evil, by contrast, is not among the things that have being nor is it among what is not in being. It has a greater nonexistence and otherness from the Good than nonbeing has. (*De diuinis nominibus* IV 19; Luibheid 1987: 84)

Based on these deliberations, Ps.-Dionysius proceeded to some bold conclusions. Some beings, whom we designate as evil, cannot nevertheless be identified with evil, because they necessarily feature some basics of goodness, such as, for example, the desire to exist. From this perspective, even the most unrepentant evildoers and demons are not completely evil, but have a spark of goodness in themselves:

> All beings, to the extent that they exist, are good and come from the Good and they fall short of goodness and being in proportion to their remoteness from the Good. In the case of other qualities such as heat or cold the things which have experienced warmth can lose warmth. Indeed there are things even which have no life and no mind. True, there is God who is on a level above being and is therefore transcendental. But with entities generally, if a quality is lost for them, or was never there in fact, it is still the case that these entities possess being and subsistence. However, that which is totally bereft of the Good never had, does not have, never shall have, never can have

**Figure 7.17** This fifth-century "Saridere mosaic" decorated a Christian church in Syria. It reflects an optimistic outlook at the created world. Zeugma Museum in Gaziantep, Turkey.
Source: Photo by the author.

any kind of being at all. Take the example of someone who lives intemperately. He is deprived of the Good in direct proportion to his irrational urges. To this extent he is lacking in being and his desire is for what has no real existence. Nevertheless he has some share in the Good, since there is in him a distorted echo of real love and of real unity. Anger too has a share in the Good to the extent it is an urge to remedy seeming evils by returning them toward what seems beautiful. Even the person who desires the lowest form of life still desires life and a life that seems good to him; thus he participates in the Good to the extent that he feels a desire for life and for what—to him at least—seems a worthwhile life. Abolish the Good and you will abolish being, life, desire, movement, everything. (*De diuinis nominibus* IV 20; Luibheid 1987: 86)

# VII.7 Freedom

Evil, thus, is nested not in objects, but is a function, or rather malfunction of rational subjects. It is an abuse of freedom. Eastern Christian theologians dedicated many folia of their writings to the phenomenon of freedom and identified many nuances in this function. They explored freedom as a part of the dialectics of human autonomy and determinism: how the divine providence is correlated with human agency.

## Dialectics of Autonomy and Determinism

Since at least Homer, the Greeks had been dealing with the same dilemma of human autonomy and determinism. This dilemma is at the core of the Greek tragedy (see Critchley 2020: 12). In probably the most dramatic story of antiquity, Oedipus did everything possible and impossible to avoid his fate, to no avail. In the collision between human agency and predestination, the former was defeated by the latter. Nevertheless, the Sophocles' drama succeeded as a theatrical work not because it demonstrated the strength of predestination, something that the ancient Greeks were aware of anyways, but because it explored human agency, howsoever helpless it appeared to be.

Three or four generations after the *Oedipus Rex* was first staged in Athens, the human agency became perceived as successfully competing with predestination, and even averting it. Aristotle, in his ethics, substantiated moral autonomy as a condition sine qua non for any human behavior. Human capacity to choose (προαίρεσις) became the basis of commonly accepted ethics: "Moral excellence is a state concerned with choice (ἕξις προαιρετική)" (*Ethica Nicomachea* VI 2). This was not yet free will in the modern sense, but it was not too far from it (see Frede 2011: 19–30). It is noteworthy that Aristotle ascribed such capacity to each human being and, thus, made it a universal category pertinent to the common humanity.

The idea of free will closer to ours emerged in Stoicism. While in Aristotle *proaeresis* was a purely intellectual function (see Gottlieb 2021), in the Stoic philosophy it became volitional, that is, connected with phsyché and its emotionality. It played a central role in the Stoicism of Epictetus (*c.* AD 55–135), for example. For him, *proaeresis* defines one's persona. Moreover, it is the only thing that should bother us as the basis of moral choices: "Among things external and independent of our free choice none concerns us" (*Dissertationes ab Arriano digestae* I 4).

Paradoxically, the Stoic idea of free will was intertwined with determinism. Stoic determinism was total (see Salles 2005): the divine powers determined every single movement of both rational and irrational beings. Stoics believed that the consequent worlds that succeed one another after *ekpyrosis* are predestined to be the same—because of the Stoic radical determinism.

Origen fiercely criticized the idea of determinism. He was the most outspoken on the issue of freedom among the early Christian theologians (see Fürst 2019). For him, the status of a human being depends completely on the choices that this human being makes: "It is within our power to devote ourselves either to a life worthy of praise or one worthy of blame" (*De principiis* III 1.1; Behr 2017: 284–5). The choosing faculty of the human nature played a crucial role in Origen's cosmogony and anthropology. The transformation of rational beings, after their creation, to angels, humans with their thick bodies, and demons, was contingent on the choices they had made.

## Two Meanings of Freedom

Origen explored the phenomenon of freedom in a small treatise, which became a part of his opus magnum, *On First Principles*. The Cappadocians regarded this small treatise so important that they included it to *Philokalia*—a selection of Origen's works (see Origen 2006). In this selection, the treatise is titled *Peri autexousiou* (Περί αὐτ-εξουσίου) (Behr 2017: 284). *Autexousion* can literally be translated as the capacity of a person to be a master of himself or herself. After Origen, *autexousion* became a subcategory of the category of will that denoted one of two major meanings of freedom. Another subcategory was *eleutheria* (ἐλευθερία) (see Hovorun 2019).

The duality of these terms followed the general line in the Eastern theological anthropology. According to this line, every human being is "wired" with a capacity that cannot be taken from him or her. This capacity is a constant of the human existence and not contingent on anything that a person does or does not. It was defined as *imago Dei* or *isotheon*. *Autexousion* is also something given to the human nature. This capacity is a feature of the human commonality. *Autexousion* is a sort of freedom that cannot be reduced or removed from the common human nature or from particular *individua*. In his or her most miserable condition, one always has the fullness of *autexousion*. This means that a person can always arise from his or her misery, if of course he or she takes a firm decision to do so.

In contrast to *autexousion*, *eleutheria* is a changeable sort of freedom. It can be reduced or increased, even though it never completely disappears. It corresponds to the category of what is assigned to individual human beings, similarly to the likeness of human individuals with God. Its fullness is equivalent to *theosis*. *Eleutheria* is contingent on the choices a person makes. Enslavement to passions, addictions, and so on diminishes the degree of *eleutheria*, as the person cannot fully control his or her own desires. Such meaning of *eleutheria* goes back to the centuries, when this word differentiated social statuses in a Greek *polis*: completely *eleutheroi* were only free citizens with full rights to vote, that is, wealthy free males. Women, children, foreigners, and even more slaves, experienced various degrees of the deficit of *eleutheria*.

Speaking mathematically, freedom in the sense of *eleutheria* is a function of the freedom in the sense of *autexousion*. The former is impossible without the latter, while the latter is possible without the former. If expressed in the terms of existentialist philosophy, *autexousion* is a foundation of human being, while *eleutheria* is a foundation of human existence. Without *eleutheria*, human life turns meaningless and purposeless. *Autexousion* without *eleutheria* causes nausea. Existential discomfort that human beings may experience comes from disbalance between *autexousion* and *eleutheria*. It happens when the degree of *eleutheria* is lower than the degree of *autexousion*, and when *autexousion* remains only an unrealized potentiality for *eleutheria*. A person is existentially whole only when his or her *eleutheria* is commensurable with *autexousion*.

Both *autexousion* and *eleutheria* stem from God. The former was embedded in the human nature at the moment of its creation, while the latter rewards a human being for his or her synergetic efforts to come closer to God. From this perspective, *autexousion* can be seen as a *common* freedom, which belongs to the entire human nature. In contrast to it, *eleutheria* is a *particular* freedom, which is provided to individual human beings depending on the way they handle their common freedom, *autexousion*.

Not all Eastern Christian writers differentiated between *autexousion* and *eleutheria* in this way, but many did. As early as in the second century, Justin claimed that God created rational beings with *autexousion* embedded in their nature: "God from the very beginning created the race of angels and men with αὐτεξούσιον" (*Apologia* II 6). Justin's disciple Tatian coined the phrase "freedom of will" (ἐλευθερία τῆς προαιρέσεως; *Oratio ad Graecos* VII 1)—based on the term *eleutheria*. It seems that this was the first time in the classical literature that this phrase was used. The pair of terms *autexousion* and *eleutheria* became heavily relied upon from the fourth century on.

For Basil of Caesarea, for example, God has created all human beings as not subordinated (ὑπεξούσιος). The freedom that the human beings have been endowed with is significantly higher than the state of subordination: *autexousion* is better than *hypexousion (Adversus Eunomium*; PG 29, 697). In the Ps.-Basilian sermon *De contubernalibus*, this kind of freedom was presented as making the human soul godlike (θεοειδές) (PG 30, 817). Gregory of Nyssa, in his sermon *On Those Who Have Died*, also praised the divine character of the *autexousion*:

> A human being has become God-like (θεοειδής) and blessed with freedom (τῷ αὐτεξ-ουσίῳ), because being a master of him- (her-)self (αὐτοκρατές) and not having another master (ἀδέσποτον) is the property of the divine beatitude. However, to move someone elsewhere by force means to deprive him (or her) of honor. If some people by their choice (ἑκουσίως) and though the free movement (κατὰ τὴν αὐτεξούσιον κίνησιν) force the human nature to something which is not appropriate, they deprive it of goodness, with which it has been endowed, and insult its honor, which equates it with God (τῆς ἰσοθέου τιμῆς). Because freedom (τὸ αὐτεξούσιον) is equal to God (ἰσόθεον). (*De mortuis non esse dolendum* 54; translation is mine)

In contrast to the permanency of *autexousion*, as was mentioned earlier, *eleutheria* fluctuates as contingent on the choices that someone makes. It comes from God as a reward for the synergetic efforts of a human being to approach God. Christ is "the only free one" (ὢν ἐλεύθερος μόνος; *Christus patiens* 1523), according to a treatise attributed to Gregory of Nazianzus. He shares his freedom with those believing in him. Basil of Caesarea also stressed the role of the Holy Spirit in supplying freedom (*De spiritu sancto* 28.69). John Chrysostom summarized the idea of freedom in Christ and the Holy Spirit in the following passage:

> For there is no man free, save only he who lives for Christ. He stands superior to all troubles, and if he does not choose to injure himself no one else will be able to do this, but he is impregnable; he is not stung by the loss of wealth; for he has learned that we brought nothing into this world, neither can we carry anything out; he is not caught by the longings of ambition or glory; for he has learned that our citizenship is in heaven; no one annoys him by abuse, or provokes him by blows; there is only one calamity for a Christian which is, disobedience to God; but all the other things, such as loss of property, exile, peril of life, he does not even reckon to be a grievance at all. And that which all dread, departure hence to the other world—this is to him sweeter than life itself. (John Chrysostom 2010: 52)

# VII.8
# Human Rights

## Esoteric Freedom

Most references to freedom in the Eastern Christian literature feature an esoteric interpretation of this category—as an internal liberty from sins and passions, regardless of the social condition of a person. This interpretation was not specifically Christian, but went back to Cynicism and Stoicism (see Lampe 2019: 121–3). For the Christians, it was a comfortable way to avoid discussions about slavery and other restrictions on personal liberties. Such an esoterization of freedom also became a cover-up for many abuses of personal freedoms in the history of Christianity.

A prominent Greek theologian of the twentieth century, Savvas Agouridis (1921–2009), stated categorically that Byzantine Christianity contributed nothing to the development of the category of human rights (see Αγουρίδης 1998: 29). He might be exaggerating, but one has to agree that although Christianity had a potentiality to challenge the ancient institute of slavery and other mechanisms of discrimination, it did not do enough to actualize this potentiality. Slavery in the Christian East continued until 1861, when it was formally abolished in the Russian Empire. During the twentieth century, the tradition of the esoterization of freedom gave the churches an excuse to collaborate with various dictatorships. This tradition contributes to authoritarianism being cherished by the churches in the twenty-first century.

The category of freedom has become almost completely a part of the ascetic discourses and for a long time was excluded from what we now can call human rights discourses. Even now the Eastern churches prefer to keep the two discourses separate from one another.[1] The rhetorics of human rights is often perceived in the Eastern Christianity as a Western construct alien to Orthodoxy.

[1]The book by Aristotle Papanikolaou (Papanikolaou 2012), which explores the connectedness between the ascetic and political theologies, is rather an exception.

# Slavery and Racism in Ancient Greece

This is, however, a misperception of the categories that constitute the core of modern human rights. As mentioned earlier, the basic category of freedom was coined in ancient Greece. Originally, it was a political and social notion. Politically, it meant the freedom of a *polis* from any external dependence and from the internal tyrannic rule. Socially, freedom meant that someone was not a slave and had financial independence. This means that only free and wealthy men were considered completely free. Other strata of a Greek *polis* featured different degrees of reduced freedom. Slaves almost completely lacked it. Women, children, and foreigners were socially marginalized. Their social location was somewhere between rich men and slaves. Political and social freedoms were connected in ancient Greece. A *polis* was free only if it was governed by free citizens. Citizens could be free only in a free *polis*: democratic and ruled not by a tyrant, but through representation (see Lampe 2019: 118–19).

When ancient Greeks began developing logical categories, they applied them to social groups. For Aristotle, slaves belonged to the category of instruments that sustain a household. Moreover, slaves were instruments to instruments—the lowest subcategory in the category of instruments: "In the arrangement of the family, a slave is a living possession; <. . .> the servant is himself an instrument for instruments." Slavery marked a distinct common nature, which was different from the common nature of masters. A slave is "by nature not his own but another's man, is by nature a slave." A characteristic feature of slave's nature is to be in complete possession by his or her master: "The slave is not only the slave of his master, but wholly belongs to him" (*Politica* I 4).

Logical categories, thus, helped making the institute of slavery ossified in the ancient societies. Classical dialectics presented slaves, women, and children as sharing in the common natures, which are inferior to the assumed common nature of free males. Unlike the former natures, the latter one was regarded as the standard of humanity. The same categories constituted a framework for nationalism and racism in antiquity. Because the ideas of nation and race are modern and should not be anachronistically ascribed to premodern times, it is more correct to speak about proto-nationalism and proto-racism in the Greco-Roman world (see Isaac 2004). As with slavery, the Aristotelian dialectics established a theoretical framework for them.

Aristotle suggested what modern scholars have called "environmental determinism" (Isaac 2006: 35–7). It means that intellectual capacities and morality of a people depend on geography and climate. This is undoubtedly a racist theory. Speaking about "the distribution of races in the habitable world," Aristotle observed that "those who live in a cold climate and in Europe" are "wanting in intelligence and skill." Therefore, they "have no political organization, and are incapable of ruling over others." At the same time, the Asians "are intelligent and inventive, but they are wanting in spirit, and therefore they are always in a state of subjection and slavery." The best of all races is the Hellenic one, which "is the best-governed of any nation, and, if it could be formed into one state, would be able to rule the world" (*Politica* VII 7).

A later pseudo-Aristotelian treatise *Physiognomics* contains racist statements about black people (called in it "Ethiopians"):

> When the hair of the head stands up stiff, it signifies cowardice, by congruity, for fright makes the hair stand on end: and very woolly hair also signifies cowardice, as may be seen in Ethiopians. (*Physiognomica* 1248)

No surprise, therefore, that black people in the Greco-Roman societies, however few they were there, were usually slaves: they embodied prejudices about both slaves and other races. It is also not a surprise that this way of applying dialectics became a justification for imperialist wars for the Greek states. These wars, according to Aristotle, should be waged against those peoples whose nature is to be ruled by others, but they do not want to submit themselves to the Greeks. He placed "the art of war" to the natural category of "acquisition." This "art" should be applied "against men who, though intended by nature to be governed, will not submit." The wars waged on the basis of this logics are "naturally just" (*Politica* I 8). Aristotle passed this logic to the young Alexander, who then would implement it in his empire. Later, the Romans, good disciples of the Greeks, used these logical insights to build their own empire, which, ironically, conquered the Greek lands.

Aristotelian logical categories, primarily those of commonality and particularity, provided a theoretical framework for the inherent inequality in the ancient societies. Because individuals in different social group shared properties, which did not apply to other groups, they were believed to be of a different nature than other groups. Slaves and free men and women, adults and children, whites and people of color, Greeks/Romans and Barbarians—all of them were believed to participate in different commonalities. Needless to say that this particularization of the common human nature is incompatible with the modern concept of the universal human rights.

This does not mean, however, that some early elements of human rights were not entertained in the ancient societies. One can discern such an element, for example, in the story about Antigone, told by Sophocles. According to this story, Antigone fought against the arbitrariness of King Creon for some rights, such as to mourn her brother Polynices (see Αγουρίδης 1998: 19). Her failure, on the one hand, demonstrated that the social and natural *taxis* was still stronger than one's aspirations for rights (see Balot 2012: 111). On the other hand, Sophocles' generation seemed to be dissatisfied with this fact, for which reason it became a topic of a successful play.

# Human Dignity and *Imago Dei*

Christian theologians faced a difficult task to deconstruct the ancient axiom about ontological divides within the humankind. This axiom was wrong from the Christian perspective, which envisaged common salvation for all human beings. Paul promoted this perspective in his famous dictum: "Here there is not Greek and Jew, circumcised and uncircumcised, barbarian, Scythian, slave, free; but Christ is all, and in all" (Col. 3:11). In the verse before this dictum, Paul spoke about "the new self," which has to correspond to "the image of its creator" (Col. 3:10).

Christian theologians after Paul counterposed the idea of human beings as created in the image of God to the pagan idea of the humanity ontologically divided to strata. There are strata in the human society, but they do not cut to the bones of humankind. On the contrary, all human beings bear in themselves the image of God. This image cannot be destroyed or diminished. Slaves, women, children, and foreigners are not less images of God than white free wealthy males. Theology of image underpinned the new Christian attitude to the old pagan stratifications. This attitude was summarized by John of Damascus, who in his treatise on the defense of icons wrote:

> Whereby we venerate one another as having a portion of God and having come to be in the image of God, humbling ourselves before one another and fulfilling the law of love. (*Orationes de imaginibus* III 37)

# Christians on Slavery

This beautiful theology of image, however, did not translate to consistent anti-slavery polemics. The institute of slavery survived the Christianization of the Roman Empire, with only a few patristic voices speaking out against it. The most eloquent of them was Gregory of Nyssa's (see Stramara 1997). In his homily on Ecclesiastes, he rebuked slavery as a sinful institution, which contradicts the Gospels and the very idea of *imago Dei*. For Gregory, slavery contradicts also the idea that all human beings "are equal in all things," that is, they share in the common nature:

> As for the person who appropriates to himself what belongs to God and attributes to himself power over the human race as if he were its lord, what other arrogant statement transgressing human nature makes this person regard himself as different from those over whom he rules? <. . .> You have forgotten the limit of your authority which consists in jurisdiction over brutish animals. Scripture says that man shall rule birds, beasts, fish, four-footed animals and reptiles (Gen. 1:26). How can you transgress the servitude bestowed upon you and raise yourself against man's freedom by stripping yourself of the servitude proper to beasts? <. . .> Man, who was created as lord over the

> earth, you have put under the yoke of servitude as a transgressor and rebel against the divine precept. You have forgotten the limit of your authority which consists in jurisdiction over brutish animals. <. . .> He who knows human nature says that the world is not an adequate exchange for man's soul. When the Lord of the earth bought man, he acquired nothing more precious. He will then proclaim this surpassing possession along with the earth, island, sea and everything in them. What is the deposit God puts down? What will he receive from the contract by which he has received possession? <. . .> How can you who are equal in all things have superiority so that as man, you consider yourself as man's ruler and say "I have servants and maidens" as if they were goats or cattle? When Ecclesiastes said that "I have servants and maidens" (2:7) he also speaks of his prosperity in flocks and herds: "I also had abundant possessions of flocks and herds," both of which were subject to his authority. (*In Ecclesiasten* IV; J.R. Wright 2019: 210)

Basil of Caesarea even more explicitly stated that slavery cannot be seen as an ontological status of human beings: "Among the human beings no one is a slave by nature" (παρὰ μὲν ἀνθρώποις τῇ φύσει δοῦλος οὐδείς) (*De spiritu sancto* XX 51). However, unlike Gregory, Basil failed to condemn slavery as an institution. Other Christian authors also stigmatized abuses of slavery, but not slavery as such (see Hart 2001). Some even advocated for this institution. Such was, for instance, Theodoret of Cyrus, who wrote against those who criticized slavery:

> The slave, on the other hand, though a slave in body, enjoys freedom of soul and has none of these worries. He does not bewail the failure of the crops or lament the scarcity of buyers; he is not pained at the sight of a creditor nor does he fear a swarm of tax-collectors; he is not forced to sit on juries; he does not fear the voice of the herald, or the judge looking with awesome eye. He takes his food, rationed no doubt, but he has no worries.
>
> He lies down to sleep on the pavement, but worry does not banish sleep: on the contrary, its sweetness on his eyelids keeps him from feeling the hardness of the ground. Wisdom, speaking in accordance with nature, said: "Sleep is sweet to the slave." He covers his body with a single garment, but his body is stronger than his master's. He eats rye bread, and never tastes anything dainty, but he enjoys his food better than his master does. His master is constantly bothered by indigestion: he takes more than enough, bolts his food, and forces it down. The slave consumes only what he needs, takes what is given to him with moderation, enjoys what he receives, digests it slowly, and it fortifies him for his work.
>
> You consider only the slavery of this man; you do not consider his health. You see the work, but not the recompense involved; you complain of toil, but forget the happiness of a carefree life. You criticize his lowly state, but fail to notice how soundly he sleeps. You should see from that the providence of God and witness the equity of His rule. When sin necessitated the division of men into rulers and slaves, God joined cares to responsibility, allotting to the master sleepless nights and more than his share

> of sickness, whereas the slave received better health, greater zest for his food, pleasant and longer sleep calculated to free his body from fatigue and make it stronger for the toils of the morrow. (*De providentia* VII 22-24; Theodoret of Cyrus 1989: 95–6)

The Roman Empire influenced the Christian attitudes to slavery, without being much influenced in return. When the empire became supposedly Christian, bishops were given the right to legalize manumission of slaves—the conferment of freedom by their masters. Sometimes such liberation was performed liturgically—as a solemn ritual. However, bishops did not feel obliged to free even their own slaves. Gregory of Nazianzus, for example, freed only two of his slaves, which became his deacons. His other slaves would receive their freedom upon his death, according to his will (*Testamentum* 157). Only a few exceptions are known when bishops freed their own slaves and helped freeing others. The Chalcedonian archbishop of Alexandria John the Almsgiver, who lived in the early seventh century, was known for buying slaves who had been maltreated by their masters, and immediately liberated them, using his right of manumission.

Slavery and its toleration by the church outlived the Roman Empire. It continued to be a social norm, for instance, in Russia. Inhuman practices of dealing with slaves and servants there were praised in the codification of social norms called *Domostroi*. It was published in the early years of Ivan the Terrible as tsar (r. 1547–84). Ivan's spiritual mentor, priest Silvester, was the compiler of the codex, which thus was perceived as guidelines endorsed by the authority of both the church and the state. It is a pietistic catalogue of dos and don'ts that a layperson was expected to do in the church, at home, and in public. It also instructed the master of a household how to deal with serfs and servants. Here is a passage about how to punish them:

> When you must whip someone, take off the culprit's shirt. Beat him in a controlled way with the lash, holding him by the hands while you think of his fault. When you have punished him, you must talk with him; there should be no anger between you. <. . .>
>
> If he sincerely repents, punish him lightly and forgive him. If the person is innocent, do not connive with the slanderer. To prevent enmity henceforth, punish appropriately and only after personal investigation. If an offender does not repent, punish him severely.

Some ascetic practices, such as containment of anger, were advised for those who were about to beat their serfs or members of the family, including children and wife. Not every kind of beating was advised. For example, pregnant women, according to the *Domostroi*, should be beaten with lash and not in belly:

> Do not box anyone's ears for any fault. Do not hit them about the eyes or with your fist below the heart. Do not strike anyone with a stick or staff or beat anyone with anything made of iron or wood. From such a beating, administered in passion or anguish, many misfortunes can result: blindness or deafness, dislocation of an arm, leg, or finger, head

injury, or injury to a tooth. With pregnant women or children, damage to the stomach could result, so beat them only with the lash, in a careful and controlled way, albeit painfully and fearsomely. Do not endanger anyone's health. (Pouncy 1994: 143–4)

# Esoteric Ethics

Even when Christian theologians found justification for slavery, they did not explain it by an ontological status pertinent to a certain social group. In this point, they differentiated themselves from the pagan traditions of antiquity. Christians unanimously criticized any ontological compartmentalization of humankind. In particular, they turned against the idea that humankind is divided to spiritual strata. This idea was promoted by dualistic groups. They had extrapolated different social statuses, known in the antiquity as nobility, merchants, and slaves, to the spiritual statuses of spiritual, emotional, and bodily persons. These types of personality are described, for instance, in the *Tripartite tractate*. It was written in the third century and discovered among other Gnostic texts in Nag Hammadi. It contains a classical differentiation between three spiritual conditions:

> The pneumatic (i.e., spiritual) group which is light from light and spirit from spirit, when its Head appears, has to hasten after him and has a body formed for its Head which has received gnosis with eagerness at the revelation. But the psychic group which is light from fire, has hesitated about receiving gnosis but hastened to him in faith. <. . .> But the hylic (from *hylē* (ὕλη)—"matter") group which is wholly foreign [to him] will be cut off as darkness by the brightness from the light. (In Puech et al. 1955: 60)

These three spiritual statuses effectively meant three different natures. Spiritual status was also an ontological status, which is predetermined and cannot be changed by one's effort or will. Church fathers, on the one hand, recognized that some people are more spiritual, and others are less. This, however, is not predetermined, but depends completely on one's will. If a person wants to become more spiritual, he or she can and should do this. This was also the point that the advocates of slavery among the Eastern Christian authors made. One can be a slave in body, but can and should be free in spirit.

Such a perception was a result of the esoterization of the Christian ethics in general and of the notion of freedom in particular. It was a reduction of the original message of the Gospel. With the help of such reduction, the church accommodated social institutions of antiquity in the ostensibly Christian empire. On the one hand, Christian theology recast the ancient institutions, such as slavery, in non-ontological terms. On the other hand, the Christian ideas of freedom and equality were recast in the esoteric terms. In result, the institute of slavery survived in the Eastern Christianity until the nineteenth century.

# Esoterized Gender Equality

The same reductionist esoterization of the original Gospels' message was applied to the gender equality. As was mentioned earlier, women in the classic antiquity were perceived not much higher than slaves. Christian theologians contested ontological difference between the two genders. Gregory of Nyssa more than other theologians of his time contributed to this point. For him, the difference between genders came to be embedded in the nature *after* it had been created. God bestowed gender on first human beings with the perspective that they would fall and would need to continue life by procreation. The difference between these two phases of the formation of human beings, for Gregory, can be observed in the two parts of the biblical verse that describes this formation: "So God created man in his own image," on the one hand, and "male and female he created them," on the other (Gen. 1:27):

> I think that by these words Holy Scripture conveys to us a great and lofty doctrine; and the doctrine is this. While two natures—the Divine and incorporeal nature, and the irrational life of brutes—are separated from each other as extremes, human nature is the mean between them: for in the compound nature of man we may behold a part of each of the natures I have mentioned,—of the Divine, the rational and intelligent element, which does not admit the distinction of male and female; of the irrational, our bodily form and structure, divided into male and female: for each of these elements is certainly to be found in all that partakes of human life. That the intellectual element, however, precedes the other, we learn as from one who gives in order an account of the making of man; and we learn also that his community and kindred with the irrational is for man a provision for reproduction. (*De opificio hominis* 16; Gregory of Nyssa 2016: 26)

For Gregory, thus, differentiation between genders, on the one hand, belongs to the irrational part of the human nature and thus is inferior to its rational part. In this point, he complied with the common wisdom which had been firmly believed by the Greeks since at least Plato. On the other hand, Gregory stood out from the rest of the classical tradition in clearly affirming that the gender difference is not a part of the human nature. In other words, being a male or a female is not an ontological difference—something that the Greco-Roman world firmly held. Therefore, there is no ontological ground to regard females as inferior to males.

At the same time, other theologians preferred to esoterize the gender equity. From this perspective, men and women can be equal only in their spiritual, but not social standing. Such approach was a compromise with the patriarchal norms of the Greco-Roman society. In result, these norms remained intact (see Cohick & Brown Hughes 2017).

How the esoterization of gender equality worked in the Late Antiquity can be demonstrated by the example of the female monasticism in the Egyptian desert. Egyptian society was, and still is, patriarchal from up to bottom. At the same time, the Egyptian desert was more inclusive than the Egyptian society. It welcomed women and people of color and treated them equally with other monks. The *Apophthegmata* contain stories and sayings of a black elder whose name was Moses. He was highly esteemed by other monks, church leaders, and politicians. The same *Apophthegmata* mentioned female voices (see Dunn 2003: 42–58), such as those by *ammas* (mothers) Theodora, Sarah, and Syncletica. Here is one of them:

> Amma Sarah said: "If I pray to God that everybody have confidence in me I will be at the door of each one, apologizing. But I shall rather pray that my heart be pure with everyone." (Sarah 5; Wortley 2014: 301)

This saying can be understood in two ways. It might mean that Amma Sarah did not care about the opinion of people. However, people at that time meant primarily men. Then what she wanted to say was that she did not care about the opinion of men. In such case, this was a very bold statement for that time.

# Patriarchy

As far as women deliberated on spiritual matters and, together with men, practiced spiritual exercises, they were regarded equal with their brethren. However, outside the ascetic framework, they were seen as a source of temptation and an instrument of demonic powers. Some monks preferred them dead, as in the following story from the *Apophthegmata*:

> There was a brother who was fighting the good fight at Scete and the enemy put him in mind of a certain most beautiful woman and was seriously afflicting him. Then, providentially, another brother came down from Egypt to Scete and, as they were speaking together, he said that the wife of so-and-so had died. It was the very woman on whose account the combatant was embattled. On hearing this, he took up his *levitôn* (a cloth) and, going up [to Egypt] by night, opened her tomb. He mopped up her bodily fluids with his *levitôn* and kept it in his cell when he came back. He would set that stench before him and do battle with his *logismos*, saying: "Look, this is the desired one you were seeking; you have her, take your fill!" In this way he tormented himself with the stench until the battle was stilled for him. (In Wortley 2013: 114–15)

It became a popular belief in many Eastern Christian cultures that women are a weak gender, through which demonic forces channel evil to the world. This belief coheres with the dualistic perception, which puts women to the evil pole of the good-evil binary. Radical dualism identifies women with evil.

Female monasticism was an institution, where women could be equal with men. Another chance for equality was a prominent political status. Although the Byzantine society was patriarchal, it allocated for women more political, social, and religious space, than the classical Roman or contemporary Western societies would allow.

There were intelligent and powerful women, whose achievements and roles were appreciated even in the patriarchal environment. Some of them played important roles in theological developments, such as the wife of Emperor Justinian Theodora (*c.* 497–548), who often extended helping hand to the anti-Chalcedonian party, the Empresses Irene Sarantapechaina (752–803) and Theodora (815–67), who restored veneration of icons et al.

An outstanding figure in the late Byzantine intellectual history was Anna Comnena (1083–1153), the daughter of Emperor Alexius I Comnenus (r. 1081–1118). She left a valuable testimony about her time in the treatise known as *Alexias*. There, she described with enthusiasm her paternal grandmother Anna Dalassena (1025–1105). During 1080–81, she was an acting regent of the empire. She continued playing a prominent political role at the court of her son Alexius I:

> One might be amazed that my father accorded his mother such high honor in these matters and that he deferred to her in all respects, as if he were turning over the reins of the empire to her and running alongside her while she drove the imperial chariot, contenting himself simply with the title of emperor. Indeed, he had already passed beyond the period of boyhood, an age especially when lust for power grows in men of such nature [as Alexius]. He took upon himself the wars against the barbarians and whatever battles and combats pertained to them, while he entrusted to his mother the complete management of [civil] affairs: the selection of civil magistrates, the collection of incoming revenues and the expenses of the government. A person who has reached this point in my text may blame my father for entrusting management of the empire to the gynaiconites (i.e., women's section of the palace). But if he had known this woman's spirit, how great she was in virtue and intellect and how extremely vigorous, he would cease his reproach and his criticism would be changed into admiration. For my grandmother was so dextrous in handling affairs of state and so highly skilled in controlling and running the government, that she was not only able to manage the Roman empire but could have handled every empire under the sun. She had a vast amount of experience and understood the internal workings of many things: she knew how each affair began and to what result it might lead, which actions were destructive and which rather were beneficial. She was exceedingly acute in discerning whatever course of action was necessary and in carrying it out safely. She was not only acute in her thought, but was no less proficient in her manner of speech. Indeed, she was a persuasive orator, neither verbose nor stretching her phrases out at great length; nor did she quickly lose the sense of her argument. What she began felicitously she would finish even more so. (*Alexias* III 7; Stearns 2008: 96–7)

# Modern Discussions on Human Rights

Only in the beginning of the nineteenth century, Eastern theologians began interpreting freedom not only as an esoteric category but also as an important political value.

The Greek liberation revolution of 1821 triggered such process of de-esoterization. Some hierarchs and theologians, mostly in what would become the independent Greek state, accepted and endorsed the liberation struggle. The leadership of the Ecumenical Patriarchate, however, continued to insist that freedom should be understood in esoteric and not political terms. They argued that the revolution substitutes the genuine freedom with its political simulacrum. Nevertheless, some Greek hierarchs and clergymen accepted and blessed this revolution. The most famous among them was the metropolitan of Old Patras Germanos Gotzias (1771–1826).

A popular preacher in the second half of the eighteenth century in *Sterea Ellada*, then under the Ottoman rule, Kosmas of Aetolia (1700/14–79), on the one hand emphasized the value of esoteric freedom. On the other hand, he referred to freedom as a political category:

> That which is desired (i.e., freedom) will come in the third generation. Your grandchildren will see it.
>
> France will liberate Greece, [while] Italy (will liberate) Epiros.
>
> The villages of the plain will suffer destruction, while people at the foot of [Mount] Kissavo will go to sleep slaves and will awaken free. ("Prophesies by St. Kosmas Aitolos," in *Pemptousia* online magazine: https://tinyurl.com/af9wy6wv [accessed on September 3, 2020])

Orthodox villagers, to whom he preached, believed that Patrokosmas—so they called him—could predict the future. Two generations later, an independent Greek state emerged in the Balkans as a fulfillment of this clairvoyance.

During the nineteenth and in the beginning of the twentieth century, the idea of political freedom, endorsed by the church, became applied to the church. As a result, some local churches renewed or received autocephaly. The institute of autocephaly embodied new theological ideas about freedom (see Hovorun 2017: 110–27). Still, during the nineteenth century, the Eastern Christianity did not appreciate the idea of personal freedom.

Only in the beginning of the twentieth century, this idea began emerging as a synthesis of esoteric and political freedoms. The most outspoken on personal freedom in his generation was Nikolay Berdyayev (1874–1948). He was born in Kyiv. During his studies in science and law at the Kyiv University of St. Vladimir, Berdyayev became involved in the Marxist activities and soon was arrested and exiled. At the turn of the century, he converted from Marxist positivism to metaphysical idealism. In 1922, he was expelled from the Soviet Russia. After staying for two years in Berlin, he moved to France, where he lived until his death in the estate in Clamart near Paris.

Freedom, for Berdyayev, is a cornerstone of individual existence. There is nothing prior to freedom—it is bottomless. Otherwise, freedom would have been predetermined, which is a contradiction in terms. In what follows, Berdyayev effectively rendered the patristic category of *autexousion* in existentialistic terms:

**Figure 7.18** Berdyayev's desk in his estate in Clamart, France.
Source: Photo by the author.

> The philosophy of freedom begins with a free act before which there is not, nor can there be, existence, being. If we were to begin with being as the basis, and recognize this primacy of being over freedom, then everything, including freedom, is determined by being. But a determined freedom is not freedom at all. (Berdyayev 1965: 147).
>
> <. . .>
>
> Freedom of the spirit which itself gives birth to consequences, which creates life, is revealed to us a bottomlessness, baselessness, as a force from out the boundless deep. We cannot feel a base, a foundation for freedom, nowhere can we find some solid element which determines freedom from within. Freedom of the spirit is a bottomless well. Our substantial nature could not be the basis of freedom. On the contrary, all nature is born of freedom. Freedom proceeds not from nature, but from God's idea and from the abyss which preceded being. Freedom is rooted in "nothingness." The act of freedom is primordial and completely irrational. (Berdyayev 1965: 136)

In tune with the long Eastern Christian tradition that goes back to Origen, Berdyayev utilized the category of freedom to explain the possibility of evil in the world. He seemingly described freedom in dualistic terms, as an irrational and dark force that existed prior to the world. However, his explanation of evil is opposite to the dualistic because he did not identify evil with matter. Berdyayev was coherent with the classical Eastern theology in denying any substantial existence for evil:

> The secret of evil is the secret of freedom. Without our understanding of freedom the irrational fact of the existence of evil in God's world cannot be understood. At the

> basis of the world lies irrational freedom, in the very depths of the abyss. And out of these depths pour the dark currents of life. This abyss hides all sorts of possibilities. This bottomless darkness of being, pre-existent before all good and all evil, cannot be rationalized, fully and completely: it always hides the possibility of the outflow of new, unilluminated energies. The light of the Logos conquers darkness, cosmic order conquers chaos, there is no life, no freedom, no meaning of the process which is taking place. Freedom is founded in the dark abyss, in nothingness, but without freedom there is no meaning. Freedom gives birth to evil as well as good. Therefore evil does not deny the existence of meaning, but rather confirms it. Freedom is not created, because it is not nature; freedom existed before the world began, it is rooted in immemorial nothingness. God is almighty over being, but not over nothingness, or over freedom. And this is why evil exists. (Berdyayev 1965: 187)

A friend and collaborator of Berdyayev in Paris, nun Maria Skobtsova (1891–1945) was skeptical about his proclamation of the absolute primacy of freedom (Скобцова 1931). At the same time, she stressed the importance of personal freedom in both spiritual and public life. She, on the one hand, counterposed the true freedom in Christ to its ritualistic and pietistic simulacra, when Christians perceive ascetic practices and rituals as substitutes for spiritual liberation. Skobtsova, thus, criticized an internal totalitarianism within the church. On the other hand, she criticized the political totalitarianism of the 1930s. She, thus, advocated for freedom in its political sense. In 1939, she warned about abuses of freedom by three major ideologies of that time: Communism, Nazism, and Fascism:

> The mountains become flat, the human herd is shepherded with an iron scourge, the very understanding of freedom is eradicated, the taste for freedom, the very idea of it disappear. It is the same to us, in whose hands this scourge is, and in what name the humankind has lost its soul? Whether the God-like human personality is subordinate to the law of class, whether it should fertilize the future proletarian paradise, or is it dissolved in a stream of the sacred German blood, whether it is sacrificed to the resurrected idol of the Roman state? What matters in all these manifestations is the denial of freedom's worth, of freedom itself, the denial of the possibility of God-chosenness for any human being. The godless world not only revealed to us its doctrines, but it showed what happens when these doctrines become embodied. It gave rise to hatred, persecution, blood, violence; it killed a human being, crippled soul, and encaged freedom. Those who now follow its calls cannot be deceived: they must know that the world is going to imprison freedom, to destroy the human personality, to kill the soul, and to rebel against the work of Christ. (Скобцова 1939: 85; translation is mine)

It was as if Maria predicted her own future. During the Nazi occupation of Paris, she together with other Orthodox activists helped Jews receive baptismal certificates and sheltered them. Eventually, this group was arrested by Gestapo. Maria Skobtsova died in the gas chamber at the Ravensbrück concentration camp (see Hackel 1965).

Maria Skobtsova envisaged a more prominent place for women in the Eastern Orthodoxy. Another female theologian in the twentieth century, Elizabeth Behr-Sigel, tried to redefine this place. She was called the "grandmother of western Orthodoxy" (Hinlicky Wilson: 1). Being born in a mixed Jewish-Lutheran family, she converted to Orthodoxy and became one of the most prominent modern theologians. She lived most of her life in France, where she was born in 1907 and died in 2005. She was a friend and a theological resource to many theological personalities of her time, including Maria Skobtsova and Metropolitan Anthony Bloom. She wrote on a variety of topics but became known mostly for her advocacy for a fuller female role in the Orthodox church. She believed that the genuine tradition of Orthodoxy does not exclude, but fully include, women:

> I recognize the authentic Tradition of the Church in a women's movement in which women express their will to be respected as free and responsible persons. It is in the dynamic of authentic Tradition, and not in the ephemeral ideologies, that we will find the source of eternal life, the source of our own true liberation. In line with and in the dynamic of this Tradition, we will invent lifestyles of community life in the family, society, and Churches. (Behr-Sigel 1977: 97–8)

# Primary Sources


| | |
|---|---|
| *Acta Archelai* | Edited by M.J. Vermes, 2001. [*Manichaean Studies* 4], Turnhout: Brepols. |
| *Acta conciliorum oecumenicorum* (ACO) | *Series prima* (ACO$_1$). Edited by E. Schwartz, R. Schieffer & J. Straub, 1927ff. Berlin: De Gruyter. |
| | *Series secunda* (ACO$_2$). Edited by R. Riedinger & H. Ohme, 1984ff. Berlin: De Gruyter. |
| Aëtius of Antioch (fl. mid-fourth century) | *Syntagmation*. Edited and translated by L.R. Wickham, 1968. "The *Syntagmation* of Aetius the Anomean." *The Journal of Theological Studies*, 19 (2), pp. 532–69. |
| Aëtius doxographer (late first–early second century AD) | *De placitis reliquiae*. Edited by H. Diels, 1879 (repr. 1965). *Doxographi Graeci*, Berlin: Reimer (repr. Berlin: De Gruyter). |
| Alcinous (second century AD) | *Didaskalikos*. Edited by O.F. Summerell & T. Zimmer, 2007. *Alkinoos, Didaskalikos. Lehrbuch der Grundsätze Platons. Einleitung, Text, Ubersetzung und Anmerkungen*, Berlin: Walter de Gruyter. Translated by J. Dillon, 2001. *Alcinous: The Handbook of Platonism*, Oxford: Clarendon Press. |
| Alexander of Alexandria (died AD 328) | *Epistula encyclica* (Ἑνὸς σώματος ὄντος). Edited by H.G. Opitz, 1940. *Athanasius Werke*, vol. 2.1, Berlin: De Gruyter, pp. 31–5. |
| Alexander of Aphrodisias (fl. late second–early third century AD) | *De mixtione*. Edited by I. Bruns, 1892. *Alexandri Aphrodisiensis praeter commentaria scripta minora* [Commentaria in Aristotelem Graeca suppl. 2.2], Berlin: Reimer. |
| | *De anima*. Edited by I. Bruns, 1887. *Alexandri Aphrodisiensis praeter commentaria scripta minora* [Commentaria in Aristotelem Graeca suppl. 2.1], Berlin: Reimer. |
| Anastasius of Sinai (died after 700) | *Viae dux*. Edited by K.-H. Uthemann, 1981. *Anastasii Sinaitae, Viae dux*, Turnhout: Brepols; Leuven University Press. |
| | *Opera*. Edited by K.-H. Uthemann, 1985. *Anastasii Sinaitae Opera*, Turnhout: Brepols; Leuven University Press. |
| | *Sermones in constitutionem hominis secundum imaginem Dei*. Edited by K.-H. Uthemann, 1985. *Anastasii Sinaitae sermones dvo in constitvtionem hominis secvndvm imaginem dei necnon opvscvla adversvs Monotheletas*, Turnhout: Brepols. |

Anaxagoras (fifth century BC)

*Fragmenta*. Edited by H. Diels & W. Kranz, 1952. *Die Fragmente der Vorsokratiker*, vol. 2, Berlin: Weidmann, pp. 32–44.

Anna Comnena (*c.* 1083–1153)

*Alexias*. Edited by A. Kambylis & D.R. Reinsch, 2001. [*Corpus Fontium Historiae Byzantinae*. Series Berolinensis XL/1], Berlin: De Gruyter.

*Anonymous Greek Chronicle* (sixteenth century)

Translated by M. Philippides, 1990. *Emperors, Patriarchs, and Sultans of Constantinople, 1373–1513. An Anonymous Greek Chronicle of the Sixteenth Century*, Brookline, MA: Hellenic College Press.

Anselm of Havelburg (*c.* 1100–58)

*Dialogi*. Edited by J.-P. Migne. [*Patrologiae cursus completus*, series Latina], vol. 188, Paris: Migne, coll. 111–204.

Anthimus the Patriarch of Jerusalem (1717–1808)

*Διδασκαλία Πατρική* [Fatherly teaching], Κωνσταντινούπολις: Πογὼς ἀπὸ τὴν Ἀρμενία, 1798.

Antony of Egypt (*c.* 251–356)

*Epistulae*. Edited and translated by S. Rubenson, 1997. *The Letters of St. Antony: Monasticism and the Making of a Saint*, Minneapolis, MN: Fortress.

Apollinaris of Laodicea (*c.* 310–90)

*Fides secundum partem* / Κατὰ μέρος πίστις. Edited by H. Lietzmann, 1904. *Apollinaris von Laodicea und seine Schule* [Texte und Untersuchungen 1], Tübingen: Mohr Siebeck, pp. 167–84. Translated by K.M. Spoerl, 1991. *A Study of the Κατὰ μέρος πίστις by Apollinarius of Laodicea*, University of Toronto, pp. 378–97.

*De unione*. Edited by H. Lietzmann, 1904. *Apollinaris von Laodicea und seine Schule* [Texte und Untersuchungen 1], Tübingen: Mohr Siebeck, pp. 185–93.

*De fide et incarnatione*. Edited by H. Lietzmann, 1904. *Apollinaris von Laodicea und seine Schule* [Texte und Untersuchungen 1], Tübingen: Mohr Siebeck, pp. 193–203.

*Anakephalaiosis* / Ἀνακεφαλαίωσις. Edited by H. Lietzmann, 1904. *Apollinaris von Laodicea und seine Schule* [Texte und Untersuchungen 1], Tübingen: Mohr Siebeck, pp. 242–6.

*Fragmenta*. Edited by H. Lietzmann, 1904. *Apollinaris von Laodicea und seine Schule* [Texte und Untersuchungen 1], Tübingen: Mohr Siebeck, pp. 204–42.

*Fragmenta in Joannem* (in catenis). Edited by J. Reuss, 1966. *Johannes-Kommentare aus der griechischen Kirche* [Texte und Untersuchungen 89], Berlin: Akademie Verlag, pp. 3–64.

Apollonius Dyscolus (fl. second century AD)

*Syntax (De constructione)*. Edited by J. Lallot, 1997. *De la construction* [Histoire des doctrines de l'Antiquité classique 19], Paris: Librairie Philosophique J. Vrin.

*Apophthegmata patrum* — Edited and translated by J. Wortley, 2013. *The Anonymous Sayings of the Desert Fathers: A Select Edition and Complete English Translation*, Cambridge: Cambridge University Press. Lund University in Sweden has developed an online platform *Monastica* that traces the transmission of the *Apophthegmata* in Greek, Latin, Arabic, Armenian, Coptic, Georgian, Slavonic, and Syriac languages: https://monastica.ht.lu.se/ (accessed on March 9, 2021).

Aristides (fl. second century) — *Apologia*. Edited by C. Vona, 1950. *L'apologia di Aristide*, Rome: Facultas Theologica Pontificii Athenaei Lateranensis, pp. 7–15.

Aristotle (384–22 BC) — *Categoriae*. Edited by L. Minio-Paluello, 1949 (repr. 1966). *Aristotelis categoriae et liber de interpretatione*, Oxford: Clarendon Press. Translated by J.K. Ackrill in J. Barnes, ed., 1984. *Complete Works of Aristotle*, Princeton, NJ: Princeton University Press, pp. 3–24.

*Physica*. Edited by W.D. Ross, 1950 (repr. 1966). *Aristotelis physica*, Oxford: Clarendon Press. Translated by R.P. Hardie & R.K. Gaye in J. Barnes, ed., 1984. *Complete Works of Aristotle*, Princeton, NJ: Princeton University Press, pp. 315–446.

*Metaphysica*. Edited by W.D. Ross, 1924 (repr. 1970). *Aristotle's Metaphysics*, 2 vols., Oxford: Clarendon Press. Translated by W.D. Ross in J. Barnes, ed., 1995. *Complete Works of Aristotle*, Princeton, NJ: Princeton University Press, pp. 1552–1728.

*De caelo*. Edited by P. Moraux, 1965. Aristote. *Du ciel*, Paris: Les Belles Lettres. Translated by J.L. Stocks in J. Barnes, ed., 1984. *Complete Works of Aristotle*, Princeton, NJ: Princeton University Press, pp. 447–511.

*De anima*. Edited by W.D. Ross, 1961 (repr. 1967). *De anima*, Oxford: Clarendon Press. Translated by J.A. Smith in J. Barnes, ed., 1984. *Complete Works of Aristotle*, Princeton, NJ: Princeton University Press, pp. 641–92.

*Ethica Nicomachea*. Edited by I. Bywater, 1894 (repr. 1962). *Aristotelis ethica Nicomachea*, Oxford: Clarendon Press. Translated by W.D. Ross (revised by J.O. Urmson) in J. Barnes, ed., 1995. *Complete Works of Aristotle*, Princeton, NJ: Princeton University Press, pp. 1729–1867.

*Physiognomica*. Edited by I. Bekker, 1831 (repr. 1960). *Aristotelis opera*, vol. 2, Berlin: Reimer (repr. Berlin: De Gruyter). Translated by T. Loveday & E.S. Forster in J. Barnes, ed., 1984. *Complete Works of Aristotle*, Princeton, NJ: Princeton University Press, pp. 1237–50.

Arnobius (the elder, fl. fourth century)

*Adversus nationes*. Edited by C. Marchesi, 1953. [*Corpus Scriptorum Latinorum Paravianum*], Turin: Paravia. Translated by G.E. McCracken in Arnobius, 1978. *The Case Against the Pagans*, New York: Paulist.

Athanasius of Alexandria (*c.* 293–373)

*Contra gentes*. Edited and translated by R.W. Thomson, 1971. *Athanasius. Contra gentes and de incarnatione*, Oxford: Clarendon Press.

*De incarnatione*. Edited and translated by R.W. Thomson, 1971. *Athanasius. Contra gentes and de incarnatione*, Oxford: Clarendon Press. More recent translation by J. Behr in Athanasius of Alexandria, 2011. *On the Incarnation*, Yonkers, NY: St. Vladimir's Seminary Press.

*Orationes contra Arianos*. Edited by K. Metzler & K. Savvidis, *Athanasius: Werke*, Band I. *Die dogmatischen Schriften*, Erster Teil, 2, Lieferung, Berlin: De Gruyter, 1998, pp. 109–75. Translated by John Henry Newman and Archibald Robertson, 1892. *Nicene and Post-Nicene Fathers*, Second Series (NPNF 2), vol. 4. Edited by Ph. Schaff & H. Wace, Buffalo, NY: Christian Literature Publishing Co.

*Tomus ad Antiochenos*. Edited by J.-P. Migne. [*Patrologiae cursus completus*, series Graeca], vol. 26, Paris: Migne, coll, pp. 796–809.

*De decretis Nicaenae synodi*. Edited by H.G. Opitz, 1940. *Athanasius Werke*, vol. 2.1, Berlin: De Gruyter, pp. 1–45.

*De synodis Arimini in Italia et Seleuciae in Isauria*. Edited by H.G. Opitz, 1940. *Athanasius Werke*, vol. 2.1, Berlin: De Gruyter, pp. 231–78.

*Historia Arianorum*. Edited by H.G. Opitz, 1940. *Athanasius Werke*, vol. 2.1, Berlin: De Gruyter, pp. 183–230.

Athenagoras (fl. second century AD)

*De resurrectione*. Edited by W.R. Schoedel, 1972. *Athenagoras. Legatio and De resurrectione*, Oxford: Clarendon Press. Translated by J.H. Crehan in Athenagoras, 1956. *Embassy for the Christians. The Resurrection of the Dead*, Westminster: Newman Press.

Augustine (354–430)

*De Trinitate*. Edited by W. J. Mountain & F. Glorie, 1968. [*Corpus Christianorum*. Series Latina 50], Turnhout: Brepols.

Babai the Great (*c.* 551–628)

*Liber de unione*. Edited by A.A. Vaschalde, 1974. *Babai Magni Liber de unione*, Louvain: Secrétariat du Corpus Scriptorum Christianorum Orientalium.

*Babylonian Talmud*

Translated by J. Neusner, 2011. *The Babylonian Talmud: Translation and Commentary*, 22 vols, Peabody, MA: Hendrickson.

Bardaisan (*c.* 154–222)

*Book of Laws of Countries*. Edited by W. Cureton, 1855. *Spicilegium Syriacum, Containing Remains of Bardesan, Meliton, Ambrose, and Mara Bar Serapion*, London: Rivingtons.

*Barnabae epistula*

Edited by F. Scorza Barcellona, 1975. *Epistola di Barnaba* [Corona Patrum, 1], Torino: Società Editrice Internationale.

Basil of Caesarea (329–79)

*De legendis gentilium libris*. Edited by F. Boulenger, 1935 (repr. 1965). *Saint Basile. Aux jeunes gens sur la manière de tirer profit des lettres Helléniques*, Paris: Les Belles Lettres. Translated by R.J. Deferrari & M.R. McGuire, 1934. [*Loeb Classical Library* 270], Cambridge, MA: Harvard University Press.

*Contra Eunomium*. Edited by J.-P. Migne. [*Patrologiae cursus completus*, series Graeca], vol. 29, Paris: Migne, coll. 497–768. Translated by M. DelCogliano & A. Radde-Gallwitz in Basil of Caesarea, 2011. *Against Eunomius*, Washington, DC: Catholic University of America Press.

*Homiliae in hexaemeron*. Edited by S. Giet, Basile de Césarée, 1968. *Homélies sur l'hexaéméron* [Sources chrétiennes 26 bis], Paris: Éditions du Cerf.

*De spiritu sancto*. Edited by B. Pruche, Basile de Césarée, 1968. *Sur le Saint-Esprit* [Sources chrétiennes 17 bis], Paris: Éditions du Cerf. Translated by S.M. Hildebrand in Basil of Caesarea, 2011. *On the Holy Spirit*, Yonkers, NY: St. Vladimir's Seminary Press.

*Epistulae*. Edited by Y. Courtonne, Saint Basile, 1957-1966. *Lettres*, 3 vols., Paris: Les Belles Lettres. Translated by R.J. Deferrari in Basil of Caesarea, 1986. *The Letters*, Cambridge, MA: Harvard University Press.

Būlus al-Būshī (*c.* 1170–1250)

*De incarnatione*. Edited by S.Kh. Samir, 1983. *Traité de Paul de Bus sur l'unité et la Trinité, l'Incarnation, et la vérité du Christianisme* (Maqaah fı al-tathlıth wa al-tajassud wasihh at al-masıhıyah) [Patrimoine Arabe Chrétien 4], Zouk Mikhail: al-Turath al-'Arabı al-Masıh.

*Chronica Nestoris*

Edited by F. Miklosich, 1978. *Chronica Nestoris: textum russico-slovenicum, versionem latinam glossarium*, München: R. Trofenik.

Clement of Alexandria (*c.* 150–215)

*Paedagogus*. Edited by C. Mondésert, Ch. Matray & H.I. Marrou, 1970. [Sources chrétiennes 158], Paris: Éditions du Cerf.

*Protrepticus*. Edited by M. Marcovich, 1995. *Clementis Alexandrini Protrepticus* [Supplements to Vigiliae Christianae 34], Leiden; Brill 1995. Translated by G.W. Butterworth, 1919. [*Loeb Classical Library* 92], Cambridge, MA: Harvard University Press.

*Stromata*. Edited by L. Früchtel, O. Stählin & U. Treu, 1960-1970. *Clemens Alexandrinus* [Die griechischen christlichen Schriftsteller 52 (15), 17], Berlin: Akademie Verlag. Translated by J. Ferguson in Clement of Alexandria, 1991. *Stromateis, Books One to Three*, Washington, DC: The Catholic University of America Press.

Clement of Rome (first century) — *Ad Corinthios*. Edited by A. Jaubert, 1971. Clément de Rome. *Épître aux Corinthiens* [Sources chrétiennes 167], Paris: Éditions du Cerf. Translated by B.D. Ehrman, 2003. [*Loeb Classical Library* 24], Cambridge, MA: Harvard University Press.

(Ps.) Clement of Rome — *Homiliae*. Edited by J. Irmscher, F. Paschke & B. Rehm, 1969. *Die Pseudoklementinen I. Homilien* [Die griechischen christlichen Schriftsteller 42], Berlin: Akademie Verlag.

*Codex Theodosianus* — Edited by Th. Mommsen, 2011. *Codex Theodosianus*, Berlin: Weidmann. Translated by C. Pharr, 1952. *The Theodosian Code and Novels and the Sirmondian Constitution*, Princeton, NJ: Princeton University Press.

*Collectio Palatina* — Edited by E. Schwartz, R. Schieffer & J. Straub, 1924-1926. *Acta Conciliorum Oecumenicorum* I 5, Berlin: De Gruyter, pp. 5–70.

*Corpus iuris civilis* — Edited by P. Krüger, R. Scholl & G. Kroll, 1877, 1904. *Corpus iuris civilis*, Berlin: Weidmann. Translated by D. Miller & P. Sarris, 2018. *The Novels of Justinian: A Complete Annotated English Translation*, Cambridge: Cambridge University Press.

Cyprian of Carthage (*c.* 200–58) — *Epistulae*. Edited by G.F. Diercks, 1994, 1996. [*Corpus Christianorum*. Series Latina, iii B & C], Turnhout: Brepols.

Cyril of Alexandria (*c.* 375–444) — *De sancta Trinitate dialogi*. Edited by G.-M. de Durand, 1976-1978. *Cyrille d'Alexandrie. Dialogues sur la Trinité*, 3 vols. [Sources chrétiennes 231, 237, 246], Paris: Éditions du Cerf.

*Thesaurus de sancta consubstantiali Trinitate*. Edited by J.-P. Migne, [*Patrologiae cursus completus*, series Graeca], vol. 75, Paris: Migne, coll. 9–657.

*Quod unus sit Christus*. Edited by G.-M. de Durand, 1964. *Cyrille d'Alexandrie. Deux dialogues christologiques* [Sources chrétiennes 97], Paris: Éditions du Cerf. Translated by J.A. McGuckin in Cyril of Alexandria, 2000. *On the Unity of Christ*, Crestwood, NY: St. Vladimir's Seminary Press.

*Commentarii in Lucam* (in catenis). Edited by J.-P. Migne. [*Patrologiae cursus completus*, series Graeca], vol. 72, Paris: Migne, coll. 476–949.

*Commentarii in Joannem*. Edited by Ph.E. Pusey, 1872. *Sancti patris nostri Cyrilli archiepiscopi Alexandrini in D. Joannis evangelium*, 3 vols., Oxford: Clarendon Press. Translated by Ph.E. Pusey & Th. Randell in Cyril of Alexandria, 1874. *Commentary on the Gospel According to S. John*, Oxford: J. Parker.

*Fragmenta in sancti Pauli epistulam ad Hebraeos.* Edited by Ph.E. Pusey, 1872. *Sancti patris nostri Cyrilli archiepiscopi Alexandrini in D. Joannis evangelium*, vol. 3, Oxford: Clarendon Press, pp. 362–423.

*Epistulae paschales sive Homiliae paschales.* Edited by W.H. Burns & P. Évieux, 1991, 1993, 1998. *Cyrille d'Alexandrie. Lettres Festales*, [Sources chrétiennes 372, 392, 434], Paris: Éditions du Cerf. Translated by Ph.R. Amidon in Cyril of Alexandria, 2009, 2013. *Festal Letters 1–30*, 2 vols, Washington, DC: Catholic University of America Press.

*Epistulae.* Translated by J. McEnerney in Cyril of Alexandria, 1987. *Letters 1–50 & Letters 51–110*, Washington, DC: Catholic University of America Press; L.R. Wickham in Cyril of Alexandria, 1983. *Select Letters edited and translated* [Oxford Early Christian Texts], Oxford: Oxford University Press.

Cyril of Jerusalem (*c.* 315–86) — *Catechesis.* Edited by W.C. Reischl & J. Rupp, 1848–1860 (repr. 1967). *Cyrilli Hierosolymorum archiepiscopi opera quae supersunt omnia*, 2 vols., Munich: Lentner (repr. Hildesheim: Olms).

Cyril Lucaris (1572–1638) — *Confessio fidei*, 1629. London: Printed for Nicolas Bourne, dwelling at the south entrance of the Royall Exchange.

David Invincible (fl. mid-sixth century) — *On Porphyry's Introduction.* Edited and translated by G. Muradyan, 2015. *David the Invincible, Commentary on Porphyry's Isagoge.* Old Armenian text with the Greek original, an English translation, introduction and notes, Leiden: Brill.

Dexippus (*c.* AD 210–73) — *In Aristotelis categorias commentarium.* Edited by A. Busse, 1888. *Dexippi in Aristotelis categorias commentarium* [Commentaria in Aristotelem Graeca 4.2], Berlin: Reimer. Translated by J. Dillon, 2014. *On Aristotle Categories*, London: Bloomsbury.

*Didaché XII apostolorum* — Edited and translated by B.D. Ehrman, 2003. [*Loeb Classical Library* 24], Cambridge, MA: Harvard University Press.

*Didascalia apostolorum* — Edited by A. Vööbus, 1978. *The Didascalia Apostolorum in Syriac* I-II [Corpus scriptorum christianorum orientalium 401, 407 (textus), 402, 408 (translatio)], Louvain: Peeters. Translated by A. Stewart-Sykes, 2009. *The Didascalia apostolorum: An English Version*, Turnhout: Brepols.

Didymus the Blind (*c.* 313–98) — *De spiritu sancto.* Edited by L. Doutreleau, 1992. *Didyme l'Aveugle. Traité du Saint-Esprit* [Sources chrétiennes 386], Paris: Édition du Cerf.

| | |
|---|---|
| Dio Cassius (*c.* 150–235) | *Historiae Romanae*. Edited by U.P. Boissevain, 1895-1901 (repr. 1955). *Cassii Dionis Cocceiani historiarum Romanarum quae supersunt*, 3 vols., Berlin: Weidmann. Translated by E. Cary & H.B. Foster, 1917. [*Loeb Classical Library* 83], Cambridge, MA: Harvard University Press. |
| Diodore of Tarsus (*c.* 330–90) | *Commentarii in Psalmos*. Edited by J.-M. Olivier, 1980. [*Corpus Christianorum*. Series Graeca, 6], Turnhout: Brepols. |
| Diogenes Laërtius (fl. third century AD) | *Vitae philosophorum*. Edited and translated by S. White, 2021. *Diogenes Laertius, Lives of Eminent Philosophers*, Cambridge: Cambridge University Press. |
| (Ps.) Dionysius Areopagita (flourished late fifth–early sixth century) | *De diuinis nominibus*. Edited by B.R. Suchla, 1990. *Corpus Dionysiacum. I: Pseudo-Dionysius Areopagita. De divinis nominibus* [Patristische Texte und Studien 33], Berlin: De Gruyter. Translated by C. Lulbheld, 1987. *Pseudo-Dionysius: The Complete Works*, Mahwah, NJ: Paulist, pp. 47–132. |
| | *De mystica theologia*. Edited by G. Heil & A.M. Ritter, 1991. *Corpus Dionysiacum. II: Pseudo-Dionysius Areopagita. De coelesti hierarchia, De ecclesiastica hierarchia, De mystica theologia, Epistulae* [Patristische Texte und Studien 36], Berlin: De Gruyter, pp. 141–50. Translated by C. Lulbheld, 1987. *Pseudo-Dionysius: the Complete Works*, Mahwah, NJ: Paulist, pp. 133–42. |
| | *De caelesti hierarchia*. Edited by G. Heil & A.M. Ritter, 1991. *Corpus Dionysiacum. II: Pseudo-Dionysius Areopagita. De coelesti hierarchia, De ecclesiastica hierarchia, De mystica theologia, Epistulae* [Patristische Texte und Studien 36], Berlin: De Gruyter, pp. 7–59. Translated by C. Lulbheld, 1987. *Pseudo-Dionysius: the Complete Works*, Mahwah, NJ: Paulist, pp. 143–92. |
| | *De ecclesiastica hierarchia*. Edited by G. Heil & A.M. Ritter, 1991. *Corpus Dionysiacum. II: Pseudo-Dionysius Areopagita. De coelesti hierarchia, De ecclesiastica hierarchia, De mystica theologia, Epistulae* [Patristische Texte und Studien 36], Berlin: De Gruyter, pp. 63–132. Translated by C. Lulbheld, 1987. *Pseudo-Dionysius: The Complete Works*, Mahwah, NJ: Paulist, pp. 193–260. |
| | *Epistulae*. Edited by G. Heil & A.M. Ritter, 1991. *Corpus Dionysiacum. II: Pseudo-Dionysius Areopagita. De coelesti hierarchia, De ecclesiastica hierarchia, De mystica theologia, Epistulae* [Patristische Texte und Studien 36], Berlin: De Gruyter, pp. 133–210. Translated by C. Lulbheld, 1987. *Pseudo-Dionysius: The Complete Works*, Mahwah, NJ: Paulist, pp. 261–90. |
| *Eisagogé / Epanagogé* (Εἰσαγωγή τοῦ νόμου / Ἐπαναγωγή) | Edited by K.E. Zachariä von Lingenthal, 1852. *Ecloga Leonis et Constantini, Epanagoge Basilii Leonis et Alexandri*, Lipsiae: Sumtibus J.A. Barthii. |

Empedocles (*c.* 490–30 BC)
: *Fragmenta.* Edited and translated by M.R. Wright, 1981. Empedocles, *The Extant Fragments*, New Haven, CT: Yale University Press.

Ephrem the Syrian (*c.* 306–73)
: *Carmina Nisibena.* Edited by E. Beck, 1963. Louvain: Secrétariat du Corpus Scriptorum Christianorum Orientalium.

Epictetus (*c.* AD 50–135)
: *Encheiridion.* Edited by G.J. Boter, 2007. *Epictetus, Encheiridion* [Bibliotheca scriptorum Graecorum et Romanorum Teubneriana], Berlin: De Gruyter.

: *Dissertationes ab Arriano digestae.* Edited by H. Schenkl, 1916. *Epicteti dissertationes ab Arriano digestae*, Leipzig: Teubner. Translated by W.A. Oldfather, 1925. [*Loeb Classical Library* 131], Cambridge, MA: Harvard University Press.

Epiphanius (*c.* 310–403)
: *Panarion.* Edited by K. Holl, 1915–1933. *Epiphanius, Bände 1-3: Ancoratus und Panarion* [Die griechischen christlichen Schriftsteller 25, 31, 37], Leipzig: Hinrichs. Translated by F. Williams in Epiphanius, 2009. *The Panarion of Epiphanius of Salamis*: Book I: Sects 1-46, Leiden: Brill; Epiphanius, 2013. *The Panarion of Epiphanius of Salamis*, Books II and III: *De Fide*, Leiden: Brill.

*Epistula ad Diognetum* (second century)
: Edited by H.-I. Marrou, 1965. *A Diognète* [Sources chrétiennes 33 bis], Paris: Éditions du Cerf, pp. 52–84. Translated by B.D. Ehrman, 2003. [*Loeb Classical Library* 25], Cambridge, MA: Harvard University Press.

*Etymologicon*
: Edited by F.W. Sturz, 1973. *Orionis Thebani Etymologicon*, Hildesheim: Olms.

Eunomius (*c.* 335–94)
: *Apologia.* Edited and translated by R.P. Vaggione in Eunomius, 1987. *The Extant Works. Text and Translation* [Oxford Early Christian Texts], Oxford: Oxford University Press.

Eusebius of Caesarea (*c.* 260–340)
: *Praeparatio Evangelica.* Edited by K. Mras, 1954, 1956. *Eusebius Werke*, Band 8: *Die Praeparatio evangelica* [Die griechischen christlichen Schriftsteller 43.1 & 43.2], Berlin: Akademie Verlag. Translated by E.H. Gifford in Eusebius, 2002. *Preparation for the Gospel*, Eugene, OR: Wipf and Stock.

: *Demonstratio evangelica.* Edited by I.A. Heikel, 1913. *Eusebius Werke*, Band 6: *Die Demonstratio evangelica* [Die griechischen christlichen Schriftsteller 23], Leipzig: Hinrichs.

: *De ecclesiastica theologia.* Edited by G.C. Hansen & E. Klostermann, 1972. *Eusebius Werke*, Band 4: Gegen Marcell. *Über die kirchliche Theologie. Die Fragmente Marcells* [Die griechischen christlichen Schriftsteller 14], Berlin: Akademie Verlag.

*Historia ecclesiastica*. Edited by G. Bardy, 1952-1958. *Eusèbe de Césarée. Histoire ecclésiastique*, 3 vols. [Sources chrétiennes 31, 41, 55], Paris: Éditions du Cerf. Translated by K. Lake, 1926. [*Loeb Classical Library* 153], Cambridge, MA: Harvard University Press.

*Vita Constantini*. Edited and translated by A. Cameron & S.G. Hall, 1999. *Life of Constantine*, Oxford: Clarendon Press.

*De laudibus Constantini*. Edited by I.A. Heikel, 1902. *Eusebius Werke*, vol. 1 [Die griechischen christlichen Schriftsteller 7], Leipzig: Hinrichs.

Eustathius of Antioch (*c*. 280–360)
*Fragmenta*. Edited by J.H. Declerck, 2002. [*Corpus Christianorum*. Series Graeca 51], Turnhout: Brepols.

Eutherius of Tiana (fl. first half of sixth century)
*Confutationes quarundam propositionum*. Edited by M. Tetz, 1964. *Eine Antilogie des Eutherios von Tyana* [Patristische Texte und Studien 1], Berlin: De Gruyter.

Evagrius Ponticus (346–99)
*Practicus*. Edited by A. & C. Guillaumont, 1971. *Évagre le Pontique. Traité pratique ou le moine* [Sources chrétiennes 170-171], Paris: Éditions du Cerf.

*Kephalaia gnostica*. Syriac version edited by A. Guillaumont, 1958. *Les six Centuries des Kephalaia Gnostica d'Évagre le Pontique* [Patrologia Orientalis 28, 1], Paris: Firmin-Didot.

*De oratione*. Edited by J.-P. Migne. [*Patrologiae cursus completus*, series Graeca], vol. 79, Paris: Migne, coll. 1165–1200.

Evagrius Scholasticus (*c*. 535–600)
*Historia ecclesiastica*. Edited by J. Bidez & L. Parmentier, 1898. *The Ecclesiastical History of Evagrius with the Scholia*, London: Methuen. Translated by M. Whitby in Evagrius Scholasticus, 2000. *The Ecclesiastical History of Evagrius Scholasticus*, Liverpool: Liverpool University Press.

Gregory Mammas (died 1459)
*Responsio ad epistulam encyclicam*. Edited by J.-P. Migne. [*Patrologiae cursus completus*, series Graeca], vol. 160, Paris: Migne, coll. 111–204.

Gregory of Nazianzus (*c*. 330–89)
*Carmina dogmatica*. Edited by J.-P. Migne. [*Patrologiae cursus completus*, series Graeca], vol. 37, Paris: Migne, coll. 397–522.

*Epistulae theologicae*. Edited by P. Gallay, 1974. *Grégoire de Nazianze. Lettres théologiques* [Sources chrétiennes 208], Paris: Éditions du Cerf. Translated by L. Wickham & F. Williams in Gregory of Nazianzus, 2002. *On God and Christ: The Five Theological Orations and Two Letters to Cledonius*, Crestwood, NY: St. Vladimir's Seminary Press.

*Testamentum*. Edited by J.B. Pitra, 1868. *Iuris ecclesiastici Graecorum historia et monumenta*, vol. 2, Rome: Congregatio de Propaganda Fide, pp. 155–9.

*Christus patiens* (dub.). Edited by A. Tuilier, 1969. *Grégoire de Nazianze. La passion du Christ* [Sources chrétiennes 149], Paris: Éditions du Cerf.

Gregory of Nyssa (*c.* 335–94)

Brill publishes Gregory's works in the *Gregorii Nysseni Opera Online*: https://dh.brill.com/scholarlyeditions/about/gnoo/ (accessed on March 27, 2021).

*Oratio catechetica*. Edited by E. Mühlenberg, 2000. *Discours Catéchétique* [Sources chrétiennes 453], Paris: Éditions du Cerf. Translated by J.H. Srawley in Gregory of Nyssa, 1903. *Catechetical Oration of Gregory of Nyssa*, Cambridge: Cambridge University Press.

*Contra Eunomium*. Edited by W. Jaeger, 1960. *Gregorii Nysseni opera*, vols. 1.1 & 2.2, Leiden: Brill. Translated by S.G. Hall in M. Brugarolas, ed., 2018. *Gregory of Nyssa: Contra Eunomium I: An English Translation with Supporting Studies*, Leiden: Brill; L. Karfíková, S. Douglass & J. Zachhuber, eds., 2007. *Gregory of Nyssa: Contra Eunomium II*, Leiden: Brill; J. Leemans & M. Cassin, eds., 2014. *Gregory of Nyssa, Contra Eunomium III*, Leiden: Brill.

*Antirrheticus adversus Apollinarium*. Edited by F. Mueller, 1958. *Gregorii Nysseni opera*, vol. 3.1, Leiden: Brill.

*De professione Christiana ad Harmonium*. Edited by W. Jaeger, 1963. *Gregorii Nysseni opera*, vol. 8.1, Leiden: Brill.

*Ad Ablabium quod non sint tres dei*. Edited by F. Mueller, 1958. *Gregorii Nysseni opera*, vol. 3.1, Leiden: Brill.

*In illud: Tunc et ipse filius*. Edited by J.K. Downing, 1986. *Gregorii Nysseni opera*, vol. 3.2, Leiden: Brill.

*De vita Mosis*. Edited by J. Danielou, 1968. *Grégoire de Nysse. La vie de Moïse* [Sources chrétiennes 1 ter], Paris: Éditions du Cerf. Translated by A.J. Malherbe & E. Ferguson in Gregory of Nyssa, 2006. *The Life of Moses*, New York: HarperOne.

*In Ecclesiasten*. Edited by P.J. Alexander, 1962. *Gregorii Nysseni opera*, vol. 5, Leiden: Brill.

*Orationes viii de beatitudinibus*. Edited by J.-P. Migne. [*Patrologiae cursus completus*, series Graeca], vol. 44, Paris: Migne, coll. 1193–301. Translated by S.G. Hall in Gregory of Nyssa, 2000. *Homilies on the Beatitudes. An English Version with Commentary and Supporting Studies*, edited by. H. R. Drobner & A. Viciano, Leiden: Brill.

*De oratione dominica orationes*. Edited by C. Boudignon, M. Cassin & J. Seguin, 2018. *Grégoire de Nysse. Homélies sur le Notre Père* [Sources chrétiennes 596], Paris: Éditions du Cerf.

*De opificio hominis*. Edited by J.-P. Migne. [*Patrologiae cursus completes*, series Graeca], vol. 44, Paris: Migne, coll. 124–256.

*De mortuis non esse dolendum*. Edited by G. Heil, 1967. *Gregorii Nysseni opera*, vol. 9.1, Leiden: Brill.

*Dialogus de anima et resurrectione*. Edited by J.-P. Migne. [*Patrologiae cursus completus*, series Graeca], vol. 46, Paris: Migne, coll. 12–160. Translated by V. Woods Callahan in Gregory of Nyssa, 1967. *Ascetical Works*, Washington, DC: The Catholic University of America Press.

Gregory Palamas (1296–1359)

*Homiliae*. Edited by Π. Χρήστου, 1985-1986. Γρηγορίου τοῦ Παλαμᾶ ἅπαντα τὰ ἔργα [Ἕλληνες Πατέρες τῆς Ἐκκλησίας 72, 76, 79], vols. 9–11, Thessalonica: Πατερικαὶ ἐκδόσεις "Γρηγόριος ὁ Παλαμᾶς."

*Pro hesychastis*. Edited by J. Meyendorff, 1973. Grégoire Palamas. *Défense des saints hésychastes* [Spicilegium Sacrum Lovaniense. Études et documents 30], Louvain: Peeters. Translated by N. Gendle in J. Meyendorff, ed., 1983. *Gregory Palamas. The Triads*, New York: Paulist.

*Orationes apologeticae*. Edited by Π. Χρήστου, 1966. *Γρηγορίου τοῦ Παλαμᾶ συγγράμματα*, vol. 2, Thessalonica: Πατερικαὶ ἐκδόσεις "Γρηγόριος ὁ Παλαμᾶς."

*Orationes antirrheticae contra Acindynum*. Edited by Π. Χρήστου, 1970. *Γρηγορίου τοῦ Παλαμᾶ συγγράμματα*, vol. 3, Thessalonica: Πατερικαὶ ἐκδόσεις "Γρηγόριος ὁ Παλαμᾶς."

Heraclitus (fl. *c.* 500 BC)

*Fragmenta*. Edited by H. Diehls & W. Kranz, 1996. *Die Fragmente der Vorsokratiker*, Zürich: Weidmann.

Herodotus (*c.* 484–*c.* 430/20 BC)

*Historiae*. Edited by N.G. Wilson, 2015. *Herodoti Historiae*, 2 vols., Oxford: Oxford University Press.

Hesiod (fl. *c.* 700 BC)

*Theogonia*. Edited and translated by G.W. Most, 2018. [*Loeb Classical Library* 57], Cambridge, MA: Harvard University Press.

*Opera et dies*. Edited and translated by G.W. Most, 2018. [*Loeb Classical Library* 57], Cambridge, MA: Harvard University Press.

Hesychius of Alexandria (fl. fifth century AD)

*Lexicon*. Edited by K. Latte, 1953. *Hesychii Alexandrini lexicon*, 2 vols., Copenhagen: Munksgaard.

Hilarius of Poitiers (*c.* 315–67)

*De synodis*. Edited by J.-P. Migne. [*Patrologiae cursus completes*, series Latina], vol. 10, Paris: Migne, coll. 479–546.

| | |
|---|---|
| *Hispellum rescript* | Translated by A.C. Johnson, P.R. Coleman-Norton & F.C. Bourne, 2012. *Ancient Roman Statutes: A Translation with Introduction, Commentary, Glossary, and Index*, Austin, TX: University of Texas Press, pp. 241–2. |
| *History of the Patriarchs of the Coptic Church of Alexandria* | Arabic text edited and translated by B. Evetts, 1907. [Patrologia orientalis I 4], Paris: Firmin-Didot. |
| Homer (fl. ninth or eigth century BC) | *Ilias*. Edited and translated by A.T. Murray, revised by W.F. Wyatt, 1925. [*Loeb Classical Library* 171], Cambridge, MA: Harvard University Press. |
| Iamblichus (*c.* 242–325 AD) | *De mysteriis*. Edited by É. des Places, 1966. *Jamblique. Les mystères d'Égypte*, Paris: Les Belles Lettres. |
| | *De anima*. Edited and translated by J.M. Dillon & J. F. Finamore, 2002. *Iamblichus. De Anima: Text, Translation, and Commentary* [Philosophia Antiqua 92], Leiden: Brill. |
| Ignatius of Antioch (died *c.* 110) | *Epistulae*. Edited by P.T. Camelot, 1969. *Ignace d'Antioche. Polycarpe de Smyrne. Lettres. Martyre de Polycarpe* [Sources chrétiennes 10], Paris: Éditions du Cerf. Translated by B.D. Ehrman, 2003. [*Loeb Classical Library* 24], Cambridge, MA: Harvard University Press. |
| Irenaeus of Lyon (*c.* 120–200) | *Adversus haereses*. Edited by A. Rousseau, B. Hemmerdinger, L. Doutreleau & Ch. Mercier, 1969-1982. [*Sources chrétiennes* 100*, 152, 210, 263, 293], Paris: Éditions du Cerf. |
| Isaac of Nineveh (died *c.* 700) | *Homiliae*. Edited and translated by S.P. Brock, 1995. [*Corpus scriptorum christianorum orientalium* 554, 555], Louvain: Secrétariat du Corpus Scriptorum Christianorum Orientalium. |
| Jerome (*c.* 347–419/20) | *Epistulae*. Edited by I. Hilberg & M. Kamptner, 1910-1918. [*Corpus scriptorum ecclesiasticorum Latinorum* 54–6], Vienna: Verlag der Österreichischen Akademie der Wissenschaften. |
| | *Vita Pauli*. Edited and translated by I.S. Kozik, 1968. *The First Desert Hero: St. Jerome's Vita Pauli*, Mount Vernon, NY: King Lithographers; Ph. Schaff & W.H. Fremantle, 2017. *The Sacred Writings of Saint Jerome*. Altenmünster: Jazzybee Verlag. |
| John Chrysostom (347–407) | *Commentarii in epistulam i ad Timotheum*. Edited by J.-P. Migne. [*Patrologiae cursus completus*, series Graeca], vol. 62, Paris: Migne, coll. 501–600. |
| | *Homilia de capto Eutropio* [Dub]. Edited by J.-P. Migne. [*Patrologiae cursus completus*, series Graeca], vol. 52, Paris: Migne, coll. 395–414. |
| John Climacus (*c.* 579–649) | *Scala paradisi*. Edited by J.-P. Migne. [*Patrologiae cursus completus*, series Graeca], vol. 88, Paris: Migne, coll. 631–1161. |

John of Damascus (*c.* 675–749)

*Dialectica*. Edited by B. Kotter, 1969. *Die Schriften des Iohannes von Damaskos*, vol. I [Patristische Texte und Studien 7]. Berlin: De Gryuter. Translated by F.H. Chase, 1958. *John of Damascus, Writings*, Washington, DC: Catholic University of America Press.

*De haeresibus*. Edited by P.B. Kotter, 1981. *Die Schriften des Johannes von Damaskos*, vol. 4 [Patristische Texte und Studien 22], Berlin: De Gruyter.

*Orationes de imaginibus tres*. Edited by P.B. Kotter, 1975. *Die Schriften des Johannes von Damaskos*, vol. 3 [Patristische Texte und Studien 17], Berlin: De Gruyter. Translated by Andrew Louth in John of Damascus, 2003. *Three Treatises on the Divine Images*, Crestwood, NY: St. Vladimir's Seminary Press.

John Philoponus (fl. sixth century AD)

*Arbiter*. Edited and translated by U.M. Lang, 2001. *John Philoponus and the Controversies Over Chalcedon in the Sixth Century: A Study and Translation of the Arbiter*, Leuven: Peeters.

*Contra Themistium*. Edited by A. van Roey, 1980. "Les fragments trithéites de Jean Philopon," *Orientalia Lovaniensia Periodica*, 11, pp. 135–63.

*In Aristotelis physicorum libros commentaria*. Edited by H. Vitelli, 1887-1888. *Ioannis Philoponi in Aristotelis physicorum libros octo commentaria*, 2 vols. [Commentaria in Aristotelem Graeca 16 & 17], Berlin: Reimer.

*De aeternitate mundi contra Proclum*. Edited by H. Rabe, 1899 (repr. 1963). *Ioannes Philoponus. De aeternitate mundi contra Proclum*, Leipzig: Teubner (repr. Hildesheim: Olms).

*In Aristotelis libros de anima commentaria*. Edited by M. Hayduck, 1897. *Ioannis Philoponi in Aristotelis de anima libros commentaria* [Commentaria in Aristotelem Graeca 15], Berlin: Reimer.

John Rufus (fifth–sixth century)

*Plerophoriae*. Syriac translation edited by F. Nau, 1912. *Jean Rufus, évêque de Maiouma. Plérophories* [Patrologia Orientalis VIII 1], Paris: Firmin-Didot.

Josephus Flavius (AD 37/38–100)

*Contra Apionem*. Edited by B. Niese, 1889 (repr. 1955). *Flavii Iosephi opera*, vol. 5, Berlin: Weidmann.

Julian (the emperor, 331/2–63)

*Contra Galilaeos*. Edited by J. Bidez, 1932. *L'empereur Julien. Oeuvres complètes*, Paris: Les Belles Lettres. Translated by W.C. Wright, 1923. [*Loeb Classical Library* 157], Cambridge, MA: Harvard University Press.

Ἀθηναίων τῇ βουλῇ καὶ τῷ δήμῳ [To the council and municipality of the Athenians]. Edited by J. Bidez, 1932. *L'empereur Julien. Oeuvres complètes*, Paris: Les Belles Lettres. Translated by W.C. Wright, 1913. [*Loeb Classical Library* 29], Cambridge, MA: Harvard University Press.

| | |
|---|---|
| | *Epistulae*. Julian, 1923. *Letters. Epigrams. Against the Galilaeans. Fragments.* Translated by Wilmer C. Wright. [*Loeb Classical Library* 157], Cambridge, MA: Harvard University Press, pp. 188–91. |
| Julian of Halicarnassus (fl. *c.* 520) | *Anathema septimum.* Edited by R. Draguet, 1924. *Julien d'Halicarnasse et sa controverse avec Sévère d'Antioche sur l'incorruptibilité du corps du Christ. Étude d'histoire littéraire et doctrinale; suivie des Fragments dogmatiques de Julien.* (Texte syriaque et traduction grecque). Universitas catholica lovaniensis. Dissertationes ad gradum magistri in Facultate theologica consequendum conscriptae. Series II 12, Louvain: Peeters. |
| Justin (*c.* 100–65) | *Apologiae* I & II. Edited by M. Marcovich, 1994. *Iustini martyris Apologiae pro Christianis* [Patristische Texte und Studiens 38], Berlin: De Gryuter. Translated by Th. Falls, 2008. *The First Apology, the Second Apology, Dialogue with Trypho, Exhortation to the Greeks, Discourse to the Greeks, the Monarchy or the Rule of God*, Washington, DC: Catholic University of America Press. |
| | *Dialogus cum Tryphone Iudaeo.* Edited by M. Marcovich, 1997. *Iustini Martyris Dialogus cum Tryphone* [Patristische Texte und Studiens 47], Berlin: De Gruyter. Translated by Th. Falls, 2008. *The First Apology, the Second Apology, Dialogue with Trypho, Exhortation to the Greeks, Discourse to the Greeks, the Monarchy or the Rule of God*, Washington, DC: Catholic University of America Press. |
| Justinian (483–565) | *Edictum rectae fidei.* Edited by E. Schwartz, R. Albertella, M. Amelotti & L. Migliardi, 1973. *Drei dogmatische Schriften Iustinians*, Milan: Giuffre. |
| Khosrovik Targmanich (between 630 and 730) | Edited and translated by Kh. Grigoryan, 2019. *Dogmatic Writings*, Yerevan: Ankyunacar. |
| Lactantius (240–320) | *De mortibus persecutorum.* Edited and translated by A. Städele, 2010. [*Fontes Christiani* 43], Turnhout: Brepols. |
| Leo I of Rome (died 461) | *Epistula ad Flavianum.* Edited by J.-P. Migne. [*Patrologiae cursus completus*, series Latina], vol. 54, Paris: Migne, coll. 751–2. |
| Leontius of Byzantium (*c.* 485–543) | *Contra Nestorianos et Eutychianos.* Edited and translated by B.E. Daley, 2017. *Leontius of Byzantium. Complete Works*, Oxford: Oxford University Press, pp. 125–268. |
| | *Deprehensio et Triumphus super Nestorianos.* Edited and translated by B.E. Daley, 2017. *Leontius of Byzantium. Complete Works*, Oxford: Oxford University Press, pp. 411–524. |
| | *Epilyseis (Solutiones Argumentorum Severi).* Edited and translated by B.E. Daley, 2017. *Leontius of Byzantium. Complete Works*, Oxford: Oxford University Press, pp. 269–312. |

*Epaporemata (Triginta Capita contra Severum)*. Edited and translated by B.E. Daley, 2017. *Leontius of Byzantium. Complete Works*, Oxford: Oxford University Press, pp. 313–36.

Libanius (314–93) — *Orationes*. Edited and translated by A. F. Norman, 1977. [*Loeb Classical Library* 452], Cambridge, MA: Harvard University Press.

*Libellus from P. Oxy, IV 658* — Edited and translated by J.R. Knipfing, 1923. "The Libelli of the Decian Persecution." *The Harvard Theological Review*, 16 (4), pp. 345–90.

*Liber pontificalis* — Edited by L. Duchesne & C. Vogel, 1957. *Liber pontificalis*, Paris: E. Thorin.

(Ps) Macarius (fourth century) — Edited by H. Berthold, 1973. *Makarios/Symeon: Reden und Briefe. Die Sammlung des Vaticanus Graecus 694 (B)* [Die griechischen christlichen Schriftsteller der ersten Jahrhunderte 55-56], Berlin: Akademie-Verlag.

Makariy Ivanov (1788–1860) — Edited by Ioann Zakharchenko, 1997. *Душеполезные поучения преподобного Макария Оптинского* [Edifying admonishions of St. Makary of Optina], Введенская Оптина пустыня.

Mansi, Giovanni Domenico (1692–1769) — 1960. *Sacrorum conciliorum nova et amplissima collectio*, Graz: Akademische Druck- und Verlagsanstalt.

Marcellus of Ancyra (*c.* 285–374) — *Fragmenta e Libro contra Asterium*. Edited by E. Klostermann, 1906 (repr. 1972). *Eusebius Werke*, vol. 4 [Die griechischen christlichen Schriftsteller der ersten drei Jahrhunderte 14], Leipzig: Teubner, pp. 185–215.

*Martyrium Pionii* — Edited and translated by É. Rebillard, 2017. *Greek and Latin Narratives About the Ancient Martyrs*, Oxford: Oxford University Press, pp. 53–79.

*Martyrium Polycarpi* — Edited and translated by B.D. Ehrman, 2003. [*Loeb Classical Library* 24], Cambridge, MA: Harvard University Press.

Maximus the Confessor (*c.* 580–662) — *Capita de caritate*. Edited by A. Ceresa-Gastaldo, 1963. *Massimo confessore. Capitoli sulla carita*, Rome: Editrice Studium. Translated by P. Sherwood in Maximus the Confessor, 1978. *The Ascetic Life. The Four Centuries on Charity*, New York, NY: Paulist Press.

*Ambigua*. Edited and translated by Maximos Constas, 2014. *On Difficulties in the Church Fathers: The Ambigua*, Cambridge, MA: Harvard University Press.

*Quaestiones ad Thalassium*. Edited by C. Laga & C. Steel, 1980, 1990. *Maximi confessoris quaestiones ad Thalassium*, 2 vols. [Corpus Christianorum. Series Graeca 7 & 22], Turnhout: Brepols.

*Disputatio cum Pyrrho*. Edited by M. Doucet, 1972. *Dispute de Maxime le Confesseur avec Pyrrhus. Introduction, texte critique, traduction et notes*, Université de Montréal, Institut d'Études Médiévales. Translated by J.P. Farrell in Maximus the Confessor, 2014. *The Disputation with Pyrrhus of Our Father Among the Saints Maximus the Confessor*, Waymart, PA: St. Tikhon's Monastery Press.

*Disputatio Bizyae cum Theodosio*. Edited by P. Allen & B. Neil, 1999. *Scripta saeculi VII vitam Maximi Confessoris illustrantia* [Corpus Christianorum. Series Graeca 39], Turnout: Brepols, pp. 73–151.

*Orationis dominicae expositio*. Edited by P. van Deun, 1991. *Maximi confessoris opuscula exegetica duo* [Corpus Christianorum. Series Graeca 23], Turnhout: Brepols, pp. 27–73.

*Capita theologica et oeconomica*. Edited by K. Hajdú & A. Wollbold, 2017. *Maximus Confessor. Capita theologica et oeconomica. Zwei Centurien über die Gotteserkenntnis* [Fontes Christiani 66], Freiburg, Basel, Vienna: Herder.

*Epistulae*. Edited by J.-P. Migne. [*Patrologiae cursus completus*, series Graeca], vol. 91, Paris: Migne, coll. 364–649.

Melito of Sardes (fl. second century)

*De pascha*. Edited and translated by S.G. Hall, 1979. *Melito of Sardis. On Pascha and Fragments*, Oxford: Clarendon Press.

Michael Critobulus (fl. fifteenth century)

*Epistula ad Mechmet II & Historiae*. Edited by D.R. Reinsch, 1983. *Critobuli Imbriotae historiae* [Corpus Fontium Historiae Byzantinae. Series Berolinensis 22], Berlin: De Gruyter.

Michael Ducas (c. 1400–after 1462)

*Historia Turcobyzantina*. Edited by V. Grecu, 1958. *Ducas. Istoria Turco-Bizantina* (1341–462) [Scriptores Byzantini 1], Bucharest: Academia Republicae Romanicae.

Michael Psellus (c. 1018–82)

*Epistulae*. Edited by S. Papaioannou, 2019. Michael Psellus, *Epistulae*, 2 vols. [Bibliotheca scriptorum Graecorum et Romanorum Teubneriana], Berlin: De Gruyter.

Nemesius of Emesa (fl. fourth century)

*De natura hominis*. Edited by M. Morani, 1987. [*Bibliotheca scriptorum Graecorum et Romanorum Teubneriana*], Leipzig: Teubner. Translated by R.W. Sharples & P.J. Van der Eijk in Nemesius, 2008. *On the Nature of Man*, Liverpool: Liverpool University Press.

Nestorius of Constantinople (died c. 451)

*Liber Heracleidis*. Edited by P. Bedjan, 1910. *Nestorius, Le livre d'Héraclide de Damas*, Paris: Letouzey. Translated by G.R. Driver & L. Hodgson in Nestorius, 1925. *The Bazaar of Heracleides*, Oxford: Clarendon Press.

Nicholas of Methone (died between 1160 and 1166)

*Orationes*. Edited by Α. Δημητρακόπουλος, 1866 (repr. 1965). Ἐκκλησιαστικὴ Βιβλιοθήκη ἐμπεριέχουσα Ἑλλήνων θεολόγων συγγράμματα, Leipzig: Τύποις Ὄθωνος Βιγάνδου, pp. 219–380.

Nilus Cabasilas (*c.* 1298–1363) — *De primatu papae*. Edited by J.-P. Migne. [*Patrologiae cursus completus*, series Graeca], vol. 149, Paris: Migne, coll. 699–728.

Origen (*c.* 185–254) — *Contra Celsum*. Edited by M. Borret, 1967-1969. *Origène. Contre Celse*, 4 vols. [Sources chrétiennes 132, 136, 147, 150], Paris: Éditions du Cerf. Translated by H. Chadwick, 2009. *Origen: Contra Celsum*, Cambridge: Cambridge University Press.

*De principiis*. Edited by H. Görgemanns & H. Karpp, 1976. *Origenes vier Bücher von den Prinzipien*, Darmstadt: Wissenschaftliche Buchgesellschaft. Translated by J. Behr, 2017. *Origen. On First Principles*, 2 vols., Oxford: Oxford University Press.

*In Leviticum*. Edited by W.A. Baehrens, 1920. *Origenes Werke*, vol. 6 [Die griechischen christlichen Schriftsteller 29], Leipzig: Teubner. Translated by G.W. Barkley in Origen, 1990. *Homilies on Leviticus, 1-16*, Washington, DC: Catholic University of America Press.

*In Jeremiam*. Edited by P. Nautin, 1976-1977. *Origène. Homélies sur Jérémie*, 2 vols. [Sources chrétiennes 232, 238], Paris: Éditions du Cerf.

*Commentarii in Johannem*. Edited by C. Blanc, 1992. *Origène. Commentaire sur Saint Jean* [Sources chrétiennes 120 bis & 385], Paris: Éditions du Cerf. Translated by R.E. Helne in Origen, 1989. *Commentary on the Gospel According to John, books 1-10*, Washington, DC: Catholic University of America Press.

*Fragmenta in Lucam* (in catenis). Edited by M. Rauer, 1959. *Origenes Werke*, vol. 9 [Die griechischen christlichen Schriftsteller 49 (35)], Berlin: Akademie Verlag.

*In epistulam Pauli ad Romanos*. Edited by Th. Heither, 1990-1996. *Origenes. Commentarii in Epistulam ad Romanos* [Fontes Christiani 2], Turnhout: Brepols.

*Orphica* — *Hymni*. Edited by W. Quandt, 1962 (repr. 1973). *Orphei hymni*, Berlin: Weidmann.

Ovid (43 BC–AD 17) — *Metamorphoses*. Translated by Ch. Martin in Ovid, 2021. *Metamorphoses*, New York: Norton.

Païsiy Velichkovsky (1722–94) — 1910. *Крины сельные или цветы прекрасные* [Rustic lilies or beautiful flowers], Русский Свято-Ильинский скит на Афоне.

Parmenides (born *c.* 515 BC) — *Fragmenta*. Edited by H. Diels & W. Kranz, 1951. *Die Fragmente der Vorsokratiker*, vol. 1, Berlin: Weidmann, pp. 227–46.

*Passio sanctorum apostolorum Petri et Pauli* — Edited and translated by D.L. Eastman, 2015. *The Ancient Martyrdom Accounts of Peter and Paul*, Atlanta, GA: Society of Biblical Literature Press.

Paul of Aleppo (*c.* 1627–69) *The Travels of Macarius, Patriarch of Antioch, in Arabic.* Edited by B. Radu, 1930. [Patrologia orientalis 22], Paris: Firmin-Didot. Translated by F.C. Belfour, 1836. London: Oriental Translation Fund.

Philo (*c.* 20 BC–AD 50) *De Abrahamo.* Edited by L. Cohn, 1902 (repr. 1962). *Philonis Alexandrini opera quae supersunt*, Berlin: Reimer; De Gruyter.

Philostorgius (*c.* 368–433) *Historia ecclesiastica.* Edited by J. Bidez, 1981. *Philostorgius, Kirchengeschichte, mit dem Leben des Lucian von Antiochien und den Fragmenten eines arianischen Historiographen.* [Die griechischen christlichen Schriftsteller der ersten drei Jahrhunderte], Berlin: Akademie Verlag. Translated by E. Walford in Sozomen and Philostorgius, 1855. *History of the Church*, London: Henry G. Bohn.

Photius (*c.* 820–tenth century) *De spiritu sancti mystagogia.* Edited and translated by J. Graves, 1983. *On the Mystagogy of the Holy Spirit by Saint Photius Patriarch of Constantinople*, Astoria, NY: Studion.

*Epistulae et Amphilochia.* Edited by B. Laourdas & L.G. Westerink, 1983-1988. *Photii patriarchae Constantinopolitani Epistulae et Amphilochia*, 6 vols. [Bibliotheca scriptorum Graecorum et Romanorum Teubneriana], Leipzig: Teubner.

Pindar (*c.* 518–438 BC) *Nemea.* Edited by H. Maehler & B. Snell, 1971. *Pindari carmina cum fragmentis*, Leipzig: Teubner.

Plato (428/7–348/7) *Euthyphro.* Edited and translated by Ch. Emlyn-Jones & W. Preddy, 2017. [*Loeb Classical Library* 36], Cambridge, MA: Harvard University Press.

*Apologia Socratis.* Edited and translated by Ch. Emlyn-Jones & W. Preddy, 2017. [*Loeb Classical Library* 36], Cambridge, MA: Harvard University Press.

*Phaedo.* Edited and translated by Ch. Emlyn-Jones & W. Preddy, 2017. [*Loeb Classical Library* 36], Cambridge, MA: Harvard University Press.

*Cratylus.* Edited and translated by H.N. Fowler, 1926. [*Loeb Classical Library* 167], Cambridge, MA: Harvard University Press.

*Theaetetus.* Edited and translated by H.N. Fowler, 1921. [*Loeb Classical Library* 123], Cambridge, MA: Harvard University Press.

*Parmenides.* Edited and translated by H.N. Fowler, 1926. [*Loeb Classical Library* 167], Cambridge, MA: Harvard University Press.

*Phaedrus.* Edited and translated by H.N. Fowler, 1914. [*Loeb Classical Library* 36], Cambridge, MA: Harvard University Press.

*Alcibiades*. Edited and translated by W.R.M. Lamb, 1927. [*Loeb Classical Library* 201], Cambridge, MA: Harvard University Press.

*Theages*. Edited and translated by W.R.M. Lamb, 1927. [*Loeb Classical Library* 201], Cambridge, MA: Harvard University Press.

*Euthydemus*. Edited and translated by W.R.M. Lamb, 1924. [*Loeb Classical Library* 165], Cambridge, MA: Harvard University Press.

*Gorgias*. Edited and translated by W.R.M. Lamb, 1925. [*Loeb Classical Library* 166], Cambridge, MA: Harvard University Press.

*Timaeus*. Edited and translated by R.G. Bury, 1929. [*Loeb Classical Library* 234], Cambridge, MA: Harvard University Press.

*Leges*. Edited and translated by R.G. Bury, 1926. [*Loeb Classical Library* 187], Cambridge, MA: Harvard University Press.

*Respublica*. Edited and translated by S.R. Slings, 2003. *Platonis Rempublicam*, Oxford: Oxford University Press.

Pliny the Younger (61/62–*c.* AD 113)

*Epistulae*. Edited by S.E. Stout, 1962. Bloomington, IN: Indiana University Press. Translated by B. Radice, 1969. [*Loeb Classical Library* 59], Cambridge, MA: Harvard University Press.

*Panegyricus*. Edited and translated by B. Radice, 1969. [*Loeb Classical Library* 59] Cambridge, MA: Harvard University Press.

Plotinus (205–270)

*Enneades*. Edited by P. Henry & H.-R. Schwyzer, 1951-1973. *Plotini opera*, 3 vols. [Museum Lessianum. Series philosophica 33-35], Leiden: Brill. Translated by A.H. Armstrong in Plotinus, 2014. *In Six Volumes*, Cambridge, MA: Harvard University Press.

Porphyry (*c.* 234–305)

*Contra Christianos*. Edited by A. von Harnack, 1916. *Porphyrius. Gegen die Christen* [Abhandlungen der preussischen Akademie der Wissenschaften, Philosoph.-hist. Kl. 1], Berlin: Reimer.

*Isagoge sive quinque voces*. Edited by A. Busse, 1887. *Porphyrii isagoge et in Aristotelis categorias commentarium* [Commentaria in Aristotelem Graeca 4.1], Berlin: Reimer. Translated by J. Barnes, 2003. *Introduction*, Oxford: Clarendon Press.

*Εἰς τὰ ἁρμονικὰ Πτολεμαίου ὑπόμνημα* [Commentary on Ptolemy's "Harmonics"]. Edited by I. Düring, 1932. *Porphyrios. Kommentar zur Harmonielehre des Ptolemaios*, Göteborg: Elanders.

*Ad Marcellam*. Edited by W. Pötscher, 1969. *Porphyrios. Πρὸς Μαρκέλλαν*, Leiden: Brill.

| | |
|---|---|
| Proclus of Constantinople (died 446) | *Tomus ad Armenios*. Edited by E. Schwartz, 1914. *Acta Conciliorum Oecumenicorum*. Series prima, IV 2, Berlin: De Gruyter, pp. 187–95. |
| | *Homiliae*. Edited and translated by N. Constas, 2003. *Proclus of Constantinople and the Cult of the Virgin in Late Antiquity* [Supplements to Vigiliae Christianae 66], Leiden: Brill, pp. 125–272. |
| Procopius (died *c.* 565) | *De bellis*. Edited and translated by H.B. Dewing, 1928. [*Loeb Classical Library* 217], Cambridge, MA: Harvard University Press. |
| *Qumran scrolls* | Available online at *The Digital Dead Sea Scrolls*: http://dss.collections.imj.org.il (accessed on February 25, 2021). |
| Ratramnus of Corbie (died *c.* 868) | *Contra Graecorum opposita Romanam Ecclesiam infamantium*. Edited by J.-P. Migne. [*Patrologiae cursus completus*, series Latina], vol. 121, Paris: Migne, coll. 223–345. |
| Rufinus (*c.* 345–410/11) | *Eusebii Historiarum continuatio*. Edited by Th. Mommsen, 1908. [*Corpus Berolinense IX* 2]. Translated by Ph. Amidon, 2016. *History of the Church*, Washington DC: Catholic University of America Press. |
| Sallustius (fourth century AD) | *De deis et mundo*. Edited by G. Rochefort, 1960. *Saloustios. Des dieux et du monde*, Paris: Les Belles Lettres. |
| *Scholia in Odysseam* | Edited by F. Pontani, 2015. *Scholia Graeca in Odysseam, Scholia ad libros ε–ζ*, vol. 3 [Pleiadi 6.3], Rome: Edizioni di storia e letteratura. |
| Severus of Antioch (*c.* 456–528) | *Epistulae*. Edited and translated by E.W. Brooks, 1903, *The Sixth Book of the Select Letters of Severus Patriarch of Antioch*, Oxford: Williams & Norgate. |
| | *Homiliae cathedrales*. Edited by M. Brière, F. Graffin, M.-A. Kugener, E. Triffaux & I. Guidi. [Patrologia Orientalis 15, 37, 57, 81, 97, 108, 112, 121, 124, 127, 138 165, 167, 169, 170, 171, 175], Paris: Firmin-Didot. |
| | *Contra impium Grammaticum*. Edited by J. Lebon, 1929, 1933, 1938, 1949, [*Corpus Scriptorum Christianorum Orientalium* 45, 46, 50, 51, 58, 59, 93, 94; 101, 102; 111, 112], Leuven: Peeters. |
| | *Epistulae ad Sergium Grammaticum*. Edited by J. Lebon, 1949. [*Corpus Scriptorum Christianorum Orientalium* 64, 65, 119, 120], Leuven: Peeters. Translated by I.R. Torrance, 2011. *Correspondence of Severus and Sergius*, Piscataway, NJ: Gorgias Press. |
| | *Ad Nephalium*. Edited by J. Lebon, 1949. [*Corpus Scriptorum Christianorum Orientalium* 64, 65, 119, 120], Leuven: Peeters. |
| | *Censura tomi Iuliani*. Edited by R. Hespel, 1964. [*Corpus Scriptorum Christianorum Orientalium* 244, 245], Leuven: Peeters. |

Severus ibn al-Muqaffaʿ (died 987) — *History of the Patriarchs of Alexandria*. Edited by Ch.F. Seybold, 1912. *Alexandrinische Patriarchen-Geschichte von S. Marcus bis Michael I 61-767*, Hamburg: Gräfe.

Simplicius of Cilicia (fl. *c.* AD 530) — *In Aristotelis categorias commentarium*. Edited by K. Kalbfleisch, 1907. *Simplicii in Aristotelis categorias commentarium* [Commentaria in Aristotelem Graeca 8], Berlin: Reimer. Translated by M. Chase, 2000-2003. *On Aristotle's Categories*, 3 vols, Ithaca, NY: Cornell University Press.

*In Aristotelis physicorum libros octo commentaria*. Edited by H. Diels, 1882, 1895. *Simplicii in Aristotelis physicorum libros octo commentaria*, 2 vols. [Commentaria in Aristotelem Graeca 9 & 10], Berlin: Reimer.

*In Aristotelis libros de anima commentaria*. Edited by M. Hayduck, 1882. *Simplicii in libros Aristotelis de anima commentaria* [Commentaria in Aristotelem Graeca 11], Berlin: Reimer.

Shenoute (*c.* 360–450) — *Discources*. Translated by D. Brakke & A.T. Crislip, 2019. *Selected Discourses of Shenoute the Great: Community, Theology, and Social Conflict in Late Antique Egypt*, Cambridge: Cambridge University Press.

Socrates Scholasticus (*c.* 380– 450) — *Historia ecclesiastica*. Edited by P. Maraval & P. Périchon, 2004-2007. *Socrate de Constantinople, Histoire ecclésiastique* [Sources chrétiennes 477, 493, 505, 506], Paris: Éditions du Cerf.

Sozomen (*c.* 380–450) — *Historia ecclesiastica*. Edited by G.Ch. Hansen, 2004. [*Fontes Christiani* 73], Turnhout: Brepols. Translated by E.Walford in Sozomen & Philostorgius, 1855. *History of the Church*, London: Henry G. Bohn.

*Stoicorum Veterum Fragmenta* — Edited by H. von Arnim & M. Adler, 2004-2010. *Stoicorum Veterum Fragmenta,* 4 vols, München: K.G. Saur.

Sylvester Syropulus (*c.* 1400–after 1464) — *Historiae*. Edited by V. Laurent, 1971. *Les Mémoires du Grand Ecclésiarque de l'Église de Constantinople Sylvestre Syropoulos sur le concile de Florence (1438-1439)*, Paris: Centre National de la Recherche Scientifique.

Symeon New Theologian (*c.* 949–1022) — *Hymni*. Edited by A. Kambylis, 1976. *Symeon Neos Theologos, Hymnen* [Supplementa Byzantina 3], Berlin: De Gruyter.

*Orationes ethicae*. Edited by J. Darrouzès, 1966-1967. *Syméon le Nouveau Théologien, Traités théologiques et éthiques* [Sources chrétiennes 122, 129], Paris: Éditions du Cerf.

| | |
|---|---|
| Symeon of Thessalonica (*c.* 1381–1429) | *Dialogus contra omnes haereses*. Edited by J.-P. Migne. [*Patrologiae cursus completus*, series Graeca], vol. 155, Paris: Migne, coll. 33–174. |
| Tatian (120–173) | *Oratio ad Graecos*. Edited and translated by M. Whittaker, 1982. *Tatian. Oratio ad Graecos and Fragments*, Oxford: Clarendon Press. |
| Themistius (*c.* 317–*c.* 390) | *De anima*. Edited by R. Heinze, 1899. *Themistii in libros Aristotelis de anima paraphrasis* [Commentaria in Aristotelem Graeca 5.3], Berlin: Reimer. Translated by R.B. Todd in Themestius, 1995. *On Aristotle On the Soul*, London: Duckworth. |
| Theodore Metochites (*c.* 1270–332) | *Γνωμικαί σημειώσεις*. Edited by K. Hult, 2002. *Theodore Metochites on Ancient Authors and Philosophy (Semeioseis gnomikai 1-26 et 71)*, Göteborg: Acta Universitatis Gothoburgensis. |
| Theodore of Raith (late sixth–early seventh century) | *Preparatio*, Edited by F. Diekamp, 1938. *Analecta Patristica* [Texte und Abhandlungen zur griechischen Patristik], Roma: Pontificium Institutum Orientalium Studiorum; Ἀ. Νίκας, 1981. *Θεόδωρος τῆς Ραϊθοῦ* [Theodore of Raith], Ἀθῆναι: Ἱ.Μ. Σινᾶ. |
| Theodore Studite (759–826) | *Adversus iconoclastas*. Edited by C.I. Dalkos, 2006. *Θεοδώρου τοῦ Στουδίτου· Λόγοι ἀντιρρητικοὶ κατὰ εἰκονομαχῶν, καὶ στίχοι τινὲς ἰαμβικοί*, Ἀθήνα: Ἴνδικτος. Translated by Th. Cattol in Theodore the Studite, 2015. *Writings on Iconoclasm*, New York; Mahwah, NJ: Newman Press. |
| | *Epistulae*. Edited by G. Fatouros, 1992. *Theodori Studitae Epistulae*, 2 vols. [Corpus Fontium Historiae Byzantinae. Series Berolinensis 31], Berlin: De Gruyter. |
| Theodoret of Cyrrus (*c.* 393–458/66) | *Historia ecclesiastica*. Edited by L. Parmentier & F. Scheidweiler, 1954. *Theodoret. Kirchengeschichte* [Die griechischen christlichen Schriftsteller 44], Berlin: Akademie Verlag. |
| | *Eranistes*. Edited by G.H. Ettlinger in Theodoret of Cyrus, 1975. *Eranistes*, Oxford: Clarendon Press. Translated by G.H. Ettlinger in Theodoret of Cyrus, 2003. *Eranistes*, Washington, DC: Catholic University of America Press. |
| | *Quaestiones in Octateuchum*. Edited by J. Petruccione and translated by R.C. Hill in Theodoret of Cyrus, 2007. *The Questions on the Octateuch*, Washington, DC: Catholic University of America Press. |
| | *De providentia*. Edited by J.-P. Migne. [*Patrologiae cursus completus*, series Graeca], vol. 83, Paris: Migne, coll. 556–773. Translated by Th.P. Halton in Theodoret of Cyrus, 1989. *On Divine Providence*, New York: Newman. |

*Epistulae*. Edited by Y. Azéma, 1955, 1964, 1965. *Théodoret de Cyr. Correspondance* [Sources chrétiennes 40, 98, 111], Paris: Éditions du Cerf.

Theophilus of Antioch (died 180)
*Ad Autolycum*. Edited by M. Marcovich, 1995. *Theophili Antiocheni ad Autolycum* [Patristische Texte und Studiens 44], Berlin: De Gryuter. Translated by R.M. Grant, 1970. Oxford: Clarendon Press.

Theophylact of Ohrid (*c*. 1055–after 1107)
*Liber de iis in quorum Latini incusantur*. Edited by J.-P. Migne. [*Patrologiae cursus completus*, series Graeca], vol. 126, Paris: Migne, coll. 222–53.

Thomas Aquinas (1224/5–74)
*Summa theologica*. Edited under the auspices of Pope Leo XIII, 1882. *Sancti Thomae de Aquino Opera omnia*, Roma: Typographia Polyglotta S.C. de Propaganda Fide. Available, together with translations, online at *Corpus Thomisticum* website: https://www.corpusthomisticum.org/ (accessed on March 29, 2021).

Thomas Cajetan (*c*. 1469–1534)
1521. *De divina institutione pontificatus romani pontificis super totam ecclesiam a Christo in Petro*, Roma: Marcellus Silber.

Tikhon of Zadonsk (1724–83)
2007. *Симфония по творениям Святителя Тихона Задонского* [Concordia of the works of St. Tikhon of Zadonsk], Москва: Дар.

*Tomus synodicus*
*Tomi synodici tres in causa Palamitarum*. Edited by J.-P. Migne. [*Patrologiae cursus completus*, series Graeca], vol. 151, Paris: Migne, coll. 655–762.

Valentinus (fl. second century AD)
*Fragmenta*. Edited by Ch. Markschies, 1992. *Valentinus gnosticus? Untersuchungen zur valentinianischen Gnosis mit einem Kommentar zu den Fragmenten Valentins* [Wissenschaftliche Untersuchungen zum Neuen Testament 65], Tübingen: Mohr Siebeck.

Virgil (70–19 BC)
*Aeneia*. Edited by R.G. Austin, 1989. Oxford, Clarendon Press. Translated by S. Ruden in Virgil, 2021. *The Aeneid*, New Haven, CT: Yale University Press.

*Vita Petri Iberi*
Edited by R. Raabe, 1895. *Petrus der Iberer, ein Charakterbild zur Kirchen- und Sittengeschichte des 5. Jahrhunderts*, Leipzig: Hinrichs.

Xenophon (*c*. 430–before 350 BC)
*Memorabilia*. Edited and translated by E.C. Marchant, O.J. Todd & J. Henderson, 2013. [*Loeb Classical Library* 168], Cambridge, MA: Harvard University Press, pp. 3–380.

*Symposium*. Edited and translated by E.C. Marchant, O.J. Todd & J. Henderson, 2013. [*Loeb Classical Library* 168], Cambridge, MA: Harvard University Press, pp. 560–663.

*Apologia Socratis*. Edited and translated by E.C. Marchant, O.J. Todd & J. Henderson, 2013. [*Loeb Classical Library* 168], Cambridge, MA: Harvard University Press, pp. 664–89.

Zeno (*c.* 495–430 BC) *Testimonia et fragmenta.* Edited by J. von Arnim, 1905. *Stoicorum veterum fragmenta*, vol. 1, Leipzig: Teubner.

*Τριῴδιον* [Triodion] 1856. *Τριῴδιον Κατανυκτικόν, περιέχον ἅπασαν τὴν ἀνήκουσαν αὐτῷ Ἀκολουθίαν τῆς Ἁγίας καὶ Μεγάλης Τεσσαρακοστῆς*, Ἐν Βενετίᾳ: ἐκ τῆς Ἐκκλησιαστικῆς Τυπογραφίας τοῦ Φοίνικος.

*Священный Собор Православной Российской Церкви* [Holy Council of the Orthodox Russian Church] 1918. *Собрание Определений и Постановлений* [Collection of definitions and decrees], Москва: Издание Соборного Совета.

新唐書 [New Book of Tang] Translated by F. Hirth, 1975. *China and the Roman Orient: Researches Into Their Ancient and Medieval Relations as Represented in Old Chinese Records*, Chicago: Ares.

# Bibliography


1959. A New Translation of the 1920 Message of the Ecumenical Patriarchate. *The Ecumenical Review*, 12(1), pp. 79–82.

Adamson, P., 2014. One of a Kind: Plotinus and Porphyry on Unique Instantiation. In R. Chiaradonna & G. Galluzzo, eds. *Universals in Ancient Philosophy*. Pisa: Edizioni della Normale, pp. 329–53.

Addey, C., 2014. *Divination and Theurgy in Neoplatonism: Oracles of the Gods*, London: Taylor & Francis.

Aerts, W. J., Bochove, T. E. V. & Harder, M. A., 2001. The *Prooimion* of the *Eisagoge*: Translation and Commentary. *Subseciva Groningana*, 7, pp. 91–155.

Afanasiev, N., 2012. *The Church of the Holy Spirit*, Notre Dame, IN: University of Notre Dame Press.

Agaiby, E., Swanson, M. N. & van Doorn-Harder, N. eds., 2021. *Copts in Modernity: Proceedings of the 5th International Symposium of Coptic Studies, Melbourne, 13-16 July 2018*, Leiden: Brill.

Aitzetmüller, R., 1975. *Das Hexaemeron des Exarchen Johannes*, Graz: Akademische Druck- u. Verlagsanstalt.

Al-Azmeh, A., 2014. *The Emergence of Islam in Late Antiquity: Allah and His People*, Cambridge: Cambridge University Press.

Alberigo, G. ed., 1991. *Christian Unity: the Council of Ferrara-Florence 1438/39*, Leuven: Leuven University Press; Peeters.

Alfeyev, H., 2000. *St. Symeon the New Theologian and Orthodox Tradition*, Oxford: Oxford University Press.

Allen, P., 1981. Greek Citations from Severus of Antioch in Eustathius Monachus. *Orientalia Lovaniensia Periodica*, 12, pp. 261–4.

Allen, P. & Hayward, C. T. R., 2004. *Severus of Antioch*, London: Routledge.

Allen, P. & Neil, B., 2002. *Maximus the Confessor and His Companions: Documents From Exile*, Oxford: Oxford University Press.

Allen, P. & Neil, B., 2020. *Greek and Latin Letters in Late Antiquity: The Christianisation of a Literary Form*, Cambridge: Cambridge University Press.

Allen, P., Dehandschutter, B., Leemans, L. & Mayer, W., 2003. *"Let Us Die That We May Live": Greek Homilies on Christian Martyrs From Asia Minor, Palestine and Syria c. 350 – c. 450* AD, London: Routledge.

Altman, M. C. ed., 2014. *The Palgrave Handbook of German Idealism*, New York: Palgrave Macmillan.

Ameriks, K. ed., 2005. *The Cambridge Companion to German Idealism*, Cambridge: Cambridge University Press.

Anastasius of Sinai, 2007. *Hexaemeron*, transl. by C. A. Kuehn & J. D. Baggarly, Rome: Pontificio Istituto Orientale.

Anatolios, K., 2018. *Creatio ex nihilo* in Athanasius of Alexandria's Against the Greeks. In G. A. Anderson & M. Bockmuehl, eds. *Creation Ex Nihilo*. Notre Dame, IN: University of Notre Dame Press, pp. 119–50.

Anaxagoras, 2007. *Fragments and Testimonia*, transl. by P. Curd, Toronto: Toronto University Press.

Anderson, G. A., 2018. *Creatio Ex Nihilo* and the Bible. In G. A. Anderson & M. Bockmuehl, eds. *Creation Ex Nihilo*. Notre Dame, IN: University of Notre Dame Press, pp. 15–36.

Ando, C., 2008. *The Matter of the Gods*, Berkeley, CA: University of California Press.

Angier, T. ed., 2019. *The History of Evil in Antiquity: 2000 BCE – 450 CE*, London: Routledge.

Aquinas, T., 2013. *Summa theologica*, New York: Cosimo Classics.

Arjakovsky, A., 2006. *Essai sur le père Serge Boulgakov (1871–1944): philosophe et théologien chrétien*, Paris: Parole et silence.

Asproulis, N., 2018. Nikos Nissiotis, the "Theology of the '60s," and Personhood. In A. Torrance & S. Paschalidis, eds. *Personhood in the Byzantine Christian Tradition: Early, Medieval, and Modern Perspectives*. London: Routledge, pp. 161–72.

Athanasius of Alexandria, 1981. *Contra gentes and De incarnatione*, ed. and transl. by R. W. Thomson, Oxford: Clarendon Press.

Athanasius of Alexandria, 2003. *The Life of Antony by Athanasius of Alexandria. The Greek Life of Antony, the Coptic Life of Antony and An Enconmium on Saint Antony by John Shmun and A Letter to the Disciples of Antony by Serapion of Thmuis*, transl. by T. Vivian & A. N. Athanassakis, Kalamazoo, MI: Cistercian Publications.

Athanasopoulos, C. ed., 2015. *Triune God: Incomprehensible but Knowable—the Philosophical and Theological Significance of St Gregory Palamas for Contemporary Philosophy and Theology*, Newcastle upon Tyne: Cambridge Scholars Publishing.

Athanasopoulos, K. G. & Schneider, C. eds., 2013. *Divine Essence and Divine Energies: Ecumenical Reflections on the Presence of God in Eastern Orthodoxy*, Cambridge: James Clarke & Co.

Athanassiadi, P. & Frede, M. eds., 2008. *Pagan Monotheism in Late Antiquity*, Oxford: Clarendon Press.

Athenagoras, 1972. *Legatio and De resurrectione*, transl. by W. R. Schoedel, Oxford: Clarendon Press.

Augustine, 2008. *The Catholic and Manichaean Ways of Life (De moribus ecclesiae Catholicae et de moribus Manichaeorum)*, transl. by D. A. Gallagher & I. J. Gallagher, Washington, DC: Catholic University of America Press.

Awad, N. G., 2015. *Orthodoxy in Arabic Terms: A Study of Theodore Abu Qurrah's Theology in its Islamic Context*, Berlin: De Gruyter.

Awad, N. G., 2018. *Umayyad Christianity: John of Damascus as a Contextual Example of Identity Formation in Early Islam*, Piscataway, NJ: Gorgias.

Ayres, L., 2004. *Nicaea and Its Legacy*, Oxford: Oxford University Press.

Baer, M., Makdisi, U. & Shryock, A., 2009. Tolerance and Conversion in the Ottoman Empire: A Conversation. *Comparative Studies in Society and History*, 51(4), pp. 927–40.

Baily, M., 1958. The People of God in the Old Testament. *The Furrow*, 9(1), pp. 3–13.
Baker-Brian, N. & Tougher, S. eds., 2020. *The Sons of Constantine,* AD *337–361*, New York: Palgrave Macmillan.
Baldry, H. C., 1952. Who Invented the Golden Age? *The Classical Quarterly*, 2(1/2), pp. 83–92.
Balot, R. K. ed., 2012. Gendered Politics, or the Self-Praise of *Andres Agathoi*. In R. K. Balot, ed. *A Companion to Greek and Roman Political Thought*. Malden, MA: John Wiley & Sons, pp. 100–17.
Balthasar, H. U. V & Daley, B. eds., 2018. *Spirit and Fire. Origen: A Thematic Anthology of the Writings*, London: Bloomsbury.
Banev, K., 2015. *Theophilus of Alexandria and the First Origenist Controversy: Rhetoric and Power*, Oxford: Oxford University Press.
Bar-Asher Siegal, M., 2013. *Early Christian Monastic Literature and the Babylonian Talmud*, Cambridge: Cambridge University Press.
Barhebraeus, 2003. *The Chronography of Gregory Abû'l Faraj the Son of Aaron, the Hebrew Physician Commonly Known as Bar Hebraeus*, transl. by E. A. W. Budge, Piscataway, NJ: Gorgias.
Barkey, K., 2005. Islam and Toleration: Studying the Ottoman Imperial Model. *International Journal of Politics, Culture, and Society*, 19(1/2), pp. 5–19.
Barnard, L. W., 1980. Marcellus of Ancyra and the Eusebians. *The Greek Orthodox Theological Review*, 25, pp. 63–76.
Barnes, J., 1984. *Complete Works of Aristotle*, Princeton, NJ: Princeton University Press.
Barnes, J., 2003. *Porphyry*. Introduction, Oxford: Clarendon Press.
Barnes, T. D., 2006. *Constantine and Eusebius*, Cambridge, MA: Harvard University Press.
Barnes, T. D., 2011. *Constantine: Dynasty, Religion and Power in the Later Roman Empire*, Chichester; Malden, MA: Wiley-Blackwell.
Barrett, A. A., 2020. *Rome Is Burning*, Princeton, NJ: Princeton University Press.
Basil of Caesarea, 1963. *Exegetic Homilies*, transl. by A. C. Way, Washington, DC: Catholic University of America Press.
Basil of Caesarea, 2011. *On the Holy Spirit*, transl. by S. Hildebrand, Yonkers, NY: St. Vladimir's Seminary Press.
Bassett, S., 2004. *The Urban Image of Late Antique Constantinople*, Cambridge: Cambridge University Press.
Bautze-Picron, C., 2018. Bagan Murals and the Sino-Tibetan World. In A. Heirman, C. Meinert & C. Anderl, eds. *Buddhist Encounters and Identities Across East Asia*. Leiden: Brill, pp. 19–51.
Beard, M., 2004. Re-reading (Vestal) Virginity. In R. Hawley & B. Levick, eds. *Women in Antiquity: New Assessments*. London: Routledge, pp. 166–77.
Bechler, Z., 1995. *Aristotle's Theory of Actuality*, Albany, NY: State University of New York Press.
Beck, E., ed., 1960. *Des Heiligen Ephraem des Syrers Hymnen de Ecclesia [Textus]*, Louvain: Secrétariat du Corpus Scriptorum Christianorum Orientalium.

Beck, H. ed., 2013. *A Companion to Ancient Greek Government*, Oxford: John Wiley & Sons.

Beck, H.-G., 1959. *Kirche und theologische Literatur im byzantinischen Reich*, München: Beck.

Beck, R., 2008. *A Brief History of Ancient Astrology*, Malden, MA: John Wiley & Sons.

Becker, A. H., 2006. *Fear of God and the Beginning of Wisdom: the School of Nisibis and Christian Scholastic Culture in Late Antique Mesopotamia*, Philadelphia, PA: University of Pennsylvania Press.

Beeley, C. A., 2011. The Early Christological Controversy: Apollinarius, Diodore, and Gregory Nazianzen. *Vigiliae Christianae*, 65(4), pp. 376–407.

Behr, J., 2017a. *Origen: On First Principles*, Oxford: Oxford University Press.

Behr, J., 2017b. *The Case Against Diodore and Theodore*, Oxford: Oxford University Press.

Behr-Sigel, É., 1977. Toward a New Community. In C. Tarasar & I. Kirillova, eds. *Orthodox Women: Their Role and Participation in the Orthodox Church*. Geneva: World Council of Churches.

Bejan, C. A., 2020. *Intellectuals and Fascism in Interwar Romania. The Criterion Association*, New York: Palgrave Macmillan.

Belfour, F. C., ed., 1836. *The Travels of Macarius, Patriarch of Antioch. Written by His Attendant Archdeacon, Paul of Aleppo, in Arabic*, London: Oriental Translation Fund.

Berchman, R. M., 2005. *Porphyry Against the Christians*, Leiden: Brill.

Berdyayev, N., 1965. *Christian Existentialism: A Berdyaev Anthology*, transl. by D. Lowrie, Sydney: Allen & Unwin.

Berthold, G. C. ed., 1985. *Maximus Confessor: Selected Writings*, New York: Paulist Press.

Biliuţă, I. F., 2007. Between Orthodoxy and the Nation. Traditionalist Definitions of Romanianness in Interwar Romania. Budapest: Central European University.

Bingaman, B. & Nassif, B. eds., 2012. *The Philokalia: A Classic Text of Orthodox Spirituality*, Oxford: Oxford University Press.

Binns, J., 2020. *The T&T Clark History of Monasticism: The Eastern Tradition*, London: T&T Clark.

Black, A., Thomas, C. M. & Thompson, T. W. eds., 2020. *Ephesos as a Religious Center Under the Principate*, Tübingen: Mohr Siebeck.

Blackstone, J., 2018. *Knowledge and Experience in the Theology of Gregory Palamas*, Oxford: Peter Lang.

Bloom, A., 1971. *Beginning to Pray*, New York: Newman Press.

Blumenthal, H. J., 1993. *Soul and Intellect*, London: Routledge.

Boddice, R. ed., 2011. *Anthropocentrism: Humans, Animals, Environments*, Leiden: Brill.

Boeri, M. D., 2018. Plato and Aristotle On What Is Common to Soul and Body. Some Remarks on a Complicated Issue. In M. D. Boeri, Y. Y. Kanayama & J. Mittelmann, eds. *Soul and Mind in Greek Thought. Psychological Issues in Plato and Aristotle*, Cham: Springer, pp. 153–76.

Boersma, H., 2018. *Seeing God: the Beatific Vision in Christian Tradition*, Grand Rapids, MI: Eerdmans.

Böhmer, J. H., 1756. *Ius ecclesiasticum protestantium: usum modernum iuris canonici iuxta seriem decretalium ostendens, & ipsis rerum argumentis illustrans, adiecto duplici indice*, Halle: Orphanotropheum.
Bolshakoff, S., 1946. *The Doctrine of the Unity of the Church in the Works of Khomyakov and Moehler*, London: SPCK.
Brakke, D. & Crislip, A. T., 2019. *Selected Discourses of Shenoute the Great: Community, Theology, and Social Conflict in Late Antique Egypt*, Cambridge: Cambridge University Press.
Bray, G. L., 2009. *We Believe in One God*, Downers Grove, IL: IVP Academic.
Briggman, A., 2019. *God and Christ in Irenaeus*, Oxford: Oxford University Press.
Brightman, F. E., 1896. *Liturgies: Eastern and Western*, Oxford: Clarendon Press.
Brimioulle, P., 2020. *Das Konzil von Konstantinopel 536*, Stuttgart: Franz Steiner.
Broadie, S., 2014. *Nature and Divinity in Plato's* Timaeus, Cambridge: Cambridge University Press.
Brock, S. P., 2006. *The Wisdom of St. Isaac of Nineveh*, Piscataway, NJ: Gorgias.
Brock, S. P., 2008. *Studies in Syriac Spirituality*, Bangalore: Dharmaram Publications.
Brock, S. P., 2018. The Early Syriac Life of Maximus the Confessor. *Analecta Bollandiana*, 91(3–4), pp. 299–346.
Brown, P., 1971. *The World of Late Antiquity: From Marcus Aurelius to Muhammad*, London: Thames and Hudson.
Brumberg-Chaumont, J., 2014. Logico-Grammatical Reflections About Individuality in Late Antiquity. In J. Zachhuber & A. Torrance, eds. *Individuality in Late Antiquity*. Farnham: Ashgate, pp. 63–90.
Buchberger, E., 2017. *Shifting Ethnic Identities in Spain and Gaul, 500–700: From Romans to Goths and Franks*, Amsterdam: Amsterdam University Press.
Buch-Hansen, G., 2010. *"It is the Spirit That Gives Life": a Stoic Understanding of Pneuma in John's Gospel*, Berlin: De Gruyter.
Bucossi, A. & Calia, A. eds., 2020. Contra Latinos *et* Adversus Graecos: *the Separation Between Rome and Constantinople from the Ninth to the Fifteenth Century*, Leuven: Peeters.
Bulgakov, S., 1988. *The Orthodox Church*, transl. by L.W. Kesich, Crestwood, NY: St. Vladimir's Seminary Press.
Bulgakov, S., 2002. *The Bride of the Lamb*, transl. by B. Jakim, Grand Rapids, MI: Eerdmans.
Bulgakov, S., 2004. *The Comforter*, transl. by B. Jakim, Grand Rapids, MI: Eerdmans.
Burgersdijk, D. P. W. & Ross, A. J. eds., 2018. *Imagining Emperors in the Later Roman Empire*, Leiden: Brill.
Burns, D. M., 2020. *Did God Care?* Leiden: Brill.
Burns, J. H. & Izbicki, T. M. eds., 1997. *Conciliarism and Papalism*, Cambridge: Cambridge University Press.
Burr, M., 1949. The Code of Stephan Dušan: Tsar and Autocrat of the Serbs and Greeks. *The Slavonic and East European Review*, 28(70), pp. 198–217.
Butterworth, G. W., 1919. *Clement of Alexandria. The Exhortation to the Greeks. The Rich Man's Salvation. To the Newly Baptized*, Cambridge, MA: Harvard University Press.

Cadenhead, R. A., 2018. *The Body and Desire*, Oakland, CA: University of California Press.

Cameron, A. & Hall, S. G. eds., 1999. *Eusebius. Life of Constantine*, Oxford: Oxford University Press.

Campbell, J. G., 2008. *Deciphering the Dead Sea Scrolls*, Malden, MA: John Wiley & Sons.

Cartwright, S., 2012. The Image of God in Irenaeus, Marcellus, and Eustathius. In S. Parvis & P. Foster, eds. *Irenaeus: Life, Scripture, Legacy*. Minneapolis: MN: Fortress, pp. 173–82.

Casiday, A. & Louth, A. eds., 2006. *Byzantine Orthodoxies. Papers from the Thirty-Sixth Spring Symposium of Byzantine Studies, University of Durham, 23–25 March 2002*, London: Routledge.

Cassin, B. ed., 2014. *Dictionary of Untranslatables*, Princeton, NJ: Princeton University Press.

Cavallera, F., 1905. *Le schisme d'Antioche, (iv-v siècle)*, Paris: A. Picard.

Chabot, J.-B., 1902. Synodicon orientale *ou recueil de synodes nestoriens*, Paris: Imprimerie Nationale.

Chaillot, C. & Belopopsky, A., 1998. *Towards Unity: the Theological Dialogue Between the Orthodox Church and the Oriental Orthodox Churches*, Geneva: Inter-Orthodox Dialogue.

Charalabopoulos, N., 2007. Two Images of Sokrates in the Art of the Greek East. In M. B. Trapp, ed. *Socrates, From Antiquity to the Enlightenment*. Aldershot: Ashgate, pp. 105–26.

Chase, F. H., 1958. *John of Damascus, Writings*, Washington, DC: Catholic University of America Press.

Chase, M., 2000–2003. *Simplicius, On Aristotle's Categories*, 3 vols, Ithaca, NY: Cornell University Press.

Chatterjee, N., 2014. Reflections on Religious Difference and Permissive Inclusion in Mughal Law. *Journal of Law and Religion*, 29(3), pp. 396–415.

Chesnut, R. C., 1976. *Three Monophysite Christologies: Severus of Antioch, Philoxenus of Mabbug and Jacob of Sarug*, Oxford: Oxford University Press.

Chiaradonna, R., 2014. Plotinus on Sensible Particulars and Individual Essences. In J. Zachhuber & A. Torrance, eds. *Individuality in Late Antiquity*. Farnham: Ashgate, pp. 47–62.

Christensen, M. J. & Wittung, J. A. eds., 2007. *Partakers of the Divine Nature: the History and Development of Deification in the Christian Traditions*, Madison, NJ: Fairleigh Dickinson University Press.

Chryssavgis, J., 2004. *John Climacus: From the Egyptian Desert to the Sinaite Mountain*, Aldershot: Ashgate.

Clark, E. A., 1992. *The Origenist Controversy: the Cultural Construction of an Early Christian Debate*, Princeton, NJ: Princeton University Press.

Clark, R., 2018. Nationalism and Orthodoxy: Nichifor Crainic and the Political Culture of the Extreme Right in 1930s Romania. *Nationalities Papers*, 40(1), pp. 107–26.

Clement of Alexandria, 2008. *Christ, the Educator*, transl. by S. P. Wood, Washington, DC: Catholic University of America Press.

Clivaz, C., 2005. The Angel and the Sweat like "Drops of Blood" (Lk 22:43-44): P69 and f13. *The Harvard Theological Review*, 98(4), pp. 419–40.

Clogg, R. ed., 1976. *The Movement for Greek Independence, 1770–1821: A Collection of Documents*, London: Macmillan.

Coetzee, M., 2014. *The Filioque Impasse: Patristic Roots*, Piscataway, NJ: Gorgias.

Cohen, W. T., 2017. *The Concept of "Sister Churches" in Catholic-Orthodox Relations Since Vatican II*, Eugene, OR: Wipf & Stock.

Cohick, L. H. & Hughes, A. B., 2017. *Christian Women in the Patristic World: Their Influence, Authority, and Legacy in the Second Through Fifth Centuries*, Grand Rapids, MI: Baker.

Coman, V., 2019. *Dumitru Stăniloae's Trinitarian Ecclesiology: Orthodoxy and the Filioque*, Lanham, MD: Lexington.

Concannon, C. W., 2017. *Assembling Early Christianity*, Cambridge: Cambridge University Press.

Conradie, E. ed., 2012. *Creation and Salvation: A Mosaic of Selected Classic Christian Theologies*, Münster: Lit.

Constas, N. P., 2002. *Proclus of Constantinople and the Cult of the Virgin in Late Antiquity*, Leiden: Brill.

Conte, P., 1989. *Il sinodo lateranense dell'ottobre 649: rassegna critica di fonti dei secolo VII-XII*, Città del Vaticano: Libreria editrice vaticana.

Costache, D., 2021. *Humankind and the Cosmos: Early Christian Representations*, Leiden: Brill.

Crainic, N., 1924. Parsifal. *Gîndirea*, (anul III, no. 8–10), pp. 181–6.

Crainic, N., 1996. *Puncte cardinale în haos*, Iaşi: Timpul.

Crainic, N., 1997. *Ortodoxie şi etnocraţie: cu o anexă, programul statului etnocratic*, Bucureşti: Albatros.

Critchley, S., 2020. *Tragedy, the Greeks and Us*, London: Profile Books.

Cunningham, J. W., 2002. *The Gates of Hell: the Great Sobor of the Russian Orthodox Church: 1917–1918*, Minneapolis, MN: University of Minnesota Press.

Cyril of Alexandria, 1983. *Select Letters*, transl. by L. Wickham, Oxford: Clarendon Press.

Cyril of Alexandria, 2000. *On the Unity of Christ*, transl. by J. A. McGuckin, Crestwood, NY: St. Vladimir's Seminary Press.

Cyril of Scythopolis, 1991. *Lives of the Monks of Palestine*, transl. by R. Price, Kalamazoo, MI: Cistercian Publications.

Dagron, G., 1974. *Naissance d'une capitale; Constantinople et ses institutions de 330 à 451*, Paris: Presses universitaires de France.

Dagron, G., 1984. *Constantinople imaginaire: études sur le recueil des Patria*, Paris: Presses universitaires de France.

Dagron, G., 1995. *Empereur et prêtre: étude sur le césaropapisme byzantin*, Paris: Gallimard.

Dagron, G., 2003. *Emperor and Priest: the Imperial Office in Byzantium*, Cambridge: Cambridge University Press.

Daley, B. E., 2017. *Leontius of Byzantium. Complete Works*, Oxford: Oxford University Press.

Damgaard, F., 2013. Propaganda Against Propaganda: Revisiting Eusebius' Use of the Figure of Moses in the *Life of Constantine*. In A. Johnson & J. Schott, eds. *Eusebius of Caesarea: Tradition and Innovations*. Washington, DC: Center for Hellenic Studies, pp. 115–29.

Davis, S., 2007. The Copto-Arabic Tradition of *Theosis*. In M. J. Christensen & J. A. Witting eds., *Partakers of the Divine Nature: the History and Development of Deification in the Christian Traditions*. Madison, NJ: Fairleigh Dickinson University Press, pp. 163–74.

Davis, M., 2011. *The Soul of the Greeks: an Inquiry*, Chicago, IL: University of Chicago Press.

de Durand, G.-M., 1976–1978. *Cyrille d'Alexandrie. Dialogues sur la Trinité*, 3 vols., Paris: Éditions du Cerf.

de los Ríos, I., 2018. Politics of the Soul in Plato's *Republic*. In M. D. Boeri, Y. Y. Kanayama & J. Mittelmann, eds. *Soul and Mind in Greek Thought. Psychological Issues in Plato and Aristotle*, Cham: Springer, pp. 111–29.

Deferrari, R. J. & McGuire, M. R., 1934. *Basil, Letters 249–368. On Greek Literature*, Cambridge, MA: Harvard University Press.

DelCogliano, M., 2010. *Basil of Caesarea's Anti-Eunomian Theory of Names*, Leiden: Brill.

DelCogliano, M., 2015. Asterius in Athanasius' Catalogues of Arian Views. *Journal of Theological Studies*, 66(2), pp. 625–50.

Deletant, D., 2006. *Hitler's Forgotten Ally: Ion Antonescu and His Regime, Romania 1940–44*, New York: Palgrave Macmillan.

Demacopoulos, G. E., 2019. *Colonizing Christianity*, New York: Fordham University Press.

Demacopoulos, G. E., 2013. *The Invention of Peter: Apostolic Discourse and Papal Authority in Late Antiquity*, Philadelphia, PA: University of Pennsylvania Press.

Denzey, N. F., 2013. *Cosmology and Fate in Gnosticism and Graeco-Roman Antiquity*, Leiden: Brill.

DesRosiers, N. P. & Vuong, L. C. eds., 2016. *Religious Competition in the Greco-Roman World*, Atlanta, GA: Society of Biblical Literature Press.

Destivelle, H., 2015. *The Moscow Council (1917–1918). The Creation of the Conciliar Institutions of the Russian Orthodox Church*, Notre Dame, IN: University of Notre Dame Press.

Diekamp, F., 1938. Analecta Patristica: *Texte und Abhandlungen zur griechischen Patristik*, Roma: Pontificium Institutum Orientalium Studiorum.

Diekamp, F., 1981. Doctrina patrum de incarnatione verbi: *ein griechisches Florilegium aus der Wende des 7. und 8. Jahrhunderts*, Münster: Aschendorff.

Diehls, H. & Kranz, W., 1996. *Die Fragmente der Vorsokratiker*, Zürich: Weidmann.

Digeser, E. D., 2000. *The Making of a Christian Empire: Lactantius & Rome*, Ithaca, NY: Cornell University Press.

Dignas, B. & Winter, E., 2007. *Rome and Persia in Late Antiquity: Neighbours and Rivals*, Cambridge: Cambridge University Press.

Dijkstra, R. ed., 2020. *The Early Reception and Appropriation of the Apostle Peter (60–800 CE): The Anchors of the Fisherman*, Leiden: Brill.
Dillon, J. M., 2014. *Dexippus. On Aristotle Categories*, London: Bloomsbury.
Dillon, J. M., 2017. *The Middle Platonists: 80 B.C. to A.D. 220*, Ithaca, NY: Cornell University Press.
Dodson, J. R. & Briones, D. E. eds., 2017. *Paul and Seneca in Dialogue*, Leiden: Brill.
Dorotheos of Gaza, 1977. *Discourses and Sayings*, transl. by E. Wheeler, Kalamazoo, MI: Cistercian Publications.
Dörrie, H., 1976. *Platonica minora*, München: Fink.
Dowley, T. & Rowland, N., 2016. *Atlas of Christian History*, Minneapolis, MN: Fortress.
Drake, H. A., 2021. The Elephant in the Room. Constantine at the Council. In Y. R. Kim, ed. *The Cambridge Companion to the Council of Nicaea*. Cambridge: Cambridge University Press, pp. 111–32.
Drecoll, V. H. & Berghaus, M. eds., 2011. *Gregory of Nyssa: The Minor Treatises on Trinitarian Theology and Apollinarism: Proceedings of the 11th International Colloquium on Gregory of Nyssa (Tübingen, 17–20 September 2008)*, Leiden: Brill.
Dunderberg, I., 2008. The School of Valentinus. In A. Marjanen & P. Luomanen, eds. *A Companion to Second-Century Christian "Heretics."* Leiden: Brill, pp. 64–99.
Dunn, M., 2003. *The Emergence of Monasticism*, Oxford: John Wiley & Sons.
Dvornik, F., 1948. *The Photian Schism, History and Legend*, Cambridge: Cambridge: University Press.
Dvornik, F., 1970. *Byzantine Missions Among the Slavs: SS. Constantine-Cyril and Methodius*, New Brunswick, NJ: Rutgers University Press.
Dvornik, F., 1979. *Byzantium and the Roman Primacy*, New York: Fordham University Press.
Dykstra, T. E., 2013. *Hallowed Be Thy Name: the Name-Glorifying Dispute in the Russian Orthodox Church and on Mt. Athos, 1912–1914*, St. Paul, MN: OCABS Press.
Dzielska, M., 2002. *Hypatia of Alexandria*, Cambridge, MA: Harvard University Press.
Eastman, D. L., 2015. *The Ancient Martyrdom Accounts of Peter and Paul*, Atlanta, GA: Society of Biblical Literature Press.
Eastman, D. L., 2019. *The Many Deaths of Peter and Paul*, Oxford: Oxford University Press.
Ebbesen, S., 2007. The Traditions of Ancient Logic-cum-Grammar in the Middle Ages—What's the Problem? *Vivarium*, 45(2/3), pp. 136–52.
Edwards, M. J., 2018. *Origen Against Plato*, London: Routledge.
Edwards, M. J., 2019. *Aristotle and Early Christian Thought*, London: Routledge.
Ehrman, B. D., Evans, C. A., Kasser, R., Meyer, M. W., Wurst, G., Schenke Robinson, G. & Gaudard, F., 2008. *The Gospel of Judas*, Washington, DC: National Geographic.
Elert, W., 1951. Theodor von Pharan und Theodor von Raithu. *Theologische Literaturzeitung*, 76(2), pp. 67–76.
Elm, S., 2004. *"Virgins of God": The Making of Asceticism in Late Antiquity*, Oxford: Clarendon Press.
Emerson, C., Pattison, G. & Poole, R. A. eds., 2020. *The Oxford Handbook of Russian Religious Thought*, Oxford: Oxford University Press.

Emmel, S., 2008. Shenoute and the Destruction of Temples in Egypt. In J. Hahn, S. E. Emmel & U. Gotter, eds. *From Temple to Church.* Leiden: Brill, pp. 162–201.

Empedocles, 1981. *The Extant Fragments*, transl. by M. R. Wright, New Haven, CT: Yale University Press.

Engberg-Pedersen, T., 2010. Setting the Scene: Stoicism and Platonism in the Transitional Period in Ancient Philosophy. In T. Rasimus, T. Engberg-Pedersen & I. Dunderberg, eds. *Stoicism in Early Christianity.* Grand Rapids, MI: Baker Academic, pp. 1–14.

Engberg-Pedersen, T., 2016. Stoicism in Early Christianity: The Apostle Paul and the Evangelist John as Stoics. In J. Sellars, ed. *The Routledge Handbook of the Stoic Tradition.* London: Routledge, pp. 29–43.

Engberg-Pedersen, T., 2018. *John and Philosophy: A New Reading of the Fourth Gospel*, Oxford: Oxford University Press.

Epiphanius, 2013. *The Panarion of Epiphanius of Salamis*, Books II and III: *De Fide*, Leiden: Brill.

Erickson, J., 2013. *Panslavism*, London: Historical Association.

Erickson, J. H., 2011. The Church in Modern Orthodox Thought: Towards a Baptismal Ecclesiology. *International Journal for the Study of the Christian Church*, 11(2–3), pp. 137–51.

Erismann, C., 2014. John Philoponus on Individuality and Particularity. In J. Zachhuber & A. Torrance, eds. *Individuality in Late Antiquity.* Farnham: Ashgate, pp. 143–60.

Eunomius, 1987. *The Extant Works*, transl. by R. P. Vaggione, Oxford: Clarendon Press.

Eusebius of Caesarea, 2017. *Against Marcellus. On Ecclesiastical Theology*, transl. by K. McCarthy Spoerl & M. Vinzent, Washington, DC: The Catholic University of America Press.

Evagrius Ponticus, 1970. The Praktikos: *Chapters on Prayer*, transl. by J. E. Bamberger, Spencer, MA: Cistercian Publications.

Evagrius Ponticus, 2015. Kephalaia Gnostika: *A New Translation of the Unreformed Text from the Syriac*, transl. by I. Ramelli, Atlanta, GA: Society of Biblical Literature Press.

Evagrius Scholasticus, 2000. *The Ecclesiastical History of Evagrius Scholasticus*, transl. by M. Whitby, Liverpool: Liverpool University Press.

Evangeliou, C. C., 2016. *Aristotle's Categories and Porphyry*, Leiden: Brill.

Evetts, B., ed., 1907. *History of the Patriarchs of the Coptic Church of Alexandria*, Paris: Firmin-Didot.

Falcasantos, R. S., 2020. *Constantinople: Ritual, Violence, and Memory in the Making of a Christian Imperial Capital*, Oakland, CA: University of California Press.

Feichtinger, J., Fillafer, F. L. & Surman, J. eds., 2019. *The Worlds of Positivism: A Global Intellectual History, 1770–1930*, New York: Palgrave Macmillan.

Fine, J. V. A., 1983. *The Early Medieval Balkans: A Critical Survey from the Sixth to the Late Twelfth Century*, Ann Arbor, MI: The University of Michigan Press.

Fletcher, W. C., 1971. *The Russian Orthodox Church Underground: 1917–1970*, Oxford: Oxford University Press.

Flewelling, R. T., 1915. *Personalism and the Problems of Philosophy: An Appreciation of the Work of Borden Parker Bowne*, New York: Methodist Book Concern.

Flewelling, R. T., 1952. *The Person or The Significance of Man*, Los Angeles, CA: W. Ritchie.

Florensky, P., 1997. *The Pillar and Ground of the Truth*, transl. by B. Jakim, Princeton, NJ: Princeton University Press.

Florovsky, G., 1960. The Ethos of the Orthodox Church. *The Ecumenical Review*, 12(2), pp. 183–98.

Florovsky, G., 1979. *Ways of Russian Theology*, transl. by R. L. Nichols, Belmont, MA: Nordland.

Florovsky, G., 1987. The Church: Her Nature and Task. In R. S. Haugh, ed., *Collected Works of Georges Florovsky*. Vaduz: Büchervertriebsanstalt, pp. 57–72.

Flower, R., 2016. *Imperial Invectives Against Constantius II*, Liverpool: Liverpool University Press.

Foltz, R., 1999. *Religions of the Silk Road: Overland Trade and Cultural Exchange From Antiquity to the Fifteenth Century*, New York: St. Martin's Press.

Fournier, É. & Mayer, W. eds., 2020. *Heirs of Roman Persecution: Studies on a Christian and Para-Christian Discourse in Late Antiquity*, London: Routledge.

Foxhall, L. & Salmon, J. eds., 2011. *When Men Were Men: Masculinity, Power and Identity in Classical Antiquity*, London: Routledge.

Frede, M., 2011. *A Free Will*, Oakland, CA: University of California Press.

Freedman, J., 2009. *The Armenian Genocide*, New York: Rosen.

Freeman, A. & Meyvaert, P. eds., 2010. *Opus Caroli regis contra synodum (Libri Carolini)*, Turnhout: Brepols.

Freibergs, G., 1981. The Medieval Latin Hexameron from Bede to Grosseteste. Los Angeles, CA: University of Southern California.

Frend, W. H. C., 2008a. *Martyrdom and Persecution in the Early Church: A Study of a Conflict From the Maccabees to Donatus*, Cambridge: James Clarke & Co.

Frend, W. H. C., 2008b. *The Rise of the Monophysite Movement: Chapters in the History of the Church in the Fifth and Sixth Centuries*, Cambridge: James Clarke & Co.

Fried, J., 2012. *"Donation of Constantine" and* "Constitutum Constantini," Berlin: De Gruyter.

Fukuyama, F., 2020. *End of History and the Last Man*, London: Penguin.

Fulgentius, 2013. *Correspondence on Christology and Grace*, transl. by R. R. McGregor & D. Fairbairn, Washington, DC: Catholic University of America Press.

Fürst, A. ed., 2019. *Freedom as a Key Category in Origen and in Modern Philosophy and Theology*, Münster: Aschendorff.

Gaddis, M., 2005. *There Is No Crime for Those Who Have Christ*, Berkeley, CA: University of California Press.

Galenus, 1969. *De temperamentis libri III*, edited by G. Helmreich & S. Beßlich, Stuttgart: Teubner.

Galvão-Sobrinho, C. R., ed. 2021. *Doctrine and Power: Theological Controversy and Christian Leadership in the Later Roman Empire*, Oakland, CA: University of California Press.

Gambaré, A., 2005. *Agony in the Grand Palace: 1974–1982*, Addis Ababa: Shama Books.

García Ruiz, M. P. & Quiroga Puertas, A. J. eds., 2021. *Emperors and Emperorship in Late Antiquity: Images and Narratives*, Leiden: Brill.

Gardner, I., 2020. *The Founder of Manichaeism: Rethinking the Life of Mani*, Cambridge: Cambridge University Press.

Gardner, I. & Lieu, S. N. C. eds., 2004. *Manichaean Texts from the Roman Empire*, Cambridge: Cambridge University Press.

Gathercole, S. J., 2007. *The Gospel of Judas: Rewriting Early Christianity*, Oxford: Oxford University Press.

Gathercole, S. J., 2014. *The Gospel of Thomas*, Leiden: Brill.

Gaunt, D., Atto, N. & Barthoma, S. O. eds., 2019. *Let Them Not Return. Sayfo: the Genocide Against the Assyrian, Syriac and Chaldean Christians in the Ottoman Empire*, New York: Berghahn.

Gavrilyuk, P., 2014. *Georges Florovsky and the Russian Religious Renaissance*, Oxford: Oxford University Press.

Geanakoplos, D. J., 1984. *Byzantium: Church, Society, and Civilization Seen Through Contemporary Eyes*, Chicago: University of Chicago Press.

Geanakoplos, D. J., 1989. *Constantinople and the West: Essays on the Late Byzantine (Palaeologan) and Italian Renaissances and the Byzantine and Roman Churches*, Madison, WI: University of Wisconsin Press.

Geffert, B. & Stavrou, T. G., 2016. *Eastern Orthodox Christianity: The Essential Texts*, New Haven, CT: Yale University Press.

Gerolymatos, A., 2003. *The Balkan Wars*, New York: BasicBooks.

Gertz, S., 2018. *Elias and David: Introductions to Philosophy. Olympiodorus: Introduction to Logic*, London: Bloomsbury.

Gill, M. L. & Lennox, J. G. eds., 2017. *Self-Motion: From Aristotle to Newton*, Princeton, NJ: Princeton University Press.

Gillet, L., 1953. *On the Invocation of the Name of Jesus*, London: The Fellowship of St. Alban and St. Sergius.

Gillet, L., 1987. *The Jesus Prayer*, Crestwood, NY: St. Vladimir's Seminary Press.

Gilman, I. & Klimkeit, H.-J., 2016. *Christians in Asia before 1500*, London: Routledge.

Giocas, A. & Ladouceur, P., 2007. The Burning Bush Group and Father André Scrima in Romanian Spirituality. *The Greek Orthodox Theological Review*, 52(1), pp. 37–61.

Gleede, B., 2012. *The Development of the Term ἐνυπόστατος from Origen to John of Damascus*, Leiden: Brill.

Goddard, H., 2020. *A History of Christian-Muslim Relations*, Edinburgh: Edinburgh University Press.

Golitsis, P., 2019. Aristotelian Attraction and Repulsion in Byzantium. *Analogia*, 7, pp. 17–42.

Görg, P. H., 2011. *The Desert Fathers: Anthony and the Beginnings of Monasticism*, San Francisco, CA: Ignatius Press.

Gottlieb, P., 2021. *Aristotle on Thought and Feeling*, Cambridge: Cambridge University Press.

Gourinat, J.-B., 2000. *La dialectique des stoïciens*, Paris: Vrin.

Graf, G., 1951. *Die Schriften des Jacobiten Habib Ibn Hidma Abu Rā'iṭa*, Louvain: Peetres.

Granger, H., 1996. *Aristotle's Idea of the Soul*, Dordrecht: Kluwer.

Grant, R. M., 1970. *Theophilus of Antioch: Ad Autolycum*, Oxford: Clarendon Press.

Green, J. B., 2008. *Body, Soul, and Human Life: the Nature of Humanity in the Bible*, Grand Rapids, MI: Baker Academic.

Greer, R. A., 1966. The Antiochene Christology of Diodore of Tarsus. *Journal of Theological Studies*, 17, pp. 327–41.

Gregory of Nazianzus, 2002. *On God and Christ: The Five Theological Orations and Two Letters to Cledonius*, transl. by F. Williams & L. Wickham, Crestwood, NY: St. Vladimir's Seminary Press.

Gregory of Nyssa, 1967. *Ascetical Works*, transl. by V. Woods Callahan, Washington, DC: The Catholic University of America Press.

Gregory of Nyssa, 2016. *On the Making of Man*, London: Aeterna Press.

Gregory, A., 2007. *Ancient Greek Cosmogony*, London: Bristol Classical Press.

Greig, J., 2020. *The First Principle in Late Neoplatonism*, Leiden: Brill.

Griffith, S. H., 1993. Reflections on the Biography of Theodore Abū Qurrah. *Parole de l'Orient*, 18, pp. 143–70.

Griffith, S. H., 2002. *The Beginnings of Christian Theology in Arabic Muslim-Christian Encounters in the Early Islamic Period*, Aldershot: Ashgate.

Griffith, S. H., 2010. *The Church in the Shadow of the Mosque: Christians and Muslims in the World of Islam*, Princeton, NJ: Princeton University Press.

Grig, L. & Kelly, G. eds., 2012. *Two Romes: Rome and Constantinople in Late Antiquity*, Oxford: Oxford University Press.

Grigoryan, Kh., 2019. *Khosrovik Targmanich. Dogmatic Writings*, Yerevan: Ankyunacar.

Grillmeier, A., 1975. *Christ in Christian Tradition. From the Apostolic Age to Chalcedon*, Atlanta, GA: John Knox Press.

Groen, B. & Bercken, W. van den, eds., 1998. *Four Hundred Years Union of Brest: 1596–1996. A Critical Re-Evaluation. Acta of the Congress Held at Hernen Castle, the Netherlands, in March 1996*, Leuven: Peeters.

Gülzow, H., 1975. *Cyprian und Novatian: der Briefwechsel zwischen der Gemeinden in Rom und Karthago zur Zeit der Verfolgung des Kaisers Decius*, Tübingen: Mohr Siebeck.

Gutas, D., 1998. *Greek Thought, Arabic Culture: the Graeco-Arabic Translation Movement in Baghdad and early 'Abbasaid Society (2nd–4th/5th–10th Centuries)*, London: Routledge.

Gwynn, D. M., 2007. *The Eusebians*, Oxford: Oxford University Press.

Hackel, S., 1965. *One, of Great Price. The Life of Mother Maria Skobtsova, Martyr of Ravensbruck*, London: Darton, Longman & Todd.

Hadjiantoniou, G. A., 1961. *Protestant Patriarch*, Richmond, VA: John Knox.

Hadot, I., 2015. *Athenian and Alexandrian Neoplatonism and the Harmonization of Aristotle and Plato*, Leiden: Brill.

Haile, G., 2012. Täklä Haymanot. In A. Casiday, ed. *The Orthodox Christian World*. London: Routledge, pp. 287–93.

Hall, S. G., 1979. *Melito of Sardis. On Pascha and Fragments*, Oxford: Clarendon Press.

Hall, R. C., 2010. *The Balkan Wars 1912–1913: Prelude to the First World War*, London: Routledge.

Halo, T., 2001. *Not Even My Name*, New York: Picador.

Halsberghe, G. H., 1972. *The Cult of* Sol Invictus, Leiden: Brill.
Halton, T. P., 1985. *The Church*, Wilmington, DE: Glazier.
Hampton, A. J. B. & Kenney, J. P. eds., 2020. *Christian Platonism: A History*, Cambridge: Cambridge University Press.
Harrison, J. R. & Welborn, L. L. eds., 2018. *The First Urban Churches 3: Ephesus*, Atlanta, GA: Society of Biblical Literature Press.
Hart, D. B., 2001. The "Whole Humanity": Gregory of Nyssa's Critique of Slavery in Light of His Eschatology. *Scottish Journal of Theology*, 54(1), pp. 51–69.
Hart, D. B., 2017. *The New Testament: A Translation*, New Haven, CT: Yale University Press.
Hart, D. B., 2019. *That All Shall Be Saved*, New Haven, CT: Yale University Press.
Harte, V. & Lane, M. eds., 2013. *Politeia in Greek and Roman Philosophy*, Cambridge: Cambridge University Press.
Hauben, H., 2017. *Studies on the Melitian Schism in Egypt (AD 306–335)*, London: Routledge.
Haugaard, W. P., 1960. Arius: Twice a Heretic? Arius and the Human Soul of Jesus Christ. *Church History*, 29(3), pp. 251–63.
Haugh, R. S., 1975. *Photius and the Carolingians: the Trinitarian Controversy*, Belmont, MA: Nordland.
Hazzard Cross, S. & Sherbowitz-Wetzor, O. eds., 1953. *The Russian Primary Chronicle*, Cambridge, MA: The Medieval Academy of America.
Heath, J. M. F., 2020. *Clement of Alexandria and the Shaping of Christian Literary Practice: Miscellany and the Transformation of Greco-Roman Writing*, Cambridge: Cambridge University Press.
Heather, P. J. & Moncur, D., 2001. *Politics, Philosophy, and Empire in the Fourth Century: Select Orations of Themistius*, Liverpool: Liverpool University Press.
Henry, P., 1950. The *Adversus Arium* of Marius Victorinus, The First Systematic Exposition of the Doctrine of the Trinity. *Journal of Theological Studies*, I(1), pp. 42–55.
Heraclitus, 1991. *Fragments*, transl. by T. M. Robinson, Toronto: University of Toronto Press.
Heynickx, R., O'Connor Perks, S. & Symons, S. eds., 2018. *So What's New About Scholasticism?: How Neo-Thomism Helped Shape the Twentieth Century*, Berlin: De Gruyter.
Hinlicky Wilson, S., 2013. *Woman, Women, and the Priesthood in the Trinitarian Theology of Elisabeth Behr-Sigel*, London: Bloomsbury.
Hoffmann, R. J., 1994. *Porphyry's Against the Christians: The Literary Remains*, New York: Prometheus Books.
Hollerich, M. J., 2021. *Making Christian History: Eusebius of Caesarea and His Readers*, Oakland, CA, University of California Press.
Hopkins, J. L., 2009. *The Bulgarian Orthodox Church: A Socio-Historical Analysis of the Evolving Relationship Between Church, Nation and State in Bulgaria*, New York: Columbia University Press.
Horky, P. S. ed., 2019. *Cosmos in the Ancient World*, Cambridge: Cambridge University Press.

Horn, C. B., 2006. *Asceticism and Christological Controversy in Fifth-Century Palestine: The Career of Peter the Iberian*, Oxford: Oxford University Press.

Horne, C. F., 1917. *The Sacred Books and Early Literature of the East*, New York: Parke, Austin and Lipscomb.

Horster, M. & Reitz, C., 2018. Handbooks, Epitomes, and *Florilegia*. In S. McGill & E. Watts, eds., *A Companion to Late Antique Literature*. Hoboken, NJ: Wiley Blackwell, pp. 431–50.

Hovannisian, R. G. ed., 2014. *Armenian Genocide: History, Politics, Ethics*, New York: Palgrave Macmillan.

Hovannisian, R. G. ed., 2017. *The Armenian Genocide: Cultural and Ethical Legacies*, London: Routledge.

Hovorun, C., 2008. *Will, Action and Freedom: Christological Controversies in the Seventh Century*, Leiden: Brill.

Hovorun, C., 2014. *From Antioch to Xi'an: An Evolution of "Nestorianism,"* Hong Kong: Chinese Orthodox Press.

Hovorun, C., 2015a. *Meta-Ecclesiology: Chronicles on Church Awareness*, New York: Palgrave Macmillan.

Hovorun, C., 2015b. Was Eastern Christianity Always Orthodox? *The Wheel*, (n. 1), pp. 2–8.

Hovorun, C., 2015c. Maximus, a Cautious Neo-Chalcedonian. In P. Allen & B. Neil, eds. *The Oxford Handbook of Maximus the Confessor*. Oxford: Oxford University Press, pp. 106–24.

Hovorun, C., 2016. Ideology and Religion. *Kyiv-Mohyla Humanities Journal*, 3, pp. 23–35.

Hovorun, C., 2017a. Is the Byzantine "Symphony" Possible in Our Days? *Journal of Church and State*, 59(2), pp. 280–96.

Hovorun, C., 2017b. *Scaffolds of the Church: Towards Poststructural Ecclesiology*, Eugene, OR: Cascade.

Hovorun, C., 2018. *Political Orthodoxies: The Unorthodoxies of the Church Coerced*, Minneapolis, MN: Fortress.

Hovorun, C., 2019a. Der Horos von 1755 und die Wiedertaufe in der Orthodoxen Kirche. *Ökumenische Rundschau*, 68(4), pp. 496–513.

Hovorun, C., 2019b. Die polyphone Theologie der Kirchenväter. Der Beitrag des Johannes von Damaskus. *Evangelische Theologie*, 79(5), pp. 393–401.

Hovorun, C., 2019c. Two Meanings of Freedom in the Eastern Patristic Tradition. In M. Welker, ed. *Quests for Freedom: Biblical, Historical, Contemporary*. Eugene, OR: Cascade, pp. 134–46.

Hovorun, C., 2020. *Philokalia*: From a Manuscript to a Movement. In P. A. Cinger & J. A. Carrascosa Fuentes, eds. *Actas II congreso internacional de estudios patrísticos*. San Juan: Editorial Universitaria UCCuyo, pp. 64–7.

Hurbanič, M., 2019. *The Avar Siege of Constantinople in 626. History and Legend*, New York: Palgrave Macmillan.

Hurvitz, N., Sahner, Ch. C., Simonsohn, U. & Yarbrough, L., eds., 2020. *Conversion to Islam in the Premodern Age: A Sourcebook*, Oakland, CA: University of California Press.

Inwood, B., 2009. Empedocles and Metempsychôsis: The Critique of Diogenes of Oenoanda. In D. Frede & B. Reis, eds. *Body and Soul in Ancient Philosophy*. Berlin: De Gruyter, pp. 71–86.

Inwood, B. & Warren, J. eds., 2020. *Body and Soul in Hellenistic Philosophy*, Cambridge: Cambridge University Press.

Irenaeus, 2012. *Against the Heresies*, transl. by D. Unger, New York: Paulist.

Isaac, B. H., 2004. *The Invention of Racism in Classical Antiquity*, Princeton, NJ: Princeton University Press.

Isaac, B. H., 2006. Proto-Racism in Graeco-Roman Antiquity. *World Archaeology*, 38(1), pp. 32–47.

Ivanovic, F., 2016. Union with and Likeness to God. In M. Edwards & E. E. D-Vasilescu, eds. *Visions of God and Ideas on Deification in Patristic Thought*. London: Routledge, pp. 118–57.

Jacob of Edessa, 2010. *Hexaemeron*, edited by J. Y. Çiçek, Piscataway, NJ: Gorgias.

Jaeger, W., 1960. *Gregorii Nysseni opera*, vols. 1.1 & 2.2, Leiden: Brill.

Jaeger, W., 1962. *Early Christianity and Greek Paideia*, Cambridge, MA: Harvard University Press.

Jay, E. G., 1980. *The Church: Its Changing Image Through Twenty Centuries*, Louisville, KY: John Knox Press.

Chrysostom, John. 2010. *Two Letters to Theodore After His Fall*, transl. by W. R. W. Stephens, Whitefish, MT: Kessinger.

Climacus, John. 1982. *The Ladder of Divine Ascent*, edited by C. Luibheid & N. Russel, New York: Paulist Press.

John of Damascus, 2003. *Three Treatises on the Divine Images*, transl. by Andrew Louth, Crestwood, NY: St. Vladimir's Seminary Press.

Johnson, L. J., 2009. *Worship in the Early Church: An Anthology of Historical Sources*, Collegeville, MN: Liturgical Press.

Johnson, L. T., 2010. *Among the Gentiles: Greco-Roman Religion and Christianity*, New Haven, CT: Yale University Press.

Johnston, S. I., 2009. *Ancient Greek Divination*, Malden, MA: John Wiley & Sons.

Jullien, F., 2009. The Great Monastery at Mount Izla and the Defence of the East Syriac Identity. In E. C. D. Hunter, ed. *The Christian Heritage of Iraq: Collected Papers From the Christianity in Iraq I-V Seminar Days*. Piscataway, NJ: Gorgias, pp. 54–63.

Justin, 2008. *The First Apology, The Second Apology, Dialogue with Trypho, Exhortation to the Greeks, Discourse to the Greeks, The Monarchy or The Rule of God*, transl. by Th. B. Falls, Washington, DC: Catholic University of America Press.

Kaegi, W. E., 2007. *Heraclius Emperor of Byzantium*, Cambridge: Cambridge University Press.

Kahlos, M., 2019. *Religious Dissent in Late Antiquity, 350–450*, Oxford: Oxford University Press.

Kaldellis, A., 2015. *The Byzantine Republic: People and Power in New Rome*, Cambridge, MA: Harvard University Press.

Kaldellis, A., 2019. *Romanland: Ethnicity and Empire in Byzantium*, Cambridge, MA: Harvard University Press.

Kalkandzhieva, D., 2017. *The Russian Orthodox Church, 1917–1948: From Decline to Resurrection*, London: Routledge.

Kaplanis, T., 2014. Antique Names and Self-Identification: *Hellenes*, *Graikoi*, and *Romaioi* from Late Byzantium to the Greek Nation-State. In D. Tziovas, ed. *Re-Imagining the Past: Antiquity and Modern Greek Culture*. Oxford: Oxford University Press, pp. 81–97.

Karfíková, L., Douglas, S. & Zachhuber, J. eds., 2008. *Gregory of Nyssa: Contra Eunomium II*, Leiden; Boston: Brill.

Katz, S. T., 2013. *Comparative Mysticism: An Anthology of Original Sources*, Oxford: Oxford University Press.

Kedourie, E., 1996. *Nationalism*, Oxford: Blackwell.

Kekelidze, K., 1918. *Tskhovreba da moqalaqoba aghmsareblisa martlisa sartsmunoebisa tsmidisa da netarisa mamisa chuenisa Maqsimesi* [Life and Citizenship of Our Holy and Blessed Father Maximus—the Holy and Blessed Confessor of the True Faith], Tbilisi.

Kenanoğlu, M., 2017. *Osmanli millet sistemi: mit ve gerçek*, Istanbul: Klasik.

Kenworthy, S. M., 2015. *Chosen For His People: A Biography of Patriarch Tikhon*, Jordanville, NY: Holy Trinity Monastery.

Khalil, S., 1999. Les versions arabes de Némésius de Ḥomṣ. In M. Pavan & U. Cozzoli, eds. *L'eredità classica nelle lingue orientali*. Roma: Istituto della Enciclopedia italiana, pp. 99–151.

Khoperia, L., 2015. The Georgian Tradition on Maximus the Confessor. In P. Allen & B. Neil, eds. *The Oxford Handbook of Maximus the Confessor*. Oxford: Oxford University Press, pp. 439–59.

King, D., 2010. *The Earliest Syriac Translation of Aristotle's "Categories,"* Leiden: Brill.

King, M. S., 2012. *Unveiling the Messiah in the Dead Sea Scrolls*, Bloomington, IN: Xlibris.

Kinzig, W., 2017. *Faith in Formulae: A Collection of Early Christian Creeds and Creed-Related Texts*, Oxford: Oxford University Press.

Knipfing, J. R. 1923. *The Libelli of the Decian Persecution*, Cambridge, MA: Harvard University Press.

Knox, J., 1980. *Marcion and the New Testament: An Essay in the Early History of the Canon*, Chicago, IL: University of Chicago Press.

Koester, H. & Osiek, C., 1999. *Shepherd of Hermas: A Commentary*, Minneapolis, MN: Fortress.

Kolb, A. ed., 2019. *Roman Roads: New Evidence, New Perspectives*, Berlin: De Gruyter.

Kominko, M., 2013. *The World of Kosmas: Illustrated Byzantine Codices of the Christian Topography*, Cambridge: Cambridge University Press.

Korner, R. J., 2017. *The Origin and Meaning of* Ekklēsia *in the Early Jesus Movement*, Leiden: Brill.

Kortschmaryk, F. B., 1971. *Christianization of the European East and Messianic Aspirations of Moscow as the "Third Rome,"* Toronto; New York: Studium Research Institute.

Koslin, A. P., 1958. *The Megali Idea: A Study of Greek Nationalism*. Baltimore, MD: John Hopkins University Press.

Kosman, A., 2017. Aristotle's Prime Mover. In M. L. Gill & J. G. Lennox, eds. *Self-Motion: From Aristotle to Newton*. Princeton, NJ: Princeton University Press, pp. 135–53.

Kotter, B., 1969. *Die Schriften des Johannes von Damaskos*, Berlin: De Gruyter.

Krawchuk, A. & Bremer, T. eds., 2014. *Eastern Orthodox Encounters of Identity and Otherness: Values, Self-reflection, Dialogue*, New York: Palgrave.

Kritikos, A., 2007. Platonism and Principles in Origen. *Bulletin of the Institute of Classical Studies*, 94(2), pp. 403–17.

Kritovoulos, M. 2019. *History of Mehmed the Conqueror*, Princeton, NJ: Princeton University Press.

Kudiyiruppil, J., 2001. *Eucharistic Ecclesiology: A Critical Study*, Changanassery: HIRS Publications.

Lactantius, 1998. *On the Deaths of the Persecutors* (De mortibus persecutorum), Armidale: Northern Antiquities Press.

Ladouceur, P., 2019. *Modern Orthodox Theology*, London: T&T Clark.

Lamoreaux, J. C., 2002. The Biography of Theodore Abū Qurrah Revisited. *Dumbarton Oaks Papers*, 56, pp. 25–40.

Lampe, P., 2019. Concepts of Freedom in Antiquity: Pagan Philosophical Traditions in the Greco-Roman World. In M. Welker, ed. *Quests for Freedom: Biblical, Historical, Contemporary*. Eugene, OR: Cascade, pp. 116–33.

Lang, U. M., 2001. *John Philoponus and the Controversies over Chalcedon in the Sixth Century: a Study and Translation of the* Arbiter, Leuven: Peeters.

Larchet, J.-C., 1998. *Maxime le Confesseur, médiateur entre l'Orient et l'Occident*, Paris: Éditions du Cerf.

Lauber, D. & Johnson, K. L. eds., 2018. *T&T Clark Companion to the Doctrine of Sin*, London: T&T Clark.

Lebon, J., 1909. *Le monophysisme Sévérien: étude historique, littéraire et théologique sur la résistance monophysite au Concile de Chalcédoine jusqu'à la constitution de l'Église jacobite*, Lovanii: J. Van Linthout.

Lenski, N., 2002. *Failure of Empire*, Berkeley, CA: University of California Press.

Lenz, J., 2007. Deification of the Philosopher in Classical Greece. In M. J. Christensen & J. A. Witting, eds., *Partakers of the Divine Nature: the History and Development of Deification in the Christian Traditions*. Madison, NJ: Fairleigh Dickinson University Press, pp. 47–62.

Lewis, W., 2020. Constantine II and His Brothers: The Civil War of AD 340. In N. Baker-Brian & S. Tougher, eds. *The Sons of Constantine*, AD 337-361. New York: Palgrave Macmillan, pp. 57–94.

Lewy, G., 2012. *Essays on Genocide and Humanitarian Intervention*, Salt Lake City, UT: University of Utah Press.

Lieburg, F. A. V. ed., 2006. *Confessionalism and Pietism: Religious Reform in Early Modern Europe*, Mainz: Von Zabern.

Lietzmann, H., 1970. *Apollinaris von Laodicea und seine Schule*, Hildesheim: Georg Olms.

Lieu, S. N. C. & Thompson, G. L. eds., 2019. *The Church of the East in Central Asia and China*, Turnhout: Brepols.

Lindholm, Ch., 2002. *The Islamic Middle East: Tradition and Change*, Malden, MA: Blackwell.

Little, L. K. ed., 2009. *Plague and the End of Antiquity: The Pandemic of 541–750*, Cambridge: Cambridge University Press.

Long, A. A., 2011. *From Epicurus to Epictetus: Studies in Hellenistic and Roman Philosophy*, Oxford: Oxford University Press.

López, A. G., 2013. *Shenoute of Atripe and the Uses of Poverty: Rural Patronage, Religious Conflict and Monasticism in Late Antique Egypt*, Berkeley, CA: University of California Press.

Lossky, V., 1974. *In the Image and Likeness of God*, Crestwood, NY: St. Vladimir's Seminary Press.

Lossky, V., 1983. *Vision of God*, Crestwood, NY: St. Vladimir's Seminary Press.

Louth, A., 1996. *Maximus the Confessor*, London: Routledge.

Louth, A., 2002. *St. John Damascene: Tradition and Originality in Byzantine Theology*, Oxford: Oxford University Press.

Louth, A., 2004. The Ecclesiology of Saint Maximos the Confessor. *International Journal for the Study of the Christian Church*, 4(2), pp. 109–20.

Louth, A., 2007a. *Greek East and Latin West: The Church, AD 681–1071*, Crestwood, NY: St. Vladimir's Seminary Press.

Louth, A., 2007b. The Place of *Theosis* in Orthodox Theology. In M. J. Christensen & J. A. Witting, eds., *Partakers of the Divine Nature: The History and Development of Deification in the Christian Traditions*. Madison, NJ: Fairleigh Dickinson University Press, pp. 32–46.

Louth, A., 2013. Man and Cosmos in St. Maximus the Confessor. In J. Chryssavgis & B. V. Foltz, eds. *Toward an Ecology of Transfiguration: Orthodox Christian Perspectives on Environment, Nature, and Creation*. New York: Fordham University Press, pp. 59–72.

Louth, A., 2015. *Modern Orthodox Thinkers: From the Philokalia to the Present Day*, Downer's Grove, IL: IVP Academic.

Lubac, H. de, 1953. *Méditation sur l'église*, Paris: Aubier.

Luhtala, A., 2005. *Grammar and Philosophy in Late Antiquity: A Study of Priscian's Sources*, Amsterdam: John Benjamins.

Luibheid, C., 1987. *Pseudo-Dionysius: The Complete Works*, Mahwah, NJ: Paulist.

Lyman, J. R., 2021. Arius and Arianism: The Origins of the Alexandrian Controversy. In Y. R. Kim, ed. *The Cambridge Companion to the Council of Nicaea*. Cambridge: Cambridge University Press, pp. 43–62.

Maclear, J. F. ed., 1995. *Church and State in the Modern Age: A Documentary History*, Oxford: Oxford University Press.

Magdalino, P., 2017. Astrology. In A. Kaldellis & N. Siniossoglou, eds. *The Cambridge Intellectual History of Byzantium*. Cambridge: Cambridge University Press, pp. 198–214.

Magny, A., 2016. *Porphyry in Fragments: Reception of an Anti-Christian Text in Late Antiquity*, London: Routledge.

Mahdi, M., 1967. Alfarabi against Philoponus. *Journal of Near Eastern Studies*, 26(4), pp. 233–60.

Maier, H., 2013. Nero in Jewish and Christian Tradition from the First Century to the Reformation. In E. Buckley & M. T. Dinter, eds. *A Companion to the Neronian Age*. Oxford: Wiley-Blackwell, pp. 385–404.

Malik, S., 2020. *The Nero-Antichrist: Founding and Fashioning a Paradigm*, Cambridge: Cambridge University Press.

Malitz, J., 2008. *Nero*, Malden, MA: John Wiley & Sons.

Manning, G., 2013. The History of "Hylomorphism." *Journal of the History of Ideas*, 74(2), pp. 173–87.

Mantzarides, G., 1996. Spiritual Life in Palamism. In J. Raitt, ed. *Christian Spirituality: High Middle Ages and Reformation*. New York: Crossroad, pp. 208–22.

Marenbon, J., 2015. *Pagans and Philosophers*, Princeton, NJ: Princeton University Press.

Marjanen, A., 2008. Montanism: An Egalitarian Ecstatic "New Prophecy." In A. Marjanen & P. Luomanen, eds. *A Companion to Second-century Christian "Heretics."* Leiden: Brill, pp. 185–212.

Marmodoro, A., 2015. Gregory of Nyssa on the Creation of the World. In B. D. Prince & A. Marmodoro, eds. *Causation and Creation in Late Antiquity*. Cambridge: Cambridge University Press, pp. 94–110.

Marrou, H.-I. ed., 1965. *A Diognète*, Paris: Éditions du Cerf.

Maspero, G., 2007. *Trinity and Man: Gregory of Nyssa's* Ad Ablabium, Leiden: Brill.

Mateo-Seco, L. F. & Maspero, G. eds., 2009. *The Brill Dictionary of Gregory of Nyssa*, Leiden: Brill.

Mattá al-Miskin, 2003. *Orthodox Prayer Life: the Interior Way*, Crestwood, NY: St. Vladimir's Seminary Press.

Maximus the Confessor, 1978. *The Ascetic Life. The Four Centuries on Charity*, transl. by P. Sherwood, New York: Paulist Press.

Maximus the Confessor, 2014. *On Difficulties in the Church Fathers: The Ambigua*, transl. by M. Constas, Cambridge, MA: Harvard University Press.

Maximus the Confessor, 2018. *On Difficulties in Sacred Scripture*, transl. by M. Constas, Washington, DC: Catholic University of America Press.

McGowan, A., 2007. *Ascetic Eucharists: Food and Drink in Early Christian Ritual Meals*, Oxford: Clarendon Press.

McGuckin, J. A., 2007. The Strategic Adaptation of Deification in the Cappadocians. In M. J. Christensen & J. A. Witting, eds. *Partakers of the Divine Nature: The History and Development of Deification in the Christian Traditions*. Madison, NJ: Fairleigh Dickinson University Press, pp. 95–114.

McGuckin, J. A., 2010. *The Harp of Glory.* Enzira Sebhat: *An Alphabetical Hymn of Praise for the Ever-Blessed Virgin Mary From the Ethiopian Orthodox Church*, Yonkers, NY: St. Vladimir's Seminary Press.

McKenna, T., 2011. Hegelian Dialectics. *Critique*, 39(1), pp. 155–72.

McKinion, S. A., 2000. *Words, Imagery, and the Mystery of Christ*, Leiden: Brill.

McPartlan, P., 1996. *The Eucharist Makes the Church*, Edinburgh: T&T Clark.
Melville-Jones, J. R., 1972. *The Siege of Constantinople 1453: Seven Contemporary Accounts*, Amsterdam: Hakkert.
Menze, V. L., 2009. *Justinian and the Making of the Syrian Orthodox Church*, Oxford: Oxford University Press.
Metselaar, M., 2019. *Defining Christ: the Church of the East and Nascent Islam*, Leuven: Peeters.
Meyendorff, John, 1974a. *Byzantine Hesychasm: Historical, Theological and Social Problems*, London: Variorum.
Meyendorff, John, 1974b. *St. Gregory Palamas and Orthodox Spirituality*, Crestwood, NY: St. Vladimir's Seminary Press.
Meyendorff, J., 1987. *Byzantine Theology: Historical Trends and Doctrinal Themes*, New York: Fordham University Press.
Meyendorff, J., 2011. *Christ in Eastern Christian Thought*, Crestwood, NY: St. Vladimir's Seminary Press.
Middleton, P. ed., 2020. *Wiley Blackwell Companion to Christian Martyrdom*, Oxford: John Wiley & Sons.
Mignucci, M., 2019. *Ancient Logic, Language, and Metaphysics: Selected Essays by Mario Mignucci*, edited by A. Falcon & P. Giaretta, London: Taylor & Francis.
Miles, R. ed., 2018. *The Donatist Schism: Controversy and Contexts*, Liverpool: Liverpool University Press.
Millar, F., 2007. *A Greek Roman Empire: Power and Belief Under Theodosius II (408–450)*, Berkeley, CA: University of California Press.
Miller, D. & Sarris, P., 2018. *The Novels of Justinian: A Complete Annotated English Translation*, Cambridge: Cambridge University Press.
Milton, G., 2009. *Paradise Lost. Smyrna 1922: The Destruction of Islam's City of Tolerance*, London: Sceptre.
Minear, P. S., 1960. *Images of the Church in the New Testament*, Philadelphia, PA: Westminster Press.
Mitralexis, S., 2017. *Ever-Moving Repose: A Contemporary Reading of Maximus the Confessor's Theory of Time*, Eugene, OR: Wipf and Stock.
Mogila, P., 1898. *The Orthodox Confession of the Catholic and Apostolic Eastern Church*, transl. by P. Lodvill, London: Thomas Baker.
Mönnich, C. W., 1950. De achtergrond van de Ariaanse christologie. *Nederlands theologisch tijdschrift*, 4, pp. 378–412.
Moosa, M., 2005. *The Maronites in History*, Piscataway, NJ: Gorgias.
Morani, M. *La tradizione armena di Nemesio di Emesa. Problemi linguistici e filologici, in Autori classici in lingue del Vicino e Medio Oriente. Atti del III, IV e V seminario sul tema "Recupero di testi classici attraverso recezioni" in 15–16 aprile 1986*, Roma: Ist. Poligrafico e Zecca dello Stato—Archivi di Stato, 1990.
Morariu, I.-M., 2020. *The "Christian Nationalism" of Nichifor Crainic*, Cluj-Napoca: Presa Universitară Clujeană.
Morris, B. & Zeevi, D., 2019. *The Thirty-Year Genocide: Turkey's Destruction of Its Christian Minorities, 1894–1924*, Cambridge, MA: Harvard University Press.

Moss, C. R., 2012. *Ancient Christian Martyrdom: Diverse Practices, Theologies, and Traditions*, New Haven, CT: Yale University Press.

Moss, C. R., 2014. *The Myth of Persecution: How Early Christians Invented a Story of Martyrdom*, New York: HarperOne.

Moss, C. R., 2019. *Divine Bodies: Resurrecting Perfection in the New Testament and Early Christianity*, New Haven, CT: Yale University Press.

Moss, Y., 2016. *Incorruptible Bodies: Christology, Society, and Authority in Late Antiquity*, Berkeley, CA: University of California Press.

Mott, J. R., 1947. *Addresses and Papers of John R. Mott. Vol. 5: The International Missionary Council*, New York: Association Press.

Mounier, E., 1938. *A Personalist Manifesto*, London; New York: Longmans, Green.

Mueller, F., 1958. *Gregorii Nysseni opera*, vol. 3.1, Leiden: Brill.

Mullett, M., 2016. *Theophylact of Ochrid: Reading the Letters of a Byzantine Archbishop*, London: Routledge.

Muradyan, G., 2015. *David the Invincible, Commentary on Porphyry's* Isagoge. *Old Armenian Text with the Greek Original, an English Translation, Introduction and Notes*, Leiden: Brill.

Murray, R., 2004. *Symbols of Church and Kingdom: A Study in Early Syriac Tradition*, Piscataway, NJ: Gorgias.

Myllykoski, M., 2015. Without Decree: Pagan Sacrificial Meat and the Early History of the *Didache*. In J. A. Draper & C. N. Jefford, eds. *The Didache: A Missing Piece of the Puzzle in Early Christianity*. Atlanta, GA: Society of Biblical Literature Press, pp. 429–54.

Naddaf, G., 2005. *The Greek Concept of Nature*, Albany, NY: State University of New York Press.

Nasrallah, J., 1974. Naẓīf Ibn Yumn: médecin, traducteur et théologien melchite du Xe siècle. *Arabica*, 21, pp. 303–12.

Nemesius, 2008. *On the Nature of Man*, transl. by R. W. Sharples & P. J. van der Eijk, Liverpool: Liverpool University Press.

Nestorius, 1925. *The Bazaar of Heracleides*, transl. by G. R. Driver & L. Hodgson, Oxford: Clarendon Press.

Nichols, A., 1989. *Theology in the Russian Diaspora: Church, Fathers, Eucharist in Nikolai Afanas'ev (1893–1966)*, Cambridge: Cambridge University Press.

Nichols, A., 2019. *Byzantine Gospel: Maximus the Confessor in Modern Scholarship*, Eugene, OR: Wipf & Stock.

Niketas Choniates, 1984. *O City of Byzantium: Annals of Niketas Choniates*, transl. by H. J. Magoulias, Detroit, MI: Wayne State University Press.

Norkus, Z., 2019. *An Unproclaimed Empire: The Grand Duchy of Lithuania from the Viewpoint of Comparative Historical Sociology of Empires*, London: Routledge.

Norman, D. L. & Petkas, A. eds., 2020. *Hypatia of Alexandria: Her Context and Legacy*, Tübingen: Mohr Siebeck.

Norris, F. W., 2006. Timothy I of Baghdad, Catholicos of the East Syrian Church, 780–823: Still a Valuable Model. *International Bulletin of Missionary Research*, 30(3), pp. 133–6.

O'Brien, D., 2008. *Empedocles' Cosmic Cycle: A Reconstruction From the Fragments and Secondary Sources*, Cambridge: Cambridge University Press.
O'Carroll, M., 1982. *Theotokos: A Theological Encyclopedia of the Blessed Virgin*, Wilmington, DE: M. Glazier.
O'Donovan, O. & O'Donovan, J. L., 1999. *From Irenaeus to Grotius: A Sourcebook in Christian Political Thought, 100–1625*, Grand Rapids, MI: Eerdmans.
Oakley, F., 2008. *Kingship: The Politics of Enchantment*, Oxford: Blackwell.
Oberdorfer, B., 2001. *Filioque: Geschichte und Theologie eines ökumenischen Problems*, Göttingen: Vandenhoeck & Ruprecht.
Obolensky, D., 1971. *The Byzantine Commonwealth: Eastern Europe, 500–1453*, New York: Praeger.
Olster, D. M., 1991. The Date of George of Pisidia's "Hexaemeron." *Dumbarton Oaks Papers*, 45, pp. 159–72.
Oort, J. V. ed., 2013. *Augustine and Manichaean Christianity: Selected Papers From the First South African Conference on Augustine of Hippo, University of Pretoria, 24–26 April 2012*, Leiden: Brill.
Origen, 1989. *Commentary on the Gospel According to John, Books 1–10*, transl. by R. E. Heine, Washington, DC: Catholic University of America Press.
Origen, 1990. *Homilies on Leviticus, 1–16*, transl. by G. W. Barkley, Washington, DC: Catholic University of America Press.
Origen, 2006. *Philocalie 21–27: sur le libre arbitre*, ed. par É. Junod, Paris: Éditions du Cerf.
Origen, 2009. *Contra Celsum*, transl. by H. Chadwick, Cambridge: Cambridge University Press.
Osler, M. J., 2005. *Atoms, Pneuma, and Tranquillity: Epicurean and Stoic Themes in European Thought*, Cambridge: Cambridge University Press.
Özyasar, Y. K., 2019. *The Ottoman Empire in the* Tanzimat *Era: Provincial Perspectives From Ankara to Edirne*, London: Routledge.
Pacella, M., 2015. Aquinas and Palamas. In C. Athanasopoulos, ed. *Triune God: Incomprehensible but Knowable—the Philosophical and Theological Significance of St Gregory Palamas for Contemporary Philosophy and Theology*. Newcastle upon Tyne: Cambridge Scholars Publishing, pp. 199–210.
Palamas, Gregory, 1983. *The Triads*, transl. by J. Meyendorff & N. Gendle, Mahwah, NJ: Paulist Press.
Palmer, G. E. H, Sherrard, Ph. & Ware, K. eds., 1990. *The Philokalia*, New York: Faber and Faber.
Papademetriou, G. C., 2004. *Introduction to St. Gregory Palamas*, Brookline, MA: Holy Cross Orthodox Press.
Papademetriou, T., 2015. *Render Unto the Sultan: Power, Authority, and the Greek Orthodox Church in the Early Ottoman Centuries*, Oxford: Oxford University Press.
Papandrea, J. L., 2011. *Novatian of Rome and the Culmination of Pre-Nicene Orthodoxy*, Eugene, OR: Pickwick.

Papanikolaou, A., 2012. *The Mystical as Political: Democracy and Non-Radical Orthodoxy*, Notre Dame, IN: University of Notre Dame Press.

Parmenides, 2011. *Fragments: A Text and Translation*, transl. by D. Gallop, Toronto: University of Toronto Press.

Parvis, S., 2006. *Marcellus of Ancyra and the Lost Years of the Arian Controversy, 325–45*, Oxford: Oxford University Press.

Parvis, S., 2021. The Reception of Nicaea and *Homoousios* to 360. In Y. R. Kim, ed. *The Cambridge Companion to the Council of Nicaea*. Cambridge: Cambridge University Press, pp. 225–55.

Patelos, C. ed., 1978. *The Orthodox Church in the Ecumenical Movement*, Geneva: World Council of Churches.

Payne, R. E., 2015. *A State of Mixture*, Berkeley, CA: University of California Press.

Pearson, B. A., 2008. Basilides the Gnostic. In A. Marjanen & P. Luomanen, eds. *A Companion to Second-Century Christian "Heretics."* Leiden: Brill, pp. 1–31.

Pelikan, J., 1984. *The Vindication of Tradition*, New Haven, CT: Yale University Press.

Pelikan, J. & Hotchkiss, V. R. eds., 2003. *Creeds and Confessions of Faith in the Christian Tradition*, New Haven, CT: Yale University Press.

Peltomaa, L. M., 2001. *The Image of the Virgin Mary in the Akathistos Hymn*, Leiden: Brill.

Penner, R. J., 2008. *The Rhetoric of God in History: Eusebius of Caesarea's Political Theology in His "Panegyric to Constantine."* Ann Arbor, MI: Dalhousie University.

Peppard, M., 2016. *The World's Oldest Church: Bible, Art, and Ritual at Dura-Europos, Syria*, New Haven, CT: Yale University Press.

Persoon, J. G. & Jezek, V., 2014. *Spirituality, Power and Revolution: Contemporary Monasticism in Communist Ethiopia*, Volos: Volos Academy for Theological Studies.

Peterson, E., 1935. *Der Monotheismus als politisches Problem. Ein Beitrag zur Geschichte der politischen Theologie im* Imperium romanum, Leipzig: Hegner.

Philippides, M., 1990. *Emperors, Patriarchs, and Sultans of Constantinople, 1373–1513: an Anonymous Greek Chronicle of the Sixteenth Century*, Brookline, MA: Hellenic College Press.

Philippides, M. & Hanak, W. K., 2020. *The Siege and the Fall of Constantinople in 1453: Historiography, Topography, and Military Studies*, London: Routledge.

Photius, 1983. *On the Mystagogy of the Holy Spirit*, transl. by J. P. Farrell, Seattle, WA: Studion Publishers.

Photius, 1985. *Photii Patriarchae Constantinopolitani epistulae et amphilochia*. Vol. 3: *Epistularum pars tertia*, edited by B. Laourdas & L. G. Westerink, Leipzig: B. G. Teubner.

Pigott, J. M., 2019. *New Rome Wasn't Built in a Day: Rethinking Councils and Controversy at Early Constantinople 381–451*, Turnhout: Brepols.

Pinker, S., 2008. *The Stuff of Thought: Language as a Window into Human Nature*, London: Penguin.

Plaxco, K., 2016. *Didymus the Blind, Origen, and the Trinity*, Milwaukee, WI: Marquette University Press.

Plested, M., 2004. *The Macarian Legacy: The Place of Macarius-Symeon in the Eastern Christian Tradition*, Oxford: Oxford University Press.

Plokhy, S., 2001. *The Cossacks and Religion in Early Modern Ukraine*, Oxford: Oxford University Press.

Plokhy, S., 2016. *The Gates of Europe: A History of Ukraine*, London: Penguin.

Plotinus, 2014. *In Six Volumes*, Cambridge, MA: Harvard University Press.

Poe, M., 1997. *"Moscow, the Third Rome": The Origins and Transformations of a Pivotal Movement*, Washington, DC: National Council for Soviet and East European Research.

Pohl, W., 2018. *The Avars: A Steppe Empire in Central Europe, 567–822*, Ithaca, NY: Cornell University Press.

Popović, J., 2013. *Notes on Ecumenism*, Alhambra, CA: Sebastian Press.

Porphyry, 2003. *Introduction*, edited by J. Barnes, Oxford: Clarendon Press.

Porter, S. E. & Pitts, A. W. eds., 2018. *Christian Origins and the Establishment of the Early Jesus Movement*, Leiden: Brill.

Pospielovsky, D., 1984. *The Russian Church Under the Soviet Regime, 1917–1982*, Crestwood, NY: St. Vladimir's Seminary Press.

Possekel, U., 1999. *Evidence of Greek Philosophical Concepts in the Writings of Ephrem the Syrian*, Leuven: Peeters.

Pouncy, C. J., 1994. *The "Domostroi": Rules for Russian Households in the Time of Ivan the Terrible*, Ithaca, NY: Cornell University Press.

Price, R., 2009. *The Acts of the Council of Constantinople of 553*, Liverpool: Liverpool University Press.

Price, R., 2016. *The Acts of the Lateran Synod of 649*, Liverpool: Liverpool University Press.

Price, R., 2018. *The Acts of the Second Council of Nicaea (787)*, Liverpool: Liverpool University Press.

Price, R., 2019. The Virgin as Theotokos at Ephesus (AD 431) and Earlier. In C. Maunder, ed. *The Oxford Handbook of Mary*. Oxford: Oxford University Press, pp. 67–77.

Price, R. & Gaddis, M., 2005. *The Acts of the Council of Chalcedon*, Liverpool: Liverpool University Press.

Pseudo-Dionysius, 1987. *The Complete Works*, transl. by C. Luibhéid & P. Rorem, Mahwah, NJ: Paulist.

Puech, H.-C., Quispel, G., van Unnik, W. C. & Cross, F. L., 1955. *The Jung Codex: A Newly Recovered Gnostic Papyrus*, London: Mowbray.

Pusey, Ph.E., 1872. *Sancti patris nostri Cyrilli archiepiscopi Alexandrini in D. Joannis evangelium*, 3 vols., Oxford: Clarendon Press.

Radde-Gallwitz, A. ed., 2017. *The Cambridge Edition of Early Christian Writings.* Vol.1: *God*, Cambridge: Cambridge University Press.

Rahmani, I. E., 2008. *The History of Tur Abdin*, Piscataway, NJ: Gorgias.

Räisänen, H., 2008. Marcion. In A. Marjanen & P. Luomanen, eds. *A Companion to Second-Century Christian "Heretics."* Leiden: Brill, pp. 100–24.

Ramelli, I., 2013. *The Christian Doctrine of* Apokatastasis, Leiden: Brill.

Ramet, S. P. ed., 1988. *Eastern Christianity and Politics in the Twentieth Century*, Durham, NC: Duke University Press.

Ramsay, W. M., 2010. *The Cities and Bishoprics of Phrygia*, La Vergne, TN: Nabu Press.

Rasmussen, A., 2019. *Genesis and Cosmos: Basil and Origen on Genesis 1 and Cosmology*, Leiden: Brill.
Rebenich, S. & Wiemer, H.-U. eds., 2020. *A Companion to Julian the Apostate*, Leiden: Brill.
Rebillard, É., 2017a. *Christians and Their Many Identities in Late Antiquity, North Africa, 200–450 CE*, Ithaca NY: Cornell University Press.
Rebillard, É., 2017b. *Greek and Latin Narratives About the Ancient Martyrs*, Oxford: Oxford University Press.
Rees, R., 2004. *Diocletian and the Tetrarchy*, Edinburgh: Edinburgh University Press.
Rescher, N., 2013. *Dialectics: A Classical Approach to Inquiry*, Berlin: De Gruyter.
Reydams-Schils, G., 1999. *Demiurge and Providence: Stoic and Platonist Readings of Plato's "Timaeus,"* Turnhout: Brepols.
Richter, D. S., 2011. *Cosmopolis: Imagining Community in Late Classical Athens and the Early Roman Empire*, Oxford: Oxford University Press.
Riedinger, R., 1976. Aus den Akten der Lateran-Synode von 649. *Byzantinische Zeitschrift*, 69(1), pp. 17–38.
Riedl, M., 2010. Truth versus Utility: The Debate on Civil Religion in the Roman Empire of the Third and Fourth Centuries. In R. Weed & J. Von Heyking, eds. *Civil Religion in Political Thought: Its Perennial Questions and Enduring Relevance in North America*. Washington, DC: Catholic University of America Press, pp. 47–65.
Rist, J., 2020. On the Platonism of Gregory of Nyssa. *Hermathena*, 169, pp. 129–51.
Rives, J. B., 1999. The Decree of Decius and the Religion of Empire. *The Journal of Roman Studies*, 89, pp. 135–54.
Roberts, L., 1970. Origen and Stoic Logic. *Transactions and Proceedings of the American Philological Association*, 101, pp. 433–44.
Roberts, A. M., 2020. *Reason and Revelation in Byzantine Antioch: The Christian Translation Program of Abdallah ibn-al-Fadl*, Oakland, CA: University of California Press.
Robertson, J. M., 2007. *Christ as Mediator: A Study of the Theologies of Eusebius of Caesarea, Marcellus of Ancyra, and Athanasius of Alexandria*, Oxford: Oxford University Press.
Robinson, J. M., 1977. *The Nag Hammadi Codices: A General Introduction to the Nature and Significance of the Coptic Gnostic Library from Nag Hammadi*, Claremont, CA: Institute for Antiquity and Christianity.
Rodriguez, J. A., 2015. *Muslim and Christian Contact in the Middle Ages: A Reader*, Toronto: University of Toronto Press.
Roggema, B. & Treiger, A. eds., 2020. *Patristic Literature in Arabic Translations*, Leiden: Brill.
Romanides, J. S., 2018. *The Ancestral Sin*, Ridgewood, NJ: Zephyr.
Romocea, C., 2011. *Church and State: Religious Nationalism and State Identification in Post-Communist Romania*, London: Continuum.
Roth, D. T., 2015. *The Text of Marcion's Gospel*, Leiden: Brill.
Roueché, M., 2012. Stephanus the Philosopher and Ps. Elias: A Case of Mistaken Identity. *Byzantine and Modern Greek Studies*, 36(2), pp. 120–38.

Rousseau, A. ed., 1969. *Irénée de Lyon. Contre les hérésies. Livre V*, Paris: Éditions du Cerf.
Rowe, C. K., 2016. *One True Life: The Stoics and Early Christians as Rival Traditions*, New Haven, CT: Yale University Press.
Rubenson, S., 1997. *The Letters of St. Antony: Monasticism and the Making of a Saint*, Minneapolis, MN: Fortress.
Rubenstein, M.-J., 2014. *Worlds Without End: The Many Lives of the Multiverse*, New York: Columbia University Press.
Runciman, S., 1961. *The Medieval Manichee*, Cambridge: Cambridge University Press.
Runciman, S., 2003. *The Great Church in Captivity: A Study of the Patriarchate of Constantinople From the Eve of the Turkish Conquest to the Greek War of Independence*, Cambridge: Cambridge University Press.
Rüpke, J., 2012. *Religion in Republican Rome: Rationalization and Ritual Change*, Philadelphia, PA: University of Pennsylvania Press.
Rüpke, J. & Woolf, G. eds., 2020. *Religion in the Roman Empire*, Stuttgart: Kohlhammer.
Russell, N., 2020. *Gregory Palamas: The Hesychast Controversy and the Debate with Islam. Documents Relating to Gregory Palamas*, Liverpool: Liverpool University Press.
Saint-Laurent, J.-N. M., 2015. *Missionary Stories and the Formation of the Syriac Churches*, Oakland, CA: University of California Press.
Sakharov, S., 1977. *His Life Is Mine*, Crestwood, NY: St. Vladimir's Seminary Press.
Sakharov, S., 1999. *Saint Silouan, the Athonite*, Crestwood, NY: St. Vladimir's Seminary Press.
Salles, R., 2005. *The Stoics on Determinism and Compatibilism*, London: Routledge.
Sample, R. L., 1979. The Christology of the Council of Antioch (268. C. E.) Reconsidered. *Church History*, 48(1), pp. 18–26.
Sassi, M. M., 2018. *The Beginnings of Philosophy in Greece*, Princeton, NJ: Princeton University Press.
Saward, J., 2007. *Perfect Fools: Folly for Christ's Sake in Catholic and Orthodox Spirituality*, Oxford: Oxford University Press.
Schachner, L. A., 2010. The Archeology of the Stylite. In D. M. Gwynn & S. Bangert, eds. *Religious Diversity in Late Antiquity*. Leiden: Brill, pp. 329–400.
Schäfer, P., 1998. *Judeophobia: Attitudes Toward the Jews in the Ancient World*, Cambridge, MA: Harvard University Press.
Schäfer, P., 2003. *The History of the Jews in the Greco-Roman World*, London: Routledge.
Scheid, J., 2014. To Honour the Princeps and Venerate the Gods: Public Cult, Neighbourhood Cults, and Imperial Cult in Augustan Rome. In J. Edmondson, ed. *Augustus*. Edinburgh: Edinburgh University Press, pp. 275–302.
Schmemann, A., 1977. *Great Lent: A School of Repentance*, Crestwood, NY: St. Vladimir's Seminary Press.
Schmidt, T. C. & Nicholas, N. eds., 2017. *Hippolytus of Rome: Commentary on Daniel and "Chronicon,"* Piscataway, NJ: Gorgias.
Schminck, A., 1986. *Studien zu mittelbyzantinischen Rechtsbuechern*, Frankfurt a. Main: Löwenklau Gesellschaft.
Scupoli, L., 1978. *Unseen Warfare: The Spiritual Combat and Path to Paradise*, Crestwood, NY: St. Vladimir's Seminary Press.

Searby, D. M. ed., 2018. *Never the Twain Shall Meet? Latins and Greeks Learning From Each Other in Byzantium*, Berlin: De Gruyter.

Sedley, D., 2007. *Creationism and Its Critics in Antiquity*, Berkeley, CA: University of California Press.

Selassie, F., 2008. *Books of Meqabyan 1–3*, Raleigh, NC: Lulu Press.

Severus ibn al Muqaffa, 1912. *Alexandrinische Patriarchen-Geschichte von S. Marcus bis Michael I 61-767. Nach der ältesten 1266 geschriebenen Hamburger Handschrift. Im arabischen Urtext herausgegeben von Christian Friedrich Seybold*, Hamburg: Gräfe.

Shaw, B. D., 2011. *Sacred Violence: African Christians and Sectarian Hatred in the Age of Augustine*, Cambridge: Cambridge University Press.

Shelton, W. B., 2014. Lactantius as Architect of a Constantinian and Christian "Victory over the Empire." In E. L. Smither, ed., *Rethinking Constantine: History, Theology, and Legacy*, Cambridge: James Clarke & Co., pp. 26–36.

Shevzov, V., 2004. *Russian Orthodoxy on the Eve of Revolution*, Oxford: Oxford University Press.

Shin, M. S., 2019. *The Great Persecution: A Historical Re-Examination*, Turnhout: Brepols.

Siecienski, A. E. ed., 2017. *Constantine: Religious Faith and Imperial Policy*, London: Taylor & Francis.

Siecienski, A. E., 2010. *The Filioque: History of a Doctrinal Controversy*, Oxford: Oxford University Press.

Simplicius, 2012. *On Aristotle Physics 8.1-5*, transl. by M. I. Bodnár, M. Chase & M. Share, London: Bloomsbury.

Sims-Williams, N., Schwartz, M. & Pittard, W. J., 2014. *Biblical and Other Christian Sogdian Texts from the Turfan Collection*, Turnhout: Brepols.

Smith, L. B., 1999. *Fools, Martyrs, Traitors: The Story of Martyrdom in the Western World*, Evanston, IL: Northwestern University Press.

Solovyov, V., 1948. *Russia and the Universal Church*, transl. by H. Rees, London: G. Bles.

Solovyov, V., 2014. *Sophia, God & a Short Tale About the Antichrist*, transl. by B. Jakim, Kettering, OH: Semantron.

Sophoulis, P., 2012. *Byzantium and Bulgaria, 775–831*, Leiden: Brill.

Sorabji, R., 1987a. Infinity and the Creation. In R. Sorabji, ed. *Philoponus and the Rejection of Aristotelian Science*. Ithaca, NY: Cornell University Press, pp. 164–78.

Sorabji, R. ed., 1987b. *Philoponus and the Rejection of Aristotelian Science*, Ithaca, NY: Cornell University Press.

Sorabji, R. ed., 1990. *Aristotle Transformed: The Ancient Commentators and Their Influence*, Ithaca, NY: Cornell University Press.

Sorabji, R., 2006. *Self: Ancient and Modern Insights on Individuality, Life, and Death*, Chicago, IL: University of Chicago Press.

Sorabji, R., 2015. Waiting for Philoponus. In A. Marmodoro & B. D. Prince, eds. *Causation and Creation in Late Antiquity*, Cambridge: Cambridge University Press, pp. 71–93.

Sozomen & Philostorgius, 1855. *History of the Church*, transl. by E. Walford, London: Henry G. Bohn.

Speake, G., 2018. *A History of the Athonite Commonwealth*, Cambridge: Cambridge University Press.

Spoerl, K. M., 1991. A Study of the Κατὰ μέρος πίστις by Apollinarius of Laodicea, University of Toronto.

Spoerl, K. M., 2021. Apollinarius and the Nicene *Homoousion*. In Y. R. Kim, ed. *The Cambridge Companion to the Council of Nicaea*. Cambridge: Cambridge University Press, pp. 282–304.

Squire, M., 2009. *Image and Text in Graeco-Roman Antiquity*, Cambridge: Cambridge University Press.

Stallman-Pacitti, C., 1991. *Cyril of Scythopolis: A Study in Hagiography as Apology*, Brookline, MA: Hellenic College Press.

Starr, S. F. 2013. *Lost Enlightenment: Central Asia's Golden Age from the Arab Conquest to Tamerlane*. Princeton, NJ: Princeton University Press.

Stearns, P. N. ed., 2008. *World History in Documents: A Comparative Reader*, New York: New York University Press.

Steenberg, M., 2008. *Irenaeus on Creation*, Leiden: Brill.

Steiner, G., 2010. *Anthropocentrism and Its Discontents: The Moral Status of Animals in the History of Western Philosophy*, Pittsburgh, PA: University of Pittsburgh Press.

Stenger, J., 2020. Pagans and Paganism in the Age of the Sons of Constantine. In N. Baker-Brian & S. Tougher, eds. *The Sons of Constantine, AD 337-361*. New York: Palgrave Macmillan, pp. 389–413.

Stephenson, P., 2004. *Byzantium's Balkan Frontier: A Political Study of the Northern Balkans, 900–1204*, Cambridge: Cambridge University Press.

Sterling, G., 2018. "The Most Perfect Work": The Role of Matter in Philo of Alexandria. In G. A. Anderson & M. Bockmuehl, eds. *Creation ex Nihilo*. Notre Dame, IN: University of Notre Dame Press, pp. 99–118.

Stern, W., 1906. *Person und Sache*, Leipzig: Barth.

Stetter, S. & Nabo, M. M. eds., 2020. *Middle East Christianity*, New York: Springer.

Stevenson, J. & Frend, W. H. C., 2012. *Creeds, Councils and Controversies*, Grand Rapids, MI: Baker Academic.

Stevenson, J. & Frend, W. H. C., 2013. *A New Eusebius*, Grand Rapids, MI: Baker Academic.

Stewart-Sykes, A. C., 2011. *On the Two Ways: Life or Death, Light or Darkness: Foundational Texts in the Tradition*, Yonkers, NY: St. Vladimir's Seminary Press.

Stramara, D. F., 1997. Gregory of Nyssa: an Ardent Abolitionist? *St. Vladimir's Theological Quarterly*, 41(1), pp. 37–60.

Stratoudaki-White, D., 2000. The Dual Doctrine of the Relations of Church and State in Ninth Century Byzantium. *The Greek Orthodox Theological Review*, 45, pp. 1–11.

Strauss, B., 2019. *Ten Caesars: Roman Emperors from Augustus to Constantine*, New York: Simon & Schuster.

Stuckrad, von, K., 2000. Jewish and Christian Astrology in Late Antiquity: A New Approach. *Numen*, 47(1), pp. 1–40.

Sturz, F. W., 1973. *Orionis Thebani Etymologicon*, Hildesheim: Olms.

Suslov, M. & Uzlaner, D. eds., 2020. *Contemporary Russian Conservatism: Problems, Paradoxes, and Perspectives*, Leiden: Brill.

Swanson, M. N., 2010. *The Coptic Papacy in Islamic Egypt: (641–1517)*, Cairo: American University in Cairo Press.

Tabbernee, W. & Lampe, P., 2008. *Pepouza and Tymion: the Discovery and Archeological Exploration of a Lost Ancient City and an Imperial Estate*, Berlin: De Gruyter.

Tabbernee, W., 1997. *Montanist Inscriptions and Testimonia: Epigraphic Sources Illustrating the History of Montanism*, Macon, GA: Mercer University Press.

Tanner, N. P. ed., 1990. *Decrees of the Ecumenical Councils: Nicaea I to Lateran V*, London: Sheed & Ward.

Teule, H. & Verheyden, J. eds., 2020. *Eastern and Oriental Christianity in the Diaspora*, Leuven: Peeters.

Theodore the Studite, 2015. *Writings on Iconoclasm*, transl. by Th. Cattoi, Mahwah, NJ: Newman.

Theodoret of Cyrus, 1989. *On Divine Providence*, transl. by Th. P. Halton, New York: Newman.

Theodoret of Cyrus, 2007. *The Questions on the Octateuch*, transl. by J. Petruccione, Washington, DC: Catholic University of America Press.

Thomas, D. ed., 2018. *Routledge Handbook on Christian-Muslim Relations*, London: Routledge.

Thomson, R. W., 1995. *The Syriac Version of the Hexaemeron*, Leuven: Peeters.

Thomson, R. W., 2012. *Saint Basil of Caesarea and Armenian Cosmology: A Study of the Armenian Version of Saint Basil's Hexaemeron and Its Influence on Medieval Armenian Views About the Cosmos*, Leuven: Peeters.

Thorsteinsson, R., 2010. Stoicism as a Key to Pauline Ethics in Romans. In T. Rasimus, T. Engberg-Pedersen & I. Dunderberg, eds. *Stoicism in Early Christianity*. Grand Rapids, MI: Baker Academic, pp. 15–38.

Tiburcio, A., 2020. *Muslim-Christian Polemics in Safavid Iran*, Edinburgh: Edinburgh University Press.

Tigchelaar, E. J. C. & García Martínez, F., 1999. *The Dead Sea Scrolls. Study Edition*, Leiden: Brill.

Todd, R. B., 1976. *Alexander of Aphrodisias on Stoic Physics: A Study of the* De mixtione, *with preliminary essays, text, transl. and commentary*, Leiden: Brill.

Tolan, J. V. ed., 2013. *Medieval Christian Perceptions of Islam*, London: Routledge.

Tollefsen, T., 2012. *Activity and Participation in Late Antique and Early Christian Thought*, Oxford: Oxford University Press.

Tollefsen, T., 2015. Christocentric Cosmology. In P. Allen & B. Neil, eds. *The Oxford Handbook of Maximus the Confessor*. Oxford: Oxford University Press, pp. 307–21.

Tollefsen, T., 2018. *St Theodore the Studite's Defence of the Icons: Theology and Philosophy in Ninth-Century Byzantium*, Oxford: Oxford University Press.

Törönen, M., 2007. *Union and Distinction in the Thought of St. Maximus the Confessor*, Oxford: Oxford University Press.

Torrance, I. R., 2011. *Correspondence of Severus and Sergius*, Piscataway, NJ: Gorgias.

Travis, H. ed., 2017. *Assyrian Genocide: Cultural and Political Legacies*, London: Taylor and Francis.

Trigg, J. W., 1995. Eustathius of Antioch's Attack on Origen: What Is at Issue in an Ancient Controversy? *The Journal of Religion*, 75(2), pp. 219–38.

Troeltsch, E. 1906. Die Bedeutung des Protestantismus für die Entstehung der modernen Welt. *Historische Zeitschrift* 97(1), pp. 1–66.

Troupeau, G., 1969. Le livre de l'unanimité de la foi de ʿAlī ibn Dāwud al-Arfādī. *Parole de l'Orient*, 5(2), pp. 197–219.

Trypanis, C. A., 1968. *Fourteen Early Byzantine Cantica*, Wien, Graz, Köln: Böhlau.

Twomey, V. & Krausmüller, D. eds., 2010. *Salvation According to the Fathers of the Church. The Proceedings of the Sixth International Patristic Conference, Maynooth/ Belfast 2005*, Dublin: Four Courts.

Usacheva, A., 2017. *Knowledge, Language and Intellection from Origen to Gregory Nazianzen*, New York: Peter Lang.

Usacheva, A., Ulrich, J. & Bhayro, S. eds., 2020. *The Unity of Body and Soul in Patristic and Byzantine Thought*, Leiden: Ferdinand Schöningh.

Uthemann, K.-H. ed., 1981. *Anastasii Sinaitae, Viae dux*, Turnhout: Brepols; Leuven University Press.

Vaggione, R. P., 2000. *Eunomius of Cyzicus and the Nicene Revolution*, Oxford: Oxford University Press.

Valliere, P., 2014. *Conciliarism: A History of Decision-Making in the Church*, Cambridge: Cambridge University Press.

Van Dam, R., 2009. *The Roman Revolution of Constantine*, Cambridge: Cambridge University Press.

Van Dam, R., 2010. *Rome and Constantinople: Rewriting Roman History During Late Antiquity*, Waco, TX: Baylor University Press.

Van Dam, R., 2021. Imperial Fathers and Their Sons. In Y. R. Kim, ed. *The Cambridge Companion to the Council of Nicaea*. Cambridge: Cambridge University Press, pp. 19–42.

van Doorn-Harder, N. ed., 2017. *Copts in Context*, Columbia, SC: University of South Carolina Press.

Van Nuffelen, P., 2013. The *Life* of Constantine: The Image of an Image. In A. Johnson & J. Schott, eds. *Eusebius of Caesarea: Tradition and Innovations*. Washington, DC: Center for Hellenic Studies, pp. 131–49.

Vanderspoel, J., 1995. *Themistius and the Imperial Court: Oratory, Civic Duty and Paideia From Constantius to Theodosius*, Ann Arbor, MI: University of Michigan Press.

Vanderspoel, J., 2020. From the Tetrarchy to the Constantinian Dynasty: A Narrative Introduction. In N. Baker-Brian & S. Tougher, eds. *The Sons of Constantine, AD 337-361*. New York: Palgrave Macmillan, pp. 23–56.

Vööbus, A., 1965. *History of the School of Nisibis*, Louvain: Secrétariat du Corpus Scriptorum Christianorum Orientalium.

Wakeley, J. M., 2018. *The Two Falls of Rome in Late Antiquity: The Arabian Conquests in Comparative Perspective*, New York: Palgrave Macmillan.

Walker, J. T., 2006. *The Legend of Mar Qardagh*, Oakland, CA: University of California Press.

Ward, B. ed., 1984. *The Sayings of the Desert Fathers: The Alphabetical Collection*, Kalamazoo, MI: Cistercian Publications.

Ward, P., 2013. *Liquid Church*, Eugene, OR: Wipf & Stock.

Wardhaugh, R. & Fuller, J., 2015. *An Introduction to Sociolinguistics*, New York: Wiley.

Ware, K., 2011. Sobornost and Eucharistic Ecclesiology: Aleksei Khomiakov and His Successors. *International Journal for the Study of the Christian Church*, 11(2–3), pp. 216–35.

Warren, J., 2004. Ancient Atomists on the Plurality of Worlds. *The Classical Quarterly*, 54(2), pp. 354–65.

Watt, J. W., 2019. *The Aristotelian Tradition in Syriac*, London: Routledge.

Watts, E. J., 2008. *City and School in Late Antique Athens and Alexandria*, Berkeley, CA: University of California Press.

Watts, E. J., 2015. *The Final Pagan Generation*, Oakland, CA: University of California Press.

Watts, E. J., 2017. *Riot in Alexandria*, Oakland, CA: University of California Press.

West, M. L., 2002. *Early Greek Philosophy and the Orient*, Oxford: Oxford University Press.

Whitehead, D. ed., 1994. *From Political Architecture to Stephanus Byzantius: Sources for the Ancient Greek Polis*, Stuttgart: F. Steiner.

Whittaker, M., 1982. *Tatian. Oratio ad Graecos and Fragments*, Oxford: Clarendon Press.

Wickes, J. T., 2019. *Bible and Poetry in Late Antique Mesopotamia: Ephrem's Hymns on Faith*, Oakland, CA: University of California Press.

Wickham, L. R., 1968. The "Syntagmation" of Aetius the Anomean. *The Journal of Theological Studies*, 19(2), pp. 532–69.

Wildberg, C., 1990. Three Neoplatonic Introductions to Philosophy: Ammonius, David and Elias. *Hermathena*, 149, pp. 33–51.

Wilken, R. L., 2003. *The Christians as the Romans Saw Them*, New Haven, CT: Yale University Press.

Williams, A. N., 1999. *The Ground of Union: Deification in Aquinas and Palamas*, Oxford: Oxford University Press.

Williams, M. A., 1999. *Rethinking "Gnosticism": An Argument for Dismantling a Dubious Category*, Princeton, NJ: Princeton University Press.

Williams, R., 2001. *Arius: Heresy and Tradition*, Grand Rapids, MI: Eerdmans.

Willjung, H., 1998. *Das Konzil van Aachen, 809*, Hannover: Hahnsche Buchhandlung.

Winston, D., 1971. The Book of Wisdom's Theory of Cosmogony. *History of Religions*, 11(2), pp. 185–202.

Winston, D., 2011. *The Wisdom of Solomon: A New Translation with Introduction and Commentary*, New Haven, CT: Yale University Press.

Wisniewski, R., 2020. *Christian Divination in Late Antiquity*, Amsterdam: Amsterdam University Press.

Wolff, R. L., 1959. The Three Romes: The Migration of an Ideology and the Making of an Autocrat. *Daedalus*, 88(2), pp. 291–311.

Wooden, A., 2019. The Limits of the Church: Ecclesiological Project of Nicolas Afanasiev, Catholic University of America, Washington, DC.

Wortley, J. ed., 2013. *The Anonymous Sayings of the Desert Fathers: A Select Edition and Complete English Translation*, Cambridge: Cambridge University Press.

Wortley, J., 2014. *Give Me a Word: The Alphabetical Sayings of the Fathers*, Yonkers, NY: St. Vladimir's Seminary Press.

Wright, J. R. ed., 2019. *Proverbs, Ecclesiastes, Song of Solomon*, Downers Grove, IL: IVP Academic.

Yacoub, J. & Ferguson, J., 2016. *Year of the Sword: The Assyrian Christian Genocide. A History*, Oxford: Oxford University Press.

Yannaras, C., 2007. *Person and Eros*, Brookline, MA: Holy Cross Orthodox Press.

Yavuz, M. H. & Blumi, I. eds., 2013. *War and Nationalism: The Balkan Wars, 1912–1913, and Their Sociopolitical Implications*, Salt Lake City, UT: The University of Utah Press.

Young, W. G., 1974. *Patriarch, Shah, and Caliph: A Study of the Relationships of the Church of the East with the Sassanid Empire and the Early Caliphates Up to 820 A.D*, Rawalpindi: Christian Study Centre.

Youssef, Y. N., 2006. *A Homily on Severus of Antioch by a Bishop of Assiut (XV Century)*, Turnhout: Brepols.

Zachhuber, J., 2014a. *Human Nature in Gregory of Nyssa*, Leiden: Brill.

Zachhuber, J., 2014b. Individuality and the Theological Debate about "Hypostasis." In J. Zachhuber & A. Torrance, eds. *Individuality in Late Antiquity*. Farnham: Ashgate, pp. 91–110.

Zachhuber, J., 2014c. Universals in the Greek Church Fathers. In R. Chiaradonna & G. Galluzzo, eds. *Universals in Ancient Philosophy*. Pisa: Edizioni della Normale, pp. 425–70.

Zachhuber, J., 2020. *The Rise of Christian Theology and the End of Ancient Metaphysics: Patristic Philosophy From the Cappadocian Fathers to John of Damascus*, Oxford: Oxford University Press.

Zaranko, A. & Louth, A. eds., 2017. *The Way of a Pilgrim: Candid Tales of a Wanderer to his Spiritual Father*, London: Pinguin.

Zhyrkova, 2017. Leontius of Byzantium and the Concept of Enhypostaton. *Forum Philosophicum*, 22(2), pp. 193–218.

Αγουρίδης, Σ., 1998. *Τα Ανθρώπινα Δικαιώματα στο Δυτικό Κόσμο* [Human Rights in the Western World], Αθήνα: Φιλίστωρ.

Γιανναρᾶς, Χ., 2006. *Τὸ πρόσωπο καὶ ὁ ἔρως* [The Person and Eros], Ἀθήνα: Δόμος.

Γιανναρᾶς, Χ., 2011. *Καταφύγιο Ἰδεῶν* [The Shelter for Ideas], Ἀθήνα:Ἴκαρος.

Γιανναρᾶς, Χ., 2016. *Ὀντολογία τοῦ προσώπου* [The Ontology of Person], Ἀθήνα:Ἴκαρος.

Γιανναρᾶς, Χ., 2018. *Ἡ Εὐρώπη γεννήθηκε ἀπὸ τὸ "Σχίσμα"* [Europe has been Born from the "Schism"], Ἀθήνα:Ἴκαρος.

Γόνης, Δ., 1996. *Ιστορία των ορθοδόξων εκκλησιών Βουλγαρίας και Σερβίας* [The History of the Orthodox Churches of Bulgaria and Serbia], Αθήνα: Συμμετρία.

Ἡλιοῦ, Φ., 1985. Συγχωροχάρτια (Β'). *Τὰ Ἱστορικά*, 2(3), pp. 3–44.

Καλαϊτζίδης, Π., 2008. *Ελληνικότητα και Αντιδυτικισμός στη «Θεολογία του '60»* [Greekness and anti-Westernism in the Theology of the 60s]. PhD thesis at the Aristotle's University of Thessaloniki.

Καρμήρης, Ἰ., 1968. *Τὰ Δογματικὰ καὶ Συμβολικὰ Μνημεία τῆς Ὀρθοδόξου Καθολικῆς Ἐκκλησίας* [The Dogmatic and Symbolic Monuments of the Orthodox Catholic Church], Graz: Akademische Druck- u. Verlagsanstalt.

Κωνσταντινίδης, Ἐ., 2000. Σταθμοὶ τῆς ἱστορικῆς πορείας τῆς ἐν Ἑλλάδι Ἐκκλησίας [Milestones in the Historical Journey of the Church in Greece]. In *Δίπτυχα τῆς Ἐκκλησίας τῆς Ἑλλάδος 2000*. Ἀθήνα: Ἀποστολικὴ Διακονία, pp. 9–27.

Μεταλληνός, Γ., 1989. *Θεολογικὸς Ἀγῶνας. 1962—Ἱστορία* [Theological Struggle, 1962—History], Ἀθήνα: Παρουσία.

Νησιώτης, Ν., 1996. Ἀπὸ τὴν αὐτοσυνειδησία μέσῳ ἐνσυνείδητης ἀλλοτρίωσης στὴν ταυτότητα [From Self-awareness Through Conscious Alienation to Identity]. *Σύναξη*, 59, pp. 19–34.

Νίκας, Ἀ., 1981. *Θεόδωρος τῆς Ραϊθοῦ* [Theodore of Raith], Ἀθῆναι: Ἱ. Μ. Σινᾶ.

Παΐσιος Ἁγιορείτης, 1999. *Πνευματικὴ Ἀφύπνιση* [Spiritual Awakening], Θεσσαλονίκη: Ἱερὸν Ἡσυχαστήριον Μοναζουσῶν «Εὐαγγελιστὴς Ἰωάννης ὁ Θεολόγος».

Παπαδόπουλος-Κεραμεῦς, Ἀ., 1908. *Γράμματα Πατριαρχῶν Κωνσταντινουπόλεως. Συμβολαὶ εἰς τὴν ἱστορίαν τῆς ἀρχιεπισκοπῆς τοῦ ὄρους Σινᾶ* [Letters of the Patriarchs of Constantinople. Contribution to the history of the archbishopric of the Mount Sinai], St. Petersburg.

*Τριῴδιον Κατανυκτικόν, περιέχον ἅπασαν τὴν ἀνήκουσαν αὐτῷ Ἀκολουθίαν τῆς Ἁγίας καὶ Μεγάλης Τεσσαρακοστῆς* [The Lenten Triodion containing every service of the Holy and Great Lent], Ἐν Βενετίᾳ: ἐκ τῆς Ἐκκλησιαστικῆς Τυπογραφίας τοῦ Φοίνικος.

Τρωϊάνος, Σ., 2007. *Οι Νεαρές του Λέοντος ΣΤ' του Σοφού* [The Novels of Leo VI the Wise], Αθήνα: Ηροδότος.

Φειδᾶς, Β., 1969. *Ὁ θεσμός τῆς Πενταρχίας τῶν Πατριαρχών* [The Institute of the Pentarchy of Patriarchs], Ἀθῆναι.

Φειδᾶς, Β., 1971. *Ἐνδημούσα σύνοδος: γένεσις καὶ διαμόρφωσις τοῦ θεσμοῦ ἄχρι τῆς Δ' Οἰκουμενικῆς συνόδου* [Endemousa Synod: The Origins and Formation of the Institution till the 4th Ecumenical Council], Ἀθῆναι.

Φειδᾶς, Β., 1991. *Βυζάντιο* [Byzantium], Ἀθήνα.

Φειδᾶς, Β., 1997. *Ἱεροὶ κανόνες καὶ καταστατικὴ νομοθεσία τῆς Ἐκκλησίας τῆς Ἑλλάδος* [Sacred Canons and Constitutional Legislation of the Church of Greece], Ἀθήνα: Σ. Ἀθανασόπουλος, Σ. Παπαδάμης & Σια.

Бердяев, Н., 1933. Вселенскость и конфессионализм [Ecumenicity and Confessionalism]. In С. Булгаков, ed. *Христианское воссоединение: экуменическая проблема в православном сознании* [Christian Reunion: An Ecumenical Problem in the Orthodox Consciousness]. Paris: YMCA, pp. 63–81.

Болотов, В., 1914. *К вопросу о Filioque* [On the Issue of Filioque], Санкт-Петербург: Тип. М. Меркушева.

Дмитриева, Л. А. ed., 1981. *Памятники литературы Древней Руси: XIII век* [Monuments of the Literature of the Ancient Rus': 13th c.], Москва: Художественная литература.

Дроздов, Ф., 1886. *Собрание мнений и отзывов Филарета . . . по делам православной церкви на востоке* [A Collection of Opinions and Responses of Filaret . . . Regarding the Situation of the Orthodox Church in the East], Санкт-Петербург: Синодальная типография.

Кекелидзе, К., 1912. Сведения грузинских источников о препод. Максиме Исповеднике [Information from the Georgian Sources on St. Maximus the Confessor]. *Труди Київської Духовної Академії*, III (9, 11), pp. 1–41, 451–86.

Митрофанов, Г., 2021. *Очерки по истории Русской Православной Церкви XX века* [Sketches of the History of the Russian Orthodox Church in the 20th Century], Москва: Практика.

Павлов, И., 2017. *Как жили и во что верили первые христиане: учение двенадцати апостолов* [How the First Christians Lived and Believed: The Teaching of the Twelve Apostles], Москва: Эксмо.

Светлов, П., 1914. *Христианское вероучение в апологетическом изложении* [Christian Teaching Exposed Apologetically], Киев: Типография С. В. Кульженко.

Священный Собор Православной Российской Церкви [Sacred Council of the Orthodox Russian Church], 1918. *Собрание Определений и Постановлений. Выпуск первый* [A Collection of Definitions and Decrees. First Issue], Москва: Издание Соборного Совета.

Синицына, Н. В., 1998. *Третий Рим. Истоки и эволюция русской средневековой концепции (XV-XVI вв.)* [The Third Rome. Sources and Evolution of the Russian Medieval Concept (15–16 cc.)], Москва: Индрик.

Скобцова, Е., 1931. Рождение и творение [Birth and Creation]. *Путь*, 30, pp. 35–47.

Скобцова, Е., 1939. На страже свободы [Safeguarding Freedom]. *Православное дело*, 1, pp. 84–95.

Соболев, С., 1935. *Новое учение о Софии Премудрости Божией* [A New Teaching about Sophia the Wisdom of God], София, 1935.

Хомяков, А., 1867. *Полное собрание сочинений* [Complete Collection of Works], Prague: Типография д-ра Ф. Скрейшовского.

Ченцова, В., 2020. *Киевская митрополия между Константинополем и Москвой. 1686* [The Kyivan Metropolia between Constantinople and Moscow. 1686], Київ: Дух і літера.

Чорноморець, Ю., 2010. *Візантійський неоплатонізм від Діонісія Ареопагіта до Геннадія Схоларія* [The Byzantine Neoplatonism from Dionysius the Areopagite to Gennadius Scholarius], Київ: Дух і літера.

# Index